...dwide Volunteering 020872

Thank you for buying one of our books. We hope you'll enjoy it and it will help you to plan a successful gap year or vacation project.

We always try to ensure our books are up to date, but contact details seem to change so quickly that it can be very hard to keep up with them. If you do have any problems contacting any of the organisations please get in touch, and either we or the Worldwide Volunteering will do what we can to help. And if you do find correct contact details that differ from those in the book, please let us know so that we can put it right when we reprint.

Please do also give us your feedback so we can go on making books that you want to read. If there's anything you particularly liked about this book – or you have suggestions about how it could be improved in the future – email us on info@howtobooks.co.uk

Good luck with your adventure.

The Publishers

www.howtobooks.co.uk

Cover and text images used with grateful thanks to:

African & Asia Venture, Dickon Verey, National Trust, Quest Overseas, Raleigh International. If there is any organisation that we have inadvertantly failed to mention please let us know and we will ensure that it is included when the book is reprinted.

Worldwide Volunteering

*Hundreds of volunteer opportunities for gap year, holiday
or vacation projects*

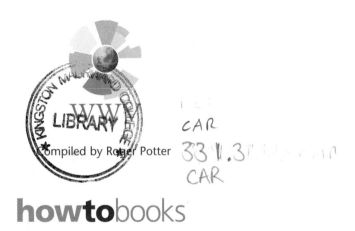

Compiled by Roger Potter

howtobooks

Published by How To Books Ltd,
3 Newtec Place, Magdalen Road,
Oxford OX4 1RE. United Kingdom.
Tel: (01865) 793806. Fax: (01865) 248780.

© Copyright 2004 Worldwide Volunteering
Database maker Worldwide Volunteering, first published 1996–2000

Fourth edition 2004

British Library Cataloguing in Publication Data
A catalogue record for this book is available from
the British Library

Cover design by Baseline Arts Ltd, Oxford
Produced for How To Books by Deer Park Productions
Typeset by Pantek Arts Ltd, Maidstone, Kent
Printed and bound by Bell & Bain Ltd, Glasgow

Contents

Foreword

Young people have enormous talent, enthusiasm and idealism. They have a real contribution to make to society and they want to make their voices heard. Volunteering is a wonderful way for them to show what they are capable of.

Volunteering is a three-way process and benefits everyone. For the individuals, groups or causes that volunteers help the value is evident. Volunteers themselves are often surprised by how much they gain from the experience: horizons are widened, doors opened, new challenges met, fresh friendships made, confidence built. I remember my own experiences with nothing but affection in every respect.

But there is a third aspect of volunteering and that is the way in which all of us gain from the altruism, co-operation and energy that volunteering releases. Society as a whole profits not only from the tangible benefits to the recipients of voluntary effort, but also from the enhanced maturity and experience that those who have volunteered bring to all other aspects of their lives. The more that people volunteer the better becomes the fabric of society. Not only that, it's fun as well – letting your life take a new outlet outside of school, college, university or even as a break from a full-time job.

No one sort of volunteer work is better than another. This new book demonstrates the enormous range of opportunities that exist around the world. There is something for everyone. The important thing is that anyone who wants to volunteer should find an opportunity to match their particular circumstances and aspirations – whether it's a week in the county next door or six months in Kathmandu.

If this guide helps you to find the right volunteering opportunity it will provide an experience you will never forget and one in which there are no losers – only winners.
Good luck!

RICHARD BRANSON

Preface

Welcome to the fourth edition of *WorldWide Volunteering*, a directory of worldwide opportunities for volunteering.

The directory creates a mass of information about some 950 volunteer organisations with over 300,000 annual volunteer opportunities throughout the UK and 214 countries worldwide. All the organisations listed have opportunities for 16 to 25-year olds, though many also have openings for younger and older volunteers. This wealth of precisely focused information makes *WorldWide Volunteering* the UK's most comprehensive directory of its kind.

You will be amazed at the enormous variety of opportunities on offer. But before going directly to directory entries you may find it helpful to spend a few moments reading this preface in order to make best use of the vast amount of information available.

Sifting through so many organisations each with its different aims and requirements can be a daunting task, but the aim of the directory is to make this process as easy as possible. First, it is crucial to build up a clear picture of exactly what sort of volunteering you are looking for, and the guide is structured to help with this.

In order to build a profile of your ideal volunteering opportunity you will need to consider a variety of questions. Which cause or group of people would you like to help? Where do you want to volunteer? How long for? Starting when? What skills do you wish to use and how much, if anything, can you afford to contribute to the cost of your project? Your responses to these and other questions will determine which organisations best suit you. The guide will pinpoint them and supply a mass of valuable information about each one.

Volunteering for all

There are many reasons why people volunteer. A motive common to all must be idealism – the wish to make a contribution to society, to do something for others or for a worthwhile cause without too much concern for personal reward.

But volunteering is not a one-way process. It is perfectly reasonable for volunteers to recognise that as well as giving, they themselves gain from the experience, and many choose to volunteer for precisely this reason.

A well-researched and well-chosen volunteer project, for instance, cannot fail to widen your experience, increase your self-confidence and offer exciting challenges. It is likely to take you to new places where you will meet new people with backgrounds and circumstances that differ widely from your own.

People are often surprised by the range of skills and interests that can be used in volunteering. Whether you are interested in accountancy or zoo-keeping there are opportunities that will allow you to use and develop your particular tastes. The starting point for many volunteers is the realisation that they have something unique to contribute!

Then there are the longer term rewards of volunteering. Employers and university admissions tutors, amongst others, increasingly value evidence of volunteering when selecting candidates for jobs and university places. They recognise the initiative and determination shown in becoming involved and demonstrating an awareness of others, and the ability to organise yourself and work as part of a team that the experience will demand.

Don't spend too much time worrying about why you want to volunteer. Far more important is the fact that you want to get involved. The purpose of this guide is to make it easier for volunteers to translate their initial enthusiasm for volunteering into a worthwhile placement.

Safety warning!

Please remember that *WorldWide Volunteering* is a reference book designed to help you to find organisations that will suit your own requirements. Whilst every effort is made to ensure that the information is correct and up to date we cannot accept responsibility for errors or omissions. Volunteers should always check with organisations in whose work they are interested.

Neither How To Books nor WorldWide Volunteering have any financial or other interest in any organisation contained in the directory. Nor does inclusion in either the database or directory guarantee the quality of any specific project, organisation or activity.

Neither How To Books nor WorldWide Volunteering can be held responsible for arrangements that individuals or groups may make with any organisation in the directory. Volunteers are strongly advised to satisfy themselves on the management, financial, safety, health and all other aspects of a project before enrolling on it.

WorldWide Volunteering

WorldWide Volunteering is a registered charity whose aim is to make it easier for young people around the world to identify and take part in appropriate volunteering projects. The publication complements the WorldWide Volunteering search and match database which is available in many schools, universities, career centres, volunteer bureaux, libraries and other information sources. The database enables volunteers to make more sophisticated searches of the information and is updated continually.

WorldWide Volunteering welcomes feedback from readers, who are invited to send comments and suggestions to WorldWide Volunteering, 7, North Street Workshops, Stoke sub Hamdon, Somerset TA14 6QR. Telephone: 01935 825588. Fax: 01935 825775. E-mail: worldvol@worldvol.co.uk, Web site: www.wwv.org.uk

Roger Potter
Director
WorldWide Volunteering

A few words for volunteers by Tom Griffiths, Founder of gapyear.com

Introduction

Volunteering, whether at home or overseas, has never been a more beneficial activity. It is encouraged by universities and valued by employers. Not only will you learn about who you really are and how you react to others, you will mature and develop a character that you probably never knew existed. It could be the most amazing, exciting and challenging time of your life.

Volunteering, however, should not be taken lightly. 'The Challenge' should be taken up in a responsible manner. No one will congratulate you for taking up a scarce place, only to drop out in a few weeks when you get bored or let others down who have come to rely on you. You should not be embarking on this journey to score 'cool points' with your mates, to impress your parents or because you think that it is deemed to be the right thing to do.

Do it because you want to. Do it because you have something to give and because you are happy to give it. Do it because of the self-satisfaction of making a difference to the lives of others. Placement organisations are not after 'shining knights' out to save the world, but young people with an infectious energy and enthusiasm to pass on to others.

Don't wait until it's too late to find that you have missed out. Where do you dream about visiting? What do you dream about doing? Whatever your answer is...that should be your placement. Now, let this book do the rest!

Life. There is no rehearsal.

Good luck.

Tom

Tom Griffiths is Founder of gapyear.com, 'gapyear magazine', author of 'Before You Go' and 'The Virgin Travellers' Handbook' and the media spokesperson for the UK Youth Travel and Gap Year industry. A previous 'Young Travel Writer of the Year' he now runs one of the largest youth travel communities in the UK.

How to use this book

Alphabetical listings

The first section of the guides (pages 3–522) lists the volunteer organisations alphabetically and gives detailed information about each one. An explanation of directory entries is given below. If you already know the name of an organisation you can go straight to its entry for further information.

Alternatively you may want to browse through the alphabetical section to familiarise yourself with the scope of volunteering on offer and the sort of information available for each organisation.

Another way of using this section is to find more information about an organisation that looks right for you once you have identified it in the cross-referencing section.

Cross-referencing

For many volunteers the cross-referencing section of the guide will be the first port of call. All organisations are listed by the cause or group of people that they help. There are 24 causes:

Addicts/Ex-addicts
Aids/HIV
Animal welfare
Archaeology
Architecture
Children
Conservation
Disabled (learning and physical)
Elderly people
Environmental causes
Health care/medical
Heritage
Holidays for disabled

Human rights
Inner city problems
Offenders/Ex-offenders
Poor/homeless
Refugees
Teaching/assisting (nursery, primary, secondary, mature, English as a foreign language – EFL)
Unemployed
Wildlife
Work camps (seasonal)
Young people

So if you think you'd really like to do something to help the homeless, turn to that particular cause in the Index by Cause on pp 541–628. Any of the organisations listed there will provide you with the opportunity to fulfil that ambition.

If you've always wanted to visit Malawi and would like to find an organisation that will take you there, turn to the Index by WorldWide Placement on pages 523–540. You will, in fact, find 26 organisations listed there that offer placements in Malawi. Now look them up in the directory section for further information.

Individual entries

Details about each organisation in the alphabetical section give you all the information you need to make contact with that organisation and in most cases a very great deal more. Entries depend entirely on information provided by individual organisations. Some are more complete than others. However, the format of each listing is identical and a complete entry will contain information under the following headings and in the following order:

Full address, contact details and name including telephone, fax and e-mail address and web site where available.

A description provided by the organisation itself outlining its aims and activities and giving volunteers a feel for the work of the organisation.

♿ This symbol appears where an organisation may be able to offer projects to those with disabilities.

📄 This symbol appears where certificates or references may be available on leaving the placement, on request to the organisation.

Number of projects worldwide and in the UK.

Starting months and **Time required**, ranging from a commitment of minimum one week to a maximum of a year or more.

Age. Indicates age limits at the start of volunteering, both lower and upper.

Details of **causes** helped.

Activities in which volunteers may be involved.

Total number of volunteer **placements** each year with this organisation.

When to apply. Note that it is always sensible to apply as early as possible. The best projects are very rapidly filled.

Whether volunteers **work alone** or **with others**.

Qualifications required if any, e.g. linguistic ability, first aid, academic qualifications etc. Also states any restrictions in nationality or geography.

Details of any specific **equipment/clothing** required.

Health requirements.

Costs to volunteers. Note that organisations are asked to state typical costs excluding travel. Costs are based on figures supplied by organisations in 2003. Always check for up-to-date details.

Benefits to volunteers. Details of accommodation provided, insurance if provided, help with travel expense, pocket money etc.

Training. Details of what, if any, training is given.

Supervision. Whether the volunteer is supervised at the placement.

Interview and selection details.

WorldWide placements listed by continent and country.

UK placements listed by region and county.

Many organisations will consider volunteers with an **offending background**. Some of these indicate this at the end of their profile entry. Contact others to check the policy.

Headings are omitted from an organisation's listing where the relevant information is not available.

Because this information is presented in a standard format from entry to entry it is possible to refine the cross-referencing facility by eliminating, for example, organisations whose start date or time commitment required do not suit the individual volunteer.

The huge variety of opportunities contained in this directory offers volunteers a really wide choice. Whether you are looking for a six-month placement in a developing country for which you will have to raise a great deal of money, or whether you want a short-term local project where all your expenses and even a pocket money allowance will be paid, there is something here for you. The important thing is to become involved, and – who knows – it could be the start of a great adventure.

A–Z Directory of Volunteer Organisations

"We are very grateful to you for including us within this excellent resource."
Ian Prior, Director, CAREFORCE

"I much appreciate your plan to include an organisation like ours which is working in remote rural areas and has very little contact with bigger cities and townships."
Bharatendu Prakash Convener, VIGYAN SHIKSHA KENDRA

"We are very grateful for the service Worldwide Volunteering provides. Volunteers are the backbone of NGOs and your database contributes to sharing what is most needed: skills and knowledge worldwide."
Kiti Mignotte, Senior Administrator, G O A L

"We would like you to record how very much we appreciate your service and for you to know that the personnel who have worked with us, through you, have brought love, joy and hope to many young lives in Romania."
Tilly & John Kimber, LITTLE JOHN'S HOUSE

15 MAY SCHOOL

245 Nguyen Trai
District 1
Ho Chi Minh City
Vietnam
T: (84 8) 837 7951
E: info@15mayschool.org
W: www.15mayschool.org
Contact: Nguyen Kim Luyen

The 15 May School is an informal school for street children and other disadvantaged children in Ho Chi Minh City. The school offers regular classes but unlike formal schools (which charge fees) children up to 18 can attend any grade according to their ability and level, without making any payment. The school's class schedule is directed towards the children's needs, offering evening classes for children who must work through the day. 25 former street or at risk children live and study at this school and approximately 250 poor children regularly attend. 15 May School offers primary schooling and secondary schooling. Promising students are awarded scholarships to attend local high schools or colleges and we are hoping also to offer university scholarships for children who pass the entrance exam. Vocational training classes are provided to give children practical skills from which they can find a job. Children also have the opportunity to attend English and performing arts classes – circus skills, singing and dancing. The art component funds the project through performances at the school and an annual fundraising event. However, the performing arts also provide a means of expression and encourage the development of the children's self-esteem through enjoyable activities. The importance of English classes is held in equal esteem. If the children cannot speak English, it is very difficult for them to find work in Ho Chi Minh City. In short the school aims to help its children 'escape their fate'. It provides them with a loving environment to live in if they need one, an education, opportunities for personal development and assistance in finding a job when they are old enough. All children at the school are encouraged to participate in the running of the project, teaching them practical skills and giving them the satisfaction of building themselves a brighter future. Volunteers are needed to help with project management, entertaining children, organising fundraising events and assisting with teaching of English classes. Long and short-term volunteers welcome all year round.

We cannot, because of nature of work accept applications from volunteers with an offending background.

Number of projects: 1 UK: 0
Starting months: January–December
Time required: 2–52 weeks (plus)
Age: 18 plus – no upper limit
Causes: Children, Poor/Homeless, Teaching/assisting (primary, secondary, EFL), Young People.
Activities: Accountancy, Administration, Arts/Crafts, Computers, Development Issues, Fundraising, Marketing/publicity, Music, Newsletter/Journalism, Research, Social Work, Teaching, Theatre/Drama.
Placements: 15+
When to apply: All year round.
Work alone/with others: With others.
Qualifications: Experience of working with children, fundraising or project management would be a bonus, but not essential.
Equipment/clothing: Just need to dress respectably as working with children.
Health requirements: No restrictions.
Costs: All costs to be covered by volunteers as school is on a small budget. School is unable to provide a work visa of any sort. Volunteers can find accommodation in a local guesthouse or a rented room in a house.
Training: No formal training.
Supervision: Help and guidance is available from other volunteers and the project manager.
Interviews: No interviews, although we do need a completed application form and CV. We can provide additional information by e-mail.
Worldwide placements: Asia (Vietnam).

1990 TRUST, THE

South Bank Technopark
90 London Road
London SE1 6LN UK
T: +44 (0) 207 717 1579
F: +44 (0) 207 717 1585
E: aadams@gn.apc.org
Contact: Mrs Audrey Adams

The 1990 Trust aims to promote good race relations, engage in policy development and articulate the needs of the Black community from a grassroots Black perspective. In so doing we will ensure that the real issues affecting the lives of people of African, Asian and Caribbean descent are addressed. Our ultimate aim is to bring about long term improvements in people's lives by fighting for the elimination of racism in all its forms. The work of The 1990

Trust is founded on the principle that Black people have an inalienable right to complete freedom, justice and equality. The very nature of our work and the environment in which we operate therefore determines our status as a civil/human rights organisation. In working to achieve our goals, we will: ensure that everything we do is informed by the views and experiences of ordinary Black people in different communities throughout the United Kingdom; embrace totally the principle of networking and aim to do so with as many organisations and individuals as relevant and possible; engage a 'community development' approach to our work of a type which enables Black people in their communities to take part in initiatives which will improve their lives economically, socially and environmentally; uphold the ideal of Asian, African and Caribbean people working together, as we view this as the most effective means of eradicating racism and racial disadvantage in the United Kingdom. Volunteers with an offending background are accepted.

Number of projects UK: 4
Starting months: January–December
Time required: 4–52 weeks
Age: 16–60

Causes: AIDS/HIV, Children, Elderly People, Environmental Causes, Human Rights, Inner City Problems, Refugees.
Activities: Accountancy, Administration, Campaigning, Community Work, Computers, Development Issues, Fundraising, Group Work, International Aid, Library/Resource Centres, Marketing/Publicity, Newsletter/Journalism, Religion, Research, Scientific Work, Social Work, Translating.
Placements: 10
When to apply: All year.
Work alone/with others: Both.
Qualifications: Specialist skills welcome i.e. law graduates, interest in immigration/race, women's issues, human rights, I.T., sustainable development.
Health requirements: Nil.
Costs: Travel.
Benefits: Standard/normal benefits.
Training: Training offered for specific jobs.
Supervision: Volunteers will be supervised.
Interviews: Interviews take place at The 1990 Trust offices.
Charity number: 1012898
Worldwide placements: Africa (Ghana, Nigeria); Central America (Jamaica); Asia (India).
UK placements: England (Leicestershire, London).

A

ABANTU FOR DEVELOPMENT

1 Winchester House
11 Cranmer Road
London
SW9 6EJ UK
T: +44 (0) 207 820 0066
F: +44 (0) 207 820 0088
E: roe@abantu.org
W: www.abantu.org
Contact: Diana Mercorios

ABANTU for Development is a non-governmental development organisation that was founded in 1991 by African women. 'ABANTU' means 'people' in several African languages. The main focus of our work is on providing training, information and advice on identifying resources which ensure long-term survival of organisations, networking and lobbying for a role in policy and decision making for refugee and African women. Our aims are: to increase the participation of Africans, especially women, in the political and economic structures of African countries; to eradicate the cultural, legal and political obstacles for women to attain economic independence and equality before the law; to ensure that the advancement of women's interests benefits the entire community; to promote and nurture public awareness of development issues with a gender perspective, which shows an understanding of women's position in society. We achieve these by: supporting African people to empower themselves through a participatory and people-centred method of training to develop skills in the area of policy analysis, economics, healthcare, the media and the environment; providing both support and networking opportunities for trainers and consultants to create an increased pool of competent Africans. ABANTU's programmes fall into four categories: training and capacity building; advocacy, public awareness and networking; research, information and publications; institutional development of ABANTU. Volunteers are taken on to support activities and projects within these four programmes usually under the supervision of the various programme officers and the line manager. ⓖ 🗋

Number of projects: varies UK: varies
Starting months: May
Time required: 12–24 weeks
Age: 16 plus – no upper limit
Causes: AIDS/HIV, Human Rights, Refugees.
Activities: Administration, Computers, Development Issues, Fundraising, Marketing/Publicity, Newsletter/Journalism, Research.
Placements: 4
When to apply: March
Work alone/with others: Both.
Qualifications: Minimum A-level.
Health requirements: Nil for UK. For Africa innoculations and anti-malarial pills.
Costs: Subsistence for all. Travel if overseas.
Benefits: London travel expenses subsidised.
Training: One week induction course.
Supervision: Line Manager and other programme officers, including the Office Manager.
Interviews: Interviews take place at our offices.
Worldwide placements: Africa (Ghana, Kenya, Nigeria).
UK placements: England (London).

ABBOT HALL ART GALLERY AND MUSEUM OF LAKELAND LIFE

Abbot Hall
Kendal
Cumbria LA9 5AL UK
T: +44 (0) 1539 722464
F: +44 (0) 1539 722494
E: ct@abbothall.org.uk
W: www.abbothall.org.uk
Contact: Mrs Cherrie Trelogan

Abbot Hall and the museums it looks after (Abbot Hall Art Gallery, Museum of Lakeland Life, Kendal Museum of National History & Archaeology and Blackwell – The Arts and Crafts House) have a particularly wide range of displays with which they are involved from fine arts through archaeology and geology to natural history and social history. There is an opportunity for people to gain experience in museum and art gallery careers. We have organised a series of structured sessions which will be delivered twice a week by museum and gallery staff. This will allow students the opportunity to combine practical skills with formal instruction and the opportunity for questions and discussion. Subjects will cover education, finance, collections management, marketing and customer care etc. ⓖ 🗋

Number of projects UK: 3
Starting months: January–December
Time required: 12–52 weeks (plus)
Age: 18 plus – no upper limit
Causes: Archaeology, Children, Conservation, Elderly People, Heritage, Teaching/assisting (nursery, primary, secondary), Young People.
Activities: Administration, Arts/Crafts, Computers, Conservation Skills, Group Work,

Manual Work, Marketing/Publicity, Newsletter/ Journalism, Research, Teaching, Technical Skills.
Placements: Many.
When to apply: All year – as early as possible.
Work alone/with others: Both.
Qualifications: English language.
Equipment/clothing: General smart appearance and a set of old clothes for messy work.
Health requirements: General good health.
Costs: Food, electricity and other power, telephone calls and transport (all within walking distance).
Benefits: Lodging for two students at a time subject to availability.
Training: Induction. A new programme of sessions is being instigated this year. Two hour-long sessions per week will be given by staff ranging from collections management to finance. These are in addition to ongoing training through practical tasks.
Supervision: One member of staff is allocated to supervise.
Interviews: Prospective volunteers are interviewed at Abbot Hall.
Charity number: 526980
UK placements: England (Cumbria).

ACET (AIDS CARE EDUCATION AND TRAINING)

1 Carlton Gardens
Ealing, London
W5 2AN UK
T: +44 (0) 208 786 7080
F: +44 (0) 208 780 0450
E: acet@acetuk.org
W: www.acetuk.org
Contact: Volunteer Co-ordinator

ACET's aim is to provide unconditional care for people living with HIV/AIDS and to reduce the number of new infections through schools' education and practical training. 🗎

Number of projects: 15 UK: 9
Starting months: January–December
Time required: 1–52 weeks
Age: 18 plus – no upper limit
Causes: AIDS/HIV, Health Care/Medical, Teaching/assisting (secondary).
Activities: Administration, Caring (general, day and residential), Cooking, Driving, Gardening/ Horticulture, Group Work, Religion, Teaching, Visiting/Befriending.
Placements: 80
When to apply: As soon as possible.
Work alone/with others: Alone.
Health requirements: Nil.
Costs: Travel to and from training.
Benefits: Travel and experience of working in the community.
Charity number: 299293

Worldwide placements: Africa (Tanzania, Uganda); Asia (Thailand); Australasia (New Zealand); Europe (Czech Republic, Ireland, Slovakia).
UK placements: England (Bedfordshire, Buckinghamshire, Essex, Hampshire, Hertfordshire, Kent, London, Northamptonshire, Surrey, E. Sussex, W. Sussex, Warwickshire, West Midlands); Scotland (Dundee City, Glasgow City); Northern Ireland (Belfast City, Derry/Londonderry); Wales (Cardiff, Newport, Vale of Glamorgan).

ACORN CHILDREN'S HOSPICE

103 Oak Tree Lane
Selly Oak
Birmingham
B29 6HZ UK
T: +44 (0) 121 248 4850
F: +44 (0) 121 248 4883
W: www.acorns.org.uk
Contact: Mrs Madelyn Coyne

Acorn Children's Hospice requires volunteers to work for a few hours a week for a minimum of a year. They could help on reception/ driving or escorting, help in the hydrotherapy pool, garden or be trained to work one to one with the children. 🗎 🗎

Number of projects UK: 2
Starting months: January–December
Time required: 1–52 weeks
Age: 17 plus – no upper limit
Causes: Children, Disabled (learning and physical), Health Care/Medical, Holidays for Disabled, Young People.
Activities: Arts/Crafts, Caring (general and day), Catering, Cooking, Counselling, Fundraising, Visiting/Befriending.
Placements: 50 approx.
When to apply: All year.
Work alone/with others: Dependant on voluntary role.
Qualifications: Willingness to work with children with disabilities.
Health requirements: Good health.
Costs: No accommodation provided.
Benefits: Training to prepare for the role.
Training: Dependent on role.
Supervision: Ongoing supervision.
Interviews: Volunteers are interviewed. References taken up and Police checks.
UK placements: England (West Midlands).

ACTION AGAINST HUNGER – OVERSEAS

4 Rue Niepce
75014 Paris
France
T: 33 1 43 35 88 88
F: 33 1 43 35 88 80
E: acf@acf.imaginet.fr

W: www.acf-fr.org
Contact: Volunteer Coordinator

Action Against Hunger – Overseas intervenes in crisis situations to bring assistance to the victims of war and famine. Our approach to emergency relief is always coupled with the long-term objective of enabling the affected population to regain their self sufficiency. The first victims of famine are nearly always the same: women, children and minority groups. Action Against Hunger combines experience and expertise to provide appropriate responses, through its four main approaches to the fight against hunger which are complemented by disaster preparedness: nutrition, food security, water, health. 📄

Number of projects: 34 UK: 0
Starting months: January–December
Time required: 52 weeks (plus)
Age: 24–60
Causes: Health Care/Medical, Poor/Homeless, Refugees.
Activities: Accountancy, Administration, Agriculture/Farming, Building/Construction, Caring – General, Community Work, Computers, Development Issues, Forestry, International Aid, Outdoor Skills, Research, Technical Skills.
Placements: 30
When to apply: All year.
Work alone/with others: With others usually.
Qualifications: Doctors, nurses, nutritionists, water engineers, agronomists, logisticians, administrators. All volunteers must have had at least one year's previous experience. Only EU or USA residents.
Equipment/clothing: Depending on location of post.
Health requirements: Certificate of good health and innoculations where necessary.
Costs: Nil.
Benefits: £500 per month after tax + travel, board and lodging.
Training: Three 3-week briefings according to technical profile. Security 1/2-day briefing for all.
Supervision: Report to Line Manager/Co-ordinator.
Interviews: Prospective volunteers are interviewed in London.
Charity number: 1047501
Worldwide placements: Africa (Angola, Burundi, Cameroon, Chad, Congo Dem Republic, Congo Republic, Côte d'Ivoire, Ethiopia, Guinea, Liberia, Mali, Mozambique, Niger, Sierra Leone, Somalia, Sudan, Tanzania, Uganda); Central America (Guatemala, Haiti, Honduras, Nicaragua); South America (Colombia); Asia (Afghanistan, Cambodia, Indonesia, Korea (North), Laos, Myanmar (Burma), Sri Lanka, Tajikistan); Europe (Bosnia-Herzegovina, Russia, Yugoslavia).

ACTION AGAINST HUNGER – UK

Unit 7b
Larnaca Works
Grange Walk
London
SE1 3EW UK
T: +44 (0) 207 394 6300
F: +44 (0) 207 237 9960
E: info@aahuk.org
W: www.aahuk.org
Contact: Volunteer Coordinator

Action Against Hunger is one of the leading international organisations in the fight against hunger and malnutrition. In over 40 countries around the world, our 320 international field-workers, sharing skills with 4500 national staff, continue to help the victims of hunger, giving them the means to prevent crisis and assisting them towards self-sufficiency. Each year, Action Against Hunger's international network brings relief to more than three million people a year. Action Against Hunger brings assistance either during the crisis itself through emergency intervention, or afterwards through rehabilitation and sustainable development programmes. Volunteers are needed in our London offices in the fundraising and communications department and for general administration, recruitment or translation work. 📄

Number of projects UK: 1
Starting months: January–December
Time required: 1–12 weeks
Age: 18 plus – no upper limit
Causes: Health Care/Medical, Human Rights, Poor/Homeless, Refugees.
Activities: Accountancy, Administration, Computers, Development Issues, Newsletter/Journalism, Research, Translating.
Placements: 20
When to apply: Up to 6 weeks in advance.
Work alone/with others: With others in the London office.
Health requirements: Nil.
Costs: Nil.
Benefits: Travel paid up to Zone 4.
Training: Not applicable to this organisation.
Supervision: Head of Department supervises.
Interviews: Prospective volunteers are interviewed in London.
Charity number: 1047501
UK placements: England (London).

ACTION AID

Hamlyn House
McDonald Road
Archway
London
N19 5PG UK
T: +44 (0) 207 561 7582
E: mail@actionaid.org.uk
Contact: Deborah Frais

Action Aid is one of the UK's largest international aid agencies, working directly with over five million of the world's poorest people in 27 countries across Asia, Africa and Latin America. We aim to improve the lives of children, families and whole communities in poorer countries. We support their needs and rights, working with local organisations and community groups so that change is appropriate and long-lasting. We work in emergency situations created by war, drought, floods, famine and the displacement of people. We also work to avert crises, particularly food shortages and famine. We work with governments and organisations to improve the policies and practices that have an impact on people living in poverty. We produce educational material for schools – used in half the schools in the UK – so that young people better understand the lives of people in developing countries. We do not send volunteers to our overseas projects. ☒ 📄

Number of projects UK: 3
Starting months: January–December
Time required: 6–52 weeks
Age: 18 plus – no upper limit
Causes: Children, Human Rights, Poor/ Homeless, Refugees.
Activities: Accountancy, Administration, Computers, Development Issues, Fundraising, International Aid, Library/Resource Centres, Marketing/Publicity, Research, Translating.
Placements: 50
When to apply: All year.
Work alone/with others: Either.
Qualifications: Depends on the task.
Health requirements: Nil.
Costs: Nil.
Benefits: Travel expenses reimbursed. For 5+ hours per day we give £3 towards lunch.
Training: Departmental training.
Supervision: Supervision undertaken by Line Manager.
Interviews: Prospective volunteers are interviewed at the office where they will work.
Charity number: 274467
UK placements: England (London, Somerset).

ACTION BENEVOLE – SWITZERLAND

Maupas 49
1004 Lausanne
Switzerland
T: 00 41 21 646 21 96
F: 00 41 21 646 18 97
E: action.benevole@span.ch
W: www.benevolat.ch
Contact: Marie-Chantal Collaud

Action Benevole promotes and has information about volunteering in Switzerland. It may well be able to put volunteers in touch with organisations which are not yet listed on the WorldWide Volunteering database.

Starting months: January–December
Time required: 1–52 weeks (plus)
Age: 16 plus – no upper limit
Causes: Addicts/Ex-Addicts, AIDS/HIV, Animal Welfare, Archaeology, Architecture, Children, Conservation, Disabled (learning and physical), Elderly People, Environmental Causes, Health Care/Medical, Heritage, Holidays for Disabled, Human Rights, Inner City Problems, Offenders/Ex-Offenders, Poor/Homeless, Refugees, Teaching/assisting (nursery, primary, secondary, mature, EFL) Unemployed, Wildlife, Work Camps – Seasonal, Young People.
Activities: Accountancy, Administration, Agriculture/Farming, Arts/Crafts, Building/ Construction, Campaigning, Caring (general, day and residential), Catering, Community Work, Computers, Conservation Skills, Cooking, Counselling, Development Issues, DIY, Driving, First Aid, Forestry, Fundraising, Gardening/Horticulture, Group Work, International Aid, Library/Resource Centres, Manual Work, Marketing/Publicity, Music, Newsletter/Journalism, Outdoor Skills, Religion, Research, Scientific Work, Social Work, Sport, Summer Camps, Teaching, Technical Skills, Theatre/Drama, Training, Translating, Visiting/Befriending, Work Camps – Seasonal.
Costs: Varies according to the project.
Worldwide placements: Europe (Switzerland).

ACTION PARTNERS

Bawtry Hall
Bawtry, Doncaster
S. Yorkshire
DN10 6JH UK
T: 01302 710750
F: 01302 719399
E: personnel@actionpartners.org.uk
W: www.actionpartners.org.uk
Contact: Susan Chalmers

Action Partners works in partnership with Christian churches and organisations in Africa and the UK, serving where the Church and Islam meet. Working in some of the most challenging regions of the world, our staff are involved in projects as diverse as health, education, development and church-related work. In the UK our staff work amongst ethnic minorities in the inner city. 📄

Number of projects: 35 **UK:** enquire
Starting months: January–December
Time required: 52 weeks (plus)
Age: 18–65
Causes: AIDS/HIV, Animal Welfare, Children, Disabled (learning and physical), Elderly People, Health Care/Medical, Inner City Problems, Poor/Homeless, Refugees, Teaching/assisting (nursery, primary, secondary, mature, EFL), Unemployed, Young People.

Activities: Accountancy, Administration, Agriculture/Farming, Arts/Crafts, Building/Construction, Caring (general, residential), Community Work, Computers, Development Issues, Gardening/Horticulture, Library/Resource Centres, Manual Work, Marketing/ Publicity, Newsletter/Journalism, Religion, Teaching, Technical Skills, Training, Visiting/ Befriending.
Placements: 8
When to apply: Six months ahead.
Work alone/with others: Both.
Qualifications: Evangelical Christians with a track record of active involvement in their local church, plus the specific requirements of each post. Only residents of the UK and certain EU countries.
Equipment/clothing: Suitable for Africa!
Health requirements: Good general health. Volunteers are required to have medicals.
Costs: Volunteers come with prayer and financial support from their home church and other friends.
Benefits: Allowances come out of total support costs as raised by volunteer. Accommodation is arranged according to situation.
Training: Orientation and other training provided as required.
Supervision: Local supervision.
Interviews: Interviews are held at our Bawtry Hall offices, near Doncaster.
Charity number: 1037154
Worldwide placements: Africa (Cameroon, Chad, Congo Dem Republic, Egypt, Ethiopia, Kenya, Nigeria, Sudan).

ACTIV FOUNDATION – RECREATION DEPARTMENT

134 Dundas Road
Inglewood
Perth
6052 Western Australia
T: 00 61 8 9370 5466
F: 00 61 8 9272 2922
E: active@wantree.com.au
W: www.active.org.au
Contact: Simon James

ACTIV Foundation is a not-for-profit, non-government organisation providing services to people with intellectual disability and their families, in the areas of accommodation, employment, respite and recreation. ACTIV Recreation provides many leisure and holiday options for people with intellectual disability to access community facilities. We are always looking for people to volunteer some time either regularly or on an ad-hoc basis. When you offer your services to ACTIV Recreation, staff will ask what your interests are and what time you have available. These are then matched with the programmes that we conduct. People visiting Perth, Western Australia, are welcome to

volunteer with us, on one or more of the programmes. Our mission statement is: 'To enable people with intellectual disability to enjoy their life and use their abilities to reach their potential and gain a greater independence.' International police clearances are required. Volunteers with an offending background may be acceptable if offences are not applicable to this line of work. 📖

Number of projects: 90 UK: 0
Starting months: January–December
Time required: 1–6 weeks
Age: 18 plus – no upper limit
Causes: Children, Disabled (learning), Elderly People, Holidays for Disabled, Young People
Activities: Arts/Crafts, Caring (general and day), Cooking, Driving, Group Work, Outdoor Skills, Sport, Summer Camps, Visiting/Befriending.
Placements: 800
When to apply: As early as possible.
Work alone/with others: With others.
Qualifications: Some driving. Caring attitude + interest in people with intellectual disability.
Health requirements: Reasonable level of fitness.
Costs: Only personal spending money.
Benefits: All food, transport, accommodation and entry to tourist attractions paid for while on programme.
Interviews: Interviews take place at our recreation centre.
Charity number: 19589
Worldwide placements: Australasia (Australia).

ADDACTION – COMMUNITY DRUG AND ALCOHOL INITIATIVES

67–69 Cowcross Street
Smithfield
London
EC1M 6BP UK
T: +44 (0) 207 251 5860
T: +44 (0) 207 251 5890
E: j.middleton@addaction.org.uk
W: www.addaction.org.uk
Contact: Julie Middleton

Addaction – Community Drug and Alcohol Initiatives would be interested in volunteers for many projects, and also possibly fundraising/administration volunteers for our central office in London. ♿ 📖

Number of projects UK: 30
Starting months: January–December
Time required: 2–10 weeks
Age: 16 plus – no upper limit
Causes: Addicts/Ex-Addicts, Offenders/Ex-Offenders.
Activities: Administration, Counselling, Fundraising, Library/Resource Centres, Marketing/Publicity, Research, Social Work, Training, Visiting/Befriending.

Placements: 40
When to apply: All year.
Work alone/with others: With others.
Health requirements: Nil.
Costs: Nil.
Benefits: Fares, travel and meals – all out of pocket expenses.
Training: 6 months structured volunteering programme.
Supervision: Volunteer co-ordinators supervise.
Charity number: 1001957
UK placements: England (Bedfordshire, Cornwall, Co Durham, Derbyshire, Devon, Essex, Leicestershire, Lincolnshire, London, Staffordshire, Suffolk, Surrey, E. Sussex, W. Sussex, West Midlands).

ADULT EDUCATION CENTRE (AEC)

P.O. Box 2056, Jinja
Plot 3 Republic Street
Njeru Town, Mukono District
Mukono Uganda
T: 256 77 403 281
E: jjuukor@yahoo.com
Contact: Jjuuko Robert

The Adult Education Centre is an indigenous NGO established in 1991, registered with the National Board for Non Governmental Organisations, Ministry of Internal Affairs. The AEC's vision is a harmonious, prosperous and learned society. The mission is to be an outstanding civil adult education agency, empowering adults with knowledge, skills and attitudes for sustainable development through training, information exchange, lobbying and advocacy. The Centre works to promote lifelong learning choices for out of school young people and adults. On going programmes include: adult basic education, specific skills development, library resource centre and management/ governance skills development. The Centre cherishes the values of volunteerism, humanism, equity, equality and honesty. The Centre's membership comprises of Ugandans interested in adult learning as a central element in socio-economic and political transformation of the needy community and country as a whole. Unfortunately, we cannot accept applications from volunteers with an offending background. ▤

Number of projects: 5 UK: 0
Starting months: January–December
Time required: 2–3 weeks
Age: 20 plus – no upper limit
Causes: Environmental Causes, Human Rights, Teaching/assisting (mature), Unemployed, Young People.
Activities: Accountancy, Administration, Community Work, Computers, Development Issues, Fundraising, Library/Resource Centres, Social Work, Technical Skills, Training.

Placements: 6
When to apply: All year – anytime so long as it gives enough time to process the papers.
Work alone/with others: Work with others.
Qualifications: Must be able to speak English.
Equipment/clothing: Uganda's weather is friendly throughout the year, we don't need any special clothing as there is neither serious winter or very hot summer.
Health requirements: No restrictions but must have a valid Yellow Fever vaccination card.
Costs: Main costs to volunteers will be food and accommodation – this is greatly reduced should volunteers stay with families of the promoters of the centre.
Benefits: The Centre is not in a position to give any direct financial benefit to international volunteers. We are only able to provide a modest honorarium to local volunteers.
Training: Induction in socio-economic and political life of the community/country as well as specifically to the local language.
Supervision: Volunteers are expected to be self motivated and are always assigned tasks and monitored through reports.
Interviews: Face to face interview not necessary so long as CV's are submitted to provide the basis for determining suitability and relevance.
Worldwide placements: Africa (Uganda).

ADVENTURE ALTERNATIVE

31 Myrtledene Road
Belfast, Down
BT8 6GQ N. Ireland
T: +44 (0) 2890 701476
F: +44 (0) 2890 701476
E: office@adventurealternative.com
W: www.adventurealternative.com
Contact: Gavin Bate

Adventure Alternative was set up by Gavin Bate, a British explorer who has climbed Mount Everest twice and uses his own expeditions to raise money for his charity Moving Mountains which supports street children in Kenya predominantly and various projects in East Africa and Nepal including hospitals, schools and community centres. The trips all tie in with Gavin's personal dream to further those objectives with many hundreds of street kids. It is very much a case of 'the right character' to work with these kids and spend time in those countries. We are not interested in big numbers of people, nor are we a big commercial machine churning out 'Gappers' for the sake of it. We want to provide an excellent experience, a really special personal experience, for every person who applies and succeeds in going. We offer really unique insights into the people and the countries on the back of Gavin's long term visits and experiences there and the friendships he has built up. We require people with initiative and the ability to make things happen rather than wait for things to happen to them. Travel and being abroad is all about that, rather than arriving just to 'do' Kenya or Nepal. We ask a lot because at the end of it all there is an awful lot to get out of it. And we never forget the power of that dream for someone ordinary to go and do something extraordinary. In Kenya – the three month gap year projects teach primary level children and work with disadvantaged kids in the slums of Nairobi, and for one month youth expeditions including street children rehabilitation camps, climbing Mt Kenya and overland safaris. Also medical electives in slum clinics and/or rural hospitals. In Nepal – teach in either Kathmandu or in a Himalayan mountain village plus extended trek to Everest Base Camp to do some conservation research. In Egypt for marine conservation work and PADI open dive course plus desert safari for 18 days. We are able to place volunteers with an offending background. Participants are simply chosen for their general character and ability. ☒ ▤

Number of projects: 3 UK: 0
Starting months: January–December
Time required: 4–12 weeks
Age: 17–25
Causes: AIDS/HIV, Children, Conservation, Environmental Causes, Health Care/Medical, Poor/Homeless, Teaching/assisting (primary, secondary, EFL), Work Camps – Seasonal, Young People.
Activities: Arts/Crafts, Community Work, First Aid, Fundraising, International Aid, Outdoor Skills, Summer Camps, Teaching, Theatre/Drama, Work Camps – Seasonal.
Placements: 120
When to apply: Apply giving enough time to raise money and at least three months prior to trip leaving in order to book air tickets.
Work alone/with others: Sometimes in large groups and sometimes in pairs.
Qualifications: None – an aptitude for good communication, teamwork and enthusiasm, lots of initiative and an open mind. English language an advantage.
Equipment/clothing: Not especially, only warm gear for the trek up to the Base Camp of Everest in Nepal.
Health requirements: Generally volunteers must get a medical certificate from their doctor for going on an expedition but there are few restrictions.
Costs: Kenya expeditions, gap year electives, Nepal elective – £1700. Egypt trip £1500. Costs excludes airfare, insurance and personal expenditure.
Benefits: All board, food and transport are supplied in-country in the fees mentioned.
Training: None to speak of but we do meet for an induction weekend for gap year participants.

Expedition members meet in Kenya and all the training is done in-country.
Supervision: In all cases we have in-country staff who are always on hand to help with any problems. All are English speaking, very friendly and very knowledgeable about their area and project. They are all personal friends of Gavin Bates.
Interviews: Interviews are held firstly over the telephone following the application form, and then later on face to face.
Worldwide placements: Africa (Egypt, Kenya); Asia (Nepal).

ADVENTURE FOUNDATION OF PAKISTAN

Adventure Foundation
Garden Avenue
National Park Area
Islamabad
44000 Pakistan
T: 00 92 51 2825805
F: 00 92 51 2272538
E: afopak@yahoo.com
W: www.adventurefoundation.org.pk
Contact: Mr Aftab Rana

Adventure Foundation of Pakistan promotes outdoor activities and 'thrill' sports for youth and other interested individuals in Pakistan. Activities include downhill skiing, rock climbing, hiking, windsurfing, bicycling, canoeing, mountaineering, and hot air ballooning. It strives to develop an 'action-orientated education system' that encourages members to achieve self-awareness; learn practical skills; appreciate Pakistan's national wilderness; participate with others in community spirit efforts; develop physical fitness. Follows the philosophy and concepts of Outward Bound. Conducts training courses at adventure training centres to prepare members for organised outings and offers advice to members who plan private excursions. Provides special training courses for disabled individuals and plans special outings to accommodate their needs. Offers courses in swimming and life saving. Is planning to establish a mountain and wilderness guides training centre. Sponsors international youth exchange programmes with other adventure sports organisations. Offers financial assistance to underprivileged members for all courses and outings. ▤

Number of projects: 1 UK: 0
Starting months: June
Time required: 3–4 weeks
Age: 21–25
Causes: Children, Conservation, Environmental Causes, Holidays for Disabled, Young People
Activities: Conservation Skills, First Aid, Group Work, Marketing/Publicity, Outdoor Skills, Summer Camps, Training.

Placements: 30
When to apply: By 15th April.
Work alone/with others: With others.
Qualifications: Outdoor/Wilderness Leadership Certificate course. Most nationalities accepted.
Equipment/clothing: Trekking/mountain boots, rock climbing shoes, sleeping bags, mat and pack.
Health requirements: Should be in general good health and be physically fit.
Costs: Return airfare Islamabad, Pakistan.
Benefits: Board and lodging plus £4 per day pocket money. Accommodation available at Adventure Training Centre of AFP at Abbottabad.
Training: Should have experience of Wilderness Leadership training.
Supervision: Supervision is undertaken by Chief Instructor of Adventure Training.
Interviews: Applicants from abroad are interviewed by post.
Worldwide placements: Asia (Pakistan).

ADVENTURE PLUS (A+)

Hill Grove Farm
Dry Lane, Crawley
Witney, Oxon
OX29 0NA UK
T: +44 (0) 1993 703308
F: +44 (0) 1993 708433
E: enquiries@adventureplus.org.uk
W: www.adventureplus.org.uk
Contact: Christine Brown

Adventure Plus (A+) was started in 1990 and is a registered non denominational Christian charity. Its aim is to reach out to young people through outdoor pursuits and adventure holidays. These take place mainly in Oxfordshire but we also run activities in the Brecon Beacons, Forest of Dean, Wye Valley, North Wales and the south coast. We currently employ a small core team of permanent staff and are supported by around 300 volunteers without whom we could not operate. We offer 'Affordable Accessible Adventure' to many children and young people by being a very low cost organisation based within 90 minutes of London, Birmingham, Bristol and Southampton. In 2002 approximately 4000 young people came through our programmes of camps and courses. We encourage campers to return each year particularly to our open summer camps held each August. We then hope they will become leaders at the age of 18. We believe that there is a real need for stimulating moral and spiritual guidance for today's young people when only too often we see the results of juvenile crime, drug and alcohol abuse. We also try to provide this in a framework of adventure and fun. Volunteers with an offending background may be accepted depending on the offences. 🗲 📄

Number of projects UK: 40
Starting months: January–December
Time required: 1–52 weeks (plus)
Age: 18 plus – no upper limit

Causes: Children, Inner City Problems, Young People.
Activities: Administration, Arts/Crafts, Catering, Cooking, First Aid, Fundraising, Group Work, Music, Outdoor Skills, Religion, Sport, Summer Camps, Teaching, Theatre/Drama, Training.
Placements: 20
When to apply: All year.
Work alone/with others: With others.
Qualifications: Nil but for outdoor pursuits governing body qualifications useful (BCU/RYA/MLTB etc).
Equipment/clothing: Provided by A+.
Health requirements: In view of our programmes we need fairly fit volunteers for outdoor work but all are welcome for office volunteering.
Costs: We ask volunteers to pay the costs of staying on our camps/courses approx £8–£15 per night.
Benefits: Training weekends offered where skills and qualifications are gained. Limited accommodation available.
Training: Training courses run throughout the year.
Supervision: Provided by staff.
Interviews: Prospective gap year volunteers are interviewed. Others are not interviewed but 2 references are followed up before a volunteer can start.
Charity number: 802659
UK placements: England (Berkshire, Cumbria, Derbyshire, Dorset, Gloucestershire, London, Oxfordshire, Shropshire); Wales (Conwy, Gwynedd, Powys).

ADVOCACY PROJECT, THE

34 Woodfield Road
London
W9 2BE UK
T: +44 (0) 207 289 5051 + minicom
T: +44 (0) 207 289 5510
E: tap@cawca.freeserve.co.uk
W: www.advocacynet.org
Contact: Becky Powell

The Advocacy Project: 1. Citizen Advocates – befriend and support people with learning difficulties. Advocates help people to express their needs, and to get the things they need. This is about civil rights, respect and empowerment. It is a one-to-one partnership and this is done in the volunteer's free time. It involves a personal commitment. 2. Management Committee members – people with a variety of skills and backgrounds are needed to support the work of the project. Various tasks – fundraising, publicity, finance. Experience not essential. Volunteers with an offending background may be accepted depending on the offence.

Number of projects UK: 1
Starting months: January–December
Time required: 52 weeks (plus)
Age: 21–68
Causes: Disabled (learning and physical), Health Care/Medical, Human Rights
Activities: Accountancy, Caring – General, Community Work, Fundraising, Marketing/Publicity, Visiting/Befriending.
Placements: 38
When to apply: All year.
Work alone/with others: On their own but there is a support group for our volunteers.
Qualifications: Experience not essential.
Health requirements: Nil.
Benefits: Out of pocket expenses reimbursed.
Training: 4 week preparation training (one evening per week).
Supervision: Monthly contact personal/phone. 2-monthly support groups.
Interviews: Interviews take place in office, community or at home.
Charity number: 1044286
UK placements: England (London).

AFPIC – ACTION FOR CHILDREN IN CONFLICT

Silverbirch House
Longworth
Abingdon
Oxon OX13 5EJ UK
T: +44 (0) 1865 821380
F: +44 (0) 1865 821384
E: info@actionchildren.org
W: www.actionchildren.org
Contact: Volunteers Co-ordinator

The mission of AfPiC is to rebuild the lives of individuals and communities damaged by conflict. This presents four different volunteer opportunities: 1. Help us with our on-going work at our head office in Longworth. We are particularly interested in volunteers who would work in marketing and promotions, general office work, volunteer recruitment and placement events. 2. We have two charity shops but intend to open more. We can offer accommodation to one or two volunteers who would like to experience this type of work. 3. In Southampton we have a project to convert an old inshore minesweeper into a 'pirate radio' station in Ireland. Volunteers to work on the refitting of the ship are very welcome. 4. In Kenya we are helping to run an orphanage for street children in Thika. Volunteers who will be expected to work there are now wanted all the year round. Volunteers may also be needed in Sierra Leone, the Balkans and India. Placement in the Balkans would be via The Balkan Sunflower Project and in India via IndiaCares who are based in Bangalore. We would happily consider volunteers with an offending background.

Number of projects: 5 UK: 2
Starting months: January–December
Time required: 2–52 weeks
Age: 16 plus – no upper limit
Causes: Children, Human Rights, Refugees, Teaching/assisting (EFL), Work Camps – Seasonal, Young People.
Activities: Administration, Building/Construction, Campaigning, Computers, Counselling, Development Issues, Driving, Fundraising, Group Work, International Aid, Marketing/Publicity, Newsletter/Journalism, Research, Work Camps – Seasonal.
Placements: 20
When to apply: All year.
Work alone/with others: With others.
Qualifications: Driving is an advantage. An interest in the charity's mission is a main requirement.
Health requirements: Nil.
Costs: Approximately £2,000 covers travel, insurance and accommodation for Kenya, Sierra Leone and India.
Benefits: 1999/2000 volunteers working on 6 month work placements in the UK received £250 per month to cover costs. Subsidised accommodation also. Accommodation provided by AfPiC.
Training: No training is required for work in the UK. Overseas – pre-briefing is essential.
Supervision: Office work – Director of Development. Retail Work – our Retail Co-ordinator. Southampton – Pirates for Peace Project Manager. Kenya and Sierra Leone – our in-country representative.
Interviews: Interviews take place either in Longworth or at a mutually convenient location.
Charity number: 1060894
Worldwide placements: Africa (Kenya, Sierra Leone, Western Sahara); Asia (India); Europe (Bosnia-Herzegovina).
UK placements: England (Oxfordshire).

AFRICA AND ASIA VENTURE

10 Market Place
Devizes, Wiltshire
SN10 1HT UK
T: 01380 729009
F: 01380 720060
E: av@aventure.co.uk
W: www.aventure.co.uk
Contact: Peter Bell

Africa and Asia Venture (AV) is for motivated, adventurous students who wish to spend part of their year out gaining cultural and work experience with youth in the developing world and have fantastic travel opportunities. Our placements are in Kenya, Tanzania, Uganda, Malawi, Botswana, India, Nepal or with our new programme in Mexico. We also have some projects available for recently qualified graduates in Malawi. Volunteers are placed in pairs as assistant teachers in selected rural schools for one term. Depending on their skills and attributes, and the requirements of the schools, volunteers assist in a variety of subjects ranging from English, science, music and vocational activities to clubs and especially sports. Schools are chosen with location, work opportunities, accommodation and security in mind, and placements do not deprive local teachers from working. Full in-country back up, support and training is provided by AV in each country. There are also a few opportunities for attachment to community-related and conservation projects. In Kenya these include working in National Parks such as Tsavo National Park. Following the placement, there are 3 weeks for independent travel and the complete programme is rounded off with an exciting group safari to game parks and places of interest such as Lake Turkana in Northern Kenya or the Zambezi River in Zimbabwe. In India the group will travel to the splendours of Rhajasthan and in Nepal to game parks or trek in the Himalayas. For details contact our Devizes office. Don't delay as we get very booked up. Africa and Asia Venture is a member of The Year Out Group.

Number of projects: 80–90 UK: 0
Starting months: Jan, Feb, Apr, May, Aug, Sep, Oct, Nov
Time required: 16–20 weeks
Age: 18–24
Causes: Children, Conservation, Environmental Causes, Health Care/Medical, Teaching/assisting (nursery, primary, secondary), Wildlife, Young People.
Activities: Arts/Crafts, Building/Construction, Caring – General, Community Work, Conservation Skills, Music, Outdoor Skills, Sport, Teaching, Theatre/Drama.
Placements: 410–430
When to apply: 9+ months before departure and preferably as early as possible.
Work alone/with others: In pairs.
Qualifications: Studied to A-level – thereafter assessment interview. Good level of spoken and written English for non British passport holders.
Health requirements: Volunteers must be in good health.
Costs: £2,500 plus air fare (£450 approx) and extra spending money (£400).
Benefits: 4-day orientation course on arrival, food and accommodation as well as final safari, charity contribution and travel including medical insurance. Accommodation is provided within schools' campus or at the projects.
Training: 4-day in-country orientation course on arrival.
Supervision: In-country support provided by our in-country director or representative.
Interviews: Interviews take place in Devizes or in regional area.

Worldwide placements: Africa (Botswana, Kenya, Malawi, Tanzania, Uganda); Central America (Mexico); Asia (India, Nepal).

AFRICA CENTRE

38 King Street
Covent Garden
London
WC2E 8JT UK
T: +44 (0) 207 836 1973
F: +44 (0) 207 836 1975
E: africacentre@gn.apc.org
W: www.africacentre.org.uk
Contact: Dr Adotey Bing

The Africa Centre is a charity established in 1961 to inform and educate the British and European public about Africa. We have over 100,000 visitors per year. Our main mission objectives are (a) to promote awareness about Africa in the UK, (b) to help empower the African Diaspora in the UK and (c) to support Africa's international aspirations. We have entertainment: music, food, exhibitions, performances and children's workshops. We give information: databases, resource room, fact sheets, courses, responses to telephone and written enquiries. Advocacy: talks, lectures, conferences, debates, radio, cultural awareness, training. We have something for everyone, especially African community groups, teachers and school children, UK NGOs working in Africa, UK national institutions, large scale employers, politicians, journalists and the media, UK business people with African connections, academics and students, African NGOs and African entrepreneurs. Volunteers with an offending background may be accepted. &

Number of projects UK: 1
Starting months: January–December
Time required: 1–52 weeks (plus)
Age: 18–70
Causes: Children, Heritage, Human Rights, Refugees, Teaching/assisting (mature), Unemployed, Young People.
Activities: Administration, Development Issues, Fundraising, Library/Resource Centres, Marketing/Publicity, Newsletter/Journalism, Research, Technical Skills.
Placements: 30
When to apply: All year.
Work alone/with others: Mixed.
Health requirements: Nil.
Costs: Accommodation and travel.
Benefits: Travel costs in London and lunch provided.
Training: None.
Supervision: The volunteer is supervised by his/her programme Co-ordinator.
Interviews: Interviews are conducted at the Centre.
UK placements: England (London).

AFRICA INLAND MISSION

2 Vorley Road
Archway, London
N19 5HE UK
T: +44 (0) 207 281 1184
F: +44 (0) 207 281 4479
E: enquiry@aim-eur.org
W: www.aim-eur.org
Contact: Angela Godfrey

Africa Inland Mission gives an opportunity for young people to be involved in cross-cultural communication and to look at the work of missionaries first-hand. Placements are made in rural schools for 8–12 months. Teams doing a practical project and church work go for seven weeks each summer.

Number of projects: 11 **UK:** 0
Starting months: Jan, Jul, Aug
Time required: 7–52 weeks
Age: 18–70
Causes: Teaching/assisting (secondary), Teaching (EFL), Young People.
Activities: Accountancy, Administration, Religion, Teaching.
Placements: 30
When to apply: September – May.
Work alone/with others: Alone, in pairs or in teams of 6–8 people.
Qualifications: Post A-level or graduates, teachers. Committed Christians.
Equipment/clothing: None needed.
Health requirements: Must be in good health.
Costs: £4,000 approx (travel , insurance, living and administration costs).
Benefits: Housing provided.
Training: 4 days of teacher training and 4 days of orientation.
Supervision: Supervision is given at the placement by a national, headteacher or church leader. Local missionary co-ordinators in most countries.
Interviews: 2 interviews for 12-month volunteers.
Worldwide placements: Africa (Central African Republic, Comoros, Kenya, Lesotho, Madagascar, Mozambique, Namibia, Seychelles, Sudan, Tanzania, Uganda).

AFRICA VOLUNTARY SERVICE OF SIERRA LEONE

PMB 717
Freetown
Sierra Leone
Contact: Franklin Alusine Sesay

Africa Voluntary Service of Sierra Leone promotes and has information about volunteering in Sierra Leone. It may well be able to put volunteers in touch with organisations which are not yet listed on the WorldWide Volunteering database.

Starting months: January–December
Time required: 1–52 weeks (plus)
Age: 16 plus – no upper limit
Causes: Addicts/Ex-Addicts, AIDS/HIV, Animal Welfare, Archaeology, Architecture, Children, Conservation, Disabled (learning and physical), Elderly People, Environmental Causes, Health Care/Medical, Heritage, Holidays for Disabled, Human Rights, Inner City Problems, Offenders/Ex-Offenders, Poor/Homeless, Refugees, Teaching/assisting (nursery, primary, secondary, mature, EFL) Unemployed, Wildlife, Work Camps – Seasonal, Young People.
Activities: Accountancy, Administration, Agriculture/Farming, Arts/Crafts, Building/Construction, Campaigning, Caring (general, day and residential), Catering, Community Work, Computers, Conservation Skills, Cooking, Counselling, Development Issues, DIY, Driving, First Aid, Forestry, Fundraising, Gardening/Horticulture, Group Work, International Aid, Library/Resource Centres, Manual Work, Marketing/Publicity, Music, Newsletter/Journalism, Outdoor Skills, Religion, Research, Scientific Work, Social Work, Sport, Summer Camps, Teaching, Technical Skills, Theatre/Drama, Training, Translating, Visiting/Befriending, Work Camps – Seasonal.
Costs: Varies according to the project.
Worldwide placements: Africa (Sierra Leone).

AFRICAN CONSERVATION EXPERIENCE

P. O. Box 9706
Solihull, West Midlands
B91 3FF UK
T: +44 (0) 970 241 5816
F: +44 (0) 870 241 5816
E: info@ConservationAfrica.net
W: www.ConservationAfrica.net
Contact: Lisa Hewston

African Conservation Experience aims: to give British people the opportunity to experience conservation in Southern Africa; to bring foreign income and information exchange for conservation in Southern Africa. Volunteers are given the opportunity for hands-on conservation work which may include research projects on endangered species, animal counts, game capture, game darting, wildlife veterinary work, wildlife rehabilitation, dolphin and whale research projects, educating local tribal children about conservation, removal of exotic vegetation, re-establishment of indigenous fauna and flora, watching and recording animal habits and movement, maintenance of game fences and roads, hiking trail construction and many other conservation related activities. It is hoped that a long-term relationship will continue between the reserve and the volunteer on research programmes, etc. in colleges, universities and UK conservation establishments.

African Conservation Experience is a member of The Year Out Group.

Number of projects: 16+ UK: 0
Starting months: January–December
Time required: 4–12 weeks
Age: 18–70
Causes: Animal Welfare, Archaeology, Children, Conservation, Environmental Causes, Teaching – Primary, Wildlife.
Activities: Agriculture/Farming, Arts/Crafts, Community Work, Conservation Skills, Manual Work, Outdoor Skills, Research, Scientific Work, Social Work, Teaching, Technical Skills, Training.
Placements: 250+
When to apply: As early as possible, all year.
Work alone/with others: Mostly in teams of up to six – sometimes alone with supervisor.
Qualifications: Driving licence and language ability preferable. Some conservation experience useful. It is essential that volunteers have enthusiasm for conservation.
No restrictions. Visas not normally necessary.
Equipment/clothing: Sleeping bag, day sack, mosquito net, water bottle, plain coloured clothing, good walking boots, binoculars useful. A full kit list is provided.
Health requirements: Volunteers must be fit and healthy.
Costs: £1795–£3900 depending on reserve, duration and timing + pocket money.
Benefits: The cost includes international flights, local transfers, food and accommodation. Staff accommodation which is a shared house with staff and other student volunteers.
Training: At the reserve.
Supervision: Work experience co-ordinator on each reserve.
Interviews: Open days held in Central England.
Worldwide placements: Africa (Botswana, South Africa, Zimbabwe).

AFRICAN CONSERVATION TRUST

P.O.Box 310
Link Hills
KwaZulu-Natal
3652 South Africa
T: +27 31 2016180
F: +27 31 2016180
E: info@projectafrica.com
W: www.projectafrica.com
Contact: Carl Grossmann

The mission of the African Conservation Trust is to provide a means for conservation projects to become self-funding, through active participation by the public. This gives ordinary people a chance to make a positive and real contribution to environmental conservation by funding and participating in the research effort as volunteers. The five projects currently being undertaken are: 'Caracal' (African Lynx)/ Brown Hyena Project in Botswana – A home range and prey use study using radio tracking on the Bushmen community owned Game Reserve, 'Dqae Qare', which is situated in the Kalahari Desert. 'Malawi Hippo Project' – Scientific study of the numbers and distribution patterns of the hippos in Lake Malawi. Working with communities to safeguard their crops and thus protect the last remaining pods of hippo. We have also begun an ecological study of the hippos of the Shire River in Liwonde National Park. 'Lake Malawi Hippo Expedition' – In April and October each year we conduct a full expedition to count and map the hippo population along the 800 kilometers of shoreline in a 6-meter semi-rigid inflatable boat. A true expedition not for the faint hearted. 'Malawi Reforestation Project' – The establishment of tree nurseries in the villages surrounding our research house. 'Research Centre Construction Project' – The construction of a permanent research base on the shore of Lake Malawi. We are unable to accept volunteers with an offending background. All projects are based in the southern section along the shores of Lake Malawi.

Number of projects: 5 **UK:** 0
Starting months: January–December
Time required: 2–52 weeks
Age: 18 plus – no upper limit
Causes: Conservation, Environmental Causes, Wildlife, Work Camps – Seasonal.
Activities: Agriculture/Farming, Building/ Construction, Conservation Skills, Cooking, Development Issues, Driving, Forestry, Research, Scientific Work, Teaching, Work Camps – Seasonal.
Placements: 120
When to apply: At least 3 months before start date.
Work alone/with others: With others.
Qualifications: No specific requirements – a driving licence and any other skills/qualifications are always welcome.
Equipment/clothing: Tent.
Health requirements: In good health – a medical questionnaire must be completed with application.
Costs: £500+, insurances, extra costs are for drinks and social and weekend excursions.
Benefits: All transport in-country covered, accommodation and food.
Training: Training is provided, any function that needs special training is given on site.
Supervision: We have a project manager that looks after all aspects of each project and the well-being of the volunteers.
Interviews: Volunteers complete a questionnaire and medical form.
Worldwide placements: Africa (Botswana, Malawi, South Africa).

AFRICAN VOLUNTEERS
P O Box 10222
Kampala
256 Uganda
T: 00 256 7769 1611
F: 00 256 4134 7797
E: a_volunteers@hotmail.com
Contact: Kironde Paul

African Volunteers was founded as a non-political, non-sectarian and non-profit-making organisation. Its membership is open to all over the age of 16, irrespective of nationality, religion, race, politics or educational qualification. We run two series of workcamps, summer and winter. The summer period starts in May and ends at the end of October and the winter workcamps run from mid-November to the end of January.

Number of projects: 10 **UK:** 0
Starting months: Jan, May, Jun, Jul, Aug, Sep, Oct, Nov, Dec
Time required: 3–6 weeks
Age: 18–70
Causes: AIDS/HIV, Animal Welfare, Archaeology, Architecture, Children, Disabled (learning and physical), Elderly People, Environmental Causes, Health Care/Medical, Heritage, Human Rights, Poor/Homeless, Refugees, Teaching/assisting (nursery, primary, secondary, mature, EFL) Wildlife, Work Camps – Seasonal, Young People.
Activities: Accountancy, Administration, Agriculture/Farming, Arts/Crafts, Building/Construction, Caring – General, Community Work, Computers, Counselling, Development Issues, First Aid, Forestry, Fundraising, Group Work, International Aid, Manual Work, Music, Outdoor Skills, Religion, Research, Social Work, Summer Camps, Teaching, Theatre/Drama, Training, Visiting/Befriending.
Placements: 100
When to apply: January, February or March.
Work alone/with others: With others.
Qualifications: No qualifications needed – English or French must be spoken.
Health requirements: Medical report is required.
Costs: US$300 registration fee.
Benefits: All travel and food costs are covered whilst in Uganda. We find and provide accommodation.
Training: Training is provided.
Supervision: Supervisors are involved.
Interviews: No interviews.
Charity number: 64193000UG
Worldwide placements: Africa (Uganda).

AFRICATRUST NETWORKS

Beaufort Chambers
Beaufort Street
Crickhowell
Powys NP8 1AA UK
T: 01873 812453
F: 01873 812453
E: wales@africatrust.gi
W: www.africatrust.gi
Contact: Mrs Sue Wintle

Africatrust Networks is an African NGO which organises residential visits to Ghana, West Africa for students either before or after their university studies. The visits include language tuition and volunteer work with disabled, orphaned and blind children and continues the earlier work of St David's (Africa) Trust. Students are encouraged to demonstrate their own team initiative in helping to develop projects with the donation funds which they will have raised. 📖

Number of projects: 6 **UK:** 0
Starting months: Jan, Sep
Time required: 14–28 weeks
Age: 18–25
Causes: Children, Disabled (learning and physical), Health Care/Medical, Teaching/assisting (nursery, primary, EFL),
Activities: Building/Construction, Caring – Residential, Community Work, Development Issues, Teaching.
Placements: 20
When to apply: At least 6 months before.
Work alone/with others: With others.
Qualifications: Preferably A levels. Swim 100m. Restrictions are only that passports must be acceptable for visa purposes in host countries.
Health requirements: Good health for insurance requirements. Advice provided on health protection.
Costs: £3250 for 2003. Reg. fee £30.
Benefits: The cost includes return air travel, UK pre-departure briefing, Fante/Twi language lessons, 2 week in country induction course, board and lodging and incountry visits/transport. 2 or 3 to a bedroom, mosquito-protection, fans but little air-conditioning. Some accommodation is with families well known to Dr. Kwansah-Filson. Concrete houses in with 'European' bathrooms with hot (sometimes) and cold running water, indoor lavatories.
Training: In UK: 6 months reading material, pre-departure lectures by past volunteers, country experts and ATN officials. **In country:** 2 weeks residential training covering language, culture etc.
Supervision: The full-time in country supervision by Dr Kwansah-Filson, Director of Africatrust Networks.
Interviews: Interviews take place in London and, possibly, South Wales.

Charity number: 90 (Gib.)
Worldwide placements: Africa (Ghana).

AFS INTERNATIONAL YOUTH DEVELOPMENT

Leeming House
Vicar Lane
Leeds W. Yorkshire
LS2 7JF UK
T: +44 (0) 113 242 6136
F: +44 (0) 113 243 0631
E: info-unitedkingdom@afs.org
W: www.afsuk.org
Contact: Sending Co-ordinator

Voluntary work opportunities in Latin America, Thailand, Ghana and South Africa. More than just travel, you can spend six months in Latin America and South Africa living with a volunteer host family, and working alongside local people on community social projects, dealing with isues such as health, education, the environment, community development and working with underprivileged children and people with disabilities. AFS is an international, voluntary, nongovernmental, nonprofit organisation that provides intercultural learning opportunities to help people develop the knowledge, skills and understanding needed to create a more just and peaceful world. AFS has been running programmes since 1947 and is the only organisation of its kind to receive a citation from the UN in recognition of its work for world youth. AFS International Youth Development is the UK partner in the international AFS network of 50 different countries worldwide. Language training and fundraising support provided. ♿ 📖

Number of projects: 60+ **UK:** 0
Starting months: Jan, Feb, Jul, Aug
Time required: 20–25 weeks
Age: 18–29
Causes: Addicts/Ex-Addicts, AIDS/HIV, Children, Disabled (learning and physical), Elderly People, Environmental Causes, Health Care/Medical, Human Rights, Inner City Problems, Poor/Homeless, Teaching/assisting (EFL), Young People.
Activities: Caring – General, Community Work, Development Issues, Group Work, Outdoor Skills, Social Work, Teaching, Theatre/Drama, Training.
Placements: 60+
When to apply: All year but at least 4 months before departure.
Work alone/with others: With others.
Qualifications: Participants must be resident in the UK.
Health requirements: Good health essential.
Costs: £2,950.

Benefits: Volunteers stay with host families or on residential projects with other volunteers.
Training: Selection, language, materials, weekend orientation.
Supervision: Local contact and office support.
Interviews: Prospective volunteers are interviewed in Manchester, Leeds or London.
Worldwide placements: Africa (Ghana, South Africa); Central America (Costa Rica, Guatemala, Honduras, Mexico, Panama); South America (Brazil, Ecuador, Paraguay, Peru, Venezuela); Asia (Thailand).

AGAPE CENTRO ECUMENICO

Segreteria
10060 Prali
Torino
Italy
T: 00 390 121 80 75 14
F: 00 390 121 80 76 90
E: campolavoro@agapecentroecumenico.org
W: www.agapecentroecumenico.org
Contact: Philipp Baumgarter

Agape Centro Ecumenico is an international ecumenical community centre in a remote part of the Italian Alps, used for national and international conferences, study camps, courses and other meetings on ecological, peace, Third World, political, cultural, theological, gays' and women's issues. An international service group made up of volunteers works alongside the resident community during the summer months. The work is varied weekly and can include kitchen duties, housework, cleaning, working in the coffee bar, laundry, baby sitting, maintenance, construction or repair work. There are opportunities for volunteers to take part in the conferences. Applicants should be willing to make a contribution to the collective life of the community. 36 hour, six days per week. 3–8 weeks, June-September. Volunteers are sometimes taken on outside the summer period. Situated 1600m high in the Alps.

Number of Projects: 1 **UK:** 0
Starting Months: Mar, Apr, Jun, Jul, Aug
Time required: 3–8 weeks
Age: 18–30
Causes: Work Camps – Seasonal.
Activities: Group Work, Manual Work, Religion, Work Camps – Seasonal.
Placements: 55
When to apply: March or sooner.
Work alone/with others: With others.
Qualifications: Basic Italian an advantage.
Health requirements: Anti-tetanus vaccination.
Costs: Travel expenses and pocket money.
Benefits: Board and lodging.
Worldwide placements: Europe (Italy).

AGE CONCERN ENGLAND (THE NATIONAL COUNCIL ON AGEING)

Astral House
1268 London Road
London
SW16 4ER UK
T: +44 (0) 208 679 8000
F: +44 (0) 208 679 6069
E: volunteering@ace.org.uk
W: www.ace.org.uk
Contact: Helen Tovey

Age Concern England is the national headquarters for over 1,400 local Age Concern groups in the UK. Each group has slightly differing policies and guidelines for volunteers. Contact your local county or large town group by telephone, available from your local telephone directory. Contact Age Concern England for a leaflet on volunteering. 🗗 🖹

Number of projects UK: 1400
Starting months: January–December
Time required: 1–52 weeks
Age: 16 plus – no upper limit
Causes: Elderly People.
Activities: Administration, Caring (general and day), Counselling, Driving, Fundraising, Research, Social Work, Training, Visiting/ Befriending.
When to apply: All year.
Work alone/with others: both.
Qualifications: References checked before volunteer can start work.
Health requirements: Nil.
Costs: Nil.
Benefits: Out of pocket expenses.
Charity number: 261794
UK placements: England (throughout); Wales (throughout).

AGE-LINK

9 Narborough Close
Ickenham
Middlesex UB10 8TN UK
T: +44 (0) 1895 676689
Contact: Mr Balraj

Age-Link needs volunteers in the Greater London area to help the elderly. A typical day would involve collecting an elderly person from their home, driving them to another family where they would have tea and be entertained, and then driving them home again.

Number of projects: 1 **UK:** 1
Starting months: January–December
Time required: 1–52 weeks
Age: 16 plus – no upper limit
Causes: Elderly People.
Activities: Driving, Fundraising, Visiting/ Befriending.

When to apply: All year.
Work alone/with others: Both.
Qualifications: Drivers especially needed.
Health requirements: Nil.
Costs: Nil.
UK placements: England (London).

AGENCY FOR VOLUNTEER SERVICE (AVS) – HONG KONG

15 Hennessy Road
Wanchai
Hong Kong
T: 852 252 73825
F: 852 286 62721
E: avs@avs.org.hk
W: www.avs.org.hk
Contact: Flora Chung Woon-fan

Agency for Volunteer Service (AVS) promotes and has information about volunteering in Hong Kong. It may well be able to put volunteers in touch with organisations which are not yet listed on the WorldWide Volunteering database. It is dedicated to playing a pro-active and pivotal role in building a civil society and caring community through the promotion and devlopment of sustainable volunteerism. Depends on different volunteer jobs.

Number of projects: 1 UK: 0
Starting months: January–December
Time required: 1–52 weeks (plus)
Age: 15 plus – no upper limit
Causes: Addicts/Ex-Addicts, AIDS/HIV, Animal Welfare, Archaeology, Architecture, Children, Conservation, Disabled (learning and physical), Elderly People, Environmental Causes, Health Care/Medical, Heritage, Holidays for Disabled, Human Rights, Inner City Problems, Offenders/ Ex-Offenders, Poor/Homeless, Refugees, Teaching/assisting (nursery, primary, secondary, mature, EFL) Unemployed, Wildlife, Work Camps – Seasonal, Young People.
Activities: Accountancy, Administration, Agriculture/Farming, Arts/Crafts, Building/ Construction, Campaigning, Caring (general, day and residential), Catering, Community Work, Computers, Conservation Skills, Cooking, Counselling, Development Issues, DIY, Driving, First Aid, Forestry, Fundraising, Gardening/Horticulture, Group Work, International Aid, Library/Resource Centres, Manual Work, Marketing/Publicity, Music, Newsletter/Journalism, Outdoor Skills, Religion, Research, Scientific Work, Social Work, Sport, Summer Camps, Teaching, Technical Skills, Theatre/Drama, Training, Translating, Visiting/Befriending, Work Camps – Seasonal.
When to apply: Anytime, placement is depending on availability and suitability of volunteer jobs.
Work alone/with others: Depends on different volunteer jobs.

Qualifications: Depends on different volunteer jobs. All accepted, preferably those who are fluent in reading Chinese and speaking Cantonese, with knowledge in Chinese word and excel processing, understanding in Chinese culture.
Equipment/clothing: Depends on different volunteer jobs.
Health requirements: Depends on different volunteer jobs.
Costs: Varies according to the project.
Benefits: Varies according to the project.
Training: Depends on different volunteer jobs.
Supervision: By the project leaders.
Interviews: Depends on different volunteer jobs.
Worldwide placements: Asia (Hong Kong).

AID TO RUSSIA AND THE REPUBLICS – ARRC

PO Box 200
Bromley Kent
BR1 1QF UK
T: +44 (0) 20 8460 6046
F: +44 (0) 20 8466 1244
E: info@arrc.org.uk
W: www.arrc.org.uk
Contact: Glen Hanna

Aid to Russia and the Republics (ARRC) was established in 1973 to help persecuted Christians in the USSR, but has evolved to meet current needs. We now support our Christian partners' humanitarian initiatives with street children and orphans, the elderly, sick and disabled, war and disaster victims, self-sustaining farms and businesses in the former Soviet Union. We also operate a child sponsorship scheme. Volunteers are essential to the running of our Bromley office and provide valuable assistance to our project partners in the former Soviet Union. In addition, overseas volunteers' feedback is useful for ongoing projects and evaluation, and for fundraising purposes. May take offenders depending on individuals' circumstances. 🖺

Number of projects: 8 UK: 1
Starting months: January–December
Time required: 2–52 weeks
Age: 18–65
Causes: Addicts/Ex-Addicts, Children, Disabled (learning and physical), Health Care/Medical, Inner City Problems, Offenders/Ex-Offenders, Teaching (EFL), Young People.
Activities: Administration, Agriculture/Farming, Caring (general and day), Community Work, Computers, Cooking, Development Issues, International Aid, Manual Work, Music, Newsletter/Journalism, Outdoor Skills, Religion, Summer Camps, Teaching, Theatre/Drama, Visiting/Befriending.
Placements: c.11
When to apply: Two months before wishing to start.

Work alone/with others: Sometimes with others.
Qualifications: Some projects require Russian language ability. Other skills – medical, children, practical can be useful.
Health requirements: Volunteers must declare any health problems before a placement. A doctor's note may be required.
Costs: ARRC Admin costs £50. Travel costs – flights £400–£750. Visa fees £25–£60. Volunteers are required to cover all costs.
Training: No formal training.
Supervision: Volunteers are placed with trusted project partners – regular phone calls/e-mail contact with ARRC office.
Interviews: At Bromley office.
Worldwide placements: Asia (Uzbekistan); Europe (Armenia, Azerbaijan, Belarus, Moldova, Russia, Ukraine, Yugoslavia).
UK placements: England (Kent).

AKHA HERITAGE FOUNDATION, THE

Postal Restant
Maesai
Chiangrai 57130 Thailand
T: 66 1 884 8111
E: akha@akha.org
W: www.akha.org
Contact: Matthew McDaniel

The Akha Heritage Foundation is set up to protect and preserve the choices of the Akha community, strengthen human rights, economics, sustainable agriculture and the cultural traditions of the Akha people. We are unable to place volunteers with an offending background. ⑤ 目

Number of projects: 1 **UK:** 0
Starting months: January–December
Time required: 2–52 weeks
Age: 16 plus – no upper limit
Causes: Children, Conservation, Elderly People, Environmental Causes, Health Care/Medical, Heritage, Human Rights, Offenders/Ex-Offenders, Poor/Homeless, Refugees, Teaching/assisting (primary, secondary, mature), Wildlife, Work Camps – Seasonal, Young People.
Activities: Administration, Agriculture/Farming, Building/Construction, Campaigning, Caring – General, Community Work, Computers, Cooking, Development Issues, First Aid, Forestry, Fundraising, International Aid, Marketing/Publicity, Newsletter/Journalism, Research, Social Work, Training, Work Camps – Seasonal.
Placements: 20+
When to apply: Any time – as soon as possible.
Work alone/with others: Both.
Qualifications: No restrictions but must be able to speak English.

Equipment/clothing: Long sleeved clothes, hat, jacket, strong mountain boots, strong alternative shoes, camera, video, pen, paper, insect repellent.
Health requirements: No diseases allowed as epidemic would be impossible to control in the close contact communitites of the hill tribe villages. This includes HIV, any form of hepatitis. Diabetes would be hard to care for as medical facilities are only in large cities.
Costs: $450 per two week project (max. one month) covers all room, food and travel. $500 fee for longer project working in the Akha villages with wells, books and schools.
Benefits: Food and lodging are provided, travel within project supplied.
Training: Training in a broad range of skills, for projects in indigenous communities.
Supervision: All volunteers work directly with AHF staff. No volunteers work alone at any time.
Interviews: Interviews are done via e-mail.
Worldwide placements: Asia (Thailand).

AKTION SÜHNEZEICHEN FRIEDENSDIENSTE E.V.

Augustr. 80
10117 Berlin
Germany
T: 00 49 30 28395 184
F: 00 49 30 28395 135
E: asf@asf-ev.de
W: www.asf-ev.de
Contact: Mrs. Jutta Weduwen

Aktion Sühnezeichen Friedensdienste (ASF) was founded in 1958 by women and men who had been active in the Protestant resistance to the Nazi Regime in Germany. Presently about 150 ASF long-term volunteers (12–18 months) and about 300 ASF short-term volunteers (2–4 weeks) are working in many countries around the world. (Long-term UK volunteers are only eligible to work in the UK and Germany.) The long-term volunteers, mostly young people aged 18–27, work in various projects including (a) educational work: together with survivors of the holocaust, at memorial centres of former concentration camps, in institutes and museums; as well as educational work in the field of human rights and anti-racism, (b) work with marginalised groups: among others with refugees, homeless persons, with elderly (mostly holocaust survivors) and disabled persons, drug addicts, persons who are mentally ill, as well as in neighbourhood centres situated in poor urban areas. The short-term volunteers are active in international groups in more than 25 summer camps working in social facilities, on Jewish cemeteries and on memorial sites of former concentration camps. Aktion Sühnezeichen Friedensdienste wants to encourage young people to overcome the feeling of powerlessness, as well as indifference and complacency, in order to contribute to a more just and peaceful world. Alternative address: Action Reconciliaton Service for Peace (ARSP), 7 Priory Row, Coventry CV1 5ES. Telephone (+44) 02476 222487. Fax (+44) 02476 63 14 48. **Contact:** Mrs. Anne Katrin Scheffbuch. 🖳 📄

Number of projects: 155 **UK:** 14 long term 2 short term
Starting months: Mar, Jun, Jul, Sep
Time required: 4–52 weeks
Age: 18 plus – no upper limit
Causes: Children, Disabled (learning), Elderly People, Health Care/Medical, Human Rights, Poor/Homeless, Refugees, Work Camps – Seasonal.
Activities: Administration, Caring (general and day), Community Work, Counselling, Development Issues, Library/Resource Centres, Research, Summer Camps, Work Camps – Seasonal.
Placements: 160
When to apply: Short term programme 2–3 weeks, starts June – August.
Long term programme, 52 weeks start September and March.
Work alone/with others: It depends on the project. During summer camps work is always performed in a group of young volunteers.
Qualifications: We expect of our volunteers a certain amount of language skills (varying with countries/projects); experience in local voluntary social or political work and above all a great deal of motivation and energy to work with ASF and in the projects. Volunteers accepted from Poland, Czech Republic, Russia, Belarus, USA, Israel, Norway, Netherlands, Begium, France and Great Britain.
Health requirements: Nil.
Costs: Before starting, each volunteer must find a financial support group to pay £8 per month.
Benefits: Travel, health insurance, board and lodging, pocket money. Depending on the project volunteers are accomodated in the project or they have a room in a flat shared with other volunteers.
Training: Before starting work in a project volunteers must participate in on arrival training organised by ASF. A midterm training and follow up is also offered to the volunteers by ASF. This does not apply to summer camps.
Supervision: No organised supervision but there is a regular meeting with a responsible contact person in the project to discuss problems and requirements.
Interviews: UK volunteers are interviewed in Coventry. For summer camps there is no personnel interview.
Worldwide placements: Europe (Czech Republic, France, Germany, Italy, Latvia, Lithuania, Netherlands, Poland, Russia).

UK placements: England (Hampshire, London, West Midlands).

ALPES DE LUMIERE

Prieure de Salagon
Mane
04300 France
T: 00 33 492 75 70 50 or 75 70 54
F: 00 33 92 75 70 51
Contact: Laurence Michel

The Association Alpes de Lumiere organises several camps around Provence dedicated to the restoration of historic buildings and the development of historic sites. These sites become recreational and cultural centres. Previous offenders are not accepted. Provence, Southern France. 📄

Number of projects: 12 **UK:** 0
Starting months: Jun, Jul, Aug, Sep
Time required: 3–52 weeks
Age: 18 plus – no upper limit
Causes: Architecture, Conservation, Environmental Causes, Heritage, Work Camps – Seasonal.
Activities: Building/Construction, Conservation Skills, Cooking, Manual Work, Summer Camps, Work Camps – Seasonal.
Placements: 160
When to apply: As early as possible.
Work alone/with others: With others (12).
Qualifications: Nil except ability to speak French or English and work under the sun.
Equipment/clothing: Sleeping bag, good shoes, old clothes (T-shirts and shorts), sun cream, anti-mosquito lotion.
Health requirements: No allergies.
Costs: Approx. €91.5 per month + pocket money + travel.
Benefits: Food, basic accommodation, trip around the area, free entry to museums and concerts.
Interviews: Applicants are not interviewed.
Worldwide placements: Europe (France).

AMERICAN FARM SCHOOL – GREEK SUMMER PROGRAM

1133 Broadway @ 26th Street
New York, NY 10010
USA
T: 00 1 212 463 8434
F: 00 1 212 463 8208
E: nyoffice@amerfarm.org
W: www.afs.edu.gr/
Contact: Ms Mary-Vicki Papaioannou

American Farm School – Greek Summer Program is a five week summer work and travel program for high-school sophomores, juniors and seniors based at the American Farm School in Thessaloniki, Greece. Every year since 1970 the

Farm School has brought 30–35 teenagers from around the US and Europe to Greece to be a part of a once in a lifetime experience living in and travelling through one of the most ancient cultures on earth. The heart of the program is a work project in a small village in northern Greece. Participants live with village families while they complete a much needed community improvement, such as a road or a foundation for a building. Outside of the time at the village, the group travels around the country to see the historical sights of Greece such as the monasteries of Meteora, the Oracle of Delphi and the Acropolis in Athens. In addition there are excursions to the vineyards at Porto Carras, the quiet fishing town of Nafplion, the island of Skiathos, and frequent stops at local beaches. The trip culminates with a two-day climb to the peak of Mount Olympus, home of the Greek gods. If you are interested in being a part of Greek Summer, please contact Ms Mary-Vicki Papaioannou. Join us for a volunteer experience that will change your life.

Reference on request
Number of projects: 1 UK: 0
Starting months: Jun
Time required: 5–6 weeks
Age: 15–18
Causes: Archaeology, Poor/Homeless, Refugees.
Activities: Building/Construction, Manual Work.
Placements: 40
When to apply: All year.
Work alone/with others: With others.
Equipment/clothing: Work clothes, leather work gloves.
Health requirements: Nil.
Costs: Application fee $500, Program fee $2,600 + return airfare to Greece.
Benefits: The cost covers all food, lodging and travel within Greece.
Training: Full construction, project, language and cultural training is provided during orientation.
Supervision: There is a Program Director, three assistant directors and four counsellors throughout the trip.
Interviews: Volunteers are interviewed either locally or by telephone.
Worldwide placements: Europe (Greece).

AMERICAN FARM SCHOOL – SUMMER INTERNATIONAL INTERNSHIP PROGRAM

1133 Broadway
New York, NY 10010
USA
T: 00 1 212 463 8433
F: 00 1 212 463 8208
E: nyoffice@amerfarm.org
Contact: The Program Coordinator

Every summer the American Farm School organises an international group to help man the agricultural and maintenance programs at the school in Greece when regular staff and students are on vacation. The work involves a 35 hour week. Other activities include a climb up Mount Olympus, trips into Thessaloniki and the islands, as well as a short stay with a family in a rural village.

Number of projects: 1 UK: 0
Starting months: Jun, Jul
Time required: 1–52 weeks
Age: 18–25
Causes: Animal Welfare.
Activities: Agriculture/Farming, Manual Work.
Placements: 30
When to apply: Any time before 30th April.
Work alone/with others: With others.
Qualifications: College enrolment.
Equipment/clothing: Everyday warm weather work clothes.
Health requirements: None.
Costs: Fare to Thessaloniki.
Benefits: Accommodation, meals and a small allowance. Participants use all available facilities at the school's campus. Dormitories, dining hall, laundry etc.
Training: Complete job and farm training provided on the site.
Supervision: Supervised by the Program Director and various farm managers.
Interviews: We do not interview applicants.
Worldwide placements: Europe (Greece).

AMERICAN HIKING SOCIETY'S VOLUNTEER VACATIONS

PO Box 20160
Washington
DC 20041-2160 USA
T: 00 1 301 565 6704
F: 00 1 301 565 6714
E: info@americanhiking.org
W: www.americanhiking.org
Contact: Shirley Hearn

For more than 20 years, American Hiking Society's Volunteer Vacations has been sending hundreds of volunteers each year into America's most special places to revitalise trails. Over the years, thousands of vacationers rake, shovel, trim, lop and chop hundreds of trail miles that, without these crews, would be unsafe for foot travel. Into its third decade of caring for America's trails, AHS Volunteer Vacations have sent more than 90 trail volunteer teams into America's national parks, forests and rangelands in 2002. Participants will restore deteriorating trails and build new ones while enjoying unique one or two week vacations. More than a programme that rehabilitates trails, AHS Volunteer Vacations is fostering public land stewardship and giving volunteers the opportunity to give back to the trails they love, and to have a great time doing it. Volunteers with an offending background are not accepted, unless supervision is provided. &

Number of projects: 90 UK: 0
Starting months: January–December
Time required: 1–52 weeks
Age: 18–70
Causes: Conservation, Environmental Causes, Work Camps – Seasonal.
Activities: Building/Construction, Conservation Skills, Forestry, Group Work, Manual Work, Outdoor Skills, Work Camps – Seasonal.
Placements: 700
When to apply: All year.
Work alone/with others: With others.
Qualifications: Nil, but international driving licence useful.
Equipment/clothing: list provided: must have backpack, sleeping bag and tent.
Health requirements: Able to hike at least 5 miles a day.
Costs: Travel and all expenses.
Benefits: Occasionally accomodation – usually volunteers camp with own equipment. Food usually provided.
Training: None. Trail maintenance experience is helpful.
Supervision: Supervised by federal land management agency ranger.
Interviews: Applicants are not interviewed.
Worldwide placements: North America: (USA).

AMERICAN JEWISH SOCIETY FOR SERVICE

15E 26th Street
New York
NY 10010 USA
T: 00 1 212 683 6178
E: info@ajss.org
W: www.ajss.org
Contact: Henry Kohn

The American Jewish Society conducts voluntary work service camps for teenagers. Volunteers are needed to work as counsellors and to help with the camps' construction work.

Number of projects: 1 UK: 0
Starting months: July
Time required: 6–7 weeks
Age: 16–18
Causes: Work Camps – Seasonal.
Activities: Building/Construction, Counselling, Manual Work, Work Camps – Seasonal.
Placements: 48
When to apply: January – May
Work alone/with others: With others.
Qualifications: Readiness to work 8 hours, 5 days/week for six weeks.
Health requirements: Good health required.

Costs: $2,500 plus pocket money and travel costs.
Benefits: Accommodation.
Training: None required.
Supervision: One to four in ratio of staff to campers.
Interviews: Interviews take place in New York City or by telephone.
Worldwide placements: North America (USA).

AMERISPAN UNLIMITED

117 South 17th Street
Suite 1401
Philadelphia
PA 19103 USA
T: 00 1 215 751 1100
F: 00 1 215 751 1986
E: info@amerispan.com
W: www.amerispan.com
Contact: Elizabeth Gregory

AmeriSpan is a company focusing on Latin America. Each year we send about 3,000 participants overseas to learn Spanish or Portuguese. Of our annual participants, almost 10% also participate in the Volunteer and Internship programme. This programme is designed to provide a first-hand experience in a Latin American country through language immersion course, homestay and volunteer/internship work in the participant's specific area of interest. Participants take four weeks of language training courses in the target language in country during the weeks prior to the start of their volunteer work. The positions available are a cooperative effort between AmeriSpan, our partner language school in the country, and the organisation itself. There are positions available in education, social work, environmental work, business, healthcare and a wide variety of other fields. & 🗎

Number of projects: 120 UK: 0
Starting months: January–December
Time required: 4–26 weeks
Age: 21–99
Causes: Children, Disabled (learning and physical), Elderly People, Environmental Causes, Health Care/Medical, Poor/Homeless, Teaching/assisting (primary, EFL).
Activities: Administration, Caring – Day, Community Work, Library/Resource Centres, Outdoor Skills, Scientific Work, Social Work, Teaching, Translating.
Placements: 200–300
When to apply: At least two months in advance.
Work alone/with others: Depends on location and position.
Qualifications: Knowledge of Spanish/Portuguese. (All positions have different requirement levels.)
Equipment/clothing: Depends on location.

Only remote locations require mosquito netting, special clothes etc. Some other positions in offices need professional dress.
Health requirements: Nil.
Costs: $350 Application and placement fee + lodging (which may or may not be included – about $75–$150 per week + language classes if needed ($1500)).
Benefits: Room and board are provided for some positions, but not all.
Training: Pre-departure preparation information, on-site orientation and training.
Supervision: Some organisations are well supervised while others lack resources for adequate supervision.
Interviews: Telephone interviews after receipt of application.
Worldwide placements: Central America (Costa Rica, Guatemala, Mexico); South America (Bolivia, Brazil, Chile, Ecuador, Peru).

AMITY READING

61 Cedar Road
Sturry
Canterbury
Kent CT2 0JG UK
T: 01227 711012
F: 01227 719364
E: philipglascoe@aol.com
W: www.amity.org, uk
Contact: Gladys Glascoe

Amity exists to help adults with special difficulties in literacy. We recruit, train and support volunteers who teach individually, in a community venue such as a library, with a club ethos and featuring social support. Gladys Glascoe pioneered this approach at the Blackfriars Settlement in 1970 and, with Philip Glascoe, founded Rathbone Reading Clubs in 1974. In 1978 they became a registered charity, Amity Reading Clubs. Our overall aim is to maintain a model of the club approach and make it available as a resource. In recent years we have provided the clubs with computers with the assistance of a grant of £22,000 from the Lottery Committee. At one time we had 20 clubs and no problem finding volunteers. Now there are countless calls for the services of volunteers and we need to raise our profile in order to make our needs known. The work is valuable, sociable and satisfying. The secretary to our management committee, who recently retired due to ill health, had been with us for twenty years. Other volunteers have been with us for several years. Volunteers with an offending background may be accepted – each case is decided on upon its merits. Volunteers are required to provide two references on their application form.

Number of projects UK: 3
Starting months: January–December
Time required: 52 weeks (plus)
Age: 18–75
Causes: Disabled (learning), Teaching/assisting.
Activities: Teaching.
Placements: 20–50
When to apply: Any time.
Work alone/with others: Work with others.
Qualifications: Ability to read and to get on with people.
Health requirements: No restrictions.
Costs: Fares if travel involved.
Benefits: Satisfactory service will lead to testimonial to use in educational or vocational applications.
Training: Initial training, ongoing tutorial support, periodic seminars. Support available on request at any time.
Supervision: Professional supervision (supervision tutors) available at all times during club sessions.
Charity number: 276011
UK placements: England (London).

Rebuilding In Bosnia

Not all volunteering placements go according to plan and many are definitely not a bed of roses – ask Neil Patterson. Neil, 24, wanted a break after two and a half years as a quantity surveyor before developing his career and changing jobs. After contacting WorldWide Volunteering, Neil spent six weeks working for the charity Action for People in Conflict (AfPiC) in Bosnia. The mission was to rebuild the lives of individuals and communities damaged by conflict. Neil's skills were certainly used to the utmost as he ended up leading the work camp and completely restructuring the organisation. Although it was a tough six weeks, Neil said that he had gained an enormous amount of confidence and had been able to contribute much more than he had ever imagined.

AMIZADE

920 William Pitt Union
Pittsburgh
PA15260 USA
T: 00 1 888 973 4443
F: 00 1 412 648 1492
E: Volunteer@amizade.org
W: http://amizade.org
Contact: Michael Sandy

Amizade encourages intercultural exploration and understanding through community driven service learning courses and volunteer programmes. In communities on five continents, over 1,000 Amizade volunteers have co-operated with community members to complete sustainable, community-identified projects that offer educational and recreational opportunities. Amizade volunteers have constructed an orphanage that houses 40 children in Bolivia, built a vocational training centre for street children in the Brazilian Amazon, and completed historical restoration and environmental preservation in the Greater Yellowstone area. Volunteers do not need any special skills, just a willingness to help. Current opportunities exist in Australia, Bolivia, Brazil, Nepal, the USA, and in several other communities around the world. Amizade offers pre-scheduled programmes for individuals and customised programmes for groups. Additionally, through a partnership with the University of Pittsburgh, the Amizade Global Service Learning centre facilitates courses that combine intercultural service and academic coursework for college credit. Volunteer programme fees range from US $475 to US $1895. The programme fee includes room and board, transportation during the programme, recreational, cultural, and educational activities, Amizade staff, and a donation to the community.

Number of projects: 7 **UK:** 0
Starting months: January–December
Time required: 1–4 weeks
Age: 14 plus – no upper limit
Causes: Animal Welfare, Architecture, Children, Conservation, Disabled (learning and physical), Elderly People, Environmental Causes, Heritage, Poor/Homeless, Teaching/assisting, Unemployed, Wildlife, Young People.
Activities: Building/Construction, Community Work, Conservation Skills, Forestry, Gardening/Horticulture, Manual Work, Sport, Visiting/Befriending.
Placements: 300
When to apply: At least 4 months before programme start date.
Work alone/with others: We offer volunteering in a group setting, working with other volunteers from around the world, as well as volunteers from the local regions.

Equipment/clothing: Varies with the programme site.
Health requirements: Volunteers are required to complete an Amizade medical form and must have had a physical examination in the previous 12 months.
Costs: Fees vary with each programme ranging from US $475 to $1,895. Excludes flight costs.
Benefits: Fees include board and lodging, project materials and costs, recreational and cultural activities, some on-site transportation, an Amizade staff contact and other administrative fees.
Training: Volunteers are sent a volunteer packet to introduce them to the region and the project in which they will participate.
Supervision: Local masons and carpenters as well as an Amizade programme director supervise the volunteers on every aspect of the programme.
Interviews: None.
Worldwide placements: North America: (USA); South America (Bolivia, Brazil); Asia (Nepal); Australasia (Australia).

AMNESTY INTERNATIONAL

99–119 Rosebery Avenue
London
EC1R 4RE UK
T: +44 (0) 207 814 6253
F: +44 (0) 207 833 1510
E: vdupont@amnesty.org.uk
W: www.amnesty.org.uk
Contact: Veronique Dupont

Amnesty International is an independent worldwide movement working for the release of prisoners of conscience; seeking fair and prompt trials for political prisoners; and working towards the end of torture and executions throughout the world. The UK section of Amnesty International has over 130,000 members and approximately 330 local groups throughout the UK. The section office is based in London and has a staff of 65 and many full-time and part-time volunteers. It is divided into six departments: administration and finance, campaigns, communications, marketing, deputy directorate and the directorate. Volunteers are allocated to a team and assist with clerical and administrative duties, such as word processing, filing, photocopying, sending faxes, helping with mailings and occasional special projects. Where a volunteer works depends upon a match between a current vacancy and the skills and experience of the volunteer. &

Number of projects UK: 100+
Starting months: January–December
Time required: 12–52 weeks (plus)
Age: 16–85
Causes: Human Rights.

Activities: Accountancy, Administration, Campaigning, Computers, Fundraising, Marketing/Publicity.
Placements: 66
When to apply: A month before starting.
Work alone/with others: Both.
Qualifications: Computer, communication skills, campaigning/fundraising experience + clerical, administrative skills, press/media experience all useful but not essential. No restrictions but volunteers from outside the UK need to have a visa allowing them to do voluntary work.
Health requirements: Nil.
Costs: Nil.
Benefits: £3.50 luncheon vouchers per day + travel costs up to £7.50 per day reimbursed.
Training: None.
Supervision: All volunteers work closely with a member of staff.
UK placements: England (London); Scotland (Edinburgh, Lothian – East, Lothian – West); Northern Ireland (Belfast City).

ANGAIA CAMPHILL DO BRASIL

36100 Juiz de Fora (Minas Gerais)
Caixa Postal 1122
Brazil
Contact: The Director

Angaia Camphill Do Brasil is part of the worldwide Camphill movement. Camphill Communities are now found all over the world and one of their main tasks is to live with and care for people with mental disabilities in a social therapeutic way which includes daily life, work, cultural activities and religious life as well as many other aspects of life.

Number of projects: 1 **UK:** 0
Starting months: January–December
Time required: 4–52 weeks
Age: 18–65
Causes: Disabled (learning and physical)
Activities: Agriculture/Farming, Arts/Crafts, Caring – Residential, Gardening/Horticulture, Manual Work, Outdoor Skills.
When to apply: All year.
Work alone/with others: With others.
Health requirements: General good health.
Costs: Travel to Brasil.
Benefits: Board and lodging.
Worldwide placements: South America (Brazil).

ANGLO-POLISH ACADEMIC ASSOCIATION [APASS]

93 Victoria Road
Leeds
LS6 1DR UK
T: 0113 275 8121
Contact: The Honorary Secretary

Anglo-Polish Academic Association (APASS) is a self-supporting fraternity of students, graduates, teachers and persons willing to teach English in Poland. The pupils are in groups of 8–10 and are Polish grammar school teenagers of roughly the same age and ability. ▨

Number of projects: 1 **UK:** 0
Starting months: June
Time required: 4–52 weeks
Age: 18–40
Causes: Teaching/assisting (secondary, mature, EFL).
Activities: Teaching.
When to apply: March-June. Send a large stamped addressed envelope and a postal order for £3.00 GBP.
Work alone/with others: Work with others.
Qualifications: Good spoken and written English.
Equipment/clothing: Educational aids – APASS will notify.
Health requirements: Statement from doctor required.
Costs: Travel costs, membership or registration fees = approximately £120.
Benefits: Assisted travel. Free board and lodging, one week tour of Poland free.
Supervision: Senior Polish teachers and leaders.
Interviews: By phone.
Worldwide placements: Europe (Poland).

ANNEE DIACONALE

SPJ
Rue du Champ de Mars 5
1050 Bruxelles
Belgium
T: 00 32 2 510 61 61
F: 00 32 2 510 61 64
E: spjad@skynet.be
Contact: Petra Rathmann or Diane Dumont

Annee Diaconale is the Belgian branch of the European Diaconal Year network which consists of a number of national Christian-based volunteering schemes. (The British branch is Time For God.) They share common standards, and a commitment to the personal development of the volunteer through this form of work. A few inner city projects. Most are in the country, so quite isolated. All projects are in the French-speaking part of Belgium.

Number of projects: 1 **UK:** 0
Starting months: Sep
Time required: 42–52 weeks
Age: 18–25
Causes: Addicts/Ex-Addicts, AIDS/HIV, Children, Disabled (learning and physical), Elderly People, Young People.
Activities: Caring (general, residential).
Placements: 20

When to apply: January/February and March.
Work alone/with others: With others generally. In some cases the volunteer is alone but there is always a support team on the project.
Qualifications: Some French, motivation to work in a social context and to live and work in a group.
Health requirements: General good health.
Costs: Travel to Belgium, health insurance and administration costs.
Benefits: Pocket money €160 per month. Accommodation provided on the project.
Training: Pre-departure training by our partner organisation plus 20 days of seminar throughout the year.
Supervision: Each branch offers support to the volunteers through both personal supervision and regular residential conferences or seminars.
Interviews: Contact with the volunteers by phone or e-mail. Our partners in other countries will interview for us.
Worldwide placements: Europe (Belgium).

ANNEE DIACONALE – STRASBOURG

8 quai Finkwiller
Strasbourg
F-67000 France
T: 00 33 388 35 46 76
F: 00 33 388 25 19 57
E: anneediaco@anneediaconale.com
W: www.anneediaconale.com
Contact: Claudie Harel

L'Annee Diaconale is the French branch of the European Diaconal Year Network which consists of a number of national Christian-based volunteering schemes. (The British branch is Time For God.) They share common standards, and a commitment to the personal development of the volunteer through this form of work. Volunteers with an offending background may be accepted but only if they are reformed characters. 56 projects in France. Four elsewhere overseas. 🔲

Number of projects: 60 **UK:** 0
Starting months: Sep
Time required: 45–49 weeks
Age: 18–25
Causes: Children, Disabled (learning), Elderly People, Health Care/Medical, Young People.
Activities: Social Work.
Placements: 60
When to apply: March
Work alone/with others: Dependent on the placement.
Qualifications: Small ability to speak and understand French and at least 'open' to spirituality.
Health requirements: Good health essential.
Costs: Registration cost of €38. Travel costs to the French border.

Benefits: Pocket money (€102 per month) board and lodging.
Training: Each branch offers support to the volunteers through both personal supervision and regular residential conferences or seminars.
Interviews: Interviews take place in the UK.
Worldwide placements: North America: (USA); Europe (Belgium, France, Germany, Hungary, Italy, Spain).

ANNUNCIATION HOUSE

1003 East San Antonio
El Paso
Texas 79901 USA
T: 00 1 915 533 4675
F: 00 1 915 351 1343
E: volunteercoordinator@
annunciationhouse.org
Contact: Ruben Garcia or Kerry Doyle

Annunciation House is an organisation that operates three houses of hospitality for the homeless poor, undocumented, internal immigrants from Mexico and refugees from Central and South America. The work we do here is the work of extending to the homeless: hospitality, shelter, meals, clothing, some basic medical care and above all, a willing ear to listen to the struggle and suffering in their lives. It is a busy and demanding work which calls for a real commitment to the people themselves. Our houses function 90 to 95% in Spanish. It has always been very important for us that volunteers understand that we do this work not only because we desire to serve the poor, but because we have come to recognise our own poverty and our own desire to feel the worthiness of life. And as we serve the homeless in their daily needs, so too do they serve and teach us through their faith, determination, strength and especially the witness of their very lives. Volunteers with Annunciation House must be willing to live in a community made up of those whom we welcome as guests as well as those who share with us the commitment of being a volunteer. As a staff, we strive to live simply and in solidarity with the poor, remaining mindful of the gospel in our daily work. Prospective volunteers who are not of US citizenship must obtain a visa before coming to volunteer with Annunciation House. On the border between El Paso, Texas and Juarez Mexico. 🔲

Number of projects: 3 **UK:** 0
Starting months: Jan, Apr, Jun, Aug, Nov
Time required: 10–52 weeks (plus)
Age: 20–64
Causes: Poor/Homeless, Refugees.
Activities: Accountancy, Administration, Building/Construction, Community Work, Computers, Cooking, Driving, Library/Resource

Centres, Newsletter/Journalism, Research, Social Work, Teaching, Translating, Visiting/Befriending.
Placements: 22
When to apply: Any time.
Work alone/with others: With others.
Qualifications: No dependants. It is essential that if you have little or no knowledge of the Spanish language, you come with a desire and commitment to learn Spanish.
Health requirements: Must be physically, mentally and emotionally healthy. Medical exam. required.
Costs: We do not require any payment or contribution. Travel and visa costs are the volunteer's responsibility.
Benefits: Board and accommodation in a shared room. All volunteers are provided with a small room in the same house in which the guests live.
Training: We hold a week long orientation for all new volunteers shortly after they arrive. After these sessions are completed, volunteers are assigned to any one of our hospitality houses.
Supervision: Each house has a co-ordinator. This person is always available to all the volunteers in the house. The new volunteer may speak with him/her at any time.
Interviews: Prospective volunteers are sometimes interviewed over the telephone.
Worldwide placements: North America: (USA); Central America (Mexico).

APARE/GEC

41 Cours Jean Jaures
Avignon
84000 France
T: 00 33 4 90 85 51 15
F: 00 33 4 90 86 82 19
E: gec@apare-gec.org
W: www.apare-gec.org
Contact: International area

Groupement Europeen des Campus organises and recruits volunteers for two activities: the European Campuses and the European Voluntary Service. The extensive network of academic workshops (campuses) is intended for all young people interested in environment and heritage. As training projects and tools of action at the service of local initiatives, they provide students with an opportunity for training and action in the real world. Under academic supervision, students, in groups of about 15, for periods of two to four weeks, are called upon to realise studies or works in support of local public or voluntary programmes. European Voluntary Service projects are open to all young people of 18 to 25 interested in participating in a 6 to 12 months voluntary service in another country. Projects are in the sphere of environment, heritage and local development. There are no charges to participate. Travel, food and lodging are covered and each volunteer receives an allowance. The European Voluntary Service represents a chance to travel, discover another country and participate in a useful activity validated by a certificate from the European Commission. ♿

Number of projects: 25–30 UK: 1 or 2
Starting months: Jan, Jul, Aug, Sep, Oct, Nov, Dec
Time required: 3–52 weeks
Age: 18–25
Causes: Archaeology, Architecture, Conservation, Environmental Causes, Heritage, Wildlife, Work Camps – Seasonal.
Activities: Campaigning, Conservation Skills, Development Issues, Group Work, Manual Work, Marketing/Publicity, Research, Scientific Work, Summer Camps, Translating, Work Camps – Seasonal.
Placements: 50–60
When to apply: Mid-June at the latest for the European Campuses, end of September at the latest for the European Voluntary Service.
Work alone/with others: With others.
Qualifications: A-level + 1 year of study minimum. Language ability.
Equipment/clothing: On some projects, working clothes.
Health requirements: Nil.
Costs: Return fare home. For campuses: registration fee €70. For voluntary service: no costs.
Benefits: Board and lodging are free during campuses. Volunteers on voluntary service are given an allowance. Individual apartment, shared flat or room with a host family – charges paid for by host organisation.
Training: Information packs and meetings.
Supervision: A person from the host organisation is responsible for supervision and personal support during the project.
Interviews: Applicants are not interviewed.
Worldwide placements: Africa (Algeria, Morocco, Tunisia); Asia (Lebanon); Europe (Austria, Belarus, Belgium, Bulgaria, Cyprus, Czech Republic, Denmark, Finland, France, Germany, Greece, Hungary, Ireland, Italy, Luxembourg, Malta, Netherlands, Norway, Poland, Portugal, Romania, Russia, Slovakia, Slovenia, Spain, Sweden, Turkey, Ukraine, Yugoslavia).
UK placements: England (Cumbria, London).

APF EVASION

Association des Paralysés de France
17 Bd Auguste Blanqui
Paris 75013 France
T: 00 33 1 40 78 69 00
F: 00 33 1 40 78 69 73
E: apfevasion@aol.com
W: www.apf.asso.fr
Contact: Pierre-Philippe Audineau

APF Evasion needs volunteers to help people with physical disabilities go on collective holidays. You will visit tourist sites, go on excursions, arrange picnics and organise entertainment in the evenings. Volunteers with an offending background may be accepted. 🗎

Number of projects: 1 **UK:** 0
Starting months: Jul
Time required: 1–4 weeks
Age: 19–35
Causes: Children, Disabled (physical), Holidays for Disabled.
Activities: Caring – Residential, Group Work, Summer Camps.
Placements: 1800
When to apply: Any time before mid-July.
Work alone/with others: With others.
Qualifications: All are welcome. We have particular need for bus drivers, lifesavers, cooks, nurses and medical students.
Health requirements: Good health and strength.
Costs: Very small.
Benefits: Travel costs within France and complete board and lodging.
Interviews: No interviews are conducted.
Worldwide placements: Europe (France).

APPALACHIAN MOUNTAIN CLUB

PO Box 298, Rf 16
Pinkham North Visitor Centre
Gorham
NH03581 USA
T: 603 466 2721 X 192
F: 603 466 2822
E: kmarion@amcinfo.org
W: www.outdoors.org
Contact: Kim Marion

Founded in 1876, the Appalachian Mountain Club, a non-profit organisation with more than 93,000 members, promotes the protection, enjoyment and wise use of the mountains, rivers and trails of the Appalachian region. We believe that the mountains and rivers have an intrinsic worth and also provide recreational opportunity, spiritual renewal and ecological and economic health for the region. We encourage people to enjoy and appreciate the natural world because we believe that successful conservation depends on this experience. Volunteers can expect to be involved in trail construction and maintenance in locations throughout the northeast, working from one day up to three weeks. Maine, New Hampshire, Massachusetts.

Number of projects: 30–40 **UK:** 0
Starting months: Jun, Jul, Aug, Sep
Time required: 1–3 weeks
Age: 16 plus – no upper limit
Causes: Conservation.
Activities: Building/Construction, Conservation Skills, Outdoor Skills, Work Camps – Seasonal.

Placements: 350
When to apply: Registration begins early April.
Work alone/with others: Work with others.
Qualifications: Enthusiasm and some previous hiking experience.
Equipment/clothing: Special clothing required – list available and will be provided upon registration.
Health requirements: Overall physical fitness is important.
Costs: Travel to the location must be provided by the volunteer. Registration fee of between $55 and $350 depending on programme length. This cost provides all food and lodging.
Benefits: Food and lodging. Bunkhouses and backcountry camping.
Training: Training provided in tool usage and safety, trail construction and maintenance.
Supervision: Volunteers are supervised during their work at all times, under 18 year olds are supervised 24 hours a day.
Interviews: Via application.
Worldwide placements: North America: (USA).

APPALACHIAN TRAIL CONFERENCE

Volunteer Trail Crew Program
1280 N. Main Street
Blacksburg
Virginia 24060 USA
T: (540) 961 5551
F: (540) 961 5554
E: crews@appalachiantrail.org
W: www.appalachiantrail.org
Contact: Heidi Hase

Help build a piece of the Appalachian National Trail! Participate in the Appalachian Trail project by joining one of the Appalachian Trail Conference's five volunteer trail crews, operated in co-operation with the National Park Service, United States Forest Service and local volunteer trail maintaining clubs. A professional crew leader directs the crew in designing and building new trail segments and rehabilitating damaged trail segments. Come on out and join us for a week or more and enjoy yourself in the outdoors while performing valuable work. May be able to accept volunteers with an offending background. Along the Appalachian Trail – Maine, Vermont, Pennsylvania, Virginia and Tennessee.

Number of projects: 5 **UK:** 0
Starting months: May, Jun, Jul, Aug, Sep, Oct
Time required: 1–6 weeks
Age: 18 plus – no upper limit
Causes: Conservation, Environmental Causes, Work Camps – Seasonal.
Activities: Building/Construction, Conservation Skills, Forestry, Gardening/Horticulture, Manual Work, Outdoor Skills.
Placements: 400+

When to apply: Ongoing – open registration/application period.
Work alone/with others: Work with others.
Qualifications: No experience necessary. Enthusiasm, physical vigor and adaptabiltiy are vital. Willingness to follow instructions and safety rules and to share equally in camp chores is essential.
Equipment/clothing: Work clothing, sturdy boots and your own basic camping gear.
Health requirements: In good health.
Costs: Travel costs to base camp.
Benefits: Shelter, food, transportation to and from work projects sites, tools, safety equipment and group camping gear.
Training: Safety, trail building and maintenance skills.
Supervision: Volunteers are supervised by the Crew Leader and Assistant Crew Leader.
Interviews: Occasionally, if so it will be done over the telephone.
Worldwide placements: North America: (USA).

APPROPRIATE TECHNOLOGY FOR TIBETANS (APTIBET)

Unit F4 & F5, Ist Floor
London Fashion Centre
89–93 Fonthill Road
London
N4 4JH UK
T: +44 (0) 208 450 8090
E: aptibet@gn.apc.org
W: www.aptibet.org
Contact: Pete Crawford

ApTibeT (Appropriate Technology for Tibetans) was founded in 1984. Over the past 15 years, ApTibeT has implemented more than 100 major development projects. ApTibeT's work has focused on a number of main areas: (a) Housing. ApTibeT has started five low cost building centres (LCBCs). Almost the full range of low environmental impact construction methods are used: stabilised mud block bricks; micro-cement roofing tiles; ferro-cement. (b) Water and sanitation. Projects aim to provide skills leading to community construction of UNICEF/WHO recommended pour flush composting latrines, generally constructed in ferro-cement. ApTibeT has also completed a number of large scale water supply projects using conventional building methods. (c) Power and household fuel. We are the major user of an indigenously produced, high quality, low maintenance and low cost wind pump. In addition, we have implemented large scale biogas and improved stove design (chula) projects. (d) Solar energy. Both solar water heating systems (SWHS) and photovoltaic (PV) energy have featured in our programmes.

(e) Agroforestry. ApTibeT works with grassroots organisations in India, Nepal and China and is developing a project in Mongolia. Volunteers with an offending background may be accepted – each case individually assessed. ♿

Number of projects: 15 UK: 0
Starting months: January–December
Time required: 8–52 weeks
Age: 18 plus – no upper limit
Causes: Conservation, Environmental Causes, Refugees.
Activities: Accountancy, Administration, Conservation Skills, Development Issues, Fundraising, International Aid, Marketing/Publicity, Newsletter/Journalism, Research.
Placements: 6–8
When to apply: All year.
Work alone/with others: Both.
Qualifications: Various skills needed in many different areas of work.
Health requirements: Nil.
Costs: Nil.
Benefits: London: Travel and £6 subsistence per day. Training for longterm/specialist work. ApTibeT may meet the cost of accommodation in some circumstances.
Training: Induction.
Supervision: Volunteers receive support sessions.
Interviews: Interviews take place in our office in London.
Charity number: 1072962
Worldwide placements: Asia (China, India, Nepal).
UK placements: England (London).

ARAB NETWORK FOR NGOS – EGYPT

5 Bahaa El-Din Karaqoush, Samalek
PO Box 15
Orman, Cairo
Egypt
T: 00 202 735 8011
F: 00 202 735 8013
Contact: Amani Kandil

Arab Network for NGOs – Egypt promotes and has information about volunteering in Egypt. It may well be able to put volunteers in touch with organisations which are not yet listed on the WorldWide Volunteering database.

Starting months: January–December
Time required: 1–52 weeks (plus)
Age: 16 plus – no upper limit
Causes: Addicts/Ex-Addicts, AIDS/HIV, Animal Welfare, Archaeology, Architecture, Children, Conservation, Disabled (learning and physical), Elderly People, Environmental Causes, Health Care/Medical, Heritage, Holidays for Disabled, Human Rights, Inner City Problems,

Offenders/Ex-Offenders, Poor/Homeless, Refugees, Teaching/assisting (nursery, primary, secondary, mature, EFL) Unemployed, Wildlife, Work Camps – Seasonal, Young People.
Activities: Accountancy, Administration, Agriculture/Farming, Arts/Crafts, Building/ Construction, Campaigning, Caring (general, day and residential), Catering, Community Work, Computers, Conservation Skills, Cooking, Counselling, Development Issues, DIY, Driving, First Aid, Forestry, Fundraising, Gardening/Horticulture, Group Work, International Aid, Library/Resource Centres, Manual Work, Marketing/Publicity, Music, Newsletter/Journalism, Outdoor Skills, Religion, Research, Scientific Work, Social Work, Sport, Summer Camps, Teaching, Technical Skills, Theatre/Drama, Training, Translating, Visiting/Befriending, Work Camps – Seasonal.
Costs: Varies according to the project.
Worldwide placements: Africa (Egypt).

ARBEITSKREIS FREIWILLIGE SOZIALE DIENSTE DER JUGEND

Stafflenbergstraße 76
Stuttgart
70184 Germany
T: 00 49 711 2159 420 417
E: fsj@diakonie.de
Contact: The Bundestutor/in

Arbeitskreis Freiwillige Soziale Dienste der Jugend organises volunteer work in the Evangelical Church of Germany. Volunteers work mostly for people who are in difficulty and in need of a helping hand, for example, with ill, handicapped or old people but work also to a certain extent in kindergartens or homes for children and young people. Throughout the one year's programme, there are seminars and discussions led by the trained group leaders. Keeping in contact with other people through the practical work and the seminars gives a chance for each volunteer to increase their personal growth and learn through new experiences.

Number of projects: 1 UK: 0
Starting months: Aug, Sep, Oct
Time required: 52 weeks
Age: 18 plus – no upper limit
Causes: Children, Disabled (learning and physical), Elderly People, Health Care/Medical, Young People.
Activities: Caring – Day, Religion.
When to apply: One year in advance.
Qualifications: Spoken German essential.
Costs: Travel.
Benefits: Board, lodging + DM300 per month and insurance.
Worldwide placements: Europe (Germany).

ARCHAEOLOGY ABROAD

31–34 Gordon Square
London
WC1H 0PY UK
T: +44 (0) 207 383 2572
E: arch.abroad@ucl.ac.uk
W: www.britarch.ac.uk/archabroad
Contact: Wendy Rix Morton

Archaeology Abroad is published twice a year and provides information about archaeological projects and field schools outside the UK. It does not provide a placement service – individuals should make contact direct with project organisers. Volunteers with an offending background might be accepted. Checked with each project directors/organisers. Sometimes European countries other than those indicated.

Number of projects: 50 UK: 0
Starting months: May, Jun, Jul, Aug, Sep, Oct, Dec
Time required: 2–52 weeks
Age: 18–75
Causes: Archaeology, Heritage.
Activities: Group Work, Manual Work, Outdoor Skills, Technical Skills.
When to apply: As soon as possible.
Work alone/with others: With others.
Qualifications: Some digs provide training but some archaeological experience preferred. Languages a plus. Any restrictions would need to be checked with each project director.
Equipment/clothing: Strong shoes, wet weather gear – otherwise according to project director.
Health requirements: Anti-tetanus advisable – otherwise depending on country.
Costs: Varies from project to project. Air fares+local travel to/from site. Registration fees often apply.
Benefits: Food, accommodation (campsite sometimes). Digs usually provide accommodation, which can range from schools/hostels or dig headquarters to camping. Volunteers frequently required to bring own sleeping bag, tent and camping equipment.
Training: We recommend that those wishing to dig abroad gain some archaeological experience/ training in their own country, if possible, prior to venturing abroad. Training excavations and Field School are listed – fees apply.
Supervision: Varies from site to site.
Interviews: Applicants are not interviewed but may need to complete a detailed application/registration form.
Worldwide placements: North America: (USA); Central America (Belize, Saint Lucia); South America (Chile, Colombia, Peru); Asia (Israel, Kazakhstan, Sri Lanka); Europe (Belgium, Cyprus, France, Georgia, Germany, Ireland, Italy, Malta, Portugal, Russia, Spain).

ARCHELON, SEA TURTLE PROTECTION SOCIETY OF GREECE

Solomou 57
Athens
GR – 10432 Greece
T: 00 30 210 523 1342
F: 00 30 210 523 1342
E: stps@archelon.gr
W: www.archelon.gr
Contact: Dina Soulantika

Since 1983 the primary objective of the Sea Turtle Protection Society of Greece, ARCHELON has been to protect the sea turtles in Greece through monitoring and research, developing and implementing management plans, raising public awareness and rehabilitating sick and injured turtles. ARCHELON is a member of the European Union for Coastal Conservation (EUCC), the European Environmental Bureau (EEB) and a partner to UNEP/Mediterranean Action Plan. Also members of ARCHELON participate in the IUCN/Marine Turtle Specialist Group and contribute to the formulation of the international strategy for the conservation of sea turtles. ARCHELON works closely with state agencies, the local authorities, institutions, other NGOs and local inhabitants in order to mitigate and reverse population reduction of sea turtles. Priority is given to the elaboration and implementation of integrated management plans in the major loggerhead nesting areas in Greece (bays of Kyparissia, Lakonikos and Crete). ARCHELON was instrumental in the establishment of the National Marine Park of Zakynthos. ARCHELON relies heavily on voluntary work. Volunteers help every year in protecting the nesting beaches and treating injured turtles. ▤

Number of projects: 5 **UK:** 0
Starting months: May, Jun, Jul, Aug, Sep, Oct
Time required: 4–24 weeks
Age: 18 plus – no upper limit
Causes: Animal Welfare, Conservation, Environmental Causes, Wildlife.
Activities: Building/Construction, Community Work, Driving, First Aid, Group Work, Manual Work, Outdoor Skills, Research, Social Work, Training.
Placements: 350–400
When to apply: At least one month in advance.
Work alone/with others: With others.
Qualifications: No special qualifications although driving licence, English language, licence to drive an inflatable boat are all appreciated.
Equipment/clothing: Camping gear (sleeping bag and tent), warm and comfortable clothes, waterproofs plus decent clothes for working with the public.
Health requirements: We supply a State of Health form to be completed by each applicant.

Costs: Once accepted, an applicant must pay a non-refundable participation fee of £40. A minimum amount of £5 per day may cover basic food needs.
Benefits: No financial assistance given. Volunteers must bring their own tents to stay on designated free campsites, restricted to Archelon volunteers.
Training: During the nesting and hatching season, fieldwork includes nest and turtle protection, public awareness, maintenance and day-to-day duties.
Supervision: Volunteers are trained and supervised by field leaders and experienced project members.
Worldwide placements: Europe (Greece).

ARCHEOLO-J

Avenue Paul Terlinden 23
1330 Rixensart
Belgium
T: 00 32 2 653 8268
F: 00 32 2 654 1917
E: archeolo-j@skymct.be
W: www.skene.be/archeolo-j
Contact: J. Gillet

Archeolo-J organises international workcamps at archaeological excavations where volunteers assist with all aspects of the excavations, digging, drawing finds and surveying the sites. ▤

Number of projects: 1 **UK:** 0
Starting months: Jul
Time required: 1–3 weeks
Age: 14–77
Causes: Archaeology, Work Camps – Seasonal, Young People.
Activities: Manual Work, Summer Camps, Work Camps – Seasonal.
Placements: 100
When to apply: Before the beginning of May.
Work alone/with others: With others.
Qualifications: Able to understand French or English.
Equipment/clothing: Wellington boots, rainclothes, sleeping equipment and air mattress.
Health requirements: No.
Costs: €220 – €495 + travel costs, drinks, insurance and €4.96 membership fee.
Benefits: Accommodation in tents + food + 1 visit to the region per week and all the activities and art material for the activities provided.
Training: On the field, with our team of archeologists, historians, group leaders.
Supervision: By our team of archeologists, historians and group leaders.
Interviews: No.
Worldwide placements: Europe (Belgium).

ARMY CADET FORCE

Holderness House
51–61 Clifton Street
London
EC2A 4DW UK
T: +44 (0) 207 467 8377
F: +44 (0) 207 467 8378
E: acfa@armycadets.com
W: www.armycadets.com
Contact: Brigadier Ian McGill CBE

The Army Cadet Force offers a rewarding job
giving a helping hand to young people between
12 and 18 years of age to develop their full
potential. It offers sound military based
principles of which we are proud – and a great
deal more. Emphasis is placed on looking after
those from disadvantaged backgrounds. Today
it continues to provide friendship, discipline,
leadership, challenging outdoor activities –
expeditions, survival techniques, adventurous
training, sport, first aid, music and vocational
education. Volunteers with an offending
background are sometimes accepted depending
on the offence.

Number of projects: 101 **UK:** 61
Starting months: January–December
Time required: 1–52 weeks
Age: 19–55
Causes: Disabled (learning and physical),
Environmental Causes, Inner City Problems,
Offenders/Ex-Offenders, Poor/Homeless,
Teaching/assisting (secondary), Unemployed,
Young People.
Activities: Administration, Campaigning,
Caring – General, Community Work,
Counselling, Driving, First Aid, Fundraising,
Group Work, Manual Work,
Marketing/Publicity, Music, Outdoor Skills,
Social Work, Sport, Summer Camps, Teaching,
Technical Skills, Training, Visiting/Befriending.
Placements: 7,000
When to apply: Any time.
Work alone/with others: With others.
Qualifications: Must be British subjects.
Equipment/clothing: Provided.
Health requirements: Reasonable level of
fitness.
Costs: Nil.
Benefits: Pocket money per day for up to 28
days per annum.
Training: Full training is given. If the volunteer
has the time he/she can do any training course
we offer.
Supervision: Each 2 or 3 volunteers will have a
supervisor, always present. Monitored by senior
members of ACF.
Interviews: Interviews take place, invariably in
County HQ.
Charity number: 305962

Worldwide placements: Africa (South Africa,
Zimbabwe); North America: (Canada, USA);
Central America (Bahamas, Barbados, Bermuda,
Jamaica, Trinidad and Tobago); Asia (India,
Nepal, Pakistan); Australasia (Australia); Europe
(Andorra, Austria, Belgium, Cyprus, Denmark,
France, Germany, Greece, Ireland, Italy,
Luxembourg, Netherlands, Norway, Poland,
Portugal, Spain).
UK placements: England (throughout);
Scotland (throughout); Northern Ireland
(throughout); Wales (throughout).

ARTEMIS CLOUDFOREST PRESERVE

Apdo 771
Cartago
5070 Costa Rica
T: 00 506 253 72 43
F: 00 506 253 72 43
Contact: Hilda M. de Pina

Artemis is a private cloudforest reserve in the
Talamanca Mountains of Costa Rica. It lies at an
elevation of approximately 8,800 ft and
comprises 25 ha of intricate, primary forest. A
cloudforest is very different from a rainforest
environment. Temperatures are much lower, and
the forest is often shrouded in mist. The flora
and fauna, adapted to these conditions, tend to
be much 'softer' than those found in the
rainforest. Tree life is dominated by the towering
white oak (up to 35m high), squat and twisted
laurels (sometimes 4m in diameter), and
carboniferous tree ferns. Among, and piled
within, these ancient trees lies an entanglement
of flowering vines, bromeliads, orchids, climbing
ferns, rich mosses and velvet fungi. With such a
collection of plants, there are virtually no bare
surfaces at all and thus the forest is very soft to
the touch. It is difficult to see mammals in the
cloudforest, but this is countered by a great
diversity of tropical birds (including tiny
hummingbirds and the quetzal – famous in
Mayan legend), singing frogs, beautiful moths
and fantastic insects – like golden beetles,
violently coloured and peculiarly shaped. There
are very few animals or insects which are
harmful in the cloudforest. The preserve is
owned by a Costa Rican/American family who
are trying to protect the cloudforest and open it
up to others whether they be visitors,
enthusiasts, school children, etc. Thus
volunteers will be needed to build a trail system
and help with the reafforestation of cleared
areas. Work of this kind gives volunteers the
chance to learn about the cloudforest
environment and simple conservation measures.
The work need not be restricted to these two
tasks. Volunteers of all backgrounds are welcome
to share their talents with the others, whether
biologists, ecologists, ornithologists, surveyors,
engineers, artists, etc. Also, from time to time,

maintenance work has to be done around the house, e.g. clearing property boundaries, fixing fences, simple gardening. The working day is approximately six hours long and volunteers work 20 days out of 28 (i.e. five days on, two days off) although both are flexible. People are taken on for at least one month. 📄

Number of projects: 1 UK: 0
Starting months: January–December
Time required: 4–8 weeks
Age: 18–40
Causes: Conservation, Environmental Causes, Teaching/assisting (primary, EFL), Wildlife.
Activities: Conservation Skills, DIY, Gardening/Horticulture, Teaching.
Placements: 20
When to apply: All year.
Work alone/with others: With others.
Equipment/clothing: Sleeping bag, hiking and rubber boots, warm old clothes, waterproofs and workgloves.
Health requirements: Nil.
Costs: Travel, insurance and minimum US$175 per week.
Benefits: Board, lodging, laundry service, hot showers, home atmosphere.
Training: Simple training for every job.
Supervision: Yes, we ensure jobs are done correctly to avoid damage to the forest.
Interviews: Brief application form.
Worldwide placements: Central America (Costa Rica).

ASARD (ASSOCIATION FOR SOCIAL ACTION AND RURAL DEVELOPMENT)

AT/PO. Raikia
District Phulbani
Orissa 762101
India
T: 00 91 6 847 64696
E: asard_raikia@rediffmail.com
Contact: Sisir Kumar Parichha

ASARD is a non-profit, non-political, non-religious organisation, working for the deprived and tribal (indigenous) people of the area. Its major aim is to make people self sufficient by developing the resources which are available to them. Ill health is a serious problem in the area largely due to illiteracy and a general lack of health education. In response to these needs, ASARD, working since 1988, has adopted a project based comprehensive approach, tackling education, health, community organisation, socio-economic development, rural technology and forestry. Many of the people are Christians, as the nearby missions play a crucial role in education. Volunteers from all over the world are needed on the work camps, where they can participate in village activities from sanitation projects, construction work, forestry and agricultural work, visiting schools and attending

village meetings. Work camp tasks are worked out upon the arrival of the volunteer, but usually last between 2–3 weeks. However, Sisir Kumar is particularly keen to host anyone interested in long-term study of development issues and would be happy to offer his experience and expertise for anyone carrying out thesis or doctoral research. Long-term volunteers are also needed. Write to Sisir Kumar allowing at least six weeks for a reply or send him an e-mail.

Number of projects: 3 UK: 0
Starting months: January–December
Time required: 2–52 weeks
Age: 16–30
Causes: Children, Conservation, Environmental Causes, Poor/Homeless, Teaching/assisting (primary), Young People.
Activities: Agriculture/Farming, Community Work, Conservation Skills, Fundraising, Group Work, International Aid, Newsletter/Journalism, Research, Social Work, Summer Camps, Visiting/Befriending, Work Camps – Seasonal.
Placements: 100
When to apply: 6 weeks before wishing to start.
Work alone/with others: With others.
Equipment/clothing: Sleeping bag, raincoat(June/July), warm clothes (Nov/Dec.), torch, water purification pills.
Health requirements: Nil.
Costs: Airfares and fortnightly donation of about US$100 (2 weeks). This is divided as follows: 25% administration, 25% community work, 50% board and lodging.
Benefits: The donation of approx $100 (2 week) includes basic local food, accommodation and transport to nearby villages.
Training: One day orientation briefing on camp schedule and facilities available.
Supervision: Volunteers are always accompanied by camp supervisors.
Interviews: Prospective volunteers are not interviewed.
Worldwide placements: Asia (India).

ASHIANA COMMUNITY SERVICE PROJECT

23–25 Grantham Road
Sparkbrook
Birmingham
B11 1LU UK
T: +44 (0) 121 773 7061
F: +44 (0) 121 766 7503
E: ashianacp@yahoo.co.uk
Contact: Andrew Hewitt

Ashiana Community Project has four projects based in the multi-racial and inner city area of Sparkbrook which seek to respond to poverty, unemployment and racism in the district. Our guiding principles are to: respond innovatively and flexibly to the diverse needs of the community; be managed by members of the local community; provide a quality service; provide a welcoming and accessible environment to all local people; ensure equal opportunities in all its aspects; work in partnership with voluntary and statutory organisations; be a non profit making organisation. We aim to: provide learning opportunities which enable people to gain their personal goals and access employment; encourage community management; create opportunities for volunteering; promote health in the community; provide access to free legal and welfare advice; raise awareness of environmental issues; promote understanding of cultural diversity. 🖫

Number of projects UK: 3
Starting months: January–December
Time required: 1–52 weeks
Age: 16 plus – no upper limit
Causes: Children, Conservation, Health Care/Medical, Human Rights, Inner City Problems, Poor/Homeless, Teaching/assisting (EFL), Young People.
Activities: Administration, Arts/Crafts, Community Work, Computers, Conservation Skills, DIY, Fundraising, Gardening/Horticulture, Group Work, Marketing/Publicity, Social Work, Teaching, Translating, Visiting/Befriending.
Placements: 100
When to apply: All year.
Work alone/with others: With others.
Costs: Contribution if possible.
Benefits: Accommodation.
UK placements: England (London, Manchester, West Midlands, S. Yorkshire).

ASIA-PACIFIC PUBLIC AFFAIRS FORUM – TAIWAN

28F, 55 Chung-Cheng 3rd Road
Kaohsiung City
800 Taiwan
T: 00 886 7 227 4736
F: 00 886 7 227559
E: appaf@mail.nsysu.edu.tw
W: www.appaf.nsysu.edu.tw
Contact: Dr Tim E.M. Wu

Asia-Pacific Public Affairs Forum promotes and has information about volunteering in Taiwan. It may well be able to put volunteers in touch with organisations which are not yet listed on the WorldWide Volunteering database.

Starting months: January–December
Time required: 1–52 weeks (plus)
Age: 16 plus – no upper limit
Causes: Addicts/Ex-Addicts, AIDS/HIV, Animal Welfare, Archaeology, Architecture, Children, Conservation, Disabled (learning and physical), Elderly People, Environmental Causes, Health Care/Medical, Heritage, Holidays for Disabled,

Human Rights, Inner City Problems, Offenders/Ex-Offenders, Poor/Homeless, Refugees, Teaching/assisting (nursery, primary, secondary, mature, EFL) Unemployed, Wildlife, Work Camps – Seasonal, Young People.
Activities: Accountancy, Administration, Agriculture/Farming, Arts/Crafts, Building/Construction, Campaigning, Caring (general, day and residential), Catering, Community Work, Computers, Conservation Skills, Cooking, Counselling, Development Issues, DIY, Driving, First Aid, Forestry, Fundraising, Gardening/Horticulture, Group Work, International Aid, Library/Resource Centres, Manual Work, Marketing/Publicity, Music, Newsletter/Journalism, Outdoor Skills, Religion, Research, Scientific Work, Social Work, Sport, Summer Camps, Teaching, Technical Skills, Theatre/Drama, Training, Translating, Visiting/Befriending, Work Camps – Seasonal.
Costs: Varies according to the project.
Worldwide placements: Asia (Taiwan).

ASOCIACION ESPANOLA DE VOLUNTARIADO

Gran Via 17A
28028 Madrid
Spain
T: 00 34 91 523 3624
F: 00 34 91 523 3726
E: aevol@rete-mail.es
Contact: Kristin Sverdrup

Asociacion Espanola de Voluntariado promotes and has information about volunteering in Spain. It may well be able to put volunteers in touch with organisations which are not yet listed on the WorldWide Volunteering database. AEVOL carries out investigations and research in the volunteering field and we need experienced translators from Spanish to French and French to English to translate our works. We also need volunteers specialised in web design and to maintain it. 🖻

Starting months: January–December
Time required: 1–52 weeks (plus)
Age: 18 plus – no upper limit
Causes: Children, Conservation, Disabled (learning and physical), Elderly People, Heritage, Teaching/assisting (secondary), Young People.
Activities: Community Work, Computers, Music, Research, Scientific Work, Social Work, Translating.
When to apply: At any time.
Qualifications: Perfect knowledge of Spanish or French for translations.
Equipment/clothing: Equipment and access to the Internet.
Costs: Varies according to the project.
Worldwide placements: Europe (Spain).

ASOCIACION FEDERACION DE ORGANIZACIONES VOLUNTARIAS (FOV) – COSTA RICA

Calle Primera Avenida 13
Apartado 7-3070
San Jose
Costa Rica
T: 00 506 222 1815
F: 00 506 223 1341
E: fedorvol@sol.racsa.co.cr
Contact: Ana Pardo

Asociacion Federacion de Organizaciones Voluntarias (FOV) promotes and has information about volunteering in Costa Rica. It may well be able to put volunteers in touch with organisations which are not yet listed on the WorldWide Volunteering database.

Starting months: January–December
Time required: 1–52 weeks (plus)
Age: 16 plus – no upper limit
Causes: Addicts/Ex-Addicts, AIDS/HIV, Animal Welfare, Archaeology, Architecture, Children, Conservation, Disabled (learning and physical), Elderly People, Environmental Causes, Health Care/Medical, Heritage, Holidays for Disabled, Human Rights, Inner City Problems, Offenders/Ex-Offenders, Poor/Homeless, Refugees, Teaching/assisting (nursery, primary, secondary, mature, EFL) Unemployed, Wildlife, Work Camps – Seasonal, Young People.
Activities: Accountancy, Administration, Agriculture/Farming, Arts/Crafts, Building/Construction, Campaigning, Caring (general, day and residential), Catering, Community Work, Computers, Conservation Skills, Cooking, Counselling, Development Issues, DIY, Driving, First Aid, Forestry, Fundraising, Gardening/Horticulture, Group Work, International Aid, Library/Resource Centres, Manual Work, Marketing/Publicity, Music, Newsletter/Journalism, Outdoor Skills, Religion, Research, Scientific Work, Social Work, Sport, Summer Camps, Teaching, Technical Skills, Theatre/Drama, Training, Translating, Visiting/Befriending, Work Camps – Seasonal.
Costs: Varies according to the project.
Worldwide placements: (Costa Rica).

ASSOCIATE MISSIONARIES OF THE ASSUMPTION

914 Main Street, 5
Worcester
MA01602 USA
T: 00 1(508) 767 1356
F: 00 1 508 767 1356
E: ama-usa@juno.com
W: www.AssumptionVolunteers.org
Contact: Beth Fleming or Sister Mary Ann Azanza, RA

Associate Missionaries of the Assumption (AMA) is a lay missionary programme, sponsored by the Religious of the Assumption. AMA is a group of women and men using their gifts and skills in service with the poor. For one year, an AMA will work in a school, hospital, parish or social service agency while living simply in a faith support community. Sites are located worldwide – US: Philadelphia, Worcester, MA and New Mexico. Mexico, Bolivia, Guatemala, Nicaragua, El Salvador, Italy, France, Spain, Ireland, England and Scotland. Attempt to match skills and geographical preference to site.

Number of projects: various **UK:** 3
Starting months: Aug
Time required: 45–52 weeks
Age: 22–45
Causes: Children, Disabled (learning and physical), Elderly People, Health Care/Medical, Inner City Problems, Poor/Homeless, Teaching/assisting (nursery, primary, secondary, EFL), Young People.
Activities: Arts/Crafts, Caring (general, residential), Community Work, Development Issues, Driving, Religion, Social Work, Teaching, Training, Visiting/Befriending.
Placements: 10–20
When to apply: Preferably before March 1, however admissions are rolling according to the start date of the accepting site.
Work alone/with others: With others – community and faith based.
Qualifications: Christian faith. 4 year college degree required. Previous voluntary work essential. Personal interview and discernment weekend required.
Health requirements: Certificate of good health – physically and psychologically.
Costs: One way fare in some cases. $10 application costs.
Benefits: One week orientation programme. On-going training and formation. Re-entry programme offered. Americorps Education Award for US sites to US citizens. Monthly stipend.
Training: One weekend for discernment One week orientation in summer.
Supervision: Supervision by site or Religious of Assumption on site or close to site.
Interviews: Worcester or another location with the Religions of the Assumption.
Worldwide placements: North America: (USA); Central America (El Salvador, Guatemala, Mexico, Nicaragua); South America (Bolivia); Asia (Japan, Philippines, Thailand); Europe (France, Ireland, Spain).
UK placements: England (London, Suffolk, E. Sussex, W. Sussex).

ASSOCIATION DE RECHERCHES ET ETUDES D'HISTOIRE RURALE

Maison du Patrimoine
21190 Saint-Romain
France
T: 00 33 380 21 28 50
Contact: M. Serge Grappin

The Association de Recherches et Etudes d'Histoire Rurale is conducting a long term research project on the archaeological, ethnological and historical development of the Saint-Romain area. The work consists of digging and restoration.

Number of projects: 1 **UK:** 0
Starting months: Aug
Time required: 4–52 weeks
Age: 17 plus – no upper limit
Causes: Archaeology, Heritage.
Activities: Manual Work.
Placements: 40
When to apply: Before 30th May.
Work alone/with others: Usually with others.
Costs: Pocket money, food and travel to campsite.
Benefits: Accommodation.
Worldwide placements: Europe (France).

ASSOCIATION DES CHANTIERS DE JEUNES (ACJ)

B.P. 171
Salé – Medina 11005
Morocco
T: 00 212 37 855350 [mob. 066949519]
F: 00 212 37 855350
E: acj.ong.maroc@caramail.com
Contact: Taki Abderrahmane

Association des chantiers de jeunes is a non-profit organisation with 14 local projects in Morocco. The following seven goals are at the core of its work; to safeguard the environment; to integrate youth in social and cultural life; to fight illiteracy; to brighten the lives of immigrant children; to develop the rural regions; to restore monuments; to institute peace and co-operation between people of different religions, sex, colour or language. ACJ co-operates with local and international organisations all over the world to help with development projects, to help citizens in precarious situations especially children and women in Morocco. ACJ organises voluntary work camps during school holidays. Please contact for latest projects. More details will be sent when applications are received. 📄

Number of projects: varies
Starting months: Apr, Jul, Aug, Dec
Time required: 1–8 weeks
Age: 16 plus – no upper limit
Causes: Archaeology, Children, Conservation, Disabled (learning and physical), Elderly People,

Environmental Causes, Heritage, Holidays for Disabled, Human Rights, Inner City Problems, Offenders/Ex-Offenders, Poor/Homeless, Teaching/assisting, Work Camps – Seasonal, Young People.
Activities: Agriculture/Farming, Arts/Crafts, Building/Construction, Campaigning, Caring – General, Community Work, Development Issues, First Aid, Forestry, Fundraising, Gardening/Horticulture, Group Work, Manual Work, Music, Research, Social Work, Sport, Summer Camps, Teaching, Technical Skills, Training, Visiting/Befriending, Work Camps – Seasonal.
Placements: 500
When to apply: From 1st April.
Work alone/with others: With others.
Qualifications: English and/or French an advantage.
Equipment/clothing: Sleeping bags, musical instruments and animation equipment.
Health requirements: No volunteers with contaminating illnesses.
Costs: Travel and €60 participation fees.
Benefits: Lodging and food.
Training: Directed by Morrocan Atisantse Ceramic training courses in Sal/1 courses – one month duration.
Supervision: By qualified responsible staff of ACJ.
Interviews: No interviews are needed.
Worldwide placements: Africa (Algeria, Morocco, Tunisia); Europe (France).

ASSOCIATION FOR VOLUNTEER SERVICES – LEBANON

PO Box 136104
Beirut
Lebanon 2039 4232
T: 00 961 1 797 247
F: 00 961 1 797 247
E: avs@avs.org.lb
W: www.avs.org.lb
Contact: Patricia Nabti

Association for Volunteer Services promotes and has information about volunteering in Lebanon. It may well be able to put volunteers in touch with organisations which are not yet listed on the WorldWide Volunteering database. ♿ 📄

Number of projects: varies **UK:** 0
Starting months: January–December
Time required: 1–52 weeks (plus)
Age: 16 plus – no upper limit
Causes: Addicts/Ex-Addicts, AIDS/HIV, Animal Welfare, Archaeology, Architecture, Children, Conservation, Disabled (learning and physical), Elderly People, Environmental Causes, Health Care/Medical, Heritage, Holidays for Disabled, Human Rights, Inner City Problems, Offenders/Ex-Offenders, Poor/Homeless, Refugees,

Teaching/assisting (nursery, primary, secondary, mature, EFL) Unemployed, Wildlife, Work Camps – Seasonal, Young People.
Activities: Accountancy, Administration, Fundraising, Library/Resource Centres, Marketing/Publicity, Newsletter/Journalism, Research, Training, Translating.
When to apply: Any time.
Work alone/with others: Both.
Qualifications: Knowledge of English required, knowledge of Arabic and French helpful. All nationalities accepted. Preference for those with some Lebanese heritage.
Health requirements: Good health required.
Costs: We do not provide transportation or living expenses. We may provide local transportation allowance.
Training: Available.
Supervision: Available.
Interviews: Required for final placement.
Worldwide placements: Asia (Lebanon).

ASSOCIATION JEAN-FREDERIC OBERLIN

Foyer Les Trois Sources
1 Rue des Jardins,
F-67420 Colroy-la-Roche
France
T: 00 33 388 97 61 09
Contact: The Director

Association Jean-Frederic Oberlin runs a small home for adults with special needs that wants to grow into a Camphill Community. It is part of the worldwide Camphill movement which was founded by the Austrian Doctor Karl König at the end of the Second World War when he was living as a refugee in Aberdeen, Scotland. The basis of work in any Camphill Community is Anthroposophy by Dr Rudolf Steiner and the first memorandum by Dr König. Camphill Communities are now found all over the world and one of their main tasks is to live with and care for people with mental disabilities in a social therapeutic way which includes daily life, work, cultural activities and religious life as well as many other aspects of life.

Number of projects: 1 UK: 0
Starting months: January–December
Time required: 40–52 weeks
Age: 14 plus – no upper limit
Causes: Disabled (learning and physical)
Activities: Agriculture/Farming, Arts/Crafts, Forestry, Gardening/Horticulture, Group Work, Manual Work, Music, Outdoor Skills.
When to apply: All year.
Work alone/with others: with others.
Equipment/clothing: Nothing special – outdoor wear.
Health requirements: Nil.
Costs: Travel to Colroy-la-Roche.

Benefits: Board and lodging.
Worldwide placements: Europe (France).

ASSOCIATION LE MAT

Le Viel Audon
07120 Balazuc
Ardeche France
T: 00 33 475 37 73 80
F: 00 33 475 37 77 90
W: http://vielaudon.free.fr
Contact: Co-ordinator

Association Le Mat undertakes restoration, reconstruction, farm and agricultural activities at the village of Viel Audon. Volunteers can choose their daily task from those offered as long as they work at least five hours per day.

Number of projects: 1 UK: 0
Starting months: January–December
Time required: 1–52 weeks
Age: 17 plus – no upper limit
Causes: Architecture, Conservation, Environmental Causes, Heritage.
Activities: Agriculture/Farming, Conservation Skills, Manual Work.
Placements: 300
When to apply: All year.
Work alone/with others: With others.
Qualifications: Lots of energy and enthusiasm. Need to know French language for daily life.
Equipment/clothing: Rucksack, sleeping bag and tent if possible, working gloves, torch, sleeping mat.
Health requirements: No restrictions.
Costs: Food (about £4 daily), £1 for insurance and joining fee of £5.
Benefits: Camping areas are provided and some beds are available. Camping area in your own tent.
Supervision: A team of young people take care of the camp. Everyone is responsible in the camp.
Interviews: No interview.
Worldwide placements: Europe (France).

ASSOCIATION OF CAMPHILL COMMUNITIES IN THE BRITISH ISLES

55 Caincross Road
Stroud
Gloucestershire GL5 4EX UK
T: +44 (0) 1453 753142
F: +44 (0) 1453 767469
E: coworker@camphill.org.uk
W: www.camphill.org.uk
Contact: William Steffan

The Association of Camphill Communities is an umbrella organisation for the 45+ Camphill Communities in the British Isles. Some of the communities are residential special schools, some provide further education and training for youngsters with learning disabilities or developmental disabilities; the majority of centres are therapeutic and mutually supportive communities with adults who have special needs. Some centres cater for people with mental health problems. People with special needs, short-term and long-term co-workers (unsalaried workers) and their families learn, live and work together in extended family settings or in supported independent accommodation. Short-term volunteers (up to twelve months) are provided with accommodation, food and a modest amount of pocket money. Volunteer co-workers are encouraged to apply direct to individual communities. All relevant details as well as information on each community and life as a volunteer are found on the Association's web site. Other similar Camphill Communities are found in 20 countries worldwide.

Number of projects: 90 **UK:** 47
Starting months: January–December
Time required: 12–52 weeks (plus)
Age: 18 plus – no upper limit
Causes: Disabled (learning and physical)
Activities: Agriculture/Farming, Arts/Crafts, Caring – General, Catering, Cooking, Gardening/Horticulture, Group Work.
Placements: 300
When to apply: All year. Open ended length of time – long term volunteering possible.
Work alone/with others: with others.
Qualifications: Good command of English.
Health requirements: Hepatitis B innoculation recommended.
Costs: Nil except travel to and from centre.
Benefits: Board, lodging and small pocket money. Live in family units with people with special needs.
Training: Provided during the volunteers working period at our centres.
Supervision: Each volunteer has a tutor who is concerned with their progress through the stay at our centres.
Interviews: Applicants are interviewed if they apply in Great Britain. Most volunteers are from abroad. References, criminal background checks and medical certificate required.
Charity number: 232402
Worldwide placements: Africa (Botswana, South Africa); North America: (Canada, USA); Asia (India); Europe (Austria, Denmark, Estonia, Finland, France, Germany, Ireland, Netherlands, Norway, Poland, Romania, Russia, Sweden, Switzerland).
UK placements: England (Bristol, Buckinghamshire, Devon, Dorset, Gloucestershire, Hampshire, Hertfordshire, Norfolk, E. Sussex, W. Sussex, West Midlands, N. Yorkshire, S. Yorkshire, W. Yorkshire); Scotland (Aberdeenshire, Dumfries and Galloway, Edinburgh, Highland, Perth and

Kinross, Stirling); Northern Ireland (Down, Tyrone); Wales (Carmarthenshire, Pembrokeshire).

ASSOCIATION OF GREATER LONDON OLDER WOMEN (AGLOW)

9 Manor Gardens
London
N7 6LA UK
T: +44 (0) 207 281 3485
E: admin@aglow.uninet.co.uk
Contact: Margaret Kennedy

Volunteers with an offending background may be accepted depending on the offence. Our members are elderly and vulnerable. 🖫

Number of projects UK: 1
Starting months: Apr, May, Jun, Jul, Aug, Sep
Time required: 1–52 weeks
Age: 18 plus – no upper limit
Causes: Elderly People.
Activities: Administration, Computers, DIY, Library/Resource Centres, Newsletter/Journalism, Research.
When to apply: As early as possible.
Work alone/with others: Working with staff.
Qualifications: Common sense.
Health requirements: Nil.
Costs: Accommodation if required. Out of pocket expenses are paid.
Benefits: Expenses reimbursed – travel and lunch.
Training: Training as necessary.
Supervision: Volunteers are always supervised.
Interviews: Interviews take place at our office.
UK placements: England (London).

ASSOCIATION OF VOLUNTEERS IN PROTECTED AREAS (ASVO)

10104–100 San José
Costa Rica
T: 00 506 57 0922
F: 00 506 23 6963
E: asvo89@sol.racsa.co.cr
Contact: Rodrigo Araya

ASVO needs volunteers to live and work with the park guards in the mountains and coastal parks of Costa Rica. The work consists of maintenance (cooking, cleaning, collecting litter, repairing buildings or trails), environmental education and general vigilance and support in case of emergency.

Starting months: January–December
Time required: 8–52 weeks
Age: 18 plus – no upper limit
Causes: Conservation, Environmental Causes.
Activities: Conservation Skills, Cooking, Manual Work.
When to apply: All year.

Qualifications: Fluent Spanish and ability to live in rural tropical conditions.
Costs: $350 per month contribution + air fare.
Benefits: Transport, food, accommodation and materials.
Worldwide placements: Central America (Costa Rica).

ASSOCIATION POUR LE VOLONTARIAT – BELGIUM

Rue Royale 11–10000
Bruxelles
Belgium
T: 00 32 2 2195370
F: 00 32 2 2193248
E: volontariat@swing.be
W: www.volontariat.be
Contact: Leon Lemercier/Helene de Callatay

Association pour le Volontariat promotes and has information about volunteering in Belgium, Brussels (French speaking part). It may well be able to put volunteers in touch with organisations which are not yet listed on the WorldWide Volunteering database. (Volunteer centre open daily by appointment only.)
Alternative e-mail address volontariat@skynet.be.

Starting months: January–December
Time required: 1–52 weeks (plus)
Age: 16 plus – no upper limit
Causes: Addicts/Ex-Addicts, AIDS/HIV, Animal Welfare, Archaeology, Architecture, Children, Conservation, Disabled (learning and physical), Elderly People, Environmental Causes, Health Care/Medical, Heritage, Holidays for Disabled, Human Rights, Inner City Problems, Offenders/Ex-Offenders, Poor/Homeless, Refugees, Teaching/assisting (nursery, primary, secondary, mature, EFL) Unemployed, Wildlife, Work Camps – Seasonal, Young People.
Activities: Accountancy, Administration, Agriculture/Farming, Arts/Crafts, Building/Construction, Campaigning, Caring (general, day and residential), Catering, Community Work, Computers, Conservation Skills, Cooking, Counselling, Development Issues, DIY, Driving, First Aid, Forestry, Fundraising, Gardening/Horticulture, Group Work, International Aid, Library/Resource Centres, Manual Work, Marketing/Publicity, Music, Newsletter/Journalism, Outdoor Skills, Religion, Research, Scientific Work, Social Work, Sport, Summer Camps, Teaching, Technical Skills, Theatre/Drama, Training, Translating, Visiting/Befriending, Work Camps – Seasonal.
Qualifications: N/a as we have a centre connecting volunteer applicants with our various associations looking for volunteers.
Costs: Varies according to the project.
Training: Training is available and organised by our association.
Interviews: Yes. First interview with us.
Worldwide placements: Europe (Belgium).

ASSOCIATION TUNISIENNE DE L'ACTION VOLUNTAIRE (ATAV)

Maison du RCD
Boulevard 9 Avril
Lakasbah
Tunis 1006
Tunisia
T: 00 216 1 564899
F: 00 216 1 573065
E: UTOJ@risala.ati.tn
Contact: Hafidh Rahoui

ATAV arranges short term workcamps and leadership training courses throughout Tunisia. Workcamp projects typically involve construction and maintenance work, providing social and medical assistance, and the protection and conservation of the natural environment, especially in rural areas. Volunteers of all nationalities can participate in the workcamps that are held throughout the summer of each year. 🗎

Number of projects: 15 UK: 0
Starting months: Jul, Aug
Time required: 1–3 weeks
Age: 18–35
Causes: Archaeology, Conservation, Environmental Causes, Poor/Homeless, Work Camps – Seasonal, Young People.
Activities: Building/Construction, Campaigning, Catering, Community Work, Conservation Skills, Development Issues, DIY, Gardening/Horticulture, Group Work, Manual Work, Training, Work Camps – Seasonal.
Placements: 500
When to apply: May or June.
Work alone/with others: With others.
Qualifications: French or Arabic speaking and open-minded.
Equipment/clothing: Suitable for outside work.
Health requirements: Good health.
Costs: Travel to Tunisia and to the location.
Benefits: Free food and accommodation.
Interviews: No interviews take place.
Worldwide placements: Africa (Tunisia).

ASSOCIAZIONE ITALIANA SOCI COSTRUTTORI – I.B.O.

Via Montebello 46/A
44100
(Ferrara) Italy
T: 00 39 0532 243279
F: 00 39 0532 245689
E: info@iboitalia.org
W: www.iboitalia.org

Contact: Dino Montanari

Associazione Italiana Soci Costruttori I.B.O. is a branch of International Building Companions and arranges construction workcamps in Europe in the summer for all nationalities. These last for three weeks. No volunteers with an offending background.

Number of projects: 50 (20 in Italy) **UK:** 0
Starting months: May, Jun, Jul, Aug, Sep
Time required: 3 weeks
Age: 18 plus – no upper limit
Causes: Addicts/Ex-Addicts, Archaeology, Children, Conservation, Disabled (physical), Environmental Causes, Poor/Homeless, Teaching/assisting, Work Camps – Seasonal.
Activities: Agriculture/Farming, Building/Construction, Cooking, Manual Work, Social Work, Summer Camps, Teaching, Theatre/Drama, Work Camps – Seasonal.
Placements: 2,000
When to apply: All year.
Qualifications: No specific qualifications.
Equipment/clothing: Working clothes, gloves, sleeping bag, heavy shoes. No specific equipment.
Health requirements: Nil.
Costs: Travel costs plus €100 for Europe.
Benefits: Board and lodging. Volunteers stay in the community where they are working.
Training: Any necessary training is given.
Supervision: There is a responsible supervisor in the workcamp.
Interviews: Prospective volunteers are not interviewed. We need an application form and doctor's certificate.
Worldwide placements: Central America (Guatemala); South America (Brazil, Peru); Europe (Albania, Andorra, Armenia, Austria, Azerbaijan, Belarus, Belgium, Bosnia-Herzegovina, Bulgaria, Croatia, Cyprus, Czech Republic, Denmark, Estonia, Finland, France, Georgia, Germany, Gibraltar, Greece, Hungary, Iceland, Ireland, Italy, Latvia, Liechtenstein, Lithuania, Luxembourg, Macedonia, Malta, Moldova, Monaco, Netherlands, Norway, Poland, Portugal, Romania, Russia, San Marino, Slovakia, Slovenia, Sweden, Switzerland, Turkey, Ukraine, Vatican City, Yugoslavia).

ASSUMPTION LAY VOLUNTEER PROGRAMME

23 Kensington Square
London
W8 5HN UK
T: +44 (0) 20 7361 361 4752
F: +44 (0) 20 7361 361 4757
E: cburns@rayouth.freeserve.co.uk
Contact: Caroline Burns

The Assumption Lay Volunteer Programme is an opportunity for those individuals who are willing to take up the challenge of living and working with people of different cultures, nationalities and traditions. We see this opportunity as a building up of the human family across all divides. It is a way of living the Gospel through service whilst working for justice and peace. As an educational organisation, we see the volunteer programme as a mutual learning – a discovery between the volunteer and those he/she encounters. It is an opportunity for the individual to stride towards reaching their fullest potential, which sometimes is not possible in our own reality. The programme offers a very good preparation and training which is spread over a six-month period of time. This provides an opportunity also for the volunteer to build up relationships with accompanying volunteers as well as with the Assumption. This is very important due to the 'family nature' of the programme. Also, on placement there is continual support and accompaniment. Debriefing is offered on return as well as other avenues of service if desired.

Number of projects: 15–18 **UK:** 3
Starting months: Sep
Time required: 52 weeks (plus)
Age: 21–50
Causes: Children, Health Care/Medical, Poor/Homeless, Teaching/assisting (nursery, primary, EFL), Young People.
Activities: Agriculture/Farming, Building/Construction, Caring – General, Community Work, Computers, Cooking, Driving, Group Work, International Aid, Manual Work, Newsletter/Journalism, Outdoor Skills, Religion, Social Work, Summer Camps, Teaching, Visiting/Befriending.
Placements: 16
When to apply: October to January.
Work alone/with others: With others.
Qualifications: No qualifications or skills needed but a willingness to do anything is essential.
Equipment/clothing: Clothing appropriate to weather and temperature of host country.
Health requirements: Volunteers must be physically and psychologically fit.
Costs: For overseas placements the cost is £700. This includes preparation training, all insurances, flights, and resettlement grants.
Benefits: Board and lodging, pocket money, all insurances for overseas volunteers and a resettlement grant.
Training: Six months, part-time.
Supervision: Co-ordinators and supervisors in situ as well as co-ordinator from sending country. UK co-ordinator will also visit.
Interviews: Informal first interview, followed by formal interview.
Charity number: 233084
Worldwide placements: Africa (Rwanda,

Tanzania); North America: (USA); Central America (El Salvador, Mexico); Asia (Philippines, Thailand).
UK placements: England (Suffolk, Tyne and Wear); Scotland (Highland, Inverclyde).

ASTOVOCT (Association Togolaise des Volontaires Chretiens au Travail)

BP 97
Route de Hanyigba
Kpalimé
Kloto Togo
T: 00 228 41 07 15
F: 00 228 41 07 15
E: astovoct@yahoo.com
Contact: Komi Edem Bansah

ASTOVOCT is a non profit-making Evangelist Presbyterian organisation, working towards the improvement of the standard of living in the rural areas of Togo. One hundred volunteers are recruited each year to work on short term workcamps for about one month to help with the building of health centres and schools, and also with tree planting and agricultural work. Volunteers have brainstorming sessions with local volunteers before going to a project. Middle-term workcamps are organised all year round. 🖺

Number of projects: 10 **UK:** 0
Starting months: January–December
Time required: 3–52 weeks
Age: 18 plus – no upper limit
Causes: Children, Conservation, Disabled (physical), Environmental Causes, Health Care/Medical, Heritage, Poor/Homeless, Teaching/assisting (nursery, primary, secondary, mature, EFL) Young People.
Activities: Agriculture/Farming, Arts/Crafts, Building/Construction, Campaigning, Community Work, Computers, Conservation Skills, Cooking, Counselling, Development Issues, Fundraising, Group Work, International Aid, Library/Resource Centres, Manual Work, Music, Outdoor Skills, Sport, Summer Camps, Teaching, Theatre/Drama, Training.
Placements: 90
When to apply: From May.
Work alone/with others: With others.
Qualifications: Good knowledge of French or English.
Equipment/clothing: Working shoes, mosquito net and sleeping mat.
Health requirements: Vaccination and certificate against yellow fever and anti-malaria pills.
Costs: Food, accommodation and travel, insurance and registration of €152 per place.
Benefits: Cultural exchange, experience in social work and working in a group. Accommodation provided.

Supervision: We have 2 camp leaders and 1 co-ordinator who supervise and direct the camp.
Interviews: Volunteers are interviewed in Togo before going to their project.
Worldwide placements: Africa (Togo).

ATD FOURTH WORLD

48 Addington Square
London
SE5 7LB UK
T: +44 (0) 207 703 3231
F: +44 (0) 207 252 4276
E: atd@atd-uk.org
W: www.atd-uk.org
Contact: Matt Davies

ATD Fourth World is an international voluntary organisation that works in England, Scotland and 24 countries on five continents (North and South America, Europe, Africa and Asia) and develops a human rights approach to overcoming extreme poverty. It works in partnership with the most disadvantaged, supporting their efforts in the fight against poverty and their struggle for dignity. It encourages public awareness of poverty through the publication of books and videos that tell the story of the poor and excluded through their own experience, providing them with a voice. It also periodically publishes newsletters through which the experience and knowledge of the core workers can be shared with everyone. A commitment of two years is normally expected except for the workcamps described below. Two-week international workcamps in France, Germany and the UK are organised during the summer.

Number of projects: 30 **UK:** 3
Starting months: January–December
Time required: 2–52 weeks (plus)
Age: 18–60
Causes: Addicts/Ex-Addicts, AIDS/HIV, Children, Health Care/Medical, Human Rights, Inner City Problems, Offenders/Ex-Offenders, Poor/Homeless, Teaching/assisting (nursery), Unemployed, Work Camps – Seasonal, Young People.
Activities: Accountancy, Administration, Arts/Crafts, Building/Construction, Campaigning, Caring – General, Catering, Community Work, Computers, Conservation Skills, Cooking, Counselling, Development Issues, DIY, Driving, Fundraising, Group Work, International Aid, Library/Resource Centres, Manual Work, Marketing/Publicity, Music, Newsletter/Journalism, Outdoor Skills, Research, Social Work, Sport, Summer Camps, Teaching, Technical Skills, Theatre/Drama, Training, Translating, Visiting/Befriending, Work Camps – Seasonal.
Placements: 40
When to apply: All year.

Work alone/with others: With others.
Qualifications: Participation in an induction weekend in London or Surrey. Mainly EC citizens and others who have a visa. ATD cannot help people get a visa.
Health requirements: Nil.
Costs: For workcamps: less than £50 if less than 2 weeks. No cost for placement.
Benefits: Coreworker volunteers: always accommodation, pocket money after 1st month; salary and National Insurance after one year. Always health insurance if overseas.
Friends: accommodation is offered when taking part in residential projects.
Training: Induction weekend (residential) at the beginning of each month. Ongoing training (a day a week) throughout.
Supervision: Volunteers always work as part of a team under close supervision and with close support of long-term coreworkers who have been working for many years in the organisation.
Interviews: Our induction weekends act as an interview.
Charity number: 209367
Worldwide placements: Europe (France, Germany).
UK placements: England (London, Surrey, W. Yorkshire); Scotland (Glasgow City, Stirling).

ATLANTIC WHALE FOUNDATION

St Martins House
59 St Martins Lane
Covent Garden
London
WC2N 4JS UK
T: +44 (0) 207 590 7919
F: +44 (0) 207 240 5795
E: edb@huron.ac.uk
W: www.whalefoundation.org
Contact: Ed Bentham

The objective is to provide low cost volunteer opportunities to work in whale and dolphin conservation, education and research. Main project areas are: Tenerife: whale and dolphin conservation. 300 volunteers from across Europe staying for 1–8+ weeks and working as naturalist research guides on the whale watching boats of Tenerife, running educational workshops, training workshops, exhibitions, environmental awareness campaigns, public art projects and courses/conferences. Aim of project: to develop Tenerife as a model of responsible whale watching as an example to the world, as a major platform for raising public awareness of cetacean conservation issues, and as an alternative way of life to whale hunting communities. Application details from web site www.whalefoundation.org.uk or send 31p stamped self addressed A4 envelope to London office. 🖺 🖹

Number of projects: 10 UK: 0
Starting months: January–December
Time required: 1–52 weeks (plus)
Age: 17 plus – no upper limit
Causes: Animal Welfare, Children, Conservation, Environmental Causes, Heritage, Human Rights, Poor/Homeless, Teaching/assisting, Wildlife, Young People.
Activities: Arts/Crafts, Building/Construction, Campaigning, Community Work, Computers, Conservation Skills, Development Issues, DIY, Fundraising, Gardening/Horticulture, Group Work, Outdoor Skills, Scientific Work, Teaching, Training.
Placements: 800–1000
When to apply: All year.
Work alone/with others: In groups.
Equipment/clothing: Depends on location – very simple lifestyle with lots of outdoor activities.
Health requirements: Nil.
Costs: £100 per week covers accommodation, half board and funds the projects.
Benefits: Projects are self funding. We can recommend organisations that might give support.
Training: Given on site.
Supervision: Supervision undertaken by a team of on site research co-ordinators.
Charity number: 38394227
Worldwide placements: Europe (Spain).

ATLANTIS WORKING GUEST

Kirkegata 32
0153 Oslo
Norway
T: +47 22 47 71 70
F: +47 22 47 71 79
E: atlantis@atlantis.no
W: www.atlantis.no

Atlantis Youth Exchange is a non-profit organisation established by the Norwegian Youth Council in 1987. Our goal is to promote respect and understanding between cultures through youth exchange. We have specialised in long-term work experience programmes for young people between 18 and 30. All programmes are based on the idea of working for free accommodation, board and pocket money. Each year we send and receive a total of 1500 young people on various programmes. We are a full member of IAPA (International Au Pair Association). Programmes are as follows – au pair in Norway and working guest within farming and tourism in Norway. 🖹

Number of projects: 1 UK: 0
Starting months: January–December
Time required: 6–12 weeks
Age: 18–30
Causes: Animal Welfare, Conservation, Environmental Causes.

Activities: Agriculture/Farming, Conservation Skills, Forestry, Gardening/Horticulture.
When to apply: 3–4 months before desired date of arrival.
Work alone/with others: Usually Working Guests are placed alone with a family or with one or maximum of two other Working Guests.
Qualifications: Agricultural experience preferred by not essential. Fluent English. No restrictions – maximum stay of up to 24 weeks for EU/EEA citizens.
Health requirements: Health certificate required.
Costs: Contact us for up to date information.
Benefits: Board and lodging with family. Pocket money (NOK825 per week).
Interviews: Via application.
Worldwide placements: Europe (Norway).

AVON WILDLIFE TRUST

The Wildlife Centre
32 Jacob's Wells Road
Bristol
BS8 1DR UK
T: 0117 917 7270
F: 0117 929 7273
E: avonwt@cix.co.uk
W: www.wildlifetrust.org.uk/avon
Contact: Volunteering Officer

The Avon Wildlife Trust aims to protect wildlife in our area, and to educate people about that wildlife. Volunteers are involved in all areas of the organisation, from administration and looking after members to education of children, leading practical days on nature reserves, working with planning applications, surveying wildlife sites etc. Volunteers with an offending background are accepted. ▤

Number of projects UK: 20
Starting months: January–December
Time required: 26–52 weeks (plus)
Age: 16 plus – no upper limit
Causes: Conservation, Environmental Causes, Teaching – Primary, Wildlife.
Activities: Administration, Agriculture/Farming, Campaigning, Computers, Conservation Skills, Driving, Forestry, Group Work, Manual Work, Teaching.
Placements: 20
When to apply: All year.
Work alone/with others: With other volunteers.
Health requirements: Nil.
Costs: Travel.
Benefits: Reimbursement of actual travel expenses.
Training: Job specific. Additional training is offered to longer term placements.
Supervision: Volunteer Officer.
Interviews: Interviews at our office in Bristol.
Charity number: 280422
UK placements: England (Bristol, Gloucestershire, Somerset).

B

BAND LTD (BRISTOL ASSOCIATION FOR NEIGHBOURHOOD DAYCARE)

81 St Nicholas Road
St Paul's
Bristol
BS2 9JJ UK
T: 0117 954 2128
F: 0117 954 1694
E: admin@BANDLtd.org.uk
W: www.BANDLtd.org.uk
Contact: Paul Dielhenn

BAND was established in 1978 in response to the Finer Joint Action Committee report. This report recognised that one of the most basic needs for working or training parents is care for school age children outside school hours. Such a facility would enable parents to work or train full time thus supporting the family unit to become stable and financially independent. Formed originally by five childcare groups the number of BAND member organisations providing afterschool and/or holiday services soon began to grow. Funding for a full time co-ordinator was secured in 1982 and by 1986 there were 12 BAND groups operating. Financial support from national and local government, trusts and charities allowed more staff to be employed by BAND. This supported the further promotion and development of new and existing groups, expansion of the range of support services offered to members and an increase in the level of networking opportunities, locally, regionally, nationally and internationally. BAND currently employs 12 staff and has around 180 autonomous full or affiliated member groups, providing services to approximately 4,000 families. Full member groups are managed by voluntary committees whose members have children attending the group. Affiliated members share BAND's overall aims and operate in the field of childcare. The continued growth in member groups and the high demand for the services they offer is clear indication that affordable, accessible, good quality, neighbourhood-based childcare remains a basic need for many parents, particularly for single parent and/or low income families. Bristol, S. Gloucestershire, Bath and NE Somerset and North Somerset. ⑤

Number of projects UK: 1
Starting months: January–December
Time required: 1–52 weeks
Age: 16 plus – no upper limit
Causes: Children, Young People.
Activities: Arts/Crafts, Cooking, Music, Outdoor Skills, Theatre/Drama.

When to apply: Holidays – particularly summer holidays.
Work alone/with others: With others.
Qualifications: Nil but driving licence and experience of working with children would be useful.
Health requirements: Nil.
Costs: Sometimes travel costs, accommodation and food.
Benefits: Sometimes travel costs.
Training: Access to BAND training programme. Groups arrange their own induction programmes.
Supervision: Supervised by senior playworker, ultimately by Manager or Chair of Group.
Interviews: Groups would arrange interviews.
Charity number: 1017307
UK placements: England (Bristol).

BANGLADESH WORK CAMPS ASSOCIATION (BWCA)

289/2, North Shajahanpur
(Work Camp Road)
Dhaka 1217 Bangladesh
T: 880 2 9358206/9356814
F: 880 2 95 5506/5483
E: bwca@bangla.net
W: www.mybwca.org
Contact: Abdur Rahman

Bangladesh Work Camps Association (BWCA) promotes international solidarity and peace through organising community development, which takes the form of national/international work camps for volunteers in rural and urban areas of Bangladesh. Projects include environment and health education, literacy, sanitation, aforestation, community work, development and construction etc. Volunteers work 30 hours per week on placements, which last for 1–6 weeks from October to February. A RTYP (Round the Year Programme) is also available to medium-term volunteers staying for a minimum period of three months. At least 50 volunteers a year are recruited onto one to five international work camps and 30 volunteers through RTYP. Volunteers must be able to speak English, be adaptable to any situation and be team-spirited. Unable to place volunteers with an offending background. BWCA projects are within different villages in Bangladesh – north, west and east surrounded by India and Myanmar. In the south covered by the Bay of Bengal. 🖹

Number of projects: 2 UK: 0
Starting months: January–December
Time required: 2–12 weeks

Age: 18–35
Causes: AIDS/HIV, Children, Conservation, Disabled (learning and physical), Elderly People, Environmental Causes, Health Care/Medical, Human Rights, Inner City Problems, Poor/Homeless, Refugees, Teaching/assisting (nursery, primary, secondary, EFL), Unemployed, Work Camps – Seasonal, Young People.
Activities: Administration, Agriculture/Farming, Building/Construction, Campaigning, Community Work, Computers, Conservation Skills, Cooking, Counselling, Development Issues, First Aid, Forestry, Fundraising, Gardening/Horticulture, Group Work, Manual Work, Newsletter/Journalism, Outdoor Skills, Research, Social Work, Sport, Summer Camps, Teaching, Training, Translating, Visiting/Befriending, Work Camps – Seasonal.
Placements: 50–100
When to apply: At least 15 days before work camp and 1 month before any 'Round the Year Programme' (RTYP) assignment starts. Work camps run from October to February, RTYP programmes run throughout the year.
Work alone/with others: Work with other local and international volunteers.
Qualifications: No academic qualifications or experience needed for work camps, for RTYP – project working experience required or skilled volunteers required depending on assignment.
Equipment/clothing: Extra 'old' work clothes for rough use.
Health requirements: Volunteers who are in excellent health only.
Costs: Travel costs to and from projects. Registration fee and food charge for RTYP. Applications will be accepted accompanied by US$25.
Benefits: Board and lodging during programme/assignment.
Training: Every project, work camp is, in it self, a training course. There is a one day orientation session before work camps or RTYP.
Supervision: Volunteers are supervised by the host organisation at the project.
Interviews: No interview required but every volunteer should send their CV along with their application.
Charity number: .215 with Department of Social Welfare
Worldwide placements: Asia (Bangladesh).

BARDOU RESTORATION PROJECT

Bardou
Mons La Trivalle
F-34390 Olargues
France
T: 00 33 467 97 72 43
Contact: Klaus and Jean Erhardt

Bardou needs volunteers to help restore and maintain 16th Century stone houses in a remote mountain hamlet. 20 hours weekly participation in community projects is expected. Volunteer work includes assisting builders in restoration and maintenance, painting of the houses, forest clearance and mountain path repair. Tending animals is also an occasional task. Volunteers needed 1st April until 1st July. Short-term visitors and study groups are accepted and will be charged an overnight fee starting at €8 per night per person. Applicants will be sent detailed directions as to how to reach Bardou by public transport. Applicants should write a letter in English giving full name, age, experience, education and cultural interests. Bardou is a meeting place for world travellers and nature lovers. Bardou is a hamlet in the Cevennes Mountains of Southern France. 🖹

Number of projects: 1 UK: 0
Starting months: Apr, May, Jun
Time required: 4–12 weeks
Age: 20–50
Causes: Animal Welfare, Architecture, Conservation, Environmental Causes, Heritage, Wildlife.
Activities: Agriculture/Farming, Arts/Crafts, Building/Construction, Conservation Skills, Forestry, Manual Work, Music, Theatre/Drama.
Placements: 4
When to apply: Any time.
Work alone/with others: Both.
Qualifications: English language, energy, attentiveness and good will. No specific skills or French are required, however a good cultural education and background are appreciated. Volunteers from the following countries are accepted: Australia, New Zealand, Canada, South Africa, European Community and United States of America.
Equipment/clothing: Recommended to bring: torch (flashlight), matches, light rain gear, sturdy shoes, alarm clock, food and sleeping bag (if possible).
Health requirements: Physically and mentally fit.
Costs: Travel costs, insurance and about €50–60 per week for food.
Benefits: Free lodging (self catering house). Breakfast on work days.
Interviews: Interviews are conducted by letter or phone.
Worldwide placements: Europe (France).

BARDSEY BIRD AND FIELD OBSERVATORY

Cristin Ynys Enlli (Bardsey Island)
Off Aberdaron
Pwllheli
Gwynedd Wales LL53 8DE UK
T: +44 (0) 7855 264151
E: staff@bbfo.freeserve.co.uk
W: www.bbfo.org.uk
Contact: Steven Stansfield

Bardsey Bird and Field Observatory is based on Bardsey Island, off the Gwynedd coast of North Wales. Volunteers can expect training in research, bird identification and ringing of birds. 🔲 📃

Number of projects UK: 1
Starting months: Mar
Time required: 2–24 weeks
Age: 18–65
Causes: Conservation, Heritage, Wildlife.
Activities: Computers, Conservation Skills, Manual Work, Outdoor Skills, Scientific Work.
Placements: 15
When to apply: Any time.
Work alone/with others: Work alone and in groups.
Qualifications: A knowledge of birds and their identification are minimum requirements.
Equipment/clothing: Waterproof clothes required.
Health requirements: There may be restrictions for overseas volunteers – more details from observatory.
Costs: £25.00 for the cost of the boat + food costs.
Benefits: Accommodation.
Training: Bird identification and ringing training offered.
Supervision: All volunteers are supervised by the Warden.
Interviews: Interviews are usually undertaken over the telephone.
UK placements: Wales (Gwynedd).

BARNARDO'S – LEASE CHILDREN'S SERVICES

Scotch House
Tanners Lane
Barkingside
Ilford
Essex IG6 1QG UK
T: +44 (0) 208 551 0011
F: +44 (0) 208 551 8267
E: celya.maxted@barnardos.org.uk
Contact: Celya Maxted

Barnardo's, the UK's biggest and best known children's charity, works with 90,000 children, young people and families. It has 300 services which provide accommodation and support for young people who have lived in local authority homes and are leaving care; youth training; day care in deprived areas; special education for children with disabilities; and fostering and adoption. We work with those affected by poverty, HIV/Aids, homelessness and child sexual abuse. We work with children and their families and provide day care and safe play areas for under fives. Volunteers with an offending background may be accepted depending on the offence. No offences against children. All applicants are police checked. 🔲 📃

Number of projects UK: 37
Starting months: January–December
Time required: 1–52 weeks
Age: 14–75
Causes: Addicts/Ex-Addicts, AIDS/HIV, Children, Disabled (learning and physical), Inner City Problems, Offenders/Ex-Offenders, Poor/Homeless, Refugees, Teaching/assisting, Work Camps – Seasonal, Young People.
Activities: Accountancy, Administration, Agriculture/Farming, Arts/Crafts, Building/Construction, Campaigning, Caring (general, day and residential), Catering, Community Work, Computers, Conservation Skills, Cooking, Counselling, Development Issues, DIY, Driving, First Aid, Forestry, Fundraising, Gardening/Horticulture, Group Work, International Aid, Library/Resource Centres, Manual Work, Marketing/Publicity, Music, Newsletter/Journalism, Outdoor Skills, Religion, Research, Scientific Work, Social Work, Sport, Summer Camps, Teaching, Technical Skills, Theatre/Drama, Training, Translating, Visiting/Befriending, Work Camps – Seasonal.
Placements: 20,000
When to apply: All year.
Work alone/with others: With others.
Qualifications: Obtaining the necessary CRB check means that we unfortuantely are unable to use volunteers from overseas – UK residents only.
Health requirements: Nil.
Costs: Normally Nil.
Benefits: Expenses reimbursed, training.
Interviews: Volunteers are interviewed at the projects in which they are to work.
Charity number: 216250
UK placements: England (throughout); Scotland (throughout); Northern Ireland (throughout); Wales (throughout).

BARNARDO'S – Midlands

Reception, Divisional Office
Brooklands, Great Cornbow
Halesowen
West Midlands B6 3AB UK
T: +44 (0) 121 550 5271
F: +44 (0) 121 550 2594
E: michael.baker@barnardos.org.uk
W: www.barnardos.org.uk
Contact: Corporate Volunteer/Development Manager

For more details of Barnardo's, see Barnardo's – Lease Children's Services, above. 🔲 📃

Number of projects UK: over 300
Starting months: January–December
Time required: 1–52 weeks (plus)
Age: 14 plus – no upper limit
Causes: AIDS/HIV, Children, Disabled (learning and physical), Offenders/Ex-Offenders, Young People.

Activities: Administration, Arts/Crafts, Caring – General, Catering, Community Work, Computers, Counselling, Development Issues, DIY, Driving, Fundraising, Gardening/ Horticulture, Group Work, Manual Work, Marketing/Publicity, Newsletter/ Journalism, Outdoor Skills, Social Work, Teaching, Technical Skills, Theatre/Drama, Training, Translating, Visiting/Befriending.
When to apply: Via web site 24 hours a day/356 days a year.
Work alone/with others: Both.
Qualifications: Although we have no restrictions on nationalities of volunteers, obtaining the necessary police check from the Home Office means that we cannot normally use volunteers from overseas.
Health requirements: Nil.
Costs: Nil.
Benefits: Travel and all expenses paid.
Training: Mandatory training is offered in core areas. Training given as needed for project work.
Supervision: Individual and group supervision available.
Interviews: Volunteers are interviewed at the projects in which they are to work.
UK placements: England (West Midlands).

BARNARDO'S – North East

Orchard House
Fenwick Terrace
Jesmond
Newcastle upon Tyne
NE2 2JQ UK
T: 0191 240 4800
F: 0191 281 9840
E: lana.kirkup@barnardos.org.uk
W: www.barnardos.org.uk
Contact: Lana Kirkup

For more details of Barnardo's, see Barnardo's – Lease Children's Services, above. Barnado's – North East was born in 1892 when the first 'Ever Open Door' house opened in Saville Row. Since then we have come a long way, meeting the ever changing needs of children, young people and their families. We positively welcome the many benefits that volunteers can bring to Barnado's. ⑤

Number of projects UK: 28
Starting months: January–December
Time required: 1–52 weeks (plus)
Age: 16–75
Causes: Addicts/Ex-Addicts, AIDS/HIV, Children, Disabled (physical), Inner City Problems, Offenders/Ex-Offenders, Poor/ Homeless, Teaching – Mature, Unemployed, Young People.
Activities: Administration, Arts/Crafts, Caring – General, Catering, Community Work, DIY, Driving, Fundraising, Gardening/Horticulture, Group Work, Library/Resource Centres, Manual

Work, Marketing/Publicity, Music, Newsletter/ Journalism, Outdoor Skills, Social Work, Sport, Teaching, Technical Skills, Theatre/Drama, Training, Visiting/Befriending.
Placements: 300
When to apply: All year.
Work alone/with others: Both.
Qualifications: Although we have no restrictions on nationalities of volunteers, obtaining the necessary CRB check from the Home Office means that we cannot normally use volunteers from overseas.
Health requirements: Nil.
Costs: Nil.
Benefits: Travel and all expenses paid.
Training: Differs from project to project but training is mainly given in working with children, child protection, health and safety, equal opportunities.
Supervision: Named person at project responsible for volunteers.
Interviews: Interviews take place either at Divisional Office or at the project.
Charity number: 216250
UK placements: England (Co. Durham, Cumbria, Northumberland, Tyne and Wear).

BARNARDO'S – North West

7 Lineside Close
Belle Vale
Liverpool
Merseyside L25 2UD UK
T: 0151 488 1100
F: 0151 488 1101
E: rachel.hodges@barnardos.org.uk
W: www.barnardos.org.uk
Contact: Rachel Hodges

For more details of Barnardo's, see Barnardo's – Lease Children's Services, above. ⑤

Number of projects UK: 300+
Starting months: January–December
Time required: 1–52 weeks (plus)
Age: 16 plus – no upper limit
Causes: AIDS/HIV, Children, Disabled (learning and physical), Holidays for Disabled, Inner City Problems, Poor/Homeless, Refugees, Young People.
Activities: Administration, Arts/Crafts, Campaigning, Caring (general and day), Community Work, Counselling, DIY, Driving, Fundraising, Gardening/Horticulture, Group Work, Manual Work, Music, Newsletter/ Journalism, Social Work, Teaching, Theatre/ Drama, Training, Visiting/Befriending.
Placements: Varies.
When to apply: All year.
Work alone/with others: Both.
Qualifications: None needed but any welcomed, depending on project e.g. driving licence, languages etc. Although we have no restrictions on nationalities of volunteers,

obtaining the necessary police check from the Home Office means that we cannot normally use volunteers from overseas.
Health requirements: Nil.
Costs: Nil.
Training: Differs with each project but training is mainly given in working with children, child protection, health and safety, equal opps. Training within retail will be given on site and other training will be addressed depending on the volunteering opportunity.
Supervision: Depends on involvement e.g. summer playschemes – daily informal supervision.
Interviews: Volunteers are interviewed at the projects in which they are to work. If the volunteer is within the area of the Regional office then the Corporate Volunteer Development Manger will interview.
Charity number: 216250
UK placements: England (Cheshire, Cumbria, Lancashire, Manchester, Merseyside).

BARNARDO'S – Northern Ireland

Divisional Office
542/544 Upper Newtownards Road
Belfast
BT4 3HE N. Ireland
T: 02890 672366
F: 02890 672399
E: alun.kane@barnardos.org.uk
W: www.barnardos.org.uk
Contact: Mr Alun Kane

For more details of Barnardo's, see Barnardo's – Lease Children's Services, above. Central to the work of Barnardo's are the roles played by our many volunteers. Across N. Ireland and 25 retail shops across N. Ireland too.   ♿ 📄

Number of projects UK: 300+
Starting months: January–December
Time required: 2–52 weeks (plus)
Age: 16 plus – no upper limit
Causes: Children, Health Care/Medical, Young People.
Activities: Administration, Community Work, Group Work, Social Work, Visiting/Befriending.
Placements: 150+
When to apply: Any time but 2 months in advance of preferred start date.
Work alone/with others: Mostly with others.
Qualifications: Varies – depending on volunteer work in question. Although we have no restrictions on nationalities of volunteers, obtaining the necessary police check from the Home Office means that we cannot normally use volunteers from overseas.
Health requirements: No specific requirements.
Costs: Board and lodging.
Benefits: Out of pocket expenses and travel reimbursed.

Training: Training is provided to all volunteers within our childrens services work.
Supervision: Yes – as appropriate.
Interviews: Interviews take place either at the projects or at the Regional office.
UK placements: Northern Ireland (throughout).

BARNARDO'S – Scotland

235 Corstorphine Road
Edinburgh
EH12 7AR UK
T: +44 (0) 131 334 9893
F: +44 (0) 131 316 4008
E: alison.mclaughlin@barnardos.org.uk
W: www.barnardos.org.uk
Contact: Alison McLaughlin

For more details of Barnardo's, see Barnardo's – Lease Children's Services, above. At Barnardo's Scotland we promote social inclusion in the face of a wide range of issues. We do this with the support of volunteers – in children's services, fundraising and in our shops. We could not raise as much money or reach as many children without volunteers. ♿ 📄

Number of projects UK: 60 in Scotland
Starting months: January–December
Time required: 1–52 weeks (plus)
Age: 16–80
Causes: Children, Young People.
Activities: Administration, Community Work, Driving, Fundraising, Social Work, Summer Camps, Visiting/Befriending.
Placements: Varies.
When to apply: All year. Search for volunteer vacancies online at www.barnardos.org.uk
Work alone/with others: Both.
Qualifications: Although we have no restrictions on nationalities of volunteers, obtaining the necessary police check means that we cannot normally involve volunteers from overseas.
Health requirements: Nil.
Costs: Nil.
Benefits: Travel and all expenses paid.
Training: Provided.
Supervision: Provided.
Interviews: Volunteers are interviewed at the projects, office or shop where they will volunteer.
UK placements: Scotland (throughout).

BARNARDO'S – Wales and South West England

11–15 Columbus Walk
Brigantine Place
Atlantic Wharf
Cardiff
CF1 5BZ UK

T: +44 (0) 29 2049 3387
F: +44 (0) 29 2048 9802
E: nickjenkin@barnardos.org.uk
W: www.barnardos.org.uk
Contact: Volunteer Co-ordinator

For more details of Barnardo's, see Barnardo's – Lease Children's Services, above. We welcome applicants and if there is one area that you would like to be involved in please contact Sian Jones for an informal chat. 🔊 📄

Number of projects UK: 350
Starting months: Jul, Aug
Time required: 4 weeks
Age: 16–75
Causes: Children, Disabled (learning and physical), Young People.
Activities: Arts/Crafts, Caring – Day, Cooking, Driving, First Aid, Outdoor Skills, Sport, Summer Camps.
Placements: 1,750
When to apply: All year.
Work alone/with others: Both.
Qualifications: Although we have no restrictions on nationalities of volunteers, obtaining the necessary police check from the Home Office means that we cannot normally use volunteers from overseas.
Health requirements: Nil.
Costs: Nil.
Benefits: Travel, meal subsistence and all expenses paid.
Training: Full training given before any volunteering is undertaken. There is usually an induction training given to prepare volunteers for their role and an opportunity to meet other workers and volunteers.
Supervision: Support and supervision is given to all volunteers.
Interviews: Volunteers are interviewed at the projects in which they are to work.
Charity number: 216250
UK placements: England (Bristol, Somerset); Wales (Anglesey, Blaenau Gwent, Bridgend, Caerphilly, Cardiff, Carmarthenshire, Ceredigion, Conwy, Denbighshire, Flintshire, Gwynedd, Merthyr Tydfil, Monmouthshire, Neath Port Talbot, Newport, Pembrokeshire, Rhondda, Cynon, Taff, Swansea, Torfaen, Vale of Glamorgan, Wrexham).

BARNARDO'S – Yorkshire

Signpost
Constance Green Centre, 24 Cheapside
Wakefield
West Yorkshire WF1 2TF UK
T: +44 (0) 1924 304100
F: +44 (0) 1924 304101
E: jo.hunt@barnardos.org.uk
W: www.barnardos.org.uk
Contact: Jo Hunt

For more details of Barnardo's, see Barnardo's – Lease Children's Services, above. Barnardo's values volunteering because everybody – the users of our services, staff and volunteers – benefits. 🔊 📄

Number of projects UK: 1
Starting months: January–December
Time required: 1–52 weeks (plus)
Age: 16–70
Causes: Children, Disabled (learning and physical), Holidays for Disabled, Offenders/Ex-Offenders, Poor/Homeless, Young People.
Activities: Driving, Group Work, Visiting/Befriending.
Placements: 200
When to apply: All year, particularly in September and April.
Work alone/with others: Occasionally with other young volunteers.
Qualifications: Individual assessment to ascertain suitability. Although we have no restrictions on nationalities of volunteers, obtaining the necessary police check from the Home Office means that we cannot normally use volunteers from overseas.
Health requirements: Not specifically.
Costs: Nil.
Benefits: All out of pocket expenses met.
Interviews: All volunteers are interviewed – each project has a screening process for volunteers.
Charity number: 216250
UK placements: England (E. Yorkshire, N. Yorkshire, S. Yorkshire, W. Yorkshire).

BEANNACHAR (CAMPHILL) LTD

Beannacher
Banchory-Devenick
Aberdeen
Aberdeenshire
AB12 5YL UK
T: +44 (0) 1224 869138
F: +44 (0) 1224 869250
E: beannachar@talk21.com
W: www.camphillsccotland.org.uk
or W: www.beannachar.co.uk.
Contact: Elisabeth Phethean

Beannachar needs volunteers to live and work with young adults with special needs. Work is to be done in the kitchen, laundry, garden and on the farm. Tasks also include making herbal medicines and candles, weaving and woodwork. 🔊

Number of projects UK: 1
Starting months: January–December
Time required: 26–52 weeks (plus)
Age: 19 plus – no upper limit
Causes: Animal Welfare, Disabled (learning and physical), Teaching/assisting, Young People.
Activities: Agriculture/Farming, Arts/Crafts, Building/Construction, Caring (general, day and

residential), Catering, Cooking, Gardening/ Horticulture, Manual Work, Music, Outdoor Skills, Sport, Teaching, Theatre/Drama, Training.
Placements: 10–12
When to apply: All year.
Work alone/with others: We all live and work together as a community.
Qualifications: Fluent English, enthusiasm and an interest in others.
Equipment/clothing: Old clothes suitable for gardening and walks, waterproofs and warm clothes.
Health requirements: Good health.
Costs: Nil.
Benefits: Organisation pays for day-to-day living costs + £35 per week. All volunteers live in and receive board and lodging.
Training: None at present. Induction talks at the beginning and foundation course once weekly throughout their stay.
Supervision: Volunteers supervised by house parent and experienced co-workers.
Interviews: Interviews take place, if possible, at the office in Aberdeen.
Charity number: 103915
UK placements: Scotland (Aberdeen City, Aberdeenshire, Angus, Argyll and Bute, Clackmannanshire, Dumfries and Galloway, Edinburgh, Lothian – East, Lothian – West, Moray, Perth and Kinross, Stirling).

BEAUFORT COMMUNITY CENTRE

Beaufort Road
Southbourne
Bournemouth
Dorset BH6 5LB UK
T: +44 (0) 1202 417143
F: +44 (0) 1202 434203
E: suemanager@aol.com
Contact: Sue Smith

The Beaufort Community Centre is an independent charity providing facilities for education, recreation and social welfare in Bournemouth. Volunteers with an offending background may be accepted. ♿ 📄

Number of projects UK: 1
Starting months: January–December
Time required: 1–52 weeks
Age: 16 plus – no upper limit
Causes: Children, Elderly People, Young People.
Activities: Administration, Arts/Crafts, Caring (general and day), Catering, Newsletter/ Journalism.
Placements: 40
When to apply: All year.
Work alone/with others: With others.
Qualifications: If working with children, volunteers must be approved by Social Services.
Health requirements: Nil.
Costs: Accommodation and food.

Benefits: Travel expenses paid.
Training: As necessary.
Supervision: Manager and administrator give support and supervision of all staff and volunteers.
Interviews: Interviews take place at the Centre in Dorset.
Charity number: 800843
UK placements: England (Dorset).

BEEHIVE SCHOOL TRUST IN MALAWI

The Grange
Naburn
York
YO19 4RU UK
T: +44 (0) 776 100 8000
E: grange@naburn.u-net.com
Contact: Lucy Bradshaw

Malawi is a beautiful Central African country and one of the poorest in the world. It has the second lowest literacy in Africa. There is a shortage of classrooms, teachers and other resources. We are building the Beehive School in Mzuzu where there is a very urgent need for help of all kinds including teachers in all the schools. Alternative Contact: Mr Niall Dorey, Co-Trustee of The Beehive School Trust, P O Box 669, Mzuzu. 📄

Number of projects: 1 **UK:** 0
Starting months: January–December
Time required: 4–52 weeks
Age: 18–75
Causes: Children, Poor/Homeless, Teaching/ assisting (nursery, primary), Young People.
Activities: Arts/Crafts, Development Issues, Fundraising, Library/Resource Centres, Outdoor Skills, Social Work, Teaching, Training, Visiting/ Befriending.
When to apply: All year but it is ideal to start in June/July.
Qualifications: Educated to 'A' level. Experience of working with young people or teaching desirable. We welcome volunteers from different backgrounds and different ethnicities.
Equipment/clothing: Any books or other learning resources would be welcomed.
Health requirements: Innoculations – refer to WHO guidance for Malawi.
Costs: No registration charges for UK nationals who do not require visas for Malawi. Subsistence costs are very low. The flight costs are the main expense.
Benefits: Volunteers may be offered free board and lodging at the discretion of the school. However it is more likely that volunteers will be helped in finding their own accommodation.
Training: Before leaving the volunteer will be given an induction pack with useful information. Our local trustee in Malawi will provide full local advice, training and support.

Supervision: The volunteer will be provided with a local 'mentor' and supervised within the school.
Interviews: We do not require an interview but if volunteers would like to discuss their placement on the phone or in person, we would be delighted to chat about it.
Worldwide placements: Africa (Malawi).

BEFRIENDERS INTERNATIONAL

Room 2, Parman House
30/36 Fife Road
Kingston upon Thames
KT1 1SY UK
T: +44 (0) 208 547 3041
F: +44 (0) 208 547 3905
E: fundraising@befrienders.org
W: www.befrienders.org
Contact: Leish Mason

Befrienders International is the umbrella organisation of The Samaritans and has branches all over the UK and in 41 countries abroad. Volunteers are only needed for their London office. 🔣 📄

Number of projects: 1 UK: 1
Starting months: January–December
Time required: 12–52 weeks (plus)
Age: 18 plus – no upper limit
Causes: Addicts/Ex-Addicts, AIDS/HIV, Disabled (learning and physical), Elderly People, Health Care/Medical, Human Rights, Inner City Problems, Offenders/Ex-Offenders, Poor/ Homeless, Refugees, Unemployed, Young People.
Activities: Administration, Community Work, Fundraising, Marketing/Publicity.
When to apply: All year.
Work alone/with others: With others.
Health requirements: Nil.
Costs: Nil.
Benefits: Reasonable travel expenses and £3 lunch substitute.
UK placements: England (London).

BELARUSSIAN ASSOCIATION OF INTERNATIONAL YOUTH WORK

220119 Belarus
P/b 64
Minsk
Belarus
T: 00 375 172 .278183
F: 00 375 172 .222714
Contact: Anna Dolgatcheva or Tanya Barinova

Belarussian Association of International Youth Work (ATM) is an independent NGO, which promotes voluntary work through participation in various youth exchanges: workcamps, study camps, seminars and Russian language courses. It is a member of the Co-ordinating Committee for International Voluntary Service (CCIVS

UNESCO), of the Belarussian Youth Council, of GATE (East-West commission of Service Civil International), and of Mobility International. One of the basic activities of ATM is the organisation of workcamps and studycamps (usual duration of three to four weeks) in Belarus in such different fields as: ecology and environment; work with children; work with disabled people; renovation/reconstruction/ archaeology; social/youth problems; peace work. ATM is realising the Anti-Chernobyl Project. ATM is also concerned with democracy education and is now implementing the TACIS democracy programme 'Common Power or Common Sense', and promoting by way of its workcamps and study camps grassroots education regarding alternative ways of living, practical experimentation with power games and discussions concerning organisational democracy. Volunteers with an offending background are accepted. All people should apply on equal grounds through the regular application process. 📄

Number of projects: 14 UK: 0
Starting months: Jul, Aug, Sep
Time required: 20–35 weeks
Age: 18–25
Causes: Archaeology, Architecture, Children, Disabled (physical), Environmental Causes, Human Rights, Work Camps – Seasonal, Young People.
Activities: Administration, Building/Construction, Community Work, Computers, Development Issues, Fundraising, Group Work, Library/Resource Centres, Newsletter/Journalism, Research, Social Work, Summer Camps, Technical Skills, Training,

Translating, Visiting/Befriending, Work Camps – Seasonal.
Placements: 150
When to apply: All year.
Work alone/with others: With others in groups of 10–20 people.
Qualifications: English, Russian desirable, computer skills.
Equipment/clothing: Personal computer if possible. Working clothing for workcamps.
Costs: Depends on each project. Ins. needed. DM100–150 reg.fee. Internal travel costs.
Benefits: Food, accommodation, cultural activities.
Interviews: Applicants are interviewed.
Worldwide placements: Europe (Belarus).

BELGIAN EVANGELICAL MISSION

P.O. Box 165
Swindon
Wilts SN5 6LU UK
T: +44 (0) 1793 882368
F: +44 (0) 1793 882368
E: bemuk@cs.com
W: www.B-E-M.org
Contact: Roy Saint

The Belgian Evangelical Mission (BEM) conducts summer evangelical campaigns in a number of towns and villages in both French and Dutch speaking Belgium. BEM has run short-term programmes since the 1970s. In the early days teams were involved, and still are today if there are sufficient volunteers for a given period. However, when numbers are low individuals can be accommodated, working in support of our church-planting projects and gaining experience of servicing the Lord in another culture. Study days are arranged in relation to the work of the Mission.

Number of projects: up to 10 UK: 0
Starting months: Jun, Jul, Aug, Sep
Time required: 3–52 weeks
Age: 18–30
Causes: Children, Young People.
Activities: Campaigning, Music, Religion, Sport, Theatre/Drama.
Placements: 10–20
When to apply: Preferably before May but definitely before the end of June.
Work alone/with others: With others under experienced leadership.
Qualifications: For long projects (e.g. 11–12 mths) language required.
Health requirements: Reasonably fit.
Costs: £50 p/w + travel.
Benefits: Accommodation arranged locally, often dormitory style accommodation in church halls etc.
Training: A booklet of notes and advice to volunteers is provided. A training element is ruled into the placement.

Supervision: Volunteers are placed in teams under the supervision of permanent staff normally based locally.
Charity number: 249192
Worldwide placements: Europe (Belgium).

BENDRIGG TRUST

Bendrigg Lodge
Old Hutton
Kendal
Cumbria LA8 0NR UK
T: +44 (0) 1539 723766
F: +44 (0) 1539 722446
E: office@bendrigg.org.uk
W: www.bendrigg.org.uk
Contact: Mrs Sue Murphy

The Bendrigg Trust is a residential activity centre for disabled and disadvantaged people. We are open throughout the year and take a very wide range of groups including people with learning disabilities, physical disabilities or sensory disabilities. We also run courses for able-bodied young people who are socially disadvantaged in any way and for minority groups. We employ a team of experienced and qualified staff to run the centre and to provide the activities. However, we need extra people to help us in a voluntary capacity in all areas of our work. The Trust uses the outdoors and the residential experience to: promote integration, encourage independence and to build self-confidence in our visitors. We also try to ensure that there are as many benefits to the volunteer as to the Bendrigg Trust. Volunteers help us in a number of ways including maintenance, grounds, catering and domestic work. We also need help for our tutorial staff in providing support for the activities we provide. These include: climbing and abseiling, canoeing, kayaking and rafting, caving, sailing, orienteering, ropes courses, aerial runway and tube-slide, arts and crafts including games and projects. We try and utilise whatever skills the volunteers have for the benefit of our visiting groups. Volunteers with an offending background are accepted providing they can be interviewed first at Bendrigg Lodge. 🔄

Number of projects UK: 1
Starting months: January–December
Time required: 1–4 weeks
Age: 16 plus – no upper limit
Causes: Children, Disabled (learning and physical), Holidays for Disabled, Inner City Problems, Unemployed, Young People.
Activities: Arts/Crafts, Caring – Residential, Catering, Cooking, Gardening/Horticulture, Group Work, Outdoor Skills.
Placements: 120
When to apply: All year.
Work alone/with others: Both.
Qualifications: Not essential but useful.

Health requirements: Nil, but any medical condition must be declared.
Costs: Initial travel to Bendrigg.
Benefits: Board and lodgings only provided.
Training: None.
Supervision: Volunteers are supervised all the time by qualified instructors and the volunteer co-ordinator.
Interviews: All interviews take place at Bendrigg Lodge.
Charity number: 508450
UK placements: England (Cumbria).

BERKS, BUCKS AND OXON WILDLIFE TRUST

The Lodge
1 Armstrong Road
Littlemore
Oxford
OX4 4XT UK
T: +44 (0) 1865 775476
F: +44 (0) 1865 711301
E: volunteers@bbowt.cix.co.uk
W: www.bbowt.org.uk
Contact: Gemma Swann

The Berkshire, Buckinghamshire and Oxfordshire Wildlife Trust is an independent registered charity and is the only voluntary organisation concerned with all aspects of wildlife conservation in these counties. We protect wildlife on over 90 nature reserves and aim to involve all people – children, adults, community groups and organisations – in taking action for local wildlife. Modern threats to wildlife include intensive farming, industrial development, house and road building, and the use of pesticides. Nature reserves are places where wildlife – especially rare and endangered wildlife – can be looked after, studied and enjoyed. Our nature reserves are carefully looked after to encourage the survival and spread of wild plants and animals. Every five years our conservationists work out new action plans for each nature reserve. The plans are individually tailored for the particular species that need to be protected on each site and identify key tasks – such as clearing ponds or creating nature trails – which are mainly carried out by local volunteers. Regular surveys ensure the plans are successful and that our nature reserves continue to be havens for local wildlife. We also need volunteers to help with administration work and help out in our shop in Wantage as well as carrying out practical conservation work. 🖹

Number of projects UK: 50 approx
Starting months: January–December
Time required: 1–52 weeks (plus)
Age: 16 plus – no upper limit
Causes: Conservation, Environmental Causes, Wildlife.

Activities: Conservation Skills, Forestry, Gardening/Horticulture, Manual Work, Marketing/Publicity, Outdoor Skills, Research.
Placements: 2,000
When to apply: All year.
Work alone/with others: With others.
Qualifications: No skills required.
Equipment/clothing: Old clothes, waterproofs, sturdy boots. We provide safety boots.
Health requirements: Any medical conditions (illness, allergy or physical disability) that may require treatment/medication or which affects the volunteer working with machinery must be notified to us in advance.
Costs: Travel costs to and from pick-up points + packed lunch.
Benefits: Tea and coffee provided and transport to the worksite.
Training: Some on the job training may be given ie. monitoring species etc.
Interviews: Prospective volunteers are not interviewed.
Charity number: 204330
UK placements: England (Berkshire, Buckinghamshire, Oxfordshire).

BERRINGTON HALL – NATIONAL TRUST

Berrington Hall
Leominster
Herefordshire HR6 0DW UK
T: +44 (0) 1568 615721
F: +44 (0) 1568 613263
E: berrington@nationaltrust.org.uk
W: www.nationaltrust.org.uk
Contact: Yvonne Osborne

Berrington Hall is a National Trust property which requires volunteer room stewards every day from April to October, particularly at weekends. Also needed are volunteer car park attendants to work on Bank Holidays. Volunteers are also required to work in the shop, March through to December, and in the garden volunteers are required all year round. Volunteer office staff required all year. Property is remote – own transport would be useful. ♿

Number of projects UK: 1
Starting months: January–December
Time required: 1–52 weeks
Age: 16–75
Causes: Conservation, Heritage.
Activities: Accountancy, Administration, Community Work, Computers, Conservation Skills, Fundraising, Gardening/Horticulture, Manual Work, Marketing/Publicity.
Placements: 100
When to apply: All year.
Work alone/with others: Both.
Health requirements: Must be fit.
Costs: Subsistence.
Benefits: Travel costs. Those who offer 40 hours of service get a volunteer card entitling them to

free entry to National Trust Properties in the UK and 10% discount in the shops. Locum flat available for short term placements.
Training: Visit to property and 'job shadowing'. Focus on customer training and any other relevant training are also offered.
Supervision: Mansion volunteers use 'buddy' system and are supervised overall by house steward. Shop volunteers are supervised by shop manager, garden volunteers by head gardener and office volunteers are supervised by the property assistant.
Interviews: Interviews take place at the property.
Charity number: 205846
UK placements: England (Herefordshire, Worcestershire).

BHARAT SEVAK SAMAJ (BSS)

Nehru Seva Kendra
Bye Pass Road
Mehrauli
New Delhi 110 030
India
T: 00 91 11 6852215/6644761/ 5719791
F: 00 91 11 5781744
E: cbssaNil@yahoo.com
Contact: Anil Dawesar

Bharat Sevak Samaj (BSS) runs a programme which includes child welfare centres, nursery schools, training camps for national reconstruction work, family planning camps and clinics, youth workcamps, seminars, workshops and library. The work also encompasses relief and reconstruction after natural calamities such as famine, drought, cyclones and earthquakes as well as the construction of houses for the Scheduled Caste (lowest) and tribes, and low cost latrines in villages.

Starting months: January–December
Time required: 2–12 weeks
Age: 14–80
Causes: Children, Conservation, Environmental Causes, Health Care/Medical, Poor/Homeless, Teaching/assisting (EFL).
Activities: Building/Construction, Caring – General, Community Work, Conservation Skills, Development Issues, Group Work, International Aid, Social Work, Teaching.
Placements: 50
When to apply: All year.
Qualifications: English or Hindi speaking.
Equipment/clothing: Suitable clothes for personal use only.
Health requirements: Responsibility of the volunteer.
Costs: Travel to India and internal travel by rail and bus. US$22 per week for food and lodging. Food is simple and healthy in tune with local conditions on BSS premises and projects.
Worldwide placements: Asia (India).

BIG SWAMP WILDLIFE PARK

PO Box 21
Bunbury
WA6231 Western Australia
T: 00 61 8 9721 8380
F: 00 61 8 9721 7509
E: sherim@bunbury.wa.gov.au
Contact: Sheri Metternick-Jones

The Big Swamp Wildlife Park is a city council owned facility established in 1986. The Park is maintained primarily by volunteers. Along with a full-time co-ordinator, two part-time animal attendants aid in the upkeep and running of the facility. Volunteers are responsible for daily kiosk operation, grounds keeping, feed preparation and enclosure maintenance. Along with core volunteers, there is community service personnel work for the dole participants. All contribute to the running of this unique wildlife park. Volunteering at the Big Swamp Wildlife Park is a great opportunity to meet new people and gain valuable experience in the areas of customer relations and wildlife care. Volunteers with an offending background are accepted but an Australian visa may prove difficult. 🖔 📖

Number of projects: 1 UK: 0
Starting months: January–December
Time required: 2–52 weeks (plus)
Age: 18 plus – no upper limit
Causes: Animal Welfare, Children, Conservation, Offenders/Ex-Offenders, Unemployed, Wildlife, Young People.
Activities: Building/Construction, Community Work, Conservation Skills, Gardening/ Horticulture, Manual Work, Outdoor Skills.
Placements: 100
When to apply: Approximately 1 week before starting.
Work alone/with others: With others.
Qualifications: English-speaking and numeracy.
Equipment/clothing: Neat, tidy clothes and enclosed shoes.
Health requirements: Nil.
Costs: All costs, including own lunch, travel, accommodation etc.
Benefits: Accommodation is not provided, however there is a YHA Hostel within 2km of the Park.
Training: Training provided.
Supervision: Volunteers are supervised at all times.
Interviews: Interviews take place on location, prior to commencement.
Worldwide placements: Australasia (Australia).

BIMINI BIOLOGICAL FIELD STATION

9300 SW 99 Street
Miami
Dade 33176 2050 USA

T: 305 274 0628
F: 305 274 0628
E: sgruber@rsmas.miami.edu
W: www.miami.edu/sharks
Contact: Dr. Samuel H. Gruber

The Bimini Biological Field Station is a small, self contained, independent research station affiliated to but not owned by the University of Miami. Most of the research involves the abundant and accessible elasmobranches fish fauna, especially the lemon shark. The marine environments can be reached from the station within minutes. These include sandy, muddy and rocky shores, sea grass and mangrove forests and coral reefs. The Gulf Stream flushed Bimini waters are considered pristine. The station is located on the south island, practically in isolation. Our primary research involves elucidation of the role of the lemon shark in a tropical marine ecosystem. This work uses the disciplines of systems ecology, molecular biology bioenergetics, life history studies, fishery biology, ethology and sensory biology. Other specific field studies by the investigators dealing with the abundant elasmobranches fauna will be willingly considered. Our small fleet consists of one 22ft CCP Aquasport, two 16ft center console Prolines, four small 16ft Carolina skiffs and two 19ft Carolina skiffs for working in very shallow water. A minimum stay of one month is necessary. We, unfortunately, cannot accept volunteers with an offending background. We are looking for volunteers primarily with a biological background. The Bimini Biological Field Station is located at Bimini, Bahamas, 42 nautical miles (85km) east of Miami, Florida USA. 🖐 📄

Number of projects: 1 UK: 0
Starting months: January–December
Time required: 4–24 weeks
Age: 20–35
Causes: Conservation, Environmental Causes, Wildlife.
Activities: Conservation Skills, Research, Scientific Work.
Placements: 50
When to apply: As early as possible as places are limited.
Work alone/with others: Both depending on project.
Qualifications: Those with an interest in biology/biology background, wanting field experience/internship, wanting to work with sharks, students involved in graduate programme looking for a research project for their degree work.
Equipment/clothing: Most equipment will be provided. A list of appropriate gear will be sent with the application.
Health requirements: In general good health disclosing any medical conditions within application form.

Costs: Air fares + $240 round trip chartered flight to Bimini. $15 Bahamas head tax. Share research costs, accommodation and meals is US$575.00 for 4 weeks. There is an additional $50/month if volunteers do an independent project. $135.00 refundable deposit.
Benefits: Fully equipped facilities. In station – a wood-frame house on a sheltered lagoon in near isolation – sleeps 22 in double bunks.
Training: Training provided.
Supervision: Volunteers are supervised by resident staff and researchers.
Interviews: Via application form.
Worldwide placements: Central America Bahamas).

BIO-EXPERIENCE

56 Cross Road
Tableview
Cape Town
7441 South Africa
T: +27 12 331 5483
F: +27 12 331 5483
E: bioexperience@absamail.co.za
W: www.bioexperience.org
Contact: Natanya Dreyer

Bio-Experience is an organisation that assists conservancies, game farms and wildlife rehabilitation centres to obtain a means of funding. Due to the expense involved in running the conservancy, wildlife rehabilitation centres and game farms, South Africans tend to neglect the ecological aspect of this type of business. The cheaper alternative is to develop these areas, an alternative that Bio-Experience is trying to prevent. Bio-Experience assists these organisations in obtaining volunteers to assist with ecological management, game management and some wildlife rehabilitation. Volunteers pay for their accommodation and this then funds the organisation. The greatest benefit is the work the volunteers do for the organisation from assisting in game counts to taking out invader plants. The value of the volunteer cannot be emphasised enough. Placements available – Nature Reserve Warmbaths Area – Nylstroom in Waterberg hosting game species, rare blue crane and various tree and grass species. Bird and Small Mammal Rehabilitation Centre in Rivona, South Africa, rehabilitating 100s of animals and mammals a year. Monkey Sanctuary and Rehabilitation Centre in Limpopo Province looking after over 500 monkeys. Animal Centre – Zoo Rehabilitation in Stellenbosch, located on a farm, interacting with exotic and rare animals. Klikop Nature Reserve – Bankenveld, big game, birdlife and small mammals in 300 ha reserve. Marine Bird Wildlife Rehabilitation in Cape Town. Plains Game Wildlife Rehabilitation Centre near Gravelotte for injured/orphaned animals. Helderberg Wildlife, Cape Town specialising in raptors and reptiles. Big Five Game Reserve and Game Lodge Management near Kruger National Park. Lion Park in Gauteng wildlife breeding and reserve. Eco Access in Gauteng assisting people with disabilities to gain access to nature, mainly children arranging outdoor activities on camps. Organic farming in Natal, empowering disadvantaged people by training and teaching them to become self-sufficient through organic farming. Klipkop Rehabilitation and Research Trust in Gauteng. ☒ ▤

Number of projects: 14 **UK:** 0
Starting months: January–December
Time required: 2–52 weeks (plus)
Age: 16–65
Causes: Animal Welfare, Children, Conservation, Disabled (learning and physical), Environmental Causes, Poor/Homeless, Teaching/assisting, Unemployed, Young People.
Activities: Agriculture/Farming, Community Work, Conservation Skills, Forestry, Gardening/Horticulture, Manual Work, Outdoor Skills, Research, Scientific Work, Teaching.
Placements: 120
When to apply: At least two months prior to wishing to volunteer.
Work alone/with others: With others.
Qualifications: No specific qualifications required, adults of all ages and anyone who enjoys the great outdoors. Some projects require fluency in English. Students welcome studying natural sciences and research students in natural environment. 16 & 17 year olds need parents to sign contract and indemnity.
Health requirements: Volunteers must be in good health and be up to date with anti-tetanus injections.
Costs: Varies between projects – from R6,000 (US$600) for organic farm to R10,000 (US$1,000) for game rehabilitation project for one month. Flights to Sth Africa. Some projects include laundry/food/travel to project in cost, please contact us for more details.
Benefits: Accommodation. Some projects include food/laundry and daily travel to project. Please contact for more details. Meals included do not include luxury items such as alcohol and soft drinks.
Training: Training offered on projects.
Supervision: All volunteers are supervised on projects.
Interviews: Through application process.
Worldwide placements: Africa (South Africa).

BIOSPHERE EXPEDITIONS

Sprats Water
Nr Carlton Colville
The Broads National Park
Suffolk NR33 8BP UK
T: 01502 583085
F: 01502 587414

E: info@biosphere-expeditions.org
W: www.biosphere-expeditions.org
Contact: Michelle Bell

Biosphere Expeditions is an award winning, non-profit making organisation running real wildlife conservation expeditions to all corners of the earth. Our projects are not tours, photographic safaris or excursions, but genuine wildlife expeditions placing people with no research experience alongside scientists who are at the forefront of conservation work. Our expeditions are open to all, there are no special skills or fitness required to join and there are no age limits whatsoever. Our expedition team members are people from all walks of life, of all ages, looking for an adventure with a conscience and a sense of purpose. Projects run worldwide, all year round, and you can join for anything from two weeks to several months. Expedition contributions vary depending on the project and at least two-thirds of your contribution benefits the project directly. We always work with the local people and scientists, teams are small and there is a dedicated expedition leader with the team at all times. Will accept volunteers with an offending background. Namibian savannah, Polish Mountains, Black Sea Coast in Ukraine, Russia's Altai Republic Mountains and Amazon in Peru. ☒ ▤

Number of projects: 5 **UK:** 0
Starting months: January–December
Time required: 2–8 weeks
Age: 14 plus – no upper limit
Causes: Animal Welfare, Conservation, Wildlife.
Activities: Administration, Conservation Skills, Development Issues, Manual Work, Research.
Placements: 200
When to apply: Any time.
Work alone/with others: Work with others.
Equipment/clothing: Kit list needed for each expedition.
Health requirements: Reasonably fit.
Costs: Expedition contribution – from £990 per 2 weeks + travel cost to country assembly point.
Benefits: Once contribution has been paid everything is all inclusive from assembly point.
Training: Full training provided.
Supervision: Expedition leader and scientists on every expedition.
Interviews: No interview.
Worldwide placements: Africa (Namibia); South America (Peru); Europe (Poland, Russia, Ukraine).
UK placements: England (Suffolk).

BIRDWATCH IRELAND

Ruttledge House
8 Longford Place
Monkstown
Co. Dublin Ireland

T: 00 353 1 280 4322
F: 00353 1 284 4407
E: bird@indigo.ie
W: www.birdwatchireland.ie
Contact: Senior Development Officer

Birdwatch Ireland undertakes research, surveys and applied conservation projects focusing on the protection of wild birds and their habitats in the Republic of Ireland. 📖

Number of projects: 5 UK: 0
Starting months: Jun, Jul, Aug, Sep, Oct, Nov
Time required: 14–26 weeks
Age: 18 plus – no upper limit
Causes: Wildlife.
Activities: Administration, Manual Work, Outdoor Skills, Research, Scientific Work.
Placements: 10
When to apply: Oct – Jan
Work alone/with others: With experienced personnel.
Qualifications: No qualification necessary but full driving licence and experience in bird conservation would be advantageous. No restrictions, but applicants from non-EU countries should ensure that they have the appropriate visa.
Equipment/clothing: Walking shoes and rainproof clothing required, binoculars helpful.
Health requirements: No health restrictions.
Costs: No fee but volunteers must pay for their own travel in Ireland and accommodation.
Benefits: Hands on practical experience.
Training: Training given if required.
Supervision: Provided by Project Officer.
Interviews: Interviews take place in Dublin unless by prior arrangement.
Worldwide placements: Europe (Ireland).

BIRMINGHAM PHAB CAMPS

2 Lenchs Green
Edgbaston
Birmingham
B5 7PX UK
T: +44 (0) 121 440 5727
E: maxine@bhamphabcamps.org.uk
W: www.bhamphabcamps.org.uk
Contact: Maxine Wallis

Birmingham PHAB Camps runs holiday camps each summer in England for equal numbers of physically disabled and able-bodied children, enabling the disabled children to integrate with their able-bodied contemporaries. There are seven camps a year, three of which cater for different age groups from 8–16 years; three are run for severely multiply-disabled children of all ages; and one for young adults aged 18 to around 25. Many children who are physically disabled have little opportunity to mix and form friendships with their peer groups, and the camps are designed to remedy this isolation and

overcome prejudice. There is a wide range of activities, from swimming and discos to seaside and theme parks in which all the children take part together as equals. The camps are run entirely by unpaid volunteers. The team includes an experienced leader and a qualified nurse. ♿

Number of projects UK: 7
Starting months: Jul, Aug
Time required: 1–1 weeks
Age: 16–40
Causes: Children, Disabled (learning and physical), Holidays for Disabled, Young People.
Activities: Arts/Crafts, Caring – General, Driving, Fundraising, Music, Outdoor Skills, Sport, Summer Camps, Theatre/Drama.
Placements: 100 approx.
When to apply: Any time but preferably around January/February.
Work alone/with others: With others.
Qualifications: Volunteers must be able to speak English.
Health requirements: Nil.
Costs: Pocket money + £10 for police check.
Benefits: Accommodation, food and transport between camp and Birmingham. All costs and accommodation taken care of. We leave and return from Birmingham and can arrange accommodation for those from outside Birmingham who may wish to stay the night before.
Training: We run a training day around the end of June where we cover all aspects of the camp and volunteers have the opportunity to meet others. Training days are given before each camp.
Supervision: Each camp is staffed by a group of volunteers some of whom will be new and others experienced. These include an experienced leader and a qualified nurse.
Interviews: No interviews but it is essential that applicants attend a training day in June.
Charity number: 502073
UK placements: England (Cheshire, Derbyshire, Hampshire, Shropshire, West Midlands, N. Yorkshire).

BIRMINGHAM YOUNG VOLUNTEERS

4th Floor
Smithfield House
Digbeth
Birmingham
B5 6BS UK
T: +44 (0) 121 622 2888
F: +44 (0) 121 622 1114
W: www.byadventurecamps.org.uk
Contact: BYV Co-ordinator

BYV Adventure Camps exists to provide summer holidays for children and young people who otherwise would not have a holiday. All the children are referred by Social Services, schools and other agencies. Volunteers who have been involved with the Adventure Camps project for a week during the summer are encouraged to become involved with the management of the project and the planning of the holidays. There are a number of committee posts to fill, such as children's co-ordinator, volunteer co-ordinator, transport co-ordinator, training co-ordinator, trusts co-ordinator etc. These posts are taken on for the year and involve a certain number of hours work outside committee meetings and reporting back at committee meetings. 📄

Number of projects UK: 2
Starting months: January–December
Time required: 1–52 weeks
Age: 17 plus – no upper limit
Causes: Children, Young People.
Activities: Administration, Arts/Crafts, Cooking, Driving, First Aid, Fundraising, Marketing/Publicity, Newsletter/Journalism, Outdoor Skills, Social Work, Sport, Summer Camps, Training, Visiting/Befriending.
Placements: 140–160
When to apply: All year round.
Work alone/with others: Both, mainly with other volunteers as a team supervising children and young people.
Qualifications: Previous experience with the young an advantage. Driving, first aid, sport, arts etc. It is essential that volunteers taking on these posts are Birmingham-based or are able to attend meetings regularly. Volunteers must be able to travel to Birmingham when required.
Equipment/clothing: Clothes suitable for camping and outdoor activities.
Health requirements: Need to know volunteers medical condition so their needs can be assessed.
Costs: £10–£50 registration fee returnable if not placed + spending money would be needed.
Benefits: All costs are met during the week's camps. There are opportunities for training, both within the project and using Birmingham City Council resources related to play, youth and

community work. Much of this training is free.
Training: Provided on pre-camp meeting.
Supervision: Via camp leaders.
Interviews: Once accepted, volunteers are invited for a pre-camp meeting.
UK placements: England (Herefordshire, Warwickshire); Wales (Gwynedd).

BLUE DOG ADVENTURES

Amwell Farmhouse
Nomansland, Wheathampstead
St Albans
Herts AL4 8EJ UK
T: 01582 831302
F: 01582 834002
E: info@bluedogadventures.com
W: www.bluedogadventures.com
Contact: Jenna Troy

Blue Dog Adventures provides people with the opportunity to experience the world and accomplish extraordinary things without spending a fortune. Blue Dog Adventures offers equestrian experiences and adventure internships all over the world. Blue Dog Adventures works strictly with organisations located in untouched regions of our planet, who want to keep them that way. All our partners support conservation and community development and many opportunities provide you with the chance to take part in conservation research, eco-training and to work with charities like the Working Horse Association in Romania. 📄

Number of projects: 12 UK: 0
Starting months: January–December
Time required: 4–24 weeks
Age: 18–75
Causes: Animal Welfare, Conservation, Environmental Causes, Wildlife.
Activities: Building/Construction, Conservation Skills, Cooking, Development Issues, Forestry, Marketing/Publicity, Outdoor Skills, Research, Scientific Work, Training.
Placements: 100

Environmental Tasks Down Under

Robbie Barnes's contact with WorldWide Volunteering took him to the other side of the world working for two months with the Australian Trust for Conservation Volunteers in three different states. The work included tree planting, weeding, animal surveys, fence and path building and plant observation. ATCV welcomes

participants from across the globe which enabled Robbie "to develop my communications skills and learn about new cultures. My work with ATCV was the most worthwhile part of my gap year. I learnt much about the damage humans are inflicting on our planet."

When to apply: Projects start monthly – apply at least 3 months before wishing to start.
Work alone/with others: Varies.
Qualifications: Depends on project.
Health requirements: Must have fully comprehensive health insurance.
Costs: Flights, comprehensive insurance and visa where required are to be covered by the volunteer.
Benefits: Costs includes board and lodging as well as training.
Training: Full training provided.
Supervision: Fully supervised.
Interviews: Application process – sometimes an interview (depends on programme).
Worldwide placements: Africa (Morocco, South Africa); North America: (Canada, USA); Central America (Costa Rica, Honduras); Asia (Turkey); Australasia (Australia); Europe (Romania, Spain, Turkey).

BLUE VENTURES

52 Avenue Road
London
N6 5DR UK
T: 0778 6854466
E: tom@blueventures.org
W: www.blueventures.org
Contact: Tom Savage

Blue Ventures is an award winning UK based not-for-profit organisation dedicated to facilitating projects that enhance global coral reef conservation and research. Since its creation Blue Ventures has co-ordinated marine projects in Madagascar, Tanzania, New Zealand, South Africa and the Comoros Islands. Healthy coral reefs are fundamental to the livelihoods of hundreds of millions of people in tropical coastal environments, as well as forming part of the crucial life support system of the biosphere. However, coral reefs worldwide are increasingly subjected to over exploitation and to degradation by anthropogenic and natural, particularly climatic impacts. Blue Ventures co-ordinates teams of marine scientists and volunteers, working hand-in-hand with local biologists, marine institutes, NGOs, and communities whose livelihoods depend on coral reefs, to carry out research, environmental awareness and conservation programmes at threatened reef habitats around the world. Despite the value of our work, many of the nations we have worked with have no resources to undertake these projects themselves. Blue Ventures continues to offer opportunities and field experiences, both in the UK and overseas, to volunteers wanting to become actively involved in marine conservation. Our teams are made up of dynamic, enthusiastic and committed volunteers,

coming from a wide range of backgrounds, cultures and experiences. We pride ourselves on this diversity. We may be able to offer placements to volunteers with an offending background. Belo-sur-Mer, Madagascar. 🔣 📄

Number of projects: 1 UK: 0
Starting months: Oct, Nov, Dec
Time required: 4–18 weeks
Age: 17–70
Causes: Animal Welfare, Conservation, Environmental Causes, Wildlife.
Activities: Building/Construction, Community Work, Conservation Skills, Fundraising, Group Work, International Aid, Outdoor Skills, Research, Scientific Work, Sport, Training.
Placements: 100
When to apply: As soon as possible.
Work alone/with others: With others.
Equipment/clothing: Personal diving equipment – mask wetsuit, snorkel and fins – all main diving equipment provided.
Health requirements: Must have doctor's certificates.
Costs: £1600 per six week project. Flight to Madagascar. Insurance and personal diving equipment.
Benefits: Diving training, scientific training, all board and lodging, food and all in field activities.
Training: Training is provided. Diving training to PADI Advanced level.
Supervision: All volunteers will be supervised by PADI Open Water Instructor, Medical Officer, Science Officer and Expedition Leader. Local staff are also on hand to provide support.
Interviews: Yes. Over the telephone.
Charity number: Currently applying.
Worldwide placements: Africa (Comoros, Madagascar, South Africa, Tanzania); Australasia (New Zealand).

BMS WORLD MISSION

P.O. Box 49
Baptist House
Didcot
Oxfordshire
OX11 8XA UK
T: +44 (0) 1235 517647
F: +44 (0) 1235 517601
E: jlegg-bagg@bms.org.uk
Contact: Jo Legg-Bagg

BMS World Mission works in partnership with Baptist churches in more than 40 countries on four continents – Africa, Asia, Latin America and Europe. We have around 200 missionaries engaged in pastoral and church planting work, engineering, teaching, agriculture, community and medical work, etc. Our aim to enable Christians in Britain to respond to the call of God by sharing with all God's people in making known the gospel of Jesus Christ throughout the whole world. BMS run three types of schemes: 1. A year out programme, called Action Teams, for young people between the ages of 18–25. Six months are spent overseas and on return the team tour around the UK sharing with Baptist churches what they have learnt and experienced. Training prior to departure overseas and on their return are seen as important parts of this programme; 2. Summer Teams are run in the months of July and August and consist of teams going overseas for between three to six weeks. Previous teams have spent time in Brazil, Uganda, Lebanon, India and Thailand, assisting in various social development projects and supporting the work of local missionaries; 3. Individual volunteers serve with BMS from between three months and two years. Volunteers are accepted with specialist and non-specialist skills, depending on the need in a particular country.

Number of projects: 40 UK: 0
Starting months: Jul, Sep
Time required: 2–52 weeks (plus)
Age: 18–25
Causes: Addicts/Ex-Addicts, AIDS/HIV, Children, Elderly People, Health Care/Medical, Human Rights, Inner City Problems, Poor/Homeless, Refugees, Teaching/assisting (nursery, primary, secondary, EFL), Unemployed, Work Camps – Seasonal, Young People.
Activities: Administration, Arts/Crafts, Building/Construction, Caring (general, day and residential), Community Work, Computers, Cooking, Development Issues, DIY, Gardening/ Horticulture, Group Work, Library/Resource Centres, Manual Work, Music, Newsletter/ Journalism, Outdoor Skills, Religion, Social Work, Sport, Summer Camps, Teaching, Technical Skills, Theatre/Drama, Training, Visiting/Befriending, Work Camps – Seasonal.
Placements: 140
When to apply: All year but the end of February for Action Teams.
Work alone/with others: With others in a team of between 4 and 10.
Qualifications: Committed Christians recommended by own church. No nationality restrictions but applicants should be UK based.
Health requirements: Reasonable health but really dependent on the country.
Costs: Gap year c. £3,100 fully inclusive (board, travel, training etc.) for year. Summer Teams £800–£1200. Individual Volunteers – depends on placement.
Benefits: A great opportunity to serve, develop and have the experience of a lifetime. Accommodation arranged at training venues and overseas in homes or flats.

Training: One month for year teams. Weekend for summer teams and individuals. Devotional, practical and adventure training.
Supervision: Team leader appointed and pastoral contact. Missionary or other church worker overseas the team.
Interviews: Interviews take place at the BMS training centre in Birmingham.
Charity number: 233782
Worldwide placements: Africa (Angola, Congo Dem Republic, Guinea, Mozambique, South Africa, Tunisia, Uganda, Zimbabwe); Central America (El Salvador, Jamaica, Nicaragua, Trinidad and Tobago); South America (Brazil); Asia (Afghanistan, Bangladesh, India, Indonesia, Kazakhstan, Lebanon, Nepal, Sri Lanka, Thailand); Europe (Albania, Belgium, Bulgaria, Croatia, Czech Republic, France, Hungary, Italy, Malta, Poland, Portugal).
UK placements: England (throughout); Scotland (throughout); Northern Ireland (throughout); Wales (throughout).

BONDWAY NIGHT SHELTER

c/o Ms Claire Simpson
CSV, 237 Pentonville Road
London
N1 9NJ UK
T: +44 (0) 171 278 6601 or +44 (0) 800 374991
Contact: Claire Simpson

Bondway Shelter is a 95 bed direct access hostel for homeless men aged 30 and over, many of whom have alcohol and mental health problems, plus long histories of homelessness. The Shelter offers a basic, but supportive, environment 24 hours a day, seven days a week. It is also the base for outreach work and a soup-run which operates every night of the year, catering for up to 200 people sleeping rough in central London. The Shelter's philosophy places minimum demands on the residents, showing a high level of tolerance in order to discourage them from returning to the streets. There are up to 17 volunteer trainees at all times, who work a 40 hour week. Duties include: assisting residents with medication and personal hygiene, liaising with outside agencies, e.g. hospitals, DSS, dental appointments etc., booking in residents, assisting residents with welfare benefit claims, collecting and distributing the post, maintaining the security of the building, preparing the food for the soup run and being responsible for the smooth running of it, assisting in the running of the duty office, handling enquiries etc., dealing with aggressive situations. No volunteers can be recruited directly by Bondway Night Shelter.

Number of projects UK: 6
Starting months: January–December
Time required: 26–52 weeks
Age: 18 plus – no upper limit

Causes: Disabled (learning), Elderly People, Poor/Homeless, Unemployed.
Activities: Administration, Caring (general, day and residential), Catering, Counselling, Driving, Training, Visiting/Befriending.
Placements: 24
When to apply: All year.
Work alone/with others: With other young volunteers.
Qualifications: Competent English. No previous experience needed.
Equipment/clothing: Old clothes for working.
Health requirements: We advise volunteers to have hepatitis and TB innoculations before starting.
Costs: Nil.
Benefits: Accommodation, meals on duty, travel expenses to the project and £62 per week.
Interviews: Interviews take place at the shelter.
UK placements: England (London).

BOTTON VILLAGE

Botton Village
Danby, Whitby
North Yorkshire
YO21 2NJ UK
T: +44 (0) 1287 660871
E: botton@camphill.org.uk
Contact: Mrs Jane Balls

Botton Village is nestled into the moorland landscape of the North York moors. It is a progressive village community of 330 people, many of whom are adults with learning disabilities, participating in the work of five bio-dynamic farms, two vegetable gardens and several high quality craft workshops. We live in thirty extended family homes of 7–16 people and together we create our rich social and cultural life. Each year, at the beginning of October for eight months, we run a half-day weekly foundation course introducing new co-workers to living and working with adults with special needs in a Camphill Community. ♿ 📖

Number of projects UK: 1
Starting months: January–December
Time required: 4–52 weeks
Age: 20–40
Causes: Children, Disabled (learning and physical).
Activities: Agriculture/Farming, Arts/Crafts, Caring (general, residential), Cooking, Forestry, Gardening/Horticulture, Music, Outdoor Skills.
Placements: 30
When to apply: All year.
Work alone/with others: Both – depending on the work.
Qualifications: Social skills as well as common sense, maturity and interest. Experience of landwork, care work or craft is very welcome.
Equipment/clothing: Waterproofs, wellington boots, warm clothing. (N.Yorkshire Moors with unfriendly weather).

Health requirements: Physically and mentally fit.
Costs: Travel costs.
Benefits: Board and lodging. Pocket money when stay is longer than 4 weeks. An experience of community living. Single room provided in extended village households.
Training: Foundation course starts in September for all new people. This offers introduction to Camphill and its work plus artistic activity course one morning and one evening each week. There is bio-dynamic land and farm training (2 years).
Supervision: Work alongside workmaster.
Interviews: Applicants are not interviewed if from outside the UK, but people can visit our community to meet us (+ vice versa) before applying, or come for a few days to experience Camphill life if they live in the UK.
Charity number: 232402
UK placements: England (N. Yorkshire).

BOYS' BRIGADE, THE

Felden Lodge
Felden
Hemel Hempstead
Hertfordshire HP3 0BL UK
T: +44 (0) 1442 231681
F: +44 (0) 1442 235391
E: enquiries@boys-brigade.org.uk
W: www.boys-brigade.org.uk
Contact: Martyn Waters

The Boys' Brigade (BB) is an interdenominational Christian based uniformed youth organisation for boys. The BB aims to communicate a live and meaningful Christian faith. The BB offers a wide ranging and progressive programme of activities in five age groupings: Anchor Boys (5–8) a programme of games, stories, crafts and music. Juniors (8–11) a programme of physical activities, team games, arts and crafts and stories. Some of this is centred around an award scheme offering over 200 activities. Company (12–15) activities based around the headings of adventure, interests, physical, leadership and community. Participation in running the local group is encouraged. Seniors (16–19) active leadership and participation in the BB and the local church, together with work in the local community. Awards include the BB President's and Queen's badges as well as the D of E scheme. AMICUS (15–22) a pilot project working with young men and young women. Members are fully involved in the management of their local group and in determining their own programmes. It is our policy to undertake criminal record checks on all new volunteers who will have supervised or non-supervised access to children or young people. These checks are free to the individual. Volunteers with an offending background may be accepted. ♿ 📖

Number of projects UK: 2000
Starting months: January–December
Time required: 13–52 weeks
Age: 16–60
Causes: Children, Young People.
Activities: Administration, Arts/Crafts, Community Work, Computers, Cooking, First Aid, Fundraising, Group Work, Music, Outdoor Skills, Religion, Sport, Summer Camps, Theatre/Drama, Training, Work Camps – Seasonal.
Placements: 15,000
When to apply: All year.
Work alone/with others: As part of a team.
Qualifications: Skills and abilities to work with children (5+) and young people (up to 22). Christian.
Equipment/clothing: The BB is a uniformed youth organisation.
Health requirements: Nil.
Costs: Annual levy of £20 payable in December, discounts for students and those on a state retirement pension.
Benefits: Some groups are able to reimburse out-of-pocket expenses. The BB in England is a Millenium Volunteers partner, volunteers aged 16–25 may be able to claim out of pocket expenses and monies for training. Volunteers usually live in the local area.
Training: Induction and training is provided for volunteers.
Supervision: Volunteers are supervised by the leader in charge of the unit. Volunteers operate within the BB code of good practice for adults working with children and young people.
Interviews: Applicants for volunteer positions are interviewed by local churches who have BB Companies. Applicants are required to supply references and complete an application form. Applications are made to the Criminal Records Bureau for disclosures.
Charity number: 305969
UK placements: England (throughout); Scotland (throughout); Northern Ireland (throughout); Wales (Blaenau Gwent, Bridgend, Caerphilly, Cardiff, Conwy, Flintshire, Monmouthshire, Neath Port Talbot, Newport, Rhondda, Cynon, Taff, Swansea, Torfaen, Vale of Glamorgan, Wrexham).

BOYS HOPE GIRLS HOPE IRELAND

Lynnwood House
Oldenway Business Park
Ballybrit
Galway Ireland
T: 00 353 91 773577
F: 00 353 91 773580
E: info@boyshope.ie
W: www.boyshope.ie
Contact: Paul O'Callaghan

Boys Hope Girls Hope Ireland admits young adolescents who are unable to remain at home

due to family circumstances such as illness, neglect or abuse. Boys Hope offers security and stability at its residential facility through the forming of trusting relationships between the staff and the young person. The young person is supported in continuing in an educational programme in the community, and encouraged to re-engage with the family of origin where appropriate. Boys Hope Girls Hope is seeking volunteers who may be college graduates of a related discipline and who are interested in broadening their experience through working with young people in a residential programme. All volunteers and staff must submit to a police check in advance of security placement.

Number of projects: 28 UK: 0
Starting months: January–December
Time required: 12–52 weeks
Age: 19–45
Causes: Children, Teaching (primary, secondary, mature, EFL), Young People.
Activities: Caring (day & residential), Outdoor Skills, Social Work, Sport, Teaching.
Placements: 4
When to apply: All year.
Work alone/with others: With full-time staff.
Qualifications: Clean driving licence, experience working with young people preferred. Volunteers should be prepared to be flexible in the work of the project. Non-EU citizens will have to satisfy immigration procedures.
Equipment/clothing: Some sports clothes and camping gear.
Health requirements: Volunteers should be in general good health.
Costs: Travel to project.
Benefits: Health insurance, board and lodging and a small allowance.
Supervision: Volunteers work alongside full-term staff.
Interviews: Interviews take place at the national office in Galway.
Charity number: CHY 11215
Worldwide placements: Europe (Ireland).

BRAENDAM FAMILY HOUSE

Thornhill
Stirling
FK8 3QH UK
T: 01786 850259
F: 01786 850738
E: braendam.house@care4free.net
W: www.braendam.org.uk
Contact: Brian Guidery

Braendam Family House offers ten-day (and weekend break) respite holidays to disadvantaged families from all over Scotland. The parents and children come together, sometimes after long periods (or the threat) of care for their children in local authority foster or institutional homes.

The parents themselves have often had similar negative experiences of family life or may have recently been in prison or in hospital. They may have special needs, learning or physical disabilities, drug or alcohol histories, violent relationships or abusive family relationships. We help them to leave all these experiences behind and face the future with renewed strength and determination. The house itself is an idyllic 17th century house that sits alone in the beautiful rural Scottish countryside with three acres of land. It combines peaceful surroundings for rest and recuperation with a safe play area and a stimulating environment for families who live with the many disadvantages of urban poverty to rebuild their lives and relationships. The atmosphere and communal life created by the staff is both very informal and relaxed as well as supportive and responsive to individual family member's skills and experiences. An enormous array of activities are laid on including visits to safari parks and other places of interest, tree-climbs, the running of a Native American 'sweat' (sauna), abseiling and hill walking, swimming, forest walks, pottery, photography, massage, animal husbandry and gardening. The role of volunteers is to support families on their holiday by: listening and talking to people and viewing them positively; stimulating and playing with children and adults; accompanying families on trips and organising practical aspects of their outing; driving the house vehicles confidently and safely; doing their share of domestic duties including cooking (most of the time we have a cook); cleaning, some DIY, serving food, shopping and making beds; encouraging families to participate in outdoor activities and raising environmental awareness; aiding parents in their parenting (if they seek it); building a relationship of trust and mutual respect with the families; working as a team to ensure that the smooth and pleasant communal life prevails; organising and taking part in fun, games, art crafts and light hearted groupwork. 📖

Number of projects UK: 1
Starting months: January–December
Time required: 26–52 weeks
Age: 18–40
Causes: Addicts/Ex-Addicts, AIDS/HIV, Children, Disabled (learning and physical), Elderly People, Holidays for Disabled, Human Rights, Inner City Problems, Offenders/Ex-Offenders, Poor/Homeless, Unemployed, Young People.
Activities: Arts/Crafts, Caring – General, Cooking, DIY, Driving, First Aid, Gardening/Horticulture, Group Work, Manual Work, Outdoor Skills, Sport, Visiting/Befriending.
Placements: 8
When to apply: All year.
Work alone/with others: Both.

Qualifications: Good English, driving licence, police check and two references. Sense of humour, commitment to helping people feel positive about who they are, positive and enthusiastic outlook.
Equipment/clothing: No special clothing or equipment needed.
Health requirements: Immunisation required from BCG, HIV/Aids, tetanus and hepatitis B. High levels of energy.
Costs: Nil.
Benefits: Travelling costs to Braendam reimbursed up to £40, free board and lodging and £30 spending money given per week.
Training: Food, hygiene and miscellaneous training given. Further fortnightly training and daily team meetings for discussion and learning. Linguistic support is available.
Supervision: 24-hour immediate day-to-day support given by skilled and experienced live-in permanent staff team.
Interviews: Telephone interview.
Charity number: SCO06647
UK placements: Scotland (Stirling).

BRATHAY EXPLORATION GROUP TRUST LTD

Brathay Hall
Ambleside, Cumbria
LA22 0HP UK
T: +44 (0) 1539 433942
F: +44 (0) 1539 433942
E: admin@brathayexploration.org.uk
W: www.brathayexploration.org.uk
Contact: The Administrator

The Brathay Exploration Group was established in 1947. It is a non-profit-making voluntary organisation running expeditions and courses aimed at increasing members' understanding of the natural environment and the people and cultures of the places visited. Volunteers with an offending background may be accepted.

Number of projects: 15 UK: 3
Starting months: Apr, May, Jun, Jul, Aug, Sep
Time required: 1–5 weeks
Age: 15–25
Causes: Conservation, Wildlife, Young People.
Activities: Conservation Skills, First Aid, Outdoor Skills, Scientific Work, Training.
Placements: 250
When to apply: As soon as possible.
Work alone/with others: With others.
Equipment/clothing: Group equipment only provided.
Health requirements: In general good health.
Costs: Expedition fee depending on destination.
Benefits: Accommodation at our base near Ambleside, mountain-style huts. On expedition, camping or hostel-type accommodation.

Training: Most expeditions organise a training/packing weekend at our base.
Supervision: All leaders are volunteers, qualified in relation to expedition destination and activities.
Interviews: Volunteers are not normally interviewed but references are taken up.
Charity number: 1061156
Worldwide placements: North America: (Canada, USA); Central America (Belize); South America (Bolivia); Asia (India).
UK placements: Scotland (Highland, Shetland Islands).

BREAK

1 Montague Road
Sheringham
Norfolk NR26 8LN UK
T: +44 (0) 1263 822161
F: +44 (0) 1263 822181
E: office@break-charity.org
W: www.break-charity.org
Contact: The Residential Volunteers Co-ordinator

Every year young people from all over the world come to Norfolk to help at BREAK'S holiday care centre for children and adults with learning and/or physical disabilities. Whether you are planning a career in a caring profession or taking a gap year from college, volunteering with BREAK is a life-enriching experience and an amazing opportunity to gain awareness of a wide range of disabilities. It's a chance to make lifelong friendships and it will look great on your CV. Residential volunteers work alongside experienced staff assisting guests who need help with meals, dressing, bathing and getting around. You also help out with a programme of activities ranging from swimming to trips out. It can be physically and emotionally demanding but it's also tremendous fun and very rewarding. In return for your commitment and enthusiasm we offer: placements of between six and fifty two weeks; free food and accommodation; travel expenses within the UK; weekly out of pocket expenses. We welcome volunteers from overseas but you do need to be able to speak English to a reasonable standard. 🔆 📄

Number of projects UK: 6
Starting months: January–December
Time required: 6–52 weeks
Age: 18–25
Causes: Children, Disabled (learning and physical), Holidays for Disabled.
Activities: Arts/Crafts, Caring (day and residential).
Placements: 40
When to apply: All year.
Work alone/with others: Usually with others.
Qualifications: Must be able to speak English to a reasonable standard.

Equipment/clothing: Casual clothing.
Health requirements: Ability to cope with physically and emotionally demanding work.
Costs: None – except travel costs to the UK for overseas volunteers.
Benefits: Board, lodging + £30 per week pocket money + travel to and from placement in UK. 1 week's paid leave is given, including return travel costs to and from a destination in the UK, for each completed 4 months of service. Each centre has separate accommodation for volunteers. This consists of shared bedrooms, common room, bathroom(s) and shared kitchen for preparation of snacks (main meals being provided by the centre's kitchen).
Training: All volunteers have an introductory induction session and receive on-the-job training.
Supervision: Volunteers are supervised by professional care staff.
Interviews: No interview required.
Charity number: 286650
UK placements: England (Norfolk).

BRECKNOCK WILDLIFE TRUST

Lion House
Bethel Square, Brecon
Powys
LD3 7AY UK
T: +44 (0) 1874 625708 and 01874 610551
F: +44 (0) 1874 610552
E: brecknockwt@cix.co.uk
W: www.waleswildlife.co.uk
Contact: Tim Breakwell

The Brecknock Wildlife Trust has established a number of important nature reserves, many of them Sites of Special Scientific Interest, either by purchase or through agreement with sympathetic land owners. These reserves are managed for wildlife by the Trust's conservation volunteers, who hold regular work parties. Volunteers with an offending background may be accepted depending on the offence. Volunteers will be based at our offices in Brecon and will be involved in our project to enhance eleven nature reserves within the old county of Brecknock. 📄

Number of projects UK: 1
Starting months: January–December
Time required: 1–52 weeks (plus)
Age: 18–26
Causes: Animal Welfare, Conservation, Environmental Causes, Teaching/assisting, Wildlife.
Activities: Administration, Campaigning, Computers, Conservation Skills, Fundraising, Library/Resource Centres, Manual Work, Marketing/Publicity.
Placements: 6
When to apply: All year.
Work alone/with others: With others.

Qualifications: Interpersonal and communication skills.
Health requirements: Nil.
Costs: Travel and subsistence including food and accommodation.
Benefits: We would help find accommodation which would have to be paid for by the volunteer.
Training: Volunteers will receive training in all relevant aspects of practical and office work.
Supervision: Volunteers will be supervised by Tim Breakwell, Reserves Project Officer.
Interviews: Interviews take place in the office.
Charity number: 239674
UK placements: Wales (Powys).

BRETHREN VOLUNTEER SERVICE

1451 Dundee Avenue
Elgin
Illinois 60120 USA
T: 00 1 (847) 742 5100 x 454
F: 00 1 (847)742 0278
E: bvs_gb@brethren.org
W: www.brethrenvolunteerservice.org
Contact: Recruitment

Brethren Volunteer Service is people giving their time and skills to help a world in need. It is a way for people to work at issues greater than themselves, recognising that their efforts may not immediately solve deep-rooted problems, but can be part of ongoing work for justice, peace, and the integrity of creation. As sponsor of the program, the Church of the Brethren exemplifies its heritage in peacemaking and service through the goals of BVS: working for peace; advocating justice; serving basic human needs; maintaining the integrity of creation. Some volunteers engage in projects that deal with immediate needs. Others work towards changing unjust systems. Sharing God's love through acts of service, volunteers bring hope to shattered lives, offer food and shelter to those in need, and build understanding between individuals, groups, nations and humanity and the world we share. BVS seeks volunteers willing to act on their commitment and values. We challenge individuals to offer themselves, their time and their talents to work which is both difficult and demanding, rewarding and joyful. &

Number of projects: 100 UK: 0
Starting months: Jan, Jun, Sep
Time required: 52 weeks (plus)
Age: 20 plus – no upper limit
Causes: Addicts/Ex-Addicts, AIDS/HIV, Children, Disabled (learning and physical), Elderly People, Environmental Causes, Health Care/Medical, Human Rights, Inner City Problems, Offenders/Ex-Offenders, Poor/Homeless, Refugees, Teaching/assisting, Unemployed, Work Camps – Seasonal, Young People.

Activities: Accountancy, Administration, Agriculture/Farming, Arts/Crafts, Building/Construction, Campaigning, Caring (general, day and residential), Community Work, Computers, Conservation Skills, Cooking, Counselling, Development Issues, Driving, Fundraising, Gardening/Horticulture, Group Work, International Aid, Manual Work, Music, Outdoor Skills, Religion, Research, Social Work, Summer Camps, Teaching, Technical Skills, Training, Translating, Visiting/Befriending, Work Camps – Seasonal.
Placements: 100 approx
When to apply: 2–4 months prior to orientation.
Work alone/with others: Both.
Qualifications: Fluent in English, willingness to examine Christian faith, commitment to goals of BVS, participation in a 3 week orientation.
Health requirements: Sound physical and mental health.
Costs: Travel to USA and back.
Benefits: Medical insurance, board and lodging, pocket money, annual retreat. Adequate housing provided.
Training: Volunteers begin their term of service by participating with 12–30 other volunteers in a 3 week BVS orientation. These are scheduled for the summer, fall and winter of each year.
Supervision: Director of BVS until arrival at project site. Project is responsible for direct supervision.
Interviews: Europeans need to be interviewed by the Geneva co-ordinator of Brethren Service.
Worldwide placements: North America: (USA).

BRIDGE CAMPHILL COMMUNITY

Main Street
Kilcullen
Co. Kildare Eire
T: 045 481597/481691
F: 045 481519
E: volunteer.thebridge@camphill.ie
W: www.camphill.org.uk
Contact: Nicola Hart

Bridge Camphill Community is a life sharing community with adults with special needs. Camphill Communities are found all over the world. One of their main tasks is to live with and care for people with learning disabilities in a social therapeutic way which includes daily life, work, cultural activities and religious life as well as many other aspects of life. Work includes care, housework, work in workshops, gardening, farming, bakery, creamery, laundry, food processing and household maintenance. &

Number of projects: 1 UK: 0
Starting months: January–December

Time required: 26–52 weeks (plus)
Age: 18 plus – no upper limit
Causes: Children, Disabled (learning and physical), Elderly People, Work Camps – Seasonal, Young People.
Activities: Caring – General, Social Work, Summer Camps, Work Camps – Seasonal.
Placements: 8–20
When to apply: Consult our web site for vacancies.
Work alone/with others: With others.
Qualifications: Energy, enthusiasm and a willingness to work. Visas should be arranged before a serious application is made.
Health requirements: Adequate to the task.
Costs: Travel to and from Ireland. (Food and accommodation and a small amount of pocket money are provided while you are here.)
Benefits: Food and accommodation and a small amount of pocket money.
Training: One year foundation course – part time approximately two hours per week.
Supervision: Each short term volunteer assigned a 'friend' from a different house/workplace. Supervision takes place informally through working and living together.
Interviews: No interview, but written application, telephone conversation, two references and police checks.
Worldwide placements: Europe (Ireland).

BRIGHT LIGHT

3 Fentiman Road
London
SW8 1LD UK
T: +44 (0) 20 7361 582 1582
E: enquiries@bright-light.org
W: www.bright-light.org
Contact: Mr Sam Wass

Africa Venture and Bright Light educational tours have joined forces to provide a unique cultural exchange project suitable for young people aged 17–25 with an interest in drama, music and dance. Their three month tours around East Africa feature four visits to local schools, working with and helping young children to produce plays and narratives in the Western tradition, and four visits to local performance troupes, learning about East Africa's unique traditions of narrative dance and oral performance. There will also be time to develop and perform a devised play, in response to your experiences, to be performed at the Bagamoyo international arts festival in Tanzania. These tours, which leave in January and May, are only for the committed. A contribution of £2440 is required to cover costs. We may be able to place volunteers with an offending background.

Number of projects: 1 UK: 0
Starting months: Jan, May

Time required: 12 weeks
Age: 17–25
Causes: Children, Teaching/assisting (primary, secondary).
Activities: Arts/Crafts, Community Work, Music, Theatre/Drama.
Placements: 36
When to apply: As soon as possible.
Work alone/with others: With others.
Qualifications: No, but we do conduct interviews.
Health requirements: No restrictions, but we do ask to be informed about any medical problems volunteers may have.
Costs: Required contribution of £2440 is required to cover costs plus flights and visas.
Benefits: All costs are paid for by us, from the initial contribution that the volunteer makes to the organisation. All accommodation is organised by us, mainly with schools we visit.
Training: There is an acclimatisation week at the start of each visit, fully trained professionals are on hand throughout the time spent in schools.
Supervision: All volunteers are fully supervised by trained professionals at all times.
Interviews: Yes around Britain.
Worldwide placements: Africa (Ethiopia, Kenya, Tanzania, Uganda).

BRISTOL FRIENDS OF THE EARTH

10–12 Picton Street
Montpelier
Bristol
BS6 5QA UK
T: +44 (0) 117 942 0129
E: info@bristolfoe.org.uk
Contact: Mandy Garrett

Number of projects: 1 UK: 1
Starting months: January–December
Time required: 1–52 weeks (plus)
Age: 14 plus – no upper limit
Causes: Children, Elderly People, Teaching/assisting, Young People.
Activities: Community Work, Group Work, Social Work.
UK placements: England (Bristol).

BRITAIN – TANZANIA SOCIETY

17 The Green
London
N14 7EH UK
E: btsenquiries@aol.com
W: www.btsociety.org
Contact: Jill Bowden

The Britain-Tanzania Society/Tanzania Development Trust (TDT) is not a volunteer-sending organisation. Projects supported by TDT are normally implemented by Tanzanian nationals – our project partners working with the ultimate beneficiaries. Members of both the UK and Tanzania chapters of the society give their services voluntarily in connection with the selection, evaluation, processing and funding of projects. We have a range of projects supported by TDT designed to relieve poverty and ignorance, to improve health and nutrition, and to promote self-reliance. Alternative contact address: Peter O. Park, Hon. Projects Officer, 45 Highsett, Hills Road, Cambridge, CB2 1NZ. Telephone: +44 (0) 1223 314835. ⑤

Number of projects: 6–10 UK: 0
Starting months: January–December
Time required: 1–52 weeks
Age: 17 plus – no upper limit
Causes: Addicts/Ex-Addicts, AIDS/HIV, Animal Welfare, Archaeology, Architecture, Children, Conservation, Disabled (learning and physical), Elderly People, Environmental Causes, Health Care/Medical, Heritage, Holidays for Disabled, Human Rights, Inner City Problems, Offenders/Ex-Offenders, Poor/Homeless, Refugees, Teaching/assisting (nursery, primary, secondary, mature, EFL) Unemployed, Wildlife, Work Camps – Seasonal, Young People.
Activities: Agriculture/Farming, Arts/Crafts, Building/Construction, Community Work, Conservation Skills, Development Issues, Forestry, Gardening/Horticulture, Library/Resource Centres, Scientific Work, Teaching, Technical Skills, Training.
When to apply: All year.
Work alone/with others: Both.
Qualifications: Any qualifications are a bonus.
Equipment/clothing: Depends on project.
Health requirements: Anti-malarial pills and necessary innoculations.
Costs: Depends on project – airfare to Tanzania.
Benefits: Depends on project.
Training: Varies according to project.
Supervision: Projects are normally implemented by Tanzanian nationals – our project partners working with the ultimate beneficiaries.
Charity number: 270462
Worldwide placements: Africa (Tanzania).

BRITISH RED CROSS – BUCKINGHAMSHIRE

123 London Road
High Wycombe
Buckinghamshire HP11 1BY UK
T: +44 (0) 1494 525361
F: +44 (0) 1494 465649
E: aashby@redcross.org.uk
Contact: Mrs Alex Ashby

The Red Cross is committed to attracting young people. Its Youth Programme offers a range of training opportunities and skills designed to inspire young people to help their local communities. Young people join either as Junior Members (5–10/11 years), Youth Members (10/11–18 years), or Pioneer Members (16–25 years). They receive free training in skills such as first aid, communication (eg reassuring a client), public speaking, leadership and rescue techniques, with the emphasis on personal development. Red Cross Youth is not all 'blood and guts'. Other training includes nursing, child care, camping and the Duke of Edinburgh Award Scheme to name but a few. All Red Cross branches nationwide have their own youth groups. There are 21 Youth, Junior and Pioneer groups in Buckinghamshire. The society attracts both individual members and school groups through its active schools programme. Volunteers with an offending background are accepted depending on the offence. ⑤ 📄

Number of projects UK: Varies.
Starting months: January–December
Time required: 1–52 weeks
Age: 14–25
Causes: Children, Disabled (learning and physical), Elderly People, Health Care/Medical, Holidays for Disabled, Teaching/assisting, Young People.
Activities: Administration, Arts/Crafts, Caring (general and day), Community Work, Driving, First Aid, Fundraising, Library/Resource Centres, Marketing/Publicity, Outdoor Skills, Summer Camps, Teaching, Training, Visiting/Befriending.
Placements: 300
When to apply: All year.
Work alone/with others: Both.
Qualifications: Nil – basic training given.
Health requirements: Nil.
Costs: Nil.
Benefits: Travel Costs paid.
Interviews: Interview location depends on the project.
Charity number: 220949
UK placements: England (Buckinghamshire).

BRITISH SPORTS TRUST, THE

Clyde House
10 Milburn Avenue
Oldbrook
Milton Keynes
MK6 2WA UK
T: +44 (0) 1908 689180
F: +44 (0) 1908 393744
E: rtulley@bst.org.uk
W: www.thebritishsportstrust.org.uk
or W: www.bst.org.uk.
Contact: Mr R. Tulley

The Central Council of Physical Recreation (CCPR) is the parent body that represents the national governing bodies of sport in the UK. In 1981 it launched the community sports leader award (CSLA) with the aim of training volunteers to assist in the organisation of safe and purposeful activities. The CCPR set up a charity 'The British Sports Trust' which now administers four sports leaders awards within one scheme. Schools, colleges, local authorities, youth associations and prisons are the main users of the following awards: Junior Sports Leader Award. 14 yrs + predominantly used in schools; Community Sports Leader Award. 16 yrs +; Basic Expedition Leader Award. 18 yrs+ leadership in the outdoors; Higher Leader Award. 18 yrs+ specialising in certain areas e.g. special needs, sports administration &

Number of projects UK: 2,600
Starting months: January–December
Time required: 1–52 weeks (plus)
Age: 14–65
Causes: Children, Conservation, Disabled (learning and physical), Elderly People, Offenders/Ex-Offenders, Teaching/assisting (nursery, primary, secondary), Unemployed, Young People.
Activities: Community Work, Conservation Skills, Development Issues, Outdoor Skills, Sport, Summer Camps, Teaching.
Placements: 48,000
When to apply: All year.
Work alone/with others: Both.
Equipment/clothing: Safe sporting clothes and footwear.
Health requirements: Nil.
Costs: Award 1:£5.50, Award 2: £11, Award 3: £22.50, Award 4: £22.50.
Benefits: Yes.
Training: Strongly recommended for tutors of courses.
Supervision: As part of our courses our volunteers work with sports/youth clubs. They are supervised by the coaches/youth workers.
Charity number: 299810
UK placements: England (throughout); Scotland (throughout); Northern Ireland (throughout); Wales (throughout).

BRITISH YOUTH FOR CHRIST

P.O. Box 5254
Halesowen
West Midlands B63 3DG UK
T: +44 (0) 121 550 8055
F: +44 (0) 121 550 9979
E: yfc@yfc.co.uk
W: www.yfc.co.uk
Contact: Christine Nightingale

British Youth for Christ is part of an international family of YFC Ministries in 120 countries worldwide. YFC in Britain was started in 1946 when evangelist Billy Graham came to this country with a passion to see young people reaching out to their peers with the good news of the gospel. Now, over 50 years later, YFC remains committed to the evangelism of young people. Our methods of outreach have changed since 1946, but the message and the heart remain the same. Our mission is to 'take good news relevantly to every young person in Britain'. Our staff and local centres are involved in a diverse number of activities including schools work, drop in centres, detached youth work on the streets, prison ministry, church-based youth work, drop-in centres, large events … the list goes on. YFC is also committed to training and releasing talented young youth workers and evangelists, which is why we offer several year-out opportunities. Volunteers can join us for a year working in sports teams (football, basketball or skateboarding), creative arts teams (drama and dance or music) or just general youth work and evangelism. During the year they receive high-quality, individualised training, as well as great 'hands on' experience. Once a volunteer has completed a year out, they can move on to the YFC Academy for a second year or even a third year of development – where the training and placement are designed around their needs and calling. We may be able to accept volunteers with an offending background, within Safe From Harm Procedure/Guidelines – Youth work. & ▤

Number of projects UK: 9
Starting months: Aug
Time required: 41–52 weeks (plus)
Age: 17–25
Causes: Children, Inner City Problems, Offenders/Ex-Offenders, Teaching/assisting, Young People.
Activities: Community Work, Conservation Skills, Group Work, Music, Religion, Theatre/Drama, Visiting/Befriending.
Placements: 80–90
When to apply: Before 25th August.
Work alone/with others: Work with other volunteers.
Qualifications: Christian faith is required. Some skills needed for theatre/music placements.
Health requirements: No restrictions.
Costs: E.T.A/Academy/Apprenticeship £2100. Sports ; Kick/Skate/Fly £2600. Creative Arts: TVB/Activate £2900.
Benefits: Cost includes comprehensive training, accommodation (including food) and work-related travel.
Training: Three weeks at start of academic year, mid year retreat and end of year 'bash', plus ongoing training throughout year (25% of time spent in study).
Supervision: Placements co-ordinators and one other staff member visits volunteers plus constructive feedback.
Interviews: Interviews are held at various locations throughout Britain.

UK placements: England (throughout); Scotland (throughout); Northern Ireland (throughout); Wales (throughout).

BSES EXPEDITIONS

at The Royal Geographical Society
1 Kensington Gore
London
SW7 2AR UK
T: +44 (0) 207 591 3141
F: +44 (0) 207 591 3140
E: bses@rgs.org
W: www.bses.org.uk
Contact: The Executive Director

All BSES Expeditions combine adventure with exciting scientific fieldwork, research and conservation in wild and trackless areas overseas. The aim is to challenge, educate and aid the self-development process of young people, principally from the UK, between 16.5 and 20 years old. Team leaders range from 25 years upwards. (Assistant leaders 21–24 years). Volunteers with an offending background are accepted in limited numbers. BSES Expeditions is a member of The Year Out Group. Specialists in youth exeditions to Arctic regions. ⓖ

Number of projects: 4 UK: 0
Starting months: Jan, Jul, Sep
Time required: 4–16 weeks
Age: 16.5–70
Causes: Archaeology, Conservation, Disabled (learning and physical), Environmental Causes, Wildlife, Young People.
Activities: Arts/Crafts, Community Work, Conservation Skills, Forestry, Fundraising, Group Work, Outdoor Skills, Research, Scientific Work.
Placements: 270
When to apply: Summer of the previous year. For gap year expeditions, approx. 18 months in advance.
Work alone/with others: With others.
Qualifications: Selection by personal interview. Leaders need to be qualified in science and/or adventure. Minimum age 16.5 (young explorers) or 21 (assistant leaders) and maximum age 20 (young explorers) and 70 (leaders).
Equipment/clothing: Basic adventure clothing e.g. boots, sleeping bag etc.
Health requirements: Must be fit.
Costs: Between £2,000–£2,900. Gap expeditions between £3,000 – £4,000.
Benefits: Advice and assistance given with fundraising, adventure and scientific education. Tents/camping equipment provided.
Training: There is a training session – usually Easter week – at Ilkley, Yorkshire.
Supervision: Leaders and assistant leaders responsible for groups of approximately 12 people.
Interviews: Interviews take place in the London office and in the volunteers' own home areas.

Charity number: 802196
Worldwide placements: Africa (Botswana, Kenya, Lesotho, Malawi, Morocco, Namibia, Tanzania, Zimbabwe); North America: (Canada, Greenland, USA); South America (Chile, Falkland Islands, Peru, South Georgia); Asia (India, Indonesia, Kyrgyzstan, Oman); Australasia (Australia, Papua New Guinea); Europe (Finland, Iceland, Norway, Russia, Sweden).

BTCV – HQ

36 St Mary's Street
Wallingford
Oxfordshire OX10 OEU UK
T: +44 (0) 1491 821600
F: +44 (0) 1491 839646
E: Information@btcv.org.uk
W: www.btcv.org
Contact: Customer Services

BTCV is the UK's largest practical conservation charity. It enables people of all ages from all sections of the community to take action in caring for their environment in towns, cities and the countryside. Every year over 130,000 volunteers take part in conservation projects that include woodland management and tree planting, pond creation and restoration, dry stone walling and footpath work. No prior experience is needed as all projects have experienced leaders. Volunteer opportunities range from day projects, both at weekends and during the week, to week long conservation holidays. Inexpensive training courses enable volunteers to develop new skills. BTCV runs an affiliation scheme for school, youth and community groups that are carrying out practical conservation work. Volunteers with an offending background are accepted at BTCV's discretion.

Number of projects: 650+ UK: 500+
Starting months: January–December
Time required: 1–52 weeks (plus)
Age: 16–85
Causes: Conservation, Environmental Causes, Heritage, Wildlife, Work Camps – Seasonal, Young People.
Activities: Agriculture/Farming, Building/Construction, Community Work, Conservation Skills, Forestry, Gardening/Horticulture, Group Work, Manual Work, Marketing/Publicity, Outdoor Skills, Summer Camps, Technical Skills, Training, Work Camps – Seasonal.
Placements: 130,000
When to apply: All year.
Work alone/with others: With other volunteers.
Qualifications: Varies.
Equipment/clothing: Waterproofs and strong boots.

Health requirements: Tetanus vaccination.
Costs: UK conservation hols £30–£100
depending on destination. International from
£280–£1500.
Benefits: Expenses generally paid.
Training: Training avalable during placement.
Supervision: All volunteers supervised by
qualified leaders.
Interviews: Applicants are not interviewed.
Charity number: 261009
Worldwide placements: Africa (Kenya, South
Africa); North America: (Canada, USA); Central
America (Mexico); South America (Ecuador);
Asia (Japan, Nepal, Thailand, Turkey);
Australasia (Australia, New Zealand); Europe
(Albania, Bulgaria, Estonia, France, Germany,
Greece, Hungary, Iceland, Ireland, Italy, Latvia,
Lithuania, Norway, Poland, Portugal, Romania,
Russia, Slovakia, Spain, Turkey).
UK placements: England (throughout);
Scotland (throughout); Northern Ireland
(throughout); Wales (throughout).

BTCV – NORTH WEST REGION

Davy Hulme Water Treatment Works
Rivers Lane
Urnston
Manchester
M41 7JB UK
T: +44 (0) 161 608 0498
F: +44 (0) 161 608 0497
E: m.desborough@btcv.org.uk
W: www.btcv.org.uk
Contact: Maria Desborough

For more details of BTCV see BTCV HQ, above.

Number of projects UK: 60–70
Starting months: January–December
Time required: 1–52 weeks
Age: 16 plus – no upper limit
Causes: Conservation, Environmental Causes,
Wildlife.
Activities: Administration, Community Work,
Computers, Conservation Skills, First Aid,
Forestry.
When to apply: All year.
Work alone/with others: With others.
Qualifications: Commitment and enthusiasm.
Equipment/clothing: Strong boots and
waterproofs.
Health requirements: Nil.
Costs: Varies.
Benefits: Free training, improved employability.
Training: Training avalable during placement.
Supervision: All volunteers supervised by
qualified leaders.
Interviews: Applicants are sometimes
interviewed.
Charity number: 261009
UK placements: England (Cheshire, Cumbria,
Lancashire, Manchester, Merseyside).

BTCV – SCOTLAND

Ballalan House
24 Allan Park
Stirling
FK8 2QG UK
T: +44 (0) 1786 479697
F: +44 (0) 1786 465359
E: stirling@btcv.org.uk
W: www.btcv.org
Contact: Peter Blackburn

For more details of BTCV see BTCV HQ, above.
BTCV Scotland is a branch of the UK's largest
environmental conservation charity. It involves
people in improving the quality of the
environment through practical conservation.
Volunteers on these projects carry out work
such as drystone dyking, footpath
construction, vegetation clearance and tree
planting. Projects last between 7 and 14 days
and are residential. Regular midweek groups
operate in Glasgow, Edinburgh, Stirling,
Aberdeen, Inverness and Broxham. Volunteers
with an offending background may be accepted
depending on circumstances. 🔊

Number of projects UK: 40 approx.
Starting months: Mar, Apr, May, Jun, Jul, Aug,
Sep, Oct
Time required: 1–2 weeks
Age: 16–70
Causes: Archaeology, Architecture,
Conservation, Environmental Causes, Heritage,
Wildlife, Work Camps – Seasonal.
Activities: Administration,
Building/Construction, Conservation Skills,
Forestry, Fundraising, Gardening/Horticulture,
Manual Work, Marketing/Publicity, Outdoor
Skills, Technical Skills, Work Camps – Seasonal.
Placements: 8,000
When to apply: Any time.
Work alone/with others: With others usually.
Equipment/clothing: Warm, waterproof, safety
boots.
Health requirements: In reasonable health.
Costs: Varies.
Benefits: Accommodation, food, insurance and
training.
Training: Training given on site.
Supervision: A leader and assistant leader on
every project.
Interviews: Applicants are not interviewed.
Charity number: 261009
UK placements: Scotland (throughout).

BTCV – SOUTH EAST/LONDON REGION

80 York Way
King's Cross
London
N1 9AG UK
T: +44 (0) 20 7361 278 4294
F: +44 (0) 20 7361 278 5095

E: London@btcv.org.uk
W: www.btcv.org
Contact: Zoe Ramsden

For more details of BTCV see BTCV HQ, above. 🖫

Number of projects UK: 1,000
Starting months: January–December
Time required: 1–52 weeks
Age: 16 plus – no upper limit
Causes: Conservation, Environmental Causes, Unemployed, Wildlife, Work Camps – Seasonal.
Activities: Building/Construction, Conservation Skills, Gardening/Horticulture, Manual Work, Outdoor Skills, Work Camps – Seasonal.
Placements: 500+
When to apply: All year.
Work alone/with others: With others.
Equipment/clothing: Strong boots and waterproofs.
Health requirements: Nil – please declare any allergies or special medical needs.
Costs: Small contribution for accommodation (approx. £13 for w/e, £40 for week).
Benefits: Food and equipment provided. Accommodation arranged on residential projects only (weekends).
Training: Health and Safety induction and introduction to site ecology.
Supervision: Volunteers are supervised by experienced trained leaders.
Interviews: Applicants are not interviewed.
Charity number: 261009
UK placements: England (Bedfordshire, Berkshire, Buckinghamshire, Essex, Hampshire, Isle of Wight, Kent, Lincolnshire, London, Norfolk, Northamptonshire, Oxfordshire, Surrey, E. Sussex, W. Sussex).

BTCV – SOUTH WEST AREA

7 Station Road
Hemyock
Cullompton
Devon
EX15 3SE UK
T: +44 (0) 1823 680061
F: +44 (0) 1823 680061
E: M.Sibley@btcv.org.uk
W: www.btcv.org
Contact: Miles Sibley

For more details of BTCV see BTCV HQ, above. 🖫

Starting months: January–December
Time required: 1–52 weeks
Age: 16 plus – no upper limit
Causes: Conservation, Environmental Causes, Heritage, Wildlife, Young People.
Activities: Administration, Community Work, Computers, Conservation Skills, Driving, First Aid, Forestry, Fundraising, Group Work, Manual Work, Outdoor Skills, Technical Skills, Training.
Placements: 40

When to apply: As soon as possible.
Work alone/with others: Mainly with others.
Qualifications: Interest in the environment.
Health requirements: Nil.
Costs: Nil.
Benefits: Skills training, environmental education, job responsibilities to add to CV.
Training: Training avalable during placement.
Supervision: All volunteers supervised by qualified leaders.
Interviews: Informal interview may be required.
Charity number: 261009
UK placements: England (Bristol, Cornwall, Devon, Dorset, Gloucestershire, Somerset, Wiltshire).

BTCV – WALES REGIONAL OFFICE

Wales Conservation Centre
Forest Farm Road
Whitchurch
Cardiff
CF14 7JJ UK
T: 02920 520990
F: 02920 522181
E: wales@btcv.org.uk
W: www.btcv.org
Contact: Regional Administrator

For more details of BTCV see BTCV HQ, above. 🖫

Starting months: January–December
Time required: 1–52 weeks
Age: 16 plus – no upper limit
Causes: Conservation, Disabled (learning and physical), Environmental Causes, Heritage, Inner City Problems, Unemployed, Wildlife.
Activities: Administration, Catering, Community Work, Computers, Conservation Skills, Driving, Forestry, Fundraising, Group Work, Manual Work, Marketing/Publicity, Outdoor Skills, Training.
Placements: 100
When to apply: All year.
Work alone/with others: With others.
Qualifications: Nil. Interest in the environment.
Equipment/clothing: Outdoor.
Health requirements: Anti-tetanus innoculation recommended.
Costs: Varies.
Benefits: Free training, improved employability. Farmhouse accommodation – approximately 12 places.
Training: Training available during placement.
Supervision: Qualified paid staff and volunteers.
Interviews: Applicants are not interviewed.
Charity number: 261009
UK placements: Wales (Anglesey, Blaenau Gwent, Bridgend, Caerphilly, Cardiff, Carmarthenshire, Ceredigion, Conwy,

Denbighshire, Flintshire, Gwynedd, Merthyr Tydfil, Monmouthshire, Neath Port Talbot, Newport, Pembrokeshire, Rhondda, Cynon, Taff, Swansea, Torfaen, Vale of Glamorgan, Wrexham).

BTCV – YORKSHIRE REGION

Bridge Mill
St George's Square
Hebden Bridge
W. Yorkshire HX7 8ET UK
T: 01422 845440
F: 01422 846453
E: L.Blezard@btcv.org.uk
W: www.btcv.org
Contact: Lisa Blezard

For more details of BTCV see BTCV HQ, above.

Number of projects UK: 1500
Starting months: January–December
Time required: 1–52 weeks (plus)
Age: 16 plus – no upper limit
Causes: Conservation, Environmental Causes, Heritage, Wildlife.
Activities: Administration, Conservation Skills, Forestry, Manual Work, Outdoor Skills, Scientific Work.
Placements: 10,000
When to apply: All year.
Work alone/with others: With others.
Equipment/clothing: Strong boots and waterproofs.
Health requirements: Anti-tetanus innoculation.
Costs: Travel to pick-up point.
Benefits: Expenses.
Training: BTCV provides all training where required/requested but not necessary to all volunteering opportunities.
Supervision: All volunteers supervised by qualified leaders.
Interviews: Applicants are not interviewed except for VO positions.
Charity number: 261009
UK placements: England (E. Yorkshire, N. Yorkshire, S. Yorkshire, W. Yorkshire).

BUNAC (BRITISH UNIVERSITIES NORTH AMERICA CLUB)

16 Bowling Green Lane
London
EC1R 0QH UK
T: +44 (0) 207 251 3472
T: +44 (0) 207 251 0215
E: enquiries@bunac.org.uk
W: www.bunac.org.uk
Contact: General Enquiries Department

BUNAC was formed in 1962 by students from various North American and Canadian Clubs at UK universities. BUNAC is a non-profit organisation committed to providing the best possible affordable opportunities in international work and travel programmes for students and young people around the world. BUNAC's programmes include two fare-paid programmes placing people either as summer-camp counsellors (Summer Camp USA) or kitchen and maintenance staff (KAMP) at US children's camps. Work Canada and Work America offer students and those in a gap year the opportunity to spend either the summer or up to one year working and travelling abroad. Work Australia and Work New Zealand offer the same opportunities but are open to anyone between 18 and 35 years old. Opportunities are also available for recent graduates to work in Ghana, South Africa, Costa Rica and Argentina. Anyone wishing to apply for programmes should first contact the enquiries department from October onwards and request a copy of 'Working Adventures Abroad'. Departures all year round, most in June or July. Volunteers with an offending background may be accepted but may be refused a visa by Embassy/High Commission in question. BUNAC is a member of The Year Out Group.

Number of projects: 12 **UK:** 0
Starting months: January–December
Time required: 8–52 weeks
Age: 18–35
Causes: Children, Disabled (learning and physical), Health Care/Medical, Teaching/assisting, Young People.
Activities: Agriculture/Farming, Arts/Crafts, Caring (general, residential), Catering, Community Work, Cooking, Counselling, First Aid, Manual Work, Music, Newsletter/Journalism, Outdoor Skills, Religion, Sport, Summer Camps, Teaching, Theatre/Drama.
Placements: 10,000
When to apply: All year.
Work alone/with others: Both.
Qualifications: Sporting/dramatic/arts skills for counsellors. Catering skills for Kamp. Work America, Summer Camp USA, Kamp: must be a undergraduate but any nationality. Work Canada: British or Irish nationalities Work Australia: British, Irish, Canadian or Dutch nationalities.
Health requirements: Medical for childcare/nursing positions.
Costs: Varies with programme.
Benefits: Some accommodation provided by employer.
Training: Orientation before departure is provided on all programmes.
Supervision: Depends on programme but back-up support in each country is provided.
Interviews: Only counsellors and Work Ghana are interviewed.
Worldwide placements: Africa (Ghana, South Africa); North America: (Canada, USA); Central

America (Costa Rica); South America (Argentina); Australasia (Australia, New Zealand).

BUNDESARBEITSGEMEINSCHAFT DER FREIWILIGENAGENTUREN – BAGFA – GERMANY

Torstr. 231
10115 Berlin
Germany
T: 00 49 30 20 45 33 66
F: 00 49 30 2809 4699
E: bagfa@bagfa.de
W: www.bagfa.de
Contact: Erik Rahu

Bundesarbeitsgemeinschaft der Freiwiligenagenturen – BAGFA promotes and has information about volunteering in Germany. It may well be able to put volunteers in touch with organisations which are not yet listed on the WorldWide Volunteering database. It is a network of volunteer centres and therefore supports the development of the infrastructure for voluntary work. BAFGA has currently 60 members and contact with about 200 volunteer centres in Germany. Main tasks are public relations and information/consulting in all matters concerning volunteer centres and their work. There is no direct negotiation of volunteers by the BAGFA office but advice on where to contact in the local community.

Starting months: January–December
Time required: 1–52 weeks (plus)
Age: 16 plus – no upper limit
Causes: Addicts/Ex-Addicts, AIDS/HIV, Animal Welfare, Archaeology, Architecture, Children, Conservation, Disabled (learning and physical), Elderly People, Environmental Causes, Health Care/Medical, Heritage, Holidays for Disabled, Human Rights, Inner City Problems, Offenders/Ex-Offenders, Poor/Homeless, Refugees, Teaching/assisting (nursery, primary, secondary, mature, EFL) Unemployed, Wildlife, Work Camps – Seasonal, Young People.
Activities: Accountancy, Administration, Agriculture/Farming, Arts/Crafts, Building/Construction, Campaigning, Caring (general, day and residential), Catering, Community Work, Computers, Conservation Skills, Cooking, Counselling, Development Issues, DIY, Driving, First Aid, Forestry, Fundraising, Gardening/Horticulture, Group Work, International Aid, Library/Resource Centres, Manual Work, Marketing/Publicity, Music, Newsletter/Journalism, Outdoor Skills, Religion, Research, Scientific Work, Social Work, Sport, Summer Camps, Teaching, Technical Skills, Theatre/Drama, Training, Translating, Visiting/Befriending, Work Camps – Seasonal.
When to apply: 9–16.00 hours Monday to Friday.

Costs: Varies according to the project.
Worldwide placements: Europe (Germany).

BUSCA

(Brigada Universitaria de Servicios Comunitarios Para la Autogestion)
Soria No. 127-9
Col. Alamos
03400, Mexico, DF
Mexico
E: busca@laneta.apc.org

BUSCA (Brigada Universitaria de Servicios Comunitarios para la Autogestion) organises volunteers to work with young local people in indigenous communities in Mexico on development projects concerned with areas such as health, education, human rights, the environment, community work etc. Volunteers live and work in teams of five or six people in hardship conditions and in a very different culture. The minimum period of work is seven weeks between 25th June and 20th August. Volunteers must be willing to share and exchange experiences. Volunteers should have initiative, as well as respect for other lifestyles and cultures. No pocket money.

Starting months: Jun, Jul
Time required: 5–7 weeks
Age: 18–26
Causes: Environmental Causes, Health Care/Medical, Poor/Homeless, Teaching/assisting, Young People.
Activities: Building/Construction, Community Work, Development Issues, International Aid, Teaching.
Placements: 20
When to apply: From February to 1st May.
Qualifications: Basic knowledge of Spanish.
Costs: Travel costs to and from Mexico + $US500 for board, lodging and transport in Mexico.
Worldwide placements: Central America (Mexico).

BUTTERWICK HOSPICE CARE

Middlefield Road
Stockton-on-Tees
Durham TS19 8XU UK
T: +44 (0) 1642 615824
F: +44 (0) 1642 617641
E: avenue@butterwick.org.uk
W: www.avenueZbutterwick.org.uk
Contact: Sharon Cuthbert

Butterwick Hospice Care's aim is to improve the quality of life for those who have a life limiting illness and their families and to help them relate positively to every challenge they may encounter during their illness and to see death as part of life's journey. Any applicants with an offending background must disclose spent convictions under the Offenders Act 1976. Adult Hospice and Children's Hospice – Stockton-on-Tees, Adult Hospice in Bishop Aukland, Co. Durham and Hospice at Home in County Durham area. Also 11 retail outlets and two coffee shops in local area. ♿ 📄

Number of projects UK: 4
Starting months: January–December
Time required: 25–52 weeks (plus)
Age: 16 plus – no upper limit
Causes: Children, Disabled (physical), Elderly People, Health Care/Medical, Teaching – Nursery, Young People.
Activities: Arts/Crafts, Caring (general, day and residential), Catering, Community Work, Computers, Cooking, DIY, Driving, Fundraising, Gardening/Horticulture, Group Work, Library/ Resource Centres, Visiting/Befriending.
Placements: 350+
When to apply: All year.

Work alone/with others: Work with others.
Qualifications: Good basic skills, enthusiasm – training can be given in certain areas. No nationality restrictions but references requested in all cases.
Health requirements: Health restrictions for certain positions – would need to enquire to find out more.
Costs: Accommodation costs not covered.
Benefits: Some travel costs are covered.
Training: On the job training provided for all positions and accredited for some positions. Induction to include, health and safety, moving and handling and food hygiene as needed.
Supervision: All volunteers are supervised and reviewed regularly.
Interviews: Interviewed on site.
Charity number: 1044816
UK placements: England (Co Durham).

C

CALEDONIA LANGUAGES ABROAD

The Clockhouse
Bonnington Mill
72 Naven Road
Edinburgh
EH6 5QG UK
T: +44 (0) 131 6217721/2
F: +44 (0) 131 621 7723
E: courses@caledonialanguages.co.uk
W: www.caledonialanguages.co.uk
Contact: Doreen Rutherford

Caledonia Languages Abroad first initiated voluntary work programmes in Peru in 1996 to enable Spanish language students to participate in the local community at the same time as improving their language skills. The main aim of our placements is still to enble people of all ages to integrate into the local community and to practically contribute to the development of local projects. The success of volunteer work placements is largely due to the commitment and enthusiasm of the individual volunteer. Whilst there are particular projects in all locations, volunteers will be expected to act on their own initiative without constant supervision and to be able to deal with unexpected situations which may arise. The lack of resources in Cuba, for example, means that imaginative use of whatever materials are available is essential. Depending on the experience and qualifications of volunteers, they may well be involved in the planning and management of projects and in the development of new programmes. In most cases, at least intermediate Spanish or Portuguese is required before volunteers can start a placement although this is variable depending on the location. ▣

Number of projects: 4 UK: 0
Starting months: January–December
Time required: 3–52 weeks (plus)
Age: 18 plus – no upper limit
Causes: Animal Welfare, Children, Conservation, Disabled (learning and physical), Environmental Causes, Poor/Homeless, Teaching/assisting (nursery, EFL), Wildlife, Young People.
Activities: Agriculture/Farming, Caring – Day, Community Work, Conservation Skills, Development Issues, Library/Resource Centres, Manual Work, Music, Teaching, Theatre/Drama.
Placements: 3–12
When to apply: All year.
Work alone/with others: Possibly either.
Qualifications: Language training is included in the price and a 3-week language course is a pre-requisite.

Equipment/clothing: No specific equipment or clothing required.
Health requirements: Volunteers must be in good health.
Costs: Depends on project. £275 for Bolivia in addition to living and study expenses. No additional fee for Costa Rica or Peru.
Benefits: Accommodation is offered with host families and/or student residences.
Training: Advice is given by local co-ordinators.
Supervision: There is an on-location co-ordinator.
Interviews: Interviews on arrival by local co-ordinators.
Worldwide placements: Central America (Costa Rica, Cuba); South America (Argentina, Bolivia, Peru).

CAMBODIA TRUST, THE

11 Friday Court
North Street
Thame, Oxon
OX9 3GA UK
T: +44 (0) 1844 214844
F: +44 (0) 1844 216269
E: office@cambodiatrust.co.uk
W: www.cambodiatrust.org.uk
Contact: Pat Yates

The Cambodia Trust is a registered UK charity, established in 1989 to provide help for Cambodia's marginalised disabled population, which includes 40,000 landmine amputees and 50,000 victims of polio and other diseases. Poverty, discrimination and lack of health care have left the country's disabled people without education or employment. These people are dependent on others and seen as a burden on society. These people are the poorest of the poor. We work to restore disabled people's mobility and self-sufficiency by providing artificial limbs and braces, physiotherapy, medical care, access to education for disabled children and access to skills training for disabled adults. We provide these services through our three rehabilitation clinics, our outreach and community work projects, and our accredited training school, where local people are trained to international standards in the prescription and fitting of artificial limbs and braces. We are currently at the stage of development of handing over clinical and management responsibility to highly trained and professional staff. For this reason we can only offer volunteer work to experienced, qualified people (eg prosthetists, orthotists, physiotherapists, occupational therapists and TEFL trainers). We may be able to place volunteers with an offending background. ♿ ▣

Number of projects: 1 with 4 sections **UK:** 0
Starting months: January–December
Time required: 1–52 weeks (plus)
Age: 16 plus – no upper limit
Causes: Children, Disabled (physical), Elderly
People, Health Care/Medical, Human Rights,
Poor/Homeless, Teaching/assisting (EFL).
Activities: Caring – General, First Aid,
International Aid, Teaching.
Placements: 3–4
When to apply: No deadlines. Length of
volunteer placement negotiated on an
individual basis and nature of work. Some
placements require a longer inducton, so will
require a longer commitment of time.
Work alone/with others: With others.
Qualifications: We can only offer volunteer
work to experienced, qualified people (eg,
prosthetists, orthotists, physiotherapists,
occupational therapists and TEFL trainers).
Health requirements: Volunteers must be in
good health.
Costs: Volunteers must be completely self-
financing unless there is a special agreement
with Cambodia Trust.
Benefits: These are discussed at the recruitment
stage.
Training: Induction programme commensurate
with the type of volunteer work being offered.
Supervision: Volunteers receive professional
supervision and support.
Interviews: Yes, the location of interview
depends on the circumstances and the type of
position volunteers are applying for.
Charity number: 1032476
Worldwide placements: Asia (Cambodia).

CAMBRIDGE CYRENIANS

4 Short Street
Cambridge
CB1 1LB UK
T: +44 (0) 1223 712501
F: +44 (0) 1223 712503
E: emma@camcyrenians.fsnet.co.uk
Contact: Emma Hooton

Cambridge Cyrenians provides a range of
accommodation and support services to single,
homeless men and women in Cambridge.
Cambridge Cyrenians recruit up to six full-time
volunteers at any one time to live and work
with residents in our community houses.
Support is provided by experienced staff
daytime, evenings and weekends. Volunteers are
responsible for the day-to-day running of the
projects and can be involved in project planning
if they choose. An offending background would
not necessarily be a bar to volunteering. ♿

Number of projects UK: 3
Starting months: January–December
Time required: 26–52 weeks

Age: 18–35
Causes: Addicts/Ex-Addicts, Offenders/Ex-
Offenders, Poor/Homeless, Unemployed.
Activities: Caring – Residential, Social Work.
Placements: 10–12
When to apply: All year.
Work alone/with others: Volunteers work with
a co-volunteer and meet up with other
volunteers regularly.
Qualifications: Good English essential.
Health requirements: General good health.
Costs: Nil.
Benefits: Travel costs up to £60 to and from the
project+ up to £60 for holidays. £44/wk pocket
money of an additional £44 for each week of
holidays (1 week due for 10 weeks work) + £10
per month leaving bonus. All bills paid, except
private phone calls. Accommodation provided
on the project, plus accommodation away from
the project for days off.
Training: There is an induction period and
training is provided once on placement. We
encourage potential volunteers to visit before
accepting a place if this is possible.
Supervision: Volunteers have fortnightly
supervision with the volunteer co-ordinator,
daily contact with several members of staff,
weekly meetings with staff and can call on staff
at any time day or night.
Interviews: Prospective volunteers are not
interviewed as such, but invited to visit if
possible.
Charity number: 261994
UK placements: England (Cambridgeshire).

CAMBRIDGE DHIVERSE (DEVELOPING HIV EDICATION, RESOURCES AND SUPPORT)

Office B
Dales Brewery, Gwydir Street
Cambridge
CB1 2LJ UK
T: +44 (0) 1223 508805
F: +44 (0) 1223 508808
E: info@dhiverse.demon.co.uk
W: www.dhiverse.org.uk
Contact: Grant Chambers

Cambridge DHIVERSE (Developing HIV
Education, Resources and Support) needs
volunteers who must live locally. This is a very
supportive environment with lots of support
networks within the organisation. ▤

Number of projects UK: 1
Starting months: January–December
Time required: 52 weeks (plus)
Age: 17–80
Causes: AIDS/HIV, Health Care/Medical, Young
People.
Activities: Administration, Counselling, Group
Work, Training, Visiting/Befriending.

Placements: 60
When to apply: All year.
Work alone/with others: With others.
Qualifications: Volunteers must live locally.
Health requirements: Nil.
Costs: Nil.
Benefits: Local travel costs and out of pocket expenses reimbursed.
Training: All prospective volunteers go through an induction weekend.
Supervision: Support is available through group convenors and staff.
Interviews: All prospective volunteers are interviewed.
UK placements: England (Cambridgeshire).

CAMP AMERICA – CAMPOWER PROGRAMME

Dept YFB2
37a Queen's Gate
London
SW7 5HR UK
T: +44 (0) 207 581 7373
T: +44 (0) 207 581 7377
E: inquiries@campamerica.co.uk
Contact: Gwen Miller

Camp America is the largest of the summer camps international exchange programmes. While we do not own or operate camps, we carefully select and monitor those where we place international staff. Last year, we placed 7,500 applicants from over 20 countries. Camps vary in size and in philosophy, and are often sited in areas of outstanding natural beauty. Children are usually 6–18. As a Campower you will be working as camp support staff. Roles range from kitchen, laundry and general maintenance work to secretarial, horse/stable care and cleaning. The Campower Extended Stay option gives you the chance to work for up to 17 weeks. There is also the opportunity for Campowers to be placed in resorts or conference facilities. The Campower Programme is an ideal option if you prefer not to work directly with children. You will be working long hours, but you will receive more pocket money than general counsellors and you will have more free evenings. Brochures and application forms can be obtained at the address listed. Volunteers with an offending background may be accepted but not with a criminal record relating to children or drugs. Records must be produced and then considered. 🖑 📄

Number of projects: 800 UK: 0
Starting months: May, Jun
Time required: 9–19 weeks
Age: 18 plus – no upper limit
Causes: Children, Young People.
Activities: Administration, Catering, Cooking, DIY, Driving, Group Work, Manual Work, Summer Camps.

Placements: 8,000
When to apply: October – April.
Work alone/with others: With others.
Qualifications: For the Campower Programme, you must be a student or intending to be a student in the autumn.
Equipment/clothing: Nothing specific – equipment provided.
Health requirements: Medical check has to be undertaken before leaving UK.
Costs: 1st deposit £40, 2nd deposit including visa/insurance fee £165.
Benefits: Free London–New York return flight, board and lodging + up to 10 weeks independent travel. Depending on the length of placement, you can earn up to US$1620!
Interviews: Interviews take place all over the UK and overseas.
Worldwide placements: North America: (USA).

CAMP AMERICA – COUNSELLOR PROGRAMME

Dept YFB1
37a Queen's Gate
London
SW7 5HR UK
T: +44 (0) 207 581 7373
F: +44 (0) 207 581 7377
E: inquiries@campamerica.co.uk
Contact: Anne Chancel

Camp America is the largest of the summer camps international exchange programmes. While we do not own or operate camps, we carefully select and monitor those where we place international staff. Last year, we placed 7,500 applicants from over 20 countries. Camps vary in size and in philosophy, and are often sited in areas of outstanding natural beauty. Children are usually aged 6–18. As a Counsellor, you can be working as a specialist instructor, and teach different groups of children specific skills such as sports or arts, or as a general bunk counsellor and assist in a variety of activities and be responsible for the supervisory care of a specific group of children. Within the Counsellor programme, there is an additional option: as a Special Needs Counsellor you will be working with physically and/or mentally disabled campers. These camps may include adults as well. Supervision and caring is a priority on a special needs camp. Brochures and application forms can be obtained at the above address. Volunteers with an offending background accepted but court records must be produced. We do not take people with a criminal record relating to children or drugs. American summer camps. 🖑 📄

Number of projects: 800 UK: 0
Starting months: May, Jun
Time required: 9–19 weeks
Age: 18 plus – no upper limit

Causes: Children, Disabled (learning and physical), Inner City Problems, Teaching/assisting, Young People.
Activities: Arts/Crafts, Caring – General, Catering, Computers, Group Work, Manual Work, Music, Outdoor Skills, Sport, Summer Camps, Teaching, Theatre/Drama.
Placements: 8,000
When to apply: End October previous year – end April.
Work alone/with others: With others.
Qualifications: Preferably sports, arts/crafts, drama etc. Special Needs Counsellors need to have prior experience with people with special needs.
Equipment/clothing: Normal clothes.
Health requirements: Medical required before leaving UK.
Costs: First deposit £40, 2nd deposit/insurance/visa fee £165.
Benefits: London – New York flights, board and lodging + pocket money.
Interviews: Interviews take place all over the UK and overseas.
Worldwide placements: North America: (USA).

CAMP BEAUMONT

Camp Beaumont Day Camp
The Old Rectory
Beeston Regis
Norfolk
NR27 9NG UK
T: +44 (0) 207 922 1234
T: +44 (0) 207 928 7733
E: info@campbeaumont.com
Contact: Catherine Swain

Camp Beaumont runs three residential year-round centres and 12 summer camps for children. Volunteers who just want to work with children need no skills. 16–18 year olds are needed as volunteers. Telephone for a recruitment pack. 🔣 📄

Number of projects: 11 **UK:** 3 perm. 8 summer
Starting months: Jun, Jul, Aug
Time required: 1–52 weeks
Age: 16–30
Causes: Children, Health Care/Medical, Teaching/assisting (nursery, primary, secondary, EFL), Work Camps – Seasonal, Young People.
Activities: Administration, Arts/Crafts, Caring (general, day and residential), Catering, Computers, Cooking, DIY, Driving, First Aid, Forestry, Gardening/Horticulture, Group Work, Manual Work, Music, Newsletter/Journalism, Outdoor Skills, Scientific Work, Sport, Summer Camps, Teaching, Technical Skills, Theatre/Drama, Translating, Work Camps – Seasonal.
Placements: 550–600
When to apply: From January.
Work alone/with others: Both.

Qualifications: Specialist skill for activity centre ideal, but not essential. Police check.
Equipment/clothing: Uniform supplied – otherwise very casual.
Health requirements: Health check.
Costs: Travel to camp.
Benefits: Board, lodging, training and living allowance. Those over 18 years are salaried employees.
Worldwide placements: Europe (France).
UK placements: England (Berkshire, Devon, Essex, Isle of Wight, Kent, London, Norfolk, Staffordshire, Surrey).

CAMPAIGNERS

Campaigners House
St Mark's Close
Colney Heath
St Albans, Hertfordshire
AL4 0NQ UK
T: +44 (0) 1727 824065
F: +44 (0) 1727 825049
E: information@campaigners.org.uk
W: www.campaigners.co.uk
Contact: John Radcliffe

Campaigners was founded in 1922 by an Anglican vicar. Every group is attached to a local church. We cater for 4–18 year olds in four different groupings. We offer a weekly meeting programme for children and young people and the programme comprises anything from sports activities, Duke of Edinburgh, Bible teaching to games and refreshments. 🔣 📄

Number of projects UK: 250
Starting months: January–December
Time required: 1–52 weeks
Age: 17–65
Causes: Children, Disabled (learning and physical), Young People.
Activities: Arts/Crafts, Caring – General, DIY, Gardening/Horticulture, Manual Work, Music, Outdoor Skills, Religion, Sport, Summer Camps, Teaching, Theatre/Drama, Visiting/Befriending.
When to apply: All year.
Work alone/with others: With others under supervision of trained youth workers.
Qualifications: Nil – Christians preferred.
Health requirements: Nil.
Costs: Nil.
Benefits: Training and possible summer camps.
Training: By youth workers.
Supervision: Supervised by trained youth workers.
Interviews: Interviews are conducted at Campaigner headquarters.
Charity number: 283171
UK placements: England (Bedfordshire, Berkshire, Buckinghamshire, Cambridgeshire, Cheshire, Cornwall, Derbyshire, Devon, Dorset, Essex, Gloucestershire, Hampshire, Herefordshire, Hertfordshire, Kent, Lancashire,

Leicestershire, London, Manchester, Merseyside, Northamptonshire, Nottinghamshire, Shropshire, Somerset, Staffordshire, Suffolk, Surrey, E. Sussex, W. Sussex, Warwickshire, West Midlands, Wiltshire, N. Yorkshire, S. Yorkshire, W. Yorkshire); Scotland (throughout); Northern Ireland (Antrim, Armagh, Belfast City, Derry/Londonderry, Down); Wales (throughout).

CAMPHILL ASSOCIATION OF NORTH AMERICA

20 Triform Road
Hudson NY
Colombia 12534 USA
T: 518 851 3260
F: 518 851 3257
E: coworker@camphill.org
W: www.camphill.org
Contact: Lauren Bratburd

Camphill is an international social movement of international communities where children, adolescents and adults with developmental disabilities, mental illness and social disadvantage can be supported in community to unfold their potential. Humanitarian physician, Dr Karl Koenig who had fled from Nazi-occupied Austria, founded Camphill in Scotland in 1939. The Camphill approach honors the spiritual integrity of every human being, regardless of ability or circumstances, and recognises the individual's need and right to lead a full life that includes material, emotional, social and spiritual needs. The Camphill approach to community living, service, outreach and support is a practical expression of the holistic worldview introduced by Rudolf Steiner PhD. It brings together education, science, healing, agriculture, the arts and civil society. Most Camphill communities are in rural settings, providing opportunities for agricultural and horticultural work supporting sustainable world ecology. Each Camphill community – whether a children's village, a community for young people finding their way into adult life, or communities that provide opportunities for adults – people live together in house communities. Members of the house community share in the daily life and tasks of the house, and engage in work at school, on the land, in one of the craft workshops or providing some other service. Celebration has a central place in the life of the community through arts, festivals and honoring special events and milestones in people's lives. Care for the earth is highly valued and considered an essential component to the well being of people and the community. We may be able to place volunteers with an offending background – each case addressed on an individual basis. 100 Camphill communities worldwide, eight are in North America, California (1), New York (2), Pennsylvania (3), Minnesota (1) and Ontario, Canada (1). 🗎

Number of projects: 100
Starting months: January–December
Time required: 12–52 weeks
Age: 19 plus – no upper limit
Causes: Children, Disabled (learning), Elderly People, Holidays for Disabled, Teaching/assisting, Young People.
Activities: Agriculture/Farming, Arts/Crafts, Building/Construction, Caring – Residential, Community Work, Cooking, Gardening/ Horticulture, Group Work, Manual Work, Music, Outdoor Skills, Social Work, Teaching, Theatre/Drama.
Placements: 150
When to apply: Rolling admissions.
Work alone/with others: Work with others.
Qualifications: Volunteers must be at least 19 years, flexible & possess a willingness to be involved in the ongoing process of community building. Strong English language skills are required.
Equipment/clothing: As many communities are agriculturally based, farm clothing is appropriate.
Health requirements: Camphill life can be physically, mentally and emotionally challenging and includes many outdoor activities. It is important have physical, mental and emotional stamina.
Costs: Travel/flights to and from Camphill is responsibility of volunteer.
Benefits: Food and accommodation, own room, medical insurance, vacation time and a modest stipend. Volunteers have their own room in a house which they would share with a number of people with developmental disabilities and a long time volunteer.
Training: Formal and on-the-job training available in providing human support, empowerment and care giving (social therapy), educating children with disabilities (curative education), ecology and biodynamic agriculture, the healing arts and therapies, and crafts.
Supervision: Each volunteers has a mentor, houseparent and workshop leader to provide support, training and supervision.
Interviews: Generally, international applicants would have a scheduled phone interview.
Charity number: 23 2235911 (EIN)
Worldwide placements: North America: (Canada, USA).

CAMPHILL COMMUNITIES, ONTARIO

7841 4th Line
Angus, Ontario
LOM 1BI Canada
T: 00 1 705 424 5363
F: 00 1 705 424 1854
E: info@camphill.on.ca
W: www.camphill.on.ca
Contact: Co-worker Care Group

For more details of Camphill Communities see Camphill Association of North America, above. Camphill Nottawasaga is a rural community on 300 acres near Barrie. It comprises several homes and workshops, a large vegetable garden and a farm. Our work is to care for each other, our homes, our gardens and our land. The aim of Camphill Ontario is to build a vital community life that offers each person the conditions for healing, growth and renewal. One year is the minimum recommended length of stay. Three month summer help possible. 100kms north of Toronto. Winter very cold (–30°C), summer hot (+35°C).

Number of projects: 1 **UK:** 0
Starting months: January–December
Time required: 12–52 weeks
Age: 19–45
Causes: Disabled (learning and physical).
Activities: Agriculture/Farming, Arts/Crafts, Building/Construction, Caring – General, Community Work, Cooking, Counselling, Driving, Forestry, Fundraising, Gardening/Horticulture, Manual Work, Music, Outdoor Skills, Religion, Social Work, Sport, Technical Skills, Theatre/Drama, Training, Visiting/Befriending.
Placements: 9–10
When to apply: All year but at least 4–6 months before coming.(Visa takes 4–5 months.)
Work alone/with others: With others, generally.
Qualifications: English speaking, being open to life in the community. 1 year is recommended or 3 month summer stay. No restrictions with UK volunteers but Canadian immigration is tough with certain nationalities.
Equipment/clothing: Good solid work clothes for all seasons. Winters very cold, summers hot.
Health requirements: Health insurance for the first 3 months.
Costs: Return travel fare, Hepatitis B vaccine, Visa costs.
Benefits: Board, lodging, pocket money C$150 per month. Health insurance after 3 months. All volunteers live on the premises in family style house communities. Everyone has their own room.
Training: No pre-placement training for short-term volunteers. All volunteers have an induction training at the beginning and then a weekly orientation course.
Supervision: Each volunteer is supervised for the first three months while they are trained. They have a three month review, then weekly mentoring from experienced co-workers.
Interviews: A personal interview or a phone interview prior to acceptance.
Charity number: 0553834.56
Worldwide placements: North America (Canada).

CAMPHILL COMMUNITY BALLYBAY

Robb Farm
Corraskea
Co. Monaghan Eire
T: 00 353 42 974 1939
F: 00 353 42 974 1359
E: bkonink@eircom.net
or E: camphillballybay@eircom.net
Contact: Betsie Konink

For more details of Camphill Communities see Camphill Association of North America, above. Camphill Community Ballybay is a rural community which works about 20 acres of land and has different craft workshops for weaving, candle making, woodwork and basket making. Everyone lives and works together in community houses varying in size from 9 to 15 people. Prospective volunteers can apply by letter.

Number of projects: 1 **UK:** 0
Starting months: January–December
Time required: 26–52 weeks (plus)
Age: 19–52
Causes: Disabled (learning)
Activities: Agriculture/Farming, Arts/Crafts, Caring (general, residential), Driving, Group Work, Manual Work, Outdoor Skills.
Placements: 15
When to apply: All year, preferably at least 6 months in advance.
Prospective volunteers can apply by letter.
Work alone/with others: Both.
Qualifications: Nil but an open attitude to our way of life. Must be able to speak reasonable English.
Equipment/clothing: Enough clothes for a year including rainwear.
Health requirements: General good health.
Costs: Travel to Ballybay only.
Benefits: Board and lodging and about £20 pocket money per week.
Training: None.
Supervision: Everybody has a mentor.
Worldwide placements: Europe (Ireland).

CAMPHILL COMMUNITY BALLYTOBIN

Callan
Co. Kilkenny Ireland
T: 00 353 56 25114
F: 00 353 56 25849
E: ballytobin@camphill.ie
Contact: Christina Dwan

For more details of Camphill Communities see Camphill Association of North America, above. The Camphill Community Ballytobin is a small rural community caring at present for 22 children and 12 adults all with disabilities. Ballytobin has a school, a garden, an organic farm, a weaving workshop and also offers many individual therapies, for example: music, coloured-light speech therapy, eurythmy, physiotherapy and horse riding! Ballytobin was established in 1979 to provide a home and school mainly for children with exceptional needs.

Number of projects: 1 UK: 0
Starting months: Jul
Time required: 4–52 weeks
Age: 19 plus – no upper limit
Causes: Children, Disabled (learning and physical), Work Camps – Seasonal.
Activities: Agriculture/Farming, Arts/Crafts, Caring (general, residential), Cooking, Gardening/Horticulture, Music, Work Camps – Seasonal.
Placements: 20–25
When to apply: Spring.
Work alone/with others: With others.
Qualifications: All skills welcome. Long-term work permits may be difficult for non-EU citizens.
Health requirements: Good general health as work with disabled children can be demanding.
Costs: Travel to Ireland.
Benefits: Full board and lodging + pocket money and expenses. Holidays if stay is over 12mths.
Training: Given just before volunteer commences.
Supervision: Volunteers work alongside experienced co-workers.
Interviews: Prospective volunteers are not interviewed but we require references, etc.
Charity number: 5861 Irish
Worldwide placements: Europe (Ireland).

CAMPHILL COMMUNITY DUNSHANE

Dunshane House
Brannockstown
Naas
Co. Kildare Eire
T: 00 353 45 483628
F: 00 353 45 483833
E: dunshane@Camphill.ie
W: www.camphill.ie
Contact: Jeannemarie Marden

For more details of Camphill Communities see Camphill Association of North America, above. The Dunshane Community caters for adolescents and young adults in need of special care. The community consists of three houses, which offer residential and day-care facilities for young people aged 15 to 22 years. The co-workers, their families and the residential students live together in extended families. With a Government FAS scheme in operation, and local volunteers giving their time to help out, there is a mutually beneficial exchange of support and service. (FAS is an Irish government funded one year work placement scheme for the long-term unemployed.)

Number of projects: 1 UK: 0
Starting months: Aug

Time required: 44–52 weeks (plus)
Age: 21–35
Causes: Disabled (learning), Teaching/assisting (secondary, mature), Young People.
Activities: Agriculture/Farming, Arts/Crafts, Building/Construction, Caring (general, residential), Catering, Community Work, Cooking, Counselling, DIY, First Aid, Gardening/Horticulture, Group Work, Manual Work, Music, Outdoor Skills, Social Work, Teaching, Theatre/Drama, Training.
Placements: 14
When to apply: May.
Work alone/with others: With others.
Qualifications: Good will and an open mind.
Equipment/clothing: Practical wear and something for special occasions.
Health requirements: Good health in general.
Costs: Travel costs.
Benefits: Board and lodging plus a small amount of pocket money.
Training: Basic in-house training.
Supervision: Due to the nature of our lifesharing community, there is much support and supervision.
Interviews: If possible interviews take place at Dunshane.
Worldwide placements: Europe (Ireland).

CAMPHILL COMMUNITY KYLE

Coolagh
Callan
Co. Kilkenny Eire
T: 00 353 56 25848
E: kyle@camphill.ie
Contact: Co-worker

For more details of Camphill Communities see Camphill Association of North America, above. Camphill Community Kyle is part of the worldwide Camphill movement.

Number of projects: 1 UK: 0
Starting months: January–December
Time required: 1–52 weeks (plus)
Age: 14 plus – no upper limit
Causes: Children, Disabled (learning and physical), Elderly People, Work Camps – Seasonal, Young People.
Activities: Caring (general, day and residential), Catering, Community Work, Group Work, Social Work.
Worldwide placements: Europe (Ireland).

CAMPHILL COMMUNITY THOMASTOWN

Jerpoint Barn
Thomastown
Co. Kilkenny Eire
T: 00 353 56 24844
E: jerpoint@camphill.ie
Contact: The Director

For more details of Camphill Communities see Camphill Association of North America, above. Camphill Community Thomastown includes two places: Jerpoint, a small residential, landbased community with adults in need of special care and The Watergarden, a coffeeshop, landscaped garden and garden centre in town, open to the public. Volunteers with an offending background may be accepted possibly – by arrangement.

Number of projects: 2 **UK:** 0
Starting months: January–December
Time required: 50–52 weeks (plus)
Age: 18 plus – no upper limit
Causes: Conservation, Disabled (learning and physical), Environmental Causes, Holidays for Disabled.
Activities: Agriculture/Farming, Arts/Crafts, Caring (general, day and residential), Catering, Conservation Skills, Cooking, DIY, Fundraising, Gardening/Horticulture, Group Work, Manual Work, Music, Outdoor Skills, Religion, Social Work, Sport.
Placements: Varies.
When to apply: All year.
Work alone/with others: With others.
Health requirements: Nil.
Costs: Travel to Thomastown only.
Benefits: All board, lodging and approx. £20 per week pocket money.
Interviews: Applicants are not interviewed but they can come on a trial visit.
Worldwide placements: Europe (Ireland).

CAMPHILL DORFGEMEINSCHAFT HAUSENHOF

Hausenhof 7
D91463 Dietersheim
Germany
T: 00 49 9164 9984 36
F: 00 49 9164 9984 10
E: ingrid.hatz@hausehof.de
W: www.hausenhof.de
Contact: Mrs Ingrid Hatz

For more details of Camphill Communities see Camphill Association of North America, above.

Number of projects: 1 **UK:** 0
Starting months: January–December
Time required: 1–52 weeks (plus)
Age: 18–30
Causes: Disabled (learning and physical), Health Care/Medical.
Activities: Agriculture/Farming, Arts/Crafts, Caring (general, day and residential), Catering, Community Work, Cooking, Driving, Gardening/Horticulture, Group Work, Manual Work, Music, Outdoor Skills, Religion, Social Work, Sport, Theatre/Drama, Training.
Placements: 15–20

When to apply: All year but as early as possible.
Work alone/with others: Mainly with others.
Qualifications: Basic knowledge of German language. No restrictions providing you hold a work and residence permit.
Health requirements: Health or medical problems must be reported when applying.
Costs: Travel costs only.
Benefits: Board and lodging. For people staying for a year or more, small wage also. Volunteers would live in house communities with 8 disabled young people, the houseparents and their own children as well as other helpers.
Interviews: Applicants are interviewed where possible but written applications are also accepted.
Worldwide placements: Europe (Germany).

CAMPHILL DORFGEMEINSCHAFT HERMANNSBERG

D88633
Heiligenberg-Hattenweiler
Germany
T: 00 49 7552 2601 00
F: 00 49 7552 2601 40
E: marg.Mentzel@hermannsberg.de
W: www.hermannsberg.de
Contact: Mrs Margaret Mentzel

For more details of Camphill Communities see Camphill Association of North America, above. Camphill Dorfgemeinschaft Hermannsberg: Living together in family-units with our friends with disabilities can be one way of getting nearer to so-called integration. The co-workers as part of the house community are involved in the care of those in need. We have a number of workshops: a candle-workshop, a small weavery, a joinery/woodworkshop, a laundry, a big paperworkshop where copybooks for many Waldorf schools in Germany are being produced. We also have a garden/estate group and about one mile up the road is our farm with three houses, stables, utility sheds etc.

Number of projects: 1 **UK:** 0
Starting months: Jan, Feb, Mar, Apr, May, Jun, Sep, Oct, Nov, Dec
Time required: 12–52 weeks
Age: 19–28
Causes: Disabled (learning).
Activities: Caring – Residential.
When to apply: Any time between September and end of June.
Qualifications: EU Nationals only. Driving Licence and some foundation in German are both a bonus.
Equipment/clothing: Normal winter/summer clothing required – also for outside work.
Health requirements: Must be physically, psychologically and mentally fit.
Costs: Travel costs only.

Benefits: Pocket money of €153 per month rising to €179 after three months + board and lodging, health insurance and all taxes. Accommodation is in family units with adults with disabilities, houseparents etc.
Training: Training on-going. There is also a three-year training course with a state-recognised examination.
Supervision: Supervision by the houseparents.
Interviews: Only those living in Germany are interviewed.
Worldwide placements: Europe (Germany).

CAMPHILL DORFGEMEINSCHAFT SELLEN E.V

Sellen 101,
D48565 Steinfurt/Burgsteinfurt
Nordrhein-Westfalen 48565 Germany
T: 00 49 2551 9366 0 or 35
F: 00 49 2551 9366 11
E: Camphill-Steinfurt@t-online.de
W: www.camphill.org.uk/diverty/germany/
sellen.htm
Contact: Mrs Lieselotte Liebeck

For more details of Camphill Communities see Camphill Association of North America, above. Camphill Dorfgemeinschaft Sellen e.v. is an institution with 51 mentally disabled people. They live in seven separate houses together with their co-worker-family. 🔥

Number of projects: 6 **UK:** 0
Starting months: May, Aug, Sep
Time required: 4–52 weeks
Age: 18–30
Causes: Disabled (learning and physical), Environmental Causes, Holidays for Disabled, Young People.
Activities: Agriculture/Farming, Arts/Crafts, Building/Construction, Caring – Residential, Catering, Cooking, Driving, Forestry, Gardening/Horticulture, Group Work, Manual Work, Music, Outdoor Skills, Social Work, Sport, Summer Camps, Theatre/Drama.
Placements: 4
When to apply: 2–3 months before wishing to start.
Work alone/with others: Both.
Qualifications: Willingness to do any kind of craftwork and look after our people (washing/dressing etc). Must be EU nationals unless they are only coming for 4 weeks and take out their own insurance.
Equipment/clothing: Working trousers and shoes.
Health requirements: A certificate for a Common Health Test is required (Gesundheits-Zeugnis).
Costs: Travel costs except in special cases.
Benefits: Board (3 meals), lodging, and €180 per month pocket money.

Training: One afternoon per week there is a special introductory course run by the staff especially for the volunteers to give them an understanding of our work with the disabled people.
Supervision: Supervised by trained responsible co-workers.
Interviews: Volunteers are interviewed by Mrs Silvia Shin, Camphill St Albans, 50 Carlisle Avenue, St Albans, Herts AL3 5LT. Telephone 01727-811228 or phone Lieselotte Liebeck at 00-49-2551 936635 and Reinhard Berger 00-49-2551 936618.
Charity number: VR705(E.V)
Worldwide placements: Europe (Germany).

CAMPHILL FARM COMMUNITY AND CAMPHILL SCHOOL

Camphill Farm Community
PO Box 301
Hermanus 7200
South Africa
T: 00 27 28 3138200
F: 00 27 28 3138210
E: camphillfarm@hermanus.co.za
Contact: The Reception Group

For more details of Camphill Communities see Camphill Association of North America, above. The Camphill School is dedicated to the care of mentally handicapped children and adolescents. It provides education and training in both a residential and day setting, spanning the ages between 5 and 20, and providing for a wide range of learning difficulties, developmental handicaps and emotional disturbances. Alternative contact details: Camphill School, P O Box 68, Hermanus, South Africa. Phone: 0027 28 313 8216. Fax: 0027 28 313 8238. e-mail: camph@intekom.co.za 📄

Number of projects: 1 **UK:** 0
Starting months: January–December
Time required: 52 weeks (plus)
Age: 20 plus – no upper limit
Causes: Children, Disabled (learning), Teaching/assisting (nursery, primary, secondary).
Activities: Agriculture/Farming, Arts/Crafts, Caring (general, day and residential), Cooking, Fundraising, Gardening/Horticulture, Group Work, Manual Work, Music, Outdoor Skills, Teaching, Technical Skills, Theatre/Drama.
Placements: 20–25
When to apply: 6–12 months before.
Work alone/with others: Both.
Qualifications: Must be able to speak English, otherwise only enthusiasm.
Equipment/clothing: Sufficient clothing, i.e. for work and formal occasions for at least one year.

Health requirements: Good health as our way of life is strenuous.
Costs: Medical ins. or costs, visa costs incl. extensions, travel costs, holiday costs.
Benefits: Board and lodging and modest pocket money.
Interviews: Prospective volunteers are not interviewed.
Charity number: 78/03803/0
Worldwide placements: Africa (South Africa).

CAMPHILL IN POLAND – WOJTOWKA

Stójków 22
Wójtówka 1
PL-57 540 Ladek Zdrój
Poland
T: 00 48 74 8146501
F: 00 48 74 8146501
Contact: Co-worker

For more details of Camphill Communities see Camphill Association of North America, above. Wspolnota Wójtówka is a village community for adults with special needs. 600 metres up in the mountains of SW Poland, a project is taking shape which should claim the attention of all. On an abandoned farm, buildings are being restored, fields reclaimed for ecological farming and a whole new approach to the mentally handicapped person is being launched. Everyone is a volunteer. Workcamps start in late May. Longer-term volunteers may join at any time. ▣

Number of projects: 1 UK: 0
Starting months: January–December
Time required: 2–52 weeks (plus)
Age: 18–26
Causes: Disabled (learning), Environmental Causes, Holidays for Disabled, Teaching (EFL), Work Camps – Seasonal, Young People.
Activities: Agriculture/Farming, Building/Construction, Community Work, Cooking, Driving, Forestry, Gardening/Horticulture, Manual Work, Outdoor Skills, Summer Camps, Technical Skills, Work Camps – Seasonal.
Placements: 10–15
When to apply: Workcamps: before 1st April.
Other volunteers: All year.
Work alone/with others: With others.
Qualifications: Nil but manual skill and/or basic knowledge of Polish + int. driving licence an advantage.
Equipment/clothing: Wellingtons, rain clothing, a pullover and general work clothing.
Health requirements: Applicants should arrange own medicinal needs and not require dental care.
Costs: All travel costs for return round trip.
Benefits: Board and lodging, pocket money for long-termers.
Interviews: Volunteers are not interviewed.
Worldwide placements: Europe (Poland).

CAMPHILL LEBENSGEMEINSCHAFT KÖNIGSMÜHLE

Schöntalstr. 9
Neustadt a.d. Weinstrasse
Rheinland-PfalzD67434 Germany
T: 00 49 6321 7289 or 7295
F: 00 49 6321 31487
Contact: Herr Ehmcke or Herr Foskett

For more details of Camphill Communities see Camphill Association of North America, above. Camphill Lebensgemeinschaft Königsmühle is a small community (four families) with 24 young disabled adults, together with our own eight children and one or more young volunteers. We live, work and 'play' together which includes basket making, candle making, wood workshop, weavery, gardening, and grape growing. ▣

Number of projects: 1 UK: 0
Starting months: Jan, Feb, Mar, Apr, May, Jun, Jul, Aug, Sep, Oct, Nov
Time required: 26–52 weeks
Age: 18–55
Causes: Disabled (learning and physical).
Activities: Caring (general, day and residential), Forestry, Fundraising, Gardening/Horticulture, Group Work, Manual Work, Music, Social Work, Theatre/Drama.
Placements: 5–6
When to apply: All year.
Work alone/with others: With others.
Qualifications: Open-minded to new impressions.
Health requirements: Nil.
Costs: Travel costs (refunded if volunteer stays a year or more).
Benefits: Board, lodging and pocket money €250 a month, medical insurance and state pension.
Training: As needed.
Supervision: Trained staff always there.
Interviews: Interviews are conducted only if possible.
Worldwide placements: Europe (Germany).

CAMPHILL RUDOLF STEINER SCHOOLS

Central Office, Murtle Estate
Murtle House,
Bieldside
Aberdeen
AB15 9EP UK
T: 01224 867935
F: 01224 868420
E: b.porter@crss.org.uk
W: www.camphillschools@org.uk
Contact: Mrs B Porter

For more details of Camphill Communities see Camphill Association of North America, above. Camphill Rudolf Steiner School is a residential school for children and youngsters in need of special care. It caters for a great variety of developmental, psychological, emotional and physical handicaps (ages 4–19 years). Adults (carers) and pupils live in houses, within the estate, of varying sizes and form the community. The pupils live in their own room or sometimes share with another pupil. They are looked after by houseparents, group parents, and other co-workers. ⬚

Number of projects: 40+ **UK:** 40
Starting months: Jan, Apr, Aug, Oct
Time required: 28–49 weeks
Age: 18 plus – no upper limit
Causes: Children, Disabled (learning and physical), Teaching/assisting, Young People.
Activities: Caring (general, residential), Cooking, Gardening/Horticulture, Group Work, Music, Outdoor Skills, Religion, Sport, Summer Camps, Teaching, Theatre/Drama, Training.
Placements: 80
When to apply: 8–12 weeks prior to school entry term (Aug, Oct, Jan, April).
Work alone/with others: With others.
Qualifications: Adequate understanding of the English language.
Equipment/clothing: For Sunday services and festivals only: girls skirts, boys no jeans.
Health requirements: Up-to-date medical health record.
Costs: Own travel expenses to Aberdeen.
Benefits: £140 pocket money per month.
Training: Induction course and on-going Foundation Training Programme.
Supervision: House parents and senior co-workers are on hand for guidance and supervision.
Interviews: Volunteer applicants are interviewed where possible. For overseas volunteers, a telephone interview will be conducted.
Charity number: SCO 15588
Worldwide placements: Africa (South Africa); North America: (Canada, USA); Europe (Finland, Germany, Norway, Sweden, Switzerland).
UK placements: Scotland (Aberdeen City, Aberdeenshire).

CAMPHILL SCHULGEMEINSCHAFT BRACHENREUTHE

Camphill Schulemeinschaft Brachenreuthe
D-88662 Uberlingen
Germany
T: 00 49 7551 80070
F: 00 49 7551 800750
E: Brachenreuthe@t-online.de
W: www.brachenreuthe.de
Contact: Bruno Wegmüller

For more details of Camphill Communities see Camphill Association of North America, above.

Camphill Schulgemeinschaft Brachenreuthe is a residential school for mentally handicapped children. It is beautifully situated in the country near Uberlingen, a medium-sized town on the Lake of Constance (Bodensee) in southern Germany. ⬚

Number of projects: 1 **UK:** 0
Starting months: January–December
Time required: 12–52 weeks
Age: 18–40
Causes: Children, Disabled (learning), Young People.
Activities: Caring (general, residential).
Placements: 15
When to apply: All year.
Work alone/with others: With others.
Qualifications: Basic knowledge of German. No restrictions but non-EU members may have difficulty in obtaining residency/work permit.
Health requirements: Free from TB and infectious diseases.
Costs: Travel expenses.
Benefits: Board, lodging (shared room) + insurance + €205 per month pocket money. We provide accommodation, single or double rooms and meals.
Training: House parents show volunteers the ropes and there is also a weekly course in curative education for volunteers.
Supervision: Volunteers work in a team headed by the house parents and, ultimately, the directors.
Interviews: Applicants are not interviewed.
Worldwide placements: Europe (Germany).

CAMPHILL SCHULGEMEINSHAFT FÖHRENBÜHL

D88633 Heiligenberg-Steigen
Bodenseekreis Germany
T: 00 49 7554 80010
F: 00 49 7554 8001 163
E: info@foehrenbuehl.de
W: www.foehrenbuehl.de (for Fohrenbuhl direct)
Contact: Richard Steel

For more details of Camphill Communities see Camphill Association of North America, above. Camphill Heimsonderschule Föhrenbühl is a school community with family-like units in which handicapped and staff live and learn together. It has a kindergarten and school with trainee course for children and young people with special needs. Alternative web sites: www.camphill.de (for German centres). www.foehrenbuehl.de (for Föhrenbühl direct) Alternative e-mail address: info@designtherapie. de (Lake of Constance area). ⬚

Number of projects: 1 **UK:** 0
Starting months: January–December
Time required: 3–52 weeks (plus)

Age: 18 plus – no upper limit
Causes: Children, Disabled (learning and physical), Teaching/assisting (nursery, primary, secondary), Young People.
Activities: Arts/Crafts, Caring (general, residential), Cooking, Gardening/Horticulture, Manual Work, Teaching.
Placements: 20
When to apply: All year.
Work alone/with others: With others.
Qualifications: German language (basic at least) is a help. Applicants with EC passport are easiest otherwise a work permit must be applied for well in advance.
Health requirements: Health certificate required proving absence of contagious diseases.
Costs: Travel costs only.
Benefits: Board and lodging (single rooms usually). After 3 weeks pocket money (€100 + per month). Furnished room is provided for the full length of stay either in the community or within easy walking distance.
Training: When wished a visit or pre-practical visit can be arranged in a Camphill Centre near to the volunteer's home. Courses are offered during volunteer period.
Supervision: Volunteers work within a house community where experienced house parents are responsible. Also school work is only under guidance of responsible teacher. A contact person is always available for questions/problems.
Interviews: Applicants are interviewed at the nearest Camphill Centre to their home address if this is practicable.
Worldwide placements: Europe (Germany).

CAMPHILL SOLTANE

224 Nantmeal Road
Glenmoore
Pennsylvania 19343 USA
T: 00 1 610 469 0933
F: 00 1 610 469 1054
E: soltane@aol.com
W: www.camphillsoltane.org
Contact: Annegret Goetze

For more details of Camphill Communities see Camphill Association of North America, above. Camphill Soltane is an intentional community based on the work of Rudolf Steiner. Essentially, it attempts to create a life-sharing community, work towards social renewal and practice awareness of each other's needs through a life of meaning and fulfilment together with mentally handicapped young men and women aged 18–25. Our students or companions live, learn and work in Camphill Soltane together with co-workers and their families, interns, 'practicants' and shorter term co-workers.

Number of projects: 1 UK: 0
Starting months: Jan, Sep
Time required: 12–52 weeks (plus)
Age: 18–25
Causes: Disabled (learning), Teaching – Secondary, Young People.
Activities: Agriculture/Farming, Caring (general, residential), Community Work, Cooking, Counselling, Driving, Gardening/Horticulture, Group Work, Manual Work, Outdoor Skills.
Placements: 10–15
When to apply: By 1st May (for Sept. start) or 1st November (Jan. start).
Work alone/with others: With other experienced workers.
Qualifications: English language. Interest and commitment to community. Experience with developmental disabilities preferred.
Health requirements: Able-bodied, healthy, no major illness or disease.
Costs: Travel costs.
Benefits: Room and board provided as well as $110 pocket money monthly.
Training: After arrival, before companions return from vacation, we have orientation sessions and common planning meetings.
Supervision: Co-working with house-parents and work masters.
Interviews: Interviews are conducted by mail or over the telephone.
Worldwide placements: North America: (USA).

CAMPHILL SPECIAL SCHOOLS (BEAVER RUN)

Camphill Special Schools, Beaver Run
1784 Fairview Road
Glenmoore
Pennsylvania 19343 USA
T: 00 1 610 469 9236
F: 00 1 610 469 9758
E: BvrRn@aol.com
W: www.beaverrun.org
Contact: Anne Sproll

For more details of Camphill Communities see Camphill Association of North America, above. Camphill Special Schools provides extended family living in a sheltered community, education, and therapy for mentally retarded and disabled children and youngsters in a wholesome, rural setting. Volunteers must be willing to serve the needs of others and work co-operatively. Rural community in driving distance from town.

Number of projects: 1 UK: 0
Starting months: Aug
Time required: 46–50 weeks
Age: 20–28
Causes: Children, Disabled (learning), Teaching/assisting, Young People.

Activities: Arts/Crafts, Caring – Residential, Community Work, Cooking, Driving, Gardening/Horticulture, Group Work, Manual Work, Music, Outdoor Skills, Social Work, Summer Camps, Teaching, Theatre/Drama.
Placements: 40–60
When to apply: 4–6 mths in advance.
Work alone/with others: With others.
Qualifications: Experience with children desirable. If possible volunteers should visit a Camphill Centre in own country.
Equipment/clothing: Bring own clothing: snowy winters, hot summers.
Health requirements: Good mental and physical health, TB screening required.
Costs: Travel.
Benefits: Board, lodging + $135 per month pocket money, vacation stipend, medical insurance.
Training: On-going training on campus. Volunteers receive some training and orientation, 3–8 hours per week.
Supervision: Special education teachers for school, house-parents for the houses, therapists for therapy.
Worldwide placements: North America (USA).

CAMPHILL VILLAGE ALPHA (WESTERN CAPE)

P. O. Box 1451
Dassenberg 7350
Western Cape South Africa
T: 00 27 21 572 2345
F: 00 27 21 572 2238
E: info@camphill.org.za
W: www.camphill.org.za
Contact: Lee Eksteen

For more details of Camphill Communities see Camphill Association of North America, above. Camphill Village (Western Cape) is a rural working community of 160 men, women and children. Some 90 adults, many of whom are ageing, have learning difficulties and special needs. There are 11 households where co-workers and villagers live together in group homes. We share our daily living and work with villagers. A warm and healthy home life is integral to the well being of our community and all co-workers share responsibility in our homes. We employ some local people from the surrounding district.

Number of projects: 1 UK: 0
Starting months: January–December
Time required: 52 weeks (plus)
Age: 18–25
Causes: Disabled (learning and physical).
Activities: Agriculture/Farming, Arts/Crafts, Caring (general, residential), Catering, Community Work, Cooking, Driving, First Aid, Gardening/Horticulture, Group Work, Manual Work, Outdoor Skills, Social Work, Sport, Visiting/Befriending.

Placements: 10
When to apply: All year.
Work alone/with others: Both.
Qualifications: Driving licence, English, good social skills, common sense, practical nature, love people. Most nationalities accepted.
Equipment/clothing: Work clothes, casual clothes and one set of informal but good clothes.
Health requirements: Need to come with health insurance.
Costs: Return ticket and transport costs within S. Africa.
Benefits: R300 per month plus full board and lodging.
Training: On-going training. 2 hours orientation per week.
Supervision: Houseparents and work masters supervise.
Interviews: Applicants are interviewed by correspondence and possibly by other friends of Camphill in UK.
Worldwide placements: Africa (South Africa).

CAMPHILL VILLAGE COMMUNITY DUFFCARRIG

Duffcarrig
Gorey
Co. Wexford Eire
T: 00 353 55 25911
F: 00 353 55 25910
E: volunteering.duffcarrig@camphill.ie
W: www.camphill.ie
Contact: The Admissions Group

For more details of Camphill Communities see Camphill Association of North America, above. Camphill Village Community Duffcarrig is a centre with adults (aged 20–77) who have a mental handicap. Duffcarrig is situated on the coast of County Wexford in the sunny south-east of Ireland, five minutes walk from the sea, and is neighbour to farms and holiday homes. The nearest town, Gorey, is three and a half miles away. Originally founded as a land-based community with young adults, Duffcarrig has changed into a place for adults of all ages which offers care for the elderly as well as for people with very special needs, some of them needing one-to-one working relation. 📖

Number of projects: 1 UK: 0
Starting months: January–December
Time required: 52 weeks (plus)
Age: 19–60
Causes: Disabled (learning and physical), Elderly People.
Activities: Agriculture/Farming, Arts/Crafts, Caring – Residential, Cooking, Gardening/Horticulture, Manual Work, Social Work.
Placements: 30
When to apply: All year.

Work alone/with others: With others.
Qualifications: Good knowledge of English language is essential. No restrictions, but for nationals of some countries it is very hard to get a visa.
Equipment/clothing: For outside workers, wellies, rainwear etc.
Health requirements: Varies from applicant to applicant.
Costs: Travel.
Benefits: Pocket money of €140 per month, food and accommodation.
Training: Leaflet and co-worker information sheet. Visit before starting if wished. Any questions answered by contact person.
Supervision: Introductory course, study groups, working together and introduction by long-term co-workers.
Interviews: Interviews are conducted by letter. 2 references and a CV must be supplied + a police statement.
Worldwide placements: Europe (Ireland).

CAMPHILL VILLAGE KIMBERTON HILLS, INC

P.O. Box 155
Kimberton
Pennsylvania 19442 USA
T: 00 1 610.935.3963
F: 00 1 610.935.8896 or 3963
E: information@camphillKimberton.org
W: www.camphillKimberton.org
Contact: The Personnel Forum

For more details of Camphill Communities see Camphill Association of North America, above. Camphill Village Kimberton Hills is a life-sharing community based on a 430 acre estate in the rolling hills of southeast Pennsylvania. There is a total population of about 120, including 42 adults with developmental disability. The community grows vegetables, fruits, meat, and produces milk and cheese from a small dairy herd. Their own baked goods and handcrafts are sold in a health food store nearby. Volunteers are required to live and work as co-workers within the community, working side by side with developmentally disabled adults. Work takes place on the dairy farm, in the bakery, coffee shop, orchards, craft workshops and in expanded family homes. 🔊

Number of projects: 1 UK: 0
Starting months: Aug
Time required: 52 weeks (plus)
Age: 19–86
Causes: Conservation, Disabled (learning), Elderly People, Environmental Causes, Holidays for Disabled, Wildlife.
Activities: Agriculture/Farming, Arts/Crafts, Caring (general, residential), Conservation Skills, Cooking, Driving,

Gardening/Horticulture, Group Work, Manual Work, Music, Social Work, Teaching, Visiting/Befriending.
Placements: 40
When to apply: At least 2 months in advance of preferred starting date.
Work alone/with others: Both.
Qualifications: Enthusiasm and idealism.
Equipment/clothing: Prepared for all seasons of temperate climate: hot summers – snowy winters.
Health requirements: Must be able to meet the physical and emotional challenges of a life-sharing working community.
Costs: Travel costs.
Benefits: Board and lodging and $100 per month pocket money. Volunteers live in homes with householders, their families and specially handicapped residents.
Training: On-the-job training at work site.
Supervision: Volunteers are supervised by long-term co-workers in the house and at work stations.
Interviews: By correspondence or telephone.
Worldwide placements: North America: (USA).

CAMPHILL VILLAGE MINNESOTA

15136 Celtic Drice
Sauk Centre
MinnesotaMN 56378 USA
T: 00 1 320.732.6365
F: 00 1 320.732.3204
E: cvmn@rea-alp.com
W: www.camphill.org
Contact: Trudy Pax

For more details of Camphill Communities see Camphill Association of North America, above. The mission of Camphill Village Minnesota is to create and sustain a community where people with and without disabilities live, work, and care for each other to foster social, cultural and agricultural renewal. This village is an intentional community of approximately 60 people, including adults with developmental disabilities. The community is based on the belief that every individual, regardless of ability, is an independent spiritual being. Developmental disabilities are treated not as illnesses, but as part of the fabric of human experience, and all members of the community are cared for in the context of a healthy home and village life. Camphill is located on a 360 acre working farm ten miles north of Sauk Centre in central Minnesota. 📧

Number of projects: 1 UK: 0
Starting months: January–December
Time required: 24–52 weeks (plus)
Age: 18 plus – no upper limit
Causes: Disabled (learning and physical).
Activities: Agriculture/Farming, Arts/Crafts,

Caring – General, Catering, Community Work, Cooking, Counselling, Driving, First Aid, Gardening/Horticulture, Group Work, Manual Work, Music, Outdoor Skills, Social Work, Theatre/Drama.
Placements: 4
When to apply: All year.
Work alone/with others: Both.
Qualifications: Language ability.
Equipment/clothing: Heavy winter outdoor gear if coming in winter.
Health requirements: Reasonable health is required.
Costs: Travel costs.
Benefits: Board, lodging and US$50 per month pocket money. Volunteers live in a family-style setting with a private room.
Training: There is an orientation course for newcomers. A volunteer may learn other skills (eg gardening, woodworking) during the course of their stay.
Supervision: We expect volunteers to be able to work independently. There is guidance of course but not always supervision.
Interviews: We ask people to visit a Camphill near them or have a telephone interview.
Worldwide placements: North America: (USA).

CAMPHILL VILLAGE TRUST – LOCH ARTHUR COMMUNITY

Stable Cottage
Beeswing
Dumfries
DG2 8JQ UK
T: 01387 760687
F: 01387 760618
E: chanarin@btinternet.com
Contact: Lana Chanarin

For more details of Camphill Communities see Camphill Association of North America, above. Work activities in Loch Arthur include farming (crops, dairy, beef and sheep), gardening, estate work, creamery, bakery, weaving workshop and housework. We hope that co-workers joining us are willing and able to participate in any of these activities, depending on where the needs are in the community at the time in question. Volunteers with an offending background may be accepted depending on the nature of the offence.

Number of projects: 1 **UK:** 1
Starting months: January–December
Time required: 26–102 weeks
Age: 18 plus – no upper limit
Causes: Disabled (learning and physical), Teaching/assisting.
Activities: Agriculture/Farming, Arts/Crafts, Caring (day & residential), Catering, Cooking, Driving, Gardening/Horticulture, Group Work, Music, Teaching.

Placements: 13
When to apply: All year – apply at least 2 months in advance.
Work alone/with others: Both.
Qualifications: Open mindedness and enthusiasm.
Equipment/clothing: Sufficient clothing for duration of stay remembering Scottish weather and rural setting.
Health requirements: Physically and mentally fit to be able to participate fully and assist less able members.
Costs: Travel to and from the community.
Benefits: Board and Lodging + pocket money.
Training: Volunteers are trained on the job.
Supervision: Volunteers are supervised by long-term members of the community.
Interviews: Volunteer applicants are not necessarily interviewed – some do visit prior to placement. 2 references and a criminal record check is required.
Charity number: 232402
UK placements: Scotland (Dumfries and Galloway).

CAMPHILL VILLAGE TRUST LTD

Gawain House
56 Welham Road
Norton, Malton
North Yorkshire YO17 9DP UK
T: 01653 694197
F: 01653 600001
E: co-worker@camphill.org.uk
W: http://www.camphill.org.uk
Contact: Andy Paton

For more details of Camphill Communities see Camphill Association of North America, above. Camphill Village Trust Ltd was established to work with people who are mentally handicapped – and this is still its principal role today. From the outset, the intention was to do this work not as a 'job' in the usual sense of the word, but as a way of life. A community of co-workers was formed who shared all the work that had to be done: teaching, caring, household tasks, gardening. Volunteers with an offending background may be accepted with full disclosure. Each case is considered individually.

Number of projects: 100 **UK:** 47
Starting months: January–December
Time required: 26–52 weeks (plus)
Age: 18–50
Causes: Disabled (learning and physical).
Activities: Administration, Agriculture/Farming, Arts/Crafts, Caring (general, day and residential), Catering, Community Work, Cooking, Counselling, DIY, Gardening/ Horticulture, Group Work, Manual Work, Music, Outdoor Skills.
Placements: 300

When to apply: All year.
Work alone/with others: With other volunteers and staff.
Qualifications: Nil, only a sense of humour.
Equipment/clothing: Varied.
Health requirements: Health record required.
Costs: Dependent on placement.
Benefits: In Britain usually Community Service Volunteer rates.
Interviews: Interviews sometimes take place at centre applied for.
Charity number: 232402
Worldwide placements: Africa (Botswana, South Africa); North America: (Canada, USA); South America (Brazil); Europe (Austria, Denmark, Estonia, Finland, France, Germany, Ireland, Netherlands, Norway, Poland, Sweden, Switzerland).
UK placements: England (Buckinghamshire, Devon, Dorset, Gloucestershire, Hampshire, Hertfordshire, Norfolk, Sussex – East, West Midlands, N. Yorkshire, W. Yorkshire); Scotland (Aberdeenshire, Angus, Argyll and Bute, Dumfries and Galloway, Highland, Moray, Perth and Kinross, Stirling); Northern Ireland (Belfast City, Down, Tyrone); Wales (Carmarthenshire, Pembrokeshire).

CAMPHILL VILLAGE USA, INC

Copake, New York
12516 USA
T: 00 1 (518) 329 4851/7924
F: 00 1 (518) 329 0377
E: cvvolunteer@taconic.net
W: www.camphill.org
Contact: Penelope Roberts

For more details of Camphill Communities see Camphill Association of North America, above. Camphill Village USA is an intentional, international community of approximately 250 people, about 110 of whom are adults with mental disabilities. Located on 800 acres of woodland and farmland 100 miles north of New York City. The Village has a large biodynamic dairy farm, and gardens, seven craft shops, a production bakery, a community centre, a gift shop, a food co-op and 20 family residences in which life is shared by 5–7 adults with disabilities and 2–4 co-workers and their families, often with children. &

Number of projects: 90 UK: 20
Starting months: January–December
Time required: 13–52 weeks (plus)
Age: 19 plus – no upper limit
Causes: Disabled (learning and physical), Work Camps – Seasonal.
Activities: Administration, Agriculture/Farming, Arts/Crafts, Building/Construction, Caring (general, residential), Catering, Cooking, Driving, Forestry, Gardening/Horticulture,

Group Work, Manual Work, Music, Newsletter/ Journalism, Outdoor Skills, Social Work, Teaching, Theatre/Drama, Training, Work Camps – Seasonal.
Placements: 80
When to apply: All year.
Work alone/with others: Both.
Qualifications: Willingness to learn, to help out, and to join in our way of life. Volunteers must be able to speak and understand English.
Equipment/clothing: Nil – winters are cold and summers can be hot.
Health requirements: Physically fit and well, strong and ambulatory.
Costs: Travel costs.
Benefits: Board, lodging + $90 per month pocket money.
Training: After arrival.
Supervision: Depends on experience. Always supervision of experienced co-workers leading to more independent responsibility if appropriate.
Interviews: Interviews take place if possible at one of our 80 Camphill centres worldwide.
Worldwide placements: North America: (USA).

CANADIAN ORGANISATION FOR TROPICAL EDUCATION & RAINFOREST CONSERVATION

Box 335
Pickering, Ontario
L1V 2P9 Canada
T: 905 831 8809
F: 905 831 4203
E: coterc@interhop.net
W: www.coterc.org
Contact: Fran Mason

Canadian Organisation for Tropical Education and Rainforest Conservation (COTERC) is a non-profit organisation and not affiliated with any universities. Consequently we must generate our own funding support. Volunteers receive a reduced rate for staying at the station. Volunteers are expected to devote the majority of their time to duties assigned by our station co-ordinator, whether they be of a more menial nature such as washing dishes, grounds keeping etc. or of a more technical nature. The type of work done will depend on what studies are being conducted at any given time and may range from census studies of indigenous wildlife to assisting in environmental education programmes with children from the local community. Volunteers may not participate in research activities depending on when they choose to go. The station manager has designed a list of projects for volunteers when there are not any students present and few scientific studies being pursued. We may be able to accept applications from volunteers with an offending background – each applicant will be individually assessed. ⬚ ⬚

Number of projects: 1 **UK:** 0
Starting months: January–December
Time required: 2–52 weeks (plus)
Age: 18 plus – no upper limit
Causes: Children, Environmental Causes, Wildlife.
Activities: Community Work, Manual Work, Research, Scientific Work.
Placements: 12+
When to apply: Any time.
Work alone/with others: With other young volunteers.
Qualifications: Able to speak Spanish would be an advantage. Must be able to take directions from Station Manager.
Equipment/clothing: Clothes needed suitable for the climate.
Health requirements: No restrictions, but we are located in a remote field station in the rainforest, 25 minutes from the nearest village by boat. The weather may be unsuitable for people with certain medical conditions.
Costs: Air fare to San José and local transportation to Tortuguero + $100.00 US per week for accommodation and food. This does not include drinks which are paid for at the station.
Benefits: Reduced rate for accommodation and food at one of the stations. Dormitory accommodation.
Training: Manager will train depending on tasks.
Supervision: Station Manager will set up programme for volunteer to ensure supervision.
Interviews: Interviewed by resumé and e-mail, follow up on telephone if needed.
Charity number: 890096183RR0001
Worldwide placements: (Costa Rica).

CANARY NATURE

St Martins House
59 St Martins Lane
Covent Garden, London
WC2N 4JS UK
T: +44 (0) 207 590 7919
T: +44 (0) 207 240 5795
E: edb@huron.ac.uk
W: www.canarynature.com
Contact: Ed Bentham

Canary Nature's objective is to support the Atlantic Whale Foundation through facilitating quality research work. Main project areas are: zodiac based bottlenose dolphin research out of Los Gigantes, Tenerife (£345 per week); yacht based programmes in the Canaries, Azores, Mediterranean and Caribbean tracking whale and dolphins (Atlantic Whale Trail project) (starting from £595 per week) and a range of educational programmes in the International Cetacean

Summer School, Los Christianos, Tenerife (courses £50/£100 per week). Application details from web site or send 31p stamped addressed A4 envelope to London office. ⬚ ⬚

Number of projects: 10 **UK:** 0
Starting months: January–December
Time required: 1–52 weeks (plus)
Age: 17 plus – no upper limit
Causes: Animal Welfare, Children, Conservation, Environmental Causes, Heritage, Human Rights, Teaching/assisting, Wildlife, Young People.
Activities: Building/Construction, Campaigning, Community Work, Conservation Skills, Development Issues, DIY, Gardening/Horticulture, Outdoor Skills, Scientific Work, Teaching, Training.
Placements: 800–1000
When to apply: All year.
Work alone/with others: In groups.
Equipment/clothing: Depends on location.
Health requirements: Nil.
Costs: Educational courses from £50. Zodiac based dolphin research £345 per week. Yacht based Atlantic Whale Trail programme from £595 per week.
Benefits: Projects are self funding. We can recommend organisations that might give support.
Training: Given on site.
Supervision: Team of on site research co-ordinators undertake supervision.
Worldwide placements: Africa (Gambia, Ghana); Central America (Costa Rica, Cuba); South America (Brazil); Europe (Spain, Turkey).

CAPE TRIBULATION TROPICAL RESEARCH STATION

PMB 5, Cape Tribulation
Queensland
4873 Australia
T: 00 61 7 4098 0063
F: 00 61 7 4098 0063 (Ring first)
E: austrop@austrop.org.au
W: www.austrop.org.au
Contact: Hugh Spencer

The Cape Tribulation Tropical Research Station is a research and conservation organisation specialising in lowland tropical ecosystems, and has been in operation since 1988. It is independent and non-affiliated, and is funded by the not-for-profit Australian Tropical Research Foundation. Station projects: ecology of flying foxes (fruit bats) and their relatives; productivity and pollination of cluster figs; development of techniques for assisted regeneration of rainforests; development of appropriate technology for the wet tropics; rainforest and reef conservation; plus a variety of projects by researchers outside the Station.

Station operates the Bat House environmental centre for visitors to area. The area has a variety of habitats from coastal reefs to tropical rainforest. Volunteers pay $US15 per day (room and board) to assist in research and Station activities, from radio-tracking bats to counting figs and constructing Station buildings and regenerating rainforest. All volunteers are expected to actively participate in the household activities of the Station. The facilities are relatively spartan. Interns pay US$20 a day – room and board (interns are only part-time volunteers, involved in specific research projects requiring input of staff time and equipment). Students pay US$25 per day (small volunteer component, the rest is research time). **How to apply:** First look at the web site, www.austrop.org.au especially the 'What's New?' pages which are fairly regularly updated. Look at the information on the Station itself and the current conservation activities. Determine whether you want to be a volunteer, an intern or a student. Then send a brief e-mail to the director, hugh@austrop.org.au – describing your interest, likely time of visiting and a brief resume. E-mail is about the only way in which you can be guaranteed of an answer. If you apply by letter send an international reply coupon and a SAE. If you don't hear from us, contact us again. (We are a small outfit and it is easy for correspondence to get lost.) The Station relies on solar power and cannot leave the fax on. If you wish to fax, call them and ask to send a fax. You will be sent the latest volunteer update which contains everything you need to know about the Station, what to bring, and what to expect. If you don't get a response, please e-mail again as e-mails do go astray. On the Coral Sea of Queensland, about 120km north of Cairns.

Number of projects: 1 UK: 0
Starting months: January–December
Time required: 2–52 weeks (plus)
Age: 20–70
Causes: Animal Welfare, Conservation, Environmental Causes, Wildlife.
Activities: Accountancy, Building/Construction, Campaigning, Conservation Skills, Forestry, Fundraising, Manual Work, Outdoor Skills, Research, Scientific Work, Technical Skills.
Placements: 50
When to apply: All year.
Work alone/with others: Both – depends on number of volunteer/others at Station.
Qualifications: Open, flexible attitude, willing actively to contribute to even the most mundane activity. Must be proficient in English.
Equipment/clothing: Seasonal – request volunteer information sheet by e-mail.
Health requirements: Area poses no significant health problems.

Costs: A$18 per day + cost of transport to and from Cape Tribulation. This is at the volunteer's expense, although every reasonable effort will be made to find cheap or free transport.
Benefits: The cost covers food (lots) and modest accommodation.
Training: Variable – depends on projects.
Supervision: Usually Director or other staff.
Interviews: E-mail contact and resume – please don't send as an attachment.
Worldwide placements: Australasia (Australia).

CARE – COTTAGE AND RURAL ENTERPRISES LIMITED

36d Newgate Street
Morpeth, Northumberland
NE61 1BA UK
T: +44 (0) 1670 511157
F: +44 (0) 1670 511080
E: carefund.north@freeuk.com
Contact: Gary Richardson

CARE is concerned with giving support, through the provision of residential accommodation and work facilities, to people who have a learning disability. This offers each person the opportunity to live a full and purposeful life. Volunteers with an offending background may be accepted depending upon the circumstances.

Number of projects: 8+ UK: 8+
Starting months: January–December
Time required: 4–52 weeks
Age: 18–60
Causes: Disabled (learning).
Activities: Arts/Crafts, Caring (general, day and residential), Cooking, Gardening/Horticulture, Visiting/Befriending.
When to apply: All year.
Work alone/with others: Volunteers provide help to staff assisting those with learning disabilities.
Qualifications: Good communication skills.
Health requirements: Nil.
Costs: None.
Benefits: Board, accommodation and full insurance provided, plus £30 per week pocket money. Accommodation is usually a single bed-sitting room in one of the residents' cottages.
Training: All volunteers go through a full induction process before commencement of any duties.
Supervision: All volunteers would have a nominated supervisor who would carry out regular supervision.
Interviews: Interviews take place in the local community.
Charity number: 250058
UK placements: England (Devon, Kent, Lancashire, Leicestershire, Northumberland, Shropshire, Sussex – West, Wiltshire).

CARE AND RELIEF FOR THE YOUNG (CRY)

Sovereign Place
Upper Northam Close, Hedge End
Southampton, Hampshire
SO30 4AA UK
T: +44 (0) 1489 788300
F: +44 (0) 1489 790750
E: ukoffice@cry.org.uk
W: www.cry.org.uk
Contact: Project Director

Care and Relief for the Young (CRY): After the downfall of Romanian dictator Nicolae Ceausescu in December 1989, pictures that shocked the world revealed thousands of neglected and abandoned children living in appalling conditions in Romanian state orphanages. Pictures that left permanent scars in most human minds – warehouses for bodies. Many of these dispossessed children still live in stark state institutions or on the streets – inhabiting the sewers, underground heating systems and Metro service tunnels of major cities. Many are killing themselves by sniffing glue to stave off hunger pangs, others sell their bodies to the preying paedophiles for a few coins. CRY – a Christian charity – has designed and initiated a long-term childcare project – a unique working partnership with the local authorities. CRY's Casa Robin Hood project in Bucharest provides a residential home for up to 60 children in small family units; a childcare training programme for Romanian childcare workers; a vocational training programme with micro business centre and street outreach. A 'model' children's home is much needed as a catalyst for improving Romanian child care methods and policy. The long term goal is to equip Romanian people to take responsibility themselves. Casa Robin Hood, set in 3/4 acre of grounds, has been completely refurbished at a cost of £400,000. Opportunities exist for volunteers who are able to give six months or more of their time in Romania, living in at the centre. There are occasional places on DIY work parties. You can visit our web site. ⓖ

Number of projects: 1 UK: 1
Starting months: January–December
Time required: 12–52 weeks (plus)
Age: 21–60
Causes: Children, Poor/Homeless, Teaching/assisting (EFL), Work Camps – Seasonal, Young People.
Activities: Administration, Arts/Crafts, Caring (general, residential), Community Work, Computers, Cooking, DIY, First Aid, Gardening/Horticulture, Group Work, International Aid, Manual Work, Marketing/Publicity, Music, Newsletter/Journalism, Outdoor Skills, Religion, Research, Social Work, Summer Camps, Technical Skills, Theatre/Drama, Training,

Visiting/Befriending, Work Camps – Seasonal.
Placements: 50
When to apply: All year.
Work alone/with others: With staff/volunteers.
Qualifications: Applicants should have an active Christian commitment.
Health requirements: Yes – as medical support is limited in Bucharest, we issue a detailed health form.
Costs: £180 per month of stay must be prepaid before departure, £130 of this is paid back locally. Travel (air fare approx. £250 return) + insurance + visa.
Benefits: Costs cover just about everything; the £130 paid back is pocket money and off-duty food. All other costs covered by the £50 we retain. Live in at Casa Robin Hood Children's Home in Romania.
Training: All volunteers receive a comprehensive pack and cultural awareness dialogue.
Supervision: Volunteers supervised by group leaders and home director.
Interviews: Once prospective volunteers have passed initial screening and telephone call. Interviews usually take place in Southampton or Scunthorpe.
Charity number: 1011513
Worldwide placements: Europe (Romania).
UK placements: England (Hampshire).

CARE CORPS

47 Potter Avenue
New Rochelle
New York
10801 USA
T: 00 1 404 979 9274 or 001 877 CARE VOL
F: 001 914 632 8494
E: carecorps@care.org
Contact: Farhana Rehman or Shelby French

CARE Corps is an international volunteer programme for people interested in learning about sustainable solutions to poverty. CARE Corps volunteers work in partnership with local people in a variety of community-based projects. This unique programme offers exciting hands-on work opportunities, meaningful cultural immersion and enriching educational sessions about global issues. Ayacucho, Peru. ⓖ 🖹

Number of projects: 1 UK: 0
Starting months: January–December
Time required: 3 weeks
Age: 17 plus – no upper limit
Causes: Children, Elderly People, Health Care/Medical, Human Rights, Poor/Homeless, Teaching/assisting (nursery, primary), Young People.
Activities: Caring – General, Community Work, Development Issues, Fundraising, Group Work, International Aid, Marketing/Publicity,

Newsletter/journalism, Sport, Teaching, Visiting/Befriending.
Placements: 169
Work alone/with others: With others.
Qualifications: Spanish is helpful but not essential. All nationalities welcome but visa restrictions make it difficult for those not living in the US or UK.
Health requirements: Depends on work placement.
Costs: US$2490 for the three week programme plus all expenses and airfares. Fundraising assistance is available.
Benefits: Cost includes all meals, domestic transport and accommodation. All volunteers live in CARE Corps house, centrally located in the town of Ayacucho.
Training: In-country orientation and a 3-week curriculum about poverty, development and CARE.
Supervision: Volunteers are supervised by CARE Corps staff and CARE project staff as needed.
Interviews: Interviews by telephone.
Worldwide placements: South America (Peru).

CAREFORCE

35 Elm Road
New Malden, Surrey
KT3 3HB UK
T: +44 (0) 208 942 3331
F: +44 (0) 208 942 3331
E: enquiry@careforce.co.uk
W: www.careforce.co.uk
Contact: The Reverend Ian Prior

Careforce serves evangelical churches and organisations by placing Christian volunteers aged 18–25 where their help is most needed in the UK and Ireland. Careforce enables volunteers to offer themselves to serve God in an area of need for a year alongside local Christians. Volunteers with an offending background are accepted. &

Number of projects: 150 UK: 150
Starting months: Sep
Time required: 44–52 weeks
Age: 18–25
Causes: Addicts/Ex-Addicts, AIDS/HIV, Children, Disabled (learning and physical), Elderly People, Inner City Problems, Offenders/Ex-Offenders, Poor/Homeless, Teaching/assisting (nursery, primary, secondary), Young People.
Activities: Administration, Arts/Crafts, Caring (general, day and residential), Community Work, Development Issues, DIY, Music, Outdoor Skills, Religion, Social Work, Sport, Teaching, Training, Visiting/Befriending.
Placements: 150
When to apply: Any time – interviews held

February – August for UK based applicants. Before 28th February for applicants outside the UK.
Work alone/with others: Mainly placed as one volunteer within a team of local workers.
Qualifications: Committed Christians. Those from overseas need to be commended by their church leader.
Health requirements: Nil.
Costs: Travel cost to interview.
Benefits: Board and lodging, insurance and travel + £30 per week pocket money. Full board and lodging provided by each placement.
Training: Careforce holds an induction course for all volunteers at the start of year otherwise local induction training is given by placement. Volunteers also attend two national Careforce conferences during their year.
Supervision: Each volunteer has a work supervisor on placement and an area Careforce staff worker is attached to all volunteers for the year.
Interviews: Interviews are conducted at various UK based centres.
Charity number: 279443
UK placements: England (throughout); Scotland (throughout); Northern Ireland (throughout); Wales (throughout).

CARETTA RESEARCH PROJECT (SAVANNAH SCIENCE MUSEUM INC)

P.O. Box 9841
Savannah, Georgia
Chatham
31412 USA
T: 912 447 8655
F: 912 447 8656
E: WassawCRP@aol.com
W: www.carettaresearchproject.org
Contact: Kris Carroll

A hands-on research and conservation project that protects the threatened loggerhead sea turtles that nest on Wassaw National Wildlife Refuge, GA. It is run in co-operation with the U.S Fish and Wildlife Service and the Wassaw Island Trust. The objectives are to: learn more about population levels, trends and nesting habits of the loggerhead sea turtle; enhance the survival of eggs and hatchlings on a nesting beach where loss to predators and beach erosion have historically been high; educate the public and involve interested individuals in the research and conservation efforts for the loggerhead sea turtle. Each research team consists of two staff and up to six volunteers per week. Wassaw Island is patrolled from dusk until dawn every night. If a turtle is observed, any existing tag numbers, unusual markings, abnormalities and carapace measurements are recorded. Turtles, with or without tag scars, are tagged appropriately. Nests in an unsafe area, are carefully relocated to a safe area, either higher in the dunes or to a hatchery. All nests are screened to protect the nests from raccoon, hog and mink depredation. After emergence, nest contents are examined, recorded and the hatching success of each nest is calculated.

Number of projects: 1 **UK:** 0
Starting months: May
Time required: 1–2 weeks
Age: 15 plus – no upper limit
Causes: Conservation, Environmental Causes, Wildlife.
Activities: Conservation Skills, Research, Scientific Work.
Placements: 96
When to apply: January.
Work alone/with others: Work with others on the same project.
Equipment/clothing: None – bug suits are helpful.
Health requirements: Wassaw Island is remote with no hospital and we do a lot of walking so we require volunteers to be in relatively good shape.
Costs: $550 US/week (Saturday–Saturday) includes food and rustic accommodation.
Benefits: Food and lodging.
Training: Training is given on data collection.
Supervision: 2 staff are present at all times and there only 6 volunteers per team.
Interviews: Interviewed by telephone.
Worldwide placements: North America (USA).

CARIBBEAN CONSERVATION CORPORATION

4424 NW 13th Street
Suite A1, Gainsville
Florida 32609 USA
T: 352 373 6441
F: 352 375 2449
E: ccc@cccturtle.org
W: www.cccturtle.org
Contact: Dan Evans

Caribbean Conservation Corporation needs volunteers to assist the scientists with several important research tasks. Participants receive specific training in mist netting, walking transects and point counts, and will work in various settings including the rainforest, rivers and canals and near the beach. Highly trained ornithologists head up the work teams for each site. Whether you are a seasoned birder looking to add some rare species to your list, or a newcomer with a strong interest in conservation, you can be an integral part of our research team. Field study goes from dawn until afternoon, with a few hours break during the warmer part of the day, when you may explore jungle nature trails, boat the intricate river systems or climb the remnants of a nearby ancient volcano. During the evenings there will be workshops, time to

explore the village of Tortuguero, write letters, exchange stories with new friends, do your own birding or simply relax by the riverside at sunset and take in the surrounding tranquil beauty.

Number of projects: 1 **UK:** 0
Starting months: Aug, Sep, Oct
Time required: 1–3 weeks
Age: 18–60
Causes: Conservation, Environmental Causes, Wildlife.
Activities: Conservation Skills, Manual Work, Research, Scientific Work.
Placements: 10–20
When to apply: Applications are accepted throughout the year.
Work alone/with others: Work in groups.
Qualifications: In good physical condition and able to speak either English or Spanish.
Equipment/clothing: Participants should wear shirts without buttons and with good quality/waterproof hiking boots.
Health requirements: Restrictions include – people who cannot walk several miles and those with heart conditions or poor eye sight.
Costs: Estimated costs, not including international airfare are US $1,210 for one week, US $1,650 for two weeks and US $1,975 for three weeks.
Benefits: Volunteers will stay in dormitory style housing on site in Tortuguero, Costa Rica. It has running water, beds and bedding provided and food is cooked for volunteers.
Training: Participants are trained on site.
Supervision: Volunteers will always work with a CCC Research Assistant during the day, but nights are free and unsupervised.
Interviews: Interviews take place over the telephone.
Worldwide placements: Central America (Costa Rica).

CARIBBEAN VOLUNTEER EXPEDITIONS

Box 388, Corning
New York 14830 USA
T: 00 1 607 962 7846
F: 00 1 607 936 1153
E: ahershcve@aol.com
W: www.cvexp.org
Contact: Ann Hersh

Caribbean Volunteer Expeditions needs volunteers to document, measure and photograph historic buildings in the Caribbean. Throughout the Caribbean and in Nepal we find many deteriorated historic structures. Other historic and architecturally valuable buildings are being torn down and replaced by more modern buildings. The purpose of Caribbean Volunteer Expeditions is to record and document these buildings and structures. Our effort adds information about styles, history, and architecture of the Caribbean. And more importantly, we hope our work will encourage the preservation of important architectural and cultural heritage.

Number of projects: Many **UK:** 0
Starting months: January–December
Time required: 1–2 weeks
Age: 17–90
Causes: Architecture, Heritage.
Activities: Building/Construction, Computers, Gardening/Horticulture, Library/Resource Centres, Research.
Placements: 20–80
When to apply: All year.
Work alone/with others: With others.
Qualifications: Nil but architecture, photography, surveying, preservation are helpful.
Health requirements: Nil.
Costs: Cost per trip = US$500–US$1500. Registration fee $150.
Benefits: Free or very inexpensive lodging.
Interviews: Applicants are not interviewed.
Charity number: 501 c3
Worldwide placements: Central America (Aruba, Bahamas, Barbados, Bermuda, Costa Rica, Dominica, Montserrat, Netherlands Antilles, Puerto Rico, Saint Christopher/Nevis, Saint Lucia, Saint Vincent/Grenadines, Trinidad and Tobago, Turks and Caicos Islands, Virgin Islands); South America (Guyana, Suriname); Asia (Nepal).

CASA DE LOS AMIGOS A.C. (CONVIVE PROGRAMME)

Ignacio Mariscal 132, Col, Tabacalera
D.F. 06030 Mexico
T: 0052 5557 050521
F: 0052 5557 050771
E: convive@casadelosamigos.org
W: www.casadelosamigos.org
Contact: Christophe Grigri

Convive is a volunteer programme of the Casa de los Amigos, a Quaker service centre in Mexico City. The programme acts as a link between non-profit social and community organisations and volunteers from Mexico and abroad. The programme places volunteers with organisations which work in a wide range of areas, including HIV/AIDS, drug addiction and alcoholism, ecology, community development, indigenous communities, street kids, children at risk, people with disabilities, women and the older people. Convive maintains contact with volunteers before, during and after their service. On arrival in Mexico, volunteers attend an orientation, which covers themes including being a volunteer and the concept of volunteer service, the social situation in Mexico and life in Mexico City, the Casa de los Amigos, and the Quaker tradition of service. They are then placed in the organisation that best fits their skills, interests and motivation. Their work is directed by the organisation in which they are working, but volunteers can always suggest and plan their own projects in consultation with the organisation. Convive personnel provide constant support during the placement and are always available to liaise if necessary. There are also regular meetings held at Casa de los Amigos, which are attended by volunteers and representatives of the organisations. Volunteers can choose to remain in contact after completing their volunteering. Convive is based on the principles of service, equality, social understanding and pacifism and considers volunteer service an experience of dedication to others. Volunteers are required to carry a sense of giving more than they receive and to undertake their service in the spirit of mutual learning. There may be placements for volunteers with an offending background – non-violent. Mexico City, Mexico. ♿ ▤

Number of projects: 2 **UK:** 0
Starting months: January–December
Time required: 6–52 weeks (plus)
Age: 18 plus – no upper limit
Causes: Addicts/Ex-Addicts, AIDS/HIV, Children, Disabled (physical), Elderly People, Environmental Causes, Health Care/Medical, Holidays for Disabled, Human Rights, Inner City Problems, Poor/Homeless, Teaching/ assisting (nursery, primary, EFL), Young People.
Activities: Accountancy, Administration, Agriculture/Farming, Arts/Crafts, Building/Construction, Campaigning, Caring (general and day), Community Work, Computers, Development Issues, Fundraising, Gardening/Horticulture, Group Work, Manual Work, Marketing/Publicity, Newsletter/ Journalism, Research, Social Work, Teaching, Training, Translating, Visiting/Befriending.
Placements: 25
When to apply: All year round.
Work alone/with others: Both.
Qualifications: Volunteers need at least a basic level of Spanish.
Health requirements: No restrictions.
Costs: Registration fee £30 initial fee, £15 monthly subsistence (food & accommodation), approx £160 a month depending on where you live. Plus airfare.
Benefits: Some organisations provide lodgings and reimburse fares for travel. Quite a few provide food. Very few give any financial support.
Training: Most organisations provide minimal training, although some give more extensive introductions to their work.
Supervision: Convive maintains contact with volunteers working in organisations, but they are supervised by a specific person within each organisation.
Interviews: Interviews are held when possible in volunteer's home town, or by phone if we do not have a contact in home town.
Worldwide placements: Central America (Mexico).

CASA GUATEMALA

30 Church Road
Upton
Wirral CH49 6JZ UK
T: +44 (0) 151 606 0729
E: pete_rachel@lineone.net
W: www.casa-guatamala.org
Contact: Peter Brown and Rachel Phelps

The Casa Guatemala orphanage is based on three sites. There is a clinic in zone 1 of Guatemala City, which extends free medical care as well as being home to the babies and youngest children. It is staffed entirely by Guatemalans (a doctor, nurse, nursery nurses and social workers). Some of the nursery work is carried out by older girls from the orphanage, providing them with an income and work experience whilst they continue their studies in the city. Also in the city is a house in zone 10: home to the girls who work in the zone 1 clinic. They live there with the support of a housemother but with more independence than when they were at the main orphanage. Here also are the main administrative offices run by a senior social worker. The final site is the largest, situated in Rio Dulce. This site is home to a varying number of children (usually around 100) aged 2–16, who are sent there by the courts due to abandonment, abuse, poverty etc. as well as to many more children whose families live in isolated villages and send their children there for education. The site provides home, food, education and healthcare free of charge to all these children. It is at this site that volunteers are placed. The orphanage receives no financial help from the government of Guatemala and depends on donations. Casa Guatemala is striving toward self-sufficiency, though, and has opened Hotel Backpackers in Rio Dulce and runs a farm and a farm shop – all profits go toward the running cost of the orphanage. An essential part of the workforce is the foreign volunteers who generously give their time, expertise and support to the project. There are many opportunities for both skilled and unskilled volunteers at Casa Guatemala. 🖳 📖

Number of projects: 1 UK: 0
Starting months: January–December
Time required: 12–52 weeks (plus)
Age: 18 plus – no upper limit
Causes: Children, Disabled (learning and physical), Health Care/Medical, Poor/Homeless, Teaching/assisting (nursery, EFL), Young People.
Activities: Administration, Agriculture/Farming, Caring – General, Social Work, Teaching.
Placements: 100
When to apply: All year.
Work alone/with others: with others.
Qualifications: Spanish an advantage., enthusiasm, teaching or child care qualifications, agriculture qualifications. Also

positions for volunteers without specific skills or qualifications.
Equipment/clothing: Tropical clothes for rainforest region + torch + batteries, sheet and sleeping bag.
Health requirements: Relevant vaccinations needed and malaria pills may be advisable.
Costs: Volunteers are requested to pay a one-off fee of US$180 regardless of length of stay. Flight extra.
Benefits: Bed and board. Basic, mixed, dormitory type accommodation with own cooking facilities (although meals are provided) showers and toilets etc.
Training: 'On the Job' training from volunteer co-ordinator.
Supervision: Carried out by volunteer co-ordinator.
Interviews: Informal, either with contacts in UK or with Director in Guatemala. References required.
Worldwide placements: Central America (Guatemala).

CAT SURVIVAL TRUST, THE

The Centre
Codicote Road
Welwyn
Hertfordshire AL6 9TU UK
T: +44 (0) 1438 716873
F: +44 (0) 1438 717535
E: cattrust@aol.com
W: www.catsurvivaltrust.org
Contact: Dr Terry Moore

The Cat Survival Trust is a conservation society for endangered species of wild cat and their habitat. In the UK we have a library and research centre which works to find ways of protecting all species in their natural habitat as well as the proximate cause of habitat destruction worldwide. We have in excess of 50 live cats in our rescue centre which are from zoos closing down, members of the public found keeping them without a licence or from people smuggling them into the country. We only breed cats from stud books where captive numbers are low. Currently we breed caracals, scottish wild cats, european lynx and snow leopards. In Argentina, we run a 10,000 acre reserve with five million trees, billions of insects and plants and hundreds of thousands of reptiles, fish, birds and mammals including five species of wild cat. Here we study the best methods of preservation of ecosystems. Volunteers help us maintain our facilities and get involved in our research work. Volunteers with offending background are not accepted. Welwyn, England. Pinalito, Misiones, North East Argentina. 📖

Number of projects: 1 UK: 1
Starting months: January–December

Time required: 1–52 weeks
Age: 17 plus – no upper limit
Causes: Animal Welfare, Conservation, Environmental Causes, Wildlife.
Activities: Administration, Building/Construction, Campaigning, Computers, Conservation Skills, Development Issues, Forestry, Fundraising, Gardening/Horticulture, Group Work, Library/Resource Centres, Manual Work, Marketing/Publicity, Newsletter/Journalism, Outdoor Skills, Research, Scientific Work, Teaching, Translating.
Placements: 20–25
When to apply: All year.
Work alone/with others: Work with others and alone.
Qualifications: Dependent on volunteer position. Spanish required for Argentina.
Equipment/clothing: Old clothes needed for many positions, but specialist clothing is provided.
Health requirements: General good health required.
Costs: All costs (excluding accommodation) including travel for Argentina to be paid by volunteer.
Benefits: Accommodation, electricity, heating and basic food in UK. Argentina accommodation only. In the UK, caravan accommodation, cooking, heating and lighting provided free. In Argentina accommodation only free.
Training: Training provided as necessary by the Trust.
Supervision: All work is supervised by the Trust.
Interviews: Initial application should include a C.V./resume indicating requested dates preferred. Applicants can be interviewed via e-mail/mail or telephone.
Charity number: 272187
Worldwide placements: South America (Argentina).
UK placements: England (Hertfordshire).

CATHEDRAL CAMPS

16 Glebe Avenue
Flitwick, Bedfordshire
MK45 1HS UK
T: +44 (0) 1525 716237
F: +44 (0) 1525 716237
E: admin@cathedralcamps.org.uk
W: www.cathedralcamps.org.uk
Contact: Mrs Shelley Bent

Cathedral Camps undertakes the conservation and restoration of cathedrals and major parish churches and their environments, including tasks that have hitherto been postponed because of a lack of resources. Volunteers are needed to work in groups of 15–25 people throughout the country. Although in cathedrals all over the country, they may not be in every county listed. ⓑ

Number of projects: 24 **UK:** 24
Starting months: Jul, Aug, Sep
Time required: 1–2 weeks
Age: 16–30
Causes: Conservation, Heritage, Work Camps – Seasonal.
Activities: Building/Construction, Conservation Skills, Work Camps – Seasonal.
Placements: 500
When to apply: February – July prior to camp starting.
Work alone/with others: With others.
Equipment/clothing: All equipment provided.
Health requirements: Fit.
Costs: £55 per week towards the cost of camp, board and lodging.
Benefits: Can be used towards Gold Duke of Edinburgh Award. Accommodation provided in choir school, church hall etc.
Training: None.
Supervision: Volunteers are supervised by camp leaders and staff at the camp.
Interviews: Applicants for volunteer positions are not interviewed but we require a reference for their first camp.
Charity number: 286248
UK placements: England (throughout); Scotland (throughout); Northern Ireland (throughout); Wales (throughout).

CATHOLIC NETWORK OF VOLUNTEER SERVICE

1410 Q Street NW
Washington DC
20009 USA
T: 202 332 6000
F: 202 332 1611
E: volunteer@cnvs.org
W: www.cnvs.org
Contact: Recruitment Co-ordinator

Catholic Network of Volunteer Service (CNVS) is an organisation of over 200 full time, Christian faith based volunteer programmes. The programmes offer volunteers the opportunity to volunteer on a full-time basis (30+ hours/week) for as little as one week to two years. Programmes place people in numerous ministries, and in over 110 countries. We are based in the US and place volunteers in all 50 states in the US. We may have placements for volunteers with an offending background, depending on the offence, but acceptance varies between programmes. ⓑ

Number of projects: 200 **UK:** 0
Starting months: January–December
Time required: 1–52 weeks (plus)
Age: 21–99
Causes: Addicts/Ex-Addicts, AIDS/HIV, Animal Welfare, Archaeology, Architecture, Children, Conservation, Disabled (learning and physical),

Elderly People, Environmental Causes, Health Care/Medical, Heritage, Holidays for Disabled, Human Rights, Inner City Problems, Offenders/Ex-Offenders, Poor/Homeless, Refugees, Teaching/assisting (nursery, primary, secondary, mature, EFL) Unemployed, Wildlife, Work Camps – Seasonal, Young People.

Activities: Accountancy, Administration, Agriculture/Farming, Arts/Crafts, Building/Construction, Campaigning, Caring (general, day and residential), Catering, Community Work, Computers, Conservation Skills, Cooking, Counselling, Development Issues, DIY, Driving, First Aid, Forestry, Fundraising, Gardening/Horticulture, Group Work, International Aid, Library/Resource Centres, Manual Work, Marketing/Publicity, Music, Newsletter/Journalism, Outdoor Skills, Religion, Research, Scientific Work, Social Work, Sport, Summer Camps, Teaching, Technical Skills, Theatre/Drama, Training, Translating, Visiting/Befriending, Work Camps – Seasonal.

Placements: 9000
When to apply: Varies between programmes.
Work alone/with others: Varies.
Qualifications: Varies between programmes.
Equipment/clothing: Varies between programmes.
Health requirements: Varies between programmes.
Costs: Varies between programmes. Generally programmes cover most expenses incurred during the year, but volunteers are responsible for some part of their travel costs as well as personal expenses beyond the basic necessities.
Benefits: Varies between programmes. Most programmes cover board and room, medical insurance and provide a very modest living allowance to cover the basic necessities.
Training: Varies by programme. Most programmes have an orientation period of around one week (for a year long volunteer) Most placement sites also offer on the job training.
Supervision: Varies by programme.
Interviews: Varies by programme.
Worldwide placements: North America: (USA).

CCUSA

Green Dragon House
64–70 High Street
Croydon, Surrey
CR0 9XN UK
T: +44 (0) 20 8688 9051
F: +44 (0) 20 8680 4534
E: info@ccusa.co.uk
W: www.ccusa.com
Contact: Jamie Mackler

CCUSA need counsellors to look after children (or adults with special needs if they prefer) and teach activities on summer camps in America.

These activities can be general or specialised and cover a massive range from soccer to jazz dance and from orienteering to pottery. Support staff work behind the scenes running the catering, secretarial and maintenance departments of the camps. Applicants must be available for nine weeks beginning between 30th May–30th June. Hours: can be working from 7am until 11 p.m. with free time during the day and one day off per week. Nine weeks actual work but five month visas allow plenty of time for travel. Volunteers with an offending background may be accepted depending on offence. Each application is taken on an individual basis. ⓖ ▤

Number of projects: 1,000 **UK:** 0
Starting months: Jun
Time required: 9–9 weeks
Age: 18–30
Causes: Children, Disabled (learning and physical), Health Care/Medical, Holidays for Disabled, Inner City Problems, Poor/Homeless, Teaching/assisting (nursery, primary, secondary), Work Camps – Seasonal, Young People.
Activities: Administration, Agriculture/Farming, Arts/Crafts, Caring (general, day and residential), Catering, Community Work, Computers, Cooking, Counselling, Driving, First Aid, Forestry, Gardening/Horticulture, Group Work, Manual Work, Music, Newsletter/ Journalism, Outdoor Skills, Religion, Social Work, Sport, Summer Camps, Teaching, Technical Skills, Theatre/Drama, Work Camps – Seasonal.
Placements: 1350 UK (7000 international)
When to apply: As soon as possible, but before April 30th.
Work alone/with others: Both.
Qualifications: Strong English Language. Love of children. Experience with children, sport, art or craft, performing art, outdoor activity, catering, secretarial, maintenance is an

advantage, but enthusiasm and the right attitude are more important for the job.
Health requirements: Good general health.
Costs: Total cost = £245 for insurance and registration deposits.
Benefits: Return flight to the USA, accommodation, 3 months comprehensive insurance, travel to camp, food, J1 working visa, 24 hour emergency service whilst in the USA and pocket money up to $1000. Up to 7 weeks free time to travel around the USA at the end.
Training: Pre-departure orientation and on the job training.
Interviews: Interviews are conducted by a regional network of interviewers all over England and Wales.
Worldwide placements: North America: (USA).

CEDAM INTERNATIONAL

One Fox Road
Croton-on-Hudson
NY 10520 USA
T: 00 1 914 271 5365
F: 00 10914 271 4723
E: cedam@aol.com
W: www.cedam.org
Contact: Susan Sammon

Cedam International is a non-profit agency organising marine expeditions to tropical locations such as Mexico, the Seychelles, the Galapagos, Kenya, Australia, Belize etc. Cedam International focuses principally on conservation, environmental education and marine research, with expert divers, photographers and biologists undertaking marine research activities. Volunteers can participate in these expeditions for short term periods. Those with scuba qualifications or skills in underwater video/photography are welcome to apply, though these skills are not essential. Expeditions are made up of teams of volunteers, scientists, divers etc and therefore a team spirit is required.

Number of projects: Currently one diving expedition per year.
Starting months: January–December
Time required: 1–2 weeks
Age: 18 plus – no upper limit
Causes: Conservation, Environmental Causes, Heritage.
Activities: Conservation Skills, Manual Work, Outdoor Skills, Sport.
When to apply: Any time.
Qualifications: Certified diver with c-card.
Equipment/clothing: Must bring own diving gear.
Health requirements: Good.
Costs: US$1,500–$4,000 depending on location.
Interviews: Volunteers submit expedition application. Expeditions are filled on a first come first served basis.

Worldwide placements: Central America (Belize, Cayman Islands, Dominica, Mexico, Turks and Caicos Islands); Asia (Indonesia); Australasia (Fiji, Palau, Papua New Guinea, Solomon Islands).

CELIA HAMMOND ANIMAL TRUST

High Street, Wadhurst
East Sussex
TN5 6AG UK
T: +44 (0) 1892 783820
F: +44 (0) 1892 784882
E: chat@ukonline.co.uk
W: www.celiahammond.org
Contact: Miss Roma Brawn

The Celia Hammond Animal Trust is a registered charity whose main objectives are the running of low cost neuter clinics for animals belonging to people unable to afford private veterinary fees. We also have a rescue/rehoming service for animals in need. Our animal sanctuary is set in 12 acres of Sussex countryside. Volunteers would be based at our animal sanctuary and the main duties would be helping to look after the animals in our care. Volunteers should have a love of animals and concern for animal welfare. Please note – there are no placements available until April 2004. Our animal sanctuary is isolated with limited public transport. ⅁

Number of projects UK: 4
Starting months: January–December
Time required: 1–52 weeks (plus)
Age: 18 plus – no upper limit
Causes: Animal Welfare, Environmental Causes, Wildlife.
Activities: Building/Construction, Driving, Fundraising, Outdoor Skills.
Placements: 15
When to apply: All year.
Work alone/with others: With other young volunteers.
Qualifications: Nil, but driving licence is useful.
Health requirements: No special Health requirements. Volunteers need to be physically fit.
Costs: All travel costs would need to be met by the volunteer.
Benefits: Board and lodging. Accommodation is available in a shared vegetarian/vegan household.
Training: Training on site.
Supervision: Supervised at all times.
Interviews: Initial interviews will be via phone or e-mail. As volunteer placements are residential, references will be required.
Charity number: 293787
UK placements: England (Sussex – East).

CENTRE FOR DEVELOPMENT SERVICES (CDS) – BANGLADESH

38/1 Block-F, Ring Road
Shyamoli
Dhaka
Bangladesh
F: 00 880 2 8115 512
E: cds@bdmail.net
Contact: Omar Faruque Chowdhury

Centre for Development Services (CDS) promotes and has information about volunteering in Bangladesh. It may well be able to put volunteers in touch with organisations which are not yet listed on the WorldWide Volunteering database.

Starting months: January–December
Time required: 1–52 weeks (plus)
Age: 16 plus – no upper limit
Causes: Addicts/Ex-Addicts, AIDS/HIV, Animal Welfare, Archaeology, Architecture, Children, Conservation, Disabled (learning and physical), Elderly People, Environmental Causes, Health Care/Medical, Heritage, Holidays for Disabled, Human Rights, Inner City Problems, Offenders/Ex-Offenders, Poor/Homeless, Refugees, Teaching/assisting (nursery, primary, secondary, mature, EFL) Unemployed, Wildlife, Work Camps – Seasonal, Young People.
Activities: Accountancy, Administration, Agriculture/Farming, Arts/Crafts, Building/Construction, Campaigning, Caring (general, day and residential), Catering, Community Work, Computers, Conservation Skills, Cooking, Counselling, Development Issues, DIY, Driving, First Aid, Forestry, Fundraising, Gardening/Horticulture, Group Work, International Aid, Library/Resource Centres, Manual Work, Marketing/Publicity, Music, Newsletter/Journalism, Outdoor Skills, Religion, Research, Scientific Work, Social Work, Sport, Summer Camps, Teaching, Technical Skills, Theatre/Drama, Training, Translating, Visiting/Befriending, Work Camps – Seasonal.
Costs: Varies according to the project.
Worldwide placements: Asia (Bangladesh).

CENTRE 63

Old Hall Lane
Kirkby
Merseyside L32 5TH UK
T: +44 (0) 151 549 1494
E: c63@mersinet.co.uk
Contact: Dave Coates

Centre 63 was set up in 1963. Volunteers are very welcome to work as part of a team in an innovative go-ahead youth organisation working in a disadvantaged estate in North Merseyside. Volunteers with an offending background may be accepted depending on the offence. 🖫 🖹

Number of projects: 2 UK: 2
Starting months: January–December
Time required: 1–52 weeks
Age: 18 plus – no upper limit
Causes: Addicts/Ex-Addicts, Children, Health Care/Medical, Inner City Problems, Poor/Homeless, Unemployed, Young People.
Activities: Administration, Arts/Crafts, Community Work, Fundraising, Group Work, Newsletter/Journalism, Outdoor Skills, Social Work, Sport, Summer Camps, Visiting/Befriending.
Placements: 5–10
When to apply: All year.
Work alone/with others: With others.
Qualifications: Sense of humour and good command of English. Good command of English essential.
Health requirements: Nil.
Costs: Nil.
Benefits: Travel expenses and lunch.
Interviews: Applicants are interviewed in Kirkby.
Charity number: 700064
UK placements: England (Merseyside).

CENTRE DE SCULPTURE

Fonderie de la Dure
Montolieu
Languedoc-Roussillon
11170 France
T: 00 33 (0)4 68 24 81 81
F: 00 33 (0)4 68 24 88 88
E: louise.sculpture@wanadoo.fr
Contact: Louise Romain

The Centre de Sculpture is a mini art centre surrounded by a beautiful natural environment in a little village. We act as a host organisation for European exchange projects (Leonardo, Youth Mobility). The work is mainly outside and typically involves environmental, simple building and maintenance work. To give you an idea – creating a trail in a small forest, path clearance, rebuilding small stonewalls, strimming, woodcutting, and riverbank maintenance, cutting down blackberry thorns, creating an organic garden, renovation of a canal. Energy, enthusiasm, adaptability, and dynamism are the order of the day. There may be placements for volunteers with an offending background depending on the offence. 🖫 🖹

Number of projects: 6 UK: 0
Starting months: Apr, May, Jun
Time required: 3–52 weeks (plus)
Age: 18 plus – no upper limit
Causes: Architecture, Conservation, Environmental Causes, Heritage, Unemployed, Wildlife, Young People.
Activities: Agriculture/Farming, Arts/Crafts, Building/Construction, Community Work, Conservation Skills, Cooking, DIY, Forestry,

Group Work, Outdoor Skills, Summer Camps, Technical Skills, Translating, Work Camps – Seasonal.
Placements: 20
When to apply: As soon as possible as places are limited.
Work alone/with others: With others.
Qualifications: We look for enthusiasm and willingness. No restrictions but it is easier to get funding for EU citizens.
Equipment/clothing: Maybe a favourite pair of boots and gloves. We provide everything else.
Health requirements: No restrictions.
Costs: Travel and pocket money. We are happy to help apply for funding for these.
Benefits: Free lodging. In small house with all mod cons. Fully equipped. Bedding provided in small bedrooms. No smoking in house.
Training: Training is provided depending on individuals needs.
Supervision: We have full time supervisor.
Interviews: Not face-to-face interview although we hope to contact via telephone or e-mail.
Worldwide placements: Europe (France).

CENTRE FOR ALTERNATIVE TECHNOLOGY

Machynlleth
Powys
SY20 9AZ UK
T: +44 (0) 1654 705950
F: +44 (0) 1654 702782
E: rick.dance@cat.org.uk
Contact: Rick Dance

Before you apply, please think about why you want to come and the reality of what we have to offer. The volunteer programme is not a course, and we do not give any formal training or instruction. Conditions are far from luxurious. You will however have the chance to learn and experience what we are doing through working, talking to people, consulting information material etc. – it is very much up to you. A variety of different work tasks might be undertaken in each volunteer week, and an element of flexibility is essential (especially dependent on the the weather). Sometimes you might simply be asked to help with whatever jobs are most urgent at the time. You may imagine that we spend all our time erecting windmills or building solar panels, but actually most of the work we do is pretty ordinary. It is likely that volunteers will work mostly in the gardens. We try to use people's skills appropriately where possible, but you may end up doing routine work. Please don't bring any animals or illegal drugs. Please note that antisocial or inappropriate behaviour might result in us requiring you to curtail your stay. The minimum age for residential participation is 18, and since we have no creche facilities it is unfortunately not possible to bring children. Please arrive on the Monday of the week you are booked, not Sunday. There is no work organised for volunteers at the weekend, but you are welcome to stay until 2pm on the Sunday at the end of your booking if you wish (and for the whole of the interim weekend if you are staying for two weeks). Travel to Machynlleth is fairly easy by car, train or bus. From Machynlleth the three mile walk to the Centre (on the Dolgellau road, A487) can be enjoyable, especially along the back road if you can find it. Buses run to nearby Pantperthog every day except Sunday. 🗎

Number of projects: 1 **UK:** 1
Starting months: Mar, Apr, May, Jun, Jul, Sep
Time required: 1–2 weeks
Age: 18 plus – no upper limit
Causes: Environmental Causes.
Activities: Building/Construction, Cooking, Gardening/Horticulture, Manual Work.
Placements: 70
When to apply: As early in the year as possible.
Work alone/with others: With others.
Equipment/clothing: Please bring a sleeping-bag, a torch, strong work clothes, boots and waterproof clothing – it rains alot. If you own steel toecap boots, please bring them as well.
Health requirements: Nil.
Costs: Short-term volunteers come to help and are asked to contribute for bed and board – £5.50 GB per day.
Benefits: Accommodation is basic Youth Hostel-style, share with other volunteers. Food & drinks are provided.
Training: We do not give any formal training or instruction.
Interviews: Applicants are not interviewed.
Charity number: 265239
UK placements: Wales (Powys).

CENTRE FOR ENVIRONMENT AND DEVELOPMENT

Godicherla Post
via Payakaraopeta
Visakhapatnam District
Andhra Pradesh 531 126 India
T: 00 91 8854 53664
F: 00 91 891 563704
E: vijaylaxmicead@yahoo.com
Contact: Ms G. Vijayalaxmi and Mr G.S.P. Kumar

Centre for Environment and Development (CEAD) is a women's development organisation which was established by a group of educated women who belong to rural remote areas. These women had gone through the problems/disadvantages in their area, observing the situation since childhood and they decided to form CEAD in order to take action. CEAD strives to develop issues like literacy, the rights of the girl-child, land development, watershed, animal and human health, savings, access to credit, gender balance and equality, women's rights, communication and media. CEAD's mission is to eliminate extreme poverty by empowering the rural poor women through a process of social mobilisation combined with creating opportunities for self-reliance. CEAD identifies crucial development issues and evolves a strategy to build local bodies to be effective in the respective areas. Issues of local areas are identified, followed up and training programmes are held to improve planning, implementation, administration, finance, organisational and individual skills. Our objectives are to sensitise members to the issue of self-esteem and dignity of work, to eliminate the middlemen's control and to secure greater bargaining power in the market. We undertake to explore land/livestock-based activities that will generate sources of income for the people in our target areas. The Nakkapalli and Payakaraopeta Blocks are continuously affected by drought and Nakkapalli Block is one of the most backward blocks in the district. People are totally landless or with marginal land. Most people migrate to other neighbouring districts in search of a livelihood. Women and children are the worst sufferers. 🕭 📄

Number of projects: 2 **UK:** 0
Starting months: January–December
Time required: 2–12 weeks
Age: 15 plus – no upper limit
Causes: AIDS/HIV, Animal Welfare, Children, Disabled (learning and physical), Elderly People, Environmental Causes, Health Care/Medical, Human Rights, Poor/Homeless, Teaching/assisting (nursery, primary, secondary), Teaching – Mature.
Activities: Community Work, Computers, Counselling, Development Issues, Forestry, Fundraising, Gardening/Horticulture, Group Work, International Aid, Newsletter/Journalism, Outdoor Skills, Research, Scientific Work, Social Work, Theatre/Drama, Training, Translating.
Placements: 25–50
When to apply: All year.
Work alone/with others: With others usually.
Qualifications: Interest in working with the poorest. Experience in animal, documentation, teaching, computer education and management a bonus.
Equipment/clothing: Casual cottons during summer and light wool mix in winter.
Health requirements: Nil. CEAD will provide boiled drinking water free or bottled mineral water and soft drinks at nominal cost.
Costs: Travel, pocket money. Board and lodging for £3 a day.
Benefits: Travel costs within the project will be reimbursed. The cost of board and lodging covers unlimited amount of tea and coffee, Indian or continental breakfast, lunch and dinner of vegetables with mutton, chicken or fish.

Interviews: Interviews do not take place.
Worldwide placements: Asia (India).

CENTRE FOR VOLUNTEERING & PHILANTHROPY (YOUTH DEVELOPMENT FOUNDATION)

P.O. Box 5191
Model Town Lahore – 54700
Pakistan
T: +92 42 5887835
F: +92 42 5887836
E: youth@wol.net.pk
W: www.youth.org.pk
Contact: Bilal Zafar

Youth Development Foundation is a non profit, non-partisan national youth organisation encouraging and helping young people to meet the challenges of adolescence and adulthood through a co-ordinated, progressive and positive series of activities and experiences which help them to become socially, morally, emotionally, physically, and cognitively competent to contribute in national development. Centre for Volunteering and Philanthropy is a project running the following volunteer projects – Youth Club Network, Young Volunteer Corps, Pakistan's Tomorrow – an after school Initiative, Youth Development Internship Programme, Local Government Public Access Initiative, Youth Friendly Organisations – a Fundraising Campaign. 📄

Number of projects: 6 **UK:** 0
Starting months: January–December
Time required: 1–15 weeks
Age: 15–29
Causes: AIDS/HIV, Children, Disabled (learning and physical), Elderly People, Environmental Causes, Health Care/Medical, Human Rights, Inner City Problems, Teaching (nursery, primary), Young People.
Activities: Administration, Campaigning, Caring – General, Community Work, Counselling, Fundraising, Marketing/Publicity, Social Work, Teaching, Theatre/Drama, Training.
Placements: 80
When to apply: Projects start on the first day of each month so applications should be placed by the 15th of the month.
Work alone/with others: Both.
Qualifications: Basic education and language proficiency.
Health requirements: Yes, there are some health restrictions – more details on request.
Costs: £500+, no registration or membership charged though.
Benefits: Some projects will cover some communication and local travelling charges.
Training: We provide basic training before starting any assignment according to the assignment.

Supervision: There is a volunteer co-ordinator to monitor and facilitate all projects.
Interviews: Interviews take place usually on the telephone, on-line or personally in our office.
Charity number: RP/687/L/S/2002/1188
Worldwide placements: Asia (Pakistan).

CENTRE GENEVOIS DU VOLONTARIAT (CGV) – SWITZERLAND

7 Avenue Pictet-de-Rochemont
1207 Geneve
Switzerland
T: 00 41 22 736 8242
F: 00 41 22 786 1118
W: www.voluntariat-ge.org
Contact: Lola Sasson

Centre Genevois du Volontariat (CGV) promotes and has information about volunteering in Switzerland. It may well be able to put volunteers in touch with organisations which are not yet listed on the WorldWide Volunteering database.

Starting months: January–December
Time required: 1–52 weeks (plus)
Age: 16 plus – no upper limit
Causes: Addicts/Ex-Addicts, AIDS/HIV, Animal Welfare, Archaeology, Architecture, Children, Conservation, Disabled (learning and physical), Elderly People, Environmental Causes, Health Care/Medical, Heritage, Holidays for Disabled, Human Rights, Inner City Problems, Offenders/Ex-Offenders, Poor/Homeless, Refugees, Teaching/assisting (nursery, primary, secondary, mature, EFL) Unemployed, Wildlife, Work Camps – Seasonal, Young People.
Activities: Accountancy, Administration, Agriculture/Farming, Arts/Crafts, Building/Construction, Campaigning, Caring (general, day and residential), Catering, Community Work, Computers, Conservation Skills, Cooking, Counselling, Development Issues, DIY, Driving, First Aid, Forestry, Fundraising, Gardening/Horticulture, Group Work, International Aid, Library/Resource Centres, Manual Work, Marketing/Publicity, Music, Newsletter/Journalism, Outdoor Skills, Religion, Research, Scientific Work, Social Work, Sport, Summer Camps, Teaching, Technical Skills, Theatre/Drama, Training, Translating, Visiting/Befriending, Work Camps – Seasonal.
Costs: Varies according to the project.
Worldwide placements: Europe (Switzerland).

CENTRE NATIONAL DU VOLONTARIAT (CNV) – FRANCE

127 rue Falguiere
Paris
F-75015 France
T: 00 33 1 406 101 61
F: 00 33 1 456 799 75
E: cnv@globenet.org
Contact: Jacqueline Couste

Centre National du Volontariat (CNV) promotes and has information about volunteering in France. It may well be able to put volunteers in touch with organisations which are not yet listed on the WorldWide Volunteering database.

Starting months: January–December
Time required: 1–52 weeks (plus)
Age: 16 plus – no upper limit
Causes: Addicts/Ex-Addicts, AIDS/HIV, Animal Welfare, Archaeology, Architecture, Children, Conservation, Disabled (learning and physical), Elderly People, Environmental Causes, Health Care/Medical, Heritage, Holidays for Disabled, Human Rights, Inner City Problems, Offenders/Ex-Offenders, Poor/Homeless, Refugees, Teaching/assisting (nursery, primary, secondary, mature, EFL) Unemployed, Wildlife, Work Camps – Seasonal, Young People.
Activities: Accountancy, Administration, Agriculture/Farming, Arts/Crafts, Building/Construction, Campaigning, Caring (general, day and residential), Catering, Community Work, Computers, Conservation Skills, Cooking, Counselling, Development Issues, DIY, Driving, First Aid, Forestry, Fundraising, Gardening/Horticulture, Group Work, International Aid, Library/Resource Centres, Manual Work, Marketing/Publicity, Music, Newsletter/Journalism, Outdoor Skills, Religion, Research, Scientific Work, Social Work, Sport, Summer Camps, Teaching, Technical Skills, Theatre/Drama, Training, Translating, Visiting/Befriending, Work Camps – Seasonal.
Costs: Varies according to the project.
Worldwide placements: Europe (France).

CENTRO CAMUNO DI STUDI PREISTORICI

Via Marconi 7
25044 Capo di Ponte
Brescia Italy
T: 00 390 364 42091
F: 00 390 364 42572
E: ccspreist@tin.it
W: www.rockart-ccsp.com
Contact: Director's Office

Centro Camuno di Studi Preistorici is a research institute concentrating on the study of prehistory and primitive art, with field projects in Europe, the Near East, Asia and Africa, and run by a non profit making cultural association. Volunteers are needed to participate in the exploration of sites and also for assisting in laboratory, archives and library. Skilled volunteers in computer editing, graphics, topography, photography and translations are welcome. There are projects all year long in

Valcamonica, Italy; from March – April in the Negev Desert, Israel; and from August – September in the Helanshan Mountains, Ningxia, China; or in Oceania. ⓖ ▣

Number of projects: 4 UK: 0
Starting months: January–December
Time required: 12–52 weeks
Age: 18 plus – no upper limit
Causes: Archaeology, Heritage, Work Camps – Seasonal.
Activities: Arts/Crafts, Computers, Fundraising, Library/Resource Centres, Manual Work, Newsletter/Journalism, Research, Scientific Work, Summer Camps, Teaching, Technical Skills, Training, Translating, Work Camps – Seasonal.
Placements: 50
When to apply: January, April, July, October.
Work alone/with others: Both.
Qualifications: Deep interest in archaeology, primitive art, anthropology or history of religions.
Equipment/clothing: Casual clothes.
Health requirements: Health insurance and good health.
Costs: All, including board, lodging, local travel and insurance.
Benefits: Knowledge and experience in prehistoric and primitive art and experience in the field. Guesthouse of rooms for 2–3 or rent an apartment or a room in the vicinity.
Training: Reading a list of brochures.
Supervision: Each volunteer has a supervisor who follows up his/her work.
Interviews: Centro Camuno di Studi Preistorici.
Worldwide placements: Africa (Egypt, Morocco); Asia (China, Israel, Jordan); Australasia (Australia, Oceania); Europe (Azerbaijan, France, Italy).

CENTRO CARAPAX

Loc. Le Venelle, C.P. 34
Massa Marittima
Grosseto 58024 Italy
T: +39 0566/94.00.83
F: +39 0566/91.23.87
E: carapax@cometanet.it
W: www.carapax.org
Contact: Veerle Vandepitte

Centro Carapax has been established for the protection, scientific research and the re-population of tortoises and recruits volunteers to work in Tuscany. Experience is not essential since motivation and a willingness to learn are sufficient. For a minimum of three weeks, volunteers will participate in the management and infrastructure and care of animals at the centre and participate in environmental education and naturalistic research. Volunteers must be at least 18 years of age and in good health. They will work in small groups under curators who are directly responsible to the

Director. Carapax works in a protected area of 15 hectares. Work is carried out over five days allowing two days off. The town Massa Marittima is an old medieval town with a cathedral. All surrounding towns are steeped in middle age history but above all Etruscan history. Volunteers must be prepared to live in the community and be able to assume responsibilities attached. ⓖ ▣

Number of projects: 1 UK: 0
Starting months: Apr, May, Jun, Jul, Aug, Sep, Oct
Time required: 3–28 weeks
Age: 18 plus – no upper limit
Causes: Animal Welfare, Conservation, Wildlife.
Activities: Building/Construction, Caring – General, Computers, Cooking, Manual Work, Outdoor Skills.
Placements: 100
When to apply: February.
Work alone/with others: With others.
Qualifications: A good knowledge of English as this is the main language spoken, German/Italian also useful. A willingness to help and a serious sense of responsibility.
Equipment/clothing: Sleeping bag, jeans to work in the bush, summer clothes, swimwear, torch, protection against the sun.
Health requirements: No persons under psychiatric care, no persons with drug or alcohol problems. We expect open communication of any problems so that we can evaluate individually (eg allergies to insect bites, heart condition etc).
Costs: Airfare or train ticket to destination, daily contribution for living costs – see web site.
Benefits: Simple accommodation and food for daily contribution paid by volunteer.
Training: Group training given.
Supervision: Volunteers are led by different curators from the centre according to the working area. Veerle Vandepitte is generaly responsible for volunteers during their stay at Carapax.
Interviews: Interviews are done via a registration form.
Worldwide placements: Europe (Italy).

CENTRO DE ATENCION INTEGRAL 'PIÑA PALMERA' A.C.

Apdo Postal 109
Carretera hacia Mazunte s/n
Playa Zipolite
Pochutla
Oaxaca 70900 Mexico
T: 00 52 958 58 43145 and 58 43173
F: 00 52 958 5843145
E: pinapalmera@laneta.apc.org
W: www.laneta.apc.org/pina/
Contact: Anna Johansson de Cano and/or the Volunteer co-ordinator

Piña Palmera is a resource and rehabilitation centre for disabled people, principally children, in a little village, Zipolite. Volunteers with some sort of medical skill, such as doctors, nurses, occupational therapists, physiotherapists, pedagogists, kindergarten teachers and psychologists are always needed. Volunteers with experience in building and construction are needed. Help is particularly needed from March to September as this is when we generally have fewer volunteers. We work with community based rehabilitation in surrounding communities. There is also a programme for lifeguards on the beach and we need experienced lifeguards and instructors in CPR. Alternative web site – www.pinapalmera.org. Zipolite, on the south coast of the state of Oaxaca in Mexico. The nearest town is Pochutla, about 14 km away, and the nearest airport is Huatulco about 40km away. 🏠 📷

Number of projects: 1 UK: 0
Starting months: January–December
Time required: 26–52 weeks
Age: 18–65
Causes: Children, Disabled (learning and physical), Health Care/Medical, Human Rights, Teaching/assisting (primary), Young People.
Activities: Administration, Agriculture/Farming, Arts/Crafts, Building/Construction, Caring (general, residential), Community Work, Computers, Cooking, Counselling, Development Issues, DIY, Driving, First Aid, Fundraising, Gardening/Horticulture, Group Work, Library/Resource Centres, Manual Work, Marketing/Publicity, Music, Newsletter/Journalism, Outdoor Skills, Social Work, Sport, Summer Camps, Teaching, Technical Skills, Theatre/Drama, Training, Translating.
Placements: 10–20
When to apply: 6 months in advance
Work alone/with others: With others.
Qualifications: Fluent spoken Spanish. Medical skills + rehabilitation experience particularly welcome.
Equipment/clothing: Very hot climate so light clothes recommended.
Health requirements: Imperative to bring all own medicines and to have appropriate vaccinations and to have health insurance.
Costs: Travel costs, insurance and personal expenses.
Benefits: Accommodation and food if volunteer stays for at least 6 months. A bed in a dormitory. Communal shower 5 minutes away and a compost-toilet next to the house.
Training: Upon arrival, volunteers go through an introduction period of about one week.
Supervision: There is a co-ordinator in each area and there is a co-ordinator for the volunteers.
Interviews: Applicants are not interviewed.
Worldwide placements: (Mexico).

CENTRO DE VOLUNTARIOS – PUERTO RICO

Fondos Unidos de Puerto Rico
Calle Los Angeles final/parada 26 1/2 Santurce
San Juan
Puerto Rico
T: 00 787 728 8500
F: 00 787 728 7099
E: c.Rodriguez@fondosunidos.org
Contact: Carmen L. Rodriguez de Lion

Centro de Voluntarios promotes and has information about volunteering in Puerto Rico. It may well be able to put volunteers in touch with organisations which are not yet listed on the WorldWide Volunteering database. Mail address – PO Box 1919114, San Juan PR 00919-1914.

Starting months: January–December
Time required: 1–52 weeks (plus)
Age: 16 plus – no upper limit
Causes: Addicts/Ex-Addicts, AIDS/HIV, Children, Disabled (physical), Elderly People, Environmental Causes, Health Care/Medical, Poor/Homeless, Young People.
Activities: Campaigning, Caring – Day, Counselling, Technical Skills, Training.
Placements: 5000
When to apply: Any time.
Work alone/with others: Either.
Health requirements: Good.
Costs: None.
Training: By institution to which the volunteers are referred.
Supervision: By institution to which the are referred.
Interviews: By institution to which the are referred.
Worldwide placements: Central America (Puerto Rico).

CENTRO MEXICANO PARA LA FILANTROPIA (CEMEFI)

Cerrada de Salvador Alvarado No. 7
Colonia EscandonDistrito Federal,
Mexico City
CP 11180 Mexico
T: 52 55 5277 6111
F: 52 55 5515 5448
E: cemefi@cemefi.org
W: www.cemefi.org
Contact: Jorge Villalobos

Centro Mexicano para la Filantropia (CEMEFI) promotes and has information about volunteering in Mexico. It may well be able to put volunteers in touch with organisations which are not yet listed on the WorldWide Volunteering database.

Starting months: January–December
Time required: 1–52 weeks (plus)

Age: 16 plus – no upper limit
Causes: Addicts/Ex-Addicts, AIDS/HIV, Animal Welfare, Archaeology, Architecture, Children, Conservation, Disabled (learning and physical), Elderly People, Environmental Causes, Health Care/Medical, Heritage, Holidays for Disabled, Human Rights, Inner City Problems, Offenders/Ex-Offenders, Poor/Homeless, Refugees, Teaching/assisting (nursery, primary, secondary, mature, EFL) Unemployed, Wildlife, Work Camps – Seasonal, Young People.
Activities: Accountancy, Administration, Agriculture/Farming, Arts/Crafts, Building/Construction, Campaigning, Caring (general, day and residential), Catering, Community Work, Computers, Conservation Skills, Cooking, Counselling, Development Issues, DIY, Driving, First Aid, Forestry, Fundraising, Gardening/Horticulture, Group Work, International Aid, Library/Resource Centres, Manual Work, Marketing/Publicity, Music, Newsletter/Journalism, Outdoor Skills, Religion, Research, Scientific Work, Social Work, Sport, Summer Camps, Teaching, Technical Skills, Theatre/Drama, Training, Translating, Visiting/Befriending, Work Camps – Seasonal.
Costs: Varies according to the project.
Worldwide placements: (Mexico).

CENTRO NACIONAL DE VOLUNTARIADO (CENAV) – PORTUGAL

Drua D. Estefania 124, 3 piso
Lisbon
1000–158 Portugal
F: 00 351 21 3142893
Contact: Segismundo Pinto

Centro Nacional de Voluntariago (CENAV) promotes and has information about volunteering in Portugal. It may well be able to put volunteers in touch with organisations which are not yet listed on the WorldWide Volunteering database.

Starting months: January–December
Time required: 1–52 weeks (plus)
Age: 16 plus – no upper limit
Causes: Addicts/Ex-Addicts, AIDS/HIV, Animal Welfare, Archaeology, Architecture, Children, Conservation, Disabled (learning and physical), Elderly People, Environmental Causes, Health Care/Medical, Heritage, Holidays for Disabled, Human Rights, Inner City Problems, Offenders/Ex-Offenders, Poor/Homeless, Refugees, Teaching/assisting (nursery, primary, secondary, mature, EFL) Unemployed, Wildlife, Work Camps – Seasonal, Young People.
Activities: Accountancy, Administration, Agriculture/Farming, Arts/Crafts, Building/Construction, Campaigning, Caring (general, day and residential), Catering, Community Work, Computers, Conservation Skills,

Cooking, Counselling, Development Issues, DIY, Driving, First Aid, Forestry, Fundraising, Gardening/Horticulture, Group Work, International Aid, Library/Resource Centres, Manual Work, Marketing/Publicity, Music, Newsletter/Journalism, Outdoor Skills, Religion, Research, Scientific Work, Social Work, Sport, Summer Camps, Teaching, Technical Skills, Theatre/Drama, Training, Translating, Visiting/Befriending, Work Camps – Seasonal.
Costs: Varies according to the project.
Worldwide placements: Europe (Portugal).

CENTRO NAZIONALE PER IL VOLONTARIATO (CNV) – ITALY

Via A. Catalani 158
55100 Lucca
Toscana Italy
T: 00 39 0583 419 500
F: 00 39 0583 419 501
E: cnv@cnv.cpr.it
Contact: Aldo Intaschi

Centro Nazionale per il Volontariato (CNV) promotes and has information about volunteering in Italy. It may well be able to put volunteers in touch with organisations which are not yet listed on the WorldWide Volunteering database.

Starting months: January–December
Time required: 1–52 weeks (plus)
Age: 16 plus – no upper limit
Causes: Addicts/Ex-Addicts, AIDS/HIV, Animal Welfare, Archaeology, Architecture, Children, Conservation, Disabled (learning and physical), Elderly People, Environmental Causes, Health Care/Medical, Heritage, Holidays for Disabled, Human Rights, Inner City Problems, Offenders/Ex-Offenders, Poor/Homeless, Refugees, Teaching/assisting (nursery, primary, secondary, mature, EFL) Unemployed, Wildlife, Work Camps – Seasonal, Young People.
Activities: Accountancy, Administration, Agriculture/Farming, Arts/Crafts, Building/Construction, Campaigning, Caring (general, day and residential), Catering, Community Work, Computers, Conservation Skills, Cooking, Counselling, Development Issues, DIY, Driving, First Aid, Forestry, Fundraising, Gardening/Horticulture, Group Work, International Aid, Library/Resource Centres, Manual Work, Marketing/Publicity, Music, Newsletter/Journalism, Outdoor Skills, Religion, Research, Scientific Work, Social Work, Sport, Summer Camps, Teaching, Technical Skills, Theatre/Drama, Training, Translating, Visiting/Befriending, Work Camps – Seasonal.
Costs: Varies according to the project.
Worldwide placements: Europe (Italy).

CERT INTERNATIONAL (CHRISTIAN EMERGENCY RELIEF TEAMS)

P.O. Box 1129
Crossville, Tennessee
Cumberland 38557 USA
T: (931) 707 9382
F: (931) 707 9406
E: cert3@frontiernet.net
Contact: Dr. Ken Daugherty

CERT International is a non-profit humanitarian organisation that provides short-term opportunities, usually lasting about two weeks, to various parts of the world. The volunteers become instruments of charitable assistance to hurting, suffering and displaced persons. CERT sends medical/dental teams assisted by lay volunteers into remote areas of the world. The basic philosophy of CERT is to go where there is little help if any available to the people. CERT teams go at the request of missionaries, indigenous pastors, other non-profit organisations that have a permanent presence in a country, national ministries of health, and occasionally corporations such as Chevron and others needing medical assistance. CERT also sends a limited number of construction teams and water well-drilling teams. Volunteers with an offending may be accepted – each case reviewed independently.

Number of projects: 10–12 UK: 0
Starting months: January–December
Time required: 2–52 weeks
Age: 18–75
Causes: Children, Health Care/Medical, Poor/Homeless.
Activities: First Aid, International Aid, Outdoor Skills, Religion, Translating.
Placements: 80–100
When to apply: At least six months prior to availability.
Work alone/with others: With others.
Qualifications: Language skills are helpful, but not required, Spanish, English, Romanian, and others depending on country being served. Willingness to serve and do whatever is needed to assist in the projects.
Equipment/clothing: In some cases – briefing manual given to team members to prepare them for their chosen area.
Health requirements: Depends on area of service and assigned projects.
Costs: Volunteers are to pay their own expenses. CERT puts together all expected expenses i.e., travel, hotel lodging. CERT does not profit in any way.
Benefits: In some cases board and lodging may be provided. It varies from tents in the jungles to modest but clean hotels.

Training: Briefing manuals are provided and upon arrival a brief orientation if given to all team members.
Supervision: Volunteers work under direction of the CERT Team Leader who is experienced and knows the particular project area.
Interviews: Normally by phone interview unless living in close proximity to CERT International offices. Character references are also required.
Worldwide placements: Africa (Congo Republic); Central America (Honduras); South America (Bolivia, Peru); Asia (China); Europe (Moldova, Romania, Ukraine).

CHALCS

Unit 5
9 Harrogate Road, Tech North
Leeds, W. Yorkshire
LS7 3NB UK
T: +44 (0) 113 262 3892
F: +44 (0) 113 295 9596
E: s.sobers@chalcs.org.uk
Contact: Anne Wiliamson

CHALCS (Chapeltown and Harehills Assisted Learning Computer School) is a seven-day week school, opening evenings and weekends, to help inner city children from the areas of Chapeltown and Harehills. The school uses computers to encourage children to achieve their full educational potential, and all usual curriculum subjects are taught. The children range in age from 7–18, and GCSE and A level support is also given. The school has 590 children attending each week and there is a waiting list of over 400. In addition to computer classes a basic literacy scheme is run to help children reach their correct reading age before moving on to the more advanced computer classes. This scheme is operated by volunteers, and more are urgently needed if we are to match demand for the classes. Children here range from 6–11 and all are behind with their reading, spelling and arithmetic. Volunteers supported by a qualified teacher run classes to help children reach their correct level of literacy. These classes operate on Thursday evenings between 6.00pm and 8.00pm and our volunteers come from a wide range of backgrounds. Leeds inner city area of Chapeltown and Harehills. 🖥 📄

Number of projects: 1 UK: 1
Starting months: January–December
Time required: 13–52 weeks
Age: 16 plus – no upper limit
Causes: Children, Inner City Problems, Teaching/assisting (primary, secondary).
Activities: Computers, Group Work, Teaching.
Placements: 37
When to apply: All year.
Work alone/with others: With others.

Qualifications: Interest in children's development.
Health requirements: Nil.
Costs: Nil except travel costs to the school.
Training: On the job.
Supervision: Supervised by a qualified teacher.
Interviews: All volunteers are police checked and interviewed at our address.
Charity number: 1001323
UK placements: England (W. Yorkshire).

CHALLENGES WORLDWIDE

13 Hamilton Place
Edinburgh, Midlothian
EH3 5BA UK
T: +44 (0) 131 332 7372
F: +44 (0) 7674 820372
E: helen@challengesworldwide.com
W: www.challengesworldwide.com
Contact: Helen Tirebuck

Contact Challenges WorldWide if you want to take some time out or a career sabbatical, to constructively contribute to human development and poverty alleviation, while adding an international aspect to your professional portfolio. This is a challenge to leave your mark and a chance to change your world.

Number of projects: 100 UK: 0
Starting months: January–December
Time required: 12–36 weeks
Age: 18–65
Causes: Addicts/Ex-Addicts, AIDS/HIV, Architecture, Children, Conservation, Disabled (learning and physical), Elderly People, Environmental Causes, Health Care/Medical, Inner City Problems, Offenders/Ex-Offenders, Teaching/assisting (nursery, primary, secondary, mature, EFL) Unemployed, Young People.
Activities: Accountancy, Administration, Agriculture/Farming, Arts/Crafts, Building/Construction, Campaigning, Caring (general and day), Community Work, Computers, Conservation Skills, Counselling, Development Issues, Forestry, Fundraising, Group Work, Library/Resource Centres, Marketing/Publicity, Music, Newsletter/Journalism, Outdoor Skills, Research, Scientific Work, Social Work, Teaching, Technical Skills, Training.
Placements: Varies.
When to apply: As soon as possible – project start dates vary – see web site.
Work alone/with others: Varies.
Qualifications: V1 – school leaver. V2 – university student/2 years post school experience. V3 – graduate/5 years post school experience. V4 – qualified professional/expert. No restrictions apart from visa arrangements in certain countries, we cannot provide insurance for non EU nationals.
Equipment/clothing: Depends on placement, we have both rural and urban projects.

Health requirements: This can depend on country and placement.
Costs: Flight, consumption beyond basic food, personal effects and free time.
Benefits: We arrange accommodation and basic food.
Training: Briefing undertaken in the UK and then induction training held when you reach placement as appropriate by host Placement Leader.
Supervision: Volunteers are placed within functional organisations and are supervised by a person appointed within that organisation.
Interviews: Interviews are held on a monthly basis in Edinburgh, Manchester and London.
Charity number: SCO28814
Worldwide placements: Africa (Gambia); Central America (Antigua and Barbuda, Belize, Dominica); South America (Ecuador); Asia (Bangladesh).

CHANGING WORLDS

11 Doctors Lane
Chaldon, Surrey
CR3 5AE UK
T: +44 (0) 1883 340960
F: +44 (0) 1883 330783
E: welcome@changingworlds.co.uk
W: www.changingworlds.co.uk
Contact: David Gill

Changing Worlds is a small organisation run by a former director of another gap-year organisation and an ex-VSO teacher. On offer are voluntary work assignments in Tanzania, Chile, India, Romania and Nepal. Placements include teaching in primary and secondary schools, supporting within orphanages, working in hospitals and helping in local businesses. Changing Worlds organises voluntary placements to work in zoos and fauna parks in Australia. Changing Worlds was founded to enable volunteers to gain a full understanding of the communities they will be part of and hopes volunteers will forge lifelong ties with these schools, orphanages and our other projects. Most placements run from September and January for three to six months. We offer flexible departure dates for those looking for a career break. Whilst in country, volunteers are backed up by the Changing Worlds representative who will help with any problems volunteers experience and will source suitable placements. Representatives are selected for their local knowledge and an understanding of life as a volunteer. Changing Worlds looks for determined and adaptable volunteers who can get on with others. Basic teaching techniques are covered at our two day residential course. Most volunteers are 18–25 although older applicants are very welcome. A Changing Worlds placement can be used as part of the service section of The Duke of Edinburgh award scheme and is well regarded by employers and universities. We can only accept those people without any previous criminal convictions. Changing Worlds is a member of The Year Out Group.

Number of projects: 4–6 **UK:** 0
Starting months: Jan, Feb, Mar, Apr, Jun, Sep
Time required: 12–26 weeks
Age: 18–35
Causes: AIDS/HIV, Animal Welfare, Archaeology, Children, Conservation, Disabled (learning and physical), Elderly People, Environmental Causes, Health Care/Medical, Heritage, Human Rights, Poor/Homeless, Refugees, Teaching/assisting (nursery, primary, secondary, mature, EFL) Wildlife, Young People.
Activities: Accountancy, Administration, Agriculture/Farming, Arts/Crafts, Caring (general, day and residential), Catering, Community Work, Computers, Conservation Skills, Counselling, Development Issues, Forestry, Group Work, Library/Resource Centres, Manual Work, Marketing/Publicity, Music, Newsletter/ Journalism, Outdoor Skills, Research, Social Work, Sport, Teaching, Technical Skills, Theatre/ Drama, Training.
Placements: Around 80
When to apply: Not less than 8 weeks before departure.
Work alone/with others: With others. We try to ensure all those going to a destination at a specific time meet at our pre departure courses. We do offer placements to individuals who are on a career break.
Qualifications: A levels or equivalent and spoken English. Relevant work skills and experience are desirable but not essential. Volunteers are expected to undertake some pre-departure research and show a willingness to gain a basic understanding of the local language. Volunteers need to speak English.
Health requirements: Nil.
Costs: Prices range from £2275 to £2245 (which includes a 12 month open air ticket) + insurance £170, + subsistence £200, + innoculations £100, + visa £0–40 + pocket money.
Benefits: The cost includes return flights, pre-departure briefings, meeting on arrival and transport to placement, accommodation and support of our overseas representative. Basic accommodation provided in schools, orphanages or similar local institutions.
Training: A 2 day residential course is held – volunteers fully briefed on the country & their placement. Training on work with children is provided as part of the course. In country orientation provided on arrival in-country that includes basic language training.
Supervision: We employ in-country representatives who welcome volunteers to the country, take them to their placements and visit them. Changing Worlds provides contact details of their representatives before departure.
Interviews: Applicants fill in our application form providing the name and address of a referee. Prospective volunteers are interviewed in Redhill, Surrey where they also take part in team exercises. We also assess written references.
Worldwide placements: Africa (Tanzania); South America (Chile); Asia (India, Nepal); Australasia (Australia); Europe (Romania).

CHANTIERS DE JEUNES PROVENCE/ COTE D'AZUR

7 Avenue Pierre de Coubertin,
La Bocca
06150 France
T: 00 33 4 93 47 89 69
F: 00 33 4 93 48 12 01
E: cjpca@club-internet.fr
W: www.club-internet.fr.st
Contact: Stéphane Victorion

Chantiers de Jeunes Provence/Cote D'Azur needs volunteers to take part in the restoration of historic monuments, rural patrimony and environmental protection. Projects consist of five hours work in the morning and organised activities such as sailing, climbing and diving in the afternoons and evenings. French camps take place on Sainte-Margerite island near Cannes, in the Alpes or in Provence. Apply with an international reply coupon and a letter written in French. About 14 volunteers per camp and about 20 camps in the summer. Projects in Italy run all year. Volunteers with an offending background may be accepted depending on the offence.

Number of projects: 6 **UK:** 0
Starting months: January–December
Time required: 1–2 weeks
Age: 14–17
Causes: Archaeology, Architecture, Conservation, Environmental Causes, Heritage, Work Camps – Seasonal, Young People.
Activities: Arts/Crafts, Building/Construction, Catering, Conservation Skills, Manual Work, Music, Sport, Summer Camps, Theatre/Drama, Work Camps – Seasonal.
Placements: 340
When to apply: All year.
Work alone/with others: With others – about 15 teenagers.
Qualifications: Volunteers must speak a little French.
Equipment/clothing: Just clothes and shoes that can get dirty (for working).
Health requirements: Normal.
Costs: Approx €304.9.
Benefits: Food, accommodation and activities.
Training: None.
Supervision: 3 professionals are always with young volunteers.

Worldwide placements: Europe (France, Italy).
UK placements: Scotland (Clackmannanshire).

CHANTIERS D'ETUDES MEDIEVALES

4 rue du Tonnelet Rouge
F-67000 Strasbourg
France
T: 00 33 3 88 37 17 20
F: 00.33.3.88.37.17.20
E: castrum@wanadoo.fr
W: http://perso.wanadoo.fr/castrum
Contact: Mélanie Rouviere

The aim of Chantiers d'Etudes Medievales is to
organise voluntary work centres for youngsters.
These working sites are devoted to the study
and restoration of monuments or sites which
date back to the Middle Ages. The working sites
are open to volunteers from all countries
without discrimination, who work together to
carry out a manual task they think useful to
society as a whole. The association is not a
travel agency. It offers you an opportunity to
meet other youngsters who share your goal.
Through its specific operations on historic sites,
you are offered not only physical exercise but
cultural enrichment as well. You have an
opportunity to give new social functions to the
monuments you help to save: parks, cultural
centres, recreation centres, etc. The outstanding
organisation of the association enables us to
welcome all volunteers, previous acquaintance
being unnecessary. Our reception is friendly
and simple. For the last 15 years the association
has welcomed each summer about 100
volunteers from over 20 countries who are
divided into 20 or 30 member teams. Through
our experience we aim to preserve this human
dimension in which individuals can still learn
to know and appreciate one another. 📖

Number of projects: 4 UK: 0
Starting months: Jul, Aug
Time required: 2–52 weeks
Age: 16–30
Causes: Archaeology, Architecture,
Environmental Causes, Heritage, Work Camps –
Seasonal.
Activities: Building/Construction, Forestry,
Gardening/Horticulture, Summer Camps, Work
Camps – Seasonal.
Placements: 80
When to apply: Before April.
Work alone/with others: With others.
Qualifications: English or French speaking,
capable of hard work.
Equipment/clothing: Old strong clothes.
Health requirements: Good health.
Costs: Approx £34 covers board and basic
accommodation for 15 days. Accommodation is
neither fancy nor hotel-style. Most often we
work on a camp-basis. Concrete (hard roof)

lodgings (houses, schools, barracks) are the rule
when available.
Benefits: Your financial contribution includes
insurance, meals and lodging.
Interviews: Applicants are not interviewed.
Worldwide placements: Europe (France).

CHANTIERS HISTOIRE ET ARCHITECTURE MEDIEVALES (CHAM)

5 et 7, rue Guilleminot
75014 Paris
France
T: 00 33 1 43 35 15 51
F: 00 33 2 43 20 46 82
E: cham@cham.asso.fr
W: www.cham.asso.fr
Contact: Louisa Crispe

Chantiers Histoire et Architecture Medievales is
dedicated to the conservation and restoration of
medieval buildings around France. Founded in
1980, we organise permanent or seasonal
volunteer sites across the country. We welcome
any motivated volunteer who wishes to
participate in historical heritage rescue and
restoration. Volunteers work on a specific
monument daily (for about six hours a day) and
six days a week with breaks. Qualified
supervisors and technicians are on hand to give
training. Around 15 volunteer conservation
camps, mainly in July and August, of which
some are teenage camps (16–18 years), others
for 17+. 20 or so sites around France.

Starting months: Apr, Jul, Aug, Oct, Nov
Time required: 2–10 weeks
Age: 16 plus – no upper limit
Causes: Architecture, Conservation, Heritage.
Activities: Building/Construction, Conservation
Skills, Manual Work.
Placements: 600
When to apply: As early as possible – March
onwards.
Work alone/with others: With others – in a
group.
Qualifications: Basic French.
Equipment/clothing: Sleeping bags, blankets
and working clothes. Mat or airbed if camping.
Health requirements: Good health essential.
Costs: Travel expenses + membership fees €30,
plus €10 daily (board and lodging).
Benefits: Board and lodging. Basic
accomodatation – camping or village hall.
Showers and toilets. Cooking facilities
(volunteers cook in turns).
Training: On site supervision.
Supervision: Leadership team.
Interviews: Volunteer applicants are not
interviewed.
Worldwide placements: Europe (France).

CHESHIRE WILDLIFE TRUST

Grebe House
Reaseheath, Nantwich
Cheshire
CW5 6DG UK
T: +44 (0) 1270 610180
F: +44 (0) 1270 610430
E: scolderley@cheshirewt.cix.co.uk
W: www.wildlifetrusts.co.uk/cheshire
Contact: Simon Colderley

Cheshire Wildlife Trust is the region's leading environmental conservation charity, incorporating Cheshire, Warrington, Halton, Tameside, Trafford, Stockport and Wirral. We safeguard local wildlife by encouraging practical conservation involving local members; defending plant and animal communities against development through the planning system; caring for over 40 nature reserves covering more than 250 hectares, including woodland, meadows, heathland, wetland, coastal dunes and much more; campaigning for wildlife and the environment; managing the county's database of over 400 sites of biological importance; providing advice on all aspects of nature conservation to local authorities, industry and business, farming and local communities; encouraging environmental education at all levels, and through WATCH, the Trust's junior wing. Cheshire, Wirral and the Met boroughs of Stockport, Tameside and Trafford. 🖰 📠

Number of projects: 20 **UK:** 20
Starting months: January–December
Time required: 2–52 weeks (plus)
Age: 16–90
Causes: Conservation, Environmental Causes, Heritage, Wildlife.
Activities: Administration, Agriculture/Farming, Building/Construction, Campaigning, Conservation Skills, Forestry, Fundraising, Gardening/Horticulture, Library/Resource Centres, Manual Work, Marketing/Publicity, Newsletter/Journalism, Research, Scientific Work, Teaching, Training.
Placements: 20
When to apply: As early as possible.
Work alone/with others: Both.
Qualifications: Varies, depending on the job.
Equipment/clothing: Nil providing health and safety requirements are satisfied.
Health requirements: Nil as long as health and safety regulations are satisfied.
Costs: Board and lodging.
Benefits: Expenses for work done in worktime (mileage) and some small research costs.
Training: Ongoing training.
Supervision: Supervision undertaken by Volunteer Co-ordinator.
Interviews: Prospective volunteers are

interviewed at our office in Nantwich.
Charity number: 214927
UK placements: England (Cheshire).

CHICKS (COUNTRY HOLIDAYS FOR INNER CITY KIDS)

Woodside Retreat
Milton Abbot
Tavistock
Devon
PL19 0QJ UK
T: +44 (0) 1822 870692
F: +44 (0) 1822 870691
E: info@chicks.org.uk
W: www.chicks.org.uk
Contact: Pamela Wakeling

CHICKS (Country Holidays for Inner City Kids) is a registered children's charity based in Devon. We provide respite breaks for under privileged children aged 8–15 years from all over the UK. Our residential holidays run for six days every Thursday to Tuesday from March until early December. We are looking for four volunteers each week to help assist the supervisors with the day-to-day care of 16 children. The activities we participate in vary from horse-riding, kayaking and canoeing, climbing and abseiling, body boarding, face painting, bike riding and adventure parks. We may be able to place volunteers with an offending background, as long as not child-related offence. 📠

Number of projects: 2 **UK:** 2 – over 48 weeks
Starting months: Mar, Apr, May, Jun, Jul, Aug, Sep, Oct, Nov, Dec
Time required: 1 week
Age: 16 plus – no upper limit
Causes: Children, Young People.
Activities: Arts/Crafts, Caring (general, residential), Group Work, Outdoor Skills, Social Work, Visiting/Befriending.
Placements: 200+
When to apply: As soon as possible.
Work alone/with others: With others.
Qualifications: No restrictions except when police checks from own country cannot be provided.
Health requirements: Possibly – assessed on an individual basis.
Costs: Travel costs covered by CHICKS up to £50.
Benefits: Free accommodation, food, police checks and activities.
Training: Informal chat on arrival. Comprehensive information pack provided.
Supervision: Two to three supervisors on each holiday.
Interviews: No interviews.
Charity number: 1080953
UK placements: England (Cornwall, Devon).

CHILD FAMILY HEALTH INTERNATIONAL

953 Mission St. #220
San Fransisco
California
94103 USA
T: +1 415 957 9000
F: +1 415 840 0486
E: students@cfhi.org
W: www.cfhi.org
Contact: Betsy Fuller Matambanadzo

Child Family Health International (CFHI) builds and strengthens sustainable healthcare services for underserved communities worldwide. CFHI does this by initiating and supporting long-term sustainable health care projects, providing short-term medical relief in times of natural disaster and conducting international health programmes abroad for medical and pre-medical students in the U.S. Each year, we provide free medical services for families and children around the world. Launched in 1992 by Dr. Evallen Jones, CFHI's success is evidenced by the phenomenal growth it has experienced over its ten-year existence. CFHI has matured into an internationally recognised organisation providing a comprehensive and sophisticated curriculum to students and volunteers. Enrolment has increased from 15 students in 1998 to over 300 in 2003. Quito, Cuenca, Santo Domingo de los Colorados and the Amazon Jungle in Ecuador. Dehra Dun, New Delhi and Bambay in India. Cape Town in South Africa. Oaxaca and Puerto Escondido in Mexico. 🖹

Number of projects: 9 UK: 0
Starting months: January–December
Time required: 4–8 weeks
Age: 21–99
Causes: Children, Conservation, Health Care/Medical.
Activities: Caring – General, Community Work, Conservation Skills, International Aid, Visiting/Befriending.
Placements: 300+
When to apply: At least three months in advance.
Work alone/with others: Varies.
Qualifications: Some programmes require Spanish ability. Participants should be pre-medical, medical or other students of the health profession.
Health requirements: None.
Costs: Travel costs, registration fees and personal expenses.
Benefits: Lodging, 2.5 meals a day, Spanish courses depending on location. Clinical rotation schedule/contacts, orientation and on-going support. Homestays or group accommodations (each person has their own room).

Training: Cultural orientation training, preparation materials prior to departure, medical rotations on a daily basis, Medical Spanish courses depending on site.
Supervision: Local co-ordinators employed at every site. All rotations done with supervision of a local medical professional.
Interviews: No.
Worldwide placements: Africa (South Africa); Central America (Mexico); South America (Ecuador); Asia (India).

CHILD WELFARE SCHEME

30 Spirit Quay
Wapping
London
E1W 2UT UK
T: +44 (0) 207 488 4394
T: +44 (0) 207 488 4394
E: triffid@compuserve.com
W: www.childwelfarescheme.org
Contact: Mrs T.J.E. Beaumont

CWS concentrates on rural and urban projects in Nepal. We have built our projects together with the local village people achieving ten daycare/health centres in remote villages and a clinic in Pokhara. We opened a college and a hostel for boys and one for girls in May 2002, for street children between the age of 14 and 22. A clinic and ambulance provide free medical care in Pokhara. A full-scale drinking water project and a smokeless stove project have also been established. Two tourist hotels have been set up to cover local overhead costs in order to create local sustainability and to ensure that all donations go straight to the physical creation of each project. The main aims and objectives are: reduce infant mortality and create awareness in local rural communities on health issues and how to prevent simple illnesses and diseases; introduce pre-primary education in a local culturally sustainable manner improving domestic health in the local village mud houses; a free medical health service for marginalised children and youths in urban areas; form a bridge for marginalised youths to bring them back to society; ensure projects are culturally and sustainably sound and ensure that all donated funds go straight to where they are intended and not on so-called 'project costs'! We particularly need doctors, medical students and nurses. All volunteers help train and assist their Nepalese colleagues. The advice and experiences of the volunteers contribute to planning current and future programmes. Alternative e-mail address: cws@wlink.cnet.com.np. We work particularly in Pokhara, Karki and Lamjung districts. 🔖

Number of projects: 16 UK: 0
Starting months: January–December
Time required: 12–40 weeks

Age: 25–60
Causes: Children, Health Care/Medical, Poor/Homeless, Teaching/assisting (nursery), Young People.
Activities: Agriculture/Farming, Caring – General, Community Work, Counselling, Development Issues, First Aid, Research, Social Work, Teaching, Technical Skills.
Placements: 9
When to apply: All year but for August September start, apply April – June. Volunteers can stay for a maximum of 40 weeks depending on start date, ie, 5 months/calendar year visa.
Work alone/with others: Sometimes alone and sometimes with other young volunteers.
Qualifications: Doctors, medical students, nurses and any volunteers who are independent, flexible, able to take initiative and open to other cultures.
Health requirements: Volunteers must be fit and healthy as there is usually a lot of walking involved.
Costs: Travel to Nepal. Visa costs (first 2 months US$30, for each month thereafter $50 per month).
Food and lodging and other miscellaneous costs (approx. US$175 per month).
Benefits: For volunteers who commit themselves for longer than 40 weeks, we pay all visa costs, board and lodging and local travel expenses.
Training: A 2-week introduction in Nepal before starting in the field project.
Supervision: Constant monitoring is done by the INGO (CWS and CWSN) and the NGO. Depending in which department you work, 1 supervisor and 1 monitor will be in constant contact.
Interviews: Interviews usually take place in London at the Secretariat.
Charity number: 1061699
Worldwide placements: Asia (Nepal).

CHILDREN IN CRISIS

5th Floor, The Tower
125 High Street, Colliers Wood
London
SW19 2JR UK
T: +44 (0) 208 542 2000
F: +44 (0) 208 542 2299
E: MarciaM@childrenincrisis.org.uk
W: www.childrenincrisis.org.uk
Contact: Marcia Montaque

Children in Crisis exists to improve the lives of children around the world affected by conflict, poverty or other hidden crisis, by working with local communities to provide education, healthcare and protection. Poland is a country of great beauty. The Haven is nestled amongst fields, forest and mountains and is in stark contrast to the children's home environment. It offers a two-

week recuperative stay in the clean air of the mountains. Children from two up to eight years old visit The Haven, where there is a wide range of recreational therapy programmes to choose from. These programmes allow the children to have fun, strengthen weakened muscles, gain self-confidence and express themselves in a safe and nurturing environment. The activities are specifically formulated to incorporate play with challenges both on personal and group levels. All of this happens in the sunshine and clean air at the foot of the Babia Gora mountain, far away from the industrial pollution of Silesia, and will increase the children's will to fight their life threatening illnesses. Variety is the key element in keeping the programme fresh for those children who return year after year to The Haven. It is also essential to allow for the wide disparity in the needs of the different children. Due to the nature of our work and particularly in view of the Child Protection Act, we are unable to accept ex-offenders. All volunteers are required to take a police check.

Number of projects: 8 UK: 0
Starting months: Jan, Feb, Mar, Apr, May, Jun, Jul, Sep, Oct, Nov, Dec
Time required: 4–12 weeks
Age: 18 plus – no upper limit
Causes: Children, Health Care/Medical, Young People.
Activities: Arts/Crafts, Caring – General, First Aid, Group Work, Outdoor Skills, Sport, Summer Camps.
Placements: 22
When to apply: All year round.
Work alone/with others: Work with others. Occasionally with Polish volunteers and local Polish Scout Association.
Qualifications: Some previous childcare – babysitting, after school clubs, youth club etc would be an advantage, although we mostly require patience and a willingness to 'muck in'. No restrictions, please note that we are unable to assist with applications for visa or permits for volunteers to visit the Haven.
Equipment/clothing: Warm clothing essential in winter.
Health requirements: No restrictions. Volunteers should consult with their medical practitioner on the necessary vaccinations required.
Costs: Flights and travel insurance plus cost of police check.
Benefits: Food and accommodation will be provided for the duration of the volunteers stay at the Haven in Poland. Volunteers are collected and returned to Krakow airport.
Training: No training provided or necessary.
Supervision: All volunteers are supervised by our English speaking Manager of the Haven, as well as other bi-lingual staff.

Interviews: All volunteers are interviewed at our office in London.
Charity number: 1020488
Worldwide placements: Europe (Poland).

CHILDREN OF THE ANDES

Oregon House
309 Kentish Town Road
London
NW5 2TJ UK
T: +44 (0) 20 7361 485 8634/0207 485 9114
F: +44 (0) 20 7361 485 8690
E: info@children-of-the-andes.org
W: www.children-of-the-andes.org
Contact: Christine Oram

Children of the Andes, a British registered charity founded in 1991, is dedicated to improving the lives of street children and child victims of violence in Colombia. We also support Colombian non-governmental organisations working for the same objectives. We raise funds and awareness, distribute grants and monitor and evaluate projects. Our work falls into four main categories: rescue and rehabilitation of street children; education, training and therapy for displaced children and parents who have fled from political violence; work in shanty towns to prevent children resorting to the streets; provision for health care and special needs. Our volunteers are exclusively UK based – in London. We can put volunteers in contact with our projects in Columbia, however, we do not offer placements there. 🖺 🖹

Number of projects: 10 **UK:** 1
Starting months: January–December
Time required: 12–52 weeks
Age: 16 plus – no upper limit
Causes: Children.
Activities: Administration, Catering, Computers, Development Issues, Fundraising, International Aid, Newsletter/Journalism, Research, Translating.
Placements: 5
When to apply: All year.
Work alone/with others: Mainly with the staff.
Qualifications: Fluency in Spanish, data input including use of word, Excel and Publisher telephone, writing, communication skills, PC skills.
Health requirements: Nil.
Costs: Board and lodging, flights and insurance costs.
Benefits: Local transport and £5 for lunch per day.
Training: We give our own training.
Supervision: Yes.
Interviews: Yes – in our offices.
Worldwide placements: South America (Colombia).
UK placements: England (London).

CHILDREN ON THE EDGE

Watersmead
Littlehampton
W. Sussex
BN17 6LS UK
T: +44 (0) 1903 850906
F: +44 (0) 1903 859296
E: office@childrenontheedge.org
W: www.childreontheedge.org.
Contact: Suzanne Handsford

Children on the Edge, a project of The Body Shop Foundation, is involved in the refurbishment of orphanages, the running of healthcare programmes, playschemes and community work. Qualified volunteers are needed occasionally for up to a year. There are also 2–4 week opportunities for unskilled volunteers. The playscheme takes part in north-east region of Iasi, Romania. 🖺

Number of projects: 5 approx. **UK:** 0
Starting months: January–December
Time required: 2–52 weeks
Age: 18 plus – no upper limit
Causes: Children, Disabled (learning and physical), Health Care/Medical, Poor/Homeless, Refugees, Teaching/assisting (secondary), Unemployed, Young People.
Activities: Administration, Arts/Crafts, Building/Construction, Caring (general, day and residential), Community Work, Cooking, First Aid, Fundraising, Group Work, International Aid, Outdoor Skills, Social Work, Sport, Summer Camps, Teaching, Theatre/Drama, Translating.
Placements: 40
When to apply: All year but beginning of January for playscheme.
Work alone/with others: With others as part of a team.
Qualifications: Childcare professionals, art and play therapists, nurses.
Health requirements: Good health.
Costs: Playscheme Volunteers: £1,200 for airfare, travel, insurance, visa, accommodation, food and equipment for children.
Benefits: Chance to help children by taking part in play, art and sports activities during the summer playscheme. Playscheme volunteers are accommodated.
Training: Briefed with information packs and videos.
Supervision: Supervised by core team on ground who lead sessions through.
Interviews: No interview. Applicants will be assessed by an application form.
Charity number: 802757R
Worldwide placements: Asia (Indonesia); Europe (Albania, Bosnia-Herzegovina, Romania, Yugoslavia).

CHILDREN'S COUNTRY HOLIDAYS FUND

42–43 Lower Marsh
Tanswell Street
London
SE1 7RG UK
T: +44 (0) 207 928 6522
F: +44 (0) 207 401 3961
E: clare@childrensholidays-cchf.org
W: www.childrensholidays-cchf.org
Contact: Clare Diggins

Children's Country Holidays Fund provides holidays for London children who have no other chance of a holiday. We need volunteers to be activity holiday/camp supervisors in the summer. The holidays are a week long, residential (in the south east) and incorporate a wide range of activities to provide a fun, safe and memorable holiday for 32 children aged 8–12. Supervisors are responsible for the care, welfare and entertainment of four children, within a larger group of 32, under an experienced leader and deputy. Quality training provided and all travel, board and accommodation costs met. Volunteers with offending backgrounds may be accepted, but not if child, sex or drug related. Each case is treated individually. All sites are located within a two hour drive of London.

Number of projects: 15–20 **UK:** 15–20
Starting months: Jul, Aug
Time required: 1–3 weeks
Age: 18–60
Causes: Children, Poor/Homeless.
Activities: Arts/Crafts, Outdoor Skills, Sport, Summer Camps.
Placements: 75.
When to apply: January–May.
Work alone/with others: With a team of 9 others, including two experienced leaders.
Qualifications: Only applicants who are resident in England and Wales and have been so for 5 years are accepted, due to the necessary Police check required.
Health requirements: In good health.
Costs: Nil. All travel, board and accommodation costs met.
Benefits: Free travel, board, food and training. Accommodation in single and dormitory rooms for volunteers and twin or dormitories for the children.
Training: Training weekend including child protection, anti-discrimination roles and responsibilities, a day in the life of a camp, working as a team, managing difficult behaviour.
Supervision: Supervision on camp by leader and deputy.
Interviews: Applicants will need to apply and if successful attend for separate interview and training.
Charity number: 206958

UK placements: England (throughout); Wales (throughout).

CHILDREN'S EXPRESS (CE) UK

Exmouth House
3–11 Pine Street
London
EC1R 0JH UK
T: +44 (0) 207 833 2577
F: +44 (0) 207 278 7722
E: enquiries@childrens-express.org
W: http://www.childrens-express.org
Contact: Helen Smeed

Children's Express is an out-of-school programme of learning and development through journalism for children aged 8 to 18. Our aim is to give young people the power and means to express themselves publicly on vital issues that affect them, and in the process to raise their self-esteem and develop their potential. CE reporters and editors research and report stories on subjects of their choice. They also accept commissions from newspapers and magazines. CE operates like a news agency by selling their stories to local, national and regional newspapers and magazines. Children's Express targets children aged 8 to 18 from inner-city areas, working with them after school, at weekends and during the holidays. The young people are the workforce, and take responsibility not only for their stories, but the way the programme is run. It is highly participatory. Every member is required to go through a one or two-day induction programme, run by specially trained editors (aged 14–18). The younger children, aged 8 – 13, are the reporters; editors are older, aged 14–18. They take responsibility for editing and overseeing the editorial activities. They work in teams of five to develop the story angle and questions. Every aspect of the story, from basic interview to impressions afterwards, is tape-recorded. Not only does this mean that the programme is open to all, regardless of academic ability, but it encourages literacy, organisation and good writing. In particular it reinforces numerous aspects of the National Curriculum. The journalists take an extraordinary degree of ownership into the process, from the initial story idea right through to seeing their names on the published article. They run the reporters' and editors' boards, determine which stories to follow, initiate research and interviews and work together in teams to realise their aims. They organise and run monthly meetings, quarterly training sessions and presentations. The adults in the programme make sure the whole process works. There are no academic requirements and no discrimination against those excluded from school or with an offending background. 🚹 📄

Number of projects UK: 4
Starting months: January–December
Time required: 1–52 weeks (plus)
Age: 14–18
Causes: Children, Inner City Problems, Young People.
Activities: Administration, Computers, Development Issues, Fundraising, Group Work, Marketing/Publicity, Newsletter/Journalism, Research, Technical Skills, Translating.
Placements: 300
When to apply: All year.
Work alone/with others: Mainly in teams.
Qualifications: Enthusiasm.
Health requirements: Nil.
Costs: Nil.
Benefits: Expenses paid on all assignments.
Interviews: No interviews but there is an application form and a day's training required (delivered by teen trainers).
Charity number: 1043300
UK placements: England (London, Tyne and Wear, West Midlands, S. Yorkshire).

CHILDREN'S OPPORTUNITIES GROUP

Children's Information Centre
6 Queen's Walk
Reading, Berkshire
RG1 7PU UK
T: +44 (0) 118 957 6686
F: +44 (0) 118 950 9500
E: cic@childrensinfo.org
W: www.childrensinfo.org
Contact: Deborah Fox

The Children's Opportunities Group project aims to provide worthwhile and meaningful volunteering opportunities for people aged 16–24. It does this by befriending disabled children/young people who would like to attend mainstream out-of-school activities such as Brownies, sports, youth clubs, visiting cinema and library etc. Volunteers are represented at the COG advisory board meetings and are invited to provide input whenever possible – all volunteers are expected to be pro-active and manage their own time spent with the young person. There are opportunities to help with training of new volunteers. Regular team meetings are held. Every three months an evaluation feedback is obtained from the child/young person and family or activity provider. Volunteers with an offending background may be accepted if the offence is not related to children. ♿ 🏠

Number of projects: 1 UK: 1
Starting months: January–December
Time required: 26–52 weeks (plus)
Age: 16–24
Causes: Children, Disabled (learning and physical), Young People.
Activities: Visiting/Befriending.

Placements: 35
When to apply: All year.
Work alone/with others: Varies.
Costs: Accommodation costs.
Benefits: Reimbursement of out of pocket expenses – travel/fares, cost of activity, drinks or snacks taken in the course of volunteering.
Training: Preparation training given on volunteering issues, project overview, disability equality, child protection issues, challenging behaviour and paediatric first aid.
Supervision: Volunteers receive regular informal supervision via telephone calls or visits. Project co-ordinator is always available.
Interviews: At the Children's Information Centre office.
Charity number: 1078331
UK placements: England (Berkshire).

CHILDREN'S TRUST, THE

Tadworth Court
Tadworth, Surrey
KT20 5RU UK
T: +44 (0) 1737 365038 or 39
F: +44 (0) 1737 373848
E: rturner@thechildrenstrust.org.uk
W: www.thechildrenstrust.org.uk
Contact: Rachel Turner

The Children's Trust can accept short or longer term full-time live in student volunteers. They will work directly with our profoundly disabled and exceptional needs children. St Margaret's School and our care and rehabilitation units require residential volunteers for six to twelve month periods to assist with the daily routine of physical care and education of our children with exceptional learning difficulties in both the school, the school's residential homes or our specialised care/rehab units and the school's residential homes. Under the guidance of teachers, or therapists and senior care staff, students will work as part of an interdisciplinary team on the individual planned programmes for the children. The Trust also requires shorter term summer scheme residential volunteers to work in our specialised nursing and therapeutic child care units. The project runs for a minimum of 13 up to 17 weeks from June to September each year and students are expected to stay for the duration of the scheme. The work involves acting as a friend to the children, carrying out basic personal care, organising games, encouraging them to take an active part in daily activities, escorting them on outings and organising evening activities. Applicants for both the above situations should expect to work a 37 1/2 hour week with two days off. Those wishing to go into the caring professions will be particularly welcomed. ♿ 🏠

Number of projects: 1 **UK:** 1
Starting months: January–December
Time required: 13–52 weeks
Age: 18 plus – no upper limit
Causes: Children, Disabled (learning and physical).
Activities: Arts/Crafts, Caring – General, Music.
Placements: 15+
When to apply: As soon as possible.
Work alone/with others: With others.
Qualifications: Previous experience with children or children with disabilities is preferable but not essential.
Equipment/clothing: Flat shoes with soft soles and comfortable clothes.
Health requirements: No eczema or open wounds and no-one with a bad back should apply.
Costs: Nil.
Benefits: Accommodation and an allowance of £51 per week is paid.
Training: Trained staff are there to assist and train.
Supervision: By trained staff.
UK placements: England (Surrey).

CHRISTIAN APPALACHIAN PROJECT

322 Crab Orchard Street
Lancaster
KY 40446 USA
T: 00 1 606 792 2219
F: 00 1 606 792 6625
E: volunteer@chrisapp.org
Contact: Kathy Kluesener

Have an adventure in beautiful Appalachia! Come and volunteer for a year or a summer with the Christian Appalachian Project. We are a non-profit, interdenominational, service organisation that assists people in Appalachia to become self-sufficient. More specifically, we serve economically, socially, and/or physically disadvantaged people in eastern Kentucky through programmes such as child development, adult education, home repair, elderly programmes, respite care, emergency outreach, summer camps, spouse abuse shelters, teen/youth centers and many more. Our volunteers live together sharing meals, prayer, and the challenge of fighting poverty as they support each other through their strong Christian motivation to serve people. Minimum age 18 for summer but 21 years for a one-year position. 🗿 🗎

Number of projects: 1 **UK:** 0
Starting months: January–December
Time required: 3–52 weeks
Age: 18 plus – no upper limit
Causes: Children, Disabled (learning and physical), Elderly People, Environmental Causes, Holidays for Disabled, Human Rights, Poor/Homeless, Teaching/assisting (nursery, mature), Unemployed, Young People.

Activities: Arts/Crafts, Building/Construction, Caring (general, day and residential), Community Work, Cooking, Counselling, Driving, Group Work, Manual Work, Social Work, Summer Camps, Teaching, Visiting/Befriending.
When to apply: Min. 7 mths in advance for 3–20 week position, 4 mths for 1yr.
Work alone/with others: Both.
Qualifications: English language, driving licence, openminded, flexible individuals.
Equipment/clothing: Depends on the job. Usually casual or rugged clothing. Not usually dress-up clothing.
Health requirements: Depends on individual case.
Costs: Return fare to Kentucky + visa costs.
Benefits: Board and lodging. Long term (1 year) volunteers receive $100 per month, health insurance and loan deferment information.
Interviews: Prospective volunteers are interviewed in Kentucky.
Worldwide placements: North America: (USA).

CHRISTIAN WELFARE AND SOCIAL RELIEF ORGANISATION

39 Soldier Street
Freetown
Sierra Leone West Africa
T: 00 232 22 229779 or 224096
F: 00 232 22 224439
E: revarhill@yahoo.com
Contact: Ms Joyor Cummings

Christian Welfare and Social Relief Organisation was established in 1980 as a non-governmental, non-political, non-profitable organisation, active in the field of rural grassroot development in the different villages where education, health and other facilities are not available. The organisation is engaged in literacy programmes caring for street children, displaced children, refugees, school drop-outs, orphans, neglected school children, and children affected by the civil war. Farming, setting up literacy classes and vocational training centres, caring for handicapped/aged/ adults/ youths are also all part of our remit. We set up mobile health centres in the different camps and assist children, youth/adults in each village to know more about their culture and the culture of the volunteer as well. The organisation is a Christian body which offers the chance to work for God and runs a variety of pro-church programmes. One such programme, CWASRO Crusaders Sierra Leone needs committed Christians and aims to bring together talented young Christian musicians and volunteers to work to achieve a common goal. Committed volunteers are sent to different villages where no church is located. Alternative address – 20 Robert Street, Freetown, Sierra Leone, West Africa. Rural villages in the districts of Bo, Bombali Freetown, Kenema including Makemi. ⓖ ▤

Number of projects: Many UK: 0
Starting months: January–December
Time required: 4–52 weeks
Age: 18–50
Causes: Animal Welfare, Children, Disabled (learning and physical), Elderly People, Health Care/Medical, Poor/Homeless, Refugees, Teaching/assisting (primary, secondary, mature, EFL), Unemployed, Work Camps – Seasonal, Young People.
Activities: Administration, Agriculture/Farming, Arts/Crafts, Caring (day & residential), Counselling, Driving, First Aid, Gardening/Horticulture, International Aid, Manual Work, Social Work, Teaching, Visiting/Befriending.
Placements: 1250
When to apply: All year.
Work alone/with others: Both.
Qualifications: Nil – but any welcome.
Equipment/clothing: Nothing special.
Health requirements: Innoculations required.
Costs: Air fare to Sierra Leone and from £300 for one month to £1,900 for 1 year.
Benefits: Accommodation, local language/group work/vocational training projects. Live and work with local people.
Training: Training offered by CWASRO and other organisations.
Supervision: Volunteers are supervised by CWASRO and representatives from other organisations.
Interviews: Through a selection process.
Worldwide placements: Africa (Sierra Leone).

CHRISTIANS ABROAD

233 Bon Marché Centre
241–251 Ferndale Road
London
SW9 8BJ UK
T: 0870 770 7990
F: 0870 770 7991
E: admin@cabroad.org.uk
W: www.cabroad.org.uk
Contact: Kevin Cusack

Christians Abroad through World Service Enquiry, is the only organisation providing expert, impartial information and advice about working and volunteering in the third world to people of all faiths or none. As World Service Enquiry, Christians Abroad provides, information on voluntary and paid opportunities, short or long-term in aid, development and mission programmes overseas – for skilled and qualified professionals and unskilled people. Our comprehensive free information guide, updated annually, is geared mainly to unskilled people without professional experience. It gives details about how to start a search for work overseas, outlines organisations with information on development issues and international organisations who recruit volunteers, with useful addresses to contact. For those considering where and how they can best use their experience abroad, World Service Enquiry also provides one to one vocational guidance. They provide a forum to discuss your interest in working overseas and possible ways forward. E-volve is our unique Internet self coaching programme, written by a leading life coach to help you access your suitability to work in development. For those already qualified with some work experience we publish a monthly job magazine, Opportunities Abroad, available on subscription, which contains up-to-date vacancies (overseas and in the UK) from international and UK agencies. We also hold a development worker database of skilled personnel seeking contracts overseas. This is available on the Internet and allows any agency to search your personal web page. Volunteers with offending backgrounds may be accepted. ⓖ ▤

Number of projects: Many UK: 0
Starting months: January–December
Time required: 1–52 weeks (plus)
Age: 16–65
Causes: AIDS/HIV, Archaeology, Children, Conservation, Disabled (learning and physical), Elderly People, Environmental Causes, Health Care/Medical, Heritage, Holidays for Disabled, Human Rights, Inner City Problems, Offenders/

Slashing And Burning In Norfolk

Following GCSEs at his local comprehensive Nick Ruff contacted British Trust for Conservation Volunteers via WorldWide Volunteering. The result was a week of conservation work at Woodbastwick Marshes on the Norfolk Broads – removing scrub and restoring open fen land, the habitat of the swallow tailed butterfly. Apart from a broken rear axle on the group's mini bus the week passed without incident and Nick "enjoyed getting to know new people" and felt that "the work was a valuable experience".

Ex-Offenders, Poor/Homeless, Refugees, Teaching/assisting (nursery, primary, secondary, mature, EFL) Unemployed, Wildlife, Work Camps – Seasonal, Young People.
Activities: Accountancy, Administration, Agriculture/Farming, Arts/Crafts, Building/Construction, Campaigning, Caring (general, day and residential), Catering, Community Work, Computers, Conservation Skills, Cooking, Counselling, Development Issues, DIY, Driving, First Aid, Forestry, Fundraising, Gardening/Horticulture, Group Work, International Aid, Library/Resource Centres, Manual Work, Marketing/Publicity, Music, Newsletter/Journalism, Outdoor Skills, Religion, Research, Scientific Work, Social Work, Sport, Summer Camps, Teaching, Technical Skills, Theatre/Drama, Training, Translating, Visiting/Befriending, Work Camps – Seasonal.
Placements: Many.
When to apply: Between 6 months -1 year in advance.
Work alone/with others: Both.
Qualifications: Language helps – esp. Portuguese, French, Spanish. No restrictions generally but some organisations require volunteers to be British nationals.
Equipment/clothing: Depends on the project.
Health requirements: Good health.
Costs: Varies from £70 to £3,000 per project.
Benefits: Vary – accommodation usually provided + often local salary.
Training: Depends on the project.
Supervision: Depends on the project.
Interviews: Applicants are not interviewed by Christians Abroad.
Charity number: 265867
Worldwide placements: Africa (Angola, Benin, Botswana, Burkina Faso, Burundi, Cameroon, Cape Verde, Central African Republic, Chad, Comoros, Congo Dem Republic, Congo Republic, Côte d'Ivoire, Egypt, Equatorial Guinea, Eritrea, Ethiopia, Gabon, Gambia, Ghana, Guinea, Guinea-Bissau, Kenya, Lesotho, Liberia, Libya, Madagascar, Malawi, Mali, Mauritius, Mayotte, Morocco, Mozambique, Namibia, Niger, Nigeria, Reunion, Rwanda, Saint Helena, Senegal, Sierra Leone, Somalia, South Africa, Sudan, Swaziland, Tanzania, Togo, Tunisia, Uganda, Zambia, Zimbabwe); North America: (Canada, USA); Central America (Antigua and Barbuda, Barbados, Belize, Costa Rica, Cuba, Dominica, Dominican Republic, El Salvador, Guatemala, Haiti, Honduras, Mexico, Netherlands Antilles, Nicaragua, Panama, Puerto Rico, Saint Christopher/Nevis, Saint Lucia, Saint Vincent/Grenadines, Trinidad and Tobago, Turks and Caicos Islands, Virgin Islands); South America (Argentina, Bolivia, Brazil, Chile, Colombia, Ecuador, French Guiana, Guyana, Paraguay, Peru, South Georgia, Suriname, Uruguay, Venezuela); Asia

(Afghanistan, Bangladesh, Bhutan, Cambodia, China, India, Indonesia, Iran, Israel, Japan, Jordan, Kazakhstan, Korea (North), Korea (South), Kyrgyzstan, Laos, Lebanon, Myanmar (Burma), Nepal, Pakistan, Philippines, Sri Lanka, Syria, Taiwan, Tajikistan, Thailand, Tibet, Turkey, Turkmenistan, Uzbekistan, Vietnam, Yemen); Australasia (Kiribati, Micronesia, Papua New Guinea, Solomon Islands, Tuvalu, Vanuatu); Europe (Albania, Austria, Belgium, Bosnia-Herzegovina, Bulgaria, Croatia, Czech Republic, Estonia, France, Germany, Hungary, Italy, Latvia, Lithuania, Macedonia, Moldova, Poland, Portugal, Romania, Russia, Slovakia, Slovenia, Spain, Turkey, Ukraine, Yugoslavia).

CHRISTIANS AWARE

2 Saxby Street
Leicester
LE2 0ND UK
T: +44 (0) 116 254 0770
F: +44 (0) 116 254 0770
E: barbarabutler@christiansaware.co.uk
W: www.christiansaware.co.uk
Contact: Barbara Butler

Christians Aware is an international and educational charity. Its main aim is to develop multi-cultural understanding and friendship locally, nationally and internationally, in a spirit of sharing. Thus new energy is generated for action towards human development and justice, through conferences, work camps, international exchanges and written resources, including a range of books and the quarterly magazine. An international visits brochure lists the group visits for the next two years. There are no experts in Christians Aware. Everyone is welcome for all conferences, courses and visits. Our written resources offer insights and suggest ways forward. We are continually reminded of the advice of Ronald Wynne who has worked for many years in Botswana: 'Do not try to teach anyone anything until you have learnt something from them.' Christians Aware recognises the importance of openness, adaptability and faith in the future. Applicants with an offending background will be assessed and interviewed.

Number of projects: varies **UK:** varies
Starting months: January–December
Time required: 2–52 weeks
Age: 16 plus – no upper limit
Causes: Children, Conservation, Environmental Causes, Health Care/Medical, Human Rights, Refugees, Teaching/assisting, Work Camps – Seasonal, Young People.
Activities: Administration, Agriculture/Farming, Arts/Crafts, Community Work, Computers, Conservation Skills, Development Issues, Fundraising, Group Work, International Aid, Manual Work, Newsletter/Journalism, Outdoor Skills, Religion, Social Work, Summer Camps,

Work Camps – Seasonal.
Placements: 75
When to apply: At any time of the year.
Work alone/with others: With other young volunteers in the country where the camp is held.
Qualifications: Particular qualities needed for particular visits will be listed in the published brochures.
Equipment/clothing: Kit list available for the tropics.
Health requirements: Innoculations for the tropics.
Costs: Each project individually priced.
Benefits: Working in the developing world & its people is an opportunity to see the world through the eyes of the hosts & to understand issues of development, justice and human rights in a new way. The experience is also an enrichment. Accommodation is normally in the home of someone from the host community. When work camps are organised a camping arrangement, in tents or a school, is normal. Participants rarely stay in hotels, but this is occasionally necessary.
Training: Preparation time is the main training. Varies from 1 full day to several separate days. Training on information on health & programme details, the culture & history of the country concerned.
Supervision: The local hosts are responsible for their guests, especially if a guest travels alone. When groups travel the group leader is responsible for keeping an eye on members and for liaison between the group and the hosts.
Interviews: Interviews and preparation take place in Leicester or London.
Charity number: 328322
Worldwide placements: Africa (Kenya, Malawi, Mauritius, South Africa, Tanzania, Uganda, Zambia, Zimbabwe); South America (Peru); Asia (Bangladesh, China, India, Japan, Sri Lanka).
UK placements: England (Leicestershire, London).

CHRYSALIS YOUTH PROJECT

The Active Centre
Stansfield Road
Airedale, Castleford
West Yorkshire
WF10 3UA UK
T: +44 (0) 1977 736284
F: +44 (0) 1977 736287
E: Chrysproj@aol.com
Contact: Neil Kennedy

Chrysalis Youth Project enables young people to participate in an enjoyable and exciting activity, which integrates formal and informal training opportunities to develop their life and other skills. The facilities at the project offer positive use of time and encourage wider links

with the community. The project bridges the gap between school and moving on into further education and/or the world of work by offering the facilities of the go kart track and an alternative programme of education leading to qualification in motor vehicle, sports and recreation, administration, life skills, basic skills and arts and crafts. Volunteers with an offending background may be accepted depending on each individual case. ⓑ ⓔ

Number of projects: 1 UK: 1
Starting months: January–December
Time required: 1–52 weeks
Age: 16–25
Causes: Children, Conservation, Disabled (learning and physical), Environmental Causes, Teaching/assisting, Unemployed, Young People.
Activities: Administration, Caring – General, Catering, Community Work, Computers, Conservation Skills, Cooking, Driving, Fundraising, Gardening/Horticulture, Group Work, Manual Work, Marketing/Publicity, Outdoor Skills, Social Work, Sport, Training.
Placements: 18
When to apply: Any time.
Work alone/with others: With others.
Health requirements: Nil.
Costs: Nil.
Benefits: Can gain experience and qualification which may aid employment prospects or career change.
Training: The project is an accredited centre with Edexcel and City and Guilds. We run many of our own training programmes. We also make use of the many courses running locally.
Supervision: All volunteers have a nominated supervisor.
Interviews: There is an interview selection process which takes place at the office.
Charity number: 1066871
UK placements: England (W. Yorkshire).

CHURCH MISSION SOCIETY – ENCOUNTER

Partnership House
157 Waterloo Road
London
SE1 8UU UK
T: +44 (0) 207 928 8681
F: +44 (0) 207 401 3215
E: debbie.james@cms-uk.org
W: www.cms-uk.org
Contact: Debbie James

The Church Mission Society (CMS) is a voluntary society within the Anglican Church, established in 1799, working in partnership with Asian, African and East European churches; sending and receiving personnel to share in and learn from each other's mission. Encounter provides exciting opportunities for

Christians to go as part of a group and live alongside national Christians in Asia, Africa or Eastern Europe, sharing their lifestyle, witness, worship, hopes and aspirations. Volunteers with an offending background may be accepted. Each case is assessed separately. ♿

Number of projects: 6 **UK:** 0
Starting months: Jul, Aug
Time required: 3–4 weeks
Age: 18–30
Causes: Children, Conservation, Disabled (learning and physical), Elderly People, Inner City Problems, Poor/Homeless, Refugees, Teaching/assisting (EFL), Work Camps – Seasonal, Young People.
Activities: Agriculture/Farming, Arts/Crafts, Building/Construction, Caring – General, Community Work, Computers, Conservation Skills, Development Issues, Forestry, Gardening/Horticulture, Group Work, Manual Work, Music, Outdoor Skills, Religion, Sport, Summer Camps, Teaching, Visiting/Befriending, Work Camps – Seasonal.
Placements: 50–60
When to apply: Before April for summer placement.
Work alone/with others: With others.
Qualifications: British residents, Christian. Any nationality accepted but need to be based in Britain for selection and training purposes.
Equipment/clothing: Varies according to location – kit list provided.
Health requirements: Health clearance required; innoculations vary according to location.
Costs: £600–£1,000. Help and advice on fundraising given.
Benefits: Training, debriefing and experienced leaders.
Training: 2 weekend pre-placement training.
Supervision: Accompanied by 2 leaders with previous overseas experience.
Interviews: Applicants are interviewed at selection weekend. Residential selection – location varies.
Charity number: 220297
Worldwide placements: Africa (Gambia, Kenya, Rwanda, Tunisia, Uganda); Asia (China, India, Lebanon, Malaysia, Pakistan, Philippines, Sri Lanka, Syria, Thailand); Europe (Georgia, Romania, Russia, Ukraine).

CHURCH MISSION SOCIETY – MAKE A DIFFERENCE (IN BRITAIN)

157 Waterloo Road
London
SE1 8UU UK
T: +44 (0) 207 928 8681
F: +44 (0) 207 401 3215
E: kathy.tyson@cms-uk.org
W: www.com-uk.org
Contact: Experience Programme Adviser

The Church Mission Society (CMS) is a voluntary society within the Anglican Church, established in 1799, working in partnership with Asian, African and East European churches; sending and receiving personnel to share in and learn from each other's mission. Make a Difference (In Britain) placements provide exciting opportunities to form cross cultural relationships and grow spiritually through being involved in a parish or project in Britain. Britain Experience placements are generally in multicultural, inner city areas. Volunteers with an offending background may be accepted – each case is assessed separately. ♿

Number of projects: 12 **UK:** 12
Starting months: Jan, Sep
Time required: 28–78 weeks
Age: 18 plus – no upper limit
Causes: Children, Disabled (learning and physical), Elderly People, Environmental Causes, Inner City Problems, Poor/Homeless, Teaching/assisting (nursery), Unemployed, Work Camps – Seasonal, Young People.
Activities: Administration, Caring – General, Community Work, Driving, Group Work, Library/Resource Centres, Manual Work, Music, Religion, Social Work, Summer Camps, Teaching, Visiting/Befriending, Work Camps – Seasonal.
Placements: 1 or 2
When to apply: All year.
Work alone/with others: With local people.
Qualifications: British residents, Christian. British volunteers only.
Health requirements: Nil.
Costs: All.
Benefits: Occasional board, lodging and pocket money. Training and re-orientation courses.
Training: 10 days at CMS Training College.
Supervision: Person to whom volunteer is responsible in parish/project is identified.
Interviews: Interviews take place in London.
Charity number: 220297
UK placements: England (Derbyshire, Lancashire, London, Manchester, West Midlands, S. Yorkshire, W. Yorkshire).

CHURCH MISSION SOCIETY – MAKE A DIFFERENCE (OVERSEAS)

157 Waterloo Road
London
SE1 8UU UK
T: +44 (0) 207 928 8681
F: +44 (0) 207 401 3215
E: alex.gough@cms-uk.org
W: www.cms-uk.org
Contact: Alex Gough

The Church Mission Society (CMS) is a voluntary society within the Anglican Church, established in 1799, working in partnership with Asian,

African and East European churches; sending and receiving personnel to share in and learn from each other's mission. Make a Difference (Overseas) provides challenging opportunities to form cross cultural relationships, to grow spiritually through contact with the national church and to gain experience in Africa, Asia and Eastern Europe. Church Mission Society Make a Difference (Overseas) placements can be arranged together with a Church Mission Society British Experience placement. Overseas locations vary each year. Volunteers with offending backgrounds may be accepted. Each case is assessed separately. &

Number of projects: 40 **UK:** 0
Starting months: Jan, Sep
Time required: 26–78 weeks
Age: 21–35
Causes: Addicts/Ex-Addicts, Children, Disabled (learning), Elderly People, Environmental Causes, Health Care/Medical, Inner City Problems, Poor/Homeless, Refugees, Teaching/assisting (nursery, primary, secondary, EFL), Unemployed, Work Camps – Seasonal, Young People.
Activities: Accountancy, Administration, Building/Construction, Caring (general, residential), Community Work, Computers, Development Issues, Driving, Group Work, Library/Resource Centres, Manual Work, Music, Religion, Social Work, Summer Camps, Teaching, Translating, Visiting/Befriending, Work Camps – Seasonal.
Placements: 15
When to apply: All year.
Work alone/with others: With local people.
Qualifications: British residents, Christian, professional qualifications/experience or graduates preferred. British volunteers only.
Health requirements: Nil.
Costs: £2,500 per annum.
Benefits: Training and reorientation courses. Occasionally board, lodging and pocket money.
Training: 10 days at CMS Training College.
Supervision: Person to whom responsible on location is identified.
Interviews: Interviews take place in London.
Charity number: 220297
Worldwide placements: Africa (Egypt, Gambia, Guinea, Kenya, South Africa, Tanzania, Uganda); Asia (Bangladesh, India, Japan, Jordan, Lebanon, Nepal, Pakistan, Palestinian Authority, Philippines, Taiwan, Yemen); Europe (Czech Republic, Romania, Russia, Ukraine).

CHURCH OF ENGLAND YOUTH SERVICE

Church House
Great Smith Street
London
SW1P 3NZ UK
T: +44 (0) 207 898 1509

F: +44 (0) 207 233 1094
E: peter@boe.demon.co.uk
Contact: Peter Ball

Church of England Youth Service ask that in the first instance enquiries should be made to the National Youth Service at Church House, as above. Depending on the time of year the enquiry is made, opportunities could be available in any part of the country. & 🖹

Starting months: January–December
Time required: 1–52 weeks
Age: 18–25
Causes: Addicts/Ex-Addicts, Children, Disabled (learning and physical), Elderly People, Inner City Problems, Poor/Homeless, Teaching/assisting, Unemployed, Young People.
Activities: Caring – General, Community Work, Counselling, Group Work, International Aid, Music, Newsletter/Journalism, Religion, Social Work, Summer Camps, Teaching, Visiting/Befriending.
When to apply: 6 months in advance.
Work alone/with others: With others.
Health requirements: Nil.
Costs: Contribution if possible.
Benefits: Board and lodging usually. Opportunities to develop new skills and experience living and working in new communities.
UK placements: England (throughout); Scotland (throughout); Northern Ireland (throughout); Wales (Anglesey, Blaenau Gwent, Bridgend, Caerphilly, Cardiff, Carmarthenshire, Ceredigion, Conwy, Denbighshire, Flintshire, Gwynedd, Merthyr Tydfil, Monmouthshire, Neath Port Talbot, Newport, Pembrokeshire, Powys, Rhondda, Cynon, Taff, Swansea, Torfaen, Wrexham).

CHURCH'S MINISTRY AMONG JEWISH PEOPLE, THE

30c Clarence Road
St Albans
Hertfordshire AL1 4JJ UK
T: 01727 833114
F: 01727 848312
E: jeremyp@cmj.org.uk
W: www.cmj.org
Contact: Jeremy Purcell

The Church's Ministry Among Jewish People has a three-fold aim: evangelism – to share the gospel widely, particularly with Jewish people; encouragement – to support and encourage Jewish believers in Jesus; education – to teach the Church about its Jewish roots.
Activities: 1. In Israel CMJ runs Christchurch guesthouse, a heritage centre and a church where messianic congregations meet and accommodation is provided for conferences and pilgrims. In Jerusalem CMJ runs The Anglican

international schools and also Shoresh Tours who run study tours of Israel. Messianic and Christian ministries encourage various contacts that help messianic groups and encourage any reconciliation work they do. Beit Bracha, a prayer centre beside Gallilee is being fitted with visitor chalets. 2. CMJ supports work in South Africa, Australia, U.S.A, Ireland and UK working with and training churches in evangelism to Jews. The Simeon Centre in North London is a base for outreach. Shalom Magazine is sent out from St Albans. Bible Come to Life exhibition is a travelling exhibition, which visits schools/ churches during the year. Volunteers are involved in the Christchurch guest house in Jerusalem where they help with the day to day running of the centres carrying out mainly domestic/maintenance or reception duties. Volunteers are expected to provide three references and may get one of our regional advisors to visit their church. Please check for availability of volunteer placements.

Number of projects: 3 **UK:** 0
Starting months: January–December
Time required: 6–52 weeks
Age: 18–70
Causes: Children, Elderly People, Poor/ Homeless, Teaching/assisting, Unemployed, Young People.
Activities: Administration, Caring – General, Catering, Cooking, DIY, Gardening/Horticulture, Manual Work, Religion.
Placements: 12
When to apply: 3 months prior to start.
Work alone/with others: With others.
Qualifications: Committed Christians involved in local church. No restrictions on nationalities of volunteers but volunteers from other countries must arrange visas if necessary.
Health requirements: Nil – good health.
Costs: Volunteers must find their fare and insurance but we can help with this and to encourage your local church to raise £35 per week towards lodging, food and domestic costs.
Benefits: Board and accommodation, pocket money. Christchurch hires apartments for female voluntary workers. Mature couples may use our contacts to hire. Single male may use small room in guest house.
Training: When practical an orientation day is provided in St Albans or Oxford. Volunteers are placed in contact with CMJ area representatives who live nearest to them.
Supervision: Volunteers are supervised by the centre directors on a continuous basis.
Interviews: Applicants are not interviewed but must complete a 6-page application form and supply 3 references all of which is sent to Israel.
Charity number: 228519
Worldwide placements: Africa (Ethiopia, South Africa); South America (Argentina); Asia (Israel).

CHURCHTOWN OUTDOOR ADVENTURE CENTRE

Lanlivery
Bodmin, Cornwall
PL30 5BT UK
T: +44 (0) 1208 872148
F: +44 (0) 1208 873377
E: lanlivery@hotmail.com
Contact: Neil Jackman

Churchtown Outdoor Adventure Centre provides outdoor, environmental and adventurous training courses accessible to everyone, regardless of degree of special need. As well as the more traditional courses, in ecology and outdoor pursuits, a new development is the provision of personal development programmes which concentrate on personal growth, encouraging a positive image of self and promoting self-confidence. Churchtown also needs volunteers to help with a day centre, working with clients from the local area. The Centre is attractively converted and well equipped with an indoor swimming pool, farm, nature reserve and attractive grounds. Sailing and canoeing take place on the nearby River Fowey and the Centre is only five miles from the coast. Ten volunteers are needed at a time to support the professional staff.

Number of projects: 1 **UK:** 1
Starting months: January–December
Time required: 1–52 weeks
Age: 18 plus – no upper limit
Causes: Animal Welfare, Children, Conservation, Disabled (learning and physical), Elderly People, Environmental Causes, Health Care/Medical, Holidays for Disabled, Teaching/ assisting (primary, secondary), Unemployed, Wildlife, Young People.
Activities: Administration, Agriculture/Farming, Arts/Crafts, Building/Construction, Caring (general, day and residential), Catering, Computers, Conservation Skills, Fundraising, Gardening/Horticulture, Group Work, Manual Work, Marketing/Publicity, Music, Outdoor Skills, Sport, Summer Camps, Teaching.
Placements: 30
When to apply: All year.
Work alone/with others: With others.
Qualifications: Enthusiasm.
Health requirements: Must be fit.
Costs: Travel costs only to and from centre.
Benefits: Full board and lodging + £25 per week for a stay of 3 or more weeks. Accommodation is in a shared house and Manor House adjacent to the main centre.
Training: Basic training in all areas including care.
Supervision: Report to team leader or care manager.
Interviews: Interviews are usually on the telephone or by application form.
UK placements: England (Cornwall).

CIRCLE OF LIFE
Senju – Dó 497-4
Ranzan
Hiki-Gun Saitama-Ken 355-0227
Japan
T: 81 0493 62 2864
Contact: Tashina Wambli

The Circle of Life is run solely by one person – Tashina Wambli. (Profile taken from letter to WorldWide Volunteering.) 'Despite getting spiritual support from many concerned people, I am quite alone in my work here. The work concerns wildlife, rescue and rehabilitation and care for abandoned and feral dogs and cats. I have no income, so I must do translating/interpretation to support the activities here. It's impossible to offer any financial payment or assistance to anyone who may want to come and help. I must purchase all medicines, treatment and equipment necessary for the rescue/rehabilitation work. The benefit I believe I receive is a 'gift-in-return' for all the world gives to me. When I was 10 years old, upon the death of my grandfather, I was adopted and cared for by a pack of wolves. I lived with them where they warmed, fed, and taught me for four years. It is a long way to come to me; there is a language barrier, no sewerage and 24 hours a day work (when the mange season begins, the going gets tough). The only requirement necessary is unlimited patience and the spiritual viewpoint that humans are not in any way superior to any other being, animal, vegetable or mineral! Circle of Life can place volunteers with an offending background so long as they are responsible concerning animals, trees, water, the universe and understand their true place within them.' Ranzan is a rural town.

Number of projects: 1 **UK:** 0
Starting months: January–December
Time required: 1–52 weeks (plus)
Age: 16 plus – no upper limit
Causes: Animal Welfare, Conservation, Environmental Causes, Wildlife.
Activities: Building/Construction, Caring – General, Conservation Skills, Cooking, Development Issues, Driving, First Aid, Forestry, Manual Work, Outdoor Skills.
When to apply: Any time.
Work alone/with others: With Director.
Qualifications: Driving licence is necessary and ideally a knowledge of Japanese. Most of all unlimited patience and affection for animals.
Equipment/clothing: Practical clothing, warm, waterproof and durable.
Health requirements: The work concerns handling injured and ill wildlife, good health of the volunteer is a neccessity.
Costs: Volunteers will have to fund accommodation, food, travel and insurances.

Benefits: No accommodation/food etc.
Training: None necessary if willing to learn from the natural world.
Supervision: Supervision by Director.
Interviews: Interviews by letter, telephone etc, to learn about each other before any decisions are made.
Worldwide placements: Asia (Japan).

CITIZENS ADVICE
Myddelton House
115–123 Pentonville Road
London
N1 9LZ UK
T: +44 (0) 207 833 7002
F: +44 (0) 20 7361 253 4341
E: andy.yuille@citizensadvice.org.uk
W: www.citizensadvice.org.uk
Contact: Andy Yuille

Five million people seek help from Citizens Advice Bureaux every year. Each bureau offers free, confidential, impartial and independent advice and helps solve problems, which are central to people's lives, including debt and consumer issues, benefits, housing, legal matters, employment and immigration. As well as giving advice, the CAB service uses its bank of client evidence to campaign for changes to local and national services and policies. There are 2000 CAB outlets in England, Wales and Northern Ireland. Each CAB is an independent charity, relying on funding from the local authority and local business, charitable trusts and individual donations. There are many ways that volunteers can get involved including: advising clients, admin and office support, campaigning/social policy, fundraising, interpreting, IT support, press/PR/publicity work, reception, research, as a trustee board member, volunteer recruitment, web site design and more. Some bureaux are also part of the CAB Millennium Volunteer Project, which provides official recognition for the time volunteered by young people aged 16–25. Volunteers with offending background accepted. Applicants should contact the Citizens Advice Bureaux volunteer recruitment hotline on 08451 264 264 or visit the Citizens Advice web site www.citizensadvice.org.uk/join-us.

Number of projects: 2000 **UK:** 2000
Starting months: January–December
Time required: 4–52 weeks (plus)
Age: 16 plus – no upper limit
Causes: Addicts/Ex-Addicts, AIDS/HIV, Children, Disabled (learning and physical), Elderly People, Health Care/Medical, Human Rights, Inner City Problems, Offenders/Ex-Offenders, Poor/Homeless, Refugees, Teaching/assisting, Unemployed, Young People.
Activities: Accountancy, Administration,

Campaigning, Community Work, Computers, DIY, Fundraising, Group Work, Library/Resource Centres, Marketing/Publicity, Research, Teaching, Technical Skills, Training, Translating.
Placements: 21000
When to apply: All year.
Work alone/with others: With others.
Qualifications: Numeracy and an ability to speak, read and write English.
Health requirements: Nil.
Costs: Nil.
Benefits: Out of pocket expenses.
Training: All volunteers receive full induction. All volunteer advisors complete the Generalist Advice Certificate Programme. Training/induction is arranged at each bureau/locally with Citizens Advice support for advisor and some other training.
Supervision: Supervision arranged locally with CAB Manager.
Interviews: Interviews take place at the individual bureau.
Charity number: 279057
UK placements: England (throughout); Scotland (throughout); Northern Ireland (throughout); Wales (throughout).

CIVILISATIONS ATLANTIQUES & ARCHEOSCIENCES

UMR 6566 Labo Anthropologie-Archeometrie
Campus de Beaulieu, CS 74 205
F-35042 Rennes
Cedex France
T: 00 33 2 23 23 61 09
F: 00 33 2 23 23 69 34
E: jean-laurent.monnier@univ-rennes1.fr
W: http://ens.univ-rennes1.fr
Contact: Dr Jean Laurent Monnier

Civilisations Atlantiques & Archeosciences needs volunteers to take part in archaeological digs in the summer. To work from 0830–1200 and 1400–1800, five and a half days a week. Alternative web addresses – http://archeologie.univ-rennes1.fr /http://www.archeologie.univ-rennes1.fr. 🔊 📖

Number of projects: 1 **UK:** 0
Starting months: Jun, Jul, Aug, Sep
Time required: 2–6 weeks
Age: 18 plus – no upper limit
Causes: Archaeology, Heritage.
Activities: Administration, Manual Work, Research.
Placements: 60
When to apply: March to April.
Work alone/with others: with others.
Qualifications: Genuine interest in prehistoric archaeology. No language necessary. No nationality restrictions but preferably archaeological students (periods of probation for example).
Equipment/clothing: Camping equipment.

Health requirements: In good health.
Costs: Food and travel.
Benefits: Board. Accommodation in tents on site.
Training: If required.
Supervision: Yes.
Interviews: Yes.
Worldwide placements: Europe (France).

CLUB DU VIEUX MANOIR

Siège National
10 rue de la Cossonnerie
F-75001 Paris
France
T: 00 33 1 45 08 80 40
F: 00 33 1 42 21 38 79
E: secretariat@clubduvieuxmanoir.asso.fr

Club du Vieux Manoir – founded in 1953 – is a volunteer association formed of young people who want to spend some of their spare-time doing rescue and restoration work (under direction) on ancient monuments and sites. On the different sites two aims are pursued: the historic monuments and places which form part of the national heritage are restored and brought to life; the participants are offered a leisure activity where they can work with their hands and at the same time learn about different techniques. The young people, divided into groups, share the day to day organisation of the camp and site: everybody lends a hand to achieve a common objective. The monuments and sites undertaken are always open to the public. Usually they belong to local councils or societies. Thus after the work is finished the building continues to be of use. Office address of Secretariat-General: Monique Dine, Directeur, Ancienne Abbaye du Moncel, 60700 – Pontpoint.

Tel: 03 44 72 33 98
Fax: 03 44 70 13 14
Number of projects: UK: 0
Starting months: January–December
Time required: 1–52 weeks
Age: 15 plus – no upper limit
Causes: Archaeology, Architecture, Conservation, Heritage, Work Camps – Seasonal.
Activities: Arts/Crafts, Building/Construction, Conservation Skills, Summer Camps, Work Camps – Seasonal.
Placements: 4,670
When to apply: All year.
Work alone/with others: With others.
Equipment/clothing: Sleeping bag and camp cooking utensils.
Health requirements: Nil.
Costs: Approx £7 per day.
Benefits: Tented accommodation in the summer months. Showers available. Sheltered accommodation during the winter months.
Training: Courses in various techniques available for youngsters from 16 years old upwards. Practical instruction given on the site.

Supervision: Group leaders, site director, technical supervision, architects, archaeologists, historians and volunteers who return regularly to the same site.
Interviews: Applicants are not interviewed.
Worldwide placements: Europe (France).

CLUB UNESCO AU MONDE DES LECTEUR (CUML)

BP 4671 Kinshasa 2
7 Rue Meteo,
Djelo Binza (Delvaux), Zone de Ngaliema
Kinshasa
Dem. Republic of Congo
Contact: Mr Lejoly Mandango

CUML, founded in 1983, is a non-governmental organisation providing voluntary assistance and services with an aim to improve the standard of living in the Democratic Republic of Congo. Volunteers of all nationalities are needed every year to help with projects in a wide variety of areas including health, agriculture, the environment, education, rural and social development and construction.

Number of projects: many UK: 0
Starting months: January–December
Time required: 3–52 weeks
Age: 18–35
Causes: Children, Conservation, Disabled (learning and physical), Elderly People, Environmental Causes, Health Care/Medical, Heritage, Poor/Homeless, Refugees, Teaching/assisting, Unemployed, Young People.
Activities: Administration, Agriculture/Farming, Arts/Crafts, Building/Construction, Caring – General, Catering, Community Work, Conservation Skills, Development Issues, First Aid, Forestry, Gardening/Horticulture, Group Work, International Aid, Social Work, Teaching.
Placements: 150
When to apply: All year.
Work alone/with others: Both.
Costs: Travel and insurance.
Benefits: Food, accommodation, pocket money and some travel expenses.
Worldwide placements: Africa (Congo Dem Republic).

COLIN GLEN TRUST

Forest Park Centre
163 Stewarts Town Road
Dunmurry, Belfast
Antrim
BT17 0HW N. Ireland
T: +44 (0) 2890 614115
F: +44 (0) 2890 601694
E: info@colinglentrust.org
W: www.colinglentrust.org
Contact: Bill McComb

Colin Glen Trust offers a wide range and variety of challenging voluntary opportunities. These are suitable for able and less able persons of all ages, on both long and short-term basis. Volunteers complement the work done by the staff and bring additional skills and fresh ideas to the Trust. Initially volunteers carried out tasks such as tree planting and general park maintenance. The Trust has now developed a volunteer programme, the aim of which is to get all sections of the community interested and involved in its projects on a more regular and formal basis. Volunteers have the opportunity to get involved with a variety of projects gaining maximum field experience. Tasks within practical conservation include tree planting, wildlife surveys, and path and woodland maintenance. Environmental education opportunities exist, working alongside education staff gaining knowledge and first hand evidence of an environmental based programme for schools and community groups. There are placements for volunteers with an offending background – we actively work with rehabilitation projects. Colin Glen Forest Park, Belfast, Co. Antrim/ Colin Glen Golf Complex, Belfast, Co. Antrim. 10 minutes from Belfast City Centre and less than a mile from Junction 3 of the M1.

Number of projects: 2 UK: 2
Starting months: January–December
Time required: 1–24 weeks
Age: 16 plus – no upper limit
Causes: Archaeology, Conservation, Environmental Causes, Unemployed, Wildlife, Young People.
Activities: Administration, Building/Construction, Campaigning, Community Work, Conservation Skills, Forestry, Gardening/Horticulture, Group Work, Manual Work, Outdoor Skills, Research, Training.
Placements: 70
When to apply: Any time.
Work alone/with others: Work with others.
Qualifications: No, we are usually able to accommodate people of various ability with suitable tasks.
Equipment/clothing: All safety equipment – boots, wet gear etc, all provided.
Health requirements: No restrictions – we will go to great lengths to accommodate anyone wishing to contribute.
Costs: We will cover cost of travel, lunch etc. No registration fee. We aim for an inclusive project irrespective of economic circumstances. Accommodation costs.
Benefits: The Trust covers travel costs and lunch. None.
Training: Training provided in gardening, nursery skills, record keeping, planning, woodland conservation and management.
Supervision: Adequate supervision provided at all times, Health and Safety is a priority.

Interviews: Yes, interviews are held at the Colin Glen Forest Park Centre.
Charity number: 26146
UK placements: Northern Ireland (Antrim, Belfast City).

COLLÈGE LYCÉE CÉVENOL INTERNATIONAL

Chambon-sur-Lignon 434000
Haute Loire
France
T: 00 33 4 71 59 72 52
F: 00 33 4 71 65 87 38
E: lecervenol@aol.com
W: www.members.aol.com|lecevenol
Contact: M. le Directeur

Collège Lycée Cévenol International Workcamp takes place in the Massif Central. The surrounding country is wooded and mountainous and provides an invigorating setting for the camp activities. The present school at Chambon-sur-Lignon has been partly built by workcamps held at the site.

Number of projects: UK: 0
Starting months: Jul
Time required: 3–3 weeks
Age: 18–30
Causes: Architecture, Environmental Causes.
Activities: Building/Construction, Manual Work.
When to apply: As early as possible.
Work alone/with others: With others.
Health requirements: Good.
Costs: €101 registration fee.
Benefits: Accommodation, food and all other facilities. Free registration.
Interviews: Applicants are not interviewed.
Worldwide placements: Europe (France).

COLORADO TRAIL FOUNDATION, THE

710 10th Street, #210
Golden, Colorado
80401–5843 USA
T: 00 1 303 384 3729
F: 00 1 303 384 3743
E: ctf@coloradotrail.org
W: www.coloradotrail.org
Contact: Suzanne Reed or Marian Polito Phillips

The Colorado Trail Foundation builds and maintains a 500 mile trail between Denver and Durango, Colorado, passing through eight mountain ranges, seven national forests, six wilderness areas and the headwaters of five river systems. All participants share in the work of setting up daily camp chores, meal preparation and clean up. Trail crews are highly participatory and volunteers join in daily camp life from helping to cook to trail building and maintenance as well as the evening camp fire. State of Colorado in the High Rockies.

Starting months: Jun, Jul, Aug
Time required: 1–10 weeks
Age: 16 plus – no upper limit
Causes: Conservation, Environmental Causes, Heritage, Wildlife.
Activities: Building/Construction, Conservation Skills, Forestry, Manual Work, Outdoor skills.
Placements: 300–500
When to apply: February to May.
Work alone/with others: With others – a trail crew.
Equipment/clothing: Tent, sleeping bag and pad, leather boots, eating utensils, work clothes and personal items.
Health requirements: Good physical condition.
Costs: Trail crew registration is $40. Must supply a tent or contact leader for a loaner. Contact crew leader for carpool and other transportation.
Benefits: Food, tools and hard hats. Leaders and base camp work 4 days/week. Wednesdays are free to explore the area.
Training: Sunday. Safety lecture and tool handling procedures with demonstrations.
Supervision: Qualified leaders.
Interviews: Applicants are not interviewed.
Worldwide placements: North America: (USA).

COMMUNITY FOR CREATIVE NON-VIOLENCE

425 2nd Street NW
Washington
DC 20001 USA
T: 00 1 202 393 1909
F: 00 1 202 783 3254
W: www.erols.com.CCNV
Contact: Fred Henry

Community for Creative Non-Violence (CCNV) works to ensure that the rights of the homeless and poor are not infringed upon and that every person has access to life's basic essentials – food, clothing, shelter and medical care. The Community is also committed to protecting the rights of the homeless, advocating on behalf of the under-served and preparing homeless men and women to re-enter mainstream society as skilled and productive citizens. CCNV has the largest shelter in the USA with a 1350-bed shelter in Washington DC. CCNV provides shelter and educational opportunities for its residents. We have thousands of volunteers from all over the world. CCNV has successfully instituted an aggressive anti-drugs campaign resulting in the largest reduction in crime in the district.

Starting months: January–December
Time required: 26–52 weeks
Age: 18 plus – no upper limit
Causes: Addicts/Ex-Addicts, AIDS/HIV, Elderly People, Health Care/Medical, Human Rights,

Inner City Problems, Offenders/Ex-Offenders, Poor/Homeless.
Activities: Administration, Arts/Crafts, Catering, Cooking, Counselling, Driving, Fundraising, Library/Resource Centres, Manual Work, Social Work.
When to apply: All year.
Work alone/with others: Work with others.
Health requirements: Good.
Costs: Fares, pocket money and USA visa.
Benefits: Board and dormitory accommodation.
Training: On job training.
Supervision: Yes.
Interviews: Written, e-mail or fax.
Worldwide placements: North America: (USA).

COMMUNITY MUSIC WALES

Unit 8, 24 Norbury Road
Fairwater
Cardiff
CF5 3AU UK
T: +44 (0) 29 2083 8060
F: +44 (0) 29 2056 6573
E: admin@communitymusicwales.org.uk
W: www.communitymusicwales.org.uk
Contact: Eileen Smith

Community Music Wales aims to make music available to people who would normally be marginalised in society e.g. people with learning difficulties, people with physical disabilities, people with mental health problems, people from ethnic minorities, young offenders. Our aim is to create and promote music-making opportunities for people of all ages, skills and experience. We only take volunteers every six months. Volunteers with an offending background are accepted. ♿ ▣

Number of projects: 144 **UK:** 100 +
Starting months: Jan, Feb, Mar, Apr, May, Jun, Jul, Aug, Sep, Oct, Nov
Time required: 1–52 weeks
Age: 14 plus – no upper limit
Causes: Addicts/Ex-Addicts, Children, Disabled (learning and physical), Elderly People, Inner City Problems, Offenders/Ex-Offenders, Poor/Homeless, Unemployed, Young People.
Activities: Administration, Community Work, Computers, Fundraising, Marketing/Publicity, Music, Training.
Placements: 2
When to apply: All year.
Work alone/with others: With others.
Qualifications: Interest in music and working in the community.
Health requirements: Nil.
Costs: None.
Benefits: Expenses paid. Accommodation can be arranged for overseas volunteers.
Training: Any training needed would be carried out at the headquarters.

Supervision: Full supervision at all times.
Interviews: Interviews take place at CMW's headquarters in Cardiff.
Charity number: 1009867
UK placements: Wales (throughout).

COMMUNITY PARTNERS' ASSOCIATION (COPA)

Green Banks
Old Hill, Longhope
Gloucestershire
GL17 OPF UK
T: +44 (0) 1452 830492
F: +44 (0) 1452 830492
E: copauk@tinyworld.co.uk
Contact: David Wilson

COPA is a small but very active charity working in poor rural villages in the Dominican Republic. In the village of La Hoya COPA has completed the construction of a school for approximately 400 children up to year eight and a pre-school. It has also built and maintains a rural clinic there. Nearby, Bombita is occupied entirely by very poor migrant Haitians where COPA has built and maintains a school for 400 children and a clinic. The aim of COPA is to provide the expertise and finance to help very poor communities to help themselves. The communities have therefore been heavily involved as volunteers in the construction. Work groups from the USA and the UK travel to the Dominican Republic for periods of two or three weeks to work alongside the local people on the building site and in the school. The COPA projects are run by two-year volunteers directed by a management team in the UK. Short term volunteers are also welcome for periods of less than one year. The teachers are all Dominican and one of the principal roles of volunteers is to support them in the classroom and also to teach English to the older students. They greatly help visiting work groups as translators. There is usually administrative work to be done for those with computer skills. COPA is a Christian organisation and expects volunteers to work in sympathy with its aims. Applications from qualified primary teachers or qualified nurses are particularly welcome for two-year contracts.

Number of projects: 4 **UK:** 0
Starting months: Jan, Feb, Mar, Apr, May, Jun, Jul, Aug, Sep, Nov, Dec
Time required: 5–52 weeks
Age: 18 plus – no upper limit
Causes: Children, Health Care/Medical, Poor/Homeless, Teaching/assisting (nursery, primary, secondary, EFL), Work Camps – Seasonal, Young People.
Activities: Administration, Building/Construction, Computers, Development Issues, Teaching, Translating, Work Camps – Seasonal.

Placements: 6
When to apply: All year.
Work alone/with others: With others.
Qualifications: A-level and ability to converse in Spanish.
Health requirements: Good health essential.
Costs: Return airfare and subsistence (approx. £200 per month) for short-term volunteers. No contribution is required from 2-year volunteers.
Benefits: Free accommodation, water and electricity.
Training: One-day pre-placement preparation on the job training by COPA staff. Written notes also given to volunteers.
Supervision: Resident COPA staff supervise short-term volunteers.
Interviews: Interviews take place in Gloucester.
Charity number: 1027117
Worldwide placements: Central America (Dominican Republic).

COMMUNITY SERVICE VOLUNTEERS

237 Pentonville Road
London
N1 9NJ UK
T: 0800 374 991
F: +44 (0) 207 837 9318
E: volunteer@csv.org.uk
W: www.csv.org.uk
Contact: Volunteers Administrator

CSV invites all people aged 16+ to experience the challenge, excitement and reward of helping people in need. Each year it places 3,000 volunteers on projects throughout the UK, working with elderly or homeless people, adults or children with disabilities, learning difficulties or mental illness, and young people who are in care or in trouble. No volunteer is ever rejected. Volunteers work hard, have fun and gain valuable experience working away from home for four to twelve months. Applications are welcome throughout the year. There are specialist projects for volunteers with disabilities (physical and learning) and CSV welcomes applications from people with disabilities. Volunteers need to be prepared to work flexible hours but not more than 40 hours per week. Specialist schemes cater for vulnerable people from disadvantaged backgrounds, such as substance misusers, homeless people, young people looked after by local authorities and young offenders, who may need special encouragement to volunteer. Opportunities are available for these volunteers to work part-time locally on one of many CSV schemes nationwide while receiving pro-rata weekly allowance, food, travel expenses and supervision. CSV is a member of The Year Out Group. Volunteers work away from their home area. 🖼 📄

Number of projects: 800 UK: 800
Starting months: January–December
Time required: 16–52 weeks
Age: 16–70
Causes: Addicts/Ex-Addicts, AIDS/HIV, Children, Disabled (learning and physical), Elderly People, Inner City Problems, Offenders/Ex-Offenders, Poor/Homeless, Young People.
Activities: Administration, Building/Construction, Caring (general, day and residential), Community Work, Cooking, Counselling, Driving, Group Work, Social Work, Visiting/Befriending.
Placements: 2, 200
When to apply: 6–8 weeks before start.
Work alone/with others: Both on their own and with others.
Qualifications: Volunteers from outside the UK are accepted but they must pay a charge (currently £543) and satisfy UK visa requirements.
Health requirements: Nil.
Costs: no costs.
Benefits: Board and lodging + £28.00 per week for 40 hour week.
Training: Depending on placement.
Supervision: Depending on placement.
Interviews: Volunteers are interviewed at the CSV office nearest to them.
Charity number: 291222
UK placements: England (throughout); Scotland (throughout); Wales (throughout).

COMMUNITY SERVICE VOLUNTEERS EDUCATION

237 Pentonville Road
London
N1 9NJ UK
T: +44 (0) 207 643 1313
T: +44 (0) 207 278 1020
E: information@csv.org.uk
Contact: Melanie Elkan

Community Service Volunteers is an organisation which offers people the opportunity to play an active part in the community by volunteering. CSV Education for citizenship is a part of CSV which encourages young people to volunteer in their schools and communities and promotes the involvement of adults volunteering in schools. The scheme, known as Adults Other Than Teachers, aims to improve links between schools and the adult community. Pupils gain a great deal from the voluntary support of adults who can offer one to one or group work time. Volunteers generally offer an hour a week to work with children in areas such as reading support, numeracy, sports, arts, crafts, music or leisure activities. Volunteers do not need to have any experience. They should be interested in children and able to

make a commitment of at least a term.
Volunteers are required to undergo a formal
recruitment procedure, including a police check.
Volunteers will apply to individual schools.
Volunteers with an offending background may
be accepted. Police check for purposes of child
protection will be carried out. Central London.

Number of projects: 40 **UK:** 40
Starting months: January–December
Time required: 10–52 weeks (plus)
Age: 18 plus – no upper limit
Causes: Children, Teaching/assisting (primary).
Activities: Arts/Crafts, Music, Sport, Teaching,
Theatre/Drama, Translating, Visiting/Befriending.
Placements: 20
When to apply: All year.
Work alone/with others: With others.
Health requirements: Nil.
Costs: Travel costs – ideally vols will live close
enough to schools to avoid travel costs.
Benefits: Accommodation depending on the
placement.
Training: Schools will provide the necessary
induction and training.
Supervision: Depending on the placement.
Interviews: Volunteers will be interviewed at
the school at which they wish to volunteer.
Charity number: 291222
UK placements: England (London).

CONCORDIA

20–22 Heversham House
Boundary Road
Hove, East Sussex
BN3 4ET UK
T: 01273 422367
F: 01273 421182
E: info@concordia-iye.org.uk
W: www.concordia-iye.org.uk
Contact: Gwyn Lewis

Short-term (2–3 weeks), Concordia runs
international volunteer projects. It also runs
volunteer projects in the UK for overseas
volunteers and needs UK volunteers to act as
project co-ordinators who must be aged 20+
and have previous workcamp or leadership
experience. Volunteers with an offending
background are accepted unless they want to
work on a children's camp and the offence was
child related. All volunteers for UK based
playscheme work must provide a certificate of
good conduct. ♿ 📄

Number of projects: 300+ **UK:** 15+
Starting months: January–December
Time required: 2–4 weeks
Age: 16–30
Causes: Animal Welfare, Archaeology, Children,
Conservation, Disabled (learning and physical),
Elderly People, Environmental Causes, Health

Care/Medical, Heritage, Holidays for Disabled,
Inner City Problems, Poor/Homeless, Refugees,
Teaching/assisting, Unemployed, Wildlife, Work
Camps – Seasonal, Young People.
Activities: Arts/Crafts, Building/Construction,
Caring (general and day), Community Work,
Conservation Skills, Cooking, Forestry,
Gardening/Horticulture, Group Work, Manual
Work, Music, Social Work, Sport, Summer
Camps, Teaching, Theatre/Drama, Work Camps
– Seasonal.
Placements: 200+
When to apply: From April for Summer
projects or as early as possible for out of season
projects.
Work alone/with others: With others in a
group of about 10–15 international volunteers.
Qualifications: Language ability for some
projects. Volunteers applying for projects
abroad must be resident in the UK. Limited
places for UK volunteers applying for projects
in the UK.
Equipment/clothing: Sleeping bag, rollmat,
strong shoes, old clothes + work gloves.
Health requirements: Volunteers must be fit
enough to undertake the (often physical) work
required.
Costs: Registration fee £80–£125 depending on
the country + travel + insurance + an annual
membership fee of £6.50/£10.
Benefits: Board and lodging, social programme.
Training: None.
Supervision: Dependent on project, country
etc. but usually there are 2 project co-ordinators
with additional supervision during the work.
Interviews: Applicants are not interviewed.
Charity number: 381668
Worldwide placements: Africa (Algeria,
Botswana, Gambia, Ghana, Kenya, Morocco,
Rwanda, South Africa, Tanzania, Togo, Tunisia,
Uganda, Zambia, Zimbabwe); North America:
(Canada, Greenland, USA); Central America
(Mexico); South America (Ecuador); Asia
(Bangladesh, India, Israel, Japan, Korea (South),
Mongolia, Nepal, Palestinian Authority,
Thailand, Turkey); Europe (Albania, Armenia,
Azerbaijan, Belarus, Belgium, Bosnia-
Herzegovina, Bulgaria, Croatia, Czech Republic,
Denmark, Estonia, Finland, France, Germany,
Greece, Italy, Latvia, Lithuania, Macedonia,
Netherlands, Norway, Poland, Romania, Russia,
Slovakia, Slovenia, Spain, Switzerland, Turkey,
Ukraine, Yugoslavia).
UK placements: England (Cheshire, Derbyshire,
Hampshire, Herefordshire, Lancashire,
Lincolnshire, London, Northumberland,
Nottinghamshire, Oxfordshire, Staffordshire, E.
Sussex, W. Sussex, West Midlands, E. Yorkshire,
S. Yorkshire); Wales (Flintshire, Gwynedd).

CONFERENCE ON TRAINING IN ARCHITECTURAL CONSERVATION (COTAC)

Building Craft College
Kennard Road
Stratford
London E15 1AH UK
T: +44 (0) 208 221 1150
F: +44 (0) 208 221 2708
E: cotac@tcp.co.uk
W: www.cotac.org.uk
Contact: Mr Richard Davies

The Conference on Training in Architectural Conservation (COTAC) was formed 30 years ago to initiate better eduation for architects who wished to work on the repair and conservation of historic buildings. It is now composed of representatives from the main conservation bodies, the relevant professions, the construction industry, government agencies and educational institutions. As it has evolved, COTAC works for the training of all disciplines and crafts concerned with building conservation: architects, surveyors, engineers, conservation officers, construction managers, facility managers and skilled craftsmen and women. We recognise that conservation is a theme that involves society at all levels as well as being a positive force for unity within the construction industry. It aims: to encourage a general appreciation of the benefits of skilled conservation amongst all sections of the building industry in the community; to identify and encourage the development of general and specialist training in conservation skills at the professional, technical and craft levels; to foster links between centres involved in both formal training and practical conservation in the UK and abroad; to assist in developing appropriate methods for monitoring training standards and specialist qualifications; to encourage funding for the development of courses and other training methods and to support students in the study of architectural conservation and associated craft skills. ♿ 📄

Number of projects: 2 UK: 2
Starting months: January–December
Time required: 4–52 weeks (plus)
Age: 18 plus – no upper limit
Causes: Architecture, Conservation, Heritage, Inner City Problems.
Activities: Administration, Arts/Crafts, Building/ Construction, Computers, Conservation Skills, Fundraising, Library/ Resource Centres.
When to apply: As soon as possible.
Work alone/with others: With a small team of consultants.
Qualifications: Reasonably literate, numerate, with common sense and the ability to apply themselves. Good competence in English essential.
Health requirements: Nil.

Costs: Nil apart from local travel and any accommodation required.
Benefits: By negotiation, some contribution to volunteers' expenses may be possible.
Training: On project.
Supervision: Depending on project.
Interviews: Prospective volunteers are interviewed at COTAC office.
Charity number: 1036263
Worldwide placements: Europe (Finland, France, Hungary, Ireland, Italy, Portugal, Spain).
UK placements: England (London).

CONNECT YOUTH

The British Council
10 Spring Gardens
London
SW1A 2BN UK
T: +44 (0) 207 389 4030
F: +44 (0) 207 389 4033
E: connectyouth.enquiries@britishcouncil.org
W: www.connectyouthinternational.com
Contact: Information Officer

Connect Youth is the British National Agency for the European Voluntary Service Scheme which is open to all young people with no qualification requirement. There is a very wide range of tasks and positive measures will enable disadvantaged young people to have access to the programme. Although you will have a say over your placement and type of work you must be prepared to work in any one of the fields ticked. You will meet volunteers from other European countries to share experiences. You will have a rewarding experience doing something useful for other communities. You will learn a lot at the same time helping yourself to develop as a person and to develop your future. You will learn new skills which make you more attractive to future employers. It is exciting and you will get to see places. You will be living in another country for quite a long time. You will learn about their customs and feel a sense of belonging to the European Union. You will make useful contacts for the future, even at European level. You will have an active part in discussing your role, place and responsibilities in the host project. At in-service training events you will have the chance to meet other EVS volunteers in your country and to discuss and reflect upon your experiences. You may be the only volunteer at your assignment or you may be working with a group of volunteers. But you will always be part of a team. THIS ENTRY IS REPEATED UNDER 'EUROPEAN VOLUNTARY SERVICE'. ♿

Number of projects: 1500+ UK: 0
Starting months: January–December
Time required: 3–52 weeks
Age: 18–25
Causes: Addicts/Ex-Addicts, AIDS/HIV, Animal

Welfare, Archaeology, Architecture, Children, Conservation, Disabled (learning and physical), Elderly People, Environmental Causes, Health Care/Medical, Heritage, Holidays for Disabled, Human Rights, Inner City Problems, Offenders/ Ex-Offenders, Poor/Homeless, Refugees, Unemployed, Wildlife, Work Camps – Seasonal, Young People.
Activities: Accountancy, Administration, Agriculture/Farming, Arts/Crafts, Building/ Construction, Campaigning, Caring (general, day and residential), Catering, Community Work, Computers, Conservation Skills, Cooking, Counselling, Development Issues, DIY, Driving, First Aid, Forestry, Fundraising, Gardening/ Horticulture, Group Work, International Aid, Library/Resource Centres, Manual Work, Marketing/Publicity, Music, Newsletter/ Journalism, Outdoor Skills, Religion, Research, Scientific Work, Social Work, Sport, Summer Camps, Teaching, Technical Skills, Theatre/ Drama, Training, Translating, Visiting/ Befriending, Work Camps – Seasonal.
When to apply: All year.
Work alone/with others: Both.
Qualifications: Connect Youth accepts applications from young people legally residing in the UK at the time of application.
Equipment/clothing: Any special equipment or clothing supplied.
Health requirements: Any special Health requirements for a specific project would be notified to prospective volunteer.
Benefits: Board and lodging + pocket money approx £20 p/w. Travel money and special equipment.
Training: You will be given preparatory training before you leave including language training and preparation for the new culture you will be living in. You will also attend an in-service training event during the course of your assignment.
Supervision: As well as a job supervisor, you will have a personal supervisor unconnected with your project to whom you can turn for personal support if needed.
Worldwide placements: Europe (Austria, Belgium, Bulgaria, Czech Republic, Denmark, Estonia, Finland, France, Germany, Greece, Hungary, Iceland, Ireland, Italy, Liechtenstein, Lithuania, Luxembourg, Malta, Netherlands, Norway, Poland, Portugal, Slovakia, Slovenia, Spain, Sweden, Turkey).

CONSEJO DE COORDINACION DE OBRAS PRIVADAS (CONDECOORD) – ARGENTINA

Avenida Santa Fe 3114
3fl B
Buenos Aires 1425
Argentina
Contact: Oscar Garcia

Consejo de Coordinacion de Obras Privadas (Condecoord) promotes and has information about volunteering in Argentina. It may well be able to put volunteers in touch with organisations which are not yet listed on the WorldWide Volunteering database.

Starting months: January–December
Time required: 1–52 weeks (plus)
Age: 16 plus – no upper limit
Causes: Addicts/Ex-Addicts, AIDS/HIV, Animal Welfare, Archaeology, Architecture, Children, Conservation, Disabled (learning and physical), Elderly People, Environmental Causes, Health Care/Medical, Heritage, Holidays for Disabled, Human Rights, Inner City Problems, Offenders/ Ex-Offenders, Poor/Homeless, Refugees, Teaching/assisting (nursery, primary, secondary, mature, EFL) Unemployed, Wildlife, Work Camps – Seasonal, Young People.
Activities: Accountancy, Administration, Agriculture/Farming, Arts/Crafts, Building/ Construction, Campaigning, Caring (general, day and residential), Catering, Community Work, Computers, Conservation Skills, Cooking, Counselling, Development Issues, DIY, Driving, First Aid, Forestry, Fundraising, Gardening/Horticulture, Group Work, International Aid, Library/Resource Centres, Manual Work, Marketing/Publicity, Music, Newsletter/Journalism, Outdoor Skills, Religion, Research, Scientific Work, Social Work, Sport, Summer Camps, Teaching, Technical Skills, Theatre/Drama, Training, Translating, Visiting/Befriending, Work Camps – Seasonal.
Costs: Varies according to the project.
Worldwide placements: South America (Argentina).

CONSERVATION TRUST, THE

305 Townsend Avenue
New Haven
06512 USA
T: 203 668 1358
F: 203 468 6296
E: interns@conservation-trust.org
W: www.conservation-trust.org
Contact: Volunteer Co-ordinator

This is a work from home volunteering opportunity. The Conservation Trust is a forward-looking environmental organisation headquartered in New Haven, CT. Consisting of a small, supported office, a programme of carefully selected Internet volunteers, and a host of members from coast to coast. We work with government, with businesses and with other non-profit making organisations to illuminate and develop methods to improve the environment and sustain strong economic growth. Our numerous successes include preserving wetlands and ecologically sensitive areas through working with developers to devise safe plans, improving water quality through practical methods of 'non-point source pollutant control', restoring river habitat for endangered northwest salmon, and co-implementing measures to prevent coastal oil spills. We are proud of ourselves and have also succeeded through the providing of leading edge support for a number of campaigns to improve humanity's relationship with the outdoors, including campaigns for sustainable forestry and grassland use, clean air requirements, and land use planning. With the help of our friends, we plan on continuing the scope of our mission and improving the quality of life on the Earth we inhabit. Depending on the situation, we may be able to place volunteers with an offending background. However, we would like to have reliable, dependable and dedicated people volunteering with us.

Number of projects: 50 **UK:** 0
Starting months: January–December
Time required: 1–52 weeks
Age: 17–75
Causes: Animal Welfare, Conservation, Environmental Causes, Wildlife.
Activities: Campaigning, Community Work, Conservation Skills, Forestry, Research, Technical Skills.
Placements: 50
When to apply: As soon as possible.
Work alone/with others: Varies.
Qualifications: Have a sincere desire to help the world around you i.e., the environment and wildlife.

Health requirements: No restrictions.
Costs: No cost as you work online from your own home. Only your time.
Benefits: Not applicable. Work from home.
Training: We will train volunteers in whatever area we assign you to work on for us. You will have the tools you need.
Supervision: All volunteer co-ordinators will perform all debriefing if needed.
Interviews: We will talk with volunteers either via e-mail or we may call you.
Charity number: 91–2073024
UK placements: England (throughout); Scotland (throughout); Northern Ireland (throughout); Wales (throughout).

CONSERVATION VOLUNTEERS AUSTRALIA

Box 423
Ballarat
Victoria 3353 Australia
T: 00 61 3 5333 1483
F: 00 61 3 5333 2166
E: info@conservationvolunteers.com.au
W: www.conservationvolunteers.com.au
Contact: Executive Director

Conservation Volunteers Australia operates conservation projects across Australia all year round. The CVA experience is an ideal way to get to know the country and its culture, and is a great 'first step' if you intend to extend your travel throughout Australia. CVA volunteers come from a wide range of ages, abilities and backgrounds. No special skills are required, as

qualified and experienced team leaders provide training and direction on site. Our projects offer the chance to learn and apply a variety of practical conservation skills whilst living and working with people of similar interest and commitment. We recommend that overseas volunteers apply for a minimum of four to six weeks. Volunteers can apply to commence from any CVA office around Australia, commencing on any Friday throughout the year.

Number of projects: 2,000 **UK:** 0
Starting months: January–December
Time required: 4–20 weeks
Age: 17–70
Causes: Conservation, Environmental Causes, Heritage, Wildlife, Young People.
Activities: Agriculture/Farming, Building/Construction, Community Work, Conservation Skills, Forestry, Gardening/ Horticulture, Group Work, Manual Work, Outdoor Skills, Research, Training.
Placements: 3,000
When to apply: 8 weeks prior to starting.
Work alone/with others: With others in teams of 6–10 under direction of CVA team leader.
Qualifications: Ability to speak and understand English. Interest in practical conservation. No prior experience necessary. No restrictions but must be able to understand English for safety reasons.
Equipment/clothing: Full list available.
Health requirements: Reasonable fitness.
Costs: From AU$27 per day, this includes food, accommodation and project related transport.
Benefits: The cost includes all food, accommodation and transport whilst working with CVA.
Training: All volunteers are briefed 1) on arrival, 2) at the start of each week and 3) daily reminders are given regarding safety.
Supervision: CVA team leaders are with volunteers throughout projects. The leaders are responsible for on-site training safety, project management and volunteer welfare.
Interviews: Applicants are not usually interviewed.
Worldwide placements: Australasia (Australia).

CONSERVATION VOLUNTEERS IRELAND

The Steward's House
Rathfarham Castle
Dublin 14
Eire
T: 00 353 1 454 7185
F: 00 353 1 4546935
E: info@cvi.ie
W: www.cvi.ie
Contact: Melanie Hamilton

Conservation Volunteers Ireland is involved in many projects all over Ireland. Volunteers interested in working with CVI need no previous skills or experience, just energy and commitment. Scenic locations and historic sites.

Number of projects: 50 **UK:** 0
Starting months: January–December
Time required: 1–1 weeks
Age: 18 plus – no upper limit
Causes: Conservation, Environmental Causes, Heritage, Wildlife.
Activities: Conservation Skills, Forestry, Group Work, Outdoor Skills, Technical Skills, Training.
Placements: 50
When to apply: All year.
Work alone/with others: With others.
Equipment/clothing: Wet weather and strong boots.
Health requirements: Good general health.
Costs: Travel and membership. Board and lodging at a reasonable cost.
Benefits: Internal travel.
Training: An induction course is provided.
Supervision: Volunteers are supervised by trained officers.
Interviews: No interviews necessary.
Charity number: 10105
Worldwide placements: Europe (Ireland).

CONSERVATION VOLUNTEERS NORTHERN IRELAND (CVNI)

159 Ravenhill Road
Belfast
BT6 0BP N. Ireland
T: +44 (0) 28 9064 5169
F: +44 (0) 28 9064 4409
E: b.belshaw@cvni.org
W: www.cvni.org.uk
Contact: Billy Celshaw

Conservation Volunteers Northern Ireland is part of BTCB. BTCV is the UK's largest practical conservation charity. It enables people of all ages from all sections of the community to take action in caring for the environment in towns, cities and the countryside. Each year over 30,000 volunteers are equipped and trained to work on thousands of environmental projects. These include the creation and protection of wildlife habitats, pond and coastal work, tree planting, drystone walling and the improvement of access to the countryside. Week-long natural breaks and weekend breaks are organised throughout the year, costing from €110 (natural breaks) and €25 for weekend breaks. BTCV is striving towards equal opportunities for all, regardless of age, class, colour, disability, employment status, ethnic or national origins, marital status, race, religious beliefs, responsibilities for children or dependents, sex, sexual orientation or unrelated criminal offences. Volunteers with an offending background are accepted but this does depend upon the type of offence and type of work.

Number of projects: Hundreds **UK:** Hundreds
Starting months: January–December
Time required: 1–52 weeks (plus)
Age: 16–80
Causes: Conservation, Environmental Causes, Unemployed, Wildlife, Work Camps – Seasonal, Young People.
Activities: Administration, Arts/Crafts, Community Work, Computers, Conservation Skills, Cooking, Driving, Forestry, Fundraising, Group Work, Library/Resource Centres, Manual Work, Marketing/Publicity, Newsletter/Journalism, Outdoor Skills, Technical Skills, Training, Work Camps – Seasonal.
Placements: 4,000
When to apply: All year.
Work alone/with others: With others.
Health requirements: Nil.
Costs: From €25 for weekend breaks, from €110 for natural breaks.
Benefits: Unemployed volunteers get £2.50 per day. Accommodation can be provided for volunteers aged 18+ on a short-term basis and by prior agreement.
Training: Volunteers receive free training at our training centre in Clandeboye Estate.
Supervision: By trained members of staff and/or volunteer officers.
Interviews: Applicants for volunteer officers (volunteers willing to give 6 months or more of their time), are interviewed but other volunteers are not interviewed although there is a volunteer questionnaire. Interviews would take place at the area office.
Charity number: 261009
UK placements: Northern Ireland (throughout).

CONTACT – MOLDOVA

83 Bucuresti Str
Chisinau
MD-2012 Moldova
T: 00 373 2 233947
F: 00 373 2 33947
E: info@contact.md
Contact: Sorin Hanganu

Contact promotes and has information about volunteering in Moldova. It may well be able to put volunteers in touch with organisations which are not yet listed on the WorldWide Volunteering database.

Starting months: January–December
Time required: 1–52 weeks (plus)
Age: 16 plus – no upper limit
Causes: Addicts/Ex-Addicts, AIDS/HIV, Animal Welfare, Archaeology, Architecture, Children, Conservation, Disabled (learning and physical), Elderly People, Environmental Causes, Health Care/Medical, Heritage, Holidays for Disabled,

Human Rights, Inner City Problems, Offenders/Ex-Offenders, Poor/Homeless, Refugees, Teaching/assisting (nursery, primary, secondary, mature, EFL) Unemployed, Wildlife, Work Camps – Seasonal, Young People.
Activities: Accountancy, Administration, Agriculture/Farming, Arts/Crafts, Building/Construction, Campaigning, Caring (general, day and residential), Catering, Community Work, Computers, Conservation Skills, Cooking, Counselling, Development Issues, DIY, Driving, First Aid, Forestry, Fundraising, Gardening/Horticulture, Group Work, International Aid, Library/Resource Centres, Manual Work, Marketing/Publicity, Music, Newsletter/Journalism, Outdoor Skills, Religion, Research, Scientific Work, Social Work, Sport, Summer Camps, Teaching, Technical Skills, Theatre/Drama, Training, Translating, Visiting/Befriending, Work Camps – Seasonal.
Costs: Varies according to the project.
Worldwide placements: Europe (Moldova).

COOK ISLANDS ASSOCIATION OF NONGOVERNMENTAL ORGANISATIONS

Post Office Box 733
Rarotonga
Cook Islands
T: 00 682 29420
F: 00 682 28420
E: spmailbox@uts.edu.au
Contact: Vereara Maeva

Cook Islands Association of Nongovernmental Organisations promotes and has information about volunteering in the Cook Islands. It may well be able to put volunteers in touch with organisations which are not yet listed on the WorldWide Volunteering database.

Starting months: January–December
Time required: 1–52 weeks (plus)
Age: 16 plus – no upper limit
Causes: Addicts/Ex-Addicts, AIDS/HIV, Animal Welfare, Archaeology, Architecture, Children, Conservation, Disabled (learning and physical), Elderly People, Environmental Causes, Health Care/Medical, Heritage, Holidays for Disabled, Human Rights, Inner City Problems, Offenders/Ex-Offenders, Poor/Homeless, Refugees, Teaching/assisting (nursery, primary, secondary, mature, EFL) Unemployed, Wildlife, Work Camps – Seasonal, Young People.
Activities: Accountancy, Administration, Agriculture/Farming, Arts/Crafts, Building/Construction, Campaigning, Caring (general, day and residential), Catering, Community Work, Computers, Conservation Skills, Cooking, Counselling, Development Issues, DIY, Driving, First Aid, Forestry, Fundraising, Gardening/Horticulture, Group Work, International Aid, Library/Resource Centres,

Manual Work, Marketing/Publicity, Music, Newsletter/Journalism, Outdoor Skills, Religion, Research, Scientific Work, Social Work, Sport, Summer Camps, Teaching, Technical Skills, Theatre/Drama, Training, Translating, Visiting/Befriending, Work Camps – Seasonal.
Costs: Varies according to the project.
Worldwide placements: Australasia (New Zealand).

CO-ORDINATING COMMITTEE FOR INTERNATIONAL VOLUNTARY SERVICE

UNESCO House
1 rue Miollis
75732 Paris Cedex 15
France
T: 00 33.1.45 68 49 36
F: 00.33.1.42 73 05 21
E: ccivs@unesco.org
W: www.unesco.org/ccivs
Contact: Simona Costanzo Sow

CCIVS was created in 1948 under the aegis of UNESCO as an international non-governmental organisation responsible for the co-ordination of voluntary service world-wide. Its 142 member organisations implement voluntary programmes in the fields of environment, literacy, preservation of cultural heritage, aid to refugees, health service, emergency relief, development, social services. These programmes are generally carried out through workcamps, consisting of a national or an international group working on a common project. Please note that workcamps and longer-term projects are not organised directly by CCIVS, and that we do not recruit volunteers directly. These activities are carried out by CCIVS member organisations who undertake the recruitment. Our new public information centre provides information to volunteers wishing to participate in a project abroad (workcamps or longer-term projects). We provide directories on voluntary work abroad (explanation of what is a workcamp, how to participate, age, qualifications, expenses and useful advice) with the addresses of the organisations the volunteer needs to contact, costing €5 (7US$, 10DM, £3.50 or seven international reply coupons). Please send international reply coupons. ♿

Starting months: January–December
Time required: 1–52 weeks
Age: 15 plus – no upper limit
Causes: Archaeology, Children, Conservation, Disabled (learning and physical), Elderly People, Environmental Causes, Health Care/Medical, Heritage, Human Rights, Refugees, Teaching/assisting, Work Camps – Seasonal, Young People.
Activities: Administration, Agriculture/Farming, Building/Construction, Campaigning, Caring – General, Community Work, Conservation

Skills, Development Issues, First Aid, Forestry, Fundraising, Group Work, International Aid, Library/Resource Centres, Manual Work, Outdoor Skills, Research, Social Work, Summer Camps, Teaching, Technical Skills, Training, Work Camps – Seasonal.
Placements: 30,000
When to apply: All year.
Work alone/with others: Dependent on the placement.
Qualifications: Dependent on the placement.
Equipment/clothing: Dependent on the placement.
Health requirements: Dependent on the placement.
Costs: Dependent on the placement.
Benefits: Dependent on the placement.
Training: Dependent on the placement.
Supervision: Dependent on the placement.
Interviews: Dependent on the placement.
Worldwide placements: Africa (Algeria, Benin, Botswana, Burkina Faso, Burundi, Cape Verde, Congo Republic, Côte d'Ivoire, Ethiopia, Ghana, Kenya, Lesotho, Liberia, Libya, Mali, Mauritius, Morocco, Mozambique, Namibia, Nigeria, Reunion, Senegal, Sierra Leone, South Africa, Swaziland, Tanzania, Togo, Tunisia, Uganda, Zambia, Zimbabwe); North America: (Canada, Greenland, USA); Central America (Costa Rica, Cuba, Dominica, El Salvador, Guadeloupe, Guatemala, Honduras, Martinique, Mexico); South America (Argentina, Bolivia, Brazil, Chile, Colombia, Ecuador, Peru, Uruguay, Venezuela); Asia (Bangladesh, Cambodia, China, India, Indonesia, Israel, Japan, Korea (South), Lebanon, Malaysia, Maldives, Nepal, Pakistan, Philippines, Singapore, Sri Lanka, Taiwan, Thailand, Turkey, Vietnam); Australasia (Australia, New Zealand); Europe (Armenia, Austria, Azerbaijan, Belarus, Belgium, Bosnia-Herzegovina, Bulgaria, Croatia, Cyprus, Czech Republic, Denmark, Estonia, Finland, France, Georgia, Germany, Gibraltar, Greece, Hungary, Iceland, Ireland, Italy, Latvia, Liechtenstein, Lithuania, Malta, Netherlands, Norway, Poland, Portugal, Romania, Russia, Slovakia, Slovenia, Spain, Sweden, Switzerland, Turkey, Ukraine, Yugoslavia).

CORAL CAY CONSERVATION LTD

The Tower
13th Floor
125 High Street Colliers Wood
London
SW19 2JG UK
T: 0870 750 0668
F: 0870 750 0667
E: info@coralcay.org
W: www.coralcay.org
Contact: Andrea Simmons

Coral Cay Conservation (CCC) is seeking volunteers to assist with tropical forest and coral reef conservation projects throughout the

Asia-Pacific region and in the Caribbean. Volunteers can spend from two weeks participating on expeditions, with monthly departures throughout the year. The aim of CCC expeditions is to help gather data for the protection and sustainable use of tropical resources, and to offer poverty alleviation and alternative livelihood opportunities for local communities. Current CCC projects are based in the Philippines, Fiji and Honduras and Malaysia. No previous experience is required. Since 1986, thousands of CCC volunteers have helped establish eight new marine reserves and wildlife sanctuaries, including the Belize Barrier Reef World Heritage Site. CCC also requires volunteers to assist in a busy administration and scientific office in London. A limited number of scholarships are awarded on a discretionary basis for volunteer staff wishing to gain industrial experience in the marine and terrestrial sciences at CCC's London offices. Presentations take place at regular pre-arranged national/international venues. Volunteers with an offending background are accepted at the discretion of CCC. Alternative e-mail address: ccc@coralcay.org. Coral Cay Conservation is a member of The Year Out Group. 🖐

Number of projects: 5 UK: 0
Starting months: January–December
Time required: 2–52 weeks (plus)
Age: 16 plus – no upper limit
Causes: Conservation, Environmental Causes, Teaching/assisting, Wildlife.
Activities: Administration, Building/Construction, Community Work, Conservation Skills, Development Issues, DIY, First Aid, Forestry, Fundraising, Group Work, International Aid, Manual Work, Marketing/Publicity, Outdoor Skills, Research, Scientific Work, Sport, Teaching, Technical Skills, Training.
Placements: 400
When to apply: 3 months in advance is advised but depending on availability of projects.
Work alone/with others: In groups.
Equipment/clothing: Own basic equipment is required.
Health requirements: Must be reasonably fit.
Costs: Non divers: £1100 for 3 weeks Qualified divers: £700 for 2 weeks Rainforest Project: £550 for 2 weeks.
Benefits: Daily trekking on forest projects. Mixed dormitory style accommodation. Mattresses and mosquito nets provided.
Training: Full expedition training is provided on site. UK pre-departure meeting to meet fellow volunteers and expedition staff. Fully accredited scientific and expedition training courses, including SCUBA training are given.
Supervision: Trained and experienced expedition staff.

Interviews: During presentations, full expedition briefings given which are may be followed by informal group interviews.
Charity number: 1025534
Worldwide placements: (Honduras); Asia (Malaysia, Philippines); Australasia (Fiji).

CORNWALL WILDLIFE TRUST

Five Acres
Allet, Truro
Cornwall
TR4 9DJ UK
T: +44 (0) 1872 273939
F: +44 (0) 1872 225476
E: cornwt@cix.compulink.co.uk
W: www.wildlifetrust.org.uk/cornwall/
Contact: Gavin Henderson

Cornwall Wildlife Trust is a member of the Wildlife Trusts, a national partnership of 47 County Trusts. The aims of the Trust are primarily to: promote nature conservation in the community; acquire and manage nature reserves; monitor biological and geological resources; liaise with local authorities to promote regard for nature conservation; offer practical advice on nature conservation to landowners. It is the Trust's policy to involve all sectors of the community, of all ages, backgrounds, abilities and disabilities towards these ends. Volunteers require no previous experience just lots of enthusiasm. They will receive on-the-job training in an informal atmosphere and, if they desire, can go on to participate more fully assisting with the organisation and running of activities/projects. Limited opportunities may also arise, for those with a longer term commitment, for NVQ training to level 2 in Landscapes and Ecosystems. Volunteers with an offending background may be accepted – each case separately assessed. 🖐 📄

Number of projects: 25+ UK: 25+
Starting months: January–December
Time required: 1–52 weeks (plus)
Age: 16–70
Causes: Conservation, Environmental Causes, Wildlife.
Activities: Computers, Conservation Skills, Driving, Forestry, Gardening/Horticulture, Manual Work, Outdoor Skills, Research, Scientific Work, Technical Skills.
Placements: 150
When to apply: All year.
Work alone/with others: With others.
Qualifications: Nil but practical skills useful.
Equipment/clothing: Casual work clothes, waterproofs, stout boots. Protective safety gear is provided.
Health requirements: Any medical conditions (illness, allergy or physical disability) that may

require treatment/medication or which affects the volunteer working with machinery must be notified to us in advance. Tetanus injections must be up to date.
Costs: Bring your own packed lunch and any accommodation costs.
Benefits: Out of pocket expenses.
Training: On-the-job training provided.
Supervision: All volunteers are supported either directly by staff supervision or with experienced volunteers.
Interviews: Interviews at our office.
Charity number: 214929
UK placements: England (Cornwall).

CORPORACION COLOMBIANA DE TRABAJO VOLUNTARIO (CCTV)

Avenida Caracas No. 63 32 Torre Oeste
Oficina 301 y 301A
Sante Fe de Bogota
Colombia
T: 00 57 1 235 01 56
F: 00 57 1 640 54 93
E: cctv@multiphone.net.co
Contact: Luz Stella Alvarez

Corporacion Colombiana de Trabajo Voluntario (CCTV) promotes and has information about volunteering in Colombia. It may well be able to put volunteers in touch with organisations which are not yet listed on the WorldWide Volunteering database.

Starting months: January–December
Time required: 1–52 weeks (plus)
Age: 16 plus – no upper limit
Causes: Addicts/Ex-Addicts, AIDS/HIV, Animal Welfare, Archaeology, Architecture, Children, Conservation, Disabled (learning and physical), Elderly People, Environmental Causes, Health Care/Medical, Heritage, Holidays for Disabled, Human Rights, Inner City Problems, Offenders/Ex-Offenders, Poor/Homeless, Refugees, Teaching/assisting (nursery, primary, secondary, mature, EFL) Unemployed, Wildlife, Work Camps – Seasonal, Young People.
Activities: Accountancy, Administration, Agriculture/Farming, Arts/Crafts, Building/Construction, Campaigning, Caring (general, day and residential), Catering, Community Work, Computers, Conservation Skills, Cooking, Counselling, Development Issues, DIY, Driving, First Aid, Forestry, Fundraising, Gardening/Horticulture, Group Work, International Aid, Library/Resource Centres, Manual Work, Marketing/Publicity, Music, Newsletter/Journalism, Outdoor Skills, Religion, Research, Scientific Work, Social Work, Sport, Summer Camps, Teaching, Technical Skills, Theatre/Drama, Training, Translating, Visiting/Befriending, Work Camps – Seasonal.
Costs: Varies according to the project.

Worldwide placements: South America (Colombia).

CORPORACION DE ACCION VOLUNTARIA VOLUNTAR – CHILE

Avenida Italia 929
Providencia
Santiago
Chile
T: 00 56 22096408
F: 00 56 22096408
E: funacion@fsoles.cl
W: www.guiasolidaria.cl
Contact: Daniela Thumala

Corporacion de Accion Voluntaria Voluntar promotes and has information about volunteering in Chile. The mission of Voluntar is to promote a volunteering culture in Chile. For that purpose, Voluntar links volunteers with social agencies. It also gives training to social agencies in volunteering management. It may well be able to put volunteers in touch with organisations which are not yet listed on the WorldWide Volunteering database.

Starting months: January–December
Time required: 1–52 weeks (plus)
Age: 16 plus – no upper limit
Causes: Addicts/Ex-Addicts, AIDS/HIV, Animal Welfare, Archaeology, Architecture, Children, Conservation, Disabled (learning and physical), Elderly People, Environmental Causes, Health Care/Medical, Heritage, Holidays for Disabled, Human Rights, Inner City Problems, Offenders/Ex-Offenders, Poor/Homeless, Refugees, Teaching/assisting (nursery, primary, secondary, mature, EFL) Unemployed, Wildlife, Work Camps – Seasonal, Young People.
Activities: Accountancy, Administration, Agriculture/Farming, Arts/Crafts, Building/Construction, Campaigning, Caring (general, day and residential), Catering, Community Work, Computers, Conservation Skills, Cooking, Counselling, Development Issues, DIY, Driving, First Aid, Forestry, Fundraising, Gardening/Horticulture, Group Work, International Aid, Library/Resource Centres, Manual Work, Marketing/Publicity, Music, Newsletter/Journalism, Outdoor Skills, Religion, Research, Scientific Work, Social Work, Sport, Summer Camps, Teaching, Technical Skills, Theatre/Drama, Training, Translating, Visiting/Befriending, Work Camps – Seasonal.
Placements: 2000
When to apply: Any start month.
Costs: Varies according to the project.
Interviews: It depends on the social agencies.
Worldwide placements: South America (Chile).

CORPORACIÓN PARA EL DESAROLLO DEL APRENDIZAJE (CDA)

Grajales 2561
Santiago Centro
Chile
T: 00 56 2 689 1633
F: 00 56 2 689 1633
E: cdachile@terra.cl
Contact: Helena Todd or Myriam Leoz

Corporación para el Desarollo del Aprendizaje (CDA) is a foundation for the treatment and stimulation of 5–18 year olds with neuro-cognitive deficit from deprived backgrounds who also attend the normal school system. The family also receives attention. Volunteers may provide auxiliary service to the children and youths, in the preparation of didactic materials, in fund raising and organisational activities, and other suitable activities according to the talents shown on their CV. Volunteers should be aware that they must not travel to the north of Chile into the mountain regions if there is any heart weakness. (We have no centres there but volunteers like to travel and visit.) ♿

Number of projects: 15 **UK:** 0
Starting months: Mar, Jul
Time required: 16–50 weeks
Age: 18–25
Causes: Children, Disabled (learning and physical), Elderly People, Health Care/Medical, Inner City Problems, Teaching/assisting (primary, secondary, EFL), Young People.
Activities: Administration, Caring – General, Community Work, Computers, First Aid, Fundraising, Group Work, Library/Resource Centres, Music, Newsletter/Journalism, Social Work, Teaching, Technical Skills, Translating, Visiting/Befriending.
Placements: 2–4
When to apply: Up to two months prior to arrival.
Work alone/with others: Depends on project – probably both.
Qualifications: None but Spanish useful – as are art and computer skills.
Equipment/clothing: Huge seasonal and geographical variations in climate. Sleeping bags, drivers licence, towels and sheets. English music/family photos etc.
Health requirements: We care for minor illnesses. Recommend wisdom teeth removed prior to travel. If spectacles are worn, please bring spare pair. Volunteers should eat well and sensibly.
Costs: The volunteer has to cover everything. We do however provide very cheap board and lodging in Santiago and Illapel. We are aiming to provide the same in Magallanes and Concepcion.
Benefits: Help to find paid TEFL positions. Paid travel with CDA Professionals to regions other than where volunteers are located, also for participation in some events in Santiago. Latin American fiction and professional articles on care available. We find cheap board and lodging for volunteers either in Santiago or the regions.
Training: 3–4 weeks at our main centre in Santiago.
Supervision: Volunteers are assigned to one therapist and have a monthly meeting with the Director.
Interviews: Applicants are interviewed only by communication by letter, fax or e-mail.
Charity number: DofL 659
Worldwide placements: South America (Chile).

CORPS VOLONTAIRES CONGOLAIS AU DEVELOPPEMENT (COVOZADE)

7 Rue Meteo
Quartier Kimpe
Commune de Ngaliema
Kinshasa
3410 Kin/Gombe Democratic Rep of Congo
F: 001 770 240 2901/2902/2985
Contact: Joseph Milamba Kasongo

We aim to increase the awareness of the social problems throughout Zaire as well as to help with the particularly deprived areas. Volunteers are needed to work on long term projects with a minimum of a three month commitment, and a maximum of a year. COVOZADE also promotes and has information about volunteering in Zaire. It may well be able to put volunteers in touch with organisations which are not yet listed on the WorldWide Volunteering database. 📄

Number of projects: 1 **UK:** 0
Starting months: January–December
Time required: 12–52 weeks
Age: 17–30
Causes: AIDS/HIV, Architecture, Children, Conservation, Environmental Causes, Health Care/Medical, Human Rights, Inner City Problems, Offenders/Ex-Offenders, Poor/Homeless, Teaching/assisting (primary, secondary), Work Camps – Seasonal, Young People.
Activities: Agriculture/Farming, Arts/Crafts, Building/Construction, Campaigning, Caring (general, day and residential), Community Work, Computers, Conservation Skills, Development Issues, Forestry, Fundraising, Group Work, Library/Resource Centres, Manual Work, Newsletter/Journalism, Outdoor Skills, Religion, Research, Scientific Work, Social Work, Summer Camps, Teaching, Technical Skills, Training, Translating, Visiting/Befriending, Work Camps – Seasonal.
Placements: 35

When to apply: All year.
Work alone/with others: With others.
Qualifications: French or English speaking. Post A-level, International Baccaleureate or university.
Equipment/clothing: Sunshade and umbrella! Our country is tropical! Camera and films etc.
Health requirements: Medical certificate confirming that the volunteer is healthy to work in a tropical country.
Costs: Travel to Kinshasa, subsistence fees as follows: 0–3 months US$500, 4–6 months US$800, 7–12 months US$1,000. Registration Fee of US$150 to be paid before arrival.
Benefits: Modest accommodation, local travel to project and pocket money.
Charity number: 73–309
Worldwide placements: Africa (Congo Dem Republic).

CORRYMEELA COMMUNITY

5 Drumaroan Road
Ballycastle
Co. Antrim BT54 6QU N. Ireland
T: 028 2076 2626
F: 028 2076 2770
E: ballycastle@corrymeela.org.uk
Contact: Oona Faloona

Corrymeela is a dispersed Christian community, founded in 1965, that is committed to the healing of social, religious, and political divisions that exist in Northern Ireland and throughout the world. Corrymeela seeks to offer a safe place in which people can meet one another as they are, and thus enable new relationships to grow. Corrymeela's work is grounded on the belief that reconciliation is central to finding new ways to live together, at both personal and societal levels. Each year Corrymeela recruits a team of ten volunteers to assist the permanent staff in the running of the Ballycastle centre. The commitment is usually for one year, starting in September, with two six-month volunteers being added in March. Full-time volunteers form an integral part of the Corrymeela programme. We try each year to include people from a range of social, religious and cultural backgrounds. Usually, about half the team are from outside Northern Ireland. Volunteers help with all aspects of the work at Ballycastle, an eight-acre residential village on the beautiful north coast of County Antrim. The work includes hosting groups, planning activities, cooking, leading discussions, assisting, housekeeping, showing visitors around, working on reception, singing, leading worship, staffing the tuck shop, driving (if you have a bus driver's licence) and much more. Volunteers have two days off in every ten days and four weeks annual holiday. Volunteers give a great deal of themselves, not only to fellow members of the team but also to those who come to the centre. At times this can lead to long working days (up to 16 hours), and the work is not always 'glamorous'. Corrymeela is definitely not a place for those who seek a regular work experience! This, together with the tensions which will be experienced by any small group living together in a community, results in a way of life that is challenging, sometimes demanding, but also unusually rewarding and enriching. Approximately 25 volunteers are also needed during each week of July/August for 1–3 weeks. Volunteers with an offending background may be accepted depending on the offence. &

Number of projects: 200–300 UK: 200–300
Starting months: Mar, Jul, Aug, Sep
Time required: 1–52 weeks
Age: 18 plus – no upper limit
Causes: Children, Disabled (learning and physical), Elderly People, Environmental Causes, Inner City Problems, Offenders/Ex-Offenders, Teaching/assisting (nursery, primary, secondary), Unemployed, Young People.
Activities: Administration, Arts/Crafts, Caring (general, residential), Community Work, Computers, Cooking, Counselling, Development Issues, Driving, Fundraising, Group Work, Manual Work, Music, Outdoor Skills, Religion, Sport, Summer Camps, Teaching, Theatre/Drama, Visiting/Befriending.
Placements: 200–300
When to apply: March (12 mth), October (6 mth)
Work alone/with others: Both.
Qualifications: Nil required but all skills helpful and valued.
Health requirements: Nil.
Costs: Travel to and from Corrymeela.
Benefits: Free board and lodging. Accommodation for 12 and 6 month volunteers is provided in a house. Volunteers share a room with another volunteer.
Training: Provided at the beginning of the placement.
Supervision: Regular meetings in group, and monthly supervisions with the Volunteer Co-ordinator.
Interviews: Interviews normally take place in Ballycastle but elsewhere also sometimes.
Charity number: XN48052A
UK placements: Northern Ireland (Antrim).

COTRAVAUX

11 rue de Clichy
Paris
75009 France
T: 00 33 1 4874 7920
F: 00 33 1 4874 1401
E: cotravaux@clubinternet.fr
Contact: National Delegate

Cotravaux directs young people from any country to the workcamp organisations, working on projects across Europe, Asia, America and Africa. Cotravaux is the co-ordination of 12 French organisatons, most of which have links with international networks.

Number of projects: Many **UK:** Many
Starting months: January–December
Time required: 2–4 weeks
Age: 14 plus – no upper limit
Causes: Archaeology, Architecture, Conservation, Disabled (learning and physical), Environmental Causes, Heritage, Human Rights, Inner City Problems, Refugees, Work Camps – Seasonal, Young People.
Activities: Catering, Community Work, Cooking, Gardening/Horticulture, Group Work, International Aid, Manual Work, Outdoor Skills, Work Camps – Seasonal.
Placements: Very many.
When to apply: Any time but during April is best because a large number of workcamps run between May to October.
Work alone/with others: With others.
Qualifications: Must be able to speak French, English or Spanish.
Equipment/clothing: Detailed in a specific info. sheet.
Health requirements: Must be in good physical and mental health.
Costs: Travel, registration, insurance.
Interviews: No, but a motivation letter could be requested or some previous volunteer experiences on some camps.
Worldwide placements: Africa (Benin, Botswana, Burkina Faso, Côte d'Ivoire, Ghana, Kenya, Lesotho, Morocco, Mozambique, Senegal, Sierra Leone, South Africa, Tanzania, Togo, Tunisia, Uganda, Zimbabwe); North America: (Canada, Greenland, USA); Central America (Costa Rica, Cuba, El Salvador, Guatemala, Mexico, Nicaragua, Panama); South America (Argentina, Bolivia, Brazil, Chile, Colombia, Ecuador, Paraguay, Peru); Asia (Bangladesh, Cambodia, China, India, Japan, Korea (South), Lebanon, Nepal, Palestinian Authority, Philippines, Sri Lanka, Thailand, Turkey, Vietnam); Australasia (Australia); Europe (Albania, Armenia, Austria, Azerbaijan, Belarus, Belgium, Bosnia-Herzegovina, Bulgaria, Croatia, Czech Republic, Denmark, Finland, France, Germany, Greece, Hungary, Ireland, Italy, Latvia, Lithuania, Macedonia, Netherlands, Norway, Poland, Portugal, Romania, Russia, Slovakia, Slovenia, Spain, Sweden, Switzerland, Turkey, Ukraine, Yugoslavia).
UK placements: England (Isle of Wight, Leicestershire); Scotland (Edinburgh); Northern Ireland (Belfast City); Wales (Cardiff).

CRESSET HOUSE CAMPHILL VILLAGE

P.O. Box 74
Halfway House
1685 Gauteng South Africa
E: cresset@iafrica.com
Contact: Anna Haberkorn

Cresset House Camphill Village is an urban village community with adults with intellectual disabilities. We have a large organic vegetable garden contract, card workshop and bakery. Between Johannesburg and Pretoria, semi-rural. 🗎

Number of projects: 1 **UK:** 0
Starting months: Jul, Aug
Time required: 52 weeks (plus)
Age: 19–50
Causes: Disabled (learning and physical), Environmental Causes, Teaching/assisting.
Activities: Agriculture/Farming, Arts/Crafts, Caring (general, residential), Community Work, Cooking, Counselling, Driving, Gardening/Horticulture, Religion, Social Work, Sport, Training.
Placements: 5–6
When to apply: February/March
Work alone/with others: Both.
Qualifications: Spoken English and willingness to help wherever needed (workshops, land, houses).
Equipment/clothing: Working clothes and good clothes for Sunday festivities.
Health requirements: Volunteers should be healthy – teeth in good condition.
Costs: Travel costs to and from RSA.
Benefits: Board, lodging, acute medical and dental costs, pocket money R380 a month.
Training: Informal training on the job.
Supervision: Volunteers are supervised by work masters and house leaders.
Interviews: Volunteers are not interviewed – only via correspondence.
Worldwide placements: Africa (South Africa).

CRIME CONCERN TRUST

London Office
89 Albert Embankment
London
SE1 7TS UK
T: +44 (0) 20 7361 820 6012
F: +44 (0) 20 7361 587 1617
E: info@crimeconcern.org.uk
W: www.crimeconcern.org.uk
Contact: Adrian Smith

Crime Concern is a national crime prevention charity specialising in youth crime, criminality prevention, high crime neighbourhoods, women's safety, business and town centre crime, rural crime and school, hospital and passenger safety. We manage around 60 projects across England and Wales, prepare crime surveys, reports and briefings and work in partnership with local authorities, police, housing and youth agencies, businesses and parish councils. Our projects are centred on London, Manchester, West Midlands, Nottingham and Bath although we have several other areas. ⑤

Number of projects: 60 **UK:** 60
Starting months: January–December
Time required: 1–52 weeks (plus)
Age: 16 plus – no upper limit
Causes: Children, Environmental Causes, Inner City Problems, Offenders/Ex-Offenders, Young People.
Activities: Administration, Community Work, Fundraising, Group Work, Social Work, Sport, Summer Camps, Visiting/Befriending.
Placements: 600–700
When to apply: Any time.
Work alone/with others: With others.
Qualifications: Interest in community work and young people. A police check will be needed for those working with young people.
Health requirements: Nil.
Costs: Accommodation.
Benefits: Expenses paid.
Training: Training as required is provided.
Supervision: Supervision as required.
Interviews: Interview is part of the selection process.
UK placements: England (Bedfordshire, Bristol, Devon, Hampshire, Kent, Leicestershire, London, Manchester, Merseyside, Northumberland, Nottinghamshire, Somerset, Staffordshire, Tyne and Wear, Warwickshire, West Midlands, Wiltshire); Wales (Cardiff, Vale of Glamorgan).

CRISIS

64 Commercial Street
London
E1 6LT UK
T: +44 (0) 207 426 3873
F: 0870 011 3336
E: micky.walsh@crisis.org.uk
W: www.crisis.org.uk
Contact: Micky Walsh

Crisis is the national charity for solitary homeless people, that works year round to help vulnerable and marginalised people get through the crisis of homelessness, fulfill their potential and transform their lives. We have a range of volunteering opportunities including drivers, navigators and sorters for FareShare, our national food redistribution service. Receptionists and hosts for Crisis Skylight, our innovative activities centre. Office roles including database work, fundraising, admin, marketing and communications. Hundreds of volunteers are needed between December 23–30 to run our five London shelters for Crisis Open Christmas. Office based work and Skylight roles will be at 64–66 Commercial Street, London. ⑤

Number of projects: 1 **UK:** 1
Starting months: Jan, Feb, Mar, Apr, May, Jun, Jul, Aug, Sep, Oct, Nov
Time required: 1–52 weeks (plus)
Age: 16–75
Causes: Poor/Homeless.
Activities: Administration, Arts/Crafts, Computers, Fundraising, Marketing/Publicity, Teaching, Theatre/Drama.
Placements: 3000
When to apply: All year.
Work alone/with others: With others.
Qualifications: Nil, except enthusiasm and commitment.
Costs: Board and lodging.
Benefits: Travel expenses provided.
Training: General induction for all volunteers – other training tends to be 'on the job'.
Supervision: Named supervisor for all volunteers.
Interviews: General for all volunteers – specific for certain roles.
UK placements: England (London).

CROSS-CULTURAL SOLUTIONS

47 Potter Avenue
New Rochelle
New York 10801 USA
T: 001 914 632 0022
F: 001 914 632 8494
E: info@crossculturalsolutions.org
W: www.crossculturalsolutions.org
Contact: Sarah Pole

Cross-cultural Solutions is a leading international volunteer organisation in the US and sends 1,000 volunteers overseas a year. We are an independent, non-religious, non-profit organisation that employs volunteer humanitarian action to empower local communities, foster cultural sensitivity and understanding, and contribute grassroots solutions to global challenges. We work in partnership with over 100 non profit humanitarian organisations around the world, including both large, international NGOs and grassroots organisations in the countries where we send volunteers. We maintain field offices in five countries and have a staff of approx 100 worldwide. In keeping with our philosophy of 'local people are the experts' each of our offices is staffed exclusively by host country nationals. Our directors are local leaders in their fields and typically have decades of development experience. The executive director and founder is Steven C Rosenthal. Since September 11th we have been playing a key role in recruitment and co-ordination of volunteers for the World Trade Center Disaster site. Through partnerships with the American Red Cross, The Salvation Army, the September 11th fund and others, our organisation has provided over 5,000 volunteers to the relief effort. CARE, one of the world's largest international humanitarian organisations, recently honored us by choosing us as its strategic partner to operate the CARE Corps Volunteer programme. We are a member of the International Volunteer Programmes Association and the New Rochelle Chamber of Commerce. Our organisation has been featured in over 300 publications and broadcasts. Asia, Africa, Latin America, Eastern Europe. 🔊 📄

Number of projects: 6 UK: 0
Starting months: January–December
Time required: 2–24 weeks
Age: 18 plus – no upper limit
Causes: Addicts/Ex-Addicts, AIDS/HIV, Children, Disabled (learning and physical), Elderly People, Environmental Causes, Health Care/Medical, Heritage, Inner City Problems, Offenders/Ex-Offenders, Poor/Homeless, Teaching/assisting (nursery, primary, secondary, mature, EFL) Unemployed, Young People.
Activities: Arts/Crafts, Caring (general, day and residential), Community Work, Computers, Counselling, Development Issues, First Aid, Fundraising, Group Work, International Aid, Library/Resource Centres, Marketing/Publicity, Music, Newsletter/Journalism, Research, Social Work, Sport, Summer Camps, Teaching, Technical Skills, Theatre/Drama, Training, Visiting/Befriending.
Placements: 1000
When to apply: All year.
Work alone/with others: With others.
Qualifications: No special skills are required. No restrictions.
Equipment/clothing: Varies.
Health requirements: Certain medical requirements to volunteer in Russia.
Costs: Programme fee begins at $1200 for one week in Peru and varies depending on country and length of stay.
Benefits: The opportunity to serve others, cross-cultural exchange, the chance to learn new skills or try out a potential career (teaching, health care), new friendships, a new perspective on the world. Dorm, hotel or house maintained by us year round in each country. Participants live with their fellow volunteers and the local staff. Housing, meals and in country transportation are included in the programme fee.
Training: None given, nor required.
Supervision: Country director and local staff provide support.
Interviews: Skills and interests survey given to match volunteer with placement, re-entry interview by phone.
Worldwide placements: Africa (Ghana, Tanzania); Central America (Costa Rica); South America (Brazil, Peru); Asia (China, India, Thailand); Europe (Russia).

CROSSLINKS

251 Lewisham Way
London
SE4 1XF UK
T: +44 (0) 208 691 6111
F: +44 (0) 208 694 8023
E: smile@crosslinks.org
W: www.crosslinks.org
Contact: Oliver Leonard

Crosslinks is an Anglican evangelical mission agency, working worldwide in partnership with churches and other agencies. It supports mission partners, study partners and projects and links these with local churches in Britain and Ireland. Our SMILE programme (Short-term Mission Involvement, Learning and Experience) gives you the opportunity to find out what it is like to take God's word to God's world. Whether you have a week or two, or six months, to spare, here is the chance for you to do something really useful for the Gospel. SMILE volunteers have been seen around the world – teaching in Tanzania, working on holiday clubs in Ireland, or studying wildlife in Portugal. There is even the opportunity to teach English in China, or to study Mandarin. Ireland has summer holiday clubs. Portugal has environmental work. China has language placements. Kenya, Tanzania and Uganda are maximum six months placements. Volunteers with an offending background will probably be accepted. 🔊

Number of projects: 6 UK: 1
Starting months: Jan, Jul, Aug, Sep
Time required: 1–52 weeks
Age: 18–65
Causes: Children, Conservation, Environmental Causes, Poor/Homeless, Teaching/assisting (primary, secondary, EFL).
Activities: Building/Construction, Conservation Skills, Development Issues, Religion, Sport, Summer Camps, Teaching.
Placements: 50
When to apply: All year.
Work alone/with others: With other young volunteers.
Qualifications: Training in TEFL (teaching English as a Foreign Language) for some placements (i.e. China).
Equipment/clothing: No specific equipment or clothings is required.
Health requirements: Good health is essential, particularly for Africa. Some innoculations recommended.
Costs: For Africa: travel costs £500 approximately and subsistence £1500 for six months.
For UK: £30 per week subsistence plus travel. Insurance necessary for all.
Benefits: Accommodation provided for overseas projects.

Training: Comprehensive pre-departure training is provided.
Supervision: All volunteers are placed near long-term overseas personnel.
Interviews: Interviews take place in London or the UK regions.
Worldwide placements: Africa (Kenya, Tanzania, Uganda); Asia (China); Europe (Ireland, Portugal).
UK placements: Northern Ireland (Antrim).

CRUSADERS

FREEPOST 544
2 Romeland Hill
St Albans
Hertfordshire AL3 4ET UK
T: 01727 855422
F: 01727 848518
E: crusoe@crusaders.org.uk
W: www.crusaders.org.uk
Contact: Jenny MacDonald

Crusaders is an international youth organisation helping churches and volunteers reach young people with the Christian message, through youth groups, holiday programmes and overseas projects. The emphasis is on relevance and on equipping volunteers with leadership training, active teaching materials and the latest specialist youth resources, through local and national support. Committed Christians are invited to volunteer as youth leaders for new or existing youth groups, as holiday staff, for short term service opportunities overseas or in the UK. Youth leaders: aged 21+. Training is given for new leaders in all the important skills. Assistant leaders: aged 17+, nominated by local leaders. Group helpers: aged 15–16 who have leadership potential and are beginning to assist the group appointed by local leaders. Training through new 'Into Action' programme. Holiday staff: roles include small group team leaders, speakers, catering staff, programme planners; anyone aged 17+, with tremendous energy and enthusiasm for young people can apply; those with gifts in specialist areas such as sports, music, etc especially welcome. CRUSOE (Crusaders Overseas Expeditions): for any committed young Christian aged 14–22 to put faith into practice in projects during Summer break. Selection w/e in February and de-brief w/e in September. Romania Project: aged 18+, to help Romanian Christians run holiday camps for young people. Fund raisers and supporters – a valuable role for volunteers. Volunteers with an offending background may be accepted depending on circumstances and subject to references. ♿

Number of projects: 511 UK: 500
Starting months: Jul, Aug, Sep
Time required: 1–5 weeks
Age: 14–80
Causes: Children, Holidays for Disabled, Poor/Homeless, Teaching/assisting, Work Camps – Seasonal, Young People.
Activities: Administration, Arts/Crafts, Building/Construction, Catering, Community Work, Cooking, Development Issues, First Aid, Fundraising, Group Work, International Aid, Manual Work, Marketing/Publicity, Music, Outdoor Skills, Religion, Social Work, Summer Camps, Teaching, Translating, Work Camps – Seasonal.
Placements: 150
When to apply: November–February for CRUSOE; May for Romania; all year for UK.
Work alone/with others: With others.
Qualifications: Varies according to vacancy. Sympathetic with Christian basis of the organisation.
Equipment/clothing: Variable.
Health requirements: Need to have good health for heavy overseas projects.
Costs: £500–£1400 to fund trip for CRUSOE scheme.
Benefits: The cost covers all needs. Accommodation is basic, some camping, some on floor in buildings and some on mattresses.
Training: Depends on project. Normally one weekend pre-placement training a minimum.
Supervision: 18s supervised by leaders.
Interviews: CRUSOE selection weekends take place in Central England, Scotland and Northern Ireland.
Charity number: 223798
Worldwide placements: Africa (Kenya, South Africa, Tunisia, Uganda, Zambia, Zimbabwe); Central America (Costa Rica, El Salvador, Guatemala, Honduras, Mexico, Nicaragua, Panama); South America (Bolivia, Brazil, Chile); Asia (India, Philippines, Thailand); Europe (France, Germany, Ireland, Lithuania, Poland, Portugal, Romania, Switzerland).
UK placements: England (Bedfordshire, Berkshire, Bristol, Buckinghamshire, Cambridgeshire, Channel Islands, Cheshire, Cornwall, Cumbria, Derbyshire, Devon, Dorset, Essex, Gloucestershire, Hampshire, Hertfordshire, Isle of Man, Isle of Wight, Kent, Lancashire, Leicestershire, Lincolnshire, London, Manchester, Merseyside, Norfolk, Northamptonshire, Northumberland, Nottinghamshire, Oxfordshire, Shropshire, Somerset, Staffordshire, Suffolk, Surrey, E. Sussex, W. Sussex, Tyne and Wear, Warwickshire, West Midlands, Wiltshire, S. Yorkshire, W. Yorkshire); Scotland (throughout); Northern Ireland (throughout); Wales (Bridgend, Caerphilly, Cardiff, Conwy, Gwynedd, Newport, Powys, Rhondda, Cynon, Taff, Vale of Glamorgan).

CUBA SOLIDARITY CAMPAIGN (CSC), THE

Red Rose Club
129 Seven Sisters Road
London
N7 7QG UK
T: +44 (0) 207 263 6452
T: +44 (0) 207 561 0191
E: tours@cuba-solidarity.org.uk
W: www.cuba-solidarity.org.uk
Contact: Simon Bull

The Cuba Solidarity Campaign works to develop understanding of Cuba and to build support for the following positions: respect for Cuba's right to sovereignty and independence; an end to the USA's trade blockade against Cuba. Twice a year CSC sends a delegation to join groups from other European countries on an international brigade. During their three weeks' stay, brigadistas work with Cubans mainly on agricultural projects. Visits to schools, hospitals, factories and places of cultural and historic interest are organised as well as meetings with representatives of Cuba's mass organisations. The brigade is an excellent opportunity to witness Cuban society at first hand. Volunteers with an offending background are accepted. Second web site: www.cubaconnect.co.uk. &

Number of projects: 2 UK: 0
Starting months: Jul, Dec
Time required: 3–52 weeks
Age: 16–75
Causes: Conservation, Environmental Causes, Human Rights, Young People.
Activities: Agriculture/Farming, Building/Construction, Conservation Skills, Development Issues, International Aid, Manual Work, Music, Outdoor Skills.
Placements: 80–100
When to apply: Any time, preferably 3–4 months prior to departure.
Work alone/with others: With others, including alongside Cuban volunteers.
Qualifications: Wish to help Cuba and Cuban people.
Health requirements: Nil.
Costs: Travel costs and contribution to accommodation, food and local travel (£850 approx).
Benefits: Will be able to see the real Cuba away from the tourist locations – experience of a lifetime. All accommodation is provided at a purpose-built centre near Havana.
Training: Participants should attend a preparation day in London where sessions are given on Cuban life, daily life on the brigade, and the volunteers can get to know each other and plan solidarity action.
Supervision: During work times there is supervision to ensure safety.

Interviews: Application form.
Worldwide placements: (Cuba).

CULTURAL CUBE LTD

16 Acland Road
Ivybridge
Devon PL21 9UR UK
T: 0870 742 6932
F: 0870 742 6935
E: info@culturalcube.co.uk
W: www.culturalcube.co.uk
Contact: Tim Swale-Jarman

Cultural Cube provides programmes and information for young people who wish to experience a different culture through travel, temporary work, volunteering, study or internship. Acceptance of volunteers with an offending background would be dependent on work to be undertaken and eligibility for the visa, if required. &

Number of projects: 4 UK: 0
Starting months: Jan, Mar, Apr, Jun, Jul, Aug, Sep, Oct
Time required: 2–8 weeks
Age: 18 plus – no upper limit
Causes: Archaeology, Conservation, Environmental Causes, Health Care/Medical, Heritage, Poor/Homeless, Teaching/assisting (nursery, primary, EFL), Work Camps – Seasonal, Young People.
Activities: Building/Construction, Caring – General, Community Work, Conservation Skills, DIY, Manual Work, Summer Camps, Teaching, Work Camps – Seasonal.
Placements: 80
When to apply: Applications are accepted at any time, participation is determined by project dates.
Work alone/with others: Work with others in Armenia and Italy. Working alone with guidance in Nepal and Brazil.
Qualifications: None for general projects in Armenia and Italy. Good level of English for Nepal Project and TEFL qualification for Brazil English Teaching project.
Health requirements: Must be in good health.
Costs: Details of the costs for each project are detailed on our web site.
Benefits: Check specific project details on web.
Training: Local training/orientation relevant to the specific project is given prior to commencement.
Supervision: Volunteers are supervised – varies according to project.
Interviews: Interviews are required for projects involving work with young people.
Worldwide placements: South America (Brazil); Asia (Nepal); Europe (Armenia, Italy).

CVSS/UNITED WAY OF JAMAICA, THE

122–126 Tower Street
Kingston
Jamaica
T: 00 (876) 92 294 24 7
F: 00 (876) 922 1033
E: vwj35@hotmail.com
W: www.unitedwayja.org
Contact: Elon E. Beckford

The CVSS/United Way of Jamaica promotes and has information about volunteering in Jamaica. It may well be able to put volunteers in touch with organisations which are not yet listed on the WorldWide Volunteering database.

Starting months: January–December
Time required: 12–52 weeks (plus)
Age: 21–99
Causes: Addicts/Ex-Addicts, AIDS/HIV, Animal Welfare, Archaeology, Architecture, Children, Conservation, Disabled (learning and physical), Elderly People, Environmental Causes, Health Care/Medical, Heritage, Human Rights, Inner City Problems, Offenders/Ex-Offenders, Poor/Homeless, Teaching/assisting (nursery, primary, secondary, mature), Unemployed, Wildlife,

Work Camps – Seasonal, Young People.
Activities: Accountancy, Administration, Agriculture/Farming, Arts/Crafts, Building/Construction, Campaigning, Caring (general, day and residential), Catering, Community Work, Computers, Conservation Skills, Cooking, Counselling, Development Issues, DIY, Driving, First Aid, Forestry, Fundraising, Gardening/Horticulture, Group Work, International Aid, Library/Resource Centres, Manual Work, Marketing/Publicity, Music, Newsletter/Journalism, Outdoor Skills, Religion, Research, Scientific Work, Social Work, Sport, Summer Camps, Teaching, Technical Skills, Theatre/Drama, Training, Translating, Visiting/Befriending, Work Camps – Seasonal.
When to apply: Any time.
Work alone/with others: With others.
Qualifications: Must be fluent in English.
Costs: Varies according to the project. Accommodation is the responsibility of the volunteer. Assistance would be given to identify suitable accommodation.
Training: Provided.
Supervision: Provided.
Worldwide placements: Central America (Jamaica).

D

D.C.F. PREMIER WORKSHOPS TRUST
211 Wick Road
Brislington
Bristol
BS4 4HP UK
T: 0117 985 1188
F: 0117 985 1188
E: dcfpremier@aol.com
W: www.members.aol.com/dcfpremier
Contact: Peter Hamar

DCF Premier Workshops Trust is open five days a week throughout the year providing a working environment for people with disabilities. We are a Christian charity open to all volunteers of any or no persuasion. Volunteers with an offending background have to be agreed by the local authority. ♿ 📖

Number of projects: 1 UK: 1
Starting months: January–December
Time required: 1–44 weeks
Age: 16–65
Causes: Disabled (learning and physical).
Activities: Arts/Crafts, Catering, Computers, Cooking, Fundraising, Gardening/Horticulture, Music, Newsletter/Journalism, Technical Skills.
Placements: 3+
When to apply: Any time.
Work alone/with others: With others.
Qualifications: Caring nature.
Health requirements: Nil.
Costs: All costs except free travel to centre.
Benefits: Occasionally 2-course lunch for £1.30, free travel to centre. Accommodation may be able to be provided.
Training: Any training which is necessary would be given.
Supervision: Always supervision at all times.
Interviews: Interviews take place at our office.
UK placements: England (Bristol).

DAKSHINAYAN
A5/108, Clifton Apartments
Charmwood Village, Eros Gardens
Surajkund Road
Faridabad – 121009
121009 India
T: 00 91 129 5253114
F: 00 91 11 6484468
E: dakshinayan@vsnl.com
W: www.linkindia.com/dax
Contact: Siddharth Sanyal

Dakshinayan aims to promote international and intercultural understanding through the Development Education Programme. The aim of the programme is to introduce concerned and sensitive individuals to rural development projects in India so that they may gain an in-depth understanding of the myth and reality of 'third world poverty'. The programme is not meant for 'helping the poor, underdeveloped' people living in Indian villages, but rather to participate in what is being done by grassroots development projects. The programme is open to both skilled and unskilled participants. Those who wish to join the programme should be seriously interested in visiting a rural development project and understanding the reality of rural India. It should not matter to them where they are placed nor to what work they are assigned. Dakshinayan has a policy of sending not more than two or three participants to a project at the same time. This facilitates better integration and interaction with the community and project. It also ensures that the natural rhythm of the project is not disturbed. 📖

Number of projects: 3 UK: 0
Starting months: January–December
Time required: 4–32 weeks
Age: 18–60
Causes: Children, Conservation, Elderly People, Environmental Causes, Health Care/Medical, Teaching/assisting (nursery, primary, EFL), Wildlife.
Activities: Administration, Agriculture/Farming, Arts/Crafts, Building/Construction, Caring – General, Community Work, Conservation Skills, Cooking, Development Issues, First Aid, Forestry, Fundraising, Gardening/Horticulture, Group Work, International Aid, Manual Work, Music, Newsletter/Journalism, Outdoor Skills, Social Work, Sport, Teaching, Technical Skills, Training, Translating, Visiting/Befriending, Work Camps – Seasonal.
Placements: 200
When to apply: 1 month prior to arrival.
Work alone/with others: Yes with other young volunteers.
Health requirements: Physically and mentally fit.
Costs: Registration fee of $50 + fares + $150 per month.
Benefits: The cost covers board and lodging.
Interviews: Prospective volunteers are screened in New Delhi before orientation.
Worldwide placements: Asia (India).

DALE VIEW, THE
Punalal P.O.
Poovachal – 695 575
Thiruvananthapuram District
Kerala State India

T: 00 91 471 882063 or 882163
F: 00 91 471 882063
E: daleview@satyam.net.in
W: www.thedaleview.org
Contact: Mr C. Das

'Be not weary in well doing' is the motto of The Dale View and it sums up the aim of the organisation. The projects vary enormously, focusing on what is needed locally and encouraging self-help. The largest project is education – a pair of schools, kindergarten and other training programmes. The fastest growing project is the Micro Credit Scheme, which encourages women to set up financial Self-Help Groups (SHGs). The Dale View loans money to the SHGs to start Income Generating Projects (IGPs). The De-Addiction Centre caters for local alcohol and substance abusers, to whom we offer a free 21-day treatment. This includes medical care, dry therapy, and group and individual counselling sessions with regular follow-up for a year. The Dale View runs environmental projects, like a watershed scheme, the digging of community wells and latrines, and a bio-gas plant programme. Dale View has helped over 370 local disabled people to start IGPs to give them mental satisfaction and financial independence. Other schemes include a creche, forestry project, plant nursery, piggery and poultry unit, and training centre. Volunteers can 'shadow' the hard working Director, but they are encouraged to partake in the projects that interest them. The language barrier prevents most volunteers from working directly with the locals, but most of the staff speak basic English. The Dale View encourages all forms of support and individual sponsorship. We hope to soon set up a hospital and a special school for physically handicapped children. We are especially interested in people with expertise in these fields, although we warmly welcome all volunteers who are able to adjust to our environment. Each case individually assessed.
Alternative e-mail address: dale_view@hotmail.com The small village of Punalal is 25kms from Trivandram, capital of Kerala State and has a moderate temperature.

Number of projects: 35 UK: 0
Starting months: Jan, Feb, May, Jul, Aug, Sep, Oct, Nov, Dec
Time required: 3–18 weeks
Age: 18–55
Causes: Addicts/Ex-Addicts, AIDS/HIV, Animal Welfare, Children, Conservation, Disabled (physical), Environmental Causes, Health Care/Medical, Human Rights, Poor/Homeless, Teaching/assisting (nursery, primary, EFL), Unemployed, Work Camps – Seasonal, Young People.
Activities: Agriculture/Farming, Building/Construction, Campaigning, Caring (day & residential), Community Work, Computers, Conservation Skills, Cooking, Counselling, Development Issues, First Aid, Forestry, Fundraising, Gardening/Horticulture, Group Work, International Aid, Marketing/Publicity, Research, Social Work, Teaching, Technical Skills, Training, Translating, Visiting/Befriending, Work Camps – Seasonal.
Placements: 15
When to apply: At least 3 months in advance.
Work alone/with others: With local volunteers.
Qualifications: Matriculation and those skilled are encouraged to help in relevant projects. No restrictions providing they have necessary visas to stay in India.
Equipment/clothing: Nil – but suitable for hot temperatures – preferably cotton clothes.
Health requirements: Only very limited healthcare is available. Volunteers must be fit to be able to thrive in Indian climate and environment.
Costs: Travel to Trivandram. US$150 per month donation.
Benefits: The donation (listed under costs) covers the cost of food and lodging. Large hostel with individual rooms and shared bathrooms.
Training: No special training is given. Volunteers are required to learn from their colleagues.
Supervision: Personal supervision by the Director and the head of the project.
Interviews: There are no interviews but details are exchanged by post and telephone to check suitability of candidates.

Restoring a Medieval Village in Southern France

At 22 Zara Owen had never been abroad before and needed a challenge...which was exactly what she got with the Bardou Restoration Project in the Cevennes Mountains. She found the placement via WorldWide Volunteering following a visit to Norfolk & Norwich Voluntary Services. "It felt like a sealed world, completely removed from clubbing, mobile phones and the internet. The confidence I brought away, encouraged me to apply for an Access Course and hopefully teacher training at University."

Charity number: 96/1978
Worldwide placements: Asia (India).

45–47 Blythe Street
London
E2 6LN UK
T: +44 (0) 207 729 1928
F: +44 (0) 207 729 1928
E: dfdtrust@aol.com
W: www.danefordtrust.fsnet.co.uk
Contact: Anthony Stevens

The Daneford Trust is a community based organisation and our priority is to increase and develop young people's activity in their local areas, both in London and in Africa, Asia and the Caribbean. We seek to work in active partnership with relevant initiatives that are being taken by organisations and individuals in local communities. Young people's work has included assisting with teaching English, youth work, office and library administration, work with people with disabilities and organising children's summer schemes. Young volunteers from London only. East London. 🖭

Number of projects: 20 UK: 5
Starting months: Jan, Apr, Sep
Time required: 12–52 weeks
Age: 18–25
Causes: Disabled (physical), Poor/Homeless, Teaching/assisting (primary, secondary), Young People.
Activities: Community Work, Teaching, Training.
Placements: 20
When to apply: All year.
Work alone/with others: Both.
Qualifications: Commitment – A levels useful, English language and Bengali useful in some cases. Volunteers only from the London Boroughs.
Equipment/clothing: No equipment needed.
Health requirements: In good health.
Costs: £1,500–4,000 depending on placement, raised with help from trust.
Benefits: Accommodation and small expenses provided. Mainly homestay, sometimes staff or hostel accommodation.
Training: 2 annual seminars. Monthly briefings, various observations and workshops as required.
Supervision: From trust whilst in UK and within project overseas.
Interviews: Yes in London office.
Charity number: 283962
Worldwide placements: Africa (Botswana, Namibia, South Africa, Zimbabwe); Central America (Barbados, Jamaica, Saint Lucia, Saint Vincent/Grenadines); Asia (Bangladesh).
UK placements: England (London).

21 St Georges Road
London
SE1 6ES UK
T: +44 (0) 207 405 5617
T: +44 (0) 207 831 6632
E: Tcrabbe@daycaretrust.org.uk
Contact: Thom Crabbe

Daycare Trust was established in 1986 to provide information on childcare services and to promote affordable, accessible, quality childcare that provides equal opportunities for all. We give free advice to parents and childcare workers, and advise and brief childcare professionals, employers, trade unions, researchers, early years workers and teachers, journalists, local authorities, TECs, politicians, policy-makers, charities and other organisations interested in childcare provision, childcare information services or family-friendly policies. Volunteers are needed to help with administrative and information work in the London office. National organisation based in London. 🖭

Number of projects: 1 UK: 1
Starting months: January–December
Time required: 4–52 weeks
Age: 16 plus – no upper limit
Causes: Children
Activities: Administration, Campaigning, Community Work, Computers, Fundraising, Library/Resource Centres, Marketing/Publicity, Newsletter/Journalism, Research.
Placements: 2–3
When to apply: All year.
Work alone/with others: It varies.
Qualifications: Graduate level.
Health requirements: Nil.
Costs: Any accommodation costs.
Benefits: Travel to and from office, £1.30 towards lunch.
Interviews: Interviews are conducted at our Holborn office.
UK placements: England (London).

100 Bridge Street
Peterborough
Cambridgeshire PE1 1DY UK
T: 01733 358100
F: 01733 358356
E: lisab@deafblinduk.demon.co.uk
W: www.deafblind.org.uk
Contact: Lisa Bloodworth

Being without both sight and hearing is hard. It puts a great strain on people. It makes simple things difficult and requires a lot of determination to live life to the full. But it does not stop people being people. Deafblind people are not totally different from everyone else. They have the same sorts of needs, interests, likes, dislikes, fears, hopes and ambitions as sighted hearing people. They want to live their lives, make choices, meet people and explore their individual interests just like everybody else. If you are reliable and have patience, you can be a great help to deafblind people. Here are some ideas: Visit and chat. Write letters. Teach a skill. Read magazines and newspapers. Be a lifeline to services such as doctors, hospitals or dentists. Take a deafblind person out and about, shopping, visiting friends, taking part in activities. Help in the Rainbow club for deafblind people. Go on holiday with Deafblind UK. Volunteer befrienders are introduced to a local voluntary activity and usually matched with a deafblind person with similar interests. 🖰 🖹

Number of projects: 1 UK: 1
Starting months: January–December
Time required: 1–102 weeks
Age: 18 plus – no upper limit
Causes: Elderly People, Holidays for Disabled.
Activities: Fundraising, Visiting/Befriending.
Placements: about 50–100
When to apply: All year.
Work alone/with others: Both.
Qualifications: Nil. Training in communication and guiding skills is given. Awareness training given. No restrictions but voluntary work is carried out in the United Kingdom.
Health requirements: Nil.
Costs: Public transport costs reimbursed. Petrol reimbursed at 27p per mile. Any accommodation costs.
Benefits: Travel costs. Further training opportunities available with nationally recognised certificates.
Training: Full training in communicating and guiding dual sensory impaired people. General deafblind awareness.
Supervision: Supervised locally by Regional Development Officer.
Interviews: Interviews take place local to the volunteer.
Charity number: 802976
UK placements: England (throughout); Scotland (throughout); Northern Ireland (throughout); Wales (throughout).

DEPARTAMENTO DE GESTION ESTRATEGICA – PANAMA

Apartado 2694
Panama 3
Panama
T: 00 507 2236612
E: Ekowalczyk@mef.go.pa
Contact: Edith A. Kowalczyk

Departamento de gestion estrategica – promotes and has information about volunteering in

Panama. It may well be able to put volunteers in touch with non government organisations which are not yet listed on the WorldWide Volunteering database. Duties to include studies of poverty, analysis of data and database of NGO's.

Starting months: January–December
Time required: 1–52 weeks (plus)
Age: 16 plus – no upper limit
Causes: Addicts/Ex-Addicts, AIDS/HIV, Animal Welfare, Archaeology, Architecture, Children, Conservation, Disabled (learning and physical), Elderly People, Environmental Causes, Health Care/Medical, Heritage, Holidays for Disabled, Human Rights, Inner City Problems, Offenders/ Ex-Offenders, Poor/Homeless, Refugees, Teaching/assisting (nursery, primary, secondary, mature, EFL) Unemployed, Wildlife, Work Camps – Seasonal, Young People.
Activities: Accountancy, Administration, Agriculture/Farming, Arts/Crafts, Building/ Construction, Campaigning, Caring (general, day and residential), Catering, Community Work, Computers, Conservation Skills, Cooking, Counselling, Development Issues, DIY, Driving, First Aid, Forestry, Fundraising, Gardening/Horticulture, Group Work, International Aid, Library/Resource Centres, Manual Work, Marketing/Publicity, Music, Newsletter/Journalism, Outdoor Skills, Religion, Research, Scientific Work, Social Work, Sport, Summer Camps, Teaching, Technical Skills, Theatre/Drama, Training, Translating, Visiting/ Befriending, Work Camps – Seasonal.
Equipment/clothing: Computers, typing machine, fax.
Costs: Varies according to the project.
Worldwide placements: Central America (Panama).

DEPDC

PO Box 10
Mae Sai
Chiang Rai 57130 Thailand
T: +66 (0) 53 733186
F: +66 (0) 53 642415
E: info@depdc.org
W: www.depdc.org
Contact: English Language Volunteer

DEPDC (Development and Education Programme for Daughters and Communities) is a community-based organisation offering education and full-time accommodation for children to prevent them from being trafficked into the sex industry or other exploitative child-labour situations. DEPDC works across borders with countries in the Mekong Sub Region on child protection and anti trafficking programmes, repatriating women and girls rescued from sex work. We also provide a free day school for 150 refugee children from

Burma, vocational training, agriculture and handicraft production, emergency rescue and shelter of children in crisis. At the core of all the activities is the full time accommodation and care for up to 100 children who would not be able to continue their education if they stayed at home. Volunteers are involved in agriculture, handicraft production, English teaching, English language correspondence, administration, PR and becoming great friends with all the children. Minimum stay of 12 weeks includes six weeks of Thai language training. Please see our web site for further information. We are unable to accept volunteers with an offending background. DEDPC is located in a small town called Mae Sai, which is the northern most town in Thailand on the border with Myanmar (Burma) and is in the Chiang Rai Province. 🗄 📄

Number of projects: 8 UK: 0
Starting months: January–December
Time required: 12–52 weeks (plus)
Age: 18 plus – no upper limit
Causes: Children, Human Rights, Teaching/assisting (EFL), Young People.
Activities: Administration, Agriculture/Farming, Arts/Crafts, Caring – General, Community Work, Cooking, Outdoor Skills, Social Work, Sport, Summer Camps, Teaching, Translating, Visiting/Befriending.
Placements: 15
When to apply: Any time.
Work alone/with others: Work with others.
Qualifications: Volunteers must be enthusiastic, have loads of initiative and be prepared to learn Thai.
Health requirements: No restrictions.
Costs: No cost once volunteers arrive. Flights and insurance to be covered by volunteer.
Benefits: Three vegetarian meals are provided as well as accommodation.
Training: Six weeks of Thai language training for a twelve week stay.
Supervision: Volunteers work as part of a team and supervise each other. Generally the oldest or most long-term volunteer orientates new volunteers.
Interviews: No interviews.
Worldwide placements: Asia (Thailand).

DEUTSCHER CARITASVERBAND – GERMANY

Verbund Freiwilligen-Zentren
Postfach 420
D-79004 Germany
T: 00 49 761 200 425
F: 00 49 761 200 751
E: Freiwilligen-Zentren@caritas.de
W: www.caritas.de
Contact: Dr Eugen Baldas

Deutscher Caritasverband promotes and has information about volunteering in Germany. It may well be able to put volunteers in touch with organisations which are not yet listed on the WorldWide Volunteering database.

Starting months: January–December
Time required: 14–52 weeks (plus)
Age: 16 plus – no upper limit
Causes: Addicts/Ex-Addicts, AIDS/HIV, Animal Welfare, Architecture, Children, Conservation, Disabled (learning and physical), Elderly People, Environmental Causes, Health Care/Medical, Heritage, Holidays for Disabled, Human Rights, Inner City Problems, Offenders/Ex-Offenders, Poor/Homeless, Refugees, Teaching/assisting (nursery, primary, secondary, mature, EFL) Unemployed, Work Camps – Seasonal, Young People.
Activities: Accountancy, Administration, Agriculture/Farming, Arts/Crafts, Building/Construction, Campaigning, Caring (general, day and residential), Catering, Community Work, Computers, Conservation Skills, Cooking, Counselling, Development Issues, DIY, Driving, First Aid, Forestry, Fundraising, Gardening/Horticulture, Group Work, International Aid, Library/Resource Centres, Manual Work, Marketing/Publicity, Music, Newsletter/Journalism, Outdoor Skills, Religion, Research, Scientific Work, Social Work, Summer Camps, Teaching, Technical Skills, Theatre/Drama, Training, Translating, Visiting/Befriending, Work Camps – Seasonal.
Costs: Varies according to the project.
Worldwide placements: Europe (Germany).

DEVON WILDLIFE TRUST

Shirehampton House
35–37 St David's Hill
Exeter
Devon EX4 4DA UK
T: 01392 279244
F: 01392 433221
E: devonwt@cix.compulink.co.uk
W: www.devonwildlifetrust.org
Contact: Dawn Lenn

Devon Wildlife Trust has opportunities for volunteer involvement in all areas of the Wildlife Trust from conservation to general office work. Volunteers play a key role in Wildlife Trust. Volunteer opportunities exist especially for environmental graduates seeking conservation 'work' experience with: Estate team – practical conservation tasks and training in range of skills. Wildlife recording – a number of schemes, e.g. operation otter, seaquest. Irregular hours and often involves working alone. Awareness – People and wildlife skills essential. Ideal for those interested in environmental education. Office – data entry, marketing, PR, fund-raising etc. Watch – children's club. Guided walks and tours. NB: Long term placements are sought after and limited. 🔾

Number of projects: 1 **UK:** 1
Starting months: January–December
Time required: 1–52 weeks (plus)
Age: 16 plus – no upper limit
Causes: Conservation, Wildlife.
Activities: Administration, Conservation Skills, Fundraising, Gardening/Horticulture, Library/ Resource Centres, Manual Work, Marketing/ Publicity, Outdoor Skills, Scientific Work.
Placements: 200
When to apply: All year.
Work alone/with others: Both. Generally with others but some wildlife recording is on a more casual working alone basis.
Qualifications: Conservation/wildlife/ environmental interests helpful.
Equipment/clothing: Provided if necessary for health and safety.
Health requirements: Nil.
Costs: Travel to work (or central pick-up point) only, and accommodation costs.
Benefits: Training provided where needed.
Training: Training is provided where needed, particularly for long-term conservation work, educational activities and local group activities.
Supervision: Volunteers are supported by a designated manager, who can be a member of staff or another volunteer.
Interviews: Selection by interview. CVs accepted. Interviews take place in the Trust HQ in Exeter.
Charity number: 213224
UK placements: England (Devon).

DEVON YOUTH ASSOCIATION

1b Costly Street
Ivybridge
Devon PL21 ODB UK
T: 01752 691511
F: 01752 895411
E: dya@dya.org.uk
W: www.dya.org.uk
Contact: Tim Todd or Jo Gunner

Devon Youth Association needs volunteers to work in youth clubs, in independent projects which we sponsor and with detached youth workers working on the streets with young people. We have a special project promoting work with girls in girls clubs, a workshop project in a deprived area, advice and information, and issue based youth work. We also have an increasing need for administrative back up by volunteers and information dissemination by way of a

newsletter which would benefit from volunteer input. Volunteers with an offending background may be accepted. We take each individual case on its merits. We have an equal opportunities policy. 🔾 📷

Number of projects: 13–14 **UK:** 13–14
Starting months: January–December
Time required: 1–52 weeks
Age: 16–25
Causes: Addicts/Ex-Addicts, AIDS/HIV, Disabled (learning and physical), Human Rights, Inner City Problems, Offenders/Ex-Offenders, Poor/ Homeless, Unemployed, Young People.
Activities: Administration, Arts/Crafts, Community Work, Computers, Counselling, DIY, Fundraising, Group Work, Library/Resource Centres, Marketing/Publicity, Music, Newsletter/ Journalism, Outdoor Skills, Social Work, Sport, Summer Camps, Theatre/Drama, Training, Visiting/Befriending.
Placements: 80
When to apply: All year.
Work alone/with others: With others.
Qualifications: Nil – enthusiasm and motivation. 'Hands-on' experience always a benefit.
Health requirements: Nil.
Costs: Accommodation if needed.
Benefits: Travel costs and out of pocket expenses.
Interviews: Interviews take place in Ivybridge, Plymouth or Exeter.
Charity number: 301028
UK placements: England (Devon).

DEYA ARCHAEOLOGICAL MUSEUM AND RESEARCH CENTRE (DAMARC)

c/o Earthwatch Europe
57 Woodstock Road
Oxford
OX2 6HJ UK
T: 01865 318831
F: 01865 311383
E: vp@earthwatch.org.uk
W: www.earthwatch.org/europe
Contact: Sandra Winnick

Deya Archaeological Museum and Research Centre organises prehistoric site excavation, cleaning, classifying, restoring, drawing, measuring pottery and bones, site surveying and photography combined with lectures. Live in Centre, help with chores, swim, sun and learning experience combined. Balearic Isles.

Number of projects: 150 **UK:** 10
Starting months: Jan, Jun, Jul, Aug, Sep, Dec
Time required: 2–6 weeks
Age: 16 plus – no upper limit
Causes: Archaeology, Conservation, Environmental Causes, Heritage, Work Camps – Seasonal.

Activities: Arts/Crafts, Building/Construction, Computers, Conservation Skills, Library/ Resource Centres, Manual Work, Outdoor Skills, Research, Scientific Work, Technical Skills, Training, Work Camps – Seasonal.
Placements: 500
When to apply: All year.
Work alone/with others: With others.
Qualifications: No restrictions providing they speak English and are over 16 years.
Equipment/clothing: Long trousers, sturdy shoes, sleeping bag and sheet.
Health requirements: Need to cope with heavy dust and lifting and carrying.
Costs: Travel, Medical insurance + from £1,195 to cover board, lodging and tuition.
Benefits: Tuition, excavation, conservation, lab experience. Bunk beds and meals to scholarship students.
Training: On site training.
Interviews: No interview.
Charity number: 327017
Worldwide placements: Europe (Spain).

DIAKONALA ARET

Svenska kyrkans Forsamlingsnamnd
S-75170 Uppsala
Sweden
T: 00 46 18 16 95 00
F: 00 46 18 16 96 18
Contact: The Director

Diakonala Aret is the Swedish branch of the European Diaconal Year network which consists of a number of national Christian-based volunteering schemes. (The British branch is Time For God.) They share common standards, and a commitment to the personal development of the volunteer through this form of work.

Number of projects: 1 UK: 0
Starting months: Aug
Time required: 42–52 weeks (plus)
Age: 18–25
Causes: Addicts/Ex-Addicts, Children, Elderly People, Young People.
Activities: Caring (general, residential), Community work, Training.
When to apply: Before April.
Qualifications: Small knowledge of Swedish and active Christian church membership.
Costs: Income tax and travel to Sweden.
Benefits: Pocket money, board, lodging, health and pension insurance.
Training: Regular residential conferences or seminars.
Supervision: Support is offered to the volunteers through both personal supervision and regular residential conferences or seminars.
Worldwide placements: Europe (Sweden).

DIAKONI AARET

Diakonissestiftelsen
Peter Bangs Vej 1
Frederiksberg
DK-2000 Denmark
T: 00 45 38 38 41 26
F: 00 45 38 87 14 93
E: diakoniaaret@diakonissen.dk
W: www.diakoniaaret.diakonissen.dk
Contact: Anne Marie Boile Nielsen

Diakoni Aaret is the Danish branch of the European Diaconal Year network which consists of a number of national evangelical Lutheran-based volunteering schemes. (The British branch is Time For God.) They share common standards, and a commitment to the personal development of the volunteer through this form of work. Support is offered to the volunteers through both personal supervision and regular residential conferences or seminars.

Number of projects: 1 UK: 0
Starting months: Sep
Time required: 48–49 weeks
Age: 18–25
Causes: Children, Elderly People, Inner City Problems, Poor/Homeless, Refugees, Teaching/ assisting (nursery), Young People.
Activities: Administration, Campaigning, Caring (general and day), Computers, Cooking, Marketing/Publicity, Music, Religion, Social Work, Summer Camps, Teaching, Training, Visiting/Befriending.
Placements: 50
When to apply: March – May.
Work alone/with others: Mostly alone attached to a counsellor.
Qualifications: Volunteers must speak a little Danish.
Health requirements: Nil.
Costs: Travel to Denmark.
Benefits: Pocket money DKr1,700 per month. Board DKr1,521 per month. Lodging + local travel costs. Dormitory/apartment shared with other volunteers /single room in family house.
Training: On arrival a week's seminar of pre-placement training is provided.
Supervision: Every volunteer has a supervisor at the placement. In January all have the possibility of evaluating at the mid-term seminar.
Worldwide placements: Europe (Denmark).

DIAKONISCHES JAHR

Diakonisches Werk der Pfalz
Karmeliterstrasse 20
67346 Speyer
Germany
T: 00 49 6232 664214
F: 00 49 6232 6642427

E: djaus@diakonie-pfalz.de
W: www.djia.de
Contact: Astrid Guhmann

Diakonisches Jahr is the German branch of the European Diaconal Year network which consists of a number of national Christian-based volunteering schemes. (The British branch is Time For God.) They share common standards, and a commitment to the personal development of the volunteer through this form of work. Each offers support to the volunteers through both personal supervision and regular residential conferences or seminars. Placements generally include residential care projects (children, elderly, disabled, learning difficulties, sick, etc.), rehabilitation/hostel work (drug abusers, ex-offenders, homeless, refugees, etc.), community support (visiting elderly, families affected by HIV/Aids, youth work, etc), and churches (assisting ministry teams, parish work, pastoral care, youth work, children). The degree of fluency in German determines to which type of placement a volunteer is assigned. Volunteers with an offending background may be accepted on the programme. Apply in your own country through our partner organisation. ♿

Number of projects: 1 **UK:** 0
Starting months: Aug, Sep
Time required: 36–52 weeks
Age: 18–27
Causes: AIDS/HIV, Children, Disabled (learning and physical), Elderly People, Health Care/Medical, Holidays for Disabled, Inner City Problems, Offenders/Ex-Offenders, Poor/Homeless, Refugees, Teaching/assisting (nursery), Young People.
Activities: Caring (general, day and residential), Community Work, Counselling, Group Work, Outdoor Skills, Religion, Social Work, Sport, Training, Visiting/Befriending.
Placements: 50
When to apply: 1st Jan–30th April at latest.
Work alone/with others: Both.
Qualifications: A willingness to serve full-time and open to working in church-related placements. Working with children and youth requires a good level of German whilst caring for the elderly and people with special needs requires less proficiency.
Volunteers from the UK, France, Denmark, Sweden, Austria, Belgium, Hungary, Estonia, Poland, the Netherlands, Italy and the USA – all countries where we have partner organisations.
Health requirements: Nil.
Costs: Travel to and from placement (paid if EVS approved).
Benefits: Pocket money, board, lodging, social insurance (includes health, pension and accident). Accommodation is arranged. 95% are housed in staff quarters of the institutions. In

some placements a furnished room or flat is rented for the volunteer.
Training: There are at least 4 one-week residential seminars for volunteers during the year, usually in groups of 15–25. One of these is an orientation.
Supervision: In each institution, there is a named supervisor who has regular meetings with the volunteer. There are also counsellors in the regional volunteer co-ordinating organisations who visit the volunteers in the placement.
Worldwide placements: Europe (Germany).

DISABLEMENT INFORMATION AND ADVICE LINES (DIAL UK)

St Catherine's
Tickhill Road
Doncaster
DN4 8QN UK
T: 01302 310123
F: 01302 310404
E: enquiries@dialuk.org.uk
W: www.dialuk.org.uk
Contact: Andy Short

Disablement Information and Advice Lines are local advice centres running telephone advice lines and drop-in information centres. There are over 100 of them across the UK. Anyone who needs disability related information may use their services: people with disabilities, their families, carers or professionals. Volunteers with an offending background may be accepted. ♿

Number of projects: 104 **UK:** 104
Starting months: January–December
Time required: 1–52 weeks (plus)
Age: 20–69
Causes: Disabled (learning and physical), Holidays for Disabled.
Activities: Administration, Campaigning, Community Work, Computers, Counselling, Fundraising, Library/Resource Centres, Social Work, Visiting/Befriending.
When to apply: All year.
Work alone/with others: Both.
Qualifications: Telephone skills, computer and word processing useful.
Health requirements: Volunteers with disabilities sought after.
Costs: Any accommodation and food costs.
Benefits: Travel expenses within reasonable distances.
Training: DIAL UK induction.
Supervision: Supervised by Line Managers.
Interviews: Interviews take place at local DIALs. Contact DIAL UK for details of local DIALs.
Charity number: 283937
UK placements: England (throughout); Scotland (throughout); Northern Ireland (throughout); Wales (throughout).

DISAWAY TRUST, THE

2 Charles Road
Merton Park
London
SW19 3BD UK
T: +44 (0) 208 543 3431
F: +44 (0) 208 543 3431
E: lynnesimpkins@hotmail.com
Contact: Lynne Simpkins

The aim of the Disaway Trust is to provide holidays for physically disabled adults who would not be able to travel alone. Our Trust provides a one-to-one carer for each holidaymaker who we try to match to a like-minded helper. We stay in regular hotels both at home and abroad and organise trips out to interesting venues. Venues change every year and are decided in the summer of the previous year. ▨

Number of projects: 1–2 **UK:** 1
Starting months: Mar, Jul, Sep, Oct
Time required: 1–2 weeks
Age: 18 plus – no upper limit
Causes: Disabled (physical), Holidays for Disabled.
Activities: Caring – Residential.
Placements: 40
When to apply: Any time after January.
Work alone/with others: Both.
Qualifications: Nil, but caring attitude, adaptable and a good sense of humour.
Health requirements: General physical health OK.
Costs: Half cost of the holiday + travel to London departures.
Benefits: Board and lodging in a hotel while on holiday.
Interviews: Volunteer applicants are not interviewed.
Charity number: 282874
Worldwide placements: North America: (Canada).
UK placements: England (Cumbria).

DISCOVER NEPAL

G.P.O. Box 20209
Kathmandu
Nepal
T: 00 977 1 4413690
F: 00 977 1 4255487
E: stt@mos.com.np
W: www.discovernepal.com.np
Contact: Bijaya Pradhan

Discover Nepal, a government-registered NGO, was established in Nepal in 1998. Our aim is to provide opportunities for the involvement of volunteers in the development process, and to contribute practically towards the socio-economic development of the country. The programme involves teaching English at a school for a period of 10–20 weeks. Apart from teaching English, in some schools, volunteers are expected to help in conducting extra-curricular activities (sports, music, art, clubs, environmental conservation etc). Volunteers with some teaching experience or experience with children would be preferred but it is not essential. The fee of £700 includes a two week orientation programme (including accommodation with breakfast and lunch), a week's trek in the Himalayas, jungle safari, sightseeing tours and 10–18 weeks stay in a boarding school. Alternative web site: www.catmando.com/discovernepal. ▨

Number of projects: 3 **UK:** 0
Starting months: Jan, Apr, Jun, Oct
Time required: 8–12 weeks
Age: 20–40
Causes: Conservation, Disabled (learning and physical), Environmental Causes, Health Care/Medical, Holidays for Disabled, Refugees, Teaching/assisting (nursery, primary, secondary), Work Camps – Seasonal, Young People.
Activities: Administration, Campaigning, Caring – Residential, Community Work, Computers, Conservation Skills, Development Issues, Forestry, Group Work, International Aid, Outdoor Skills, Research, Social Work, Sport, Summer Camps, Teaching, Technical Skills, Training, Visiting/Befriending, Work Camps – Seasonal.
Placements: 20–30
When to apply: Two months before the programme begins.
Work alone/with others: With other young volunteers.
Qualifications: Minimum GCSE, good English language skills.
Equipment/clothing: Warm clothes required for winter season.
Health requirements: Yes.
Costs: £900 (US$2,000) for education programme + air fares and personal expenses.
Benefits: All board and lodging at school + 12 days orientation, 12 days lodging, 1 week trekking, jungle safari and sightseeing. Free accommodation at school. Accommodation is also provided during the orientation and trek.
Training: 2 week orientation programme.
Supervision: Volunteers are supervised by authorities at place of voluntary assignment and Discover Nepal also monitors their activities.
Interviews: Prospective volunteers are not interviewed but they must meet our selection criteria.
Worldwide placements: Asia (Nepal).

DIVINE ONKAR MISSION

66–67 Dudley Road
Wolverhampton
West Midlands WV2 3BY UK
T: 01902 453453
F: 01902 459911
E: support@divine-onkar.org.uk
W: www.divine-onkar.org.uk
Contact: Tersam Lal

The Divine Onkar Mission was initiated in 1991 and registered in 1992 with the Charity Commission. The aims of this charity are the advancement of education, medical and agricultural development in third world countries especially in India. We are currently running projects in the following areas of India:
1. Leprosy aid. We support a leper colony in Delhi, funding all costs for their treatment and rehabilitation.
2. Orphanage/boarding school. In Behar State, we are running the project for children whose parents have been victims of leprosy and other deadly diseases.
3. General hospital. We provide medical care free of charge for the poor whom we select from remote jungle areas. Some 300/400 patients are seen of whom 50–60 receive eye operations to correct cataract and other eye defects.
4. In Orissa state we are funding similar projects for children and widows. The mortality rate amongst young males is very high.
A large area of land has been donated by the locals who want paid work in return for cultivating and developing the land.
Volunteers with an offending background may be accepted. 📋

Number of projects: 4 UK: 1
Starting months: Aug, Sep
Time required: 4–52 weeks
Age: 18–75
Causes: Animal Welfare, Children, Disabled (physical), Elderly People, Health Care/Medical, Holidays for Disabled, Teaching/assisting (nursery, primary, secondary, mature, EFL) Work Camps – Seasonal.
Activities: Administration, Agriculture/Farming, Building/Construction, Community Work, Computers, Counselling, Development Issues, First Aid, Forestry, Fundraising, International Aid, Marketing/Publicity, Music, Newsletter/Journalism, Research, Social Work, Teaching, Technical Skills, Theatre/Drama.
Placements: 5
When to apply: March or April.
Work alone/with others: With other young volunteers.
Qualifications: Driving licence would be an advantage but not essential.
Health requirements: Nil.

Costs: Travel to project.
Benefits: Board and lodging. Accommodation is provided in India by Divine Onkar Mission.
Training: As required.
Supervision: All volunteers must keep strictly within the boundary of the law of the country and must consult and get agreement from Divne Onkar Mission officials of anything they are unsure of.
Interviews: Prospective volunteers are interviewed in our office in Wolverhampton.
Charity number: 1074527
Worldwide placements: Asia (India).
UK placements: England (West Midlands).

DOLPHIN RESEARCH CENTER

58901 Overseas Highway
Gras Key, FL
Monroe 33050-6019 USA
T: 00 1 305 289 1121 EXT. 230
F: 00 1 305 743 7627
E: drc-vr@dolphins.org
W: www.dolphins.org
Contact: Mary Ackroyd

Dolphin Research Center is pleased to offer volunteer opportunities designed for individuals who would like to donate their efforts to assist the various departments of our organisation. Although volunteers do not work directly with the dolphins, participants do encounter many unique opportunities for learning about various aspects of the daily operations of a marine mammal care facility. The responsibilities typically handled by our volunteers all represent vital aspects of our operations. Volunteers may find themselves helping to prepare our dolphins' meals or caring for our family of exotic birds. Volunteers are utilised to monitor visitors and answer their questions and also assist staff in conducting public interactive programmes. Volunteers are involved with facility maintenance such as trash collection, recycling, painting and landscaping projects. Volunteers also help with administrative projects such as computer data entry and the preparation of bulk mailings. Our volunteer resources department is staffed throughout the year. Our non-local volunteers work 40 hours per week and a 4–8 week commitment is preferred. Within our volunteer resources department, we offer an Intern Programme. Regular internships involving concentration in a specific department, are normally 3–4 months in length, and are offered during the summer, fall and winter terms. Middle of the Florida Keys near Marathon.

Number of projects: 1 UK: 0
Starting months: January–December
Time required: 4–12 weeks
Age: 18 plus – no upper limit

Causes: Animal Welfare, Conservation, Wildlife.
Activities: Conservation Skills, Group Work, Manual Work.
Placements: 100
When to apply: At least 3 months before wishing to start.
Work alone/with others: With other volunteers of all ages over 18.
Qualifications: Applicants should be fluent in English, be able to work as part of a team as well as independently and should be able to appropriately interface with guests and co-workers.
Equipment/clothing: Swimsuits.
Health requirements: Many activities involve manual labour and exposure to sun, heat and the marine environment. Therefore, applicants should have a high level of mobility, be in good mental health and have the ability to lift at least 30lbs.
Costs: All travel costs and living expenses +US $35 programme fee. It is best but not essential if they are able to rent a car while they are here. Total costs depend on air fares and length of stay – US$1,500–$4,000.
Benefits: A variety of learning opportunities are available for self motivated individuals. We send confirmed volunteers a list of housing options for them to pursue and we send a room mate questionnaire to those wishing to share expenses.
Training: We do on-the-job training.
Supervision: Volunteer resource staff supervise the volunteers Monday to Friday. Other staff are available to provide necessary assistance at the weekends.
Interviews: Prospective volunteers are interviewed by telephone after submitting a completed volunteer application.
Worldwide placements: North America: (USA).

DORSET ASSOCIATION FOR THE DISABLED

c/o Weymouth Outdoor Education Centre
Knightsdale Road
Weymouth
Dorset DT4 0HS UK
T: 01305 761840 (9 am 12 noon) + answerphone
F: 01305 761840
E: info@dorsetdisabled.co.uk
W: www.dorsetdisabled.co.uk
Contact: Angela Barnsley

The Dorset Association for the Disabled was set up to provide additional services and social amenities for disabled people, complementing and supplementing the services provided by the statutory welfare authorities. The Association also embraces Tapes for the Handicapped who provide talking magazines of local interest to those disabled people who unfortunately are also housebound. Branch committees run social clubs and outings and some also run handicraft groups. They provide a visiting service to housebound people and an advisory service to the disabled members and families in a wide variety of spheres. Annual holidays are organised to a number of resorts and many members treat these events as reunions with other branches. Funds are raised by branches through flag days, sales of work, coffee mornings, car boot sales, etc. and from the generosity of the public in donations and covenants. Acceptance of volunteers with an offending background would depend on the offence committed. ♿ 📄

Number of projects: a few **UK:** a few
Starting months: May, Jun, Sep
Time required: 1–4 weeks
Age: 18–70
Causes: Disabled (physical), Holidays for Disabled.
Activities: Caring – General.
Placements: 300
When to apply: March
Work alone/with others: With other volunteers.
Health requirements: Fit and healthy.
Costs: Travel to and from pick up point for holiday.
Benefits: No financial support but board and lodging given on holiday.
Interviews: Interviews conducted in Weymouth, Dorset.
Charity number: 202524
UK placements: England (Devon, Dorset, Somerset).

DORSET WILDLIFE TRUST

Brooklands Farm
Forston
Dorchester
Dorset DT2 7AA UK
T: 01305 264620
F: 01305 251120
E: dorsetwt@cix.compulink.co.uk
Contact: The Director

The Dorset Wildlife Trust aims to achieve now and for the future a county, and through the Wildlife Trusts, a United Kingdom, that is richer in wildlife, managed on sustainable principles. This aim will be achieved by: acquiring and managing nature reserves; acquiring data on habitats and species; promoting conservation and management of important wildlife sites by their existing landowners; influencing decisions on land use; increasing awareness of the value of wildlife. This work creates volunteering opportunities in practical estate work, recording and monitoring, formal and informal education projects for people of all ages, developing and facilitating community projects, raising awareness of the need to conserve wildlife through art, design and creative writing, raising money and membership, as well as administration and building maintenance. The more complex the task, the longer the placement should be.

Number of projects: 40 UK: 40
Starting months: January–December
Time required: 2–52 weeks
Age: 18–80
Causes: Conservation, Environmental Causes.
Activities: Administration, Agriculture/Farming, Community Work, Computers, Conservation Skills, Forestry, Fundraising, Library/Resource Centres, Manual Work, Marketing/Publicity, Newsletter/Journalism, Outdoor Skills, Research, Scientific Work, Teaching.
Placements: 400
When to apply: All year.
Work alone/with others: With others.
Qualifications: Varies according to projects.
Equipment/clothing: Equipment supplied.
Health requirements: Varies according to projects.
Costs: Food and sometimes accommodation.
Benefits: All expenses reimbursed. Informal training; work experience, chance to help wildlife. Limited accommodation on one reserve only.
Training: No formal training but we do invite placement volunteers for an informal introduction.
Supervision: Volunteers are usually assigned to one named person for supervision.
Charity number: 200222
UK placements: England (Dorset).

DORSET YOUTH AND COMMUNITY SERVICE

Princes House
Princes Street
Dorchester
Dorset DT1 1TP UK
T: 01305 225291
F: 01305 225293
E: d.m.higton@dorset-cc.gov.uk
W: www.dorsetyouth.org.uk
Contact: Derek Higton

Dorset Youth and Community Service supports young people aged 12–21 in their transition from childhood to responsible adulthood, encourages their social development and individual fulfilment, and helps them participate fully in society. Youth work in Dorset is critically informed by a set of beliefs which include a commitment to equal opportunity, and to young people as partners in learning and in decision making. It also aims to develop within young people a sense of both

their rights and responsibilities as citizens. Youth work in Dorset offers a comprehensive range of flexible educational programmes and projects in which young people choose to be involved. The Service encourages young people to be both critical and creative in responding to their world, and widens their experiences within it. The programmes and projects also provide opportunities for relaxation, meeting friends and having fun. Youth work in Dorset complements and supports learning in school and college and contributes to social welfare and community development. It offers to all a constructive and educational use of leisure time. It helps young people achieve and fulfil their potential and make choices about their lives, offering them information, advice and support. It works with other agencies to encourage society to be responsive to young people's needs, especially those young people who are vulnerable. 🖺

Number of projects: 70 UK: 70
Starting months: January–December
Time required: 12–52 weeks (plus)
Age: 18–25
Causes: Young People.
Activities: Arts/Crafts, Community Work, Counselling, Group Work, Music, Social Work.
Placements: 200
When to apply: All year.
Work alone/with others: Both.
Health requirements: Nil.
Costs: Any accommodation.
Benefits: Training opportunities are available.
Training: The Service has an induction process for all volunteers.
Supervision: All volunteers are supervised as necessary by professionally qualified staff.
Interviews: Volunteers are interviewed at the youth centre in which they will work.
UK placements: England (Dorset).

DUKE OF EDINBURGH'S AWARD, THE

Head Office
Gulliver House, Madeira Walk
Windsor
Berkshire SL4 1EV UK
T: 01753 727400
E: info@theaward.org
W: www.theaward.org
Contact: Country/Regional Officer

The Duke of Edinburgh's Award is more than a well known and respected charity. For the 100,000+ young people who enter for an Award each year, it can provide an opportunity to try things other than the 'usual' and be something more than simply 'normal'. To qualify for a Bronze, Silver or Gold Award, a young person must meet the challenge in four sections –

service, expeditions, physical recreation and skills. For Gold they must also undertake a residential project. For over 45 years the Award's programme of personal development activities has been opening doors for young people from all walks of life; from academic high-flyers to excluded under-achievers; from those forging a career path to the unemployed; and from the naturally adventurous to those just willing to have a go at something challenging. The Award relies heavily on volunteers to help guide young people through their Awards. These include specialist skills instructors and assessors, leaders and mentors. Volunteering is at the heart of the Award Programme too, with all participants having to undertake community service projects over set periods of time. Due to the generous support from the Award's supporters, there are many projects that the Award is currently involved with which will help to meet this challenge. These include developing the Award among groups of young people that would otherwise not have the opportunity to undertake the Award, such as those on probation, the homeless or those with special needs. Volunteers with an offending background are accepted. ♿ 📄

Number of projects: 10,000+ UK: 10,000 award groups
Starting months: January–December
Time required: 12–78 weeks
Age: 14–25
Causes: Addicts/Ex-Addicts, AIDS/HIV, Animal Welfare, Archaeology, Children, Conservation, Disabled (learning and physical), Elderly People, Environmental Causes, Health Care/Medical, Heritage, Holidays for Disabled, Inner City Problems, Offenders/Ex-Offenders, Poor/Homeless, Refugees, Teaching/assisting (nursery, primary), Unemployed, Wildlife, Work Camps – Seasonal, Young People.
Activities: Administration, Agriculture/Farming, Arts/Crafts, Building/Construction, Campaigning, Caring (general, day and residential), Catering, Community Work, Computers, Conservation Skills, Cooking, Counselling, DIY, Driving, First Aid, Forestry, Fundraising, Gardening/Horticulture, Group Work, Library/Resource Centres, Manual Work, Music, Newsletter/Journalism, Outdoor Skills, Social Work, Sport, Summer Camps, Teaching, Technical Skills, Theatre/Drama, Training, Translating, Visiting/Befriending, Work Camps – Seasonal.
Placements: 200,000
Work alone with others: With other young volunteers.
Equipment/clothing: Equipment may be needed only in the expedition section.

Health requirements: No requirements.
Costs: Depends on choice of travel and destination. Accommodation costs.
Training: Is provided with an Award group.
Supervision: Award group leader has clear responsibilities.
Interviews: Award group leader will see all volunteers for that group.
Worldwide placements: Africa (Benin, Botswana, Burkina Faso, Cameroon, Comoros, Côte d'Ivoire, Egypt, Gabon, Gambia, Ghana, Guinea, Guinea-Bissau, Kenya, Lesotho, Madagascar, Malawi, Mali, Mauritius, Namibia, Nigeria, Saint Helena, Senegal, Seychelles, Sierra Leone, South Africa, Swaziland, Tanzania, Togo, Uganda, Zambia); North America: (Canada, USA); Central America (Antigua and Barbuda, Bahamas, Barbados, Bermuda, Cayman Islands, Costa Rica, Dominica, Grenada, Jamaica, Mexico, Montserrat, Saint Lucia, Saint Vincent/Grenadines, Trinidad and Tobago, Turks and Caicos Islands, Virgin Islands); South America (Argentina, Brazil, Ecuador, Falkland Islands, Guyana, Peru); Asia (Bahrain, Brunei, China, Hong Kong, India, Indonesia, Israel, Japan, Jordan, Kuwait, Macao, Malaysia, Mongolia, Nepal, Pakistan, Qatar, Saudi Arabia, Singapore, Sri Lanka, Taiwan, Thailand, United Arab Emirates); Australasia (Australia, Fiji, New Zealand); Europe (Austria, Azerbaijan, Belgium, Cyprus, Czech Republic, Denmark, Estonia, Finland, France, Germany, Gibraltar, Greece, Hungary, Ireland, Italy, Lithuania, Luxembourg, Malta, Monaco, Netherlands, Portugal, Slovenia, Spain, Switzerland, Turkey, Yugoslavia).
UK placements: England (throughout); Scotland (throughout); Northern Ireland (throughout); Wales (throughout).

DURHAM WILDLIFE TRUST

Rainton Meadows
Chilton Moore
Houghton-Le-Spring
Tyne and Wear DH4 6PU UK
T: 0191 5843112
F: 0191 5843934
E: durhamwt@cix.co.uk
W: www.wildlifetrust.org.uk/durham/
Contact: Karen Fisher

Durham Wildlife Trust is a member of the Wildlife Trusts, a national partnership of 47 County Trusts. The aims of the Trust are primarily to: promote nature conservation in the community; acquire and manage nature reserves; monitor biological and geological resources; liaise with local authorities to promote regard for nature conservation; offer practical advice on nature conservation to landowners. It is the Trust's policy to involve all sectors of the community, of all ages, backgrounds, abilities and disabilities towards these ends. Volunteers require no previous experience just lots of enthusiasm. They will receive on-the-job training in an informal atmosphere and, if they desire, can go on to participate more fully, assisting with the organisation and running of activities/projects. Limited opportunities may also arise for those with a longer term commitment.

Volunteers with an offending background may be accepted, each case separately assessed.

Number of projects: 1 **UK:** 1
Starting months: Jan, Feb, Mar, Apr, May, Jun, Jul, Aug, Sep, Oct, Nov
Time required: 1–52 weeks (plus)
Age: 16–75
Causes: Conservation, Environmental Causes, Unemployed, Wildlife.
Activities: Community Work, Computers, Conservation Skills, Driving, Forestry, Gardening/Horticulture, Group Work, Manual Work, Outdoor Skills, Research, Scientific Work, Technical Skills, Training.
Placements: 150

When to apply: All year.
Work alone/with others: With others.
Qualifications: Nil but practical skills useful.
Equipment/clothing: Casual work clothes, waterproofs, stout boots. Protective safety gear is provided.
Health requirements: Any medical conditions (illness, allergy or physical disability) that may require treatment/medication or which affects the volunteer working with machinery must be notified to us in advance. Tetanus injections must be up to date.
Costs: Bring your own packed lunch.
Benefits: Out of pocket expenses. Volunteer room. Toilet/washing/showers/locker room. Kitchen/catering facilities.
Training: 2–4 hour induction on health and safety issues. On the job training in an informal atmosphere.
Supervision: Supervised by our staff and other volunteers. Risk assessments carried out on site.
Interviews: Interviews at our office.
UK placements: England (Co Durham).

E.I.L.

287 Worcester Road
Malvern
Worcs WR14 1AB UK
T: 01684 562577/ 0800 0184015
F: 01684 562212
E: info@eiluk.org
W: www.eiluk.org
Contact: Karen Morris or Neil Humpage

EIL specialises in intercultural learning and education. We are part of a federation and there are partner organisations throughout the world. The core of our work involves travelling to different countries and experiencing their cultures through homestays. Both individuals and groups ask us to arrange homestay experiences. Our volunteering opportunities, for young UK volunteers, are mainly concentrated within Europe. In 2000 we were the UK's biggest sending organisation for the European Union's EVS programme (European Voluntary Service). We have contacts with many different projects throughout the European Union. It is possible to specify a country and also the type of work that one wishes to do. However, the fewer restrictions that are imposed on a volunteering experience the greater the likelihood of our being able to place you. Volunteers usually go for between six months and one year. Shorter programmes, for between three weeks and three months are available for some young people. EIL has contacts with other organisations in different parts of the world, but these often have higher costs for volunteers. Volunteers with an offending background are accepted. 📧 📄

Number of projects: Thousands UK: 7
Starting months: January–December
Time required: 3–52 weeks
Age: 18–25
Causes: Addicts/Ex-Addicts, AIDS/HIV, Archaeology, Children, Conservation, Disabled (physical), Elderly People, Environmental Causes, Health Care/Medical, Heritage, Holidays for Disabled, Human Rights, Inner City Problems, Poor/Homeless, Refugees, Teaching/assisting, Unemployed, Wildlife, Work Camps – Seasonal, Young People.
Activities: Administration, Arts/Crafts, Building/Construction, Campaigning, Caring (general, day and residential), Catering, Community Work, Computers, Conservation Skills, Cooking, Development Issues, DIY, Gardening/Horticulture, Group Work, Library/Resource Centres, Manual Work, Marketing/Publicity, Music, Newsletter/ Journalism, Outdoor Skills, Research, Social Work, Sport, Summer Camps, Teaching, Theatre/Drama, Training, Visiting/Befriending, Work Camps – Seasonal.
Placements: 120
When to apply: All year.
Work alone/with others: Generally with other volunteers.
Qualifications: EU Citizens resident in the UK only.
Health requirements: Some projects may have restrictions but not all.
Costs: Nil. All costs paid by European Union.
Benefits: Travel, board, lodging, medical insurance, pocket money (£25 per week). Varies according to project.
Training: Meeting in UK and induction in country of project.
Supervision: Personal mentor provided by project.
Interviews: Interviews take place in Malvern, although interviews nearer volunteers' homes are sometimes possible.
Worldwide placements: Europe (Austria, Belgium, Cyprus, Czech Republic, Denmark, Estonia, Finland, France, Germany, Greece, Hungary, Iceland, Ireland, Italy, Latvia, Lithuania, Luxembourg, Netherlands, Norway, Poland, Portugal, Romania, Slovakia, Slovenia, Spain, Sweden, Switzerland).
UK placements: England (Hampshire, Herefordshire, London, Merseyside, Worcestershire).

EARTHCARE

G.P.O. Box 11546
Hong Kong
T: (852) 25780434
F: (852) 25780522
E: care@earth.org.hk
W: www.earth.org.hk
Contact: NG Wai Yee

Earthcare – a local Chinese charity aims to promote a green lifestyle, green business, environmental conservation, humane education, healthy lifestyle and the protection of animals. Established in November 1993, Earthcare became a registered charity in 1994. We advised the authorities in Guizhou, a Chinese province with severe shortage of water, on water recycling systems, reforestation and reconstruction of the eco-system. We co-operated with international organisations in investigations into the trafficking and illegal sales of rhino horns in China. Our efforts prompted the Chinese Government to take immediate action to combat these large-scale criminal activities and the Agriculture and Fisheries Department of Hong Kong to announce a series of measures to strengthen its protection of endangered species. In late 1994 we were the first to advocate the use of herbal alternatives to replace animal medicine due to the years of friendship between one of our founders and doctors. The Association of Chinese Medicine and Philosophy, IFAW and Earthcare succeeded in persuading the Chinese authorities to reduce by one third its bear farms over the next three years. During the last few years we have been concentrating on raising awareness of the threats to wildlife, in particular, tiger, marine turtle, elephant, rhino, sharks and bears due to human encroachment and trade in their body parts. We also actively promote sustainable energy resources, solar power, responsible pet ownership, no-kill sanctuary and anti-bull fighting. Volunteers with offending background may be accepted, each case assessed individually.

Number of projects: 2 UK: 0
Starting months: January–December
Time required: 1–12 weeks
Age: 14 plus – no upper limit
Causes: Animal Welfare, Children, Conservation, Elderly People, Environmental Causes, Health Care/Medical, Holidays for Disabled, Teaching (primary, secondary), Wildlife, Young People.
Activities: Accountancy, Administration, Agriculture/Farming, Building/Construction, Campaigning, Computers, Conservation Skills, Cooking, Development Issues, Driving, First Aid, Fundraising, Gardening/Horticulture, Group Work, Library/Resource Centres, Manual Work, Marketing/Publicity, Newsletter/Journalism, Outdoor Skills, Research, Scientific Work, Social Work, Summer Camps, Teaching, Technical Skills, Training, Translating, Visiting/Befriending.
Placements: 600
When to apply: All year/ depending on when project starts.
Work alone/with others: Work with others.
Health requirements: No restrictions.
Costs: Travel costs, living costs. No membership or registration fees required.
Benefits: Volunteers could apply for free lodging in the Animal Orphanage of Earthcare.
Training: Depends on project.
Supervision: Ongoing.
Interviews: No.
Worldwide placements: Asia (China, Hong Kong).

EARTHWATCH

267 Banbury Road
Oxford
OX2 7HT UK
T: 01865 318831
F: 01865 311383
E: vp@earthwatch.org.uk
W: www.earthwatch.org/europe
Contact: The Volunteer Programme

Earthwatch is an international charity which sponsors environmental and cultural research by sending paying volunteers to help scientists on their expeditions around the world. The volunteers' time and money has enabled scientists on 1,800 projects in 104 countries to conduct research into a wide variety of issues, from vanishing musical traditions to global warming and dolphin intelligence. Earthwatch gives people the chance to do more than just read about the environment. Volunteers do not need any special skills, just two weeks of their time and curiosity. Volunteers are guaranteed a safe, well organised experience with like-minded people working alongside world experts. Many of the volunteers are single or have had children and are now retired.

Number of projects: 120+ UK: 9
Starting months: January–December
Time required: 1–4 weeks
Age: 16–90
Causes: Animal Welfare, Archaeology, Architecture, Conservation, Environmental Causes, Health Care/Medical, Wildlife.
Activities: Computers, Conservation Skills, Research, Scientific Work, Technical Skills.
Placements: 1,000
When to apply: All year.
Work alone/with others: With others.
Equipment/clothing: Depending on project – most equipment provided.
Health requirements: Depending on project/location.
Costs: £85–£2199 per trip + travel costs (Optional membership £30).
Benefits: Small grants available from Earthwatch. Ranges from camping to comfortable hotels depending on the project. All arranged in advance for volunteers.
Training: All volunteers are sent a detailed project briefing explaining the aims of the project, volunteer tasks etc.
Supervision: Volunteers are supervised at all times by the project staff.
Interviews: Applicants are not interviewed.
Charity number: 327017
Worldwide placements: Africa (Cameroon, Ghana, Kenya, Madagascar, Mauritius, Namibia, South Africa, Tanzania); North America: (Canada, USA); Central America (Bahamas, Belize, Bermuda, Costa Rica, Dominica, Jamaica,

Mexico, Puerto Rico, Virgin Islands); South America (Argentina, Brazil, Chile, Ecuador, Falkland Islands, Peru); Asia (China, India, Israel, Japan, Malaysia, Mongolia, Nepal, Philippines, Sri Lanka, Thailand, Vietnam); Australasia (Australia, New Zealand); Europe (Czech Republic, Estonia, Hungary, Iceland, Ireland, Italy, Romania, Russia, Spain).
UK placements: England (Hampshire, London, Oxfordshire, Tyne and Wear); Scotland (Ayrshire – East, Ayrshire – North, Ayrshire – South, Dumfries and Galloway, Inverclyde, Renfrewshire, Renfrewshire – East); Wales (Blaenau Gwent, Monmouthshire, Newport, Torfaen).

ECO-CENTRE CAPUT INSULAE-BELI

Beli 4
Beli
Island of Cres 51559 Croatia
T: 00 385 51 840525
F: 00 385 51 840525
E: caput.insulae@ri.tel.hr
W: www.caput-insulae.com
Contact: Gordana Pavokovic

The main objectives of this volunteer programme are protecting the natural, cultural and historical heritage of Cres Island especially Tramuntana – the northern part of the island, and the little village of Beli and its surroundings in which most of our programmes are situated. The island of Cres is the biggest island in the Adriatic Sea with only eight inhabitants per square km but 1300 species of plants, 29 reptile species, nine species of snakes (non-venomous), 17 species of mammals, 200 marshes and ponds with 21 species of dragonflies and 200 species of birds of which 90 are breeding on the island. The historical heritage of Cres goes back deep into the Stone Age. It is strewn with undiscovered remains in which a rich history is found. The centre deals with programmes of eco-tourism, education, protection of cultural and historical heritage, conservation of the eurasian griffons and a volunteer centre which is concerned with all of the above. Island of Cres, northern part of the Adriatic Sea, Croatia. 📄

Number of projects: 5 UK: 0
Starting months: Jan
Time required: 2–48 weeks
Age: 18 plus – no upper limit
Causes: Animal Welfare, Archaeology, Conservation, Environmental Causes, Heritage, Wildlife, Work Camps – Seasonal.
Activities: Agriculture/Farming, Arts/Crafts, Building/Construction, Caring (general, day and residential), Community Work, Computers, Conservation Skills, Cooking, Forestry, Group Work, Manual Work, Outdoor Skills, Research,

Summer Camps, Visiting/Befriending, Work Camps – Seasonal.
Placements: 360
When to apply: Two weeks before arrival.
Qualifications: Knowledge of English language is required.
Equipment/clothing: Shoes for rocky terrain, wind jacket, working clothes and, if desired, binoculars.
Health requirements: Good health and physical condition is required.
Costs: Travel to the Island of Cres, £4 daily for subsistence, £80 weekly contribution to the project.
Benefits: Accommodation is provided.
Training: Education about biodiversity and history of the island of Cres.
Supervision: Every volunteer group has a co-ordinator.
Interviews: No interview.
Worldwide placements: Europe (Croatia).

ECOVOLUNTEER PROGRAM

Wildwings, First Floor
577/579 Fishponds Road
Fishponds
Bristol BS16 3AF UK
T: 0117 965 8333
F: 0117 937 5681
E: wildinfo@wildwings.co.uk
W: www.ecovolunteer.org.uk
Contact: Melanie Saunders

Ecovolunteer represents an international network of projects and agencies which operate working conservation holidays all around the world. Many of the projects are set in wild and remote destinations, but also include a number in Europe and in the UK. Ecovolunteers link opportunities, conservation projects get extra manpower and nature enthusiasts get the chance to participate actively. Being a volunteer on the projects is a rewarding and unforgettable experience. A holiday with a mission, ideal for a gap year trip or as part of your round the world epic. Work with wolves in Eastern Europe, with rhinos in Africa, with wild horses on the vast steppes in Mongolia, or in the tropical rainforest in South America. Just examples of the many exciting projects available. All the project details and bookings are available online. Please download extensive project files for each project for free from the web site. Volunteers with an offending background may be accepted. 📄

Number of projects: 30 UK: 1
Starting months: January–December
Time required: 1–26 weeks
Age: 18 plus – no upper limit
Causes: Animal Welfare, Conservation, Environmental Causes, Wildlife.

Activities: Conservation Skills, Outdoor Skills, Research, Scientific Work.
Placements: Approx 500
When to apply: All year, as early as possible before the project is fully booked.
Work alone/with others: Work with others.
Qualifications: Different skills/qualifications may be needed for different projects.
Equipment/clothing: Any equipment needed is provided.
Health requirements: Good health and condition are necessary.
Costs: Different for each project – check web site – no membership or registration fees.
Benefits: Depends on the project: tents, field stations, vessel or small local accommodation.
Training: As far as necessary, for participation in a specific project, on the spot training is provided as part of the participation in the project.
Supervision: Local specialist conservationist and/or researchers from local NGOs.
Interviews: No interviews but on some projects a letter of motivation and a curriculum vitae is required.
Worldwide placements: Africa (Kenya, Malawi, Swaziland, Zimbabwe); Central America (Mexico); South America (Brazil, Colombia, Ecuador); Asia (India, Indonesia, Kyrgyzstan, Malaysia, Mongolia, Thailand); Australasia (New Zealand); Europe (Bulgaria, Croatia, Italy, Poland, Romania, Russia, Spain, Turkey).
UK placements: Scotland (Moray).

ECUMENICAL NETWORK FOR YOUTH ACTION

U Nas 9
CZ-147 00 Prague 4
Czech Republic
T: 00 420 2 472 7390
F: 00 420 2 472 7390
E: enya@ecumenical.org
Contact: Cath Moss

Ecumenical Network for Youth Action (ENYA) is an exciting membership/partnership based movement of churches and related organisations, including youth organisations groups, women's networks, diaconal projects, children's rights and protection activists, social movements, justice, peace, reconciliation and environmental groups, NGOs/INGOs combined with individual members from over 50 countries around the world. Volunteers with an offending background may be accepted but not in all circumstances. It depends on the offence and the nature of the project. ▣

Number of projects: 15–20 UK: 2
Starting months: January–December
Time required: 2–52 weeks
Age: 15 plus – no upper limit

Causes: Addicts/Ex-Addicts, AIDS/HIV, Children, Human Rights, Inner City Problems, Offenders/Ex-Offenders, Poor/Homeless, Refugees, Unemployed, Work Camps – Seasonal, Young People.
Activities: Administration, Arts/Crafts, Building/Construction, Campaigning, Caring – Residential, Community Work, Computers, Development Issues, DIY, Fundraising, Group Work, International Aid, Newsletter/Journalism, Outdoor Skills, Religion, Social Work, Summer Camps, Technical Skills, Training, Visiting/Befriending, Work Camps – Seasonal.
Placements: 50
When to apply: All year.
Work alone/with others: With others.
Qualifications: An openness to others, their cultures and traditions and religions. If working with children's projects, clearance papers from justice authorities are needed. We welcome all young people and look forward to the diversity of inter-cultural exchanges.
Equipment/clothing: Any special equipment would be provided by us.
Health requirements: Nil.
Costs: Varies depending on the placement and the length of time. Average £50 per week.
Benefits: Depends on project. Generally volunteers are not provided with any financial benefits and need to contribute to their accommodation and food costs unless from Eastern or Central Europe. Accommodation varies, depending on the placement. Ranges from tents in the summer to home accommodation in the winter.
Training: There is always an orientation meeting at the beginning of any placement and occasional evaluations throughout the placement period.
Supervision: We have trained supervisors in each project placement.
Interviews: Interviews are in person by a member of the ENYA national committee and by telephone with the Volunteer Co-ordinators.
Charity number: ICO: 65998871
Worldwide placements: Africa (Cameroon, Congo Dem Republic, Egypt, South Africa, Zimbabwe); North America: (Canada, USA); Central America (Antigua and Barbuda, Cuba, Jamaica); South America (Brazil); Asia (Hong Kong, India, Israel, Pakistan, Thailand); Australasia (Australia, Fiji); Europe (Albania, Armenia, Austria, Belarus, Bulgaria, Croatia, Czech Republic, Denmark, Estonia, Finland, France, Georgia, Germany, Greece, Hungary, Ireland, Latvia, Lithuania, Malta, Moldova, Poland, Portugal, Romania, Russia, Slovakia, Slovenia, Switzerland, Ukraine, Yugoslavia).
UK placements: England (Manchester, Oxfordshire, Tyne and Wear); Scotland (Edinburgh, Fife, Perth and Kinross); Northern Ireland (Antrim, Belfast City).

EDINBURGH CYRENIANS
Norton Park
57 Albion Road
Edinburgh
Midlothian EH7 5QY UK
T: 0131 475 2354
F: 0131 475 2355
E: director@cyrenians.org.uk
W: www.cyrenians.org.uk
Contact: Des Ryan

Residential volunteers offer peer support and mentoring for young people who are vulnerable to long-term homelessness. Living in a community household, volunteers help to uphold the house rules and to promote a positive environment through which residents will progess in their lives. Lots of fun, activity, challenge, learning and a fair bit of hard work! The City Community offer all the leisure and cultural opportunities provided by Edinburgh. The Farm – about ten miles out of town – offers therapy of organic gardening, chickens, goats and talking to tomatoes. We may be able to accept volunteers with an offending background. Cyrenian Farm, 12 Humble Holdings, West Lothian EH27 8DS – therapeutic community for young homeless people. City Community, 107a Ferry Road, Edinburgh – urban therapeutic community in cultural capital city. ♿ ▤

Number of projects: 2 **UK:** 2
Starting months: January–December
Time required: 20–40 weeks
Age: 18–35
Causes: Animal Welfare, Conservation, Environmental Causes, Poor/Homeless, Refugees, Unemployed, Young People.
Activities: Agriculture/Farming, Caring – Residential, Conservation Skills, Cooking, DIY, Gardening/Horticulture, Group Work, Outdoor Skills, Visiting/Befriending.
Placements: 12
When to apply: All year.
Work alone/with others: With others.
Qualifications: No qualifications/skills are required except a working ability in English.
Equipment/clothing: All provided.
Health requirements: Good.
Costs: No cost.
Benefits: Travel. board and lodging, pocket money, holiday allowance and leaving grant. Accommodation is provided within the communities. We also offer a time off flat for use when volunteers have free time.
Training: Induction training and regular session training.
Supervision: Regular professional supervision.
Interviews: Guest visit and interview if volunteers are from the UK.
Charity number: SCO 11052

UK placements: Scotland (Edinburgh, Lothian – East, Lothian – West, Midlothian).

EDUCATION CENTRE FOR HELPLESS CHILDREN (ECHC)
Dhapasi-4
Kathmandu
Nepal
T: 00 977 1 355209
E: echc@wlink.com.np
W: www.echcnepal.org
Contact: Saraswoti Shrestha

The Education Centre for Helpless Children (ECHC) was established in 1998 as a non-governmental organisation. Its mission is for the education, accommodation, food and health of orphaned and helpless children. At the head office 30 children are being given a new ray of hope. The ECHC provides a homely atmosphere and makes arrangements for their basic school education. The main objectives are: to provide shelter, health and education to helpless children; to help helpless children to become self-reliant in the future; to save children from deprivation of the basic child rights; to help children realise their fundamental rights. The long-term goal of the ECHC is to enable these children to stand on their own feet and lead a normal social life. The volunteers are expected to help with all activities including formal and informal education, and to assist in the management of the organisation. Volunteers will be met at the airport on arrival. Dhapasi village in Kathmandu city.

Number of projects: 4 **UK:** 0
Starting months: January–December
Time required: 4–15 weeks
Age: 16–60
Causes: Children, Health Care/Medical, Human Rights, Teaching/assisting, Work Camps – Seasonal.
Activities: Development Issues, Fundraising, Newsletter/Journalism, Research, Social Work, Teaching, Training, Work Camps – Seasonal.
Placements: 12
When to apply: All year.
Work alone/with others: Yes.
Qualifications: Working knowledge of English.
Health requirements: Nil.
Costs: Registration fee £100, Membership and training fee £100 + travel.
Benefits: Food and accommodation.
Training: Office management, teaching, etc.
Supervision: We provide intensive guidance and supervision.
Interviews: No interviews.
Charity number: 582
Worldwide placements: Asia (Nepal).

EDUCATIONAL CENTER VERA

28 Suite, 51 House
Liteiny pr
St Petersburg
191104 Russia
T: 7 812 275 75 81/84/87
F: 7 812 272 31 75
E: veraspb@online.ru
W: www.eduvera.spb.ru
Contact: Vadim Amelchenko

Educational Center VERA deals with tuition of foreign languages, mainly English. Our center is located in the very center of the city.
We teach English in our center, in some secondary schools, and in different organisations. During the summer, we organise children's camps in Russia and Finland with tuition of English by native-speakers. We can help with visa processing and support volunteers during their stay. You are welcome! We unfortunately are not able to accept volunteers with an offending background. ⌨ ▤

Number of projects: 2–3 UK: 0
Starting months: January–December
Time required: 2–48 weeks
Age: 20–60
Causes: Children, Refugees, Teaching (EFL).
Activities: Summer Camps, Teaching.
Placements: 5–10
When to apply: 2 months before wishing to arrive. Russia stays from 8 weeks to 48 weeks all year. Finland stays from 2 weeks to 4 weeks during the summer.
Work alone/with others: Work with others.
Qualifications: The more qualifications in teaching English volunteers have, the better.
Health requirements: No restrictions.
Costs: Travel city card for metro, bus, train trollybus costs $12 per month. Air fare. Lunch (MacDonalds – $3–$5).
Benefits: Breakfast, dinner and lodging.
Training: Consultation before tuition. Methodical support offered at any time.
Supervision: Supervised by the VERA center.
Interviews: Interviews are done via e-mail.
Worldwide placements: Europe (Finland, Russia).

EIN YAEL LIVING MUSEUM

P. O. Box 9679
Jerusalem 91094
Israel
T: 00 972 26451866
Contact: Mr Eli Vaknin

The Ein Yael Living Museum is situated in the Rephaim Valley of Jerusalem. The project combines experimentation in the techniques of traditional agriculture with crafts such as pottery, weaving, mosaic, basketry and construction as practised in various historical periods. The research in these fields is an attempt to understand the way ancient man interacted with his environment. Volunteers are needed for the building of workshops, to act as guides for child visitors and to help with research and archaeological excavations on the site. Jerusalem.

Number of projects: 1
Starting months: January–December
Time required: 2–52 weeks
Age: 16 plus – no upper limit
Causes: Archaeology, Conservation, Heritage.
Activities: Arts/Crafts, Building/Construction, Conservation Skills, Manual Work, Research.
When to apply: All year.
Worldwide placements: Asia (Israel).

ELEPHANT NATURE PARK

209/2 Sridorn Chai Road
Chiang Mai
501000 Thailand
T: +66(0)53818754
F: +66(0)53818755
E: info@thaifocus.com
W: www.thaifocus.com/elephant
Contact: Sangduen Chailert

Elephant Nature Park helps elephants in need. We have a farm which has two orphaned infants. We are funded by volunteer contribution. Volunteers are offered a unique chance to get close to elephants and will learn about the root cause of their problems. We also go out in the jungle to help injured or sick elephants. Often this is their only source of treatment. Team work is essential as is an easy going pleasant character. Volunteers are required to work hard for six days per week. Projects start the first and third Monday of each month. Extensions of more than two weeks are only considered after the completion of two weeks. North Thailand.

Number of projects: 1 UK: 0
Starting months: January–December
Time required: 1–2 weeks
Age: 18 plus – no upper limit
Causes: Animal Welfare, Conservation, Environmental Causes, Teaching/assisting, Unemployed, Wildlife.
Activities: Agriculture/Farming, Catering, Community Work, Conservation Skills, DIY, Forestry, Manual Work, Outdoor Skills, Research.
Placements: 200
When to apply: 2 months before volunteers wish to arrive.
Work alone/with others: Work alone.
Health requirements: No restrictions – volunteers should check with GP for vaccinations.
Costs: Travel costs and US$249 per week contribution.

Benefits: Accommodation.
Training: On the job training provided.
Supervision: Local staff supervise.
Interviews: At office on arrival.
Worldwide placements: Asia (Thailand).

ELI SHENHAV: JNF

11 Zvi Shapira Street
Tel Aviv
Israel
T: 00 972 3 2561129
E: elis@kkl.org.il
Contact: Eli Shenhav

Eli Shenhav needs volunteers to work on an excavation of a Roman theatre three miles from Caesarea and a Roman theatre in Shuni. Working hours are from 5.30 am – noon, five days a week.

Number of projects: 1 UK: 0
Starting months: Jul
Time required: 1–52 weeks
Age: 14 plus – no upper limit
Causes: Archaeology
Activities: Administration, Conservation Skills, Research.
Placements: 17
When to apply: As early as possible.
Costs: Board and accommodation at approx £10 per day.
Worldwide placements: Asia (Israel).

EMMAUS INTERNATIONAL

183 bis, rue Vaillant-Couturier
BP 91
94140 Alfortville
France
T: (00 33)1 48 93 29 50
F: (00 33)1 43 53 19 26
E: contact@emmaus-international.org
W: www.emmaus-international.org
Contact: The Secretary

The Emmaus movement started in Paris in 1949 and there are now some 442 Emmaus communities in 42 countries. These communities try to provide a meaning to life for those without one – that meaning being to help others in need. Each community is autonomous and independent of race, sex, religion, politics, age etc. Living conditions are usually simple and the work is hard. The activities of European Emmaus groups are recycling, sorting and resale of second-hand items. The benefits are given to Emmaus social action. Although in Eastern Europe, Africa, Asia and the Americas, Emmaus never sends volunteers to the third world countries because they employ local people on the spot. Volunteers with offending backgrounds are accepted. ⓐ ▤

Number of projects: 5 approximately UK: 0
Starting months: Jun, Jul, Aug, Sep
Time required: 2–10 weeks
Age: 18 plus – no upper limit
Causes: Work Camps – Seasonal.
Activities: Community Work, Cooking, Manual Work, Summer Camps, Work Camps – Seasonal.
Placements: 500
When to apply: February/March
Work alone/with others: With others.
Qualifications: Spoken English or language of project country.
Health requirements: Generally in good health.
Costs: All costs except food and accommodation.
Benefits: Accommodation and food. Volunteers are accommodated in tents or dormitory-style rooms.
Training: Depending on project.
Supervision: A responsible supervisor is in charge of volunteers and also the friends of the communities which organise the camps.
Interviews: Applicants are not interviewed.
Worldwide placements: Europe (Denmark, Germany, Italy, Poland, Portugal).

EMMS INTERNATIONAL

7 Washington Lane
Edinburgh
EH11 2HA UK
T: 0131 313 3828
F: 0131 313 4662
E: info@emms.org
W: www.emms.org
Contact: Mr Robin G.K. Arnott

EMMS International assists seven Christian hospitals and clinics in Africa, Asia and the Middle East to obtain volunteers for occasional support and general maintenance work. Vacancies occur regularly at any time of the year. Enquiries should be made to us.

Number of projects: 9 UK: 0
Starting months: January–December
Time required: 4–52 weeks
Age: 18 plus – no upper limit
Causes: Children, Disabled (learning and physical), Elderly People, Health Care/Medical, Work Camps – Seasonal.
Activities: Administration, Building/Construction, Caring – General, DIY, Gardening/Horticulture, Manual Work, Religion, Teaching, Technical Skills, Work Camps – Seasonal.
Placements: 10
When to apply: Any time.
Work alone/with others: With others.
Qualifications: Nil but experience and/or skill valuable.
Equipment/clothing: Provided by the hospitals/clinics.

Health requirements: Fit and in good health.
Costs: Return travel to the country involved
and possibly some accommodation costs.
Benefits: Board and lodging provided in
Nazareth hospital flats. In other hospitals
accommodation is generally in compound.
Training: None.
Supervision: Hospital would provide this.
Interviews: Applicants for volunteer projects
are not interviewed.
Charity number: SC 015000
Worldwide placements: Africa (Malawi); Asia
(India, Israel, Nepal).

ENDEAVOUR TRAINING

Sheepbridge Centre
Sheepbridge Lane
Chesterfield
Derbyshire S41 9RX UK
T: 0870 770 3250
F: 0870 770 3254
E: colin.matchett@endeavour.org.uk
W: www.endeavour.org.uk
Contact: Colin Matchett

Endeavour has a number of targeted youth
programmes to support disaffected young
people. This work is supported by Endeavour
volunteers working alongside project workers, for
which training is provided. Endeavour and its
network of volunteers also provide opportunities
for these young people to continue participating
in exciting developmental opportunities as
members of Endeavour, after completing a
targeted youth programme. Participating in
activities as well as putting something back into
the community. Volunteers with an offending
background are accepted. Applicants have to
become members. 🔊 📄

Number of projects: 9+ UK: 7+
Starting months: January–December
Time required: 1–52 weeks
Age: 16–26
Causes: Young People.
Activities: Arts/Crafts, Community Work,
Fundraising, Group Work, Outdoor Skills,
Summer Camps.
Placements: 180+
When to apply: Any time.
Work alone/with others: With others.
Qualifications: Membership of Endeavour.
Caring, dependable.
Health requirements: Nil.
Costs: Membership is free in return for
voluntary work + some travel cost.
Benefits: Some expenses and training provided
in return for voluntary support of projects.
Access to exciting challenges and opportunities
for members.
Training: Volunteers have to participate in
training and events before participating on
projects with at risk groups.

Supervision: Volunteers receive support and
supervision from project workers and senior
volunteers.
Interviews: References are checked and
volunteers undergo vetting procedures before
acceptance.
Charity number: 275061
UK placements: England (Co Durham,
Derbyshire, Leicestershire, Nottinghamshire,
Tyne and Wear, Warwickshire, West Midlands,
S. Yorkshire).

ENVIRONMENTAL LIAISON CENTRE INTERNATIONAL

P O Box 72461
Nairobi
Kenya
T: 00 254 2 576 114 or 576119
F: 00 254 2 562175
E: barbarag@elci.org
W: www.elci.org
Contact: Barbara Gemmill

Objective – To make information a useful tool
to measurably improve the environment.
Organisation – The Environment Liaison Centre
International (ELCI) is an international NGO
established in Nairobi. ELCI works with
partners throughout the world. In particular it
works in five thematic areas: forests, water,
energy, agriculture and access to information.
For each thematic area, a variety of approaches
and projects are implemented. These are based
at the local, national and regional levels, with
cost-cutting initiatives concentrated at
international flora. ELCI focuses on the local-
global linkages especially with those initiatives
that bring policy or ideas to the grassroots
levels or to bring 'on the ground' case studies or
lessons learned to the decision-making people.
The main aspects of this work are
communication, information generation and
dissemination aimed at environmental
conservation and sustainable use of natural
resources. In addition it focuses on the link
between civil society and the United Nations
Environment Programme (UNEP) encouraging a
stronger advisory role of the NGOs in UNEP
decision-making. Founded in 1974.
As of February 2002 – 92 non govermental and
community based organisations worldwide.

Number of projects: 0 UK: 2
Starting months: January–December
Time required: 20–40 weeks
Age: 20 plus – no upper limit
Causes: Environmental Causes.
Activities: Agriculture/Farming, Computers,
Conservation Skills, Development Issues,
Forestry, Fundraising, Newsletter/Journalism,
Research.
Placements: 3

When to apply: All year.
Work alone/with others: Both.
Qualifications: Qualification in environmental or development. Some experience in one of the following – Forest conservation, agricultural biodiversity, sustainable development, world summit on sustainable development, water conservation, energy, environment law.
Health requirements: Good health required vaccinations. Malaria does not occur in Nairobi.
Costs: Return travel to Nairobi. Subsistence in Nairobi approx £50 per week plus start up costs.
Benefits: Will assist to find suitable accommodation within the volunteer's budget.
Training: Training is not available except work where necessary. Volunteers will have the opportunity to observe United Nations Environment Programme, International Advocacy Work around UNEP and other international processes.
Supervision: Volunteer will be placed in a project and will be supervised by that project co-ordinator. In development projects – supervision undertaken by the Director.
Interviews: Prospective volunteers are not interviewed but e-mail communication is used for screening.
Worldwide placements: Africa (Kenya).

EQUINOCCIAL SPANISH SCHOOL

Reina Victoria 1325 y
Lizardo Garcia
Quito Ecuador
T: (593) 2 256 4488
F: (593) 2 256 4488
E: service@ecuadorspanish.com
W: www.ecuadorspanish.com
Contact: Sandra Navarrete

Equinoccial Spanish School is responsible for promoting the volunteer programmes, contacting international organisations interested in sending volunteers to Ecuador, and working with foundations of a social and ecological nature that work in Ecuador. As we are responsible for promoting volunteer programmes, we establish contact with volunteers before they come to Ecuador so that their trip runs as smoothly as possible.
Once the volunteers arrive in Ecuador, we pick them up from the airport, take them to their home stay families and take them to school on their first day. While at the school, we introduce them to the foundation that will receive them and we co-ordinate the orientation process. Volunteer programmes – Ecological – teaching English. Volunteers who stay for more than six months receive free food, housing and transport. Cost of working in field conservation is $30 daily for food and housing. Social-Community – working with children,

tutoring and mentoring @£12 per day. Health – three centres. Volunteers work supporting doctors and nurses in the North and South. We can arrange home stays with Ecuadorian families in a residential neighbourhood close to the school or in the quieter northern Quito. This gives volunteers the opportunity for additional Spanish practice. Staying with a family is one of the best ways to complement your Spanish instruction and is a great way to learn about typical food, traditions and culture. The service includes three meals per day, a private room and laundry once a week, at the cost of $15/day. Quito, Maquipucuna, Casa de la Ninez, San Jose. 🦽 📄

Number of projects: 5 UK: 0
Starting months: January–December
Time required: 4–24 weeks
Age: 18 plus – no upper limit
Causes: Children, Conservation, Environmental Causes, Health Care/Medical, Teaching/assisting (EFL), Young People.
Activities: Caring – General, Community Work, Conservation Skills, First Aid, Teaching.
Placements: Varies.
When to apply: As soon as possible.
Work alone/with others: With others.
Qualifications: Some basic Spanish language skills are an advantage.
Health requirements: In general good health.
Costs: Programme costs vary from US$112 per week for standard programme to $426 per week for explorer programme. Flight, visa and insurance paid for by volunteer.
Benefits: Transport from Quito airport. Study materials. Use of library. Home stay accommodation. Free food if staying over six months.
Training: Orientation process.
Supervision: We maintain contact with volunteers while they are working on their project and ensure they are taken care of.
Interviews: Via e-mail and application form.
Worldwide placements: South America (Ecuador).

ESCUELA DE ENFERMERIA – STELLA MARIS

Apartado Postal 28
Zacapu
Michoacan
CP 58670 Mexico
T: 001 52 436 36 31300
F: 001 52 436 36 31300
E: stellamariszac@hotmail.com
Contact: Sister Theresa Avila

Stella Maris is a private nursing school whose student body is made up of many students from very poor areas. Volunteers are needed to help with general school maintenance and act as secretaries or, if qualified, to be teaching nurses or doctors. Stella Maris is a school of nursing for native Indian girls with limited resources, with the goal of preparing qualified nurses who can improve health care in the towns and pueblos in this region. Nursing teachers and supervisors are urgently needed, as well as a volunteer librarian. Our students usually come from poor families, and we strive to make their education as inexpensive as possible. Volunteer workers help us realise this goal. Sister Theresa Avila, a registered nurse and a Catholic nun from Southern California, founded the school in 1967. Part-time instructors from the community constitute the school faculty, each holding other full-time jobs concomitantly. The school has an average of 90 students, both male and female. The students have a number of places where they can develop their clinical skills; a 40-bed government hospital well equipped and professionally staffed, a ten-bed general hospital, a Red Cross, and a number of rural public health clinics. Students also affiliate in large hospitals in three different cities outside of Zacapu. We prefer a period of no less than six months from volunteers. Board and lodging and a small monthly stipend are offered to volunteers. The lodging school has electricity, running water and indoor toilets. We seek volunteers for service as community health assistants, clinical supervisors, and teachers in English and nursing subjects, a librarian and those with general backgrounds who are simply willing to tackle a variety of jobs. Some ability to communicate in Spanish is helpful and fluency is essential for classroom teaching. Volunteers are expected to fulfil their commitment and full obligations of their service. Please contact Sister Theresa Avila for more details. ♿ 📄

Number of projects: 1 UK: 0
Starting months: January–December
Time required: 26–52 weeks
Age: 14 plus – no upper limit
Causes: Children, Health Care/Medical, Poor/Homeless, Teaching/assisting (nursery, primary, secondary, EFL).
Activities: Administration, Caring – General, First Aid, Teaching, Training.
Placements: 1–6
When to apply: All year.
Work alone/with others: With others.
Qualifications: Preferably knowledge of Spanish, driving licence, typing, organising skills.
Equipment/clothing: School supplies working equipment.
Health requirements: Vaccinations are available here free of charge. Our doctors here give free service to volunteers.

Costs: Travel.
Benefits: Accommodation, food and small monthly allowance. Accommodation is simple but clean and comfortable.
Training: Since the school has a variety of work, volunteers choose where they feel most comfortable, we then train on the job.
Supervision: Sister Theresa works closely with volunteers.
Interviews: Via telephone and e-mail.
Worldwide placements: Central America (Mexico).

ESPACO T

Avenida de Franca 256
Centro Comercial Capitolio
Salas 5, 12, 22, 23
Porto
4050-276 Portugal
T: 00 351 22 830 2432
F: 00 351 22 830 5593
E: espacot@espacot.pt
W: www.espacot.pt
Contact: Jorge Oliveira

Espaco t (Association for Support and Social and Community Integration) takes care of people with multiple physical, psychological and social problems. This Association provides them with artistic activities including photography, theatre, painting, physical education, music, dance, tai-chi-chuan and journalism. In the social area, Espaco t has a UNIVA (Unity of Insertion in the Active Life) whose main aim is promoting employment. We also have a phone line which informs about Espaco t's activities and which also supports people in crisis and distress. About 30 volunteers are taken on annually to help with cultural activities. Volunteers with an offending background are accepted. ♿ 📄

Number of projects: 1 UK: 0
Starting months: Jan
Time required: 2–4 weeks
Age: 18–60
Causes: Addicts/Ex-Addicts, AIDS/HIV, Disabled (learning and physical), Offenders/Ex-Offenders, Poor/Homeless, Teaching/assisting, Unemployed.
Activities: Arts/Crafts, Community Work, Group Work, Music, Newsletter/Journalism, Social Work, Sport, Teaching, Theatre/Drama.
Placements: 30
When to apply: Any time.
Work alone/with others: With others.
Qualifications: Knowledge of Portuguese, Spanish or Italian and some artistic or social work expertise.
Health requirements: Good health essential, both physically and mentally.
Costs: All costs.

Benefits: We can help the volunteers to find a room.
Training: The team will brief the volunteer about the Association's activities.
Supervision: Director, psychologist and the social-cultural animator will be responsible for the supervision of volunteers.
Interviews: Interviews are conducted either by telephone or at the Association offices.
Worldwide placements: Europe (Portugal).

ESTONIAN VOLUNTEER CENTRE (EVC)

Endla 4
Talinn 10142
Estonia
T: 00 372 626 3372
F: 00 372 626 3310
E: merleh@ngo.ee
Contact: Merle Helbe

Estonian Volunteer Centre promotes and has information about volunteering in Estonia. It may well be able to put volunteers in touch with organisations which are not yet listed on the WorldWide Volunteering database.

Starting months: January–December
Time required: 1–52 weeks (plus)
Age: 16 plus – no upper limit
Causes: Addicts/Ex-Addicts, AIDS/HIV, Animal Welfare, Archaeology, Architecture, Children, Conservation, Disabled (learning and physical), Elderly People, Environmental Causes, Health Care/Medical, Heritage, Holidays for Disabled, Human Rights, Inner City Problems, Offenders/Ex-Offenders, Poor/Homeless, Refugees, Teaching/assisting (nursery, primary, secondary, mature, EFL) Unemployed, Wildlife, Work Camps – Seasonal, Young People.
Activities: Accountancy, Administration, Agriculture/Farming, Arts/Crafts, Building/Construction, Campaigning, Caring (general, day and residential), Catering, Community Work, Computers, Conservation Skills, Cooking, Counselling, Development Issues, DIY, Driving, First Aid, Forestry, Fundraising, Gardening/Horticulture, Group Work, International Aid, Library/Resource Centres, Manual Work, Marketing/Publicity, Music, Newsletter/Journalism, Outdoor Skills, Religion, Research, Scientific Work, Social Work, Sport, Summer Camps, Teaching, Technical Skills, Theatre/Drama, Training, Translating, Visiting/Befriending, Work Camps – Seasonal.
Costs: Varies according to the project.
Worldwide placements: Europe (Estonia).

ETUDES ET CHANTIERS (UNAREC)

3, rue des Petits Gras
Delegation internationale UNAREC
Clermont-Ferrand
63000 France
T: 00 33 4 73 36 52 28
F: 00 33 4 73 36 46 65
Contact: François Ribaud

Etudes et Chantiers is a non-profit and non-governmental organisation, organised locally by regional organisations and federated with a national union (UNAREC). All associations lead permanent actions to help deprived areas and people with work for local communities: 120 staff and 100 volunteers lead these projects all around the year. In ten regions of France and 29 countries in the world, Etudes et Chantiers invites you in practical action to build and enrich communities and environment ('spaces of life').

Number of projects: 60 UK: 0
Starting months: Jun
Time required: 2–24 weeks
Age: 14 plus – no upper limit
Causes: Conservation, Environmental Causes, Heritage, Work Camps – Seasonal.
Activities: Building/Construction, Conservation Skills, Forestry, International Aid, Social Work, Work Camps – Seasonal.
Placements: 800
When to apply: Before end of May.
Work alone/with others: With other international volunteers in a group of 12–15.
Equipment/clothing: Work clothes, sleeping bag, good shoes, boots, gloves, suncream.
Health requirements: Nil.
Costs: Registration and insurance €91.5. Travel/camp fees: (13–16yr) €366; (17–18yr) €137; Adults over 18 free.
Benefits: Board and lodging, leisure activities. Accommodation provided – usually in tents.
Interviews: We do not interview applicants for voluntary work.
Worldwide placements: Europe (France).

EUROPEAN VOLUNTARY SERVICE

The British Council
Connect Youth
10 Spring Gardens
London
SW1A 2BN UK
T: +44 (0) 207 389 4030
F: +44 (0) 207 389 4033
E: connectyouth.enquiries@britishcouncil.org
Contact: Information Officer

Connect Youth is the British national agency for the European Voluntary Service Scheme which is open to all young people with no qualification requirement. There is a very wide range of tasks and positive measures will enable disadvantaged young people to have access to the programme. Although you will have a say over your placement and type of work you must be prepared to work in any one of the fields ticked. You will meet volunteers from other European countries to share experiences. You will have a rewarding experience doing something useful for other communities. You will learn a lot, at the same time helping yourself to develop as a person and to develop your future. You will learn new skills which make you more attractive to future employers. It is exciting and you will get to see places. You will be living in another country for quite a long time. You will learn about their customs and feel a sense of belonging to the European Union. You will make useful contacts for the future, even at European level, and also have an active part in discussing your role, place and responsibilities in the host project. At in-service training events you will have the chance to meet other EVS volunteers in your country and to discuss and reflect upon your experiences. You may be the only volunteer at your assignment or you may be working with a group of volunteers. But you will always be part of a team. This entry is repeated under 'Connect Youth'. ♿

Number of projects: 100+ **UK:** 0
Starting months: January–December
Time required: 3–52 weeks
Age: 18–25
Causes: Addicts/Ex-Addicts, AIDS/HIV, Animal Welfare, Archaeology, Architecture, Children, Conservation, Disabled (learning and physical), Elderly People, Environmental Causes, Health Care/Medical, Heritage, Holidays for Disabled, Human Rights, Inner City Problems, Offenders/Ex-Offenders, Poor/Homeless, Refugees, Unemployed, Wildlife, Work Camps – Seasonal, Young People.

Activities: Accountancy, Administration, Agriculture/Farming, Arts/Crafts, Building/Construction, Campaigning, Caring (general, day and residential), Catering, Community Work, Computers, Conservation Skills, Cooking, Counselling, Development Issues, DIY, Driving, First Aid, Forestry, Fundraising, Gardening/Horticulture, Group Work, International Aid, Library/Resource Centres, Manual Work, Marketing/Publicity, Music, Newsletter/Journalism, Outdoor Skills, Religion, Research, Scientific Work, Social Work, Sport, Summer Camps, Teaching, Technical Skills, Theatre/Drama, Training, Translating, Visiting/Befriending, Work Camps – Seasonal.
When to apply: All year.
Work alone/with others: Both.
Qualifications: Only EU citizens.
Equipment/clothing: Any special equipment or equipment supplied.
Health requirements: Any special Health requirements for a specific project would be notified to prospective volunteer.
Costs: Nil.
Benefits: Board and lodging + pocket money approx £20 per week. Travel money and special equipment.
Training: You will be given preparatory training before you leave including language training and preparation for the new culture you will be living in. You will also attend an in-service training event during the course of your assignment.
Supervision: As well as a job supervisor, you will have a personal supervisor unconnected

with your project whom you can turn to for personal support if needed.

Worldwide placements: Europe (Austria, Belgium, Bulgaria, Cyprus, Czech Republic, Denmark, Estonia, Finland, France, Germany, Greece, Iceland, Ireland, Italy, Latvia, Liechtenstein, Lithuania, Luxembourg, Malta, Netherlands, Norway, Portugal, Romania, Slovakia, Slovenia, Spain, Sweden, Turkey).

EVANGELISCHE KIRCHE IN OSTERREICH

Diakonie Osterreich
Trautsongasse 8
A-1080 Wien
Austria
T: 00 43 1 409 80 01
F: 00 43 1 409 80 01 20
E: bischof@okr-evang.at
Contact: Mag. Waltraut Kovacic

Evangelische Kirche – Diakonie Osterreich is the Austrian branch of the European Diaconal Year network which consists of a number of national Christian-based volunteering schemes. (The British branch is Time For God.) They share common standards, and a commitment to the personal development of the volunteer through this form of work.

Number of projects: 5 UK: 0
Starting months: January–December

Time required: 26–52 weeks
Age: 18–25
Causes: Children, Disabled (learning and physical), Elderly People, Health Care/Medical, Holidays for Disabled, Human Rights, Refugees, Teaching/assisting (nursery, primary, secondary), Unemployed, Young People.
Activities: Caring (general, day and residential), Social Work.
Placements: 10–15
When to apply: Before March to start the following school year – September onwards.
Work alone/with others: with other employees.
Qualifications: Fluent German. Personal active Christian faith.
Health requirements: Must be in good health.
Costs: Travel costs to the Austrian border or location of placement.
Benefits: Board and lodging, pocket money (€180 per month), social insurance. Volunteers usually share an apartment together with others, in single bedrooms.
Supervision: We offer support to the volunteers through both personal supervision and regular residential conferences or seminars.
Interviews: Written interviews, meetings with the person in charge of the volunteers.
Worldwide placements: Europe (Austria).

F

FAIRBRIDGE

207 Waterloo Road
London
SE1 8XD UK
T: +44 (0) 207 928 1704
F: +44 (0) 207 928 6016
E: info@fairbridge.org.uk
W: www.fairbridge.org.uk
Contact: Personnel Officer

Fairbridge works with disaffected young people aged 13–25 in 13 of the UK's inner cities. It offers a long-term personal development programme which focuses on the development of personal and social skills. As participants progress, they also build a balanced portfolio of secondary skills such as independent living skills, recreation and community skills and work-based skills. Various vehicles are used to deliver the programme, from challenging outdoor activities to the arts and workplace environments. Each young person tailors the programme to their individual needs by selecting from a wide range of courses and is supported by a mentor to develop a personal action plan. Volunteers contribute to all aspects of programme delivery within Fairbridge, depending on individual skills and the needs of the particular Fairbridge team. Responsibilities could include recruitment of young people for the programme, project delivery, mentoring, fundraising or administrative duties. Volunteers with an offending background will be considered. ♿

Number of projects: 13 **UK:** 13
Starting months: January–December
Time required: 4–52 weeks (plus)
Age: 18–65
Causes: Addicts/Ex-Addicts, Conservation, Inner City Problems, Offenders/Ex-Offenders, Poor/Homeless, Unemployed, Young People.
Activities: Administration, Arts/Crafts, Community Work, Conservation Skills, Cooking, Counselling, Driving, First Aid, Fundraising, Group Work, Marketing/Publicity, Music, Newsletter/Journalism, Outdoor Skills, Sport, Theatre/Drama, Training.
Placements: 60–80
When to apply: All year.
Work alone/with others: Both.
Qualifications: Driving licence and first aid an advantage.
Health requirements: Nil.
Costs: none.
Benefits: Travel, subsistence, training.
Training: Depending on the position, volunteers will be interviewed and expected to participate in an induction process. A budget is available for further training.
Supervision: Volunteers will be supervised by a head of department and appraised regularly.
Interviews: Volunteer applicants are always recruited and interviewed at the relevant team centre (details of centres can be obtained from Central Office).
Charity number: 206807
UK placements: England (Bristol, Hampshire, Kent, London, Manchester, Merseyside, Tyne and Wear, West Midlands, N. Yorkshire); Scotland (Edinburgh, Glasgow City); Wales (Cardiff).

FARM SANCTUARY

P O Box 150
Watkins Glen
NY14891 USA
T: 00 1 607 583 4512
F: 00 1 607 583 2041
E: education@farmsanctuary.org
W: www.farmsanctuary.org
Contact: Michelle Waffner

Farm Sanctuary is a national, non-profit organisation dedicated to ending farm animal abuse. Farm Sanctuary works to stop abusive animal agricultural practices by providing hands-on rescue, rehabilitation and permanent shelter for abused and neglected farm animals. We also educate the public and encourage individuals to adopt a lifestyle that fosters the protection of farm animals and to initiate investigative, legal and legislative campaigns to prevent cruelty to farm animals at factory farms, stockyards and slaughterhouses. Volunteers are involved in the day to day operations at Farm Sanctuary. They are generally assigned to shelter, administration and/or education departments where responsibilities may include: shelter: cleaning barns, maintaining farm grounds and assisting with animal care. Administration: filing, assisting with mailings and other projects, data entry, office cleaning and recycling education: staffing and maintaining visitor centre, conducting tours and assisting with education events. Watkins Glen, NY and Orland, CA. ♿ 📄

Number of projects: 2 **UK:** 0
Starting months: January–December
Time required: 4–12 weeks
Age: 16 plus – no upper limit
Causes: Animal Welfare.

Activities: Agriculture/Farming, Campaigning, Manual Work.
Placements: 40
When to apply: A few months before available date.
Work alone/with others: With other young volunteers.
Qualifications: Commitment to animal rights and vegetarianism. A desire to stop farm animal abuse.
Health requirements: Manual labour outside and in the barns. People with lifting restrictions may have trouble.
Costs: Travel, food and personal expenses.
Benefits: Accommodation is provided in a shared house with up to six volunteers at any one time.
Training: Volunteers will be trained as needed.
Supervision: Volunteers live and work fairly independently.
Interviews: By telephone.
Worldwide placements: North America: (USA).

FEDERACIO CATALANA DE VOLUNTARIAT SOCIAL (FCVS) – SPAIN

Pere Verges 1, 11e
08020 Barcelona
Spain
T: 00 34 933 141 900
F: 00 34 933 141 108
E: direccio@federacio.net
W: www.federacio.net
Contact: Ramon Bartomeus

Federacio Catalana de Voluntariat Social (FCVS) promotes and has information about volunteering in Catalonia (Catalunya), Spain. It may well be able to put volunteers in touch with organisations that are not yet listed on the WorldWide Volunteering database. There are about 300 volunteering organisations that are members of the Federation, working in all fields of the social action. The Federation belongs to several international networks – IAVE, AVA and CEV.

Starting months: January–December
Time required: 4–52 weeks (plus)
Age: 16 plus – no upper limit
Causes: Addicts/Ex-Addicts, AIDS/HIV, Disabled (learning and physical), Elderly People, Holidays for Disabled, Human Rights, Inner City Problems, Poor/Homeless, Refugees, Teaching/assisting, Work Camps – Seasonal, Young People.
Activities: Administration, Arts/Crafts, Campaigning, Caring (general, day and residential), Catering, Community Work, Counselling, Development Issues, First Aid, Fundraising, Group Work, International Aid, Library/Resource Centres, Manual Work, Marketing/Publicity, Newsletter/Journalism, Research, Social Work, Summer Camps, Teaching, Technical Skills, Training,

Visiting/Befriending, Work Camps – Seasonal.
Costs: Varies according to project.
Worldwide placements: Europe (Spain).

FEDERACION DE INSTITUCIONES PRIVADAS DE ATENCION A NINOS – VENEZUELA

Edificio Las Fundaciones, Piso 7
Avenida Andres Bello
Caracas
Venezuela
T: 00 58 2 578 0028
F: 00 58 2 578 0948
E: fipan-voluntariado@cantv.net
Contact: Aida Blasco

Federacion de Instituciones Privadas de Atencion a Ninos promotes and has information about volunteering in Venezuela. It may well be able to put volunteers in touch with organisations which are not yet listed on the WorldWide Volunteering database.

Starting months: January–December
Time required: 1–52 weeks (plus)
Age: 16 plus – no upper limit
Causes: Addicts/Ex-Addicts, AIDS/HIV, Animal Welfare, Archaeology, Architecture, Children, Conservation, Disabled (learning and physical), Elderly People, Environmental Causes, Health Care/Medical, Heritage, Holidays for Disabled, Human Rights, Inner City Problems, Offenders/Ex-Offenders, Poor/Homeless, Refugees, Teaching/assisting (nursery, primary, secondary, mature, EFL) Unemployed, Wildlife, Work Camps – Seasonal, Young People.
Activities: Accountancy, Administration, Agriculture/Farming, Arts/Crafts, Building/Construction, Campaigning, Caring (general, day and residential), Catering, Community Work, Computers, Conservation Skills, Cooking, Counselling, Development Issues, DIY, Driving, First Aid, Forestry, Fundraising, Gardening/Horticulture, Group Work, International Aid, Library/Resource Centres, Manual Work, Marketing/Publicity, Music, Newsletter/Journalism, Outdoor Skills, Religion, Research, Scientific Work, Social Work, Sport, Summer Camps, Teaching, Technical Skills, Theatre/Drama, Training, Translating, Visiting/Befriending, Work Camps – Seasonal.
Costs: Varies according to the project.
Worldwide placements: South America (Venezuela).

FEDERATION OF CITY FARMS AND COMMUNITY GARDENS

The Green House,
Hereford Street,
Bedminster
Bristol
BS3 4NA UK

T: 0117 923 1800
F: 0117 923 1900
E: admin@farmgarden.org.uk
W: www.farmgarden.org.uk
Contact: Laura Murgatroyd

The Federation of City Farms and Community Gardens (FCFCG) was established in 1980 to provide representation, advice and information for its members. There are up to 2,000 young people who volunteer on City Farms and Gardens throughout the UK. The FCFCG does not place volunteers directly, but will put people in touch with their nearest City Farm or Garden. City Farms and Community Gardens are all very different. They vary in size from a quarter of an acre to 90 acres. Some have extensive community buildings as well as farm buildings, many specialise in rare breeds of animals and poultry, some have riding stables, others are adventure playgrounds with areas for gardens or animals. Young people volunteer in many ways. Activities include helping to run summer playschemes, sporting activities if projects have a sports pitch, help with fundraising, showing animals, animal care, conservation, supporting people with learning difficulties, horticulture. There are many different things happening at City Farms and Gardens which means that there are a variety of ways to become involved as a volunteer. We are a member of the European Federation of City Farms (EFCF) which supports 880 farms in 9 countries. If young people are interested they should contact us and we will put them in touch with EFCF. ♿ 📖

Number of projects: 250 **UK:** 250
Starting months: January–December
Time required: 1–52 weeks
Age: 14 plus – no upper limit
Causes: Animal Welfare, Architecture, Children, Conservation, Disabled (learning and physical), Elderly People, Environmental Causes, Inner City Problems, Unemployed, Wildlife, Young People.
Activities: Accountancy, Administration, Agriculture/Farming, Arts/Crafts, Building/Construction, Community Work, Computers, Conservation Skills, Forestry, Fundraising, Gardening/Horticulture, Group Work, Manual Work, Marketing/Publicity, Newsletter/Journalism, Outdoor Skills, Sport, Teaching.
Placements: 2,000
When to apply: All year.
Work alone/with others: With others.
Equipment/clothing: Provided if needed.
Health requirements: Nil.
Costs: Nil.
Benefits: Expenses usually covered.
Training: Dependent on the individual project that takes the volunteer on.
Supervision: Dependent on the individual

project that takes the volunteer on.
Interviews: Dependent on the individual project that takes the volunteer on.
Worldwide placements: Europe (Belgium, Denmark, France, Germany, Netherlands, Norway, Spain, Sweden).
UK placements: England (Bristol, Cambridgeshire, Essex, Gloucestershire, Hampshire, Kent, Lancashire, Leicestershire, Lincolnshire, London, Manchester, Merseyside, Norfolk, Nottinghamshire, Oxfordshire, Tyne and Wear, West Midlands, E. Yorkshire, N. Yorkshire, S. Yorkshire, W. Yorkshire); Scotland (Dunbartonshire – West, Edinburgh, Glasgow City); Northern Ireland (Armagh, Derry/Londonderry); Wales (Swansea, Torfaen).

FELLOWSHIP OF RECONCILIATION (F.O.R.)

Task Force on Latin America and Caribbean
2017 Mission Street , #305
San Francisco
CA 94110 USA
T: 00 1 (415) 495 6334
F: 00 1 (415) 495 5628
E: forlatam@igc.org
W: www.forusa.org
Contact: John Lindsay-Poland

The Fellowship of Reconciliation invites you to: join in efforts on behalf of Latin America and the Caribbean's poor majority; develop ties with groups working for non violent social change; contribute to intercultural understanding and respect; immerse yourself in Latin American culture; learn about the impact of US culture and politics in the region; have fun! Volunteers with an offending background are accepted. ♿

Number of projects: 12 **UK:** 0
Starting months: January–December
Time required: 12–52 weeks (plus)
Age: 21–99
Causes: Human Rights, Teaching/assisting.
Activities: Administration, Teaching, Training, Translating.
Placements: 6
When to apply: At least two months prior to date of beginning service.
Work alone/with others: With host group.
Qualifications: Fluent in Spanish. Committment to goals of host organisation, all of which are peace and justice groups. Volunteers may be of any nationality but we prefer volunteers living or staying in the US.
Equipment/clothing: Bring enough for own living situation, or purchase in-country.
Health requirements: Physically and psychologically well.
Costs: Travel, insurance, board and lodging + $60 registration fee.
Benefits: Host organisations help volunteers

find appropriate housing.
Training: None, however background
information is provided.
Supervision: Volunteers work with host groups
– capacity for supervision varies. Often the
volunteer is part of a team.
Interviews: Interviews take place in California
or by phone.
Worldwide placements: Central America
(Mexico, Nicaragua, Panama, Puerto Rico);
South America (Argentina, Bolivia, Chile,
Ecuador, Paraguay, Peru).

FERNE ANIMAL SANCTUARY

Wambrook
Chard
Somerset TA20 3DH UK
T: 01460 65214
F: 01460 65214
E: info@ferneanimalsanctuary.org
W: www.ferneanimalsanctuary.org
Contact: Mrs J.B. Wheadon

Ferne Animal Sanctuary provides refuge for
unwanted animals. General sanctuary work
involved. We unfortunately cannot accept
applications from volunteers with an offending
background. Chard, Somerset. 🕿 📖

Number of projects: 1 UK: 1
Starting months: January–December
Time required: 1–52 weeks (plus)
Age: 14 plus – no upper limit
Causes: Animal Welfare.
Activities: Agriculture/Farming, Caring –
General, Fundraising, Gardening/Horticulture,
Visiting/Befriending.
Placements: 60–70
When to apply: Any time.
Work alone/with others: Work with other
young members of staff.
Qualifications: None required.
Equipment/clothing: Wellington boots and
waterproof clothing in wet weather.
Health requirements: It would depend on
what kind of voluntary work was being
undertaken.
Costs: Travel costs as we are not on a bus route,
so the ability to get to and from the sanctuary
under one's own steam is essential. No
accommodation provided so this would have to
also be funded.
Benefits: No financial support offered. Benefit
of working in the country air to help unwanted
animals.
Training: Health and Safety training and 'on-
the-job' training.
Supervision: Volunteers always work with a
member of staff.
Interviews: Interviews are held at the
sanctuary.
UK placements: England (Somerset).

FFESTINIOG RAILWAY COMPANY

Harbour Station
Porthmadog
Gwynedd LL49 9NF UK
T: 01766 516035
F: 01766 516006
E: tricia.doyle@festrail.co.uk
W: www.festrail.co.uk
Contact: Tricia Doyle

The world famous Ffestiniog Railway runs from
the sea at Porthmadog into the mountains of
Snowdonia to Blaenau Ffestiniog. The railway
was originally built to carry slate from the
quarries at Blaenau Ffestiniog down to the ships
at the port of Porthmadog. Originally operated
by gravity and horses and then by steam, the
railway now winds its way up the valley with
the passengers enjoying some unique views.
The railway closed down in 1946 due to the
decline in the demand for slate. However the
line reopened in 1954 thanks to the time and
dedication of volunteers. Volunteers still play a
major role on the Ffestiniog Railway. Thousands
of volunteers give up their free time to come
and work on the railway and give their
continued support. There are many different
types of jobs to do, from serving passengers on
our buffet cars to working on locomotives,
tracks, buildings, gardens or restoring carriages.
There is always something to keep you busy. 📖

Number of projects: 1 UK: 1
Starting months: January–December
Time required: 1–52 weeks
Age: 16–77
Causes: Conservation, Heritage.
Activities: Administration, Building/
Construction, Catering, Conservation Skills, DIY,
Gardening/Horticulture, Group Work, Manual
Work, Marketing/Publicity, Outdoor Skills.
Placements: 1,000+
When to apply: As soon as possible.
Work alone/with others: Usually with other
volunteers.
Qualifications: No restrictions but for the
safety of all, a good comprehension of English
required.
Equipment/clothing: Yes – details on
application.
Health requirements: Yes – details on
application.
Costs: Hostel £3.50 per night self catering.
Benefits: Free Ffestiniog Railway travel and
coffe/tea, soft drinks discounts on duty.
Training: A safety induction pack is sent from
'Safety Critical' sections.
Supervision: This varies by section but normal
distribution is one staff to five volunteers. On
special working parties, some work is on a one-
on-one basis.
Interviews: Applicants may be interviewed.
UK placements: Wales (Gwynedd).

FIDESCO

BP 137
6 rue Pablo Neruda
Bagneux
France
T: 00 33 1 41 17 48 20
F: 00 33 1 46 55 71 29
E: fidesco@emmanuel-info.com
W: www.fidesco-international.org
Contact: Carole Elbhar

Fidesco is a Roman Catholic foundation for international solidarity. FIDESCO was founded in France in 1980 and sends volunteers to work on development projects and evangelisation in 30 countries in the world.

Number of projects: 100+ UK: 0
Starting months: Sep, Oct, Nov, Dec
Time required: 52 weeks (plus)
Age: 21–99
Causes: AIDS/HIV, Children, Disabled (learning and physical), Elderly People, Health Care/Medical, Poor/Homeless, Teaching/assisting (nursery, primary, secondary, mature), Work Camps – Seasonal, Young People.
Activities: Accountancy, Administration, Agriculture/Farming, Building/Construction, Community Work, Computers, Development Issues, Fundraising, Manual Work, Marketing/Publicity, Newsletter/Journalism, Religion, Scientific Work, Social Work, Summer Camps, Teaching, Technical Skills, Training.
Placements: 140+
When to apply: September – January.
Work alone/with others: With other young volunteers.
Qualifications: Driving licence, language ability (depending on the project country), – any qualifications welcome.
Health requirements: Nil.
Training: 4 weekends and 2 weeks during the summer.
Supervision: A visit once a year and a report every 3 months.
Charity number: Assoc 1901
Worldwide placements: Africa (Benin, Burkina Faso, Cameroon, Côte d'Ivoire, Gabon, Guinea, Kenya, Madagascar, Namibia, Rwanda, Senegal, South Africa, Sudan, Tanzania, Togo, Tunisia, Zambia); Central America (Dominican Republic, Haiti); South America (Brazil, Colombia, Peru, Venezuela); Asia (Cambodia, Indonesia, Israel, Kazakhstan, Philippines, Taiwan, Thailand); Europe (Cyprus).

FIRST CONTACT

Candidates and Vocations Department
Church Army
Marlowe House, 109 Station Road
Sidcup
DA15 7AD UK

T: +44 (0) 20 8309 3506
F: +44 (0) 20 8309 3500
E: first.contact@churcharmy.org.uk
W: www.year-out.org.uk
Contact: Ray Khan

First Contact is a year out scheme, which seeks to place volunteers alongside a trained Church Army evangelist. Church Army have five areas of focus, which are: children and young people, homelessness, church planting, older people, area Evangelism. The mission statement of Church Army is 'Sharing Faith through Words and Action'. At First Contact we seek to share the good news of God's love as seen in Jesus Christ. First Contact is useful for those who wish to explore or test a calling for full time ministry. Volunteers are placed in teams for a year. The work varies from place to place but generally includes: some work in schools, work with young people, involvement in a local church, music and drama where appropriate. The volunteers have two residential training conferences, expenses for which are paid by Church Army. This is a chance to reflect on some of the experiences gained during their placement, and to meet up with other First Contact volunteers in different teams, as well as those who are on the Oasis Trust Frontline Teams. In selecting volunteers, we seek to find those whom God is calling to work in full time ministry. We are looking for active Christian young people who are enthusiastic about their faith and interested in sharing it with others. Volunteers with an offending background might be accepted. Each case is looked at individually, but any offence relating to children or young people would mean the volunteer not being accepted on the scheme. ♿

Number of projects: 6 UK: 6
Starting months: Sep
Time required: 30–46 weeks
Age: 18 plus – no upper limit
Causes: Children, Elderly People, Inner City Problems, Poor/Homeless, Young People.
Activities: Campaigning, Caring – Residential, Community Work, Group Work, Music, Outdoor Skills, Religion, Teaching, Theatre/Drama.
Placements: Up to 25
When to apply: Before 30th April.
Work alone/with others: With others.
Qualifications: An active Christian faith and a desire for others to experience relationship with Jesus. No restrictions but will need to abide by any necessary visa requirements laid down by the Home Office.
Equipment/clothing: No specific clothing or equipment needed.
Health requirements: No restrictions.
Costs: Volunteers are responsible for finding their own pocket money although a small bursary is available.

Benefits: Board and lodging, travel to and from the placement each term.
Training: Two residential training conferences and on-the-job training from a qualified church army evangelist. Opportunities to attend vocational conferences.
Supervision: Volunteers are supervised by their line manager locally with pastoral visits from the project co-ordinators.
Interviews: Interviews take place either in the candidates home or in Sheffield. Candidates accepted for the First Contact scheme must also assent to enhanced clearance using the Police Criminal Records Bureau.
Charity number: 226226
UK placements: England (throughout); Scotland (Scottish Borders); Northern Ireland (throughout); Wales (Cardiff, Monmouthshire, Powys).

FLORIDA PARK SERVICE

3900 Commonwealth Blvd MS 535
Tallahassee
Florida 32399 USA
T: 00 1 850 488 8243
F: 00 1 850 487 3947
W: www.dep.state.fl.us/parkes
Contact: Phil Werndli

Florida Park Service needs volunteers to work in its national parks. Florida – ISS State Parks. & ▤

Number of projects: 1 **UK:** 0
Starting months: January–December
Time required: 1–40 weeks
Age: 16 plus – no upper limit
Causes: Archaeology, Architecture, Environmental Causes, Wildlife, Work Camps – Seasonal.
Activities: Building/Construction, Community Work, Conservation Skills, Forestry, Gardening/ Horticulture, Manual Work, Outdoor Skills.
Placements: 6,000
When to apply: All year.
Work alone/with others: With others.
Qualifications: Varies with project.
Equipment/clothing: Varies with project.
Health requirements: Nil.
Costs: Travel, subsistence.
Benefits: Some lodging, some camping, tools and supplies.
Training: All the training that is needed is given.
Supervision: Varies according to project and park staff.
Interviews: Interviews at individual state parks.
Worldwide placements: North America: (USA).

FLYING ANGEL CLUB

76 Queen Victoria Street
Fremantle
6160 Western Australia

T: 00 61 8 9335 5000
F: 00 61 8 9335 5321
E: fangelc@starwon.com.au
Contact: Mr Jim Cross

Flying Angel Club is the commonly used name of the British and International Sailors' Society and The Missions to Seamen which is the Anglican Church's ministry to seafarers of all races and creeds. The people who make up the Missions to Seamen include volunteers who work in the Society's centres and those who raise funds for its work, as well as chaplains and other full-time staff. Fremantle, port for Perth, the capital city of W. Australia.

Number of projects: 1 **UK:** 0
Starting months: January–December
Time required: 1–52 weeks
Age: 18–60
Causes: Inner City Problems, Poor/Homeless, Young People.
Activities: Administration, Catering, Driving, Marketing/Publicity, Religion, Social Work, Visiting/Befriending.
Placements: 20
When to apply: All year.
Work alone/with others: No, mostly with older volunteers.
Qualifications: Ordinary driving licence and, if possible, a bus driving licence.
Health requirements: Good general health.
Costs: Travel to Fremantle, Australia.
Benefits: Subsidised board and lodging.
Worldwide placements: Australasia (Australia).

FOCUS (BRIDGE AND CHALLENGE PROGRAMMES)

Komtech House
255–257 London Road
Headington, Oxford
Oxon OX3 9EH UK
T: 01865 308488
E: headoffice@focus-charity.co.uk
Contact: Denise Barrows

Focus (Bridge and Challenge Programmes) was set up by Cambridge students in 1988 and aims to challenge the way people see themselves, to provide opportunities for people to focus on their abilities and interests, and gain in self-confidence. We achieve our aims by running a wide variety of team based projects, bringing together a wide range of people to understand and appreciate each other: local teenagers aged 12 – 16 who need a break; adults with a physical disability; adults with learning disabilities; students. We provide week-long adventure camps for an integrated group of mentally and physically handicapped adults and socially disadvantaged children. Teams of very different people are challenged to work together on activities ranging from building a medieval encampment to hot air ballooning. Progress is built on by a programme of year-round projects including weekend mini-camps and long-term team challenges. There is also a new SCOPE project, challenging teams of teenage schoolchildren to organise their own community projects. &. 📄

Number of projects: 10+ **UK:** 10+
Starting months: Mar, Apr, May, Jun, Jul, Aug
Time required: 1–6 weeks
Age: 18 plus – no upper limit
Causes: Children, Disabled (learning and physical), Elderly People, Holidays for Disabled, Poor/Homeless, Young People.
Activities: Caring – Residential, Community Work, First Aid, Fundraising, Group Work, Outdoor Skills, Social Work, Summer Camps, Training.
Placements: 400
When to apply: For Easter camps apply by March at the latest. For Summer camps apply by June at the latest.
Work alone/with others: Normally in teams.
Qualifications: Willingness to work hard, help others + make the camps FUN! Police profiling possible.
Equipment/clothing: Warm clothing and fancy dress (if possible).
Health requirements: Nil.
Costs: May include travel to/from camp sites.
Benefits: Board and lodging normally provided on camps.
Charity number: 1028637
UK placements: England (Cambridgeshire, Nottinghamshire, Oxfordshire).

FOOD FOR THE HUNGRY UK

44 Copperfield Road
Bassett
Southampton
Hampshire SO16 3NX UK
T: 023 8090 2327
F: 023 8090 2327
E: uk@fhi.net
W: www.uk.fhi.net
Contact: Doug Wakeling

Food for the Hungry is an international Christian relief and development organisation. Our primary emphasis is on long-term development among the extremely poor, recognising their dignity, creativity and ability to solve their own problems. Volunteers with offending backgrounds will probably be accepted.

Number of projects: 1–2 **UK:** 0
Starting months: Aug
Time required: 4 weeks
Age: 19–65
Causes: Children, Conservation, Elderly People, Health Care/Medical, Poor/Homeless,

Unemployed, Work Camps – Seasonal, Young People.
Activities: Agriculture/Farming, Building/Construction, Community Work, Conservation Skills, Gardening/Horticulture, Religion, Visiting/Befriending, Work Camps – Seasonal.
Placements: 20
When to apply: Any time before mid-March.
Work alone/with others: With leaders and field staff.
Qualifications: Christian commitment and willingness to work alongside Ugandan nationals.
Equipment/clothing: Summer clothes.
Health requirements: Travel vaccinations and anti-malarial tablets.
Costs: £1000 total.
Benefits: Lodging in Uganda, training before going, de-briefing on return.
Training: Prospective volunteers attend a selection and orientation weekend in Bournemouth.
Supervision: Supervised by experienced team leaders and local staff.
Interviews: Prospective volunteers attend a selection and orientation weekend in Bournemouth.
Charity number: 328273
Worldwide placements: Africa (Uganda).

FOREIGN LANGUAGES CENTRE

Peschanaya Street 89-107
Barnaul 656049
Russia
T: 07 385 2 243974
F: 07 385 2 261704
E: denisenkolaura@mail.ru
Contact: Mrs Larissa Denissenko

Foreign Language Teaching Centre was set up in 1989. There are adult and children departments. Class sizes are between 10 and 14 students and students are aged between 9 and 15 years, teaching elementary to advanced levels. A teacher is expected to use their own initiative, language teaching techniques and follow the Centre's teaching curricula. Some preparation of cross cultural material – customs and traditions of English speaking people is expected. Volunteers aged between 25 and 45 years wishing to stay 12–24 weeks are welcomed. The Centre also organises summer linguistic 'YES' camps. The aim of the 'YES' camp is to broaden children's outlook by means of socio-cultural activities, and develop and increase their motivation in learning English. Most of the children who go to the camp attend English courses during the year at the centre. There are eight groups in the camp with 10–12 children in each group. At the head of each group is a counsellor, either a teacher of English from our centre or a student from the Pedagogical University (the Faculty of Foreign Languages). Volunteers help local counsellors conduct 1 hour 20 minute planned English lessons every day. Volunteers spend all day with the children and are involved in all indoor and outdoor activities. Volunteers aged between 20 and 30 years wishing to stay 7–10 weeks are welcomed. Volunteers should note that living standards are generally lower than in Western Europe and North America, so adaptability and flexibility are essential. Camp is located in the Altai Region, in the south-western part of Siberia. Our summer camp is 40km from Barnaul and Barnaul is 220 km from Novosibirsk.

Number of projects: 3 UK: 0
Starting months: Jun, Jul
Time required: 7–24 weeks
Age: 20–45
Causes: Children, Teaching/assisting (nursery, primary, secondary, EFL).
Activities: Conservation Skills, Counselling, Summer Camps, Teaching.
Placements: 3
When to apply: Closing date is the 20th April.
Work alone/with others: With others.
Qualifications: English native speakers, student of colleges and universities, experience of working with children. For teaching in Centre a 4 year diploma is needed, TESOL or ESL teaching certificate. No restrictions but must be native English speaking.
Health requirements: Unable to accept volunteers with AIDS, tuberculosis or veneral diseases.
Costs: Flights to Russia and home, $100 per month subsistence. There are no membership or registration fees.
Benefits: Full board and lodging included in subsistence fee.
Supervision: Supervision of volunteers is conducted by the director of YES camp.
Interviews: Usually via telephone and e-mails.
Worldwide placements: Europe (Russia).

FORENINGEN STAFFANSGAARDEN

Box 66
Furugatan 1
82060 Delsbo
Sweden
T: 00 46 653 16850
F: 00 46 653 10968
E: staffansgarden@user.bip.net
Contact: Matti Remes

Foreningen Staffansgaarden is a community for mentally handicapped adults in Sweden. A volunteer can help in many ways, including working in the bakery, the wood workshop, the garden, weaving, farming, cooking and cleaning

or merely by participating in daily life with the handicapped adults. Volunteers with an offending background are accepted. Delsbo, 300 km north of Stockholm. 🔲 📖

Number of projects: 1 UK: 0
Starting months: January–December
Time required: 26–52 weeks (plus)
Age: 18 plus – no upper limit
Causes: Disabled (learning)
Activities: Agriculture/Farming, Arts/Crafts, Caring (general, day and residential), Community Work, Cooking, Driving, Forestry, Gardening/Horticulture, Group Work, Music, Outdoor Skills, Religion, Social Work, Sport, Theatre/Drama, Training.
Placements: 10
When to apply: All year.
Work alone/with others: Both.
Qualifications: Swedish speaking is a big plus and driving licence is also preferred.
Equipment/clothing: Warm clothing for the winter.
Health requirements: Stable mental health.
Costs: Fare to Staffansgaarden.
Benefits: Board and lodging + pocket money and insurance + fare home after 6 months. Single bedroom in house together with 4 handicapped and about 3 other co-workers.
Training: None.
Supervision: The volunteer always has a house parent or workshop master to help in the daily task.
Interviews: Applicants are not interviewed.
Worldwide placements: Europe (Sweden).

FOREST SCHOOL CAMPS

75 St Thomas's Road
London
N42 QJ UK
T: +44 (0) 20 7361 354 2713
E: gensec@fsc.org.uk
W: www.fsc.org.uk
Contact: The Secretary

Forest School Camps is a national organisation for young people which aims to encourage the idea that socially necessary work should be undertaken by volunteers on behalf of the general community.

Number of projects: 80 UK: 80
Starting months: Mar, Apr, May, Jul, Aug
Time required: 1–2 weeks
Age: 18 plus – no upper limit
Causes: Children, Disabled (learning and physical), Work Camps – Seasonal.
Activities: Arts/Crafts, Caring – General, Manual Work, Music, Outdoor Skills, Sport, Summer Camps, Work Camps – Seasonal.
Placements: 750–800
When to apply: Jan. Feb. March.
Work alone/with others: Work as part of

camping community – mostly in small groups.
Qualifications: None but personal/professional references requested.
Equipment/clothing: Lightweight tent if possible.
Health requirements: Health status not necessarily a factor unless it impairs ability to contribute to the group.
Costs: All costs plus contribution towards food and expenses.
Training: Weekend training near Cambridge – one weekend must be attended before becoming a staff member of Forest School Camps.
Supervision: We are all volunteers. Those more experienced guide and support those less so.
Interviews: Interview not required but references requested.
Worldwide placements: Europe (France, Ireland).
UK placements: England (Berkshire, Cornwall, Cumbria, Derbyshire, Devon, Essex, Gloucestershire, Herefordshire, Lancashire, Lincolnshire, London, Norfolk, Somerset, Staffordshire, E. Sussex, W. Sussex, Warwickshire, West Midlands, N. Yorkshire, S. Yorkshire, W. Yorkshire); Scotland (Scottish Borders); Wales (throughout).

FORO DEL SECTOR SOCIAL – ARGENTINA

Federacion de Asociaciones Civiles Y Fundaciones
Maipu 972, Pido 1
Buenos Aires
1006 Argentina
T: 00 54 4311 5001
F: 00 54 4311 5001
E: foro@arnet.com.ar
Contact: Maria Rosa S. de Martini

Foro del Sector Social promotes and has information about volunteering in Argentina. It may well be able to put volunteers in touch with organisations which are not yet listed on the WorldWide Volunteering database.

Starting months: January–December
Time required: 1–52 weeks (plus)
Age: 16 plus – no upper limit
Causes: Addicts/Ex-Addicts, AIDS/HIV, Animal Welfare, Archaeology, Architecture, Children, Conservation, Disabled (learning and physical), Elderly People, Environmental Causes, Health Care/Medical, Heritage, Holidays for Disabled, Human Rights, Inner City Problems, Offenders/Ex-Offenders, Poor/Homeless, Refugees, Teaching/assisting (nursery, primary, secondary, mature, EFL) Unemployed, Wildlife, Work Camps – Seasonal, Young People.
Activities: Accountancy, Administration, Agriculture/Farming, Arts/Crafts, Building/Construction, Campaigning, Caring (general, day and residential), Catering, Community Work, Computers, Conservation Skills, Cooking, Counselling, Development Issues, DIY, Driving, First Aid, Forestry, Fundraising, Gardening/Horticulture, Group Work, International Aid, Library/Resource Centres, Manual Work, Marketing/Publicity, Music, Newsletter/Journalism, Outdoor Skills, Religion, Research, Scientific Work, Social Work, Sport, Summer Camps, Teaching, Technical Skills, Theatre/Drama, Training, Translating, Visiting/Befriending, Work Camps – Seasonal.
Costs: Varies according to the project.
Worldwide placements: South America (Argentina).

FORUM FOR FRIVILLIGT SOCIALT ARBETE – SWEDEN

Box 49005
100 28 Stockholm
Sweden
T: 00 46 8 665 5600
F: 00 46 8 783 6692
E: ludvig.sandberg@socialforum.a.se
Contact: Volunteer Director

Forum for Frivilligt Socialt Arbete promotes and has information about volunteering in Sweden. It may well be able to put volunteers in touch with organisations which are not yet listed on the WorldWide Volunteering database.

Starting months: January–December
Time required: 1–52 weeks (plus)
Age: 16 plus – no upper limit
Causes: Addicts/Ex-Addicts, AIDS/HIV, Animal Welfare, Archaeology, Architecture, Children, Conservation, Disabled (learning and physical), Elderly People, Environmental Causes, Health Care/Medical, Heritage, Holidays for Disabled, Human Rights, Inner City Problems, Offenders/Ex-Offenders, Poor/Homeless, Refugees, Teaching/assisting (nursery, primary, secondary, mature, EFL) Unemployed, Wildlife, Work Camps – Seasonal, Young People.
Activities: Accountancy, Administration, Agriculture/Farming, Arts/Crafts, Building/Construction, Campaigning, Caring (general, day and residential), Catering, Community Work, Computers, Conservation Skills, Cooking, Counselling, Development Issues, DIY, Driving, First Aid, Forestry, Fundraising, Gardening/Horticulture, Group Work, International Aid, Library/Resource Centres, Manual Work, Marketing/Publicity, Music, Newsletter/Journalism, Outdoor Skills, Religion, Research, Scientific Work, Social Work, Sport, Summer Camps, Teaching, Technical Skills, Theatre/Drama, Training, Translating, Visiting/Befriending, Work Camps – Seasonal.
Costs: Varies according to the project.
Worldwide placements: Europe (Sweden).

FOUNDATION BURGER FUR BURGER – GERMANY

Stiftung Buerger Fuer Buerger
Singestr. 109
D-10179 Berlin
Germany
T: 00 49 30 243 1490
F: 00 49 30 243 149 49
E: info@buerger-fur-buerger.de
W: www.buerger-fur-buerger.de
Contact: Bernhard Schulz

Foundation Burger fur Burger (Citizens for Citizens) promotes and has information about volunteering in Germany. It may well be able to put volunteers in touch with organisations which are not yet listed on the WorldWide Volunteering database.

Starting months: January–December
Time required: 1–52 weeks (plus)
Age: 16 plus – no upper limit
Causes: Addicts/Ex-Addicts, AIDS/HIV, Animal Welfare, Archaeology, Architecture, Children, Conservation, Disabled (learning and physical), Elderly People, Environmental Causes, Health Care/Medical, Heritage, Holidays for Disabled, Human Rights, Inner City Problems, Offenders/Ex-Offenders, Poor/Homeless, Refugees, Teaching/assisting (nursery, primary, secondary, mature, EFL) Unemployed, Wildlife, Work Camps – Seasonal, Young People.
Activities: Accountancy, Administration, Agriculture/Farming, Arts/Crafts, Building/Construction, Campaigning, Caring (general, day and residential), Catering, Community Work, Computers, Conservation Skills, Cooking, Counselling, Development Issues, DIY, Driving, First Aid, Forestry, Fundraising, Gardening/Horticulture, Group Work, International Aid, Library/Resource Centres, Manual Work, Marketing/Publicity, Music, Newsletter/Journalism, Outdoor Skills, Religion, Research, Scientific Work, Social Work, Sport, Summer Camps, Teaching, Technical Skills, Theatre/Drama, Training, Translating, Visiting/Befriending, Work Camps – Seasonal.
Costs: Varies according to the project.
Worldwide placements: Europe (Germany).

FOUNDATION FOR SUSTAINABLE DEVELOPMENT

59 Driftwood Court
San Rafael
California 94901 USA
T: 00 1 415 482 9366
F: 00 1 415 482 9366
W: www.fsdinternational.org
Contact: Alicia Robb

Foundation for Sustainable Development (FSD) hosts internship programmes in Latin America and Africa. Programmes include family homestays and orientation and de-briefing sessions. Most programmes included group travel at some point during the programme. Interns are completely immersed – one intern per host family and internship organisation. Volunteers with an offending background may be accepted providing visas are obtainable.

Number of projects: 100 UK: 0
Starting months: January–December
Time required: 8–52 weeks
Age: 18 plus – no upper limit
Causes: Animal Welfare, Children, Conservation, Disabled (learning and physical), Elderly People, Environmental Causes, Health Care/Medical, Human Rights, Inner City Problems, Poor/Homeless, Refugees, Teaching/assisting (nursery, primary, secondary, mature, EFL) Wildlife, Work Camps – Seasonal, Young People.
Activities: Administration, Agriculture/Farming, Arts/Crafts, Building/Construction, Caring (general, day and residential), Community Work, Computers, Conservation Skills, Cooking, Counselling, Development Issues, First Aid, Forestry, Fundraising, Gardening/Horticulture, International Aid, Library/Resource Centres, Manual Work, Marketing/Publicity, Music, Newsletter/Journalism, Outdoor Skills, Research, Scientific Work, Social Work, Sport, Summer Camps, Teaching, Technical Skills, Theatre/Drama, Training, Translating, Visiting/Befriending, Work Camps – Seasonal.
Placements: 75+
When to apply: By 1st March for summer. Otherwise two months prior to expected departure.
Work alone/with others: Alone.
Qualifications: Spanish for all Latin American programmes except Ecuador. Good grades for college students.
Health requirements: No restrictions.
Costs: Varies – generally $2,000 plus airfares.
Benefits: In-country travel, room and board, most in-country expenses and trips.
Training: In-country orientation session.
Supervision: Host organisation supervisor, in-country co-ordinator.
Interviews: Only application forms.
Worldwide placements: Africa (South Africa, Tanzania, Uganda); Central America (Nicaragua); South America (Bolivia, Ecuador, Peru).

FOUNDATION TO ENCOURAGE POTENTIAL OF DISABLED PERSONS

195/197 Ban Tanawan, Moo 8
Chiang Mai
50300 Thailand
T: 053 852172
F: 053 240935

E: assist@loxinfo.co.th
W: www.infothai.com/disabled
Contact: Don Willcox

The Foundation to Encourage the Potential of Disabled Persons is a legally registered, private, non-governmental foundation established in 1993 by disabled polio survivor Sunan Willcox and her husband Don. The Foundation has achieved a distinguished record of fiscal integrity and responsibility. In 1999, Thai Minister Chuan Leekpai presented our founder with Thailand's 'Volunteer of the Year' award. The purpose of the foundation is to promote and encourage the health, education, employment and dignity of northern Thailand's disabled persons. Unfortunately (unlike many western nations), Thai disabled persons remain locked into a negative social stigma that continues to teach that disability is a payback for evil deeds in former lives. Thai perception of disability is that people with disabilities are mentally inferior, that they spread bad luck and are not accepted in the work place. The foundation set up Thailand's first Disabled Centre in 1998 called 'Look What We Can Do'. The centre provides free English classes, computer classes and guitar lessons. It also provides business start up support. The foundation also set up the Chiang Mai Disabled Centre Wheelchair Clinic to provide free mobility to needy children and adults. Additional services include financially supporting corrective surgery, providing prosthesis, providing educational and employment opportunities, providing social activities and disabled transport, promoting disabled access and publishing Thai language books. We unfortunately cannot place volunteers with an offending background. We are located in the centre of Chiang Mai City, which is Thailand's second largest city directly at the foot of the scenic mountains and 800km north of Bangkok with it's own unique culture. 🗎

Number of projects: 1 **UK:** 0
Starting months: January–December
Time required: 20–52 weeks
Age: 18 plus – no upper limit
Causes: Children, Disabled (learning and physical), Elderly People, Health Care/Medical, Teaching/assisting (mature), Young People.
Activities: Caring – General, Community Work, Computers, Fundraising, Manual Work, Music, Teaching, Training, Visiting/Befriending.
Placements: 10–15
When to apply: Any time.
Work alone/with others: Sometimes work with others. Our staff vary in age from 20–60 years, but most are 20–35 years.
Qualifications: We appreciate volunteers willing to learn Thai and also those who play guitar, keyboard or can sew. Welding is also helpful.

Equipment/clothing: Digital camera is helpful.
Health requirements: No restrictions.
Costs: 1500–3000 BAHT/US$60–75 per month depending on accommodation requirements. Plus airfare, visa and insurance.
Benefits: We can provide a bicycle or the use of a motorcycle. Accommodation is in local guesthouses, but volunteers must fund this and their food.
Training: None provided.
Supervision: Volunteers are supervised by two co-ordinators. All staff speak English.
Interviews: Generally e-mail communication ahead of arrival and/or acceptance.
Charity number: 54 Chiang Mai
Worldwide placements: Asia (Thailand).

FOUR CORNERS SCHOOL OF OUTDOOR EDUCATION

P.O. Box 1029,
95 W. 600 S. (shipping orders only)
Monticello
UT84535, USA
T: 00 1 435 587 2156
F: 00 1 435 587 2193
E: fcs@fourcornersschool.org
W: www.fourcornersschool.org
Contact: Rosie O'Connor

Four Corners School, located in a 160,000 square mile region known as the Colorado Plateau, aims to increase participants' awareness and sensitivity to the physical and cultural heritage. The school teaches outdoor skills, natural sciences and land stewardship by creating a community of individuals who share their interests through informal, relaxed, hands-on experiences. Most programmes are in Arizona, N. Mexico, Utah and Colorado.

Number of projects: 35+ **UK:** 0
Starting months: Mar, Apr, May, Jun, Jul, Aug, Sep, Oct
Time required: 1–2 weeks
Age: 18 plus – no upper limit
Causes: Archaeology, Conservation, Environmental causes, Teaching/assisting, Wildlife.
Activities: Conservation Skills, Manual Work, Outdoor Skills, Research, Scientific Work, Teaching.
Placements: 60+
When to apply: 60 days prior to a scheduled programme.
Work alone/with others: With others – usually 8–12 to a programme.
Equipment/clothing: Yes – depends on time of year, location and programme.
Health requirements: Yes – physical fitness essential.
Costs: Tuition fees, travel costs.

Benefits: Lodging, meals, transportation, guides/experts, group equipment and park fees.
Training: None required.
Supervision: The expert and trip leader provides supervision.
Interviews: Applicants are not interviewed.
Worldwide placements: North America: (USA).

FOUR HOMES OF MERCY, THE

Bethany
Jerusalem 9119
Palestine
PO Box 19185 Jerusalem 91191
T: 02 6282076
F: 02 6274871
E: homes4@netvision.net.il
W: www.fourhomesofmercy.com
Contact: Henrietta Siksek Farradj

The Four Homes of Mercy of Arab Orthodox Invalids Homes Charitable Society are a Christian Arab organisation, with nearly all of us belonging to the Arab (Greek) Orthodox Church. All members are women. Founded in 1940 by Katherine George Siksek, who was born and died in the Old City of Jerusalem and saw the miseries of those times. A group of helpful women continued the service that was started up to help the invalids. We have a team of doctors, matron, educational nurses, nursing advisors, staff nurses and aid nurses, also domestic and maintenance staff. Our patients are from Palestine, none yet from warring areas because of blockades around towns and villages. We unfortunately cannot accept volunteers with an offending background. Number of volunteers may not exceen ten. Sections available for volunteer assistance: crippled children, invalid's men and women and invalid teenagers. The next eight months is undergoing updating, please consult before making any arrangements. Bethany is 7 km from Jerusalem to the South East West Bank area. 🗎

Number of projects: 2 UK: 0
Starting months: January–December
Time required: 1–8 weeks
Age: 20–60
Causes: Disabled (physical), Elderly People, Health Care/Medical, Poor/Homeless, Teaching (EFL).
Activities: Building/Construction, Caring (general, residential), Community Work, Gardening/Horticulture, Social Work, Teaching, Visiting/Befriending.
Placements: 8+
When to apply: All year.
Work alone/with others: Varies.
Qualifications: Occupational therapists, recreational, teachers of English for beginners and people with nursing skills.
Equipment/clothing: Casual wear for manual workers or overalls for painters. In winter –

jumpers and boots as weather can be cold.
Health requirements: In good health.
Costs: Flight costs and insurances.
Benefits: Pocket money for transport. Board and lodging offered. Accommodation is similar to camp life.
Training: None except in the form of advice for the specific job.
Supervision: Supervision is done by head nurses and main advisors for manual work.
Interviews: No interview. We correspond with volunteers, and need a church certificate and recommedation from an organisation we recognise, or a principal's recommendation.
Charity number: 159
Worldwide placements: Asia (Palestinian Authority).

FOYER THÉRAPEUTIQUE DE RUZIERE

Chateau de Ruzière
F 03160 Bourbon-l'Archambault
France
T: 00 33 4 70 67 00 23
F: 00 33 4 70 47 35 41
E: assoc.ruziere@wanadoo.fr
Contact: The Director

Foyer Thérapeutique de Ruziere is a training and social therapeutic community for adolescents and young people with special needs. It is based in a beautiful large country house and is a friend of the Camphill Community organisation. 🗎

Number of projects: 1 UK: 0
Starting months: January–December
Time required: 52 weeks plus
Age: 18–30
Causes: Disabled (learning)
Activities: Agriculture/Farming, Caring – Residential, Cooking, Gardening/Horticulture, Manual Work, Theatre/Drama.
Placements: 5
When to apply: All year.
Work alone/with others: Both.
Qualifications: Must speak French.
Health requirements: Healthy.
Costs: Travel to the Centre.
Benefits: Food and accommodation.
Training: Prior training is not needed.
Supervision: Yes.
Interviews: Interview is required.
Worldwide placements: Europe (France).

FRENCH ENCOUNTERS

63 Fordhouse Road
Bromsgrove
WorcestershireB60 2LU UK
T: 01527 873645
F: 01527 832794
E: admin@frenchencounters.co.uk
W: www.frenchencounters.com

Contact: Soula Callow, Patsy Musto and Joan Glover

French Encounters is a small independent family company specialising in French language field trips for schools. The programme, based in two chateaux centres in Normandy, is designed to give maximum linguistic and educational benefit to children in the 10–13 age range. Some older groups – GCSE and A-level projected. We are looking for gap year students who need to work in France, who have stamina, enthusiasm and a sense of humour and adventure. They need to be reliable, responsible and calm in crises. They work from mid-February to mid-June. They will work as animateurs/couriers, giving commentaries, organising activities and entertainments, and giving general assistance to the director of the programme. Volunteers with an offending background may be accepted but no racists, rapists or known drug addicts. Normandy.

Number of projects: 2 UK: 0
Starting months: Feb, Mar, Apr, May
Time required: 12–17 weeks
Age: 18–25
Causes: Children, Teaching/assisting, Young People.
Activities: Caring – General, First Aid, Group Work, Music, Outdoor Skills, Sport, Teaching, Theatre/Drama, Training.
Placements: 8
When to apply: Before 25th September.
Work alone/with others: Both – individual responsibility + teamwork.
Qualifications: A-Level French or equivalent, experience with pre-teens, enthusiasm, good general educational background.
Health requirements: Good general health, stamina and energy essential.
Costs: Nil – except personal travel for pleasure.
Benefits: Full board and lodging + £70 per week approx. + weekend allowance, transport to and from Normandy and comprehensive insurance.
Training: 2 weeks on-site training. Detailed handbook provided well in advance of start of season. English Speaking Board professional presentation skills training and assessment provided. First Aid training also.
Supervision: Adult directrice in overall charge with additional supervision by owner/director.
Interviews: Interviews take place at the head office in Bromsgrove.
Worldwide placements: Europe (France).

FRIEDENSDORF INTERNATIONAL (PEACE VILLAGE INTERNATIONAL)

Aktion Friedensdorf e.V.
Lanterstrasse 21
Dinslaken 46539
Germany
T: 00 49 20644974 0
F: 00 49 20644974 999
E: info@friedensdorf.de
W: www.friedensdorf.de
Contact: Dept. 0211

For 35 years Friedensdorf International has worked with wounded children from war-torn and crisis areas including Afghanistan, Vietnam, Romania, Angola, Armenia, Georgia, Kasachstan and Tadzhikistan who need medical treatment in European hospitals. After appropriate treatment the children live in the Peace Village care station in Oberhausen for rehabilitation until they return to their native countries and to their families. The children range from one year up to 12 years of age. About 15 volunteers work in the village every year. Volunteers are required all the year round to take care of the children in the Peace Village. The work includes all kind of day care occupations with those children who have already finished their treatment in hospital and need to wait for their return flight home or with children whose treatment is interrupted for a while. Duties include all kinds of day care occupations, such as helping children with their meals, toileting, changing clothes etc. Learning German is necessary. Most of our staff members do not speak English. Of course, the communication with the children is done in German. Please note – if interested in volunteering in Sri Lanka – please contact Mr. Diatmar Doering at sport@panlanka.net.

Number of projects: 1 UK: 0
Starting months: January–December
Time required: 12–52 weeks
Age: 18–70
Causes: Children, Disabled (learning and physical), Health Care/Medical.
Activities: Caring – General, Catering, First Aid.
Placements: 15
When to apply: All year (minimum period of volunteering 3 months) but as early as possible as we receive very many requests from people wanting to help us voluntarily.
Work alone/with others: With others.
Qualifications: Experience as social worker desirable but not essential. No special skills needed except a love for children. Basic knowledge and ability of German language.
Health requirements: Free from infectious illnesses. Health insurance must be valid for Germany. Several children arrive with Hepatitis A, B or C. Detailed information is given about viruses. Each volunteer must decide whether they should be injected before arrival.
Costs: All except board and accommodation.
Benefits: Board and accommodation. Accommodation provided in a room with other volunteers.
Training: As required.

Supervision: Yes, volunteers are supervised.
Worldwide placements: Asia (Sri Lanka);
Europe (Germany).

FRIENDS OF BIRZEIT UNIVERSITY (FoBZU)

1 Gough Square
London
EC4A 3DE UK
T: +44 (0) 20 7361 832 1340
F: +44 (0) 20 7361 832 1349
E: fobzu@fobzu.org
W: www.fobzu.org
Contact: Dan Richards

Every year since the late 1970s, the Palestinian
Friends of Birzeit University (BZU) has
organised international 'workcamps' based on
its own campus which is one of the best
examples of modern Arab architecture in the
area. From January 1988 to April 1992 the
campus was closed by Israeli military order and
students were banned from the campus.
However, even during this time, BZU managed
to arrange workcamps in off-campus locations.
In August/September 1992 workcamps were
once again held on the university campus.
Two workcamps are held each summer, usually
during July and August. They are two weeks
long and each one accommodates 30
international volunteers, of whom half are from
the UK. The camps are an opportunity for
volunteers from Europe and North America to
experience the local situation at first hand and
to contribute to improving the local conditions
of life. Tasks range from helping farmers with
their harvest to building basic sanitation
facilities in refugee camps. Some of the work is
symbolic in nature – showing solidarity with
the community – and some is much-needed
support which will really benefit the local
people. Whilst the work is highly rewarding,
participants should be prepared for strenuous
activity. In addition to the work, a wide range
of visits, meetings and cultural events are
arranged. The social life of the workcamp is
very enjoyable. The political situation
sometimes makes organisation of the
programme difficult but alternative
arrangements can usually be made. Volunteers
must be aware that they are travelling to an
area of unrest and must behave accordingly.
There have not, however, been any serious
incidents involving volunteers attending the
workcamps. 15 miles north of Jerusalem on the
occupied West Bank. 🖥 📄

Number of projects: 1–2 UK: 1
Starting months: Jun, Jul
Time required: 2–2 weeks
Age: 20–58
Causes: Children, Conservation, Environmental

Causes, Human Rights, Poor/Homeless,
Refugees, Work Camps – Seasonal, Young
People.
Activities: Administration, Agriculture/Farming,
Building/Construction, Campaigning,
Community Work, Computers, Conservation
Skills, Development Issues, Fundraising, Manual
Work, Marketing/Publicity, Newsletter/
Journalism, Translating, Work Camps – Seasonal.
Placements: 20
When to apply: Before 22nd May.
Work alone/with others: With others.
Equipment/clothing: Clothes for manual
outdoor work in the heat – culturally
conservative dress. No shorts.
Health requirements: Reasonably fit.
Costs: For workcamps: £18 application fee, £80
Reg. fee to include food and accommodation,
£200 approx return flight to Tel Aviv and about
£3 per day for extra travel and expenses.
Benefits: Board and lodging.
Interviews: Interviews take place in London.
Send an A4 stamped (31p) addressed envelope.
Charity number: 279026
UK placements: England (London).

FRIENDS OF ISRAEL EDUCATIONAL TRUST

P O Box 7545
London
NW2 2QZ UK
T: +44 (0) 20 7361 435 6803
F: +44 (0) 207 794 0291
E: foi_asg@msn.com
W: www.foi-asq.org
Contact: John D. A. Levy

Friends of Israel Educational Trust seeks to
develop critical interest in the land, peoples and
cultures of Israel. The Foundation organises an
extensive lecture programme around the UK
and has created a variety of hands-on working
programmes in Israel for students, academics,
clergy and other selected British groups. Bridge
in Britain programme is a gap year scheme. In
addition we offer occasional awards to graduate
students of art schools, or young Christian
clergy, young farmers or young horticulturalists.
These are short-term placements.

Number of projects: 5 UK: 0
Starting months: Jan, Feb
Time required: 24–30 weeks
Age: 18–20
Causes: Inner City Problems, Teaching/assisting
(primary, secondary, EFL), Work Camps –
Seasonal, Young People.
Activities: Arts/Crafts, Music, Sport, Summer
Camps, Teaching, Theatre/Drama, Work Camps
– Seasonal.
Placements: 12
When to apply: 1st July.

Work alone/with others: Both.
Qualifications: Nil. Require talented, personable good all-rounders. UK nationals only.
Health requirements: Good physical and mental health.
Costs: Only cost is entertainment and travel when not on our programme.
Benefits: Travel + insurance for 6 months; 5 months board and lodging carefully planned. Free time not planned. We provide bed and board, or funds to cover self-catering accommodation, on all placement programmes.
Training: No training. Pre-departure briefing by Trust staff and previous volunteers.
Supervision: Avoiding suffocation, we have professional co-ordinators on every programme who take general responsibility for organising placements and monitoring progress.
Interviews: Interviews take place in London.
Charity number: 271983
Worldwide placements: Asia (Israel).

FRIENDS WEEKEND WORKCAMP PROGRAM

1515 Cherry Street
Philadelphia
PA 19102 USA
E: info@quakerinfo.org
Contact: Programme Organiser

Friends Weekend Workcamp Program offers short term projects within inner city Philadelphia which combine physical work with discussions on urban poverty.

Number of projects: 1 **UK:** 0
Starting months: Jan, Feb, Mar, Apr, May, Oct, Nov, Dec
Time required: 1–52 weeks
Age: 16 plus – no upper limit
Causes: Elderly People, Inner City Problems.
Activities: Building/Construction, Community Work, Counselling, DIY, Manual Work, Social Work.
Placements: 200
When to apply: As early as possible.
Work alone/with others: With others.
Qualifications: Spoken English.
Costs: Donation of $35 per w/e.
Benefits: Board and lodging.
Worldwide placements: North America: (USA).

FRIENDSHIP CLUB NEPAL

P. O. Box 11276
Maharajgunj
Kathmandu
Nepal
E: fcn@ccsl.com.np
W: http://members.aol.com/jacusa/fcn.html
Contact: Prakash Babu Paudel

Friendship Club Nepal is a non-profit making organisation that works towards helping the poor people in rural areas of Nepal. Volunteers are recruited to work throughout the year for both short term (few weeks) and long term (few months) periods. Volunteers can assist with teaching English in schools or colleges for 3–5 hours a day, six days a week, or as project visitors in rural areas to conduct research and help with community building projects. Volunteers require no special skills or experience but should have a willingness to experience very basic living conditions. In return they will have the chance to experience the real Nepal. Volunteers with an offending background must provide full details, after which each case is considered separately. In village areas. 🖺

Number of projects: Many **UK:** 0
Starting months: January–December
Time required: 2–22 weeks
Age: 18 plus – no upper limit
Causes: Conservation, Environmental Causes, Health Care/Medical, Teaching/assisting (nursery, primary, secondary, EFL), Work Camps – Seasonal, Young People.
Activities: Agriculture/Farming, Building/Construction, Conservation Skills, Development Issues, Forestry, Gardening/Horticulture, Manual Work, Outdoor Skills, Teaching, Work Camps – Seasonal.
Placements: 200
When to apply: As early as possible all year.
Work alone/with others: With other young volunteers.
Qualifications: Spoken English.
Health requirements: Nil but applicants should be aware of necessary medication in local areas.
Costs: $120 registration fee plus flights and visas.
Benefits: All board and lodging provided. Medium/long-term volunteers receive pocket money too.
Worldwide placements: Asia (Nepal).

FRISAM – NORWAY

Kongensgt 9
0153 Oslo
Norway
E: terje.skjeldam@frisam.dep.no
Contact: Terje Skjeldam

FRISAM promotes and has information about volunteering in Norway. It may well be able to put volunteers in touch with organisations which are not yet listed on the WorldWide Volunteering database.

Starting months: January–December
Time required: 1–52 weeks (plus)
Age: 16 plus – no upper limit

Causes: Addicts/Ex-Addicts, AIDS/HIV, Animal Welfare, Archaeology, Architecture, Children, Conservation, Disabled (learning and physical), Elderly People, Environmental Causes, Health Care/Medical, Heritage, Holidays for Disabled, Human Rights, Inner City Problems, Offenders/ Ex-Offenders, Poor/Homeless, Refugees, Teaching/assisting (nursery, primary, secondary, mature, EFL) Unemployed, Wildlife, Work Camps – Seasonal, Young People.
Activities: Accountancy, Administration, Agriculture/Farming, Arts/Crafts, Building/ Construction, Campaigning, Caring (general, day and residential), Catering, Community Work, Computers, Conservation Skills, Cooking, Counselling, Development Issues, DIY, Driving, First Aid, Forestry, Fundraising, Gardening/Horticulture, Group Work, International Aid, Library/Resource Centres, Manual Work, Marketing/Publicity, Music, Newsletter/Journalism, Outdoor Skills, Religion, Research, Scientific Work, Social Work, Sport, Summer Camps, Teaching, Technical Skills, Theatre/Drama, Training, Translating, Visiting/Befriending, Work Camps – Seasonal.
Costs: Varies according to the project.
Worldwide placements: Europe (Norway).

FROME VALLEY PROJECT

Dorset Countryside
The Barracks
Bridport Road, Bridport Road
Dorchester
Dorset DT1 1RN UK
T: 01305 268731
F: 01305 266920
E: J.Penney@dorsetcc.gov.uk
Contact: Jenny Penney

Frome Valley is a Downs and Valleys Project to conserve, sustain and enhance the special character and diversity of landscape and wild life through the Frome Valley; to improve the opportunities for informal access and recreation within the Frome Valley; to ensure the provision of interpretative and educational material and information which will lead to greater understanding and enjoyment of the countryside; to contribute to the quality of life for local people, in particular through support for community initiatives and schemes which promote sustainable tourism in the economy. Volunteers with an offending background may be accepted depending on the offence. West Dorset. [symbols]

Number of projects: 1 UK: 1
Starting months: Jan, Feb, Mar, Sep, Oct, Nov, Dec
Time required: 1–52 weeks
Age: 16 plus – no upper limit
Causes: Conservation, Disabled (learning and

physical), Environmental Causes, Unemployed, Wildlife, Young People.
Activities: Administration, Conservation Skills, Group Work, Manual Work, Newsletter/Journalism, Outdoor skills, Research.
Placements: 10
When to apply: All year.
Work alone/with others: Groups.
Qualifications: Huge enthusiasm, artistic design talent and practical skills for outdoor work. Previous experience not necessary.
Equipment/clothing: Sturdy boots and old clothes + gardening gloves if possible.
Health requirements: Nil.
Costs: Local people will be required to travel to site.
Benefits: Work experience.
Training: Under the Ranger's Supervision (Health and Safety is a high priority).
Supervision: By Ranger.
Interviews: Interview to ascertain suitability at our office.
UK placements: England (Dorset).

FRONTIER

50–52 Rivington Street
London EC2A 3QP UK
T: +44 (0) 207 613 2422
T: +44 (0) 207 613 2992
E: info@frontier.ac.uk
W: www.frontier.ac.uk
Contact: Harriet Woodhouse

Frontier is a non profit-making organisation which brings together the conservation needs of developing countries with the commitment and enthusiasm of volunteers from around the world. As ecological crises are multiplying and the resources to deal with them diminishing, Frontier brings people of all ages and backgrounds to the forefront of conservation research enabling them to become involved in vital scientific work in the field. Since Frontier's inception in 1989, well over 450,000 hours of research have been undertaken by volunteers in threatened areas of Tanzania, Madagascar, Vietnam, Uganda and Mozambique. Working alongside scientists and conservation organisations from these countries, each Frontier project represents a unique and valuable scientific investigation. Volunteers are recruited for 10 or 20 week projects implementing a research programme which draws on their strengths as an expeditionary team. Volunteers are also recruited to take part in 28 day expeditions combining expedition management training with the conservation of endangered wildlife and threatened habitats. Once in country, volunteers are encouraged to participate in every part of the project. This will include anything from data collection, surveys and communication with the local population to the collection of supplies. In short everything involved in a conservation research expedition undertaken in tough and often inhospitable conditions. The 'hands on' experience Frontier offers is such that many of our volunteers subsequently move on to work in conservation related fields. Each Frontier project is self funded, the expeditionary team contributing to the cost of the expedition. Comprehensive advice on fundraising is offered to all volunteers. Frontier are a member of The Year Out Group. Projects are currently running in Madagascar, Tanzania and Vietnam.

Number of projects: 6 **UK:** 0
Starting months: Jan, Apr, Jul, Oct
Time required: 4–52 weeks
Age: 17 plus – no upper limit
Causes: Animal Welfare, Conservation, Environmental Causes, Wildlife.
Activities: Administration, Building/Construction, Community Work, Computers, Conservation Skills, Cooking, Development Issues, DIY, Forestry, Fundraising, Gardening/Horticulture, Group Work, International Aid, Outdoor Skills, Research, Scientific Work, Teaching, Technical Skills, Training.
Placements: 300+
When to apply: All year, preferably 6 months in advance. Contact office for free information pack and application form.
Work alone/with others: With others in groups of 15–30.
Qualifications: None required.
Equipment/clothing: Depends on location – kit list provided.
Health requirements: Reasonably fit and healthy.
Costs: Volunteers are asked to raise from £2,300 for a 10 week project, from £4,000 for a 20 week project, and £1,850 for a 28 day expedition (excluding flights and visa costs).
Benefits: No prior experience or skills are necessary as full training is provided leading to BTEC qualification, which is equivalent to and A level, in Tropical Habitat Conservation or Expedition Management (Biodiversity Research). All accommodation is provided by way of basic conditions on a base camp.
Training: Pre-expedition health and safety, basic first aid techniques and conservation methods training is given.
Supervision: Supervised by a team of 5–6 field staff experienced in logistics, training, research and health and safety. Also a fully qualified dive officer, where appropriate.
Interviews: Interview days are held at the London office after receiving an application form. For those unable to attend there is a possibility of a telephone interview.
Worldwide placements: Africa (Madagascar, Tanzania); Asia (Vietnam).

FRONTIERS FOUNDATION/OPERATION BEAVER

419 Coxwell Avenue
Toronto
Ontario M4L 3B9 Canada
T: 00 1 (416) 690 3930
F: 00 1 (416) 690 3934
E: frontiersfoundation@on.aibn.com
W: www.frontiersfoundation.org
Contact: Marco A Guzman

Frontiers Foundation is a non-profit, non-denominational voluntary service organisation supporting the advancement of economically and socially disadvantaged communities in Canada and overseas through the Operation Beaver Programme:
– Voluntary service programme for people from Canada and around the world, interested in volunteering their time to help others help themselves.
– Partnership between the host communities in Canada on community-based development projects, such as building and/or renovating homes, or organising activities for local youth/children at various recreation and/or educational centres.
– Volunteers and members of the host communities exchange and share cross-cultural information and experiences and learn from each other.
– Host communities, families or groups actively participate in the development projects. A contractual arrangement is worked out with Frontiers Foundation defining each group's responsibilities.
– Still others offer their skills at the national or regional levels by supporting programme development or office management.
Purpose:
– To contribute to the relief of poverty by supporting tangible community development projects which have enduring significance.
– To foster understanding and sharing of culture and experience through cross cultural exchanges between various peoples of Canada and other volunteers from around the world.
– To support the needs and goals identified by the requesting communities.
– To promote development through the hands of those people who know and understand their own needs, and those of their communities. We do not aspire to change their way of life, but to work in partnership with requesting communities.

Number of projects: 3 **UK:** 0
Starting months: Jan, Jun, Jul, Aug, Sep
Time required: 12–52 weeks
Age: 18–81
Causes: Children, Poor/Homeless, Teaching/assisting, Young People.

Activities: Building/Construction, Community Work, Group Work, Outdoor Skills, Sport, Teaching.
When to apply: At least 3 months in advance.
Work alone/with others: Both.
Qualifications: Housing construction related skills preferred but not necessary. Volunteers must be able to adapt to very primitive conditions. All nationalities welcome but sometimes we have to set a limiting quota from any one country.
Equipment/clothing: Back-pack and sleeping bag. No need to take work boots.
Health requirements: Volunteers are usually in good physical condition.
Costs: Travel to Canada.
Benefits: Board, lodging, insurance, local travel and pocket money.
Training: A general introduction to: history and purpose of Frontiers Foundation, construction safety, nature of project, native people and administrative details.
Supervision: Regional Co-ordinators supervise the projects.
Interviews: Interviews take place in Toronto and other major cities in Canada and Europe.
Charity number: 13037-3970
Worldwide placements: North America: (Canada); Central America (Haiti); South America (Bolivia).

FRYLANDS WOOD SCOUT CAMP

Featherbed Lane
New Addington
Croydon CR0 9AA UK
T: +44 (0) 208 657 1154
F: +44 (0) 208 657 4069
E: mark.bourne@talk21.com
W: www.frylandswood.co.uk
Contact: Mark Bourne

Volunteers at Frylands help to run activities such as climbing, archery, rifle shooting, go karts, assault course, mountain bikes etc. They also assist and maintain the site. Our visitors vary from scouts, cubs, guides, brownies, schools, special needs children and teenage youth groups. We are unable to offer placements to volunteers with an offending background. Surrey just outside of Croydon, South east London, 45 minutes from central London on public transport. ▨

Number of projects: 1 UK: 1
Starting months: Jun, Jul, Aug
Time required: 4–16 weeks
Age: 16–25
Causes: Children, Conservation, Work Camps – Seasonal, Young People.
Activities: Arts/Crafts, Building/Construction, Cooking, DIY, Outdoor Skills, Sport, Summer Camps, Training, Work Camps – Seasonal.

Placements: 6
When to apply: Any time.
Work alone/with others: Varies.
Qualifications: None required but may be useful.
Health requirements: None.
Costs: Transport to project.
Benefits: Board and lodging.
Training: Training given for activities and first aid.
Supervision: Supervision is the responsibility of both the camp site manager and deputy manager.
Interviews: No interviews.
Charity number: 1001668
UK placements: England (Surrey).

FULCRUM

Unit 7
Luccombe Farm Business Centre
Milton Abbas
Dorset DT11 0BD UK
T: 01258 881399
F: 01258 881300
E: office@fulcrum-challenge.org
W: www.fulcrum-challenge.org
Contact: John Hunt

Fulcrum Challenge is a new and exciting educational youth initiative for A-level, GNVQ and Scottish Highers students. Fulcrum Challenge operates across the country and schools in each and individuals area are invited to nominate students who must submit a completed application form to Fulcrum Challenge. Fulcrum Challenge operates in other areas with other sponsors. Only 24 places are available each Challenge. Financial day is organised for the students. The group spends two weeks in a remote area of the world, living and working with local communities on environmental and cultural activities.
The group must take part in an environmental project in their home area in co-operation with Countryside Agency. All students are invited to take part in a bi-annual Leadership Conference. The five phases are designed to bring together bright young people from all backgrounds, in order to learn how to work both as a group and in other communities, develop leadership and business skills, study natural and scientific topics and develop close personal links at home and abroad. ASDAN award given to participants who complete the necesary documented work.

Number of projects: Up to 20 UK: Up to 20
Starting months: Feb, Mar, Apr, Aug, Sep, Oct, Nov
Time required: 3–4 weeks
Age: 16–18
Causes: Children, Conservation, Environmental Causes, Heritage, Poor/Homeless, Wildlife, Young People.

Activities: Accountancy, Administration, Agriculture/Farming, Arts/Crafts, Building/Construction, Caring (general, residential), Community Work, Computers, Conservation Skills, Cooking, Counselling, Development Issues, DIY, First Aid, Forestry, Fundraising, Gardening/Horticulture, Group Work, International Aid, Library/Resource Centres, Manual Work, Marketing/Publicity, Music, Newsletter/Journalism, Outdoor Skills, Religion, Research, Scientific Work, Social Work, Sport, Teaching, Technical Skills, Theatre/Drama, Training, Visiting/Befriending.
Placements: Up to 400
When to apply: Only through Heads of school and then by invitation or direct contact
Work alone/with others: As a team.
Qualifications: A-level, GNVQ or Scottish Highers. No restrictions but they must be in the UK educational system.
Equipment/clothing: Suitable for selection, environmental, overseas programmes.
Health requirements: Must be fit and take the recommended medical treatments for the overseas phase.
Costs: With charitable sponsorship £1,500 raised by their own initiative. Individual participation £2750.
Benefits: Certain programmes are support funded by major companies.
Training: Not applicable.
Supervision: Experienced leaders and instructors are used on all stages.
Interviews: There is a three-day Introduction to Leadership Weekend for participants.
Charity number: 1072830
Worldwide placements: Africa (Botswana, Kenya, Namibia, South Africa, Tunisia, Zimbabwe); South America (Argentina, Guyana, Paraguay, Venezuela); Asia (Bangladesh, China, Hong Kong, India, Malaysia, Mongolia, Nepal, Oman, Philippines, Thailand, Tibet, United Arab Emirates, Vietnam).
UK placements: England (Berkshire, Cheshire, Co Durham, Cumbria, Dorset, Herefordshire, Kent, Lancashire, London, Manchester, Merseyside, Northumberland, Shropshire, Staffordshire, Surrey, E. Sussex, W. Sussex, Tyne and Wear, Warwickshire, West Midlands, Worcestershire, N. Yorkshire); Scotland (throughout); Northern Ireland (throughout).

FUNDACION ANISA, A.C.

1101 Ollie Avenue 5709
Calexico
92231 USA
T: 00 1 1 52 686 566 7152
E: frazelle09@yahoo.com
W: www.fundacionanisa.org
Contact: Frederick Frazelle

The Anisa Foundation promoted two programmes. The volunteers' input is very necessary, both in planning and implementation stages. The first programme involves promoting and managing the programme at village or rural community level. For this tutors are needed who can speak and read Spanish and who can assist the village tutors accomplish their task of training the members of their group in junior high rural education. This includes animal husbandry, pig management, poultry, training in basic health and literacy as well as other skills to enable the group in the village to plan and achieve the goals they have defined as 'sustainable development'. The other programme involves giving conferences at universities, colleges and schools on virtues and development as requested. The foundation is now offering a post – B.A. programme in Health Education and needs volunteers to help with some of the classes. It also has another programme which trains tutors to provide early childhood education to parents of small children – the American S.T.E.P. programme. Volunteers with an offending background may be accepted. Each application individually assessed. Alternative address in Mexico – Narciso de Mendoza 546, Colonia Magisterial, Mexicali, Baja California, 21290. In the desert northwest of Mexico, between Mexicali, Tijuana and Ensenada in the state of Baja California, Mexico which is on the southern border of the USA. ⓑ 📄

Number of projects: 2 UK: 0
Starting months: January–December
Time required: 4–52 weeks
Age: 18 plus – no upper limit
Causes: Children, Conservation, Environmental Causes, Health Care/Medical, Teaching/assisting (secondary, mature), Young People.
Activities: Administration, Agriculture/Farming, Community Work, Computers, Conservation Skills, Development Issues, First Aid, Fundraising, International Aid, Marketing/Publicity, Social Work, Teaching, Training.
Placements: 1 or 2
When to apply: As early as possible.
Work alone/with others: Varies depending on maturity and ability to take responsibility.
Qualifications: Volunteers should be able to speak and write Spanish with a reasonable degree of fluency, should have a valid drivers licence and be computer literate. Only volunteers who can obtain a Mexican tourist card can be accepted.
Equipment/clothing: No specific equipment or clothing is required. It would be very helpful if the volunteer had a vehicle and insurance.
Health requirements: For summer time volunteering in the low desert areas, the volunteer should be able to take the heat.

Costs: Travel + US$400 per month for food and $50 for extra travel + personal expenses.
Benefits: We assist volunteers in finding a suitable apartment. Sometimes hospitality is available.
Training: All necessary training in the junior high programme is provided by the foundation staff.
Supervision: The volunteers' work is closely supervised.
Interviews: Interviews by e-mail and on arrival.
Worldwide placements: Central America (Mexico).

FUNDACION CHOL-CHOL

Regalil, Camino Labrenza-Imperial, Km 3
Casilla 14, Nueva Imperial
Temuco
9 Region Chile
T: 56 45 614007
F: 56 45 614008
E: info@chol-chol.org
W: www.cholchol.org
Contact: Johanna Perez Vega

The Fundacion Chol-Chol is a non-profit, non-governmental, human-development organisation created in 1971 with the initial goal of 'ending world hunger' which has been developed into a series of sustainable, hands-on training programmes. We work with individuals from the most impoverished indigenous communities of Chile, who are interested in exploring their potential for building self-reliance and self-sufficiency, improving their economic, social and technical plights, and supporting the rebirth of many traditional Mapuche cultural ways. Currently, we work to create and support change that is self-sustainable for indigenous, rural women by acting as a bridge to integrated education. Furthermore, we support financial independence everyday through the management of a rotating, micro-credit fund. Finally, given the fact that most of our beneficiaries live far away from those markets in which they could sell their woven textiles, the Fundacion accepts responsibility for the sale of the beneficiary products. We look forward to the time when the Mapuche community groups interact directly with national and/or international textile salespeople. We generally would not be able to accept volunteers with an offending background, unless under particular perusal of the case by the Volunteer Co-ordinator. Ninth region of Chile.

Number of projects: 2 **UK:** 0
Starting months: January–December
Time required: 12–72 weeks
Age: 18 plus – no upper limit
Causes: Conservation, Health Care/Medical, Poor/Homeless, Teaching/assisting (nursery, mature).

Activities: Agriculture/Farming, Arts/Crafts, Building/Construction, Development Issues, First Aid, Fundraising, Gardening/Horticulture, Group Work, Manual Work, Outdoor Skills, Research, Social Work, Teaching, Technical Skills, Training, Translating.
Placements: 10
When to apply: Any time.
Work alone/with others: Work with others.
Qualifications: The most important skill required is Spanish proficiency because we have proved that without it the whole volunteer experience becomes frustrating and not at all rewarding.
Equipment/clothing: Only during winter regarding wet weather clothing/ warm clothing and boots. May be specific items to enhance performance as defined in the co-ordinator programme – more details with application.
Health requirements: No restrictions.
Costs: Flight costs, bus to Temuco US$9.09. One month home stay (room and board) US$112–150. Home stay (room only) US$70 plus food @US$100 approx. Rent apartment and food US$240. Bus to Fundacion US$21.
Benefits: Accommodation in Saniago, Temuco and Nueva Imperial. Free lunch on work days. The foundation will contribute up to $800 to the cost of international travel for volunteer doctors who remain with us for more than three months.
Training: No formal training but the volunteer will receive orientation training on the Mapuche indigenous culture when needed.
Supervision: Supervision undertaken by Programme Co-ordinator or Programme Head, this will be done regularly and will evaluate assignment and work process. Volunteer Co-ordinator is also in close contact.
Interviews: Interviews are held by phone or by contact in the country.
Worldwide placements: South America (Chile).

FUNDACION ECUATORIANA DE TRABAJO

Quito y Ricaurte (esquina)
Casilla 13–01–131
Quito
Ecuador
T: 00 593 5 63920
F: 00 593 5 631 351
Contact: Betty Amen de Arteaga

Fundacion Ecuatoriana de Trabajo promotes and has information about volunteering in Ecuador. It may well be able to put volunteers in touch with organisations which are not yet listed on the WorldWide Volunteering database.

Starting months: January–December
Time required: 1–52 weeks (plus)
Age: 16 plus – no upper limit

Causes: Addicts/Ex-Addicts, AIDS/HIV, Animal Welfare, Archaeology, Architecture, Children, Conservation, Disabled (learning and physical), Elderly People, Environmental Causes, Health Care/Medical, Heritage, Holidays for Disabled, Human Rights, Inner City Problems, Offenders/Ex-Offenders, Poor/Homeless, Refugees, Teaching/assisting (nursery, primary, secondary, mature, EFL) Unemployed, Wildlife, Work Camps – Seasonal, Young People.
Activities: Accountancy, Administration, Agriculture/Farming, Arts/Crafts, Building/Construction, Campaigning, Caring (general, day and residential), Catering, Community Work, Computers, Conservation Skills, Cooking, Counselling, Development Issues, DIY, Driving, First Aid, Forestry, Fundraising, Gardening/Horticulture, Group Work, International Aid, Library/Resource Centres, Manual Work, Marketing/Publicity, Music, Newsletter/Journalism, Outdoor Skills, Religion, Research, Scientific Work, Social Work, Sport, Summer Camps, Teaching, Technical Skills, Theatre/Drama, Training, Translating, Visiting/Befriending, Work Camps – Seasonal.
Costs: Varies according to the project.
Worldwide placements: South America (Ecuador).

FUNDACION GOLONDRINAS

Avenida Isabel La Católica 1559
Quito
Ecuador
T: 00 593 2 226 602
E: manteca@uio.satnet.net
W: www.ecuadorexplorer.com/golondrinas
Contact: Maria-Eliza Manteca Oñate, President or Mónica Yépez, Secretary

The Fundación Golondrinas is a privately managed, non-profit organisation founded in 1991. The primary site is a small farming village in Northern Ecuador where volunteers work often alongside locals on a farm and tree nursery using the principles of permaculture. This method demonstrates the advantages of farming one area of land economically and productively for an indefinite period of time, as opposed to the 'slash and burn' techniques currently used by the locals. This is rapidly and irrevocably destroying the cloudforest, which 25 years ago covered the surrounding mountains, now bare and largely infertile. Not only is the foundation hoping to improve the productivity of the land but its goal is to rescue the old ways of farming which the local people once used in order to maintain an aspect of their culture that is becoming lost. Volunteers are needed for a number of jobs, including planting, harvesting and general farm maintenance. There is a need for volunteers willing to stay a minimum of six months to act

in one of the following positions: volunteer co-ordinator, teacher of environmental sustainability with local children, scientific researcher, administrative assistant or marketing representative in the office in Quito. The contribution for those volunteers wishing to stay six months or so is negotiable. The work is interesting and diverse and gives a rare opportunity to become truly involved in Ecuadorian rural life. You may also get the chance to visit the 18,000 hectares of protected virgin cloudforest, owned by the project. Here there is a cabin overlooking 40 miles of undamaged forest where a range of wildlife may be seen. Lower down in the reservation is a further site where two cabins and a tree nursery are located. This is an excellent location in which to do scientific research and studies.

Number of projects: 1 UK: 0
Starting months: January–December
Time required: 4–12 weeks
Age: 18–33
Causes: Conservation, Environmental Causes.
Activities: Agriculture/Farming, Building/Construction, Conservation Skills, Forestry, Manual Work, Outdoor Skills.
Placements: 60
When to apply: Any time but three months in advance if possible.
Work alone/with others: With others.
Qualifications: Spanish is absolutely essential.
Equipment/clothing: A pair of working gloves, a penknife, insect repellent, sleeping bag, rubber boots, long trousers, longsleeve shirt, waterproof jacket.
Health requirements: Nil but work is physical so good health is necessary.
Costs: US$240/month includes accomm. food ($200/m if more than 3 mths). Health insurance. Accommodation in the Reserve lodges in Guallupe Hostel.
Training: Not necessary.
Supervision: On the field supervised by 2 experienced staff. In Quito volunteers are briefed in the office.
Interviews: Prospective volunteers are not interviewed but a general briefing is given before work starts and volunteers are required to sign a statement of the rules of the foundation.
Charity number: 213
Worldwide placements: South America (Ecuador).

FUTURE IN OUR HANDS KENYA (FIOHK)

PO Box 4037
Kisumu
Kenya
T: 00 254 35 40522
E: fiohk@hotmail.com
Contact: Rom Wandera

Future in our Hands Kenya needs volunteers to work in many areas such as: 1. Environment – to encourage environmental concern through planting of trees in schools and within the community; educate on the dangers of improper waste disposal and environmental upgrading through proper planning. 2. Health – we strive to reduce the mortality rate of the underprivileged in the community who have no access to medication. In particular, through the provision of basic health care and the establishment of community based health centres, we give help and hope to the children and the elderly. 3. Education – we seek sponsorship for the disadvantaged children within the communities to enable them to pursue education. Encourage communities to set up education centres in the remote areas of our country. In urban areas set up a centre to educate the school drop-outs, especially girls who are forced out of education due to early pregnancy, child labour and excessive poverty. 4. Women's Co-operative – Educate and initiate credit unions consisting of groups of 12 women. Encourage the poor women to develop a culture of saving and borrowing from their own individual group savings. 5. Water and sanitation – help to provide safe and clean water to communities which have no access to it. 🔣 🔣

Starting months: May, Jun
Time required: 5–52 weeks
Age: 16–45
Causes: AIDS/HIV, Children, Environmental Causes, Teaching/assisting (nursery, primary).
Activities: Administration, Campaigning, Community Work, Counselling, Development Issues, Fundraising, International Aid, Newsletter/Journalism, Social Work, Teaching.
Placements: 5
When to apply: Before 30th March.
Work alone/with others: With other young volunteers.
Qualifications: English language.
Health requirements: Nil.
Costs: Travel.
Benefits: We offer boarding facilities in an apartment.
Training: One-week orientation training when volunteers are shown areas of work.
Supervision: Volunteers should expect to work with minimal or no supervision.
Interviews: No interviews necessary.
Charity number: S/H.ND.5241
Worldwide placements: Africa (Kenya).

FUTURE IN OUR HANDS TANZANIA, THE

P.O. Box 147
Bunda
Tanzania
Contact: Mr Sylivester N. Nyinyimbe

The Future in Our Hands (FIOHT) is a non-governmental organisation and has no political or religious affiliations. Established early 2002. The aims of FIOHT are as follows – i) To promote environmental conservation activities, because our future depends on a healthy environment. ii) To promote sustainable development projects, which will help the community to improve the living standard. iii) To alleviate poverty in the community in a sustainable way. iv) To work in co-operation with like-minded organisations/institutions both in Tanzania and overseas. The FIOHT activities are focused on sustainable environment conservation and development projects, e.g. tree planting, tree seedlings nursery, alternative technology, health education, income generating activities, women development, water and sanitation etc. Volunteers are needed to become involved in project planning and management in FIOHT programmes in order to share or exchange skills, education, knowledge and experience in different fields of work and life. Once in Tanzania, volunteers will spend one week planning the work programme to cover the entire period of stay. Volunteers have a variety of programmes to choose from. We are unable to place volunteers with an offending background. Tanzania, Mara Region, Bunda District, Bunda Town, east of Lake Victoria and west of Serengeti National Park. 🔣

Number of projects: 1 UK: 0
Starting months: January–December
Time required: 5–24 weeks
Age: 20–45
Causes: AIDS/HIV, Children, Conservation, Environmental Causes, Health Care/Medical, Inner City Problems, Poor/Homeless, Teaching/assisting, Young People.
Activities: Accountancy, Administration, Agriculture/Farming, Community Work, Computers, Conservation Skills, Counselling, Development Issues, DIY, First Aid, Forestry, Fundraising, Gardening/Horticulture, International Aid, Library/Resource Centres, Manual Work, Newsletter/Journalism, Outdoor Skills, Research, Scientific Work, Social Work, Teaching, Technical Skills, Training, Visiting/Befriending.
Placements: Varies.
When to apply: Apply any time, the earlier the better.
Work alone/with others: Both.
Qualifications: Various skills, knowledge and experience are required for different fields of activities.
Equipment/clothing: Mosquito net required.
Health requirements: Malaria innoculations are advised.
Costs: Travel costs, subsistence,

accommodation, meals, medication, leisure and emergency cases costs are to be covered by the volunteer. These would depend on ones lifestyle but tend to average between £1500 and £2000 per month.
Benefits: Successful participants receive certificates and cheap tourism costs. The Co-ordinator will arrange accommodation with the volunteer.
Training: On site.
Supervision: Supervision takes place by the Co-ordinator from FIOHT.
Interviews: No interviews but C.V and photo are required from prospective volunteers. Do not come without confirmation from Co-ordinator from FIOHT.
Charity number: Officially recognised by the Government
Worldwide placements: Africa (Tanzania).

FYD (FRIENDS FOR YOUNG DEAF PEOPLE)

East Court Mansion
College Lane
East Grinstead
W. Sussex RH19 3LT UK
T: 01342 323444 minicom 01342 312639
F: 01342 410232
E: fyd.egho@charity.vfree.com
W: www.fyd.org.uk
Contact:

The aim of FYD is to promote an active partnership between deaf and hearing people which will enable young deaf people to develop themselves and become active members of society. FYD will work to ensure that the partnership is created through friendship. Deaf people take the lead in shared responsibility as volunteers and staff work together to achieve the aim. Positive role models are provided for both deaf and hearing people. The partnership focuses on work with young people. Deaf and hearing young people share in activities which promote effective communication and self confidence. Deaf and hearing young people

train together to develop a variety of personal, leadership and work skills. The partnership acknowledges deafness as a key issue. Deaf and hearing people can choose how they can communicate through 'total communication'. Deaf people overcome disadvantage by developing skills and hearing people become more aware so that both can be equal partners with equal opportunities. Volunteers with an offending background are accepted unless it contravenes The Children Act.

Number of projects: 22 **UK:** 22
Starting months: January–December
Time required: 1–52 weeks
Age: 15–50
Causes: Children, Disabled (physical), Teaching (secondary, mature), Unemployed, Work Camps – Seasonal, Young People.
Activities: Administration, Arts/Crafts, Community Work, Computers, Counselling, Development Issues, Driving, First Aid, Fundraising, Group Work, Marketing/Publicity, Newsletter/Journalism, Outdoor Skills, Research, Sport, Summer Camps, Teaching, Theatre/Drama, Training, Visiting/Befriending, Work Camps – Seasonal.
Placements: 200–500
When to apply: All year.
Work alone/with others: With others.
Qualifications: It is preferred that a volunteer should go through the FYD training programme.
Health requirements: Nil.
Costs: Nil.
Benefits: 25p per mile or 2nd class public transport. Free accommodation and meals.
Training: FYD training programme.
Interviews: Interviews are carried out at our training programme (7 per year) and at our regional bases in the Midlands and the south of England.
Charity number: 1045011
Worldwide placements: Australasia (Australia, New Zealand).
UK placements: England (throughout).

GALWAY ASSOCIATION, THE

Blackrock House
Salthill
Galway
Ireland
T: 00 353 91 528122
F: 00 353 91 528150
E: volunteers@galwayca.ie
W: www.galwayca.ie
Contact: Tony Cunningham

The Galway Association needs volunteers who share their time, energy and enthusiasm with the children and adults who use our services. No particular qualifications are required, just a willingness to make a reliable commitment. Volunteers are involved in Friendship Schemes by becoming a friend to a person with a learning disability. Volunteers provide valuable assistance with leisure pursuits such as swimming, horseriding, social outings, recreation, specific programmes and projects to mention but a few! Western region of Ireland. &

Number of projects: 1 UK: 0
Starting months: January–December
Time required: 12–52 weeks (plus)
Age: 16 plus – no upper limit
Causes: Disabled (learning)
Activities: Arts/Crafts, Caring (general, residential), Community Work, Computers, Gardening/Horticulture, Music, Outdoor Skills, Sport.
Placements: 100
When to apply: All year.
Work alone/with others: Both.
Qualifications: Good conversational English.
Health requirements: Nil.
Costs: Travel and subsistence.
Training: Individual induction and group training.

Supervision: Volunteers are supervised by co-ordinator of volunteers plus individual staff supervisor.
Interviews: Volunteers are interviewed in Galway.
Charity number: 6306
Worldwide placements: Europe (Ireland).

GAP ACTIVITY PROJECTS

GAP House
44 Queen's Road
Reading
Berkshire RG1 4BB UK
T: 0118 959 4914 or 0118 956 2902 (brochures)
F: 0118 957 6634
E: volunteer@gap.org.uk
W: www.gap.org.uk
Contact: Jane Turner

GAP arranges voluntary work overseas for school-leavers taking a year out before going on to higher education, further training or employment. Work placements are all of charitable or educational value and last on average five months. This can form a core of worthwhile experience and the basis for travel in a busy year out schedule. GAP sees the year out as the ideal opportunity for young people to broaden their experience of the world while making a personal contribution to other communities. A constructive and exciting GAP project can be undertaken for less than £1,500. A variety of voluntary work opportunities exist in over 34 countries. There may be placements for those with an offending background, depending on the offence. Alternative e-mail address: volunteer@gap.org.uk. Gap Activity Projects are a member of The Year Out Group. Refer to web site. &

Number of projects: 600+ UK: 0
Starting months: Jan, Feb, Mar, Apr, May, Jul, Aug, Sep, Oct

A Dream Come True – Teaching in The Philippines

"A visit to my local Volunteer Bureau led to the start of a new life for me," writes Sheryl Thompson. After years of illness, she fulfilled her dream of working abroad when she found a placement with Little Children of the World through WorldWide Volunteering. Sheryl's anxieties soon faded when she was welcomed to her project at Dumaguete, where she taught pre-school children, tutored basic English and maths and helped out wherever needed. "My experience as a volunteer in the Philippines has given me a new direction in life. It has changed me as a person."

Time required: 18–52 weeks
Age: 17–19
Causes: AIDS/HIV, Animal Welfare, Archaeology, Children, Conservation, Disabled (learning and physical), Elderly People, Environmental Causes, Health Care/Medical, Heritage, Inner City Problems, Poor/Homeless, Refugees, Teaching/assisting (nursery, primary, secondary, mature, EFL) Wildlife, Work Camps – Seasonal, Young People.
Activities: Administration, Agriculture/Farming, Arts/Crafts, Building/Construction, Caring (general, day and residential), Community Work, Computers, Conservation Skills, Cooking, Driving, First Aid, Forestry, Gardening/Horticulture, Group Work, Library/Resource Centres, Music, Outdoor Skills, Research, Scientific Work, Social Work, Sport, Summer Camps, Teaching, Theatre/Drama, Visiting/Befriending, Work Camps – Seasonal.
Placements: 1, 550
When to apply: Any time after GCSEs. The earlier the better.
Work alone/with others: Alone or in pairs.
Qualifications: Students in their year out between school and higher education, further training or employment. Must hold a UK or Irish passport.
Equipment/clothing: According to placement.
Health requirements: Volunteers may be required to produce confirmation of fitness to travel overseas. Projects in some countries require a medical examination.
Costs: £750 + £40 registration fee + air fare, insurance and TEFL course (if necessary).
Benefits: Board and accommodation plus pocket money in most cases. Business Partnership Scheme.
Training: Dependent on placement. TEFL if necessary, co-ordinated by GAP and paid for by volunteer.
Supervision: All placements chosen because they are appropriate and challenging. Hosts, be it on site or staying with a family, look after volunteers. GAP has overseas agents in the host country and a project manager who will visit at least once.
Interviews: Interviews take place in Reading, Leeds, Edinburgh, Belfast or Dublin. The interview is GAP's opportunity to match candidates to projects. We have something for everyone on a year out. (Academic qualifications/predictions do not affect selection.)
Charity number: 272761
Worldwide placements: Africa (Lesotho, South Africa, Swaziland, Tanzania, Zambia); North America: (Canada, USA); Central America (Mexico, Trinidad and Tobago); South America (Argentina, Brazil, Chile, Ecuador, Falkland Islands, Paraguay); Asia (China, Hong Kong, India, Israel, Japan, Macao, Malaysia, Nepal, Thailand, Vietnam); Australasia (Australia, Fiji,

New Zealand, Vanuatu); Europe (Germany, Hungary, Poland, Romania, Russia).

GAP CHALLENGE

at World Challenge Expeditions
Black Arrow House
2 Chandos Road
London
NW10 6NF UK
T: +44 (0) 20 8728 7274 or 7200
F: +44 (0) 20 8961 1551
E: welcome@world-challenge.co.uk
W: www.world-challenge.co.uk
Contact: Nicola Stopforth

Gap Challenge is part of World Challenge Expeditions who have been providing overseas opportunities for young people since 1989. Applicants should have a high degree of motivation and commitment and be prepared for a challenge. Placements last six weeks to nine months and run to ten destinations across the world. With a 12-month return flight, there is plenty of opportunity for independent travel afterwards. Placements include teaching, carework, conservation, eco-tourism and agricultural work. Paid work is available in Canada in hotels or mountain lodges. The flexible Gap Challenge programme has a range of worthwhile and rewarding voluntary placements to select from in a number of destinations. Apart from those listed, other exciting placements include paid hotel work and ski instructor courses in Canada, farming in Australia and medical support in Peru or Costa Rica. There are also opportunities to take part in other programmes organised by World Challenge Expeditions, ranging from an 8 day First Challenge expedition in Morocco to a 6-week Team Challenge expedition to the Andes and Amazon (see World Challenge Expeditions entry). All applicants are required to attend a 2-day selection course. These are held throughout the year. There is also a Skills Training course before departure where Gap Challengers receive information and briefings from qualified staff and a chance to meet ex-Gap Challengers. Gap Challenge are a member of The Year Out Group. 🅰 🄱

Number of projects: 33 UK: 0
Starting months: Jan, Mar, Apr, Jun, Sep, Nov
Time required: 6–36 weeks
Age: 18–24
Causes: Children, Conservation, Disabled (learning and physical), Environmental Causes, Health Care/Medical, Teaching/assisting (primary, secondary, EFL), Wildlife.
Activities: Agriculture/Farming, Caring (general, residential), Community Work, Conservation Skills, Forestry, Gardening/Horticulture, Outdoor Skills, Scientific Work, Social Work, Sport, Teaching.

Placements: over 450
When to apply: Any time up to a month before departure.
Work alone/with others: Usually in pairs or small groups.
Qualifications: 3 A-levels or equivalent preferred for teaching posts. No restrictions although Gap Challengers need to participate in a selection course and skills training course based in the UK (Derbyshire) or the USA (Boston).
Equipment/clothing: Gap Challenge provides information on suitable clothing.
Health requirements: All applicants are asked to disclose pre-existing conditions.
Costs: Costs vary accordingly. Voluntary work placements such as teaching + conservation costs around £1800 inc a 12-mth return flight, skills training pre-departure, transfer to placement, Orientation course in country + 24-hr emergency back up from WCE.
Benefits: The cost includes training, return flights and travel, in-country support and London 24-hour emergency back-up.
Training: All participants attend the Skills Training Course before their placement.
Supervision: Every country has support from in-country agents and there is a 24-hour emergency back-up and support from Gap Challenge Headquarters in London.
Interviews: Two-day Selection Courses take place at our Leadership and Development Centre throughout the year.
Worldwide placements: Africa (South Africa, Tanzania); North America: (Canada); Central America (Belize, Costa Rica, Mexico); South America (Ecuador, Peru); Asia (Malaysia, Nepal); Australasia (Australia, New Zealand).

GAP SPORTS ABROAD

39 Guinions Road
High Wycombe
Buckinghamshire HP13 7NT UK
T: +44 (0) 1494 769090
F: +44 (0) 1494 769090
E: info@gapsportsabroad.co.uk
W: www.gapsportsabroad.co.uk
Contact: James Burton

Gap Sports Abroad (GSA) is leading the way in the gap year industry for sports associated placements. Priding itself on its variety of unique coaching positions currently available in Ghana (West Africa) a volunteer will be hard pressed to find another organisation to rival the GSA experience. And while volunteers are experiencing the coaching opportunity of their lifetime, they will also be addressing the importance of sports development in third-world communities. But don't let the word 'sport', in Gap Sports Abroad put you off! GSA can provide any volunteer with the opportunities that the other leading gap year

companies can offer, from teaching in rural Africa to medical experiences and broadcast journalism. With well-established links in Ghana's most prestigious sports academies, GSA volunteers will be exposed to some of Africa's finest raw talent in football, tennis, boxing and basketball. Because of the variety of GSA positions available, volunteers with any level of sporting background can have the chance to coach in Ghana, be it at an under 12 youth club or shadowing a premier league head coach. Gap year volunteers can feel safe and secure when taking their step into the daunting world of a developing country. GSA has a well-experienced and friendly support team permanently living in Ghana. Not only will they help volunteers feel settled and comfortable, they will also be in charge of a variety of social activities that make GSA placements truly memorable. GSA also encourages its volunteers to explore Ghana and what it has to offer independently. With its dense forests, wild savannah and beautiful beaches, not to mention the capital's vibrant market place and authentic nightlife, there is certainly a lot to keep you busy. Because of the sought after sports placements GSA offer, volunteers will gain an extremely unique gap year opportunity. There is no fear of missing out on what you want to do as GSA gives volunteers the freedom to tailor-make their own experience – affiliated to the Duke of Edinburgh Awards, you can use your time away towards gaining your Gold Award. Take this coaching opportunity in your gap year, and you will take away the gap year experience of your lifetime. Placements currently available in Ghana are – football coaching, basketball coaching, tennis coaching, boxing experience, teaching, art and design, medical, journalism, sports psychology, physiotherapy and sports tours. Placement in Accra in Ghana.

Number of projects: 22 UK: 0
Starting months: January–December
Time required: 5–52 weeks
Age: 16–65
Causes: Children, Health Care/Medical, Teaching/assisting (nursery, primary, secondary, mature, EFL) Unemployed, Work Camps – Seasonal, Young People.
Activities: Arts/Crafts, Caring – General, Community Work, Computers, Development Issues, Fundraising, International Aid, Marketing/Publicity, Newsletter/Journalism, Outdoor Skills, Religion, Sport, Summer Camps, Teaching, Theatre/Drama, Visiting/Befriending.
Placements: 60
When to apply: One month before departure.
Work alone/with others: Varies.
Qualifications: Any relevant skills to the placements we offer is an advantage but not

essential. It will help us in putting people in the right level of placement.
Equipment/clothing: Nothing specific. However, we will organise clothing for our volunteers if it is needed. i.e. medical clothing.
Health requirements: No restrictions.
Costs: Placement cost, flights, insurance, vaccinations, personal spending money and visas.
Benefits: Food and accommodation, staff support in country of placment as well as on going support from the UK before and after the trip. We provide full board at a football academy where our support team are based. This in in the capital, Accra and is located near to all our placements. Volunteers will share a room at the academy, or we can organise accommodation in local guest houses.
Training: Training is provided.
Supervision: We have a 24 hour support team in Ghana who are available to take care of any volunteers needs.
Interviews: We may conduct a telephone interview to find out any further information we require.
Worldwide placements: Africa (Ghana).

GENCTUR (Tourism and Travel Agency Ltd)

Istiklal Cad.
Zambak Sok. 15/AK.5
Beyoglu
80080 Istanbul
Turkey
T: 00 90 212 249 25 15
F: 00 90 212 249 25 54
E: workcamps.in@genctur.com
W: www.genctur.com
Contact: Zafer Yilmaz

Genctur needs volunteers of all ages over 18 to take part in international workcamps in small Turkish villages or towns (rarely big towns or cities), involving work such as constructing or repairing, painting and white washing schools and village centres. Also digging water trenches, forestry, festival organisation, environmental development work, helping with people with a disability, practising English with children etc. Camp language is English. ▤

Number of projects: 25–40 **UK:** 0
Starting months: Jun, Jul, Aug, Sep
Time required: 2–8 weeks
Age: 18 plus – no upper limit
Causes: Environmental Causes, Teaching/assisting (primary, secondary), Work Camps – Seasonal.
Activities: Agriculture/Farming, Arts/Crafts, Building/Construction, Community Work, Counselling, Forestry, Manual Work, Social Work, Summer Camps, Teaching, Work Camps – Seasonal.

Placements: 300
When to apply: April – September through partner organisations in the country.
Work alone/with others: With others.
Equipment/clothing: Additional information is supplied to the applicants.
Health requirements: Nil.
Costs: All costs + £35 registration fee for the participant applying from a country where there is no partner.
Benefits: Board and lodging.
Training: None.
Supervision: Orientation meeting before each camp starts.
Interviews: Applicants for volunteer projects are not interviewed.
Worldwide placements: Asia (Turkey); Europe (Turkey).

GENERAL UNION OF VOLUNTARY SOCIETIES IN JORDAN, THE

PO Box 910236
Amman
Jordan
T: 00 962 6 634 001
F: 00 962 6 659 973
E: guvs@accessme.com
Contact: Abdullah El-Khatib

The General Union of Voluntary Societies in Jordan promotes and has information about volunteering in Jordan. It may well be able to put volunteers in touch with organisations which are not yet listed on the WorldWide Volunteering database.

Starting months: January–December
Time required: 1–52 weeks (plus)
Age: 16 plus – no upper limit
Causes: Addicts/Ex-Addicts, AIDS/HIV, Animal Welfare, Archaeology, Architecture, Children, Conservation, Disabled (learning and physical), Elderly People, Environmental Causes, Health Care/Medical, Heritage, Holidays for Disabled, Human Rights, Inner City Problems, Offenders/Ex-Offenders, Poor/Homeless, Refugees, Teaching/assisting (nursery, primary, secondary, mature, EFL) Unemployed, Wildlife, Work Camps – Seasonal, Young People.
Activities: Accountancy, Administration, Agriculture/Farming, Arts/Crafts, Building/Construction, Campaigning, Caring (general, day and residential), Catering, Community Work, Computers, Conservation Skills, Cooking, Counselling, Development Issues, DIY, Driving, First Aid, Forestry, Fundraising, Gardening/Horticulture, Group Work, International Aid, Library/Resource Centres, Manual Work, Marketing/Publicity, Music, Newsletter/Journalism, Outdoor Skills, Religion, Research, Scientific Work, Social Work, Sport,

Summer Camps, Teaching, Technical Skills, Theatre/Drama, Training, Translating, Visiting/Befriending, Work Camps – Seasonal.
Costs: Varies according to the project.
Worldwide placements: Asia (Jordan).

GENESIS II CLOUDFOREST PRESERVE

Apartado 655
7050 Cartago
Costa Rica
T: 00 506 381 0739
F: 00 506 381 0739
E: volunteer@genesis-two.com
Contact: Co-owner

Genesis II Cloudforest Preserve is a privately owned cloudforest at the 7500 foot/2360 metre level in the Talamanca Mountains of central Costa Rica. From its inception it has been intended and operated as a preserve for academic research and recreational (non hunting) pleasure. Within its 95 acre boundaries can be found up to 120 species of birds plus many types of ferns, orchids, fungi, and its major tree: the towering white oak. While the terrain is quite rugged, the forest is very benign. No known very venomous reptiles, plants or insects and the climate is generally best described as 'moistly soft'. There are two distinct seasons here. January to May is our dry season (summer). June to December is our wet or rainy season (winter). At most times during the year, the early mornings are clear and sunny. However, during the wet season it clouds over by 9–10 am and usually rains by noon. Occasionally during this season, we may experience several continuous days of cloud and drizzle; depressing but not serious. If you choose to come during the wet season you should be prepared to work in cool, rainy conditions. To provide access to the forest for the birdwatchers, ornithologists and naturalists, we have provided a small, first class trail system of about three km. Each unit is 29 days long with a week separation between each. Opportunities now exist for volunteers to stay for more than one unit (but this should be agreed to before coming). We also can accept students on placement as part of their degree programme (with formal agreement from their supervisor and department). Cost in these situations is similar to regular volunteers. Volunteers with an offending background who are motivated may be accepted. This can be a very testing experience. We need volunteers who are totally willing – no rebels. 📄

Number of projects: 1 UK: 0
Starting months: Jan, Feb, Mar, Apr, May, Jun, Jul, Aug, Sep, Oct
Time required: 4–52 weeks
Age: 21–99

Causes: Conservation, Environmental Causes, Work Camps – Seasonal.
Activities: Building/Construction, Conservation Skills, Forestry, Manual Work, Outdoor Skills, Work Camps – Seasonal.
Placements: 60
When to apply: All year.
Work alone/with others: Mostly with others.
Qualifications: Willingness and a preference for studying environment and conservation. Camping/hiking/surveying skills.
Equipment/clothing: List of equipment supplied.
Health requirements: No vegans. Prefer non-smokers. Volunteers need to be physically fit.
Costs: US$600 for room, board, and laundry. Other costs are volunteer's responsibility, e.g. travel, insurance, pocket money.
Benefits: Board lodging and laundry. Simple cabins with electric light.
Training: Given by co-owner or supervisor.
Supervision: Given by co-owner or supervisor.
Interviews: Volunteer applicants are not interviewed.
Worldwide placements: Central America (Costa Rica).

GHANA NETWORK OF VOLUNTEER SERVICE

P.O.Box TA 167 Taifa
Accra
Taifa
TA 167 Ghana
T: 223 21 407803
E: service_gnvs@yahoo.com
W: www.geocities.com/service_gnvs
Contact: Emmanuel Odonkor Corletey

Ghana Network of Volunteer Service is a non-governmental organisation with a distinctive approach to development. We are looking for volunteers who are open, resilient, and committed. Interest from those who can take initiative to assist the needy in nursery, primary and secondary schools. Volunteers may be accepted with offending background.

Number of projects: 10 UK: 0
Starting months: January–December
Time required: 4–24 weeks
Age: 18–35
Causes: Children, Teaching/assisting (nursery, primary, secondary, EFL), Young People.
Activities: Administration, Caring – General, Community Work, Group Work, Teaching, Training, Translating.
Placements: 100
When to apply: Throughout year.
Work alone/with others: Work with others.
Qualifications: Volunteers must be able to speak English.
Health requirements: No restrictions.
Costs: Travel to Ghana. $200 for the initial

month and additional $70 for each subsequent month. This covers accommodation, airport pick up breakfast and lunch only.
Benefits: Accommodation, airport pick up free tour visit, breakfast and lunch.
Training: No.
Supervision: Responsibility of GNVS to supervise.
Interviews: No interview.
Charity number: ch/gh006610
Worldwide placements: Africa (Ghana).

GIRLGUIDING UK

17–19 Buckingham Palace Road
London
SW1W 0PT UK
T: +44 (0) 207 834 6242
F: +44 (0) 207 828 8317
E: chq@girlguiding.org.uk
W: www.girlguiding.org.uk
Contact: Marketing and External Relations

Girlguiding UK as part of a worldwide movement, enables girls and young women to fulfil their potential and to take an active and responsible role in society through its distinctive, stimulating and enjoyable programme of activities delivered by trained volunteer leaders. Its vision is to be recognised as the leading organisation for girls and women and to widen and increase its membership. Guiding is about enjoyment, challenge and excitement for girls and young women from five to 25. It provides an opportunity to make friends, enjoy activities and achieve whatever a girl's abilities might be. Events and activities take place across the UK and there are a growing number of opportunities for international expeditions and activities. 🚹

Number of projects: Many UK: Many
Starting months: January–December
Time required: 1–52 weeks (plus)
Age: 14–65
Causes: Young People.
Activities: Arts/Crafts, Community Work, First Aid, Fundraising, Group Work, Music, Outdoor Skills, Summer Camps, Theatre/Drama, Training.
Placements: 661,000
When to apply: All year.
Work alone/with others: Both.
Equipment/clothing: Yes – uniform.
Health requirements: No. ·
Costs: Membership subscription.
Benefits: Most expenses such as travel, accommodation etc. are reclaimable.
Training: Varies according to project.
Supervision: As a volunteer organisation, volunteers are supervised by other volunteers through our established structures and under the guidance of approved policies such as 'Safe From Harm'.

Interviews: Through application.
Charity number: 306016
Worldwide placements: Africa (Egypt, Ethiopia, Ghana, Malawi, Tanzania, Tunisia, Uganda, Zimbabwe); North America: (USA); South America (Brazil); Asia (Bahrain, Brunei, China, Indonesia, Japan, Kuwait, Malaysia, Nepal, Oman, Pakistan, Qatar, Saudi Arabia, Singapore, Taiwan, Turkey, United Arab Emirates); Europe (Belgium, Cyprus, Czech Republic, France, Germany, Greece, Italy, Luxembourg, Netherlands, Norway, Poland, Portugal, Romania, Russia, Spain, Switzerland, Turkey).
UK placements: England (throughout); Scotland (throughout); Northern Ireland (throughout); Wales (throughout).

GIRLS VENTURE CORPS AIR CADETS

Phoenix House
3 Handley Square, Finningley Airport
Doncaster
South Yorkshire DN9 3GH UK
T: 01302 775019
F: 017302 775020
E: gvcachq1@btopenworld.com
W: www.gvcac.org.uk
Contact: Mrs B Layne MBE

The Girls Venture Corps Air Cadets is a voluntary uniformed youth organisation for girls between the ages of 11 and 20 years. It offers a challenging and worthwhile programme, introducing its members to a wide range of activities which help to give them a wider outlook and a greater sense of purpose. Great emphasis is placed upon leadership and initiative training, and camps and courses for this purpose are held annually. The Corps makes a great contribution to the community. Members help either individually or as a group on various community projects and service to others plays an important part in a cadet's training. Because of its origins, the Corps is slanted towards 'air-mindedness' and is unique among youth organisations in offering air experience flights arranged with flying clubs. Solo Flying Scholarships are awarded when funds permit. The organisation seeks co-operation with local authorities, schools, employers and all concerned with the welfare of youth. 🚹

Number of projects: 60 UK: 60
Starting months: January–December
Time required: 1–52 weeks
Age: 18–60
Causes: Young People.
Activities: Administration, Arts/Crafts, Catering, Community Work, Cooking, Driving, First Aid, Fundraising, Group Work, Newsletter/Journalism, Outdoor Skills, Sport, Summer Camps, Training.

Placements: 260
When to apply: All year.
Work alone/with others: both.
Qualifications: Only enthusiasm.
Equipment/clothing: Depends on activities pursued.
Health requirements: For flying, yes.
Costs: Travel costs. The cost could be any amount depending on project/commitment.
Benefits: Travel costs might be paid by the region. Accommodation provided for camps/courses only.
Training: Training is provided in units.
Supervision: All volunteers are supervised at unit, region and national levels.
Interviews: Interviews take place either at local, regional or national level, depending on type of project.
Charity number: 306109
UK placements: England (Cambridgeshire, Co Durham, Essex, Hampshire, Isle of Wight, Kent, Leicestershire, London, Norfolk, Nottinghamshire, Somerset, Staffordshire, Suffolk, Surrey, Sussex – East, Tyne and Wear, West Midlands, S. Yorkshire).

GLAMORGAN WILDLIFE TRUST

Fountain Road
Tondu
Bridgend
CF32 OEH UK
T: 01656 724100
F: 01656 729880
E: information@wtsww.cix.co.uk
W: www.wildlifetrust.org.uk/wtsww/
Contact: Linda Wood

Glamorgan Wildlife Trust is a member of the Wildlife Trusts, a national partnership of 47 County Trusts. The aims of the Trust are primarily to: promote nature conservation in the community; acquire and manage nature reserves; monitor biological and geological resources; liaise with local authorities to promote regard for nature conservation; offer practical advice on nature conservation to landowners. It is the Trust's policy to involve all sectors of the community, of all ages, backgrounds, abilities and disabilities towards these ends. Volunteers require no previous experience just lots of enthusiasm. If they desire, can go on to participate more fully assisting with the organisation and running of activities/projects. Limited opportunities may also arise, for those with a longer term commitment, for NVQ training to level 2 in Landscapes and Ecosystems. Volunteers with an offending background may be accepted – each case separately assessed. ⅏ ▤

Number of projects: 10 UK: 10
Starting months: January–December
Time required: 1–52 weeks (plus)

Age: 16 plus – no upper limit
Causes: Conservation, Environmental Causes, Wildlife.
Activities: Computers, Conservation Skills, Driving, Forestry, Gardening/Horticulture, Manual Work, Outdoor Skills, Research, Scientific Work, Technical Skills.
Placements: 250
When to apply: All year.
Work alone/with others: With others.
Equipment/clothing: Casual work clothes, waterproofs, stout boots. Protective safety gear is provided.
Health requirements: Any medical conditions (illness, allergy or physical disability) that may require treatment/medication or which affects the volunteer working with machinery must be notified to us in advance. Tetanus injections must be up to date.
Costs: Bring your own packed lunch.
Benefits: Negotiable.
Training: They will receive on-the-job training in an informal atmosphere,.
Supervision: By qualified staff.
Interviews: Interviews at our office.
Charity number: 200653
UK placements: Wales (Bridgend, Caerphilly, Cardiff, Merthyr Tydfil, Neath Port Talbot, Rhondda, Cynon, Taff, Swansea, Vale of Glamorgan).

GLENCREE PEACE AND RECONCILIATION CENTRE

Glencree
Enniskerry
Co. Wicklow Ireland
T: 00 353 2829711/2766025
F: 00 353 276085
E: volunteering@glencree-cfr.ie
W: www.glencree.cfr.ie
Contact: Naoise Kelly

Glencree is a unique organisation in the Republic of Ireland, dedicated to peace-building, offering secluded facilities and programme resources to political, religious, youth and community groups. We provide facilities devoted to peace-building and reconciliation within the island of Ireland, between Britain and Ireland, and beyond. The resources of the centre are available to all sides involved in the conflict; to all individuals and groups who wish to work for peace in an atmosphere which is welcoming and inclusive; and to the victims of the conflict who face the huge challenge of coming to terms with their loss and suffering. Glencree is helped and supported by ten international volunteers and a small core of professional staff. Volunteers with an offending background may be accepted, depending on the offence. Each case can be discussed individually. ⅏ ▤

Number of projects: 1 UK: 0
Starting months: January–December
Time required: 2–12 weeks
Age: 18 plus – no upper limit
Causes: Work Camps – Seasonal.
Activities: Catering, Cooking,
Gardening/Horticulture, Manual Work, Work
Camps – Seasonal.
Placements: 20
When to apply: All year.
Equipment/clothing: Old clothes for
manual/gardening work.
Health requirements: Nil.
Costs: Travel and approximately €32 per day
food and accommodation – shared hostel style
accommodation.
Training: No training – information supplied.
Supervision: Volunteers will work alongside
Glencree volunteers under management
supervision.
Interviews: No interviews.
Worldwide placements: Europe (Ireland).

GLOBAL ACTION NEPAL

Baldwins
Eastlands Lane
Cowfold
West Sussex RH13 8AY UK
T: 01403 864704
F: 01403 864088
E: info@gannepal.org
W: www.gannepal org
Contact: Chris Sowton

Global Action Nepal was founded in 1996 to
improve the education of children in Nepal,
and to raise communities' awareness of
environment, health and sanitation issues. GAN
believes that the people of Nepal have the right
to the most basic level of healthcare, sanitation
and education, and that they deserve to be in
control of their own destiny. GAN's projects
and work are always closely in harness with
grass roots level needs, focusing on community
led, participatory development. It does not seek
to change the culture or people of Nepal but to
provide them with the tools to enable them to
help themselves. As a charity, where the sharing
of ideas and direct contact with local
communities is so important, GAN is very
dependent on hard-working, dedicated and
open-minded volunteers. The success of many
of our projects in Nepal involves working in
government schools for sustainable, long-term
improvement that will last well beyond the
length of the six months that each volunteer
spends in Nepal. Volunteers will spend the
majority of their time working on our CITE
(Clinic for the Improvement of Teachers of
English) programme, which enables Nepali
English Teachers to work better within their
classrooms and gives them the skills and

training which they lack. GAN offers full
training and support to volunteers, and aims to
keep costs as low as possible while maximising
the use of their time spent in Nepal. They will
accept someone with an offending background
but it depends on detail of offence – would
consider on case-by-case basis. Several districts
of Nepal, including Kathmandu, Lalitpur and
Pokhara (urban and more rural areas).

Number of projects: 2 UK: O
Starting months: Sep, Oct, Nov
Time required: 24 weeks
Age: 18–60
Causes: Teaching/assisting (nursery, primary,
secondary, mature, EFL).
Activities: Arts/Crafts, Community Work,
Development Issues, Teaching, Training.
Placements: 32
When to apply: As soon as possible.
Work alone/with others: With others.
Qualifications: Native or very high level of
spoken English. Need a good standard of
English (due to the nature of the work).
Equipment/clothing: Jumpers and strong
shoes.
Health requirements: Must be in good health
because of Nepal's geography.
Costs: £1,850 which includes return flight from
UK, transportation in Nepal, accommodation,
training, registration and programme fee, minor
medical costs, insurance and visa fees.
Benefits: Nepali language and culture, teaching
skills and working with adults. Board and
benefits included in costs.
Training: Is provided.
Supervision: Staff in the central office and field
regularly check up on volunteers and give
support to them – especially at the beginning
when most supervision is needed.
Interviews: Yes – usually in London, but
alternative arrangements have been made.
Worldwide placements: Asia (Nepal).

GLOBAL CITIZENS NETWORK

130 N. Howell Street
St Paul
Minnesota 55104 USA
T: 00 1 651 644 0960
E: info@globalcitizens.org
W: www.globalcitizens.org
Contact: Kim Schneider

Global Citizens Network seeks to create a
network of people who are committed to the
shared values of peace, justice, tolerance, cross-
cultural understanding and global co-operation;
to the preservation of indigenous cultures,
traditions and ecologies; and to the
enhancement of the quality of life around the
world. GCN sends small teams of volunteers to
rural communities around the world where the

volunteers immerse themselves in the daily life of the community. Trips last one, two or three weeks, depending on the site, and each team is led by a trained GCN team leader. The team works on projects initiated by people in the local community, for the benefit of the community. Such projects could include setting up a library, teaching business skills, building a health clinic, or planting trees to reforest a village. A unique and integral component of your experience includes daily activities of cross-cultural learning. You may test your skills at making tortillas, visit a nearby tea factory or the family farm, learn a local dance and discover the history and rich traditions of the area. People of all ages, backgrounds and experiences travel with GCN. Families are welcome to join our teams. Although there is really no typical day on a Global Citizens Network trip, volunteers stay in local homes or as a group in a community centre. Meals are either eaten together with your host family or communally prepared and shared with your project hosts. After breakfast, you join your team along with community members to work together on projects under the direction of the local leadership. As a volunteer, you immerse yourself in the more relaxed pace and adjust to life in a developing community. During the afternoon, you either continue working on a project or may participate in an activity which promotes cross-cultural understanding. Each evening you will join other team members and the team leader to go over the day's events and talk about what you have learned. &

Number of projects: 6 UK: 0
Starting months: January–December
Time required: 1–3 weeks
Age: 18 plus – no upper limit
Causes: Children, Conservation, Environmental Causes, Health Care/Medical, Teaching/assisting, Young People.
Activities: Building/Construction, Community Work, Conservation Skills, Cooking, Development Issues, Group Work, Manual Work, Outdoor Skills, Teaching, Visiting/Befriending.
Placements: 100
When to apply: 2–4 months before the trip or until teams are full.
Work alone/with others: With others – teams of 6–8 volunteers work alongside local volunteers.
Qualifications: Nil – only an open mind and sensitivity to new cultures. No restrictions. Children as young as five are accepted, providing they are accompanied by an adult.
Equipment/clothing: Dependent on site – very casual dress since most projects generally involve manual labour.
Health requirements: Must be in good health.

Some sites are very rural and remote – no water, electricity etc.
Costs: Programme costs range from US$600–$1650. Airfare additional.
Benefits: Costs include board, lodging, local transport, orientation materials and a donation to project. Accommodation varies but generally volunteers do homestays or stay in a local community centre.
Training: Orientation manual sent out pre-trip and in-country orientation meetings on site.
Supervision: A trained team leader accompanies each team of volunteers.
Interviews: Prospective volunteers are not interviewed.
Worldwide placements: Africa (Kenya); North America: (USA); Central America (Guatemala); Asia (Nepal).

GLOBAL EXCHANGE

2017 Mission St
Suite 303
San Fransisco
California 94110 USA
T: 415 255 7296
F: 415 255 7498
E: mexico@globalexchange.org
W: www.globalexchange.org
Contact: Carleen Pickard

Global Exchange is a human rights organisation dedicated to promoting environmental, political and social justice around the world. Since our founding in 1988, we have been striving to increase global awareness among the US public while building international partnerships around the world. We are unable to accept applications from those with offending background. Mexico, state of Chiopas. Generally in Southern areas near to San Crisobal de las Casas. &

Number of projects: 1 UK: 0
Starting months: January–December
Time required: 2–8 weeks
Age: 23–99
Causes: Children, Environmental Causes, Human Rights, Poor/Homeless, Refugees.
Activities: Campaigning.
Placements: 35
When to apply: Applications are accepted throughout the year.
Work alone/with others: Alone.
Qualifications: Volunteers must be fluent in Spanish and have the ability to deal with sensitive situations as well as other cultures.
Health requirements: Must be in good physical and mental health.
Costs: Volunteers are responsible for travel costs to San Cristobol and means to support themselves – estimated $150–300 per month including housing, food and all travel.

Benefits: Accommodation is in the community.
Training: Orientation to human rights observation.
Supervision: No supervision when in community.
Interviews: Interview with co-ordinator is necessary. In some cases this can be done over the telephone.
Worldwide placements: Central America (Mexico).

GLOBAL HANDS, NEPAL

P. O. Box 489
Zero k.m.
Pokhara
Kaski Nepal
T: 00 977 061 30266
E: insight@fewnet.com.np
Contact: Ms Maniari Shrestha

The kingdom of Nepal which is situated in the lap of Central Himalaya with a rich cultural heritage, is a land of ancient history and colourful cultures. Insight Nepal was established as an institution with a view to introducing the diverse geographical and cultural environment of Nepal to the participants, and to foster an awareness and cultural understanding. Global Hands is a short term volunteer programme which is designed for those people who want to come to Nepal with a desire to explore, experience and discover a unique way of life. The main objective of this programme is to provide opportunities to those who have limited time and budget, but are keenly interested in gaining experiences by sharing their ideas and skills with local community service groups, and to reach the people who are in need. Placements will be in the different areas of Pokhara and Kathmandu valleys. 🔽 📋

Number of projects: 2 UK: 1
Starting months: January–December
Time required: 4–6 weeks
Age: 18–70
Causes: AIDS/HIV, Children, Conservation, Disabled (physical), Environmental Causes, Health Care/Medical, Poor/Homeless, Teaching/assisting (primary, secondary, mature, EFL).
Activities: Administration, Agriculture/Farming, Arts/Crafts, Community Work, Computers, Conservation Skills, Fundraising, Social Work, Teaching, Training, Visiting/Befriending, Work Camps – Seasonal.
Placements: 40
When to apply: 8 weeks in advance.
Work alone/with others: Alone or in pairs.
Qualifications: Minimum 'A' level. Flexibility and willingness to be immersed in another culture.
Equipment/clothing: It depends on the season. However, Insight Nepal will inform before their arrival.

Health requirements: Immunisation against certain diseases.
Costs: US$40 application fee + US$400 programme fee (Nepal) or US$500 fee (India) + visa fee + return travel. Programme fee includes a 3 day orientation training.
Benefits: The cost covers homestay accommodation, 2 meals a day and a 3-day orientation training.
Training: Basic Nepali language training.
Supervision: Yes.
Interviews: No.
Worldwide placements: Asia (India, Nepal).

GLOBAL SERVICE CORPS

300 Broadway, Suite 25
San Fransisco
California 94133 USA
T: 415 788 3666
F: 415 788 7324
E: gsc@earthisland.org
W: www.globalservicecorps.org
Contact: Rick Lathrop

The aims of Global Service Corps GSC) are simply to create opportunities for young adults and adults to live and work in developing nations on projects to serve Earth's people and the environment supporting them. These projects are designed to address global issues at the grass-roots level through the mutual transfer of skills and the promotion of cross-cultural understanding. Our goals are to provide developing communities with the means to function more sustainably as well as to enrich the experiences of participants in challenging situations. In Thailand, GSC's project site is in the Kanchanaburi region west of Bangkok where project work revolves around healthcare work in a local hospital and also the teaching of English at local schools and monasteries. In Arusha, Tanzania, GSC's twin programmes are in HIV/AIDS education and sustainable agriculture development. In 2002, GSC initiated new programmes for the future health professionals, giving participants the opportunity to shadow doctors and visit local health facilities. Also, in Tanzania, GSC started summer camps for local teenagers to raise awareness of HIV and AIDS through the use of integrated curriculum. Both short-term and long-term volunteers have the opportunity to demonstrate initiative in their project work. Long-term volunteers, moreover, are given flexibility to guide their own work, and to assume positions of greater responsibility. Since a primary belief of GSC is that its programmes benefit from capitalising on the expertise of its participants, long-term participants are especially given leeway in sculpting their own work through the long-term agreement. In this way, GSC welcomes creative input from volunteers in the way of new ideas to incorporate into their projects. Generally we are unable to accept volunteers with an offending background. Kanchanaburi, Thailand's second largest province, about two hours west of Bangkok bordering Myanmar (Burma) within easy reach of the Kwai River bridge. Arusha, a town in Northern Tanzania, close to the Olduvai Gorge. &

Number of projects: 4 UK: 0
Starting months: January–December
Time required: 3–12 weeks
Age: 18–70
Causes: AIDS/HIV, Conservation, Environmental Causes, Health Care/Medical, Teaching (primary, secondary, mature, EFL), Young People.
Activities: Agriculture/Farming, Development Issues, First Aid, Gardening/Horticulture, Manual Work, Summer Camps, Teaching, Training.
Placements: 100
When to apply: Ideally three months but, at least two months before programme start.
Work alone/with others: Work with others.
Qualifications: Unless you are participating in a Thailand health care project, then you'd have to have a science or medical background or have prior hospital experience.
Equipment/clothing: None. Except to dress sensibly and not loudly or outlandishly. Participants on the Tanzania sustainable agriculture projects should be physically fit and dressed for the part.
Health requirements: None generally, those on prescription medication are responsible for maintaining an adequate supply of medication for the duration of the trip. Any health or dietary requirements should be revealed in writing at the time of application.
Costs: Airfare to and from project site, travellers insurance, and any other travel related and personal expenses in addition to GSC programme fee.
Benefits: All homestays, meals, on-site project transportation, and safari/jungle excursions.
Training: In the form of training manuals and supplementary materials mailed to pre-trip participants. In Tanzania, on site, four day training sessions are provided to participants, hosted by GSC.
Supervision: GSC's in-country staff in both Thailand and Tanzania will provide the requisite guidance and supervision of volunteers.
Interviews: Registered participants are sent a Participant Background Information Questionnaire in which they provide answers to the interview questions.
Worldwide placements: Africa (Tanzania); Asia (Thailand).

GLOBAL VISION INTERNATIONAL

Amwell Farm House
Nomansland, Wheathamstead
St Albans
Hertfordshire AL4 8EJ UK
T: 01582 831300
F: 01582 834002
E: tabitha@gvi.co.uk
W: www.gvi.co.uk
Contact: Tabitha Cooper

Global Vision International (GVI) is a non-political, non-religious organisation, which specialises in providing overseas expeditions, research projects and independent voluntary work to the general public. Through its alliance with aid reliant environmental organisations throughout the world, GVI volunteers fill a critical void in the fields of environmental research, conservation, education and community development. 'GVI promotes sustainable solutions for a rapidly changing world by matching you, the general public, with the international environmentalists, researchers and pioneering educators'. GVI runs expeditions to worthwhile projects all over the world. Some of GVI's current partners include Rainforest Concern, The Endangered Wildlife Trust, the South African National Parks Board and the Dian Fossey Gorilla Fund International. No previous experience is necessary, as full training is given. While our priority is the success of the project, we realise that it is your contribution that ultimately achieves this very success. Between 40 and 60% of your financial contribution goes directly to your particular project and the remaining funds are used to ensure that GVI keeps assisting   aid-reliant projects well into the future. GVI expeditions are designed with you, the volunteer, in mind. They incorporate worthwhile, pioneering projects with dramatic locations, excellent training and fun professional staff. &

Number of projects: 20 UK: 0
Starting months: Jan, Feb, Mar, Apr, May, Jun, Jul, Aug, Sep, Oct, Nov
Time required: 2–52 weeks
Age: 18 plus – no upper limit
Causes: Animal Welfare, Children, Conservation, Environmental Causes, Teaching/assisting (nursery, primary, secondary, mature, EFL) Wildlife, Young People.
Activities: Campaigning, Community Work, Conservation Skills, Development Issues, First Aid, Fundraising, Group Work, International Aid, Manual Work, Marketing/Publicity, Outdoor Skills, Research, Scientific Work, Social Work, Sport, Teaching, Technical Skills, Training.

Placements: 500
When to apply: As early as possible.
Work alone/with others: Varies depending on project.
Qualifications: Spoken English – any other qualifications are an added bonus. No restrictions but volunteers must speak English.
Equipment/clothing: Specific clothing required – volunteers will receive detailed information pack.
Health requirements: General medical prior to departure + relevant immunisation.
Costs: Varies – from £500 for projects, from £1,550 for expeditions – flights and insurance not included.
Benefits: The volunteer contribution covers food and accommodation (often quite basic), project equipment and training materials.
Training: All necessary science training on site.
Supervision: Numbers are dependent on project – but staff members are always on hand.
Interviews: Some projects are first come, first served, others have an application/selection process.
Worldwide placements: Africa (South Africa, Swaziland); Central America (Mexico, Panama); South America (Ecuador); Asia (China, Malaysia, Nepal, Thailand); Australasia (New Zealand).

GLOBAL VOLUNTARY SERVICE ASSOCIATION

P O Box AC 348 Art Centre
Accra
Ghana
T: 0045 2521 9073
E: gvsa20@yahoo.com
Contact: Samuel K. Attah

Global Voluntary Service Association's aims are: 1. To invite people of all social, ethnic and economic backgrounds to Ghana to participate in development projects and cultural exchange programmes. 2. To provide voluntary services to benefit local communities. 3. To create mutual understanding and respect by working together on a common goal. 4. To develop and appreciate our cultural values. 5. To encourage global interest in voluntary and development work. Types of work placement: GVSA arrange individual voluntary placements according to volunteers' experiences and interests. We are in contact with a range of organisations, schools and institutions that need volunteers for long and short-term programmes (three weeks to six months). The placements can, for example, be teaching mathematics and English, health sector, kindergarten, institutions, family planning, gender issues and homeless children. Alternative address:
GVSA
Kvintus Alle 7, 1–106

2300 Kobenhavn S
Denmark
Telephone: 00 45 33 253143 We have projects in all ten regions of Ghana.

Number of projects: 10+ **UK:** 0
Starting months: January–December
Time required: 3–24 weeks
Age: 18–50
Causes: Addicts/Ex-Addicts, AIDS/HIV, Animal Welfare, Archaeology, Architecture, Children, Conservation, Disabled (learning and physical), Elderly People, Environmental Causes, Health Care/Medical, Heritage, Holidays for Disabled, Human Rights, Inner City Problems, Offenders/Ex-Offenders, Poor/Homeless, Refugees, Teaching/assisting (nursery, primary, secondary, mature, EFL) Unemployed, Wildlife, Work Camps – Seasonal, Young People.
Activities: Administration, Caring (general and day), Community Work, Development Issues, Forestry, Manual Work, Outdoor Skills, Research, Social Work, Summer Camps, Teaching, Technical Skills, Theatre/Drama, Training, Visiting/Befriending, Work Camps – Seasonal.
Placements: 30
When to apply: Eight weeks before starting.
Qualifications: Depending on the project. No specific skill is required.
Equipment/clothing: Jeans, long sleeved shirt and sweater.
Health requirements: Vaccinations needed.
Costs: US$250 covers administration cost. US$150 per month covers all food and accommodation.
Benefits: Accommodation with host families. Experience West Africa's rich culture and exclusive places of interest.
Training: On-the-job training. Programme information is sent 6 weeks before programme starts and 3 days orientation on arrival in Ghana.
Supervision: Is being taken by the placement.
Interviews: No interviews.
Worldwide placements: Africa (Ghana).

GLOBAL VOLUNTEER NETWORK

P.O.Box 2231
Wellington
6001 New Zealand
T: ++64 4 569 9080
F: 0064 8326 7788
E: info@volunteer.org.nz
W: www.volunteer.org.nz
Contact: Colin Salisbury

The Global Volunteer Network currently has volunteer positions available through our partner organisations in China, Ghana, Ecuador, Nepal, Uganda and Romania. Our vision is to support the work of local community organisations in developing countries through the placement of international volunteers. We currently have teaching English opportunities in China. You could teach at primary, secondary and university level in either rural or urban school. We have environmental opportunities in Ecuador. Volunteer interns participate in research, education, community service, station maintenance, plant conservation and agro-forestry activities carried out by the Jatun Sacha, Bilsa and Guandera biological stations. We have teaching opportunities throughout Ghana. Volunteers have the chance to participate in the development of Ghana's young people. You can teach at pre-school, primary and secondary schools. We have educational and community aid programmes available in Nepal. You can be involved in areas such as teaching English, environmental awareness, health and sanitation issues, or a home stay programme. We have opportunities to join a Christian Mission in Romania. They run four group homes for disabled orphans. There are chances to teach, counsel, and help with feeding, cooking and cleaning depending on your skills and experience. In Uganda, volunteers can take part in several programmes including the training and educating of HIV/AIDS orphans, primary healthcare, prevention and counselling for HIV/AIDS, mother's empowerment or community development projects. We are unable to accept volunteers with previous criminal convictions. China – Shandong Province. Ecuador – Jatun Sacha, Bilsa, Guandera biological stations. Ghana. Nepal. Uganda – Kampala, Romania – Galati County. 📄

Number of projects: 5 UK: 0
Starting months: January–December
Time required: 2–52 weeks
Age: 18–70
Causes: AIDS/HIV, Children, Conservation, Disabled (learning and physical), Environmental Causes, Health Care/Medical, Teaching/assisting (nursery, primary, secondary, mature), Wildlife, Young People.
Activities: Arts/Crafts, Caring – Residential, Community Work, Conservation Skills, Development Issues, Forestry, Group Work, Research, Teaching.
Placements: 250
When to apply: 3–6 months prior to the time you wish to volunteer.
Work alone/with others: Varies between projects.
Qualifications: Some programmes require recognised qualifications such as the health programmes where you are required to have medical experience. Most nationalities accepted.
Equipment/clothing: Suitable clothing for the conditions. Varies between programmes.

Health requirements: Some projects require a medical/doctors certificate.
Costs: Application fee US$250. The application fee covers administration, marketing, programme information, communication and direct support of our partner organisations.
Benefits: Varies between projects.
Training: On site training before you start, this varies between projects.
Supervision: All volunteers have regular supervision.
Interviews: Varies between projects but there are no face to face interviews.
Charity number: WN/1194442
Worldwide placements: Africa (Ghana, Uganda); South America (Ecuador); Asia (China, Nepal); Europe (Romania).

GLOBAL VOLUNTEERS

375 E. Little Canada Road
St Paul, MN
55117
USA
T: 00 1 651 407 6100
F: 00 1 651 482 0915
E: e-mail@globalvolunteers.org
W: www.globalvolunteers.org
Contact: Volunteer Co-ordinators

Global Volunteers is in consultative status with the United Nations. More than 150 teams of volunteers are mobilised each year to live and work with local people on human and economic development projects identified by the community as important to their long-term development. In this way, the volunteers' energy, creativity and labour are put to use and at the same time they gain a genuine, first-hand understanding of how other people live day to day. Our experience, since inception in 1984 enables us to offer you:
– genuine opportunities to serve
– immediate acceptance by host communities
– continuity of programme from year to year
– experienced team leaders and programme consultants
– informed insight into other cultures
– the joy of travelling and working with a team of like-minded people. New Zealand project is in the Cook Islands.

Number of projects: 19 UK: 0
Starting months: January–December
Time required: 1–3 weeks
Age: 18 plus – no upper limit
Causes: Children, Conservation, Environmental Causes, Health Care/Medical, Heritage, Human Rights, Poor/Homeless, Teaching/assisting (primary, secondary, mature, EFL), Young People.

Activities: Agriculture/Farming, Building/Construction, Caring (general, day and residential), Community Work, Computers, Conservation Skills, Development Issues, Gardening/Horticulture, Group Work, International Aid, Manual Work, Summer Camps, Teaching, Technical Skills, Training.
Placements: 2,000
When to apply: All year.
Work alone/with others: With others in a team.
Qualifications: Native English speaker for English teaching projects. English fluency required for all other projects.
Equipment/clothing: No special requirements.
Health requirements: Good physical and mental health.
Costs: All costs. (2003 costs range $650 to $2,595 (US) excluding air fares.)
Benefits: Accommodation, food, ground transportation, project materials and team leader.
Training: Orientation training is provided for the team on site as well as a pre-trip volunteer booklet and teaching manual (for teaching sites).
Supervision: Volunteers serve as a team with an experienced team leader in charge. Volunteers under 18 are supervised by their guardian.
Interviews: Applicants for volunteer projects are not interviewed.
Worldwide placements: Africa (Ghana, Tanzania); North America: (USA); Central America (Costa Rica, Jamaica, Mexico); South America (Ecuador); Asia (China, India, Vietnam); Australasia (Oceania); Europe (Greece, Ireland, Italy, Poland, Romania, Spain, Ukraine).

GLOUCESTERSHIRE WILDLIFE TRUST

Dulverton Building
Robinswood Hill Country Park
Reservoir Road
Gloucester
GL4 6SX UK
T: 01452 383333
F: 01452 383334
E: sarahk@gloucswt.cix.co.uk
W: www.gloucestershirewildlifetrust.co.uk
Contact: Sarah Killingback

The Gloucestershire Wildlife Trust was formed in 1961 by local people, including Sir Peter Scott, who wanted a better future for the county's wildlife. A variety of programmes and initiatives have been developed to help achieve the Trust's aim of caring for the wildlife and wild places of Gloucestershire. The Trust is a registered independent charity. It has a membership of over 7,500 people with more than 300 active volunteers and 15 corporate partners from the world of industry and commerce. The Trust manages 71 nature reserves in Gloucestershire which are homes to the county's rarest flora and fauna. Most of the reserves are open to the public or by permit. The Trust employs a small professional staff which carries out the increasingly technical work associated with conserving wildlife in the face of growing economic and demographic pressures. The Trust is run by a Board of Trustees elected annually by the members. The Conservation Centre is the hub of all Trust activities providing information, advice, education and a huge range of environmental and wildlife materials, activities etc in the Wildlife Shop. Events and talks are held for people of all ages and last year 3,500 school children took part in the Trust's Learning for Life education programme.The Trust's vision is to continue to use its knowledge and expertise to help the people and organisations of Gloucestershire to enjoy, understand and take action to protect the wildlife and habitats of town and countryside. Volunteers with an offending background may be accepted, each case is reviewed separately.

Number of projects: 1 UK: 1
Starting months: January–December
Time required: 12–52 weeks
Age: 16–85
Causes: Children, Conservation, Environmental Causes, Heritage, Teaching/assisting (primary), Wildlife.
Activities: Administration, Building/ Construction, Campaigning, Conservation Skills, Forestry, Fundraising, Library/Resource Centres, Manual Work, Marketing/Publicity, Newsletter/Journalism, Outdoor Skills, Research, Scientific Work, Teaching.
Placements: 10
When to apply: All year.
Work alone/with others: Either.
Qualifications: We will endeavour to find work suitable to your level of training, experience and aspirations, although we cannot automatically guarantee a place.
Equipment/clothing: For outdoor practical conservation work, steel toe-capped footwear is ESSENTIAL, waterproof clothing is advised.
Health requirements: For practical outdoor work, volunteers are only accepted with a level of fitness that allows them to perform the work safely.
Costs: Volunteers will be expected to arrange transport to and from their allocated place of work, for which mileage will be paid.
Benefits: Agreed out of pocket expenses will be paid.
Training: Training will be provided in order that volunteers can carry out their work to a set standard. Other training available to longer term volunteers.
Supervision: All volunteers are managed and supervised by the Trusts Volunteers Manager in the first instance.

Interviews: An informal interview is held to access what work or training options volunteers can do.
Charity number: 232580
UK placements: England (Gloucestershire).

GOAL

7 Hanson Street
London
W1W 6TE UK
T: +44 (0) 207 631 3196
F: +44 (0) 207 631 3197
E: info@goal-uk.org
W: www.goal.ie
Contact: Venetia Bellers

GOAL is an international relief and development agency, dedicated to the objective of alleviating the suffering of the poorest of the poor in the third world. The organisation was founded in 1977 by a sports journalist John O'Shea and four of his friends. GOAL believes that every human being has a right to the fundamentals of life, i.e. food, water, shelter, literacy and medical attention. It is non-denominational and non-political and its resources are targeted at the most vulnerable in the developing world. GOAL has responded to every major natural and man-made disaster and catastrophe over the past 25 years. At present GOAL is operational in 20 countries, while we provide financial support to a whole range of indigenous groups and missionaries who share our philosophy in many other deprived countries. Since our inception GOAL has sent in excess of 900 volunteers to work in third world regions while £125 million has been spent by the agency, reaching those in greatest need. GOAL has managed to keep its administration costs to a minimum – under 5% over the last 25 years. The organisation is directly accountable to the Irish tax payer and is audited each year by Arthur Andersen and Company. In addition to emergency relief and development activities GOAL's work is very heavily centred on street children. In our efforts to assist the poor, GOAL receives support from, among others, the governments of Ireland, the UK, the USA, Holland and Sweden as well as from the EU, the UN and the general public. Volunteers with offending backgrounds are not accepted – host countries insist on police records for visa purposes. ▣

Number of projects: 100 UK: 0
Starting months: January–December
Time required: 52 weeks (plus)
Age: 21–99
Causes: AIDS/HIV, Children, Disabled (learning and physical), Health Care/Medical, Human Rights, Poor/Homeless, Refugees, Teaching/assisting (primary).
Activities: Accountancy, Administration,

Building/Construction, Catering, Community Work, Development Issues, First Aid, Fundraising, International Aid, Newsletter/Journalism, Sport, Teaching.
Placements: 6–7
When to apply: Any time.
Work alone/with others: With others.
Qualifications: Mainly medical staff, nurses, midwives, doctors, administrators, accountants.
Languages: French, Spanish and Portuguese.
Health requirements: Medical examination prior to being recruited.
Costs: Nil.
Benefits: Subsistence while abroad, small holiday allowance, travel to and from project destination.
Training: Volunteers holding EU passports are sent on weeklong APSO training in Dublin prior for departure to the field.
Interviews: Interviews take place in London or Dublin.
Charity number: 1002941
Worldwide placements: Africa (Angola, Ethiopia, Kenya, Mozambique, Sierra Leone, Swaziland, Uganda); Central America (Honduras); Asia (India, Philippines, Vietnam); Europe (Bosnia-Herzegovina, Yugoslavia).

GOOD SHEPHERD FOUNDATION

c/o The Fountain of Life Centre
3/199 M.6 Soi Chalermprakiet 3
Pattaya 3rd Road, Naklua
Pattaya, Chonburi, 20150
Thailand
T: 038 424 173
E: joangormleyrgs@yahoo.com
W: www.care4kids
Contact: Joan Gormley

The focus of the work is to provide the poor with opportunities. They have several projects in SE Asia helping women to earn money without working in the bars and sex-industry. They offer girls the chance to gain qualifications and skills which will break the cycle of poverty. In Pattaya the sisters have two schools, adult and children, which provide education, medical care, counselling, practical skills, e.g., sewing and hairdressing, and school certificate (non-formal education) which many have missed. They need volunteers, and because of the culture and circumstances would prefer females, to teach English for four hours each day. They provide accomodation above the school, which is one of the reasons they prefer women. As this is a charity they are unable to provide expenses. They also offer the chance to find out about Thai culture and language. The sisters also run projects in Bankok, NonKhai and KonKhaen which vounteers will be able to visit. Pattaya is on the coast, two hours drive from Bangkok. ♿

Number of projects: 1 UK: 0
Starting months: January–December
Time required: 24–52 weeks
Age: 18–50
Causes: Children, Teaching/assisting (mature, EFL), Young People.
Activities: Community Work, Counselling, Teaching.
Placements: 12
When to apply: All year round.
Work alone/with others: With others.
Qualifications: All who can get a visa and who speak fluent English.
Health requirements: None.
Costs: Flights, approx. £450. Transfer to Pattaya by bus, £2. Weekly expenses, £25–£40. Visa run every three months, approx. £40.
Benefits: Free accommodation.
Training: Training is provided – one week induction into Thai language and customs, following outgoing volunteer.
Supervision: Volunteers are independent but have regular meetings with the sisters.
Interviews: Volunteers can have an informal interview in the UK Contact: nancy_wilkie@hotmail.com.
Worldwide placements: Asia (Thailand).

GRAIL, THE

125 Waxwell Lane
Pinner
Middlesex HA5 3ER UK
T: +44 (0) 208 866 2195/0505
F: +44 (0) 208 866 1408
E: grailcentre@compuserve.com
Contact: Volunteer Co-ordinator

The Grail Volunteer Programme has been running for more than 20 years. It arose out of an idea to recruit from friends and contacts of the resident community at The Grail Centre, but international listing has increasingly drawn people worldwide. The Grail is not a high profile charity but has an international network of contacts through its publishing, women's groups and conferences. The centre, a listed building with extensions, circa 1600, set in 10 acres of wooded garden is less than 45 minutes from central London. At the heart of the organisation is a permanent community of Christian women. The focus is non-denominational, open, offering short and long term hospitality, courses and workshops designed to heal and restore people caught up in the pressures of life today. Prospective volunteers write a letter enclosing stamped envelope or international reply coupon. UK applicants may visit if they wish. Vegetarians catered for, but not dietary preferences. The Grail regrets being unable to accept volunteers with offending backgrounds. 📄

Number of projects: 1 UK: 1
Starting months: January–December
Time required: 12–52 weeks
Age: 20–60
Causes: Conservation, Elderly People, Environmental Causes, Human Rights, Young People.
Activities: Administration, Arts/Crafts, Caring – General, Catering, Computers, Conservation Skills, Cooking, DIY, Driving, Fundraising, Gardening/Horticulture, Group Work, Library/Resource Centres, Manual Work, Music, Newsletter/Journalism, Outdoor Skills.
Placements: 9 or 10
When to apply: While there may be unexpected last minute vacancies, early applications are more likely to be successful. Candidates may apply up to 9 months in advance.
Work alone/with others: Both.
Qualifications: Basic spoken English, positive attitude. Applicants of all nationalities are free to apply but it is increasingly difficult for some foreign nationals to gain entry.
Health requirements: Good health.
Costs: Travel to and from Pinner + any home visits or holidays + insurance.
Benefits: Board, lodging + £21.50 pocket money per week. 1 English lesson per week + occasional bonuses. Accommodation in single rooms in several different locations on campus.
Training: In service training only.
Supervision: Paid staff employed.
Charity number: 221076
UK placements: England (London).

GRANGEMOCKLER CAMPHILL COMMUNITY

Temple Michael
Carrick-on-Suir
Co. Tipperary Eire
T: 00 353 51 647202
F: 00 353 51 647253
E: grangemockler@camphill.ie
Contact: Astrid Teppan

Grangemockler Camphill Community is part of the developing international Camphill movement. Founded in 1940, much of the inspiration came from and continues to be found in the teachings of Rudolf Steiner. Camphill Communities offer those in need of special care – children, adolescents and adults – a sheltered environment in which their education, therapeutic and social needs can be met. There are about 40 people living in four houses in our community. For the majority of us this is our home, where we will probably live for several years, or perhaps even for our lifetime. For those of you coming to stay with us for some time it is an opportunity for new experiences. All new volunteers receive €40 pocket money per week plus €20 is set aside each week collectable when leaving or going on holidays. Our lives are not governed by rules, but everyone is expected to take as full a part as possible in all realms of our lives. This includes cooking, gardening, folk dancing, milking, eurythmy, cleaning, film shows, weaving, cutting toe nails, meetings, mucking out pigs, celebrating festivals etc. Everyone has a day off each week. This could be accurately termed a 'personal day'. Camphill is not a job but a way of life and as such goes on 24 hours/day, seven days a week. We recognise, however, that we need time for ourselves and that this is not always easy to find, unless it is written into our timetable. Weekends are not days off but time we can use to meet each other in different ways. Our care for those people with special needs does not extend only into the working realm. To go for a walk or to play a game together on a Saturday afternoon is all part of our lives. 🔲 📄

Number of projects: 1 **UK:** 0
Starting months: January–December
Time required: 1–52 weeks (plus)
Age: 18 plus – no upper limit
Causes: Disabled (learning)
Activities: Agriculture/Farming, Arts/Crafts, Building/Construction, Caring (general, day and residential), Catering, Cooking, First Aid, Forestry, Gardening/Horticulture, Group Work, Manual Work, Music, Sport, Theatre/Drama.
Placements: 16
When to apply: All year. No restriction on length of stay.
Work alone/with others: With others.
Equipment/clothing: Wellies and a raincoat.
Health requirements: Nil.
Costs: Return travel costs to community if stay is short.
Benefits: €40 per week + €20 put aside for payment at end of stay or for holidays. Rooms in our community houses.
Training: An introductory course held here.
Supervision: Human interest by people living here.
Interviews: Applicants are not interviewed but long-term applicants, if affected, will be asked for a short handwritten CV, 2 referees and a police check.
Worldwide placements: Europe (Ireland).

GREAT GEORGES PROJECT – THE BLACKIE

The Blackie
Great George Street
Liverpool
L1 5EW UK
T: 0151 709 5109
F: 0151 709 4822
E: staff@theblackie.org.uk
W: www.theblackie.org.uk
Contact: The Duty Officer

Great Georges Project (The Blackie) is a centre for experimental work in the arts, sport, games and education of today. First started in 1968 as an arts centre or artists' studio. The basic principle is the provision of creative opportunities for all. The Blackie – 'A bridge across troubled waters ... linking artists and communities' – was founded in 1968. And what might have seemed almost fortuitous at that time can now be seen as essential ingredients in determining the character of Britain's first community arts project. The proximity of the Blackie to Britain's oldest established African-Caribbean community – and to Europe's oldest Chinatown – has meant that cultural diversity is celebrated as a natural phenomenon. The siting of the Blackie adjoining a residential neighbourhood and yet close to the city centre has meant that both residents and visitors to the city find it accessible – and it is natural that playgroups and community enterprises should take their place alongside concerts and exhibitions. In the heart of Liverpool. 🔲 📄

Number of projects: 1 **UK:** 1
Starting months: January–December.
Time required: 4–52 weeks
Age: 18 plus – no upper limit
Causes: Addicts/Ex-Addicts, Children, Disabled (learning), Inner City Problems, Offenders/Ex-Offenders, Poor/Homeless, Teaching/assisting, Young People.
Activities: Administration, Arts/Crafts, Cooking, DIY, Fundraising, Gardening/Horticulture, Music, Newsletter/Journalism, Sport, Teaching, Theatre/Drama, Visiting/Befriending.
Placements: 60–100
When to apply: All year.
Work alone/with others: With others.
Qualifications: Huge sense of humour, working knowledge of English.
Equipment/clothing: Sleeping bag, jeans, tough shoes and clothes.
Health requirements: Nil.
Costs: £18.50 per week. £1.50 covers cost and £17 covers food.
Benefits: Board and lodging.
Training: On the job training.
Supervision: General supervision by manager on individual projects.
Interviews: Self-selected.
Charity number: 9018509
UK placements: England (Merseyside).

GREAT NORTH AIR AMBULANCE

The Imperial Centre
Grange Road
Darlington
DL1 5NQ UK
T: 01325 487263
E: info@greatnorthairambulance.co.uk

W: www.greatnorthairambulance.co.uk
Contact: John Everson

The Great North Air Ambulance is a Charity that depends heavily on the generosity of the people from the area which it serves. It receives no funding whatsoever from the government. The helicopters are deployed by the Ambulance Service and cover a full range of accident and medical emergencies. To date GNNAA has responded to over 4500 calls for help and transported 3700 patients. We are unable to accept volunteers with an offending background. North East Yorkshire and North Yorkshire. ♿ 📄

Number of projects: 1 UK: 1
Starting months: January–December
Time required: 1–52 weeks (plus)
Age: 16 plus – no upper limit
Causes: Health Care/Medical.
Activities: Administration, Community Work, Fundraising, Marketing/Publicity, Newsletter/Journalism.
Placements: 100
When to apply: Any time.
Work alone/with others: With others.
Health requirements: Nil.
Costs: Volunteer will have to pay for own travel expenses and accommodation.
Supervision: Supervision is undertaken by area managers.
Interviews: Interviews are held locally.
Charity number: 1092204
UK placements: England (E. Yorkshire, N. Yorkshire).

GREEK DANCES THEATRE

8 Scholiou Str.
Plaka
Athens
GR-10558 Greece
T: 00 30 210 3244395
F: 00 30 210 3246921
E: grdance@hol.gr
W: http://users.hol.gr/~grdance
Contact: Adamantia Angeli

The Dora Stratou Greek Dances Theatre was established in 1953 as The Living Museum of Greek Dance. This is a non-profit institution subsidised by the Ministry of Culture and the National Tourist Organisation. Daily performances in its 1,000-seat garden theatre on Philopappou Hill, opposite the Acropolis. An ensemble of 80 dancers, musicians and folk singers. A collection of 2,500 village-made costumes, jewels and other works of folk art, worn on stage. Courses, lectures and workshops on dance and folk culture; field research programmes in dance ethnography and dance sociology; study group, courses and workshops on Ancient Greek dance; archives of dance

books, field recordings, films. Series of records, cassettes, videocassettes and books on dance in Greek, English and other languages. Costume copies made to order. 📄

Number of projects: 5 UK: 0
Starting months: January–December
Time required: 4–10 weeks
Age: 16–66
Causes: Heritage, Teaching/assisting (primary, secondary, EFL), Young People.
Activities: Arts/Crafts, Computers, Library/Resource Centres, Music, Newsletter/Journalism, Research, Summer Camps, Teaching, Theatre/Drama, Translating.
Placements: 15
When to apply: All year.
Work alone/with others: With other young volunteers.
Health requirements: Nil.
Costs: Travel to Athens and subsistence.
Interviews: Prospective volunteers are not interviewed.
Worldwide placements: Europe (Greece).

GREENFORCE

11–15 Betterton Street
Covent Garden
London
WC2H 9BP UK
T: 0870 770 2646
F: 0870 770 2647
E: info@greenforce.org
W: www.greenforce.org
Contact: Andrew Eden/ Alex Cormack

'Work on the wild side!'
Greenforce needs volunteers to work on environmental biodiversity and marine surveys throughout the world. Full training provided in the UK then with host country experts, prior to leaving on the expedition. All locations are very remote, volunteers should be prepared to spend 10 weeks out of regular contact.
Projects range from animal tracking in Africa, setting up Fiji's first marine park to working in the Amazon rainforest helping to conserve endangered wildlife. Contact Greenforce for the latest projects. Enthusiasm, a sense of humour and the ability to cope with basic conditions are more important than experience or exam results. All training is provided on expedition, including free BSAC diver training for marine volunteers. Groups sizes are strictly controlled to minimise our impact on the environment. The Royal Geographical Society's YET Code of Practice and the UNESCO Scientific Guidelines are adhered to. Satellite phone back-up and air evacuation plans are in place to give all participants peace of mind. Paid staff positions are first offered to suitable ex-volunteers. On each expedition, one person is chosen to stay

on for the next expedition, free. You are chosen by the staff on your expedition. All staff are eligible for a long service bonus after two years. So a Greenforce expedition can be an incredible experience and also, if you wish, the start to a career in conservation. Come to one of the monthly open evenings in Covent Garden where slides and videos explain each project. Check out our web site for further details. Greenforce are a member of The Year Out Group. Accommodation is living in local houses, cooking local food, working with the local community. &

Number of projects: 20 UK: 0
Starting months: Jan, Apr, Jul, Oct
Time required: 10–10 weeks
Age: 18 plus – no upper limit
Causes: Animal Welfare, Children, Conservation, Environmental Causes, Wildlife, Work Camps – Seasonal, Young People.
Activities: Building/Construction, Community Work, Conservation Skills, Development Issues, Forestry, Group Work, International Aid, Manual Work, Outdoor Skills, Research, Scientific Work, Social Work, Teaching, Training, Visiting/Befriending, Work Camps – Seasonal.
Placements: 300
When to apply: Average 6 months before departure, but late space often available.
Work alone/with others: With others.
Qualifications: No formal qualifications required – all training provided.
Equipment/clothing: All technical equipment provided including diving kit. Volunteers are sent a list of personal kit to bring.
Health requirements: Declaration of fitness to participate required. Health issues will be referred to our consultant physician for approval and insurers will be informed. All marine volunteers to pass fitness to dive medical.
Costs: £2,550 for 10 week expedition Zambia, Peru. £2750 for 10 week marine expedition Bahamas, Borneo, Fiji.
Benefits: Conservation of wildlife and endangered habitats. Information given free to local management authorities. Local community interaction and environmental education. All accommodation in the UK and in-country is included.
Training: Distance learning packs, UK training weekend, lectures in host country university. Dr or MSc level of training staff in field. Medical, scientific and survival training are also provided. Free traineeship programme and long-service funding for staff.
Supervision: One full time member of staff per 4 volunteers. Therefore, assuming there are 16 volunteers on camp, there are 4 members of staff.

Interviews: Open evenings are held twice a month in Covent Garden, London.
Charity number: 3321466
Worldwide placements: Africa (Uganda, Zambia); Central America (Bahamas); South America (Peru); Asia (Brunei, India, Malaysia); Australasia (Fiji).

GREENHILL YMCA NATIONAL CENTRE

Donard Park
Newcastle
Co. Down BT33 0GR N. Ireland
T: 028 4372 3172
F: 028 4372 6009
E: tim@ymca-ire.dnet.co.uk
Contact: Ken Byatt

The Greenhill YMCA National Centre is an outdoor education centre which needs volunteers to act as domestic staff and cooks, instructors in outdoor pursuits such as canoeing, hill walking, archery, etc., and tutors in personal development. An interest in community relations would be an advantage. All suitable applicants will have to complete an applications form with photo. All suitable applicants will have to have two references taken up and undergo police vetting for criminal record and offences towards children. East coast at the foot of the Mourne Mountains, 1/2 mile from the sea. &

Number of projects: 1 UK: 1
Starting months: Jun, Sep
Time required: 8–52 weeks
Age: 18–40
Causes: Children, Human Rights, Inner City Problems, Offenders/Ex-Offenders, Teaching/assisting (primary, secondary), Unemployed, Work Camps – Seasonal, Young People.
Activities: Administration, Arts/Crafts, Caring – General, Catering, Community Work, Computers, Cooking, Driving, First Aid, Gardening/Horticulture, Group Work, Manual Work, Music, Outdoor Skills, Religion, Social Work, Sport, Summer Camps, Teaching, Technical Skills, Work Camps – Seasonal.
Placements: 14
When to apply: As early as possible.
Work alone/with others: Both.
Qualifications: Group/youth work, social work, outdoor pursuits experience welcomed. The Centre is a Christian centre and welcomes applications from those who agree with or are not opposed to the Christian faith.
Equipment/clothing: Personal clothing.
Health requirements: Physically and mentally fit.
Costs: Return travel to centre.
Benefits: Board, lodging in shared rooms and pocket money of £45 per week.
Training: One week local orientation after specialist training as assistant instructor.

Supervision: Day to day – Senior Instructor. Overall – Programme Manager.
Interviews: Overseas volunteers are not interviewed but they must include a Police character reference when returning their application. Only long-term Irish volunteers are interviewed.
Charity number: XN 45820
UK placements: Northern Ireland (Down).

GREENPEACE

Canonbury Villas
London
N1 2PN UK
T: +44 (0) 207 865 8272
F: +44 (0) 207 865 8200
E: emma.barfoot@uk.greenpeace.org
W: www.greenpeace.org.uk
Contact: Emma Barfoot

Greenpeace sometimes needs volunteers to help with office duties which are mainly routine. At Head Office in London. 🖾

Number of projects: many **UK:** many
Starting months: January–December
Time required: 1–52 weeks
Age: 18 plus – no upper limit
Causes: Conservation, Environmental Causes.
Activities: Administration, Computers, Conservation Skills, Fundraising, Marketing/Publicity, Research.
Placements: Not known.
When to apply: All year.
Work alone/with others: With others.
Qualifications: Office experience.
Equipment/clothing: Depends on the job.
Health requirements: Nil.
Costs: Nil.
Benefits: Travel to Greenpeace within central London and £3.80 off lunch in staff canteen.
Training: Induction by manager on site.
Supervision: Each volunteer is placed with a supervisor (manager) who is responsible for inducting and designating work to the volunteer.
Interviews: At our Head Office.
UK placements: England (London).

GROUNDWORK (IRELAND)

Garden Level
21 Northumberland Road
Dublin 4
Rep of Ireland
T: 00 353 1 6604530
F: 00 353 1 6604571
E: grndwork@iwt.ie
W: www.groudwork.ie
Contact: Barbara Henderson

Groundwork's primary aim is to carry out important nature conservation projects in Ireland which would otherwise not be done, and thereby to facilitate persons wishing to make a practical voluntary contribution to nature conservation in Ireland. Groundwork's aim is essentially to act as a bridge between the many people who want to work for conservation and the many conservation tasks that urgently need to be carried out. Secondary aims of Groundwork are to facilitate international cultural exchange by recruiting volunteers from outside Ireland and to increase the volunteers' appreciation of the importance of nature conservation and their appreciation of the areas in which they are working. Killarney National Park, Co. Kerry; Glenveagh National Park, Co. Donegal. 🖾

Number of projects: 2 **UK:** 0
Starting months: Jun
Time required: 1–2 weeks
Age: 17–65
Causes: Conservation, Environmental Causes, Work Camps – Seasonal.
Activities: Conservation Skills, Group Work, Manual Work, Work Camps – Seasonal.
Placements: 200
When to apply: April/May onwards.
Work alone/with others: With others.
Equipment/clothing: Waterproof boots and clothing.
Health requirements: Volunteers MUST be in good health and free from serious medical conditions.
Costs: €25 registration fee for one week, €40 for 2 weeks.
Benefits: Board and lodging.
Training: On evening of arrival volunteers are given a talk and shown a video of work practices.
Supervision: 2 leaders for each workcamp and 2 supervisors.
Interviews: Applicants are not interviewed.
Worldwide placements: Europe (Ireland).

GROUNDWORK UK

85–87 Cornwall Street
Birmingham
B3 3BY UK
T: +44 (0) 121 236 8565
F: +44 (0) 121 236 7356
E: dpeace@groundwork.org.uk
W: www.groundwork.org.uk
Contact: Amanda Smith

Groundwork is a leading environmental regeneration charity making sustainable development a reality in the UK's poorest neighbourhoods. We work in partnership with local people, local authorities and businesses to bring about economic and social regeneration by improving the local environment. From small community projects to major national programmes, Groundwork uses the environment as a means of engaging and motivating local people to improve their quality of life. Groundwork is a federation of over 40 Groundwork Trusts, each a partnership between the public, private and voluntary sectors and each delivering holistic solutions to the challenges faced by poor communities. Volunteers with an offending background may be accepted depending on the nature of the offence and support required by that individual. ♿ 📖

Number of projects: 44 UK: 44
Starting months: January–December
Time required: 1–52 weeks
Age: 16–25
Causes: Children, Conservation, Disabled (learning and physical), Environmental Causes, Inner City Problems, Refugees, Unemployed, Wildlife, Young People.
Activities: Administration, Agriculture/Farming, Arts/Crafts, Catering, Community Work, Computers, Conservation Skills, Driving, Fundraising, Gardening/Horticulture, Group Work, Manual Work, Marketing/Publicity, Music, Newsletter/Journalism, Outdoor Skills, Research, Summer Camps, Technical Skills, Theatre/Drama, Training.
Placements: 40,000
When to apply: All year.
Work alone/with others: With others.
Qualifications: Enthusiasm, motivation and an ability to get on with people.
Equipment/clothing: Normally supplied.
Health requirements: Depends on the project.
Costs: Travel to local office.
Benefits: Travel and subsistence allowance normally offered.
Training: Depending on the project.
Supervision: Depending on the project.
Interviews: Interviews take place at local offices where volunteers are to be placed.
Charity number: 291558
UK placements: England (Berkshire, Buckinghamshire, Cheshire, Cornwall, Co Durham, Cumbria, Derbyshire, Devon, Hertfordshire, Kent, Lancashire, Leicestershire, Lincolnshire, London, Manchester, Merseyside, Nottinghamshire, Staffordshire, Surrey, Tyne and Wear, West Midlands, E. Yorkshire, N. Yorkshire, S. Yorkshire, W. Yorkshire); Northern Ireland (Belfast City, Derry/Londonderry, Down); Wales (Bridgend, Caerphilly, Merthyr Tydfil, Rhondda, Cynon, Taff, Wrexham).

GROUPE ARCHEOLOGIQUE DU MESMONTOIS

Mairie de Malain
21410 Pont de Pany
France
T: 00 33 3 80 30 05 20 or 00 33 3 80 23 66 08
F: 00 33 3 80 75 13 48

E: malain_gam@hotmail.com
Contact: M. Roussel

Groupe Archeologique du Mesmontois undertakes archaeological digs and restoration work. Volunteers are needed to help with tasks which include sketching, photographing the finds, model making and restoration. Cote D'Or, 10 minute train journey from Dijon. 📖

Number of projects: 2 UK: 0
Starting months: Jul
Time required: 1–4 weeks
Age: 17 plus – no upper limit
Causes: Archaeology, Architecture, Conservation, Environmental Causes, Heritage.
Activities: Arts/Crafts, Building/Construction, Conservation Skills, Cooking, Library/Resource Centres, Manual Work, Research, Scientific Work, Technical Skills.
Placements: 30
When to apply: Before May.
Work alone/with others: With others.
Qualifications: Care and patience.
Equipment/clothing: Sleeping bag.
Health requirements: Anti-tetanus innoculation.
Costs: €15 per week (£10 per week approximately) towards board and lodging.
Benefits: Board and lodging, speak French.
Training: Yes.
Supervision: Yes.
Interviews: Applicants for volunteer projects are not interviewed.
Worldwide placements: Africa (Algeria, Congo Republic, Egypt, Morocco, Tunisia); North America: (Canada, USA); Central America (Guadeloupe, Martinique); South America (Argentina, Chile); Asia (Hong Kong, Japan); Australasia (Australia); Europe (Austria, Belgium, Czech Republic, Denmark, Finland, France, Germany, Hungary, Ireland, Italy, Luxembourg, Netherlands, Poland, Portugal, Romania, Slovakia, Spain, Sweden, Switzerland, Ukraine, Yugoslavia).

GRUPPI ARCHEOLOGICI D'ITALIA

via Tacito 41
I-00193 Rome
Italy
T: 00 390 6 6874028
F: 00 390 6 6896981
E: gruppiarch@gruppiarcheologici.org
Contact:

Gruppi Archeologici D'Italia needs volunteers to work on archaeological excavations in Italy. Six hours work per day, six days per week. Placements involve lectures and excursions.

Number of projects: 1 UK: 0
Starting months: January–December
Time required: 2–52 weeks

Age: 16 plus – no upper limit
Causes: Archaeology
Activities: Administration, Conservation Skills, Research, Scientific Work.
Placements: 1,000
When to apply: 15th June.
Work alone/with others: With others.
Qualifications: Previous archaeological experience desirable.
Costs: €200 – €2582 for 2 weeks board and accommodation + fares.
Worldwide placements: Europe (Italy).

GRUPPO VOLUNTARI DELLA SVIZZERA ITALIANA

CP 12
Arbedo
CH-6517 Switzerland
T: 00 41 91 857 4520/79 354 0161
F: 00 41 91 692 7272
E: fmari@vtx.ch
Contact: Mari Federico

Gruppo Voluntari Della Svizzera Italiana takes 15 volunteers per camp to take part in work camps helping mountain communities, clearing woods etc. Four hours work per day. Maggia, Fusio and Borgogne, Switzerland.

Number of projects: 8 **UK:** 0
Starting months: Jun, Jul, Aug, Sep
Time required: 1–16 weeks
Age: 18 plus – no upper limit
Causes: Conservation, Elderly People, Environmental Causes.
Activities: Agriculture/Farming, Community Work, Conservation Skills, Driving, Gardening/Horticulture, Social Work, Summer Camps.
Placements: 60
When to apply: As early as possible.
Work alone/with others: With others.
Qualifications: Spoken Italian, German, French, English or Spanish. There may be restrictions on nationalities of volunteers.
Equipment/clothing: No special equipment needed.
Health requirements: Nil.
Costs: £2.50 approx per day to cover board and accommodation + travel costs and out-of-hours activities.
Benefits: Accommodation is included.
Training: On site.
Supervision: Yes.
Interviews: Interviews take place in Switzerland, Mexico, Honduras or Brasil.
Worldwide placements: North America: (Canada, USA); Central America (Guatemala, Honduras, Mexico); South America (Brazil); Asia (Philippines); Europe (Austria, Belarus, Belgium, Cyprus, Czech Republic, Finland, France, Germany, Greece, Hungary, Iceland, Ireland, Italy, Liechtenstein, Luxembourg, Netherlands,

Norway, Poland, Portugal, Russia, Slovakia, Spain, Sweden, Switzerland, Turkey, Yugoslavia).

GSM – Gençlik Servisleri Merkezi/ Youth Services Centre

Beyindir Sok 45/9
Kizilay-Ankara
06650 Turkey
T: (00 90) 312 417 1124/417 2991
F: (00 90) 312 425 8192
E: gsm@gsm-youth.org
W: www.gsm-youth.org
Contact: Ertugrul Senoglu

GSM has been organising activities for young people at national and international levels since 1985. The main areas in which GSM specialise are international voluntary workcamps, international youth camps and international youth exchange projects. Our main objectives are: to strengthen the youth power against the dangers of war, social and racial discrimination and for peace; to contribute to young people's social, cultural and artistic development and to promote development of common understanding, friendship and solidarity among young people; to encourage young people to participate in administration, planning and production to give them the consciousness of the democratic life; thereby contributing to the enrichment of the democratic culture in our country; to develop international friendship and to promote cultural exchanges among young people by making contacts with youth organisations; to sensitise young people towards their social and natural environment and to contribute to and widen the preservation of natural environment. GSM has a very democratic structure related to its aims, so is open to the participation of young people from various backgrounds. There are five people who have been working formally in GSM. Apart from these five people who work professionally, there are more than 25 young people who are students in different universities in Ankara and work voluntarily in GSM throughout the year.

Number of projects: 30 **UK:** 3
Starting months: Jul, Aug, Sep
Time required: 2–2 weeks
Age: 18–28
Causes: Archaeology, Architecture, Conservation, Environmental Causes, Work Camps – Seasonal, Young People.
Activities: Conservation Skills, Summer Camps, Visiting/Befriending, Work Camps – Seasonal.
Placements: 550
When to apply: 1st October – 15th June.
Work alone/with others: With others.
Qualifications: English is essential.
Equipment/clothing: Sleeping bags, swimming wear etc.

Health requirements: Nil – Health insurance is provided.
Costs: Registration fee plus travel.
Benefits: All board and lodging and sightseeing tours.
Training: None.
Supervision: During working hours supervisors will be with the volunteers.
Interviews: Interviews for those going abroad from Turkey take place in our office.
Worldwide placements: Africa (Morocco); Australasia (Australia); Europe (Austria, Belarus, Belgium, Bosnia-Herzegovina, Bulgaria, Croatia, Czech Republic, Denmark, Estonia, Finland, France, Germany, Ireland, Italy, Netherlands, Norway, Poland, Portugal, Romania, Russia, Slovakia, Spain, Sweden, Switzerland, Turkey).
UK placements: England (London, Manchester, Oxfordshire, West Midlands).

GUATEMALA SOLIDARITY NETWORK

20 Felday Road
London
SE13 7HJ UK
T: +44 (0) 20 8690 9640
E: gsn_mail@yahoo.com
W: www.guatemalasolidarity.org.uk
Contact: Alyson King

Guatemala Solidarity Network – Some 24 communities in five regions of Guatemala are involved in a process of denouncing state-sponsored acts of violence which took place in the early 1980s. It is hoped that an investigation by the Attorney General's Office will result, leading to trials against the military high command involved in implementing a plan of genocide in Guatemala. Some of the communities involved in collecting evidence have already received threats and others fear reprisals for their participation in the process. As a result, international accompaniment has been requested. It is hoped that there will be a permanent accompaniment presence in each region for the communities and individual witnesses, even if a continuous presence cannot be assured for each community. What does the accompanier do? Acts as an observer and a physical presence, most likely for communities and witnesses from one particular region, and writes reports on relevant issues, gets information out about any intimidations, threats or acts of violence against members of the communities, keeps in touch with Guatemala solidarity organisations in their own countries via an accompaniment co-ordinator based in Guatemala. The ideal accompanier will have: good Spanish – to understand daily conversation, as well as in meetings, and be able to report this accurately in both verbal and written form, availability for a minimum of three months and financial resources, experience of living and or working in a developing country, preferably in Latin America, in-depth understanding of the situation in Guatemala, particularly relating to human rights and the issues affecting the communities, cultural sensitivity towards rural Mayan communities, patience and adaptability – life in Guatemala can be unpredictable and frustrating, maturity to work in a highly sensitive situation where discretion and good judgement will be essential and which is emotionally challenging, good health and fitness – living conditions can be difficult in a tropical climate with poor sanitation, commitment to contributing to on-going solidarity work with Guatemala in the UK. GSN assists by screening potential accompaniers and assisting them in arrangements as detailed above. Guatemala Central America. 🔲

Number of projects: 1 UK: 0
Starting months: January–December
Time required: 12–52 weeks (plus)
Age: 18–80
Causes: Human Rights, Refugees.
Activities: Development Issues, International Aid, Outdoor Skills.
Placements: Varies.
When to apply: Six months prior to desired start date.
Work alone/with others: Both.
Qualifications: Spanish to a reasonable level is a must. Volunteers could commit to one month (self funded) in language school in Guatemala or Mexico prior to their placement if they do not speak Spanish. No nationality restrictions, although volunteers from communist countries may have difficultites getting a visa for Guatemala.
Health requirements: Reasonable health required for difficult placements in jungle.
Costs: Cost of airfare plus any language tuition if needed. Approx $100 per month while there + $50/month provided by partner organisation. We may be able to offer assistance with seeking grants.
Benefits: Accommodation in Guatemala City is arranged but funded by volunteers, although living in Guatemala is not expensive.
Training: Full briefing prior, three day training in Guatemala on arrival.
Supervision: No formal supervision as such, volunteers are expected to be self-reliant, with help on hand from partner organisations in Guatemala as needed.
Interviews: Interviews can be held in London or elsewhere, sometimes done by telephone.
Worldwide placements: Central America (Guatemala).

GURT RESOURCE CENTER FOR NGO DEVELOPMENT – UKRAINE

PO Box 126
Kyiv
01025 Ukraine
T: 00 380 44 552 10 52
F: 00 380 44 552 10 52
E: info@gurt.org.ua
W: www.gurt.org.ua
Contact: Vasylyna Dybaylo

Gurt Resource Center for NGO Development promotes and has information about volunteering in Ukraine. It may well be able to put volunteers in touch with organisations which are not yet listed on the WorldWide Volunteering database.

Starting months: January–December
Time required: 6–52 weeks (plus)
Age: 20–80
Causes: Addicts/Ex-Addicts, AIDS/HIV, Animal Welfare, Archaeology, Architecture, Children, Conservation, Disabled (learning and physical), Elderly People, Environmental Causes, Health Care/Medical, Heritage, Holidays for Disabled, Human Rights, Inner City Problems, Offenders/Ex-Offenders, Poor/Homeless, Refugees, Teaching/assisting (nursery, primary, secondary, mature, EFL) Unemployed, Wildlife, Work Camps – Seasonal, Young People.
Activities: Accountancy, Administration, Agriculture/Farming, Arts/Crafts, Building/Construction, Campaigning, Caring (general, day and residential), Catering, Community Work, Computers, Conservation Skills, Cooking, Counselling, Development Issues, DIY, Driving, First Aid, Forestry, Fundraising, Gardening/Horticulture, Group Work, International Aid, Library/Resource Centres, Manual Work, Marketing/Publicity, Music, Newsletter/Journalism, Outdoor Skills, Religion, Research, Scientific Work, Social Work, Sport, Summer Camps, Teaching, Technical Skills, Theatre/Drama, Training, Translating, Visiting/Befriending, Work Camps – Seasonal.
Costs: Varies according to the project.
Worldwide placements: Europe (Ukraine).

GWENT WILDLIFE TRUST

16 White Swan Court
Church Street
Monmouth
Gwent NP25 3NY UK
T: 01600 715501
F: 01600 715832
E: jrabjohns@gwentwildlife.cix.co.uk
Contact: Jessica Rabjohns

Gwent Wildlife Trust is a member of the Wildlife Trusts, a national partnership of 47 County Trusts. The aims of the Trust are primarily to: promote nature conservation in the community; acquire and manage nature reserves; monitor biological and geological resources; liaise with local authorities to promote regard for nature conservation; offer practical advice on nature conservation to landowners.
It is the Trust's policy to involve all sectors of the community, of all ages, backgrounds, abilities and disabilities towards these ends. Volunteers require no previous experience just lots of enthusiasm. If so desired, they can go on to participate more fully assisting with the organisation and running of activities/projects. Limited opportunities may also arise, for those with a longer term commitment, for NVQ training to level 2 in Landscapes and Ecosystems.
Volunteers with an offending background may be accepted – each case separately assessed. 🖥 📄

Number of projects: UK: Varies
Starting months: January–December
Time required: 1–52 weeks (plus)
Age: 16 plus – no upper limit
Causes: Conservation, Environmental Causes, Wildlife.
Activities: Campaigning, Computers, Conservation Skills, Driving, Forestry, Gardening/Horticulture, Manual Work, Outdoor Skills, Scientific Work, Technical Skills.
When to apply: All year.
Work alone/with others: With others.
Equipment/clothing: Outdoor clothes.
Health requirements: Anti-tetanus. immunisation. Any medical conditions (illness, allergy or physical disability) that may require treatment/medication or which affects the volunteer working with machinery must be notified to us in advance.
Costs: Food and accommodation.
Benefits: Out of pocket expenses.
Training: Volunteers receive on-the-job training in an informal atmosphere and an appropriate induction.
Supervision: All work is supervised by the Volunteers Support Officer, appropriate member of Trust staff or from Trust local group.
Interviews: Interviews at our office.
UK placements: Wales (Blaenau Gwent, Caerphilly, Merthyr Tydfil, Monmouthshire, Newport, Torfaen).

H

HABITAT FOR HUMANITY INTERNATIONAL

Human Resources Department
121 Habitat Street
Americus
Georgia 31709-3498 USA
T: 00 1 229 924 6935
F: 00 1 229 924 0641
E: VSD@Habitat.org
W: www.habitat.org
Contact: Volunteer Co-ordinator

Habitat for Humanity International is a movement of individuals and groups working in partnership to build houses with those who otherwise would be unable to afford decent shelter. Habitat partners volunteer their construction and administrative skills with the vision of eliminating poverty housing from the face of the earth. Three month internship programme is available any time within the year. Apply by sending resumé and cover letter and write/e-mail for an application form. ⌗

Number of projects: 2000+ UK: 3
Starting months: January–December
Time required: 1–52 weeks (plus)
Age: 18–89
Causes: Architecture, Children, Poor/Homeless, Teaching/assisting (nursery), Work Camps – Seasonal, Young People.
Activities: Accountancy, Administration, Building/Construction, Computers, DIY, Fundraising, Group Work, Marketing/Publicity, Newsletter/Journalism, Research, Summer Camps, Teaching, Technical Skills, Training, Work Camps – Seasonal.
Placements: 300 approx.
When to apply: All year.
Work alone/with others: With other volunteers in a community.
Qualifications: Driver's licence is a plus. Degree not mandatory but preferred. Must obtain B-1 visa. No restrictions unless restricted by visa.
Health requirements: Depends on job/work environment.
Costs: Travel costs to and from Habitat.
Benefits: Housing and $75 per week (grocery allowance).
Training: Training is on the job.
Supervision: Supervised by managers at all levels.
Interviews: We conduct interviews by telephone before accepting applicants.
Worldwide placements: North America: (USA).

HACKNEY INDEPENDENT LIVING TEAM

Richmond House
1A Westgate Street
Hackney
London
E8 3RL UK
T: +44 (0) 208 985 5511 ext 222
F: +44 (0) 208 533 2029
E: volunteers@hilt.org.uk
Contact: Alison Bell

Hackney Independent Living Team helps people with learning difficulties to live as part of the community and as independently as possible, to choose how they live and what they do, to be in control of their own lives, and to be able to make plans for the future. Volunteers introduce service users to new activities and international culture through everyday life. They also enable service users to have a better quality of life by doing activities that are not just about daily living. Volunteers enable service users to go out and do things they cannot do without support. For example, making new friends at the pub, or doing other varied leisure and educational activities. Volunteers contribute to project planning and development as they bring new ideas and ask questions about the way things are done. This means that services are constantly being evaluated and improved. It can be frustrating sometimes for volunteers as they do not always understand why things have to keep be done in a certain way. However, it is a great learning experience. Will accept volunteers with an offending background if it does not relate to offences to people. London Borough of Hackney, Clapton, Stoke Newington, Dalston, Victoria Park.

Number of projects: 10–20 UK: 10–20
Starting months: January–December
Time required: 26–52 weeks
Age: 18–65
Causes: Disabled (learning and physical).
Activities: Arts/Crafts, Caring – General, Cooking, Gardening/Horticulture, Sport, Teaching, Visiting/Befriending.
Placements: 13
When to apply: Any time.
Work alone/with others: Both.
Qualifications: Interest in working wih people with learning difficulties.
Good level of conversational English. All – visas permitting for voluntary work.
Equipment/clothing: Nil.
Health requirements: No restrictions.

Costs: Food and travel.
Benefits: Free accommodation plus £55 weekly
expenses and zone 1–2 travelcard and out of
pocket expenses.
Training: Induction various – on epilepsy,
manual handling, health and safety and food
hygiene.
Supervision: Each volunteer has a supervisor
who has regular contact and supervision every
two weeks.
Interviews: At HILT office.
Charity number: 25852R
UK placements: England (London).

HAIFA UNIVERSITY, DEPT OF ARCHAEOLOGY

Mount Carmel 31905
Israel
T: 97250 677994
F: 972 4 8279876
E: assawir@research.haifa.ac.il
Contact: Prof, Dr Adam Zertal/Haim Cohen

El Ahwat, one of the most recent and surprising
discoveries in the field of Biblical archaeology
in Israel, is situated on a high hill overlooking
the Mediterranean coast, ca. 12km east of
Caesarea. The site was discovered in 1992, being
excavated since 1993. The site is a large fortified
town enclosed by a stone-built city wall 5–6
metres wide. The lines of the wall are wavy in
design, having 10–12 tower-like projections
along its perimeter. The area within the town is
divided into four quarters by dividing-walls two
meters wide. According to the pottery found,
the site was founded near the end of the 13th
century BC. It was a short-lived site – only 50
years – and then abandoned, never to be settled
again. In 1995 indications were revealed which
connected the site to the big island of Sardinia
in the Western Mediterranean. Architectural
elements of the Nuragic culture of Sardinia were
unearthed in the site, and there is a possibility
to connect the place with the Shardana, one of
the well-known tribes among the sea peoples.
These were tribes who attacked the empires of
the late bronze age in the Mediterranean and
destroyed them. Working days – Sunday to
Thursday. Work starts at noon on Sunday. El-
Ahwat, Central Israel, 18km east of
Mediterranean Sea. 🗒 📷

Number of projects: 1 UK: 0
Starting months: Jul, Sep
Time required: 1–4 weeks
Age: 16–70
Causes: Archaeology.
Activities: Scientific Work.
Placements: 20
When to apply: Before 1st June.
Work alone/with others: With others.
Equipment/clothing: Hat, high boots, anti-sun

cream, all other simple clothing for a hot
summer.
Health requirements: Good general health.
Costs: Travel to Israel and US$200 per week in
the dig, includes everything.
Benefits: Meals are served in the kibbutz dining
room. Participants will have free use of the
kibbutz swimming pool. Each weekday
afternoon there is a free guided tour by bus to
sites and places of interest in the area (Caesarea,
Megiddo etc). The campers will stay in a
kibbutz nearby. There are well equipped rooms
for four, with bathrooms, kitchen and frigidaire
for each floor.
Worldwide placements: Asia (Israel).

HALLEY VOLUNTEER CENTRE – MAURITIUS

Halley Movement
PO Box 250
Curepipe
Mauritius
T: 00 230 674 6504
F: 00 230 677 8544
E: halley@intnet.mu
W: www.halleymovement.org
Contact: Mahendranath Busgopaul

Halley Volunteer Centre promotes and has information about volunteering in Mauritius. It may well be able to put volunteers in touch with organisations which are not yet listed on the WorldWide Volunteering database. 📄

Starting months: January–December
Time required: 1–52 weeks (plus)
Age: 16 plus – no upper limit
Causes: AIDS/HIV, Children, Elderly People, Environmental Causes, Human Rights, Poor/ Homeless, Teaching – Primary, Young People.
Activities: Campaigning, Caring – General, Community Work, Computers, Counselling, Development Issues, Group Work, Newsletter/Journalism, Research, Social Work, Teaching, Training.
When to apply: All year.
Qualifications: University graduate. Prior experience in volunteering will be an advantage. Good command of either English or French languages. Ready to work odd hours.
Equipment/clothing: The organisation's equipment will be put at the disposal of the volunteer.
Health requirements: Volunteers should be medically fit. A medical certificate needs to be produced.
Costs: Foreign volunteers need to secure their own air travel.
Benefits: Accommodation may be arranged for volunteers.
Training: On the spot training based on qualifications may be conducted.
Supervision: A programme officer will be in charge of monitoring and supervision.
Interviews: Interviews for foreign students will be carried out electronically.
Worldwide placements: Africa (Mauritius).

HAMPSHIRE AND ISLE OF WIGHT WILDLIFE TRUST

Woodside House
Woodside Road
Eastleigh
Hampshire SO50 4ET UK
T: 023 80 613636
F: 023 80 68 8900
E: annettef@hwt.org.uk
W: www.hwt.org.uk
Contact: Annette Forrest

Hampshire and Isle of Wight Wildlife Trust. Prospective volunteers are invited to contact the Volunteers Officer for further discussion. ♿

Number of projects: varies **UK:** varies
Starting months: January–December
Time required: 1–52 weeks (plus)
Age: 16 plus – no upper limit
Causes: Conservation, Environmental Causes, Wildlife.
Activities: Administration, Computers,

Conservation Skills, Driving, Forestry, Fundraising, Gardening/Horticulture, Manual Work, Marketing/Publicity, Outdoor Skills, Research, Scientific Work, Technical Skills.
When to apply: All year.
Work alone/with others: With others.
Qualifications: Depends on the project.
Equipment/clothing: Casual work clothes, waterproofs, stout boots for outdoor work. Protective safety gear is provided.
Health requirements: Anti-tetanus innoculation recommended.
Costs: Food, accommodation and travel.
Benefits: Volunteers Officer will provide information on expenses.
Training: Some training – dependent upon task.
Supervision: Senior volunteer or staff.
Interviews: By telephone or at the Eastleigh office.
UK placements: England (Hampshire, Isle of Wight).

HAMPTON HOUSE

Tonmead Road
Lumbertubs
Northampton
Northants NN3 8JX UK
T: 01604 403733
F: 01604 413832
Contact: Colin Knowlton

Hampton House is a residential service, part of SCOPE. (Scope is the organisation for people with cerebral palsy.) Volunteers with an offending background are not generally accepted. ♿ 📄

Number of projects: 1 **UK:** 1
Starting months: January–December
Time required: 26–52 weeks (plus)
Age: 16–25
Causes: Disabled (learning and physical).
Activities: Arts/Crafts, Caring (day & residential), Computers, DIY, Gardening/Horticulture, Music.
Placements: 3–6
When to apply: All year.
Work alone/with others: Both.
Qualifications: Some practical skills and ability in DIY and gardening.
Health requirements: Nil, other than fitness to undertake the work required.
Costs: Nil.
Benefits: Travel costs in the UK to and from placement paid. Meals + pocket money up to £23 per week.
Interviews: Interviews take place at Hampton House.
Charity number: 208231
UK placements: England (Northamptonshire).

HCJB UK

131 Grattan Road
Bradford
West Yorkshire BD1 2HS UK
T: 01274 721 810
F: 01274 741302
E: airwave@hcjb.org.uk
W: www.HCJB.org
Contact: Ray Thurgood

HCJB began in 1931 as the first ever Christian Missionary radio station. Today, with our partners, we broadcast to some 85% of the world's surface by shortwave, FM, AM, satellite, TV and the Internet in well over 100 languages. Whilst Ecuador, where we started, is still our main broadcasting centre, we also work with local Christians in some 70 different countries throughout the world and broadcast in well over 100 different languages every day. As well as the radio work we have Hydro Electric power stations to supply the electricity for our transmitters and a television station which broadcasts to the three main cities in Ecuador. We also have a large amount of medical work in Ecuador, with two hospitals (one in Quito, the capital city, and one in the jungle at Shell), eight clinics which give medical and dental treatment to the poorer areas, a mobile medical caravan which visits the remotest areas with medical help and we also put in fresh clean water supplies to remote villages high in the mountains and in the jungle. HCJB is international and interdenominational. At present we need for 3–12 months: radio presenters and producers, sound and electronic engineers, IT specialists, electrical civil and water engineers, doctors, surgeons, nurses, physio-therapists, occupational therapists and all grades of medical professionals. We also need administrators, photographers, desk-top publishing experts, graphic artists etc. Volunteers with an offending background are accepted depending upon the individual case. ☒ ▤

Number of projects: Several UK: 1
Starting months: January–December
Time required: 2–52 weeks
Age: 18–65
Causes: Environmental Causes, Health Care/Medical, Young People.
Activities: International Aid, Religion, Scientific Work, Technical Skills, Training.
Placements: Several.
When to apply: 1st January for summer. Any time – others.
Work alone/with others: Usually with others.
Qualifications: Spanish desirable. We expect all applicants to be sympathetic to and in agreement with our Christian beliefs. Spanish is essential for medical work.
Equipment/clothing: Nurse's uniforms.

Health requirements: Some vaccinations required.
Costs: All costs including travel and maintenance, food and accommodation.
Benefits: Opportunity to gain experience in the volunteer's specialism in a Latin American environment; experience of working in a Christian missionary organisation. Accommodation arranged by HCJB but paid for by the volunteer.
Training: Given as necessary.
Supervision: Supervised by HCJB missionaries in the field.
Interviews: Interviews take place in Bradford.
Charity number: 263449
Worldwide placements: South America (Ecuador).
UK placements: England (W. Yorkshire).

HEBRIDEAN WHALE AND DOLPHIN TRUST, THE

28 Main Street
Tobermory, Isle of Mull
Argyll PA75 6UN UK
T: 01688 302620
F: 01688 302728
E: hwdt@sol.co.uk
W: www.hwdt.org
Contact: Fiona Quarmby

The Hebridean Whale and Dolphin Trust is a registered charity, which has pioneered the study of whales, dolphins and porpoises found in the waters of the Hebrides. Using study techniques that neither harm nor seriously disturb the animals, the research work we undertake provides those who manage Scotland's wildlife and habitats with the information they need to achieve effective conservation. The research also provides the materials for our work in environmental education, helping to raise public awareness around the UK and educate visitors to this outstanding area about the wildlife, which exists right on our doorstep. HWDT Marine Outreach Project – HWDT requires volunteer – 1st Mate, education assistant and research assistant from March to November to assist on board our education and research vessel. We also have short-term opportunities available for paying volunteers. HWDT Discovery Centre – HWDT HQ in Tobermory, Mull requires volunteers to work throughout the year. Tasks include environmental interpretation, fundraising, administration, computer support and web design. HWDT Ardnamurchan Land-Based Survey Project – based at Ardnamurchan lighthouse, volunteers are required between July and September. Tasks include marine mammal observation, using a theodolite, assisting with the analysis and writing up of data, environmental interpretation and public talks. HWDT Bottlenose Dolphin Project – based on the Isle of Islay, volunteers are required to carry out a variety of research and education tasks. Volunteers will need to be able to fit into a small team and live in a remote community. We are based in Tobermory in the Isle of Mull. Mull is one of the inner Hebridean islands off the west coast of Scotland. Projects are also on the mainland peninsular of Ardnamurchan to the north of Mull, & on the Isle of Islay to the south of Mull. 🖹

Number of projects UK: 4
Starting months: January–December
Time required: 1–52 weeks
Age: 18 plus – no upper limit
Causes: Children, Conservation, Environmental Causes, Wildlife.
Activities: Administration, Arts/Crafts, Community Work, Computers, Conservation Skills, Library/Resource Centres, Marketing/Publicity, Newsletter/Journalism, Outdoor Skills, Research, Scientific Work.
Placements: 60
When to apply: Any time, as long as volunteers have definite dates they are available. The Marine Outreach project is very popular so to avoid disappointment, applications should be made early in the year.
Work alone/with others: Mainly with others.
Qualifications: No, however a background in biology and an interest in marine life are beneficial. Most volunteers are university students who are studying for marine-based degrees, but this is not always the case. A good grasp of the English language is essential.
Equipment/clothing: No, specialist equipment is provided.
Health requirements: None known at present.
Costs: Volunteers must fund their own accommodation, this can be about £50 per week. They are responsible for covering their own travel costs and subsistence costs. There are no membership or registration fees necessary.
Benefits: None from the trust. Students can sometimes claim from their university.
Training: All necessary training is provided.
Supervision: There is one member of staff who supervises each project. All volunteers on that project are responsible to that member of staff.
Interviews: Telephone interviews.
Charity number: SCO22403
UK placements: Scotland (Argyll and Bute).

HELP (Humanitarian Educational Long Term Projects)

60 The Pleasance
Edinburgh
EH8 9TJ UK
T: 0131 556 9497
F: 0131 650 6383

E: 9627860@sms.ed.ac.uk
W: www.eusa.ed.ac.uk/societies/help
Contact: Sarah Beslee or Jonathan Crampin

HELP (Scotland) is an Edinburgh University society and a charitable organisation that has now been running for 11 years. It began in 1990 by a student called Ben Carey who established the society in order to support a community based project in the village of Mellcote in southern India. Since then the organisation has grown and developed and thousands of people within Edinburgh and across the world have been involved. AIMS: 1. To support community led initiatives, working together with people to help them achieve their goals of development. 2. To provide new knowledge, skills and experience to students. 3. To promote international understanding through projects that are focused on building friendship, trust and respect between HELP volunteers and people across the world.
India: Mellcote and Manali.
Tanzania: Titye.
South Africa: Boitumelang.
Uganda: Kampala.

Number of projects: 15–20 **UK:** 0
Starting months: Jul, Aug, Sep
Time required: 4–10 weeks
Age: 18–25
Causes: Children, Conservation, Environmental Causes, Teaching/assisting (EFL), Work Camps – Seasonal.
Activities: Building/Construction, Community Work, Conservation Skills, Development Issues, Forestry, Fundraising, Group Work, International Aid, Manual Work, Outdoor Skills, Social Work, Summer Camps, Teaching, Work Camps – Seasonal.
Placements: 150–200
When to apply: Co-ordinator deadline end of November.
Volunteer deadline end of January
Work alone/with others: With others.
Qualifications: None specific but enthusiasm, adaptability essential. Volunteers must also be enterprising.
Health requirements: Nil.
Costs: Approx £210 board and lodging + air fare, insurance, own money = £600+.
Benefits: Advice on fundraising, travel, medical care, equipment. Discounts on medical supplies, travel and camping items. Usually very basic accommodation – sleeping on floor in sleeping bags – included in cost of project.
Training: Aids awareness programme for African camps plus voluntary Swahili lessons.
Supervision: Co-ordinator in overall control of project but usually same aged peer only with more experience of travelling abroad etc.
Interviews: Applicants may be interviewed in Edinburgh.

Worldwide placements: Africa (Malawi, Mozambique, South Africa, Tanzania, Uganda, Zambia, Zimbabwe); Central America (Mexico); South America (Bolivia, Ecuador, Peru); Asia (India, Nepal, Pakistan, Philippines).

HELP THE AGED

207–221 Pentonville Road
London
N1 9UZ UK
T: +44 (0) 207 278 1114
F: +44 (0) 207 278 1116
E: info@helptheaged.org.uk
W: www.helptheaged.org.uk
Contact: Kate Chalk

Help The Aged: Each shop has one or two paid shop managers and a team of volunteer helpers. We are always looking for people who can spare a morning from 9.00am to 1.00 pm, afternoon from 12.50 p.m. to 5.00 p.m. or a full day each week to work in their local shop. You can become involved in all aspects of shop work from sorting and pricing stock to window dressing, operating the till and serving customers. Facilities are provided for making tea and coffee. Volunteers with an offending background may be accepted. It would be left to the Area Manager's decision. ⬛

Number of projects: 350 shops **UK:** 350 shops
Starting months: January–December
Time required: 2–52 weeks
Age: 16 plus – no upper limit
Causes: Elderly People.
Activities: Fundraising.
When to apply: All year.
Work alone/with others: With others.
Health requirements: Nil.
Costs: Food, accommodation and travel costs.
Benefits: Full training.
Training: We will train you in all aspects of shop work and in Help The Aged's work.
Supervision: Supervised.
Interviews: Interviews take place at the shop.
Charity number: 272786
UK placements: England (throughout); Scotland (Edinburgh, Lothian – East, Lothian – West); Northern Ireland (throughout); Wales (Conwy).

HELP THE HANDICAPPED HOLIDAY FUND

147a Camden Road
Tunbridge Wells
Kent TN1 2RA UK
T: 01892 547474
F: 01892 524703
E: info@3hfund.org.uk
W: www.3hfund.org.uk
Contact: Margaret James

Help The Handicapped Holiday Fund specialises in holidays for physically disabled people and respite for their carers. Volunteers are required to help care for the disabled guests on the holidays with full back up of a leader and nurse on each holiday. Holiday venues vary from year to year. We run 6 x 1 week holidays – 5 in the UK and 1 abroad. Please either contact the office or go to the web site for more details. Varies from year to year with choice of holiday venues. ⬛ ▤

Number of projects: 6 **UK:** 5
Starting months: Apr, May, Jun, Jul, Aug, Sep
Time required: 1 week
Age: 18–65
Causes: Disabled (physical), Holidays for Disabled.
Activities: Caring – General.
Placements: 100
When to apply: As early as possible.
Work alone/with others: Generally with others – always with a back-up.
Qualifications: An interest in caring, or experience of caring.
Health requirements: In good health, physically fit.
Costs: Travel to and from coach at Tunbridge Wells.
Benefits: Board, accommodation and travel from Tunbridge Wells.
Challenging but rewarding work with people with disabilities.
Training: Training will be given to new helpers on the activity holiday.
Supervision: Team leaders and nurses.
Interviews: Volunteer applicants are not interviewed, but all applicants will have to undergo police checks because the work is with children and/or vulnerable adults.
Charity number: 286306
Worldwide placements: Europe (Spain).
UK placements: England (Cumbria, Isle of Wight, Norfolk, Sussex – West).

HENSHAW'S SOCIETY FOR THE BLIND

John Derby House
88–92 Talbot Road
Old Trafford
Manchester
M16 0GS UK
T: 0161 872 1234
E: info@hsbp.org.uk
Contact: Mrs Linda Norbury

Henshaw's Society for the Blind is a registered charity providing a wide range of residential, nursing, education, training, leisure and community care services for people of all ages who are blind or partially sighted across northern England and Wales.

Number of projects: 1 **UK:** 1
Starting months: January–December
Time required: 1–52 weeks (plus)
Age: 18 plus – no upper limit
Causes: Children, Disabled (physical), Young People.
Activities: Administration, Caring – Day, Visiting/Befriending.
When to apply: All year.
UK placements: England (Cheshire, Manchester).

HEREFORDSHIRE NATURE TRUST

Lower House Farm
Ledbury Road
Tupsley
Hereford
HR1 1UT UK
T: 01432 356872
F: 01432 275489
E: herefordwt@cix.co.uk
W: www.herefordwt.cix.co.uk
Contact: Steve Roe

For well over 30 years, the Herefordshire Nature Trust, a registered charity, has been playing a key role in protecting this heritage and conserving the wildlife of our county. We own and manage over 46 nature reserves. These encompass the best of the county's natural heritage and include sites that date back to Saxon times and beyond, like Lea and Pagets Wood, home of the endangered dormouse, and the flood-plain hay meadows of the lower Lugg valley, one of the few remaining places where the fritillary still grows. We carry out surveys of the wildlife of the county. We influence land use by giving advice on conservation to statutory bodies, landowners and all with an interest in the countryside. We encourage a wider understanding of nature conservation by education and publicity and place special importance on our WATCH groups for children. Despite the Trust's work and despite increasing interest in conservation and a national commitment to conserving biodiversity, many habitats are still under threat; hedgerows are still being destroyed; and a recent survey by the Trust has shown that 70% of the county's herb-rich grasslands have been lost in the last 15 years. 🚹

Number of projects: variable **UK:** variable
Starting months: Jan, Feb, Mar, Apr, May, Jun, Jul, Aug, Sep, Nov, Dec
Time required: 1–52 weeks (plus)
Age: 16–70
Causes: Conservation, Environmental Causes, Wildlife.
Activities: Conservation Skills, Outdoor Skills, Scientific Work.
Placements: 15

When to apply: All year.
Work alone/with others: Both.
Qualifications: Conversational English required. No restrictions on nationalities.
Equipment/clothing: Safety clothing provided as appropriate.
Health requirements: Some restrictions when using machinery.
Costs: Food, accommodation and travel.
Benefits: Experience of nature conservation projects, with possible qualifications depending on duration of placement.
Training: Depends on duration of placement.
Interviews: Interviews take place at Herefordshire Nature Trust offices.
Charity number: 220173
UK placements: England (Herefordshire).

HERTFORDSHIRE ACTION ON DISABILITY

The Woodside Centre
The Commons
Welwyn Garden City
Herts AL7 4DD UK
T: 01707 324581
F: 01707 371297
E: info@hadnet.co.uk
W: www.hertsaction.dial.pipex.com
Contact: Mrs A. Waterfield

For over 30 years the HAD has aimed to meet the needs of the disabled in Hertfordshire with services including financial support, counselling, equipment, exhibitions and hire, and driving instruction in a fully adapted car. The association also has its own hotel at Clacton-on-Sea. About 100 volunteers are needed annually to assist disabled people on holiday for two-week periods from March to November. Free return coach travel is provided to and from the Woodside Centre to Clacton. Further details (an information pack and Holiday Fact Sheets 1–10) can be obtained by sending a 75p postage stamp to the above address. Volunteers are also needed at the Woodside Centre for general office duties and meeting and greeting disabled people coming for assistance. Volunteers with an offending background may be accepted. 🚹 📄

Number of projects: numerous **UK:** numerous
Starting months: Jan, Feb, Mar, Apr, May, Jun, Jul, Aug, Sep, Oct, Nov
Time required: 2–52 weeks (plus)
Age: 18–70
Causes: Disabled (physical), Elderly People, Holidays for Disabled.
Activities: Administration, Caring (general, residential), Fundraising, Library/Resource Centres.
Placements: 300

When to apply: As early as possible.
Work alone/with others: With others.
Health requirements: Nil.
Costs: Nil.
Benefits: Travel and board if volunteering for hotel in Clacton.
Training: Induction + how we expect our guests to be treated.
Supervision: Hotel manager and assistant manager will supervise.
Interviews: Interviews take place at the Woodside Centre and at Clacton.
Charity number: 1059015
UK placements: England (Hertfordshire).

HERTFORDSHIRE AND MIDDLESEX WILDLIFE TRUST

Grebe House
St Michael's Street
St Albans
Hertfordshire AL3 4SN UK
T: 01727 858901
F: 01727 854542
E: jago.moles@hmwt.org
W: www.wildlifetrusts.org/herts
Contact: Jago Moles

Hertfordshire and Middlesex Wildlife Trust is a member of the Wildlife Trusts, a national partnership of 48 County Trusts. The aims of the Trust are primarily to: promote nature conservation in the community; acquire and manage nature reserves; monitor biological and geological resources; liaise with local authorities to promote regard for nature conservation; offer practical advice on nature conservation to landowners. It is the Trust's policy to involve all sectors of the community, of all ages, backgrounds, abilities and disabilities towards these ends. Volunteers require no previous experience just lots of enthusiasm. If they desire, volunteers can go on to participate more fully assisting with the organisation and running of activities/projects. Volunteers with an offending background may be accepted – each case separately assessed. ⬚ ⬚

Number of projects: 1 **UK:** 1
Starting months: January–December
Time required: 1–52 weeks (plus)
Age: 16–75
Causes: Children, Conservation, Environmental Causes, Wildlife.
Activities: Agriculture/Farming, Building/Construction, Community Work, Conservation Skills, Forestry, Fundraising, Manual Work, Marketing/Publicity, Scientific Work.
When to apply: All year.
Work alone/with others: Both.
Equipment/clothing: Casual work clothes,

waterproofs, stout boots for outdoor work. Protective safety gear is provided.
Health requirements: Anti-tetanus innoculation recommended.
Costs: Food, accommodation and travel.
Benefits: Out of pocket expenses.
Training: On-site training.
Supervision: Supervision by Reserves staff.
Interviews: Yes.
UK placements: England (Hertfordshire, London).

HESTIA NATIONAL VOLUNTEER CENTRE PRAGUE

YMCA Palace
Na Porici 12
Praha 1, 115 30
Czech Republic
T: + 420 224 872 077
F: + 420 224 872 076
E: osozanaka@hest.cz
W: www.hest.cz
Contact: Olga Sozanska

Hestia National Volunteer Centre Prague promotes and has information about volunteering in the Czech Republic. It may well be able to put volunteers in touch with organisations which are not yet listed on the WorldWide Volunteering database. Centre offers trainings and education, consultations, supervision and affiliation for volunteers and professionals.

Starting months: January–December
Time required: 4–52 weeks
Age: 18–25
Causes: Addicts/Ex-Addicts, AIDS/HIV, Animal Welfare, Archaeology, Architecture, Children, Conservation, Disabled (learning and physical), Elderly People, Environmental Causes, Health Care/Medical, Heritage, Holidays for Disabled, Human Rights, Inner City Problems, Offenders/Ex-Offenders, Poor/Homeless, Refugees, Teaching/assisting (nursery, primary, secondary, mature, EFL) Unemployed, Wildlife, Work Camps – Seasonal, Young People.
Activities: Accountancy, Administration, Agriculture/Farming, Arts/Crafts, Building/Construction, Campaigning, Caring (general, day and residential), Catering, Community Work, Computers, Conservation Skills, Cooking, Counselling, Development Issues, DIY, Driving, First Aid, Forestry, Fundraising, Gardening/Horticulture, Group Work, International Aid, Library/Resource Centres, Manual Work, Marketing/Publicity, Music, Newsletter/Journalism, Outdoor Skills, Religion, Research, Scientific Work, Social Work, Sport, Summer Camps, Teaching, Technical Skills, Theatre/Drama, Training, Translating, Visiting/Befriending, Work Camps – Seasonal.

When to apply: Any time.
Qualifications: EU Countries – European Volunteer Service Programme.
Costs: Varies according to the project.
Worldwide placements: Europe (Czech Republic).

HiPACT

PO Box 770
York House, Empire Way
Wembley
Middlesex HA9 0RP UK
T: +44 (0) 20 8900 0770
F: +44 (0) 20 8900 0330
E: enquiries@hipact.ac.uk
W: www.hipact.ac.uk
Contact: Lucy Hicks

HiPACT is an association of British Universities committed to widening participation in Higher Education and promoting modern education for practical development. They have been invited to help manage several universities in Nigeria. The programme is far reaching, involving academic and administrative staff as well as volunteers. Volunteer projects run for one month during the summer in a variety of locations and may involve peer teaching, teaching computer skills, helping to market the public-private partnership they are establishing, or supporting permanent staff on projects. HiPACT runs summer schools in the UK to motivate children into attending higher education institutions. Volunteers are asked to spend at least a week teaching in the summer schools as a way of preparing them for the Nigeria projects. If volunteers stay for the whole three weeks admin costs will be refunded. Nigeria, West Africa. 🔥

Number of projects: 4 UK: 1
Starting months: Jun, Jul, Aug
Time required: 4–8 weeks
Age: 18 plus – no upper limit
Causes: Teaching/assisting, Young People.
Activities: Administration, Group Work, Teaching, Training.
Placements: 60
When to apply: January to June.
Work alone/with others: Work with others.
Qualifications: Volunteers ideally should be undergraduates, postgraduates or young professionals.
Health requirements: Volunteers should contact their own GP re: vaccinations.
Costs: Contribution of £75 administration and accommodation fee week towards the cost of British training week and Summer School. International volunteers pay for cost of flights, visa and spending money.
Benefits: Accommodation with local families , usually those of civil servants, teachers and chefs.

Training: Weekend of workshop training before students arrive.
Supervision: Logistical and administrative support by local co-ordinating officers.
Interviews: No.
Worldwide placements: Africa (Nigeria).
UK placements: England (Leicestershire).

HOGGANVIK LANDSBY

N-5583 Vikedal
Norway
T: 00 47 52 760 274
F: 00 47 52 760 408
E: holandb@online.no
W: www.camphill.no/hogganvik
Contact: Medarbeider Ansvarlig

Hogganvik Landsby is a Camphill village community with adults in need of a protected environment. Hogganvik is part of the worldwide Camphill movement with centres for children, adolescents and adults. Hogganvik is a small community (about 40–45 people), we live as a community together. We share work, cultural and social houselife together. Work is mainly land based (forest, farm and garden) but there is also work in the home and in a small woodwork shop. Volunteers with an offending background are not ususally accepted but each case is taken up individually. West coast of Norway about 1 hour by car from Haugesund, beautiful landscape. 🔥 📖

Number of projects: 1 UK: 0
Starting months: January–December
Time required: 12–52 weeks
Age: 19–50
Causes: Disabled (learning).
Activities: Agriculture/Farming, Arts/Crafts, Caring – Residential, Forestry, Gardening/Horticulture.
Placements: 6
When to apply: In good time.
Work alone/with others: With others in the village.
Qualifications: It is not always easy for people to learn Norwegian which is a necessity after a few weeks.
Equipment/clothing: Outside workclothes, free time clothes and some clothes which are respectable.
Health requirements: HIV and TB free and an openness about health problems. Health certificates required.
Costs: Travel.
Benefits: Board, lodging and modest pocket money.
Training: For volunteers who are staying for a year, there is an introduction course and the possibility to take curative/social therapeutic training.
Supervision: Close daily contact with experienced co-workers.

Interviews: Volunteers are not usually interviewed.
Worldwide placements: Europe (Norway).

HOLIDAYS FOR THE DISABLED

Flat 4
62 Stuart Park
Edinburgh
EH12 8YE UK
T: 0131 339 8866
E: AliWalker1@aol.com
Contact: Alison Walker

Holidays for the Disabled recruits volunteers annually to help with holidays for the disabled. A large scale annual holiday for all ages of physically handicapped people is provided. The organisation runs a wide range of interesting holidays in the UK and abroad. In addition to holidays at fixed locations there are boating and camping trips. Activities on the holidays include discotheques, swimming, horse riding, wheelchair sports, barbecues and banquets. 🔊 🗎

Number of projects: 1 **UK:** 1
Starting months: May, Jun, Jul, Aug, Sep
Time required: 1–2 weeks
Age: 18–35
Causes: Disabled (physical), Holidays for Disabled.
Activities: Caring – General, First Aid, Gardening/ Horticulture, Manual Work, Music, Outdoor Skills, Social Work, Sport, Summer Camps.
When to apply: All year.
Work alone/with others: Both.
Qualifications: No special qualifications.
Equipment/clothing: Outdoor holiday clothes.
Health requirements: Healthy and strong.
Costs: Helpers are asked for contribution of 40% of overseas holidays and 25% of UK holidays. This can be anything from £50 – £300 depending on the location.
Training: Receive training at the start of the holiday.
Supervision: Yes during holiday.
Interviews: No.
UK placements: Scotland (Edinburgh, Lothian – East, Lothian – West).

HOME FARM TRUST, THE

Merchants House
Wapping Road
Bristol
BS1 4RW UK
T: 0117 930 2600
F: 0117 922 5938
E: marketing@hft.org.uk
W: www.hft.org.uk
Contact: Suzi Walton

HFT is a national charity and leading provider of care, opportunities and quality of life within the community for people with a learning disability. HFT's commitment and expertise means that people, no matter what their disability, are helped to develop their potential. Established in 1962, today HFT provides services for over 800 people, an advocacy project, supported employment services and a carer support service offering support and guidance to thousands of families. Our approach to care is centred on the needs and wishes of the people we are here to help. We give people a say in the kind of home they want, the activities, training and work they pursue and help them achieve greater levels of independence. People can be helped to acquire new skills and improve their self confidence and are encouraged to participate in the community. Families also play a very valuable role within HFT's philosophy, supporting the work of HFT. 🔊 🗎

Number of projects: 14 **UK:** 14
Starting months: Jan, Feb, Mar, Apr, May, Jun, Jul, Aug, Sep, Oct, Nov
Time required: 1–52 weeks (plus)
Age: 18–64
Causes: Disabled (learning).
Activities: Arts/Crafts, Caring (general, day and residential), Computers, Counselling, Development Issues, Fundraising, Gardening/Horticulture, Music, Outdoor Skills, Sport, Training, Visiting/Befriending.
When to apply: All year.
Work alone/with others: With others.
Qualifications: HFT requires a police check on all volunteers.
Health requirements: Nil but a risk assessment of the placement would be carried out.
Costs: All own costs including travel and board.
Benefits: Subsistence + some travel costs would be paid whilst travelling with residents.
Training: Depends on the placement.
Supervision: Volunteers are supervised by relevant staff.
Interviews: Interviews take place at the project/shop/office.
Charity number: 313069
UK placements: England (Bedfordshire, Bristol, Cambridgeshire, Cheshire, Cornwall, Derbyshire, Devon, Essex, Gloucestershire, Herefordshire, Hertfordshire, Kent, Lancashire, London, Manchester, Merseyside, Nottinghamshire, Oxfordshire, Staffordshire, Suffolk, Surrey, Warwickshire, Worcestershire, N. Yorkshire, S. Yorkshire, W. Yorkshire).

HOPE AND HOMES FOR CHILDREN

East Clyffe
Salisbury
Wiltshire SP3 4LZ UK
T: 01722 790111
F: 01722 790024

E: hhc@hopeandhomes.org
W: www.hopeandhomes.org
Contact: Mrs Caroline Cook

Hope and Homes for Children was started and is run by Colonel Mark Cook OBE and his wife Caroline. Our aim is 'To give hope to children who have nowhere to live, due to war or disaster, by providing them with a home.' The aims are very clear and very specific; to provide homes for orphaned children in areas afflicted by war or disaster; to support the economies of these areas by using local builders and resources; to ensure that our homes are run and maintained by people in the country concerned, respecting local customs and traditions; to insist that the homes are for children of any race, colour or creed. This is a cornerstone of our activities, and we will only embark on projects where this philosophy will be respected. We are in dire need of physiotherapists to help in a home for children in Romania.

Number of projects: 14 UK: 0
Starting months: January–December
Time required: 24–52 weeks
Age: 25–60
Causes: Children, Disabled (learning and physical), Poor/Homeless, Refugees, Teaching/assisting (nursery, primary, EFL), Young People.
Activities: Administration, Arts/crafts, Caring (general, day and residential), Cooking, Group work, Music, Social work, Sport, Teaching, Training.
Placements: 25
When to apply: Any time – normally six months to one year before but sometimes we need volunteers quite urgently.
Work alone/with others: In pairs and with/alongside local staff.
Qualifications: Must love children and have infinite patience. Must have good childcare qualifications.
Health requirements: Must be fit.
Costs: £500+. Volunteers would normally fundraise for their required expenses within the country.
Benefits: Accommodation, return flight and insurance.
Training: Volunteers must already have good childcare qualifications.
Supervision: We have a Project Director in country.
Interviews: Interviews take place at our office in Salisbury.
Charity number: 1040534
Worldwide placements: Europe (Albania, Bosnia-Herzegovina, Croatia, Romania).

HOPE UK

25F Copperfield Street
London
SE1 0EN UK
T: +44 (0) 207 928.0848
F: +44 (0) 207 401 3477
E: s.brighton@hopeuk.org
W: www.hopeuk.org
Contact: Sarah Brighton

Hope UK needs volunteers to become local representatives of Hope UK by being involved in alcohol and other drug-related education which involves working with young people and children. This is mostly preventative work and takes at least six months to train. Volunteers with an offending background may be accepted. ♿

Number of projects: varies UK: varies
Starting months: January–December
Time required: 26–52 weeks (plus)
Age: 18 plus – no upper limit
Causes: Addicts/Ex-Addicts, Children, Conservation, Health Care/Medical, Inner City Problems, Offenders/Ex-Offenders, Teaching/assisting (nursery, primary), Young People.
Activities: Caring – General, Conservation Skills, Fundraising, Group Work, Summer Camps, Teaching, Theatre/Drama, Training.
Placements: Varies.
Work alone/with others: Both.
Qualifications: Nil but this is a Christian organisation.
Health requirements: Nil.
Costs: accommodation and food.
Benefits: Training, support, expenses all provided.
Training: A training course accredited by Open College Network Group or individual face-to-face meetings and sessions.
Supervision: Training co-ordinator, 2 regional representatives, part time office support and volunteers assigned to member of staff.
Interviews: Interviews take place either at our head office or at an appropriate place near where the applicant lives.
Charity number: 1044475
UK placements: England (throughout); Scotland (throughout); Northern Ireland (throughout); Wales (throughout).

HORIZON COSMOPOLITE

3011 Notre Dame West
Montreal
Quebec HYC 1N9 Canada
T: 00 1 514 935 8436
F: 00 1 514 935 4302
E: info@horizoncosmopolite.com
W: www.horizoncosmopolite.com
Contact: Jonathan Paquet

Horizon Cosmopolite is a Canadian based organisation helping young and less young people to go abroad for internships, volunteer work and Spanish immersion programmes. In the last six years we have sent more than 1000 individuals who have had the chance to get involved in social projects, environmental protection projects and teaching opportunities. Volunteers do not need to be Canadian to apply. They choose the project that meets their objectives and apply. Volunteers with offending backgrounds are accepted if they can get a passport and a visa. UK: Monkey Sanctuary in Cornwall. ⬚ ⬚

Number of projects: 25 approx. **UK:** 1
Starting months: January–December
Time required: 1–52 weeks
Age: 18–78
Causes: Animal Welfare, Children, Conservation, Disabled (learning), Environmental Causes, Health Care/Medical, Poor/Homeless, Teaching/assisting (nursery, primary, secondary, mature, EFL) Wildlife, Work Camps – Seasonal, Young People.
Activities: Agriculture/Farming, Arts/Crafts, Community Work, Computers, Conservation Skills, Development Issues, Forestry, Gardening/Horticulture, International Aid, Library/Resource Centres, Manual Work, Marketing/Publicity, Music, Social Work, Teaching, Theatre/Drama, Work Camps – Seasonal.
Placements: 250 + groups
When to apply: Three months before departure date.

Work alone/with others: With other young volunteers.
Qualifications: English speaking, motivation, autonomy, sense of responsibility. Generally no restrictions.
Equipment/clothing: We highly recommend certain types of clothes in certain countries (i.e. Nepal, India).
Health requirements: Nil.
Costs: Participants pay all the costs related to their programme (travel, vaccinations etc.) plus administrative fees and participation fees. (Our web site has up to date prices.)
Benefits: No financial support except for special Canadian internships from the Government for Canadian volunteers. All accommodation is arranged by the local organisation.
Training: Pre-departure booklet and pre-departure orientation day (culture shock, adaptation process, health abroad, cross cultural communication, globalisation) and private meetings with past participants.
Supervision: Abroad: volunteers are welcomed and taken care of by the hosting NGO.
Interviews: Usually in Montreal – or by telephone.
Charity number: FL618-3
Worldwide placements: Africa (Benin, Ghana, Mali, Senegal, Togo, Tunisia); Central America (Costa Rica, Guatemala, Honduras); South America (Chile); Asia (Bangladesh, India, Nepal, Philippines, Thailand); Europe (Estonia, France, Germany, Norway, Portugal).
UK placements: England (Cornwall).

IAVE BOLIVIA

Avenida Las Americas No. 346
Santa Cruz
Bolivia
T: 00 591 3 351474 or 351473
F: 00 591 3 377775
E: mimi@cotas.com.bo
Contact: Mercedes Ortiz de Gasser

IAVE promotes and has information about volunteering in Bolivia. It may well be able to put volunteers in touch with organisations which are not yet listed on the WorldWide Volunteering database.

Starting months: January–December
Time required: 1–52 weeks (plus)
Age: 16 plus – no upper limit
Causes: Addicts/Ex-Addicts, AIDS/HIV, Animal Welfare, Archaeology, Architecture, Children, Conservation, Disabled (learning and physical), Elderly People, Environmental Causes, Health Care/Medical, Heritage, Holidays for Disabled, Human Rights, Inner City Problems, Offenders/Ex-Offenders, Poor/Homeless, Refugees, Teaching/assisting (nursery, primary, secondary, mature, EFL) Unemployed, Wildlife, Work Camps – Seasonal, Young People.
Activities: Accountancy, Administration, Agriculture/Farming, Arts/Crafts, Building/Construction, Campaigning, Caring (general, day and residential), Catering, Community Work, Computers, Conservation Skills, Cooking, Counselling, Development Issues, DIY, Driving, First Aid, Forestry, Fundraising, Gardening/Horticulture, Group Work, International Aid, Library/Resource Centres, Manual Work, Marketing/Publicity, Music, Newsletter/Journalism, Outdoor Skills, Religion, Research, Scientific Work, Social Work, Sport, Summer Camps, Teaching, Technical Skills, Theatre/Drama, Training, Translating, Visiting/Befriending, Work Camps – Seasonal.
Costs: Varies according to the project.
Worldwide placements: South America (Bolivia).

IAVE JAPAN

Rm 305, Gyoen Heights
1–6 Naito-cho
Shinjuku-ku
Tokyo
160-0014 Japan
T: 00 81 3 3351 5130
F: 00 81 3 3351 5131
E: iave@gray.plala.or.jp
W: http://www8.plala.or.jp/iavej/

Contact: Akiko Seto

Iave Japan promotes and has information about volunteering in Japan. It may well be able to put volunteers in touch with organisations which are not yet listed on the WorldWide Volunteering database.

Starting months: January–December
Time required: 1–52 weeks (plus)
Age: 16 plus – no upper limit
Causes: Addicts/Ex-Addicts, AIDS/HIV, Animal Welfare, Archaeology, Architecture, Children, Conservation, Disabled (learning and physical), Elderly People, Environmental Causes, Health Care/Medical, Heritage, Holidays for Disabled, Human Rights, Inner City Problems, Offenders/Ex-Offenders, Poor/Homeless, Refugees, Teaching/assisting (nursery, primary, secondary, mature, EFL) Unemployed, Wildlife, Work Camps – Seasonal, Young People.
Activities: Accountancy, Administration, Agriculture/Farming, Arts/Crafts, Building/Construction, Campaigning, Caring (general, day and residential), Catering, Community Work, Computers, Conservation Skills, Cooking, Counselling, Development Issues, DIY, Driving, First Aid, Forestry, Fundraising, Gardening/Horticulture, Group Work, International Aid, Library/Resource Centres, Manual Work, Marketing/Publicity, Music, Newsletter/Journalism, Outdoor Skills, Religion, Research, Scientific Work, Social Work, Sport, Summer Camps, Teaching, Technical Skills, Theatre/Drama, Training, Translating, Visiting/Befriending, Work Camps – Seasonal.
Costs: Varies according to the project.
Worldwide placements: Asia (Japan).

IAVE CÔTE D'IVOIRE

04 BP 686
Abidjan 04
Cote d'Ivoire
T: 00 225 20 21 35 40
F: 00 225 20 21 35 40
Contact: Angela N'Guessan Yaba

Iave Côte D'Ivoire promotes and has information about volunteering in Côte D'Ivoire. It may well be able to put volunteers in touch with organisations which are not yet listed on the WorldWide Volunteering database.

Starting months: January–December
Time required: 1–52 weeks (plus)
Age: 16 plus – no upper limit
Causes: Addicts/Ex-Addicts, AIDS/HIV, Animal Welfare, Archaeology, Architecture, Children,

Conservation, Disabled (learning and physical), Elderly People, Environmental Causes, Health Care/Medical, Heritage, Holidays for Disabled, Human Rights, Inner City Problems, Offenders/Ex-Offenders, Poor/Homeless, Refugees, Teaching/assisting (nursery, primary, secondary, mature, EFL) Unemployed, Wildlife, Work Camps – Seasonal, Young People.
Activities: Accountancy, Administration, Agriculture/Farming, Arts/Crafts, Building/Construction, Campaigning, Caring (general, day and residential), Catering, Community Work, Computers, Conservation Skills, Cooking, Counselling, Development Issues, DIY, Driving, First Aid, Forestry, Fundraising, Gardening/Horticulture, Group Work, International Aid, Library/Resource Centres, Manual Work, Marketing/Publicity, Music, Newsletter/Journalism, Outdoor Skills, Religion, Research, Scientific Work, Social Work, Sport, Summer Camps, Teaching, Technical Skills, Theatre/Drama, Training, Translating, Visiting/Befriending, Work Camps – Seasonal.
Costs: Varies according to the project.
Worldwide placements: Africa (Côte d'Ivoire).

ICA UK

PO Box 171
Manchester
M15 5BE UK
E: gbowman@gn.apc.org
W: www.ica-uk.org.uk
Contact: The VSP Co-ordinator

The Volunteer Service Programme of the ICA UK is a highly participatory programme for all those interested in volunteering overseas. It offers short courses for the orientation, training and preparation of volunteers, and a small number of placements each year, with local development organisations world-wide, on projects that emphasise community participation and self-help initiative. The programme has trained and placed over 300 UK volunteers since 1981. It is now run in the UK and the Netherlands by a network of returned volunteers. 🔥

Number of projects: 50 UK: 0
Starting months: January–December
Time required: 39–52 weeks
Age: 18 plus – no upper limit
Causes: AIDS/HIV, Children, Conservation, Elderly People, Environmental Causes, Health Care/Medical, Human Rights, Inner City Problems, Poor/Homeless, Refugees, Teaching/assisting (nursery, primary, mature, EFL), Unemployed, Young People.
Activities: Accountancy, Administration, Agriculture/Farming, Arts/Crafts, Campaigning, Community Work, Computers, Conservation Skills, Development Issues, Driving, Forestry, Fundraising, Gardening/Horticulture, Group

Work, International Aid, Library/Resource Centres, Marketing/Publicity, Newsletter/Journalism, Research, Social Work, Teaching, Technical Skills, Theatre/Drama, Training, Translating.
Placements: 16
When to apply: At any time.
Work alone/with others: With host organisations.
Qualifications: None required.
Health requirements: Nil.
Costs: Variable according to placement. Generally £2,000–£4,000 total including training, travel, insurance etc.
Benefits: Scholarships of up to £500 available.
Training: Orientation weekend and foundation course. Required pre-departure training takes place only between May and October.
Supervision: Depends on placement.
Interviews: Prospective volunteers are oriented at volunteer orientation weekends in the UK throughout the year.
Charity number: 293086
Worldwide placements: Africa (Burkina Faso, Cameroon, Côte d'Ivoire, Egypt, Gambia, Ghana, Kenya, Mali, Mauritania, Namibia, Nigeria, Reunion, Senegal, South Africa, Tanzania, Uganda, Zambia, Zimbabwe); North America: (Canada, USA); Central America (Belize, Costa Rica, El Salvador, Guatemala, Honduras, Mexico, Netherlands Antilles, Nicaragua); South America (Brazil, Chile, Colombia, Ecuador, Peru, Suriname, Venezuela); Asia (Bangladesh, Cambodia, China, Hong Kong, India, Indonesia, Japan, Jordan, Korea (South), Lebanon, Malaysia, Nepal, Pakistan, Philippines, Sri Lanka, Taiwan, Thailand); Australasia (Australia); Europe (Belgium, Bosnia-Herzegovina, Croatia, Netherlands, Portugal, Russia).

ICADS, INSTITUTE FOR CENTRAL AMERICAN DEVELOPMENT STUDIES

Apartado 300–2050 (Costa Rica)
San Pedro Montes de Oca
Costa Rica
T: 011 506 225 0508
F: 011 506 234 1337
E: icads@netbox.com
W: www.icadscr.com
Contact: S.N. Kinghorn

The Institute for Central American Development Studies (ICADS) is a centre for study, research and analysis of Central American social and environmental issues. We focus on economic development, agriculture, human rights, gender issues, education, public health and the environment. Volunteers with an offending background will not be accepted. Alternate address: Dept 826 P.O.Box 025216 (USA), Miami 33102-5216, Florida, USA. Location is in the central Costa Rican valley, beaches, rainforests and mountains. 🔥

Number of projects: 25 UK: 0
Starting months: January–December
Time required: 4–24 weeks
Age: 18 plus – no upper limit
Causes: Addicts/Ex-Addicts, Children, Conservation, Disabled (learning and physical), Elderly People, Environmental Causes, Health Care/Medical, Heritage, Human Rights, Inner City Problems, Poor/Homeless, Teaching/assisting (primary, EFL), Unemployed, Wildlife, Young People.
Activities: Agriculture/Farming, Building/Construction, Caring (general, day and residential), Community Work, Computers, Conservation Skills, Counselling, Development Issues, Forestry, Fundraising, Gardening/Horticulture, Group Work, International Aid, Marketing/Publicity, Newsletter/Journalism, Religion, Research, Social Work, Teaching, Theatre/Drama, Translating.
Placements: Varies.
When to apply: All year.
Work alone/with others: Both.
Qualifications: Most projects need volunteers to be able to speak Spanish at different levels. Intensive Spanish classes are available.
Health requirements: In good health – vaccinations for the Central American area needed.
Costs: Travel.
Benefits: Accommodation, breakfast and dinner and laundry service.
Training: Training provided depending on each project.
Worldwide placements: Central America (Costa Rica).

IJAW YOUTH LINK PROJECT

76 Falcon Road
Battersea
London
SW11 2LR UK
T: +44 (0) 20 7361 223 2181
F: +44 (0) 20 7361 223 2181/020 7652 677
E: ijawyouthlink@btconnect.com
Contact: Stanley Ebikinei-Eguruze

IJAW Youth Link Project is run entirely by volunteers who are the most valued resource at the project. We have a drop-in centre for the general public. The drop-in centre offers computer training, weekend (supplementary) school for African languages/homework support, legal support services, accommodation referral services for young people and asylum seekers/refugees who are homeless, support/assistance for Start up community organisations, international youth exchange and advice and assistance on business and charities, African indoor games, and volunteering opportunities. We need volunteers in our London office, in Amsterdam and also in Nigeria. In Nigeria we need volunteers in Beyelsa State in the Niger Delta. This area, which produces over 95% of the Nigerian oil/gas revenue, has very poor and neglected people. There is very little or no portable drinkable water, electricity, transportation, housing, medicare and educational facilities and their environment is devastated by oil/gas exploration and exploitation. Volunteers with an offending background may be accepted subject to appropriate checks. Based in Bayelsa State in the Niger Delta, Southern Nigeria.

Number of projects: 2 UK: 1
Starting months: January–December
Time required: 12–52 weeks
Age: 18–60
Causes: Addicts/Ex-Addicts, AIDS/HIV, Children, Conservation, Disabled (learning and physical), Elderly People, Environmental Causes, Health Care/Medical, Heritage, Human Rights, Inner City Problems, Offenders/Ex-Offenders, Poor/Homeless, Refugees, Teaching/assisting (nursery, primary, secondary, mature, EFL) Unemployed, Wildlife, Work Camps – Seasonal, Young People.
Activities: Administration, Agriculture/Farming, Arts/Crafts, Building/Construction, Campaigning, Caring (general and day), Catering, Community Work, Computers, Conservation Skills, Counselling, Development Issues, DIY, Driving, First Aid, Forestry, Fundraising, Group Work, International Aid, Library/Resource Centres, Manual Work, Marketing/Publicity, Music, Newsletter/Journalism, Outdoor Skills, Research, Social Work, Sport, Teaching, Technical Skills, Theatre/Drama, Training, Translating, Visiting/Befriending, Work Camps – Seasonal.
Placements: 11
When to apply: As early as possible.
Work alone/with others: With other young volunteers.
Qualifications: No qualifications required but interest and commitment.
Equipment/clothing: No special equipment required.
Health requirements: Innoculations need to be checked out with volunteer's own doctor.
Costs: Travel to Nigeria or Amsterdam. Subsistence between £100 and £200 per month depending on the city/area.
Benefits: Board and lodging plus pocket money whilst serving in Nigeria.
Training: Induction to the project and introduction to Nigeria.
Supervision: A volunteer Project Manager is available and he reports to the management committee.
Interviews: Interviews at our Battersea London office.
Charity number: 1026307

Worldwide placements: Africa (Nigeria); Europe (Netherlands).
UK placements: England (London).

IJGD Internationale Jugendgemeinschaft Dienste eV.

Kaiserstrasse 43
D-53113 Bonn
Germany
T: 00 49 228 2280011
F: 00 49 228 2280024
E: djia@ev-freiwilligendienste.de
W: www.ijgd.de
Contact: The Secretary General

The IJGD needs volunteers to work on summer projects such as environmental protection, the restoration of educational centres, and to assist with city fringe recreational activities. 30 hours per week of work.

Number of projects: 12 **UK:** 0
Starting months: Jun, Jul, Aug, Sep
Time required: 3–52 weeks
Age: 16–25
Causes: Archaeology, Conservation, Elderly People, Environmental Causes, Work Camps – Seasonal.
Activities: Arts/Crafts, Building/Construction, Conservation Skills, Forestry, Gardening/Horticulture, Manual Work, Social Work, Work Camps – Seasonal.
Placements: 6,000 short and long-term.
When to apply: As soon as possible.
Work alone/with others: With others.
Qualifications: Knowledge of German only required on social projects.
Costs: Travel expenses.
Benefits: Free board and accommodation and insurance.
Training: None.
Supervision: Group leaders and work instructors.
Interviews: Usually no interview.
Worldwide placements: Africa (Morocco, Sierra Leone, Togo, Tunisia, Zimbabwe); North America: (USA); Central America (Mexico); Asia (India, Indonesia, Japan, Korea (South), Nepal); Europe (Armenia, Belarus, Belgium, Bulgaria, Czech Republic, Denmark, Estonia, Finland, France, Germany, Greece, Italy, Lithuania, Netherlands, Poland, Russia, Slovakia, Spain, Turkey, Ukraine).

ILOS-TANZANIA

Oysterbay
Karume Road
P O Box 6995
Dar es Salaam
Tanzania
T: 00 255 022 245 1079
F: 00 255 022 211 2572
E: ilos-tz@cc.udsm.ac.tz

Contact: Mr Stan Tinsh Bash

ILOS is a non-government organisation which deals with the 'education for human development without borders'. It was established in 1989 with its main office in Dar es Salaam. From here it runs other centres countrywide including Dar es Salaam, Zanzibar, Arusha, Mwanza, Kagera, Kigoma, Iringa and Morogoro. The education programmes range from kindergarten, primary, secondary to adult education. We offer language training and translation programmes to adults, organisations and various diplomatic missions such as UNDP, USAID, UNHCR, UNICEF, NORAD, SIDA, WHO. The languages are English, French, German, Spanish, Italian, Portuguese, Arabic, Kiswahili, Japanese and any other according to demand. The main aim on language training is to bring the world to work closely together without any language barriers. Moreover, ILOS is the authorised examination centre for Cambridge University in Tanzania. It runs student exchange programmes with some schools in UK, France, USA, Switzerland, Germany and Japan. ILOS formal programmes are meant to promote education for girls, especially those orphaned by HIV/AIDS. These children are exempted from paying school fees in order that they may study at ILOS English Medium Nursery Schools countrywide, ILOS Primary School in Zanzibar and ILOS Secondary School in Dar es Salaam. ILOS was (1994–6) an implementing partner with UNHCR running the education programmes for refugees children in northern Tanzania. Presently it is engaged in the rehabilitation programmes for the most affected areas by refugee influx. These programmes include: renewable energy, environment, water supply and sanitation, health care and counselling, women empowerment, promotion of handicraft and heritage, education on HIV/AIDS and agriculture. Volunteers are placed in schools or in one of the integrated community service programmes. In order to get these programmes sustainable, we also need volunteers with fundraising skills and computer skills to assist in the management. Dar es Salaam, Zanzibar, Arusha, Mwanza, Kagera, Kigoma, Morogoro, Shinyanga and Iringa.

Number of projects: 5 **UK:** 0
Starting months: Jan, Feb
Time required: 12–52 weeks
Age: 22–45
Causes: AIDS/HIV, Architecture, Children, Conservation, Environmental Causes, Health Care/Medical, Heritage, Poor/Homeless, Refugees, Teaching/assisting (nursery, primary, secondary, mature, EFL) Work Camps – Seasonal, Young People.
Activities: Administration, Agriculture/Farming, Arts/Crafts, Community Work, Computers, Conservation Skills, Cooking, Counselling,

Development Issues, First Aid, Fundraising, Gardening/Horticulture, International Aid, Library/Resource Centres, Manual Work, Marketing/Publicity, Music, Outdoor Skills, Scientific Work, Social Work, Sport, Summer Camps, Teaching, Technical Skills, Theatre/Drama, Training, Translating, Work Camps – Seasonal.
Placements: 10
When to apply: September–November.
Work alone/with others: With other young volunteers.
Qualifications: Driving licence, language ability. Teachers need a first degree in order to obtain a work permit. Other community services volunteers need a diploma/qualification in the relevant field.
Equipment/clothing: Formal clothing during work sessions but during free time casual clothing is all right.
Health requirements: Should be physically fit.
Costs: Return air fare, health and personal insurance.
Benefits: $100 per month paid to volunteers for meals and other needs. Accommodation also provided with basic needs: furniture, fridge, cooker, utensils, iron, running water, electricity etc.
Training: Swahili and cultural orientation training provided.
Supervision: Volunteers are paired to local staff and there is head of the programme who supervises, i.e. headmistress, field officer, co-ordinator etc.
Interviews: Interviews are by telephone or with special arrangement in the UK or in the USA.
Charity number: S.16350
Worldwide placements: Africa (Tanzania).

INDEPENDENT LIVING ALTERNATIVES

Trafalgar House
Grenville Place
London
NW7 3SA UK
T: +44 (0) 208 906 9265
F: +44 (0) 208 906 9265
E: mail@I-L-A.fsnet.co.uk
W: www.I-L-A.fsnet.co.uk
Contact: Tracey Jannaway

Independent Living Alternatives is a voluntary organisation managed by people with disabilities. It aims to facilitate freedom in living for people with physical disabilities in the London Boroughs. ILA recruits full time volunteers to enable people who require physical support to be independent in the community to take full control of their own lives. ILA recruits and places voluntary personal care assistants to provide support, such as cooking, cleaning, driving, etc., on a one to one

basis through a philosophy of equality and interdependency. ILA needs full time volunteers, who have four months to spare, to provide physical support to people with physical disabilities in the London area. In return volunteers receive £63.50 per week living expenses and free accommodation (no bills). No experience is necessary. Volunteers receive on-demand support as and when required and are able to participate in the running of the organisation and to attend workshops on volunteering issues. ILA also provides support, advocacy and advice to disabled people and campaigns to raise the awareness of disability issues around independent living. It produces the publications 'A Strategy for Independent Living in London' and 'Independent Living Through Personal Assistance'. Volunteers with an offending background will be accepted depending on when, where, how etc. London and Cumbria. 🖰 🗈

Number of projects: 20 UK: 20
Starting months: January–December
Time required: 21–52 weeks
Age: 18 plus – no upper limit
Causes: Disabled (physical).
Activities: Caring – General, Counselling, Driving, Social Work.
Placements: 50
When to apply: All year.
Work alone/with others: Alone but live with others on time off.
Qualifications: Driving licence useful and English essential but no experience necessary.
Health requirements: Nil.
Costs: No direct costs, but enquire.
Benefits: Accommodation + £63.50 per week + expenses.
Training: On-site with service user. All training is provided to new volunteers.
Supervision: On demand by phone/in person/Internet. Regular volunteer meetings.
Interviews: Interviews are conducted in ILA London office – can be by phone if neccesary.
Charity number: 802198
UK placements: England (Cumbria, Essex, London).

INDEPENDENT LIVING SCHEMES, LEWISHAM SOCIAL CARE AND HEALTH

Lewisham Social Care and Health
John Henry House
299 Verdant Lane
Catford
London SE6 1TP UK
T: +44 (0) 208 314 7239
F: +44 (0) 208 314 3013
E: ken.smith@lewisham.gov.uk
W: www.lewisham.gov.uk
Contact: Kenneth Smith

Independent Living enables severely disabled people to hold on to their civil rights. Volunteer helpers help this process by working directly for the person they are assisting. Each disabled person (ILS User) has two or three volunteers working directly for him or her. Assistance with bodily functions, i.e. eating, toileting, bathing is required but the volunteers can also help to facilitate social activity. Volunteers can find their experience is of value in getting paid work in the caring professions and, importantly, teaches them that people are disabled by their environment rather than by their impairment. Volunteers with an offending background are accepted – police checks made anyway. We will try to sponsor visas or work permits if required by UK Government. Preferred minimum placement is six months. Placements can be extended up to two years. (Personal callers only by appointment.) London Borough of Lewisham, SE London. ♿ 📄

Number of projects UK: 3
Starting months: January–December
Time required: 26–52 weeks (plus)
Age: 17 plus – no upper limit
Causes: Disabled (physical), Human Rights.
Activities: Caring – General, Community Work, Cooking.
Placements: 12
When to apply: All year.
Work alone/with others: On their own but as part of a team of 2 or 3.
Health requirements: Must be capable of lifting without harming user or themselves.
Costs: No cost to volunteer.
Benefits: Accommodation, £23 pocket money +£37 food per week + £15 per month clothing/leisure. All bills paid including free local telephone calls. Free membership of Lewisham libraries and discounts on Lewisham leisure facilities. Furnished accommodation provided free, shared with other volunteers assisting the same disabled person. All bills paid including local telephone calls. Internet access not allowed at accommodation – Internet access is free at all Lewisham libraries.
Training: By disabled person being assisted.
Supervision: Support available from Lewisham Social Care and Health.
Interviews: Interviews are conducted in ILS London office.
UK placements: England (London).

INDIA DEVELOPMENT GROUP (UK) LTD

68 Downlands Road
Purley
Surrey CR8 4JF UK
T: +44 (0) 208 668 3161
F: +44 (0) 208 660 8541
E: idguk@clara.co.uk

W: www.welcome.to/idg
Contact: Mr Surur Hoda

The India Development Group (UK) Ltd (IDG) aims to alleviate rural poverty in India by trying to enhance personal income through village-based mini industries, using appropriate and sustainable forms of technology. To this end IDG (UK) Ltd has helped to set up two associate organisations in India: (a) The Appropriate Technology Development Association (ATDA – founded in 1975) is a research and implementation agency; (b) The Schumacher Institute of Appropriate Technology (SIAT – founded in 1988) provides training in equipment using such technology and other service areas identified as the greatest needs for rural people, such as social forestry, weaving, primary health care etc. (c) IDG (India chapter) is currently carrying out women's empowerment project funded by National Lotteries Charities Board, 3 year of 5 year funded project.

Number of projects: 5 **UK:** 0
Starting months: January–December
Time required: 12–52 weeks (plus)
Age: 18–65
Causes: AIDS/HIV, Environmental Causes, Health Care/Medical, Human Rights, Poor/Homeless, Teaching/assisting (nursery, primary, secondary), Unemployed, Young People.
Activities: Agriculture/Farming, Building/Construction, Community Work, Development Issues, First Aid, Forestry, Fundraising, Social Work, Teaching, Technical Skills, Training.
Placements: Changes each year.
When to apply: All year.
Work alone/with others: With others or alone, depending on project.
Qualifications: Preferably at least A level. Specialist/vocational qualifications and skills relevant to projects preferred.
Equipment/clothing: May be specific to project.
Health requirements: Volunteers must be in good health.
Costs: £110 approx. per month + air fare to India, visas, innoculations etc.
Benefits: Friendly project teams, secure living environment, meet other volunteers, experience different culture, learn new language etc. Accommodation in IDG guesthouse.
Training: General briefing.
Supervision: Supervisors/project team are provided in the area of specialisation.
Interviews: Interviews take place at our office in England.
Charity number: 291167
Worldwide placements: Asia (India).

INDIAN ASSOCIATION OF VOLUNTEER EFFORT

People's House Paryavaran Complex
Shidulla Jab
New Delhi
110030 India
T: 00 91 1 1689 5091
F: 00 91 1 1689 4407
E: pidt.@del6.vsnl.net.in
Contact: Indira Dasgupta

Indian Assocation of Volunteer Effort promotes
and has information about volunteering in
India. It may well be able to put volunteers in
touch with organisations which are not yet
listed on the WorldWide Volunteering database.

Starting months: January–December
Time required: 1–52 weeks (plus)
Age: 16 plus – no upper limit
Causes: Addicts/Ex-Addicts, AIDS/HIV, Animal
Welfare, Archaeology, Architecture, Children,
Conservation, Disabled (learning and physical),
Elderly People, Environmental Causes, Health
Care/Medical, Heritage, Holidays for Disabled,
Human Rights, Inner City Problems, Offenders/
Ex-Offenders, Poor/Homeless, Refugees,
Teaching/assisting (nursery, primary, secondary,
mature, EFL) Unemployed, Wildlife, Work
Camps – Seasonal, Young People.
Activities: Accountancy, Administration,
Agriculture/Farming, Arts/Crafts, Building/
Construction, Campaigning, Caring (general,
day and residential), Catering, Community
Work, Computers, Conservation Skills,
Cooking, Counselling, Development Issues,
DIY, Driving, First Aid, Forestry, Fundraising,
Gardening/Horticulture, Group Work,
International Aid, Library/Resource Centres,
Manual Work, Marketing/Publicity, Music,
Newsletter/Journalism, Outdoor Skills, Religion,
Research, Scientific Work, Social Work, Sport,
Summer Camps, Teaching, Technical Skills,
Theatre/Drama, Training, Translating,
Visiting/Befriending, Work Camps – Seasonal.
Costs: Varies according to the project.
Worldwide placements: Asia (India).

INDIAN VOLUNTEERS FOR COMMUNITY SERVICE (IVCS)

12 Eastleigh Avenue
Harrow
Middlesex HA2 OUF UK
T: +44 (0) 208 864 4740
E: enquiries@ivcs.org.uk
W: www.ivcs.org.uk
Contact: Jyoti Singh

This Indian Volunteers for Community Service
programme is intended for members of IVCS
over the age of 18 who are interested in going
to India but want to be more than just tourists.

It gives them an opportunity to meet rural
Indians and learn about their culture. Under
this scheme, project visitors can spend up to six
months living in a rural development project in
India, experiencing life in the local community
and participating in rural development work.
Orientation Project is situated 120 miles east of
Delhi in Uttar Pradesh.

Number of projects: 22 UK: 0
Starting months: Jan, Feb, Mar, Sep, Oct, Nov
Time required: 3–26 weeks
Age: 18–65
Causes: Children, Conservation, Environmental
Causes, Health Care/Medical, Poor/Homeless,
Teaching/assisting (nursery, primary,
secondary, EFL).
Activities: Accountancy, Administration,
Agriculture/Farming, Arts/Crafts, Computers,
Conservation Skills, Development Issues,
Forestry, Fundraising, Gardening/Horticulture,
Group Work, International Aid, Library/
Resource Centres, Marketing/Publicity, Music,
Newsletter/Journalism, Research, Teaching.
Placements: 50
When to apply: 4 months before intended
departure date.
Work alone/with others: Both.
Qualifications: None necessary.
Health requirements: Innoculations necessary.
Costs: Applicants pay all their own travel and
personal expenses, membership £15.
Orientation in UK and three weeks orientation
in India £160. Further stays at projects in India
£3 a day board and lodging.
Benefits: Opportunity to absorb the culture of
India and learn about rural life and
development work. Basic accommodation,
shared, on projects.
Training: Orientation day (London) and 3
weeks orientation in India.
Supervision: Project staff supervise volunteers
during 3 week orientation. After that there is no
specific supervision.
Interviews: Prospective volunteers are
interviewed in London or for overseas
applicants, by telephone and must attend an
orientation day in London.
Charity number: 285872
Worldwide placements: Asia (India).

INFORMATION FOR ACTION

P. O. Box 1040
West Leederville
6901 Western Australia
T: 00 61 8 9228 0395
E: rowland@informaction.org
W: www.informaction.org
Contact: Dr Rowland Benjamin

Information is a free automated lobbying
service for anyone interested in the
environment. The web site enables people to

contact their leaders (governments and companies worldwide) easily and quickly and ask them to respect the environment. The work volunteers do on the web site writing about issues, drafting letters, advertising the web site and updating changes of contacts names and addresses depends on their level of skill and interest in the environment. It may include scanning; word processing; programming; data entry; creating animations; creating sound files; searching the net, our own database, CD Roms, telephone directory or local library for politicians' or company directors' contact details. We are currently engaged in increasing our subjects, letters and contacts; writing an environment awareness game/quiz for kids; linking with like-minded groups; advertising; and maintaining the web site. Our goal is basically to increase lobbying pressure on the world's leaders, support direct action and provide ideas for individual change. Inner city Perth, W. Australia.

Number of projects: 1 **UK:** 0
Starting months: January–December
Time required: 2–50 weeks
Age: 20–70
Causes: Conservation, Environmental Causes, Wildlife.
Activities: Administration, Campaigning, Computers, Conservation Skills, Library/ Resource Centres, Newsletter/Journalism, Research, Scientific Work.
Placements: 10
When to apply: All year.
Work alone/with others: Both.
Qualifications: Basic computer skills to build the web pages and/or volunteers with environmental knowledge to help update the information and add new subjects.
Health requirements: Alert and intelligent.
Costs: Travel, accommodation, food.
Training: Provided.
Supervision: Ongoing supervision.
Interviews: Prospective volunteers are only interviewed by telephone or e-mail.
Worldwide placements: Australasia (Australia).

INNISFREE VILLAGE

5505 Walnut Level Road
Crozet
Virginia 22932 USA
T: 00 1 (434) 823 5400
F: 00 1 (434) 823 5027
E: innisfreevillage@prodigy.net
W: www.avenue.org/innisfree
Contact: Nancy Chappell

Innisfree Village is a lifesharing community with adults who have mental disabilities and the volunteers who come from all over the world to share a year of their lives with us.

Volunteers also work in our weavery, woodshop, bakery, kitchen and gardens. We are on a 550 acre farm in central Virginia, close to Charlottesville, a University town.

Number of projects: 1 **UK:** 0
Starting months: January–December
Time required: 52 weeks
Age: 21–65
Causes: Disabled (learning and physical), Health Care/Medical, Teaching/assisting, Work Camps – Seasonal.
Activities: Agriculture/Farming, Arts/Crafts, Caring (general, residential), Cooking, Counselling, Driving, Gardening/Horticulture, Group Work, Manual Work, Social Work, Sport, Teaching, Training, Work Camps – Seasonal.
Placements: 15
When to apply: All year.
Work alone/with others: With others.
Qualifications: Related experience or college graduates, fluent English, patience, good sense of humour. No nationality restrictions – dependent on ability to get B1/2 visa.
Equipment/clothing: No particular needs.
Health requirements: Chest x-ray to prove free from TB.
Costs: Travel costs return to USA.
Benefits: Board/lodging, US$215 per month, medical insurance (not pre-existing conditions), 15 days holiday. Own room in a shared house with 1–2 volunteers and 2–6 residents (co-workers).
Training: One month orientation. Training in Medical Assistance, CPR and First Aid is given.
Supervision: After one month volunteers are working in teams of 2–4. Support by long-term staff at all times.
Interviews: Applicants are not interviewed – there is a one month trial period.
Worldwide placements: North America: (USA).

INSIGHT NEPAL

P.O. Box 489
Zero K.M.
Pokhara
Kaski Nepal
T: 00 977 061 30266
E: insight@fewanet.com.np
W: www.insightnepal.org
Contact: Naresh M. Shrestha

Insight Nepal was established with a view not only to introduce participants to Nepal's diverse geographical and cultural environment, but also to establish and foster an awareness and understanding of cultural differences through experience. This placement scheme is designed to leave the participant with more than photographs. The participant will learn about the world by working to make it better. Insight Nepal believes that serving others is one of the most worthwhile human endeavours. The main objective of the programme is to provide opportunities to those who are keenly interested in gaining a cultural experience by contributing their time and skills to benefit worthwhile community service groups throughout the kingdom. Our second objective is to help those who are looking for an opportunity to reach people and community groups who are in need of their skills. Placements will be located in the different areas of Pokhara and Kathmandu valleys. 🔊 📄

Number of projects: 1 **UK:** 0
Starting months: January–December
Time required: 4–12 weeks
Age: 18–70
Causes: AIDS/HIV, Children, Disabled (physical), Environmental Causes, Health Care/ Medical, Teaching/assisting (nursery, primary, secondary, mature, EFL).
Activities: Administration, Agriculture/Farming, Community Work, Computers, Counselling, Development Issues, Fundraising, Music, Outdoor Skills, Research, Social Work, Sport, Teaching, Technical Skills, Training.
Placements: 60
When to apply: 3 months in advance for the 3 month programmes.
6 weeks in advance for the 4–6 week programmes
Work alone/with others: Alone or in pairs.
Qualifications: Minimum A level or equivalent.
Equipment/clothing: We will notify you about equipment.
Health requirements: Physically fit and immunised against certain diseases.
Costs: US$40 application fee (non refundable) US$800 programme fee for 3 months or US$400 programme fee (for Nepal) or US$500 programme fee (for India) 4–6 weeks + visa fee + fares + insurance.
Benefits: Full board and accommodation. 1 week language/cultural training. 1 week village trip. 3-day jungle safari (for 3 month participants).
Training: Volunteers will be provided with a short Nepali language training course.
Supervision: Insight Nepal organise supervision of volunteers during placement period, as and when necessary.
Interviews: Through application form.
Worldwide placements: Asia (India, Nepal).

INSTITUT D'HISTOIRE

Université du Mans
Avenue O. Messiaen
Le Mans
F-72017 France
T: 00 33 2 43 83 31 64
F: 00 33 2 43 83 31 44
E: www@univ-lemans.fr
Contact: Annie Renoux

Institut d'Histoire needs volunteers to assist on archaeological digs. Eight hour day, five and a half day week.

Number of projects: 1
Starting months: Jul
Time required: 3–52 weeks
Age: 18 plus – no upper limit
Causes: Archaeology, Heritage.
Activities: Manual Work, Technical Skills.
Placements: 20
When to apply: April
Work alone/with others: With others.
Qualifications: Knowledge of French or English.
Health requirements: Good health.
Benefits: Board and lodging provided free.
Worldwide placements: Europe (France).

INSTITUTE FOR EARTH EDUCATION

Cedar Cove
Box 115
Greenville
West Virginia 24945 USA
T: 00 1 304 832 6404
F: 00 1 304 832 6077
E: IEE1@aol.com
W: www.eartheducation.org
Contact: Office Co-ordinator

The Institute for Earth Education is for people who want to live more lightly on the earth's environment. We are concerned with environmental issues and need help in building Cedar Cove, shipping educational details and teaching by doing – from the ground up. Organic gardening is not a theory here, it is a daily activity from early spring until early winter. Volunteers with an offending background may be accepted (visas permitting) on a case by case basis. Greenville, West Virginia, USA. 📄

Number of projects: 1 **UK:** 0
Starting months: January–December
Time required: 8–52 weeks (plus)
Age: 18 plus – no upper limit
Causes: Conservation, Environmental Causes.
Activities: Agriculture/Farming, Building/Construction, Gardening/Horticulture, Manual Work.
Placements: 6
When to apply: All year.
Work alone/with others: With other young volunteers.
Qualifications: Spoken English.
Equipment/clothing: Outdoor clothing.
Health requirements: No requirements.
Costs: Travel and personal expenses.

Benefits: We give $20 per week for food and we provide housing.
Training: Limited training is given. Guidance given at all times.
Supervision: Supervision available Monday-Friday, 9am – 5pm.
Interviews: No interviews but recommendations required.
Worldwide placements: North America: (USA).

INSTITUTE FOR ENVIRONMENT AND DEVELOPMENT STUDIES – BANGLADESH

5/12–15 Eastern View (5th Floor)
50 D.I.T. Extension Road
G.P.O. Box No. 3691
Dhaka – 1000
Bangladesh
T: 00 880 2 935 4128
F: 00 880 2 831 5394
E: iedsfoeb@accesstel.net
Contact: Mr Amir Hossain Chowdhury

Institute for Environment and Development Studies is an organisation and a federation of grass root organisations/associations that deals with various environmental issues of land, water and air. It is committed to the preservation, restoration and rational use of the environment. IEDS was founded in 1985 and is registered with Social Welfare Ministry of the Government of Bangladesh. The Institute was awarded the consultative status of UN ECOSOC in 2000. IEDS was given the Membership of International Federation of Organic Agriculture Movements (IFOAM) in 2003. The institute mainly campaigns by writing articles in the press and by creating publicity. Other than that, the organisation sometimes organises field projects related to the environment and pressurises the Bangladesh government with great success. IEDS also concentrates on human rights abuse in the sub-continent. Volunteers are always needed to help with a wide variety of campaigns/projects.

Number of projects: Many UK: 0
Starting months: January–December
Time required: 2–50 weeks
Age: 16–40
Causes: Children, Conservation, Disabled (learning and physical), Environmental Causes, Human Rights, Poor/Homeless, Refugees, Teaching/assisting (primary), Unemployed, Wildlife, Young People.
Activities: Administration, Agriculture/Farming, Campaigning, Community Work, Computers, Conservation Skills, Development Issues, Forestry, Fundraising, International Aid, Library/Resource Centres, Manual Work, Newsletter/Journalism, Research, Social Work, Training.

Placements: 5–7
When to apply: All year.
Work alone/with others: Both.
Qualifications: Basic orientation and commitment to the environment.
Equipment/clothing: Depends on project.
Health requirements: Innoculations required for Bangladesh.
Costs: Fares and living costs. Accommodation either in homestays with families or at village lodges etc.
Training: On-the-job training.
Supervision: Experienced group leaders (local) are present at all camps and permanent staff manage the service.
Interviews: Are conducted by a team of campaigners.
Charity number: J-01947
Worldwide placements: Asia (Bangladesh).

INSTITUTE OF SOCIAL ECOLOGY AND TOURISM

Baikalskaya Str.279
Irkutsk
664050 Russia
T: 00 3952 259 215 or 430 417
E: bienru@bbc.ru
Contact: Alexander Vlassov

Institute of Social Ecology and Tourism runs international ecological work camps on the shores of Lake Baikal and welcomes volunteers of all nationalities. Each workcamp runs for two weeks beginning 1 May until 3 October. We hope to see you on the shores of Lake Baikal this summer. There is something for everyone to enjoy in the region. We can arrange a visa support for you within three days. It will be valid for three weeks and costs US$10. If you wish to stay here longer it is possible to extend your visa.

Number of projects: 1 UK: 0
Starting months: May, Jun, Jul, Aug, Sep
Time required: 2–8 weeks
Age: 17 plus – no upper limit
Causes: Conservation, Environmental Causes.
Activities: Agriculture/Farming, Building/Construction, Conservation Skills, Forestry, Gardening/Horticulture, Group Work, International Aid, Manual Work, Outdoor Skills, Summer Camps, Work Camps – Seasonal.
When to apply: All year.
Work alone/with others: With others.
Health requirements: Good health.
Costs: US$200 per workcamp of 2 weeks. Thereafter each week costs US$70. Return travel from your country to Irkutsk.
Benefits: All transfers, accommodation in the camp, full board, guide service.
Interviews: No interview.
Worldwide placements: Europe (Russia).

INSTITUTO DA JUVENTUDE

Av. da Liberdade 194
6th Floor
1250 Lisboa
Portugal
T: 00 351 213 179200 or 170200 or 536947
E: carlos.rapoula@ipj.pt
Contact: Mr Carlos Rapoula

Instituto da Juventude organises around 37
international workcamps each summer.
Volunteers are needed to assist with construction
and reconstruction work, protection of the
natural environment and the protection and
restoration of Portugal's cultural heritage.

Number of projects: 1 UK: 0
Starting months: Apr, May, Jun, Jul, Aug
Time required: 2–52 weeks
Age: 18 plus – no upper limit
Causes: Conservation, Environmental Causes,
Heritage, Work Camps – Seasonal.
Activities: Building/Construction, Conservation
Skills, Manual Work, Work Camps – Seasonal.
Placements: 740
When to apply: February or March.
Work alone/with others: With others.
Benefits: Board and lodging.
Worldwide placements: Europe (Portugal).

INTEGRATED SOCIAL DEVELOPMENT EFFORT (ISDE)

House #485
Road #01, Block-B
Chandgoan R/A
Chittagong – 4212
Bangladesh
T: 00 880 31 671727
F: 00 880 31 610774
E: isde@abnetbd.com
Contact: S. M. Nazer Hossain

ISDE was established by some like-minded
young people of Cox's Bazar, Bangladesh, in
1987 as a private, non-profit, non-
governmental voluntary, development
organisation to fight illiteracy, ignorance,
poverty and hunger and to improve the health
of the community people. Initially it was a local
voluntary youth organisation but after the
devastating cyclone of 1991 ISDE participated
in rescue, relief and rehabilitation for the
victims with the support of a number of
national and international organisations.
Resulting from that, it has developed into a
professional development organisation to serve
the poorest of the poor. The following is a
synopsis of the activities we are involved in:
Micro-credit for income and employment
generation for women.
Non-formal education programme: this is
responsible for a large increase in the literacy
rate in the operational areas.
Community-based primary health care
programme: for preventative and curative
maternal and child health service in 5000
households. Participatory social forestry
programme: For this coastal disaster prone zone
of the country, social forestation is most
important.
Nutrition education and homestead gardening
programme: 90 village nurseries for year-round
vegetable production.
Safe water supply and sanitation programme.
Disaster preparedness and response programme.
Coastal embankment maintenance programme.
NGO networking and partnership programme:
to build better understanding on gender,
environment and human rights.
Tribal community development programme: to
develop the indigenous tribal ethnic
community.
Human rights and legal education programme.
Coastal fisheries community development.
STD/AIDS prevention and education.
Fisheries and livestock development
programme.
Regenerative agriculture programme.
Rural volunteer programme.
Action against child and women trafficking.
Disability and development programme. S.E.
Bangladesh, close to the Hindu Kush-Himalayas
region, the Bay of Bengal and Myanmar
(Burma). 🖫

Number of projects: 10 in Bangladesh UK: 0
Starting months: January–December
Time required: 2–52 weeks
Age: 20–38
Causes: AIDS/HIV, Children, Conservation,
Environmental Causes, Health Care/Medical,
Heritage, Human Rights, Poor/Homeless,
Teaching/assisting (nursery, primary, secondary,
mature, EFL) Unemployed, Young People.
Activities: Administration, Agriculture/Farming,
Arts/Crafts, Building/Construction, Caring –
General, Community Work, Conservation
Skills, Counselling, Development Issues,
Forestry, Gardening/Horticulture, Group Work,
International Aid, Manual Work, Outdoor Skills,
Social Work, Teaching, Technical Skills, Training.
Placements: 20
When to apply: All year.
Work alone/with others: Foreign volunteers
work with a local counterpart.
Qualifications: None required but any
specialisation or skill in relevant fields are
welcomed and encouraged. Most nationalities
accepted.
Equipment/clothing: Blanket and personal
clothing is required.
Health requirements: Malaria prophylactics
and usual travel pills required.
Costs: All travel costs. Registration fees of
US$100. Food costs.

Benefits: Accommodation, local travel costs, cooking facilities. The lodging is provided through ISDE's own hostel or sometimes with ISDE's staff members' families.
Training: ISDE provides basic orientation on Bangla language and local culture also.
Supervision: The director is the overall supervisor. Team managers of each project supervise the volunteer.
Interviews: No interviews – but CVs are required before a volunteer is accepted.
Charity number: FDR-803
Worldwide placements: Asia (Bangladesh).

INTER-ACTION TRUST

HMS President (1918)
Victoria Embankment
London
EC4Y 0HJ UK
T: +44 (0) 207 583 2652
T: +44 (0) 207 583 2840
Contact: Charlotte

Inter-Action Trust is an educational charity which trains inner city and deprived young people in media, computer and office skills. 🖹

Number of projects: 1 UK: 1
Starting months: January–December
Time required: 1–52 weeks
Age: 16 plus – no upper limit
Causes: Inner City Problems, Young People.
Activities: Administration, Manual Work, Training.
When to apply: All year.
Work alone/with others: With others.
Health requirements: Nil.
Costs: Food, accommodation and travel.
Benefits: Expenses and lunch allowance.
UK placements: England (London).

INTERCULTURAL YOUTH EXCHANGE

Latin American House
Kingsgate Place
London
NW6 4TA UK
T: +44 (0) 207 681 0983
T: +44 (0) 207 681 0983
E: info@icye.co.uk
W: www.icye.co.uk
Contact: Miguel Gonzalez

Inter-Cultural Youth Exchange – UK (ICYE-UK) aims to promote peace, cultural understanding and youth empowerment through opportunities for international exchange and voluntary work overseas. A nationally recognised charity working in the area of youth development, ICYE-UK sends individuals who want to broaden their horizons, develop personally and make a difference to live and work with communities throughout the world for a year or six months. Placements include drug rehabilitation programmes, working with street children, human rights projects, and HIV programmes. Participants gain valuable work experience, learn a new language and develop important vocational, interpersonal and cultural skills through their experience abroad. ICYE-UK is part of a worldwide federation of independent youth organisations established in 1949 with a head office in Berlin and national offices in over 30 different countries. The organisation has consultative status with UNESCO, and works in partnership with the European Commission's 'Youth for Europe' Programme, the Council of Europe (European Youth Directive) and Mobility International. In addition ICYE has been recognised as an 'International Peace Messenger' by the United Nations General Assembly. We particularly encourage applications from individuals who have experienced some form of social exclusion as a result of class, ethnicity, sexuality and disability etc. 🖹

Number of projects: 600 UK: 0
Starting months: Jan, Jul
Time required: 26–52 weeks
Age: 18–30
Causes: Addicts/Ex-Addicts, AIDS/HIV, Children, Conservation, Disabled (learning and physical), Elderly People, Environmental Causes, Health Care/Medical, Human Rights, Poor/Homeless, Refugees, Teaching/assisting (nursery, primary, secondary, EFL), Young People.
Activities: Administration, Agriculture/Farming, Arts/Crafts, Caring (general, day and residential), Community Work, Conservation Skills, Development Issues, Fundraising, Group Work, International Aid, Newsletter/Journalism, Outdoor Skills, Social Work, Teaching, Training, Translating.
Placements: 50
When to apply: September to March (late applications accepted).
Work alone/with others: With others.
Qualifications: Maturity and flexibility. Must be a UK resident. Other applicants should apply through their national committee, see separate international web site (www.icye.org) for details.
Health requirements: Nil.
Costs: £2,850–£3,150 for outside Europe. Free within Europe.
Benefits: The cost covers preparation, training, seminars, flight, insurance, board, lodging and pocket money. Accommodation in host families (Latin America, Africa, Europe) or provided by work project (Africa, Asia, Europe).
Training: Preparation weekend in UK before departure and orientation and language course upon arrival in host country.
Supervision: Volunteers normally have a supervisor at project plus a mentor/contact

person from our partner organisation in host country.
Interviews: Open days and interviews arranged in London on a regular basis.
Charity number: 1039310
Worldwide placements: Africa (Egypt, Ghana, Kenya, Morocco, Mozambique, Nigeria, Uganda); Central America (Costa Rica, Honduras, Mexico); South America (Bolivia, Brazil, Colombia); Asia (India, Japan, Korea (South), Nepal, Taiwan, Thailand, Turkey); Australasia (New Zealand); Europe (Austria, Belgium, Denmark, Estonia, Finland, France, Germany, Iceland, Italy, Poland, Portugal, Sweden, Switzerland, Ukraine).

INTERNASJONAL DUGNAD

Nordahl Brunsgate 22
0165 Oslo
Norway
T: 00 47 22113123
F: 00 47 22207119
E: ivs@ivsgbsouth.demon.co.uk
Contact:

Internasjonal Dugnad organises workcamps for volunteers in Norway. NB. All volunteers must apply through:
The Regional Co-ordinator
International Voluntary Service (IVS – South)
Old Hall
East Bergholt
Nr Colchester
Essex CO7 6TQ
T: 01206 298215
F: 01206 299043
E: ivs@ivsgbsouth.demon.co.uk.

Number of projects: 1 **UK:** 0
Starting months: January–December
Time required: 1–16 weeks
Age: 17 plus – no upper limit
Causes: Conservation, Environmental Causes, Heritage, Work Camps – Seasonal.
Activities: Conservation Skills, Group Work, Manual Work, Outdoor Skills, Technical Skills, Work Camps – Seasonal.
When to apply: All year.
Work alone/with others: With others.
Equipment/clothing: Any equipment needed would be supplied.
Health requirements: Nil.
Costs: Fares to Norway.
Interviews: Apply to Steve Davies at IVS-South for details.
Worldwide placements: Europe (Norway).

INTERNATIONAL CHINA CONCERN

P. O. Box 20
Morpeth
NE61 3YP UK
T: 00 44 1670 505622

F: 00 44 1670 505622
E: info@IntlChinaConcern.org
W: www.IntlChinaConcern.org
Contact: Richard Hubbard

International China Concern began in January 1993 after the executive director, Mr David J. Gotts travelled to an orphanage in Southern China to see the conditions that many of China's orphans are living in. At that time it was known that there were few organisations involved in relief work with Chinese orphans and so it was decided that an organisation would be set up to encourage those in the West and those in Asia to support these needy children. Initially the main work of ICC was to organise teams of lay and professional people, such as doctors, nurses, physiotherapists and occupational therapists, to visit orphanages in China and to be involved in the rehabilitation of disabled children and also train local workers. This work continues and international teams travel to the orphanages in China every few months. ICC also acts as a channel through which finances, medicines, clothing and rehabilitation equipment can be given to China's orphanages. Much has been done in the last few years. Since 1993 International China Concern has taken teams of people from all around the world, to serve in China's orphanages. These teams are made up of people from different backgrounds, cultures, ages and experience – but all have a heart to care for China's disadvantaged. Each trip lasts approximately two weeks and starts with orientation and team building. This allows team members to start to build relationships and lays the foundation for the practical ministry. Once in China you will work in small groups with specific children. They will range in ages and abilities, from babies to older disabled children. The trips take place three or four times a year and build on the work carried out by the permanent ICC team based at the orphanage. You do not have to be a professional – just willing to become Jesus' hands and feet. If you can hug a child, play with a child, pray with a child or help meet their basic needs, then you qualify. If you have medical, nursing or therapy background you can be sure it will be fully utilised during your stay. Over the last few years, dramatic changes have taken place in the lives of the children touched by ICC Short Term Teams. Each team builds on the one before, making lasting and solid changes, physically, emotionally and spiritually. Past team members describe their time in China as – 'enriching, ministering, touching, hilarious, everlasting' ... 'may be the most important two weeks of my life' ... 'a life changing experience'. In China, Guangxi and Hunan Province. 🚻 📷

Number of projects: 4 **UK:** 0
Starting months: January–December

Time required: 2–52 weeks
Age: 16–75
Causes: Children, Disabled (learning and physical), Health Care/Medical, Holidays for Disabled, Poor/Homeless, Teaching/assisting (nursery, primary, secondary), Work Camps – Seasonal, Young People.
Activities: Accountancy, Administration, Caring (general, day and residential), Computers, Development Issues, Fundraising, Group Work, Music, Outdoor Skills, Religion, Social Work, Summer Camps, Teaching, Technical Skills, Training, Translating.
Placements: 150
When to apply: Up to 2 month before start date.
Work alone/with others: With others.
Qualifications: Christian commitment. No restrictions, applicants under 18 years may be considered if accompanied.
Equipment/clothing: Nothing special.
Health requirements: ICC requires a health form to be completed with application.
Costs: Short term (16 days) £650 (excl. flight to HK). Medium/long term budgets available. All volunteers are expected to be self-financing. Accommodation is in Chinese standard hotel inside China. YMCA dormitory for 4 in Hong Kong.
Training: 2 days orientation takes place in Hong Kong before a team commences.
Supervision: ICC staff lead teams.
Interviews: Short-term volunteers only need references. Volunteers must have Christian commitment.
Charity number: 1068349
Worldwide placements: Asia (China, Hong Kong).

INTERNATIONAL ECOLOGICAL CAMP

P.O. Box 52
665718 Bratski-18
Irkutsk Region
Russia
T: 00 3953 364301
F: 00 3953 451579
E: tatyana@bratsk.esir.ru
Contact: Belyakova Lyudmila

International Ecological Camp organises voluntary service workcamps and cultural programmes in Siberia which give volunteers the opportunity to come to the heart of Russia and learn the legends, ideas and priorities of the Russians; the reality behind the news stories. Free time is spent swimming in nearby lakes, enjoying the campfire and the forest, sightseeing and experiencing local culture. Food is either cooked by the group or enjoyed at the cafe. The camp is on the bank of the Bratsk sea. Each workcamp lasts for one month and accommodates 30 people. Travel either by plane Moscow-Bratsk or by plane Moscow-Irkutsk and then train to Bratsk. Volunteers will be met at Bratsk airport or train station. If you decide to travel through Irkutsk we encourage you to visit Lake Baikal.

Number of projects: 1
Starting months: Jun, Jul, Aug
Time required: 4–12 weeks
Age: 19 plus – no upper limit
Causes: Children, Conservation, Environmental Causes, Heritage, Teaching/assisting (EFL), Work Camps – Seasonal.
Activities: Conservation Skills, Forestry, Teaching, Translating.
Placements: 80
When to apply: All year.
Work alone/with others: With others.
Qualifications: Volunteer workers none. Volunteer leaders needed to lead the work-camps must be fluent in Russian, interested in or experienced with the Russian language and culture and they must be TEFL qualified. Will apply for a visa once they have full name, date of birth and number of passport. No restrictions.
Costs: The price of the programme is $160 for 2 weeks and $240 per 4-week workcamp, which includes accommodation, 3 meals a day and a cultural programme every day.
Benefits: Volunteers are met at the airport or at the train station. Accommodation and meals provided. Accommodation is basic but comfortable in vacation cabins situated on the seashore.
Interviews: No interviews.
Worldwide placements: Europe (Russia).

INTERNATIONAL EXCHANGE CENTER

35 Ivor Place
London
NW1 6EA UK
T: +44 (0) 207 724 4493
E: isecinfo@btconnect.com
Contact: Patricia Santoriello

International Exchange Center needs camp leaders/sports instructors to work in children's summer camps on the Baltic Sea, and in other locations looking after children aged 8–15 years. 🖹

Number of projects: 1 UK: 0
Starting months: Jul, Aug
Time required: 4–12 weeks
Age: 18–40
Causes: Children, Young People.
Activities: Arts/Crafts, Music, Sport, Summer Camps, Translating.
Placements: 20
When to apply: 2 months in advance.
Work alone/with others: With other volunteers.

Qualifications: Energetic and friendly. Basic knowledge of local language helpful.
Health requirements: Some camps require medical certificate.
Costs: Application fee $50 plus cost of travel to camp.
Benefits: Board, lodging and pocket money equal to local counsellors.
Interviews: Applicants are not interviewed.
Worldwide placements: Europe (Latvia, Lithuania, Russia, Ukraine).

INTERNATIONAL NEPAL FELLOWSHIP

69 Wentworth Road
Harborne
Birmingham
B17 9SS UK
T: +44 (0) 121 427 8833
F: +44 (0) 121 428 3110
E: jmackay@inf.org.uk
W: www.inf.org.uk
Contact: Judith Mackay

INF is a Christian organisation and only requires volunteers who have a specific Christian commitment. INF's aim is to bring long-term sustainable benefits to people living mainly in western regions of Nepal. There are a range of health and development projects. There are placements available up to three years. Western regions of Nepal. ▤

Number of projects: 5 **UK:** Nil
Starting months: January–December
Time required: 12–52 weeks (plus)
Age: 21–99
Causes: Addicts/Ex-Addicts, Disabled (physical), Health Care/Medical, Teaching – Primary.
Activities: Administration, Caring – General, Community Work, Library/Resource Centres, Newsletter/Journalism, Religion, Research, Scientific Work, Social Work, Teaching, Technical Skills, Training.
When to apply: All year.
Work alone/with others: Both.
Qualifications: No restrictions, except we only process EU applicants in the UK. All other nationalities should apply to Nepal – recruit@inf.org.np.
Health requirements: Good health essential, climate and conditions are harsh.
Costs: All costs including travel.
Training: Where appropriate.
Supervision: Volunteers are always supervised.
Interviews: No.
Worldwide placements: Asia (Nepal).

INTERNATIONAL OTTER SURVIVAL FUND

Broadford
Isle of Skye
IV9 9AQ Scotland

T: 01471 822487
F: 01471 822487
E: iosf@otter.org
W: www.otter.org
Contact: Grace Yoxon

The International Otter Survival Fund (IOSF) is the only organisation in the world dedicated to the conservation of all 13 species of otter. Otters are semi-aquatic members of the family Mustelidae. As they use both land and aquatic habitats they are very important biological and environmental indicators. The Eurasian otter is the only species found in Europe where its range formerly extended from the Arctic to the Mediterranean and from Ireland in the west to the eastern seaboard of Asia. However, numbers are now seriously depleted in most of Europe. The islands off the northwest coast of Scotland are still a stronghold for otters and continuous studies are being carried out by IOSF. If you wish to volunteer, contact us for details of our ongoing research projects and surveys into the behaviour of otters on the Isle of Skye and elsewhere in the Hebrides. Scotland: Isle of Skye and other Hebridean islands – we survey different islands each year.

Number of projects UK: 4
Starting months: May, Jun, Jul, Aug, Sep
Time required: 1–1 weeks
Age: 17–70
Causes: Animal Welfare, Wildlife.
Activities: Outdoor Skills, Scientific Work.
Placements: 60
When to apply: Any time.
Work alone/with others: Generally with other volunteers of all ages.
Qualifications: Nil but a general interest in wildlife and the environment. Must also be willing to work in all weathers.
Equipment/clothing: No technical equipment but outdoor and walking gear.
Health requirements: Good level of fitness required. Projects require walking over rough ground.
Costs: Varies, from £250.
Training: Yes.
Supervision: All are supervised.
Interviews: Interviews are not held.
Charity number: SCO03875
UK placements: Scotland (Western Isles).

INTERNATIONAL VOLUNTARY SERVICE (IVS – N. IRELAND)

122 Great Victoria Street
Belfast
Co. Antrim BT2 7BG N. Ireland
T: 028 9023 8147
F: 028 9024 4356
E: colin@dnet.co.uk
W: www.ivsni.dnet.co.uk
Contact: Colin McKinty

The primary object of IVS-NI is to afford opportunities by which men and women, in a spirit of friendship, international understanding and voluntary discipline, without regard to their race, religion, creed or politics are encouraged and enabled to give to the community, either individually or in groups, effective voluntary service. IVS-NI is a membership organisation and that means that our members – participants who have been involved in any or all of the activities, or those who agree with our aims – dictate the work and the direction that IVS-NI takes. Our membership therefore is vital, not only because it lets us know that the work we are involved in is relevant and worthwhile. As a member of IVS-NI, you would have the opportunity to have your say in the future of IVS-NI. Even if you only sympathise with our aims, and do not wish to participate in activities, your support would be welcome. Please note that work in Croatia and Bosnia is not workcamps but work with refugees. The minimum age for Africa and Asia is 21. Volunteers with an offending background are accepted. ♿

Number of projects: 400–500 **UK:** 100 approx.
Starting months: January–December
Time required: 2–52 weeks
Age: 18 plus – no upper limit
Causes: Archaeology, Architecture, Children, Conservation, Disabled (learning and physical), Elderly People, Environmental Causes, Heritage, Holidays for Disabled, Human Rights, Inner City Problems, Offenders/Ex-Offenders, Poor/Homeless, Refugees, Teaching/assisting (nursery, primary), Unemployed, Wildlife, Work Camps – Seasonal, Young People.
Activities: Administration, Building/Construction, Campaigning, Caring – General, Catering, Conservation Skills, Development Issues, Fundraising, Gardening/Horticulture, Manual Work, Summer Camps, Teaching, Training, Work Camps – Seasonal.
Placements: 100
When to apply: April onwards for workcamps.
Work alone/with others: Normally in an international group.
Equipment/clothing: Dependent on work.
Health requirements: Nil.
Costs: Travel costs; registration fee; membership. Apply to branch in own country.
Benefits: International workcamps: board and lodging.
Long and medium term: board, lodging + pocket money.
Training: Interview plus preparation day detailing issues that are relevant to inter-cultural exchanges.
Supervision: Workcamp leader at project.
Interviews: Interviews may be held in Belfast, depending on the project.
Charity number: 48740
Worldwide placements: Africa (Algeria, Ghana, Morocco, Namibia, Senegal, Sierra Leone, Swaziland, Tanzania, Togo, Tunisia, Uganda, Zimbabwe); North America: (Canada, Greenland, USA); Asia (Bangladesh, India, Japan, Kazakhstan, Korea (South), Lebanon, Malaysia, Mongolia, Nepal, Sri Lanka, Thailand, Turkey); Australasia (Australia); Europe (Armenia, Austria, Azerbaijan, Belarus, Belgium, Bosnia-Herzegovina, Bulgaria, Croatia, Czech Republic, Denmark, Estonia, Finland, France, Georgia, Germany, Gibraltar, Greece, Hungary, Iceland, Ireland, Italy, Latvia, Lithuania, Macedonia, Netherlands, Norway, Poland,

'PEAK' – "Holidays For Young People With Eczema & Asthma"

Kerry Harris participated as a volunteer in the Rugby 2001 PEAK holiday at Bilton Grange and had such a good time that she is returning next year. "Everyone seemed to settle in very quickly and soon both volunteers and children were having a good time. I was a little nervous to start with as this was my first PEAK holiday and most of the volunteers had done at least one holiday before." The children were severe sufferers of eczema and asthma and Kerry was to cope with very young children having to be creamed and taking their medication. "I will never forget how one child cried at me because he hated the feeling of being covered in cream. It makes you realise just how lucky we are. My advice to anyone who is thinking of doing any volunteering is definitely go for it. It may only be a week that you can give up, but you will come away with a different outlook on life. This experience has certainly boosted my confidence and I can't wait to back again next year."

Portugal, Romania, Russia, Slovakia, Slovenia, Spain, Sweden, Switzerland, Turkey, Ukraine, Yugoslavia).
UK placements: Northern Ireland (throughout).

INTERNATIONAL VOLUNTARY SERVICE (IVS – NORTH)

Castlehill House
21 Otley Road
Leeds
West Yorkshire LS6 3AA UK
T: 0113 230 4600
F: 0113 230 4610
E: ivsgbn@ivsgbn.demon.co.uk
W: www.ivs-gb.org.uk
Contact: Col Collier

International Voluntary Service works for peace, justice and international understanding through voluntary work. It brings together groups of international volunteers to work on projects of importance to community groups. Volunteers live and work together. Accommodation can be basic and the volunteers live communally, sharing the cooking and household tasks of the project. Summer projects usually are short-term and usually last between two and four weeks with groups of 6–16 international volunteers. In many workcamps volunteers are working alongside local volunteers. Medium and long-term opportunities are for 3+ months. ♿

Number of projects: 750+ UK: 20
Starting months: January–December
Time required: 2–14 weeks
Age: 16–65
Causes: AIDS/HIV, Archaeology, Children, Conservation, Disabled (learning and physical), Elderly People, Environmental Causes, Heritage, Holidays for Disabled, Human Rights, Poor/Homeless, Refugees, Work Camps – Seasonal, Young People.
Activities: Administration, Arts/Crafts, Building/Construction, Caring – General, Community Work, Conservation Skills, Development Issues, Fundraising, Gardening/Horticulture, Manual Work, Summer Camps, Theatre/Drama, Visiting/Befriending, Work Camps – Seasonal.
Placements: 300+
When to apply: Most of the projects take place over the summer, June to September and applications for these are best made as soon as our Summer Directory is printed in early April. Autumn, winter and spring projects can be applied for during these seasons.
Work alone/with others: With others.
Qualifications: Non specific skills or qualifications are required but some projects will ask for a letter of motivation.

Equipment/clothing: Work clothes and sleeping bag.
Health requirements: Volunteers with a disability need to inform placement officer when applying.
Costs: Membership of IVS, placement/registration fee, travel to project and pocket money.
Benefits: Basic accommodation and food supplied.
Training: Preparation days before leaving for project.
Supervision: Work is supervised by professional workers. No supervision in leisure time.
Interviews: Volunteers may be required to attend orientation for certain locations.
Charity number: 275424
Worldwide placements: Africa (Morocco, Tunisia); North America: (Canada, Greenland, USA); Asia (Israel, Japan, Lebanon, Mongolia, Palestinian Authority, Turkey); Australasia (Australia); Europe (Albania, Armenia, Austria, Azerbaijan, Belarus, Belgium, Bosnia-Herzegovina, Bulgaria, Croatia, Czech Republic, Denmark, Estonia, Finland, France, Georgia, Germany, Gibraltar, Greece, Hungary, Iceland, Ireland, Italy, Latvia, Liechtenstein, Lithuania, Luxembourg, Macedonia, Malta, Moldova, Netherlands, Norway, Poland, Portugal, Romania, Russia, Slovakia, Slovenia, Spain, Sweden, Switzerland, Turkey, Ukraine, Yugoslavia).
UK placements: England (throughout); Scotland (Inverclyde, Lanarkshire – North, Lanarkshire – South, Lothian – East, Lothian – West, Midlothian, Moray, Perth and Kinross, Renfrewshire, Renfrewshire – East, Scottish Borders, Shetland Islands, Stirling, Western Isles); Northern Ireland (throughout); Wales (throughout).

INTERNATIONAL VOLUNTARY SERVICE (IVS – SCOTLAND)

7 Upper Bow
Edinburgh
EH1 2JN UK
T: 0131 226 6722
F: 0131 226 6723
E: ivs@ivsgbscot.demon.co.uk
W: www.ivs-gb.org.uk
Contact: Jackie Purves

IVS is a voluntary organisation that exists to provide opportunities for voluntary work for all people, both in this country and abroad, in the belief that this will further international understanding and lead to a more just and peaceful world. IVS is the British branch of Service Civil International, a world-wide organisation with groups in over 30 countries. Full information sheet provided for each project. ♿ 📖

Number of projects: 750 UK: 45
Starting months: January–December
Time required: 1–52 weeks
Age: 16–75
Causes: Archaeology, Children, Conservation, Disabled (learning and physical), Environmental Causes, Heritage, Holidays for Disabled, Human Rights, Inner City Problems, Offenders/Ex-Offenders, Poor/Homeless, Refugees, Unemployed, Work Camps – Seasonal, Young People.
Activities: Administration, Agriculture/Farming, Arts/Crafts, Building/Construction, Campaigning, Caring (general, day and residential), Community Work, Conservation Skills, Development Issues, DIY, Forestry, Fundraising, Gardening/Horticulture, Group Work, International Aid, Manual Work, Marketing/Publicity, Music, Newsletter/Journalism, Outdoor Skills, Social Work, Sport, Summer Camps, Work Camps – Seasonal.
Placements: 400
When to apply: All year.
Work alone/with others: With others.
Qualifications: Nil unless specified for special projects.
Equipment/clothing: Sleeping bag and working clothes.
Health requirements: Existing medical conditions may not be covered by our insurance.
Costs: All travel, registration and membership fees of £50–£135 per volunteer project.
Benefits: Board, lodging and insurance cover supplied, and also various social outings.
Training: Preparation days/weekends are optional.
Supervision: Supervision of work provided at all projects.
Interviews: No interview necessary.
Charity number: 275424
Worldwide placements: Africa (Morocco, Tunisia); North America: (Canada, Greenland, Saint Pierre-Miquelon, USA); Asia (Bangladesh, India, Israel, Japan, Mongolia, Nepal, Palestinian Authority, Sri Lanka, Thailand, Turkey); Australasia (Australia); Europe (Albania, Armenia, Austria, Azerbaijan, Belarus, Belgium, Bosnia-Herzegovina, Bulgaria, Croatia, Cyprus, Czech Republic, Denmark, Estonia, Finland, France, Georgia, Germany, Gibraltar, Greece, Hungary, Iceland, Ireland, Italy, Latvia, Liechtenstein, Lithuania, Luxembourg, Macedonia, Malta, Moldova, Netherlands, Norway, Poland, Portugal, Romania, Russia, Slovakia, Slovenia, Spain, Sweden, Switzerland, Turkey, Ukraine, Yugoslavia).
UK placements: England (throughout); Scotland (throughout); Northern Ireland (throughout); Wales (throughout).

INTERNATIONAL VOLUNTARY SERVICE (IVS – SOUTH)

Old Hall
East Bergholt
Nr Colchester
CO7 6TQ UK
T: 01206 298215
F: 01206 299043
E: ivs@ivsgbsouth.demon.co.uk
W: www.ivsgbn.demon.co.uk
Contact: Steve Davies

IVS aims to promote peace, justice and international understanding through voluntary work. IVS is the British branch of Service Civil International (SCI), a world-wide organisation with branches in over 30 countries. Our main activity is the organisation of workcamps. Workcamps help to support communities by bringing volunteers to work on useful projects. At the same time they offer opportunities to meet new people, learn new skills and have fun. Each workcamp is different, but what they all have in common is that volunteers live and work together in an international group, learning about others' lifestyle and cultures. This experience can have a great impact on people, and influence the rest of their lives. The work varies enormously and can include any of the following: campaigning on issues related to the third world, racism and peace education, working with people with disabilities, children or elderly people in their homes at day centres or on holiday, ecological and environmental work, women only camps, artistic and cultural camps. Where and when? The length of a workcamp can range between two and four weeks. In return for the work, volunteers receive basic food and accommodation free. The workcamp group will normally be made up of between 6 and 20 volunteers from almost as many countries. The volunteers will live and work together sharing the organisation of work and domestic arrangements such as cooking and cleaning. Workcamps take place wherever there is a project that can benefit from the assistance of volunteers. Most workcamps run between June and September and details of these are provided in our Summer Workcamp Listing. Other camps take place throughout the year. Volunteers with an offending background are accepted if referred. ♿

Number of projects: 700 UK: 40
Starting months: January–December
Time required: 2–21 weeks
Age: 18 plus – no upper limit
Causes: Children, Conservation, Disabled (learning and physical), Elderly People, Environmental Causes, Inner City Problems, Poor/Homeless, Refugees, Work Camps – Seasonal, Young People.

Activities: Administration, Arts/Crafts, Building/Construction, Campaigning, Caring – General, Community Work, Conservation Skills, Development Issues, Fundraising, Gardening/Horticulture, Group Work, International Aid, Manual Work, Outdoor Skills, Social Work, Visiting/Befriending, Work Camps – Seasonal.
Placements: 300
When to apply: All year but for summer programme from April 1st.
Work alone/with others: with others.
Health requirements: Nil.
Costs: Dependent on type of work – travel to work camp.
Benefits: Board and lodging.
Interviews: No interviews take place.
Charity number: 275424
Worldwide placements: Africa (Algeria, Morocco, Tunisia); North America: (Canada, Greenland, Saint Pierre-Miquelon, USA); Asia (Japan, Turkey); Australasia (Australia); Europe (Albania, Armenia, Austria, Azerbaijan, Belarus, Belgium, Bosnia-Herzegovina, Bulgaria, Croatia, Czech Republic, Denmark, Estonia, Finland, France, Georgia, Germany, Gibraltar, Greece, Hungary, Iceland, Ireland, Italy, Latvia, Liechtenstein, Lithuania, Luxembourg, Macedonia, Malta, Moldova, Netherlands, Norway, Poland, Romania, Russia, Slovakia, Slovenia, Spain, Sweden, Switzerland, Turkey, Ukraine, Yugoslavia).
UK placements: England (throughout); Scotland (throughout); Northern Ireland (throughout); Wales (throughout).

INTERNATIONAL VOLUNTEER PROGRAM

7106 Sayre Drive
Oakland
California CA 94611 USA
T: 00 1 510 339 1107
F: 00 1 510 339 0729
E: rjewell@ivpsf.org
W: www.ivpsf.org
Contact: Rebecca Jewell

Be more than a tourist with the International Volunteer Program. IVP provides six-week volunteer placements in the United States (California). Each summer, volunteers from North America and Western Europe travel to the other side of the Atlantic to be more than a tourist by helping non-profit organisations with their work, meanwhile experiencing a new culture and often a new language. Learn about a new country. The International Volunteer Program is a unique opportunity to immerse oneself in a new culture. Learn more about yourself. As a volunteer, you'll learn more about yourself and the role you want to play in this world. The goal of this program is to encourage

volunteers to also return to their home communities and find ways to make differences in the lives of those around them. Lend a helping hand. Volunteers will be present to help others in a real way. Whether in a retirement home, summer camp, or home for the blind, volunteers find that they have been a real help both to their host agencies and to their clients. Unfortunately, we don't have programs during other times of the year.
Costs – £900 includes – The round trip ticket from London to San Francisco or Los Angeles (depending on destination agency). This ticket will be valid for six to eight weeks. If the volunteer chooses to stay for an additional two weeks after their placement is finished, they are responsible for their own travel during these two weeks.
– Transport to the association from the airport to their placement.
– Room and meals during 6 weeks (accommodations include host families, dorms or on-site lodging; meals include breakfast lunch and dinner).
– Certificate of completion from La Société Française de Bienfaisance Mutuelle.
History- IVP was founded in 1991 by La Société to incorporate the important goals of that organization of helping San Francisco, Bay Area community and encourage cultural exchanges between France and the United States. The program has since expanded to include the UK.
USA: California – Napa Valley, Big Bear, Long Beach, San Francisco, Los Angeles. ♿

Number of projects: 10 UK: 0
Starting months: Jul, Aug
Time required: 6–6 weeks
Age: 18 plus – no upper limit
Causes: Addicts/Ex-Addicts, AIDS/HIV, Animal Welfare, Children, Conservation, Disabled (learning and physical), Elderly People, Environmental Causes, Health Care/Medical, Holidays for Disabled, Human Rights, Inner City Problems, Poor/Homeless, Refugees, Work Camps – Seasonal, Young People.
Activities: Arts/Crafts, Building/Construction, Caring – Residential, Cooking, Counselling, Development Issues, First Aid, Gardening/Horticulture, Group Work, International Aid, Music, Outdoor Skills, Social Work, Summer Camps, Theatre/Drama, Translating, Work Camps – Seasonal.
Placements: 35
When to apply: Before 15 April.
Work alone/with others: Usually with other young volunteers, when available.
Equipment/clothing: Depending on the placement. Clothing requirements will be notified at the same time as the placement information is provided.

Health requirements: None.
Costs: £900 (or US$1500 or €1350) plus personal expenses e.g. stamps, phone calls and independent travel.
Benefits: The cost covers return ticket from London to San Francisco or Los Angeles, transportation to the placement and food and lodging for the six weeks.
Training: Provided by the host agency.
Supervision: Volunteers are supervised by staff of the host agency.
Interviews: Interviews by telephone.
Worldwide placements: North America: (USA).

INTERNATIONALE BEGEGNUNG IN GEMEINSCHAFTSDIENSTEN e.V.

Schlosserstrasse 28
Stuttgart
D-70180 Germany
T: 00 49 711 6491128
F: 00 49 711 6409867
E: IBG-workcamps@t-online.de
W: www.workcamps.com
Contact: Christoph Meder or Alejandro Garcia

Internationale Begegnung in Gemeinschaftsdiensten needs volunteers to attend international youth workcamps in Germany. Projects include restoring an old castle, environmental protection, children's playschemes, arts and remedial projects. Each workcamp consists of a group of about 15 people aged 18–30 from all over the world. Opportunities are available in Africa, the Americas, Asia and many other countries in Europe for non-British nationals. Our current programme will be sent on receipt of two international reply coupons. Besides workcamps we have long-term stays up to one year as well. The registration fee is €130 + insurance.

Number of projects: 4 UK: 0
Starting months: Jun, Jul, Aug, Sep
Time required: 1–52 weeks
Age: 18–27
Causes: Archaeology, Children, Conservation, Disabled (learning and physical), Elderly People, Environmental Causes, Holidays for Disabled, Inner City Problems, Poor/Homeless, Refugees, Teaching/assisting (primary, EFL), Unemployed, Wildlife, Work Camps – Seasonal, Young People.
Activities: Agriculture/Farming, Arts/Crafts, Building/Construction, Community Work, Computers, Conservation Skills, Forestry, Gardening/Horticulture, Manual Work, Music, Social Work, Theatre/Drama, Work Camps – Seasonal.
Placements: 400
When to apply: April – July
Work alone/with others: Group of 10–20 international people.
Equipment/clothing: Working clothes/boots/sleeping bag.

Health requirements: Nil.
Costs: €130 registration fee + travel costs.
Benefits: Board and lodging and parts of leisure activities.
Interviews: Applicants for volunteer projects are not interviewed.
Worldwide placements: Europe (Germany).

INTERNATIONALER BAUORDEN – DEUTSCHER ZWEIG

Postfach 14 38
Liebigstr 23
D-67551 Worms
Germany
T: 00 49 62 41 37900 and 37901
F: 00 49 62 41 37902
E: bauorden@t-online.de
W: http://ibo-d.bei.t-online.de
Contact: Peter Runck

Internationaler Bauorden – Deutscher Zweig (IBO) was founded in 1953. It aims to realise more justice by building international friendships and social workcamps. IBO's motto is 'we help build'. We help through building and renovation works on homes for children, orphans, the elderly, people with disabilities and by building meeting centres for young people. IBO concentrates on people in need of help. The volunteers work on the sites for up to eight hours a day, 40 hours a week. The groups are international.

Number of projects: 80 UK: 0
Starting months: May, Jun, Jul, Aug, Sep, Oct
Time required: 3–4 weeks
Age: 18–25
Causes: Children, Disabled (learning and physical), Elderly People, Holidays for Disabled, Poor/Homeless, Refugees, Work Camps – Seasonal, Young People.
Activities: Building/Construction, Manual Work, Work Camps – Seasonal.
Placements: 250
When to apply: As early as possible.
Work alone/with others: With others.
Equipment/clothing: Working clothes, closed shoes.
Health requirements: Nil.
Costs: Travel costs to the camp.
Benefits: Board and lodging.
Training: None.
Supervision: On the project by the responsible person.
Worldwide placements: Europe (Albania, Armenia, Austria, Belarus, Belgium, Croatia, Czech Republic, Denmark, France, Georgia, Germany, Greece, Hungary, Italy, Lithuania, Moldova, Netherlands, Poland, Portugal, Romania, Russia, Slovakia, Slovenia, Spain, Ukraine).

INTERNATIONALER BUND e.V.

Freiwilliges Soziales Jahr
Orber Straße 19
60386 Frankfurt am Main
Germany
T: 00 49 69 28 21 71
F: 00 49 69 91 39 63 65
E: fsj-frankfurt@internationler-bund.de
W: www.fsj-info.de.vu
Contact: Mr Winfried A. Burkard

Internationaler Bund can offer you work in the Federal Republic of Germany. You can work as a volunteer in a hospital, residential home for the aged or a home for handicapped people.
As a volunteer you will assist the staff in all duties which can be performed by non-skilled volunteers: washing the patients, helping them to get dressed and to take their meals, running of errands etc. You'll be fully integrated into the work-flow. Like the rest of the staff, you will be required to work 38.5 hours per week, including some weekends. Your work may be early or late day shift. After six months service you are entitled to two weeks leave. Programmes start in early April and September and you can stay for a period of six or 12 months. In individual cases, exceptions to this schedule may be agreed upon. During your stay you will be given the opportunity to get to know both the country and its people and to extend your knowledge of the German language.
When applying please send
1. application sheet
2. handwritten curriculum vitae
3. three photos
4. medical certificate
5. certificate giving evidence of your knowledge of German and
6. last school leaving certificate.

Number of projects: 25 UK: 0
Starting months: Apr, Sep
Time required: 26–52 weeks
Age: 16–27
Causes: Disabled (learning and physical), Elderly People, Health Care/Medical.
Activities: Caring – General.
Placements: 120
When to apply: All year.
Work alone/with others: With others.
Qualifications: Some knowledge of German.
Health requirements: In good health.
Costs: Travel.
Benefits: €150 per month + board and accommodation. Single room accommodation will be provided and costs incurred for the renting of a room will be refunded.
Training: Learning by doing. With other volunteers, particularly Germans, you will attend day or weekend seminars in order to exchange experiences and to discuss a number

of related subjects.
Supervision: By full-time staff colleague.
Interviews: An interview will be held in Frankfurt or London prior to your acceptance.
Worldwide placements: Europe (Germany).

INTERSERVE

On Track Programme
325 Kennington Road
London
SE11 4QH UK
T: +44 (0) 207 735 8227
T: +44 (0) 207 587 5362
E: enquiries@isewi.org
Contact: Dave Taylor

Interserve is an international, interdenominational, evangelical Christian fellowship of about 450 committed Christians who have a desire to share their faith, as well as their skills, in another culture. Interserve's long-term partners work in the countries of Asia, the Gulf, Middle East, and North Africa, undertaking a range of roles. On Track enables short-term volunteers to assist, or work along-side partners already in place. On Track is a short-term service programme run by Interserve and has two aims: to encourage an interest in cross-cultural Christian service overseas; to provide an opportunity for Christians to experience living, working, and sharing their faith in a cross-cultural environment. Open to those aged 18 years and over, On Track has a variety of programmes including school leavers, summer vacation programme, student electives, new graduates, and professional/skilled workers. Programmes vary in length from two to 12 months and examples of the type of activities undertaken range from teaching, including TEFL, to health, development, administration, engineering and care work. Volunteers with an offending background may be accepted – each application is assessed on an individual basis.

Number of projects: 200 UK: 0
Starting months: January–December
Time required: 9–52 weeks
Age: 18–75
Causes: Addicts/Ex-Addicts, AIDS/HIV, Children, Conservation, Disabled (learning and physical), Elderly People, Health Care/Medical, Inner City Problems, Poor/Homeless, Refugees, Teaching/assisting (nursery, primary, secondary, mature, EFL) Unemployed, Young People.
Activities: Accountancy, Administration, Agriculture/Farming, Arts/Crafts, Building/Construction, Caring (general, day and residential), Catering, Community Work, Computers, Conservation Skills, Counselling, Development Issues, First Aid, Forestry, Gardening/Horticulture, International Aid, Marketing/Publicity, Newsletter/Journalism,

Religion, Social Work, Teaching, Technical Skills.
When to apply: 5 months prior to intended departure date.
Work alone/with others: Both.
Qualifications: Depends on the placement. UK Residents only.
Equipment/clothing: Depends on the placement.
Health requirements: Good health and able to cope with overseas travel and life.
Costs: Volunteers are responsible for all expenses/costs which vary and include £10 application fee, £50 for weekend training, £50 placement fee plus £15 per month after the first 3 months.
Benefits: Pastoral care. Accommodation will be found but the cost will be the volunteer's responsibility.
Interviews: Prospective volunteers are interviewed in London.
Charity number: 2789773
Worldwide placements: Africa (Egypt); Asia (Afghanistan, Bahrain, Bangladesh, China, India, Jordan, Kyrgyzstan, Lebanon, Mongolia, Nepal, Oman, Pakistan, Turkey, Yemen); Europe (Turkey).

INTERXCHANGE GAMBIA

31 Clarkson Street
Banjul
PMB 303 SERREKUNDA The Gambia
West Africa
T: +00220 224661/909040
F: +00220 228004
E: interxchange@e-mail.com
Contact: Sadibou Kamaso

Interxchange Gambia was established basically to promote and facilitate social, cultural and educational travel amongst students aimed at increasing understanding through culture education and exchange visit programmes. Our programmes include: Volunteer Work Abroad – this programme aims to give students, youths and seniors the opportunity to volunteer their time to assist local NGOs in the Gambia in various projects enabling them to gain African work experience. Interxchange Gambia places volunteers with these local NGOs for durations of two months to two years in health, education, eco-tourism, water and sanitation, environmental studies, small scale industries and other community projects. Volunteer opportunities include – HIV/AIDS projects, women in development, culture/tourism/eco-tourism, water/sanitation, environmental issues/ disaster relief, community development, health/medical/research, teaching pre-school/secondary, communication/marketing, child survival development, speech therapy, audio and visual projects, physical and mental disability.

cultural and exchange visits – sightseeing and cultural tours facilitated by full participation of schools and registered youth groups, linguistic courses alongside drumming and dancing lessons – jointly co-ordinated with Gamspirit (experienced tourism and travel firm) giving international students the opportunity to quickly grasp certain cultural norms and feel a part of the Gambian society, home stays in Gambia – share experiences and cultures while staying with a family, summer camping programmes – cultural sports and tour packages during summer holidays for both national and international students and youths.
Volunteers can expect:
– airport pickup
– cultural and medical orientation upon arrival for the first five days
– food and accommodation throughout placement period
– a suitable work placement to suit the volunteer's career
– certificates at the end of the placement.
Volunteers with offending background may be accepted. 🦽 📄

Number of projects: 12 **UK:** 0
Starting months: January–December
Time required: 8–52 weeks
Age: 16–35
Causes: AIDS/HIV, Children, Conservation, Disabled (learning and physical), Environmental Causes, Health Care/Medical, Refugees, Teaching/assisting (nursery, primary, secondary, mature, EFL) Wildlife, Work Camps – Seasonal, Young People.
Activities: Accountancy, Administration, Agriculture/Farming, Campaigning, Caring (general and day), Community Work, Computers, Conservation Skills, Cooking, Counselling, Development Issues, First Aid, Forestry, Fundraising, Gardening/Horticulture, Group Work, International Aid, Library/Resource Centres, Marketing/Publicity, Newsletter/Journalism, Outdoor Skills, Research, Social Work, Sport, Summer Camps, Teaching, Technical Skills, Theatre/Drama, Training, Visiting/Befriending, Work Camps – Seasonal.
Placements: 18
When to apply: All year round.
Work alone/with others: With others.
Qualifications: Secondary school/college graduation – some projects require experiences in that specific area.
Health requirements: No health restrictions except critical conditions – medical reports to be submitted with application.
Costs: £500: this fee includes food and accommodation with host families/individual apartment rental throughout the placement, medical and cultural orientation and ongoing

support services. It also includes monthly allowances depending on area of stay.
Benefits: Accommodation with host families or apartments, food, allowance of £20 per month, certificates at the end of the placement.
Training: Four to five days medical and cultural orientation upon arrival.
Supervision: Supervision done by host organisations.
Interviews: On arrival in the Gambia – but all necessary information would be provided prior to volunteer's arrival.
Worldwide placements: Africa (Gambia).

INVOLVEMENT VOLUNTEERS

P.O. Box 218
Port Melbourne
Victoria 3207 Australia
T: 00 61 3 9646 5504 or 9392
F: 00 61 3 9646 5504
E: ivworldwide@volunteering.org.au
W: www.volunteering.org.au
Contact: Mr Tim B. Cox

Involvement Volunteers is a registered, not for profit organisation, that creates programmes of suitable, unpaid, individual volunteer placements related to the natural environment and social service within the community. Volunteers participate as individuals or in groups of individuals or in teams around the world, around the calendar. Placements are available in a wide variety of situations, i.e. National Parks, and bird observatories; private landholdings and flora and fauna reserves; community based social service organisations for the benefit of both young and old as well as physically or medically disadvantaged people. Volunteers are required to speak and understand the English language for safety reasons. Volunteers gain valuable experience arranging their own visas as required; locally purchasing their air tickets and suitable travel insurance with some advice to suit their travel and volunteering programme. A police check is required for some placements. 🖹

Number of projects: Hundreds **UK:** 5
Starting months: January–December
Time required: 2–52 weeks
Age: 16–75
Causes: Animal Welfare, Archaeology, Architecture, Children, Conservation, Disabled (learning and physical), Elderly People, Health Care/Medical, Heritage, Holidays for Disabled, Refugees, Teaching/assisting (nursery, primary, secondary, mature, EFL) Wildlife, Work Camps – Seasonal.
Activities: Administration, Agriculture/Farming, Arts/Crafts, Building/Construction, Caring (general, residential), Computers, Conservation Skills, DIY, Driving, First Aid, Forestry,

Gardening/Horticulture, Library/Resource Centres, Manual Work, Marketing/Publicity, Music, Newsletter/Journalism, Outdoor Skills, Research, Scientific Work, Social Work, Sport, Summer Camps, Teaching, Training, Translating, Work Camps – Seasonal.
Placements: 600
When to apply: As early as possible.
Work alone/with others: Both.
Qualifications: Must speak and understand English. Specific qualifications and potential interest are not necessary except in specific cases i.e. teaching.
Equipment/clothing: Sleeping bag, removable-washable inner sheet bag, towel, long sleeved shirts, trousers, shorts, sun hat, cool and wet weather gear + strong walking or working boots. Backpack with overnight bag for spares in case of misplaced backpack while travelling.
Health requirements: As suitable for the site.
Costs: Registration fee A$242, A$430+$100 multiple placement fee, £230+$100 single placement fee.
Benefits: Opportunities to travel and explore as individuals or in group or team activities while gaining practical and cultural experience related to activities in life while assisting others in need of assistance. Accommodation varies from living with host families, camping, dormitories or own arrangements.
Training: No training necessary.
Supervision: Volunteers are supervised by the placements.
Interviews: Applicants are not formally interviewed.
Worldwide placements: Africa (Kenya, South Africa, Togo); North America: (USA); Central America (Mexico); South America (Argentina, Ecuador); Asia (Cambodia, China, India, Korea (South), Lebanon, Malaysia, Nepal, Thailand, Turkey, Vietnam); Australasia (Australia, Fiji, New Zealand); Europe (Estonia, Finland, France, Germany, Greece, Italy, Spain, Turkey).

INVOLVEMENT VOLUNTEERS – DEUTSCHLAND

Naturbadstr. 50
D-91056 Erlangen
Germany
T: 00 49 9135 8075
F: 00 49 9135 8075
E: ivde2@t-online.de
Contact: Marion Mayer

Involvement Volunteers – Deutschland is the European office of Involvement Volunteers which is based in Australia. It enables people to participate in voluntary activities related to conservation. An updated task list can be received via e-mail all year through. Volunteers with an offending background are accepted. ♿ 🖹

Number of projects: 200 UK: 0
Starting months: January–December
Time required: 2–52 weeks
Age: 17–35
Causes: Animal Welfare, Archaeology,
Architecture, Children, Conservation, Disabled
(learning and physical), Elderly People,
Environmental Causes, Health Care/Medical,
Heritage, Inner City Problems, Poor/Homeless,
Refugees, Teaching/assisting (nursery, primary,
EFL), Wildlife, Work Camps – Seasonal, Young
People.
Activities: Administration, Agriculture/Farming,
Building/Construction, Caring (general, day and
residential), Community Work, Conservation
Skills, Development Issues, Forestry,
Gardening/Horticulture, Group Work, Manual
Work, Outdoor Skills, Research, Scientific Work,
Social Work, Summer Camps, Teaching, Work
Camps – Seasonal.
Placements: 500
When to apply: 2–3 months in advance of
departure.
Work alone/with others: Both, depending on
preference and availability.
Qualifications: Nil for most placements,
sometimes special skill is requested by host.
Health requirements: Nil.
Costs: €120 initial fee+ A$340confirmation fee
for IV Australia+travel +A$60.
Benefits: 90% free board and lodging. Others
pay A$10–50 per week.
Interviews: Volunteer applicants are not
interviewed. A CV and detailed questions
concerning planned travel route are basis for
schedule.
Charity number: VR1246
Worldwide placements: Africa (Ghana, Kenya,
South Africa); North America: (USA); Asia
(India, Indonesia, Lebanon, Malaysia, Sri Lanka,
Thailand); Australasia (Australia, Fiji, New
Zealand, Papua New Guinea); Europe (Austria,
Estonia, Finland, Germany, Greece, Italy, Latvia,
Lithuania, Spain).
UK placements: England (London).

INVOLVEMENT VOLUNTEERS UNITED KINGDOM (IVUK)

7 Bushmead Avenue
Kingskerswell
Nr Newton Abbot
Devon TQ12 5EN UK
T: 01803 872594
F: 01803 403514
E: ivengland@volunteering.org.au
W: www.volunteering.org.au
Contact: Mrs Ratcliffe

Involvement Volunteers United Kingdom offers
various countries where volunteers have the
choice of many placements, including
conservation, teaching, farm work, historical

settlements, plant nurseries, Social services etc.
to choose from.

UK placements:
Farm UKI001 – IVP Rural dairy farm in
Yorkshire. Approx 30 minutes away from large
town. Accommodation and food is provided.
Volunteers will live with the family.
Farm UKI002 – IVP A typical Welsh farm of 40
hectares with a traditional mix of sheep, cattle
and ponies, dogs, cats etc. There is a small
riding/pony trekking centre during the summer
months. Accommodation and food is provided.
Live with the family. Conservation UK1004 –
IVP To assist the warden with conservation
tasks, which would include help in the gardens,
assisting in historical house. Accommodation is
provided but volunteers would be expected to
provide their own food and cook it. Also,
volunteers are required to bring a sleeping bag
or bedding. There are only a few places at the
site and a period of two to three months is
recommended; however they will where
possible take volunteers for one month. Social
Service UK1005 – IIVP or SIVP. A respite care
and holiday centre for 60 people with physical
disabilities (so their carers can have a short
holiday). Volunteers live-in, assist full time staff
with care and companionship of disabled guests
who are happy to enjoy a holiday themselves.
Volunteers take the disabled people to visit
interesting places. Having just arrived in the
UK, IV volunteers meet interesting people from
many parts of the country, who can tell them
what to see and where to go. Two weeks.
(Available between February and November,
and run from Saturday to Saturday.) Social
Services UKI006-IVP. Retreat therapy centre.
Potential long-term placement at this Christian
based retreat offering meditation, recreation
(especially music) and healing therapies. The
volunteer can assist with the gardening or in
the house where they can help with the
catering, washing, and guest rooms for those
taking part in the therapy activities.
Accommodation and food is provided. Within
reasonable distance of London. ♿

Number of projects: Hundreds UK: 4
Starting months: January–December
Time required: 2–52 weeks
Age: 18 plus – no upper limit
Causes: Animal Welfare, Archaeology,
Architecture, Children, Conservation, Disabled
(learning and physical), Elderly People,
Environmental Causes, Heritage, Holidays for
Disabled, Teaching/assisting (nursery, primary,
secondary, mature, EFL) Wildlife, Work Camps –
Seasonal, Young People.
Activities: Agriculture/Farming,
Building/Construction, Caring (general, day and
residential), Catering, Community Work,
Conservation Skills, Cooking, DIY, Forestry,

Group Work, International Aid, Manual Work, Outdoor Skills, Social Work, Summer Camps, Teaching, Technical Skills, Training, Visiting/Befriending, Work Camps – Seasonal.
Placements: 80+
When to apply: All the year round.
Work alone/with others: Both.
Qualifications: No qualifications needed but any will help. Teaching needs TEFL course.
Equipment/clothing: Depends on placement.
Health requirements: Travelling vaccinations.
Costs: Registration fee £80, and programme fee of £90 for a single placement, £130 for more than one placement and a placement fee of £25 for each placement. Travel costs.
Benefits: Board and lodging usually paid unless volunteering in a poor country.
Accommodation is usually provided unless the project is in a poor country.
Training: Training is provided by placement.
Supervision: Placement provide supervision.
Interviews: No interviews – volunteers have to send a CV with registration form.
Worldwide placements: Africa (Botswana, Kenya, Namibia, South Africa, Togo, Zambia); North America: (USA); Central America (Mexico); South America (Argentina, Brazil, Ecuador, Venezuela); Asia (Bangladesh, Cambodia, China, India, Japan, Korea (South), Lebanon, Malaysia, Mongolia, Nepal, Thailand, Vietnam); Australasia (American Samoa, Australia, Fiji, New Zealand, Papua New Guinea, Samoa); Europe (Austria, Estonia, Finland, France, Germany, Greece, Italy, Latvia, Poland, Spain, Turkey, Ukraine).
UK placements: England (Kent, Surrey, S. Yorkshire); Wales (Pembrokeshire).

IONA COMMUNITY, THE

Iona Abbey
Isle of Iona
Argyll PA76 6SN UK
T: 01681 700404
F: 01681 700460 or 603
E: Ionacomm@iona.org.uk
W: www.iona.org.uk
Contact: The Staff Co-ordinator

The Iona Community is an ecumenical Christian Community, founded in 1938 by the late George MacLeod (Very Rev. Lord MacLeod of Fuinary) and committed to seeking new ways of living the Gospel in today's world. The Iona Community maintains three centres on Iona and Mull: Iona Abbey and the MacLeod Centre on Iona, and Camas Adventure Centre on the Ross of Mull. The islands' work focuses around welcoming guests to join in the common life of work, worship and recreation. There is a resident group living and working all year round on Iona, but the centres can only run with the support of the volunteers from the beginning of March to the end of October.

There are up to 35 volunteers here at any one time coming for six or more weeks at a time. Types of jobs on offer: kitchen assistant, housekeeping assistant, general assistant, children's worker, abbey assistant, driver, shop assistant, office assistant, gardener and maintenance assistant. Posts for Camas Adventure Camp include cook, programme workers (outdoors), gardener and general assistant. Volunteers with an offending background accepted. 🖐
Number of projects UK: 3
Starting months: Mar, Apr, May, Jun, Jul, Aug, Sep, Oct
Time required: 6–14 weeks
Age: 18 plus – no upper limit
Causes: Addicts/Ex-Addicts, AIDS/HIV, Children, Disabled (learning and physical), Elderly People, Holidays for Disabled, Human Rights, Inner City Problems, Offenders/Ex-Offenders, Poor/Homeless, Refugees, Teaching/assisting (nursery, primary, secondary, mature), Work Camps – Seasonal, Young People.
Activities: Administration, Arts/Crafts, Caring – General, Catering, Cooking, Development Issues, Driving, First Aid, Gardening/Horticulture, Manual Work, Outdoor Skills, Religion, Summer Camps, Teaching, Work Camps – Seasonal.
Placements: 130
When to apply: Previous autumn.
Work alone/with others: With others.
Qualifications: Drivers must be 25 or more. We require commitment to community life and to exploring/being open to Christian faith.
Health requirements: Nil.
Costs: All paid by Iona community.
Benefits: Reasonable travel expenses within Britain, board, lodging and weekly allowance.
Training: As you work.
Supervision: Volunteers work as part of a team and have regular team meetings and reflection sessions with their line manager.
Interviews: Applicants are not interviewed.
Charity number: SCO03794
UK placements: Scotland (Argyll and Bute).

IRACAMBI ATLANTIC RAINFOREST RESEARCH AND CONSERVATION CENTER

Fazenda Iracambi
Rosario da Limeira
Minas Gerais 36878-000 Brazil
T: +55 32 3721 1436
F: +55 32 3722 4909
E: iracambi@iracambi.com
W: www.iracambi.com
Contact: Robin Le Breton

The Iracambi Atlantic Rainforest Research and Conservation Center's mission statement is to make the conservation of the forest more attractive than its destruction. We welcome volunteers to come and help in our ongoing projects. Current projects include: land use mapping of the rainforests around Iracambi, with a view to rehabilitation of forest and linking up forest islands. GIS and survey database maintenance. Marketing of our forest programme (see web site for details). Trail clearing and signposting, tree planting and nursery maintenance. We have a special need for volunteers who are fluent in Portuguese and who have experience with working with children to help in our environmental education programmes with the local children. We are always keen to accept volunteers who are computer literate especially databases and web site management. We may be able to place volunteers with an offending background. Brazil – Rosario da limeirs, near Muriae, State of Minas Gerais – about 350 km north east of Rio de Janeiro. 🔊 📄

Number of projects: 1 **UK:** 0
Starting months: January–December
Time required: 12–26 weeks
Age: 18 plus – no upper limit
Causes: Conservation, Environmental Causes.
Activities: Administration, Computers, Driving, Forestry, Fundraising, Gardening/Horticulture, Manual Work, Marketing/Publicity, Newsletter/Journalism, Research, Teaching, Translating.
Placements: 50
When to apply: Any time.
Work alone/with others: Work with others.
Qualifications: None required, but the ability to speak Portuguese and driving skills are an advantage. Certain nationalities require a Brazilian visa.
Equipment/clothing: Work gloves and waterproof clothing are recommended.
Health requirements: No restrictions.
Costs: International and local travel. Board and lodging US$500 for three months or less, US$150 per month thereafter.
Benefits: Full board and lodging is provided within the costs.
Training: None.
Interviews: No.
Worldwide placements: South America (Brazil).

IRONBRIDGE GORGE MUSEUMS, THE

The Wharfage
Ironbridge
Telford
Shropshire TF8 7AW UK
T: 01952 583003
F: 01952 588016
E: info@ironbridge.org.uk
W: www.ironbridge.org.uk
Contact: Lisa Wood

The Ironbridge Gorge Museums require

volunteers to help with a huge variety of activities in all the different sections of the museums. Most opportunities are with the Blists Hill Open Air Museum. Demonstrators, clad in Victorian style costume, are required to work in exhibits. Shropshire. 🔊

Number of projects: 1 **UK:** 1
Starting months: January–December
Time required: 2–52 weeks
Age: 16 plus – no upper limit
Causes: Animal Welfare, Children, Heritage, Young People.
Activities: Arts/Crafts, Gardening/Horticulture, Manual Work, Research, Theatre/Drama.
Placements: 60
When to apply: January for main season, but all year for general volunteering.
Work alone/with others: Normally with others.
Qualifications: Good spoken English.
Equipment/clothing: Sensible black/dark shoes/boots.
Health requirements: No.
Costs: All expenses – accommodation, food and travel.
Benefits: Training, costume and equipment provided, lunch vouchers and free entry to other museums.
Training: Induction training and hands-on training is carried out in-house.
Supervision: Volunteers are never expected to work alone. They have a staff mentor, volunteer co-ordinator plus duty officer on hand 7 days a week.
Interviews: Wherever possible we have an informal meeting to assess suitability.
Charity number: 503717-R
UK placements: England (Shropshire).

ITALIAN FOUNDATION FOR VOLUNTARY SERVICE (FIVOL), THE

Via Nazionale, 39-00184
Rome
Italy
T: 00 39 06 474 811
F: 00 39 06 4814617
E: info@fivol.org
W: www.fivol.org
Contact: Stefania Mancini

The Italian Foundation for Voluntary Service (FIVOL) promotes and has information about volunteering in Italy. It may well be able to put volunteers in touch with organisations which are not yet listed on the WorldWide Volunteering database.

Starting months: January–December
Time required: 1–52 weeks (plus)
Age: 16 plus – no upper limit
Causes: Addicts/Ex-Addicts, AIDS/HIV, Animal Welfare, Archaeology, Architecture, Children, Conservation, Disabled (learning and physical),

Elderly People, Environmental Causes, Health Care/Medical, Heritage, Holidays for Disabled, Human Rights, Inner City Problems, Offenders/Ex-Offenders, Poor/Homeless, Refugees, Teaching/assisting (nursery, primary, secondary, mature, EFL) Unemployed, Wildlife, Work Camps – Seasonal, Young People.
Activities: Accountancy, Administration, Agriculture/Farming, Arts/Crafts, Building/Construction, Campaigning, Caring (general, day and residential), Catering, Community Work, Computers, Conservation Skills, Cooking, Counselling, Development Issues, DIY, Driving, First Aid, Forestry, Fundraising, Gardening/Horticulture, Group Work, International Aid, Library/Resource Centres, Manual Work, Marketing/Publicity, Music, Newsletter/Journalism, Outdoor Skills, Religion, Research, Scientific Work, Social Work, Sport, Summer Camps, Teaching, Technical Skills, Theatre/Drama, Training, Translating, Visiting/Befriending, Work Camps – Seasonal.
Costs: Varies according to the project.
Worldwide placements: Europe (Italy).

i-to-i INTERNATIONAL PROJECTS

9 Blenheim Terrace
Leeds
LS2 9HZ UK
T: 0870 333 2332
F: 0113 242 2171
E: info@i-to-i.com
W: www.i-to-i.com
Contact: The i Venture Co-ordinator

Intensive TEFL Courses: 40 hour (one weekend) TEFL courses at venues nation-wide which give you an i to i TEFL certificate. Refreshments provided. Extensive guidance on work opportunities abroad. 20 hour optional home study grammar module provided at no additional cost. Fees: £195. Online TEFL courses available. 40 hour courses accessible from all over the world. You are assigned your own tutor and you work throughout the course in your time, in your own home. Fees £195. i-Venture: Voluntary projects operated by i-to-i. Volunteers work on school projects teaching English in Russia, Sri Lanka, India, Mongolia, Thailand, Nepal, China, Cambodia, Vietnam, Ghana, Costa Rica, Honduras, Guatemala, El Salvador, Ecuador and Bolivia. Placements are flexible and last for two weeks to six months. TEFL training is provided in the UK before departure. Field staff, board and lodging included in most circumstances. Conservation projects and working holidays in Australia, Costa Rica, Honduras, Ecuador, Bolivia, Ghana, Mongolia, India, Thailand, South Africa, Sri Lanka, Ireland, El Salvador, Guatemala, Cambodia and Vietnam. Board and lodging in most circumstances, in-country orientation and

support plus fun-in-the-sun. Age range: 17+. Costs from £750. Working holidays include care work, health, journalism and heritage work. £195 deposit must be sent with the application form. On application we send you a large amount of information about our projects and TEFL course and provide pre-departure briefing and preparation. Volunteers with an offending background are accepted. i-to-i are a member of The Year Out Group. &

Number of projects: 350 UK: 0
Starting months: January–December
Time required: 2–26 weeks
Age: 17–70
Causes: Animal Welfare, Children, Conservation, Environmental Causes, Inner City Problems, Poor/Homeless, Teaching/assisting (primary, secondary, mature, EFL), Wildlife, Work Camps – Seasonal, Young People.
Activities: Agriculture/Farming, Conservation Skills, Fundraising, Marketing/Publicity, Social Work, Teaching, Training, Work Camps – Seasonal.
Placements: 2000.
When to apply: All year.
Work alone/with others: Both.
Qualifications: i to i TEFL course which is 2 days in the UK or Ireland or i-to-i online TEFL certificate. Fluent English speakers. No nationality restrictions but must be fluent English speakers.
Equipment/clothing: Teaching materials (ie. TEFL toolkit, Grammar Awareness Module etc.) supplied to teaching volunteers. Other necessities can be purchased through the i-shop.
Health requirements: Good health.
Costs: For 3 months from £995. Deposit £195.
Benefits: For the fee, volunteers are guaranteed (in most circumstances) food, accommodation, 15 hrs teaching per week, support from UK and weekend TEFL training in UK prior to departure and in-country support.
Training: TEFL training weekend, or online TEFL, country briefing CD ROM and Venture Pack – a comprehensive pack on how to survive abroad.
Supervision: Co-ordinators abroad, in the capital (generally) look after welfare of volunteers. They pick up from airport and visit during volunteer's stay.
Interviews: We require a reference and secondary application form following the initial application.
Worldwide placements: Africa (Ghana, South Africa); Central America (Costa Rica, El Salvador, Guatemala, Honduras); South America (Bolivia, Ecuador); Asia (Cambodia, China, India, Mongolia, Nepal, Sri Lanka, Thailand, Vietnam); Australasia (Australia); Europe (Russia).

J

JACOB'S WELL

2 Ladygate
Beverley
E. Yorkshire HU17 8BH UK
T: 01482 881478
F: 01482 865452
E: thejacobswell@aol.com
Contact: Mrs J Johnston

Jacob's Well Appeal is a Christian charity which was founded in 1982 to send medical aid to Poland. The work in Romania is almost entirely based in the Neuropsychiatric Hospital in Siret which contains some 500 children of all ages. It is understaffed with local women working as carers for the children. The culture, attitudes and eating patterns are all very different to those in England. Siret is very remote and modern facilities such as telephones, transport, water supply and indoor toilets are scarce and unreliable. The climate is continental with wide temperature swings. Many young people have made a valuable contribution with the children during a gap year before or after university.

Number of projects: 1 UK: 0
Starting months: January–December
Time required: 4–13 weeks
Age: 18–68
Causes: Children, Disabled (learning and physical).
Activities: Caring – General.
Placements: 60
When to apply: At least 6 months in advance.
Work alone/with others: With other volunteers.
Qualifications: Not essential but physiotherapists, nurses, teachers for special needs have priority.
Equipment/clothing: No specialist clothing or equipment required.
Health requirements: Volunteers need to be fit and healthy.
Costs: £10 – £15 p/w – local family accommodation + travel expenses (approx £250).
Interviews: Interviews are mostly conducted in Beverley, E. Yorkshire. Occasionally in London.
Charity number: 515235
Worldwide placements: Europe (Romania).

JAGRITI FOUNDATION

6401 East Ocean Boulevard
Long Beach
California 90803 USA
T: 562 621 0024
F: 805 969 4122
E: info@jagritifoundation.org
W: www.jagritifoundation.org
Contact: Michele Andina

Jagriti Foundation 'supports the work of grassroots women's groups around the globe'. Founded in 1998, a group of American and European women who had travelled to Nepal, and wanted to make a difference to often brutal conditions that women faced in many countries of the world, and end their fears of being trafficked and raped. The Jagriti Foundation provides women opportunities for cultural exchange with women's organisations around the world. It encourages women to come together to share their ideas and skills. It fosters universal communication and seeks the impetus of other women's awakenings. The organisations are dedicated to strengthening the position of women in their societies through income generation, women's rights and legal change, access issues, education, agricultural improvements and other activities. The Jagriti Foundation works directly with these organisations in ways that support their own goals and objectives, understanding that these women's organisations know the best way to make change within their community. Many organisations need technical assistance or other skills that are difficult or expensive to access locally. Some need a committed advocate, friend or volunteer who will help to promote their issues locally, nationally or even internationally – Bridging Worlds. Individuals must have a demonstrated capacity for being responsible and mature citizens. This is not a programme intended for immature travellers. There is very little supervision or guidance, and therefore our Bridging Worlds volunteers are screened for their maturity, independence and experience as well as ability to function in new cultures and environments.

Number of projects: Varies UK: 0
Starting months: January–December
Time required: 8–24 weeks
Age: 20–70
Causes: Children, Human Rights, Young People.
Activities: Accountancy, Administration, Computers, Development Issues, Fundraising, Marketing/Publicity, Newsletter/Journalism, Research, Teaching, Technical Skills.
Placements: 10
When to apply: All year.
Work alone/with others: Sometimes work with other volunteers – depends on host organisation.
Qualifications: Prefer volunteers who have completed their A level exams or someone with extensive skills to share.

Health requirements: Volunteers must be healthy enough to travel and contribute their promised skill to the host women's organisation.
Costs: Volunteers cover all their own costs. Travel – air fare. Accommodation, with or without food and laundry costs to be covered @ US$100–$500 per month.
Benefits: Accommodation, food and laundry services are provided. However there is a charge made to cover these costs which varies between host organisations and length of stay.
Training: We provide an orientation booklet on what to expect and information on the country. The host organisation is responsible for orientating the volunteer.
Supervision: Host organisation is responsible for supervision.
Interviews: Yes, we try to interview all volunteers in person (we have advisors in many countries to assist with this task) and if an in-person interview is not possible we conduct telephone interviews, in this case we require extensive references.
Charity number: 330893866
Worldwide placements: Asia (Afghanistan, India, Nepal, Pakistan).

JAKARTA INTERNATIONAL ASSOCIATION FOR VOLUNTEER EFFORT (JIAVE)

Bina Murni Oannekia Educational Foundation
Binataro Java
Jakarta Selatan
15221 Indonesia
T: 00 62 21 735 9061
F: 00 62 21 572 7409
Contact: Nurhayati Hasan

Jakarta International Association for Volunteer Effort (JIAVE) promotes and has information about volunteering in Indonesia. It may well be able to put volunteers in touch with organisations which are not yet listed on the WorldWide Volunteering database.

Starting months: January–December
Time required: 1–52 weeks (plus)
Age: 16 plus – no upper limit
Causes: Addicts/Ex-Addicts, AIDS/HIV, Animal Welfare, Archaeology, Architecture, Children, Conservation, Disabled (learning and physical), Elderly People, Environmental Causes, Health Care/Medical, Heritage, Holidays for Disabled, Human Rights, Inner City Problems, Offenders/Ex-Offenders, Poor/Homeless, Refugees, Teaching/assisting (nursery, primary, secondary, mature, EFL) Unemployed, Wildlife, Work camps – Seasonal, Young People.
Activities: Accountancy, Administration, Agriculture/Farming, Arts/Crafts, Building/Construction, Campaigning, Caring

(general, day and residential), Catering, Community Work, Computers, Conservation Skills, Cooking, Counselling, Development Issues, DIY, Driving, First Aid, Forestry, Fundraising, Gardening/Horticulture, Group Work, International Aid, Library/Resource Centres, Manual Work, Marketing/Publicity, Music, Newsletter/Journalism, Outdoor Skills, Religion, Research, Scientific Work, Social Work, Sport, Summer Camps, Teaching, Technical Skills, Theatre/Drama, Training, Translating, Visiting/Befriending, Work Camps – Seasonal.
Costs: Varies according to the project.
Worldwide placements: Asia (Indonesia).

JAPAN YOUTH VOLUNTEER ASSOCIATION (JYVA)

3–1 Yoyogi-Kamizono-cho
Shibuya
Tokyo
151–0052 Japan
F: 00 81 3 3460 0386
E: jyva@blue.ocn.ne.jp
Contact: Yoshitsugu Sukenari

Japan Youth Volunteer Association (JYVA) promotes and has information about volunteering in Japan. It may well be able to put volunteers in touch with organisations which are not yet listed on the WorldWide Volunteering database.

Starting months: January–December
Time required: 1–52 weeks (plus)
Age: 16 plus – no upper limit
Causes: Addicts/Ex-Addicts, AIDS/HIV, Animal Welfare, Archaeology, Architecture, Children, Conservation, Disabled (learning and physical), Elderly People, Environmental Causes, Health Care/Medical, Heritage, Holidays for Disabled, Human Rights, Inner City Problems, Offenders/Ex-Offenders, Poor/Homeless, Refugees, Teaching/assisting (nursery, primary, secondary, mature, EFL) Unemployed, Wildlife, Work Camps – Seasonal, Young People.
Activities: Accountancy, Administration, Agriculture/Farming, Arts/Crafts, Building/Construction, Campaigning, Caring (general, day and residential), Catering, Community Work, Computers, Conservation Skills, Cooking, Counselling, Development Issues, DIY, Driving, First Aid, Forestry, Fundraising, Gardening/Horticulture, Group Work, International Aid, Library/Resource Centres, Manual Work, Marketing/Publicity, Music, Newsletter/Journalism, Outdoor Skills, Religion, Research, Scientific Work, Social Work, Sport, Summer Camps, Teaching, Technical Skills, Theatre/Drama, Training, Translating, Visiting/Befriending, Work Camps – Seasonal.
Costs: Varies according to the project.
Worldwide placements: Asia (Japan).

JATUN SACHA FOUNDATION

Eugenio de Santillán y Maurian Casilla 17 12
867 Quito
Ecuador
T: 00 593 2 243 2173
F: 00 593 2 245 3583
E: volunteer@jatunsacha.org
W: www.jatunsacha.org
Contact: Gabriela Cadena

The Jatun Sacha Foundation offers opportunities for volunteers and interns to participate in research, education, community service, station maintenance, plant conservation, and agroforestry activities carried out by the Jatun Sacha, Bilsa and Guandera biological stations. The Jatun Sacha Biological Station is a 2,000 hectares reserve located in the tropical rainforest region of the Upper Napo of Amazonian Ecuador. Bilsa is a 3,000 hectares reserve containing some of the last premontane tropical wet forest of the northwestern coastal province of Esmeraldas. This forest has been catalogued as a 'Hot Spot', being the third priority for conservation in the world. Guandera, at altitudes of 3,100–3,600 meters conserves more than 1,000 hectares of tropical wet montane forest and páramo highlands in the northern Andes of the Carchi province. The newest reserve, Congal Biological reserve and Sustainable Aquiculture Center is located in the province of Esmeraldas, near the area of Muisne. The Tito Santos Dry Forest Reserve is located in the province of Manabi on the coastal area of Ecuador. This 2000 hectare reserve contains dry, humid and semi-humid forest. There is also access to the beach from the reserve. All four reserves are owned and operated by The Jatun Sacha Foundation, a private, non-profit Ecuadorian organisation founded in 1989 to promote biological conservation, research, education and community programmes. Guandera: Prov. of Carchi, nr city of San Gabriel, Andes Highlands. Jatun Sacha: Prov. of Napo, nr city of Tena in Ecuadorian Amazon. Bilsa, nr Quinindé & Congal, nr Muisne, on Ecuadorian Coast Tito Santos Res. nr Bahia & beautiful Canoa beach. 📄

Number of projects: 5 UK: 0
Starting months: January–December
Time required: 2–24 weeks
Age: 17–60
Causes: Conservation, Environmental Causes, Teaching (EFL), Wildlife.
Activities: Agriculture/Farming, Community Work, Conservation Skills, Forestry, Gardening/Horticulture, Manual Work, Research, Scientific Work, Teaching.
Placements: 385
When to apply: Two or three months in advance of starting.
Work alone/with others: With others.
Qualifications: We require energetic and dynamic people. Spanish is not required but it is strongly recommended to have at least a basic knowledge of the language.
Equipment/clothing: Rubber boots, torch, rainponcho or raincoat, biodegradable soap and shampoo.
Health requirements: With the application form we require a recent health certificate and also a medical insurance certificate.
Costs: Application fee US$30 + US$300 per month for food and lodging – shared rooms, in some cases no electricity. Bed, mattress, blankets, sheets and mosquito nets provided.
Benefits: Experience working in the tropical forests of Ecuador.
Training: Provided on site.
Supervision: By volunteer co-ordinator and reserves directors.
Interviews: No interviews. Just e-mail or telephone.
Worldwide placements: South America (Ecuador).

JESUIT EUROPEAN VOLUNTEERS (JEV)

Kaulbachstr. 31a
Munich
Bavaria D-80539 Germany
T: 00 49 89 2386 2200
F: 00 49 89 2805348
E: team@jev-online.de
W: www.jev-online.de
Contact: Stefanie Langel

Jesuit European Volunteers is a full-time lay volunteer organisation grounded in the principles of Ignatian spirituality, which enables young men and women (ages 18–30) the opportunity to complete one or two years of service experience with the focus on peace and justice. As a way of integrating Christian faith, volunteers work full-time with the poor and marginalised in various placements: with the homeless, the mentally and physically disabled, with addicted persons, refugees and asylum seekers and with abused/abandoned persons. It is expected that Jesuit Volunteers open their minds and hearts to conscientiously helping the poor, committed to the Church's mission of promoting justice in the service of faith. Volunteers live on a simple stipend in an intentional community with four to five other JEVs, where they can explore together the root causes of social injustice and further their personal development. Each community is supported by a Jesuit and/or a former volunteer. The values of the Jesuit European Volunteers are confirmed in these four tenets: social justice, Ignatian spirituality, community living and simple lifestyle. Germany: Berlin, Hamburg, Leipzig, Nuremburg. Austria:Wien, Graz. Bosnia: Tuzla. Belgium: Brussels. Romania: Lipova, Temesvar. Mexico: Mexicalli, Tijuana, Hidalgo, Mexico City. Venezuela. 📄

Number of projects: 40–50 **UK:** 0
Starting months: Sep
Time required: 48–52 weeks (plus)
Age: 18–30
Causes: Addicts/Ex-Addicts, Children, Disabled (learning and physical), Elderly People, Health Care/Medical, Human Rights, Inner City Problems, Poor/Homeless, Refugees, Unemployed, Young People.
Activities: Arts/Crafts, Caring (general, day and residential), Community Work, Cooking, Counselling, Development Issues, Social Work, Teaching, Visiting/Befriending.
Placements: 40–50
When to apply: September–February for Bosnia, Romania or Mexico placements September–May for Germany, Austria or Belgium projects.
Work alone/with others: Work and live with other young volunteers.
Qualifications: German is a requirement for the application process. For some placements a driving licence is needed. Language skills may be needed depending on the project and the country. A Christian background is essential. No restrictions but German is required and a visa is necessary.
Health requirements: Applicants must have strong physical endurance.
Costs: No costs except travel to the orientation week in Germany. All volunteers outside Germany and Austria are required to do fundraising for their project.
Benefits: Travel from Germany to the placements, travel for retreats during the year, room and board, insurance and €100 per month.
Training: Volunteers will participate in various retreats throughout the year, will have support people in the work placements as well as for group dynamics in the community.
Supervision: There is a community support person in town who comes once a week to visit the volunteers for the required 'community meeting'.
Interviews: Interviews with ex-volunteers or Jesuits. We try to find people nearest the applicant's home.
Worldwide placements: Central America (Mexico); South America (Venezuela); Europe (Austria, Belgium, Bosnia-Herzegovina, Germany, Romania).

JESUIT VOLUNTEER COMMUNITY: BRITAIN

23 New Mount Street
Manchester
M4 4DE UK
T: 0161 832 6888
F: 0161 832 6958
E: staff@jvc.u-net.com

W: www.jesuitvolunteers-uk.org
Contact: Rachel Saum

The Jesuit Volunteer Community: Britain (JVC) is a registered charity, part of the Trust for Roman Catholic Purposes. We exist to offer young people, aged between 18 and 35, a one year developmental programme. In offering this programme, JVC aims to enable young people to become more reflective, grow in self-awareness, develop a greater understanding of the needs of others (particularly those who are marginalised in Britain today) in order to promote Christian values. This aim is achieved through four core experiential themes:
– living in community
– working in areas of social need
– leading a simple lifestyle
– integrating life and faith within a Christian context.
During the year volunteers work in placements such as homeless hostels, alcohol and drug dependency units, local community schemes, Citizens Advice Bureaux, centres of mental and physical disability, projects to help refugees. We ask for a commitment to exploring the above four values, for which we supply resources and information, and a series of residential events throughout the year. Volunteers with offending backgrounds are accepted. Inner city areas of Birmingham, Liverpool, Manchester and Glasgow. &

Number of projects: 13 **UK:** 4
Starting months: Sep
Time required: 47 weeks
Age: 18–35
Causes: Addicts/Ex-Addicts, AIDS/HIV, Children, Disabled (learning and physical), Elderly People, Human Rights, Inner City Problems, Offenders/Ex-Offenders, Poor/Homeless, Refugees, Teaching/assisting, Unemployed, Young People.
Activities: Administration, Arts/Crafts, Campaigning, Caring (general and day), Community Work, Computers, Development Issues, Driving, Fundraising, Group Work, Library/Resource Centres, Outdoor Skills, Religion, Research, Social Work, Sport, Training, Visiting/Befriending.
Placements: 21
When to apply: January–July.
Work alone/with others: With others.
Health requirements: JVC cannot accept anyone with a personal history of problems with alcohol or drug use unless he/she has completed rehabilitation or ceased drug or alcohol misuse for a minimum of two years.
Costs: Nil.
Benefits: Self-catering accommodation, £55 per week pocket money and some travel costs.
Training: A 5-day residential orientation.
Supervision: Each volunteer has a work

supervisor with a supervision session at least once a month. JVC provide supervision of the programme overall.
Interviews: A residential interview takes place in Manchester.
Charity number: 230165
Worldwide placements: Europe (Austria, France, Germany, Ireland, Poland, Slovakia, Switzerland).
UK placements: England (Manchester, Merseyside, West Midlands); Scotland (Glasgow City).

JEUNESSE EN MISSION

BP 40
Kpalime
Togo
T: 00 228 47.10.12
F: 00 228 47.10.12
E: hadzi36@hotmail.com
Contact: Yawo Selom Hadzi

Jeunesse en Mission works in three main areas: Evangelism: Jeunesse en Mission organises Christian summer camps. Formation: prepare and equip the young in different mission schools. Aid: help at times of natural catastrophes and crisis. Volunteers with an offending background are accepted – we believe that God changes people. The mission station is at Agou-Nyoogbo which is 120km from Lome.

Number of projects: 2 **UK:** 0
Starting months: Jul, Aug
Time required: 1–4 weeks
Age: 16–50
Causes: Conservation, Health Care/Medical, Teaching (EFL), Work Camps – Seasonal, Young People.
Activities: Arts/Crafts, Building/Construction, Community Work, Computers, Conservation Skills, First Aid, Fundraising, Gardening/Horticulture, Group Work, Manual Work, Outdoor Skills, Religion, Summer Camps, Teaching, Translating, Work Camps – Seasonal.
Placements: 60
When to apply: Before the end of June.
Work alone/with others: With others.
Qualifications: Driving licence if possible and a little French.
Equipment/clothing: Everyday clothes for hot and cold temperatures.
Health requirements: Necessary vaccinations and anti-malarial prophylactic.
Costs: Travel, cost of living and registration fee.
Benefits: The volunteer will receive a small present as a memoir at the end of their service.
Interviews: There are no interviews.
Worldwide placements: Africa (Togo).

JEWISH CARE

Stuart Young House
221 Golders Green Road
London
NW11 9DQ UK
T: +44 (0) 208 922 2408
F: +44 (0) 208 922 2401
E: jover@jcare.org
Contact: Juliette Overlander

Jewish Care is the Jewish Community's largest welfare charity. In total we provide support for over 5000 elderly, physically disabled, mentally ill and visually impaired people and their families. Volunteer projects for young people include a summer experience programme for sixth formers, a student work placement programme and a gap year programme. During the course of the year, student volunteers of 14–18 years are warmly welcomed to our team of volunteers. They work with our resources, befriending members and running small groups. In addition young people visit elderly, lonely and isolated people living on their own. London and South East.

Number of projects: 1 **UK:** 0
Starting months: January–December
Time required: 1–52 weeks
Age: 14 plus – no upper limit
Causes: Disabled (learning and physical), Elderly People.
Activities: Arts/Crafts, Caring – General, Community Work, Group Work, Music, Visiting/Befriending.
Placements: 2,500
When to apply: All year.
Work alone/with others: Both.
Health requirements: No.
Costs: Accommodation and food costs.
Benefits: Travel expenses reimbursed.
Training: All volunteers are offered an 'Introduction to Jewish Care' training day.
Supervision: All volunteers know who to contact if needed. They are each allocated a volunteer co-ordinator.
Interviews: Interviews take place at Head Office in Golders Green.
Charity number: 802559
UK placements: England (Essex, London, Sussex – East).

JEWISH LADS' AND GIRLS' BRIGADE

3 Beechcroft Road
London
E18 1LA UK
T: +44 (0) 208 989 5743/8990
F: +44 (0) 208 518 8832
E: office@jlgb.org
W: www.jlgb.org
Contact: Richard Weber

Jewish Lads' and Girls' Brigade has three separate but interlinked divisions. The uniformed JLGB runs weekly local groups and national one-week summer camps for children aged 8–11 and 11–16. Volunteers are needed to help run activities or look after the general welfare of the young people and to organise voluntary service projects and other activities all year. It also organises weekend activities and courses throughout the year. The JLGB is the only Jewish operating authority for the Duke of Edinburgh's Award, which it also offers to pupils in Jewish and state schools throughout the UK, as part of its 'Outreach Kiruv Project'. Young people working for the Award – or taking part in any other activities organised by 'Outreach' are not required to join the uniformed JLGB. The JLGB's National Lottery-funded project, 'Hand-in-Hand', offers the opportunity for 14–17 year olds to volunteer, in a wide range of projects, in their local community. Volunteers with an offending background may not be accepted. 🖮 🖹

Number of projects: 1 UK: 1
Starting months: January–December
Time required: 1–52 weeks
Age: 14 plus – no upper limit
Causes: Children, Disabled (learning), Work Camps – Seasonal.
Activities: Administration, Arts/Crafts, Caring – General, Community Work, Computers, Conservation Skills, First Aid, Fundraising, Group Work, Marketing/Publicity, Music, Newsletter/Journalism, Outdoor Skills, Social Work, Sport, Summer Camps, Theatre/Drama, Training, Visiting/Befriending.
Placements: 250
When to apply: Any time.
Work alone/with others: With others.
Qualifications: Nil – references checked.
Health requirements: Medical form to be completed.
Costs: Contribution towards the camps and other activities, but no-one prevented from helping on grounds of financial difficulty.
Benefits: Food, accommodation as appropriate.
Interviews: Interviews take place in London and in provincial centres.
Charity number: 286950
UK placements: England (Berkshire, Cheshire, Dorset, Essex, Hertfordshire, London, Manchester, Merseyside, Nottinghamshire, Surrey, Sussex – East, West Midlands); Scotland (Edinburgh, Glasgow City); Wales (Cardiff).

JLGB HAND-IN-HAND

Head Office
3 Beechcroft Road
London
E18 1LA UK

T: +44 (0) 208 530 8220
F: +44 (0) 208 530 3327
E: hand-in-hand@jlgb.org
W: www.handinhand.8m.com
Contact: Raina Gee

JLGB Hand-in-Hand is a national network of Jewish volunteers, aged 14–24, involved in a variety of projects working with both Jewish and non-Jewish charities. Hand-in-Hand is one of the services offered by the Jewish Lads and Girls Brigade to young people. A new initiative for Hand-in-Hand is Millennium Volunteers (MV), which we are now offering to all our volunteers aged 16–24. Volunteers can accrue their MV hours working in the whole range of projects for Hand-in-Hand, which makes it a very exciting way of completing their MV. JLGB Hand-in-Hand also run the Young Citizens Project for 14–15 year olds, which is pre-MV and volunteers only have to volunteer for 50 hours for their award. Volunteers work individually or in groups in a variety of placements – befriending, running camps and activities, newsletter design, campaigning, working with disabled people, gardening, web site design, entertainment and peer education projects – among other things. Volunteers are encouraged to select activities which interest them and match the amount of time commitment they are prepared to make. They can volunteer on a regular or on a one-off basis. JLGB Hand-in-Hand also run regular training sessions on a variety of different subjects including sign language, CSLA – Community Sports Leaders Award, drug awareness sessions for a small fee.
Alternative Address – Northern Office, 27 Bury Old Road, Prestwich, M25 0EY. Tel No. 0161 720 9199. The project is now a national project with offices in London and Manchester. 🖮 🖹

Number of projects: 80 UK: 80
Starting months: January–December
Time required: 1–52 weeks (plus)
Age: 14–24
Causes: AIDS/HIV, Animal Welfare, Children, Conservation, Disabled (learning and physical), Elderly People, Environmental Causes, Poor/Homeless, Teaching/assisting.
Activities: Administration, Arts/Crafts, Campaigning, Caring – General, Community Work, Computers, Conservation Skills, First Aid, Fundraising, Gardening/Horticulture, Group Work, Marketing/Publicity, Music, Newsletter/Journalism, Outdoor Skills, Religion, Sport, Summer Camps, Theatre/Drama, Training, Visiting/Befriending.
Placements: 300
When to apply: All year.
Work alone/with others: Both.
Qualifications: No restrictions but all volunteers must be Jewish.

Health requirements: Nil.
Costs: All out of pocket expenses are paid for volunteers while they are volunteering. There may be costs for residential and training courses although there are grants available.
Training: Whatever is necessary.
Supervision: Adult supervision.
Interviews: Prospective volunteers are interviewed at home or wherever suits them, school, club etc.
Charity number: 286950
UK placements: England (Berkshire, Buckinghamshire, Essex, Hertfordshire, London, Manchester, Merseyside, E. Yorkshire, W. Yorkshire); Scotland (Glasgow City); Wales (Cardiff).

JOHN MUIR AWARD

41 Commercial Street
Edinburgh
EH6 6SD UK
T: 0845 458 2910
F: 0845 458 2910
E: info@johnmuiraward.org
W: www.johnmuiraward.org
Contact: David Picken

The John Muir Award encourages young and old to 'Discover, Explore and Conserve' a wild place. There are also courses on environmental youthwork. John Muir, born in 1838 in the small Scottish port of Dunbar, emigrated with his family as a child to the USA. In his adopted homeland he became a founding father of the world conservation movement, and devoted his life to safeguarding the world's landscapes for future generations. Since 1983, the John Muir Trust, guided by Muir's charge to 'do something for wildness and make the mountains glad', has dedicated itself to making Muir's message a reality within the United Kingdom. By acquiring and sensitively managing key wild areas, the Trust sets out to show that the damage inflicted on the wild over the centuries can be repaired; that the land can be conserved on a sustainable basis for the human, animal, and plant communities which share it; and the great spiritual qualities of wilderness, of tranquillity and solitude, can be preserved as a legacy for those to come. 🖼 📄

Number of projects: 2 UK: Varies
Starting months: January–December
Time required: 1–1 weeks
Age: 14–50
Causes: Conservation, Environmental Causes, Heritage, Unemployed, Work Camps – Seasonal, Young People.
Activities: Arts/Crafts, Conservation Skills, Forestry, Group Work, Manual Work, Outdoor Skills, Summer Camps, Training, Work Camps – Seasonal.

Placements: 1,000
When to apply: All year.
Work alone/with others: With others.
Qualifications: No previous skills – ability to work in a group.
Equipment/clothing: Boots/wellies, warm old clothes and waterproofs.
Health requirements: Some sites are remote, require long walk-in, isolated.
Costs: Approx. £100 for one week's residential.
Benefits: Discovering and exploring wild places and conserving them.
Training: Yes, standard courses.
Supervision: Structured support and supervision.
Interviews: Volunteer applicants are interviewed in Edinburgh.
Charity number: CR 42964
Worldwide placements: North America: (USA).
UK placements: England (Cumbria); Scotland (throughout); Wales (throughout).

JOINT ASSISTANCE CENTRE

G17/3 DLF Qutab Enclave Phase 1
Gurgaon
122002 Haryana India
T: 0091 11 835 2141
F: 0091 11 463 2517
E: jacusa@juno.com
Contact: N K Jain

The international volunteer programmes of JAC are intended to provide opportunities for visiting friends from abroad to see India and learn about its people and their concerns while travelling. Programmes run all year around in different parts of the country. An individual schedule is devised for each person or group to meet their needs. Arrangements have to be made at least 30 days in advance of arrival in India in order to plan properly. Volunteers working with children will be placed in one location at a school or a home for children for a period of three months or longer. These volunteers should be prepared to learn some basic Hindi language preferably starting before they leave for India. Participation in work camps in Indian villages: These programmes involve work with villagers on such activities as sanitation projects, building construction, plant nurseries and other agricultural work, literacy and women's welfare, health projects including use of local herbal medicine, environmental awareness campaign etc. (1–4 weeks). Working with children in schools and orphanages (12 weeks minimum). Helping in JAC office in New Delhi doing office work, and research for cultural exchange, disaster preparedness and other programmes. Preparing and attending conferences on development, disasters and environmental issues. Taking part in environmentally oriented treks in the Himalayan area. Participation in yoga, meditation and natural health care training programme. Participation in individually designed projects based on special skills involving a long term commitment in such areas as medicine, journalism and engineering.

Number of projects: 1
Starting months: January–December
Time required: 4–26 weeks
Age: 18 plus – no upper limit
Causes: Children, Conservation, Elderly People, Environmental Causes, Health Care/Medical, Poor/Homeless, Teaching/assisting (nursery, primary, secondary, EFL), Work Camps – Seasonal, Young People.
Activities: Administration, Agriculture/Farming, Arts/Crafts, Building/Construction, Caring (general and day), Community Work, Conservation Skills, Forestry, Fundraising, Group Work, International Aid, Manual Work, Marketing/Publicity, Social Work, Summer Camps, Teaching, Training, Work Camps – Seasonal.
When to apply: At least 3 months in advance.
Qualifications: Personal faith in God.
Health requirements: Vegetarian, no alcohol, tobacco or drugs allowed.
Costs: £75per month + travel, insurance and pocket money. Registration fee £15.
Benefits: The cost include food, accommodation and administrtion fee.
Worldwide placements: Asia (India).

JOSSÅSEN LANDSBY

N 7550 Hommelvik
Norway
T: 00 47 73 9799900
F: 00 47 73 978840
E: landsby@online.no
Contact: Birgit Hammer or Thomas Bresges

Jossåsen Landsby is a Camphill Village community with adults. The purpose of the trust is to create working communities where people who are mentally and physically handicapped, working together with workshop leaders, volunteers and houseparents can find satisfaction in purposeful work in the security of a family setting. In this village, 40 km east of Trondheim, about 55 people live in five family units. There is a weavery where we also spin, a book workshop, a wood workshop, a farm with gardening in the summer and work in the forest in the winter. We also have cows, sheep, chickens etc. Like all Camphill communities Jossåsen functions on voluntary non-salary basis. Experience has shown that volunteer work is most valuable if you stay long enough to give you the opportunity to share in the responsibilities of living and working with

people who are handicapped. Therefore it is recommended that volunteers come to Jossåsen for one year or longer. However, exceptions are made for working holidays in the summer. Bear in mind that the Norwegian climate needs warm clothing for the winter and boots etc but in the summer it can be warm. The habitual use of drugs and alcohol is not in harmony with life in a Camphill community. We do not want private TV either, because it may have a negative influence on the common activities we try to create together. Life in the community can provide many lasting rewards for anyone who is willing to approach that life with goodwill, a degree of tolerance and openhearted interest and enthusiasm. People with offending backgrounds may be accepted but the 'issue' must be made clear beforehand so that we can talk openly about it. We cannot accept everybody but we are willing to consider each case separately. 40km east of Trondheim. 📖

Number of projects: 1 UK: 0
Starting months: January–December
Time required: 25–52 weeks
Age: 18 plus – no upper limit
Causes: Disabled (learning and physical), Elderly People.
Activities: Agriculture/Farming, Arts/Crafts, Building/Construction, Caring (general and day), Catering, Community Work, Cooking, Forestry, Gardening/Horticulture, Manual Work, Music, Sport, Theatre/Drama.
Placements: 6–8
When to apply: All year.
Work alone/with others: Both.
Qualifications: None specifically but volunteers must have an interest in anthroposophy.
Equipment/clothing: Warm clothes.
Health requirements: Normal health is enough.
Costs: Travel.
Benefits: Board and lodging and NKr1,500 per month pocket money.
Training: Introduction training course.
Interviews: Volunteers are interviewed by phone and letter.
Worldwide placements: Europe (Norway).

JUBILEE OUTREACH YORKSHIRE

14 Jubilee Way
Windhill
Shipley
West Yorkshire BD18 1QG UK
T: 01274 531999
F: 01274 531396
E: joy@jiffytrucks.co.uk
W: www.joyworld.org.uk
Contact: Dr Kathy Tedd

JOY have been sending urgent supplies and teams of volunteers to help the needy of Romania since the beginning of 1990. From the very beginning we realised the problems of aid going on to the black market and so have only used tried and trusted contacts. So, although we have greatly improved the living conditions in many orphanages by renovation, our aim is to support the struggling families, and keep the children of the poorest families with their parents, by providing essential aid through Christian doctors and pastors. While Western European aid pours into the orphanages which the state already subsidises, there is little or no help for the families struggling to stay together. JOY aims to try to stem the flow of children into the orphanages from families unable to cope, setting up self help groups, supporting soup kitchens and medical provisions, day care for the disabled and provision for street children. 🔆 📄

Number of projects: 3 UK: 0
Starting months: Mar
Time required: 2–52 weeks (plus)
Age: 18 plus – no upper limit
Causes: Children, Disabled (learning and physical), Elderly People, Health Care/Medical, Poor/Homeless, Teaching (EFL), Unemployed, Work Camps – Seasonal, Young People.
Activities: Arts/Crafts, Building/Construction, Caring – Day, Cooking, DIY, Driving, Fundraising, International Aid, Manual Work, Music, Religion, Summer Camps, Work Camps – Seasonal.
Placements: 60
When to apply: Varies – worth asking any time.
Work alone/with others: Always in a team.
Qualifications: Drivers need to be 25 with clean licence and truck/van driving experience. For projects, practical building skills ideal.
Equipment/clothing: Depends on the project – generally not.
Health requirements: Must have had triple antigen vaccine as a baby and be up to date with tetanus and polio innoculations.
Costs: Minimum £350 for 2 weeks.
Benefits: The cost covers travel, board and insurance. Very basic accommodation provided.
Training: If required.
Supervision: With the team leader.
Interviews: Interviews take place at the office in Shipley, W. Yorkshire.
Charity number: 1004231
Worldwide placements: Europe (Romania).
UK placements: England (W. Yorkshire).

JUBILEE PARTNERS

Box 68
Comer
GA 30629 USA

T: 00 1 706 783 5131
F: 00 1 706 783 5134
E: jubileep@igc.org
W: www.jubileepartners.org
Contact: Robbie Buller

Jubilee Partners is a Christian community dedicated to serving poor and oppressed people. The community's work includes several areas of service: resettling refugees, peace-making, fund raising and working against the death penalty. Volunteers teach English as a second language to refugees among other things. Southern US.

Number of projects: 1 UK: 0
Starting months: Jan, Jun, Sep
Time required: 12–28 weeks
Age: 19–80
Causes: Children, Human Rights, Offenders/Ex-Offenders, Poor/Homeless, Refugees, Teaching/assisting (EFL).
Activities: Administration, Building/Construction, Caring (general and day), Cooking, Driving, Gardening/Horticulture, Library/Resource Centres, Manual Work, Religion, Teaching, Visiting/Befriending.
Placements: 30
When to apply: Anytime, preferably 6 mths prior to start of terms.
Work alone/with others: With others.
Qualifications: Nil. Construction/maintenance skills welcomed. Must be able to obtain a visa without assistance from Jubilee. Coming to Jubilee as a volunteer does not make one eligible for a visa.
Health requirements: Must be able to do physical work.
Costs: Transportation and insurance costs.
Benefits: Board, accommodation and community allowance of $15 per week. Must be willing to participate in the spiritual life of the community. Accommodation in two-person rooms along a hall. Shared bath. Similar to dormitory.
Training: None prior to arrival. One week of orientation and teacher training provided upon arrival.
Supervision: Volunteer is expected to be a self-starter and to work with the minimum of supervision. Some work is individual, some done in groups. There is a work supervisor, a teaching supervisor, and a volunteer programme supervisor at Jubilee.
Interviews: Applicants are not usually interviewed but must submit a written spiritual journey after contacting the volunteer co-ordinator to express interest. References may be required.
Worldwide placements: North America: (USA).

K

KAIROS DWELLING

2945 Gull Road
Kalamazoo
Michigan MI 49048 USA
T: 00 1 616 381 3688
F: 00 1 616 388 8016
E: kairosdwelling1@juno.com
Contact: Sr Maureen Merry

Kairos Dwelling is an interfaith sponsored home that provides physical care, emotional support and spiritual sustenance for terminally ill persons and their loved ones in a loving and compassionate environment. When people are living with a terminal disease, it is important to have fewer distressing symptoms, the security of a caring environment and the assurance that they and their families will not be abandoned. The guest's psychological comfort will arise from arranging for special activities of interest as well as periods of peaceful withdrawal, as determined by the guest's physical state of care. It is our expectation that the guest's physical comfort will come under the direction of the pain control management of local hospices, agencies and physicians. As an ecumenical endeavour, we value the importance of the spiritual journey in one's life. Spiritual support will come from the guest's personal preference of how his or her needs are to be met. It is our hope that support from all faith communities will be available as the needs arise. The environment is a home setting with an extended family of volunteers whose main focus is unconditional love and compassionate service. Kairos Dwelling is a home that can accommodate four guests. It is not a hospice, nursing home or assisted living facility. Room, meals and 24 hour nursing care will be provided by trained volunteers at no charge. Priority will be given to those in the greatest need. &

Number of projects: 1 UK: 0
Starting months: January–December
Time required: 6–52 weeks (plus)
Age: 18 plus – no upper limit
Causes: AIDS/HIV, Elderly People, Health Care/Medical, Poor/Homeless.
Activities: Caring (general, residential), Cooking, Group Work.
Placements: 100
When to apply: All year.
Work alone/with others: With others most of the time.
Qualifications: Communication skills, listening, bending, stretching, working on feet, having compassion and presence. No nationality restrictions but it is important to speak and understand English well.
Health requirements: No contageous illness and able to do normal activities of daily living with ease.
Costs: All travel costs, health insurance, expenses and spending money.
Benefits: We provide housing and meals.
Training: 16 hours of training given.
Supervision: Direct supervision by the Director or Volunteer Co-ordinator.
Interviews: Telephone or personal interviews.
Worldwide placements: North America: (USA).

KENT KIDS MILES OF SMILES

Footprints
Stodmarsh Road
Canterbury
Kent CT3 4AP UK
T: 01227 780796
F: 01227 764480
E: admin@footprint-holidays.org.uk
W: www.miles-of-smiles.org.uk
Contact: Linda George

The aim of Kent Kids Miles of Smiles as stated in the charity's deed trust is 'to generally assist in the well-being, comfort and happiness of sick and disabled children and to establish and run a holiday centre in the Kent area'. We hope that we are able to raise awareness in people that a sick and/or disabled child is no different to any other child in the fact that when on holiday they like to participate in all the activities enjoyed by able children and we are here to enable this. We accommodate seven children (between the ages of 3 and 19 inclusive) per week and the week's fun includes visits to local attractions (we have our own mini-bus) and also activities in the house and gardens at Footprints. On the outskirts of the small town of Fordwich, a few miles from the city of Canterbury.

Number of projects: 1 UK: 1
Starting months: January–December
Time required: 1–12 weeks
Age: 17 plus – no upper limit
Causes: Children, Disabled (physical), Holidays for Disabled.
Activities: Caring (general, day and residential).
Placements: 60
When to apply: Any time but as early as possible as police checks are essential.
Work alone/with others: With others.
Health requirements: Must be fit and healthy.

Costs: Incidental expenses, food and accommodation.
Training: All necessary training, e.g. lifting of children, will be given on site at induction meetings. These take place before commencement of voluntary time.
Supervision: Regular supervision sessions during the week.
Interviews: Prospective volunteers are interviewed at Footprints.
Charity number: 1018320
UK placements: England (Kent).

KENT WILDLIFE TRUST

Tyland Barn
Sandling
Maidstone
Kent ME14 3BD UK
T: 01622 662012
F: 01622 671390
E: kentwildlife@cix.co.uk
Contact: Debbie Davey

Kent Wildlife Trust is a member of the Wildlife Trusts, a national partnership of 47 County Trusts. The aims of the Trust are primarily to: promote nature conservation in the community and secure a better future for the wildlife of Kent; acquire and manage nature reserves; monitor biological and geological resources; liaise with local authorities to promote regard for nature conservation; offer practical advice on nature conservation to landowners. It is the Trust's policy to involve all sectors of the community, of all ages, backgrounds, abilities and disabilities towards these ends. Volunteers require no previous experience just lots of enthusiasm. They will receive on-the-job training in an informal atmosphere and, if they desire, can go on to participate more fully, assisting with the organisation and running of activities/projects. Volunteers with an offending background may be accepted, each case separately assessed.

Number of projects: 1 UK: 1
Starting months: January–December
Time required: 1–52 weeks (plus)
Age: 16 plus – no upper limit
Causes: Conservation, Environmental Causes, Wildlife.
Activities: Conservation Skills.
When to apply: Any time.
Work alone/with others: With others.
Health requirements: Anti-tetanus innoculation recommended.
Costs: Food and accommodation costs – travel to project.
Training: On the job training given.
Supervision: Always supervised.
Charity number: 239992
UK placements: England (Kent).

KENYA VOLUNTARY DEVELOPMENT ASSOCIATION

P O Box 48902
00100 GPO
Nairobi
Kenya
T: 00 254 2 225379 or 247393
F: 00 254 2 225379
E: kvdakenya@yahoo.com
Contact: Opimbi Osore

Kenya Voluntary Development Association needs volunteers to work on projects in villages aimed at improving amenities in Kenya's rural and needy areas, working alongside members of the local community. The work may involve digging foundations, building, making building blocks, roofing, environmental projects etc. All volunteers are accepted whatever their background providing they are interested in changing other people's lives by volunteering. We are an indigenous, non-political, non-sectarian and non-profit making organisation founded in 1962 and registered as an NGO. The location of the office is next to Nakumat Checkpoint at Gilfilian House, 4th Floor, Room 411, Kenyatta Avenue, Nairobi (opposite 680 Hotel). 🖥 📄

Number of projects: 12 UK: 0
Starting months: Feb, Apr, Jul, Aug, Oct, Dec
Time required: 12–52 weeks (plus)
Age: 17 plus – no upper limit
Causes: Conservation, Poor/Homeless, Work Camps – Seasonal.
Activities: Building/Construction, Conservation Skills, Work Camps – Seasonal.
Placements: 200+
When to apply: Ideally 8 weeks in advance but anytime before starting.
Work alone/with others: With others who are local volunteers and community members.
Qualifications: Nil. For mid/long-term volunteers, professionals are preferred.
Equipment/clothing: Strong work boots, sleeping bag or blanket, mosquito net, mug, plate, spoon, fork, knife, malaria tablets, clothes for working in, toilet paper and any other necessary personal effects.
Health requirements: Malaria pills and any other innoculations etc.
Costs: Camp for three weeks-US$220 which covers food, accommodation, clearance and preparation during a the orientation course. For two camps US$400. Long-term stay for more than three weeks $250 for entire stay with volunteers meeting subsistence costs.
Benefits: Food and very basic accommodation (classroom). Familiarisation with Kenyan culture, creating friendships, self-realisation and making a change in a needy community. We arrange safaris for interested volunteers.

Training: Our volunteers are not given pre-training as such but they are given orientation which includes demonstration of what is to be done and what to expect.
Supervision: Camps are led by camp facilitator and the project officer.
Interviews: No interviews other than exchange of views and interest.
Worldwide placements: Africa (Kenya).

KERALA LINK

7 Newland Place
Banbury
Oxfordshire OX16 5BU UK
E: mayfieldhowson@yahoo.co.uk
Contact: Caroline Mayfield Howson

Kerala Link is a very small organisation sending self-funding volunteers to work at a school in Kerala, India for children with learning disabilities. Kerala Link, a non-profit charitable organisation, was set up in 2001 after the co-ordinator and her family spent several months working at the school. Setting up Kerala Link is a way to continue to support these needy children. The co-ordinator knows each child and member of staff personally and hopes that volunteers will find that a placement will be like joining a family for which they will be thoroughly prepared. Volunteers will bring a variety of skills to their placement, perhaps in arts, crafts, music, sport or drama. They will select appropriate projects on which to work with the children, liaising with the staff at all times, and bring funding to cover the cost of materials. The pre-departure weekend training prepares volunteers for working with children with special educational needs, and provides help with ideas for projects and a language base. ⌖

Number of projects: 1 UK: 0
Starting months: January–December
Time required: 12–52 weeks (plus)
Age: 18 plus – no upper limit
Causes: Children, Disabled (learning), Teaching/assisting.
Activities: Arts/Crafts, Teaching, Technical Skills, Theatre/Drama.
Placements: 6
When to apply: All year.
Work alone/with others: Both – it varies.
Qualifications: Volunteers should bring their particular skills to the project. These might be in arts and craft, music, dance, drama, sport etc. A willingness to learn the local language is required. No restrictions but must be able to travel to the UK for pre-departure training.
Equipment/clothing: Volunteers fund their own projects and may need to provide materials specific to their skill.
Health requirements: None.
Costs: Volunteers pay a fee which covers their accommodation, airport pick-up and

communication costs. Volunteers are responsible for their own flight, visa, insurance and food costs.
Benefits: Self catering accommodation and food.
Training: Kerala Link provides pre-departure weekend training courses for which there is a separate charge.
Supervision: A Kerala Link co-ordinator at the placement is a permanent contact locally. At school, a volunteer is responsible at all times to the head teacher or the school administrator.
Interviews: Interview in Banbury, Oxfordshire.
Worldwide placements: Asia (India).

KIBBUTZ REPRESENTATIVES

1a Accommodation Road
London
NW11 8ED UK
T: +44 (0) 208 458 9235
F: +44 (0) 208 455 7930
E: enquiries@kibbutz.org.uk
Contact: Volunteer Co-ordinator

Kibbutz Representatives needs volunteers to work on kibbutzim to help the community as a whole, but also experience the alternative lifestyle. They may be working anywhere – agriculture, industry or services. Volunteers do not get a choice of kibbutz. ⌖ ▤

Number of projects: 1 UK: 0
Starting months: January–December
Time required: 8–32 weeks
Age: 18–42
Causes: Animal Welfare, Children, Conservation, Elderly People, Work Camps – Seasonal, Young People.
Activities: Agriculture/Farming, Catering, Community Work, Conservation Skills, Cooking, Forestry, Gardening/Horticulture, Group Work, Manual Work.
Placements: 3,000
When to apply: For July and August it is essential to apply before Easter. For the rest of the year, 5–6 weeks in advance.
Work alone/with others: Both but mainly with others.
Qualifications: No restrictions, however volunteers from some countries may need visas.
Health requirements: Volunteers must be physically and mentally healthy, free from chronic conditions.
Costs: Travel package cost and insurance and £60 application fee.
Benefits: Board, lodging, leisure facilities, occasional excursions round country + an allowance.
Training: Training available if required.
Supervision: Supervised at all times.
Interviews: Interviews take place in London or Manchester.

Charity number: 294564
Worldwide placements: Asia (Israel).

KIDS' CAMPS: Camps for Students with an Intellectual Disability Inc.

City West Lotteries House
2 Delhi Street
West Perty
6005 Australia
T: 00 61 8 9420 7247
F: 00 61 8 9420 7248
E: enquiries@kidscampsinc.com
Contact: Robert Evans

Kids' Camps Inc. provides residential camps for school-aged children (6–18 years) who live at home and are walking unassisted, i.e. no wheelchairs, and who have an intellectual disability (Downs syndrome, autism etc.). Camps are for two days or six days. Volunteer camp leaders care for up to three children, taking responsibility for their safety, welfare, personal hygiene etc. and also encouraging them to join in recreational activities in the programme. One or two paid staff supervise the group, supporting, assisting, advising and co-ordinating the volunteer staff. Qualities needed to be a volunteer leader are:
– genuine liking for children
– sense of responsibility and understanding of duty of care issues in the daily care of children
– good communication skills with kids, other leaders and staff
– sense of humour, patience and ability to have FUN
– initiative as necessary.
A booklet, 'An Introduction to Volunteering with Kids' Camps' is available plus orientation and information sessions. Feedback is encouraged by Kids' Camps during camps. Volunteers with an offending background would not be accepted if the charges are associated with abuse/assault or serious injury or children. Western Australia, mainly Perth City and environs.

Number of projects: 1 UK: 0
Starting months: January–December
Time required: 1–52 weeks (plus)
Age: 18 plus – no upper limit
Causes: Children, Disabled (learning), Holidays for Disabled.
Activities: Caring – Residential, Summer Camps, Visiting/Befriending.
Placements: 130
When to apply: All year.
Work alone/with others: With other young volunteers.
Qualifications: Good English speaking skills.
Health requirements: General good health and fitness.
Costs: Travel to camp.
Benefits: Accommodation, food and entertainment.

Training: Interview and pre-camp orientation, 4–6 hours.
Supervision: Paid experienced staff offer support, assistance, advice to volunteers.
Interviews: Interviews take place in the Kids' Camps office in West Perth, W. Australia.
Worldwide placements: Australasia (Australia).

KIDS' CLUBS NETWORK

Bellerive House
3 Muirfield Crescent
London
E14 9SZ UK
T: +44 (0) 207 512 2112
T: +44 (0) 207 512 2010
E: information.office@kidsclubs.org.uk
W: www.kidclubs.org.uk
Contact: Anne Longfield

Out of school kids clubs. Kids' Clubs Network provide play and care opportunities for primary school age children before and after school during term time and all day long during school holidays. Children are collected from school at the end of the day by playworkers, escorted safely to the club where they are offered tea and play activities until they are collected by parents. Whilst at the club children are able to enjoy a range of activities including arts and crafts, sports and games, drama, music, books and trips out. Kids' Club Network is the national organisation for out of school care and can give details of local clubs. Volunteers with an offending background connected with violence or possible abuse will not be accepted. Volunteers' records will be checked by the police including for all spent convictions. Volunteers may not be able to commence work at a club without first receiving a clear police check. &

Number of projects: 3, 400 UK: 3, 400
Starting months: January–December
Time required: 1–52 weeks
Age: 16 plus – no upper limit
Causes: Children, Teaching/assisting (primary).
Activities: Arts/Crafts, Caring (general and day), Community Work, Fundraising, Marketing/Publicity, Outdoor Skills, Sport, Summer Camps, Teaching.
When to apply: All year.
Work alone/with others: Both.
Qualifications: Sensitivity, judgement, energy, arts, crafts, sports. Police check also mandatory.
Health requirements: Check locally.
Costs: Out of pocket expenses usually.
Benefits: Dependent on the club.
Training: Dependent on each particular club (see Ofsted Out of School Care Standards).
Supervision: Dependent on the club.
Interviews: Each club interviews its own applicants.

Charity number: 288285
UK placements: England (throughout); Scotland (throughout); Northern Ireland (throughout); Wales (throughout).

KINGS CROSS – BRUNSWICK NEIGHBOURHOOD ASSOCIATION

Marchmont Community Centre
62 Marchmont Street
London
WC1N 1AB UK
T: +44 (0) 207 278 5635
E: kcbna@aol.com
Contact: Maggie Morgan

Kings Cross Brunswick Neighbourhood Association is involved in a volunteer pool called South Camden Volunteers Project. Volunteers with an offending background are not normally accepted except in exceptional circumstances when a person is known.

Number of projects: 1 **UK:** 1
Starting months: January–December
Time required: 1–52 weeks
Age: 14 plus – no upper limit
Causes: Elderly People.
Activities: Arts/Crafts, Campaigning, Driving, Gardening/Horticulture, Training.
When to apply: All year.
Interviews: Interviews take place at the office in London.
Charity number: 1001872
UK placements: England (London).

KITH AND KIDS

The Irish Centre
Pretoria Road
London
N17 8DX UK
T: +44 (0) 208 801 7432
F: +44 (0) 208 885 3035
E: projects@kithandkids.org.uk
W: www.kithandkids.org.uk
Contact: Dan Cary

Kith and Kids supports children and adults who have a variety of learning and/or physical disabilities on a variety of social, stimulating and creative activities. Activities include weekend afternoon activities, half term outings, week long holiday projects, summer camp, befriending and advocacy schemes. On each of the activities we link up two volunteers to each of our members and they support them whilst involved in the activities available. Volunteers with an offending background may be accepted but a police check is made. Most of our activities throughout the year are based in Tottenham, North London. ♿ 📷

Number of projects: 6 **UK:** 6
Starting months: January–December

Time required: 1–52 weeks
Age: 14 plus – no upper limit
Causes: Children, Disabled (learning and physical), Health Care/Medical, Holidays for Disabled, Young People.
Activities: Administration, Arts/Crafts, Caring (general, day and residential), Catering, Community Work, Computers, Cooking, First Aid, Fundraising, Group Work, Music, Outdoor Skills, Sport, Summer Camps, Theatre/Drama, Visiting/Befriending.
Placements: 300
When to apply: All year.
Work alone/with others: With others.
Equipment/clothing: None required.
Health requirements: No health restrictions.
Costs: Volunteers need to find and pay for their own accommodation except on our camp in the summer. Travel expenses up to £75 per week offered.
Benefits: On our week long projects we are able to offer up to £75 expenses. Accommodation provided for the week of the summer camp – not for other activities.
Training: Before our projects we always offer at least three days training.
Supervision: There are always at least three co-ordinators on each of our projects and a great deal of support and feedback opportunities.
Interviews: Interviews take place at our office in Tottenham.
Charity number: 265496
UK placements: England (London).

KOINONIA PARTNERS

1324 Georgia Highway 49 South
Americus
Georgia 31709 USA
T: 00 1 229 924 0391
F: 00 1 229 924 6504
E: volunteer@koinoniapartners.org
W: www.koinoniapartners.org
Contact: Ellie Castle

Koinonia Partners is a non-profit Christian organisation working in the rural south of the USA to attack poverty and racism. Koinonia attempts to promote self-sufficiency for low-income neighbourhoods and to fight inequality in this region. Koinonia operates a large farm and bakery. All income from the operation is used to fund community organising, youth education, and housing. We are trying to make our neighbourhood a model of a self-sufficient, inter-racial, empowered community. Volunteers support our full-time staff in many different areas: the farm, garden, youth programme, office, maintenance, bakery and products business. Volunteers also share weekly study sessions that focus on justice, racism, environmentalism, community, and issues of faith. Koinonia supports volunteers with housing, community development centre, food, access to field trips, social events, transportation and small weekly stipend. &

Number of projects: 1 UK: 0
Starting months: January–December
Time required: 1–52 weeks
Age: 18–80
Causes: Addicts/Ex-Addicts, Children, Conservation, Elderly People, Environmental Causes, Poor/Homeless, Teaching/assisting, Young People.
Activities: Administration, Agriculture/Farming, Building/Construction, Community Work, Computers, Conservation Skills, Cooking, Development Issues, Forestry, Fundraising, Gardening/Horticulture, Library/Resource Centres, Manual Work, Marketing/Publicity, Newsletter/Journalism, Outdoor Skills, Religion, Summer Camps, Teaching, Visiting/Befriending.
Placements: 50
When to apply: As early as possible.
Work alone/with others: With others in different areas of Koinonia.
Qualifications: Willing to explore the Christian faith and life. Applicants must speak English and volunteers must obtain a tourist visa.
Equipment/clothing: Clothing only.
Health requirements: Good to excellent health.
Costs: Tourist visa and travel expenses.
Benefits: Board, lodging and and stipend for food and extra costs.
Training: Orientation and on-the-job experience.
Supervision: Supervision provided by volunteer co-ordinator and department supervisors.
Interviews: Applicants for volunteer projects are not interviewed.
Worldwide placements: North America: (Canada, USA); Asia (Bangladesh, Japan, Korea (South), Thailand).
UK placements: England (Lancashire, London).

KOREA COUNCIL OF VOLUNTEER ORGANIZATIONS (KCVO)

100–043, 32–3 Ka, Nam-San-Dong
Choong-Ku
Seoul
Korea
T: 00 82 2 755 6734
F: 00 82 2 755 6735
E: volun@peacenet.or.kr
Contact: Young Hoon Suh

Korea Council of Volunteer Organizations (KCVO) promotes and has information about volunteering in S. Korea. It may well be able to put volunteers in touch with organisations which are not yet listed on the WorldWide Volunteering database.

Starting months: January–December
Time required: 1–52 weeks (plus)
Age: 16 plus – no upper limit
Causes: Addicts/Ex-Addicts, AIDS/HIV, Animal Welfare, Archaeology, Architecture, Children, Conservation, Disabled (learning and physical), Elderly People, Environmental Causes, Health Care/Medical, Heritage, Holidays for Disabled, Human Rights, Inner City Problems, Offenders/Ex-Offenders, Poor/Homeless, Refugees, Teaching/assisting (nursery, primary, secondary, mature, EFL) Unemployed, Wildlife, Work Camps – Seasonal, Young People.
Activities: Accountancy, Administration, Agriculture/Farming, Arts/Crafts, Building/Construction, Campaigning, Caring (general, day and residential), Catering, Community Work, Computers, Conservation Skills, Cooking, Counselling, Development Issues, DIY, Driving, First Aid, Forestry, Fundraising, Gardening/Horticulture, Group Work, International Aid, Library/Resource Centres, Manual Work, Marketing/Publicity, Music, Newsletter/Journalism, Outdoor Skills, Religion, Research, Scientific Work, Social Work, Sport, Summer Camps, Teaching, Technical Skills, Theatre/Drama, Training, Translating, Visiting/Befriending, Work Camps – Seasonal.
Costs: Varies according to the project.
Worldwide placements: Asia (Korea (South)).

KOREA YOUTH VOLUNTEER CENTER (KYVC)

142 Woomyeon-Dong
Seocho-ku
Seoul
S. Korea
T: 00 82 2 578 4104
F: 00 82 2 2188 8889
E: kyvc@youthnet.re.kr
Contact: Dr Choi, Chung Ok

Korea Youth Volunteer Center (KYVC) promotes and has information about volunteering in S. Korea. It may well be able to put volunteers in touch with organisations which are not yet listed on the WorldWide Volunteering database.

Starting months: January–December
Time required: 1–52 weeks (plus)
Age: 16 plus – no upper limit
Causes: Addicts/Ex-Addicts, AIDS/HIV, Animal Welfare, Archaeology, Architecture, Children, Conservation, Disabled (learning and physical), Elderly People, Environmental Causes, Health Care/Medical, Heritage, Holidays for Disabled, Human Rights, Inner City Problems, Offenders/Ex-Offenders, Poor/Homeless, Refugees, Teaching/assisting (nursery, primary, secondary, mature, EFL) Unemployed, Wildlife, Work Camps – Seasonal, Young People.
Activities: Accountancy, Administration, Agriculture/Farming, Arts/Crafts,

Building/Construction, Campaigning, Caring (general, day and residential), Catering, Community Work, Computers, Conservation Skills, Cooking, Counselling, Development Issues, DIY, Driving, First Aid, Forestry, Fundraising, Gardening/Horticulture, Group Work, International Aid, Library/Resource Centres, Manual Work, Marketing/Publicity, Music, Newsletter/Journalism, Outdoor Skills, Religion, Research, Scientific Work, Social Work, Sport, Summer Camps, Teaching, Technical Skills, Theatre/Drama, Training, Translating, Visiting/Befriending, Work Camps – Seasonal.
Costs: Varies according to the project.
Worldwide placements: Asia (Korea (South)).

KOREAN ASSOCIATION OF VOLUNTEER CENTERS (KAVC)

c/o Songpa-GU Volunteer Center
62–2 Samjeon-Dong
Songpa-Gu
Seoul
138-180 S. Korea
T: 00 82 2 410 37978
F: 00 82 2 2202 1104
E: spvol@unitel.co.kr
Contact: Kyun-Oak Kim

Korean Association of Volunteer Centers (KAVC) promotes and has information about volunteering in Korea. It may well be able to put volunteers in touch with organisations which are not yet listed on the WorldWide Volunteering database.

Starting months: January–December
Time required: 1–52 weeks (plus)
Age: 16 plus – no upper limit
Causes: Addicts/Ex-Addicts, AIDS/HIV, Animal Welfare, Archaeology, Architecture, Children, Conservation, Disabled (learning and physical), Elderly People, Environmental Causes, Health Care/Medical, Heritage, Holidays for Disabled, Human Rights, Inner City Problems, Offenders/Ex-Offenders, Poor/Homeless, Refugees, Teaching/assisting (nursery, primary, secondary, mature, EFL) Unemployed, Wildlife, Work Camps – Seasonal, Young People.
Activities: Accountancy, Administration, Agriculture/Farming, Arts/Crafts, Building/ Construction, Campaigning, Caring (general, day and residential), Catering, Community Work, Computers, Conservation Skills, Cooking, Counselling, Development Issues, DIY, Driving, First Aid, Forestry, Fundraising, Gardening/Horticulture, Group Work, International Aid, Library/Resource Centres, Manual Work, Marketing/Publicity, Music, Newsletter/Journalism, Outdoor Skills, Religion, Research, Scientific Work, Social Work, Sport, Summer Camps, Teaching, Technical Skills, Theatre/Drama, Training, Translating, Visiting/Befriending, Work Camps – Seasonal.
Costs: Varies according to the project.
Worldwide placements: Asia (Korea (South)).

KRISTOFFERTUNET

Hans Collins vej 5
N 7053 Ranheim
Norway
T: 00 47 73 82 68 60
F: 00 47 73 82 68 51
E: adm@kristoffertunet.no
W: www.kristoffertunet.no
Contact: Lars Ursin

Kristoffertunet is an urban community project with adults in need of special care. At the moment there are 30 people living in the community, including volunteers and co-workers with their families. We live together in three big houses, work in the houses, the gardens, the farm, the weavers and the pottery workshop. Each house has their meals together and we gather for cultural and festive events. Kristoffertunet takes part in a trust which has recently bought an old group of farm buildings – all of which are/will be ecologically based. Furthermore, there will be workshops both for us and the local artists and craftsmen, a gallery as well as a hall for cultural events, and for the use of the local community. These buildings are situated just beside the houses we live in. To make our plans a reality and to make this an area the people of Trondheim can benefit from, a lot of voluntary work will be needed. We welcome applications from everyone who would like to live and work in our community, for a short or long period of time. We seek new co-workers who want to live in one of our community houses and who will take part in the cultural life and other activities of the community. We offer you free food and lodging, pocket money and new challenges and opportunities in a young and developing environment. Kristoffertunet is part of the European Voluntary Service Programme. Kristoffertunet is beautifully placed in natural surroundings by the sea. It is situated by the city Trondheim – seven minutes by train from the city centre. Trondheim is a city of 150,000 inhabitants and gives ample opportunities for cultural life.

Number of projects: 1 UK: 0
Starting months: January–December
Time required: 26–78 weeks
Age: 18–30
Causes: Addicts/Ex-Addicts, Disabled (learning).
Activities: Agriculture/Farming, Building/Construction, Caring – General, Cooking, Gardening/Horticulture.
Placements: 6
When to apply: Any time.
Work alone/with others: With others.
Qualifications: We seek volunteers who are interested in music, drama, textile work, bio-dynamic farming and pottery.
Equipment/clothing: No special requirements.

Health requirements: No special requirements.
Costs: Travel (depends on the duration of your stay).
Benefits: Board, lodging and pocket money.
Training: Language and introduction training.
Supervision: Mentor, house responsible and workshop leader all supervise.
Interviews: You are encouraged to submit our application form, which you will find on our web page.
Worldwide placements: Europe (Norway).

KWA MADWALA PRIVATE GAME RESERVE

P.O. Box 192
Hectorspruit
Mpumalanga 1330 South Africa
T: + 27 13 792 4526
F: + 27 13 792 4219
E: kwamadwala@abccomp.co.za
W: www.kwamadwala.co.za
Contact: Mr Conrad van Eyssen

The Kwa Madwala Private Game Reserve is a Big 5 Reserve on the south side of the world-renowned Kruger National Park. We have various luxury lodges and combined accommodation with a game experience. One of the things we do is the gap year experience. We supply two different courses: a 90-day gap year experience or a 25-day gap year experience. Please visit our web site and read students' testimonials. All correspondence to: kwamadwala@abccomp.co.za. We may be able to accept volunteers with an offending background. South of Kruger National Park, Lowveld, Mpumalanga, South Africa.

Number of projects: 1 UK: 0
Starting months: Jan, Apr, Dec
Time required: 4–12 weeks
Age: 16 plus – no upper limit
Causes: Conservation.
Activities: Accountancy, Administration, Agriculture/Farming, Building/Construction, Conservation Skills, Cooking, First Aid, Group Work, Marketing/Publicity, Outdoor Skills, Research, Summer Camps, Training, Work Camps – Seasonal.
Placements: 200
When to apply: As soon as possible.
Work alone/with others: With others.
Health requirements: In good health.
Costs: Travel costs and pocket money.
Benefits: Transfers from/to airport, all board and lodging and activities.
Training: Training is provided in conservation, ranger and tracker training is done with FEGASA registered guides.
Supervision: Supervision is given by FEGASA guides.
Interviews: Interviewed via e-mail.
Worldwide placements: Africa (South Africa).

LA RIOBE

53 Avenue Pasteur
93260 Les Lilas
France
T: 00 33 1 48 97 07 83 (7pm 9pm)
E: la-riobe@wanadoo.fr
Contact: Ms Genevieve Gleyze

La Riobe organises in August an archaeological dig, on a Gallo-Roman site 72km east of Paris. The work to be done includes digging, cleaning and restoring the finds and making an inventory on a computer of the finds and scientific research. 72km east of Paris.

Number of projects: 1 UK: 0
Starting months: Aug
Time required: 2–4 weeks
Age: 18 plus – no upper limit
Causes: Archaeology
Activities: Group Work, Manual Work, Research, Summer Camps.
Placements: 20–25
When to apply: As early as possible.
Work alone/with others: Teamwork.
Qualifications: Adequate French to be understood.
Equipment/clothing: Sleeping bag, working clothes, sun hat and rainwear.
Health requirements: Proof of anti-tetanus injection.
Costs: €35 for subscription and insurance and €9 per day for food.
Interviews: Applicants are not interviewed.
Worldwide placements: Europe (France).

LA SABRANENQUE

Centre International
Rue de la Tour de L'Oume
F-30290 Saint Victor la Coste
France
T: 00 33 4 66 50 05 05
F: 00 33 4 66 50 12 48
E: info@sabranenque.com
W: www.sabranenque.com
Contact: Marc Simon

La Sabranenque volunteer restoration projects offer the opportunity to become directly and actively involved in the preservation and reconstruction of monuments dating often from the Middle Ages. Volunteers learn traditional construction techniques on-the-job from experienced technicians, experience daily life in Mediterranean villages, and share in a multi-cultural project with participants coming from a variety of countries and backgrounds. 📖

Number of projects: 3 UK: 0
Starting months: Mar, Apr, May, Jun, Jul, Aug, Sep, Oct
Time required: 2–52 weeks
Age: 18–65
Causes: Architecture, Conservation, Heritage.
Activities: Building/Construction, Conservation Skills.
Placements: 150
When to apply: Any time.
Work alone/with others: With others.
Health requirements: Nil.
Costs: Approximately £80 per week for food and accommodation in France. £180 for 10 day project including food and accommodation in Italy plus travel.
Benefits: Board and lodging in furnished rooms of restored houses.
Training: On-site.
Supervision: Our team of experienced restoration technicians.
Interviews: Applicants are not interviewed.
Worldwide placements: Europe (France, Italy).

LAKELAND ARTS TRUST

Abbott Hall Art Gallery
Kendal
CumbriaLA9 5AL UK
T: +44 (0) 1539 722464
F: +44 (0) 1539 722494
E: ct@abbothall.org.uk
Contact: Mrs Cherrie Trelogan

Lakeland Arts Trust needs volunteer research assistants, reception staff, events helpers and coffee shop staff to work in the Kendal Museum, Abbot Hall Art Gallery, the Museum of Lakeland Life and Industry and Blackwell. Hours are from 9am to 5pm Monday to Friday and weekends in July, August and September or at any time during the year subject to availability. Although we welcome volunteers for at least a week, we prefer a minimum stay of three months. ♿

Number of projects UK: 3
Starting months: Feb, Mar, Apr, May, Jun, Aug, Sep, Oct, Nov, Dec
Time required: 1–12 weeks
Age: 18 plus – no upper limit
Causes: Archaeology, Architecture, Children, Heritage.
Activities: Administration, Marketing/Publicity, Research.
Placements: 20 approx.
When to apply: As early as possible.
Work alone/with others: Both.

Qualifications: Graduates or undergraduates wishing to gain museum experience.
Health requirements: Nil.
Costs: Accommodation costs, food and travel.
Benefits: Accommodation may be available free of charge – very limited. Students are most welcome if they can find their own acommodation with friends/relatives or in local hostels.
Training: Induction will be given.
Supervision: Volunteers are supervised by the education department but may work with other members of staff at the Lakeland Arts Trust.
Interviews: All applicants should be available for interview in Kendal.
UK placements: England (Cumbria).

Placements: 200
When to apply: All year.
Work alone/with others: With others.
Equipment/clothing: Not necessarily but outdoor practical work would require suitable clothing, boots etc.
Health requirements: Nil – any medical problems must be disclosed in case some areas of work are unsuitable.
Costs: Travel costs and subsistence.
Interviews: Prospective volunteers are interviewed either at our main office, Bolton office or at our larger reserves.
Charity number: 229325
UK placements: England (Lancashire, Manchester, Merseyside).

LANCASHIRE WILDLIFE TRUST

Cuerden Park Wildlife Centre
Shady Lane, Baber Bridge
Preston
Lancashire PR5 6AU UK
T: 01772 324129
F: 01772 628849
E: lancswt@cix.co.uk
W: www.wildlifetrust.org.uk/lancashire
Contact: Tim Mitcham

Lancashire Wildlife Trust is the leading regional charity committed to the protection and promotion of all native wildlife within the 'old' county of Lancashire. Lancashire's magnificent coastline, fells and river valleys form a region rich in diversity. From the splendour of our wading birds, badgers, barn owls and dragonflies to the estuaries, woods, meadows and wetlands where they live – the Trust is working on their behalf. Lancashire, Greater Manchester and Merseyside, north of the River Mersey. 🔲 🔲

Number of projects: 1 **UK:** 1
Starting months: January–December
Time required: 6–52 weeks (plus)
Age: 16–75
Causes: Conservation, Environmental Causes, Wildlife.
Activities: Community Work, Conservation Skills, Forestry, Fundraising, Outdoor Skills.

LANKA JATHIKA SARVODAYA SHRAMADANA SANGAMAYA (INC)

Damsak Mandira
98 Rawatawatte Road
Moratuwa
Sri Lanka
T: 00 94 1 647159 or 655255
F: 00 94 1 656512
E: sarsed@lanka.ccom.lk
W: www.sarvodaya.org
Contact: Dr Vinya Ariyaratne

Lanka Jathika Sarvodaya Shramadana Sangamaya was founded in 1958. The movement is a large non-governmental people's self development effort covering nearly 10,000 villages, providing the possibility of realising the well-being of all, be they human beings, animals or plants. It also creates awareness among deprived communities and mobilises latent human and material potential for the satisfaction of basic human needs in a manner that ensures sustainable development and develops strategies and implements action programmes. Services of the volunteers are taken on the availability of vacancies in the fields of agriculture, bio-diversity and environment, appropriate technology, information technology, economic activities, health care, pre-school activities and legal aid programmes based at grass-roots level to satisfy

Restoring a Medieval Village in Southern France

At 22 Zara Owen had never been abroad before and needed a challenge…which was exactly what she got with the Bardou Restoration Project in the Cevennes Mountains. She found the placement via WorldWide Volunteering following a visit to

Norfolk & Norwich Voluntary Services. "It felt like a sealed world, completely removed from clubbing, mobile phones and the internet. The confidence I brought away, encouraged me to apply for an Access Course and hopefully teacher training at University."

the basic human needs and gradually work upwards to national and international levels. Applicants should have an awareness of their responsibility to improve human conditions wherever needed and an ability to work in sometimes difficult circumstances. They should also have a commitment to the promotion of peace and international understanding that leads to the equitable distribution of the world's resources according to need. Services of volunteers are initially taken for six months or less and on the performance of work, extensions are granted. Volunteers with an offending background may be accepted depending on the nature of the offence. 🗎

Number of projects: 1 UK: 0
Starting months: January–December
Time required: 4–52 weeks
Age: 21–35
Causes: Children, Disabled (learning and physical), Elderly People, Health Care/Medical, Human Rights, Refugees, Teaching/assisting (nursery, mature).
Activities: Agriculture/Farming, Building/Construction, Community Work, Computers, First Aid, Fundraising, Gardening/ Horticulture, Marketing/Publicity, Newsletter/ Journalism, Research, Social Work, Teaching, Technical Skills.
Placements: 30
When to apply: Six months ahead of date of arrival.
Work alone/with others: With others.
Qualifications: No special skills required and academic qualifications are optional.
Health requirements: Good health.
Costs: Rs500 per day plus travel, medical and insurance costs. (This includes the payment for accommodation.)
Training: Basic local language training and prior visits to the projects and programme sites.
Supervision: Supervised by the person in charge of the project/programme as and when necessary.
Worldwide placements: Asia (Sri Lanka).

L'ARCHE – KILKENNY

Fair Green Lane
Callan
Co. Kilkenny Ireland
T: 00 353 (0)56 25957
F: 00 353 (0)56 25946
E: kilkenny@larche.ie
W: www.larche.ie
Contact: The Assistants Co-ordinator

L'Arche provides residential care for adults with learning disabilities. L'Arche communities are places where people with and without learning disabilities live and work together in a simple way, to build community in the spirit of Jesus –

places which offer a way of life that is not competitive nor dependent on material success and intellectual achievement – places that heal rather than divide. L'Arche communities provide a family atmosphere within small homes that are well integrated into the local neighbourhood. L'Arche workshops provide different kinds of work where each person can find fulfilment and opportunity for growth. L'Arche's spiritual life is particularly important, and all homes offer a life of prayer which members can share as they wish. L'Arche is a Christian community, ecumenical in spirit, striving to live a life of simplicity in the spirit of the Gospels. September start is preferred but other months are possible. Volunteers with an offending background are not generally accepted. Highland project in Inverness. ♿

Number of projects: 119 UK: 7
Starting months: January–December
Time required: 8–52 weeks (plus)
Age: 21–70
Causes: Disabled (learning).
Activities: Arts/Crafts, Caring (general, day and residential), Community Work, Cooking, DIY, Driving, Gardening/Horticulture, Group Work, Religion.
Placements: 10
When to apply: All year.
Work alone/with others: With other young volunteers.
Qualifications: Reasonably fluent in spoken English. No restrictions but volunteers need a reasonable fluency in spoken English.
Health requirements: Hepatitis B and HIV negative documentation.
Costs: Travel to Kilkenny.
Benefits: Board, lodging and pocket money of approximately IR£180 per month.
Training: In-house training is provided after arrival.
Supervision: Volunteers are accountable to their house leader/work leader and director.
Interviews: Interviews are generally not held – correspondence and references on paper. Also contact by telephone.
Charity number: 7979
Worldwide placements: Africa (Burkina Faso, Côte d'Ivoire, Uganda, Zimbabwe); North America: (Canada, USA); Central America (Dominican Republic, Haiti, Honduras, Mexico); South America (Brazil); Asia (India, Japan, Philippines); Australasia (Australia, New Zealand); Europe (Belgium, Denmark, France, Germany, Hungary, Ireland, Italy, Netherlands, Poland, Slovenia, Spain, Switzerland).
UK placements: England (Kent, London, Merseyside, Sussex – West); Scotland (Edinburgh, Highland); Northern Ireland (Belfast City).

L'ARCHE – UK

10 Briggate
Silsden
Keighley
West Yorkshire BD20 9JT UK
T: 01535 656186
F: 01535 656426
E: info@larche.org.uk
W: www.larche.org.uk
Contact: John Peet

L'Arche provides residential care for adults with learning disabilities. L'Arche communities are places where people with and without learning disabilities live and work together in a simple way, to build community in the spirit of Jesus – places which offer a way of life that is not competitive nor dependent on material success and intellectual achievement – places that heal rather than divide. L'Arche communities provide a family atmosphere within small homes that are well integrated into the local neighbourhood. L'Arche workshops provide different kinds of work where each person can find fulfilment and opportunity for growth. L'Arche's spiritual life is particularly important, and all homes offer a life of prayer which members can share as they wish. L'Arche is a Christian community, ecumenical in spirit, striving to live a life of simplicity in the spirit of the Gospels. Volunteers with an offending background are not generally accepted. UK communities in Kent, Inverness, Liverpool, Lambeth, Bognor Regis, Brecon, Edinburgh and Preston. Worldwide address list available.

Number of projects: 100+ UK: 8
Starting months: January–December
Time required: 52 weeks (plus)
Age: 18–65
Causes: Disabled (learning).
Activities: Arts/Crafts, Caring (general, day and residential), Community Work, Cooking, Gardening/Horticulture, Group Work, Religion, Social Work.
Placements: 60–70
When to apply: As early as possible.

Work alone/with others: With others.
Qualifications: No nationality restrictions. No restriction on duration of stay.
Health requirements: In good health physically, mentally and emotionally to cope with the demands of caring duties.
Costs: Travel and personal expenses.
Benefits: Board and lodging + pocket money. Own single room in a L'Arche house living as a member of the community.
Training: Continuing programme.
Supervision: Each volunteer is assigned a personal mentor and is supervised regularly by the community leader.
Interviews: Process which involves correspondence and references on paper and a trial period.
Charity number: 264166
Worldwide placements: Africa (Burkina Faso, Côte d'Ivoire, Zimbabwe); North America: (Canada, USA); Central America (Dominican Republic, Haiti, Honduras, Mexico); South America (Brazil); Asia (India, Japan, Philippines); Australasia (Australia, New Zealand); Europe (Belgium, Denmark, France, Germany, Hungary, Ireland, Italy, Netherlands, Poland, Slovenia, Spain, Switzerland).
UK placements: England (Kent, Lancashire, London, Merseyside, Sussex – West); Scotland (Edinburgh, Highland); Wales (Powys).

L'ARCHE MOBILE

151 South Ann Street
Mobile
Alabama AL 36604 USA
T: 251 438 2094
F: 251 438 2094
E: larchmob@hotmail.com
W: www.2.acan.net/~/larchmob/
Contact: Dennis O'Keefe

L'Arche Mobile needs volunteers to live, work and share their lives with people with disabilities (primary diagnosis – mental health problems). Duties include sharing the daily

Endangered Deer in Chile

Jeannie Worthington deferred her place at Sheffield to read medicine. Through WorldWide Volunteering she joined a Raleigh International project in Chile. Her time was spent surveying the endangered Huemule deer, working on community projects and teaching in the small village of Lago Verde, and trekking in the Andes. Jeannie believes, "The experience increased my confidence and diplomatic skills. I wish I could repeat it all again and would recommend it to anyone as a chance to prepare mentally and emotionally for what lies ahead."

tasks of making a home together, cooking, cleaning, yardwork, celebrating, repairs etc. &

Number of projects: 1 **UK:** 0
Starting months: January–December
Time required: 12–52 weeks
Age: 18–62
Causes: Disabled (learning and physical), Elderly People.
Activities: Caring (general, residential), Community Work, Cooking, DIY, Driving, Group Work, Manual Work, Visiting/Befriending.
Placements: 15
When to apply: All year.
Work alone/with others: With others.
Qualifications: A desire to live in a community. English speaking.
Equipment/clothing: Just cotton to help with the humidity.
Health requirements: Capable of some lifting work.
Costs: Travel to and from L'Arch Mobile, medical and dental insurance for first 4 months.
Benefits: Board and lodging. Pocket money after 1 month, health insurance after 4 months if committed to 6 months.
Training: None.
Supervision: Orientation, regular meetings with the head of house, regular meetings with the assistant director. Team meetings. Assistant meetings. Evaluations after 1st and 3rd month trial and annually.
Interviews: Interviews are conducted on site.
Worldwide placements: North America: (USA).

LASALLIAN DEVELOPING WORLD PROJECTS

405 Beulah Hill
London
SE19 3HB UK
T: +44 (0) 208 670 1612
F: +44 (0) 208 761 7357
E: terry@dlsnet.demon.co.uk
W: www.dlsnet.demon.co.uk
Contact: John Deeney

We provide opportunities for young people to give personal and practical service to the educationally deprived in developing countries. Projects normally involve building, instruction and social contact. Teams of up to 12 people work to develop school or youth facilities, usually in rural or small town areas. Volunteers fund themselves and make a small contribution towards the cost of building materials. We are a Christian organisation but also work with and for those who profess other faiths. To date we have not accepted volunteers with an offending background.

Number of projects: 4–5 **UK:** 0
Starting months: Jul
Time required: 5–5 weeks
Age: 18 plus – no upper limit
Causes: Children, Teaching/assisting (primary, secondary, EFL), Work Camps – Seasonal, Young People.
Activities: Building/Construction, Cooking, Development Issues, Fundraising, Group Work, International Aid, Manual Work, Teaching, Work Camps – Seasonal.
Placements: 50
When to apply: April-May of the previous year.
Work alone/with others: Yes with other young volunteers.
Qualifications: Volunteers need to be eligible for a visa in the country of placement.
Health requirements: Must be able to work in a tropical climate.
Costs: Total cost £1200.
Benefits: The cost includes travel, insurance, food, lodging, training + contribution to project materials. Simple shared accommodation with rest of group.
Training: 3-day sessions prior to departure.
Supervision: Experienced group leaders. Local co-ordinators advise.
Interviews: Prospective volunteers are interviewed in London, the north of England or Glasgow.
Charity number: 232632
Worldwide placements: Africa (Ethiopia, Ghana, Kenya, Mozambique, Uganda); Asia (Philippines, Sri Lanka).

LATIN AMERICAN LANGUAGE CENTER

PMB 123
7485 Rush River Drive, Suite 710
Sacramento
CA 95831–5260 USA
T: 00 1 916 447 0938
F: 00 1 916 428 9542
E: lalc@madre.com
W: www.madre.com/lalc
Contact: Susan Shores

Learn Spanish while volunteering! Assist with the training of Costa Rican public school teachers in ESL and computers. Assist local health clinics, social services agencies and environmental projects. Enjoy learning Spanish in the morning, volunteer work in the afternoon/evening.
Spanish classes of 2–4 students plus group learning activities; conversations with middle class homestay families (one student or couple per family). Homestays and most volunteer projects are in a small town near the capital, San Jose. &

Number of projects: 10 **UK:** 0
Starting months: January–December

Time required: 2–52 weeks (plus)
Age: 18 plus – no upper limit
Causes: Children, Conservation, Health Care/Medical, Poor/Homeless, Teaching/assisting.
Activities: Building/Construction, Caring (general, day and residential), Community Work, Computers, Conservation Skills, Cooking, Group Work, Manual Work, Social Work, Teaching, Technical Skills, Training.
Placements: Between 20 and 100
When to apply: All year.
Work alone/with others: With others.
Qualifications: Minimum 2-week enrollment in spanish language courses required at our school. Volunteers need to be able to speak Spanish and be aware of Costa Rican culture.
Health requirements: Volunteers should be in good health.
Costs: Minimum cost: 2 weeks tuition US$715. Airport departure tax (approx.US$14) and some volunteer programmes ask for donation or charge for supplies.
Benefits: On most programmes volunteers are given meals, lodging and transportation.
Training: Spanish language training, Costa Rican culture and various on-the-job training depending on the particular programme.
Supervision: All volunteers are supervised by project or programme manager.
Interviews: Prospective volunteers are interviewed by the director of the school and referred to a community volunteer programme that is appropriate for the volunteer's skills, education, background and interests.
Worldwide placements: Central America (Costa Rica).

LATIN LINK

Short Term Experience Projects (Step/Stride)
175 Tower Bridge Road
London
SE1 2AB UK
T: +44 (0) 207 939 9000
T: +44 (0) 207 939 9015
E: stride.uk@latinlink.org
W: www.latinlink.org
Contact: Jo Hassoun or Laurence East

STEP projects aim to give young people the chance to live and work alongside a Latin American church community and help out in a basic building programme. In 2000 we had Steppers working on ten different projects, building orphanages, classrooms for local schools and church community centres amongst other things. In 2001 we continued our programme working in Bolivia, Brazil, Ecuador, Peru, Argentina and Mexico. There are two types of projects. Summer projects run for four to eight weeks from mid-July until early

September and usually take place in all the countries mentioned above. Spring projects run for four months from the middle of March until mid-July. On these projects there is the option to stay on for a further seven weeks and join a summer project in the same country. STRIDE placements are for a minimum of six months and a maximum of two years. Candidates are placed on individual projects which match their particular skills and gifts. Stride volunteers depart for Latin America in September each year. Alternative e-mail address stride.uk@latinlink.org
Alternative web site www.stepteams.org. &

Number of projects: 12–15 UK: 0
Starting months: Mar, Jul, Aug, Sep
Time required: 4–52 weeks (plus)
Age: 17–65
Causes: AIDS/HIV, Children, Disabled (learning and physical), Elderly People, Health Care/ Medical, Inner City Problems, Offenders/Ex-Offenders, Poor/Homeless, Refugees, Teaching/ assisting (nursery, primary, secondary, EFL), Young People.
Activities: Accountancy, Administration, Arts/ Crafts, Building/Construction, Caring – General, Community Work, DIY, Group Work, International Aid, Manual Work, Music, Religion, Social Work, Teaching, Theatre/Drama, Translating.
Placements: 100–150
When to apply: For Spring: October–December Summer: February-May. Stride: January–April.
Work alone/with others: Both.
Qualifications: Christian commitment. Spanish or Portuguese is helpful but not essential.
Equipment/clothing: Equipment list provided.
Health requirements: Each volunteer must prove medical fitness to Latin Link's consultant.
Costs: Minimum £1,320.
Benefits: Step: Accommodation is arranged by local Latin Link workers. Teams usually live together as a unit. Accommodation may be very basic.
Stride: Individuals usually live with a Latin American family.
Training: Step: A training weekend + written briefing materials. Team leaders have an additional 2-day training course.
Stride: a 4-day orientation course in early September.
Supervision: Teams and individuals are supervised by local Latin Link workers and local Christian leaders.
Interviews: We hold individual interviews at our selection day.
Charity number: 1020826
Worldwide placements: Central America (Costa Rica, Honduras, Mexico, Nicaragua); South America (Argentina, Bolivia, Brazil, Colombia, Ecuador, Peru).

LEA RIVERS TRUST

The Lock Office
Gillender Street
London
E3 3JY UK
T: +44 (0) 20 7361 515 3337
F: +44 (0) 20 7361 515 3338
E: emma.harrington@leeriverstrust.co.uk
W: www.leariverstrust.co.uk
Contact: Emma Harrington

Lea Rivers Trust is an environmental organisation working to improve the environment of the Lower Lea Valley in East London, through practical projects with volunteers, environmental education with schools, community development, leisure and recreation. Our programme includes conservation work on riverside areas, planting and looking after trees, clearing vegetation, creating new wildlife habitat as well as building footpaths, steps and terracing steep slopes. We also run a river maintenance team who clear rubbish from the waterways of the Lea, using a variety of tools and purpose-built boats. They also remove debris from mudbanks and the riverbed, and plant reedbeds for wildlife. We welcome volunteers in this programme, during the week and on some weekends, with a minimum commitment of just one day to see if it suits you. Longer term placements are welcomed. Volunteers can learn conservation skills and how to operate boats and equipment, as well as achieving the satisfaction of having helped improve the 'urban countryside'. &

Number of projects: 1 UK: 1
Starting months: January–December
Time required: 1–52 weeks
Age: 16–80
Causes: Children, Conservation, Environmental Causes, Heritage, Teaching/assisting (primary, secondary), Wildlife, Young People.
Activities: Arts/Crafts, Community Work, Conservation Skills, Manual Work, Outdoor Skills, Scientific Work, Teaching, Theatre/Drama, Training.
Placements: 150
When to apply: All year.
Work alone/with others: With others.
Equipment/clothing: Old clothes, strong footwear.
Health requirements: Clean bill of health.
Costs: Travel, food and accommodation.
Benefits: Chance to learn conservation skills and make a difference to the environment.
Training: On the job training.
Supervision: All volunteers are supervised by a member of staff.
Charity number: 1075368
UK placements: England (London).

LEAN ON ME

Suite 7A Cowell Park
47 Old Main Road
Hillcrest
3610 Kwazulu Natal South Africa
T: 27 31 765 3129
F: 27 31 765 1818
E: claude@wah.co.za
W: www.wecare4africa.com
Contact: Claude Fourie

Lean on Me serves the local Kwazulu/Natal community and assists with finances in an AIDS orphanage and a community creche. Volunteers are welcomed for any skills they may bring, such as music lessons with the children, to painting, fixing vehicles etc. Volunteers are offered a budget to travel with the children and share life changing experiences with them. Kwazulu/Natal, South Africa.

Number of projects: 2 **UK:** 0
Starting months: January–December
Time required: 4–12 weeks
Age: 17 plus – no upper limit
Causes: AIDS/HIV, Children, Disabled (learning and physical), Health Care/Medical, Human Rights, Teaching/assisting (nursery, primary, EFL), Unemployed, Young People.
Activities: Administration, Agriculture/Farming, Arts/Crafts, Building/Construction, Campaigning, Caring (general, day and residential), Catering, Community Work, Computers, Cooking, Counselling, Development Issues, DIY, First Aid, Fundraising, Gardening/Horticulture, Group Work, International Aid, Manual Work, Marketing/Publicity, Music, Outdoor Skills, Social Work, Sport, Teaching, Technical Skills, Theatre/Drama, Training, Visiting/Befriending.
Placements: 120
When to apply: Any time.
Work alone/with others: Work with others.
Qualifications: None needed – any skills welcome.
Health requirements: No restrictions.
Costs: Flights and payment for accommodation.
Benefits: Board and lodging. Activity budget to spend on doing things with the children.
Training: First aid training offered.
Supervision: Programme manager supervises volunteers.
Interviews: No interview, but applications are screened.
Worldwide placements: Africa (South Africa).

LEBENSGEMEINSCHAFT ALT SCHÖNOW

Alt Schönow 5
D-14165 Berlin (Zehlendorf)
Germany
T: 00 49 30 845 718 0
F: 00 49 30 845 718 99
E: info@camphill-alt-schoenow.de
W: www.camphill-alt-schoenow.de
Contact: The Director

Lebensgemeinschaft alt Schönow is an urban adult Camphill community. We have four houses and 30 people with disabilities. We work creatively at weaving, laundry, fence-workshop and the garden.

Number of projects: 1 **UK:** 0
Starting months: January–December
Time required: 1–52 weeks
Age: 18 plus – no upper limit
Causes: Disabled (learning).
Activities: Agriculture/Farming, Arts/Crafts, Caring (general, residential), Community Work, Cooking, Gardening/Horticulture, Music, Outdoor Skills.
When to apply: All year.
Work alone/with others: With others.
Qualifications: Willingness to live and work with people with disabilities.
Health requirements: Nothing specific.
Costs: Only travel costs.
Benefits: Community experience. Volunteers live in our houses.
Training: Introduction course.
Supervision: Volunteers work and live with supervisors of the houses.
Worldwide placements: Europe (Germany).

LEE ABBEY COMMUNITY

Lee Abbey
Lynton
Devon EX35 6JJ UK
T: 01598 752621
F: 01598 752619
E: personnel@leeabbey.org.uk
W: www.leeabbey.org.uk
Contact: Personnel

Lee Abbey is a Christian holiday and conference centre run by a community working for the renewal and refreshment of the church. The Community has a branch in London which is a hostel for international students. Other branches are in Knowle West (Bristol), Aston (Birmingham) and Blackburn. These communities help in urban priority areas. Volunteers with an offending background for minor offences will be considered.

Number of projects: 1 **UK:** 1
Starting months: January–December
Time required: 52 weeks (plus)
Age: 18–60
Causes: Children, Inner City Problems, Young People.
Activities: Accountancy, Administration, Agriculture/Farming, Catering, Computers, Cooking, Forestry, Gardening/Horticulture, Manual Work, Marketing/Publicity, Outdoor Skills, Religion, Summer Camps.
Placements: 80
When to apply: All year.
Work alone/with others: With others.
Qualifications: Nil but agricultural or catering experience useful.
Health requirements: Good, physically and mentally.
Costs: Travel expenses to Lee Abbey – no other costs.

Benefits: Board and lodging + allowance.
Training: None at present.
Supervision: Each person is on a team and is supported by a team leader. We also supply pastoral support.
Interviews: Interviews take place at Lynton, Devon.
Charity number: 227322
UK placements: England (Devon, Lancashire, London, West Midlands).

LEICESTER CHILDREN'S HOLIDAY CENTRE

Quebec Road
Mablethorpe
Lincolnshire LN12 1QX UK
T: 01507 472444
F: 01507 472444
E: helen@lanzetta.freeserve.co.uk
W: www.leicschildsholsmablethorpe.com
Contact: Mrs Eagle-Lanzetta

Leicester Children's Holiday Centre provides summer holidays for groups of 30 girls and 30 boys from socially deprived backgrounds in the Leicester area. The two week camps are held from May through to the end of August each year. We prefer people who are able to work the whole season, or stay at least one month. Volunteers are expected to work a six day week on our outdoor programme of activities. (Proof of no convictions for all volunteers.) Lincolnshire coast seaside resort. 🖫

Number of projects: 1 UK: 1
Starting months: May, Jun, Jul, Aug
Time required: 4–16 weeks
Age: 18–35
Causes: Children, Poor/Homeless.
Activities: Arts/Crafts, Caring (general, residential), Catering, First Aid, Music, Sport, Summer Camps, Theatre/Drama.
Placements: 16–20
When to apply: 1st January with s.a.e.
Work alone/with others: As a team.
Qualifications: Spoken English. + certificate of good conduct if position offered. No nationality restrictions but must be able to speak English.
Health requirements: Must be fit.
Costs: Travel costs.
Benefits: Board, accommodation (shared room with one other) and national minimum wage based on 48 hours per week less deductions for food and accommodation.
Training: We provide a 2-week on-site training programme for volunteers based on the NVQ with a certificate.
Supervision: Supervised by senior staff members at the start.
Interviews: Interviews take place at the centre in Mablethorpe, Lincolnshire or by telephone for overseas volunteers.

Charity number: 217976
UK placements: England (Lincolnshire).

LEPROSY MISSION, THE

80 Windmill Road
Brentford
Middlesex TW8 0QH UK
T: +44 (0) 20 8326 6767
F: +44 (0) 20 8326 6777
E: friends@tlmint.org
W: www.leprosymission.org
Contact: Personnel Support Administrator

The Leprosy Mission or TLM is an international Christian charity working in over 30 countries of the developing world. Since its beginnings in 1874, TLM has been seeking to relieve the terrible suffering of people affected by leprosy through treatment, acceptance and prayer. Today leprosy can be cured with multidrug therapy or MDT, and deformities can be prevented with early treatment. The challenge facing TLM is to reach the many untreated sufferers with help – about 600,000 new cases of leprosy develop each year – and to care for people with or at risk of deformity – numbering over four million worldwide. TLM's aim is to minister in the name of Jesus Christ to the physical, mental and spiritual needs of leprosy sufferers; to assist in their rehabilitation; and to work towards the eradication of the disease. To this end we work in partnership with churches, governments and other charities around the world, depending on the prayer and finances of our Christian supporters. Volunteers with an offending background may be accepted – each person is assessed individually. 🖫

Number of projects: Numerous UK: 0
Starting months: January–December
Time required: 6–8 weeks
Age: 20–30
Causes: Health Care/Medical.
Activities: Community Work, Religion.
Placements: 12
When to apply: At least 9 months in advance.
Work alone/with others: With trained personnel.
Qualifications: 4th yr medic. students + nurses, physios, O.Ts, chiropodists. Christian commitment.
Equipment/clothing: Will advise – depends on country.
Health requirements: Good health.
Costs: Travel expenses.
Benefits: Board and lodging.
Supervision: Senior medical staff.
Interviews: Interviews are conducted in the National Council.
Charity number: 211432
Worldwide placements: Africa (Nigeria, Uganda); Asia (India, Nepal, Thailand).

LES AMIS DE CHEVREAUX CHATEL

Rue de chateau
39190 Chevreaux
Jura FRANCE
T: 00 33 3 84 85 95 77
F: 00 33 3 84 85 95 77
E: accjura@free.fr
W: http://accjura.free.fr
Contact: Sebastien Suchet

Les Amis de Chevreaux Chatel runs two workcamps for young people at the mediaeval castle of Chevreaux. The work varies between stonework, archaeology, woodwork, lime masonry, carpentry, clearing, citizenship, landscaping, and enjoying the sunshine. Of the three weeks, 15 days are devoted to working and restoring, the rest is for leisure pursuits. Carpentry is in July and archaeology in August. Clearing and stoneworking, reconstruction of ruins are in both July and August. Volunteers should bring a typical 'thing' from their country (recipe, object, flag, map etc) and a musical instrument if they play one. 100km from Lyon, 40km from Bourg-en-Bresse, 25km from Lons-le-Saunier.

Number of projects: 1 UK: 0
Starting months: Jul, Aug
Time required: 3–6 weeks
Age: 18–25
Causes: Conservation, Heritage, Work Camps – Seasonal.
Activities: Arts/Crafts, Building/Construction, Conservation Skills, Manual Work, Outdoor Skills, Summer Camps, Work Camps – Seasonal.
Placements: 50
When to apply: As early as possible.
Work alone/with others: With others.
Qualifications: No skills required but motivation and goodwill.
Equipment/clothing: Sleeping bag, strong work shoes, working clothes, waterproof clothes, pullovers, swimsuit, torch.
Health requirements: Anti-tetanus injection is essential.
Costs: Total registration cost with insurance is €50 + travel costs.
Benefits: Tent, sanitary and kitchen equipment and a washing machine are all provided + food and the cost of leisure activities: swimming pool, equestrian centre, volley ball, badminton and football. Lodged on site in tents.
Training: Technical supervision by professional builders, architects, stone masons, archaeologists.
Interviews: Send CV and a goodwill letter.
Worldwide placements: Europe (France).

LES AMIS DE LA TERRE – BENIN

03 BP 1162 Jericho
Cotonou
Benin

T: 00 33 32 88 84
F: 00 33 32 88 84
E: dasven.foe@intnet.bj
Contact: Venance Dassi

Les Amis de la Terre is the Benin office of Friends of the Earth, an organisation which, for the past 20 years, has been working towards creating positive solutions to many of the environmental problems threatening this planet. FOE is committed to empowering local communities and people to get actively involved in the debate to protect the environment through environmental education, public awareness, campaigning and so on. Volunteers are always needed to help with a wide variety of projects.

Number of projects: 1 UK: 0
Starting months: January–December
Time required: 1–52 weeks (plus)
Age: 14 plus – no upper limit
Causes: Conservation, Environmental Causes, Heritage.
Activities: Conservation Skills, Forestry, International Aid, Manual Work, Outdoor Skills
Worldwide placements: Africa (Benin).

LES AMIS DE LA TERRE – BURKINA FASO

01 B.P. 5648
Ouagadougou
Burkina Faso
T: 00 226 306936
Contact: The Director

Les Amis de la Terre is the Burkina Faso office of Friends of the Earth, an organisation which, for the past 20 years, has been working towards creating positive solutions to many of the environmental problems threatening this planet. FOE is committed to empowering local communities and people to get actively involved in the debate to protect the environment, through environmental education, public awareness, campaigning and so on. Volunteers are always needed to help with a wide variety of projects.

Number of projects: 1 UK: 0
Starting months: January–December
Time required: 1–52 weeks (plus)
Age: 14 plus – no upper limit
Causes: Conservation, Environmental Causes, Heritage.
Activities: Conservation Skills, Forestry, International Aid, Outdoor Skills.
Worldwide placements: Africa (Burkina Faso).

LES AMIS DE LA TERRE – TOGO

B.P. 20 190 'Caisse'
Lomé
Togo

T: 00 228 222 1731
F: 00 228 222 1732
E: adt-togo@cafe.tg
W: www.foei.org
Contact: Mensah Todzro

Les Amis de la Terre was founded in 1990 and is the Togo office of Friends of the Earth (FOE), an organisation dedicated to creating solutions to the environmental problems threatening this planet. FOE is committed to empowering local communities to get actively involved in protecting the environment through environmental education, public awareness, campaigning and so on. At the national level, Les Amis de la Terre Togo works with issues such as desertification, phosphate mining, health, gender, water resources, debt and environment. Every summer the group holds international work camps to construct schools and plant trees, among other activities. Volunteers are always needed to help on a wide variety of projects.

Number of projects: 1 UK: 0
Starting months: January–December
Time required: 1–52 weeks (plus)
Age: 14 plus – no upper limit
Causes: AIDS/HIV, Children, Conservation, Environmental Causes, Health Care/Medical, Wildlife, Work Camps – Seasonal, Young People.
Activities: Administration, Agriculture/Farming, Building/Construction, Campaigning, Community Work, Development Issues, Forestry, Fundraising, Gardening/Horticulture, Group Work, International Aid, Library/Resource Centres, Manual Work, Outdoor Skills, Summer Camps, Translating, Work Camps – Seasonal.
Placements: 75 (non-Togolese)
When to apply: Any time.
Work alone/with others: Group work (July–September). Individual work (October – June).
Qualifications: General.
Health requirements: Good health.
Costs: Room and board to be covered by the volunteer.
Training: No, unless provided on the job or through other organisations.
Supervision: Yes.
Interviews: No, selection is made by correspondence or through other organisations.
Worldwide placements: Africa (Togo).

LESOTHO WORKCAMPS ASSOCIATION

P.O.Box 12783
Masero – 100
Lesotho
T: 00 266 8848061
Contact: Mrs. M. Makotoko

Lesotho Work Camps Association organises volunteers to take part in voluntary workcamps in co-operation with local communities involving manual work, including building, installing water supplies, constructing roads, planting trees, soil conservation etc. The camps consist of groups of up to 25 people, mainly students and those out of work from Lesotho and abroad. A leader and a work supervisor are appointed in each camp but decisions are made communally. Eight hours work per day, five days per week. We have workcamps in June/July (winter) and January/December (summer). We are unable to accept volunteers with an offending background.

Number of projects: 1 UK: 0
Starting months: Jan, Jun, Jul, Dec
Time required: 4–8 weeks
Age: 16 plus – no upper limit
Causes: Conservation, Poor/Homeless, Unemployed, Work Camps – Seasonal.
Activities: Building/Construction, Conservation Skills, Forestry, Work Camps – Seasonal.
Placements: Varies.
When to apply: Anytime.
Work alone/with others: Work with others.
Equipment/clothing: Sleeping bag.
Health requirements: Good.
Costs: Workcamp fee.
Benefits: Free food and accommodation.
Training: Leadership training provided.
Supervision: Supervision undertaken by a skilled person.
Interviews: Orientation before attending a workcamp.
Worldwide placements: Africa (Lesotho).

LINCOLNSHIRE WILDLIFE TRUST

Banovallum House
Manor House Street
Horncastle
Lincolnshire LN9 5HF UK
T: 01507 526667
F: 01507 525732
E: lincstrust@cix.compulink.co.uk
W: www.lincstrust.co.uk
Contact: Dave Bromwich or Mary Edwards

The Lincolnshire Wildlife Trust, formed in 1948, is a charity dedicated to safeguarding the countryside and wildlife of the historic county. It is one of a network of Wildlife Trusts that together form the largest voluntary organisation in the UK devoted to all aspects of wildlife protection. The Lincolnshire Trust is the largest voluntary organisation in the county with over 18,000 members. Its junior wing is the Wildlife Watch Club which provides environmental activities for children aged between 8 and 15 years. The activities and policies of the Trust are based on its extensive records of plants and animals and of the wild places in Lincolnshire where they occur. In 1996 this data was used to compile a special report on the state of the county's wildlife habitats and endangered species. The Trust's 99 nature reserves provide the most tangible and best-known results of its work. They are enjoyed by perhaps half a million people each year. To achieve its objectives the Trust relies heavily on the commitment and support of members. Much of the work is undertaken by volunteers with the support of field staff and a small administrative staff at the headquarters office. Many hundreds of volunteers work for the Trust in activities as diverse as running sales points, managing nature reserves, conducting surveys of plants and animals. fundraising and checking planning lists. ♿

Number of projects: 105 **UK:** 105
Starting months: January–December
Time required: 1–52 weeks (plus)
Age: 16 plus – no upper limit
Causes: Conservation, Environmental Causes, Wildlife.
Activities: Computers, Conservation Skills, Driving, Forestry, Gardening/Horticulture, Manual Work, Outdoor Skills, Research, Scientific Work, Teaching.
Placements: 1,000
When to apply: All year.
Work alone/with others: With others.
Qualifications: Nil but any are a bonus.
Equipment/clothing: Sensible outdoor clothes.
Health requirements: General good health.
Costs: Food and travel costs.
Benefits: Improvement to CVs and good preparation for college. Accommodation at Gibraltar Point NNR, Gibraltar Road, Skegness.
Training: No training required.
Supervision: All volunteers are supervised by trained staff.
Interviews: Informal.
Charity number: 218895
UK placements: England (Lincolnshire).

LINK OVERSEAS EXCHANGE

25 Perth Road
Dundee
DD1 4LN UK
T: 01382 203192
F: 01382 226087
E: info@linkoverseas.org.uk
W: www.linkoverseas.org.uk
Contact: Mrs Vicky Greaves

Link Overseas Exchange was established in 1991 and has since sent around 400 volunteers overseas. In 2003 we sent up to 60 volunteers to a range of projects in India, Nepal, Sri Lanka and China. All volunteer locations are carefully screened, are ethical and have a genuine need for volunteers. Link volunteers primarily help

to teach and develop young people's English speaking skills, working at grass-roots level in schools or community projects. A particular feature of Link's programme is its unique culture-to-culture approach and its emphasis on bringing communities together through greater understanding both here in the UK and overseas. Link volunteers have the opportunity to become completely integrated into local culture providing a unique insight into a different way of life. Link provides full support for its volunteers at every stage of the experience. If volunteers are prepared to commit themselves fully the benefits from their time overseas are considerable. Most volunteers gain considerably in maturity and confidence and their experience often gives them greater direction and purpose in later life. Link is as much about eduation and preparing for work as it is volunteering and travelling. If our programme sounds interesting why not drop us a line and we will send you an application form and more information. Volunteers with an offending background may be accepted depending on circumstances. ♿

Number of projects: 20 **UK:** 0
Starting months: Feb, Aug
Time required: 20–26 weeks
Age: 17–25
Causes: Archaeology, Children, Disabled (learning and physical), Elderly People, Human Rights, Inner City Problems, Poor/Homeless, Refugees, Teaching/assisting (nursery, primary, secondary, EFL), Unemployed, Young People.
Activities: Arts/Crafts, Caring – Day, Community Work, Computers, Development Issues, Music, Outdoor Skills, Social Work, Sport, Teaching, Theatre/Drama, Visiting/Befriending.
Placements: 60–70
When to apply: All year round.
Work alone/with others: Usually in pairs.
Qualifications: Formal qualifications not necessarily required.
Health requirements: Medical advice available about immunisations required.
Costs: £2,250 to include flights, visas, food and accommodation, insurance, pre-departure training, UK back-up and overseas support, debriefing on return.
Benefits: Valuable + practical experience proven to enhance academic and career prospects. Provided by the host organisations on site.
Training: All Link volunteers attend a 4-day residential preparation course in order to prepare them as fully as possible for the experience ahead.
Supervision: Whilst overseas volunteers are supported by a network of Link representatives and receive a visit by a UK-based Link

representative once during their stay and contact by e-mail/phone with Link in Scotland. **Interviews:** Interviews are conducted at regular selection days in Scotland for groups of 6–8 candidates. **Charity number:** SCO 22028 **Worldwide placements:** Asia (China, India, Nepal, Sri Lanka).

LIPU the Italian League for Bird Protection

LIPU-UK
Fernwood
Doddington Road
Whisby
Lincolnshire LN6 9BX UK
T: 01522 689030
E: info@lipu-uk.org
W: www.lipu-uk.org
Contact: David Lingard

LIPU-UK is the British branch of the Italian bird conservation and protection body. We have over 1500 members and supporting friends and have been raising awareness of conservation challenges in Italy since our foundation in 1989. In addition funds are raised to enable conservation projects to succeed in Italy and the total raised exceeds a third of a million pounds. Traditionally we have supported the spring anti-poaching camps both financially and with volunteer participants. The camp is on the strait between Sicily and Calabria where millions of birds are concentrated during their migration. In the past, thousands have been shot and LIPU is determined to fight this illegal practice. The situation has improved over the years but the camps have to continue lest complacency takes over and allows the poachers to resume the scale of previous slaughter. Throughout the year various other activities are suitable for volunteers and current details can be supplied on request. We are unable to place volunteers with an offending background. Spring-time there is an anti-poaching camp on the Straits of Messina. Other projects occur throughout the country and can range from office support to reserve management.

Number of projects: varies **UK:** 0
Starting months: Mar, Apr, May, Jun, Jul, Aug, Sep
Time required: 1–4 weeks
Age: 18 plus – no upper limit
Causes: Animal Welfare, Conservation, Wildlife.
Activities: Fundraising, Research.
Placements: 2–15
When to apply: As soon as available.
Work alone/with others: Work with others.
Qualifications: Bird identification is useful as is some knowledge of Italian (useful but not essential).

Equipment/clothing: Some equipment may be needed depending on project.
Health requirements: Not normally any restrictions.
Costs: Travel costs incurred to be covered by volunteer, subsistence by the organisation.
Benefits: Accommodation and subsistence is normally provided.
Training: As required.
Supervision: Working as one member of a team with experienced team members.
Interviews: Normally considered via e-mail.
Charity number: 1081826
Worldwide placements: Europe (Italy).

LISLE INC.

900 County Road # 269
Leander
TX 78641
USA
T: 00 1 512 259 7621
F: 00 1 512 259 0392
E: lisle@io.com
W: www.lisle.utoledo.edu.
Contact: Mark Kinney

Lisle broadens global awareness and increases appreciation of cultures through programmes which bring together persons of diverse religions, cultural, social, political and racial backgrounds, to interact, and to consider reflectively their experience. While on field assignments, small groups go out for several days for varied assignments with sponsoring agencies. Volunteers with an offending background are accepted. 🔊

Number of projects: 3 **UK:** 0
Starting months: Mar, Jun, Jul
Time required: 2–4 weeks
Age: 17–85
Causes: Children, Conservation, Environmental Causes, Health Care/Medical, Heritage, Human Rights, Work Camps – Seasonal, Young People.
Activities: Agriculture/Farming, Arts/Crafts, Building/Construction, Caring – General, Community Work, Conservation Skills, Gardening/Horticulture, Manual Work, Visiting/Befriending.
When to apply: Before 1st April.
Work alone/with others: With others.
Equipment/clothing: Depends on location.
Health requirements: Nil.
Costs: Airfare to programme + programme fee which covers board and lodging.
Benefits: Learn about other cultures by actually living and participating in that culture.
Interviews: Applicants for volunteer projects are not interviewed.
Worldwide placements: Central America (Costa Rica); Asia (India, Malaysia); Europe (Poland, Turkey).

LITTLE BROTHERS (Friends of the Elderly

25 Bolton Street
Dublin 1
Ireland
T: 00 353 1 873 1855
F: 00 353 1 873 1617
E: ireland@little-brothers.org
W: www.petits-freres.org
Contact: Niamh Macken

Little Brothers works for the elderly to alleviate loneliness and isolation by providing friendship, social contact and opportunities for participating in community activities. Each year Little Brothers takes a group of elderly on holiday to France and also to various parts of Ireland for short breaks. As many of our elderly have little variety in their lives, a holiday can do wonders for their physical and mental well-being. Dublin city suburbs and inner city. ♿ 📄

Number of projects: 1 UK: 0
Starting months: January–December
Time required: 26–52 weeks
Age: 18 plus – no upper limit
Causes: Disabled (learning), Elderly People, Holidays for Disabled.
Activities: Caring – General, Catering, Community Work, Computers, Cooking, Social Work, Theatre/Drama, Visiting/Befriending.
Placements: 120
When to apply: All year.
Work alone/with others: With other young volunteers.
Qualifications: Good working fluency in spoken and written English. Love for the elderly.
Health requirements: Nil.
Costs: Return travel to Ireland.
Benefits: Living allowance (for food) and free accommodation.
Training: On the spot training.
Supervision: Volunteers are supervised by their co-ordinator and the board.
Interviews: Interviews are held by telephone. An international application form is available. Two referees are required.
Charity number: CHY 12003
Worldwide placements: Europe (Ireland).

LITTLE CHILDREN OF THE WORLD

361 County Road 475
Etowah
Tennessee 37331 USA
T: 00 1 423 263 2303
F: 00 1 423 263 2303
E: lcotw@tds.net
W: www.littlechildren.org
Contact: Dr Doug Elwood

Little Children of the World is a non-profit international and interdenominational Christian service organisation dedicated to creating caring communities for the world's homeless or neglected children. As a volunteer with LCW you can use your creativity to benefit children who are victims of poverty and neglect, of whom there are more than 150 million worldwide. They are God's children too and desperately need our help. Child advocacy is a new worldwide mission frontier, but so far a neglected one. Here is an opportunity to invest a portion of your life in helping to rescue children from the dire effects of poverty, neglect and abuse. As an LCW volunteer you can serve for as long a period as you like (at least one month) and you can serve in whatever capacity best suits your own personality, talents and training. You can do what you do best, and do it for a worthy cause. Serving the needs of the poor is, in fact, what Christian service is all about. Volunteers with an offending background are not accepted Dumaguete City, Philippines. 15 communities on Negros Island in central Philippines, with multiple child services. 📄

Number of projects: 1 UK: 0
Starting months: January–December
Time required: 4–52 weeks (plus)
Age: 18 plus – no upper limit
Causes: Children, Disabled (learning and physical), Poor/Homeless.
Activities: Arts/Crafts, Caring (general and day), Community Work, Development Issues, Group Work, International Aid, Music, Outdoor Skills, Social Work, Teaching.
Placements: 25–40
When to apply: All year.
Work alone/with others: Yes.
Qualifications: We are flexible but applicants must be at least 18 years old.
Equipment/clothing: Nothing special but we do ask that volunteers dress modestly.
Health requirements: Must be free of any communicable diseases.
Costs: Travel costs, food. We ask for a donation of US$10 per week for use of dormitory.
Benefits: International experience. Volunteers use a dormitory at Mission House. The house has e-mail, cable television, kitchen etc.
Training: No training is provided. Orientation is by web site and handbook.
Supervision: Volunteers are assigned to local staff for supervision.
Interviews: Prospective volunteers are not interveiwed – communications are by e-mail or regular post.
Worldwide placements: Asia (Philippines).

LITTLE JOHN'S HOUSE

2 The Square
Merton
Okehampton
Devon EX20 3EE UK
T: 01805 603623
F: 01805 603623
E: mags_liviu@onetel.net.uk
W: www.littlejohnshouse.org
Contact: John and Tilly Kimber

Little John's House (previously Orphan Aid –
Romania) has the sole objective of relieving the
suffering of sick and handicapped children in
Romania; improving their living standards and
bringing love and purpose into their lives.
Little John's House provides a secure home for
up to six children with special needs and
operates as a centre for respite care, serving the
communities of Cisnadioara, Cisnadie and
Sibiu. The main activity involves a summer
school which, between the months of June and
September, receives up to 150 children of mixed
abilities who are unable to attend any schooling
and who are often 'imprisoned' in a single
room (their home) for months on end!
Cisnadioara, Sibiu, Romania.

Number of projects: 1 UK: 0
Starting months: Jul, Aug, Sep
Time required: 1–6 weeks
Age: 18–65
Causes: Children, Disabled (learning and
physical), Health Care/Medical.
Activities: Administration, Arts/Crafts,
Building/Construction, Caring – General,
Cooking, DIY, International Aid, Manual Work,
Music.
Placements: 70
When to apply: All year.
Work alone/with others: With others.
Qualifications: Those with and without
qualifications. Special needs teachers, nursery
nurses, play specialists and any who feel they
can cope with disabled children, to provide a
fun time of working in music, art, drama, etc.
Health requirements: Innoculations before
leaving.
Costs: Airfare to Romania + contribution to
food.
Benefits: Accommodation.
Training: Clear guidelines are sent to each
volunteer detailing the work required and
expected standard of behaviour.
Supervision: All volunteers are supervised by
resident English director.
Interviews: Two references required.
Charity number: 1002714
Worldwide placements: Europe (Romania).

LIVING OPTIONS

Fennes
Farm Road, Bracklesham Way
Chichester
West Sussex PO20 8JT UK
T: 01243 672989
F: 01243 672989
E: livingoptions@hotmail.com
Contact: Gill Donovan

Living Options is a registered national charity
whose aims are to provide opportunities for
young people who are physically disabled to
live in small groups in the community. A
volunteer may be asked to: (a) assist in meeting
the more personal needs of the disabled person,
such as washing, bathing, toileting, dressing,
etc as appropriate, (b) accompany students to
lectures and on other outings of both an
academic and social nature, (c) assist with the
domestic tasks of the project, such as cooking,
cleaning, washing of clothes etc., (d) seek to
improve self-awareness and knowledge of the
needs of people who are disabled, by personal
experience, reading, attending training courses
(if available) and discussion of these, (e) attend,
and be prepared to contribute to project
meetings. Working hours are determined by the
project manager, who reserves the right to vary
them according to the needs of the residents. A
rota is arranged and displayed on the project
notice board. From time to time you may be
asked to attend a project meeting when off
duty. It is vital to the smooth running of the
project that these meetings are attended by all
residents and volunteers. Volunteers with an
offending background are accepted.

Number of projects UK: 3
Starting months: January–December
Time required: 16–52 weeks
Age: 18–30
Causes: Disabled (physical).
Activities: Arts/Crafts, Caring (general,
residential), Cooking, Group Work, Music.
Placements: 30+
When to apply: All year.
Work alone/with others: With other
volunteers under supervision of manager.
Health requirements: Nil.
Costs: Nil.
Benefits: Board, lodging plus personal
allowance. CSV rates plus some travel expenses.
Some accommodation at project houses, some at
other houses – always with other volunteers.
Some shared rooms but most have single rooms.
Training: Monthly training courses on a variety
of subjects are held in project.
Supervision: Volunteer and house meetings.
Interviews: Interviews are not held.
Charity number: 299206
UK placements: England (Sussex – West).

LLANELLI CENTRE PROJECT

2 Station Road
Llanelli
Carmarthenshire SA15 1AB UK
T: 01554 771595
E: averillsioux@aol.com
Contact: Mrs Averill Rees

The Llanelli Centre Project is an independent charity funded youth organisation which opened in 1989. It aims to meet the needs of young people. It is open seven days a week, usually from 10.00am – 10.00pm and employs four full-time workers as well as students in training and volunteers. Activities are used as a basis for building up better relationships with young people, and there is a focus on empowerment to help them gain control over their own lives. We run an advocacy and information service with young people dealing with issues such as: homelessness, drugs misuse, alcohol misuse, unplanned pregnancy, contraception, relationship difficulties (peers, parents, school, police etc) and basic skills training. We are currently developing a motor project with the help of National Lottery funding. Other services provided are opportunities for young people to repay their offences by voluntary special activity orders and community service orders. All volunteers are accepted subject to police checks. Restrictions are on those with offences against children. ♿

Number of projects: 1 UK: 1
Starting months: January–December
Time required: 1–52 weeks
Age: 16–30
Causes: Addicts/Ex-Addicts, Children, Health Care/Medical, Offenders/Ex-Offenders, Poor/Homeless, Teaching/assisting, Unemployed, Young People.
Activities: Administration, Arts/Crafts, Building/Construction, Computers, Cooking, Counselling, DIY, Driving, Fundraising, Group Work, Music, Outdoor Skills, Social Work, Sport, Visiting/Befriending.
Placements: 20
When to apply: As soon as possible.
Work alone/with others: With others.
Qualifications: References and police clearance.
Health requirements: Nil.
Costs: Travel costs, accommodation and food.
Benefits: We will help find accommodation.
Training: Induction training, introduction to staff team, members, policies, procedures etc.
Supervision: Volunteers always work under the supervision of a qualified worker.
Interviews: Interviews take place at the Llanelli Centre Project (by appointment please).
Charity number: 1002011
UK placements: Wales (Carmarthenshire).

LONDON CITY MISSION

175 Tower Bridge Road
London
SE1 2AH UK
T: +44 (0) 207 407 7585
T: +44 (0) 207 403 6711
E: lcm.uk@btinternet.com
W: www.lcm.org.uk
Contact: Phil Moore

London City Mission has a varied programme of voluntary work within the Greater London and inner city areas which includes Christian community work, open air meetings, door-to-door visits, working with homeless people, running youth camps and children's clubs. Alternative telephone number: 0207 234 3583. ♿

Number of projects: 6 UK: 6
Starting months: Aug, Sep
Time required: 1–52 weeks
Age: 18–30
Causes: Children, Elderly People, Inner City Problems, Poor/Homeless, Teaching (EFL), Young People.
Activities: Caring (general and day), Community work, Religion.
Placements: 150
When to apply: Start month for year out scheme September.
Short-term summer programmes during August/September.
Work alone/with others: With others and full-time staff.
Qualifications: Committed Christians with membership of an evangelical church. Predominantly EU residents.
Health requirements: Good health required.
Costs: Donation (if possible) towards board and lodging.
Benefits: Board and lodging. (Pocket money and travel for Long Term placement.) Basic accommodation provided: Mattress on church floor (1–2 weeks). Hostel accommodation (1 year scheme).
Training: Continuous training on the job.
Supervision: All volunteers supervised by full-time long-term staff.
Interviews: One formal and one informal.
Charity number: 247186
UK placements: England (London).

LONDON WILDLIFE TRUST

Harling House
47–51 Great Suffolk Street
London
SE1 0BS UK
T: +44 (0) 207 261 0447
T: +44 (0) 207 261 0538
E: enquiries@wildlondon.org.uk
W: www.wildlondon.org.uk
Contact: Support Services

London Wildlife Trust looks after 60 nature reserves and raises awareness of nature conservation issues in London. The Trust achieves this through: community involvement. We organise over 600 free events every year. Land management: workdays on our reserves often appeal to volunteers. Effective communication – we provide a popular wildlife information service. Education – our education work is targeted at all ages. Campaigning – the London Wildlife Trust speaks up for wildlife whenever it is under threat in London. Nature reserves in London including a wildlife garden centre. 🅰

Number of projects: 6 UK: 6
Starting months: January–December
Time required: 1–52 weeks (plus)
Age: 14 plus – no upper limit
Causes: Conservation, Environmental Causes, Wildlife, Young People.
Activities: Campaigning, Conservation Skills, Gardening/Horticulture, Group Work, Outdoor Skills.
When to apply: All year.
Work alone/with others: Both.
Equipment/clothing: Robust outdoor clothing.
Health requirements: Nil.
Costs: Travel, food and accommodation.
Benefits: Transport costs.
Training: Not applicable.
Supervision: Volunteers will be supervised by nature reserve officers/staff. If tools are being used there will be a health and safety talk.
Interviews: Interviews take place at the site/nature reserve in question.
Charity number: 283895
UK placements: England (London).

LONDON YOUTH

Bridge House
Bridge House Quay
Prestons Road
London
E14 9QN UK
T: +44 (0) 20 7361 537 2777
F: +44 (0) 20 7361 537 7072
E: tracie.trimmer@londonyouth.org.uk
Contact: Tracie Trimmer

London Youth exists to meet the needs of both voluntary and statutory youth groups across Greater London. Our aim is to support and improve the range, quality and safety of youth work opportunities that are available to young people. We do this primarily by working with those who work with young people. We also work directly with young people giving them access to a range of learning opportunities and challenging experiences, which promote their personal and social development. 📖

Number of projects: 500 UK: 500
Starting months: January–December
Time required: 1–52 weeks (plus)
Age: 16 plus – no upper limit
Causes: Children, Disabled (learning and physical), Young People.
Activities: Caring – Residential, Community Work, Outdoor Skills, Sport.
Placements: 3000+
When to apply: All year.
Work alone/with others: With other young volunteers.
Qualifications: No restrictions but preference is for UK citizens (for police checking reasons).
Costs: Travel, food and accommodation.
Benefits: Some out of pocket expenses may be payable depending on the placement.
Supervision: All volunteer placements are supervised by project co-ordinators/leaders.
Interviews: Interviews take place at the location of the placement.
Charity number: 303324
UK placements: England (Buckinghamshire, London, Sussex – East).

LOS NIÑOS

287 G. Street
Chula Vista
California 91910 USA
T: 00 1 619 426 9110
E: andy@losninosinternational.org
W: www.losninosinternational.org
Contact: Andy Schaefer

Los Niños is a charitable organisation founded to provide food, clothing, shelter, education and affection for children in orphanages and poor communities in the Mexican border cities of Tijuana and Mexicali. Volunteers assist by undertaking jobs in education, nutrition, construction, as youth consellors or in other areas of community development.

Number of projects: 1 UK: 0
Starting months: January–December
Time required: 1–6 weeks
Age: 16 plus – no upper limit
Causes: Children, Poor/Homeless, Teaching/assisting.
Activities: Caring – General, Counselling, Teaching.
Placements: 1200
When to apply: All year.
Qualifications: Fluent in Spanish.
Costs: Programme fee to include board and lodging. Visa to cross US/Mexican border daily.
Worldwide placements: North America: (USA); Central America (Mexico).

LOTHLORIEN (ROKPA TRUST)

Corsock
Castle Douglas
Kirkcudbrightshire DG7 3DR UK
T: 01644 440602
E: lothlorien1@btopenworld.com
W: www.lothlorien.tc
Contact: Project Manager

Lothlorien is a therapeutic community where
people with mental health problems can develop
their potential through living alongside people
who are relatively well, in an atmosphere
friendship, acceptance and mutual support.
Lothlorien is situated in an isolated rural area in
south west Scotland. It consists of a large log
house with 13 bedrooms and communal living
areas. It is set in 17 acres of grounds which
include organic vegetable gardens, woodland,
workshops and outbuildings. A volunteer
placement at Lothlorien offers a valuable
opportunity for personal growth and will be of
particular interest to those considering a career in
a helping profession. There are places for four
live-in volunteers who play a key role in creating
a warm, accepting atmosphere through which
everyone in the community feels valued. On the
practical level, volunteers along with all the
community members, work in the vegetable
gardens, participate in domestic tasks and
undertake maintenance work on the house and in
the grounds. A staff team of three provide
continuity and an administrative structure which
facilitates the community in functioning
effectively. The staff also offer individual and
group supervision to the volunteers. We have
vacancies on a regular basis. Volunteers receive
free room and board, pocket money of £30 per
week plus a monthly travel allowances. We
require a minimum commitment of six
months.

Number of projects: 1 UK: 1
Starting months: January–December
Time required: 26–52 weeks
Age: 21–99
Causes: Health Care/Medical.
Activities: Building/Construction, Caring –
Residential, Gardening/Horticulture, Manual
Work.
Placements: 4
When to apply: All year.
Work alone/with others: With others.
Qualifications: Nil but important to have an
interest in the welfare of others.
Health requirements: Applicants need to be in
good health.
Costs: Travel costs to come for an interview are
paid.
Benefits: Board and lodging + £30 per week.
Training: Ongoing in-service training given.
Supervision: Regular individual and group
supervision for volunteers.

Interviews: Interviews take place at the project.
UK placements: Scotland (Dumfries and
Galloway).

LOTUS EYES INTERNATIONAL SCHOOL

P. O. Box 13557
New Baneshwor
Kathmandu
Nepal
E: leis@ccsl.com.np
W: www.leis-nepal.np
Contact: Ms Pushpa Pradhan

Lotus Eyes International School is a co-
educational English medium school. The school
is staffed by fully qualified, highly motivated
and professional teachers who are strongly
committed to providing quality education and
training to our children in order to increase
their self-confidence, to prepare them for their
careers and to fulfil their duty to their country.
The school's aim is to build up the mental and
physical education of the country whilst
serving the wider community to the greatest
possible extent. It is our policy to maintain the
cultural identity of all Nepal's communities,
and we are proud and privileged to be a school
at which a modern education system can exist
side by side and in harmony with our country's
rich traditional heritage. Volunteers are
welcomed to provide the students at Lotus Eyes
with the invaluable experience of learning from
native English speakers and to provide funding
for the education of children from poor
families. Volunteers will see Nepal's natural
beauty as they raft the Trisuli river, ascend into
the Himalayan mountains and canoe Phewa
Lake in scenic Pokhara. Volunteers will be
exposed to Nepal's art, culture and traditional
crafts and have the opportunity to learn the
Nepali language. Volunteers can witness and
participate in our traditional lifestyle, see the
festivals and admire the ancient and beautiful
Hindu and Buddhist temples. Near Balaju,
Kathmandu.

Number of projects: 1 UK: 0
Starting months: January–December
Time required: 4–12 weeks
Age: 18–60
Causes: Children, Elderly People,
Teaching/assisting (nursery, primary, secondary,
mature, EFL) Young People.
Activities: Administration, Caring – Day,
Computers, Fundraising, Social Work, Teaching.
Placements: 10
When to apply: All year – there is no specific
date during which applications should be
submitted, volunteers may simply apply at their
earliest convenience.
Work alone/with others: With other young
volunteers.

Qualifications: Applicants must have completed high school education. No restrictions provided that the volunteer speaks fluent English.
Equipment/clothing: School-appropriate dress (i.e. decent clothing).
Health requirements: No restrictions.
Costs: Programme fee of $750 plus registration fee of $50. This includes Nepli language tutoring, room and board in school and various excursions. Costs of any other activities outside school are not included.
Benefits: Accommodation and two meals a day (Nepali food). Excursions included in the cost: a rafting trip, Annapurna-Himalayan (basic camp) trek, sightseeing, a trip to Chitwan National Park/jungle and a trip to Pokhara.
Training: Nepali language training provided.
Supervision: The principal and other teachers are available at all times.
Interviews: Volunteers are not interviewed.
Worldwide placements: Asia (Nepal).

LOUIS ROUSSEL

28 rue du Bourg
F-21000 Dijon
France
T: 00 33 (0)3 80 23 6608
F: 00 33 (0)3 60 75 1348
E: malain_gam@hotmail.com
Contact: M. Roussel

Louis Roussel recruits volunteers to participate in the restoration and archaeological excavation of a medieval chateau and a Gallo-Roman site near Dijon in July. In addition to restoring and digging, the jobs to be done may include sketching the finds, model making and restoration. Eight hours work per day and five days per week. Site near Dijon.

Number of projects: 1 UK: 0
Starting months: Jul
Time required: 1–4 weeks
Age: 18 plus – no upper limit
Causes: Archaeology, Conservation, Heritage.
Activities: Conservation Skills.
Placements: 20
When to apply: Before the end of May.
Work alone/with others: Both.
Qualifications: Experience. in digging, photography, sketching, model making or restoration an advantage.
Health requirements: Tetanus vaccination.
Costs: €15 per week.
Benefits: Free accommodation. Dormitory, or tent if preferred.
Training: Instructions given during work.
Supervision: Volunteers will be supervised.
Interviews: No interviews.
Worldwide placements: Europe (France).

LUBBOCK LAKE LANDMARK

The Museum of Texas Tec. University
Box 43191
Lubbock
Texas 79409-3191 USA
T: 00 1 806 742 1117
F: 00 1 806 742 1136
E: lubbock.lake@.ttu.edu
W: www.ttu.edu/~museum/lll/field.html
Contact: Dr Eileen Johnson

The Lubbock Lake National Historic and State Archaeological Landmark is an archaeological preserve on the outskirts of Lubbock, Texas. Located in a meander of an ancient valley, Yellowhouse Draw, the preserve contains a well-stratified concurrent cultural, faunal and geological record that spans the past 12,000 years. Over 100 archaeological activity areas have been excavated from five major stratigraphic units, representing all of the major time periods of North American archaeology. The programme is aimed at the excavation and interpretation of data and requires the assistance of 50 volunteers a year. Volunteers are needed to work in the field and laboratory. Crew members come for a 6–9 week period. Crew members are expected to help with daily kitchen and camp chores, including cooking duties. The Lubbock Lake Landmark is open to the public on a daily basis, through exhibits in the Interpretative Centre and guided tours of the excavation areas. Volunteers have the opportunity to assist with special programmes and tours for the public. Alternative telephone number 00 1 806 742 2479.

Number of projects: 1 UK: 0
Starting months: Jun, Jul, Aug
Time required: 6–13 weeks
Age: 18 plus – no upper limit
Causes: Archaeology, Heritage.
Activities: Cooking, Manual Work, Outdoor Skills, Research, Scientific Work.
Placements: 50
When to apply: By 1st June.
Work alone/with others: With others.
Qualifications: Fluent English, no experience required – willingness to learn and work as team player.
Equipment/clothing: All supplied except hand tools.
Costs: Travel to Lubbock Lake, international health/accident insurance, local transport, personal costs and supplies.
Benefits: Board/lodging in 6-person wooden-floored tents, major equipment and field supplies.
Training: None.
Supervision: In the field the crew chief provides supervision. In the lab, lab assistant provides daily supervision.

Interviews: Applicants are not interviewed.
Worldwide placements: North America: (USA).

LUCCA LEADERSHIP TRUST

P.O. Box 34958
London
SW6 2WR UK
T: +44 (0) 207 736 3155
T: +44 (0) 207 691 9614
E: info@luccaleadership.org
W: www.luccaleadership.org
Contact: Mr Michael Harper

The Lucca Leadership Trust runs unique week long Foundation Programmes in transformational leadership for young people aged 16–28 and mentors subsequent community based projects with the aim of uplifting their community. Participants are required to submit a project proposal during the application process, which is developed into an implementable action plan during the programme. In this way, the project acts as a practical focus for their learning. Participants are allocated a mentor for a year after the programme. Where possible, the mentor is located within their home country to provide advice and help overcome any difficulties that are encountered. The aim of the Programme is to inspire in the hearts and minds of young people the belief that they can make a difference in the world, and to equip them with the knowledge and skills required to become transformational leaders. Throughout the Programme, the emphasis is to teach people how to think, not what to think. Through tuition, practical experience, reflection and dialogue, participants are given the opportunity to cultivate personal awareness, discover effective decision making techniques and develop strong communication and project management skills. In this way, the Programme develops the three key abilities leaders require to bring about transformation – awareness, communication and leading through one's own example. Together, these abilities provide leaders with the strength and steadiness to become a platform for the growth and transformation of others.
If the applicant can show evidence of community work and a desire to make a positive difference for thie community, then their offending background may not exclude then from successfully applying to the Programme. Villa Boccella, in Tuscany. ♿ 📄

Number of projects: 2 UK: 2
Starting months: Jun, Aug
Time required: 1–52 weeks
Age: 16–28
Causes: Addicts/Ex-Addicts, AIDS/HIV, Animal Welfare, Archaeology, Architecture, Children, Conservation, Disabled (learning and physical), Elderly People, Environmental Causes, Health Care/Medical, Heritage, Holidays for Disabled, Human Rights, Inner City Problems, Offenders/Ex-Offenders, Poor/Homeless, Refugees, Teaching/assisting (nursery, primary, secondary, mature, EFL) Unemployed, Wildlife, Work Camps – Seasonal, Young People.
Activities: Accountancy, Administration, Agriculture/Farming, Arts/Crafts, Building/Construction, Campaigning, Caring (general, day and residential), Catering, Community Work, Computers, Conservation Skills, Cooking, Counselling, Development Issues, DIY, Driving, First Aid, Forestry, Fundraising, Gardening/Horticulture, Group Work, International Aid, Library/Resource Centres, Manual Work, Marketing/Publicity, Music, Newsletter/Journalism, Outdoor Skills, Religion, Research, Scientific Work, Social Work, Sport, Summer Camps, Teaching, Technical Skills, Theatre/Drama, Training, Translating, Visiting/Befriending, Work Camps – Seasonal.
Placements: 70
When to apply: End of April to end of May.
Work alone/with others: Varies.
Equipment/clothing: Dependent upon projects choice.
Health requirements: No restrictions.
Costs: Travel costs. €525 for Leadership Programme and £200 for the 4 day Leadership Programme.
Benefits: Some bursaries covering the cost of the Programmes and travel are available. Accommodation is included at the beautiful Villa Boccella, in Tuscany, Northern Italy.
Training: Transformation Leadership project planning training throughout the Leadership Programme.
Supervision: Minimum participant to staff ratio of 4:1 throughout the Leadership Programme.
Interviews: No interviews, although a thorough application form needs to be completed.
Worldwide placements: Europe (Italy).

M

MEDICO – MEDICAL EYE & DENTAL INTERNATIONAL CARE ORGANIZATION

2955 Dawn Drive, Ste. D
George Town
Williamson 78628 USA
T: (512) 930 1893
F: (512) 869 7500
E: director@medico.org
W: www.medico.org
Contact: Lynda Peters

MEDICO is a humanitarian aid organization whose mission is to serve areas of Central America where there is little or no access to medical care. Volunteers serving with MEDICO find it extremely rewarding to reach out to those in need in a culture unlike their own. Personal rewards are too numerous to mention. Serving with others from across the US and various other countries is another part of the rewarding experience. MEDICO is diverse in its programmes which include volunteer mission teams, special surgical teams, establishing water sanitation projects, elementary school dental fluoride programmes, shipments of school and medical supplies, medical seminars and bringing children to the US for necessary medical attention when not obtainable in Central America. MEDICO's vision is to continue its current programme of providing the opportunity of humanitarian service to the under-served in the hope of touching the hearts of the volunteers and inspiring them to see the importance of service not only on an international level but in their own communities. MEDICO welcomes all medical professional as well as lay volunteers, translators in the Spanish language and medical students. An executive director and a national board of directors prepare project planning and management, but input from all volunteers who serve on a team is requested by filling out a trip evaluation form. Each team works with a host organisation that provides in-country logistics for each of the work sites. A new perspective on life can be felt after serving on a MEDICO team. Service weeks begin and end on a Saturday. One-week trips are scheduled six times a year. We are unable to accept volunteers with an offending background. Central America – mainly Honduras. ▨

Number of projects: 6 UK: 0
Starting months: January–December
Time required: 1 week
Age: 18 plus – no upper limit
Causes: Children, Elderly People, Health Care/Medical, Young People.
Activities: First Aid, International Aid, Translating.
Placements: 125
When to apply: Six months to one year in advance.
Work alone/with others: With others.
Qualifications: Spanish language helpful but not essential. All medical professionals must provide current medical licence. All volunteers should have the desire to help those less fortunate. Diversity is welcomed.
Equipment/clothing: MEDICO provides equipment – general clothing and medical scrubs for clinic times.
Health requirements: Volunteers must be in good health with no major health problems.
Costs: US$630 which covers hotel, transportation, food, immigration/airport taxes, travel insurance etc. Plus airfares.
Benefits: Food, accommodation, travel insurance, transport are included in trip fee.
Training: On site training. Volunteers will assist professionals in various areas – no expertise necessary.
Supervision: Each team has two experienced team leaders. Most of team made up of adults.
Interviews: No. Volunteres will be asked to fill out an application form.
Worldwide placements: (Honduras).

M.E.E.R. e.V.

Germany
T: 00 49 30 8507 8755
F: 00 49 30 8507 8755
E: meer@infocanarias.com
W: www.M-E-E-R.org
Contact: Fabian Ritter

During the last decades a new kind of encounter of humans and cetaceans (the biological order of whales and dolphins) has developed: whale watching – the observation of whales and dolphins in their natural environment. Whale watching today is promoted as an important means of increasing the environmental awareness of the public – if it happens within a context of awareness and ecological sustainability. The sea in the southwest of the island of La Gomera (Canary Islands) is one of the most outstanding places in the world where humans can meet cetaceans in the wild. In the relative vicinity of the coast more than 15 cetacean species can be sighted and research is possible under extraordinarily good conditions. The Canary Islands meanwhile show a rapid and alarming expansion of the whale watching industry. With its project M.E.E.R. La Gomera, the German nonprofit association M.E.E.R. wants to guarantee that the encounters between humans and cetaceans happen with respect and consideration. We aim to realise this through the combination of ecological whale watching tourism, research and public work. Since 1995 whale watching boats operating off the island serve as platforms for the collection of scientific data. The investigation of the abundance and distribution of cetaceans as well as their interactions with boats is the main subject of this research. The results of the study are applied to the further development of whale watching regulations and management. In 2001, the project M.E.E.R. La Gomera was honoured with the international environmental award 'Umwelt & Tourismus 2001', which is granted by the German association of travel and tour operators (DRV) since 1987. As was said during the bestowal, the project 'realises new ways of co-operation of research and tourism in an exemplary and innovative way'. In 2003 the association M.E.E.R. e.V published its scientific report 'Interactions of Cetaceans with Whale Watching Boats', which is based on the findings of the project M.E.E.R. La Gomera. La Gomera, Canary Islands, Spain.

Number of projects: 1 UK: 0
Starting months: Mar, Apr, May, Sep, Oct
Time required: 2 weeks
Age: 18–80
Causes: Conservation, Wildlife.
Activities: Research, Scientific Work.
Placements: 20–40
When to apply: As early as possible.
Work alone/with others: With other volunteers.
Qualifications: Ability to speak English is necessary, Spanish is helpful. Experience in behavioural research or photography is welcome. Courses in German possible according to participants' nationalities.
Equipment/clothing: Camera, dictaphone, laptop computer helpful but not essential. No special clothing.
Health requirements: Volunteers should discuss existing illness, health problems in advance of booking.
Costs: Approx €750–850 per 2 weeks. Accommodation, full training programme and all research expenses included. Travel and food not included.
Benefits: Accommodation, 7 whale watching research trips, 3 working meetings, lectures, scientific supervision, certificate of attendance, donation to M.E.E.R. e.V., typically close encounters with cetaceans.
Training: Scientific programme for introduction to behavioural research. Practical

and theoretical work from data collection to data handling. Slide presentaions and videos. The course may be accepted at certain universities.
Supervision: Scientific supervision is provided.
Interviews: No interviews.
Worldwide placements: Europe (Spain).

MADVENTURER

Adamson House
Newcastle upon Tyne
Northumberland NE1 1SG UK
T: 0191 261 1996
E: team@madventurer.com
W: www.madventurer.com
Contact: Volunteer Co-ordinator

Madventurer brings together adventurous travel and development projects to offer people a unique experience. Madventurer's ethos is 'developing together'. It aims to further the needs of communities in the developing world, whilst at the same time enabling people to gain experience through work and adventurous travel. Part of your payment to Madventurer is donated to the Mottey African Development (MAD) Foundation, a trust set up to support a wide range of development projects in the developing world. Madventurer was set up in 1999 by John Lawler. John's first experience of Africa was as a teacher in Ghana during his gap year. In recognition of his contribution to the village in which he taught, John was installed as Torgbui Mottey I aka Chief of Development. Madventurer is a continuation of his work in Ghana. Volunteers have the opportunity to get involved in the planning of their own development projects as well as the chance to lead a project once they have successfully completed an expedition as a volunteer. There are also opportunities to act as a MAD rep for their school/college/university by telling people about their own MAD experience and inviting others to get involved. MAD expeditions allow you to undertake both community projects and adventure travel hand in hand. The projects are sustainable and are chosen by the community for maximum benefit. The adventure section enables you to explore remote and 'difficult to reach' regions. Such an expedition may help your future career prospects, providing you 'soft skills' such as initiative, decision-making and problem solving. Employers see people who have undertaken community projects as well-rounded team players who are looking for a challenge. May accept volunteers with an offending background, although in some cases we ask volunteers to attend an interview depending on their application form. West Africa – Kenya, Uganda, Tanzania, East Africa, South Africa, Peru, Bolivia Guatemala, Latin America.

Number of projects: 30 **UK:** 0
Starting months: January–December
Time required: 4–12 weeks
Age: 17 plus – no upper limit
Causes: Architecture, Children, Conservation, Environmental Causes, Health Care/Medical, Poor/Homeless, Teaching/assisting (nursery, primary, secondary), Young People.
Activities: Agriculture/Farming, Arts/Crafts, Building/Construction, Community Work, Computers, Conservation Skills, Development Issues, Forestry, Fundraising, Group Work, International Aid, Music, Newsletter/Journalism, Outdoor Skills, Sport, Summer Camps, Teaching, Theatre/Drama.
Placements: 200
When to apply: 6 weeks before departure.
Work alone/with others: Varies.
Qualifications: There are no specific qualifications or skills required.
Equipment/clothing: This is dependent on project chosen. A full Equipment/clothing list is provided to all volunteers.
Health requirements: Volunteers will fill out an application form giving details of their health and any medication taken – this will be assessed to ensure volunteers are physically fit to undertake all activities.
Costs: Expedition fee – £1180 covers food, accommodation & in country transport overseas. Volunteers will be given advice on flights, visas, insurance and spending money.
Benefits: Accommodation and food within costs. We offer advice on fundraising to volunteers. We can also organise various fundraising activities through related university societies. Accommodation varies with each project from staying with an indigenous family to log cabin style dormitories.
Training: One weeks training is provided in whichever field the volunteer has chosen – this is done in-country.
Supervision: Each group of volunteers are assigned a MAD rep (or two depending on group size). The rep is with the group at all times.
Interviews: Some volunteers are interviewed at Newcastle office.
Worldwide placements: Africa (Kenya, South Africa, Tanzania, Uganda); Central America (Guatemala); South America (Bolivia, Peru).

MAGNET YOUNG ADULT CENTRE

81a Hill Street
Newry
Co. Down BT34 1DG N. Ireland
T: 028 3026 9070
F: 028 3026 8132
E: magnet@magnetyoungadults.co.uk
W: www.magnetyoungadults.co.uk
Contact: Colette Ross

Magnet Young Adult Centre is a registered charity group who provide facilities primarily, but not exclusively for 16–25 year olds from Newry and the surrounding rural areas in a neutral and non-alcoholic environment. The Centre is managed by a voluntary group of 16–25 year olds who represent various youth groups, schools and training schemes along with a team of paid and voluntary staff. Our facilities include: social area with coffee bar; rehearsal space for musicians; guitar, bass, drum and keyboard lessons; young women's/girls' groups; young men's group; live music; youth information centre; drama; Duke of Edinburgh Award Scheme; art projects; creative writing; study space; computer and photocopying services; and lots more! Depending on the time of year, the Centre also runs outdoor activities; pottery classes; personal development courses; live music events; festival/street entertainment; workshops on a wide range of issues (e.g. drugs, community relations, sex education); European youth exchanges; and, entertainment nights with table quizzes, videos, etc. Newry in County Down. 🔊

Number of projects: 1 **UK:** 1
Starting months: January–December
Time required: 8–52 weeks
Age: 16 plus – no upper limit
Causes: Unemployed, Young People.
Activities: Administration, Arts/Crafts, Community Work, Computers, Fundraising, Group Work, Music, Theatre/Drama, Training.
Placements: 20
When to apply: All year.
Work alone/with others: With others.
Qualifications: Interest in the area of work.
Health requirements: Nil.
Costs: Meals, travel and accommodation.
Benefits: Experience, training and accreditation where possible.
Training: No pre-placement training other than discussion to determine suitability of placement and role of volunteer. Induction is usually completed within 2 days of starting.
Supervision: Regular contact with supervisor on a daily basis with formal supervision at least once a month depending on time commitment.
Charity number: XO/284/91
UK placements: Northern Ireland (Down).

MAISON EMMANUEL

1561 Chemin Beaulne
Val-Morin
QuebecJOT 2RO Canada
T: 00 1 819 322 3718
F: 00 1 819 322 6930
E: info@maisonemmanuel.org
W: www.maisonemmanuel.org
Contact: Eileen Lutgendorf

Maison Emmanuel Inc (Centre Educatif) is a life sharing intentional community based on anthroposophy, as developed by the Austrian educator Rudolf Steiner, and modelled on the Camphill communities existing worldwide. We are approximately 50 people living and working together, including 22 children, adolescents and adults in need of special care, in the beautiful Laurentians, 100 km north of Montreal. House-parents, their children and young co-workers live together in family like settings. The rhythmic structure of the household, school, workshops (garden, small farm, pottery, weaving, bakery, ceramics, candle-making, woodwork) create the warm, supportive environment of community living. Shared meals, seasonal festivals, plays, birthday celebrations and outings, help create bonds of friendship and responsibility where everyone learns to care and provide for the needs of others. A programme of expansion and social integration has started in the centre of nearby Val David with the establishment of two adult residences and the building of a bakery, with a boutique for Maison Emmanuel's crafts. Training for new co-workers and a foundation course is provided. There is also the beginning of a Waldorf School in nearby Val David with a kindergarten and 1st grade. We are always open to enquiries (individuals and families) to take on or share responsibilities for our houses and/or workshops. Many people from different countries come to help for about a year at a time. Life is intense and very rewarding. We welcome your inquiry by letter or e-mail, or come and visit us (with prior appointment). Volunteers with an offending background might not be eligible for a visa. In any case assault or child abuse offenders would not be acceptable. 100 km North of Montreal in the Laurentian Mountains. French population in the surrounding communities. 🔊 📄

Number of projects: 1 UK: 0
Starting months: January–December
Time required: 48–52 weeks (plus)
Age: 21–99
Causes: Disabled (learning and physical), Holidays for Disabled, Work Camps – Seasonal.
Activities: Agriculture/Farming, Arts/Crafts, Caring (general, residential), Cooking, Driving, Gardening/Horticulture, Group Work, Manual Work, Music, Newsletter/Journalism, Summer Camps, Theatre/Drama, Work Camps – Seasonal.
Placements: 25
When to apply: All year.
Work alone/with others: With other young volunteers.
Qualifications: French is an asset.
Equipment/clothing: Warm clothes for our winters, and work clothes.

Health requirements: Doctor's certificate of good health.
Costs: Travel costs.
Benefits: The use of a car, 4 weeks vacation, medical needs are covered, pocket money plus vacation pay. Accommodation provided – mostly single rooms.
Training: First aid – crisis intervention, working with the intellectually disabled.
Supervision: Each house has an experienced person in a supervisory position.
Interviews: No interviews but 3 written letters of reference are required.
Charity number: 1/9028850R
Worldwide placements: North America: (Canada).

MANIC DEPRESSION FELLOWSHIP

Castle Works
21 St Georges Road
London
Surrey SE1 6ES UK
T: +44 (0) 207 793 2600
T: +44 (0) 207 793 2639
E: mdf@mdf.org.uk
W: www.mdf.org.uk
Contact: Michelle Rowett

Manic Depression Fellowship was set up in 1983 to help people with manic depression, their relatives, friends and others who care through the establishment of self-help groups; to educate the public and caring professions through the provision of information; and to encourage research for the better treatment of manic depression. Volunteers support the work of the administrative staff in head office. This can involve telephone work, wordprocessing, preparing letters and filing. Volunteers should already have some basic office experience and skills, and be willing to undertake a variety of tasks as part of a team.

Number of projects: 1 UK: 1
Starting months: January–December
Time required: 4–52 weeks (plus)
Age: 16–60
Causes: Health Care/Medical.
Activities: Administration.
When to apply: Three months in advance.
Qualifications: Basic office skills and experience. Volunteers should also have an understanding of mental illness.
Health requirements: Nil.
Costs: Travel to London, food and accommodation.
Benefits: Travelcard expenses within London reimbursed.
Training: Given.
Supervision: Given.
Interviews: Yes – at our office.
UK placements: England (London, Surrey).

MANSFIELD OUTDOOR CENTRE

Manor Road
Lambourne End
Romford
Essex RM4 1NB UK
T: +44 (0) 208 500 3047
F: +44 (0) 208 559 8481
E: noel.forest@aston-mansfield.org.uk
W: www.aston-mansfield.org.uk
Contact: Noel Forrest

Mansfield Outdoor Centre supports people of all ages and backgrounds, particularly those who are most vulnerable. We encourage everyone to take responsibility for their own physical, spiritual and psychological health so that they can make a full contribution to society and benefit from its rewards. The Outdoor Centre promotes the well-being of the people of Newham and other surrounding areas by a wide variety of programmes.
The Centre offers a range of training programmes to groups of young people or adults using an outdoor environment and a variety of activities. Safe opportunities for: working as a member of a team, achieving personal goals, gaining self-respect, taking responsibility for your actions. A working farm: introduction to a variety of animals, hands-on experience caring for them, fears overcome and confidence gained, environmental awareness widened. Working with special needs: mental health problems (all ages), physical difficulties (especially wheelchairs), emotional and behavioural challenges. Facilities and activities available include: climbing wall, rope courses, swimming pool and access to lake, orienteering in Hainault Forest, canoeing and dinghy sailing, archery and problem solving exercises. Volunteers are required to help with all the above. The duration of stay can be discussed individually. Daily volunteers needed all year. Volunteers with an offending background are accepted provided that the offence is not one which would cause a danger to the young people we work with. Essex countryside, ten miles from the E. London city suburbs. 🗎

Number of projects: 20 UK: 20
Starting months: January–December
Time required: 2–26 weeks
Age: 18–40
Causes: Addicts/Ex-Addicts, AIDS/HIV, Animal Welfare, Children, Conservation, Disabled (learning and physical), Environmental Causes, Human Rights, Inner City Problems, Offenders/Ex-Offenders, Poor/Homeless, Refugees, Teaching/assisting (primary, secondary, mature), Unemployed, Wildlife, Work Camps – Seasonal, Young People.
Activities: Agriculture/Farming, Conservation Skills, DIY, First Aid, Gardening/Horticulture, Group Work, Manual Work, Outdoor Skills, Religion, Social Work, Sport, Summer Camps, Teaching, Training, Work Camps – Seasonal.
Placements: 10
When to apply: All year.
Work alone/with others: Always with others.
Qualifications: A need to speak English.
Equipment/clothing: Old clothes, all specialist equipment is provided.
Health requirements: The work demands that volunteers are fit and healthy.
Costs: Residential facilities are only available from end of June to beginning Sept. Otherwise no costs.
Benefits: £20 per week. Food allowance for summer camp volunteers. Travel costs within England at start and finish.
Training: Variety of in-house training. Where necessary or affordable external training will be provided.
Supervision: This is compulsory and delivered by the appropriate person.
Interviews: If possible we invite prospective volunteers to come and see our site and the work we do before they work for us.
Charity number: 220085
UK placements: England (Essex).

MAR – BULGARIAN YOUTH ALLIANCE FOR DEVELOPMENT

P.O Box 201
BG 1000 Sofia
Bulgaria
T: 00 359 2 980 2037
F: 00 359 2 973 1361
E: mail@mar.bg
W: www.mar.bg
Contact: Roumen Yakimov

MAR – Bulgarian Youth Alliance for Development is an independent, non-governmental and non-profit organisation dedicated to the building of civil society through the initiatives of youth. Established in 1992, MAR was the first to organise international youth workcamps in Bulgaria and welcomes each year hundreds of volunteers from all over the world.
Aims of the organisation:
– to strengthen the international contacts and multi-understanding among young people from all over the world, stimulating their awareness of other cultures and lifestyles.
– to promote among young people the idea of voluntary work.
– to facilitate the individual growth, acquisition of skills and sense of responsibility of the volunteers as well as to give them an opportunity to create new ideas for work, living and learning.
– to support community initiatives and assist in community development.

Changing an Outlook on Life – Teaching in Nepal

Caroline Williams knew nothing of the Sermathang Project in Nepal until WorldWide Volunteering sent her a list of volunteering opportunities in that country. Caroline, 18, had the chance of a gap year after being offered a place at Cardiff University to study medicine and wanted to volunteer overseas.
Sermathang village, 70 miles from Kathmandu was certainly different. The

project was set up by ex-volunteers to ensure the continuing education of children in this traditional village high in the Himalayas – a perfect example of volunteering breeding volunteering. "Being so isolated was one of the best aspects," she said. "It was somewhere where the culture and lifestyle are so different and untouched by the outside world.......It completely changes your outlook on life."

MAR organises international workcamps in Bulgaria in the field of environmental protection, social actions, archaeological excavations, restoration and conservation work. Different regions of Bulgaria.

Number of projects: 15 **UK:** 0
Starting months: Jun, Jul, Aug, Sep
Time required: 2–3 weeks
Age: 16–30
Causes: Archaeology, Children, Conservation, Disabled (learning and physical), Environmental Causes, Heritage, Wildlife, Work Camps – Seasonal, Young People.
Activities: Arts/Crafts, Caring – General, Community Work, Forestry, Group Work, Manual Work, Social Work, Sport, Work Camps – Seasonal.
Placements: 300
When to apply: March, April, May and June.
Health requirements: Nil.
Costs: Registration fee of £129.
Benefits: Full board and lodging given.
Training: Technical leaders are present to lead the working process.
Supervision: Camp leaders and technical leaders constantly monitor the work and the safety of the volunteers.
Interviews: No interviews.
Worldwide placements: Europe (Bulgaria).

MARIANIST VOLUNTARY SERVICE COMMUNITIES (MVSC)

P.O. Box 9224
Wright Bros. Branch
Dayton
Ohio OH 45409 USA
T: +1 513 229 4630
F: +1 513 229 2772
E: mvsc@udayton.edu
Contact: Laura Libertore

Number of projects: 1 **UK:** 0
Starting months: January–December

Time required: 1–52 weeks (plus)
Age: 14 plus – no upper limit
Causes: Children, Elderly People, Young People.
Activities: Administration, Agriculture/Farming, Catering, Community Work, Cooking, Forestry, Gardening/Horticulture.
Worldwide placements: North America: (USA).

MARIE CURIE CANCER CARE

89 Albert Embankment
London
SE1 7TP UK
T: +44 (0) 207 7599 7768
T: +44 (0) 207 7599 7180
E: volunteering@mariecurie.org.uk
Contact: Clair Bryan or Jessica Bourne

Marie Curie Cancer Care is a comprehensive cancer care charity, helping people with cancer and their families throughout the UK. Marie Curie provides free practical nursing care at home and specialist care at ten hospices across the UK and conducts research into the causes and treatment of cancer. We provide education and training in cancer and palliative care for doctors, nurses and other healthcare professionals. We would not be able to operate as effectively as we do without the valuable contribution of volunteers. Volunteers are involved in every part of our organisation, on a yearly basis volunteers contribute over 1,000,000 hours to us. Like those who use our services, our volunteers come from all sections of the community. Volunteers are matched to opportunities based on their preference, skills, abilities and experience. There are many ways that you can get involved in our work as a volunteer. The three main areas are shops, hospices and fundraising. If you would like to find out more about what you can offer the charity and what the charity can offer you, please contact Clair Bryan or Jessica Bourne or refer to the Marie Curie web site at www.mariecurie.org.uk.

Number of projects: over 100 **UK:** over 100
Starting months: January–December
Time required: 1–52 weeks
Age: 16 plus – no upper limit
Causes: Health Care/Medical.
Activities: Administration, Fundraising.
When to apply: All year.
Work alone/with others: Either on their own or with other volunteers.
Qualifications: No nationality restrictions, relevant visa must be provided. There may be some age restrictions where law dictates.
Costs: Travel, meals and accommodation.
Benefits: Experience only.
Training: The aim of training is to enable the volunteer to develop their skills and knowledge to enable them to perform their role effectively. Requirements will vary in relation to the role and area of involvement.
Supervision: The nature and complexity of the role will determine the regularity and format of supervision. Supervision can be delivered in a 'one-to-one' session, in a small group, by telephone or via e-mail.
Interviews: A selection meeting may be set up. This meeting allows discussion of available options and provides an opportunity to make the best use of the individuals presented skills and abilities to the benefit of both parties.
UK placements: England (throughout); Scotland (throughout); Northern Ireland (throughout); Wales (throughout).

MARINE CONSERVATION SOCIETY (MCS)

9 Gloucester Road
Ross-on-Wye
Herefordshire HR9 5BU UK
T: 01989 566017
F: 01989 567815
E: info@mcsuk.org
W: www.mcsuk.org
Contact: Ann Hunt

Volunteer opportunities for a minimum of one week are only available occasionally, and only for those with marine science qualifications.

Number of projects: 1 **UK:** 1
Starting months: January–December
Time required: 1–52 weeks
Age: 20 plus – no upper limit
Causes: Conservation, Wildlife.
Activities: Administration, Computers.
When to apply: All year.
Work alone/with others: With others.
Qualifications: Marine science qualifications – at or post university.
Health requirements: Reasonable.
Costs: all costs including accommodation.

Supervision: Yes.
Interviews: Interview takes place at our office.
UK placements: England (Herefordshire).

MARITIME VOLUNTEER SERVICE (MVS)

202 Lambeth Road
London
SE1 7JW UK
T: +44 (0) 207 928 8100
T: +44 (0) 207 401 2537
E: hg@mvs.org.uk
Contact: The Secretary,

In recent years many people from our island nation have looked on with disquiet and a feeling of helplessness as the Royal Navy, its reserve forces and the British merchant fleet have declined substantially in size. One group of volunteers has acted to redress this trend. The MVS, founded in 1994, is a team of men and women who are determined to maintain, foster and pass on to the next generation that rich vein of maritime skills which underpins our national way of life. Members of the MVS come from a wide variety of backgrounds, ranging from former members of the Royal Navy and its reserves through merchant seafarers to ordinary citizens with no more than a keenness to learn about the sea and its ways. The MVS has already established itself with nearly fifty units around the coast of the United Kingdom. Their purpose is to provide a nucleus of trained people to support existing naval and civil authorities when needed and in so doing to advance the awareness of the local community of the importance of maritime skills and knowledge. The MVS has gained the recognition of the Royal Navy, a tribute to the important role it plays in the education and training of young people in nautical skills. Close association between the Navy and the MVS is seen as contributing to the Government's 'New Deal' initiative by enriching the pool of training opportunity in the community and helping young people to get jobs.

Number of projects: 1 **UK:** 1
Starting months: January–December
Time required: 1–52 weeks (plus)
Age: 18–65
Causes: Environmental Causes, Unemployed, Work Camps – Seasonal, Young People.
Activities: Accountancy, Administration, Catering, Cooking, Driving, First Aid, Fundraising, Newsletter/Journalism, Outdoor Skills, Sport, Technical Skills, Training.
Placements: 1,000
When to apply: All year.
Work alone/with others: Work in units.
Qualifications: Nil – MVS provides qualifications. British volunteers only.
Equipment/clothing: MVS is a uniformed service.

Health requirements: Medical certificate required for afloat.
Costs: HQ Membership £15 p.a., local £50 approx subject to unit.
Interviews: Prospective volunteers are interviewed by their local unit.
Charity number: 1048454
UK placements: England (Cornwall, Co Durham, Cumbria, Devon, Dorset, Essex, Gloucestershire, Hampshire, Kent, Lancashire, Lincolnshire, Merseyside, Norfolk, Northumberland, Somerset, Suffolk, E. Sussex, W. Sussex, N. Yorkshire); Scotland (throughout); Wales (Anglesey, Blaenau Gwent, Bridgend, Caerphilly, Cardiff, Carmarthenshire, Ceredigion, Conwy, Denbighshire, Flintshire, Gwynedd, Merthyr Tydfil, Monmouthshire, Neath Port Talbot, Newport, Pembrokeshire, Rhondda, Cynon, Taff, Swansea, Torfaen, Vale of Glamorgan, Wrexham).

MARLBOROUGH BRANDT GROUP

1A London Road
Marlborough
Wiltshire SN8 1PH UK
T: 01672 514078
F: 01672 514922
E: mbguk@talk21.com
Contact: Mrs Penelope O'Neill

One of the aims of the Marlborough Brandt Group is to increase understanding between different cultures by maintaining a link with a community in a developing country. For the last 20 years there has been a constant flow of people in both directions between Marlborough in Wiltshire and Gunjur, a village of about 12, 500 people in the Gambia, West Africa. The Gambia is one of the world's poorest nations, and is a predominantly Muslim country, so the way of life there is very different from our own. Every year at least two Gambians come to Marlborough for three months to gain experience in a particular field, staying with local families. At the same time, two young people, usually post graduates, go to Gunjur for a similar period of time to work with a partner NGO or at the local schools. They stay in family compounds and live as Gambians. They are expected to pay £40 per month for accommodation with a Gambian family. For this they can expect a small house, all food and washing and we recommend them to raise £1,500 for the three months. This includes airfares, insurance and other personal expenses. Going to Gunjur provides a unique opportunity to experience African life from the inside, in an environment where you have plenty of friends from the day you arrive. Our volunteers are profoundly affected by the experience, and many become involved in development issues in later life. Gunjur, 50 km south of Banjul, the capital of the Gambia. &

Number of projects: 1 UK: 0
Starting months: Sep
Time required: 12–52 weeks
Age: 18–60
Causes: Teaching/assisting (secondary), Young People.
Activities: Community Work, Development Issues, Gardening/Horticulture, Library/Resource Centres, Sport, Teaching.
Placements: 4
When to apply: By 1 January.
Work alone/with others: As a group.
Qualifications: Post graduates preferred with interest/experience in development issues. No restrictions but school leavers only from the UK.
Health requirements: Good general health important as medical facilities limited.
Costs: Administration fee £200; Air fare + insurance approx £800. About £1,500 covers all including £130 charged for the induction and Mandinka lessons on arrival.
Benefits: Food, accommodation. Volunteers live with families in family compounds.
Training: We provide an induction programme in Marlborough for a weekend.
Supervision: Volunteers are supervised in the school in which they work and the responsibility of TARUD, our partner organisation in the Gambia.
Interviews: There is a preliminary briefing in December before starting, followed by interviews. Interviews are held in Marlborough.
Charity number: 1001398
Worldwide placements: Africa (Gambia).

METHODIST CHURCH – North Lancashire District, The

122 Lancaster Road
Cabus, Garstang
Preston
Lancashire PR3 1JE UK
T: 01995 603261
W: www.northlancsmethodist.org.uk
Contact: Rev John A Maiden

The North Lancashire District of the Methodist Church stretches from South Ribble in the south to the boundary of Cumbria in the north and from the Fylde coast in the west to the Yorkshire border in the east, and, indeed, takes in a tiny bit of West Yorkshire. It covers almost all of the administrative county of Lancashire. The district is made up of 16 circuits with almost 130 churches. There are 63 presbyteral ministers in the district and 13 other staff, either deacons or lay workers. There are churches in every sort of area, town centre, inner town or city, suburban, small town and rural. In some parts of the district there are large ethnic communities, Indian, Pakistani and Bangladeshi. The tasks and duties, which might be available for volunteers, would come mainly in our larger churches in the urban areas. There are a number of community projects involving children, the elderly and, indeed various sections of the community. In Preston there is a night shelter for the homeless, while in other places work is done with this group with addicts. Elsewhere those who can help develop children's and youth work will perhaps find opportunities. Anyone interested in what we might be able to offer is advised to contact the individual church through Revd. John Maiden. More information as and when projects are set up.

Number of projects: 1 UK: 1
Starting months: January–December
Time required: 1–52 weeks
Age: 14 plus – no upper limit
Causes: Children, Elderly People, Offenders/Ex-Offenders, Poor/Homeless, Unemployed, Young People.
Activities: Administration, Caring – General, Community Work, Group Work, Social Work, Visiting/Befriending.
When to apply: Any time.
Work alone/with others: Usually with others.
Qualifications: This can depend on project.
Equipment/clothing: Dependent on project.
Health requirements: Dependent on project.
Costs: Travel, food and sometimes accommodation depending on local availability.
Training: Training provided as appropriate.
Supervision: Supervision is always provided.
Interviews: Yes, volunteers are normally interviewed.
UK placements: England (Lancashire).

MID-AFRICA MINISTRY (CMS)

c/o Christian Mission Society, Youth Office
Partnership House
157 Waterloo Road
London
SE1 8UU UK
T: +44 (0) 207 261 1370
T: +44 (0) 207 401 2910
E: info.mam@cms-uk.org
W: www.midafricaministry.org
Contact: Dr Bill Hawes

A Christian Mission Society works in partnership with the Anglican Church in Rwanda, Burundi, South West Uganda, Eastern Congo and Congo Brazzaville. From time to time, the overseas Church requests short-term assistance or is able to accommodate offers from those who are unable to go overseas for as long as two years or who wish to test whether they are being called to Africa longer-term or who are over 65. The minimum period of time for such

service is usually six months although three months is sufficient for some medical assignments; an academic year is often the requirement for teaching posts. Medicine and teaching are the most common disciplines. Offers of service need to be on a self-funded basis although MAM does have a discretionary fund and is happy to help those volunteers unable to raise all their funds. Volunteers usually live in difficult or basic conditions which is part of the 'culture shock'. Accommodation, water and electricity supply (if any!), food, health facilities, leisure activities can all be guaranteed to be very different from back home but so also can the compensations be similarly guaranteed. Volunteers are expected to be involved in the life and worship of the local Anglican Church where they work overseas; there is a requirement of obedience to the local Anglican Church and its decisions. Whilst MAM is not the employer, volunteers are expected to follow its advice, requests and decisions.

Number of projects: many UK: 0
Starting months: January–December
Time required: 4–52 weeks (plus)
Age: 18–70
Causes: Health Care/Medical, Teaching/assisting (primary, secondary, EFL), Young People.
Activities: Accountancy, Administration, Agriculture/Farming, Building/Construction, Caring – General, Catering, Community Work, Computers, Library/Resource Centres, Music, Religion, Social Work, Sport, Teaching, Technical Skills, Theatre/Drama, Training, Visiting/Befriending, Work Camps – Seasonal.
Placements: 20
When to apply: All year. For summer camps by 1st March.
Work alone/with others: With others.
Qualifications: Professional skills required and also some without professional qualifications. No nationality restrictions but UK based volunteers are generally required.
Equipment/clothing: Yes if medical.
Health requirements: All volunteers subject to satisfactory medical examination for tropical countries.
Costs: Airfare £600–£1,000; subsistence £150 a month; medical and travel insurance £120 p.a. Discretionary fund available. Most volunteers are self-funded or funded by churches etc.
Training: One week orientation in Britain.
Supervision: Under the care of the Diocesan Bishop of the area.
Interviews: Prospective volunteers are interviewed, usually in the London office.
Charity number: 220297
Worldwide placements: Africa (Burundi, Congo Dem Republic, Rwanda, Uganda).

MILLENNIUM ELEPHANT FOUNDATION

Randeniya
Hiriwadunna
Kegalle
Sri Lanka
T: +94 35 65377
F: +94 35 66572
E: elefound@sltnet.lk
W: www.eureka.lk/elefound
Contact: Carminie Samarasinghe

The Millennium Elephant Foundation is dedicated to the care and protection of elderly and disabled elephants in Sri Lanka. We operate a mobile vet unit that travels across the country treating ill or injured elephants. We also have strong community development goals and provide free English lessons for people from low-income backgrounds. Standard volunteer placements run for three months and are available in the following focus areas –
1. MEF – raising awareness and fundraising
2. Mobile vet unit
3. English teaching
4. Maximus paper recycling
5. Ecological farming
For more information – please visit our web site. We may be able to place volunteers with an offending background – each application individually assessed. MEF operates in rural villages outside Kegalle town. Mobile vet unit operates throughout the country. English teaching programmes operate from local Buddhist temple. 📄

Number of projects: 1 UK: 0
Starting months: January–December
Time required: 4–26 weeks
Age: 18 plus – no upper limit
Causes: Animal Welfare, Children, Conservation, Environmental Causes, Teaching/assisting (primary, secondary, mature, EFL), Wildlife.
Activities: Administration, Conservation Skills, Development Issues, Fundraising, Newsletter/Journalism, Teaching.
Placements: 30
When to apply: Any time.
Work alone/with others: With others.
Qualifications: Enthusiasm, computer literacy preferred and dedication.
Equipment/clothing: Rarely.
Health requirements: Volunteers must be reasonably fit as the work if often physically demanding.
Costs: Placement fee of £1000 for three months, includes visa, accommodation, meals, programme implementation and airport collection – enquire for more details. Plus flights and insurance.
Benefits: Food, accommodation, visa airport pickup are included in programme fee. Onsite volunteer bungalow that accommodates up to 11 volunteers at a time, meals are provided at local restaurant. Bungalow has western style bathroom, shared bedrooms, kitchenette, living area and garden area.
Training: Onsite safety training and guidance is given by volunteer programme manager and site managers.
Supervision: Volunteers are expected to work independently to a certain degree but guidance/supervision is provided by volunteer manager, site manager and elephant keepers (mahouts).
Interviews: Interviewed via telephone. Prospective volunteers also correspond extensively with the volunteer programme manager via e-mail prior to arrival.
Charity number: 457
Worldwide placements: Asia (Sri Lanka).

MILTON KEYNES RESOURCE CENTRE

1 Fletchers Mews
Neath Hill
Milton Keynes
Buckinghamshire MK14 6HW UK
T: 01908 660364
F: 01908 231407
E: annmarie.sweeney@scope.org.uk
Contact: Annmarie Sweeney

Milton Keynes Resource Centre is a day service providing IT, core skills, art, relaxation, DT and we conform to the Scope Mission Statement. Scope exists to provide support and services for people with physical disabilities and their families. Volunteers with an offending background may be accepted if they are an exception under the Rehabilitation Act 1974. ♿

Number of projects: 1 UK: 1
Starting months: January–December
Time required: 1–52 weeks (plus)
Age: 16 plus – no upper limit
Causes: Disabled (physical).
Activities: Administration, Arts/Crafts, Caring – Day, Computers, Cooking, Gardening/Horticulture, Training.
Placements: 16–18
When to apply: All year.
Work alone/with others: With others.
Qualifications: No specific skills are required.
Health requirements: Reasonably good health.
Costs: Some travel, food and accommodation.
Benefits: Reasonable travel costs.
Training: Health and safety, and local induction.
Supervision: Overseen by an appropriate member of staff.
Interviews: Prospective volunteers are interviewed at the Centre. References are required as is a CRB check.
UK placements: England (Buckinghamshire).

MIND

50 Oole Road
Cleethorpes
North East Lincolnshire DN35 8LR UK
T: 01472 602502
E: mind.office@virgin.net
Contact: Martin Skelton

MIND is the leading mental health charity in
England and Wales, working for a better life for
people diagnosed, labelled or treated as
mentally ill. The Grimsby and Cleethorpes
office provides a number of services for people
living in the community. We also promote
mental health issues locally and have recently
begun to raise the awareness of MIND in the
area. We need more volunteers with ideas and
new skills to join us and take us forward. Due
to the sensitive nature of our work we may not
always be able to place volunteers who have
offended. Based within the Grimsby/
Cleethorpes area of North East Lincolnshire. 📖

Number of projects UK: 4
Starting months: January–December
Time required: 6–52 weeks
Age: 18–80
Causes: Disabled (learning), Elderly People,
Health Care/Medical, Inner City Problems.
Activities: Administration, Caring – General,
Community Work, Computers, Cooking,
Counselling, Driving, Fundraising, Gardening/
Horticulture, Group Work, Music, Newsletter/
Journalism, Social Work, Theatre/Drama,
Training, Visiting/Befriending.
Placements: 20–30
When to apply: As soon as possible.
Work alone/with others: With others.
Qualifications: No nationality restrictions but
will need basic English language skills.
Health requirements: No restrictions.
Costs: Travel, training and food and
accommodation.
Benefits: Reasonable travel and out of pocket
expenses are paid.
Training: We have an induction programme
and various training opportunities throughout
the year.
Supervision: The volunteers co-ordinator and
services manager provides supervision and
ongoing assessment of volunteers.
Interviews: Interviews held at our Oole Road
office in Cleethorpes.
Charity number: 507014
UK placements: England (Lincolnshire).

MINISTÈRE DE LA CULTURE – sous DIRECTION DE L'ARCHÉOLOGIE

4 rue d'Aboukir
Paris
75002 France
T: 00 33 1 4015 80 00
F: 00 33 1 4015 7700
W: www.culture.gouv.fr/fouilles
Contact: M. le Directeur

Each year in May we issue a brochure which
lists the archaeological workcamps for
volunteers in France. This lists all the different
programmes for the year. The list is also
accessible on our web site. 📖

Number of projects: 200 UK: 0
Starting months: May, Jun, Jul, Aug, Sep, Oct
Time required: 2–26 weeks
Age: 16 plus – no upper limit
Causes: Archaeology, Work Camps – Seasonal.
Activities: Group Work, Manual Work, Outdoor
Skills, Scientific Work.
Placements: 300 approx.
When to apply: Any time.
Work alone/with others: Work in a team.
Qualifications: None required but any
appreciated.
Equipment/clothing: Work shoes and clothes
for outside work.
Health requirements: Anti-tetanus and polio
innoculations.
Costs: Travel to the project.
Benefits: Board and lodging.
Interviews: No interview. Contact us by letter
or telephone.
Worldwide placements: South America (French
Guiana); Europe (France).

MINORITY RIGHTS GROUP INTERNATIONAL

International Secretariat
379 Brixton Road
London
SW9 7DE UK
T: +44 (0) 207 978 9498
T: +44 (0) 207 738 6265
E: minorityrights@mrgmail.org
W: www.mrgmail.org
Contact: The Director

Minority Rights Group International (MRG) is a
non-governmental organisation (NGO) working
to secure rights for ethnic, religious and
linguistic minorities worldwide, and to promote
co-operation and understanding between
communities. Founded in the 1960s MRG has
over 30 years' experience of promoting the
rights of marginalised, non-dominant groups
within society. MRG seeks to link local and
international human rights initiatives. Local
practical experience influences MRG's policy
representations and vice versa. MRG
concentrates on processes and group capacity-
building rather than individual complaints.
MRG advocacy work aims to raise awareness of
minority rights issues among international

audiences and promote positive change at national and international levels. MRG continually develops partnerships which are essential to our work. We currently work with over 60 partner organisations throughout the world who are involved in a range of activities. An international agency with consultative status with the United Nations Economic and Social Council (ECOSOC).

Number of projects: several **UK:** 1
Starting months: January–December
Time required: 16–52 weeks
Age: 18 plus – no upper limit
Causes: Human Rights, Refugees.
Activities: Development Issues, Fundraising, Marketing/Publicity, Religion, Research, Training, Translating.
When to apply: Our use of volunteers is limited by available space and by the fact that we like to have a definite project for volunteers. So apply any time.
Work alone/with others: Alone under supervision and team working too.
Qualifications: University degree or above. Interest in human rights, minority rights, international development and conflict resolution.
Costs: All costs including housing, meals, transport.
Supervision: Depends on project.
Interviews: Interviews take place at our office by the deputy director or head of department.
UK placements: England (London).

MISSION AVIATION FELLOWSHIP

Castle House
Castle Hill Avenue
Folkestone
Kent CT20 2TN UK
T: 01303 850950
F: 01303 852 800
E: heather.faulkner@maf-uk.org
W: www.maf-uk.org
Contact: Heather Faulkner

Mission Aviation Fellowship is a Christian agency whose mission is to fly light aircraft in developing countries so that people in remote areas can receive the help they need. Our professional staff team includes pilots, engineers, radio technicians, computer specialists, builders and administrators. We operate over 150 aircraft in more than 30 countries and carry medicines, doctors, food, aid workers, patients and missionaries. Unfortunately we are unable to place volunteers with an offending background. Normally Tanzania (Dodoma) and Uganda (Entebbe). Others e.g. Kenya, Mongolia, Bangladesh, Chad. 🖹

Number of projects: Varies **UK:** 0
Starting months: Jul, Aug

Time required: 3 weeks
Age: 18–80
Causes: Addicts/Ex-Addicts, AIDS/HIV, Children, Disabled (learning and physical), Elderly People, Environmental Causes, Poor/ Homeless, Refugees, Unemployed, Young People.
Activities: Building/Construction, DIY, Group Work, International Aid, Manual Work, Religion, Technical Skills.
Placements: 20
When to apply: Winter/Spring – October to May.
Work alone/with others: With others as we send volunteers in teams.
Qualifications: Interest in Christian mission needed. Skills required depend on project applied to. May require DIY, building or painting expertise. British passport normally required.
Equipment/clothing: Depends on placement – more information on application.
Health requirements: Must be fit and healthy for overseas travel and for the work being undertaken.
Costs: Depends on project – please contact us for more information.
Benefits: Details supplied on application as projects vary. Accommodation provided and insurance.
Training: Briefing weekend prior to departure.
Supervision: Each team has an experienceed leader. Overseas staff are also involved in supervision.
Interviews: Normally in Ashford in Kent, or Folkestone in Kent.
Charity number: 1064598
Worldwide placements: Africa (Chad, Kenya, Tanzania, Uganda); Asia (Bangladesh, Mongolia).

MISSION AVIATION FELLOWSHIP – WHAT 4

Ingles Manor
Castle Hill Avenue
Folkestone
Kent CT20 2TN UK
T: 01303 850950
F: 01303 852800
E: what4@maf-uk.org
Contact: The Rev. Dave Barker

WHAT 4 is the youth division of the registered charity, Mission Aviation Fellowship UK. We are a Christian agency whose mission is to fly light aircraft in developing countries so that people in remote areas can receive the help they need. What 4 exists to introduce young people to the work of MAF worldwide and involve young people in projects, both in the UK as well as overseas in East Africa and parts of Asia where MAF operates. For further details please contact the MAF office. 🖹

Number of projects: 8 UK: 7
Starting months: January–December
Time required: 1–52 weeks (plus)
Age: 14 plus – no upper limit
Causes: Children, Elderly People, Young People.
Activities: Agriculture/Farming, Community Work, Manual Work, Outdoor Skills, Religion.
Placements: 210
When to apply: Anytime.
Work alone/with others: Both.
Training: In place.
Supervision: In place.
Interviews: Required.
Worldwide placements: Africa (Kenya, Tanzania, Uganda).
UK placements: England (Kent).

MISSION RAINFOREST FOUNDATION

The Centre
Codicote Road
Welwyn
Hertfordshire AL6 9TU UK
T: 01438 716873 or 716478
F: 01438 717535
E: cattrust@aol.com
W: www.catsurvivaltrust.org
Contact: Dr Terry Moore

The Mission Rainforest Foundation operates a 10,000-acre reserve in Pinalito, North East Argentina, which is now registered as a Provincial Park. The park was purchased in 1992 with public and NGO donations and contains five million trees, billions of insects, hundreds of thousands of plants, birds, fish, reptiles and mammals. 54 plants in the forest have been used by the local community for generations as natural medicines and there are many of the original plant stocks of fruit and nuts from which the commercial hybrids now produce some of the world's supermarket food. The Foundation has plans to purchase more land in other countries. Volunteers have been involved and are involved in the running of the reserve and there are plans for more reserves elsewhere. Pinalito, North East Argentina.

Number of projects: 1 UK: 0
Starting months: January–December
Time required: 1–52 weeks
Age: 16 plus – no upper limit
Causes: Conservation, Human Rights.
Activities: Administration, Campaigning, Computers, Conservation Skills, Development Issues, Fundraising, Library/Resource Centres, Research, Scientific Work, Technical Skills, Translating.
Placements: 12
When to apply: Any time.
Work alone/with others: Both.
Qualifications: Qualifications required for the task/s to be undertaken. In Argentina, spoken Spanish is important.
Equipment/clothing: All specialist equipment is provided, but personal equipment must be provided by the volunteer.
Health requirements: Good general health required.
Costs: All living and travelling costs must be paid by the volunteer.
Benefits: Accommodation electricity and basic food provided.
Training: Provided.
Supervision: Provided.
Interviews: Interviews held at Welwyn Head Office.
Charity number: 272187
Worldwide placements: South America (Argentina).

MISSIONARY CENACLE VOLUNTEERS

P.O. Box 35105
Cleveland
Ohio 44135-0105 USA
T: 00 1 800 221 5740
F: 00 1 216 671 2320
E: cenaclevol@aol.com
W: www.tmc3.org
Contact: Shaun Witmer

Since 1916, the Missionary Cenacle Volunteers have been 'Helping Catholics Become Apostles' through faith-based voluntary service, for long-term (nearly one year or more, for 21+ year olds) and summer (18+ year olds) service terms. Our volunteers serve throughout the US and (if Spanish speaking) in Central America. Volunteers work on our missions with Missionary Cenacle family members and others, while participating in community life and an active prayer life. The Missionary Cenacle family is a Catholic missionary family devoted to fostering the vocation of the laity to become apostles, by growing spiritually while serving God and others among the spiritually abandoned and materially poor in such ministries as: parish/youth ministry, health care, education, social work and other ministries including teaching, building maintenance, cooking, religious education, clerical/office work, child care, teacher's aide, working with elderly, homeless, and persons with physical and developmental disabilities. Our Trinita summer family programme lies in the beautiful mountains of western Connecticut. For 2–6 weeks we need young and adult Catholics (couples included) to share their gifts of faith, fellowship, music, arts and crafts, laughter, and recreation to provide a rewarding faith experience for disadvantaged inner-city families from New York, New Jersey, Connecticut and Pennsylvania. For long-term service you will receive housing, food, health insurance and a small monthly stipend for personal expenses. Room and board is provided for our summer sites. All applicants go through a background check and criminal history search; an offending background could negatively impact an applicant's chances of acceptance into the programme. ♿

Number of projects: 20–25 **UK:** 0
Starting months: January–December
Time required: 3–52 weeks (plus)
Age: 18 plus – no upper limit
Causes: Children, Disabled (learning and physical), Elderly People, Health Care/Medical, Inner City Problems, Offenders/Ex-Offenders, Poor/Homeless, Refugees, Teaching/assisting (primary), Young People.
Activities: Administration, Arts/crafts, Caring (general, residential), Community Work, Computers, Cooking, Counselling, Driving, Group Work, Manual Work, Music, Religion, Social Work, Sport, Summer Camps, Teaching, Training, Translating, Visiting/Befriending.
Placements: 75
When to apply: February – May and year round.
Work alone/with others: Yes usually.
Qualifications: Summer: ability to work with youth. Long-term: college degree, driving licence, comfortable working at Roman Catholic Church sites.
Equipment/clothing: Clothing based on local climate/weather.
Health requirements: Some sites require physical ability to do manual work or heavy lifting – but not all sites.
Costs: Return travel to site in USA or Central America + personal expenses.
Benefits: Board and lodging for short and long-term volunteers. Long-term also offers pocket money. Housing provided for all programmes, often with Catholic religious priests, brothers and nuns or with other volunteers.
Training: A one-week programme orientation and varying on-site training depending on work site.
Supervision: Supervisors are provided at every work site to assist, orientate and train volunteers in their work.
Interviews: All volunteers are interviewed in person when possible, but at least by phone when necessary.
Worldwide placements: North America: (USA); Central America (Costa Rica, Mexico, Puerto Rico).

MISSIONS INTERNATIONAL

P.O.Box 3246
Diego Martin
Trinidad and Tobago
T: 868 632 3500

E: missions-international@usa.net
W: www.missions-international.com
Contact: Dr. Brian Lushington

Missions International aims to bring the message of the cross to hurting people. Current projects include – Working successfully with Cuban people who are desperately in need of medical supplies and toiletries. We ensure that all donations reach their destination. The construction and equipping of a free clinic in Chaguanas, Trinidad. Rural church assistance programme. Sending overseas missions teams to Latin America and Caribbean countries. Church planting in all the Caribbean islands. Evangelistic crusades in villages, towns and cities in Tobago and Guyana. Conducting religious instruction through schools in Trinidad and Tobago. Providing medical equipment and supplies to humanitarian organisations. Food distribution to the poor. Evangelistic outreaches into Venezuela. Volunteers with an offending background may be accepted. Trinidad and Tobago, Guyana and Barbados. ♿

Number of projects: 30–40 **UK:** 0
Starting months: January–December
Time required: 1–52 weeks
Age: 15 plus – no upper limit
Causes: Addicts/Ex-Addicts, AIDS/HIV, Children, Disabled (physical), Elderly People, Health Care/Medical, Poor/Homeless, Teaching/assisting, Work Camps – Seasonal, Young People.
Activities: Administration, Arts/Crafts, Building/Construction, Caring – General, Community Work, Computers, First Aid, International Aid, Manual Work, Music, Religion, Social Work, Sport, Summer Camps, Teaching, Training, Work Camps – Seasonal.
Placements: 120
When to apply: Any time.
Work alone/with others: Work with others.
Equipment/clothing: We are in the Caribbean so light cotton clothing is best.
Health requirements: No restrictions.
Costs: Volunteers to fund – accommodation, meals, transportation to and from the airport and transport to and from project on a daily basis – cost around $20.00 US per day per person. Accommodation is in a comfortable modern dormitory with hot and cold water.
Benefits: We can offer some assistance with lodging and meals.
Training: Depends on the project but we will provide training where needed.
Supervision: Project managers and co-ordinators will supervise volunteers.
Interviews: No interview.
Charity number: M1789(95)
Worldwide placements: Central America (Barbados, Trinidad and Tobago); South America (Guyana).

MISTA V SRDCI (PLACES IN THE HEART FOUNDATION) – CZECH REPUBLIC

Jugoslavskych Partyzanu 11
1600 Praha 6
Czech Republic
T: 00 42 2 311 8390
F: 00 42 2 311 5269
Contact: Petr Marek

Mista v Srdci (Places in the Heart Foundation) promotes and has information about volunteering in the Czech republic. It may well be able to put volunteers in touch with organisations which are not yet listed on the WorldWide Volunteering database.

Starting months: January–December
Time required: 1–52 weeks (plus)
Age: 16 plus – no upper limit
Causes: Addicts/Ex-Addicts, AIDS/HIV, Animal Welfare, Archaeology, Architecture, Children, Conservation, Disabled (learning and physical), Elderly People, Environmental Causes, Health Care/Medical, Heritage, Holidays for Disabled, Human Rights, Inner City Problems, Offenders/Ex-Offenders, Poor/Homeless, Refugees, Teaching/assisting (nursery, primary, secondary, mature, EFL) Unemployed, Wildlife, Work Camps – Seasonal, Young People.
Activities: Accountancy, Administration, Agriculture/Farming, Arts/Crafts, Building/ Construction, Campaigning, Caring (general, day and residential), Catering, Community Work, Computers, Conservation Skills, Cooking, Counselling, Development Issues, DIY, Driving, First Aid, Forestry, Fundraising, Gardening/Horticulture, Group Work, International Aid, Library/Resource Centres, Manual Work, Marketing/Publicity, Music, Newsletter/Journalism, Outdoor Skills, Religion, Research, Scientific Work, Social Work, Sport, Summer Camps, Teaching, Technical Skills, Theatre/Drama, Training, Translating, Visiting/Befriending, Work Camps – Seasonal.
Costs: Varies according to the project.
Worldwide placements: Europe (Czech Republic).

MITRANIKETAN

Mitraniketan P.O.
Thiruvananthapuram
Vellanad
Kerala 695-543 India
T: 00 91 472 2882045
F: 00 91 472 2882015
E: kvmitra@satyam.net.in
W: www.mitraniketan.org
Contact: K. Viswanathan

Mitraniketan is well-known in India and abroad as a Kerala-based voluntary non-governmental organisation that has pioneered people-centred holistic rural development for improving the quality of life and living of village communities. It strives to promote rural development with a human face. Mitraniketan has a resident community engaged in a variety of development activities. It has an unmistakable international presence in a Kerala-setting and promotes a lifestyle that is essentially spartan. It is an education-based community which imparts community-based education which is participative by nature and emphasises dignity of labour. It promotes sustainable agriculture and farming practices that are environment and farmer friendly. A variety of vocations for rural employment are promoted at Mitraniketan, with efficiency-additions through appropriate science and technology inputs. Mitraniketan also strives to promote and enhance rural human resource development capabilities that can foster a participative culture and work-ethic. It seeks to blend tradition with modernity and indigenous knowledge systems with other knowledge systems. In its development-update and innovative endeavours, a like-minded fraternity resident in and outside Mitraniketan lends devoted support. Major activities include: residential tribal school project; community education centre for rural youth; farm science centre; appropriate rural technology centre; library and documentation centre; animal science section; social science research under projects of development nature; health centre; research and development in simple technologies useful for villagers. Average temperature 28 degrees C. 🔊 📄

Number of projects: 1 UK: 0
Starting months: January–December
Time required: 1–52 weeks
Age: 18–60
Causes: Animal Welfare, Children, Environmental Causes, Health Care/Medical, Teaching/assisting (nursery, primary, secondary, mature, EFL) Young People.
Activities: Agriculture/Farming, Building/Construction, Community Work, Computers, Development Issues, Fundraising, Gardening/Horticulture, International Aid, Library/Resource Centres, Manual Work, Marketing/Publicity, Newsletter/Journalism, Research, Scientific Work, Social Work, Sport, Teaching, Training.
Placements: 100
When to apply: All year.
Work alone/with others: With other young volunteers.
Qualifications: English language and special skills for some projects – for other projects no skills required.
Equipment/clothing: Ordinary clothing.
Health requirements: Nil.

Costs: Rs250 (US$5.50) per day for board and lodging in Mitraniketan guest house. Travel to India.
Training: One-day campus tour and orientation.
Supervision: We have a volunteers' co-ordinator.
Interviews: There are no interviews but bio-data is checked.
Charity number: 11 of 1967
Worldwide placements: Asia (India).

MOKOLODI NATURE RESERVE

P O Box 170
Gabarone
Botswana
T: 00 267 3161955/6
F: 00 267 315488
E: volunteers@mokolodi.com
W: www.mokolodi.com
Contact: 'Puso' J.R.B. Kirby

The Mokolodi Nature Reserve lies in the heart of Botswana bush but only 14 kms from the capital Gaborone. The Reserve extends to over 10,000 acres. It was started in 1994 and is fully stocked with a varied population of species indigenous to S.E. Botswana. The three founding pillars of the Reserve are the reintroduction and propagation of rare and endangered indigenous species, environmental education and community involvement. An education centre has been established, using the 'outdoor classroom', to instil in children from all over Botswana a love of nature and an understanding of the importance of conserving wildlife for Botswana and the world. In 2001, 11,000 children visited the centre. One day these children will have the vote. Mokolodi is home to over a third of Botswana's white rhino population, and has a breeding programme aimed at the eventual reintroduction of the species to all parts of Botswana. This programme was recently instrumental in reintroducing the white rhino to the Delta region of Botswana, re-establishing the Big 5 in Botswana's most famous destination. The Reserve has one of only two wild animal orphanages in the country and is home to Botswana's only Cheetah Transit Station, created in order to relocate 'problem' cheetahs brought in from private game farms and cattle ranches. A joint venture with the Serendib Orphanage cares for four young orphan elephants, who are being trained in an educational project firstly to disprove the long-standing myth that it is impossible to train African elephants and secondly, to show young people the potential value of these beasts both in tourism and otherwise. Volunteers are needed to help in the following areas: marketing and fundraising; education centre; animal sanctuary; conservation/field work assistant; permaculture gardens; park maintenance and development; community development Mokolodi Nature Reserve is situated on the main Lobatse Road just 15 km away from the capital of Botswana, Gaborone. Mokolodi is 30 minutes away from Gaborone International airport and is also very close to the South African border. ♿ 📄

Number of projects: 1 UK: 0
Starting months: January–December
Time required: 2–24 weeks
Age: 15 plus – no upper limit
Causes: AIDS/HIV, Animal Welfare, Archaeology, Architecture, Children, Conservation, Environmental Causes, Teaching/assisting (nursery, primary, secondary, mature), Wildlife, Work Camps – Seasonal, Young People.
Activities: Accountancy, Administration, Arts/Crafts, Building/Construction, Caring – General, Catering, Community Work, Computers, Conservation Skills, Development Issues, Driving, First Aid, Forestry, Fundraising, Gardening/Horticulture, Group Work, International Aid, Library/Resource Centres, Manual Work, Marketing/Publicity, Music, Newsletter/Journalism, Outdoor Skills, Research, Scientific Work, Summer Camps, Teaching, Technical Skills, Theatre/Drama, Training, Work Camps – Seasonal.
Placements: 24 long term
When to apply: All year.
Work alone/with others: Both.
Qualifications: University degree preferable but otherwise people with specific skills and experience. No nationality restrictions. We now offer short term programmes. Volunteers under 18 years must have letter of parental consent. Long term volunteers should be at least 21 years.
Equipment/clothing: Volunteers are required to either purchase uniform items from us (see web for costs) or to bring their own uniform in line with our uniform policy.
Health requirements: Good health. Government requirements can be obtained from the Botswana Embassy.
Costs: Short term volunteers pay fee towards their stay – check web site. Long term volunteers to pay refundable deposit of 4800PULA on arrival – check web site. Flight and insurance costs.
Benefits: Thatched accommodation for 12 is available for long term volunteers. Shared tent accommodation for 10 has been constructed with bush showers and kitchen facilities for short term volunteers. 12 month or more stay – allowance of 300PULA per month.
Training: Short term volunteers are allocated supervisor and will receive training relevant to particular placement.

Long term volunteers are recruited on the basis that they will not need training, but are able to provide training to local staff.
Supervision: Supervised/overseen by senior management.
Interviews: Prospective volunteers are interviewed mostly by e-mail.
Worldwide placements: Africa (Botswana).

MONDOCHALLENGE

Galliford Building, Gayton Road
Milton Malsor
Northampton
Northants NN7 3AB UK
T: 01604 858225
F: 01604 859323
E: info@mondochallenge.org
W: www.mondochallenge.org
Contact: Anthony Lunch

MondoChallenge sends volunteers to community based projects in a range of countries. The organisation is based on the success of the Nepal volunteer programme that has been running since 1990, and has resulted in the building of a new school in the Himalayas, pupil exchanges and greater sustainability of mountain communities. A substantial UK support organisation exists around this project. The Tanzanian programme revolves around the Maasai tribe in Arusha, situated close to Mount Kilimanjaro. Teaching, community development and cultural programmes are available, all aimed at helping sustain the indigenous way of life. There are also programmes in Pangani, on the coast, and in Arusha at primary schools near Mount Meru. In the Gambia, the volunteer project is based in a small village school 30km from Banjul. It is close to the wonderful Gambian beaches, amongst the best in Africa! In Chile we are working in small towns north of Santiago in beautiful mountain settings. In India, the programmes are in the Darjeeling/Kalimpong region, situated in the beautiful foothills of the Himalayas. They are all based in primary or secondary schools. The Nepalese projects are in attractive locations in or close to Kathmandu. Volunteers initially make contact mainly via the Internet, or by phone. The recruitment process is informal but demanding and references are needed. Some of the postings are rural and fairly remote whilst others are town based. The project director and founder, Anthony Lunch, did VSO in The Gambia and served as a member of the VSO Council for seven years. He has wide experience of international business and has worked for government, local authorities and private businesses. Arusha, Pangani and Longido in Tanzania. Kunkujang near Banjul in the Gambia. Monte Grande in Chile. Bomet in

Ghana. Dhulikhel and Kathmandu in Nepal. Darjeeling and Kalimpong in India.

Number of projects: 25 UK: 0
Starting months: January–December
Time required: 5–26 weeks
Age: 18–60
Causes: Children, Conservation, Environmental Causes, Poor/Homeless, Teaching/assisting (nursery, primary, secondary, mature, EFL) Unemployed, Wildlife, Young People.
Activities: Accountancy, Administration, Agriculture/Farming, Arts/Crafts, Building/ Construction, Computers, Conservation Skills, Fundraising, Group Work, Marketing/Publicity, Newsletter/Journalism, Teaching, Theatre/ Drama.
Placements: 150+
When to apply: All year.
Work alone/with others: With other volunteers.
Qualifications: Minimum A level or equivalent.
Health requirements: Physically fit.
Costs: Contribution to project costs in country £500–£800 plus board (approx. £50 per month) plus travel (approximately £500).
Training: Orientation and training in country. Briefing and basic training in the UK.
Supervision: Volunteers are supervised by our in-country managers and by the headteachers.
Interviews: Interviews in London, Edinburgh, Manchester and Northampton.
Worldwide placements: Africa (Gambia, Kenya, Tanzania); South America (Chile); Asia (India, Nepal, Sri Lanka).

MONGOLIAN YOUTH DEVELOPMENT CENTRE

Room #12
MYF Building
Baba-Toiruu-44
Ulaanbaatar
Mongolia
T: 00 976 11 314433
F: 00 976 11 323 921
E: volunteers@mydc.org.mn
W: www.mydc.org.mn
Contact: D. Bayarjargal

The Mongolian Youth Development Centre was established in 1995 as a non-governmental organisation working to assist Mongolian youth through the transition process from childhood to adulthood by providing opportunities for them to become fully participating members of society. This we aim to achieve through social, educational, cultural and physical activities. MYDC would like to help young people to develop their capacities and to be comfortable in a rapidly changing and developing world. We target 14–24 year olds. This is a very significant time due to the rapid sexual, physical and emotional change, and we believe that it is most important, during this period of adolescence and throughout the transition into young adulthood, that adults provide the support and assistance that they need to develop their full potential. Recent research (The Mongolian Adolescent Needs Assessment UNICEF/ Government of Mongolia) found that Mongolian adolescents have limited knowledge about the issues that most affect them, and that they have limited options and capacity to put forward their views and express their feelings and ideas. There are very few programmes, information and activities for young people or their families that are relevant to youth. There are very few youth centres and very few options for out of school activities. It is these issues that the MYDC would like to address. It is the policy of MYDC to have young people working with young people. Our staff are young – 90% of them aged between 20 and 26 years and they respond eagerly to training and are enthusiastic. No. 🔲

Number of projects: 5 UK: 0
Starting months: January–December
Time required: 2–52 weeks
Age: 16–40
Causes: AIDS/HIV, Children, Disabled (learning and physical), Environmental Causes, Health Care/Medical, Human Rights, Offenders/Ex-Offenders, Poor/Homeless, Teaching/assisting (nursery, primary, secondary, mature, EFL) Work Camps – Seasonal, Young People.
Activities: Administration, Agriculture/Farming, Arts/Crafts, Building/Construction, Caring – General, Community Work, Computers, Cooking, Counselling, Development Issues, First Aid, Fundraising, Gardening/Horticulture, Group Work, International Aid, Library/Resource Centres, Manual Work, Marketing/Publicity, Music, Newsletter/Journalism, Research, Social Work, Summer Camps, Teaching, Training, Translating, Work Camps – Seasonal.
Placements: 150–200
When to apply: 2 or 3 months before planning to arrive.
Work alone/with others: Sometimes with others and at other times alone.
Qualifications: Volunteers must speak either English or Russian. They should have at least 2 or 3 years experience in doing voluntary work.
Equipment/clothing: Depends on the season. It is very cold in the winter and warm in the summer. Clean and practical casual clothing would be appropriate. Equipment necessary depends on the project and specific skills. Please check in advance.
Health requirements: No restrictions but bring any medicines that you take regularly, they may be hard to find in Mongolia.
Costs: Volunteers pay for their travel, accommodation and food.

Training: Orientation training is provided.
Supervision: Mongolian Youth Development Centre staff supervise.
Interviews: No interviews.
Charity number: 49
Worldwide placements: Asia (Mongolia).

MONGOLIAN YOUTH VOLUNTEER ORGANIZATION

P.O. Box 159
Ulaanbaatar 210646a
Mongolia
T: 00 976 99197774
F: 00 976 11320616
E: infomongolia@yahoo.com
W: www.owc.org.mn/myvo
Contact: Mr Gankhuyag

Mongolian Youth Volunteer Organization is a non-governmental organisation, which was established in 1999 and is working to assist Mongolian youth by providing social, educational, cultural and physical activities and opportunities. At the start of the new millennium many in Mongolia have hopes for the future but most of them find themselves marginalised, economically disadvantaged and oppressed. Whatever your background or circumstances your actions can make a positive contribution to the society. Your involvement may be for a short or long time – whatever you decide, you can contribute constructively. Each year we are recruiting volunteers who want to experience the unique tradition of nomadic people and exposure to alternative and different lifestyles in Mongolia. We will arrange a guide and transport for the Naadam festival (a celebration of Mongolian culture and sport) and for those keen on horse or camel riding, we will arrange a 5–11 day tour to Karakhorum, the Gobi Desert and many exciting places. Alternative e-mail address – myvo@owc.org.mn Mongolia's bustling capital city, Ulaanbaatar, lies in a pituresque valley surrounded by four peaks. Buddhist monastries nestled in the urban landscape provide an interesting insight to the religious origins of the country. 🔲

Number of projects: 12 UK: 0
Starting months: January–December
Time required: 2–52 weeks
Age: 17–45
Causes: Conservation, Health Care/Medical, Teaching/assisting (nursery, primary, secondary, mature, EFL).
Activities: Community Work, Conservation Skills, Development Issues, First Aid, International Aid, Newsletter/Journalism, Outdoor Skills, Social Work, Teaching, Theatre/Drama, Training.
Placements: 100

When to apply: Three to four months before planning to arrive.
Work alone/with others: Alone and with others.
Qualifications: Pleased to accept anyone willing to be a volunteer.
Equipment/clothing: Depends on the season. It is very cold in winter and warm in the summer. Clean and practical casual clothing would be appropriate. Equipment necessary depends on project and specific skills. Please check in advance.
Health requirements: Of good health and full of energy.
Costs: Volunteers pay for their travel accommodation and food. US$250 co-ordination fee, $200-300 per month for accommodation and $3.50 – $5 per day for food.
Benefits: Food and accommodation arranged but paid for by volunteer.
Training: Orientation training is provided. Volunteers wishing to stay 6 months to 1 year will be offered a Mongolian language course for two weeks.
Supervision: Mongolian Youth Volunteer Organisation staff will supervise.
Interviews: No interviews.
Worldwide placements: Asia (Mongolia).

MONKEY SANCTUARY, THE

Looe
Cornwall PL13 1NZ UK
T: 01503 262532
E: info@monkeysanctuary.org
W: www.monkeysanctuary.org
Contact: Lauren Goodchild

The Monkey Sanctuary is the home of a social colony of woolly monkeys. It was established in 1964 and has received world-wide recognition as the first place where this beautiful species of monkey survived and bred outside its own habitat in the South American rainforests. All of the woolly monkeys in the colony have been born at the Sanctuary and among them are a few who belong to the fifth generation. The Sanctuary has now begun a rescue centre for other primates. Over the course of a year the Sanctuary receives several dozen people for voluntary work, with up to four or five at any one time. Volunteers stay for periods of two to four weeks and are invited to stay with the Sanctuary team in their home on site. We hope volunteers will come because they share our concern for animal welfare, conservation and a need to continue questioning people's attitude to other animals. Volunteers help in various ways, making and serving teas for the visitors, serving in the Sanctuary shop and kiosk, preparing monkey foods (a main volunteer responsibility year round), domestic help,

gardening, sweeping paths and public areas and general maintenance. Volunteers with an offending background accepted. To apply, please write to Lauren Goodchild and enclose SAE or e-mail.

Number of projects: 1 UK: 1
Starting months: January–December
Time required: 2–4 weeks
Age: 18–75
Causes: Animal Welfare, Conservation, Environmental Causes, Wildlife.
Activities: Building/Construction, Conservation Skills, DIY, Gardening/Horticulture, Manual Work.
Placements: 120
When to apply: 3 or more months in advance of preferred stay.
Work alone/with others: Both.
Qualifications: No qualifications are needed but relevant skills welcomed. Interest in animal welfare and conservation essential. No restrictions but all volunteers must speak and understand a high degree of English.
Health requirements: Only if it may cause possible problem with safety around the monkeys.
Costs: We ask all volunteers for a voluntary donation towards the Monkey Sanctuary Trust (Reg. Charity no 1038022), suggested amount £35 a week waged, £30 unwaged.
Benefits: The chance to learn about and from, this beautiful species of monkey. Volunteers can live in with the Sanctuary team.
Training: Provided on arrival.
Supervision: Volunteers work closely with sanctuary keepers but will not be supervised during many aspects of their work.
Interviews: Applicants for volunteer positions are not interviewed.
Charity number: 1038022
UK placements: England (Cornwall).

MONTGOMERYSHIRE WILDLIFE TRUST

Collott House
20 Severn Street
Welshpool
Powys SY21 7AD UK
T: 01938 555654
F: 01938 556161
E: montwt@cix.co.uk
W: www.wildlifetrust.org.uk/montwt
Contact: Jen Barr

Montgomeryshire Wildlife Trust is a member of the Wildlife Trusts, a national partnership of 47 County Trusts. The aims of the Trust are primarily to: promote nature conservation in the community; acquire and manage nature reserves; monitor biological and geological resources; liaise with local authorities to promote regard for nature conservation; offer practical advice on nature conservation to landowners. It is the Trust's policy to involve all sectors of the community, of all ages, backgrounds, abilities and disabilities towards these ends. Volunteers require no previous experience just lots of enthusiasm. If they desire, can go on to participate more fully, assisting with the organisation and running of activities/projects. Volunteers with an offending background may be accepted – each case separately assessed.

Number of projects: 1 **UK:** 1
Starting months: January–December
Time required: 1–52 weeks (plus)
Age: 18 plus – no upper limit
Causes: Conservation, Environmental Causes, Wildlife.
Activities: Conservation Skills.
Work alone/with others: Both.
Equipment/clothing: Casual work clothes, waterproofs, stout boots for outdoor work. Protective safety gear is provided.
Health requirements: Anti-tetanus innoculation required.
Costs: Accommodation and food.
Benefits: Out of pocket expenses.
Training: Limited training budget available.
Supervision: By assigned member of staff.
Interviews: Preferably face to face (necessary for jobs working with vulnerable people).
UK placements: Wales (Powys).

MOSCOW NATIONAL VOLUNTEER CENTER, THE

B. Komsomolskaya per
303982 Moscow, 8/7
Russia
T: 00 70 95 203 7870
F: 00 70 95 973 1870
E: volunteer_centre@hotmail.com
Contact: Galina Bedrenkova

The Moscow National Volunteer Center promotes and has information about volunteering in Russia. It may well be able to put volunteers in touch with organisations which are not yet listed on the WorldWide Volunteering database.

Starting months: January–December
Time required: 1–52 weeks (plus)
Age: 16 plus – no upper limit
Causes: Addicts/Ex-Addicts, AIDS/HIV, Animal Welfare, Archaeology, Architecture, Children, Conservation, Disabled (learning and physical), Elderly People, Environmental Causes, Health Care/Medical, Heritage, Holidays for Disabled, Human Rights, Inner City Problems, Offenders/Ex-Offenders, Poor/Homeless, Refugees, Teaching/assisting (nursery, primary, secondary, mature, EFL) Unemployed, Wildlife, Work Camps – Seasonal, Young People.

Activities: Accountancy, Administration, Agriculture/Farming, Arts/Crafts, Building/Construction, Campaigning, Caring (general, day and residential), Catering, Community Work, Computers, Conservation Skills, Cooking, Counselling, Development Issues, DIY, Driving, First Aid, Forestry, Fundraising, Gardening/Horticulture, Group Work, International Aid, Library/Resource Centres, Manual Work, Marketing/Publicity, Music, Newsletter/Journalism, Outdoor Skills, Religion, Research, Scientific Work, Social Work, Sport, Summer Camps, Teaching, Technical Skills, Theatre/Drama, Training, Translating, Visiting/Befriending, Work Camps – Seasonal.
Costs: Varies according to the project.
Worldwide placements: Europe (Russia).

MOUNT KAILASH SCHOOL CHARITABLE TRUST

58 Kenwyn Street
Truro
Cornwall TR1 3DB UK
T: 01872 222278
E: karekari@hotmail.com
Contact: Mrs Karenza Adhikari

Mount Kailash School is for the education of poor and needy Tibetan refugees and Nepalese children. At present there are 250 children, 12 classrooms, 30 staff and ever expanding facilities. One of the very important aims and objectives of the school is to preserve the ancient Tibetan and Nepalese cultures where there is an emphasis on drama and dance. Volunteers are desperately needed to help at all levels of every day life as well as helping/ teaching the children. Experience with children aged 3–16 and teaching is preferred. Gap year volunteers should note that some of the students they are teaching may be older than themselves (students may be 20 years old if they did not start their education in infancy). Volunteers with an offending background are not accepted except in exceptional circumstances.
Alternative address:
Jane Osborne-Fellows
White Lodge
Shortlanesend
Truro, Cornwall TR4 9DU

Number of projects: 1 **UK:** 0
Starting months: January–December
Time required: 4–20 weeks
Age: 18–70
Causes: Children, Health Care/Medical, Human Rights, Poor/Homeless, Refugees, Teaching/assisting (nursery, primary, secondary, EFL), Young People.
Activities: Arts/Crafts, Caring (general, residential), Computers, Development Issues, First Aid, Fundraising, Gardening/Horticulture,

Group Work, International Aid, Outdoor Skills, Religion, Social Work, Sport, Teaching, Technical Skills, Theatre/Drama.
Placements: 10 approx.
When to apply: Any time, 3 months in advance. School year starts mid-Feb.
Work alone/with others: Both. Volunteers should note that they may be the only volunteer teacher at the school when they are there.
Qualifications: A-levels or above. Also urgent places for qualified English or science teachers for 1 year.
Equipment/clothing: Modest clothing – also suitable clothing for climatic changes.
Health requirements: Good health needed.
Costs: Travel, insurance, visa, airport tax and general spending money.
Benefits: Qualified teachers get £30 approx. per month + board, lodging. Volunteers will live at the school in their own room (or shared with another teacher) within the dormitory area and eat with the principal's family who live on top of the dormitory.
Training: None.
Supervision: Volunteers are given duties by the school principal.
Interviews: Interviews take place in Truro, Cornwall. If distance is a problem then interviews may be done by telephone and sending CV is acceptable.
Charity number: 1015291
Worldwide placements: Asia (Nepal).

MOUNTAINS TO SOUND GREENWAY TRUST

1011 Western Avenue, Suite 606
Seattle
Washington 98105 USA
T: 206 812 0122
F: 206 382 3414
E: volunteer@mtsgreenway.org
W: www.mtsgreenway.org
Contact: Kelly Kirkland

Mountains to Sound Greenway Trust provides young people with an opportunity to learn about the environment, and how they can make a difference in their community. In addition to improving the landscape along the Interstate 90 corridor, volunteers meet new friends, work hard, and have fun camping in the Cascade Mountains. The two week international adult session will include the following projects: Trail work: Rattlesnake Mountain is being conserved to protect the wildlife habitat, preserve working forests and provide recreation opportunities. Last summer, volunteers worked on the first two miles of this trail leading to the scenic Rattlesnake Ledge. This summer, volunteers will work on the top of the mountain, building connecting sections of a new 11 mile trail that will lead from Rattlesnake Lake to Snoqualmie Point. Road removal: Abandoned logging roads on Bessemer Mountain are eroding away, sending large quantities of soil, gravel and debris into our streams. Since 1995 the community has worked to remove logging roads and improve wildlife habitat and water quality. The process of logging road removal starts with heavy machinery pulling the roads back up the mountain to restore the original shape of the hillside. Then volunteers will follow, spreading hay, seed and compost to prevent future erosion and create a trail on the old road bed. This programme is in co-operation between the Greenway Trust and Earth Corps. For more information about the project, please visit www.mtsgreenway.org/volunteer/usa-sci.htm. We may be able to place volunteers with an offending background, assessed on a case-by-case basis. Seattle, Washington, USA. Volunteers work in the beautiful Cascade Mountains, about 40 miles east of Seattle. The Trust will provide transport for volunteers from Seattle to work site. 🔲

Number of projects: 1 UK: 0
Starting months: Jul
Time required: 2–4 weeks
Age: 16–35
Causes: Conservation, Environmental Causes, Work Camps – Seasonal.
Activities: Building/Construction, Conservation Skills, Forestry, Gardening/Horticulture, Manual Work, Outdoor Skills, Sport, Summer Camps, Work Camps – Seasonal.
Placements: 100+
When to apply: Applications must be recieved before June 15th.
Work alone/with others: With others.
Qualifications: No experience necessary, but volunteers should expect to work hard, get dirty, live outdoors in a variety of weather conditions and have fun!.
Equipment/clothing: Volunteers are asked to provide their own basic outdoor gear, including appropriate clothing, a sleeping bag, pad, and eating utensils. All other camp gear will be provided.
Health requirements: There are no standard restrictions, anyone in good health should be able to complete this project.
Costs: Travel/airfare to Seattle, travel and health insurance also to be covered by volunteer.
Benefits: Room and board (through homestays or camping) are available. Travel from Seattle to work site. No monetary compensation is provided. Volunteers live and work in a backcountry camp (no running water or electricity) and sleep in tents.
Training: All training with tools, camping skills and other project skills is provided.

Supervision: Project leaders from Earth Corps are trained environmental resoration professionals who will provide safety, project procedure talks and oversee all field components of the programme.
Interviews: There is no interview process, just an application required.
Worldwide placements: North America: (USA).

MOUVEMENT TWIZA

B.P. 77
Rue Chiguer Hamadi No. 23
Hay Es-Salam
Khemisset
15000 Morocco
T: 00 212 7 55.30.68
F: 00 212 7 55.73.15
E: twiza@iam.net.ma
Contact: Lahcen Azaddou

Mouvement Twiza organises summer workcamps for volunteers to participate in a range of socio-cultural activities including work in the slums and in schools and construction work. Volunteers with an offending background are accepted.

Number of projects: 5 **UK:** 0
Starting months: Jul, Aug, Sep
Time required: 3–4 weeks
Age: 18–35
Causes: AIDS/HIV, Archaeology, Architecture, Children, Conservation, Disabled (learning), Environmental Causes, Inner City Problems, Poor/Homeless, Teaching/assisting (mature, EFL), Unemployed, Work Camps – Seasonal, Young People.
Activities: Accountancy, Administration, Building/Construction, Campaigning, Caring – Day, Community Work, Computers, Conservation Skills, Cooking, Development Issues, First Aid, Forestry, Gardening/ Horticulture, Group Work, International Aid, Library/Resource Centres, Manual Work, Newsletter/Journalism, Outdoor Skills, Research, Social Work, Summer Camps, Teaching, Training, Translating, Visiting/Befriending, Work Camps – Seasonal.
Placements: 500
When to apply: April/May.
Work alone/with others: With others.
Qualifications: None is necessary, although any qualifications are welcomed.
Equipment/clothing: Working clothes.
Health requirements: Healthy.
Costs: Living allowance.
Benefits: Accommodation and food.
Interviews: No interviews but an introductory round table meeting aimed at introducing volunteers to each other and the presentation of the organised work.
Worldwide placements: Africa (Morocco).

MUNDO GUATEMALA

Mundo Guatemala, S.A.
Res. Las Jacarandas #12-B
Antigua Guatemala
Sacatepequez Guatemala
T: ++502 832 3896
F: ++ 502 832 3896
E: info@mundo-guatemala.com
W: www.mundo-guatemala.com
Contact: Mrs Elke Sagniewicz

Mundo Guatemala offers open-minded travellers and volunteers a real encounter with the people and sights of Guatemala.
Our aim is:
– to promote socio-sustainable tourism through direct fundraising
– to raise awareness of the needs and problems of the country
– to develop alternative tourism products avoiding negative impact on population, nature, wildlife etc
– to provide learning experience through helping people in need
– to help overcome cross-cultural differences.
We work with approximately 15 – 20 projects. Amongst them are NGOs, hospitals, day care centres, orphanages, street workers and wildlife/street animal rescue centres. Volunteer involvement in project planning and management varies from project to project, but active volunteers can be sure that their ideas and enthusiasm are always appreciated. Around Antigua and all over Guatemala.

Number of projects: 15–20 **UK:** 0
Starting months: January–December
Time required: 4–52 weeks
Age: 18 plus – no upper limit
Causes: AIDS/HIV, Animal Welfare, Children, Disabled (physical), Elderly People, Health Care/Medical, Teaching/assisting, Wildlife.
Activities: Caring (general and day), Community Work, Computers, Group Work, Library/Resource Centres, Marketing/Publicity, Social Work, Teaching.
Placements: 25–30
When to apply: At least three months prior to departure.
Work alone/with others: With others mainly.
Qualifications: Medical background is a plus, so is social work or teaching. Language skills are a must. General interest to help others and an openess to learn about cross-cultural differences.
Health requirements: Restrictions on any contagious diseases.
Costs: Cost for standard 6 week programme (2 weeks Spanish, 4 weeks volunteering) US$640. 8 weeks (4 weeks Spanish, 4 weeks volunteering) US$960. One off placement fee US$75, 50% goes to the project. Plus travel.

Benefits: Some projects offer cost free or discounted accommodation for long-term volunteers, most projects do not have a budget to pay volunteers. Included in costs in homestay with Guatemalan family, includes private room and 3 meals per day except Sunday. Additional accommodation can be booked during placement @ US$65 per week.
Training: During the language course the volunteer is introduced to cross-cultural differences through volunteer co-ordinator, and training on the job is provided on the project. We recommend all volunteers to show an interest and be active.
Supervision: We keep in touch with all volunteers throughout their placement, scheduled meetings 1–2 per month, or upon request. Direct supervision by project leaders and volunteers must hand in weekly reports.
Interviews: Prospective volunteers are screened only through evaluating their curriculum and motivation letter and upon arrival.
Worldwide placements: Central America (Guatemala).

MUSEUM NATIONAL D'HISTOIRE NATURELLE

Lab. de Prehistoire
1 rue Rene Panhard
F-75013 Paris
France
T: 00 33 1 43 31 62 91
F: 00 33 1 43 31 22 79
E: dewever@mnhn.fr
Contact: Professor Henry de Lumley

Museum National D'Histoire Naturelle organises volunteers to take part in archaeological digs in France. To work eight and a half hours per day, six days per week. 📖

Number of projects: 1 **UK:** 0
Starting months: Mar, Apr, Jun, Jul, Aug
Time required: 2–13 weeks
Age: 18 plus – no upper limit
Causes: Archaeology.
Activities: Research, Scientific Work.
Placements: 80
When to apply: From February.
Work alone/with others: With others.
Qualifications: Students or researchers in prehistory, archaeology or natural science.
Equipment/clothing: Nil except Mont Bego where warm clothes and camping equipment are needed.
Health requirements: No – good health need for Bego.
Costs: Travel costs. No remuneration.
Benefits: Subsistence.
Interviews: Applicants are not interviewed.
Worldwide placements: Europe (France).

MUSLIM AID

P.O. Box 3
London
NW1 7UB UK
T: +44 (0) 207 387 7171
T: +44 (0) 207 387 7474
E: info@muslimaid.org
W: www.muslimaid.org
Contact: Mr E. Mohammed

Muslim Aid, founded in 1985 in the shadow of the raging famine in Ethiopia, has extended its humanitarian work to over 48 countries in Aisa, Africa, Middle East and Europe. It reaches out to the most vulnerable, poverty stricken and desperate people and provides them the basic necessities of life – food, shelter, medicine, clean water and skills to earn a living. Besides emergency relief, Muslim Aid aims to provide short and long term programmes to help people out of the poverty trap and thus give them dignity and self-respect. 🖐

Number of projects: 1 **UK:** 0
Starting months: January–December
Time required: 1–52 weeks (plus)
Age: 14 plus – no upper limit
Causes: Children, Elderly People, Poor/Homeless, Refugees, Young People.
Activities: Administration, Campaigning, Computers, Fundraising, International Aid, Marketing/Publicity, Translating.
Placements: 20
When to apply: All year.
Work alone/with others: Sometimes with other young volunteers.
Qualifications: Nil required.
Equipment/clothing: No specific equipment required.
Health requirements: No Health requirements.
Costs: Travel costs.
Charity number: 295224
Worldwide placements: Asia (Afghanistan, Bahrain, Bangladesh, Bhutan, Brunei, India, Indonesia, Iran, Iraq, Jordan, Kuwait, Lebanon, Malaysia, Myanmar (Burma), Oman, Pakistan, Palestinian Authority, Qatar, Saudi Arabia, Singapore, Turkey, United Arab Emirates, Yemen).

MUSTARD SEED EVANGELISM & PRAYER FELLOWSHIP

Box 40, Ejisu, A/R
Ejisu
Ashanti 00233 Ghana
T: 002335133510
E: bamankwaa78@yahoo.com
Contact: Benjamin Amankwaa

Mustard Seed Evangelism and Prayer Fellowship (MSEPF) is a Christian organisation committed to spreading the gospel of Christ, well equipped for real-world Christian ministry, which is both biblical and missional, prepared to share the gospel of Christ in a world of monumental need. Furthermore, MSEPF undertakes voluntary community services in many areas, which means we work with volunteers from different backgrounds who are prepared to share the many visions of MSEPF in Ghana. Volunteers are welcome at any time to join with these committed people to serve the world with services within the limitation and/or region of your concern. What are you waiting for – life is too short to waste, come join us for a better service. More information on how to apply, please contact the president, Benjamin Amankwaa. We are unable to accept volunteers with an offending background. Kumasi, Ashanti – Ghana. ☒ ☒

Number of projects: 9 **UK:** 0
Starting months: January–December
Time required: 4–52 weeks (plus)
Age: 15–30
Causes: Disabled (physical), Elderly People, Environmental Causes, Teaching/assisting (nursery, primary, secondary, mature).
Activities: Agriculture/Farming, Caring (general, day and residential), Community Work, Counselling, Development Issues, Gardening/Horticulture, Group Work, Religion, Social Work, Teaching, Training, Visiting/Befriending, Work Camps – Seasonal.
Placements: 26
When to apply: Any time.
Work alone/with others: Varies.
Qualifications: Yes – more details on request.
Health requirements: Volunteers should be in good health.
Costs: Registration fee of US$20 required for confirmation of a place. Volunteers will have to fund travel, accommodation and food.
Benefits: This can vary.
Training: General training is provided.
Supervision: Volunteers are grouped and are supervised by group leaders.
Interviews: Interviews are held.
Worldwide placements: Africa (Ghana).

MUYAL LIANG TRUST

53 Blenheim Crescent
London
W11 2EG UK
T: +44 (0) 207 229 4774
E: Jjulesstewart@cs.com
Contact: Jules Stewart

The Muyal Liang Trust was founded in 1980 and in 1989 it received India's National Award for Child Welfare. The Trust administers a school (DPCA) in Sikkim for orphans and poor children. The primary aim is to provide the children with a working knowledge of English and other subjects. The school is adjacent to Pemayangtse, a 17th Century Buddhist monastery in the Himalayan foothills. Volunteers are offered board and lodging at the monastery. The current maximum stay is eight weeks as Sikkim is a restricted area for foreigners. Volunteers can apply for an extended permit, which may be granted on a case-by-case basis. All enquiries should be directed to Jules Stewart. Yongda Hill, Drakchung Dzong, West Sikkim, India. ☒

Number of projects: 1 **UK:** 0
Starting months: Mar, Apr, May, Jun, Jul, Aug, Sep, Oct, Nov, Dec
Time required: 8 weeks
Age: 18 plus – no upper limit
Causes: Children, Teaching/assisting (primary, secondary, EFL).
Activities: Teaching.
Placements: 25–40
When to apply: All year.
Work alone/with others: Work alone.
Qualifications: A-level minimum.
Equipment/clothing: Warm clothing needed for winter mountain environment. Waterproofs for summer monsoon.
Health requirements: Nil.
Costs: Travel costs only: Flight to Delhi or Calcutta plus domestic flight (approx £280) or train (£100).
Benefits: Board and lodging provided. Ensuite room in the monastery.
Supervision: Volunteers must be independent.
Interviews: Interviewed in London.
Worldwide placements: Asia (India).

NABC – CLUBS FOR YOUNG PEOPLE

371 Kennington Lane
London
SE11 5QY UK
T: +44 (0) 207 793 0787
T: +44 (0) 207 820 9815
E: office@nacyp.org.uk
W: www.nacyp.org.uk
Contact: Euan Eddie

NABC-CYP is an association of about 2,000 clubs for young people throughout the UK, which provides informal educational training and leisure time activities for young people aged between 8 and 25.
It is one of the largest and most influential parts of the voluntary youth service.

Number of projects: 2.000 UK: 2,000
Starting months: January–December
Time required: 1–1 weeks
Age: 18 plus – no upper limit
Causes: Children, Disabled (learning and physical), Environmental Causes, Human Rights, Inner City Problems, Unemployed, Work Camps – Seasonal, Young People.
Activities: Arts/Crafts, Community Work, Counselling, Development Issues, First Aid, Fundraising, Group Work, Newsletter/Journalism, Sport, Summer Camps, Theatre/Drama, Training, Work Camps – Seasonal.
Placements: 23,000
When to apply: All year.
Work alone/with others: With others.
Qualifications: Driving licence useful but not essential. Sports qualifications very useful.
Health requirements: Nil.
Costs: Limited – every attempt would be made to minimise costs.
Benefits: Reasonable expenses, travel, board, lodging etc.
UK placements: England (throughout); Scotland (throughout); Northern Ireland (throughout); Wales (throughout).

NADEZHDA JOB CENTRE

P.O. Box 273
Woodstock
Cape Town
7915 South Africa
T: +27 21 447 4774
F: +27 21 447 4774
E: nadezhdajobcentre@hotmail.com
Contact: Claudette Julies

Nadezhda Job Centre is based in Cape Town. We have been in operation for four years under the auspices of a national network called Arise. We were registered in July 2002 as a company not for gain. Nadezhda is the Russian word for 'HOPE'. A board of seven people who continuously give advice and guidance manages us. Due to the great unemployment rate in our country, we started to use volunteerism to build a bridge into getting the unemployed busy. We place volunteers both employed and unemployed, skilled and unskilled at community projects. We also assist the unemployed to find work by providing them with job seeking skills as well as placing them at projects where they can develop some skills, training and development. We are also entering a new phase of corporate volunteering. Businesses often approach us if they are in need of staff and volunteers, which is great for the unemployed because they get experience and references. There may be placements for volunteers with an offending background depending on the offence.

Number of projects: 15 **UK:** 0
Starting months: January–December
Time required: 2–40 weeks
Age: 18 plus – no upper limit
Causes: Addicts/Ex-Addicts, AIDS/HIV,
Children, Disabled (learning and physical),
Elderly People, Health Care/Medical, Poor/
Homeless, Teaching/assisting (nursery, primary,
secondary, mature), Unemployed, Young People.
Activities: Accountancy, Administration, Arts/
Crafts, Caring – General, Fundraising, Group
Work, Outdoor Skills, Religion, Social Work,
Sport, Summer Camps, Teaching.
Placements: 50
When to apply: All year.
Work alone/with others: Work with others.
Qualifications: Usually depends on vacant
voluntary position. No restrictions but we look
for those with a Christian faith.
Equipment/clothing: Depends on the position.
Health requirements: No restrictions.
Costs: The cost depends on the duration of the
stay as well as how many volunteers come at
the same time. More details with application.
Benefits: Due to the fact that most projects are
understaffed and have a lack of finances we are
unable to pay volunteers any sort of
remuneration. We will inform volunteers about
the cost of accommodation and car hire during
their application. We can arrange
accommodation according to volunteers needs
and money available.
Training: When volunteers arrive in Cape
Town there is a short orientation session.
Supervision: Supervision is done at the project
and we will regularly keep in contact.
Interviews: Yes – overseas volunteers are
usually interviewed via e-mail and we request
reference letters from church leaders and former
employer/lecturer.
Charity number: 005-757
Worldwide placements: Africa (South Africa).

NANSEN HIGHLAND

Redcastle Station
Muir-of-Ord
Ross-shire IV6 7RX Scotland UK
T: 01463 871255
F: 01463 870258
E: Nansen@highlandhq.freeserve.co.uk
W: www.nansenhighland.co.uk
Contact: Bart Lafere

Nansen Highland is a non-governmental
organisation and registered charity, motivated
in its aims by the humanitarian and
adventurous deeds of the explorer Fridtjof
Nansen. Nansen Highland runs a day training
centre to promote life skills, work skills and
independence skills for young adults with
learning difficulties. Volunteers are required to
assist with the training for the young adults.
Responsibilities may include basic English and
numeracy skills, job-seeking skills, practical and
general maintenance work, social skills, and
being able to work with a team. There may also
be duties related to the general administration
of the project and meetings with external
bodies. Placements are considered after
receiving clean police check and application
form. Alternative e-mail – Volunteers co-
ordinator/residential co-ordinator –
paula.logan@nansenhighland.co.uk Scottish
Highlands: Evanton, Nr Dingwall (residential)
and Muir of Ord, Nr Inverness (day). ⊠ ▤

Number of projects: 2 **UK:** 2
Starting months: January–December
Time required: 13–52 weeks
Age: 21–99
Causes: Children, Disabled (learning and
physical), Teaching/assisting (mature), Young
People.
Activities: Administration, Arts/Crafts, Caring
(general and day), Catering, Computers,
Cooking, Counselling, DIY, First Aid, Group
Work, Manual Work, Music, Outdoor Skills,
Social Work, Sport, Teaching, Technical Skills,
Training.
Placements: 3
When to apply: All year – 3–4 months in
advance.
Work alone/with others: Both.
Qualifications: Experience teaching young
people with special needs, outdoor education,
farmwork or conservation desirable. Ability to
motivate young people and fit in with the
community. Good spoken English, clean
driving licence preferred, social work
qualification.
Health requirements: Good mental and
physical health.
Costs: Travel and insurance costs.
Benefits: Board and lodging.
Training: Full induction given.
Supervision: All supervision by the
management.
Interviews: Prospective volunteers are
interviewed in person or on the telephone.
Police check is made.
Charity number: SCO28479
UK placements: Scotland (Highland).

NATIONAL ASSOCIATION OF NGO'S – ZIMBABWE

19 Selous Avenue 3rd Street
PO Box CY 250
Causeway
Harare
Zimbabwe
T: 00 263 4 708 761
F: 00 263 4 794 973

E: info@nango.org.zw
W: www.nango.org.zw
Contact: Jonah Mudehwe

National Association of Non-governmental Organizations (NANGO) promotes and has information about volunteering in Zimbabwe. It may well be able to put volunteers in touch with organisations which are not yet listed on the WorldWide Volunteering database.

Starting months: January–December
Time required: 1–52 weeks (plus)
Age: 16 plus – no upper limit
Causes: Addicts/Ex-Addicts, AIDS/HIV, Animal Welfare, Archaeology, Architecture, Children, Conservation, Disabled (learning and physical), Elderly People, Environmental Causes, Health Care/Medical, Heritage, Holidays for Disabled, Human Rights, Inner City Problems, Offenders/Ex-Offenders, Poor/Homeless, Refugees, Teaching/assisting (nursery, primary, secondary, mature, EFL) Unemployed, Wildlife, Work Camps – Seasonal, Young People.
Activities: Accountancy, Administration, Agriculture/Farming, Arts/Crafts, Building/Construction, Campaigning, Caring (general, day and residential), Catering, Community Work, Computers, Conservation Skills, Cooking, Counselling, Development Issues, DIY, Driving, First Aid, Forestry, Fundraising, Gardening/Horticulture, Group Work, International Aid, Library/Resource Centres, Manual Work, Marketing/Publicity, Music, Newsletter/Journalism, Outdoor Skills, Religion, Research, Scientific Work, Social Work, Sport, Summer Camps, Teaching, Technical Skills, Theatre/Drama, Training, Translating, Visiting/Befriending, Work Camps – Seasonal.
Costs: Varies according to the project.
Worldwide placements: Africa (Zimbabwe).

NATIONAL ASSOCIATION OF TOY AND LEISURE LIBRARIES

68 Churchway
London
NW1 1LT UK
T: +44 (0) 207 387 9592
E: admin@natll.ukf.net
Contact: Administrator

Number of projects: 1 UK: 1
Starting months: January–December
Time required: 1–52 weeks
Age: 14 plus – no upper limit
Causes: Children, Elderly people, Unemployed, Young people.
Activities: Administration, Arts/Crafts, Community Work.
Costs: Food, travel and accommodation.
UK placements: England (London).

NATIONAL ASSOCIATION OF YOUTH THEATRES

Arts Centre
Vane Terrace
Darlington
DL3 7AX UK
T: 01325 363330
F: 01325 363313
E: naytuk@aol.com
W: www.nayt.org.uk
Contact: Stuart Hawkes

National Association of Youth Theatres (NAYT) was founded in 1982. NAYT is the flagship membership organisation for youth theatre practice in England, supporting the development of youth theatre activity through programmes of training advocacy and participation. NAYT is currently undertaking a regional development programme, funded by the DfES and Arts Council of England. The programme seeks to increase levels of support, for youth theatre, provide access to training and provide new opportunities for the sharing of the best practice. The Arts Council of England, funded by Big Youth Theatre Festival is NAYT's annual showcase event. Held in July and set in Epping Forest and attracting groups from the UK and beyond, the Festival brings together young people to perform, workshop and celebrate their involvement in youth theatre. Incorporating our AGM, workshop weekend brings together practitioners from across the country for two days of workshops, debate and networking. ARTiculation is a three-year partnership with NCH, funded by the Lloyds/TSB Foundation. ARTiculation will see the arts introduced into the mainstream of NCH's work with some of the country's most marginalised young people. ARTiculation was the winner of the Annual Charity Award, Arts and Culture. The Big Youth Festival is based at the Scout Association, Gilwell Park, Chingford in London. ⑤

Number of projects: 1 UK: 1
Starting months: Jul
Time required: 1–2 weeks
Age: 16–25
Causes: Children, Young People.
Activities: Administration, Arts/Crafts, Group Work, Theatre/Drama.
Placements: 20–30
When to apply: April.
Work alone/with others: With others.
Equipment/clothing: T-shirts provided, otherwise need to bring all clothing, toiletries, bedding, torch etc.
Health requirements: Good health.
Costs: Accommodation, food and travel within the UK are paid for.
Benefits: Food and accommodation.
Training: Training offered relevant to tasks

required to carry out as part of a festival team member.
Supervision: Fully supervised.
Interviews: Application form and telephone contact.
UK placements: England (Co Durham, Essex, London).

NATIONAL ASTHMA CAMPAIGN

PEAK
Providence House
Providence Place
London
N1 0NT UK
T: +44 (0) 207 704 5892
T: +44 (0) 207 704 0740
W: www.asthma.org.uk
Contact: Patrick Ladbury

Would you like to go windsurfing, canoeing, ice-skating and ten-pin bowling? Try your hand at jewellery making, T-shirt designing and modelling? Do you have any spare time this summer? Do you enjoy working with children and young people? Have you a sense of humour? The National Asthma Campaign run unique holidays (PEAK) in specialised centres giving children, teenagers and young adults (age range 6–18 years) with asthma (and other medical conditions) the chance to enjoy adventurous and social activities with their peers. For many it is the first time away from home and the holidays give them an opportunity to develop new skills, self-confidence and experience some independence. All holidays are staffed by volunteers. Volunteers are drawn from a wide background: some are doctors and nurses, others have personal experience of eczema or asthma; some have a background in sports or childcare; others wish to learn some new skills. Leaders take responsibility for a group of 4 or 5 children who share a room. During the day you will work with another member of staff and a group of youngsters, supporting and encouraging them through a range of activities. Participation is a vital part of the week. Activities are led by volunteers or qualified instructors who do the teaching and in the evening staff work together to provide a range of social activities. In this way PEAK holidays provide an understanding environment with sympathetic, approachable staff where children, teenagers, and young adults alike can relax, have fun and learn more about their asthma themselves. The gains and rewards from volunteering for a project like this are tremendous and clearly difficult to explain. PEAK is looking for applicants with maturity combined with a sense of humour and fun, able to supervise and support children and teenagers. PEAK is also looking for volunteers to help run its new family weekends during the winter. The weekends are held in hotels and aim to teach parents and their children more about asthma. 🚹 📖

Number of projects: 7 UK: 7
Starting months: Apr, May, Jul, Aug
Time required: 1–3 weeks
Age: 18–60
Causes: Children, Health Care/Medical, Holidays for Disabled, Young People.
Activities: Caring (general, residential), Group Work, Sport, Summer Camps.
Placements: 90
When to apply: September to March/April.
Work alone/with others: With others.
Qualifications: Ability to get on with others in a group environment and lots of energy!
Health requirements: Must be in reasonably good health.
Costs: Nil.
Benefits: All travel expenses, board and lodging and training weekend.
Gain knowledge of asthma and eczema, help children gain confidence about their condition and meet others.
Training: Training weekend covering child protection, medical conditions, child play and holiday planning.
Supervision: One full time PEAK manager attends all holidays.
Interviews: References and police checks required.
UK placements: England (Buckinghamshire, Cumbria, Essex, Northamptonshire, Nottinghamshire, Suffolk); Scotland (Edinburgh, Lothian – East, Lothian – West); Northern Ireland (Antrim).

NATIONAL AUTISTIC SOCIETY, THE

4th Floor, Castle Heights
72 Maid Marian Way
Nottingham
Nottinghamshire NG1 6BJ UK
T: 0115 9113360
F: 0115 9113362
E: claire.rintoul@nas.org.uk
W: www.nas.org.uk
Contact: Claire Rintoul

The National Autistic Society's Volunteering Network is currently setting up befriending schemes throughout the UK. Volunteers over the age of 18 years are welcome to apply. Training, support and accreditation opportunities are offered to all befrienders. Outside the volunteering network, there are limited opportunities for volunteers to work on special projects with children with autism. Most of this work is in special schools. Some offices and units may also be able to accommodate volunteers. 🚹

Number of projects: 16 UK: 16
Starting months: January–December

Time required: 25–52 weeks
Age: 18 plus – no upper limit
Causes: Children, Disabled (learning).
Activities: Administration, Visiting/Befriending.
Placements: 150
When to apply: All year.
Work alone/with others: With others.
Health requirements: Nil.
Costs: Food and accommodation.
Benefits: Travel expenses reimbursed.
Training: Training provided for befrienders. This training occurs once or twice a year and is compulsory before a volunteer can become a befriender.
Supervision: 6-weekly support meeting, annual appraisal, telephone support, supervision from co-ordinator.
Charity number: 269425
UK placements: England (Bedfordshire, Berkshire, Cheshire, Cumbria, Essex, Isle of Wight, Leicestershire, London, Manchester, Nottinghamshire, Surrey); Scotland (Glasgow City); Northern Ireland (Belfast City); Wales (Cardiff, Vale of Glamorgan).

NATIONAL CENTRE FOR VOLUNTEERS – ENGLAND, THE

Regent's Wharf
8 All Saints Street
London
N1 9RL UK
T: 00 44 171 520 8900
F: 00 44 171 520 8910
E: centrevol@aol.com
Contact: Christopher Spence

The National Centre for Volunteers promotes and has information about volunteering in England. It may well be able to put volunteers in touch with organisations which are not yet listed on the WorldWide Volunteering database.

Starting months: January–December
Time required: 1–52 weeks (plus)
Age: 16 plus – no upper limit
Causes: Addicts/Ex-Addicts, AIDS/HIV, Animal Welfare, Archaeology, Architecture, Children, Conservation, Disabled (learning and physical), Elderly People, Environmental Causes, Health Care/Medical, Heritage, Holidays for Disabled, Human Rights, Inner City Problems, Offenders/Ex-Offenders, Poor/Homeless, Refugees, Teaching/assisting (nursery, primary, secondary, mature, EFL) Unemployed, Wildlife, Work Camps – Seasonal, Young People.
Activities: Accountancy, Administration, Agriculture/Farming, Arts/Crafts, Building/Construction, Campaigning, Caring (general, day and residential), Catering, Community Work, Computers, Conservation Skills, Cooking, Counselling, Development Issues, DIY, Driving, First Aid, Forestry, Fundraising,

Gardening/Horticulture, Group Work, International Aid, Library/Resource Centres, Manual Work, Marketing/Publicity, Music, Newsletter/Journalism, Outdoor Skills, Religion, Research, Scientific Work, Social Work, Sport, Summer Camps, Teaching, Technical Skills, Theatre/Drama, Training, Translating, Visiting/Befriending, Work Camps – Seasonal.
Costs: Varies according to the project.
UK placements: England (throughout).

NATIONAL CENTRE FOR YOUNG PEOPLE WITH EPILEPSY

St Piers Lane
Lingfield
Surrey RH7 6PW UK
T: 01342 832243
F: 01342 834639
E: gbennet@ncype.org.uk
W: www.ncype.org.uk
Contact: Gwilym Bennet

NCYPE (National Centre for Young People with Epilepsy) is a non-maintained residential special school for children and young adults who have learning difficulties, epilepsy and other neurological disorders. Situated on the Surrey, Sussex and Kent borders we are just 30 miles from Brighton and 20 miles from London. NCYPE has built up a worldwide reputation for the excellence of its educational, care and medical facilities. Working at NCYPE provides an ideal opportunity for practical experience of living with and caring for children and young adults with various disabilities in an environment offering support and education. Rural setting. Near large village. 40 minutes by rail to London. ▤

Number of projects: 1 UK: 1
Starting months: Jan, Apr, Sep
Time required: 16–52 weeks
Age: 18–65
Causes: Children, Disabled (learning and physical), Health Care/Medical, Holidays for Disabled, Teaching/assisting (primary, secondary), Young People.
Activities: Agriculture/Farming, Arts/Crafts, Caring (general, day and residential), Catering, Computers, Cooking, Counselling, First Aid, Gardening/Horticulture, Group Work, Music, Outdoor Skills, Sport, Teaching.
Placements: 20–30
When to apply: All year – but mainly term time only.
Work alone/with others: With trained staff.
Qualifications: Maturity of approach. Our students can be very demanding. Must have a good level of spoken English.
Equipment/clothing: Try to set an example in dress but volunteers must 'muck in' with all sports, personal care etc.

Health requirements: Reasonable fitness required. Manual lifting would be part of the job in some areas.
Costs: Nil.
Benefits: Travel to and from project each term/half term. Full board and lodging. £25 per week pocket money. Large staff accommodation, single room and plenty of friends. Single bedroom in hostel.
Training: Full induction on arrival. Training is given in appropriate areas and all volunteers are encouraged to participate each half term in in-service training days with the other members of staff.
Supervision: Line manager of relevant department plus director responsible for co-ordination of volunteers and support from personnel.
Interviews: No.
Charity number: 311877
UK placements: England (Surrey).

NATIONAL COUNCIL FOR VOLUNTARISM IN ISRAEL, THE

4 Ha'Arbaa
PO Box 20428
Tel Aviv 67012
Israel
T: 00 972 3 561 4144
F: 00 972 3 561 3343
Contact: Dr Baruch Levy

The National Council for Voluntarism in Israel promotes and has information about volunteering in Israel. It may well be able to put volunteers in touch with organisations which are not yet listed on the WorldWide Volunteering database.

Starting months: January–December
Time required: 1–52 weeks (plus)
Age: 16 plus – no upper limit
Causes: Addicts/Ex-Addicts, AIDS/HIV, Animal Welfare, Archaeology, Architecture, Children, Conservation, Disabled (learning and physical), Elderly People, Environmental Causes, Health Care/Medical, Heritage, Holidays for Disabled, Human Rights, Inner City Problems, Offenders/Ex-Offenders, Poor/Homeless, Refugees, Teaching/assisting (nursery, primary, secondary, mature, EFL) Unemployed, Wildlife, Work Camps – Seasonal, Young People.
Activities: Accountancy, Administration, Agriculture/Farming, Arts/Crafts, Building/Construction, Campaigning, Caring (general, day and residential), Catering, Community Work, Computers, Conservation Skills, Cooking, Counselling, Development Issues, DIY, Driving, First Aid, Forestry, Fundraising, Gardening/Horticulture, Group Work, International Aid, Library/Resource Centres, Manual Work, Marketing/Publicity, Music, Newsletter/Journalism, Outdoor Skills,
Religion, Research, Scientific Work, Social Work, Sport, Summer Camps, Teaching, Technical Skills, Theatre/Drama, Training, Translating, Visiting/Befriending, Work Camps – Seasonal.
Costs: Varies according to the project.
Worldwide placements: Asia (Israel).

NATIONAL COUNCIL OF SOCIAL SERVICE (NCSS) – SINGAPORE

7 Maxwell Road 05-01
Annex B MND Complex
Singapore 069111
Singapore
F: 00 65 221 0625
E: feedback@nvc.org.sg
W: www.nvc.org.sg
Contact: Tan Chee Koon

National Council of Social Service (NCSS) promotes and has information about volunteering in Singapore. It may well be able to put volunteers in touch with organisations which are not yet listed on the WorldWide Volunteering database.

Starting months: January–December
Time required: 1–52 weeks (plus)
Age: 16 plus – no upper limit
Causes: Addicts/Ex-Addicts, AIDS/HIV, Animal Welfare, Archaeology, Architecture, Children, Conservation, Disabled (learning and physical), Elderly People, Environmental Causes, Health Care/Medical, Heritage, Holidays for Disabled, Human Rights, Inner City Problems, Offenders/Ex-Offenders, Poor/Homeless, Refugees, Teaching/assisting (nursery, primary, secondary, mature, EFL) Unemployed, Wildlife, Work Camps – Seasonal, Young People.
Activities: Accountancy, Administration, Agriculture/Farming, Arts/Crafts, Building/Construction, Campaigning, Caring (general, day and residential), Catering, Community Work, Computers, Conservation Skills, Cooking, Counselling, Development Issues, DIY, Driving, First Aid, Forestry, Fundraising, Gardening/Horticulture, Group Work, International Aid, Library/Resource Centres, Manual Work, Marketing/Publicity, Music, Newsletter/Journalism, Outdoor Skills, Religion, Research, Scientific Work, Social Work, Sport, Summer Camps, Teaching, Technical Skills, Theatre/Drama, Training, Translating, Visiting/Befriending, Work Camps – Seasonal.
Costs: Varies according to the project.
Worldwide placements: Asia (Singapore).

NATIONAL COUNCIL ON SOCIAL WELFARE OF THAILAND, THE

Mahidol Building
Rajavithi Road
Bangkok 10400
Thailand

T: 00 66 2 246 0077
F: 00 66 2 247 6279
E: info@ncswt.or.th
W: www.ncswt.or.th
Contact: Prapasna Auychai

The National Council on Social Welfare of
Thailand under Royal patronage promotes and
has information about volunteering in
Thailand. It may well be able to put volunteers
in touch with organisations which are not yet
listed on the WorldWide Volunteering database.

Starting months: January–December
Time required: 1–52 weeks (plus)
Age: 16 plus – no upper limit
Causes: Addicts/Ex-Addicts, AIDS/HIV, Animal
Welfare, Archaeology, Architecture, Children,
Conservation, Disabled (learning and physical),
Elderly People, Environmental Causes, Health
Care/Medical, Heritage, Holidays for Disabled,
Human Rights, Inner City Problems, Offenders/
Ex-Offenders, Poor/Homeless, Refugees,
Teaching/assisting (nursery, primary, secondary,
mature, EFL) Unemployed, Wildlife, Work
Camps – Seasonal, Young People.
Activities: Accountancy, Administration,
Agriculture/Farming, Arts/Crafts, Building/
Construction, Campaigning, Caring (general,
day and residential), Catering, Community
Work, Computers, Conservation Skills,
Cooking, Counselling, Development Issues,
DIY, Driving, First Aid, Forestry, Fundraising,
Gardening/Horticulture, Group Work,
International Aid, Library/Resource Centres,
Manual Work, Marketing/Publicity, Music,
Newsletter/Journalism, Outdoor Skills, Religion,
Research, Scientific Work, Social Work, Sport,
Summer Camps, Teaching, Technical Skills,
Theatre/Drama, Training, Translating, Visiting/
Befriending, Work Camps – Seasonal.
Costs: Varies according to the project.
Worldwide placements: Asia (Thailand).

NATIONAL FEDERATION OF 18 PLUS GROUPS OF GREAT BRITAIN

8–10 Church Street
Newent
Gloucestershire GL18 1PP UK
T: 01531 821210
F: 01531 821474
E: office@18plus.org.uk
W: www.18plus.org.uk
Contact: Volunteer Co-ordinator

You can get out of 18 Plus what you put into it
and what better way than to get involved in the
running of your group. 18 Plus is run by its
members for its members so you have a say in
what you want to do. A wide range of training is
available to every member and topics including
self confidence, self development and team skills
are taught by highly experienced tutors. While

this can cost hundreds of pounds to employers,
we charge our members a very minimal fee.
With the new skills and experience gained many
of our members have furthered their career
prospects. Joining 18 Plus opens you up to a
multitude of different opportunities, friendships,
sports, trips and holidays, nightlife, charity and
community work. Volunteers with an offending
background are accepted providing they
conduct themselves within the aims and ideals
of the federation.

Number of projects: 1 UK: 1
Starting months: January–December
Time required: 1–52 weeks
Age: 18–36
Causes: Conservation, Disabled (learning and
physical), Elderly People, Environmental
Causes, Heritage, Poor/Homeless, Wildlife,
Young People.
Activities: Accountancy, Administration,
Arts/Crafts, Campaigning, Community Work,
Computers, Conservation Skills, Development
Issues, First Aid, Fundraising, Group Work,
Library/Resource Centres, Marketing/Publicity,
Music, Newsletter/Journalism, Outdoor Skills,
Research, Sport, Summer Camps, Training.
Placements: 1,000 aprox
When to apply: All year.
Work alone/with others: With others.
Health requirements: Nil.
Costs: £25 per annum. Food and
accommodation.
Interviews: Prospective volunteers are not
interviewed.
UK placements: England (Bedfordshire,
Berkshire, Bristol, Buckinghamshire,
Cambridgeshire, Cheshire, Cornwall, Co
Durham, Derbyshire, Devon, Dorset, Essex,
Gloucestershire, Hampshire, Herefordshire,
Hertfordshire, Kent, Lancashire, Leicestershire,
Lincolnshire, London, Manchester, Merseyside,
Norfolk, Northamptonshire, Northumberland,
Nottinghamshire, Oxfordshire, Rutland,
Shropshire, Somerset, Staffordshire, Suffolk,
Surrey, E. Sussex, W. Sussex, Tyne and Wear,
Warwickshire, West Midlands, Wiltshire,
Worcestershire, E. Yorkshire, N. Yorkshire, S.
Yorkshire, W. Yorkshire).

NATIONAL STAR COLLEGE

Ullenwood
Cheltenham
Gloucestershire GL52 9QU UK
T: 01242 527631
F: 01242 222234
E: rgreenwe@natstar.ac.uk
W: www.natstar.ac.uk
Contact: Richard Greenwell

The National Star College of Further Education is
a residential specialist college for students with a

physical or sensory disability. The college is a registered charity. The college offers volunteers the opportunity to develop personal skills through working alongside our professional carers and lecturers. Volunteers are provided with accommodation, meals and laundry facilities as well as 'pocket money' to cover incidental personal expenditures. Certain travel costs are also reimbursed as well as college transport provided. Volunteers may also use the college's facilities such as computers, swimming pool, gymnasium, sports fields, bathing lake and recreation areas. For more information on the college and our international volunteer programme in 2003 we had 30 volunteers from 16 countries – visit our web site – www.natstar.ac.uk 'volunteer'. We are unable to place volunteers with an offending background. Ullenwood, 5km from Cheltenham. 🖹

Number of projects: 1 UK: 1
Starting months: Sep
Time required: 6–38 weeks
Age: 18–28
Causes: Children, Disabled (physical).
Activities: Caring (general, residential), Teaching.
Placements: 40
When to apply: April.
Health requirements: No restrictions.
Costs: Travel to UK if not resident in UK. Cost of CRB check (criminal record check), health insurance (teeth/eyes).
Benefits: Accommodation, meals, travel in UK, pocket money £45 a week £2, £300 a year.
Training: Two weeks full time training before students arrive.
Supervision: Supervised at all times with students.
Interviews: No interview.
Charity number: 220239
UK placements: England (Gloucestershire).

NATIONAL TRUST, THE

Working Holidays
P O Box 39
Bromley
Kent BR1 8XL UK
T: +44 (0) 20 8315 1111
E: enquiries@thenationaltrust.org.uk
W: www.nationaltrust.org.uk/volunteers
Contact: Working Holidays

The National Trust has special projects, not only in general countryside conservation, but also construction, archaeology, botany, working with a group from another country and shortbreaks.

Number of projects: 400 **UK:** 400
Starting months: January–December
Time required: 1–52 weeks
Age: 17–70

Causes: Conservation, Environmental Causes, Wildlife, Work Camps – Seasonal.
Activities: Building/Construction, Conservation Skills, Forestry, Gardening/Horticulture, Manual Work, Work Camps – Seasonal.
Placements: 4,000
When to apply: All year.
Work alone/with others: With others.
Qualifications: Enthusiasm only.
Equipment/clothing: Stout footwear, waterproofs and sleeping bag.
Health requirements: Physically fit.
Costs: Approx £45–£90 per week. Travel and pocket money not included.
Benefits: Accommodation, all meals. Admission card (1 year) to National Trust properties after 40 hours voluntary work. Accommodation in National Trust basecamps – purpose designed, self catering hostels for groups.
Training: No pre-placement training – support literature is provided.
Supervision: Fully supervised by qualified National Trust wardens.
Interviews: Applicants for volunteer projects are not interviewed.
Charity number: 205846
UK placements: England (throughout); Northern Ireland (throughout); Wales (throughout).

NATIONAL VOLUNTEER ACTIVITY PROMOTION CENTER (NVAPC) – JAPAN

Shin-Kasumigaseki Bldg
3-3-2 Kasumigaseki
Chiyoda-ku
Tokyo
Japan
T: 00 81 3 3581 7858
Contact: Toshiaki Wada

National Volunteer Activity Promotion Center (NVAPC) promotes and has information about volunteering in Japan. It may well be able to put volunteers in touch with organisations which are not yet listed on the WorldWide Volunteering database.

Starting months: January–December
Time required: 1–52 weeks (plus)
Age: 16 plus – no upper limit
Causes: Addicts/Ex-Addicts, AIDS/HIV, Animal Welfare, Archaeology, Architecture, Children, Conservation, Disabled (learning and physical), Elderly People, Environmental Causes, Health Care/Medical, Heritage, Holidays for Disabled, Human Rights, Inner City Problems, Offenders/ Ex-Offenders, Poor/Homeless, Refugees, Teaching/assisting (nursery, primary, secondary, mature, EFL) Unemployed, Wildlife, Work Camps – Seasonal, Young People.
Activities: Accountancy, Administration, Agriculture/Farming, Arts/Crafts, Building/ Construction, Campaigning, Caring (general,

day and residential), Catering, Community
Work, Computers, Conservation Skills,
Cooking, Counselling, Development Issues,
DIY, Driving, First Aid, Forestry, Fundraising,
Gardening/Horticulture, Group Work,
International Aid, Library/Resource Centres,
Manual Work, Marketing/Publicity, Music,
Newsletter/Journalism, Outdoor Skills, Religion,
Research, Scientific Work, Social Work, Sport,
Summer Camps, Teaching, Technical Skills,
Theatre/Drama, Training, Translating,
Visiting/Befriending, Work Camps – Seasonal.
Costs: Varies according to the project.
Worldwide placements: Asia (Japan).

NATIONAL VOLUNTEER CENTER OF THE FIJI COUNCIL OF SOCIAL SERVICES, THE

256 Waimanu
PO Box 13476
Suva
Republic of Fiji Islands
T: 00 679 312 649
F: 00 679 302 396
E: fcoss@is.com.fj
Contact: Hassan M. Khan

The National Volunteer Center (NVC) of the Fiji
Council of Social Services (FCOSS) promotes
and has information about volunteering in Fiji.
It may well be able to put volunteers in touch
with organisations which are not yet listed on
the WorldWide Volunteering database.

Starting months: January–December
Time required: 1–52 weeks (plus)
Age: 16 plus – no upper limit
Causes: Addicts/Ex-Addicts, AIDS/HIV, Animal
Welfare, Archaeology, Architecture, Children,
Conservation, Disabled (learning and physical),
Elderly People, Environmental Causes, Health
Care/Medical, Heritage, Holidays for Disabled,
Human Rights, Inner City Problems, Offenders/
Ex-Offenders, Poor/Homeless, Refugees,
Teaching/assisting (nursery, primary, secondary,
mature, EFL) Unemployed, Wildlife, Work
Camps – Seasonal, Young People.
Activities: Accountancy, Administration,
Agriculture/Farming, Arts/Crafts, Building/
Construction, Campaigning, Caring (general,
day and residential), Catering, Community
Work, Computers, Conservation Skills,
Cooking, Counselling, Development Issues,
DIY, Driving, First Aid, Forestry, Fundraising,
Gardening/Horticulture, Group Work,
International Aid, Library/Resource Centres,
Manual Work, Marketing/Publicity, Music,
Newsletter/Journalism, Outdoor Skills, Religion,
Research, Scientific Work, Social Work, Sport,
Summer Camps, Teaching, Technical Skills,
Theatre/Drama, Training, Translating, Visiting/
Befriending, Work Camps – Seasonal.
Costs: Varies according to the project.
Worldwide placements: Australasia (Fiji).

NATIONAL VOLUNTEER CENTRE – BOTSWANA

Botswana
T: 00 267 3 26021
F: 00 267 3 26020
E: orampa@cf.mega.bw
Contact: Martha Rampa

National Volunteer Centre promotes and has
information about volunteering in Botswana. It
may well be able to put volunteers in touch
with organisations which are not yet listed on
the WorldWide Volunteering database.

Starting months: January–December
Time required: 1–52 weeks (plus)
Age: 16 plus – no upper limit
Causes: Addicts/Ex-Addicts, AIDS/HIV, Animal
Welfare, Archaeology, Architecture, Children,
Conservation, Disabled (learning and physical),
Elderly People, Environmental Causes, Health
Care/Medical, Heritage, Holidays for Disabled,
Human Rights, Inner City Problems, Offenders/
Ex-Offenders, Poor/Homeless, Refugees,
Teaching/assisting (nursery, primary, secondary,
mature, EFL) Unemployed, Wildlife, Work
Camps – Seasonal, Young People.
Activities: Accountancy, Administration,
Agriculture/Farming, Arts/Crafts,
Building/Construction, Campaigning, Caring
(general, day and residential), Catering,
Community Work, Computers, Conservation
Skills, Cooking, Counselling, Development
Issues, DIY, Driving, First Aid, Forestry,
Fundraising, Gardening/Horticulture, Group
Work, International Aid, Library/Resource
Centres, Manual Work, Marketing/Publicity,
Music, Newsletter/Journalism, Outdoor Skills,
Religion, Research, Scientific Work, Social Work,
Sport, Summer Camps, Teaching, Technical
Skills, Theatre/Drama, Training, Translating,
Visiting/Befriending, Work Camps – Seasonal.
Costs: Varies according to the project.
Worldwide placements: Africa (Botswana).

NATIONAL VOLUNTEER CENTRE – NIGERIA

14 Bende
Umuahia
Abia State Nigeria
T: 00 234 88 221 900
F: 00 234 88 221 900
E: iave.nig@phca.linkserve.com
Contact: Rose Ekeleme

National Volunteer Centre promotes and has
information about volunteering in Nigeria. It
may well be able to put volunteers in touch
with organisations which are not yet listed on
the WorldWide Volunteering database.
It also places volunteers who so desire in other
volunteer centres. It co-ordinates activities of

volunteers. Interaction with groups, sharing of ideas enriches members. Currently networking with Watchman Humanitarian Organization (WHO) – who offer free services for people awaiting trial, especially women and youth who have been abandoned by their relations.
Address:
Ugochi Chambers
14 Bende Road
Umuahia, Abia State
Nigeria
Contact Bernard Ikwunagum – Co-ordinator. 📖

Starting months: January–December
Time required: 1–52 weeks (plus)
Age: 16 plus – no upper limit
Causes: Addicts/Ex-Addicts, AIDS/HIV, Animal Welfare, Archaeology, Architecture, Children, Conservation, Disabled (learning and physical), Elderly People, Environmental Causes, Health Care/Medical, Heritage, Holidays for Disabled, Human Rights, Inner City Problems, Offenders/Ex-Offenders, Poor/Homeless, Refugees, Teaching/assisting (nursery, primary, secondary, mature, EFL) Unemployed, Wildlife, Work Camps – Seasonal, Young People.
Activities: Accountancy, Administration, Agriculture/Farming, Arts/Crafts, Building/Construction, Campaigning, Caring (general, day and residential), Catering, Community Work, Computers, Conservation Skills, Cooking, Counselling, Development Issues, DIY, Driving, First Aid, Forestry, Fundraising, Gardening/Horticulture, Group Work, International Aid, Library/Resource Centres, Manual Work, Marketing/Publicity, Music, Newsletter/Journalism, Outdoor Skills, Religion, Research, Scientific Work, Social Work, Sport, Summer Camps, Teaching, Technical Skills, Theatre/Drama, Training, Translating, Visiting/Befriending, Work Camps – Seasonal.
When to apply: Anytime of the year. Placements could be for six months or more.
Work alone/with others: Work with others.
Costs: Varies according to the project.
Training: Minimal training is offered due to costs.
Supervision: Supervision through training and during stay.
Interviews: Interviews are held throughout the year.
Worldwide placements: Africa (Nigeria).

NATIONAL VOLUNTEER SERVICE – PAPUA NEW GUINEA

PO Box 4073 Bokoko
Bokoko
111 NCD Papua New Guinea
F: 00 675 325 8756
Contact: Margaret Sete

National Volunteer Service promotes and has information about volunteering in Papua New Guinea. It may well be able to put volunteers in touch with organisations which are not yet listed on the WorldWide Volunteering database.

Starting months: January–December
Time required: 1–52 weeks (plus)
Age: 16 plus – no upper limit
Causes: Addicts/Ex-Addicts, AIDS/HIV, Animal Welfare, Archaeology, Architecture, Children, Conservation, Disabled (learning and physical), Elderly People, Environmental Causes, Health Care/Medical, Heritage, Holidays for Disabled, Human Rights, Inner City Problems, Offenders/Ex-Offenders, Poor/Homeless, Refugees, Teaching/assisting (nursery, primary, secondary, mature, EFL) Unemployed, Wildlife, Work Camps – Seasonal, Young People.
Activities: Accountancy, Administration, Agriculture/Farming, Arts/Crafts, Building/Construction, Campaigning, Caring (general, day and residential), Catering, Community Work, Computers, Conservation Skills, Cooking, Counselling, Development Issues, DIY, Driving, First Aid, Forestry, Fundraising, Gardening/Horticulture, Group Work, International Aid, Library/Resource Centres, Manual Work, Marketing/Publicity, Music, Newsletter/Journalism, Outdoor Skills, Religion, Research, Scientific Work, Social Work, Sport, Summer Camps, Teaching, Technical Skills, Theatre/Drama, Training, Translating, Visiting/Befriending, Work Camps – Seasonal.
Costs: Varies according to the project.
Worldwide placements: Australasia (Papua New Guinea).

NATIVE ENGLISH

Rua São Benedito
306 Bairro Lixeira
Cuiabá
Mato Grosso 78.008-100 Brazil
T: +55 65 321 8656
E: steve@nativeenglish.com.br
W: www.nativeenglish.com.br
Contact: Mr Steven B Robinson

Our philosophy is to generate a greater understanding of the modern Brazilian reality, provide native English-speaking nationals with a unique, unforgettable tailor-made gap experience, create greater awareness of both social, cultural and indigenous issues through international co-operation, and promote sustainable ecological, social, cultural and indigenous projects within the Brazilian central west. We have local community projects – a local NGO street-children orphanage – Projeto Nossa Casa – this aims to retrieve street children from difficult areas placing them into care away from the constant danger of Brazilian urban violence and decadence. We are renovating a dilapidated former telegraph building to create a local museum for artefacts. Other projects include appeals for funding and setting up and running a group with fee-paying tourists to enable sustainable income. We have a permanent TEFL teaching project at a local primary/secondary school and are directly responsible for the English language education of about 260 children between the ages of seven and 17 years of age. Volunteers have full access to a whole range of eco-tourist activities – piranha fishing, alligator spotting, boat trips down river, horse riding and bush walking. In return, they teach basic conversational English to the lodge staff deep within the UNESCO world biosphere – the Pantanal Wetlands. These staff have little access to traditional educational methods as they live in remote lodges within the national park. Volunteers help in evenings with everyday English phrases. Native English is very much aware of the sheer logistics involved in maintaining this ambitious project, but feels this is a real chance for volunteers to make a difference and come away with a sense of a job well done, as well as a look into another world, based on different values, and different social patterns. Head office in state capital of Cuiaba – Mato Grasso, central west of Brazil. Permanent secondary projects up to 300km from base in state at local Indian people-nation reserves, National Parks and Pantanan ecological UNESCO biosphere. ♿ 📷

Number of projects: 6 UK: 0
Starting months: January–December
Time required: 1–24 weeks
Age: 18–55
Causes: Children, Conservation, Environmental Causes, Human Rights, Poor/Homeless, Teaching/ assisting (primary, secondary, mature), Wildlife, Young People.
Activities: Arts/Crafts, Building/Construction, Campaigning, Community Work, Computers, Conservation Skills, Development Issues, Fundraising, Group Work, International Aid, Newsletter/Journalism, Social Work, Teaching, Training, Visiting/Befriending.
Placements: 25
When to apply: Up to one month before intended start dates.
Work alone/with others: With others.
Qualifications: No qualifications – just a get up and help attitude, a humble approach and a willingness to listen as much as to speak. We only ask that volunteers be able to speak English competently as a first or second language and can enter Brazil on a tourist visa without being barred.
Health requirements: No restrictions.
Costs: £180 administration fee and £180 per month fully inclusive. Flights and insurance

extra costs to volunteer. Policy to charge absolute minimum – a 90 day stay costs equivalent to US $12 per day.
Benefits: Full board & lodging in volunteer house with maid service – washing cleaning and ironing. 3 meals/day. Airport pick up & drop-off. Transport around city and to projects. 24 hour access to Internet and satellite TV. Director – 24hrs a day support.
Training: None – we are based at the location and work from references and past experience resumes plus CV's.
Supervision: Supervision is undertaken by the director.
Interviews: Interviews are held over the internet via e-mail.
Worldwide placements: South America (Brazil).

NATUUR 2000

Bervoetstraat 33
B-2000 Antwerpen
Belgium
T: 00 32 3 231 26 04
F: 00 32 3 233 64 99
E: natuur2000@pandora.be
W: www.home.pi.be/~n2000
Contact: Julius Smeyers

Natuur 2000 organises nature study and nature conservation activities for young people aged between 8 and 25 including birdwatching camps, management of nature reserves, etc. It also runs an environmental information centre for young people. 📷

Number of projects: 10 UK: 0
Starting months: Jun, Jul, Aug, Sep
Time required: 2–4 weeks
Age: 16–23
Causes: Conservation, Environmental Causes, Work Camps – Seasonal, Young People.
Activities: Administration, Computers, Conservation Skills, Cooking, Driving, Library/ Resource Centres, Newsletter/Journalism, Scientific Work, Summer Camps, Work Camps – Seasonal.
Placements: 20
When to apply: Before 15th May.
Work alone/with others: With others.
Qualifications: Experience in field biology – environmental conservation.
Equipment/clothing: Usually rucksack, sleeping bag, isomat, boots, eating and washing gear.
Health requirements: Medical papers required.
Costs: Travel to/from Belgium, participation fee and insurance.
Benefits: Accommodation, food.
Worldwide placements: Europe (Belgium).

NAUTICAL TRAINING CORPS

39 Chesham Road
Brighton
E. Sussex BN22 1NB UK
T: 01273 676836
F: 01273 625066
E: NauticalTrainingCorps@bigfoot.com
Contact: Mrs Grace Nash

Nautical Training Corps trains young people, with and without disabilities, in nautical disciplines including rifle shooting, bands, boatwork, adventure activities and all other aspects of naval life. 🔊

Number of projects: 5 UK: 5
Starting months: January–December
Time required: 3–52 weeks
Age: 18 plus – no upper limit
Causes: Children, Disabled (learning and physical), Young People.
Activities: Sport, Teaching, Technical Skills.
When to apply: All year.
Work alone/with others: With others.
Qualifications: Nautical youth work or business experience.
Health requirements: Nil.
Costs: Nil.
Benefits: Travel expenses.
Charity number: 306084
UK placements: England (Hampshire, London, Surrey, E. Sussex, W. Sussex).

NCH ACTION FOR CHILDREN

Supporter Helpline
Chesham House, Church Lane
Berkhamstead
Herts HP4 2AX UK
T: 0845 7626579
E: supphelp@nch.org.uk
W: www.nch.org.uk
Contact: Gary Day

NCH Action for Children relies on the support of people across the United Kingdom to help us make a difference to the lives of vulnerable children, young people and their families. A very important way in which people support our work is by giving time to NCH through a range of voluntary activities such as, volunteering in one of our 480 projects, organising house to house and street collections, helping to put on fundraising and awareness raising events and volunteering in one of our shops. Prospective volunteers should contact the supporter helpline address, where information packs on local projects will be sent out. We may be able to place volunteers with an offending background depending on offence and volunteer placement involved. Throughout the UK. 🔊 📄

Number of projects: 480 UK: 480
Starting months: January–December
Time required: 1–52 weeks
Age: 16 plus – no upper limit
Causes: Children, Young People.
Activities: Caring – General, Community Work, Counselling, Group Work, Social Work, Visiting/Befriending.
Placements: Varies.
When to apply: Any time.
Work alone/with others: with others.
Qualifications: Dependent on volunteering placement.
Health requirements: No restrictions.
Costs: Accommodation, food and travel.
Benefits: None provided.
Training: If required.
Supervision: By NCH staff.
Interviews: No.
Charity number: 215 301
Worldwide placements: Europe (Ireland).
UK placements: England (throughout); Scotland (throughout); Northern Ireland (throughout); Wales (throughout).

NEDERLANDES ORGANISATIES VRIJWILLIGERSWERK

PO Box 2877
Utrecht
NL-3500 GW The Netherlands
T: 00 31 30 2 31 98 44
F: 00 31 30 2 34 38 96
E: algameen@nov.nl
Contact: Theo van Loon

Nederlandes Organisaties Vrijwilligerswerk promotes and has information about volunteering in Holland. It may well be able to put volunteers in touch with organisations which are not yet listed on the WorldWide Volunteering database.

Starting months: January–December
Time required: 1–52 weeks (plus)
Age: 16 plus – no upper limit
Causes: Addicts/Ex-Addicts, AIDS/HIV, Animal Welfare, Archaeology, Architecture, Children, Conservation, Disabled (learning and physical), Elderly People, Environmental Causes, Health Care/Medical, Heritage, Holidays for Disabled, Human Rights, Inner City Problems, Offenders/Ex-Offenders, Poor/Homeless, Refugees, Teaching/assisting (nursery, primary, secondary, mature, EFL) Unemployed, Wildlife, Work Camps – Seasonal, Young People.
Activities: Accountancy, Administration, Agriculture/Farming, Arts/Crafts, Building/Construction, Campaigning, Caring (general, day and residential), Catering, Community Work, Computers, Conservation Skills, Cooking, Counselling, Development Issues, DIY, Driving, First Aid, Forestry, Fundraising,

Gardening/Horticulture, Group Work, International Aid, Library/Resource Centres, Manual Work, Marketing/Publicity, Music, Newsletter/Journalism, Outdoor Skills, Religion, Research, Scientific Work, Social Work, Sport, Summer Camps, Teaching, Technical Skills, Theatre/Drama, Training, Translating, Visiting/Befriending, Work Camps – Seasonal.
Costs: Varies according to the project.
Worldwide placements: Europe (Netherlands).

NEHEMIAH PROJECT, THE

47 Tooting Bec Gardens
Streatham
London
SW16 1RF UK
T: +44 (0) 20 8769 3444
F: +44 (0) 20 8773 7419
E: enquiries@nehemiahproject.org.uk
W: www.nehemiahproject.org.uk
Contact: Alistair Hardy

The Nehemiah Project is a Christian charity working with drug addicts and alcoholics in south London. We operate three houses where men with addictions can come firstly to find refuge and then start to work on the root issues causing their problems. Each house is a therapeutic community where men can come and experience the love and acceptance of a 'family', often for the first time. The men will also go through a structured programme including group therapy, drug education, key working and 12 step groups. As well as the various groups, all the residents will benefit from work-training and informal mentoring. After the programme, graduates have the opportunity to join a business run by the Nehemiah Project and to move into our move-on accommodation. Volunteers usually come to the Project for a period of a year during which time they become involved in all aspects of the ministry. All volunteers doing this receive training on our leadership training programme to enable them to develop new skills as well as help run the formal aspects of the programme. The Nehemiah Project is a highly successful ministry to those with addictions. It is very intensive and focused. All those who join the team must be committed to the aims of the project and willing to work within our Christian ethos. Volunteers with an offending background may be accepted. Clapham and Streatham in London. 🖹

Number of projects: 1 UK: 1
Starting months: January–December
Time required: 52 weeks (plus)
Age: 21–60
Causes: Addicts/Ex-Addicts, Inner City Problems, Offenders/Ex-Offenders, Poor/Homeless.

Activities: Caring (general, residential), Counselling, Religion.
Placements: 4
When to apply: All year.
Work alone/with others: This is a team ministry and all work done as part of team and with other young volunteers.
Qualifications: No qualifications or skills needed. Must be fluent in English.
Health requirements: Nil.
Costs: Nil – only pocket money for personal expenses.
Benefits: Board and lodging.
Training: Weekly training in the addiction field and on-the-job mentoring.
Supervision: Two weekly support groups plus frequent formal supervision.
Interviews: Interviews take place in London.
UK placements: England (London).

NEIGE ET MERVEILLES

F-06430 St Dalmas de Tende
France
T: 00 33 4 93 04 62 40/0493876433
F: 00 33 4 93 04 88 58/0493877751
E: doc@neige-merveilles.com
W: www.neige-merveilles.com
Contact: Recruitment Department

Neige et Merveilles need volunteers to take part in international workcamps which take place between April and October. Work 27 hours per week. 🖹

Number of projects: 1 UK: 0
Starting months: Apr, May, Jun, Jul, Aug, Sep, Oct
Time required: 2–24 weeks
Age: 18 plus – no upper limit
Causes: Children, Environmental Causes, Teaching/assisting (primary, secondary, mature), Work Camps – Seasonal.
Activities: Administration, Building/Construction, Forestry, Group Work, Manual Work, Social Work, Sport, Summer Camps, Teaching, Training, Visiting/Befriending, Work Camps – Seasonal.
Placements: 4
When to apply: All year.
Work alone/with others: With others.
Equipment/clothing: For mountains and outside work.
Health requirements: Good health.
Costs: Membership fee €8 + enrolment and insurance fees €62 + travel.
Training: On site.
Supervision: Yes.
Worldwide placements: Europe (France).

NES AMMIM (Communal Village in Israel)

68 Melbourn Road
Royston
Herts SG8 7DG UK
T: 01763 230210
F: 01763 230210
E: pjennings@royston1999.freeserve.co.uk
Contact: Peter Jennings

Nes Ammim is an international Christian community in Israel's northwest Galilee. It aims to contribute to the creation of a new relationship between Jews and Christians following centuries of alienation and ignorance. The name Nes Ammim means 'a banner to or for the nations' and is taken from two quotations in the Book of Isaiah (11:10 and 62:10). It recently celebrated its silver jubilee as a community after being established in the sixties by a group of Christians who had lived through the horrors of World War II and the Nazi holocaust in continental Europe. Nes Ammim is the product of a dream – a dream of a radically new and positive relationship between Christians and Jews based upon mutual trust and respect. This excludes any thought of missionary activity directed at the Jewish people. The founders of Nes Ammim believe that such a relationship is not only possible, but absolutely essential. Surrounded by Jewish kibbutzim and Muslim and Druze villages, Nes Ammim is an ecumenical Christian community whose members and volunteers represent a broad spectrum of Protestant tradition. It is a learning, serving, working and worshipping community. Its main commercial business is to grow roses for export. It grows avocados too and shares in the tourist industry with its guest house and youth hostel. It runs an annual work and information programme for young European students and puts very special demands upon its residents who need to be mature 'card-carrying Christians'. We emphasise the word 'mature' because in the settlement there are Christians from many denominations and any volunteer needs a fairly wide range of biblical scholarship and post-Reformation church history in Europe. Volunteers with offending backgrounds would probably have visa difficulties with Israel.

Number of projects: 1 **UK:** 0
Starting months: January–December
Time required: 26–52 weeks
Age: 21–30
Causes: Work Camps – Seasonal.
Activities: Administration, Building/Construction, DIY, Gardening/Horticulture, Marketing/Publicity, Religion, Work Camps – Seasonal.
Placements: 20

When to apply: 1 year in advance.
Work alone/with others: With others.
Qualifications: Broad Christian theological awareness. Any volunteer needs a fairly wide range of biblical scholarship and post-Reformation church history in Europe. No restrictions but Israeli visas must be obtained.
Equipment/clothing: Dress as for a sunny English summer!
Health requirements: Medical/dental certificates needed.
Costs: Costs of travel to the village in Israel.
Benefits: Board, lodging and pocket money. Shared accommodation in 2s and 4s.
Training: Training is provided on arrival when assignment takes place.
Supervision: Supervision by professional workers/leaders in various assignments.
Interviews: Interviews generally by telephone but, if requested, take place in Royston, Herts.
Worldwide placements: Asia (Israel).

NETWORK DRUGS ADVICE PROJECTS (YOUTH AWARENESS PROG.)

Abbey House
361 Barking Road
Plaistow
London
E13 8EE UK
T: +44 (0) 207 474 2222
T: +44 (0) 207 473 5399
E: headoffice@in-volve.org.uk
Contact: Ken Williams

In-volve's Youth Awareness Programme (YAP) is a specialist comprehensive drugs service for young people. YAP provides: drug education in schools and other settings; counselling for drug users under 25 years of age, with a focus on under 16's; literature, CDs and other drugs information resources for young people; an on-site service for 'raves'; a range of diversionary projects including graffiti and music; outreach work. Volunteers are involved in all aspects of our work except counselling. Volunteers are encouraged to contribute to and develop areas of work in which they are interested with the support of project workers. Volunteers with an offending background would be accepted provided that the offences would not make them a risk to work with young people. London boroughs, Newham, Merton, Sutton, Haringey, Enfield, Hillingdon and Birmingham. 🦽 📄

Number of projects: 11 **UK:** 11
Starting months: January–December
Time required: 26–52 weeks (plus)
Age: 16–25
Causes: Addicts/Ex-Addicts, Children, Disabled (learning), Health Care/Medical, Offenders/Ex-Offenders, Teaching – (primary, secondary), Unemployed, Young People.

Activities: Arts/Crafts, Campaigning, Community Work, First Aid, Group Work, Music, Teaching, Theatre/Drama, Training.
Placements: 200
When to apply: All year.
Work alone/with others: With others.
Qualifications: LOCF + NVQ.
Health requirements: Current users of illegal drugs are not accepted. Ex-users are encouraged to take part.
Costs: Nil except travel to work on unauthorised business, accommodation and food costs.
Benefits: Travel and training are paid for by the organisation. The training is accredited and many volunteers go on to paid employment in a related area of work.
Training: Volunteers are required to undertake extensive training.
Interviews: Prospective volunteers are interviewed at project offices in each area of activity.
Charity number: 803244
UK placements: England (London).

NEVE SHALOM/WAHAT AL-SALAM

Doar Na Shimshon 99761
Israel
T: 00 972 2 912222
F: 00 972 2 9912098
E: rita@nswas.com
W: www.nswas.com
Contact: Volunteer Organiser

Neve Shalom/Wahat al-Salam was founded in 1972. It is a co-operative village of Jews and Palestinian Arabs of Israeli citizenship. Members are demonstrating the possibility of coexistence by developing a community based on mutual acceptance, respect and co-operation on a daily basis whilst each individual remains faithful to his/her own cultural, national and religious identity. Limited number of places for volunteers wishing to live and work in the community. Work may involve general maintenance work around the village, looking after children in the kindergarten and nursery or helping out at the community's guest house. 35 km from Jerusalem and Tel Aviv-Jaffa.

Number of projects: 1 UK: 0
Starting months: January–December
Time required: 12–52 weeks
Age: 18–30
Causes: Children.
Activities: Administration, Agriculture/Farming, Building/Construction, Caring – General, DIY, Gardening/Horticulture.
Placements: 5
When to apply: 6–12 months in advance
Work alone/with others: With others.
Qualifications: At least a basic knowledge of

English, Arabic or Hebrew.
Equipment/clothing: Personal equipment as desired.
Health requirements: We require that applicants be in good health. Please specify any health problems you may have when applying.
Costs: Travel and insurance.
Benefits: Board, accommodation and approx £30 per month pocket money. Volunteers receive a simply furnished single room (sharing kitchen and bathroom).
Training: Training is offered.
Supervision: Volunteers are supervised.
Interviews: No interviews.
Worldwide placements: Asia (Israel).

NEW HOPE RURAL COMMUNITY TRUST

P.O.Box – 176
Ashford
Kent TN24 9WD UK
T: 01233 611281
F: 01233 611281
E: nhrct@ukonline.co.uk
Contact: Daniel Parisipogula

New Hope Rural Community Trust is a registered charity run by volunteers. Its main objective is to relieve poverty and sickness and in particular to support the work of the New Hope Rural Leprosy Trust in Orissa state, India, by assisting with the provision of equipment and facilities required by the Trust to function. About 4–5 volunteers a year are recruited to work on and observe the various programmes run by New Hope India. Areas of work include: leprosy eradication programme, working with disabled children, and community health and educational programmes. Volunteers are needed to help with nursing, working with people with learning difficulties, health care, educational work, computing, teaching and using management skills. Help is needed all year round for a period of 2–3 months. During the summer we have children's polio surgeries and cataract operations in the winter. We are unable to take volunteers with an offending background. State of Orissa and Andrapradesh State.

Number of projects: 20 UK: 0
Starting months: January–December
Time required: 4–8 weeks
Age: 18 plus – no upper limit
Causes: AIDS/HIV, Children, Disabled (learning and physical), Elderly People, Environmental Causes, Health Care/Medical, Poor/Homeless, Teaching/assisting, Young People.
Activities: Agriculture/Farming, Arts/Crafts, Caring (general, day and residential), Community Work, Computers, Conservation Skills, Cooking, Development Issues, DIY, Fundraising, Manual Work, Music, Outdoor Skills, Sport, Teaching, Visiting/Befriending.

Placements: 5–10
When to apply: Anytime.
Work alone/with others: Work with others.
Qualifications: Applicants should have skills relevant to the area for which they wish to volunteer. We would like volunteers who can work in remote areas and ability to fundraise.
Equipment/clothing: Summer/winter clothes depending on season. Any medication you might need.
Health requirements: No restrictions.
Costs: All expenses and travel costs to India – also we would like volunteers to fundraise prior to visit and donate the money to a project in India. A contribution towards food is appreciated.
Benefits: Basic accommodation. Meals are basic and free, although a contribution towards food is appreciated.
Training: Mainly observation, following the Lozar traditional culutre. Basic brief on working with the children and learning about the project work.
Supervision: Ongoing.
Interviews: No interviews – contact us in the UK.
Charity number: 1002694
Worldwide placements: Asia (India).

NEW ZEALAND CONSERVANCY TRUST

Karuna Falls
RD4 Coromandel
New Zealand
T: 00 64 7 866 6735
E: networkers@eartheal.org.nz
W: www.eartheal.org.nz
Contact: Bryan Innes

Our focus is on the benefit to the volunteers. Our specific interest is in promotion of the learning of sustainable living skills. We teach permaculture design. We also teach teaching skills to environmentalists. We arrange educational/study opportunities for travellers to New Zealand. These can be in the form of volunteering, paid courses or a combination of the two. e-mail contact works best for us. Prospective volunteers tell us of their experience and interests. We suggest a programme. It is fine-tuned through negotiation. Fixed and variable costs can then be quoted. Examples of programmes of past volunteers:
Primary school, secondary school teaching/assisting.
Special education service psychological assistance.
Marine laboratory assistance.
Organic farming internship, landscape architecture internship. &

Number of projects: Varies UK: 0

Starting months: January–December
Time required: 4–52 weeks
Age: 18 plus – no upper limit
Causes: Architecture, Children, Conservation, Environmental Causes, Teaching/assisting (nursery, primary, secondary), Wildlife.
Activities: Administration, Agriculture/Farming, Arts/Crafts, Building/Construction, Campaigning, Community Work, Computers, Conservation Skills, Cooking, DIY, Forestry, Gardening/Horticulture, Group Work, Library/Resource Centres, Manual Work, Marketing/Publicity, Music, Outdoor Skills, Research, Teaching, Technical Skills.
Placements: 15
When to apply: All year.
Work alone/with others: Both.
Qualifications: Must be able to communicate in English, be independent and self-responsible.
Equipment/clothing: Depends on programme.
Health requirements: Depends on programme.
Costs: Set-up fee NZ$675. All travel costs. Board costs (NZ$150 per week) usually provided free.
Benefits: Depending on programme – usually free board and accommodation. Sometimes other benefits. Accommodation usually with a family.
Training: Depends on the programme – usually consistent with prior experience.
Supervision: Volunteers are always supervised – given more responsibility and independence as they show ability to handle it.
Worldwide placements: Australasia (New Zealand).

NICARAGUA SOLIDARITY CAMPAIGN

129 Seven Sisters Road
London
N7 7QG UK
T: +44 (0) 207 272 9619
T: +44 (0) 207 277 5476
E: nsc@nicaraguasc.org.uk
W: www.nicaragua.org.uk
Contact: Helen Yuill

Nicaragua Solidarity Campaign organises work and study tours to Nicaragua. Volunteers live and work with Nicaraguan fair trade producers of coffee and sesame for two weeks. This is followed by a study tour programme visiting other areas of Nicaragua for a week. Volunteers with an offending background are accepted. &

Number of projects: 1 UK: 0
Starting months: Feb, Jul, Aug
Time required: 1–3 weeks
Age: 18–70
Causes: Conservation, Environmental Causes, Human Rights.
Activities: Community Work, Conservation Skills, Development Issues, International Aid, Manual Work.

Placements: 25
When to apply: 3 months before departure.
Work alone/with others: With other volunteers and local people.
Qualifications: Fit and adaptable – no specialist skills required.
Costs: £1,100 includes air fares, insurance, accommodation, all meals and co-ordination costs.
Benefits: Gain an understanding of the impact of fluctuations of commodity prices on producers (especially coffee) and the benefits of fair trade. Basic accommodation with local families for work programme. Hotels/hostels for study tour.
Training: Weekend preparation training.
Supervision: NSC representative in Nicaragua and designated people in the community where the group is working.
Interviews: Interviews are conducted as near as possible to where applicants live.
Worldwide placements: Central America (Nicaragua).

NICHS

547 Antrim Road
Belfast
Antrim BT15 3BU N. Ireland
T: 028 9037 0373
F: 028 9078 1161
E: nichs@wtvinternet.com
Contact: Paddy Doherty

NICHS is a community relations youth organisation which exists to provide opportunities for young people and to promote understanding and an acceptance of cultural difference between divided and segregated communities in Northern Ireland. The organisation achieves its aims by working with young people, in particular from socially disadvantaged and deprived backgrounds, through various programmes. NICHS was established in 1972 by a group of seminarians in Liverpool. Its original objectives were to provide a holiday for young Protestants and Catholics who were directly caught up in and lived in the areas worst hit by the extreme violence which was affecting Northern Ireland at that time. Since these early days NICHS has grown and developed to become a professional youth organisation working with approximately 500 young people per year. NICHS has a limited number of places for volunteers from outside Northern Ireland to assist in the implementation of residentials for young people during August. In order to prepare for the residentials, potential volunteers must attend an induction event, usually held in Northern Ireland and in the north of England. Volunteers with criminal records are considered on merits and nature of offence. &

Number of projects UK: 4
Starting months: Aug
Time required: 2–52 weeks (plus)
Age: 18 plus – no upper limit
Causes: Children, Young People.
Activities: Arts/Crafts, Caring – Residential, Catering, Community Work, Cooking, Driving, First Aid, Group Work, Music, Outdoor Skills, Sport, Summer Camps.
Placements: 60–80
When to apply: January.
Work alone/with others: With others.
Qualifications: No specific skills or qualifications necessary, experience desirable. Most of our volunteers are from Northern Ireland. Some restrictions – check with office on application.
Health requirements: Nil but individuals need to be generally fit and active.
Costs: Nil except travel to N. Ireland, some assistance given with travel costs.
Benefits: Volunteers can claim half of all travel to a maximum of £50. Board + lodging provided free. Accommodation provided free of charge for residential volunteers.
Training: Volunteers must attend and successfully complete an induction event which deals with policy issues, child care issues and good practice in youth work, among other things.
Supervision: All volunteers are supervised and supported by either staff or more experienced co-ordinating volunteers.
Interviews: Interviews take place at various locations throughout the UK.
Charity number: XN48644
Worldwide placements: Europe (Ireland).
UK placements: Northern Ireland (Belfast City, Down).

NIGHTINGALES CHILDREN'S PROJECT

Meriden Lodge
11 Colin Road
Preston
Paignton
Devon TQ3 2NR UK
F: 01803 527233
E: a6nat@yahoo.com
W: www.nightingaleschildrensproject.org.uk
Contact: Reg and Julia Bale

Nightingales Children's Project was set up by David Savage from Torbay, South Devon in 1992. He went to Romania to work in an orphanage where he found babies and children with no nappies, no bathrooms, no comforts. Since that time the organisation has helped David to build bathrooms and toilets, have the orphanage fully decorated and equipped and send a continuous stream of volunteers to love, help and stimulate the children with play and learning. Some of the children were HIV positive and David realised a special need for these children, who were not accepted for education by state schools. Nightingales raised £20,000 to have a small boarding school built in the grounds of the orphanage and 23 children live and are taught there in a loving family atmosphere. They will stay there until they die. Volunteers work mainly in the orphanage but do have contact with the HIV children. The school has also opened its door to 70 children of some of the most poverty stricken families in Cernavoda. They have a hot meal and some schooling every day. Volunteers work in teams of two. There is an apartment where they stay, up to ten at a time, so they have to mix well. They also have to be dedicated and work very hard. They have to take it in turns to do house duties i.e. cleaning and cooking for everyone. Volunteers stay for a minimum of one month but can stay longer. All in all, the work is hard but very rewarding. Volunteers with an offending background may occasionally be accepted, depending on the offence. Please apply by post and send an A5 stamped addressed envelope for information and application form. Cernavoda in Romania.

Number of projects: 1 UK: 0
Starting months: January–December
Time required: 4–12 weeks
Age: 18–60
Causes: AIDS/HIV, Children, Disabled (learning and physical), Teaching/assisting, (nursery).
Activities: Arts/Crafts, Caring – Day, Music, Teaching.
Placements: 100
When to apply: Four months before required placement.
Work alone/with others: With others.
Qualifications: A love and understanding of children – some with HIV and special needs. No restrictions but volunteers have to be interviewed in the UK.
Health requirements: Various medical tests required and Hepatitis A and B, polio, tetanus innoculations etc.
Costs: Flight Gatwick-Bucharest approx £250, Transfers £25.
Benefits: Accommodation and food provided for £2.50 per day. Personal rewarding/learning experience.
Training: No pre-placement training needed.
Supervision: Resident director and volunteer supervisor in Cernavoda.
Interviews: Interviews take place with the nearest regional co-ordinator to the applicant. All interviews are conducted in the UK.
Charity number: 1047698
Worldwide placements: Europe (Romania).

NOMAD TRUST, THE

15a Monks Road
Lincoln
Lincolnshire LN2 5HL UK
T: 01522 883703
F: 01522 883702
E: office@nomadtrust.org.uk
Contact: Brenda Shiels

The Nomad Trust is a homeless charity offering emergency accommodation, care and support to the homeless and other individuals in need. We run a night shelter, a day centre, a charity shop and a life skills project. There are opportunities for volunteers in all our projects where there is a great diversity of skills required/taught. We are able to accept volunteers with an offending background. City of Lincoln. 🔲 📄

Number of projects UK: 4
Starting months: January–December
Time required: 1–24 weeks
Age: 18 plus – no upper limit
Causes: Addicts/Ex-Addicts, Offenders/Ex-Offenders, Poor/Homeless, Teaching – Mature.
Activities: Administration, Caring – General, Catering, Computers, Cooking, Fundraising, Teaching, Training.
Placements: 50
When to apply: Any time.
Work alone/with others: Work with others – sometimes with other volunteers.
Health requirements: Night shelter/Day centre are smoking environments so unsuitable for asthmatics.
Costs: Accommodation costs if needed to be covered by volunteer. Local travel costs are paid and meals are provided while on duty.
Benefits: Local travel and meals while on duty.
Training: On site training in retail/administration, cooking and customer service.
Supervision: Full supervision by paid trained staff.
Interviews: Interviews are held at 15a Monk Road, Lincoln.
Charity number: 517252
UK placements: England (Lincolnshire).

NON-GOVERNMENTAL ORGANIZATIONS' COORDINATING COMMITTEE – ZAMBIA

1st Floor, Bible House
PO Box 37839
Freedom Way
Lusaka
Zambia
E: Ngocc@zamnet.zm
Contact: Grace Kanyanga

NGOCC – Non-Governmental Organizations' Coordinating Committee promotes and has information about volunteering in Zambia. It may well be able to put volunteers in touch with organisations which are not yet listed on the WorldWide Volunteering database.

Starting months: January–December
Time required: 1–52 weeks (plus)
Age: 16 plus – no upper limit
Causes: Addicts/Ex-Addicts, AIDS/HIV, Animal Welfare, Archaeology, Architecture, Children, Conservation, Disabled (learning and physical), Elderly People, Environmental Causes, Health Care/Medical, Heritage, Holidays for Disabled, Human Rights, Inner City Problems, Offenders/Ex-Offenders, Poor/Homeless, Refugees, Teaching/assisting (nursery, primary, secondary, mature, EFL) Unemployed, Wildlife, Work Camps – Seasonal, Young People.
Activities: Accountancy, Administration, Agriculture/Farming, Arts/Crafts, Building/Construction, Campaigning, Caring (general, day and residential), Catering, Community Work, Computers, Conservation Skills, Cooking, Counselling, Development Issues, DIY, Driving, First Aid, Forestry, Fundraising, Gardening/Horticulture, Group Work, International Aid, Library/Resource Centres, Manual Work, Marketing/Publicity, Music, Newsletter/Journalism, Outdoor Skills, Religion, Research, Scientific Work, Social Work, Sport, Summer Camps, Teaching, Technical Skills, Theatre/Drama, Training, Translating, Visiting/Befriending, Work Camps – Seasonal.
Costs: Varies according to the project.
Worldwide placements: Africa (Zambia).

NORFOLK WILDLIFE TRUST

Bewick House
22 Thorpe Road
Norwich
Norfolk NR1 1RY UK
T: 01603 625540
F: 01603 630593
E: admin@norfolkwildlifetrust.org.uk
W: www.wildlifetrust.org.uk/norfolk
Contact: Ian Forster

Norfolk Wildlife Trust is a member of the Wildlife Trusts, a national partnership of 47 County Trusts. The aims of the Trust are primarily to: promote nature conservation in the community; acquire and manage nature reserves; monitor biological and geological resources; liaise with local authorities to promote regard for nature conservation; offer practical advice on nature conservation to landowners. It is the Trust's policy to involve all sectors of the community, of all ages, backgrounds, abilities and disabilities towards these ends. Volunteers require no previous experience just lots of enthusiasm. If they desire, can go on to participate more fully assisting with the organisation and running of activities/projects. Limited opportunities may also arise, for those with a longer term commitment. 🖰 📄

Number of projects: 1 UK: 1
Starting months: January–December
Time required: 1–52 weeks (plus)
Age: 14 plus – no upper limit
Causes: Conservation.
Activities: Conservation Skills, Forestry, Fundraising, Marketing/Publicity.
When to apply: All year.
Work alone/with others: Both.
Equipment/clothing: Depending on activity.
Health requirements: Anti-tetanus innoculation recommended.
Costs: Food, accommodation.
Benefits: Out of pocket expenses.
Training: Training will be given applicable to tasks.
Supervision: Volunteers are supervised.
Interviews: Interviews will take place.
UK placements: England (Norfolk).

NORTHUMBERLAND WILDLIFE TRUST

The Garden House
St Nicholas Park
Jubilee Road
Newcastle upon Tyne
NE3 3XT UK
T: 0191 284 6884
F: 0191 284 6794
E: mail@northwt.org.uk
W: www.wildlifetrust.org.uk/northumberland
Contact: Tom Andrews

Northumberland Wildlife Trust uses approximately 500 active volunteers per year. Projects include:
Species surveying: otters, red squirrels, water voles.
Botanical surveying.
Ornithological surveying.
Practical conservation tasks.
Otters and rivers project.
School workshops.
Community composting and recycling.
Environmental education.
Marketing, communications and fundraising support.
Administrative and reception tasks.
Wildlife gardening.
Campaigns and policy work. Projects are undertaken across Newcastle, North Tyneside and Northumberland. 🖰 📄

Number of projects: 25 UK: 25
Starting months: January–December
Time required: 1–52 weeks (plus)
Age: 16 plus – no upper limit

Causes: Children, Conservation, Environmental Causes, Wildlife.
Activities: Administration, Campaigning, Community Work, Computers, Conservation Skills, Fundraising, Gardening/Horticulture, Group Work, Library/Resource Centres, Manual Work, Marketing/Publicity, Newsletter/ Journalism, Outdoor Skills, Scientific Work, Summer Camps, Teaching.
Placements: 500
When to apply: All year.
Work alone/with others: With others.
Qualifications: Dependent upon activity.
Equipment/clothing: Outdoor clothes.
Health requirements: Dependent upon activity.
Costs: Food and accommodation.
Benefits: Out of pocket expenses.
Training: Available.
Supervision: Always provided.
Interviews: Yes, in all circumstances.
Charity number: 221819
UK placements: England (Northumberland, Tyne and Wear).

NORWOOD RAVENSWOOD

Broadway House
80–82 The Broadway
Stanmore
Middlesex HA7 4HB UK
T: +44 (0) 208 954 4555 or 020 8420 6810
F: +44 (0) 208 420 6800
E: norwoodravenswood@nwrw.org
Contact: Robyn Goldfarb or Carole Levy

Norwood Ravenswood provides a comprehensive range of professional child care services for Jewish children and their families, and also adults with learning difficulties. We act as the authoritative voice of child care in the Jewish community, offering services which are sensitive to religious, cultural, linguistic and racial issues. We seek men and women to work closely with our professional staff, helping families and adults with learning disabilities with their day-to-day problems, as a vital part of our services. We provide support, monitoring and training; help in our nine charity shops; drive and escort children to and from therapy; help children in schools and nurseries; work at the Norwood Family Centre and Buckets and Spades Lodge; assist parents of children with special needs after school and in the holidays; raise funds, send out appeals, distribute collection boxes; join one of our outings groups; work in a residential home for adults with learning difficulties; work in Unity, a youth club for children and adolescents, 5–18, with learning disabilities. London: Hendon, Stamford Hill, Edgware, Redbridge. Charity shops at Golders Green, Southgate, Finchley, Borehamwood, Barkingside, Burnt Oak, Edgware, Ilford.

Number of projects: 1 **UK:** 1
Starting months: January–December
Time required: 1–52 weeks
Age: 15 plus – no upper limit
Causes: Children, Disabled (learning and physical), Teaching/assisting (nursery, primary).
Activities: Caring (day & residential), Driving, Fundraising, Marketing/Publicity, Summer Camps, Visiting/Befriending.
Placements: 600
When to apply: No restrictions.
Work alone/with others: With others.
Qualifications: Driving licence useful.
Equipment/clothing: Dependent on assignment. In shops jeans/trainers acceptable. In Hackney only, modest dress for ladies in accordance with religious ethics i.e. skirt and covered arms.
Health requirements: Nil.
Costs: Food and accommodation.
Benefits: Local travel expenses paid.
Training: No pre-placement training given or needed.
Supervision: Dependent on task/client assigned. Supervision is offered by volunteer co-ordinators and by staff at resources where volunteers are helping.
Interviews: Interviews take place at our office or shops.
Charity number: 1059050
UK placements: England (Essex, London).

NOTTINGHAMSHIRE WILDLIFE TRUST

The Old Ragged School
Brook Street
Nottingham
NG1 1EA UK
T: 0115 9588242
F: 0115 9243175
E: adicks@nottswt.cix.co.uk
Contact: Alan Dicks

Nottinghamshire Wildlife Trust is a member of the Wildlife Trusts, a national partnership of 47 County Trusts. The aims of the Trust are primarily to: promote nature conservation in the community; acquire and manage nature reserves; monitor biological and geological resources; liaise with local authorities to promote regard for nature conservation; offer practical advice on nature conservation to landowners. It is the Trust's policy to involve all sectors of the community, of all ages, backgrounds, abilities and disabilities towards these ends. Volunteers require no previous experience just lots of enthusiasm. If they desire, they can go on to participate more fully assisting with the organisation and running of activities/projects. Limited opportunities may also arise, for those with a longer term commitment, for NVQ training to level 2 in

Landscapes and Ecosystems. Volunteers with an offending background may be accepted – each case separately assessed.

Number of projects: 1 **UK:** 1
Starting months: January–December
Time required: 1–52 weeks (plus)
Age: 14 plus – no upper limit
Causes: Environmental Causes, Wildlife.
Activities: Administration, Agriculture/Farming, Conservation Skills, Forestry, Gardening/Horticulture, Manual Work, Research.
Work alone/with others: Both.
Equipment/clothing: Casual work clothes, waterproofs, stout boots for outdoor work. Protective safety gear is provided.
Health requirements: Anti-tetanus cover recommended.
Costs: Food and accommodation.
Benefits: Out of pocket expenses.
UK placements: England (Nottinghamshire).

NOUVELLE PLANETE

Chemin de la Forêt
CH-1042 Assens
Switzerland
T: 00 41 21 881 23 80
F: 00 41 21 882 10 54
E: info@nouvelle-planete.ch
W: www.nouvelle-planete.ch
Contact: Philippe Randin

Nouvelle Planète is a non-profit organisation founded on Albert Schweitzer's example and ethics. It works with local communities and organisations. It supports definite projects which are run by dynamic partners without government intermediaries. The main regions of activity are: environmental protection, appropriate technology and social work (for women, street children, leprosy patients etc.). One of our principal goals is to set up direct relations between northern and southern groups, villages and schools. We organise youth camps each year in southern countries. The groups of 20 volunteers work on particular projects with groups of local young people for 3–4 weeks in July and August. Individuals in the group and the group collectively must organise fundraising activities prior to departure to fund project costs and their travel. Volunteers with an offending background may be accepted if they co-operate with the preparation activities during the previous six months.

Number of projects: 15 **UK:** 0
Starting months: Jul
Time required: 3–4 weeks
Age: 17–30
Causes: Children, Disabled (physical), Environmental Causes, Poor/Homeless, Work Camps – Seasonal, Young People.
Activities: Agriculture/Farming, Community

Work, Forestry, Fundraising, Group Work, Manual Work, Summer Camps, Work Camps – Seasonal.
Placements: 400
When to apply: October before following July departure.
Work alone/with others: With other young volunteers.
Qualifications: English-speaking for the projects in India and Philippines. French for others. No nationality restrictions but volunteers must live in Switzerland or Europe. There are monthly meetings in Switzerland.
Health requirements: Nil.
Costs: Travel costs.
Benefits: Board and lodging plus local transport costs. Accommodation provided.
Training: For the 6 months preceding departure, the groups meet regularly.
Supervision: Volunteers are welcomed by someone from Nouvelle Planete and supervised by him.
Interviews: Prospective volunteers are not interviewed.
Worldwide placements: Africa (Burkina Faso, Gabon, Madagascar, Uganda); Asia (India, Philippines, Vietnam).

NUESTROS PEQUEÑOS HERMANOS

1210 Hillside Terrace
Alexandria
VA22302 USA
T: 703 836 1233
F: 703 836 3554
E: olbsus@olbsus.org
W: www.nphamigos, org
Contact: Frank J Krafft

Nuestros Pequeños Hermanos has cared for thousands of orphaned and abandoned children since 1954. Through the generosity of a worldwide network of support, the children have been provided with food, clothing, shelter, medical care and an education. Children of all ages are embraced by this loving family, Nuestros Pequeños Hermanos, which in English means 'Our little brothers and sisters'. Some children have been abandoned, others have lost one or both parents, and many have physical and emotional scars. The children are encouraged to share their time, talents and belongings with others. Every child has a job, from dusting and mopping to cooking and farming. The older children give a year or more of service as house directors, medical assistants, craft apprentices, office staff and other important roles. The children find pride in contributing to their family's survival. There are a variety of volunteer positions available in each of our homes. You look for an up-to-date list on our web site. Volunteers are asked to give a minimum of one year and may serve in a variety of positions, including house parents, nurses, physicians, therapists, teachers, secretaries, gardeners, kitchen help, librarians, or assistants in the clinics. Because of the difficulties surrounding training, language and accommodation for short-term volunteers, most positions require a strict commitment of one year. The short-term summer volunteer opportunities are in Haiti, Honduras and Guatemala. These involve teaching English, music, dance, athletics and arts and crafts. Job placements in Latin American homes will depend a great deal on a degree of fluency in Spanish. For technical and manual labour positions, a minimal knowledge of Spanish is required. We are unable to accept volunteers with an offending background. Belize, Dominican Republic, El Salvador, Guatemala, Haiti, Honduras, Mexicom and Nicaragua. 🖹

Number of projects: 8 **UK:** 0
Starting months: Jan, Jul
Time required: 12–52 weeks (plus)
Age: 21–65
Causes: Children, Disabled (learning and physical), Health Care/Medical, Inner City Problems, Teaching/assisting (EFL).
Activities: Administration, Caring (general, day and residential), Community Work, Counselling, First Aid, Fundraising, International Aid, Research, Scientific Work, Social Work, Teaching, Training, Translating, Visiting/Befriending.
Placements: Varies.
When to apply: Anytime.
Work alone/with others: With others.
Qualifications: Some positions require Spanish/ English/German/French fluency. Haitian staff speak Creole -most volunteers can learn enough Creole in two months to communicate. Check web site for more details.
Health requirements: In good health, once accepted as a volunteer, you will be asked to submit a completed health statement with your doctor's signature.
Costs: Air travel. Food and accommodation are provided as a small monthly stipend given to full time volunteers.
Benefits: Food, accommodation and small monthly stipend.
Training: If required.
Supervision: Supervised by trained staff.
Interviews: Application form can be downloaded from web site, which will be submitted to Volunteer Co-ordinator.
Worldwide placements: Central America (Belize, Dominican Republic, El Salvador, Guatemala, Haiti, Honduras, Mexico, Nicaragua).

O

OASIS TRUST

115 Southwark Bridge Road
London
SE1 0AX UK
T: +44 (0) 20 7361 450 9000
F: +44 (0) 20 7361 450 9001
E: enquiries@oasistrust.org
W: www.oasisteams.org
Contact: Becca Gibson

Oasis is an innovative organisation working in
partnership in 12 countries, across four
continents, to deliver global, community, youth
and church action initiatives that tackle social
issues that matter. Built on a Christian
foundation, it operates regardless of race,
religion or creed. One in 12 people in
Zimbabwe will be an AIDS orphan by 2005.
Oasis Global Action operates projects with some
of the world's poorest children. In the UK over
1,600 sleep rough on the streets every night.
Oasis Community Action works with the
homeless and excluded. Each week
approximately 240 young people stop going to
church. Oasis Youth Action exists to inspire the
leaders of tomorrow and young people of today.
Less than 8% of people in the UK go to church.
Oasis Church Action believes the future of the
church is your responsibility. Volunteers with
an offending background may be accepted
depending on the offence. ☒

Number of projects: 6 UK: 3
Starting months: Mar, Jul, Sep, Oct
Time required: 2–43 weeks
Age: 18–30
Causes: Children, Elderly People, Health Care/
Medical, Inner City Problems, Poor/Homeless,
Teaching/assisting, Young People.
Activities: Administration, Arts/Crafts, Caring –
General, Community Work, Counselling, Group
Work, Manual Work, Music, Religion, Sport,
Teaching, Technical Skills, Theatre/Drama,
Training, Visiting/Befriending.
Placements: 310 approx
When to apply: Between September and end of
June. Places are limited so early applications
advisable.
Work alone/with others: Both – dependent on
the project.
Qualifications: Christian commitment. For
overseas placements some languages may be
required.
Health requirements: Nil.
Costs: Dependent on project.
Benefits: Board and lodging, pocket money on
some projects, travel to overseas placements.

Accommodation is provided in consultation
with Oasis staff, unless otherwise stated. It
varies from living with a family, to having your
own flat. Oasis staff always check
accommodation is of a suitable standard before
a volunteer is placed.
Training: All volunteers are trained before
going to their placement. This is generally in
the form of residential training and can last
from a few days to two weeks. On some projects
volunteers also receive ongoing training during
the duration of their project.
Supervision: Volunteers are supervised by Oasis
staff who will meet with them on a regular
basis. They are also supervised by someone in
their placement.
Interviews: Applicants are interviewed at various
selection/interview weekends in London.
Charity number: 1026487
Worldwide placements: Africa (Kenya,
Mozambique, South Africa, Tanzania, Uganda,
Zimbabwe); South America (Brazil, Peru); Asia
(India); Europe (France, Germany, Portugal,
Romania).
UK placements: England (London,
Manchester); Scotland (Glasgow City).

OCEANIC SOCIETY EXPEDITIONS

230-E
Fort Mason
San Francisco, California
94123 USA
T: 415 441 1106
F: 415 474 3395
E: office@oceanicsociety.org
W: www.oceanic-society.org
Contact: Maroy Englund

Oceanic Society Expeditions was established in
1969 as a non-profit conservation organisation
with a primary mission to protect marine
wildlife and habitats worldwide through an
integrated programme of scientific research,
environmental education and volunteerism.
Our environmental approach is to collaborate
with local communities in conservation
initiatives, and to promote sustainable
economies as an alternative to those that are
destructive to wildlife and natural habitats.
Research expeditions contribute directly to
environmental protection by supporting
conservation-directed research. We conduct and
fund field research as a basis for creating and
maintaining nature reserves and sanctuaries
and for recommending solutions to
environmental problems. No experience is

necessary to participate. Participants receive a pre-trip research plan to prepare for the project and training on-site by our staff to make observations and record data. In the evenings, researchers give lectures and/or slide presentations on the ecology, biology and behaviour of the animals under study. Participants become research assistants, working side by side with the field researcher. You will help with performing specific tasks such as logging information onto data sheets, recording data produced by scientific equipment and collecting environmental data. Some work is hands-on in nature, such as bird banding and measuring nesting sea turtles. Most research tasks are rotated and specific research components are optional and will depend on your interests. Will accept volunteers with an offending background. Alaska, Izu Peninsula – Japan, Vancouver, Baja – Mexico, Turneffe Atoll-Belize, Amazon.

Number of projects: 25 **UK:** 0
Starting months: January–December
Time required: 1–3 weeks
Age: 16 plus – no upper limit
Causes: Animal Welfare, Conservation, Environmental Causes, Wildlife.
Activities: Conservation Skills, Research, Scientific Work.
Placements: 325
When to apply: Al year round.
Work alone/with others: Work with others.
Qualifications: No specific qualifications.
Equipment/clothing: Clothing and equipment lists provided for each individual programme.
Health requirements: Must be in general good health, some vaccinations are recommended/required for certain areas of travel.
Costs: Varies between US$500–3000. Some programmes include airfare, accommodation, meals, transfer fees and equipment.
Benefits: Some programmes offer airfare, accommodation, meals, transfer fees and equipment.
Training: On-site training appropriate to progamme including photography, data entry and environmental data.
Supervision: Oceanic Society researchers or naturalist oversees group activities.
Interviews: No.
Worldwide placements: North America: (Canada, USA); Central America (Bahamas, Belize, Dominican Republic, Honduras, Mexico); South America (Guyana, Peru, Suriname).

OCHIL TOWER SCHOOL

140 High Street
Auchterarder
Perthshire PH3 1AD UK

T: 01764 662416
F: 01764 662416
E: office@ochiltowerschool.org.uk
W: www.ochiltowerschool.org.uk
Contact: Margaret Snellgrove

Ochil Tower School cares for approximately 35 children aged 7–18 years who live and attend school on either a daily, weekly or fortnightly basis. They all have a variety of difficulties, problems and challenges. We are interested essentially in having people join Ochil Tower who can commit themselves for a minimum of one year, not necessarily for the child's sense of security, stability and potential progress but also giving volunteers time to settle in to this particular way of life. The children go home once a fortnight for the weekend. You will have time off then from Friday evening through to Sunday afternoon. You will also have one day off within the fortnight. The children have 14 weeks holiday a year. Some training days may occur at the beginning of a holiday period, which you would need to attend. There may be placements for volunteers with an offending background depending on offence. Auchterarder is a royal burgh and is situated in central Scotland. The cities of Edinburgh, Glasgow and Dundee are all about 45 miles away. Perth and Dunblane are 15 miles away. Gleneagles station is $2\frac{1}{2}$ miles away. ♿ ▤

Number of projects: 1 **UK:** 1
Starting months: Aug
Time required: 40–52 weeks (plus)
Age: 18–65
Causes: Children, Disabled (learning), Teaching/assisting, Young People.
Activities: Arts/Crafts, Caring – Residential, Teaching.
Placements: 12
When to apply: January.
Work alone/with others: With others.
Qualifications: Good grasp of English, as most of our children have communication difficulties. Patience, willingness and enthusiasm. We as an organisation impose no nationality restrictions, however, volunteers coming from non EU countries can have problems to obtain visas.
Equipment/clothing: Outdoor walking gear.
Health requirements: It is important that volunteers tell us of any physical or mental health problems so that we have a clear picture of your strengths and weaknesses when placing you in the community.
Costs: Travel to Ochil Tower School must be met by volunteer.
Benefits: Board and lodging +£28 pocket money and holiday money.
Training: Induction week, first aid, health and safety – 4 hours weekly – crisis intervention, behaviour and background training to name but a few.

Supervision: Regular supervision and tutoring undertaken.
Interviews: If volunteer is in the country we do interview, otherwise assessment/interview takes place in induction week.
Charity number: SC006091
UK placements: Scotland (Perth and Kinross).

OCKENDEN

Constitution Hill
Woking
Surrey GU22 7UU UK
T: 01483 772012
E: thembi.mutch@ockenden.org.uk
W: www.ockenden.org.uk
Contact: Thembi Mutch

Ockenden International was set up in 1951. We have evolved into a specialist agency that deals with overseas refugees, delivering long-term development solutions. We are secular, non political and work in some of the harshest environments in the world. A vital part of our work is carried out by volunteers. We rely on them, and in return try to treat them equally to members of staff, offering training (internal and external), travel expenses and interesting and necessary work. In return we ask for enthusiasm and commitment. We need a communications officer to research tasks for communications – contact office for more details and specifications required. Woking, Surrey. ⓑ 📄

Number of projects: 8 **UK:** 1
Starting months: January–December
Time required: 12–52 weeks (plus)
Age: 21–65
Causes: AIDS/HIV, Refugees.
Activities: Administration, Library/Resource Centres, Newsletter/Journalism, Research.
Placements: 10
When to apply: As soon as possible
Work alone/with others: Both.
Qualifications: Familiarity and competence with MS word/databases, filing , Internet, cultural sensitvity and awareness, language aptitude.
Health requirements: No restrictions.
Costs: Accommodation and food costs.
Benefits: Travel to work within the UK.
Training: Varies as necessary.
Supervision: Supervision undertaken by volunteers co-ordinator.
Interviews: Interviews in Woking.
UK placements: England (Surrey).

OCKENDEN INTERNATIONAL

Kilmore House
20 Prior Road
Camberley
Surrey GU15 1DQ UK
T: 01276 709709
F: 01276 709707
Contact: Mrs Mary Dixon

Ockenden International is a charity registered in 1955, providing support for refugees, displaced people and the disadvantaged both at home and overseas. In the UK this consists of the provision of a home in Camberley, Surrey, for the physically and/or mentally disabled. The core clients are refugees both from Vietnam and Cambodia. Tasks include helping residents lead as normal as possible a life and develop their abilities and confidence so that they are able to interact in the community. This will include domestic and direct care tasks. ⓑ

Number of projects: 1 **UK:** 1
Starting months: January–December
Time required: 26–52 weeks
Age: 18 plus – no upper limit
Causes: Disabled (learning and physical), Refugees, Young People.
Activities: Arts/Crafts, Caring (general, day and residential), Catering, Community Work, Cooking, DIY, Driving, Gardening/Horticulture, Group Work.
Placements: 6
When to apply: All year.
Work alone/with others: With others.
Qualifications: English speaking and reading. Driving licence useful.
Health requirements: Good health.
Costs: Nil.
Benefits: Up to £35 per week for reasonable expenses. Board and accommodation provided on site free. 23 days holiday per year pro rata. Twin rooms, kitchen, shower/toilet.
Training: Induction course.
Supervision: Senior care supervision.
Interviews: Wherever possible, volunteers are interviewed at Kilmore.
Charity number: 10533720
UK placements: England (Surrey).

ONE to ONE, SRI LANKA

55A Dharmapala Mawatha
Colombo 3
WP Sri Lanka
T: 00 94 77 398353
F: 00 94 1 448526
E: one2one@sri.lanka.net
Contact: Danusha Samerawickreme

One to One is a volunteer and student placement organisation dedicated to providing volunteers and students with systematic assistance to give their best to their charity work and placement studies in Sri Lanka. We aim to blend the requirements of the volunteers/students with those of the deserving segment of society secluded in the furthest rural areas of Sri Lanka. We also expect to benefit the participating volunteers by providing them with consistant and comprehensive assistance for their volunteer/placement work (including material assistance). Trained supervisors would monitor the work of the volunteers/students providing them with the ideal environment to serve the poor with maximum efficiency. We would also provide the volunteers/students with the necessary security to serve without fear. They have 24-hour recourse to the One to One management to deal with any problem. Our vision is to provide volunteers/students and the needy with a memorable experience they would cherish forever. We are linked with some of the best companies in Sri Lanka for those who select their placements in other avenues than serving community. We offer insight progammes for youth travel and learning about people and cultures of Sri Lanka. Students/volunteers can choose to work as a group or get individual placements in their selected fields. You can choose from wanting to serve the rural areas or get your own experience by working in the city. The head office is based in Colombo, the commercial capital of Sri Lanka. 📋

Number of projects: 15 **UK:** 0
Starting months: Jan, Apr, Jul, Oct
Time required: 12–24 weeks
Age: 17–45
Causes: Children, Conservation, Elderly People, Health Care/Medical, Poor/Homeless, Teaching/assisting (nursery, primary, secondary, mature, EFL) Wildlife, Work Camps – Seasonal, Young People.
Activities: Arts/Crafts, Caring – General, Catering, Community Work, Computers, Cooking, Library/Resource Centres, Marketing/Publicity, Music, Newsletter/Journalism, Religion, Social Work, Teaching, Work Camps – Seasonal.
Placements: 50
When to apply: Our programmes run year round. Most courses commence in January, April, July, October.
Work alone/with others: On their own.
Qualifications: No specific qualifications required. Those who wish to do placements in selected fields.
Equipment/clothing: Dress according to Sri Lankan culture, especially when working in rural areas.
Health requirements: No restrictions.
Costs: Volunteers/students should obtain their airline tickets, and bear their travel insurance and personal expenses while on placement.
Benefits: Half board and lodging, airport transfers, 7-day island tour, free e-mail and 2 overseas calls free on arrival and departure, 24 hr emergency contact. Relations visiting volunteers could get complimentary accommodation and tours on discounted rates. Volunteers live in recommended homes within the placement areas.

Training: Orientation training on arrival.
Supervision: Monthly visits by managers to placements.
Interviews: Interviews conducted by telephone.
Worldwide placements: Asia (Sri Lanka).

ONEWORLD VOLUNTEER

2458 River Road
Guilford
Vermont VT 05301 USA
T: 00 1 802 257 0152
F: 00 1 802 257 2784
E: info@oneworldvolunteer.org
W: www.oneworldvolunteer.org
Contact: John Lee

OneWorld Volunteer can arrange a variety of volunteer opportunities around the world. A volunteer placement may involve working in a rain forest reserve, an agroforestry project, a migratory bird or sea turtle sanctuary, an animal rescue shelter, a rural school or an environmental education programme. In most cases, volunteers live with a host family. In other cases meals and lodging are provided at a project site. Each volunteer placement is individually arranged. Most placements are available throughout the year for varying lengths of time. We work with applicants to find out as much as we can about their goals, skills and expectations. Our goal is to match people with situations which are most appropriate for them. We want the experience to be positive for everyone involved – the volunteer as well as the staff and community at a particular placement site.
We provide volunteers with
– health and immunisation recommendations
– consular information, safety tips, information on medical facilities
– assistance making flight arrangements
– a recommended clothing and equipment list
– a briefing packet with information regarding: volunteer job description, supervisor and other contact people, phone/fax, mailing address, meals and lodging, transportation in country etc.
– all the information necessary to prepare for, travel to and participate in a particular volunteer placement.
Volunteers with an offending background may be accepted depending on circumstances and visa restrictions. 📶 📋

Number of projects: 25 approx. **UK:** 0
Starting months: January–December
Time required: 4–52 weeks (plus)
Age: 18 plus – no upper limit
Causes: Animal Welfare, Children, Conservation, Environmental Causes, Teaching/assisting (primary, secondary, EFL), Wildlife.
Activities: Agriculture/Farming, Arts/Crafts,

Building/Construction, Computers, Conservation Skills, Forestry, Gardening/ Horticulture, Manual Work, Research, Scientific Work, Teaching.
Placements: 50
When to apply: 3–4 months prior to starting.
Work alone/with others: Both.
Qualifications: Depends on the project. Some need no more than energy and enthusiasm, others need Spanish or teaching experience or biology.
Health requirements: One of our projects requires negative TB.
Costs: Travel expenses, application and placement fees, board and lodging.
Benefits: None.
Training: On site training.
Supervision: Volunteers have a project supervisor.
Interviews: Generally on the telephone or by e-mail.
Worldwide placements: North America: (Canada); Central America (Belize, Costa Rica, Cuba, Guatemala, Mexico, Puerto Rico); South America (Ecuador); Asia (Nepal, Thailand); Australasia (Australia).

OPEN HOUSES NETWORK

Goetheplatz 9B
99423 Weimar
Germany
T: 00 49 3643 502390
F: 00 49 3643 851117
E: info@openhouses.de
W: www.openhouses.de
Contact: Bert Ludwig

Open Houses Network dates back to the mid-eighties when a group of young people voluntarily undertook to restore village churches in danger of decay. Commitment to these churches united people who enjoyed the freedom that came with the work. As a result, the buildings were revived – through exhibitions, concerts, making music together or sitting round the camp fire. The rooms were once again filled with life, something which mere craftsmen's works could not achieve. In the meantime, although rooms free of political and ideological pressure are no longer so urgently required, places where people can meet without economic constraint and far from bureaucracy, institutionalisation, nepotism and society's exclusions have become rare. Though a simple concept – one where people came together for a common purpose – it seems all the same a difficult one to put into practice. The tightrope walk between public activities in a monetary or functional sense and the retreat to privacy is far from easy and tackling red tape and financial restrictions necessitates permanent effort. 'Public space' is less and less

understood as common property, and is constantly being cut down. 'Public property' seems to have gone out of fashion and places of common responsible work are now rare. The Open Houses Network aims to create and protect such places. In this process, we do not want to be the doers, but instead people who have a vision, who want to initiate something, and who achieve through co-operation with others. We see the projects, activities and opportunities we provide as offers – offers which lead to common commitment, meetings and change. Eastern Germany including Saxony, Thuringia, Mecklenburg county. & 📄

Number of projects: 7 UK: 0
Starting months: January–December
Time required: 2–45 weeks
Age: 16 plus – no upper limit
Causes: Archaeology, Architecture, Conservation, Environmental Causes, Heritage, Unemployed, Work Camps – Seasonal, Young People.
Activities: Administration, Arts/Crafts, Building/Construction, Conservation Skills, Driving, Forestry, Fundraising, Gardening/ Horticulture, Group Work, Manual Work, Music, Outdoor Skills, Social Work, Summer Camps, Theatre/Drama, Work Camps – Seasonal.
Placements: 70
When to apply: All year. There are more projects between April and September than in the winter.
Work alone/with others: With other young people.
Qualifications: Nil required but any skills such as crafts, artistic and drawing talent are very welcome.
Equipment/clothing: Sleeping bag, working clothes.
Health requirements: Nil.
Costs: Travel costs. For Western European volunteers and volunteers from USA, Canada, South Korea, Japan and Australia there is a participation fee of approx. €25 per week. No charges for E. European volunteers.
Benefits: Board and lodging.
Training: Introductory training and evaluation.
Supervision: By a social worker.
Charity number: 600 AG Sommerda
Worldwide placements: Europe (Germany).

OPENMINDPROJECTS

No 168, MOO 1
Meaung Mee Nonkhai 43000
Nongkhai
Nongkhai Province 43000 Thailand
T: 0 66 1 799 1052
E: info@openmindprojects.nu
W: www.openmindprojects.nu
Contact: Sven Mauleon

Openmindprojects arrange for volunteers to act as coaches in our learning projects for underprivileged poor and young. Openmindprojects develop cost effective computer and e-learning methods for the third world. For more information please visit our web site www.openmindproject.nu. We are unable to place volunteers with an offending background. Isan in the north east of Thailand around Bangkok. 📄

Number of projects: 8 **UK:** 0
Starting months: January–December
Time required: 4–52 weeks (plus)
Age: 18–70
Causes: Children, Poor/Homeless, Teaching/assisting (primary, secondary, EFL), Young People.
Activities: Community Work, Computers, Development Issues, Fundraising, International Aid, Teaching, Technical Skills, Training.
Placements: 20–30
When to apply: Any time.
Work alone/with others: Varies.
Qualifications: English language and computer skills.
Health requirements: No restrictions.
Costs: Insurance, travel. Fee to cover accommodation, local transport, meals and introduction training.
Benefits: Accommodation and meals included in fee.
Training: Induction training on arrival.
Supervision: Volunteers are supported and supervised by local Openmindprojects staff.
Interviews: Volunteers are asked to submit information about themselves requested by us.
Worldwide placements: Asia (Thailand).

OPERATION MOBILISATION – GLOBAL CHALLENGE

Quinta
Weston Rhyn
Oswestry
SY10 7LT UK
T: 01691 773388
F: 01691 778378
E: global.challenge@uk.om.org
W: www.uk.om.org
Contact: Roger Taylor

Operation Mobilisation (OM) is an interdenominational, evangelical Christian missionary organisation with work in over 80 countries. Short-term opportunities usually involve some kind of evangelistic work, sometimes combined with social work. There are more short term events in the summer, but there are all year round opportunities. ♿

Number of projects: over 100 **UK:** 19
Starting months: January–December
Time required: 1–6 weeks

Age: 17 plus – no upper limit
Causes: Addicts/Ex-Addicts, AIDS/HIV, Children, Disabled (learning and physical), Elderly People, Health Care/Medical, Inner City Problems, Offenders/Ex-Offenders, Poor/ Homeless, Refugees, Teaching (EFL), Young People.
Activities: Building/Construction, Community Work, Group Work, International Aid, Manual Work, Music, Outdoor Skills, Religion, Social Work, Sport, Summer Camps, Teaching, Visiting/Befriending.
Placements: 180
When to apply: At least one month in advance. Some campaigns have limited places, and it is first come first served for places.
Work alone/with others: Always working in teams with oversight by experienced people, usually long term OM staff.
Qualifications: Enthusiasm to help with the Great Commission. No nationality restrictions, but must be resident in the UK. Residents of other countries apply through the local Operations Mobilisation office.
Equipment/clothing: A Bible. You may be asked to bring a sleeping bag and musical instruments are always welcome.
Health requirements: Please advise of any problems when applying, and we will do our best to find a suitable team, although this may not always be possible.
Costs: From £95.00 per week (one week at Easter in Switzerland) to £1170(three months in Tunisia) plus travel and visas. All costs include accommodation and food.
Benefits: Basic accommodation and food are included in costs.
Training: All events include training and orientation.
Supervision: By people with local experience, usually long term OM staff.
Interviews: None. Four page application form to be completed and reference from church leader required.
Worldwide placements: Africa (Guinea, Senegal, Sierra Leone, Togo); Central America (Costa Rica, El Salvador, Guatemala, Mexico, Nicaragua, Panama); South America (Argentina, Brazil, Uruguay); Asia (Israel, Jordan, Kazakhstan, Lebanon, Malaysia, Nepal, Turkey, Uzbekistan); Europe (Albania, Belgium, Bosnia-Herzegovina, Bulgaria, Croatia, Estonia, France, Greece, Ireland, Italy, Macedonia, Malta, Moldova, Poland, Portugal, Romania, Russia, Spain, Switzerland, Turkey, Ukraine, Yugoslavia).
UK placements: England (London, West Midlands); Scotland (Western Isles).

OPERATION NEW WORLD

4 Eccleston Square
London
SW1V 1NP UK

T: +44 (0) 20 7361 931 8177
F: +44 (0) 20 7361 931 9589
E: al@operationnewworld.co.uk
W: www.operationnewworld.co.uk
Contact: Anne Leonard

The Operation New World programme aims to motivate and train unemployed young people so that they are able to get out of 'Benefits' and into worthwhile jobs. Since we began in 1995, over 90% of the trainees found jobs or took up full time education shortly afterwards. The beneficiaries are unemployed young people from all parts of the UK, from a variety of disadvantaged backgrounds. Most are disadvantaged by poverty and are from broken homes with a pattern of drifting from one temporary address to another. Some need help urgently in order to get restarted and avoid drifting into drink or drug related problems. They may have lost their first job or have never had a job because they lack the motivation or qualifications to do something permanent. They are coaxed into volunteering for the Operation New World programme because it offers a fresh start in life allied to environmental issues which are of great interest to this age group. Part 1: Once trainees enrol on a part-time study course, we provide residential outdoor training which aims to bond participants into a self support group so that they help each other to stay on-course. This is achieved through teamwork, solving problems together and learning practical skills such as first aid, map reading, navigation and verbal presentation. Part 2: This is followed by a 12-week part-time course at a supporting college in numeracy and computer skills; practical environmental studies and personal development. Part 3: Once trainees have completed Parts 1 and 2, they qualify for two weeks residential fieldwork in a remote destination, usually a nature reserve in Europe or in the UK. This is an intensive experience requiring discipline and hard work and is what makes the whole scheme work. Each day starts at 6am with classes and conservation work until dark, then lectures, presentations and written reports in the evening. Trainees practise presentation skills to help in job interviews, each giving a verbal report of his/her work at the end of each day. There are no luxuries. Everyone takes turns to prepare food, chop wood and perform other duties for the rest of the group. This experience provides young people with new skills and gives them a support group they did not have before. The increase in their self-respect empowers them to take a new course in life and become more active members of society and their positive response is reflected in the outstanding results achieved so far. Volunteers with an offending background are accepted. 🖹

Number of projects UK: 3
Starting months: Feb, Oct, Nov
Time required: 14–16 weeks
Age: 18–25
Causes: Conservation, Environmental Causes, Poor/Homeless, Unemployed, Wildlife, Young People.
Activities: Conservation Skills, First Aid, Forestry, Outdoor Skills.
Placements: 60+
When to apply: All year.
Work alone/with others: With other young volunteers.
Qualifications: GCSEs. Volunteers must be unemployed, UK and possibly EC nationalities.
Equipment/clothing: Outdoor clothing.
Health requirements: Applicants must be able to carry out fieldwork. May entail difficult walking conditions.
Costs: None (apart from UK travel to college or airport). Food and accommodation.
Benefits: UK expenses. Travel to foreign location. BTec certificate in Environmental Studies.
Training: BTec Certificate in Environmental Studies.
Supervision: Qualified college lecturers and TA/regular army volunteers.
Interviews: Interview takes place at the Outdoor Training Camp.
Worldwide placements: Europe (France, Spain, Sweden).
UK placements: England (Surrey).

ORANGUTAN FOUNDATION, THE

7 Kent Terrace
London
NW1 4RP UK
T: +44 (0) 20 7361 724 2912
F: +44 (0) 20 7361 706 2613
E: info@orangutan.org.uk
W: www.orangutan.org.uk
Contact: Cathy Whibley

The Orangutan Foundation is a conservation organisation that actively conserves the orangutan and its habitat whilst conducting long term research on the ecology of orangutans and their rainforest habitat. In the UK we deliver an educational programme and fundraise and increase public awareness. We actively lobby governments and with our education programme we hope that steps will be taken to protect orangutans and save them from extinction. In 1997 through the influence of Dr. Galdikas, we were instrumental in securing a one third (100,00 hectare) increase in the size of Tanjung Puting National Park. In addition to this, Dr. Galdikas successfully lobbied the Indonesian government for a wildlife reserve in Central Kalimantan.

Lamandu is the new orangutan release site consisting of 76,000 hectares of expired logging concession. So far in 2002, 16 rehabilitated organgutans have been released into this protected area. Another vital development took place in 1998 when the Foundation, in conjunction with the Ministry of Forestry, founded an urgently needed Orangutan Care Centre in Central Kalimantan. This provides a quarantine area and a clinic for the treatment and rehabilitation of orangutans. Our current projects are:

Maintaining Camp Leakey, the orangutan research site established in 1971 by Dr. Galdikas.

Rescuing orphaned and injured orangutans and rehabilitating them ready for life in the wild. Educating young Indonesians on the value of the Indonesian rainforest and their importance in terms of the survival of the endangered wild orangutan. Providing funds for additional monitoring units to work with police in patrolling the park. Restoring illegally logged and otherwise degraded rainforest, as well as former slash-and-burn fields, by planting light tolerant canopy species in areas adjacent to the park. Devising an eco-development programme, stimulating non-timber related industries, in the locality of the park for up to 100 people. The Orangutan Foundation is a partner of the United Nations Environmental Programme, Great Ape Survival Project (GrASP). Kalimantan, Indonesian Borneo based in Tanjung Puting National Park. 📄

Number of projects: 1 UK: 0
Starting months: Apr, Jun, Aug, Oct
Time required: 6 weeks
Age: 18 plus – no upper limit
Causes: Conservation, Environmental Causes, Wildlife.
Activities: Building/Construction, Conservation Skills, Development Issues, DIY, Forestry, Group Work, Manual Work, Outdoor Skills.
Placements: 48
When to apply: September/October.
Work alone/with others: Work with others.
Qualifications: Must be able to speak English or Indonesian, have an ability to work in a team and a high level of fitness essential.
Equipment/clothing: Equipment lists are sent out once teams are selected.
Health requirements: Volunteers must be fit and healthy, you will be working in hot and humid conditions. You must have necessary innoculations and be vaccinated against certain diseases. A medical form must be completed by volunteer before departure.
Costs: Must be member of Orangutan Foundation – £8 for students, £15 others. £500 or US$700 for 6 weeks. Volunteers must fund and pay for travel expenses to and from

Indonesia. Estimated total cost including travel, insurance etc £1500–£2000.
Benefits: Provides invaluable practical support for the Orangutan Foundation. Cost covers food and accommodation.
Training: There is a briefing day for applicants in the UK, training isn't necessary.
Supervision: There is a vounteer co-ordinator who arranges the work while volunteers are in Indonesia. The Orangutan Foundation is not responsible for volunteers whilst they are on the programme.
Interviews: Interviews are held in our London office/over the telephone for international applicants.
Charity number: 1042194
Worldwide placements: Asia (Indonesia).

ORES FOUNDATION FOR MARINE ENVIRONMENT RESEARCH

P.O. Box 1252
4502 Solothurn
Switzerland
T: 0041 32 623 63 54
F: 0041 32 623 63 54
E: info@ores.org
W: www.ores.org
Contact: Ursula Tscherter

Ores Foundation for Marine Environment Research – the unique coastal ecosystem in the St. Lawrence estuary in Eastern Canada – is known for the abundance and diversity of its marine life. Little is known about its complexity and its inhabitants, specifically baleen whales such as blue, fin, humpback and minki whales as well as toothed whale species such as harbour porpoise, beluga and sperm whales. Ores centre personnel have been studying the feeding and breathing ecology of St Lawrence whales since 1978 and have developed and introduced minimally intrusive research methods, which are labour intensive. Funding support and help with research is needed for ongoing studies. Two programmes are offered: the General Interest Course (GIC) and the Internship Course (ISC). The GIC is open to anybody (with academic or non-academic background) who wishes to take part in a unique learning and working experience and who wishes to broaden his knowledge of the ocean world generally and of the intriguing whales in particular. The ISC is open to anybody who has completed the introductory course and who would like to deepen the experience by joining the research team for a longer period of time. Participants share in all the on-water research tasks and functions, first by observing and listening to Ores personnel at work and then by taking over step-by-step themselves, as they feel comfortable and gain competence. Unfortunately we cannot accept

volunteers with an offending background. Alternative address – Field Station during summer – Ores centre for Marine Environment Research PO Box 117 Bergeronnes, Qc, GOT 1GO. Canada Research station site is in Bergeronnes, a little village at the northshore of the St Lawrence Estuary in Eastern Canada about 200km northeast of Quebec. ♿ 📄
Constant debriefings throughout the course.

Number of projects: 1 **UK:** 0
Starting months: Jul, Aug, Sep
Time required: 2–12 weeks
Age: 18 plus – no upper limit
Causes: Conservation, Wildlife.
Activities: Computers, Conservation Skills, Cooking, Driving, Group Work, Research, Scientific Work, Teaching.
Placements: 50
When to apply: As early as possible, especially during first half of the year of participation.
Work alone/with others: With others.
Qualifications: None needed except for English language skills.
Health requirements: No restrictions except back problems.
Costs: Introductory course £700 food £60/ Internship course 6 week – £1550, 12 week £2750 plus both programmes travelling £600.
Benefits: Stay at Parc Bon campgrounds equipped with washrooms, showers, a laundry room and telephone. Tents with heating system, cooking tent. Other programmes volunteers stay in cabins for 3–4 people.
Training: It is not assumed that participants have any experience. First observe and listen, then think and how and why, then take over step-by-step as you feel confident and competent.
Supervision: Ores personnel constantly supervise the work on the water and in the lab.
Interviews: No interview.
Worldwide placements: North America: (Canada).

ORGANISATION FOR RURAL EDUCATION AND DEVELOPMENT

P O Box 58
Tarkwa
Western Region 58 Ghana
T: 00 233 22 402800
F: 00 233 22 402800
E: ored@hotmail.com
Contact: Joseph Kofi Kekrebesi

Organisation for Rural Education and Development has been in existence since 1995. It is a non-profit making organisation. Our main aim is to provide basic infrastructure and facilities for rural schools with the help of the communities. We provide buildings and

furniture. We also provide library and books to most deprived schools in the rural areas. We educate parents on the need to send their children and wards to school. So far eight communities have benefitted from the organisation. We also provide accommodation for teachers and this coupled with training and incentive packages attracts teachers to these rural communities. Our organisation has also placed much emphasis on sexually transmitted diseases and HIV/AIDS. In 1999 four volunteers from Switzerland contributed enormously to the HIV/AIDS education programme. They stayed for three months and their impact was tremendous. Besides local training and workshops, the organisation has sponsored four members of staff to attend conferences on education and HIV/AIDS in Southern and Eastern Africa. We are hoping to work on the production of computers to rural schools. In the Western and Central regions of Ghana.

Number of projects: 8 **UK:** 0
Starting months: Jan, Mar, Jun, Sep
Time required: 4–52 weeks
Age: 14–40
Causes: Addicts/Ex-Addicts, AIDS/HIV, Children, Conservation, Elderly People, Health Care/Medical, Heritage, Poor/Homeless, Refugees, Teaching/assisting (nursery, primary, secondary, mature, EFL) Work Camps – Seasonal, Young People.
Activities: Accountancy, Administration, Agriculture/Farming, Arts/Crafts, Caring (general and day), Community Work, Conservation Skills, Counselling, Development Issues, Forestry, Group Work, International Aid, Library/Resource Centres, Research, Social Work, Sport, Summer Camps, Teaching, Technical Skills, Training, Visiting/Befriending, Work Camps – Seasonal.
Placements: 40
When to apply: December, February, April and August.
Work alone/with others: With other young volunteers.
Qualifications: A-Level. Must speak at least English and be able to cope with different cultures.
Equipment/clothing: Normal summer clothing is good for volunteers.
Health requirements: Must be healthy and physically fit.
Costs: Registration fee US$90, Membership fee annually US$40, subsistence $500 annually, plus travel costs to Ghana and the project.
Interviews: Questionnaires are sent to volunteers to complete and these are assessed prior to acceptance.
Charity number: 60219
Worldwide placements: Africa (Ghana).

OSMIJEH – Bosnia and Herzegovina

Nasselje Lamele b.b.
75320 Gracanica Boznia and Herzegovina
T: 00 387 35 787 281
F: 00 387 35 787 281
E: osmijeh@hotmail.com
Contact: Hamdija Kujundzic

Osmijeh promotes and has information about volunteering in Boznia and Herzegovina. It may well be able to put volunteers in touch with organisations which are not yet listed on the WorldWide Volunteering database.

Starting months: January–December
Time required: 1–52 weeks (plus)
Age: 16 plus – no upper limit
Causes: Addicts/Ex-Addicts, AIDS/HIV, Animal Welfare, Archaeology, Architecture, Children, Conservation, Disabled (learning and physical), Elderly People, Environmental Causes, Health Care/Medical, Heritage, Holidays for Disabled, Human Rights, Inner City Problems, Offenders/Ex-Offenders, Poor/Homeless, Refugees, Teaching/assisting (nursery, primary, secondary, mature, EFL) Unemployed, Wildlife, Work Camps – Seasonal, Young People.
Activities: Accountancy, Administration, Agriculture/Farming, Arts/Crafts, Building/Construction, Campaigning, Caring (general, day and residential), Catering, Community Work, Computers, Conservation Skills, Cooking, Counselling, Development Issues, DIY, Driving, First Aid, Forestry, Fundraising, Gardening/Horticulture, Group Work, International Aid, Library/Resource Centres, Manual Work, Marketing/Publicity, Music, Newsletter/Journalism, Outdoor Skills, Religion, Research, Scientific Work, Social Work, Sport, Summer Camps, Teaching, Technical Skills, Theatre/Drama, Training, Translating, Visiting/Befriending, Work Camps – Seasonal.
Costs: Varies according to the project.
Worldwide placements: Europe (Bosnia-Herzegovina).

OUTREACH INTERNATIONAL

Bartletts Farm
Hayes Road
Compton Dundon
Somerset TA11 6PF UK
T: 01458 274957
F: 01458 274957
E: projects@outreachinternational.co.uk
W: www.outreachinternational.co.uk
Contact: James Chapman

Outreach requires enthusiastic, energetic people wishing to immerse themselves in Mexican, Ecuadorian or Cambodian culture for a minimum period of three months. We encourage all volunteers to learn Spanish on their placement and to learn Khmer in Cambodia. Projects are always local initiatives so volunteers are genuinely needed to help run local charities and work in placements set up to meet local needs. These placements include: orphanages for children aged one to fifteen, running a feeding programme for homeless street children, assisting a special needs school, working with disabled children (ideal for medical students) teaching English, games, music and art. Also conservation work includes work with turtles, coral reef and protected crocodiles. The projects are all carefully selected. In Mexico they are on the Pacific Coast and in Ecuador in the rainforest or in the Andes. In Cambodia we also have projects working with disabled landmine and polio victims. Volunteers are needed to teach English, computer skills, art and crafts. Artists are particularly needed, as are people with an interest in sports. Physiotherapists are needed to give therapy to young land mine victims. We also need volunteers to assists with HIV awareness project. With skills taught by volunteers, young Cambodians can earn themselves a living. Cambodia is a remarkable country with little infrastructure. Outreach volunteers can make a significant difference to the lives of young Khmer people. It is a warm, loving country where volunteers are made to feel very welcome. Also conservation projects include working with marine mammals, working on a coral reef, sea turtle conservation and running a crocodile protection scheme. In Ecuador conservation work includes working in the heart of the rainforest. We run comprehensive fundraising awareness courses and put volunteers in touch with grant giving bodies. We have unusual opportunities in Mexico for those interested in dance and the performing arts. Outreach International is a member of The Year Out Group. Mexico – Pacific coast mainly. Exotic and stunning location but working with humble communities in simple conditions. In Cambodia most projects are in Phnom Penh but some are in rural locations. In Ecuador in Quito, the Amazon or cloudforest. ♿

Number of projects: 40 Mexico, 10 Cambodia, 12 Ecuador. **UK:** 0
Starting months: Jan, Jun, Sep
Time required: 12–40 weeks
Age: 18–40
Causes: Children, Conservation, Disabled (learning), Environmental Causes, Poor/Homeless, Teaching/assisting (primary, secondary, mature, EFL), Wildlife, Young People.
Activities: Agriculture/Farming, Arts/Crafts, Conservation Skills, Development Issues, Music, Research, Scientific Work, Sport, Teaching, Theatre/Drama.

Placements: 100
When to apply: 6–12 months before wishing to begin project.
Work alone/with others: Work with one other volunteer but often live with three or four volunteers. Normally 25 volunteers in country at any one time but working on different projects in similar location. Socialising takes place at weekends when trips are often organised.
Qualifications: A levels, degree for some projects. Enthusiasm and energy are more important than formal qualifications. Volunteers are selected from the UK only.
Equipment/clothing: Nothing specific.
Health requirements: Must be in good health.
Costs: £3100 to cover flights, insurance, food, weekend expeditions, full intensive Spanish course & all other project related costs including full 24 hr support & back up.
Benefits: Learn Spanish. Benefit host community. Experience full immersion in Mexican, Ecuadorian or Cambodian culture. Comfortable volunteer house or staying with local families.
Training: Offered in Mexico, Ecuador, Cambodia and in UK before departure.
Supervision: All projects have an overseas, local project manager. Additionally overseas director based in country – assisted by in country representative. In Cambodia projects are managed by an expatriate and supported by a full time Outreach representative.
Interviews: Interviews in London, Derby, Bristol or Somerset.
Worldwide placements: Central America (Mexico); South America (Ecuador); Asia (Cambodia).

OXFAM

62 Cotham Hill
Bristol
BS6 6JX UK
T: 01179 734335
F: 01179 731449
E: mbmclaughl@oxfam.org.uk
Contact: Mandi Boyd McLaughlin

Oxfam was founded in 1942 and is now one of the largest agencies working with development issues around the world. Its work overseas has two dimensions: as well as being able to respond to emergencies, Oxfam works with local people in their quest for basic rights – health, education, a decent standard of living, etc. It funds numerous small-scale projects, which are usually the initiative of the local people – real grass-roots development. In the UK and Ireland, work is constantly going on in the fields of campaigning and public education, raising awareness and raising issues with influential people. Most of the money needed to fund all this work is raised by volunteers and the famous Oxfam shops provide most of this money, as well as giving the volunteer useful skills and experience in the workplace. As the majority of these shops are run entirely by volunteers, positions of responsibility are shared among volunteers and so opportunities can exist, for the right person, to make a substantial contribution to shop management. Volunteers with a prison record are accepted. ♿

Number of projects: 800 UK: 800
Starting months: January–December
Time required: 1–52 weeks
Age: 14 plus – no upper limit
Causes: Animal Welfare, Children, Disabled (physical), Elderly People, Environmental Causes, Health Care/Medical, Human Rights, Poor/Homeless, Refugees.
Activities: Accountancy, Administration, Development Issues, Driving, Fundraising, Marketing/Publicity, Technical Skills, Training.
Placements: 27,000
When to apply: All year.
Work alone/with others: With others.
Qualifications: Generally nil but for training, driving etc. yes. We welcome volunteers from all ethnic backgrounds. No restrictions on nationalities.
Health requirements: Nil.
Costs: Accommodation and food.
Benefits: Travel expenses can be reimbursed.
Training: Pre-placement and on-the-job training is provided as necessary.
Supervision: Depending on the role, a supervisor is allocated as appropriate.
Interviews: Volunteer applicants are interviewed at the shop or locally.
Charity number: 202918
UK placements: England (throughout); Scotland (throughout); Northern Ireland (throughout); Wales (throughout).

OXFORD CENTRE FOR ENABLEMENT, CONTINUING DISABILITY MANAGEMENT SERVICE

Oxford Centre for Enablement
Nuffield Orthopaedic Centre, Windmill Road
Headington, Oxford
OX3 7LD UK
T: 01865 737260
F: 01865 227294
E: barbara.martin@noc.anglox.nhs.uk
Contact: Mrs Barbara Martin

The Continuing Disability Management Service, part of the Oxford Centre for Enablement is sited at the Nuffield Orthopaedic Centre in Headington, Oxford. It is a specialist service for people with disabilities. The aims of the unit are to encourage self-sufficiency and to foster interests among the clients; to forge links between them, their relatives and friends, volunteers, community workers and other clients; to work together for social interaction and life-enhancing activities, so as to improve their opportunities and welfare.

Number of projects: 1 **UK:** 1
Starting months: January–December
Time required: 1–52 weeks
Age: 17–65
Causes: Disabled (physical), Health Care/Medical, Holidays for Disabled.
Activities: Caring (general and day), Computers, Cooking, Fundraising, Gardening/Horticulture.
Placements: 30
When to apply: All year.
Work alone/with others: Both.
Qualifications: Excellent communication skills, initiative, sensitivity to caring needs.
Equipment/clothing: Flat shoes. Aprons provided if needed.
Health requirements: Usually none but medical details must be submitted.
Costs: Find own accommodation and possible contribution if carers go on holiday.
Benefits: Rewarding and satisfying.
Training: Only induction is provided and training for assisting with meals.
Supervision: Voluntary services organiser available 9–12, five days a week.
Interviews: Interviews take place at the Oxford Centre for Enablement.
Charity number: 278109
UK placements: England (Oxfordshire).

OXFORD KILBURN CLUB

45 Denmark Road
Kilburn
London
NW6 5BP UK
T: +44 (0) 20 7361 624 6292
F: +44 (0) 20 7361 372 6598
E: enquiries@okclub.org.uk
W: www.okclub.org.uk
Contact: Richard Springer

This club operates under a charity named the Oxford Boys' Club Trust, but is known as the OK Club locally. The club aims to meet the spiritual, physical, social, educational and recreational needs of young people and their families living in the area, and it runs a range of youth and children's clubs in the afternoons and evenings. It is also involved in schools work, work with local churches and other youth organisations in the area. The volunteer's job is to assist in all areas of the club which aims to help children and young people in this neighbourhood. Volunteers may be required to do any number of activities from attending club nights, visiting children in their homes, organising small after school clubs for junior children, giving support to children with special needs, participating in club holidays, organising activities and relating to individuals in the 8–18 years age group. Accommodation is provided on-site in a communal house, and pocket money is given to volunteers. The club is run by Christians and one of its aims is to present the gospel of Jesus Christ to the children in the area. South Kilburn. &

Number of projects: 1 **UK:** 1
Starting months: Sep
Time required: 52 weeks (plus)
Age: 18–29
Causes: Children, Inner City Problems, Refugees, Teaching/assisting, Young People.
Activities: Administration, Arts/Crafts, Community Work, Cooking, DIY, Fundraising, Music, Religion, Social Work, Sport, Summer Camps, Theatre/Drama.
Placements: 3
When to apply: By March for September start
Work alone/with others: Both but mostly with others.
Qualifications: Enthusiasm, commitment and Christianity.
Equipment/clothing: Casual and sporting clothes and equipment.
Health requirements: Nil.
Benefits: Board and lodging, travel costs and pocket money (£25 per week) + food. On-site residential block. Own room and communal facilities.
Training: Induction training covering basic health and safety, youth work, introduction to organisation policy and procedure etc.
Supervision: Supervised by senior youth worker, meet fortnightly.
Interviews: Interviews take place at the Oxford Kilburn Club.
Charity number: 306108
UK placements: England (London).

PACT CENTRE FOR YOUTH LTD

The Firehouse
21 Gordon Street
Paisley
Renfrewshire PA1 1XD UK
T: 0141 849 1149 or 0141 884 8199
F: 0141 849 1149
Contact: David Palmer

PACT is Paisley Action of Churches Together. The Youth Section has taken over the Old Fire Station and is transforming it into a Centre for Youth to serve the town of Paisley and the surrounding District. There will be a wide variety of facilities and amenities open to all young people whatever their background, creed, etc. The centre is served by full-time and part-time employed and voluntary staff. On the ground floor there is a youth centre with an emphasis on a discotheque/live bands arena, alcohol-free bar and cafe. The centre will encourage young people in personal (health, fitness and employment-potential) and social development and focus on training in the arts and performing arts. First floor will have a Youth Advice Centre, a point of first reference for any young person who will be put in touch with the particular resource needed. Also on this floor there will be accommodation for homeless young people. Paisley district. 📄

Number of projects: 1 UK: 1
Starting months: January–December
Time required: 1–52 weeks (plus)
Age: 18–35
Causes: Addicts/Ex-Addicts, Children, Disabled (learning and physical), Inner City Problems, Offenders/Ex-Offenders, Unemployed, Young People.
Activities: Arts/Crafts, Counselling, Fundraising, Group Work, Library/Resource Centres, Music, Newsletter/Journalism, Sport, Technical Skills.
Placements: 5–10
When to apply: Any time.
Work alone/with others: With others.
Health requirements: Nil.
Costs: Travel only.
Training: As required.
Supervision: Yes.
Interviews: Interviews take place at the Firehouse.
Charity number: SCO24331
UK placements: Scotland (Glasgow City).

PADDINGTON ARTS

32 Woodfield Road
London
W9 2BE UK
T: +44 (0) 207 286 2722
T: +44 (0) 207 286 0654
E: info@padarts.idps.co.uk
Contact: Steve Shaw

Paddington Arts started in 1983, under the umbrella of the Paddington Farm Trust – a community organisation committed to bridging the gap between city and country life, and now the proud owner of a residential centre and 42 acre farm in Somerset. Trips to the farm have played a key part in our development, not only because of the burst of energy and creativity unleashed by going out of one's usual environment, but because our early trips provided the ideas and experiences for a children's television series, 'Running Loose', which was a popular hit with young people, and helped us set up regular dance and drama workshops in London, which have been running ever since. In 1992 we were able to acquire our own building in the area. This has enabled us to develop other workshops, such as video, scriptwriting, music and design, as well as providing us with much needed office equipment and rehearsal space. In 1997 we redeveloped our building to include a dance/drama studio, a video edit suite and a large hall for rehearsals and performances. Volunteers with an offending background are accepted. ♿ 📄

Number of projects: 1 UK: 1
Starting months: Jan, Apr, May, Sep, Oct
Time required: 1–52 weeks
Age: 15–26
Causes: Children, Disabled (learning and physical), Unemployed, Young People.
Activities: Arts/Crafts, Marketing/Publicity, Newsletter/Journalism, Theatre/Drama, Training.
Placements: 20
When to apply: All year.
Work alone/with others: With others.
Health requirements: Nil.
Costs: Food and accommodation.
Benefits: Travel expenses.
Training: Provided as necessary.
Supervision: Supervision is given.
Interviews: Interviews take place at Paddington Arts.
Charity number: 298879
UK placements: England (London).

PAHKLA CAMPHILLI KULA

Prillimae
Rapla Maakond
Eesti EE 79702
Estonia
T: 00 372 48 34430
F: 00 372 48 97231
Contact: The Director

Pahkla Camphilli Küla is a Camphill land-based
rural community for adults with special needs. 📖

Number of projects: 1 UK: 0
Starting months: January–December
Time required: 52 weeks
Age: 20–50
Causes: Disabled (learning).
Activities: Agriculture/Farming, Arts/Crafts,
Caring – General, Cooking, Driving, Gardening/
Horticulture, Group Work, Manual Work,
Outdoor Skills, Social Work.
Placements: 2
When to apply: All year.
Work alone/with others: With others.
Equipment/clothing: Normal everyday clothes
for Estonian climate.
Health requirements: Nil.
Costs: Return travel to Estonia.
Benefits: Board and lodging.
Training: Not necessary.
Supervision: We expect independent people
who can do work responsibly after being
introduced to it.
Worldwide placements: Europe (Estonia).

PALESTINIAN ASSOCIATION FOR VOLUNTARY EFFORTS

PO Box 1828
Nablus
Palestine
T: 00 9729 237 6655
F: 00 9729 237 6655
E: fhassoneh@nethouse.net
Contact: Ferial Hassoneh

Palestinian Association for Voluntary Efforts
promotes and has information about
volunteering in Palestine. It may well be able to
put volunteers in touch with organisations
which are not yet listed on the WorldWide
Volunteering database.

Starting months: January–December
Time required: 1–52 weeks (plus)
Age: 16 plus – no upper limit
Causes: Addicts/Ex-Addicts, AIDS/HIV, Animal
Welfare, Archaeology, Architecture, Children,
Conservation, Disabled (learning and physical),
Elderly People, Environmental Causes, Health
Care/Medical, Heritage, Holidays for Disabled,
Human Rights, Inner City Problems, Offenders/
Ex-Offenders, Poor/Homeless, Refugees,
Teaching/assisting (nursery, primary, secondary,
mature, EFL) Unemployed, Wildlife, Work
Camps – Seasonal, Young People.
Activities: Accountancy, Administration,
Agriculture/Farming, Arts/Crafts, Building/
Construction, Campaigning, Caring (general,
day and residential), Catering, Community
Work, Computers, Conservation Skills,
Cooking, Counselling, Development Issues,
DIY, Driving, First Aid, Forestry, Fundraising,
Gardening/Horticulture, Group Work,
International Aid, Library/Resource Centres,
Manual Work, Marketing/Publicity, Music,
Newsletter/Journalism, Outdoor Skills, Religion,
Research, Scientific Work, Social Work, Sport,
Summer Camps, Teaching, Technical Skills,
Theatre/Drama, Training, Translating,
Visiting/Befriending, Work Camps – Seasonal.
Costs: Varies according to the project.
Worldwide placements: Asia (Palestinian
Authority).

PAPUA NEW GUINEA CHURCH PARTNERSHIP

Partnership House
157 Waterloo Road
London
SE1 8XA UK
T: +44 (0) 207 928 8681
E: pngcpluxton@aol.com
Contact: Chris Luxton

Number of projects: 1 UK: 0
Starting months: January–December
Time required: 26–52 weeks
Age: 20–59
Causes: Teaching/assisting.
Activities: Teaching.
Worldwide placements: Australasia (Papua
New Guinea).

PARISH OF EAST HAM NIGHT SHELTER

St. Bartholomews Church & Centre
292B Barking Road
East Ham
London E6 3BA UK
E: gordon116@vxtras.com
W: www.newhamnightshelter.fsbusiness.co.uk
Contact: Mr. Gordon P Owen

Time is the most precious gift you can offer to
give anyone. Night shelters are usually opened
for the homeless for five months of the winter
season by seven ecumenical churches in
partnership with Turnaround – Newham
renewal programme. Whether you have
professional expertise to offer e.g. cooking, chef
skills, counselling, or a general helping hand –
your time is welcome. Even if it is only one
Friday evening, there are ways to spend this
precious time to help to rebuild someone's life
away from the damaging streets. The project is

now in its ninth year and runs from 1st November to 28th March and caters for up to 30 homeless people. From next winter plans are in hand for a permanant all-year round night shelter in Newham for which volunteers are needed and would be valued. Underground – (District Line) – East Ham. Bus: 5, 15, 101, 147. 📧

Number of projects: 1 **UK:** 1
Starting months: Jan, Feb, Mar, Nov, Dec
Time required: 1–20 weeks
Age: 18 plus – no upper limit
Causes: Elderly People, Poor/Homeless.
Activities: Caring – General, Catering, Newsletter/Journalism.
When to apply: Any time.
Work alone/with others: With other volunteers.
Qualifications: No experience needed.
Equipment/clothing: Old clothes for working.
Health requirements: Reasonable good health.
Costs: Food and accommodation.
Training: Handbook and course.
Supervision: Monitored by co-ordinators.
Interviews: Interviews take place at the shelter in October and November.
UK placements: England (London).

PARTNERSHIP FOR SERVICE LEARNING, THE

815 Second Avenue
Suite 315
New York
NY 10017 USA
T: 00 1 212 986 0989
F: 00 1 212 986 5039
E: pslny@aol.com
W: www.ipsl.org
Contact:

The Partnership for Service-Learning, founded in 1982, is an incorporated not-for-profit consortium of colleges, universities, service agencies and related organisations united to foster and develop programmes linking community service and academic study. We hold that the joining of study and service: is a powerful means of learning; addresses human needs that would otherwise remain unmet, promotes intercultural/international literacy, advances the personal growth of students as members of the community, gives expression to the obligation of public and community service by educated people, sets academic institutions in right relationship to the larger society. We design and administer off-campus programmes combining service and academic study open to all qualified students and recent graduates for the semester, year, summer or January intersession overseas or in North Dakota (with Native Americans). We are governed by an International Board of Trustees including college presidents, deans and the executives of national education and service organisations. We also advise on the development of service-learning, making known the opportunities and experience of service-learning through research and publications, and hold international conferences open to college and university personnel, service agency supervisors and students, and attended by our directors from the various programme locations. Since 1982 nearly 4,000 students from over 300 colleges and universities have participated in our programmes for academic credit recognised by the students' home institutions. Although all over the UK, it may not be in every county listed. ♿

Number of projects: 1
Starting months: January–December
Time required: 26–52 weeks
Age: 18 plus – no upper limit
Causes: Addicts/Ex-Addicts, AIDS/HIV, Children, Disabled (learning and physical), Elderly People, Health Care/Medical, Holidays for Disabled, Inner City Problems, Offenders/Ex-Offenders, Poor/Homeless, Refugees, Teaching/assisting (nursery, primary, secondary, mature, EFL) Unemployed, Young People.
Activities: Arts/Crafts, Caring (general, day and residential), Community Work, Development Issues, Fundraising, Music, Sport, Teaching, Theatre/Drama.
When to apply: All year.
Qualifications: One year's study of relevant language for Mexico, Ecuador and France.
Costs: $3,000 + insurance, travel expenses and spending money.
Benefits: The cost covers board and accommodation + support and study expenses.
Worldwide placements: North America: (USA); Central America (Jamaica, Mexico); South America (Ecuador); Asia (India, Israel, Philippines); Europe (Czech Republic, France).
UK placements: England (throughout); Scotland (throughout); Northern Ireland (throughout); Wales (throughout).

PATTAYA ORPHANAGE

384 Moo 6
Sukhumvit Road
Pattaya City
Cholburi 20150 Thailand
T: (038) 716628
F: (038) 716629
E: volunteer@redemptorists.or.th
W: www.pattayaorphanage.net
Contact: Mr Derek Franklin

The Pattaya Orphanage is home to over 170 young Thai orphans, aging from newborn to university students. We provide a home for these children who have no families of their own, or for those whose families are too poor to look after them. Our other projects include a school for blind children, a school for deaf children, a home for the elderly and a home for street children. Our outreach worker visits the streets every night to try and persuade young children to join our home, away from a life of drugs, begging and prostitution. Our school for deaf children provides pre-school education such as sign language, lip reading and maths, which will enable these young children to go on to full time education at a regular school for deaf. Our school for the blind educates 170 children in life skills needed to become independent members of society. We may have placements for volunteers with an offending background depending on the offence. All volunteers are individually screened and are required to have a criminal background check. Pattaya is on the East Coast of Thailand. 📄

Number of projects: 5 **UK:** 0
Starting months: January–December
Time required: 26–52 weeks
Age: 18 plus – no upper limit
Causes: Children, Disabled (physical), Elderly People, Poor/Homeless, Teaching/assisting (EFL), Young People.
Activities: Caring (general, day and residential), Group Work, Social Work, Teaching.
Placements: 40
When to apply: As soon as possible.
Work alone/with others: Varies.
Health requirements: Must have health advice from GP in own country.
Costs: Volunteers to pay for own airfare, medical insurance and living expenses.
Benefits: We provide accommodation and food.
Training: Orientation on arrival and work description training.
Supervision: Supervision undertaken by on-site volunteer co-ordinator.
Interviews: May be invited to London for interview, or interviewed via telephone.
Worldwide placements: Asia (Thailand).

PAX CHRISTI

St Joseph's
Watford Way
London
N4 4TY UK
T: +44 (0) 208 203 4884
E: paxchristi@gn.apc.org
Contact: Pete Dunn

Pax Christi organises volunteers to work in an international team to provide hospitality and support for young people and children at summer camps. ♿

Number of projects: 5 **UK:** 4
Starting months: Jul, Aug

Time required: 3–4 weeks
Age: 19–30
Causes: Children, Young People.
Activities: Arts/Crafts, Community Work, Cooking, Driving, Music, Outdoor Skills, Sport, Summer Camps, Theatre/Drama.
When to apply: From February.
Work alone/with others: With others.
Qualifications: References checked.
Health requirements: Nil.
Costs: Own travel costs to either London or Northern Ireland + £5 registration fee.
Benefits: Board and lodging.
Interviews: Applicants are not interviewed.
UK placements: England (London); Northern Ireland (Belfast City, Tyrone).

PEACE BRIGADES INTERNATIONAL – COLOMBIA PROJECT

1a Waterlow Road
London
N19 5NJ UK
T: +44 (0) 207 687 0257
T: +44 (0) 207 272 4448
E: emma@pbicolombia.org
W: www.peacebrigades.org/colombia.html
Contact: Emma Eastwood

Peace Brigades International (PBI) has maintained a team of international observers/accompaniers in Colombia, since 1994. Our objective is to protect the political space of those human rights defenders and displaced communities who suffer repression of their non-violent work in defence of human rights. PBI works under petition of local organisations and is not affiliated to any religious or political group. We may be able to place volunteers with an offending background; case-by-case assessment. It will depend on offence and whether or not this restricts ability to gain Colombian visa. Colombia – Bogota, Barrancabermeja, Uraba, Medellin.

Number of projects: 1 **UK:** 0
Starting months: January–December
Time required: 52 weeks (plus)
Age: 25–99
Causes: Human Rights, Poor/Homeless Children, Young People
Activities: Administration, Computers, Community Work, Group Work, International Aid.
Placements: 40
When to apply: All year round.
Work alone/with others: With others.
Qualifications: Fluent Spanish. Experience working in non governmental organisations, social, human rights, groups etc. Most nationalities accepted.
Health requirements: We assess this case by case but volunteers need to be physically fit and able.

Costs: Nothing, travel board, lodging, end of placement grant, monthly stipend and paid holiday are all included.
Benefits: Travel, food and accommodation, insurance are all covered.
Training: Distance learning course and one week seminary prior to departure, continued training when in field.
Supervision: Project supervised by project committee of which volunteers are a part-horizontal organisation with non hierarchical structure.
Interviews: Yes, if in Spain face to face interviews are held, if not by telephone.
Worldwide placements: Columbia, Indonesia, Mexico, Guatemala.

PEACEWORK

209 Otey Street
Blacksburg
VA24060 USA
T: 01 540 953 1376
F: 540 953 0300
E: mail@peacework.org
W: www.peacework.org
Contact: Steve Darr

Peacework arranges international volunteer projects and service learning programmes for colleges, universities, schools, campus ministries and service organisations seeking to expand their knowledge and understanding of the global community. Projects combine meaningful volunteer service with opportunities to experience cultures and customs of people in different countries. We work in schools, orphanages and children's homes, clinics and medical services, agriculture, community development and housing. We are open to explore project possibilities in all countries, though we have current programmes in Belize, Honduras, Dominican Republic, Guatemala, Mexico, United States (Native Americans), Russia, Czech Republic, Vietnam and Kenya. Promoting peace and understanding through service and cross-cultural exchange, Peacework organises approximately 60 project trips and over 600 volunteers every year. We may be able to offer placements to volunteers with an offending background, depending on offence. &

Number of projects: 60 UK: 0
Starting months: January–December
Time required: 1–3 weeks
Age: 16 plus – no upper limit
Causes: Conservation, Health Care/Medical, Poor/Homeless, Teaching/assisting (primary, secondary), Young People.
Activities: Agriculture/Farming, Community Work, Development Issues, Group Work, Manual Work, Social Work, Teaching.
Placements: 500–600

When to apply: Two months before start of project.
Work alone/with others: With others.
Qualifications: No – though building skills and foreign languages are helpful.
Health requirements: No restrictions.
Costs: Volunteers pay for all costs. Projects normally range from US$500–$900. Plus airfare, health and travel insurance.
Benefits: Accommodation in country.
Training: Training on-site by our local partners.
Supervision: We require a group leader among the volunteers, the group leader will be on hand for supervision.
Interviews: No interview – group leaders are interviewed.
Worldwide placements: Africa (Kenya); North America: (USA); Central America (Belize, Dominican Republic, Guatemala, Honduras, Mexico); South America (Guyana); Asia (Vietnam); Europe (Czech Republic, Russia).

PENNINE CAMPHILL COMMUNITY

Boyne Hill
Chapelthorpe
Wakefield
West Yorkshire WF4 3JH UK
T: 01924 255281
F: 01924 240257
E: student@pennine.org.uk
W: www.pennine.org.uk
Contact: Steve Hopewell

Pennine offers further education and training for young people with learning difficulties or disabilities. Pennine is part of the Camphill movement founded in 1939 in Scotland by Dr Karl Konig. Since then over 80 centres in 17 countries have been established providing schooling, further education and working communities for adults. We are approximately 24 co-workers and their families. There is always a strong international element with co-workers coming from many different countries. About half of the co-workers live at the Pennine on a permanent basis and half have come for a year or more to help. There are no separate staff rooms apart from your own room. Co-workers and students take their meals together in the houses. Some will have helped with the growing of the produce, cooking the meal or perhaps just laying the tables. Personal preferences and experiences are obviously taken into account when arranging activities but an underlying strength of the co-worker group is the wish to help the needs of those we care for. Working at the Pennine is more a way of life and living with and sharing in interests with the students often blurs what is free time and what is work. It is a common wish that we live in a community where each works towards a common aim, to help each other's potential and awaken a sense of responsibility and interest in the world and for each other. Volunteers with an offending background may be accepted in special circumstances. Wakefield. ▤

Number of projects: 1 UK: 1
Starting months: January–December
Time required: 26–52 weeks
Age: 18 plus – no upper limit
Causes: Disabled (learning), Teaching/assisting (mature), Young People.
Activities: Agriculture/Farming, Arts/Crafts, Building/Construction, Caring – General, Catering, Cooking, DIY, Gardening/Horticulture, Manual Work, Outdoor Skills, Teaching, Training.
Placements: 15–20
When to apply: All year.
Work alone/with others: With others.
Health requirements: Nil.
Costs: Initial travel to Wakefield.
Benefits: Board and lodging + £25 per week with additional holiday money. We have four houses where the co-workers and students live alongside each other. Own room, shared mealtimes and dining facilities.
Training: Brochures and information provided. Visits welcomed or contact with people who have volunteered in the past. An induction programme covering working essentials and our core philosophy.
Supervision: Supervision and assistance is always available.
Interviews: Prospective volunteers are interviewed at the Pennine community, Wakefield.
Charity number: 274192
UK placements: England (W. Yorkshire).

PERSONAL OVERSEAS DEVELOPMENT LIMITED

7 Rosbury House
Putney
London SW15 2EY UK
T: 07880 707736
E: info@thepodsite.co.uk
W: www.thepodsite.co.uk
Contact: Mr Mike Beecham

Personal Overseas Development (PoD) co-ordinates career breaks, time off and gap years for people from the UK wishing to volunteer their time and skills where they are needed. We arrange placements for people looking to do something worthwhile in their gap year out or break from work. We provide opportunities for voluntary work with development charities or similar organisations in a developing world environment. Our current programme locations are in Africa and South America. Through every project that PoD is involved with we aim to ensure benefits for the volunteers, our partners in these countries and most importantly the

local population. Projects are flexible in length and type of work, so if volunteers have specific requests we are often able to accommodate them. Unfortunately, we are unable to place volunteers with an offending background. The East Usambara Mountains near Tanga in Tanzania and Cusco and surroundings in Peru. ▤

Number of projects: 2 UK: 0
Starting months: Jan, Apr, Sep
Time required: 12–24 weeks
Age: 17 plus – no upper limit
Causes: Children, Disabled (learning and physical), Health Care/Medical, Poor/Homeless, Teaching/assisting (nursery, primary, secondary, EFL).
Activities: Caring – General, International Aid, Marketing/Publicity, Social Work, Teaching.
Placements: 50–100
When to apply: Three months before starting.
Work alone/with others: With others.
Qualifications: No, just suitable references.
Health requirements: Due to remoteness of projects, volunteers must be in good health.
Costs: Flights to Tanzania and Peru are usually between £400–£3600. Visa about £40 for Tanzania and free for Peru. All other costs are included in programme fee of £2500.
Benefits: Accommodation and food. In Tanzania, volunteers are housed in a purpose built mud hut village or rented tin roof local accommodation. In Peru volunteers live in rented flats or apartments. Volunteers live with other volunteers.
Training: A weekend pre-departure training offered and a four to six day training programme on arrival, tailored to chosen project.
Supervision: Volunteers live together in groups of two to twelve and are with supervisors a couple of miles away. A meeting is held every week during the project phase, more often if problems arise.
Interviews: Interviews are only held if references leave questions as to the suitability of the volunteer. Interviews would then be held at a mutually accessible hotel location.
Worldwide placements: Africa (Tanzania); South America (Peru).

PETADISTS COMMUNITY ORGANISATION

37 Pentland House
Stamford Hill
London
N16 6RP UK
T: +44 (0) 208 802 4987
E: petadism@btconnect.com
Contact: Mr Peter Amadi

We run an African Development Education Centre (ADEC) which makes education resource materials that facilitate teaching as well as learning. We make, for example, educational calendars focusing on issues like race education, health education, political education, road safety education, refugee welfare education etc. We publish a total of 13 different calendars. We also indulge in activities such as employment training activities. Unemployed people will be taught all the skills involved in making the education resource materials such as desktop publishing skills, designing skills, marketing skills, administration skills, finance skills, computer aided design and other employment skills. We have a branch in Africa that does all the activities listed above as well. &

Number of projects: 1 **UK:** 1
Starting months: January–December
Time required: 8–20 weeks
Age: 17–60
Causes: Conservation, Environmental Causes, Health Care/Medical, Human Rights, Inner City Problems, Poor/Homeless, Refugees, Teaching (primary, secondary, mature, EFL), Unemployed, Wildlife, Young People.
Activities: Accountancy, Administration, Agriculture/Farming, Building/Construction, Community Work, Computers, Conservation Skills, Counselling, Development Issues, Fundraising, Group Work, International Aid, Marketing/Publicity, Music, Newsletter/Journalism, Sport, Teaching, Training, Visiting/Befriending, Work Camps – Seasonal.
Placements: 50
When to apply: All year.
Work alone/with others: With other young volunteers.
Qualifications: Computer literacy skills.
Health requirements: Nil.
Costs: Travel to West Africa.
Benefits: Accommodation.
Training: Induction on the project, way of life of the people, cultural differences etc.
Supervision: Supervision is provided both from London and locally in the country.
Interviews: Interviews take place in London.
Charity number: 1017691
Worldwide placements: Africa (Cameroon, Gambia, Ghana, Nigeria).
UK placements: England (London).

PGL TRAVEL

Alton Court
Penyard Lane
Ross-on-Wye
Herefordshire HR9 5GL UK
T: 01989 767833
F: 01989 767760
E: pglpeople@pgl.co.uk
W: www.pgl.co.uk/people
Contact: PGL People Team

PGL Travel is Europe's leading provider of activity holidays and courses for children. School groups visit our centres in the UK, France and Spain between February and October. We also run summer camps for unaccompanied children during the Easter and summer holidays. People are needed to help run our 25 activity centres. Positions available include childcare worker, activity instructor, catering staff and support staff. All applicants must gain satisfactory disclosure from the Criminal Records Bureau before an offer of employment can be taken up. A police record for certain offences will not necessarily prevent you from working at PGL, but you must declare any offences on your application form. &

Number of projects: 29 **UK:** 19
Starting months: Feb, Mar, Apr, May, Jun, Jul, Aug, Sep, Oct
Time required: 6–37 weeks
Age: 18 plus – no upper limit
Causes: Children, Young People.
Activities: Administration, Agriculture/Farming, Caring – General, Catering, Computers, Cooking, Driving, First Aid, Manual Work, Outdoor Skills, Sport, Summer Camps, Theatre/Drama, Training, Work Camps – Seasonal.
Placements: 2,500
When to apply: From September.
Work alone/with others: Both.
Qualifications: Varies according to job. Applications will only be accepted from candidates with a legal right to work in the UK (i.e. EC and Commonwealth).
Equipment/clothing: Supplied.
Health requirements: Nil.
Costs: Occasionally, travel to project.
Benefits: Food, accommodation + approx. £50 per week. Travel in Europe normally provided too.
Training: Full training will be provided for all positions.
Supervision: Staff report to a line manager.
Interviews: Applicants are not generally interviewed but will be expected to complete a probationary period.
Worldwide placements: Europe (France, Spain).
UK placements: England (Devon, Herefordshire, Isle of Wight, Lancashire, Oxfordshire, Shropshire, Surrey, Sussex – West, Worcestershire); Scotland (Perth and Kinross); Wales (Powys).

PHAB ENGLAND

Summit House
Wandle Road
Croydon
Surrey CRO 1DF UK

T: +44 (0) 208 667 9443
E: info@phabengland.org.uk
W: www.phabengland.org.uk
Contact: Philip Lockwood

PHAB England exists to integrate people with and without physical disabilities. It has 300 or so clubs throughout the country who meet on a regular basis. Local volunteers are always welcome. Volunteers with an offending background are accepted. ♿ 📄

Number of projects: 5 UK: 5
Starting months: January–December
Time required: 1–52 weeks
Age: 16 plus – no upper limit
Causes: Children, Disabled (physical), Holidays for Disabled, Young People.
Activities: Administration, Driving, Newsletter/ Journalism, Outdoor Skills.
Placements: 20
When to apply: All year.
Work alone/with others: With others.
Qualifications: Driving licence.
Health requirements: Nil.
Costs: Travel costs.
Benefits: Financial assistance in respect of holidays.
Interviews: Interviews are conducted local to the project, i.e. all over England.
Charity number: 283931
UK placements: England (throughout).

PHAB Northampton

Bushland Road
Headlands
Northampton
Northamptonshire NN3 2HP UK
T: 01604 405693
E: phabbers@care4free.net
Contact: Mr J N Franks

PHAB Northampton is a local charity providing social activities for people with and without physical disabilities. It is dedicated to promoting the integration of disabled and able-bodied people, at all levels of society, on equal terms. The club has its own club premises in a former school canteen. ♿

Number of projects: 1 UK: 1
Starting months: January–December
Time required: 1–52 weeks
Age: 14 plus – no upper limit
Causes: Children, Disabled (learning and physical), Young People.
Activities: Administration, Driving, Newsletter/Journalism, Outdoor Skills.
When to apply: All year.
Work alone/with others: Varies.
Equipment/clothing: The club provides all equipment.
Health requirements: All disabilities are

accepted as members.
Costs: 50p subscription weekly for members.
Training: No training offered.
Supervision: Volunteers with a lot of caring experience provide supervision.
Interviews: Volunteers are required to complete an application form and provide full medical hisory.
UK placements: England (Northamptonshire).

PHAB SW

P.O. Box 58
Chard
Somerset TA20 3YT UK
T: 01460 234422
F: 01460 234422
E: hazelapps@hotmail.com
Contact: Mrs H. Apps

PHAB SW promotes and encourages people with and without physical disabilities to come together on equal terms, to achieve complete integration within the wider community. PHAB organises: clubs which belong to and are run by disabled and abled bodied people; area, divisional, and national structures for support, development, training, events; training through working with PHAB in the community through workshops and conferences; special emphasis on work with children and young people, through junior PHAB clubs; residential holidays; links and exchanges with similar groups; an information service for booklets, films and speakers. ♿

Number of projects: Many UK: Many
Starting months: January–December
Time required: 1–52 weeks
Age: 17 plus – no upper limit
Causes: Children, Disabled (physical), Elderly People, Young People.
Activities: Administration, Arts/Crafts, Community Work, Fundraising, Group Work, Newsletter/Journalism, Summer Camps, Training.
When to apply: All year.
Work alone/with others: Both.
Health requirements: No requirements.
Costs: Nil.
Benefits: If on the holidays, volunteers are included in the accommodation with the whole group.
Training: All junior holidays have a training session.
Supervision: All volunteers are supervised by a group leader, administrator of the project and medical appointee.
Interviews: Applicants are interviewed somewhere convenient to the volunteer.
UK placements: England (Bristol, Channel Islands, Cornwall, Devon, Dorset, Gloucestershire, Hampshire, Isle of Wight, Somerset, Wiltshire).

PHILIPPINE NATIONAL VOLUNTEER SERVICE COORDINATING AGENCY (PNVSCA)

Room 301, Cabrera Building 1
130 Timog Avenue
Quezon City
The Philippines
T: 00 63 2 922 8635
Contact: Dr. Virginia P. Davide

Philippine National Volunteer Service Coordinating Agency (PNVSCA) promotes and has information about volunteering in the Philippines. It may well be able to put volunteers in touch with organisations which are not yet listed on the WorldWide Volunteering database.

Starting months: January–December
Time required: 1–52 weeks (plus)
Age: 16 plus – no upper limit
Causes: Addicts/Ex-Addicts, AIDS/HIV, Animal Welfare, Archaeology, Architecture, Children, Conservation, Disabled (learning and physical), Elderly People, Environmental Causes, Health Care/Medical, Heritage, Holidays for Disabled, Human Rights, Inner City Problems, Offenders/ Ex-Offenders, Poor/Homeless, Refugees, Teaching/assisting (nursery, primary, secondary, mature, EFL) Unemployed, Wildlife, Work Camps – Seasonal, Young People.
Activities: Accountancy, Administration, Agriculture/Farming, Arts/Crafts, Building/ Construction, Campaigning, Caring (general, day and residential), Catering, Community Work, Computers, Conservation Skills, Cooking, Counselling, Development Issues, DIY, Driving, First Aid, Forestry, Fundraising, Gardening/Horticulture, Group Work, International Aid, Library/Resource Centres, Manual Work, Marketing/Publicity, Music, Newsletter/Journalism, Outdoor Skills, Religion, Research, Scientific Work, Social Work, Sport, Summer Camps, Teaching, Technical Skills, Theatre/Drama, Training, Translating, Visiting/Befriending, Work Camps – Seasonal.
Costs: Varies according to the project.
Worldwide placements: Asia (Philippines).

PHOENIX YCP LTD

Unit 14
Bluestone Business Centre
Moyraverty Road West
Craigavon
BT65 5HE N. Ireland
T: 028 3832 7614
F: 028 3832 7614
Contact: Pearl Snowden

Phoenix YCP organises cross community youth work with children aged between 7 and 13 years such as indoor/outdoor games, drama,

music, art/crafts, environmental work, discussion groups, swimming, day trips, residentials. Lurgan, Co. Armagh. &

Number of projects: 1 UK: 1
Starting months: Jul, Aug
Time required: 4–52 weeks
Age: 18 plus – no upper limit
Causes: Children.
Activities: Arts/Crafts, Music, Sport, Summer Camps, Theatre/Drama.
Placements: 40
When to apply: Between 1st September and 30th April.
Work alone/with others: With others.
Qualifications: Must have previous experience working with children.
Costs: Travel expenses + €65 for board, lodging and a social programme.
Interviews: Applicants are not interviewed.
Charity number: XN 75547
UK placements: Northern Ireland (Armagh).

PIONEER MADAGASCAR

Suite 7
1a Beethoven Street
London
W10 4LG UK
T: +44 (0) 208 960 6629
F: +44 (0) 208 962 0126
E: azafady@easynet.co.uk
W: www.madagascar.co.uk
Contact: Pioneer Co-ordinator

Pioneer Madagascar has been set up by Azafady, a registered UK-based charity and a Madagascar-based NGO. Through Pioneer Madagascar, volunteers can experience working with a grass-roots organisation combating the problems of extensive deforestation and extreme poverty on this unique island. The programme focuses on integrated conservation and development initiatives which work closely with the Malagasy people. Each scheme lasts ten weeks, places are limited and approximately 75% of the costs go directly to running the projects. During placements volunteers will learn to speak basic Malagasy and gather skills relevant to working in the field of development, conservation and sustainable livelihoods. Our projects are led by some of the most competent conservationists and development workers on the island; they are based on communities' expressed needs and therefore provide an insight for volunteers into real on-the-ground work – they are not set up simply for volunteers. Volunteers will work on an extensive array of projects from beach surveys of endangered turtles to the building of wells. Further details and application form can be found on our web site. Volunteers with an offending background may be accepted subject to the application process. South East Madagascar in the region of Fort Dauphin. ♿ ▤

Number of projects: 4 UK: 0
Starting months: Jan, Apr, Jul, Oct
Time required: 10–10 weeks
Age: 18–65
Causes: Animal Welfare, Children, Conservation, Environmental Causes, Health Care/Medical, Wildlife.
Activities: Agriculture/Farming, Building/ Construction, Community Work, Conservation Skills, Development Issues, Forestry, Manual Work, Outdoor Skills, Research, Scientific Work, Social Work, Technical Skills.
Placements: 60
When to apply: As soon as possible.
Work alone/with others: With others.
Equipment/clothing: No specific equipment required although certain equipment may be of use.
Health requirements: No health/medical restrictions however all applicants are subject to a selection process where overall suitability will be accessed.
Costs: Volunteers are expected to raise a 'minimum donation' of £2000 and expected to pay flight £800, insurance £100, visa £40 and medical preparations.
Benefits: Support is given for fundraising. Basic accommodation provided.
Training: All training necessary for conservation and development projects is provided in the field.
Supervision: On arrival at the project, full supervision is provided during the week.
Interviews: There is no formal interview. Applicants are subject to a selection process which may result in an informal interview by phone or in the London office.
Charity number: 1079121
Worldwide placements: Africa (Madagascar).

PLAN INTERNATIONAL

5–6 Underhill Street
Camden
London
NW1 7HS UK
T: +44 (0) 20 7361 485 6612
F: +44 (0) 20 7361 485 2107
E: dora.sankoh@plan-international.org
W: www.plan-international.org.uk
Contact: Dora Sankoh

Plan International is a child sponsorship charity helping to create lasting improvements in the lives of children, their families and communities in the developing world. Our projects include immunisation, education, sanitation, agro-forestation, Aids awareness, credit schemes and improving farming techniques. Although our work is centred

abroad, our volunteers in the UK help with administration in various departments including finance, enrolment, marketing and communications. Please feel free to ring for further details. Volunteers with an offending background may be accepted – each case would be considered separately. ♿

Number of projects: 1 UK: 1
Starting months: January–December
Time required: 1–52 weeks
Age: 16 plus – no upper limit
Causes: AIDS/HIV, Children, Teaching/assisting.
Activities: Computers, Development Issues, International Aid, Research.
Placements: 35
When to apply: All year.
Work alone/with others: With other young volunteers.
Qualifications: Literate and numerate.
Health requirements: Nil.
Costs: Food and accommodation.
Benefits: Travel reimbursed up to £5 per day. £3.00 per day for lunch if more than 5 hours worked.
Training: None.
Supervision: 2 members of staff look after the volunteers full time.
Interviews: Interviews take place in our London office.
Charity number: 276035
Worldwide placements: Africa (Benin, Burkina Faso, Cameroon, Egypt, Ethiopia, Ghana, Guinea, Guinea-Bissau, Kenya, Malawi, Mali, Niger, Senegal, Sierra Leone, Sudan, Tanzania, Togo, Uganda, Zambia, Zimbabwe); Central American (Dominican Republic, El Salvador, Guatemala, Haiti, Honduras, Nicaragua); South America (Bolivia, Brazil, Colombia, Ecuador, Paraguay, Peru); Asia (Bangladesh, China, India, Indonesia, Nepal, Pakistan, Philippines, Sri Lanka, Thailand, Vietnam); Europe (Albania).
UK placements: England (London).

PLATFORMA PARA LA PROMOCION DEL VOLUNTARIADO EN ESPANA

C/Amador de los Rios
5 Bajo
Madrid 28010
Spain
T: 00 34 91 319 99 98
F: 00 34 91 319 99 99
Contact: Kristin Maso

Platforma para la Promocion del Voluntariado en Espana promotes and has information about volunteering in Spain. It may well be able to put volunteers in touch with organisations which are not yet listed on the WorldWide Volunteering database.

Starting months: January–December
Time required: 1–52 weeks (plus)

Age: 16 plus – no upper limit
Causes: Addicts/Ex-Addicts, AIDS/HIV, Animal Welfare, Archaeology, Architecture, Children, Conservation, Disabled (learning and physical), Elderly People, Environmental Causes, Health Care/Medical, Heritage, Holidays for Disabled, Human Rights, Inner City Problems, Offenders/Ex-Offenders, Poor/Homeless, Refugees, Teaching/assisting (nursery, primary, secondary, mature, EFL) Unemployed, Wildlife, Work Camps – Seasonal, Young People.
Activities: Accountancy, Administration, Agriculture/Farming, Arts/Crafts, Building/Construction, Campaigning, Caring (general, day and residential), Catering, Community Work, Computers, Conservation Skills, Cooking, Counselling, Development Issues, DIY, Driving, First Aid, Forestry, Fundraising, Gardening/Horticulture, Group Work, International Aid, Library/Resource Centres, Manual Work, Marketing/Publicity, Music, Newsletter/Journalism, Outdoor Skills, Religion, Research, Scientific Work, Social Work, Sport, Summer Camps, Teaching, Technical Skills, Theatre/Drama, Training, Translating, Visiting/Befriending, Work Camps – Seasonal.
Costs: Varies according to the project.
Worldwide placements: Europe (Spain).

POINTS OF LIGHT FOUNDATION – USA, THE

1400 I Street NW
Washington
DC 20005 USA
T: 00 1 202 729 8000
F: 00 1 202 729 8100
E: info@pointsoflight.org
W: www.pointsoflight.org
Contact: Mei Cobb

The Points of Light Foundation promotes and has information about volunteering in the United States of America. It may well be able to put volunteers in touch with organisations which are not yet listed on the WorldWide Volunteering database.

Starting months: January–December
Time required: 1–52 weeks (plus)
Age: 16 plus – no upper limit
Causes: Addicts/Ex-Addicts, AIDS/HIV, Animal Welfare, Archaeology, Architecture, Children, Conservation, Disabled (learning and physical), Elderly People, Environmental Causes, Health Care/Medical, Heritage, Holidays for Disabled, Human Rights, Inner City Problems, Offenders/Ex-Offenders, Poor/Homeless, Refugees, Teaching/assisting (nursery, primary, secondary, mature, EFL) Unemployed, Wildlife, Work Camps – Seasonal, Young People.
Activities: Accountancy, Administration, Agriculture/Farming, Arts/Crafts, Building/Construction, Campaigning, Caring (general, day and residential), Catering, Community Work, Computers, Conservation Skills, Cooking, Counselling, Development Issues, DIY, Driving, First Aid, Forestry, Fundraising, Gardening/Horticulture, Group Work, International Aid, Library/Resource Centres, Manual Work, Marketing/Publicity, Music, Newsletter/Journalism, Outdoor Skills, Religion, Research, Scientific Work, Social Work, Sport, Summer Camps, Teaching, Technical Skills, Theatre/Drama, Training, Translating, Visiting/Befriending, Work Camps – Seasonal.
Costs: Varies according to the project.
Worldwide placements: North America: (USA).

PORTAL DO VOLUNTARIO-Brazil

Rua Jardim Botanico
674/210 – Jardim Botanico
Rio de Janeiro – RJ
CEP 22461 – 000 Brazil
T: (21) 2512 1221/2512 4870
F: (21) 2512 1221/2512 4870
E: liara.pv@comunitas.org.br
W: www.portaldovoluntario.org.br
Contact: Volunteer Co-ordinator

Portal do Voluntario promotes and has information about volunteering in Brazil. It may well be able to put volunteers in touch with organisations which are not yet listed on the WorldWide Volunteering database.

Starting months: January–December
Time required: 1–52 weeks (plus)
Age: 16 plus – no upper limit
Causes: Addicts/Ex-Addicts, AIDS/HIV, Animal Welfare, Archaeology, Architecture, Children, Conservation, Disabled (learning and physical), Elderly People, Environmental Causes, Health Care/Medical, Heritage, Holidays for Disabled, Human Rights, Inner City Problems, Offenders/Ex-Offenders, Poor/Homeless, Refugees, Teaching/assisting (nursery, primary, secondary, mature, EFL) Unemployed, Wildlife, Work Camps – Seasonal, Young People.
Activities: Accountancy, Administration, Agriculture/Farming, Arts/Crafts, Building/Construction, Campaigning, Caring (general, day and residential), Catering, Community Work, Computers, Conservation Skills, Cooking, Counselling, Development Issues, DIY, Driving, First Aid, Forestry, Fundraising, Gardening/Horticulture, Group Work, International Aid, Library/Resource Centres, Manual Work, Marketing/Publicity, Music, Newsletter/Journalism, Outdoor Skills, Religion, Research, Scientific Work, Social Work, Sport, Summer Camps, Teaching, Technical Skills, Theatre/Drama, Training, Translating, Visiting/Befriending, Work Camps – Seasonal.
Costs: Costs vary according to the project.
Worldwide placements: South America (Brazil).

POW TRUST, THE

295a Queenstown Road
Battersea
London SW8 3NP UK
T: +44 (0) 20 7361 720 9767
F: +44 (0) 20 7361 948 0477
W: www.161restaurant.co.uk
Contact: Mr Peter Sainsbury

The POW Trust was established in 1992 by a group of five people with the specific intention of helping the afflicted and socially excluded in society. Recognising unemployment as one of the most significant factors resulting in social exclusion, the Trust always regarded finding employment for the socially excluded as one of its primary aims. The Trust has recently acquired Al's Bar and Restaurant, renaming it 161 Bar and Restaurant to reflect its new ownership. It enables us to offer employment directly to the socially excluded and equally important it is the embodiment of a successful business, which can flourish while pursuing humanitarian and socially responsible aims. The Trust is determined to undertake further projects similar to 161. As well as being an employer of the socially excluded the Trust operates a vigorous policy of helping the socially disadvantaged. The Trust funds and operates a legal department supporting those whom it perceives to have suffered a material miscarriage of justice, especially where legal aid or private funding is not available. We may be able to accept volunteers with an offending background. 🔗 📄

Number of projects: several **UK:** several
Starting months: January–December
Time required: 1 week
Age: 16 plus – no upper limit
Causes: Human Rights, Inner City Problems, Offenders/Ex-Offenders, Poor/Homeless, Unemployed.
Activities: Accountancy, Administration, Campaigning, Catering, Development Issues, Fundraising, Group Work, Social Work, Visiting/Befriending.
Placements: 20
When to apply: Any time.
Work alone/with others: Work with others.
Health requirements: No restrictions.
Costs: Travel costs and possible accommodation.
Benefits: There may be help with travel costs and possible accommodation for full time volunteers.
Training: On the spot training if required.
Supervision: POW management.
Interviews: Interviews are held in Battersea.
Charity number: 3381186
UK placements: England (London).

POWER – THE INTERNATIONAL LIMB PROJECT

Cutlers Court
Copyground Lane
High Wycombe
BucksHP12 3HE UK
T: 01494 464922
F: 01494 464933
E: power4limbs@lineone.net
W: www.power4limbs.org
Contact: Mrs Sarah Hodge

Power's mission is to establish sustainable services providing high quality artificial limbs to victims of conflict to restore their mobility, self-respect and quality of life, and to give first-class professional training in prosthetics and orthotics in low-income countries. Power is a small organisation set up in 1994. It is a member of the British Overseas NGOs for Development (BOND), The UK Working Group on Landmines, The International Campaign to Ban Landmines and the UK/EC NGO Network. It exists to help all who are motor-disabled and disadvantaged by so being. At present the only voluntary opportunities we have are short-term in the UK or for very experienced people overseas. However, applications from well-motivated people are always welcome, particularly if they are able to meet some expenses themselves. 🔗

Number of projects: 2 **UK:** 1
Starting months: January–December
Time required: 13–52 weeks
Age: 18–65
Causes: Disabled (physical).
Activities: Accountancy, Administration, Computers, Development Issues, Social Work.
Placements: 2
When to apply: All year.
Qualifications: 'A' level abilities. Computer literacy.
Health requirements: Must be in good health.
Costs: Travel – return air fares.
Benefits: Board and lodging. Pocket money.
Training: None.
Supervision: Volunteers are supervised by country director or administrator.
Interviews: Prospective volunteers are interviewed in Henley-on-Thames.
Charity number: 1059996
Worldwide placements: Africa (Mozambique); Asia (Laos).
UK placements: England (Oxfordshire).

PRETOMA SEA TURTLE PROTECTION PROGRAMME OF COSTA RICA

1203–1100 Tibas
San Jose
Costa Rica

T: (506) 241 6017
F: 506) 236 6017
E: info@tortugamarina.org
W: www.tortugamarina.org
Contact: Randall Arauz

PRETOMA is a non profit Civil Association, established in 1997 (CJ 3-002-212657), with headquarters in San Jose, Costa Rica. Our organisation is made up of biologists, naturalists, conservationalists, and citizens concerned with the plight of the sea turtles and the marine habitat in general. Our mission is to protect, conserve, and restore the populations of sea turtles that use the marine environment of Costa Rica to nest, feed or migrate. We seek to protect the diverse habitats along the Central American isthmus and international waters upon which turtle populations depend. Our volunteer projects are designed to:
1. Teach participants about the condition of endangered sea turtle populations.
2. Give participants hands-on-experience in helping restore turtle populations in Costa Rica.
3. Allow volunteers to work directly with locals in coastal communities and experience their culture.
4. Help build an international community of youth and people of all ages dedicated to responsible use of marine resources and protection of marine ecosystems.
Volunteers learn to sight, handle, measure and check the health of turtles on the beach at night when they nest, and record data collected. They also learn to tag flippers of the nesting turtles with internationally recognised tags. They also count eggs and transfer them from the beach to the PRETOMA hatchery near the station, where the eggs are monitored and protected until they hatch after a 45–55 day incubation period. Volunteers also release the hatchlings into the sea and investigate the hatchery nests after hatching occurs to determine hatching success rates and record this data. We unfortunately cannot accept volunteers with an offending background. Small villages on the Pacific coast of Costa Rica.

Number of projects: 1 UK: 0
Starting months: Jul, Aug, Sep, Oct, Nov, Dec
Time required: 1–20 weeks
Age: 18 plus – no upper limit
Causes: Animal Welfare, Conservation, Environmental Causes, Wildlife.
Activities: Community Work, Conservation Skills, Research, Scientific Work, Teaching.
Placements: 15–40
When to apply: Anytime between July and 1 December.
Work alone/with others: Work with others.
Qualifications: Willingness to work and live closely with other participants is a must. Spanish language skills are useful but not required.

Equipment/clothing: A list of recommended equipment is in the volunteer section of our web site, www.tortugamarina.org.
Health requirements: Bring any personal medication.
Costs: Varies depending on accommodation – see web site for more details. Flights and insurance.
Benefits: Accommodation and food included in programme cost. Stay at the PRETOMA station house in a small town – depending on numbers, rooms may be shared. There is a large communal room and shared bathroom facilities. Open air restaurant. Meals included in costs unless volunteers stay with host family.
Training: Volunteers learn to sight, handle, measure and check the health of turtles and record data collected. Also tagging, eggs, hatchery and releasing hatchlings training.
Supervision: Undertaken by two marine biology students, they teach techniques, explain accommodation, manage shifts and the project. Volunteers work as part of a team and are encouraged to foster a friendly station environment and to get to know the community.
Interviews: Generally via e-mail. Application form sent to volunteers who know when they would like to participate.
Worldwide placements: Central America (Costa Rica).

PRINCE'S TRUST, THE

18 Park Square East
London
NW1 4LH UK
T: +44 (0) 207 543 1234
T: +44 (0) 207 543 7423
E: info@princes-trust.org.uk
W: www.princes-trust.org.uk
Contact: The European Programme Team

More than 1.5 million young people in the UK are finding life particularly tough, facing problems like poverty, unemployment, discrimination, underachievement, family breakdown, homelessness and personal crisis. The European Programme aims to help them regain self-esteem, confidence, motivation and skills through the development of European projects and grant giving. European awards enable less confident young people to take the opportunity to go to another European country and take part in voluntary projects run by other organisations. This provides a structured experience with the challenge of inter-cultural learning. Applicants must be aged 18–25 and not be in full-time education or employment. We encourage applications from those who are long-term unemployed, have no or low educational qualifications, are in care or have left care, or have an offending background. Placements are available in a variety of European countries such as Poland, France, Sweden, Hungary and Italy. &

Number of projects: 3 UK: 0
Starting months: January–December
Time required: 2–3 weeks
Age: 18–25
Causes: Addicts/Ex-Addicts, AIDS/HIV, Animal
Welfare, Archaeology, Architecture, Children,
Conservation, Disabled (learning and physical),
Elderly People, Environmental Causes, Health
Care/Medical, Heritage, Holidays for Disabled,
Human Rights, Inner City Problems, Offenders/
Ex-Offenders, Poor/Homeless, Refugees,
Teaching/assisting (nursery), Unemployed,
Wildlife, Work Camps – Seasonal, Young
People.
Activities: Agriculture/Farming, Arts/Crafts,
Building/Construction, Caring (general, day and
residential), Community Work, Conservation
Skills, DIY, Forestry, Gardening/Horticulture,
Manual Work, Music, Outdoor Skills, Social
Work, Summer Camps, Teaching,
Theatre/Drama, Work Camps – Seasonal.
Placements: 100–200
When to apply: All year.
Work alone/with others: With others.
Qualifications: Applications encouraged from
those with no or low academic qualifications.
Must be resident in the UK.
Health requirements: Nil.
Costs: Nil.
Benefits: You are supported in the UK in
preparing to go abroad. You are supported on
your placement by a worker from your host
country and when you return to the UK you
will receive help with follow-on work such as
writing a CV, finding new opportunities etc.
Accommodation provided by the voluntary
work placement, e.g. youth hostel.
Training: Depends on the project.
Supervision: This varies on different
placements but there is supervision on all
projects.
Interviews: Prospective volunteers are
interviewed by a local assessor.
Charity number: 1018177
Worldwide placements: Europe (Albania,
Andorra, Armenia, Austria, Azerbaijan, Belarus,
Belgium, Bosnia-Herzegovina, Bulgaria, Croatia,
Cyprus, Czech Republic, Denmark, Estonia,
Finland, France, Georgia, Germany, Gibraltar,
Greece, Hungary, Iceland, Ireland, Italy, Latvia,
Liechtenstein, Lithuania, Luxembourg,
Macedonia, Malta, Moldova, Monaco,
Netherlands, Norway, Poland, Portugal,
Romania, Russia, San Marino, Slovakia,
Slovenia, Spain, Sweden, Switzerland, Turkey,
Ukraine, Yugoslavia).

PRINCESS MARINA CENTRE

Chalfont Road
Seer Green
Nr Beaconsfield

Buckinghamshire HP10 2QR UK
T: 01494 874231
F: 01494 871001
E: sue.dorman@virgin.net
Contact: John Inker

Princess Marina Centre (PMC) is a residential
centre which is part of Scope Eastern Region.
Scope exists to provide support and services for
people with cerebral palsy and their families.
The ongoing volunteer projects at PMC are
designed to support staff already working with
individuals to give greater scope for widening
opportunities. Volunteers provide escorts to a
range of social and educational venues, world of
work initiatives, therapy classes etc. We also
have opportunities for those wishing to use DIY
or gardening skills on our large site. Our arts
and crafts staff/tutors are always short of
assistance. People with an offending background
may be accepted depending on the offence. 🖹

Number of projects: 1 UK: 1
Starting months: January–December
Time required: 4–26 weeks
Age: 16 plus – no upper limit
Causes: Disabled (physical).
Activities: Arts/Crafts, Caring – Residential,
DIY, Driving, Gardening/Horticulture,
Visiting/Befriending.
Placements: 30+
When to apply: All year.
Work alone/with others: Both.
Qualifications: Driving licence an advantage.
Health requirements: Good health.
Costs: Travel to and from the Centre.
Benefits: CSV's receive £23 per week + full
board, students receive £50 per week + full
board.
Interviews: Interviews take place at the Centre.
Charity number: 208231
UK placements: England (Buckinghamshire).

PRO INTERNATIONAL

Bahnhofstrasse 26 A
D-35037 Marburg/L
Germany
T: 00 49 6421 65277
F: 00 49 6421 64407
E: pro-international@lahn.net
W: www.pro-international.de
Contact: Andreas Kunz

Following the concept of 'peace through
friendship' Pro International organises
international vacation workcamps. On these
camps, 10 to 15 volunteers from different
countries participate. They work about 5–6 hours
a day, except weekends, on public or social
projects and spend their time together.
More details/photos/links available about projects
in Germany – www.campinformation. info. We
are only responsible for our camps in Germany. 🖺

Number of projects: 38 camps in Germany
UK: 0
Starting months: Feb, Mar, Apr, May, Jun, Jul,
Aug, Sep, Oct
Time required: 2–4 weeks
Age: 16–26
Causes: Children, Conservation, Environmental
Causes.
Activities: Building/Construction, Conservation
Skills, Social Work.
Placements: 400 only in Germany.
When to apply: As early as possible.
Work alone/with others: With others.
Health requirements: No restrictions.
Costs: Travel and approx. €65 to cover
administration.
Benefits: Food and accommodation. Basic
accommodation (usually several bedrooms in
buildings/hostels, self catering of the groups
with own kitchen).
Training: None.
Supervision: No.
Interviews: No.
Worldwide placements: Europe (Germany).

PRO VOBIS VOLUNTEER CENTER – Romania

Dorobantilor 99/32
Cluj Napoca, 3400
Romania
T: 00 40 64 412 897
F: 00 40 64 412 897
E: volunteer_center_cluj@hotmail.com
Contact: Loana Popovici

Pro Vobis Volunteer Center promotes and has
information about volunteering in Romania. It
may well be able to put volunteers in touch
with organisations which are not yet listed on
the WorldWide Volunteering database.

Starting months: January–December
Time required: 1–52 weeks (plus)
Age: 16 plus – no upper limit
Causes: Addicts/Ex-Addicts, AIDS/HIV, Animal
Welfare, Archaeology, Architecture, Children,
Conservation, Disabled (learning and physical),
Elderly People, Environmental Causes, Health
Care/Medical, Heritage, Holidays for Disabled,
Human Rights, Inner City Problems, Offenders/
Ex-Offenders, Poor/Homeless, Refugees,
Teaching/assisting (nursery, primary, secondary,
mature, EFL) Unemployed, Wildlife, Work
Camps – Seasonal, Young People.
Activities: Accountancy, Administration,
Agriculture/Farming, Arts/Crafts, Building/
Construction, Campaigning, Caring (general,
day and residential), Catering, Community
Work, Computers, Conservation Skills,
Cooking, Counselling, Development Issues,
DIY, Driving, First Aid, Forestry, Fundraising,
Gardening/Horticulture, Group Work,

International Aid, Library/Resource Centres,
Manual Work, Marketing/Publicity, Music,
Newsletter/Journalism, Outdoor Skills, Religion,
Research, Scientific Work, Social Work, Sport,
Summer Camps, Teaching, Technical Skills,
Theatre/Drama, Training, Translating,
Visiting/Befriending, Work Camps – Seasonal.
Costs: Varies according to the project.
Worldwide placements: Europe (Romania).

PROBELIZE SERVICE CORPS

264 East 10th Street
No 5
New York
NY 10009 USA
T: 877 733 7378
F: 406 252 3973
E: info@probelize.org
W: www.probelize.org
Contact: Nick Bryngleson

ProBelize provides university students the
opportunity to experience the wonders of Belize
while contributing to the growth of small
communities through integrated academic,
adventure, and development work programmes.
Situated on the Caribbean coast of Belize, we
offer these unique cross-cultural experiences
year round through the NGO partnership and
group programmes. Our multiple programme
options allow volunteers to contribute to the
growth of the rural communities through
building projects, basic medical services,
teaching in rural communities, establishing
micro-businesses, NGO internships and many
others. Development sees building schools,
community centres, houses and computing
facilities, installing drinking water systems and
irrigation canals. ProBelize maintains a home
base in each community, which is open 24
hours a day for volunteers needing medical
care, academic support, telephones or a
comfortable meeting place. We cannot accept
volunteers with an offending background.
Located in the Hopkins Village on the South
Central Caribbean coast of Belize. The small
rural village is in between, bordered by white
sandy beaches and a national wildlife and
nature reserve.

Number of projects: 2 UK: 0
Starting months: January–December
Time required: 4–52 weeks
Age: 18 plus – no upper limit
Causes: Archaeology, Architecture, Children,
Conservation, Disabled (learning), Elderly
People, Environmental Causes, Health Care/
Medical, Heritage, Human Rights, Poor/
Homeless, Teaching/assisting (nursery,
secondary, mature), Unemployed, Young People.
Activities: Accountancy, Administration,
Agriculture/Farming, Arts/Crafts, Building/

Construction, Caring (general, day and residential), Community Work, Computers, Conservation Skills, Counselling, Development Issues, Fundraising, International Aid, Library/ Resource Centres, Manual Work, Marketing/ Publicity, Music, Newsletter/Journalism, Research, Social Work, Teaching, Technical Skills, Theatre/Drama.
Placements: 120
When to apply: 2 months prior to the start of project.
Work alone/with others: Work with others.
Qualifications: True desire to do volunteer work and to learn about the amazing culture of Belize.
Health requirements: No restrictions.
Costs: US$1900 for four weeks and $300 each additional week after the first four weeks.
Benefits: Full room and board, funding of your NGO development project, 24 hour home base and support staff, trips to local events and archaeological sites of interest.
Training: On site training provided for specific projects.
Supervision: 24 hour on site staff managing the experiences of the volunteers and ensuring their safety.
Interviews: Yes, via e-mail or telephone, or in the New York office.
Worldwide placements: Central America (Belize).

PROGRAM-BELL PRIVATE SCHOOL OF ENGLISH

61–701 Poznan
ul Fredry 1
pok.22–26
Poland
T: 00 48 61 85 19 250
F: 00 48 61 530 612
E: office@program-bell.edu.pl
Contact: Anna Gebka-Susa

Program-Bell Private School of English needs teachers of English to teach groups of 10–12 children and teenagers for three hours per day; and supervisors to organise activities and look after children at language camps. Duties include being responsible for the children 24 hours a day. 📖

Number of projects: 10–12 UK: 0
Starting months: Jun, Jul, Aug
Time required: 2–6 weeks
Age: 22–99
Causes: Children, Teaching/assisting (EFL).
Activities: Summer Camps, Teaching.
Placements: 6–8
When to apply: By April 15th.
Work alone/with others: Both.
Qualifications: TEFL preferred and experience of working with children.

Equipment/clothing: Summer clothing including a sweater; teaching materials.
Health requirements: Health certificate from family doctor required.
Costs: Travel costs.
Benefits: Full board and lodging. Wages by arrangement. Accommodation is provided for the short periods between camps. During camps instructors are provided with full board and accommodation.
Training: Three day training before the start of the camps.
Supervision: Volunteers work under the supervision of a Polish camp leader.
Interviews: Applicants are usually interviewed in London or on the phone.
Worldwide placements: Europe (Poland).

PROJECT FAUNA FOREVER (TReeS)

Jr Lambayeque 488
Puerto Maldonado
Madre de Dios Peru
E: faunaforever@yahoo.co.uk
W: www.faunaforever.com
Contact: Karen Tailby

Project Fauna Forever aims are:
1. To investigate the long term changes in wildlife abundance and biomass species diversity, and community structure in areas subject to constant pressure from tourists and activities directly related, and in comparable areas well away from the influence of this activity. It builds upon the results of a study previously undertaken in the area from 1997–1998 in the rainforests of the Tambopata area.
2. Determine acceptable levels of change in faunal populations around jungle lodges based on the opinions of tourists, lodge personnel, neotropical fauna specialists etc.
3. Identify appropriate tourist management techniques, including trail-use carrying capacities and optimum tourist group size, for consideration by tour companies and protected area managers.
4. Determine detailed levels of beta diversity, that is to say the degree to which species diversity changes between geographically close locations.
5. Develop long-term fauna monitoring database and Geographical Information System for Tambopata enabling information from past and future fauna studies in Tambopata to be integrated and compared.
6. Train local biologists and students from the National Amazon University of Madre de Dios (UNAMAD) and the National University San Antonio Abad of Cusco (UNSAAC), in methodologies for monitoring wild fauna populations, including database and GIS management.

7. Divulge results and recommendations to tour operators, local authorities and institutions, the local population, and the scientific community through radio programmes, public seminar and a peer reviewed scientific article in English to be published in an appropriate international journal. Tambopata region of South Eastern Peru. The protected areas are the Tambopata Nature Reserve created in 2001 in an area of 274, 690 hectares and the Bahuaja Sonene National Park, created in 1996 and extended in 2001in a current area of 1.09 million hectares. 🗎

Number of projects: 1 **UK:** 0
Starting months: Nov
Time required: 11–52 weeks (plus)
Age: 18–80
Causes: Conservation, Environmental Causes, Wildlife.
Activities: Conservation Skills, Outdoor Skills, Research, Scientific Work.
Placements: 24
When to apply: Applications to be received by August.
Work alone/with others: With others.
Qualifications: Basic knowledge of Spanish would help the volunteer gain more out of their time in Peru. Volunteers should have a good sense of humour, adventurous spirit and the ability to endure often challenging conditions and sometimes basic living conditions.
Equipment/clothing: Clothing for rainforest conditions – full list can be found on our web site www.faunaforever.com.
Health requirements: Volunteers need to be fit and in good health.
Costs: International flights, flights in-country US$150 return Lima to Puerto Maldonado and travel insurance.
Benefits: All food, accommodation in hotels, hostels or in the project house and travel from joining project in Puerto Maldonado until the end of the project will be covered.
Training: Full training will be provided on survey techniques and subject identification.
Supervision: Each survey group will be headed by an experienced survery co-ordinator. Volunteers should be fairly independent.
Interviews: No interviews although application details are assessed prior to acceptance of the volunteer on the project.
Charity number: TReeS No 298054
Worldwide placements: South America (Peru).

PROJECT TRUST

Hebridean Centre
Isle of Coll
Argyll PA78 6TE UK
T: 01879 230 444
F: 01879 230 357
E: info@projecttrust.org.uk
W: www.projecttrust.org.uk
Contact: The Director

Project Trust sends school leavers from the United Kingdom overseas as volunteers for twelve months. Since 1967 it has sent over 4000 volunteers to 53 different countries. Project Trust aims to give young people a better understanding of the world outside Europe through living and working overseas. Project Trust offers a year's placement to young people who at the time of application are in full time secondary education and are between 17 and 19 years at the time of going overseas. Projects fall into the following categories:
English language assistants – schools, colleges and universities.
Care Work – helping in children's homes, with the disabled or homeless.
Assisting in health and community development projects – in hospitals or with aid organisations.
Education projects – teaching or assisting in primary and secondary schools.
Outdoor activity projects – in outward bound schools.
Our selection course and training courses are accredited for the residential section of the Gold Duke of Edinburgh award.
The overseas projects count in the service section of the Gold Duke of Edinburgh award. Project Trust is a member of The Year Out Group.

Number of projects: 95 approx **UK:** 0
Starting months: Jan, Aug, Sep
Time required: 50–52 weeks
Age: 17–19
Causes: AIDS/HIV, Animal Welfare, Children, Conservation, Disabled (learning and physical), Elderly People, Environmental Causes, Health Care/Medical, Inner City Problems, Offenders/Ex-Offenders, Poor/Homeless, Refugees, Teaching/assisting (nursery, primary, secondary, mature, EFL) Wildlife, Young People.
Activities: Arts/Crafts, Building/Construction, Caring (general, residential), Community Work, Computers, Conservation Skills, Development Issues, Newsletter/Journalism, Outdoor Skills, Social Work, Sport, Teaching.
Placements: 200
When to apply: 6–18 months before departure date.
Work alone/with others: Normally in pairs.
Qualifications: Applicants must be taking 3 A-levels, Highers or equivalent qualifications, EU passport holders only.
Health requirements: Fit and healthy.
Costs: £3,850 for 2004 school leavers for 12 months and £3,350 for the 8 month winter programme (departing January 2004, £3,650 for those departing January 2005). This covers selection, training, insurance, flights, medical accommodation and food.
Benefits: Food/lodging/insurance, travel from UK to project and £40 per month pocket money.

Training: One week's residential training on the Isle of Coll before departure.
Supervision: Local representative in every country – close relationship with a personal desk officer based in the UK who makes 1 visit a year.
Interviews: An optional interview is available near the applicant's home. All applicants then attend a 5-day selection course on the Isle of Coll.
Charity number: 306088
Worldwide placements: Africa (Botswana, Egypt, Lesotho, Malawi, Morocco, Namibia, South Africa, Swaziland, Uganda, Zimbabwe); Central America (Cuba, Dominican Republic, Honduras); South America (Brazil, Chile, Guyana, Peru); Asia (China, Hong Kong, Japan, Jordan, Korea (South), Malaysia, Sri Lanka, Taiwan, Thailand, Vietnam).

PROPERU SERVICE CORPS

264 East 10th Street
No 5
New York
NY 10009 USA
T: 877 733 7378
F: 406 252 3973
E: info@properu.org
W: www.properu.org
Contact: Nick Bryngelson

ProPeru provides university students the opportunity to experience the wonders of Peru while contributing to the growth of small communities through integrated academic, adventure, and development work programmes. Situated in the Sacred Valley of the Incas, we offer these unique cross-cultural experiences year round through the Semester in Peru, NGO Partnership and Group Programmes. Our multiple programme options allow volunteers to contribute to the growth of the rural communities through building projects, basic medical services, teaching in rural communities, establishing micro-businesses, NGO internships and many others. Development sees building schools, community centres, houses and computing facilities, installing drinking water systems and irrigation canals. ProPeru maintains a home base in each community, which is open 24 hours a day for volunteers needing medical care, academic support, telephones or a comfortable meeting place. We cannot accept volunteers with an offending background. All our projects are located in one of the two locations. Specifically in the Sacred Valley they are located in Urubamba and the Amazon Basin in the Manu National Park.

Number of projects: 2 UK: 0
Starting months: January–December

Time required: 4–52 weeks
Age: 18 plus – no upper limit
Causes: Archaeology, Architecture, Children, Conservation, Disabled (learning), Elderly People, Environmental Causes, Health Care/ Medical, Heritage, Human Rights, Poor/ Homeless, Teaching/assisting (nursery, primary, secondary, mature), Unemployed, Young People.
Activities: Accountancy, Administration, Agriculture/Farming, Arts/Crafts, Building/ Construction, Caring (general, day and residential), Community Work, Computers, Conservation Skills, Counselling, Development Issues, Fundraising, International Aid, Library/ Resource Centres, Manual Work, Marketing/Publicity, Music, Newsletter/ Journalism, Research, Social Work, Teaching, Technical Skills, Theatre/Drama.
Placements: 120
When to apply: 2 months prior to the start of the project.
Work alone/with others: Work with others.
Qualifications: True desire to do volunteer work and to learn about the amazing culture of Peru.
Health requirements: No restrictions.
Costs: US$1900 for four weeks and $300 each additional week after the first four weeks.
Benefits: Full room and board, intensive Spanish classes, full funding of your NGO development project, 24 hour access to ProPeru home base and support staff, Trips to local events and archeological sites of interest.
Training: On site training provided for specific projects.
Supervision: 24 hour on site staff managing the experiences of the volunteers and ensuring their safety.
Interviews: Yes via e-mail or on the telephone, or in the New York office.
Worldwide placements: South America (Peru).

PSYCHIATRIC REHABILITATION ASSOCIATION

Bayford Mews
Bayford Street
London
SW2 2DE UK
T: +44 (0) 208 985 3570
F: +44 (0) 208 986 1334
Contact: John Wilder

The Psychiatric Rehabilitation Association has pioneered a comprehensive range of rehabilitation and after-care projects for the mentally ill since the Association was formed at the time of the 1959 Mental Health Act. Current projects include day centres, industrial education units, evening groups, group home accommodation, an evening restaurant club, shopwork training experience and various other activities including an art sudio and gallery. An Internet suite and an exercise project have just been opened in PRA'S hackney day centre. PRA evening centres were set up in response to a need for discharged patients to expand their social lives and leisure activities in a relaxed and friendly climate. Social isolation is a frequent consequence of mental illness, and is not conducive to recovery. Meeting with others, sharing experiences, and making plans for the future is an important rehabilitative facility appreciated by those who participate in the groups. Those attending have a history of chronic schizophrenia or depressive illness. Hospitals, social services and GPs refer patients and ex-patients whom they consider would benefit from this support. There is also a substantial element of self referral. The association is currently seeking additional volunteers for the teams working in these groups and day centres. There are no specific qualifications required to be a volunteer, although you should be a caring person with common sense, stability, stamina and patience. You should have the ability to share creative ideas and an enthusiasm for the enjoyment afforded by life outside the institution. Availability of volunteers will vary. However, we would ask that volunteers honour any commitment made to the association and, if this is not possible, that enough notice is given to allow alternative arrangements to be made. Regrettably, we are unable to refund expenses. However, we offer the opportunity to work directly with people suffering and recovering from mental illness. In house theoretical training will be provided in addition to the practical aspect of volunteering. Volunteers with an offending background may be accepted depending on the offence. London boroughs of Tower Hamlets, Hackney, Islington, Haringey.   🔊 📄

Number of projects: 22 UK: 22
Starting months: January–December
Time required: 42–52 weeks (plus)
Age: 25–60
Causes: Disabled (learning), Elderly People, Health Care/Medical, Holidays for Disabled, Unemployed.
Activities: Arts/Crafts, Campaigning, Caring (general and day), Catering, Computers, Cooking, Development Issues, DIY, Fundraising, Gardening/Horticulture, Group Work, Manual Work, Music, Outdoor Skills, Sport, Teaching, Training, Translating.
Placements: 15
When to apply: All year.
Work alone/with others: Both. Volunteer work is supervised by the groupworker.
Qualifications: Adequate spoken English essential. A-level or equivalent preferred – not essential.

Health requirements: Nil but no contagious diseases.
Costs: Living costs.
Benefits: Reimbursement of costs incurred while taking part in a specific project. Non-residential based in London.
Training: Training provided.
Supervision: Supervision provided.
Interviews: Volunteers are interviewed at head office and references are requested.
Charity number: 292944
UK placements: England (London).

PUBLIC FOUNDATION VOLUNTEER HOUSE SOROS-KAZAKSTAN

171, Tulebaeva Street
Almay
Kazakstan 480091
T: 00 7 3272 581 361
F: 00 7 3272 581 361
E: nbirzhan@volunteer.samal.kz
W: www.volunteer.freenet.kz
Contact: Executive Director

Public Foundation Volunteer House Soros – Kazakstan promotes and has information about volunteering in Kazakstan founding and developing a network of volunteer teams in 14 cities in Kazakhstan. This net is known as Sun World (Kyn Alemy in Kazakh). Volunteer club of VH assists for devloping projects involving young volunteers in a public process, a positive reform of society, holding seminars, training programmes, summer camps and ecological actions. There are publishing activities, too. VH issues its bulletin in August for creating a positive image of volunteerism. It may well be able to put volunteers in touch with organisations which are not yet listed on the WorldWide Volunteering database. Akmola, Aktobe, Atyrau, East Kazakhstan, Karaganda, Kostanai, Kyzylorda, Mangghystau, South Kazakhstan, West Kazakhstan and Zhambyl. 🔊 📄

Number of projects: UK: 0
Starting months: January–December
Time required: 1–45 weeks
Age: 14–60
Causes: Addicts/Ex-Addicts, AIDS/HIV, Animal Welfare, Archaeology, Architecture, Children, Conservation, Disabled (learning and physical), Elderly People, Environmental Causes, Health Care/Medical, Heritage, Holidays for Disabled, Human Rights, Inner City Problems, Offenders/Ex-Offenders, Poor/Homeless, Refugees, Teaching/assisting (nursery, primary, secondary, mature, EFL) Unemployed, Wildlife, Work Camps – Seasonal, Young People.
Activities: Accountancy, Administration, Agriculture/Farming, Arts/Crafts, Building/Construction, Campaigning, Caring (general, day and residential), Catering,

Community Work, Computers, Conservation Skills, Cooking, Counselling, Development Issues, DIY, Driving, First Aid, Forestry, Fundraising, Gardening/Horticulture, Group Work, International Aid, Library/Resource Centres, Manual Work, Marketing/Publicity, Music, Newsletter/Journalism, Outdoor Skills, Religion, Research, Scientific Work, Social Work, Sport, Summer Camps, Teaching, Technical Skills, Theatre/Drama, Training, Translating, Visiting/Befriending, Work Camps – Seasonal.
Placements: 250
When to apply: Any time.
Work alone/with others: Both.
Qualifications: In general our volunteers are students from different universities, senior pupils, and usually adults with university degrees.
Equipment/clothing: There is office equipment and publishing software.
Health requirements: Unlimited.
Costs: Varies according to the project.
Benefits: Through VH's activities people have been spreading the opportunities to devlop Kazakhstan society. Accommodation is provided.
Training: Provide training about Kazakhstan.
Supervision: Yes through regional volunteer network.
Interviews: Usually via telephone or e-mail.
Worldwide placements: Asia (Kazakhstan).

Q

QUAKER VOLUNTARY ACTION (QVA)

Friends Meeting House
6 Mount Street
Manchester
M2 5NS UK
T: 0161 8191634
F: 0161 8191634
E: mail@qva.org.uk
W: www.qva.org.uk
Contact: Sue Dixon

Quakers are a religious movement who believe that there is something of God in everyone. Religion for them is the way you live your life. This is manifested in many social and political concerns. Since the 17th century Quakers have involved themselves in humanitarian causes, endeavouring to identify the causes of conflict, oppression and inequality. In place of conflict, they try to foster understanding between individuals and nations and a respect for life. You do not have to be a Quaker to be a QVA volunteer, in fact, most volunteers are not. QVA projects are for groups of about 8–15 volunteers from different backgrounds, nationalities, cultures and abilities living and working together on a project (for 1–4 weeks or longer) which aims to meet a community need. The location of projects varies each season. We accept volunteers with an offending background. 🔲 📄

Number of projects: some, with a few Quaker projects **UK:** 4
Starting months: Jun, Jul, Aug, Sep
Time required: 1–4 weeks
Age: 18–70
Causes: Children, Conservation, Disabled (learning and physical), Elderly People, Environmental Causes, Holidays for Disabled, Inner City Problems, Offenders/Ex-Offenders, Poor/Homeless, Unemployed, Work Camps – Seasonal.
Activities: Arts/Crafts, Building/Construction, Caring (general, day and residential), Community Work, Conservation Skills, Cooking, Gardening/Horticulture, Group Work, Manual Work, Social Work, Theatre/Drama, Visiting/Befriending, Work Camps – Seasonal.
Placements: 40
When to apply: April – June for summer.
Work alone/with others: With others.
Qualifications: Dependent on project.
Equipment/clothing: Sleeping bag.
Health requirements: No.
Costs: Reg.fee £35–£60 for UK projects, £75–£100 for projects abroad. Travel + pocket money.

Benefits: Accommodation and food.
Training: Some training offered at the start of projects.
Supervision: Volunteers are always supervised and work in teams.
Interviews: Applicants are not interviewed.
Charity number: 237698
Worldwide placements: Africa (Morocco, South Africa); North America: (Canada, Greenland, Saint Pierre-Miquelon, USA); Central America (Mexico); Asia (Japan, Turkey); Europe (Belarus, Belgium, Bulgaria, Czech Republic, Denmark, Estonia, Finland, France, Germany, Greece, Hungary, Ireland, Italy, Netherlands, Poland, Slovakia, Spain, Turkey).
UK placements: England (throughout); Scotland (throughout); Northern Ireland (throughout); Wales (throughout).

QUEST OVERSEAS

32 Clapham Mansions
Nightingale Lane
London
SW4 9AQ UK
T: +44 (0) 208 673 3313
F: +44 (0) 208 673 7623
E: e-mailus@questoverseas.com
W: www.questoverseas.com
Contact: Michael Amphlet

Quest Overseas is a small organisation providing an all encompassing three month experience in South America or Africa for gap year students and eight week summer expeditions for university students. We are a young and dedicated team of travel addicts who are intent on making your gap year the most fulfilling experience you can hope for.
We have been running successful projects and expeditions overseas for over seven years for small teams of up to 16 gap year students with departures from December through to April. We also run 6–8 week summer expeditions and five week summer projects leaving every July for both gap year and university students. Apply early to secure a place on the project of your choice. Three month expeditions to South America... Combine learning or improving your Spanish for three weeks on a 'one to one' tuition course in Quito, Ecuador, with a month working on a community project (looking after children in Peru) or on one of three conservation projects (in the heart of the Amazon or Bolivian Rainforest or in 15,000 acres of prime Ecuadorian Cloud Forest) before completing a mind-blowing and challenging six week expedition through Peru, Bolivia and

Chile. Alternatively, in Africa... Spend six weeks working with either local communities in Tanzania building schools and medical centres or in game reserves in Swaziland, undertaking ecological surveys, trail building and conservation work before an adventurous six week expedition through Mozambique, Botswana and Zambia. Only gap year students between school and university. Students receive a fundraising pack and year-round advice and support in raising the necessary funds. Students need to be responsible, motivated and get on well with others whilst having a good understanding of the word FUN. We are a Founder Member of the Year Out Group.

Number of projects: 7 **UK:** 0
Starting months: Jan, Feb, Mar, Apr, Jul, Dec
Time required: 6–13 weeks
Age: 18–23
Causes: Animal Welfare, Children, Conservation, Environmental Causes, Teaching/assisting (nursery, primary), Wildlife.
Activities: Arts/Crafts, Building/Construction, Community Work, Conservation Skills, Forestry, Group Work, Manual Work, Music, Outdoor Skills, Sport, Teaching.
Placements: 240
When to apply: 3–18 mths prior to departure. Early application recommended

Work alone/with others: With others.
Qualifications: A-levels – confirmed place/deferred entry to university. British and EU students.
Equipment/clothing: Rucksack, sleeping bag, walking boots.
Health requirements: Volunteers must not suffer from any significant medical problems.
Costs: £1,980–£3,985 + international flights, insurance and pocket money.
Benefits: The cost covers all costs and includes substantial donations to project sites. Accommodation always supplied. It varies between hostels, guest houses and camping with occasional hammocks.
Training: A 3-day preparation and expedition training weekend is held 3 months prior to departure.
Supervision: Project leader accompanies volunteers for the entire 13 weeks and is joined for the 6-week expedition by a highly qualified experienced expedition leader.
Interviews: Selection Interview in London, followed by preparation and expedition training weekend for successful applicants.
Worldwide placements: Africa (Botswana, Mozambique, Namibia, South Africa, Swaziland, Tanzania, Zambia); South America (Bolivia, Chile, Ecuador, Peru).

QUIT

Ground Floor
211 Old Street
London
EC1V 9NR UK
T: +44 (0) 20 7361 251 1551
F: +44 (0) 20 7361 251 1661
E: info@quit.org.uk
W: www.quit.org.uk
Contact: Karen Bowden

QUIT® is the UK's only charity whose main aim is to offer practical help to people who want to stop smoking. Runs a telephone helpline and offers down-to-earth advice about stopping smoking for good. Volunteers are required to help with administration, fundraising and public relations. Based in Central London well served by public transport. ♿

Number of projects: 1 UK: 1
Starting months: January–December
Time required: 4–52 weeks (plus)
Age: 18 plus – no upper limit
Causes: Addicts/Ex-Addicts, Teaching/assisting, Young People.
Activities: Administration, Computers, Counselling, Fundraising, Group work, Training.
Placements: 2–5
When to apply: All year.
Qualifications: Good administration and word processing skills.
Costs: Food and accommodation costs.
Benefits: Travel expenses reimbursed.
Training: Training is given.
Supervision: All volunteers are supervised.
Interviews: Yes.
UK placements: England (London).

R

RADNORSHIRE WILDLIFE TRUST

Warwick House
High Street
Llandrindod Wells
PowysLD1 6AG UK
T: 01597 823298
F: 01597 824812
E: radnorshirewt@cix.co.uk
W: www.waleswildlife.co.uk
Contact: The Director

Radnorshire Wildlife Trust is a member of the
Wildlife Trusts, a national partnership of 47
County Trusts. The aims of the Trust are
primarily to: promote nature conservation in
the community; acquire and manage nature
reserves; monitor biological and geological
resources; liaise with local authorities to
promote regard for nature conservation; offer
practical advice on nature conservation to
landowners. It is the Trust's policy to involve all
sectors of the community, of all ages,
backgrounds, abilities and disabilities towards
these ends. Volunteers require no previous
experience just lots of enthusiasm. If they
desire, can go on to participate more fully
assisting with the organisation and running of
activities/projects. Limited opportunities may
also arise, for those with a longer term
commitment, for NVQ training to level 2 in
Landscapes and Ecosystems. Volunteers with an
offending background may be accepted – each
case separately assessed. 🦽 📄

Number of projects: 1 UK: 1
Starting months: January–December
Time required: 1–52 weeks (plus)
Age: 14 plus – no upper limit
Causes: Conservation, Environmental Causes,
Wildlife.
Activities: Conservation Skills.
Work alone/with others: Both.
Equipment/clothing: Casual work clothes,
waterproofs, stout boots for outdoor work.
Protective safety gear is provided.
Health requirements: Anti-tetanus
innoculations recommended.
Costs: Living costs.
Benefits: Out of pocket expenses.
Training: Training is given.
Supervision: Volunteers are supervised.
Interviews: Volunteers are interviewed.
UK placements: Wales (Powys).

RAINFOREST CONCERN

27 Lansdowne Crescent
London
W11 2NS UK
T: +44 (0) 207 229 2093
T: +44 (0) 207 221 4094
E: info@rainforestconcern.org
W: www.rainforestconcern.org
Contact: Fiona Dalrymple

Our main objective is to protect threatened
rainforests and the vast biodiversity of life they
contain. We assist the communities living close
to our projects by promoting health and
environmental education programmes and
encourage alternative forms of income
generation to take the emphasis away from
slash and burn agriculture. We also encourage
research programmes to investigate the
biological value of tropical forests and have a
research station based at one of our reserves in
Ecuador which caters for under and post
graduate studies. We invite volunteers to
become involved with our work either in
London or on our projects in Ecuador and
Costa Rica. In Ecuador we have a volunteer
programme which runs all year round and
involves an element of research or physical
labour such as trail maintenance, reforestation
and organic horticulture depending on the time
of year and projects being undertaken at that
time. The cost of staying at one of our reserves
reduces per day if you stay for six weeks or
more. The other projects where we regularly
take on volunteers for short periods (as little as
two weeks) are in Costa Rica and Panama. Here
we have a coastal reserve with the chief purpose
of protecting the leatherback turtle. The work
includes protecting the beaches from poachers,
monitoring and tagging turtles and clearing
trails. However these opportunities are only
available for the egg laying season between the
first week of February and the last week of
August of each year. Tandayapa and Santa Lucia
Reserves in NW Ecuador. Yachana Reserve, Rio
Napo, Amazon Basin, Ecuador. Pacuare Nature
Reserve, Caribbean coast, Costa Rica. Soropta
Project, Caribean coast, Panama.

Number of projects: 6 UK: 0
Starting months: January–December
Time required: 1–52 weeks (plus)
Age: 18 plus – no upper limit
Causes: Animal Welfare, Children,
Conservation, Environmental Causes, Teaching
(EFL), Wildlife.

Activities: Community Work, Conservation Skills, Forestry, Gardening/Horticulture, Group Work, International Aid, Manual Work, Outdoor Skills, Research, Scientific Work, Translating.
Placements: 100+
When to apply: All year.
Work alone/with others: Both.
Qualifications: Nil but biologists and geologists are particularly welcome.
Equipment/clothing: Please contact us for the kit list.
Health requirements: Reasonable level of fitness required.
Costs: Ecuador US$8 per night, Costa Rica US$100 per week towards food and accommodation. Travel.
Benefits: Costs include all accommodation and 3 substantial meals a day.
Supervision: Minimal.
Interviews: Informal phone interview and CV.
Charity number: 1028947
Worldwide placements: Central America (Costa Rica, Panama); South America (Ecuador); Asia (Sri Lanka).

RALEIGH INTERNATIONAL

Raleigh House
27 Parsons Green Lane
London
SW6 4HZ UK
T: +44 (0) 207 371 8585
T: +44 (0) 207 371 5116
E: info@raleigh.org.uk
W: www.raleigh.org.uk
Contact: Helen Aikman

Raleigh International inspires people from all backgrounds and nationalities to discover their full potential by working together on challenging environmenal projects around the world. Going on expedition with Raleigh, whether you're a staff member over 20 or a volunteer under 25, is a unique experience. We're a leading youth development charity and our voluntary projects overseas facilitate that development in our volunteers. Volunteer staff are certainly involved in liaising with project partners (eg UNDP, the British Embassy, Sight Savers International) and the other volunteers take ownership of the project planning and management once they arrive in country. The expeditions are part of a longer programme of training weekends and workshops prior to expedition that concentrate on global issues and your own personal development. Our support with fundraising before expedition is also unrivalled. We run national fundraising events for volunteers, give you a personal co-ordinator in head office and also have a

network of UK groups that can support you. Once you have fundraised for us we can buy you a six month return flight so you can travel independently after expedition finishes. Take your first steps to a challenge of a lifetime and contact us on 020 7371 8585! Raleigh International is a member of The Year Out Group. & 🏛

Number of projects: 12 UK: Varies
Starting months: January–December
Time required: 10–12 weeks
Age: 17 plus – no upper limit
Causes: Animal Welfare, Children, Conservation, Disabled (learning and physical), Elderly People, Environmental Causes, Health Care/Medical, Inner City Problems, Offenders/Ex-Offenders, Poor/Homeless, Teaching/assisting (primary, secondary), Unemployed, Wildlife, Young People.
Activities: Administration, Agriculture/Farming, Arts/Crafts, Building/Construction, Caring – General, Community Work, Conservation Skills, Cooking, Development Issues, DIY, First Aid, Forestry, Fundraising, Gardening/Horticulture, Group Work, International Aid, Manual work, Marketing/Publicity, Outdoor Skills, Research, Scientific Work, Social Work, Sport, Teaching, Technical Skills, Training, Translating.
Placements: 1,400
When to apply: All year round.
Work alone/with others: With others. For expeditions individuals will work in groups of 10–14.
Qualifications: No qualifications for 17–25 year olds. 25 + can go as staff, various qualifications needed, please call to discuss. No US nationals.
Equipment/clothing: Only personal kit required. Raleigh will advise on this and provides high-tech specialist equipment.
Health requirements: Individually assessed.
Costs: Volunteers from 17–25 fundraise £3,500 for the charity as a whole. Over 25's fundraise £1100.
Benefits: Once volunteers have fundraised a target for Raleigh, they provide flights (valid for 6 months), insurance and accommodation, all in-country costs and all training in the UK. Doctors, accountants, mountain leaders are all provided too.
Training: For 17–25's a three day residential and one weeks expedition training in country. 25+ staff development week, and a week incountry prior to the start of the expedition.
Supervision: Volunteers staff members – about 3 to every small project group supervise volunteers. These staff are all qualified to British standards for the positions which they have taken up.

Interviews: For 17–25's there are no interviews. It is a self selection process, the first part being an introduction day. These are held once a month around the country. 25 years+ two day staff assessment weekend part of which is an interview.
Charity number: 1047653
Worldwide placements: Africa (Ghana, Namibia); Central America (Belize, Costa Rica, Nicaragua); South America (Chile); Asia (Malaysia).

RATHBONE

4th Floor, Churchgate House
56 Oxford Street
Manchester
M1 6EU UK
T: 0161 238 6327
F: 0161 238 6356
E: advice@rathbonetraining.co.uk
W: www.rathbonetraining.co.uk
Contact: Special Education Advice Line Co-ordinator

Rathbone works to improve opportunities for people who have limited access to services, many of whom have moderate learning difficulties and other special needs. Our clients are mainly young people and adults trying to achieve independence, either through first time employment or through newly acquired living skills. Rathbone presents opportunity in the form of stepping stones which people can choose at different stages in their lives to suit their individual needs. We also have a special education advice line which takes on volunteers to man our freephone service. The line advises parents of children with special needs on educational issues and procedures. We also take on administration volunteers to aid office work. We now have an Asian Advice Line (0800 085 4528) and would be interested to hear from anyone who wishes to volunteer for this service. We need to hear from anyone who a good command of English but may also be fluent in one or more of the following languages – Gujerati, Urdu, Punjabi, Hindi and Bengali. For further details phone the Asian line 0800 085 4528 and speak to Rifiat Jadwat. 🖬

Number of projects: 70+ **UK:** 70 approx
Starting months: January–December
Time required: 4–52 weeks (plus)
Age: 16 plus – no upper limit
Causes: Children, Disabled (learning and physical), Offenders/Ex-Offenders, Teaching/assisting (EFL), Young People.
Activities: Administration, Caring (general, residential), Community Work, Computers,

Counselling, Fundraising, Group Work, Marketing/Publicity, Teaching, Training, Visiting/Befriending.
Placements: 15–20
When to apply: All year.
Work alone/with others: With others.
Health requirements: Nil.
Costs: Food and accommodation.
Benefits: Travel expenses paid.
Training: 5-day training on education, law and listening skills.
Supervision: Volunteers are paired with a more experienced volunteer.
Interviews: Interviews take place in various locations.
Charity number: 287120
UK placements: England (Berkshire, Buckinghamshire, Cumbria, Derbyshire, Hertfordshire, Leicestershire, London, Manchester, Northamptonshire, Nottinghamshire, Shropshire, Surrey, Tyne and Wear, Warwickshire, West Midlands, S. Yorkshire, W. Yorkshire); Scotland (Ayrshire – East, Ayrshire – North, Ayrshire – South, Dunbartonshire – East, Dunbartonshire – West, Edinburgh, Fife, Glasgow City, Highland, Lothian – East, Lothian – West, Perth and Kinross, Stirling); Wales (Bridgend, Caerphilly, Cardiff, Carmarthenshire, Monmouthshire, Newport, Pembrokeshire, Rhondda, Cynon, Taff, Torfaen, Vale of Glamorgan).

CROSS EUROPEAN VOLUNTARY SERVICE

Over the last 35 years, thousands of 16–27 year olds in Germany have taken part in a national volunteering scheme enabling them to 'give' a year's service in a social setting. The German Red Cross is one of the largest 'agents' of this scheme and is now looking for British young people to take part. They should be over 18 and interested in spending a year in Germany working in social settings such as hospitals, special schools and services for elderly or disabled people, as part of their 'European Voluntary Service'. Duties may include care services such as washing, dressing, toileting etc., medical services such as taking blood pressure, changing dressings etc. and social services such as befriending, playing games, reading or going for walks with patients/clients. Successful applicants will have the opportunity to:
– gain challenging and recognised work experience,
– experience a different country, culture and language,
– meet new people,
– discover new talents and skills.

Volunteers with an offending background would need to be individually assessed (depending on project). ⑤

Number of projects: Varies UK: 30
Starting months: January–December
Time required: 26–52 weeks
Age: 18–26
Causes: Addicts/Ex-Addicts, AIDS/HIV, Children, Disabled (learning and physical), Elderly People, Health Care/Medical, Refugees, Teaching/assisting, (nursery).
Activities: Administration, Arts/Crafts, Caring (general, day and residential), Community Work, Cooking, First Aid, Group Work, Music, Outdoor Skills, Social Work, Sport, Teaching, Training, Visiting/Befriending.
Placements: 1300
When to apply: Currently accepting applications all year.
Work alone/with others: With others in a team.
Qualifications: Working knowledge of German desirable but not essential and an interest in care/social work. We are targeting young people who may have less opportunity to access internatonal volunteering programmes (e.g. not the traditional 'gap year' student). No nationality restrictions but easier if UK resident.
Health requirements: Nil.
Costs: Nil.
Benefits: Board, lodgings, pocket money, health cover and insurance covered by the project.
Training: Written information is given. One day pre-departure training, 25 seminar days during year and in-house training in most projects.
Supervision: Allocated contact person in host project, Red Cross group leader in region. Regular contact.
Interviews: Prospective volunteers are interviewed in London, Liverpool or Glasgow.
Worldwide placements: Europe (Germany).
UK placements: England (Kent, Lancashire, Merseyside).

REDEMPTORIST VOCATIONAL SCHOOL FOR THE DISABLED

P O Box 1
Pattaya City
Cholburi 20260 Thailand
T: (038) 716628
F: (038) 716629
E: volunteer@redemptorists.or.th
W: www.rvsd.ac.th
Contact: Mr Derek Franklin

Redemptorist Vocational School for the Disabled has educated thousands of young physically disabled Thai adults since 1984. Students study electronic repair, computer sciences or computer business in English. The school realises that English is the main international language so all students are taught English. The Computer Business in English course is taught totally in English – computers, accountancy and business. The school also has a job placement agency that guarantees 100% of graduating students employment when they leave. The school charges no fees, and accepts only those who are unable to afford any other vocational school. The school also provides food, medical health and sports equipment, all for free. There may be placements for volunteers with an offending background, all volunteers are individually screened. Pattaya is on the east coast of Thailand, south of Bangkok. 📄

Number of projects: 1 UK: 0
Starting months: Apr, Oct
Time required: 26–52 weeks
Age: 18 plus – no upper limit
Causes: Disabled (learning), Teaching/assisting (EFL), Young People.
Activities: Computers, Teaching, Translating.
Placements: 20
When to apply: As soon as possible.
Work alone/with others: Varies.
Qualifications: Ability to speak, read and write fluent English. Computer knowledge is desired.
Health requirements: Advice from own GP.
Costs: Travel costs and insurance.
Benefits: Food and accommodation.
Training: Orientation by head of English department.
Supervision: On site supervisor.
Interviews: London or via telephone.
Worldwide placements: Asia (Thailand).

REFUGEE COUNCIL, THE

3 Bondway
London
SW8 1SJ UK
T: +44 (0) 207 820 3112
T: +44 (0) 207 820 3005
E: chris.badman@refugeecouncil.org.uk
W: www.refugeecouncil.org.uk
Contact: Chris Badman

The Refugee Council is a charity which gives practical support to asylum seekers and refugees and promotes their rights in Britain and abroad. It acts as a representative for many different agencies and organisations involved in refugee issues. Its members and associate members include international development agencies, refugee service providers, regional refugee organisations, as well as a large number of local refugee community groups. The practical help we give includes: advice and information to individual refugees and to other advisers, support to refugee community organisations, and training for jobs. We play a central role in representing refugees' interests to governments and policy-makers, and we provide a forum for organisations involved with refugees to meet and formulate policy and advocacy on refugee issues. The work of the Refugee Council is currently delivered through five divisions whose respective directors report to the Refugee Council's Chief Executive: The Operations Group; The Communications Group; The Resources Group; The Development Group; The Regions. Offices in London, Leeds, Birmingham and Ipswich.

Number of projects: 5 UK: 4
Starting months: January–December
Time required: 12–52 weeks (plus)
Age: 18 plus – no upper limit
Causes: Human Rights, Poor/Homeless, Refugees, Teaching (EFL).
Activities: Administration, Campaigning, Cooking, Development Issues, Driving, Group Work, Marketing/Publicity, Research, Teaching, Translating, Visiting/Befriending.
Placements: 100
When to apply: As soon as possible.
Work alone/with others: Varies.
Qualifications: None essential.
Health requirements: Varies according to placement.
Costs: Travel and subsistence.
Training: One day induction plus ongoing training days.
Supervision: Volunteers are assigned a supervisor. Amount of supervision depends on placement.
Charity number: 1014576
UK placements: England (London, Suffolk, West Midlands, W. Yorkshire).

REFUGEE TRUST

73a Blessington Street
Dublin 7 Ireland
T: 00 353 1 8820108
F: 00 353 1 8820633
E: refugeetrust@eircom.net
W: www.refugeetrust.org
Contact: Vincent O'Reilly

In 1999 Refugee Trust celebrated its 10th anniversary. Refugee field operations principally provide for programme interventions which build upon the identification of humanitarian needs in the context of major emergencies, but with the targeting of particular groups that are more likely to be overlooked in the larger UN/donor led operations. Thus, for example, our operations in Montenegro, our assistance to returning Kosovar Albanian refugees into the war damaged city of Pec and our concentration and support in Rwanda to child headed households and our primary goal of 'developing

programmes which ensure in design, and implementation and appreciation of the needs of individuals and families and in particular the elderly and the disabled'. A noteworthy feature of our work is the establishment of alliances with other organisations, and the signing of Memorandums of Understanding with War Child as well as important partnership alliance funding from both Trocaire and Net Aid. These alliances result in a reduction of resource duplication while providing opportunities for inter-agency learning and working together.

Number of projects: 3
Starting months: January–December
Time required: 1–52 weeks (plus)
Age: 14 plus – no upper limit
Causes: Children, Elderly People, Poor/ Homeless, Refugees, Young People.
Activities: Caring – General, Community Work, Group Work, Social Work.
Worldwide placements: Europe (Ireland).
UK placements: England (throughout); Scotland (throughout); Northern Ireland (throughout); Wales (throughout).

RELIEF FUND FOR ROMANIA

54–62 Regent Street
London
W1B 5RE UK
T: +44 (0) 207 437 6978
T: +44 (0) 207 494 1740
E: mail@relieffundforromania.co.uk
W: www.relieffundforromania.co.uk
Contact: Edward Parry

Almost all volunteers are needed in UK charity shops, very few are sent to Romania. The minimum age depends on maturity assessed at interview.
Volunteers with an offending background are considered.

Number of projects: Varies UK: Varies
Starting months: January–December
Time required: 1–52 weeks
Age: 18 plus – no upper limit
Causes: Children, Poor/Homeless.
Activities: International Aid.
Interviews: Interviews take place at charity shops – usually S.E. England.
Charity number: 1046737
Worldwide placements: Europe (Romania).
UK placements: England (London).

RESPONSIBLE ECOLOGICAL SOCIAL TOURS PROJECT (REST)

109/79 Mooban Yucharon Pattana
Ladphroao Soi 18
Ladyao
Chatuchak
Bangkok10900 Thailand

T: + 66 2 938 7007
F: +66 2 938 5275
E: rest@asiaaccess.net.th
W: www.ecotour.in.th
Contact: Ms Jaranya Daengnoy

Responsible Ecological Social Tours Project (REST) is a non- governmental organisation (NGO), established in 1994. We have been working with various communities in the North and South of Thailand. Our aim is to organise, manage and develop programmes for tourists who are interested in learning about Thai communities and their relationship with the natural environment by spending time with participating host families. REST's role is to support the development of CBST (Community Based Sustainable Tourism) in these communities by providing technical assistance and training, but ultimately the management of these projects lies with the communities.
REST'S policy:
To strengthen local communities through capacity and confidence building so that they have total control over tourism development in their area.
To provide community information to tourists, to help them to gain a wider understanding of this type of tourism that focuses on learning and a cultural exchange process.
To behave appropriately with an appreciation for local customs and regulations.
To buy and use local products and services in order to support and stimulate the local community.
To be aware of the impact of tourism in the local society, culture and environment.
Volunteers with an offending background may be accepted. Samut Songkram, Petchaburi, Tak Nort, Mae Hong Son Chaing Mai, Na, Chiang Rai South, Phang Nga, Phuket, Nakhon Si Thammarat.

Number of projects: 4 UK: 0
Starting months: January–December
Time required: 2–52 weeks
Age: 20–60
Causes: Children, Conservation, Environmental Causes, Teaching/assisting (primary, secondary, mature).
Activities: Arts/Crafts, Community Work, Development Issues, First Aid, Fundraising, Gardening/Horticulture, Group Work, Music, Research, Social Work, Sport, Teaching, Training, Visiting/Befriending, Work Camps – Seasonal.
Placements: 10–20
When to apply: All year round.
Qualifications: Language ability and willing to learn new culture.
Equipment/clothing: Personal belongings and own medicine.
Health requirements: No restrictions.

Costs: No financial support given. Accommodation is homestay in the village and sometimes in the REST office at BKK.
Training: Rural, Thai culture, participatory development, community study by mapping focus group and interview. On the job training.
Supervision: Field visit every 2 weeks.
Interviews: Yes if possible at the REST office.
Worldwide placements: Asia (Thailand).

RESULTS EDUCATION

13 Dormer Place
Leamington Spa
Warwickshire CV32 5AA UK
T: 01926 435430
F: 01926 435110
E: resultsuk@gn.apc.org
W: www.resultsinternational.org.uk
Contact: Sheila Davie

Results Education is an international campaign group working to end hunger and poverty. Our volunteers educate themselves on development issues and then act to educate the public, the media and specifically politicians as to the possibility of ending poverty within our lifetimes. By developing relationships with their MPs, MEPs and the media, our volunteers seek to generate the political will to end poverty throughout the world. Each month Results organises a telephone conference call with a development expert providing our volunteers with ongoing access to up-to-date development information. This knowledge is then transformed into action by our 18 volunteer groups throughout the UK with the support of our head office in Leamington Spa. We are continually seeking to expand our work and take on new volunteers in all parts of the country. Similarly, volunteers living in the Leamington area may like to consider providing administrative assistance in our head office. Joining Results provides a framework within which you can channel your concerns for those living in poverty in a focused and positive way. ⓑ

Number of projects: 20 UK: 20
Starting months: January–December
Time required: 16–52 weeks (plus)
Age: 18–25
Causes: AIDS/HIV, Children, Health Care/ Medical, Human Rights, Poor/Homeless, Young People.
Activities: Campaigning, Development Issues, Fundraising, Group Work, International Aid.
Placements: 70–100
When to apply: All year.
Work alone/with others: With others.
Qualifications: No restrictions but must be official residents or able to reside in the UK.
Health requirements: Nil.
Costs: Food and accommodation.

Training: Coaching and skills training will be given to enable the volunteer to develop the necessary skills to fulfil the tasks and responsibilities.
Reading material also provided.
Supervision: Supervision by Results staff.
Interviews: Prospective volunteers are interviewed in person at the national office.
Worldwide placements: North America: (Canada, USA); Central America (Mexico); Asia (Japan); Australasia (Australia); Europe (Germany).
UK placements: England (Berkshire, Buckinghamshire, Cheshire, Dorset, Essex, London, Manchester, Nottinghamshire, Sussex – East, Warwickshire, West Midlands, N. Yorkshire, S. Yorkshire, W. Yorkshire); Scotland (Edinburgh, Lothian – East, Lothian – West, Scottish Borders); Wales (Blaenau Gwent).

REYKJAVIK RED CROSS VOLUNTEER CENTER

Hverfisgata 105
101 Reykjavik
Iceland
T: 00 354 551 8800
F: 00 354 562 5317
E: sjalfbodamidlun@deild.redcross.is
Contact: Huldis S.Haraldsdottir

Reykjavik Red Cross Volunteer Center promotes and has information about volunteering in Iceland. It may well be able to put volunteers in touch with organisations which are not yet listed on the WorldWide Volunteering database. Alternative e-mail address: urkir@deild.redcross.is

Starting months: January–December
Time required: 1–52 weeks (plus)
Age: 16 plus – no upper limit
Causes: Addicts/Ex-Addicts, AIDS/HIV, Animal Welfare, Archaeology, Architecture, Children, Conservation, Disabled (learning and physical), Elderly People, Environmental Causes, Health Care/Medical, Heritage, Holidays for Disabled, Human Rights, Inner City Problems, Offenders/Ex-Offenders, Poor/Homeless, Refugees, Teaching/assisting (nursery, primary, secondary, mature, EFL) Unemployed, Wildlife, Work Camps – Seasonal, Young People.
Activities: Accountancy, Administration, Agriculture/Farming, Arts/Crafts, Building/Construction, Campaigning, Caring (general, day and residential), Catering, Community Work, Computers, Conservation Skills, Cooking, Counselling, Development Issues, DIY, Driving, First Aid, Forestry, Fundraising, Gardening/Horticulture, Group Work, International Aid, Library/Resource Centres, Manual Work, Marketing/Publicity, Music, Newsletter/Journalism, Outdoor Skills,

Religion, Research, Scientific Work, Social Work, Sport, Summer Camps, Teaching, Technical Skills, Theatre/Drama, Training, Translating, Visiting/Befriending, Work Camps – Seasonal.
Costs: Varies according to the project.
Worldwide placements: Europe (Iceland).

RICHMOND FELLOWSHIP

2nd and 3rd Floors
5 Portland Place, Pritchard Street
Bristol
BS2 8RH UK
T: 0117 989 2525
F: 0117 989 2626
E: rosemary.earnes@richmondfellowship.org.uk
W: www.richmondfellowship.org.uk
Contact: Rosemary Earnes

The Richmond Fellowship has worked in the field of mental health since 1959. Runs more than 150 community-based projects in the UK working with people of all ages. The projects include intensive rehabilitation programmes, supported housing projects, group homes and workshops for people with mental health problems, schizophrenia, addiction and emotional problems. Work in the projects focuses on helping residents to regain personal stability, the ability to make good relationships and to find and keep a job. The Fellowship also runs its own college and provides a comprehensive range of training options for its own staff and for people involved in mental health work. Volunteers are needed to work within some of the projects, supervised by project staff, assisting the residents and helping in the day-to-day running of the house. As well as assisting with the basic necessities of life, some volunteers also become involved in activities such as gardening, cooking, art, music, drama and sport. Whilst we recognise the important role played by our volunteers, not all of our projects are able to accept volunteers. Throughout the UK.

Number of projects: 80 UK: 80
Starting months: January–December
Time required: 1–52 weeks (plus)
Age: 18–65
Causes: Addicts/Ex-Addicts, Disabled (learning)
Activities: Arts/Crafts, Caring – Day, Community Work, Cooking, Driving, Fundraising, Gardening/Horticulture, Group Work, Music, Sport, Theatre/Drama, Training.
Placements: 5
When to apply: All year.
Work alone/with others: With others.
Qualifications: No restrictions – only able to accept 18 years and over.
Health requirements: In reasonable good health.
Costs: Travel, food and accommodation.

Benefits: Reasonable expenses reimbursed.
Training: On-the-job training is provided plus 'in-house' training courses.
Supervision: Supervision meeting every 2 weeks.
Charity number: 200453
UK placements: England (Bedfordshire, Berkshire, Bristol, Cambridgeshire, Channel Islands, Cheshire, Cornwall, Co Durham, Devon, Dorset, Essex, Herefordshire, Hertfordshire, Isle of Man, Kent, Lancashire, Leicestershire, Lincolnshire, London, Manchester, Merseyside, Northamptonshire, Northumberland, Nottinghamshire, Oxfordshire, Rutland, Staffordshire, Suffolk, Surrey, E. Sussex, W. Sussex, Tyne and Wear, Warwickshire, West Midlands, Wiltshire, Worcestershire, E. Yorkshire, N. Yorkshire, S. Yorkshire, W. Yorkshire).

RIGHT HAND TRUST

24 School Street
Wolverhampton
West MidlandsWV1 4LF UK
T: 01902 428824
F: 01902 428824
E: mail@righthandtrust.org.uk
W: www.righthandtrust.org.uk
Contact: Mike Freeman, MBE

The Right Hand Trust offers placements in Africa and sometimes in the Windward Islands as guests of the local Anglican Church. The purpose of the placements is to enable the volunteers to integrate into the local community as much as possible. In doing this they will benefit from a cross-cultural experience in a Christian environment. Activities in the placement are usually centred around teaching at a local school although the volunteers in recent years have been involved in a wide range of other activities with the church and community as their focus. The volunteers have a lifestyle as close to that of the host community as possible. Applicants are welcome from every Christian denomination and no particular level of commitment is expected, though communicant status in a home church is encouraged. This away year enables volunteers to grow in the Faith. The Trust publishes a news sheet – the Bush Telegraph – available to all enquirers (please send an A4 SAE – 44p). The view of the great majority of those who have participated in the project is that they have had a life-enriching, perhaps life-changing experience which they will value for a long time. Most believe that they have received more than they could give. There is an opportunity to meet returned volunteers and to find out more about us. Write for details!

Number of projects: 11 UK: 0
Starting months: Jul
Time required: 32 weeks
Age: 18–30
Causes: AIDS/HIV, Children, Health Care/Medical, Poor/Homeless, Refugees, Teaching/assisting (nursery, primary, secondary, EFL), Unemployed, Young People.
Activities: Administration, Building/Construction, Community Work, DIY, Library/Resource Centres, Music, Religion, Social Work, Sport, Teaching, Technical Skills, Theatre/Drama, Training, Visiting/Befriending.
Placements: 50
When to apply: Before 1st July (late entrants possible until 20th August).
Work alone/with others: In pairs (same gender).
Qualifications: A-levels or vocational training (low-tech). Christian commitment.
Equipment/clothing: Nothing expensive.
Health requirements: No known medical problems. Full range of preventative injections.
Costs: Approx. £2,900 for flights, accommodation, insurance, training etc. + cost of food (£1–£2 per day).
Benefits: Free basic accommodation and extensive research development.
Training: This includes a 5-day induction in July, a placements weekend in September, and a week-long cross-cultural training course in early January upon arrival abroad. This is followed by a short acclimatisation course in January in individual countries.
Supervision: Local representative and host Diocese.
Interviews: Interviews take place in the West Midlands during a Glimpse of Africa weekend – normally the last weekend of each month.
Charity number: 1014934
Worldwide placements: Africa (Gambia, Kenya, Lesotho, Malawi, Namibia, Rwanda, Saint Helena, Swaziland, Tanzania, Uganda, Zambia, Zimbabwe); Central America (Grenada, Saint Vincent/Grenadines).

ROADPEACE

P O Box 2579
London
NW10 3PW UK
T: +44 (0) 20 8838 5102
F: +44 (0) 20 8838 5103
E: webmaster@roadpeace.org
W: www.roadpeace.org
Contact: Alan Moran

RoadPeace is currently building its web presence through the introduction of a number of web based projects which provide interesting opportunities for volunteers with appropriate web based skills (ranging from authorship and design through to application and development in PHP and XML). RoadPeace exists to represent the interests of bereaved and injured road crash victims, to help and support them and work to stop the injustices suffered by them. Much of our work is also directed at road danger reduction and research, since we believe that to continue to tolerate this preventable mass disaster is unacceptable. RoadPeace is celebrating its 10th anniversary with the launch of a new web site, which we hope to develop with time to a truly helpful and interesting site. There may be placements for volunteers with an offending background subject to negotiation. Based in London though there may be limited opportunities in regional groups. 🖾 📗

Number of projects: 2 UK: 2
Starting months: January–December
Time required: 12–52 weeks (plus)
Age: 18 plus – no upper limit
Causes: Children, Disabled (physical), Elderly People, Health Care/Medical.
Activities: Administration, Campaigning, Computers, Research, Technical Skills.
Placements: 3
When to apply: As soon as possible.
Work alone/with others: With others.
Qualifications: Some knowledge of web based working required. Working familiarity and desktop office applications (Windows/Linux) essential. Understanding of HTML and web authoring is a distinct advantage. No nationality restrictions. We may not, however, have the resources to support visa/immigration applications.
Equipment/clothing: Access to Internet computer essential.
Health requirements: No restrictions.
Costs: Some travel costs (to attend meetings) may be incurred. Food and accommodation.
Benefits: A limited budget is available to support volunteers in their work.
Training: Subject to negotiation. Free technical documentation is available to all volunteers.
Supervision: Web based products are managed by the webmaster who acts in the position of technical lead and project manager on behalf of RoadPeace.
Interviews: Where possible volunteers will be interviewed at our London office.
Charity number: 1020364
UK placements: England (London).

ROSSY CENTRE FOR HUMAN RIGHTS AND DEVELOPMENT

Divine Abosso House
Ikot-Ekpene Road, Km1
P O Box 287, Ohokobe Noume, Ibeku
Umuahia
Abia State Nigeria
E: Rchrd2000@yahoo.com
Contact: Mrs Rosemary Chi Okpara

Rossy Centre for Human Rights and Development has as its aims:
1. to promote community project initiative,
2. to facilitate the advancement anddevelopment of the community through voluntary efforts,
3. to spread to the general public knowledge about voluntary efforts and to devise workable strategies to achieve our aims,
4. to make the community a better place to live,
5. to empower the community youths, women and the development union towards the development of their community through their voluntary efforts,
6. to educate the people that hospitals, schools, market stalls, water, electricity and other social amenities can be provided through their voluntary efforts,
7. to teach that life and property of the community can be protected by forming youthful vigilante groups to take care of the security aspect of the people.
We work with community youth organisations, a service corp of young graduates, town union (ruling body of every community), schools and training centres.
Abia State, SE Nigeria
Rives State, S. Nigeria
Bayelsa State, Niger Delta.

Number of projects: 6 UK: 0
Starting months: Feb
Time required: 39–52 weeks
Age: 18–55
Causes: AIDS/HIV, Children, Disabled (learning and physical), Elderly People, Health Care/Medical, Human Rights, Offenders/Ex-Offenders, Poor/Homeless, Refugees, Unemployed, Young People.
Activities: Community Work, Computers, Counselling, Development Issues, First Aid, Library/Resource Centres, Manual Work, Music, Newsletter/Journalism, Outdoor Skills, Religion, Research, Social Work, Technical Skills, Training.
Placements: 370
When to apply: Before the third week of January.
Work alone/with others: With other young volunteers.
Qualifications: No qualifications necessary but any skilled volunteers very welcome. No restrictions providing volunteers have required travelling/residential documents.
Equipment/clothing: Yes – further details from the organisation.
Health requirements: There may be some restrictions.
Costs: Membership fee £2. Travel costs £1689. Subsistence £250.
Benefits: Board and lodging.
Training: We train unskilled volunteers and brief all necessary about the projects and how best to do them.

Supervision: Each project has a co-ordinator and supervisor who supervise volunteers and ensure the quality of the job.
Interviews: Interviews take place at our headquarters in Nigeria.
Charity number: 022325
Worldwide placements: Africa (Nigeria).

ROTARACT CLUB OF SOUTH PERTH

PO Box 817
South Perth
WA 6151 Australia
E: southperth@rotoract.org
W: www.rotaract.org/southperth
Contact: Simone Collins

Rotaract is a non-profit, non-political international volunteer service organisation for students and young professional aged 18–30 years. There are over 7,000 Rotaract clubs in 154 countries worldwide. The Rotaract Club of South Perth is Western Australia's oldest Rotaract Club. We organise a variety of hands on and fundraising projects and events in the local community and overseas, and we offer professional development and the chance to socialise and network with likeminded individuals. 18–30 year olds visiting Perth interested in gaining a different perspective of our city are welcome to volunteer with us during their stay. Volunteer involvement ranges from brainstorming ideas, planning and implementing projects, professional development seminars, or social events to participating in a range of activities, both large and small. We are unable to accept volunteers with an offending background. Most projects are done locally in Perth, Western Australia. 🖪

Number of projects: Numerous **UK:** 0
Starting months: January–December
Time required: 30–50 weeks
Age: 18–30
Causes: Environmental Causes, Young People.
Activities: Community Work, Fundraising, International Aid, Manual Work, Marketing/Publicity, Newsletter/Journalism, Visiting/Befriending.
Placements: 20
When to apply: At anytime.
Work alone/with others: Always with others.
Qualifications: Good teamwork and communication skills are necessary. Driving licence helps but is not mandatory.
Health requirements: No restrictions.
Costs: Travel to and from Australia. Food costs. One off joining fee of A\$20. Yearly membership fee around A\$60.
Benefits: Board available. Short term (2 weeks) home hosting available to international members of Rotaract visitng Perth.

Training: Whatever is required – done on an individual basis.
Supervision: We are all volunteers ourselves – a more experienced volunteer supervises newer volunteers.
Interviews: Yes – must attend three meetings and one project for us to assess their commitment and ability to work with other volunteers.
Worldwide placements: Australasia (Australia).

ROYAL MENCAP SOCIETY

123 Golden Lane
London
EC1Y ORT UK
T: +44 (0) 121 7077877 helpline 08088081111
E: shirley.potter@mencap.org.uk
W: www.mencap.org.uk
Contact: Shirley Potter and Jo Sullivan

Mencap is the largest learning disability charity in the UK. Mencap's mission is to improve the lives and opportunities of children and adults with learning disabilities, their families and carers. Mencap's vision is a world where everyone with a learning disability has an equal right to choice, opportunity and respect, with the support that they need. Mencap is a membership organisation; membership is open to all approved and properly constituted groups. There are volunteering opportunities across the organisation in local groups, campaigning, fundraising, with children and young people, at Gateway clubs (leisure and sports). Volunteering with all ages from children to the elderly. Throughout the country there are over 700 local groups and clubs offering a wide range of activities for varying age groups, covering leisure, sports, arts, and other recreational activities. They are a bridge into the local community giving groups and individuals the opportunity to take part in community activities as any other person or group would. Our volunteers are CRB (criminal record bureau) checked. To welcome, help and support our volunteers in their roles we offer accessible information, support and training on things such as health and safety awareness, being an advocate, a supporter and a campaigner. 🖪 📄

Number of projects UK: 700
Starting months: January–December
Time required: 1–52 weeks
Age: 14 plus – no upper limit
Causes: Children, Disabled (learning), Elderly People, Young People.
Activities: Administration, Arts/Crafts, Campaigning, Caring (general and day), Community Work, Driving, Fundraising, Music, Sport, Theatre/Drama, Visiting/Befriending.
Placements: Hundreds

When to apply: All year.
Work alone/with others: with others.
Qualifications: Nil but references checked.
Health requirements: Nil.
Costs: Nil except expenses.
Training: A variety of training is provided.
Supervision: Supervision undertaken.
Interviews: Applicants are interviewed, generally at the placement site.
UK placements: England (throughout); Northern Ireland (throughout); Wales (throughout).

ROYAL NATIONAL INSTITUTE FOR THE BLIND

224 Great Portland Street
London
W1N 6AA UK
T: +44 (0) 207 388 1266
E: helpline@rnib.org.uk
W: www.rnib.org.uk
Contact: Katie Maeda

Number of projects: 1 UK: 1
Starting months: January–December
Time required: 1–52 weeks
Age: 14 plus – no upper limit
Causes: Children, Disabled (physical), Elderly People, Health Care/Medical, Young People.
Activities: Caring – General, Community Work, Group Work, Social Work, Visiting/Befriending.
UK placements: England (throughout); Scotland (throughout); Northern Ireland (throughout); Wales (throughout).

ROYAL SOCIETY FOR THE PROTECTION OF BIRDS

Volunteer Unit
The Lodge
Sandy
Bedfordshire SG19 2DL UK
T: 01767 680551
F: 01767 683262
E: volunteers@rspb.org.uk
W: www.rspb.org.uk
Contact: Kate Tycer

RSPB volunteers interested in natural history and conservation are needed for a variety of conservation-related tasks on bird reserves throughout the UK. The work varies from season to season and from reserve to reserve, but can include practical management tasks, work with visitors, species protection and survey/monitoring work. Ornithological knowledge is less important than a genuine interest in conservation, enthusiasm and a willingness to work as part of a team. There is a four week maximum stay for the first time volunteer, but long term placements are available by arrangement.

Minimum age for volunteers from overseas is 18, and must possess a good standard of spoken English. There is a £10 administration fee for overseas volunteers. More information sent with confirmation of booking.

Number of projects: 32 UK: 32
Starting months: January–December
Time required: 1–52 weeks
Age: 16–80
Causes: Conservation, Environmental Causes, Wildlife.
Activities: Agriculture/Farming, Building/Construction, Conservation Skills, Forestry, Gardening/Horticulture, Manual Work, Outdoor Skills, Scientific Work.
Placements: 500
When to apply: Any time – write for a brochure or see www.rspb.org.uk/helprspb/volunteering
Work alone/with others: With others.
Qualifications: If volunteers are from outside the UK, minimum age is 18.
Equipment/clothing: Waterproof clothing, wellington boots, old clothes, sleeping bag (a detailed list will be sent with booking confirmation).
Health requirements: Physical management tasks require physically fit volunteers, although you will only be expected to undertake tasks within your capabilities. Visitor work does not require a high level of physical fitness but it is necessary on a few sites.
Costs: Food, pocket money and travel to and from the reserve.
Benefits: Accommodation.
Training: As appropriate to task.
Supervision: Supervision is by reserve staff.
Interviews: For long-term placements only.
UK placements: England (Cumbria, Devon, Dorset, Essex, Gloucestershire, Kent, Lancashire, Norfolk, Somerset, Staffordshire, Suffolk, W. Yorkshire); Scotland (Highland, Orkney Islands, Perth and Kinross, Shetland Islands); Wales (Anglesey, Pembrokeshire, Powys).

SALVATION ARMY

101 Newington Causeway
London
SE1 6BN UK
T: +44 (0) 207 367 4944
T: +44 (0) 207 367 4711
E: colin.johnson@salvationarmy.org.uk
W: www.salvationarmy.org.uk
Contact: Major Colin Johnson

There is no voluntary work at the Salvation Army Headquarters and prospective volunteers should contact their local hostel or branch through the telephone directory. We have our own officers and trained resettlement workers so volunteers would only be involved in helping by doing the mundane tasks.

Number of projects: 1 UK: 1
Starting months: January–December
Time required: 1–52 weeks
Age: 18 plus – no upper limit
Causes: Addicts/Ex-Addicts, Inner City Problems, Offenders/Ex-Offenders, Poor/Homeless, Refugees.
Activities: Administration, Catering, Cooking, Religion, Social Work, Technical Skills.
Placements: 100
When to apply: All year.
Work alone/with others: With others.
Health requirements: Nil.
Costs: Food and accommodation.
Benefits: Varies.
Training: Many courses run 'in house'.
Supervision: Mainly by trained Salvation Army officers.
UK placements: England (throughout); Scotland (throughout); Northern Ireland (throughout); Wales (throughout).

SAMARITANS, THE

The Upper Mill
Kingston Road
Ewell
Surrey KT17 2AF UK
T: +44 (0) 208 394 8300
F: +44 (0) 208 394 8301
E: admin@samaritans.org
W: www.samaritans.org
Contact: Martin Oneill

The Samaritans provide confidential emotional support to anyone who is in despair or suicidal 24 hours a day, 365 days a year throughout the UK and the Republic of Ireland. Most contacts are by telephone but people can talk to us face to face or correspond by letter or e-mail. The 19,600 people who provide this service are all volunteers and all of the 203 branches are independent charities, responsible for raising their revenue and capital costs. The Samaritans depend on public donations for over 95% of their income. Funds are raised in the branches from public collections, events, companies and charitable trusts. A growing number of branches run charity shops. The Samaritans take volunteers from all walks of life and are non-judgemental. Contact your local Samaritan branch for an application form.

Number of projects: 203 UK: 203 branches
Starting months: January–December
Time required: 2–52 weeks
Age: 18 plus – no upper limit
Causes: Addicts/Ex-Addicts, AIDS/HIV, Disabled (learning and physical), Elderly People, Health Care/Medical, Human Rights, Inner City Problems, Offenders/Ex-Offenders, Poor/Homeless, Refugees, Unemployed, Young People.
Activities: Administration, Fundraising, Marketing/Publicity, Training.
When to apply: All year.
Work alone/with others: Others.
Qualifications: Over 18 years old.
Health requirements: No restrictions.
Costs: Cost to and from work place, food and accommodation.
Benefits: Expenses will be paid.
Training: If required.
Supervision: Yes.
Charity number: 219432
Worldwide placements: Europe (Ireland).
UK placements: England (throughout); Scotland (throughout); Northern Ireland (throughout); Wales (throughout).

SAMASEVAYA

National Secretariat
Anuradhapura Road
Talawa
Sri Lanka
T: 0094 2576266
F: 0094 25 76266
E: samasev@sltnet.lk.
Contact: Samson Jayasinghe

– works for peace through development.
– believes in the concept of settling disputes and conflicts by mutual understanding. It tolerates views of all parties involved.
– believes that all humanity is one brotherhood of man. It is against all types of injustice, hatred, violence whether it be national, communal, racial, religious or political.

– believes in the concept of self reliance and in the total development of the individual. All individuals must collectively make decisions, plan, act and execute on a just basis.
– believes in the concept that all humanity by its own strength, labour and hard work should unite to achieve progress towards self sustainability. Samasevaya helps the poorest in their best interests in the humblest form to attain both social and economic goals.
– believes in the rights of women and that all men and women have a very important role in the transformation of the social economic position of women. We provide loans, making them socially mobilised, and also with scientific knowledge in agriculture and other income generating activities.
– believes and takes an active interest in the environment. It believes that the environment has to be bequeathed to future generations intact.
Present activities are: 1. Educational programme on self reliance, 2. Educational programme on national harmony. 3. Samasevaya Children's foundation. 4.Educational programme on the environment. 5. Upliftment of women.
The workcamps provide the opportunity for young people of various nationalities and communities to live together for a short period. Volunteers with offending backgrounds are accepted. ♿ 📄

Number of projects: 17 **UK:** 0
Starting months: January–December
Time required: 1–48 weeks
Age: 16 plus – no upper limit
Causes: Children, Conservation, Environmental Causes, Human Rights, Poor/Homeless, Refugees, Teaching/assisting (primary, secondary, mature, EFL), Unemployed, Work Camps – Seasonal, Young People.
Activities: Agriculture/Farming, Community Work, Conservation Skills, Development Issues, First Aid, Forestry, Fundraising, Gardening/Horticulture, Group Work, Library/ Resource Centres, Manual Work, Marketing/ Publicity, Music, Scientific Work, Social Work, Sport, Summer Camps, Teaching, Training, Work Camps – Seasonal.
Placements: 25
When to apply: All year.
Work alone/with others: Both.
Qualifications: Usually nil.
Health requirements: Nil.
Costs: Everything except accommodation. Food costs US$4 per day approx.
Benefits: We are able to provide simple accommodation – a bed in a room. Common bathrooms and toilets are used.
Training: No pre-placement training given.
Supervision: We have an informal flexible

arrangement. Volunteers are very free and work with one of the officers. The National Executive Committee is responsible for volunteers.
Interviews: There is no interview.
Charity number: S 371
Worldwide placements: Asia (Sri Lanka).

SANWILD WILDLIFE TRUST

P.O. Box 418
Letsitele
0885 South Africa
T: +27 (0) 15 3451878
F: +27 (0) 15 3451878
E: sanwild@pixie.co.za
W: www.sanwild.org
Contact: Louise Joubert

Sanwild Wildlife Trust was founded by Louise Joubert in 2000. Louise's original exposure to the unethical and inhumane practices in the wildlife industry has made her an outspoken critic of the South African game industry and her determination to change the status quo brought her to develop Sanwild. Sanwild was established to function as a sanctuary, set in 2262 ha of land, primarily for wild animals injured or orphaned through game captures, operations and hunting. The fact that Sanwild is the only sanctuary in South Africa where both the land and the wild animals are protected by a registred non-profit trust makes it unique – a true sanctuary in all respects. No wild animal at Sanwild may ever be hunted, traded or sold and you may rest assured that all the animals encountered in the sanctuary during your visit will remain in a protected area for the duration of their natural lives. The main purpose of the sanctuary is to rehabilitate wild animals to become independent and free-ranging, suitable for release back into the wild. Sanwild comprises some of the best wildlife habitat in South Africa. We are able to place volunteers with an offending background. Between Phalaborwa and Tzaneen in the Limpopo Province, South Africa. Very close to major tourist attractions such as the Kruger National Park, Bourkes Luck's Potholes and Blyde River Canyon. Also close to Mojadji Reserve.

Number of projects: 1 **UK:** 0
Starting months: Mar, Apr, May, Jun, Jul, Aug, Sep, Oct, Nov, Dec
Time required: 2–52 weeks (plus)
Age: 18–70
Causes: Animal Welfare, Conservation, Environmental Causes, Wildlife.
Activities: Administration, Building/ Construction, Campaigning, Caring – General, Computers, Conservation Skills, Cooking.
Placements: 60
When to apply: As soon as possible.
Work alone/with others: Work alone.

Equipment/clothing: Cool clothes in summer, bathing costume, sunscreen, hat, warm clothes in winter.
Health requirements: No restrictions.
Costs: Volunteers to fund their air fares and air fares to and from Phalaborwa Airport – SA Airlink, optional day trips to places of interests, accommodation, curios or meals.
Benefits: Optional day trips to places of interest, full board and lodging at Sanwild including all meals and cold drinks – no alcholic beverages included in daily rates.
Training: Anti-poaching procedures, animal and spoor identification, bird and tree identification, fencing, bush encroachment eradication, basic veterinary procedures, animal feeding, African beadworking, claypot sculpture & tribal dancing.
Supervision: Game rangers supervise.
Interviews: No interviews.
Charity number: NPO 011–266
Worldwide placements: Africa (South Africa).

SAO CAMBODIA

Bawtry Hall
Bawtry
Doncaster
DN10 6JH UK
T: 01302 714004
F: 01302 710027
E: admin@sao-cambodia.org
W: www.sao-cambodia.org
Contact: Ivor Greer

SAO Cambodia is a UK based Christian mission serving the Cambodian people in the name and Spirit of Jesus Christ, helping relieve poverty and distress and stimulating prayer for the nation and church. We are active solely in Cambodia and are in partnership with International Co-operation for Cambodia. All our members and volunteers must have active commitment to the Christian faith. They are commissioned to join us by their home churches. Because of the nature of the work our members and volunteers usually need relevant skills and experience. Cambodia is a very poor developing country, only very slowly recovering from the ravages of the Khmer Rouge 'Killing Fields' of the 1970s when about two million people died, a quarter of the population.

Number of projects: 9 in Cambodia **UK:** 0
Starting months: January–December
Time required: 13–52 weeks (plus)
Age: 18–60
Causes: Children, Disabled (physical), Health Care/Medical, Poor/Homeless, Teaching/assisting (EFL), Young People.
Activities: Accountancy, Administration, Agriculture/Farming, Arts/Crafts, Building/Construction, Caring – General, Community

Work, Computers, Development Issues, DIY, Driving, Forestry, Manual Work, Music, Outdoor Skills, Religion, Social Work, Sport, Teaching, Technical Skills, Training, Translating, Visiting/Befriending.
Placements: Varies.
When to apply: All year.
Work alone/with others: It varies.
Qualifications: Nil but the more qualifications the better.
Health requirements: Robust health.
Costs: All costs are met by volunteers.
Benefits: We have a pooled support system. Arranged accommodation on field. Separate quarters.
Training: Relevant preparation. UK orientation, field orientation, language training when appropriate.
Supervision: Full management and pastoral supervision given.
Interviews: Preliminary exploratory interviews take place in Gravesend, Kent or at Bawtry, South Yorkshire. Further interviews are normally in London. Thorough referencing is undertaken.
Charity number: 293382
Worldwide placements: Asia (Cambodia).

SAVANNAH CAMPS AND LODGES & TAITA DISCOVERY CENTRE

Head Office
P.O. Box 48019
Nairobi
Kenya
T: 254 2 331191/229009
F: 254 2 330698
E: eaos@africaonline.co.ke
W: www.savannahcamps.com/tdc
Contact: Steve Turner

Savannah Camps and Lodges and Taita Discovery Centre are tucked in the heart of the vast and arid Tsavo thorn bush wilderness of southeastern Kenya. It stretches 170,000 acres. It is unspoiled, private and community owned land that is the core of the Tsavo Kasigau Wildlife Corridor (TKWC). Our vision is to build the largest private wildlife sanctuary in East Africa, creating a vital corridor for almost one thousand elephants as well as all other wildlife to migrate between precious sources of water in the adjacent Tsavo East and Tsavo West National Parks. Formerly known as the Taru Desert, the Tsavo area is truly one of the world's most unique ecological treasures. Tsavo offers the last best hope for the survival in the wild of large mammals that need space like the elephant, lion, cheetah, giraffe and herds of antelope and other prey species. Tsavo is also home to the Pancake Tortoise, the Taita Falcon, an endemic race of legless lizard as well as innumerable beetles, butterflies, frogs, snakes,

birds and chameleons. Our partners include the Kenya Wildlife Service, the African Wildlife Foundation, Earthwatch Institute, Wildlife Works Inc, Africa Adventure Company and other private corporations as well as local community leaders and volunteers. With their help we work towards our goals:
To enlighten both Kenyans and foreigners about the immense bio-diversity, endemic species and natural wonders of this wilderness and instil the desire to preserve it.
To offer volunteers the opportunity to acquire as much knowledge as possible about every aspect of the Tsavo environment.
To promote the expansion and preservation of land through improved management practices and the introduction of income generating, environmentally sustainable micro-enterprises.
To assist in the funding and implementation of infrastructure improvements to local schools, hospitals and other village resources.
Cannot accept volunteers with an offending background at present. Kenya – Coast Province, Taita Taveta District, nearest town – Voi, nearest village – Maungu. Rukinga Ranch/Taita Ranch close to Mount Kasigau. Area sometimes known as the Taru Desert. 🔥 📄

Number of projects: 1 **UK:** 0
Starting months: January–December
Time required: 2–52 weeks
Age: 18–80
Causes: Animal Welfare, Children, Conservation, Environmental Causes, Heritage, Poor/Homeless, Teaching/assisting (primary, secondary), Wildlife.
Activities: Agriculture/Farming, Arts/Crafts, Building/Construction, Community Work, Computers, Conservation Skills, Development Issues, DIY, Forestry, Gardening/Horticulture, Manual Work, Newsletter/Journalism, Research, Scientific Work, Sport, Teaching, Technical Skills, Training.
Placements: 55
When to apply: Any time.
Work alone/with others: Both.
Qualifications: Volunteers must be mature, self-motivated, independent, hard working, have common sense, be self confident and well organised.
Equipment/clothing: Binoculars, walking shoes, sun hat – necessary. Laptop very useful.
Health requirements: The site is a long way from a good hospital. We have an airstrip so a flying doctor can land.
Costs: All costs are borne directly by the volunteer at present. This includes the flying doctor, insurance and travel to and from site.
Benefits: Accommodation. Also volunteers can expect to be taken on game drives and walks including assent of Mount Kasigau.
Training: There is some training for some tasks.

Supervision: Can provide supervision. Volunteers must listen to and follow instructions.
Interviews: On interview. Applicants submit an application form. We reserve the right to turn away volunteers who prove unsuitable at any time.
Worldwide placements: Africa (Kenya).

SAVE THE EARTH NETWORK

P O Box CT 3635
Cantonments
Accra
Ghana
T: 00 233 21 669625
F: 00 233 21 667791
E: ebensten@yahoo.com
Contact: Ebenezer Mensah

Save The Earth Network is an organisation formed in 1998 dedicated to promoting sustainable development and international solidarity through voluntary work in Ghana. We aim at contributing positively to help reduce poverty, hunger, malnutrition, diseases, illiteracy, drug abuse, unemployment and environmental degradation which are increasingly becoming the order of the day in most parts of the developing world. We are a membership-based organisation and a networking tool for social and economic development organisations, groups and activists. We welcome new ideas from volunteers. Projects in Accra and also in towns and villages 20–60 miles from Accra in the Eastern, Greater Accra and Central regions of Ghana. 📄

Number of projects: 21 **UK:** 0
Starting months: January–December
Time required: 4–52 weeks
Age: 18–60
Causes: Addicts/Ex-Addicts, AIDS/HIV, Children, Conservation, Environmental Causes, Health Care/Medical, Human Rights, Inner City Problems, Poor/Homeless, Teaching/assisting (nursery, primary, secondary, mature, EFL) Unemployed, Work Camps – Seasonal, Young People.
Activities: Administration, Agriculture/Farming, Arts/Crafts, Building/Construction, Caring – General, Community Work, Computers, Conservation Skills, Cooking, Counselling, Development Issues, Forestry, Gardening/Horticulture, Group Work, Manual Work, Social Work, Summer Camps, Teaching, Technical Skills, Training, Work Camps – Seasonal.
Placements: 30
When to apply: All year.
Work alone/with others: With others.
Qualifications: Volunteers should understand English. A visa is required.
Equipment/clothing: Volunteers should bring mosquito net and summer clothing.

Health requirements: Volunteers should take malaria prophylactics and be in good health.
Costs: Participation fee of US$250 per month includes board and lodging.
Training: Training on the job.
Supervision: Volunteers are supervised by experienced leaders.
Interviews: No interviews.
Charity number: G3533
Worldwide placements: Africa (Ghana).

SAVIO HOUSE RETREAT CENTRE

Ingersley Road
Bollington
Macclesfield
Cheshire SK10 5RW UK
T: 01625 573256
F: 01652 560221
E: gill@saviohouse.org.uk
W: www.saviohouse.org.uk
Contact: Gill McCambridge

Savio House is a Retreat and Conference Centre run by the Salesians of Don Bosco – a Roman Catholic Order working for youth all over the world. It is situated in a valley outside Macclesfield on the edge of the Peak District, between Bollington and Rainow, surrounded by fields, hills and woodland. School groups from all over the Northwest and Midlands, usually year 10 or 11 (aged 14–16) but also some younger groups, come for a residential retreat lasting three days. The retreat takes place in an atmosphere of joy and friendship. The programme is adapted to the needs of the group and usually includes time for relaxation, sharing of life experiences, reconciliation, affirmation and celebration. Prayer and liturgy are designed to be creative and involve the young people to the full. Schools find that the advantages gained by the young people more than compensate for the loss of study time. Countless letters from young people themselves convince us that their time at Savio has been an important part of their faith journey. Many groups and organisations of a religious, charitable or educational nature use the facilities at Savio for meetings and weekend conferences. We put on day retreats for Confirmation candidates in the local deanery and leavers days for some of the local primary schools. Many schools come to Savio with year groups or individual forms and lead their own day retreats or courses. These are an excellent way to improve friendships among the young people and build good relationships with staff. We have facilities to take youth groups with a barn that can take up to 32, including staff, with comfortable dormitory accommodation and self-catering facilities. The cottage has room for 23. We also have outreach work in

operation. Because of child protection reasons, all prospective volunteers have to police checked and must inform us of any previous convictions (including those spent) Bollington, Macclesfield. &
Number of projects: several UK: 1
Starting months: Sep
Time required: 42 weeks
Age: 18–30
Causes: Children, Young People.
Activities: Arts/Crafts, Group Work, Music, Religion, Theatre/Drama.
Placements: 7
When to apply: As soon as possible.
Work alone/with others: Work as part of a team.
Qualifications: Fluency in English, a willingness to work and learn.
Health requirements: No restrictions.
Costs: No cost once at the Centre.
Benefits: Board and lodging, £40.00 (€56) per week pocket money and travel expenses paid for trips home 5 time a year. Volunteers live in community – own room with shared meals and shared living space.
Training: Training is offered in team building exercises, group work skills, first aid, health and safety, child protection and 'in house' induction.
Supervision: Volunteers are supervised once fortnightly.
Interviews: Interviews are held at Savio House and applicants are asked to work on a retreat with us, so they can get a real insight into the work we do.
Charity number: 233779
UK placements: England (Cheshire).

SCOPE – Midlands Region

2nd Floor, Talbot House
Market Street
Shrewsbury
Shropshire
SY1 1LG UK
T: 01527 550909
F: 01527 550808
E: midlands.team@scope.org.uk
W: www.scope.org.uk
Contact: Mrs Nancy Evans

Scope exists to provide support and services for people with cerebral palsy and their families. Cerebral palsy is damage to parts of the brain which results in physical impairment affecting movement. It is not a disease or an illness. It is most commonly the result of failure of a part of the brain to develop, either before birth or in early childhood. Scope is an organisation for people with cp. We originally started in life in 1952 as The National Spastics Society. Scope is about opening doors. It is about enabling people with cp to gain access to the opportunities that everyone needs to make the best use of their abilities. Our education services provide training and support for children and adults with cp, and also for parents and helpers. Our living options services provide accommodation, personal support, training, opportunities for further education, personal development and advocacy for adults with cp and other physical and learning disabilities. We run residential and small group homes, supported independent living schemes and day and respite services. Scope is also involved in a Supported Employment Programme which not only provides information for people with cp but also employs people through the scheme. Scope also has two national sources of information for people with cp. There is a freephone Cerebral Palsy helpline that is open seven days a week and there is a library and information unit, which responds to both telephone and written enquiries. There are 35 local affiliated groups in this area, some of whom provide services and support groups. Volunteers with an offending background may be accepted for some work. ⬚ ⬚

Number of projects: Many **UK:** Many
Starting months: Jan, Feb, Mar, Apr, May, Jun, Jul, Aug, Sep, Oct
Time required: 2–52 weeks (plus)
Age: 15–65
Causes: Children, Disabled (learning and physical), Work Camps – Seasonal.
Activities: Administration, Agriculture/Farming, Caring (general, day and residential), Community Work, Computers, Driving, Fundraising, Gardening/Horticulture, Library/ Resource Centres, Newsletter/Journalism, Outdoor Skills, Work Camps – Seasonal.
Placements: Hundreds.
When to apply: All year.
Work alone/with others: Both but usually with others.
Health requirements: Nil unless it affects the individual's ability to perform the agreed tasks.
Costs: Nil.
Benefits: Out of pocket expenses – normally 30p per mile (own car) or bus, rail fares. Lunch allowance.
Training: To be discussed.
Supervision: To be discussed.
Interviews: Interviews take place at project location.
UK placements: England (Buckinghamshire, Derbyshire, Herefordshire, Leicestershire, Nottinghamshire, Oxfordshire, Shropshire, Staffordshire, Warwickshire, West Midlands, Worcestershire).

SCOPE – The North Region

Unit B, Moor Park Business Centre
Thornes Moor Road
Wakefield
West Yorkshire WF2 8PF UK
T: 01924 366711
F: 01924 366764
E: northeastandyorkshire@scope.org.uk
W: www.scope.org.uk
Contact: Jesse Harris

Scope exists to provide support and services for people with cerebral palsy and their families. Cerebral palsy is damage to parts of the brain which results in physical impairment affecting movement. It is not a disease or an illness. It is most commonly the result of failure of a part of the brain to develop, either before birth or in early childhood. Scope is an organisation for people with cp. We originally started in life in 1952 as The National Spastics Society. Scope is about opening doors. It is about enabling people with cp to gain access to the opportunities that everyone needs to make the best use of their abilities. Our education services provide training and support for children and adults with cp, and also for parents and helpers. Our living options services provide accommodation, personal support, training, opportunities for further education, personal development and advocacy for adults with cp and other physical and learning disabilities. We run residential and small group homes, supported independent living schemes and day and respite services. Scope is also involved in a Supported Employment Programme which not only provides information for people with cp but also employs people through the scheme. Scope also has two national sources of information for people with cp. There is a freephone Cerebral Palsy helpline that is open seven days a week and there is a library and information unit, which responds to both telephone and written enquiries. There are 35 local affiliated groups in this area, some of whom provide services and support groups. Volunteers with an offending background may be accepted for some work. ⬚ ⬚

Number of projects: Many **UK:** Many
Starting months: Jan, Feb, Mar, Apr, May, Jun, Jul, Aug, Sep, Oct
Time required: 2–52 weeks (plus)
Age: 15–85
Causes: Children, Disabled (learning and physical), Work Camps – Seasonal.
Activities: Administration, Agriculture/Farming, Caring (general, day and residential), Community Work, Computers, Driving, Fundraising, Gardening/Horticulture, Library/ Resource Centres, Newsletter/Journalism, Outdoor Skills, Work Camps – Seasonal.

Placements: Hundreds.
When to apply: All year.
Work alone/with others: Both but usually with others.
Health requirements: Nil unless it affects the individual's ability to perform the agreed tasks.
Costs: Nil.
Benefits: Out of pocket expenses – normally 30p per mile (own car) or bus, rail fares. Lunch allowance.
Training: Training given suitable to placement.
Supervision: Supervised.
Interviews: Interviews take place at project location.
UK placements: England (Cheshire, Co Durham, Cumbria, Lancashire, Manchester, Merseyside, Northumberland, Tyne and Wear, N. Yorkshire, S. Yorkshire, W. Yorkshire).

SCOPE – West Region

Olympus House
Brittania Road
Patchway
Bristol
BS34 5TA UK
T: 0117 906 6333
Contact: Mike Shepherd

Scope exists to provide support and services for people with cerebral palsy and their families. Cerebral palsy is damage to parts of the brain which results in physical impairment affecting movement. It is not a disease or an illness. It is most commonly the result of failure of a part of the brain to develop, either before birth or in early childhood. Scope is an organisation for people with cp. We originally started in life in 1952 as The National Spastics Society. Scope is about opening doors. It is about enabling people with cp to gain access to the opportunities that everyone needs to make the best use of their abilities. Our education services provide training and support for children and adults with cp, and also for parents and helpers. Our living options services provide accommodation, personal support, training, opportunities for further education, personal development and advocacy for adults with cp and other physical and learning disabilities. We run residential and small group homes, supported independent living schemes and day and respite services. Scope is also involved in a Supported Employment Programme which not only provides information for people with cp but also employs people through the scheme. Scope also has two national sources of information for people with cp. There is a freephone Cerebral Palsy helpline that is open seven days a week and there is a library and information unit, which responds to both telephone and written enquiries. There are 35 local affiliated groups in this area, some of

whom provide services and support groups. Volunteers with an offending background may be accepted for some work. 🖥 📖

Number of projects: Many UK: Many
Starting months: Jan, Feb, Mar, Apr, May, Jun, Jul, Aug, Sep, Oct
Time required: 2–52 weeks (plus)
Age: 15–65
Causes: Children, Disabled (learning and physical), Work Camps – Seasonal.
Activities: Administration, Agriculture/Farming, Caring (general, day and residential), Community Work, Computers, Driving, Fundraising, Gardening/Horticulture, Library/Resource Centres, Newsletter/Journalism, Outdoor Skills, Work Camps – Seasonal.
Placements: Hundreds.
When to apply: All year.
Work alone/with others: Both but usually with others.
Equipment/clothing: Not usually.
Health requirements: Nil unless it affects the individual's ability to perform the agreed tasks.
Costs: Nil.
Benefits: Out of pocket expenses – normally 30p per mile (own car) or bus, rail fares. Lunch allowance.
Interviews: Interviews take place at project location.
Charity number: 208231
UK placements: England (Cornwall, Devon, Dorset, Gloucestershire, Somerset, Wiltshire).

SCOTTISH CHURCHES WORLD EXCHANGE

St Colm's International House
23 Inverleith Terrace
Edinburgh
EH3 5NS UK
T: 0131 315 4444
F: 0131 315 2222
E: we@stcolms.org
W: www.worldexchange.org.uk
Contact: The Rev. Robert S. Anderson

Scottish Churches World Exchange sends 50 volunteers each year to work in the developing world and assists congregations/groups planning their own short term visits/exchanges. Placements are arranged through partner churches and agencies of the Church of Scotland, the Catholic Church, the Scottish Episcopal Church and the United Reformed Church. We take volunteers of all denominations, experiences and of all ages. Volunteers have worked in Guatemala, El Salvador, Romania, Palestine/Israel, Pakistan, India, South Africa, Kenya, Malawi, Thailand and Lebanon. The volunteers work in health, education, development, church/community and administration according to their skills and experiences. Volunteers are expected to raise money for the World Exchange Travel Fund. This pays for travel/insurance, preparation courses before departure, debriefing weekend upon return and contributes to costs while the volunteer is overseas. (Other overseas costs are borne by the host organisation overseas.) In our volunteer placements we hope there is something of value for the volunteers themselves, for the host and for the Scottish churches. The time as a volunteer should be a time of growth in terms of both maturity and faith. ⑤

Number of projects: 50 **UK:** 0
Starting months: Jan, Aug, Sep
Time required: 12–48 weeks
Age: 17–75
Causes: Children, Disabled (learning and physical), Elderly People, Health Care/Medical, Human Rights, Poor/Homeless, Refugees, Teaching/assisting (nursery, primary, secondary, mature, EFL) Young People.
Activities: Accountancy, Administration, Agriculture/Farming, Building/Construction, Caring – General, Community Work, Computers, Cooking, Driving, Forestry, Fundraising, International Aid, Manual Work, Marketing/Publicity, Music, Religion, Social Work, Teaching, Technical Skills, Translating, Visiting/Befriending.
Placements: 50
When to apply: Applications are welcome throughout the year.
Work alone/with others: With others.
Qualifications: Member of Scottish church or United Reformed Church, UK.
Health requirements: Have to pass medical – depending on location.
Costs: Raising £2,500 fundraising towards cost.
Benefits: Food, accommodation and pocket money are provided by the host and SCWE. Training and resettlement programme with a small resettlement grant.
Training: SCWE provides preparation courses which are held twice a year before departure.
Supervision: We provide support while the volunteers are overseas.
Interviews: Interviews take place in Edinburgh.
Charity number: SCO20905
Worldwide placements: Africa (Kenya, Malawi, Nigeria, Rwanda, Zimbabwe); Central America (Guatemala); Asia (India, Lebanon, Pakistan); Europe (Romania).

SCOTTISH COMMUNITY FOUNDATION (THE CALEDONIAN CHALLENGE)

27 Palmerston Place
Edinburgh
EH12 5AP UK
T: 0131 225 9810
F: 0131 225 9818
E: toby@scottishcomfound.org.uk
W: www.scottishcomfound.org.uk
Contact: Toby Trustram Eve

The Caledonian Challenge is the most gruelling annual fundraising event of its kind. Teams of four, each representing companies from throughout the UK and beyond, all walk 54 miles of the West Highland Way over a 24 hour period in June. The event is the largest of its kind in the Highlands, raising a large amount of money for the support of local charities throughout Scotland and is set to become Scotland's largest charitable fundraising event. Volunteers are needed as support and back-up to help administer this annual event. Every sort of administrative activity is needed, both before the event and during the 24 hours. Volunteers with an offending background will be assessed individually. The West Highland Way – Fort William to Ardlut (West Coast of Scotland).

Number of projects: 1 **UK:** 1
Starting months: Jun
Time required: 1–4 weeks
Age: 16–80
Causes: Addicts/Ex-Addicts, AIDS/HIV, Animal Welfare, Children, Conservation, Disabled (learning and physical), Elderly People, Environmental Causes, Health Care/Medical, Heritage, Inner City Problems, Poor/Homeless, Teaching/assisting, Unemployed, Wildlife, Young People.
Activities: Administration, Conservation Skills, First Aid, Fundraising, Group Work, Manual Work, Marketing/Publicity, Outdoor Skills.
Placements: 200
When to apply: All year.
Work alone/with others: With other young volunteers.
Equipment/clothing: Waterproofs and sun protection.
Health requirements: Nil.
Costs: Travel, accommodation and board.
Benefits: During the event weekend, accommodation and board are provided.
Training: Varied training on location.
Supervision: Full supervision at all times.
Interviews: Interviews take place in Edinburgh.
UK placements: Scotland (Argyll and Bute, Dunbartonshire – East, Highland, Stirling).

SCOTTISH WILDLIFE TRUST

Cramond House
Kirk Cramond
Cramond Glebe Road
Edinburgh
EH4 6NS UK
T: 0131 312 7765
F: 0131 312 8705
E: enquiries@swt.org.uk
W: www.swt.org.uk
Contact: Glenn Rudman

Scottish Wildlife Trust is Scotland's leading voluntary body for nature conservation which works to protect, enhance and promote enjoyment of all aspects of our natural heritage. We own and manage over 120 wildlife reserves from the Borders to Orkney. We protect 7,000 wildlife sites. We own large areas of public greenspace in Cumbernauld and Irvine which is enjoyed by local people and benefits wildlife. Among our major campaigns, our Peat Project has already led to more gardeners choosing peat-free alternatives which save peat bogs. Volunteers are vital to our work and undertake a huge range of tasks including administraion, surveying wildlife, fundraising, managing reserves and staging events. All of the volunteering opportunities with SWT can be viewed on the web site at www.swt.org.uk or by calling the telephone number. Volunteers with offending backgrounds may be accepted but checks would be made when working with children. 🅑 📄

Number of projects: 50 UK: 50 in Scotland
Starting months: January–December
Time required: 1–52 weeks (plus)
Age: 16–75
Causes: Children, Conservation, Environmental Causes, Teaching/assisting (nursery, primary, secondary, mature), Wildlife.
Activities: Administration, Arts/Crafts, Campaigning, Computers, Conservation Skills, Development Issues, Driving, Fundraising, Group Work, Library/Resource Centres, Manual Work, Newsletter/Journalism, Outdoor Skills, Research, Teaching, Translating.
When to apply: All year.
Work alone/with others: Either.
Qualifications: Driving licence sometimes required. Other skills depend on type of project. A reasonable standard of English would be required (lower intermediate and above).
Equipment/clothing: No special clothing. Equipment provided.
Health requirements: Dependent on the project.
Costs: Travel, food and accommodation (some projects have accommodation).
Benefits: Working in some inspiring locations. Some training courses are paid for.
Training: On the job training available. Other relevant training may also be available.
Supervision: Volunteers are always appointed a line manager.
Interviews: Interviews or informal chats are usually conducted – depending on the project.
Charity number: SC 005792
UK placements: Scotland (throughout).

SCOUT ASSOCIATION, THE

Gilwell Park
Bury Road
Chingford
London
E4 7QN UK

T: +44 (0) 20 8433 7100
F: +44 (0) 20 8433 7103
E: development@scout.org.uk
W: www.scoutbase.org.uk
Contact: Field Development Service

The aim of the Scout Association is to promote the development of young people in achieving their full physical, intellectual, social, and spiritual potentials, as individuals, as responsible citizens and as members of their local, national and international communities. The method of achieving the aim of the Scout Association is by providing an enjoyable and attractive scheme of progressive training, based on the Scout Promise and Law, guided by adult leadership. The Scout Association is the country's largest co-educational youth movement, with over 640,000 voluntary members in the UK. A major priority of the Scout Association's aim and method is youth involvement. Children and young people take part in the progressive training scheme from 6–20 years. From 18 years young people can become leaders, who enable an attractive range of activities for young people which are run by young people. Youth involvement also influences the decision making process of the Scout Association, as more young people join committees which form policies affecting the future of the Scout Association in the UK. A core part of the progressive training scheme in the UK is community involvement, with young people donating their time to help others. This is an integral part of all progressive awards of the Scout Association. On an international level, Scouts are encouraged to learn more about the world environment. More than 13,000 Scouts travel abroad each year, and many complete development projects whilst overseas. These are often run in partnership with Scout Associations from different countries. All projects are planned by young people, under the guidance of leaders. Decisions on travel, accommodation, finance, etc. are taken by young people. Volunteers with an offending background may be accepted – each case is assessed individually. 🅑

Number of projects: 10,000 UK: 10,000
Starting months: January–December
Time required: 1–52 weeks (plus)
Age: 16–65
Causes: Children, Conservation, Disabled (learning and physical), Environmental Causes, Inner City Problems, Unemployed, Work Camps – Seasonal, Young People.
Activities: Accountancy, Arts/Crafts, Catering, Community Work, Computers, Conservation Skills, Cooking, Counselling, Development Issues, Driving, First Aid, Fundraising, Group Work, International Aid, Marketing/Publicity, Music, Newsletter/Journalism, Outdoor Skills,

Religion, Sport, Summer Camps, Theatre/
Drama, Training, Work Camps – Seasonal.
Placements: 30,000
When to apply: All year.
Work alone/with others: With others.
Qualifications: Volunteer opportunities only
for Scouts.
Equipment/clothing: Appropriate for activity.
Health requirements: Good health appropriate
to activity/role undertaken.
Costs: This depends on level/degree of
involvement and activities involved in.
Benefits: Arrangements can be made to pay
costs.
Training: Not applicable.
Supervision: None.
Interviews: Interviews take place locally.
Charity number: 306101
Worldwide placements: Africa (Gambia,
Ghana, Kenya, Malawi, Morocco, Namibia,
Saint Helena, Seychelles, Sierra Leone, South
Africa, Tanzania, Uganda, Zimbabwe); North
America: (USA); Central America (Anguilla,
Antigua and Barbuda, Belize, Bermuda, Cayman
Islands, Costa Rica, Dominica, Mexico,
Montserrat, Saint Lucia, Saint Vincent/
Grenadines, Trinidad and Tobago, Turks and
Caicos Islands, Virgin Islands); South America
(Argentina, Brazil, Chile, Falkland Islands); Asia
(India, Japan, Mongolia, Nepal, Sri Lanka,
Turkey); Australasia (Australia, Kiribati, Papua
New Guinea, Solomon Islands, Tonga, Tuvalu,
Vanuatu); Europe (Albania, Belarus, Bosnia-
Herzegovina, Bulgaria, Croatia, Czech Republic,
Estonia, Hungary, Latvia, Lithuania, Macedonia,
Poland, Romania, Russia, Slovakia, Slovenia,
Turkey, Ukraine, Yugoslavia).
UK placements: England (throughout);
Scotland (throughout); Northern Ireland
(throughout); Wales (throughout).

SCRIPTURE UNION HOLIDAYS

207–209 Queensway
Bletchley
Milton Keynes
Buckinghamshire MK2 2EB UK
T: 01908 856177
F: 01908 856012
E: holidays@scriptureunion.org.uk
W: www.scriptureunion.org.uk
Contact: Jeff Bowden

Scripture Union needs activity holiday
voluntary instructors to work throughout the
summer to help organise Christian activity
holidays for young people and carry out
residential work. Volunteers work on sites for
up to ten days in Britain and overseas. You will
work with, befriend and take responsibility for a
small group of young people or children,
present the Gospel in varying ways – stories,

drama, games etc. – take part in teaching,
outdoor activities, arts and crafts, sports and
special interests with the children and young
people, join in daily prayer and worship within
a team, work hard with others on the team,
prepare material to use with the children and
young people, have fun and much, much,
more. Volunteers with an offending background
may be accepted depending on offence. ♿

Number of projects: 109 UK: 107
Starting months: Jul, Aug
Time required: 1–52 weeks
Age: 18–60
Causes: Children, Disabled (learning and
physical), Holidays for Disabled, Teaching/
assisting (nursery, primary, secondary), Young
People.
Activities: Accountancy, Administration, Arts/
Crafts, Catering, Computers, Cooking,
Counselling, First Aid, Group Work, Music,
Outdoor Skills, Religion, Sport, Summer Camps,
Teaching.
Placements: 5,000
When to apply: All year. Summer deadline is
1st July.
Work alone/with others: With others.
Qualifications: Christian + qualifications in
outdoor activities, sports, First aid, life saving,
disabled. Must be fluent in English.
Equipment/clothing: Sleeping bag or sheets
and towels.
Health requirements: Good general health.
Costs: Contribution of £25–£160 depending on
location (some grants available).
Benefits: Youthwork training provided, working
in a Christian team environment.
Accommodation mainly in independent
schools.
Training: Day/weekend orientation course.
Supervision: All volunteers work under a team
leader.
Interviews: Application form and references
taken up.
Charity number: 213422
Worldwide placements: Africa (South Africa,
Uganda, Zimbabwe); Australasia (Australia);
Europe (Hungary, Switzerland, Ukraine).
UK placements: England (Berkshire, Cheshire,
Cumbria, Devon, Gloucestershire, Hampshire,
Herefordshire, Hertfordshire, Kent, Merseyside,
Norfolk, Northamptonshire, Shropshire,
Somerset, Staffordshire, Suffolk, Sussex – West,
Tyne and Wear, Wiltshire, Worcestershire, N.
Yorkshire); Wales (Powys, Swansea).

SEA CADET CORPS

202 Lambeth Road
London
SE1 7JF UK
T: +44 (0) 207 928 8978
T: +44 (0) 207 928 8914

E: tsmith@sea-cadets.org
W: www.sea-cadets.org
Contact: Administration Department

Young people with relevant qualifications may be needed to instruct for Sea Cadet Corps. Prospective volunteers should contact their local branch.

Number of projects: 400 UK: 400
Starting months: January–December
Time required: 8–52 weeks
Age: 18–55
Causes: Young People.
Activities: Outdoor Skills, Sport.
When to apply: All year.
Work alone/with others: with others.
Qualifications: Instructor level qualifications RYA, mountaineering, diving, engineering or similar.
Equipment/clothing: Dependent on qualifications.
Health requirements: Nil.
Costs: Nil.
UK placements: England (throughout); Scotland (throughout); Northern Ireland (throughout); Wales (throughout).

SECMOL (Students' Educational & Cultural Movement of Ladakh)

P O Box 4
Leh
Ladakh194 101 India
T: 91 1982 252 421, 253 012
E: secmol@rediffmail.co
Contact: Becky

SECMOL is a Ladakhi founded and run organisation, whose work is mainly reforming the local government schools and also creating local media and addressing various issues as they come up. We have some changes rolling in the school system – teacher training and medium of instruction – and now our two big areas of work are adapting the national Indian textbooks to make them locally relevant (for which volunteers could help write or illustrate) and mobilising villagers to improve their local schools. At the same time we have about 10 to 30 students aged 18–22 years living at our campus for an alternative education so they can get back on the academic track. Some have made a commitment to become teachers themselves, and some are being trained in media, video, photography and reporting. Volunteers can have a mutually enriching experience just interacting with our students. The campus is totally solar heated and solar powered. We have cows and chickens too! We would especially like to hear from volunteers who know skating and hockey. In Ladakh, a culturally Tibetan corner of India at 11,500 feet in the Himalayas.

Number of projects: 1 UK: 0
Starting months: January–December
Time required: 4–52 weeks
Age: 16–75
Causes: Teaching/assisting (secondary, EFL), Work Camps – Seasonal, Young People.
Activities: Computers, Library/Resource Centres, Manual Work, Newsletter/Journalism, Sport, Summer Camps, Teaching, Training, Translating, Visiting/Befriending.
Placements: 3–10
When to apply: Any time.
Work alone/with others: Depends if other volunteers are here at the same time.
Qualifications: Volunteers with no special skills are welcome for short term stays for cultural exchange, conversation and shared work with our students. Volunteers with computer, video, photography, writing and illustration skills are required for longer stays.
Equipment/clothing: Nothing special. Modest clothing as in the rest of India plus some warm clothes for chilly nights or winters.
Health requirements: The high altitude is not a problem for most visitors unless they have heart, lung or blood problems. Resting for the first day and a half is generally all that is needed.
Costs: Travel to Ladakh. Short term volunteers pay Rs150 (about $3) per day for room and board. Long term volunteers may make different arrangements.
Benefits: Accommodation and food are arranged at a reasonable rate. Stay at our solar heated and powered campus with our students, 18–22 year olds, who are getting alternative education.
Training: None provided.
Supervision: Casual supervision.
Interviews: No interview but will correspond via e-mail.
Worldwide placements: Asia (India).

SEDEPAC

Apartado Postal 27-054
06760 Mexico DF
Mexico
F: 00 52 5 584 3985
E: sedepac@laneta.apc.org
Contact: Ricardo Olvera

Sedepac is a Mexican non-government organisation which needs volunteers to work in remote rural villages in Mexico improving and constructing schools or other community facilities and to help with agricultural projects. In turn, the volunteer learns about local culture, women's issues, local politics and indigenous life in Mexico. All SEDEPAC placements are in indigenous areas. Participants fly to Mexico City, arriving on or before June 30th. Orientation takes place in Zilitla, a ten-hour bus ride from Mexico City. The programme ends in mid-August. Applicants fill out an application form in Spanish, which is evaluated by Sedepac. Other British young volunteers have participated in the past. Sedepac should have their adddresses. Contact them via e-mail for testimonials from past participants. 🖹

Number of projects: 1 **UK:** 0
Starting months: Jun, Jul, Aug
Time required: 7–52 weeks (plus)
Age: 18–26
Causes: Children, Conservation, Environmental Causes, Heritage, Human Rights, Poor/ Homeless, Teaching/assisting (nursery, primary, secondary, mature), Work Camps – seasonal, Young People.
Activities: Agriculture/Farming, Arts/Crafts, Building/Construction, Community Work, Conservation Skills, Cooking, Development Issues, Forestry, Gardening/Horticulture, Group Work, International Aid, Manual Work, Music, Outdoor Skills, Social Work, Sport, Teaching, Visiting/Befriending, Work Camps – Seasonal.
Placements: 40
When to apply: Before 1st April.
Work alone/with others: In groups of 10–12.
Qualifications: Must speak fluent Spanish. Each year we accept approximately 10 Europeans/British, 15 North Americans and 15 youths from Mexico and other Latin American countries.
Health requirements: Necessary innoculations, otherwise none.
Costs: All travel expenses + US$450 approx to cover board, lodging, insurance + orientation.
Benefits: Limited scholarships available some years.
Worldwide placements: Central America (Mexico).

SEEABILITY

Reigate Road
Leatherhead
Surrey KT22 8NR UK
T: 01372 389414
F: 01372 389416
E: JuliaGallagher@seeability.org
W: www.seeability.org
Contact: Julia Gallagher

Seeability is the trading name of the Royal School for the Blind. Volunteers are needed to help realise the potential of people who are blind and have other disabilities. Volunteers with an offending background may be accepted depending on the nature of the offence. Each application is judged individually. Criminal record checks are required as well as two personal references. 🦽 🖹

Number of projects: 7 **UK:** 7
Starting months: January–December
Time required: 24–52 weeks
Age: 18–75
Causes: Disabled (learning and physical), Elderly People, Holidays for Disabled, Young People.
Activities: Administration, Arts/Crafts, Caring (general, day and residential), Computers, DIY, Driving, Fundraising, Gardening/Horticulture, Group Work, Library/Resource Centres, Marketing/Publicity, Music, Sport, Theatre/ Drama, Visiting/Befriending.
When to apply: All year.
Work alone/with others: Mixed.
Qualifications: Oral and written English must be good.
Health requirements: Generally good health. Volunteers must inform us of any ill health.
Costs: Cost of travel between home and Seeability.
Benefits: Out of pocket expenses + lunch where appropriate.
Training: Introduction to Seeability, introduction to visual impairment, visual impairment level 1, valued and positive lifestyles.
Interviews: Interviews take place at the Leatherhead campus.
Charity number: 255913
UK placements: England (Devon, Hampshire, Somerset, Surrey, Sussex – East).

SENEVOLU

P.O. Box 26 557 P.A./Dakar
Dakar
Senegal
T: 00221 550 48 85
F: 00221 855 71 72
E: senevolu@mypage.org
W: www.senevolu.mypage.org
Contact: Magueye Sy

Senevolu is a Senegalese not-for-profit organisation founded to promote community tourism and volunteer work in Senegal. Senevolu offers a variety of programmes and services including home stays, volunteer opportunities, language programmes, trips and workshops. The minimum stay is one month and is available all year long. During the first five days volunteers will stay at a hostel for an orientation period. This orientation includes an immersion in the Senegalese culture, language courses (French/Wolof) and excursions in the surroundings of Dakar. After the orientation period, volunteers will move to a host family where they will participate in all-day activities, trips, celebrations, and ataya – the ritual in Senegal. From Monday to Friday volunteers will work with non governmental organisations, public services, community projects and primary schools. During the weekends volunteers can participate in cultural workshops (African dancing, cooking, djembe, kora and batik). Senevolu will also be able to design excursions for groups of at least five people during the weekends. Dakar, Senegal. 🖹

Number of projects: 25 UK: 0
Starting months: January–December
Time required: 4–52 weeks
Age: 18–70
Causes: Addicts/Ex-Addicts, AIDS/HIV, Animal Welfare, Archaeology, Architecture, Children, Conservation, Disabled (learning and physical), Elderly People, Environmental Causes, Health Care/Medical, Heritage, Holidays for Disabled, Human Rights, Inner City Problems, Offenders/Ex-Offenders, Poor/Homeless, Refugees, Teaching/assisting (nursery, primary, secondary, mature, EFL) Unemployed, Wildlife, Work Camps – Seasonal, Young People.
Activities: Accountancy, Administration, Agriculture/Farming, Arts/Crafts, Building/Construction, Campaigning, Caring (general, day and residential), Catering, Community Work, Computers, Conservation Skills, Cooking, Counselling, Development Issues, DIY, Driving, First Aid, Forestry, Fundraising, Gardening/Horticulture, Group Work, International Aid, Library/Resource Centres, Manual Work, Marketing/Publicity, Music, Newsletter/Journalism, Outdoor Skills, Religion, Research, Scientific Work, Social Work, Sport, Summer Camps, Teaching, Technical Skills, Theatre/Drama, Training, Translating, Visiting/Befriending, Work Camps – Seasonal.
Placements: 50
When to apply: Any time.
Work alone/with others: With others.
Qualifications: Basic French skills are necessary.
Health requirements: No restrictions.
Costs: Programme fee €525 covers 5 day bed and breakfast orientation period, transfer to your host family, full board with host family, volunteer placement and Senevolu support. €250 for one further month, €375 for two month stay + flights and insurance.
Benefits: Full board and accommodation with host family included in costs.
Training: 5 day orientation period in Dakar.
Supervision: All volunteers have a personal supervisor.
Interviews: No interviews – communication via e-mail, post and telephone prior to arrival – volunteers will receive all details about their placement.
Worldwide placements: Africa (Senegal).

SENSE
The National Deafblind and Rubella Association

11–13 Clifton Terrace
Finsbury Park
London
N4 3SR UK

T: +44 (0) 207 272 7774
T: +44 (0) 207 272 6012
E: holiday@sense.org.uk
W: www.sense.org.uk
Contact: Dana Franklin

Sense holidays are for people of varying ages, from the very young to older people all of whom have a sensory impairment and other difficulties. This means people who are: Deafblind (hearing and visually impaired); Visually impaired with one or more additional disability; Hearing impaired with one or more additional disability. Additional disabilities may include, for example, a learning disability or cerebral palsy. A number of Sense holidaymakers use wheelchairs or may need help with mobility. Sense has organised holidays since 1984. The aim is simply for holidaymakers to have fun in a supportive environment, while at the same time gaining new experiences and meeting new people. Importantly, our holidays also give parents and carers a chance to have a well earned break. Holidays generally last for about a week and take place through the summer months, mostly during the school break. Every holiday is managed by one (or more) experienced, skilled holiday leaders, backed up by a team of volunteers. The ratio of volunteers to holidaymakers is generally at least one to one and usually more. As a group everyone is on holiday together – although Sense holidays may not be as relaxing as holidays you may have experienced in the past! Placement subject to references and disclosure from Criminal Records Bureau. ♿

Number of projects: 22 UK: 22
Starting months: Jul, Aug
Time required: 1–2 weeks
Age: 18 plus – no upper limit
Causes: Children, Disabled (learning and physical), Holidays for Disabled.
Activities: Caring (general, day and residential), Group Work, Summer Camps.
Placements: 150
When to apply: Before April (preferably), but applications are accepted throughout the summer.
Work alone/with others: with others.
Health requirements: Nil.
Costs: Cash for personal needs.
Benefits: Accommodation, food and training.
Training: Information day to attend.
Supervision: All holidays have one or more skilled and experienced leader.
Charity number: 289868
UK placements: England (Berkshire, Bristol, Buckinghamshire, Cambridgeshire, Channel Islands, Cheshire, Cornwall, Cumbria, Derbyshire, Devon, Dorset, Essex, Gloucestershire, Herefordshire, Hertfordshire, Isle of Man, Kent, Lancashire, Leicestershire, Lincolnshire, Manchester, Merseyside, Norfolk,

Northamptonshire, Nottinghamshire, Oxfordshire, Rutland, Shropshire, Somerset, Staffordshire, Suffolk, Surrey, E. Sussex, W. Sussex, Tyne and Wear, Warwickshire, West Midlands, Wiltshire, Worcestershire, E. Yorkshire, N. Yorkshire, S. Yorkshire, W. Yorkshire); Northern Ireland (Fermanagh); Wales (Carmarthenshire, Conwy, Pembrokeshire).

SENSE SCOTLAND

5th Floor
45 Finnieston Street
Clydeway Centre
Glasgow
G3 8JU UK
T: 0141 564 2444
F: 0141 564 2443
E: info@sensescotland.org.uk
W: www.sensescotland.org.uk
Contact: Margaret Watson

Sense Scotland is part of Sense, the National Deafblind and Rubella Association. We provide a number of direct services to people who, at birth or from an early age, have impairments to both sight and hearing whether or not they have other disabilities; impairment to sight with other disabilities, and impairment to hearing with other disabilities. The services we provide include respite, day care, holidays, community homes, information and support for families. Our volunteers enable Sense Scotland to provide our clients with services such as playdays and holidays. They can also provide support to our staff or could help out in one of our shops or on a collecting day. Volunteers also help during our summer playscheme, which runs Monday to Friday during the school holidays. Playdays are one-afternoon activity sessions during the school holidays where volunteers help with painting, baking, music playing or visits to the park. The holidays are 7 or 8 day breaks where volunteers are paired with a client whom they befriend for that week, assisting with care needs of bathing, dressing, feeding as well as other activities such as visits to the zoo, swimming, canoeing etc. Volunteers with an offending background may be accepted, depending on the offence. Throughout Scotland. &

Number of projects: 21 UK: 21
Starting months: January–December
Time required: 1–52 weeks
Age: 16 plus – no upper limit
Causes: Children, Disabled (learning and physical), Health Care/Medical, Holidays for Disabled, Young People.
Activities: Arts/Crafts, Caring (general, residential), Cooking, Driving, First Aid, Fundraising, Group Work, Outdoor Skills,

Summer Camps, Visiting/Befriending.
Placements: 50
When to apply: All year – for holidays apply by May.
Work alone/with others: With other volunteers and staff.
Health requirements: Nil.
Costs: Nil.
Benefits: Travel expenses. Holiday volunteers receive accommodation, food etc.
Training: There is a specific volunteer training programme for the holiday programme volunteers, plus regular induction programmes throughout the year.
Supervision: Holiday volunteers are supervised by the holiday leader on their holiday.
Interviews: Interviews take place at our premises
Charity number: SCO22097
UK placements: Scotland (Aberdeenshire, Angus, Argyll and Bute, Ayrshire – East, Ayrshire – North, Ayrshire – South, Dumfries and Galloway, Dunbartonshire – East, Dunbartonshire – West, Fife, Glasgow City, Inverclyde, Lanarkshire – North, Lanarkshire – South, Moray, Perth and Kinross, Renfrewshire, Renfrewshire – East, Scottish Borders, Stirling).

SERMATHANG PROJECT

Galliford Building
Gayton Road, Milton Malsor
Northampton
Northants NN7 3AB UK
T: 01604 858225
F: 01604 859323
E: info@yangrima.org
W: www.yangrima.org
Contact: Anthony J. Lunch

The Sermathang Project was set up to support villages in the Helambu region of Nepal, and notably Yangrima School in Sermathang. Over many years the project flourished and we built a new school for 150 pupils. However, in 2001, the school was forced to close by Maoist terrorists who were set upon gaining political ground in this region. They deemed the school too successful! Overnight, 150 kids lost their education, although we were able to place 45 of them in school in Kathmandu, thanks to generous sponsors. Our volunteer programme, which had sent over 100 volunteers to Sermathang and surrounding villages, had to change course when this happened. We have since been working in schools in Kathmandu, notably the Nikketan school for Street Children, Deneb school and others. The programme regularly sends 20 or so volunteers a year to Nepal and, through its associate, MondoChallenge, to other countries. Just down the mountain range in Darjeeling, we send volunteers to work in the beautiful hills around

Kalimpong. The ex-head teacher of Yangrima School runs the programme for us.

Number of projects: 5 **UK:** 0
Starting months: Feb, Apr, Jul, Oct
Time required: 6–15 weeks
Age: 18–60
Causes: Children, Teaching/assisting (primary, secondary, EFL), Unemployed, Young People.
Activities: Community Work, Sport, Teaching.
Placements: 15
When to apply: Flexible.
Work alone/with others: With others.
Qualifications: A-levels or a degree for graduate volunteers.
Equipment/clothing: Normal clothing plus clothing suitable for trekking.
Health requirements: Innoculations. Volunteers must be in good health as some projects are in fairly remote locations (no electricity or running water).
Costs: £1,300 approx. Travel £450 approx. Subsistence £10 per week = £120 approx. Registration/video £25, Help with fundraising for Nepalese teacher salaries = £700.
Benefits: Board and lodging. Trekking, Nepali language classes and cultural orientation in Nepal.
Training: Briefing notes and discussion before departure. Briefing and cultural awareness in Nepal.
Supervision: Project Manager: – Ram Krishna in Nepal
Interviews: Interviews take place in London or Northampton.
Charity number: 1087024
Worldwide placements: Asia (India, Nepal).

SERVICE ARCHEOLOGIQUE DE DOUAI

191 Rue St. Albin
59500 Douai
France
T: 00 33 3 27 71 38 90
F: 00 33 3 27 71 38 93
E: arkeos@wanadoo.fr
W: www.arkeos.org
Contact: The Director

Service Archeologique de Douai conducts archaeological excavations in the medieval town of Douai. Volunteers are needed to assist with the excavations and drawing of maps. Volunteers with an offending background accepted. 🗎

Number of projects: 1 **UK:** 0
Starting months: Jul, Aug
Time required: 2–8 weeks
Age: 18 plus – no upper limit
Causes: Archaeology, Work Camps – Seasonal.
Activities: Technical Skills, Work Camps – Seasonal.
Placements: 50

When to apply: 15th June
Qualifications: Spoken English or French.
Equipment/clothing: Working clothes including sunhat, suncream and rainwear.
Health requirements: Innoculation against tetanus.
Costs: Registration fee of €23, all expenses including pocket money, except accommodation.
Benefits: Accommodation.
Interviews: Applicants are not interviewed.
Worldwide placements: Europe (France).

SERVICE D'ARCHEOLOGIE DU CONSEIL GENERAL DE VAUCLUSE

4, rue Saint-Charles
84909 Avignon Cedex
France
T: 00 33 4 90 86 33 33
Contact: Michel-Edouart Bellet

Service d'Archeologie du Conseil General de Vaucluse needs volunteers to participate in excavations on various sites with the aim of protecting, researching and documenting archaeological sites throughout Vaucluse. Recent excavations have included the prehistoric and medieval sites and the Gallo-Roman towns of Vaison-la-Romaine, Cavaillon, Orange, Apt and Avignon. Volunteers should be prepared to do hard physical work: 40 hours per week.

Number of projects: 1 **UK:** 0
Starting months: Mar, Apr, Jun, Jul, Aug
Time required: 1–52 weeks
Age: 18 plus – no upper limit
Causes: Archaeology, Conservation, Heritage.
Activities: Conservation Skills.
When to apply: As early as possible.
Qualifications: Fluent French essential and some archaeological experience desirable.
Benefits: Accommodation, food and insurance.
Worldwide placements: Europe (France).

SERVICE PROTESTANTE DE LA JEUNESSE – ANNEE DIACONALE

Rue de Champ de Mars 5
1050 Brussels
Belgium
T: 00 32 2 513 2401
E: spjad@skynet.be
Contact: Diane Dumont

Volunteers must be able to work as part of a team, but expect to spend some time on their own, after settling in to the project. In some projects, they will have shared accommodation and should expect to receive weekend visits from the other volunteers. Other projects are in the countryside and can be quite isolated, but someone who is quite happy to stay in their project during the week, can usually get away at weekends to visit Belgium (it's a very small country!) and the other volunteers or to take part in hobbies and sports. Ask us. &

Number of projects: 1 UK: 0
Starting months: Sep
Time required: 42–52 weeks
Age: 18–25
Causes: Children, Disabled (learning), Elderly People.
Activities: Arts/Crafts, Caring (general, residential), Group Work, Social Work, Summer Camps.
Placements: 20
When to apply: January/February.
Work alone/with others: With others.
Qualifications: Basic knowledge of French essential.
Equipment/clothing: None but a car or a bike can be useful on some projects, in view of the geographical situation.
Health requirements: Each case examined on its own merits.
Costs: €15 euros application fee; insurance and travel costs.
Benefits: Board, lodging, laundry + €99 per month.
Training: In situ.
Supervision: A mentor is assigned to each volunteers within the project but SPJ team is always available for advice and support. Several seminars held during the year where we evaluate volunteer's experiences and generally get to know them better.
Interviews: Volunteer applicants are interviewed by phone, but may required to visit the project beforehand.
Worldwide placements: Europe (Belgium).

SERVICE REGIONAL DE L'ARCHEOLOGIE

6 rue de la Manufacture
Orleans
Lioret 4503 ORLEANS Cedex. France
T: 02 38 78 85 41
F: 02 38 78 12 92
E: damien.leroy@culture.gouv.fr
Contact: Damien Leroy

Situated 12 km north of Vendome, the site of 'Clos des Gues' is on the river Loire. Found in 1997 and work began in 2001. It is a fifth century neolithical site. Volunteers with offending backgrounds are accepted France – Departement de Loir-et-Cher – Commune de Pezou – Site du 'Clos des Gues'. & ▤

Number of projects: 1 UK: 0
Starting months: Jul
Time required: 1–4 weeks
Age: 18 plus – no upper limit
Causes: Archaeology, Conservation, Heritage.
Activities: Administration, Conservation Skills,

Research.
Placements: 20
When to apply: Any time.
Work alone/with others: With others.
Equipment/clothing: Work clothes and protective footwear, tent and sleeping bag.
Health requirements: No special diets and anti tetanus vaccination compulsory.
Costs: €25 and registration fee.
Benefits: Full board. Accommodation is in tents.
Training: If requested.
Supervision: Yes.
Interviews: Send application letter and CV.
Worldwide placements: Europe (France).

SERVICES FOR OPEN LEARNING

North Devon Professional Centre
Vicarage Street
Barnstaple
Devon EX32 7HB UK
T: 01271 327319
F: 01271 372890
E: sol@enterprise.net
W: www.sol.org.uk
Contact: Mr G. Yeo

Services for Open Learning (SOL) was set up in 1991, as a non-profit organisation by its present Director, Grenville Yeo, who for 13 years had been deputy head of a large comprehensive school in Barnstaple, and had had much experience organising visits and exchanges, including one he set up with Hungary in 1987. The need to support teachers in countries where the demand for English has suddenly mushroomed following the political changes of 1989/90, and where resources were limited, was the driving force behind SOL. We began offering courses in England at much lower prices than commercial schools, and to work in close harmony with schools and their needs. Its structure: SOL operates in seven countries. Each has its own in-country co-ordinator, who is a qualified teacher of English. They are the link between the main office in Barnstaple, and the teachers taking groups to England. Hungary is our most active country. Teacher recruitment: Since 1992 SOL has recruited qualified native-speaking teachers for schools in the indicated countries. This ensures that SOL's help reaches a great many more students than can afford to travel to England. In 2002/03 around 30 such teachers were placed, including some in higher education. &

Number of projects: 40 UK: 0
Starting months: Sep
Time required: 42–52 weeks (plus)
Age: 21–65
Causes: Teaching/assisting (primary, secondary, mature, EFL).

Activities: Teaching.
Placements: 40
When to apply: Anytime but main recruiting is in the spring for September.
Work alone/with others: Alone.
Qualifications: Degree or teaching certificate and TEFL qualification or experience. Must be native English speakers.
Health requirements: Good health essential.
Costs: Return travel to destination country only.
Benefits: Accommodation in independent flat and local salary. In Romania free health care cover too.
Training: 3-day in-country induction programme the week before term.
Supervision: In-country co-ordinators maintain contact and provide a permanent link/support.
Interviews: Interviews usually take place in mainland Britain, usually in geographical areas.
Charity number: 1019182
Worldwide placements: Europe (Belarus, Croatia, Czech Republic, Hungary, Romania, Slovakia).

SHAD – Wandsworth

5 Bedford Hill
Balham
London
SW12 9ET UK
T: +44 (0) 208 675 6095
F: +44 (0) 208 673 2118
E: shadwand@aol.com
W: www.shad.org.uk
Contact: Volunteer Development Officer

SHAD is Support and Housing Assistance for People with Disabilities. Much of the success of SHAD is a result of its ability to recruit full-time volunteers. Volunteers come from all over Britain and Europe. Overseas volunteers are welcome providing they are able to meet their own travel expenses to this country. Volunteers are an essential part of the SHAD set up and we have enjoyed a very positive working relationship with them over the years: they are people who are responsive, sensitive, vibrant and giving. We hope that we can offer them a new perspective on disability, the possibility of personal/professional development and the opportunity of a busy social life in London. We ask volunteers to stay at least four months each. They usually work with a SHAD member on a twenty four hour rota. A volunteer's job is to act as a physical facilitator to a disabled person. They provide physical assistance, enabling a person to get on with their life in a way which suits them. Volunteers act on the direction of the disabled person they are working for and are not expected to initiate actions or decisions themselves. It is SHAD's belief that disabled persons should have control over the decisions which affect every aspect of their lives. Volunteers do not act as care workers. They are recruited so that we can 'borrow their arms and legs' along with their time and energy, to enable our members to lead a full life. We are very fortunate indeed to have such a committed response from so many volunteers every year. Volunteers with an offending background are accepted. Wandsworth. ♿ 📄

Number of projects: 1 UK: 1
Starting months: January–December
Time required: 16–26 weeks
Age: 18–35
Causes: Disabled (physical).
Activities: Caring – General, Community Work.
When to apply: 2 months before starting or immediate start.
Work alone/with others: Both in a team and alone.
Qualifications: Clean driving licence and good English language. Some non-driving placements.
Health requirements: Physically fit.
Costs: Overseas volunteers pay travel expenses to UK.
Benefits: Accommodation + £60 per week + expenses. Volunteers 'live out' in their own flat with other volunteers and 'sleep over' during their shift.
Training: Training is given – back care and manual handling training.
Interviews: Applicants are interviewed at SHAD's office or over the telephone for overseas applicants.
Charity number: 1001264
UK placements: England (London).

SHAFTESBURY SOCIETY

16–20 Kingston Road
South Wimbledon
London
SW19 1JZ UK
T: +44 (0) 208 239 5555
F: +44 (0) 208 239 5552
E: Personnel@shaftesburysoc.org.uk
W: www.shaftesburysociety.org
Contact: Personnel Department

The Shaftesbury Society exists to enable people in great need to achieve security, self-worth and significance and through this to show Christian care in action. Shaftesbury provides whole life services for people with a physical and/or learning disability. These include residential care, respite and domiciliary care services. We run three non-maintained schools and two colleges for pupils and students with a disability. We also support people who are disadvantaged and/or on a low income. We do this, in part, by helping churches respond to local community needs. Our services include Shaftesbury's Community Worker Scheme, day care services for older people, affordable furniture, and services for people who are long-term unemployed or homeless. In these ways, Shaftesbury is working every day to help individuals to reach their full potential, make more of their own choices, and live more independent lives. Now one of the country's leading Christian charities, Shaftesbury works in some 100 centres across the country with more than 2,000 staff and volunteers supporting over 2,000 people with disabilities and hundreds of others in need each year. As a charity, we rely on voluntary donations to sustain and grow our work. Units based in different locations. ⑤

Number of projects: 90+ UK: 90+
Starting months: January–December
Time required: 1–52 weeks (plus)
Age: 18 plus – no upper limit
Causes: Children, Disabled (learning and physical), Elderly People, Holidays for Disabled, Inner City Problems, Poor/Homeless, Unemployed, Young People.
Activities: Administration, Arts/Crafts, Caring (general, day and residential), Catering, Community Work, Computers, Cooking, Development Issues, Driving, Fundraising, Gardening/Horticulture, Group Work, Manual Work, Marketing/Publicity, Music, Newsletter/Journalism, Outdoor Skills, Religion, Sport, Technical Skills, Theatre/Drama, Training.
Placements: 80
When to apply: All year.
Work alone/with others: Both.
Qualifications: Contact unit to find out – depends on type of work applying for.
Equipment/clothing: Contact unit to find out.
Health requirements: Depends on type of work. Some units will involve assisting to move residents.
Costs: Contact unit to find out.
Benefits: Travel expenses, board and lodging etc, depending on type of unit, i.e. residential or not. This depends on the unit where the volunteer is placed and what is available.
Training: Training may be available.
Supervision: Volunteers are supervised.
Interviews: Yes.
Charity number: 221948
UK placements: England (Derbyshire, Dorset, Essex, Gloucestershire, Hampshire, Herefordshire, Hertfordshire, Kent, Lancashire, Lincolnshire, London, Manchester, Northamptonshire, Surrey, E. Sussex, W. Sussex, Wiltshire, Worcestershire, E. Yorkshire, N. Yorkshire, S. Yorkshire, W. Yorkshire).

SHARE HOLIDAY VILLAGE

Smiths Strand
Lisnaskea
Fermanagh BT92 OEQ N. Ireland
T: 028 6772 2122
F: 028 6772 1893
E: katie@sharevillage.org
W: www.sharevillage.org
Contact: Katie Furfey

Share is a registered charity providing a lakeside residential activity centre, promoting integration between able-bodied and people with disabilities of all ages, backgrounds and abilities. We welcome over 10,000 people each year, and run a wide range of outdoor sports and creative arts workshops. There is an indoor pool complex on site and a theatre with workshops for pottery, ceramics and dance. We place ten over 50 year old volunteers each year. Volunteers with offending background may be accepted. Share is located on the shores of Lough Erne in Co. Fermanagh in the North of Ireland. ⑤ 🖹

Number of projects: 1 UK: 1
Starting months: Mar, Apr, May, Jun, Jul, Aug, Sep, Oct
Time required: 2–52 weeks
Age: 18–70
Causes: Disabled (learning and physical), Elderly People, Holidays for Disabled, Work Camps – Seasonal, Young People.
Activities: Administration, Arts/Crafts, Caring (general, day and residential), Catering, Cooking, Gardening/Horticulture, Music, Outdoor Skills, Sport, Summer Camps, Theatre/Drama, Work Camps – Seasonal.
Placements: 200
When to apply: Any time but preferably October – March.
Work alone/with others: With others.
Qualifications: For some positions we require volunteers with skills and experience in outdoor sports or swimming or creative arts.
Health requirements: Good health.
Costs: Nil except travel to Share.
Benefits: Short-term volunteers (1–4 weeks) get out of pocket travel expenses to Share – max. £10 per week.
For long-term volunteers we provide out of pocket expenses of £40 per week.
Food and accommodation provided. Volunteers are provided with accommodation in 2 shared houses. All linen supplied.
Training: Basic training and hands-on training is provided in all areas: outdoor activites, housekeeping, arts etc.
Supervision: The volunteer co-ordinator is available to provide support. During working hours volunteers are directly supervised by trained staff.

Interviews: Interview in person if possible for long term placements or by phone if not possible.
Charity number: NI 112023
UK placements: Northern Ireland (Fermanagh).

SHATIL

Capacity Building Center for Social Change Organizations
POB 53395
Jerusalem
Israel 91533
T: 00 972 2 6723597
F: 00 972 2 6735149
E: volunteer@shatil.nif.org.il
Contact: Brenda Needle-Shimoni

Shatil, the New Israel Fund's Capacity-Building Center for Social Change Organizations, co-ordinates a volunteer placement project that matches volunteers and interns with organizations working to strengthen democracy and promote social justice by safeguarding civil and human rights, promoting Jewish-Arab co-existence, advancing the status of women, fostering tolerance and religious pluralism, bridging social and economic gaps, assisting citizen efforts to protect the environment, and increasing government accountability. Volunteers placed by Shatil work side by side with Israeli activists, learn to apply professional skills, and gain first-hand knowledge of the complexities and challenges facing Israeli society. Note: For summer camps volunteers are needed for 2–4 weeks. Short-term placements of 6–7 weeks are now available throughout the year and otherwise volunteers are needed for a minimum of 12 weeks. Throughout the country in rural and city areas. ♿

Number of projects: 85 UK: 0
Starting months: January–December
Time required: 2–52 weeks (plus)
Age: 19–65
Causes: AIDS/HIV, Children, Conservation, Disabled (learning and physical), Environmental Causes, Health Care/Medical, Heritage, Human Rights, Inner City Problems, Poor/Homeless, Teaching/assisting (primary, secondary, EFL).
Activities: Administration, Campaigning, Caring – General, Community Work, Computers, Conservation Skills, Counselling, Development Issues, Fundraising, Library/Resource Centres, Marketing/Publicity, Newsletter/Journalism, Research, Scientific Work, Social Work, Summer Camps, Teaching, Theatre/Drama, Translating.
Placements: 216
When to apply: All year.
Work alone/with others: Both – usually on their own.

Qualifications: Responsibility, strong writing and teaching skills, good intercultural communication skills, conversant in Hebrew and/or Arabic is a plus, but not a requirement. Opportunities for English speakers as well. Research or teaching skills also a bonus.
Health requirements: Nil.
Costs: Subsistence and travel to Israel. In rural areas housing (home hospitality) often provided.
Benefits: Possibly board and lodging. If a volunteer is fluent in Hebrew or Arabic and willing to volunteer long term (6+ months), subsistence stipends are available.
Training: Training and on-going supervision is provided by the host organisations as well as by Shatil, once volunteers are placed.
Supervision: All organisations are required to provide on-going supervision, training and feedback to volunteers, so as to enable them to complete their tasks.
Interviews: Prospective volunteers are interviewed on arrival in Israel.
Worldwide placements: Asia (Israel).

SHEFFIELD WILDLIFE TRUST

Wood Lane House
52 Wood Lane
Sheffield
S. Yorkshire S6 5HE UK
T: 0114 231 0120
F: 0114 231 0120
E: sheffield@cix.co.uk
Contact: John Griffiths or Lynn Smith

Sheffield Wildlife Trust is a member of the Wildlife Trusts, a national partnership of 47 County Trusts. The aims of the Trust are primarily to: promote nature conservation in the community; acquire and manage nature reserves; monitor biological and geological resources; liaise with local authorities to promote regard for nature conservation; offer practical advice on nature conservation to landowners. It is the Trust's policy to involve all sectors of the community, of all ages, backgrounds, abilities and disabilities towards these ends. Volunteers require no previous experience just lots of enthusiasm. If they desire, can go on to participate more fully assisting with the organisation and running of activities/projects. Limited opportunities may also arise, for those with a longer term commitment, for NVQ training to level 2 in Landscapes and Ecosystems. Volunteers with an offending background may be accepted – each case separately assessed.

Number of projects: 1 UK: 1
Starting months: January–December
Time required: 1–52 weeks (plus)
Age: 14 plus – no upper limit

Causes: Conservation, Environmental Causes, Wildlife.
Activities: Conservation Skills.
Work alone/with others: Both.
Equipment/clothing: Casual work clothes, waterproofs, stout boots for outdoor work. Protective safety gear is provided.
Health requirements: Anti-tetanus innoculation recommended.
Costs: Nil.
Benefits: Out of pocket expenses.
UK placements: England (S. Yorkshire).

SHEILING COMMUNITY, THE

Park Road
Thornbury
Bristol BS35 1HW UK
T: 01454 412194
F: 01454 411860
E: mail@sheilingschool.org.uk
Contact: Ms. Silke Woodward

The Sheiling Community embraces around 250 adults and children some of whom have special needs. We occupy a 50 acre rural estate and a 100 acre mixed organic farm which supplies much of our food. Young volunteers, 'co-workers', children 'trainees' and 'companions' live together in small family houses and share daily life in the realms of education, training, work, social and cultural activities. The philosophy that forms the basis of both the educational work and the striving for 'social renewal through community living' is inspired by Rudolf Steiner (1861–1925) whose teachings open up an understanding of the spiritual nature of man in the world. Our cultural life includes the celebration of Christian festivals. We ask volunteers simply to come with an open mind and willingness to participate in a therapeutic lifestyle. Further information and literature is available on request. ♿ 📄

Number of projects: 35 UK: 35
Starting months: January–December
Time required: 26–52 weeks
Age: 18 plus – no upper limit
Causes: Children, Disabled (learning), Teaching/assisting (primary, secondary, mature).
Activities: Agriculture/Farming, Arts/Crafts, Caring (general, residential), Gardening/Horticulture, Group Work, Music, Teaching, Training.
Placements: 30
When to apply: All year.
Work alone/with others: In a community with others.
Health requirements: Yes – questionnaire provided.
Costs: Initial travel to project.
Benefits: Accommodation, food and pocket money of £22 per week paid.

UK placements: England (Dorset).

SHEKINAH CARE FOUNDATION

P.O. Box 11693
Dorspruit
Pietermaritzburg
Kwa Zulu 3206 South Africa
T: 27 33 3963333
F: 27 33 396 1249
E: snellr@iafrica.com
Contact: Rev. Roy Snell

Short term treatment – Objectives – To provide rehabilitation tailored to specific needs which include Christian and moral guidance, to provide guidance to those people who suffer through being closely related to the afflicted, to increase public understanding of alcoholism and drug dependence – its nature and treatment – to promote the tenets that the alcohol and drug dependent can and should be helped and that alcoholism and drug dependence is a public health and social problem – therefore a social responsibility. Long term treatment – Objectives – To provide a non-threatening and safe environment in a therapeutic community, which has clearly defined boundaries/rules and regulations which enhance recovery, to provide a programme which offers total rehabilitation and restructuring of the drug dependent in terms of body/soul and spirit, to operate on the principles of self and mutual help and not only to focus on the drug problem and drug related lifestyle, to foster personal responsibility for improvement and for changing to a healthy positive drug-free lifestyle. Kedron Grove Retirement Estate – to assist retired ministers, missionaries and full time church workers with a home of their own and to use their talents and skills during retirement in the community at their own pace and ability. Shekinah Rural Development – to establish an eco-friendly manufacturing and training type operation on the farm in Islington, to establish community development, to establish agricultural projects, to establish a long term recovery programme for people afflicted with alcohol and drug dependence, to establish a tourism enterprise in and around the farm which has a conference and training facility. Kwa Zulu in Natal. 📄

Number of projects: 4 UK: 0
Starting months: January–December
Time required: 12–52 weeks
Age: 21–65
Causes: Addicts/Ex-Addicts, Children, Health Care/Medical, Poor/Homeless, Teaching/assisting (primary), Teaching – Secondary, Unemployed, Young People.

Activities: Accountancy, Administration, Agriculture/Farming, Building/Construction, Catering, Community Work, Computers, Cooking, Counselling, Gardening/Horticulture, Manual Work, Religion, Social Work, Teaching, Training.
Placements: 2
When to apply: Any time.
Work alone/with others: Work with others.
Qualifications: Driving licence, English language and a caring nature.
Equipment/clothing: Winter clothes – depending on the time of year, towels and work clothes.
Health requirements: Not really – just to be strong and healthy.
Costs: Flight to Durban airport and personal expenses within South Africa to be covered by volunteer. Transport to and from airport and free board and lodging provided.
Benefits: Transport to and from Durban airport and full board and lodging.
Training: Training sessions twice a week provided by our senior staff.
Supervision: Volunteers will be supervised by senior staff.
Interviews: Interviews conducted via e-mail.
Charity number: 000 280
Worldwide placements: Africa (South Africa).

SHELTER

88 Old Street
London
EC1V 9HU UK
T: +44 (0) 207 505 2097 or 2134
T: +44 (0) 207 505 2164
E: info@shelter.org.uk
W: www.shelter.org.uk
Contact: Dick Tapsall or Sarah McLean

Over more than three decades Shelter has provided a life-line to those facing the misery of homelessness and bad housing. We help approximately 118,000 families and individuals and we are the only national provider of free, specialist housing advice for people in desperate housing need. Volunteering activities include: telephone advice work; casework support, court monitoring and accommodation search in the Housing Aid Centres; assisting and befriending resettled families; helping in a Shelter shop; administrative, information gathering and report writing office tasks; campaigning, fundraising, research, information gathering, media and IT support; administration in the HQ office in Old Street; organising one-off fundraising events such as the BT Swimathon, the Marathon etc. These events involved hundreds of volunteers; participating in an event organising committee such as Shelter's City Club. ▣

Number of projects: 47 **UK:** 47
Starting months: January–December
Time required: 1–52 weeks
Age: 16 plus – no upper limit
Causes: Poor/Homeless.
Activities: Administration, Campaigning, Fundraising, Social Work.
Placements: 200–250
When to apply: All year.
Work alone/with others: With others.
Health requirements: Nil.
Costs: Food and accommodation.
Benefits: Travel expenses and lunch costs reimbursed.
Training: Yes.
Supervision: Yes.
Interviews: Yes.
Charity number: 263710
UK placements: England (Lancashire, Leicestershire, Lincolnshire, London, Manchester, Merseyside, Norfolk, Northamptonshire, Northumberland, Nottinghamshire, Oxfordshire, Rutland, Shropshire, Somerset, Staffordshire, Suffolk, Surrey, E. Sussex, W. Sussex, Tyne and Wear, Warwickshire, West Midlands, Wiltshire, Worcestershire, E. Yorkshire, N. Yorkshire, S. Yorkshire, W. Yorkshire); Scotland (throughout).

SHIN SHIZEN JUKU

Tsurui Mura
Akan Gun
085-1207 Hokkaido
Japan
T: 00 81 154 64 2821
Contact: Hiroshi Mine

The Shin Shizen Juku (SSJ) (New Nature School) needs volunteers to help teach English to both adults and children. There are usually about five volunteers working at the school at any one time, in the winter time, less people. Those with some knowledge of Japanese will find it helpful, though it is not essential. Volunteers need to acquire a tourist visa to work at the school. A work permit is not necessary. A working holiday visa is better for people from the UK, France, Australia, New Zealand and Canada. For anyone who can teach for a period of six months or more, we provide a salary (allowance). Hokkaido is the most northern Japanese island. We are on the Eastern side, 45 minutes from the city. ▣

Number of projects: 1 **UK:** 0
Starting months: January–December
Time required: 6–52 weeks
Age: 18 plus – no upper limit
Causes: Teaching/assisting (EFL).
Activities: Agriculture/Farming, Cooking, Driving, Teaching.
Placements: 20–30

When to apply: All year, 1 to 2 months before wishing to start. Volunteers are especially needed and most welcome between January and March.
Work alone/with others: With others usually.
Qualifications: English speakers only. International driving licence. Loving heart, honesty and responsibility. Enthusiastic spirit for teaching English to Japanese people.
Equipment/clothing: In winter temperature is -20C (some days). Warm clothing is a must.
Health requirements: Nil.
Costs: Airfare and money for free time.
Benefits: Board, lodging and food only.
Training: None.
Supervision: Not applicable.
Interviews: Prospective volunteers are not interviewed.
Worldwide placements: Asia (Japan).

SHROPSHIRE WILDLIFE TRUST

193 Abbey Forgate
Shrewsbury
Shropshire SY2 6AH UK
T: 01743 284280
F: 01743 284281
E: shropshirewt@cix.co.uk
W: www.shropshire wildlife trust.org.uk
Contact: The Director

Shropshire Wildlife Trust is a member of the Wildlife Trusts, a national partnership of 47 County Trusts. The aims of the Trust are primarily to: promote nature conservation in the community; acquire and manage nature reserves; monitor biological and geological resources; liaise with local authorities to promote regard for nature conservation; offer practical advice on nature conservation to landowners. It is the Trust's policy to involve all sectors of the community, of all ages, backgrounds, abilities and disabilities towards these ends. Volunteers require no previous experience just lots of enthusiasm. If they desire, can go on to participate more fully assisting with the organisation and running of activities/projects. Limited opportunities may also arise, for those with a longer term commitment, for NVQ training to level 2 in Landscapes and Ecosystems. Volunteers with an offending background may be accepted – each case separately assessed. ♿

Number of projects: 1 UK: 1
Starting months: January–December
Time required: 1–52 weeks (plus)
Age: 14 plus – no upper limit
Causes: Conservation, Environmental Causes, Wildlife.
Activities: Conservation Skills.
Placements: 200
Work alone/with others: Both.

Equipment/clothing: Casual work clothes, waterproofs, stout boots for outdoor work. Protective safety gear is provided.
Health requirements: Anti-tetanus innoculation recommended.
Costs: Accommodation and food.
Benefits: Out of pocket expenses.
Training: Yes.
Supervision: Yes.
Interviews: Yes.
UK placements: England (Shropshire).

SIERRA CLUB OUTINGS

85 Second Street, 2nd Floor
San Francisco
CA 94105 USA
T: 00 1 415 977 5522
F: 00 1 415 977 5795
E: national.outings@sierraclub.org
W: www.sierraclub.org/outings/national
Contact: Sierra Club National Outings

Sierra Club Outings offers service trips that combine wilderness travel and adventure with conservation projects. Most trips last between 7 and 10 days. Typical projects include trail maintenance and restoration, revegetation, archaeology and wildlife research and monitoring. Volunteers generally camp out and enjoy one or more free days to explore the surrounding area. Work is done in a group setting, often in conjunction with National Park Service/ US Forest Service or other societies/park groups. Although in W. Europe, Sierra Club may not be in every country shown.

Number of projects: 80–90 yearly **UK:** 0
Starting months: Feb, Mar, Apr, May, Jun, Jul, Aug, Sep, Oct, Nov
Time required: 1–3 weeks
Age: 18 plus – no upper limit
Causes: Animal Welfare, Archaeology, Conservation, Environmental Causes, Wildlife.
Activities: Conservation Skills, Forestry, Manual Work, Outdoor Skills.
Placements: 1000
When to apply: As early as possible – duration of stay from one week to three weeks plus.
Work alone/with others: With others.
Qualifications: We have a service trip that accepts children as young as seven years. Generally, however, 18 is the minimum age unless accompanied by an adult/guardian and with leader approval.
Equipment/clothing: All camping equipment. Cooking gear/commissary is not required, we provide that.
Costs: Average US$295-750 per trip of 7–10 days which typically includes all meals. Participants usually bring their own camping gear and are responsible for transportation to and from the work site.

Training: Yes.
Supervision: Yes.
Worldwide placements: North America: (USA);
Central America (Puerto Rico).

SIGN – The National Society for Mental Health and Deafness

13 Station Road
Beaconsfield
Buckinghamshire HP9 1YP UK
T: 01494 816777
F: 01494 812555
E: info@signcharity.org.uk
W: www.signcharity.org.uk
Contact: Steve Powell

Sign aims to offer a range of support to deaf
people who have experienced mental health
difficulties and who are striving to live
independently. We offer long-term supportive
accommodation and continuing care in the
community. Our first day care facility opened
in the autumn of 1995 and is based on the
clubhouse principle whereby people join as
members (as opposed to 'clients' or 'patients')
and are needed as contributors to a programme
that cannot function without their input. Sign
believes that to achieve a high quality of service
it is essential that the language and culture of
deaf people should be recognised, respected and
understood. We have therefore developed
mental health training programmes specifically
for deaf people whose preferred language is
British Sign Language thereby promoting better
opportunities for deaf people to work in
services offering care and support to deaf
clients. Each housing project has a befriender
programme which provides worthwhile
voluntary work with training and monitoring
for a large number of deaf and hearing people
(who have the communication skills necessary).
Fundraising, marketing and public relations
volunteers are also required. A variety of
opportunities exist in these areas, from general
office duties to organising events, liaising with
the media and writing publicity material for
example. Please contact Sign on 01494 816777
to find out more. 🏠 📷

Number of projects: 8 UK: 8
Starting months: January–December
Time required: 1–52 weeks
Age: 16 plus – no upper limit
Causes: Children, Disabled (learning and
physical), Elderly People, Health Care/Medical,
Poor/Homeless, Unemployed, Young People.
Activities: Administration, Campaigning,
Caring (general, day and residential), Catering,
Community Work, Computers, Cooking,
Counselling, Development Issues, DIY, Driving,
Fundraising, Gardening/Horticulture,

Marketing/Publicity, Research, Social Work,
Training, Translating, Visiting/Befriending.
Placements: 20
When to apply: All year.
Work alone/with others: Both – generally with
a deaf resident.
Qualifications: Projects: Ability to
communicate with deaf people. Head Office:
Nil.
Health requirements: Nil.
Costs: Local travel costs will be reimbursed.
Accommodation and food costs.
Benefits: Valuable work experience in field of
mental health and deafness.
Training: Offered where required.
Supervision: All volunteers are supervised by
their line manager.
Interviews: Interviews take place at the
location where the volunteer wishes to work.
Charity number: 1011056
UK placements: England (Buckinghamshire,
London, Manchester, E. Yorkshire, N. Yorkshire,
S. Yorkshire, W. Yorkshire).

SIMON COMMUNITY (IRELAND)

St Andrew's House
28–30 Exchequer Street
Dublin 2
Ireland
T: 00 353 1 671 1606
F: 00 353 1 671 1098
E: catri.okane@simoncommunity.com
W: www.simoncommunity.com
Contact: Catri O'Kane

Established in Ireland in 1969, the Simon
Communities of Ireland is an organisation
which provides accommodation and care to
homeless people and also campaigns to raise
awareness about homelessness and works
towards its eradication. We offer a variety of
accommodation that includes emergency
shelters, supported housing projects and also
transitional housing. We can offer you a
placement where you will learn about the issues
of homelessness and social exclusion and also
issues around empowerment and good practice.
Full-time volunteers will work with paid staff in
one of the above settings, as part of the team.
The work includes: to befriend the residents;
communicating and relating with residents who
may have alcohol, drug or mental health
problems; general housekeeping duties;
providing physical care to older or infirm
residents, i.e. bathing, dressing, shaving etc; to
work as part of a team; to be involved in
decision making; administrative duties;
arranging recreational activities; accompanying
residents to medical appointments; advocating
on behalf of residents. Cork, Dublin, Dundalk
and Galway.

Number of projects: 4 UK: 0
Starting months: January–December
Time required: 26–52 weeks
Age: 18 plus – no upper limit
Causes: Elderly People, Poor/Homeless,
Unemployed.
Activities: Administration, Caring (general,
residential), Catering, Cooking, Group Work,
Visiting/Befriending.
Placements: 100 approx.
When to apply: All year.
Work alone/with others: With others.
Qualifications: No nationality restrictions
providing they have excellent spoken and
written English.
Health requirements: Physically fit.
Costs: Travel costs.
Benefits: Board and lodging + insurance + €80
per week approximately. Free fully furnished
accommodation. Volunteers can live in the
house for an extra two weeks after having
completed their volunteering.
Training: On-the-job training, supervision,
support and feedback provided.
Supervision: Each project has paid staff
members responsible for the supervision and
support of volunteers. Weekly one-to-one and
team meetings.
Interviews: Interviews take place at our office
in Dublin.
Charity number: 8273
Worldwide placements: Europe (Ireland).

SIMON COMMUNITY, THE

P.O. Box 1187
London
NW5 4HW UK
T: +44 (0) 207 485 6639
T: +44 (0) 207 482 6305
E: thesimoncommunity@yahoo.com
W: www.waterlow.com/simon/
Contact: Community Leaders

The Simon Community is a small registered
charity living and working with the homeless
and rootless in London. Volunteers are involved
in the running of the shelter and residential
houses, as well as the office. A genuine desire to
help homeless people and some understanding
of the problems of the homeless is essential.
Although volunteers have to commit
themselves to a minimum of three months, it is
preferred if they can commit themselves for
longer. Volunteers with an offending
background are accepted. Each application form
is judged individually. North London. ♿ 📄

Number of projects UK: 4
Starting months: January–December
Time required: 13–52 weeks (plus)
Age: 19 plus – no upper limit
Causes: Addicts/Ex-Addicts, Disabled (learning),
Elderly People, Poor/Homeless.

Activities: Administration, Campaigning,
Caring (general, residential), Cooking, Driving,
Fundraising, Group Work, Social Work.
Placements: 30
When to apply: Minimum of 1 month in
advance.
Work alone/with others: Mostly with others.
Qualifications: Excellent command of English.
Driving licence useful. Volunteers from outside
the UK must be a minimum of 20 years old.
Health requirements: Nil.
Costs: Travel to 24 hour interview and to
London, when accepted, for volunteers from
the UK. All other expenses paid.
Benefits: £32.50/week pocket money. £150
extra for 2 weeks off every 3 months, leaving
allowance. Live in position: separate house for
volunteers on time off.
Training: Induction and training in relevant
areas is given, eg first aid, food hygeine, mental
health, alcohol, drugs, social security etc.
Supervision: Regular meetings with project
leader and regular team meetings.
Interviews: No formal interviews. Volunteer
applicants from the UK attend a 24 hour
session where people from all the projects
answer informal questions about their
experience, reasons for wanting to come etc.
Charity number: 293938
UK placements: England (London).

SIOUX INDIAN YMCAs

Box 218
Dupree
South Dakota 57623 USA
E: sioux-newsletter@energetic.com
Contact: The Programme Director

Number of projects: 1 UK: 0
Starting months: Jun, Jul, Aug
Time required: 12–52 weeks
Age: 18 plus – no upper limit
Causes: Children, Elderly People, Young People.
Activities: Arts/Crafts, Community Work,
Counselling, First Aid, Sport, Summer Camps.
When to apply: As early as possible.
Qualifications: Previous camp experience.
Costs: Travel and personal expenses.
Benefits: Board and lodging.
Worldwide placements: North America: (USA).

SKILLS ACROSS THE WORLD

1 Glebe Street
Glebe
Sydney 2037 Australia
T: +61 2 9571 8347
F: +61 2 9571 9703
E: amelia@dsf.org.au
W: www.saw.worldskills.org
Contact: Amelia Manion

Skills Across the World's (SAW) mission is to work and live together through the sharing of skills and culture. We facilitate teams of trades people to address community needs through the transferring of skills to local volunteers. We may be able to place volunteers with an offending background, each application individually assessed. Currently our projects are located in the Western Regions of Kenya near Lake Victoria. 🚻 📄

Number of projects: 1–3 UK: 0
Starting months: January–December
Time required: 12–20 weeks
Age: 20–75
Causes: Poor/Homeless, Teaching/assisting, Unemployed, Young People.
Activities: Building/Construction, Community Work, Outdoor Skills, Teaching, Technical Skills.
Placements: 4–6
When to apply: Throughout the year.
Work alone/with others: With others.
Qualifications: We mainly focus on volunteers with trade skills but we also consider volunteers who have other skills to offer.
Health requirements: In general good health.
Costs: Volunteers are asked to cover airfares to the projects site. Additional costs including allowance SAW would work with potential volunteers to seek sponsorship. Vaccination costs and tools.
Benefits: Travel insurance and accommodation. Volunteers are hosted by the communities in which they work.
Training: Training is provided.
Supervision: A team leader is provided for each volunteer, as well as consistent contact with the office.
Interviews: We try to interview where possible.
Worldwide placements: Africa (Kenya).

SKILLSHARE INTERNATIONAL

126 New Walk
Leicester LE1 7JA UK
T: 01162541862
F: 01162542614
E: info@skillshare.org
W: www.skillshare.org
Contact: People and Organisational Development

Skillshare International is an international charity working for sustainable development in partnership with the people and communities of Africa and Asia. We do this by sharing and developing skills, facilitating organisational effectiveness, and supporting organisational growth. We work in ten countries in Africa and Asia, including Botswana, Kenya, Lesotho, Mozambique, Namibia, Swaziland, South Africa, Tanzania, Uganda and India. One of the ways in which Skillshare International supports the work of its programme partners is through the provision of development workers and health trainers who share their skills, experience and knowledge with the local people so that when their placement is over, the skills remain. Our development workers and health trainers work with local organisations in accordance with their needs in areas such as agriculture, community development, education, engineering and planning, environmental conservation, health care, HIV/AIDS, income generation and vocational training. Some of the beneficiaries of our work include low income groups, marginalised groups, people living with HIV and AIDS, rural communities, women, young people and children. Skillshare International also helps organisations to develop and grow, and secure project funding. At the heart of all we do is a commitment to working for sustainable development-lasting change in accordance with the people, the country and the region as a whole. 🚻 📄

Number of projects: 90 UK: 0
Starting months: January–December
Time required: 52 weeks (plus)
Age: 22–65
Causes: Addicts/Ex-Addicts, AIDS/HIV, Architecture, Children, Disabled (learning and physical), Environmental Causes, Health Care/Medical, Offenders/Ex-Offenders, Poor/Homeless, Teaching – (nursery, primary, secondary, mature, EFL), Young People.
Activities: Administration, Building/Construction, Community Work, Computers, Development Issues, Forestry, Fundraising, Group Work, International Aid, Research, Social Work, Teaching, Training.
Placements: 25
When to apply: 6–12 months before departure.
Work alone/with others: Depends on the project.
Qualifications: Fully qualified health professionals with a minimum of 2 years post-qualification experience. Contracts range from 1 to 2 years. Doctors, midwives, health visitors, occupational/physio/speech therapists.
Health requirements: Nil.
Benefits: Housing, food, insurance, airfare and visas, monthly allowance, pre-departure orientation, local support, paid leave, pre-departure lump sum and resettlement grant on return, language training as required, national insurance cover.
Training: Residential pre-departure orientation course.
Supervision: Country office supervises.
Interviews: Selection day in the UK or in the country offices.
Charity number: 1067006

Worldwide placements: Africa (Botswana, Kenya, Lesotho, Mozambique, Namibia, South Africa, Swaziland, Tanzania, Uganda); Asia (India).

SKYLIGHT CIRCUS IN EDUCATION

Broadwater Centre
Smith Street
Rochdale
OL16 1HE UK
T: 01706 650676
F: 01706 713638
E: admin@skylight-circus-arts.org.uk
Contact: Jim Riley or Justine Marsh

Skylight Circus in Education is a school for circus arts, a centre for excellence providing circus arts training, a community arts resource, a provider of community animateur training and a circus training performance company. It is a registered charity. ⑤

Number of projects: 1 **UK:** 1
Starting months: January–December
Time required: 1–52 weeks
Age: 16 plus – no upper limit
Causes: Disabled (learning and physical), Teaching/assisting (nursery, primary, secondary), Young People.
Activities: Administration, Manual Work, Teaching.
When to apply: All year.
Health requirements: Nil.
Costs: Food and accommodation.
UK placements: England (N. Yorkshire).

SLOVAK ACADEMIC INFORMATION AGENCY SERVICE CENTER FOR THE THIRD SECTOR

SAIA-SCTS
The Slovak Academic Information Agency-Service Center for Third Sector
Ruzova Dolina 6, P.O. Box 42
820 05 Bratislava 25
Slovakia
T: +421 2 554 10 396, +421 2 554 10 397
F: +421 2 554 10 382
E: saia@saia.sk
W: www.saia.sk
Contact: Paula Jojart

Slovak Academic Information Agency Service Center for the Third Sector promotes and has information about volunteering in Slovakia. It may well be able to put volunteers in touch with organisations which are not yet listed on the WorldWide Volunteering database.

Starting months: January–December
Time required: 1–52 weeks (plus)
Age: 16 plus – no upper limit
Causes: Addicts/Ex-Addicts, AIDS/HIV, Animal Welfare, Archaeology, Architecture, Children,

Conservation, Disabled (learning and physical), Elderly People, Environmental Causes, Health Care/Medical, Heritage, Holidays for Disabled, Human Rights, Inner City Problems, Offenders/Ex-Offenders, Poor/Homeless, Refugees, Teaching/assisting (nursery, primary, secondary, mature, EFL) Unemployed, Wildlife, Work Camps – Seasonal, Young People.
Activities: Accountancy, Administration, Agriculture/Farming, Arts/Crafts, Building/Construction, Campaigning, Caring (general, day and residential), Catering, Community Work, Computers, Conservation Skills, Cooking, Counselling, Development Issues, DIY, Driving, First Aid, Forestry, Fundraising, Gardening/Horticulture, Group Work, International Aid, Library/Resource Centres, Manual Work, Marketing/Publicity, Music, Newsletter/Journalism, Outdoor Skills, Religion, Research, Scientific Work, Social Work, Sport, Summer Camps, Teaching, Technical Skills, Theatre/Drama, Training, Translating, Visiting/Befriending, Work Camps – Seasonal.
Costs: Varies according to the project.
Worldwide placements: Europe (Slovakia).

SLOVAK HUMANITARIAN COUNCIL

Blumentalska 19
816 13 Bratislava
Slovak Republic
T: 00 421 7 5542 3661
F: 00 421 7 5542 3661
E: shr@changenet.sk
Contact: Eva Lysicanova

Slovak Humanitarian Council promotes and has information about volunteering in Slovakia. It may well be able to put volunteers in touch with organisations which are not yet listed on the WorldWide Volunteering database.

Starting months: January–December
Time required: 1–52 weeks (plus)
Age: 16 plus – no upper limit
Causes: Addicts/Ex-Addicts, AIDS/HIV, Animal Welfare, Archaeology, Architecture, Children, Conservation, Disabled (learning and physical), Elderly People, Environmental Causes, Health Care/Medical, Heritage, Holidays for Disabled, Human Rights, Inner City Problems, Offenders/Ex-Offenders, Poor/Homeless, Refugees, Teaching/assisting (nursery, primary, secondary, mature, EFL) Unemployed, Wildlife, Work Camps – Seasonal, Young People.
Activities: Accountancy, Administration, Agriculture/Farming, Arts/Crafts, Building/Construction, Campaigning, Caring (general, day and residential), Catering, Community Work, Computers, Conservation Skills, Cooking, Counselling, Development Issues, DIY, Driving, First Aid, Forestry, Fundraising, Gardening/Horticulture, Group Work, International Aid, Library/Resource Centres,

Manual Work, Marketing/Publicity, Music, Newsletter/Journalism, Outdoor Skills, Religion, Research, Scientific Work, Social Work, Sport, Summer Camps, Teaching, Technical Skills, Theatre/Drama, Training, Translating, Visiting/Befriending, Work Camps – Seasonal.
Costs: Varies according to the project.
Worldwide placements: Europe (Slovakia).

SLOVENE PHILANTHROPY

Levstikova 22
1000 Ljuibljana
Slovenia
T: 00 386 1 42 12600
F: 00 386 1 42 12 605
E: slovenska.filantropija@guest.arnes.si
Contact: Dr Arnica Mikus Kos

Slovene Philanthropy promotes and has information about volunteering in Slovenia. It may well be able to put volunteers in touch with organisations which are not yet listed on the WorldWide Volunteering database.

Starting months: January–December
Time required: 1–52 weeks (plus)
Age: 16 plus – no upper limit
Causes: Addicts/Ex-Addicts, AIDS/HIV, Animal Welfare, Archaeology, Architecture, Children, Conservation, Disabled (learning and physical), Elderly People, Environmental Causes, Health Care/Medical, Heritage, Holidays for Disabled, Human Rights, Inner City Problems, Offenders/Ex-Offenders, Poor/Homeless, Refugees, Teaching/assisting (nursery, primary, secondary, mature, EFL) Unemployed, Wildlife, Work Camps – Seasonal, Young People.
Activities: Accountancy, Administration, Agriculture/Farming, Arts/Crafts, Building/Construction, Campaigning, Caring (general, day and residential), Catering, Community Work, Computers, Conservation Skills, Cooking, Counselling, Development Issues, DIY, Driving, First Aid, Forestry, Fundraising, Gardening/Horticulture, Group Work, International Aid, Library/Resource Centres, Manual Work, Marketing/Publicity, Music, Newsletter/Journalism, Outdoor Skills, Religion, Research, Scientific Work, Social Work, Sport, Summer Camps, Teaching, Technical Skills, Theatre/Drama, Training, Translating, Visiting/Befriending, Work Camps – Seasonal.
Costs: Varies according to the project.
Worldwide placements: Europe (Slovenia).

SOLBORG LANDSBY

N 3520 Jevnaker
Norway
T: 00 47 3213 2480
F: 00 47 3213 2020
E: vidaraasen@camphill.no
Contact: Karen Nesheim

Solborg is part of the worldwide Camphill village organisation. We are 50 people – co-workers and their families and adults with learning difficulties, living together in five family houses of about ten people each. Each house has also one or two volunteer co-workers who have usually come for one year's experience, from many different lands. We work together in the houses, on the land with bio-dynamic agriculture and horticulture and in craft workshops – woodworkshop, weavery, bakery. Free time is occupied with a wide variety of social activities – folk dancing, drama, lectures, concerts, games, choir and co-worker meetings. We expect that volunteers are prepared to learn Norwegian and to join in with all aspects of our life, which is based upon the philosophy of Dr Rudolf Steiner. Drugs and alcohol, and the use of these, are not permitted and will lead to dismissal if this is breached. We are one hour's drive north of Oslo, surrounded by forest, on the border of the local community. 15 minutes drive to the nearby town – lakes and mountains are nearby as a recreation area.

Number of projects: 1 UK: 0
Starting months: January–December
Time required: 52–52 weeks (plus)
Age: 18–25
Causes: Disabled (learning), Environmental Causes.
Activities: Agriculture/Farming, Caring (general, residential), Catering, Cooking, Forestry, Gardening/Horticulture, Group Work, Outdoor Skills, Theatre/Drama.
Placements: 7
When to apply: All year.
Work alone/with others: With others.
Qualifications: Willingness to learn Norwegian.
Equipment/clothing: Work clothes. Adequate summer and winter clothing suitable for Norwegian climate. No sheets or towels required.
Health requirements: Good physical and mental health. TB innoculated. No alcohol or drugs allowed.
Costs: Return fare.
Benefits: Food, lodging, medical insurance and tax, 1400 NKR in pocket money per month. 3 weeks paid holiday is included for those who stay 1 year.
Interviews: Interviews are helpful and take place in Norway.
Worldwide placements: Europe (Norway).

SOLIDARITÉ JEUNESSE

01 BP 5648
Ouagadougou 01
5648 Burkina Faso
T: 00 226 33 71 17
F: 00 226 33 71 17
E: moctar.kouanda@messrs.gov.bf
Contact: Moctar Kouanda

Volunteers with an offending background are accepted.

Number of projects: 15 **UK:** 0
Starting months: Jun
Time required: 3–52 weeks
Age: 18–40
Causes: Addicts/Ex-Addicts, AIDS/HIV, Architecture, Children, Conservation, Disabled (learning and physical), Environmental Causes, Health Care/Medical, Human Rights, Offenders/ Ex-Offenders, Refugees, Teaching/assisting (nursery, primary, secondary), Wildlife, Work Camps – Seasonal, Young People.
Activities: Administration, Building/Construction, Campaigning, Caring – General, Community Work, Conservation Skills, Development Issues, Fundraising, Gardening/Horticulture, Group Work, Newsletter/Journalism, Outdoor Skills, Social Work, Sport, Summer Camps, Teaching, Translating, Work Camps – Seasonal.
Placements: 120
When to apply: By the end of January.
Work alone/with others: With others.
Qualifications: No qualifications needed for the workcamps.
Equipment/clothing: Depending on the work.
Health requirements: Nil.
Costs: Travel, registration, food and medical insurance or costs.
Interviews: Volunteers are not interviewed.
Charity number: 198/92
Worldwide placements: Africa (Burkina Faso).

SOLIDARITÉS JEUNESSES

10 rue du 10 mai 1945
Paris
75010 FRANCE
T: 00 33 1 55 26 88 77
F: 00 33 1 53 26 03 26
E: bienvenue@solidaritesjeunesses.org
W: www.solidaritesjeunesses.org
Contact: Roel Forceville

Solidarités Jeunesses organises international workcamps in France as well as in over 70 countries worldwide. They work in co-operation with partner agencies in these countries, and exchange volunteers through each other. On workcamps, volunteers work on a wide variety of projects such as conservation, protection of the environment, construction, renovation of historical sites, social and community work etc. Volunteers are expected to work for about five to six hours each day on the projects.

Number of projects: 400 approx. **UK:** 30 approx.
Starting months: January–December
Time required: 2–52 weeks
Age: 15–30
Causes: Conservation, Disabled (physical), Heritage, Holidays for Disabled, Inner City Problems, Offenders/Ex-Offenders, Poor/ Homeless, Unemployed, Work Camps – Seasonal, Young People.
Activities: Administration, Arts/Crafts, Building/Construction, Community Work, Conservation Skills, Manual Work, Summer Camps, Work Camps – Seasonal.
Placements: 2,000
When to apply: All year.
Work alone/with others: With others.
Qualifications: None.
Equipment/clothing: None specifically.
Health requirements: Nil.
Costs: Registration of €75 – €150 and travel costs.
Benefits: Full board and lodging, pocket money sometimes (3–12 mths only), occasionally fares.
Worldwide placements: Africa (Algeria, Benin, Botswana, Burkina Faso, Cameroon, Côte d'Ivoire, Egypt, Ghana, Kenya, Lesotho, Libya, Mauritania, Morocco, Mozambique, Namibia, Niger, Nigeria, Senegal, Sierra Leone, South Africa, Tanzania, Togo, Tunisia, Uganda, Zambia, Zimbabwe); North America: (Canada, Greenland, USA); Central America (Guatemala, Honduras, Martinique, Mexico, Nicaragua); South America (Argentina, Bolivia, Brazil, Ecuador, Peru); Asia (Bangladesh, Cambodia, China, India, Indonesia, Israel, Japan, Jordan, Korea (South), Lebanon, Mongolia, Nepal, Palestinian Authority, Thailand, Turkey, Vietnam); Australasia (Australia, Fiji); Europe (Albania, Andorra, Armenia, Austria, Azerbaijan, Belarus, Belgium, Bosnia-Herzegovina, Bulgaria, Croatia, Cyprus, Czech Republic, Denmark, Estonia, Finland, France, Georgia, Germany, Gibraltar, Greece, Hungary, Iceland, Ireland, Italy, Latvia, Lithuania, Luxembourg, Macedonia, Malta, Moldova, Netherlands, Norway, Poland, Portugal, Romania, Russia, Slovakia, Slovenia, Spain, Sweden, Switzerland, Turkey, Ukraine, Yugoslavia).
UK placements: England (Dorset, Essex, Oxfordshire, E. Sussex, W. Sussex, West Midlands); Scotland (throughout); Wales (throughout).

SOMERSET WILDLIFE TRUST

Fyne Court
Broomfield
Bridgwater
Somerset TA5 2EQ UK
T: 01823 451587
F: 01823 451671
E: somwt@cix.co.uk
W: www.wildlifetrust.org.uk/somerset
Contact: The Director

Somerset Wildlife Trust is a member of the Wildlife Trusts, a national partnership of 47 County Trusts. The aims of the Trust are primarily to: promote nature conservation in the community; acquire and manage nature reserves; monitor biological and geological resources; liaise with local authorities to promote regard for nature conservation; offer practical advice on nature conservation to landowners. It is the Trust's policy to involve all sectors of the community, of all ages, backgrounds, abilities and disabilities towards these ends. Volunteers require no previous experience just lots of enthusiasm. If they desire, they can go on to participate more fully assisting with the organisation and running of activities/projects. Limited opportunities may also arise, for those with a longer term commitment, for NVQ training to level 2 in Landscapes and Ecosystems. Volunteers with an offending background may be accepted – each case separately assessed. ⑤

Number of projects: 1 **UK:** 1
Starting months: January–December
Time required: 1–52 weeks (plus)
Age: 14 plus – no upper limit
Causes: Conservation, Environmental Causes, Wildlife.
Activities: Conservation Skills.
Work alone/with others: Both.
Equipment/clothing: Casual work clothes, waterproofs, stout boots for outdoor work. Protective safety gear is provided.
Health requirements: Anti-tetanus innoculation recommended.
Costs: Food and accommodation.
Benefits: Out of pocket expenses.
Training: Given as appropriate.
Supervision: Yes.
Interviews: At Fyne Court.
UK placements: England (Somerset).

SOUTHCARE INC.

54 Bickley Crescent
Manning
Perth
6152 W. Australia
T: 00 61 8 9450 6233
F: 00 61 8 9450 2324
E: cvs_southcare@hotmail.com
Contact: Jodie Crane

Southcare's mission statement is to 'Offer caring services to residents of the City of South Perth, assisting them to enhance their quality of life'. The objectives of Southcare are to help to develop a community in which fellow members care and assist one another; establish and provide caring services for those who are disadvantaged by age, disability, unemployment, poverty, social or familial stress; link volunteers from within member organisations and elsewhere to participate in the delivery of appropriate services; and

promote and make these services available to all members of the local community. Volunteers are involved in: second hand clothing store, low cost food store, emergency relief/financial counselling, New Horizons Day Centre for the elderly, community visitors scheme, nursing home/hostel visiting, volunteer driving, young disabled group, aboriginal elders group, organising fundraising events. Volunteers with an offending background may be accepted, depending on the crime. We have close to 100 volunteers currently working for our agency. We are always on the lookout for more. The City of South Perth, Western Australia. ⑤

Number of projects: 11 **UK:** 0
Starting months: January–December
Time required: 4–52 weeks (plus)
Age: 18 plus – no upper limit
Causes: Disabled (learning and physical), Elderly People, Poor/Homeless, Unemployed.
Activities: Administration, Arts/Crafts, Caring (general, day and residential), Community Work, Computers, Cooking, Driving, Fundraising, Manual Work, Visiting/Befriending.
Placements: 100
When to apply: All year.
Work alone/with others: Both.
Qualifications: Spoken English, driving licence preferable, non-judgmental attitude with different cultures.
Health requirements: Nil.
Costs: All costs except those incurred in the course of volunteering which are partly reimbursed.
Benefits: Travel allowance.
Training: All volunteers receive orientation to the agency. Some programmes continue to receive ongoing training throughout the year.
Supervision: Some one-to-one. Others through phone calls etc. All volunteers are supervised at some level.
Interviews: Interviews take place at the offices in South Perth.
Worldwide placements: Australasia (Australia).

SOUTHERN AFRICA RESOURCE CENTRE (SARC)

Brunswick Court
Bristol
BS2 8PE UK
T: 0117 941 1442
E: info@african-initiatives.org.uk
Contact: David Mowat

SARC was set up in 1989 to educate the public in the southwest of England in the fields of art, culture, history and current affairs of southern Africa; and to manage and develop Bristol's link with Beira, a port on the coast of Mozambique. Opportunities for self-funded volunteers to participate in medical, architectural, administrative and possibly teaching placements in Beira. In Bristol there are also opportunities for volunteers to help with educational, cultural, commercial and social projects; administrative work; campaigning; press and public relations, and production of materials. Beira, Mozambique and Bristol.

Number of projects: 1 **UK:** 0
Starting months: January–December
Time required: 12–52 weeks (plus)
Age: 18 plus – no upper limit
Causes: Architecture, Health Care/Medical, Teaching/assisting.
Activities: Administration, Marketing/Publicity, Newsletter/Journalism, Teaching.
When to apply: All year.
Qualifications: For Beira, knowledge of Portuguese useful.
Costs: All costs including travel, insurance, board and accommodation.
Worldwide placements: Africa (Mozambique).

SOVA – CROYDON YOUNG PEOPLE'S PROJECT

Cornerstone House
14 Willis Road
Croydon
CRO 2XX UK
T: +44 (0) 20 8665 5668
F: +44 (0) 20 8665 1972
E: mail@sova.org.uk
Contact: Pauline McGrath

SOVA is a national charity that believes that everybody is touched by crime. We specialise in training volunteers from local communities to work with offenders, their families and young people in trouble. We promote voluntary action in the penal field by recruiting, training and deploying volunteers to work alongside the primary statutory and voluntary agencies serving the criminal justice system. Volunteers with an offending background are accepted providing a time period of two years has elapsed since the offence, and the acceptance also depends on the seriousness of the offence. ♿ 📄

Number of projects: 53 **UK:** 53
Starting months: January–December
Time required: 52 weeks
Age: 18 plus – no upper limit
Causes: Inner City Problems, Offenders/Ex-Offenders, Refugees, Teaching/assisting (mature), Young People.
Activities: Counselling, Group Work, Visiting/Befriending.
Placements: Varies.
When to apply: All year.
Work alone/with others: Both.
Health requirements: Nil.
Costs: Nil.
Benefits: All expenses paid.

Training: All volunteers attend an 8-session accredited training course.
Supervision: Compulsory.
Interviews: Interviews usually take place at the office where the project is based.
Charity number: 269040
UK placements: England (Derbyshire, Essex, Hampshire, Kent, Lincolnshire, London, Manchester, Surrey, E. Yorkshire, S. Yorkshire); Wales (Conwy, Powys).

SOVA MILLENNIUM VOLUNTEERS

Carver House
4 Carver Street
Sheffield
South Yorkshire S1 4FS UK
T: 0114 273 9389
F: 0114 275 2357
E: info@sovamv.fsnet.co.uk
Contact: Jenny Naylor & Sarah Knightley

SOVA Millennium Volunteers aims to encourage young people's involvement in their local communities through voluntary work. We want to encourage young people to think up innovative and original ways of volunteering in Sheffield. The project also provides young people with the opportunity to participate in existing voluntary and youth organisations work as volunteers. We offer practical support, information and advice to young people interested in volunteering as well as helping to promote good practice in organisations which utilise volunteers. We aim to recognise and reward young people for their outstanding contributions in their local communities through our nationally recognised MV awards system. Volunteers with an offending background are accepted. In and around Sheffield. ♿ 📄

Number of projects: 67 **UK:** 67
Starting months: January–December
Time required: 1–52 weeks
Age: 16–24
Causes: Addicts/Ex-Addicts, Animal Welfare, Children, Conservation, Disabled (learning and physical), Elderly People, Environmental Causes, Health Care/Medical, Heritage, Human Rights, Inner City Problems, Offenders/Ex-Offenders, Poor/Homeless, Refugees, Teaching/assisting (EFL), Unemployed, Wildlife, Young People.
Activities: Administration, Agriculture/Farming, Arts/Crafts, Campaigning, Caring (general and day), Catering, Community Work, Computers, Conservation Skills, Cooking, Counselling, Development Issues, DIY, Driving, First Aid, Forestry, Fundraising, Gardening/Horticulture, Group Work, Library/Resource Centres, Manual Work, Marketing/Publicity, Music, Newsletter/Journalism, Outdoor Skills, Research, Social Work, Sport, Teaching, Theatre/Drama, Translating, Visiting/Befriending.

Placements: 270
When to apply: All year.
Work alone/with others: Varies.
Qualifications: Depends on the project.
Equipment/clothing: Depends on the project.
Health requirements: Nil.
Costs: Food and accommodation.
Benefits: Expenses are reimbursed, including travel, meals, childcare and carer costs.
Training: Depends on the project. All volunteers can access training including first aid, sport coaching awards, child protection and mentor training through SOVA MV.
Supervision: Regular contact and supervision with SOVA MV staff and support from placement staff where you are volunteering.
Interviews: Informal consultation process in our offices in Carver House.
Charity number: 1073877
UK placements: England (S. Yorkshire).

SPEYSIDE HANDICAPPED HOLIDAY TRUST

Badaguish Outdoor Centre
Aviemore
Inverness-shire PH22 1QU UK
T: 01479 861285
F: 01479 861258
E: info@badaguish.org
W: www.badaguish.org
Contact: The Volunteer Director

The Badaguish Centre provides activity holidays for children and adults with learning, physical and multiple disabilities. Each person is encouraged to take part in all offered activities to have as many new experiences as possible. The weekly programme is put together with the special needs people to encourage independence and choice. Volunteers are involved in direct care of clients, helping with activities like canoeing, walking, biking, climbing etc. There are some domestic duties. They will work as part of a small team (five care staff) and always work under the supervision of full-time care staff. Our aim is to give each person a positive and exciting experience at Badaguish. 🚿 📄

Number of projects: 1 UK: 1
Starting months: Apr, May, Jun, Jul, Aug, Sep
Time required: 2–26 weeks
Age: 16–60
Causes: Children, Disabled (learning and physical), Holidays for disabled.
Activities: Caring (general, residential), Outdoor Skills.
Placements: 2 volunteers at a time.
When to apply: All year.
Work alone/with others: Volunteers work with full-time care staff.

Qualifications: No particular qualifications or skills needed.
Health requirements: No medical restrictions.
Costs: No fees. Volunteers pay their own travel expenses.
Benefits: Full lodging, part board and approx. £30 pocket money per week.
Training: Short induction training and volunteers take part in all staff training.
Supervision: Full-time staff work with volunteers.
Interviews: If a volunteer wishes to stay for more than 4 weeks we prefer them to come to the centre for an interview – but this is not always necessary.
UK placements: Scotland (Highland).

SPRINGBOARD YOUTH INFORMATION SHOP

Foothold Youth Enterprise Agency
Lord Arthur Rank Centre
Trostre Park
Llanelli
DyfedSA14 9RA UK
T: 01554 749161
F: 01554 756700
E: lyjanka@sprinboardwales.co.uk
Contact: Jill Methley

Springboard will provide a starting point from which young people can gain personal confidence, social competence and general life skills, and experience success and a sense of achievement. These skills will be developed through a range of challenging opportunities which will enable young people to bring about change for themselves, improve the quality of their lives and the lives of the communities in which they live. The overarching principle is to equip young people with skills which will assist them to compete efficiently in the employment market. We will achieve the aims of Springboard through the following objectives: the organisation of a programme of individual and group activities and challenges which will be undertaken on a contract basis; participation in projects designed to bring about change in the local community; opportunities to gain measurable skills which contribute towards recognised qualifications; engaging in enterprising employment-related activities in partnership with new businesses created in Foothold. Projects under discussion include: clearing, planning and planting a series of different types of garden in a large wasteland behind the main Foothold building; a mobile rural enterprise project; a disability project involving Enterprise; a youth information shop in conjunction with Welsh Youth Agency; a detached youthwork project housed in Llanelli, possibly in conjunction with the youth information shop (using the same premises);

Intereg project with an unemployment project in Wexford, Eire. [symbols]

Number of projects: 1 **UK:** 1
Starting months: January–December
Time required: 4–52 weeks
Age: 16–30
Causes: Conservation, Disabled (physical), Environmental Causes, Holidays for Disabled, Inner City Problems, Unemployed, Wildlife, Young People.
Activities: Administration, Building/Construction, Community Work, Conservation Skills, Development Issues, Fundraising, Gardening/Horticulture, Group Work, Manual Work, Outdoor Skills, Training.
Placements: 20+
When to apply: Any time.
Work alone/with others: Both.
Health requirements: Nil.
Costs: Food and accommodation.
Benefits: Travel costs.
Interviews: Interviews take place at Springboard (Llanelli).
Worldwide placements: Europe (Ireland).
UK placements: Wales (Carmarthenshire, Pembrokeshire).

SPRINGBOARD FOR CHILDREN

132 Friary Road
Peckham
London SE15 5UW UK
T: +44 (0) 207 6356 797
T: +44 (0) 207 6356 797
E: info@springboard.org.uk
W: www.springboard.org
Contact: Janet Bristow

Springboard for Children provides the highest levels of literacy support for disadvantaged children with learning difficulties in inner city primary schools. We employ a unique blend of specialist teachers and trained volunteers who devise individual learning programmes for each child and provide one-to-one literacy teaching. Our work helps children realise their potential in the classroom and we are determined to provide these with life enhancing skills for the ever increasing number of children. We may be able to place volunteers with an offending background, but all volunteers must be cleared by CRB for work with children. Southwark and Lambeth in London. [symbols]

Number of projects: 8 **UK:** 8
Starting months: Jan, Apr, Sep
Time required: 48–52 weeks (plus)
Age: 18 plus – no upper limit
Causes: Children, Inner City Problems, Teaching/assisting (primary), Young People.
Activities: Administration, Fundraising, Teaching.
Placements: 30

When to apply: Any time.
Work alone/with others: With others.
Qualifications: If English is not first language volunteers must have good English skills. No nationality restrictions, but must obtain appropriate visa.
Health requirements: No restrictions.
Costs: Board and lodging provided, pocket money and assistance with travel to and from placements.
Benefits: Full time volunteers are provided with board and lodging, pocket money, and assistance with travel to and from placements. Part time volunteers can claim travel expenses.
Training: Induction training at the beginning of placement and on the job coaching throughout placement.
Supervision: Every volunteer has an identified supervisor for their work.
Interviews: Interviews are held in London.
Charity number: 1034446
UK placements: England (London).

ST JOHN AMBULANCE

27 St John's Lane
London
EC1M 4BU UK
T: +44 (0) 207 235 5231
T: +44 (0) 207 235 0796
W: www.sja.org.uk
Contact: James Hilder

Number of projects: 1 **UK:** 1
Starting months: January–December
Time required: 1–52 weeks
Age: 16–65
Causes: Disabled (physical), Elderly People, Health Care/Medical, Teaching/assisting (primary), Young People.
Activities: Accountancy, Administration, Caring (general and day), Community Work, Driving, First Aid, Outdoor Skills, Summer Camps, Teaching, Training, Visiting/Befriending.
When to apply: All year.
UK placements: England (throughout); Scotland (throughout); Northern Ireland (throughout); Wales (throughout).

ST JUDE'S RANCH FOR CHILDREN

P.O. Box 60100
Boulder City
Nevada 89006-0100 USA
T: 00 1 702 294 7100
F: 00 1 702 294 7171
E: bccampus@stjudesranch.org
Contact: Teresa Hein

St Jude's Ranch for Children is a non-profit, non-sectarian residential child-care facility founded in 1967. It serves boys and girls, 6–18 (admitted only before they reach 14) who are neglected, abused or homeless or who have had difficulty functioning satisfactorily while living at home. The Ranch does not accept the physically or mentally handicapped or severely emotionally disturbed. Children live in cottages of six where they are supervised by 'cottage parents' and attend the local public schools. The director of 24 years, Fr Herbert A. Ward, is an Episcopal priest and conducts services according to the Episcopal tradition. The Ranch is financially supported in part by Episcopalians, and through special grants and many generous donors. St Jude's needs summer volunteers with life-saving certification to assist with their swimming and recreation programmes (including camping, arts and crafts, music and dramatics). Other full-time positions may be available for volunteers with specific education and/or experience dealing with emotionally disturbed or behaviourally disordered children. Volunteers must be mature, responsible and take strong initiative. They are expected to act at all times as role models in behaviour, manners, speech and values. No alcohol, drugs, heavy metal music, or inappropriate posters are permitted. Attendance at religious services is required. Service students are considered part of the staff, and are expected to accept the judgment and follow directions of the professional staff as to what is an appropriate response to children, their problems and behaviour. Southern Nevada, six miles from Hoover Dam, 20 miles from Las Vegas. 📖

Number of projects: 1 UK: 0
Starting months: January–December
Time required: 6–52 weeks
Age: 21–30
Causes: Children, Conservation, Teaching/assisting (primary, secondary), Work Camps – Seasonal, Young People.
Activities: Administration, Arts/Crafts, Caring – Residential, Computers, Conservation Skills, Counselling, Gardening/Horticulture, Outdoor Skills, Religion, Social Work, Teaching, Visiting/Befriending, Work Camps – Seasonal.
Placements: 3

When to apply: As early as possible – at least 2 months before starting.
Work alone/with others: With others.
Qualifications: A level, driving licence, language ability. Some experience in working with at-risk youth.
Health requirements: good health.
Costs: Travel to the Ranch.
Benefits: Food and lodging provided + $200 pocket money per month. Room supplied.
Training: An orientation period is given.
Supervision: All volunteers have a direct supervisor. Weekly staff meetings and opportunities for daily discussion with supervisors guide the students in their work.
Interviews: Applicants are interviewed by telephone or fax.
Worldwide placements: North America: (USA).

STAFFORDSHIRE WILDLIFE TRUST

Coutts House
Sandon
Staffordshire ST18 0DN UK
T: 01889 508534
F: 01889 508422
E: staffswt@cix.co.uk
Contact: The Director

Staffordshire Wildlife Trust is a member of the Wildlife Trusts, a national partnership of 47 County Trusts. The aims of the Trust are primarily to: promote nature conservation in the community; acquire and manage nature reserves; monitor biological and geological resources; liaise with local authorities to promote regard for nature conservation; offer practical advice on nature conservation to landowners. It is the Trust's policy to involve all sectors of the community, of all ages, backgrounds, abilities and disabilities towards these ends. Volunteers require no previous experience just lots of enthusiasm. If they desire, they can go on to participate more fully assisting with the organisation and running of activities/projects. Limited opportunities may

Two Months Teaching in Kathmandu

For Diane Clasby two months teaching at the Stamford International School in Kathmandu "was the best thing I could have done with my year out." Diane's journey started with WorldWide Volunteering in her college library. Once in Nepal she found the children "so eager to learn" and also "spent a lot of time helping the teachers. I will never forget the friends I have made and all the special times I have had." Diane's volunteering experience in Nepal led to a change of course at Plymouth University where she is now studying Environmental Science and "can't wait to get back out in the world again and do some really worthwhile work."

also arise, for those with a longer term commitment, for NVQ training to level 2 in Landscapes and Ecosystems. Volunteers with an offending background may be accepted – each case separately assessed.

Number of projects: 1 UK: 1
Starting months: January–December
Time required: 1–52 weeks (plus)
Age: 14 plus – no upper limit
Causes: Conservation, Environmental Causes, Wildlife.
Activities: Conservation Skills.
Work alone/with others: Both.
Equipment/clothing: Casual work clothes, waterproofs, stout boots for outdoor work. Protective safety gear is provided.
Health requirements: Anti-tetanus innoculation recommended.
Costs: Food and accommodation.
Benefits: Out of pocket expenses.
UK placements: England (Staffordshire).

STIFTUNG HUMANUS-HAUS

Beitenwil
CH 3076 Worb 2
Switzerland
T: 00 41 31 838 11 11
F: 00 41 31 839 7579
E: humanushaus@choroi.org
Contact: The Director

Number of projects: 1 UK: 0
Starting months: January–December
Time required: 1–52 weeks
Age: 14 plus – no upper limit
Causes: Disabled (learning).
Activities: Caring (general, residential).
Worldwide placements: Europe (Switzerland).

STRATHSPEY RAILWAY COMPANY LTD

Aviemore Station
Dalfaber Road
Aviemore
Inverness-shire PH22 1PY UK
T: 01479 810725
F: 01479 812220
E: laurence.grant@strathspey-railway.freeserve.co.uk
W: www.strathspeyrailway.co.uk
Contact: Laurence Grant or G. Law

The Strathspey Railway operates a steam railway in the Highlands of Scotland. At present services run between Aviemore, Boat of Garten and Broomhill but work is being undertaken to extend the line to Grantown-on-Spey. The railway employs seven full time staff and the rest of the workforce is made up of volunteers. The main areas of work are:
1. Operating the service – drivers, firemen, guards, ticket inspectors, booking office and shop staff.

2. Workshop staff – repairs to locomotives, carriages and wagons.
3. Permanent way – track repair and maintenance. Also construction work on the extension.
4. Signalling and telephones.
The railway was set up in 1972 and commenced operating a public service in 1978. A train service has been operated every summer since then. Much of the work is carried out by volunteers at weekends and during their holidays. Volunteers have come from South Africa, California, Wales, England as well as many parts of Scotland.

Number of projects: 1 UK: 1
Starting months: January–December
Time required: 1–52 weeks
Age: 16–70
Causes: Heritage.
Activities: DIY, Group Work, Manual Work, Outdoor Skills.
Placements: 100
When to apply: All year – as soon as possible.
Work alone/with others: Normally with others.
Qualifications: Nil – training given on the job.
Equipment/clothing: Safety footwear and appropriate clothing for work to be undertaken (i.e. overalls).
Health requirements: Some work is deemed safety critical. Volunteers should be fit and healthy for the work.
Costs: Membership £10 under 18s /OAPs, others £16. Hostel costs £2.50 for members.
Benefits: Reduced rate travel on the railway, (75% off normal fare). Railway hostel – like a very basic youth hostel, i.e. sleeping accommodation, showers, toilets, kitchen/dining room and lounge. Cost: £2.50 per night.
Training: Training on the job.
Supervision: Railway staff supervise, directly to start with. When volunteer demonstrates that they can carry out task without supervision, they are allowed to get on with the job.
Interviews: Prospective volunteers are not interviewed.
UK placements: Scotland (Highland).

STUDENT ACTION INDIA (SAI)

c/o HomeNet
Office 20
30–38 Dock Street
Leeds
LS10 1JF UK
T: 07071 225 866
F: 07071 225 866
E: info@studentactionindia.org.uk
W: www.studentactionindia.org.uk
Contact: Stuart Cameron

Student Action India (SAI) is a non-governmental development organisation run by young people for young people. We aim to promote awareness of development issues through providing development opportunities for volunteers in India, thus simultaneously improving the development of young people in India. Volunteers work with Indian development organisations in the areas of education (formal and non-formal), researching and administering projects, nursing and medicine, women's income generation and with deaf, dumb and blind children. Our placements also include two supervisors who research new placements, support the volunteers and communicate with the executive committee in the UK. Volunteers assist our partner organisations and during their placement are required to communicate frequently with the UK via the supervisors. Volunteers are involved in organising their own placements and returned volunteers can continue to work for SAI. We promote development education in the UK via our Development in Action Project. Return volunteers can use their knowledge and experience gained in India to increase the understanding of development issues in the UK. In the UK SAI is run entirely by returned volunteers, comprising a co-ordinator and executive committee. Fundraising advice will be given to volunteers and comprehensive training including an introduction to Hindi as part of the programme. 'I learnt that development is also a personal process' (quote by a volunteer). We have placements in Delhi, Indore, Mumbai, Bangalore and the surrounding area.

Number of projects: 7 UK: 0
Starting months: Jun, Sep
Time required: 12–24 weeks
Age: 18 plus – no upper limit
Causes: Children, Disabled (physical), Health Care/Medical, Teaching/assisting (EFL), Young People.
Activities: Accountancy, Administration, Arts/Crafts, Community Work, Computers, Development Issues, Fundraising, Marketing/Publicity, Newsletter/Journalism, Outdoor Skills, Research, Teaching, Theatre/Drama.
Placements: 30
When to apply: Any time before 30th March.
Work alone/with others: With others, minimum of 2 per placement.
Qualifications: None but TEFL qualifications, knowledge of Hindi, some computer skills and experience in development work an advantage. Anyone with relevant experience may apply. Willingness to learn and flexibility to cope with a range of challenges. Should speak English or Hindi and must be able to travel to India.
Equipment/clothing: General equipment for travel and work in India.

Health requirements: Must be reasonably fit and healthy.
Costs: Membership fee £9 waged, £7 unwaged. Placement fee and accommodation £475 for two months, £950 for 5 months plus flights and insurance.
Benefits: Placement fee covers lodging during placement. Either in an SAI apartment or staying with an Indian family.
Training: Training weekend in the UK.
Supervision: Two co-ordinators in India arrange the orientation week and support the volunteers throughout their placements. We also have an Indian advisor and further support and supervision from our partner organisations.
Interviews: Group and individual interviews take place in the UK.
Charity number: 1037554
Worldwide placements: Asia (India).

STUDENT CONSERVATION ASSOCIATION INC.

689 River Road
P.O. Box 550
Charlestown
NH 03603–0550 USA
T: 00 1 (603)543 1700
F: 00 1 (603) 543 1828
E: internships@sca-inc.org
W: www.sca-inc.org
Contact: Recruitment Office

The Student Conservation Association, Inc.(SCA) is the oldest and largest provider of national and community service opportunities in conservation in the United States. It involves the efforts of student and adult volunteers in the stewardship of public lands and natural and cultural resources in the US. SCA recruits and trains over 2,200 high school student and adult volunteers annually to help conserve the parks, forest, wildlife refuges and other public and private lands of the United States. SCA volunteers put their energy and talents to work with natural and cultural resource management agencies such as the National Park Service, US Forest Service, Bureau of Land Management, US Fish and Wildlife Service, as well as other federal, state, local and private agencies. The work projects completed at these various sites include visitor services and environmental education, trail maintenance and construction, GIS/GPS, archaeology, engineering, geology and range management. The work done by SCA volunteers is vital to the agencies and parks in which they serve. Because of budget staffing limitations the various projects that participants complete might otherwise never be completed, if not for the dedication and hard work of the high school and adult volunteers placed around the country each year.

Number of projects: 2,000 UK: 0
Starting months: January–December
Time required: 4–16 weeks
Age: 16 plus – no upper limit
Causes: Conservation, Environmental Causes.
Activities: Building/Construction, Computers, Conservation Skills, Forestry, Gardening/Horticulture, Manual Work, Outdoor Skills, Research, Scientific Work, Teaching, Training.
Placements: 2,200
When to apply: All year but by 15th March for high school students.
Work alone/with others: With other young volunteers.
Qualifications: 18+ yrs must have high school diploma, speak and write English fairly well. Otherwise willing to work hard.
Equipment/clothing: Hiking gear, i.e. boots, backpack etc.
Health requirements: Medical certificate confirming good health signed by physician is required.
Costs: All travel costs (except part travel costs within the US), application fees and any personal supplies needed while in residence.
Benefits: High school: food and shelter is provided. College: weekly stipend, some travel, housing, food, uniform allowance.
Training: Each site will specify what if any training is provided or required in the job description.
Supervision: High school: volunteers are supervised by 1–2 adult crew leaders who have knowledge and experience in all fields including working with teenagers.
College: volunteers work alongside other volunteers and agency personnel.
Interviews: High school volunteers are not interviewed. College volunteers are interviewed by telephone unless other arrangements can be made.
Worldwide placements: North America: (USA).

STUDENTS PARTNERSHIP WORLDWIDE

17 Dean's Yard
London
SW1P 3PB UK
T: +44 (0) 207 222 0138
T: +44 (0) 207 223 0008
E: spwinformation@gn.apc.org
W: www.spw.org
Contact: Claudia Codsi

Students Partnership Worldwide is concerned with AIDS, gender, hygiene, conservation, nutrition. SPW offers you four–nine month programmes tackling these challenging issues affecting rural communities in Africa and Asia. Uniquely, you will be working with local partners of your own age. You will use informal methods to influence young people – AIDS workshops, community health days, street drama, environmental action. Each year 500 young people become SPW volunteers. Students Partnership Worldwide is a member of The Year Out Group. 📖

Number of projects: 5 UK: 0
Starting months: Jan, Feb, Mar, Apr, Sep, Oct, Nov
Time required: 16–48 weeks
Age: 18–28
Causes: AIDS/HIV, Children, Conservation, Disabled (learning and physical), Environmental Causes, Health Care/Medical, Teaching/assisting (nursery, primary, secondary, EFL), Young People.
Activities: Agriculture/Farming, Arts/Crafts, Caring – General, Community Work, Conservation Skills, Counselling, Development Issues, Group Work, Library/Resource Centres, Outdoor Skills, Sport, Teaching, Theatre/Drama, Training.
Placements: 500
When to apply: Early application advised.
Work alone/with others: All volunteers work in pairs/groups with British and local volunteers – for example Ugandans of similar age and stage in life.
Qualifications: Enthusiasm, commitment and interest.
Costs: £2,600 – £2,900.
Benefits: Self-catering basic accommodation + subsistence allowance.
Training: Briefing in London. 4–6 week training in-country on language, culture, actual technologies, lesson plans etc.
Supervision: In-country office to train and supervise the volunteers. Placement visits before the volunteers arrive and whilst they are there.
Charity number: 292492
Worldwide placements: Africa (South Africa, Tanzania, Uganda, Zambia, Zimbabwe); Asia (India, Nepal).

SUDAN VOLUNTEER PROGRAMME

34 Estelle Road
London
NW3 2JY UK
T: +44 (0) 207 485 8619
T: +44 (0) 207 485 8619
E: davidsvp@aol.com
W: www.svp-uk.com
Contact: David Wolton

Sudan Volunteer Programme works with undergraduates and graduates who are native English speakers (regional or national accents are not a problem) and are prepared to give their summer vacation (or at least three months at other times of the year) to our urgent cause. Most will have experience of work or travel abroad and some will have experience of teaching English. TEFL certificates and Arabic are helpful but are not mandatory. We do not take gap year students. Volunteers with offending backgrounds may be accepted. Northern centres away from the civil war.

Number of projects: 1 UK: 0
Starting months: Jan, Jul, Aug, Sep, Oct
Time required: 12–52 weeks (plus)
Age: 19–65
Causes: Teaching/assisting (mature, EFL), Young People.
Activities: Sport, Teaching.
Placements: 40
When to apply: All year.
Work alone/with others: Mainly in pairs.
Qualifications: Undergraduates or graduates. Native English speakers, travel experience.
Health requirements: Medical check and vaccinations required.
Costs: Each volunteer has to raise the cost of their airfare to Sudan, about £466 plus £60 for first three months insurance and travel expenses in the UK for interviews. It is wise to take some cash – about £150.
Benefits: Free lodging, pocket money, medical and accident insurance. The schools and colleges provide accommodation which we inspect.
Training: Briefing session by TEFL teacher and ex-volunteers plus extensive reading and what-to-take lists.
Supervision: Co-ordinator and office in Khartoum. e-mail access in the British Council.
Interviews: Prospective volunteers are interviewed in London.
Charity number: 1062155
Worldwide placements: Africa (Sudan).

SUFFOLK WILDLIFE TRUST

Brooke House, The Green
Ashbocking
Ipswich
Suffolk IP6 9JY UK
T: 01473 890089
F: 01473 890165
E: christinel@suffolkwildlife.cix.co.uk
W: www.wildlifetrust.org/suffolk
Contact: Christine Luxton

Suffolk Wildlife Trust aims to conserve wildlife and wildlife habitats in the county. We do this through:
– education of young people and adults,
– managing 57 nature reserves,
– influencing decision makers,
– working with communities, other groups and individual volunteers,
– raising public awareness about issues affecting wildlife.
We need the help of volunteers in all aspects of our work, helping with everything from stuffing envelopes to tending the sheep flock. For people wishing to undertake a minimum of a week's work we offer the opportunity to carry

out vital practical work on important wildlife sites. Unfortunately we cannot provide transport except for the two midweek teams which visit Trust reserves to undertake vital management work. We may also be able to provide opportunities for groups to carry out coppicing in ancient woodlands during the winter months by arrangement. Volunteers with an offending background are accepted on projects supervised by staff and individuals – not groups. ♿

Number of projects: 600 UK: 600
Starting months: Jan, Feb, Mar, Apr, Jul, Aug, Sep, Oct, Nov, Dec
Time required: 1–2 weeks
Age: 16–70
Causes: Conservation, Wildlife, Work Camps – Seasonal.
Activities: Agriculture/Farming, Conservation Skills, Manual Work, Outdoor Skills, Work Camps – Seasonal.
When to apply: All year.
Work alone/with others: Both.
Qualifications: Must understand English.
Equipment/clothing: Outdoor work clothes, work boots and waterproofs.
Health requirements: Must have up-to-date tetanus protection. Be fit for physical work.
Costs: Travel costs. Food and accommodation. We cannot provide accommodation but may be able to identify or provide a camping site.
Training: None.
Supervision: Volunteers will report to and be supervised by a member of staff.
Interviews: Prospective volunteers are interviewed by telephone only.
Charity number: 262777
UK placements: England (Suffolk).

SUNSEED TRUST, THE

P.O. Box 2000
Cambridge
CB4 3US UK
T: 01926 421 380
F: 01923 421 380
E: sunseedspain@arrakis.es
W: www.sunseed.org.uk
Contact: Xandra Gilchrist

The Sunseed Trust has three aims: 1. To find ways to help people living in poverty on degraded land (mainly desert fringes). 2. To live an ecological lifestyle. 3. To raise concern and action about these matters. In our simple, residential research centre in Spain, we have the driest, sunniest climate in Europe, while living in an oasis. We germinate, grow and plant dry-land trees; grow organic food; grow crops with very little water; recycle our own wastes to nourish trees; develop new solar cookers, solar stills etc; cook; publicise ourselves; educate;

fundraise; maintain our own buildings and a Moorish irrigation line; and enjoy life. The work is done by volunteers, from raw beginners to experts, under the guidance of skilled voluntary staff. Up to 35 people live on the project at a time. We also run a Solar Family aiming to become self-sufficient in water and energy (implementing Sunseed's innovations). We welcome volunteers, part-time for one week+, or full time (at slightly less cost) for five weeks +. They need not be qualified or experienced. Families also welcome. Sister charity Sunseed Tanzania. Send £1 for a booklet: £5 for full information on longer-term breaks. Volunteers with an offending background are acceptable in small numbers if individually suitable. Mainly Spain, also UK and East Africa. 🔊

Number of projects: 1 UK: 0
Starting months: January–December
Time required: 1–52 weeks
Age: 16 plus – no upper limit
Causes: Conservation, Environmental Causes, Teaching – Secondary, Work Camps – Seasonal.
Activities: Administration, Agriculture/Farming, Building/Construction, Catering, Computers, Conservation Skills, Cooking, Development Issues, DIY, Forestry, Fundraising, Gardening/ Horticulture, Group Work, Manual Work, Marketing/Publicity, Newsletter/Journalism, Outdoor Skills, Research, Scientific Work, Technical Skills, Translating, Work Camps – Seasonal.
Placements: 200 approx.
When to apply: All year.
Work alone/with others: Either.
Qualifications: Enthusiasm.
Equipment/clothing: Reasonably strong shoes. Full list of seasonal requirements available on inquiry.
Health requirements: Any problems must be advised in advance.
Costs: Travel and subsistence. £49–£96 per week (includes travel insurance but not travel).
Benefits: Full board + lodging. A tiny expense allowance for staff. Training, challenge, convivial community and advice re undergraduate grants.
Training: On the job training given.
Supervision: Health and safety are very important and volunteers are supervised by project leader.
Interviews: Longer-term applicants are interviewed in the UK.
Charity number: 292511
Worldwide placements: Europe (Spain).

SURREY WILDLIFE TRUST

School Lane
Pirbright
Woking
Surrey GU24 0JN UK

T: 01483 488055
F: 01483 486505
E: surreywt@cix.co.uk
W: www.surreywildlifetrust.co.uk
Contact: The Director

Surrey Wildlife Trust is a member of the Wildlife Trusts, a national partnership of 47 County Trusts. The aims of the Trust are primarily to: promote nature conservation in the community; acquire and manage nature reserves; monitor biological and geological resources; liaise with local authorities to promote regard for nature conservation; offer practical advice on nature conservation to landowners. It is the Trust's policy to involve all sectors of the community, of all ages, backgrounds, abilities and disabilities towards these ends. Volunteers require no previous experience just lots of enthusiasm. If they desire, they can go on to participate more fully assisting in the organisation and running of activities/projects. Limited opportunities may also arise, for those with a longer term commitment, for NVQ training to level 2 in Landscapes and Ecosystems. Volunteers with an offending background may be accepted – each case separately assessed.

Number of projects: 1 UK: 1
Starting months: January–December
Time required: 1–52 weeks (plus)
Age: 16 plus – no upper limit
Causes: Conservation, Environmental Causes, Wildlife.
Activities: Administration, Conservation Skills, Development Issues, Forestry, Fundraising, Library/Resource Centres, Marketing/Publicity, Newsletter/Journalism, Teaching, Technical Skills.
Work alone/with others: Both.
Equipment/clothing: Casual work clothes, waterproofs, stout boots for outdoor work. Protective safety gear is provided.
Health requirements: Anti-tetanus innoculation recommended.
Costs: Food and accommodation.
Benefits: Out of pocket expenses.
UK placements: England (Surrey).

SURVIVAL INTERNATIONAL

6 Charterhouse Buildings
London
EC1M 7ET UK
T: +44 (0) 20 7361 687 8700
F: +44 (0) 20 7361 687 8701
E: info@survival-international.org
W: www.survival-international.org.
Contact: Clara Braggio

Survival International is a worldwide organisation supporting tribal peoples. It stands for their right to decide their own future and helps them protect their lives, lands, and human rights. 🔲 📄

Number of projects: 1 UK: 1
Starting months: January–December
Time required: 12–52 weeks (plus)
Age: 16–70
Causes: Human Rights.
Activities: Administration, Campaigning, Fundraising, Library/Resource Centres, Marketing/Publicity, Research, Translating.
Placements: 20
When to apply: All year.
Work alone/with others: Both.
Qualifications: Computer literacy useful but not essential.
Health requirements: Nil.
Costs: Food and accommodation.
Benefits: Travel expenses within Greater London can be paid.
Training: No pre-placement training provided.
Supervision: Working under supervision of relevant department e.g. membership co-ordinator.
Interviews: Interviews take place in London.
Charity number: 267444
UK placements: England (London).

SWALLOWS IN DENMARK

Osterbrøgade 49
DK-2100 Copenhagen Ø
Denmark
T: 00 45 35 26 17 47
F: 00 45 35 38 17 46
E: svalerne@svalerne.dk
W: www.Svalerne.dk
Contact: Mikael Lassen

Swallows in Denmark is a non-profit volunteer organisation. Our aim is to support grassroot level movements in Bangladesh and India. The Swallows is also supported by the Danish agency for development – Danida. Swallows in Denmark is a member of the Emmaus International Community founded by Abbe Pierre. The purpose of the camp is to participate in solidarity work for grassroot level movements in the developing countries. Furthermore the camp is a get-together for a lot of people from different countries. The main purpose of the Swallows Camp is to organise a second-hand market. It is our special summer income-generating activity. About 20 international participants will be selected from all over the world. The official language of the camp will be English. The work involves collecting, sorting and selling various items such as paper, books, clothes, furniture, electronic items and household things. The participants are organised in different day-to-day teams. Monday to Saturday are working days. Saturday will be the day of the fleamarket. Sunday is a

day off and there is one afternoon off during the week. During the camp there are many opportunities for you to explore Copenhagen where there are a lot of things to do during the summer and many of these activities are either free or very cheap. In the evenings there are social activities at the camp. No policy on accepting volunteers with an offending background.

Number of projects: 1 UK: 0
Starting months: Jun, Jul
Time required: 2–4 weeks
Age: 18 plus – no upper limit
Causes: Poor/Homeless, Work Camps – Seasonal.
Activities: Arts/Crafts, DIY, Driving, Fundraising, Group Work, International Aid, Manual Work, Summer Camps, Visiting/Befriending.
Placements: 30
When to apply: Before 1st May.
Qualifications: Knowledge of English preferred.
Equipment/clothing: Working clothes/rainclothes.
Costs: Volunteers will need to cover their own travel expenses and pocket money (work is unpaid).
Benefits: Board and accommodation.
Interviews: Applicants are not interviewed.
Worldwide placements: Asia (Bangladesh, India); Europe (Denmark).

SWAYTHLING DETACHED YOUTH WORK PROJECT

The Methodist Church
284 Burgess Road, Swaythling
Southampton
Hampshire SO16 3BE UK
T: 02380 554936
F: 02380 554936
E: smc@prsucefd.demon.co.uk
Contact: The Project Manager

The Swaythling Youth Project was established in 1979. It arose from the recognition by members of the Methodist Church and local people, that a number of local young people were in need of help, advice and support. The aim of the project is to work with young people aged between 16 and 25 years in the Swaythling area. The work takes place in the streets, in cafes, pubs and in young people's homes. The workers offer a confidential service providing support, information, advice, or just a listening ear. The project also has responsibility for the Youth Centre in Swaythling. This was re-opened under a centre manager appointed by Southampton City Council in 2002. The building (as of September 2002) is being used for various activities. We now have SOUND BASE, a digital music and also run SKYPP (Swaythling Kids and Young Peoples Project) which is detached and building based work with the 8–13 year age group. For specific details, phone Cathy the project manager. N.E. Southampton (Swaythling, Hampton Park Bassett Mansbridge). ♿ 📄

Number of projects: 1 UK: 1
Starting months: January–December
Time required: 12–52 weeks
Age: 21–99
Causes: Children, Inner City Problems, Offenders/Ex-Offenders, Poor/Homeless, Unemployed, Young People.
Activities: Community Work, Counselling, Group Work, Outdoor Skills, Summer Camps, Training.
When to apply: All year.
Work alone/with others: With others.
Qualifications: Youth work experience preferred, driving licence useful, patience and staying power.
Equipment/clothing: Waterproof clothing, strong walking shoes. We are a detached youth work project.
Health requirements: Nil.
Costs: Travel, subsistence, accommodation.
Benefits: Out of pocket expenses.
Training: Yes if required.
Supervision: Yes.
Interviews: No.
UK placements: England (Hampshire).

SYLVIA-KOTI

Kyläkatu 140
15700 Lahti
Finland
T: 00 358 3 8831 30
F: 00 358 3 8831 315
E: sylvia-koti@kolumbus.fi
Contact: Eric Kaufmann

Sylvia-Koti is a Camphill community for developmentally disabled children and youngsters. 10km south of Lahti Centre.

Number of projects: 1 UK: 0
Starting months: Aug
Time required: 52 weeks (plus)
Age: 19–45
Causes: Children, Disabled (learning and physical), Teaching/assisting (nursery, primary, secondary), Young People.
Activities: Arts/Crafts, Caring (general, day and residential), Cooking, Gardening/Horticulture, Group Work, Social Work, Teaching, Training.
Placements: 40
When to apply: By 30th April.
Work alone/with others: With others.
Qualifications: It would be useful to learn Finnish.
Health requirements: Healthy.
Costs: Travel.

Benefits: Board/lodging and around £100 monthly pocket money. Own room in one of our house communities.
Training: Generally it is an on-going and on-the-job training guided by experienced co-workers.
Supervision: Volunteers work with more experienced co-workers.
Interviews: Applicants are interviewed by letter only.
Worldwide placements: Europe (Finland).

SYNDICAT MIXTE MONTAIGU-ROCHESERVIERE

35 Avenue Villebois-Mareuil
B.P. 44
Montaigu Cedex
85607 France
T: 00 33 2.51.46.45.45
F: 00 33 2.51.46.45.40
E: julie_legree@yahoo.co.uk
W: www.explomr.com/english
Contact: Mme Julie Legrée

The Syndicat Mixte Montaigu-Rocheservière is a local government organisation. The English teaching section of the Syndicat Mixte plays an active role in 29 different villages in the Montaigu/Rocheserviere and St Fulgent area. Five teaching posts are available; four in primary schools with pupils between 9 and 11. Each teacher is allocated seven different schools and approximately 200 pupils. The fifth post, working as an assistant in the Montaigu Collège or Lycée, involves teaching pupils aged 15-21 for 20 hours a week. No work in French school holidays or weekends. This is an extremely good training for a future teaching career which would particularly appeal to conscientious hard-working francophiles. Rural environment.

Number of projects: 1 UK: 0
Starting months: Sep
Time required: 32 weeks
Age: 18–25
Causes: Teaching/assisting (primary, secondary, EFL).
Activities: Teaching.
Placements: 5
When to apply: As early as possible.
Work alone/with others: With others in a team.
Qualifications: A level French, interest in teaching and children, experience of staying in France. British nationality.
Health requirements: Students contribute to French national insurance system.
Costs: Travel costs to and from UK plus insurance (third party). Accommodation with local host families.
Benefits: Salary of €259 per month (before national insurance deductions).

Training: 10 days in-house training including training lessons in schools.
Supervision: British born resident project co-ordinator who is permanently available on a professional and social basis.
Interviews: Applicants are interviewed in July in the UK.
Worldwide placements: Europe (France).

T

TACKLEAFRICA

58 Cardigan Street
London
SE11 5PF UK
T: 07956 592 478
E: info@tackleafrica.org
W: www.tackleafrica.org
Contact: Sam Gordon

TackleAfrica is a new charity that aims to use the popularity of football in Africa to raise the understanding and awareness of HIV/AIDS among young people in local communities. Our first project in 2003 will see us put together a team of 20 for a six month football tour from West to East Africa. We are organising football matches and tournaments with local partner NGOs in Senegal, Mali, Burkina Faso, Ghana, Ethiopia, Kenya, Uganda and Tanzania that will form the focal point in the AIDS awareness events. The success of the project depends on putting together a committed, hard working team who realise that the real work begins when the final whistle of each match is blown. We are looking for pioneering, adventurous, self-motivated and understanding volunteers who will make the project as successful as possible. In return we are offering a fantastic adventure and a genuine chance to make a positive impact in the fight against the spread of HIV/AIDS in Africa. Unfortunately, we are unable to place volunteers with an offending background. ♿

Number of projects: 1 UK: 0
Starting months: Sep
Time required: 26–26 weeks
Age: 21–30
Causes: AIDS/HIV, Young People.
Activities: Campaigning, Sport.
Placements: 20
When to apply: Applications to be received on or before 21 January.
Work alone/with others: With others.
Qualifications: The ability to speak French is an advantage.
Health requirements: No, but volunteers need to be physically fit.
Costs: Total cost £3,000 covers all travel, food, accommodation, visas and insurance. This cost is paid in three instalments – £500 deposit on application.
Benefits: Food, accommodation, visas, insurance and travel included in cost. Accommodation is largely in tents with some guest houses.
Training: Training is provided – three to four weekend training sessions prior to departure.
Supervision: One tour leader, two deputies and expedition leader will supervise.
Interviews: Interviews will be held in London – no fixed address.
Charity number: 1094439
Worldwide placements: Africa (Burkina Faso, Ethiopia, Ghana, Kenya, Mali, Senegal, Tanzania, Uganda).

TAMBOPATA JUNGLE LODGE

Jr Gonzalees Prada 269
Tambopata
Puerto Maldonado, Madre de Dios
Peru, South America
T: 00 51 82 613097
F: 00 51 82 571397
E: tplpem@terra.com.pe
W: www.tambopatalodge.com
Contact: Carlo Aguilar Perez

Tambopata Jungle Lodge needs nature guides to lead nature walks for tourists and accompany them during their stay at a jungle lodge in the rain forest of Southern Peru within the Tambopata-Candamo. Working hours required may be any time between 4 am and 8 p.m. as the tour programme dictates. Those taken can either work 20 days per month and get around £100 per month or work for just ten days per month and get the other 20 days free for research etc. 📄

Number of projects: 1 UK: 0
Starting months: January–December
Time required: 13–52 weeks
Age: 18–55
Causes: Environmental Causes, Wildlife.
Activities: Forestry, Gardening/Horticulture, Research, Scientific Work.
When to apply: From February to August.
Work alone/with others: With others.
Qualifications: Nature studies qualified students and scientists. English and any other language speakers. (German is a really great help in the lodge.)
Health requirements: In good health.
Costs: Travel to Lima.
Benefits: Room, board, £100 and return air travel between Lima or Cusco and Puerto Maldonado.
Training: If required.
Supervision: Yes.
Worldwide placements: South America (Peru).

TANZED

80 Edleston Road
Crewe
Cheshire CW2 7HD UK
T: 01270 509994
E: zoe50johnson@yahoo.com
W: www.tanzed.org
Contact: Zoe Johnson

Tanzed recruits volunteer teachers to send to
Tanzania for up to twelve months at a time to
assist with the teaching of English in rural
primary schools by teaching along side the
Tanzanian teachers. Tanzed teachers also
provide seminars to assist the Tanzanian
teachers in improving their English. We plan
and implement a project within the
community, currently the setting up of libraries
in schools to benefit all members of the village.
Unfortunately we are unable to accept
volunteers with an offending background.
Tanzania, East Africa – the Morogoro region –
rural villages with no running water or
electricity. ▤

Number of projects: 1 UK: 0
Starting months: Jan, Mar, Jun
Time required: 26–52 weeks
Age: 21–55
Causes: AIDS/HIV, Children, Teaching/assisting
(primary, EFL).
Activities: Development Issues,
Library/Resource Centres, Teaching, Training.
Placements: 12–20
When to apply: All year round.
Work alone/with others: With others.
Qualifications: Degree and teaching
qualification or experience.
Health requirements: Need to be fit as village
life can be hard.
Costs: £1750. Excludes airfare.
Benefits: Monthly expenses to cover living
costs. Accommodation in brick houses provided
by the community sharing with other
volunteers.
Training: Induction in the UK plus two weeks
intensive training on arrival in Tanzania.
Supervision: Monitored monthly by in country
co-ordinators plus support from Tanzanian
teachers.
Interviews: Interviews are held in the UK.
Charity number: 1064659
Worldwide placements: Africa (Tanzania).

TAPOLA CAMPHILL YHTEISO

SF 16350 Niinikoski
Finland
T: 00 358 (0)3 882450
F: 00 358 (0)3 8824528
E: beatek@kolumbus.fi
W: www.kolombus.fi/tapolan
Contact: Beate Matthey-Kraus

Tapola Camphill Yhteiso is member of the
international Camphill movement. We are a
residential life-sharing community with adults
with learning disabilities, where disabled and
able-bodied people life and work together. The
community tries to foster mutual
interdependence and independence among its
members and strives for environmental and
ecological viability. Tapola's work is in the field
of anthroposophical social therapy. No specific
knowledge or previous work experience is
required. Activities include everyday household
chores, farming, gardening, weaving, woodwork
and baking. Everybody participates in the
activities according to his/her ability. A
volunteer would take part in the daily activities
with other co-workers and residents. Their help
will be asked for in the cultural life of the
community (music, plays, etc). Tapola has six
different households. Co-workers and residents
live together in these houses like a big family.
Responsibilities are shared. Alternative web
sites: www.lahti.fi and www.orimattila.fi. ▤

Number of projects: 1 UK: 0
Starting months: January–December
Time required: 24–52 weeks (plus)
Age: 18 plus – no upper limit
Causes: Disabled (learning), Environmental
Causes.
Activities: Agriculture/Farming, Arts/Crafts,
Caring (general, day and residential),
Community Work, Computers, Cooking,
Counselling, Forestry, Gardening/Horticulture,
Group Work, Music, Newsletter/Journalism,
Outdoor Skills, Social Work, Theatre/Drama.
Placements: 6–8
When to apply: All year, although most
volunteers start in July or August.
Work alone/with others: Usually with others.
Qualifications: Interest in people, care work,
environmental question, handicraft and social
skills are preferred. A willingness to learn
Finnish and acceptance that drugs and alcohol
are forbidden.
Equipment/clothing: Clothes suitable for
northern climate. Special work clothes are
provided.
Health requirements: Good health, no dust or
hay-fever allergies.
Costs: €340 is monthly board and lodging cost
for all residents.
Training: Training given on the job.
Supervision: Communication between
community members as much as possible.
Interviews: CV, health certificate, letters, phone
calls or by e-mail.
Worldwide placements: Europe (Finland).

TASK BRASIL

P.O. Box 4901
London
SE16 3PP UK
T: +44 (0) 207 394 1177
T: +44 (0) 207 394 7713
E: info@taskbrasil.org.uk
W: www.taskbrasil.org.uk
Contact: Kathryn Matthews

Task Brasil is a UK based charity running programmes for street children in Brazil, most of whom have been either orphaned or abandoned. Deprived of any alternative, these children 'escape' to the streets where they 'settle in' and attempt to carry on with their lives. Nationally: to create media awareness; to encourage interested parties to become project sponsors and donors; to recruit volunteers; to organise all fund-raising events; to establish links in other British cities; to establish regular transport for donated items to Brazil; to co-ordinate the projects in Brazil. In Brazil: to run programmes and home(s) for street children; to provide access to psychological and medical assistance and a secure and loving home for the children; to promote family planning awareness for both the children/teenagers and their families; to arrange an educational structure and sporting activities for the children; to set up training schemes for older children; to provide alternatives to combat drug and sexual abuse among the children; to maintain a training programme for those directly involved with the children; to heighten public awareness; to organise covenants and fund-raising. Task Brasil is concerned with: the needs of children living and working on Brazil's streets; encouraging family ties; training and educating the children in useful and beneficial skills; giving the children an awareness of and a sense of pride in their own cultural roots; helping the children enter the mainstream of society and to learn the value of life; making the children aware of family planning and diseases, e.g. AIDS; helping to change attitudes of the Brazilian public towards the street children. Task Brasil has recently been donated a small farm, which is currently being developed into a new project for street teenagers – the Epsom College Farm. This project involves agricultural and ecological work. One hour away from the city of Rio de Janeiro. 🖹

Number of projects: 2 UK: 1
Starting months: January–December
Time required: 2–52 weeks (plus)
Age: 21–60
Causes: Addicts/Ex-Addicts, Children, Environmental Causes, Health Care/Medical,

Human Rights, Inner City Problems, Offenders/Ex-Offenders, Poor/Homeless, Teaching (nursery, primary, EFL), Young People.
Activities: Accountancy, Administration, Agriculture/Farming, Arts/Crafts, Building/ Construction, Campaigning, Caring (general, day and residential), Computers, Conservation Skills, Cooking, Development Issues, Driving, Fundraising, Gardening/ Horticulture, Group Work, Library/Resource Centres, Marketing/ Publicity, Newsletter/ Journalism, Outdoor Skills, Research, Social Work, Sport, Technical Skills, Theatre/Drama, Translating.
Placements: 25 approx.
When to apply: All year.
Work alone/with others: Both.
Qualifications: Administration, fundraising, PR all useful for UK volunteers.
Creative workshops, sports, TEFL, childcare, literacy and numeracy for Brazil volunteers.
Health requirements: Nil.
Costs: from £1,200 (inclusive of air tickets, accommodation and meals).
Benefits: Fares or petrol. Rio de Janeiro – accommodation is located outside the children's home within Task Brasil premises, there are two basic apartments.
Epsom College Farm – there is a separate volunteer house. All accommodation is shared.
Training: None.
Supervision: Volunteers are supervised by the volunteer leader. Weekly meetings are held.
Interviews: Interviews take place in SE London.
Charity number: 1030929
Worldwide placements: South America (Brazil).
UK placements: England (London).

TEACHING AND PROJECTS ABROAD

Gerrard House
Rustington
W. Sussex BN16 1AW UK
T: 01903 859911
F: 01903 785779
E: info@teaching-abroad.co.uk
W: www.teaching-abroad.co.uk
Contact: Dr Peter Slowe

The aims of Teaching and Projects Abroad are to help people in developing countries and Eastern Europe learn English, provide volunteers with good work experience and provide all parties with cultural exchange. There are many students and graduates in Britain and Ireland who would like to spend some time abroad doing a useful job in an interesting part of the world. You choose your own country, dates and activities. Teaching and Projects Abroad makes sure that you have good back-up wherever you go. We have staff in all sixteen countries where we work. This means you'll have no worries about accommodation or meals, no worries about needing expensive TEFL qualifications, no worries about not being a qualified teacher or other professional, no worries about local travel, exchanging money or confirming air tickets. The money you pay Teaching and Projects Abroad is for setting you up in a job with adequate supervision, making sure you have good food, accommodation and insurance and being there to help. Over ten years, more than 8,000 volunteers have been placed for teaching and the widest range of other placements including medical (200+ places), journalism, accountancy, law, business, marketing, engineering, conservation and dissertations. Volunteers with an offending background are accepted. Teaching and Projects Abroad is a member of The Year Out Group. ⑤

Number of projects: 80 **UK:** 0
Starting months: January–December
Time required: 4–52 weeks
Age: 17–70
Causes: Animal Welfare, Archaeology, Architecture, Children, Conservation, Disabled (learning and physical), Environmental Causes, Health Care/Medical, Poor/Homeless, Refugees, Teaching/assisting (nursery, primary, secondary, mature, EFL) Wildlife, Work Camps – Seasonal, Young People.
Activities: Accountancy, Agriculture/Farming, Arts/Crafts, Caring (general and day), Community Work, Conservation Skills, Development Issues, Marketing/Publicity, Newsletter/Journalism, Sport, Summer Camps, Teaching, Technical Skills, Theatre/Drama, Work Camps – Seasonal.
Placements: 2000
When to apply: All year.
Work alone/with others: Always a local community of our volunteers. Placements can be shared if desired.
Qualifications: Gap year, graduates or undergraduates career breakers, recently retired. Native or near-native English speakers.
Health requirements: Nil.
Costs: Prices are from £895 (without travel). All prices are for up to 3 months. After 3 months we charge for extra months up to a maximum of 12 months.
Benefits: Board and lodging with local families always chosen and approved by our own local staff.
Training: Optional open days and TEFL courses.
Supervision: We have an office and our own paid staff at each destination. Each volunteer also has a supervisor at their placement.
Interviews: Applicants are not usually interviewed but visitors to our offices are most welcome by arrangement.
Worldwide placements: Africa (Ghana, South Africa, Togo); Central America (Mexico); South America (Bolivia, Chile, Peru); Asia (China, India, Mongolia, Nepal, Sri Lanka, Thailand); Europe (Romania, Russia, Ukraine).

TEARFUND

100 Church Road
Teddington
Middlesex TW11 8QE UK
T: 0845 355 8355
F: +44 (0) 208 943 3594
E: transform@tearfund.org
W: www.tearfund.org
Contact: Mia Palmer

The purpose of Tearfund's programme, 'Transform', is to serve Jesus Christ by enabling those who share evangelical Christian beliefs to bring good news to the poor. Proclaiming and demonstrating the gospel for the whole person through the support of Christian relief and development. Working through a worldwide network of evangelical Christian partners. The work is a mix of practical tasks and developing relationships with local people. All the teams take time to look beyond the surface. You'll come back understanding why people are poor and what the church can do. Encouraging partnership in prayer and support from Christians in Britain and Ireland. Seeking at all times to be obedient to biblical teaching. Our main criteria being that they are committed Christians and members of a local church, adaptable and team players. ⑤

Number of projects: 50 **UK:** 5
Starting months: Apr, Jul, Dec
Time required: 2–16 weeks
Age: 18–75
Causes: Addicts/Ex-Addicts, AIDS/HIV, Children, Conservation, Health Care/Medical, Human Rights, Inner City Problems, Poor/ Homeless, Teaching/assisting, Work Camps – Seasonal, Young People.
Activities: Arts/Crafts, Building/Construction, Caring – General, Community Work, Conservation Skills, Development Issues, DIY, Group Work, Social Work, Summer Camps, Teaching, Technical Skills, Work Camps – Seasonal.
Placements: 500
When to apply: February for international, May for UK. By November for Easter and 4 month trips.
Work alone/with others: In teams.
Qualifications: Christian. Unskilled welcome. UK residents only. No restriction on maximum age of volunteer subject to health clearance.
Health requirements: Candidates need to pass a medical check.
Costs: Approx £1500 international summer, £2500 4 months, £1200 2 weeks, £140 UK summer.

Benefits: Orientation, travel, accommodation, food, insurance but not personal spending money. Also the knowledge that Tearfund works with local partners with vast experience and has been running trips since 1972. Basic – mattress on floor, school classrooms or very simple guest houses.
Training: Residential orientation.
Supervision: We provide team leaders and work alongside national organisations.
Interviews: Interviews take place at regional selection venues.
Charity number: 265464
Worldwide placements: Africa (Burkina Faso, Ethiopia, Ghana, Kenya, Lesotho, Malawi, Nigeria, Rwanda, South Africa, Tanzania, Uganda, Zambia); Central America (Dominican Republic, Mexico, Nicaragua); South America (Brazil, Peru); Asia (Bangladesh, India, Lebanon, Thailand); Europe (Portugal).
UK placements: England (Merseyside).

TEES VALLEY WILDLIFE TRUST

Bellamy Pavilion
Kirkleatham Old Hall, Kirkleatham
Redcar
Cleveland TS10 5NW UK
T: 01642 759900
F: 01642 480401
E: teesvalleywt@cix.co.uk
W: www.wildlifetrusts.org/teesvalley
Contact: Steve Ashton

Tees Valley Wildlife Trust is an independent voluntary nature conservation organisation first set up in 1979. It is a member of the Wildlife Trusts, a national partnership of 47 County Trusts. The aims of the Trust are primarily to: promote nature conservation in the community; acquire and manage nature reserves (we currently manage in excess of 130 hectares of land); monitor biological and geological resources; liaise with local authorities to promote regard for nature conservation; offer practical advice on nature conservation to landowners. It is the Trust's policy to involve all sectors of the community, of all ages, backgrounds, abilities and disabilities towards these ends. Volunteers require no previous experience just lots of enthusiasm. They will receive on-the-job training in an informal atmosphere and, if they desire, can go on to participate more fully, assisting with the organisation and running of activities/projects. Volunteers with an offending background may be accepted – each case separately assessed. Boroughs of Stockton-on-Tees, Middlesbrough, Redcar and Cleveland, and Hartlepool. 🦽 📄

Number of projects: 20 **UK:** 20
Starting months: January–December
Time required: 1–52 weeks (plus)

Age: 16 plus – no upper limit
Causes: Conservation, Environmental Causes, Teaching/assisting, Wildlife.
Activities: Administration, Building/Construction, Community Work, Computers, Conservation Skills, Forestry, Gardening/Horticulture, Group Work, Manual. Work, Outdoor Skills, Teaching
Placements: 1–2
When to apply: All year.
Work alone/with others: With others.
Qualifications: Nil but practical skills useful.
Equipment/clothing: Casual work clothes, waterproofs, stout boots. Protective safety boots, gloves etc provided.
Health requirements: Any medical conditions (illness, allergy or physical disability) that may require treatment/medication or which affect the volunteer working with machinery must be notified to us in advance. Tetanus injections must be up to date.
Costs: Food and accommodation.
Benefits: Out of pocket expenses.
Training: Introduction session.
Supervision: Constant supervision.
Interviews: Interviews at our office.
Charity number: 511068
UK placements: England (Co Durham, N. Yorkshire).

TEJO (Tutmonda Esperantista Junulara Org.)

Nieuwe Binnenweg 176
3015 BJ Rotterdam
The Netherlands
T: 00 31 10 436 1044
F: 00 31 10 436 1751
E: info@tejo.org
W: www.tejo.org
Contact: The Director

TEJO needs volunteers to join workcamps in various European countries arranged by TEJO, the World Organisation of Young Esperantists. All camps include Esperanto lessons for beginners. TEJO's principal objectives are to serve the interests of young speakers of Esperanto throughout the world, and to spread the use and practical application of the international language in youth circles. TEJO is concerned with present-day youth problems, especially those requiring international understanding and co-operation. It is completely neutral in regard to nationality, race, sex, religion and politics with the exception of cases in which human rights are violated. The organisation has 41 national sections in all parts of the world. TEJO and its national sections organise frequent meetings, conferences, seminars and congresses. A number of young activists from all over the world serve every year for short periods in order to acquire organisational experience. Opportunities exist in Europe but not necessarily in all countries listed.

Number of projects: 1–2
Starting months: Jun, Jul, Aug
Time required: 2–5 weeks
Age: 18–30
Causes: Archaeology, Architecture, Conservation, Heritage, Work Camps – Seasonal.
Activities: Building/Construction, Conservation Skills, Gardening/Horticulture, Group Work, Outdoor Skills, Summer Camps, Work Camps – Seasonal.
Placements: 10–50
When to apply: All year.
Work alone/with others: With others.
Qualifications: Basic knowledge of Esperanto or interest in learning Esperanto.
Health requirements: Nil.
Costs: Travel costs – sometimes a small registration fee.
Benefits: Board and lodging.
Worldwide placements: Asia (Turkey); Europe (Albania, Andorra, Armenia, Austria, Azerbaijan, Belarus, Belgium, Bosnia-Herzegovina, Bulgaria, Croatia, Cyprus, Czech Republic, Denmark, Estonia, Finland, France, Georgia, Germany, Gibraltar, Greece, Hungary, Iceland, Ireland, Italy, Latvia, Liechtenstein, Lithuania, Luxembourg, Macedonia, Malta, Moldova, Monaco, Netherlands, Norway, Poland, Portugal, Romania, Russia, San Marino, Slovakia, Slovenia, Spain, Sweden, Switzerland, Turkey, Ukraine, Vatican City, Yugoslavia).
UK placements: England (throughout); Scotland (throughout); Northern Ireland (throughout); Wales (throughout).

TEL AVIV UNIVERSITY – YAVNEH-YAM PROJECT

Department of Classics
69978 Ramat Aviv
Tel Aviv
Israel
T: 00 972 3 6409938
F: 00 972 3 6406243
E: fischer@post.tau.ac.il
W: www.tau.ac.il./yaveyam
Contact: Professor Moshe Fischer

Tel Aviv University needs volunteers to take part in archaeological excavations at the ancient port site of Yavneh Yam. Volunteers are recruited for two week periods in July and August. It is possible to stay for more than one period. Previous archaeological experience is an advantage but not essential. Groups of volunteers are particularly welcome. 🗎

Number of projects: 1 UK: 1
Starting months: Jun, Jul, Aug
Time required: 2–8 weeks

Age: 16 plus – no upper limit
Causes: Archaeology.
Activities: Research, Scientific Work.
Placements: 40–50
When to apply: January–May, deadline May 31.
Work alone/with others: With others in groups of 4–5 people.
Qualifications: Not important.
Equipment/clothing: Working clothes and shoes and bathing equipment.
Health requirements: Normal good health. Insurance necessary, will be checked on arrival!.
Costs: Food and accommodation (approx. US$350 per week).
Benefits: Evening courses and trips with emphasis on archaeology and history of Israel.
Training: No special training needed.
Interviews: Applicants are not interviewed.
Worldwide placements: Asia (Israel).

TEL DOR EXCAVATION PROJECT

Institute of Archaeology
Hebrew University
Mt Scopus
Jerusalem
Israel 91905
T: 00 972 2 5881304
F: 00 972 2 5825548 Attn Tel Dor
E: dor-proj@h2.hum.huji.ac.il
W: http://www.hum.huji.ac.il
Contact: Dr Ilan Sharon

Tel Dor was a major Canaanite, Phoenician, Hellenistic and Roman port and trading emporium on the Carmel coast. The Centre of Nautical and Regional Archaeology at Dor (CONRAD), housed in a historic glass-factory, on the grounds of Kibbutz Nasholim, is home of the Tel Dor excavation project and museum. The 2003 season will be a limited 'expert season'. Volunteers are needed during season (July) for excavation and assisting the scientists and professionals in their tasks. Restoration, conservation, exhibit preparation and maintenance, analysis of the finds, and conservation work on the building go on year-round. 🖒 🗎

Number of projects: 1 UK: 0
Starting months: Jul, Aug
Time required: 2–6 weeks
Age: 17 plus – no upper limit
Causes: Archaeology, Architecture, Heritage, Work Camps – Seasonal.
Activities: Administration, Computers, Outdoor Skills, Research, Scientific Work, Training, Work Camps – Seasonal.
Placements: 100
When to apply: All year untill 30th June.
Work alone/with others: With others.
Qualifications: Not needed.
Equipment/clothing: Hat, sun screen lotion, strong shoes.

Health requirements: Volunteers must hold health and personal possessions (theft and damage) insurance for Israel.
Costs: All costs including accommodation, food, insurance.
Training: Lectures and tours are given during the day.
Supervision: One area manager working with about 20 volunteers.
Interviews: Applicants are not interviewed.
Worldwide placements: Asia (Israel).

TERRENCE HIGGINS TRUST LIGHTHOUSE, THE

The Terrence Higgins Trust
52–54 Grays Inn Road
London
WC1X 8JU UK
T: +44 (0) 207 831 0330
T: +44 (0) 207 816 4561
E: thtlondonvols@tht.org.uk
W: www.tht.org.uk
Contact: Volunteer Co-ordinator

The Terrence Higgins Trust Lighthouse was founded in 1983 to inform, advise and help people affected by HIV and AIDS. Today, we are the UK's largest HIV and AIDS voluntary organisation, providing a range of high quality services which are responsive to the needs of people living with or affected by HIV and AIDS. You will be joining 1,000 other volunteers and 80 staff who work in partnership to achieve our mission. Our volunteers and staff come from all sections of the community and are committed to providing services to anyone affected by HIV and AIDS. All aspects of selection and training are covered by our equal opportunities policy, which ensures that selection for volunteering or training is based on personal ability. Our mission is to: reduce the spread of HIV; provide services which improve the health and quality of life of those affected; campaign for greater public understanding of the personal, social and medical impact of HIV and AIDS. Volunteers with an offending background may be accepted. Volunteers are asked to self disclose certain unspent convictions. ♿

Number of projects: 1 UK: 1
Starting months: January–December
Time required: 26–52 weeks
Age: 18–75
Causes: Addicts/Ex-Addicts, AIDS/HIV, Health Care/Medical.
Activities: Administration, Campaigning, Caring – General, Computers, DIY, Driving, Fundraising, Gardening/Horticulture, Training, Translating, Visiting/Befriending.
Placements: 150
When to apply: All year.
Work alone/with others: Both.

Costs: Must be resident in London as accommodation not provided, unless willing to pay for accommodation and food.
Benefits: Travel and lunch expenses and insurance.
Training: We ask all volunteers to attend an initial orientation event to help volunteer and THT to match skills and interests. Basic skills training (2 days). We also provide ongoing training as well as regular information updates.
Supervision: Support through volunteer group and regular meetings.
Interviews: Interviews take place in London.
Charity number: 288527
UK placements: England (London, Oxfordshire, E. Sussex, W. Sussex, West Midlands, W. Yorkshire).

THE LEAP OVERSEAS LTD

Windy Hollow
Sheepdrove
Lambourne
Berkshire RG17 7XA UK
T: 0870 240 4187
F: 01488 71311
E: info@theleap.co.uk
W: www.theleap.co.uk
Contact: Guy Whitehead

The Leap is a company dedicated to the gap year industry, providing British students and employees taking a career sabbatical with the opportunity to carry out work placements in some of the most exclusive and coveted destinations in the world. What makes us unique? Our product. We specialise in overseas voluntary work placements focused on tourism, combined with a strong emphasis on conservation and community issues. All placements are in bush camps, safari lodges, private ranches and boutique hotels, located on coveted game parks, bush locations, conservation zones and coastal hideaways. Volunteers are involved in a variety of activities including hospitality, food and beverage, maintenance as well as involvement with community and conservation projects. They will be helping the professionals provide activities such as game walks, horse and camel safaris, deep-sea fishing etc.

Number of projects: 80 UK: 0
Starting months: January–December
Time required: 12 weeks
Age: 18–60
Causes: Animal Welfare, Children, Conservation, Environmental Causes, Teaching/assisting, Wildlife.
Activities: Administration, Agriculture/Farming, Building/Construction, Community Work, Conservation Skills, Cooking, Development Issues, DIY, Driving, Forestry, Manual Work, Outdoor Skills, Teaching.
Placements: 15 per country.
When to apply: As early as possible.
Work alone/with others: Work with others.
Qualifications: A level, going on to a degree. In some cases cooking, driving and riding are an advantage. We need individuals who are committed, enthusiastic and motivated, who work in a team and are prepared to get stuck in.
Equipment/clothing: Boots, rucksack, waterproof jacket, mosquito net and normal clothes.
Health requirements: We offer medical advice.
Costs: £1950–£2100 not including flights. Ring for a brochure detailing a breakdown of costs.
Benefits: 24 hour back up, local living allowance, airport pick up and transfer to and from project, full board and accommodation.
Training: We provide full training.
Supervision: We provide 24 hour back up, both in country and in the UK, by professional, knowledgable and experienced staff with excellent in country knowledge.
Interviews: Interviews are held on the training course.
Worldwide placements: Africa (Botswana, Kenya, Malawi, Namibia, South Africa, Tanzania, Uganda, Zambia); Asia (Nepal, Sri Lanka).

THISTLE CAMPS

The National Trust for Scotland
Wemyss House
28 Charlotte Square
Edinburgh
EH2 4ET UK

T: 0131 243 9470
F: 0131 243 9593
E: conservationvolunteers@nts.org.uk
W: www.thistlecamps.org.uk
Contact: Julia Downes

Thistle Camps are open to all volunteers over 18 years of age. (Some camps are open to those over 16 as well but these are limited.) They provide opportunities for you to see new places, meet new people and contribute to the conservation of Scotland's wild places. All volunteers are expected to work a 9–5 day and help out with domestic duties when not on site. A day off is programmed to visit nearby places of interest. Volunteers must be prepared for physically demanding tasks and bad weather. Thistle Camps are sponsored by Total Fina Elf.

Number of projects: 37 UK: 37
Starting months: Mar, Apr, May, Jun, Jul, Aug, Sep, Oct, Nov
Time required: 1–3 weeks
Age: 16 plus – no upper limit
Causes: Archaeology, Conservation, Environmental Causes, Heritage, Wildlife, Work Camps – Seasonal.
Activities: Building/Construction, Conservation Skills, Gardening/Horticulture, Group Work, Manual Work, Outdoor Skills, Summer Camps, Training, Work Camps – Seasonal.
Placements: 400
When to apply: January – September
Work alone/with others: With others.
Qualifications: Willingness to work hard and mix in.
Equipment/clothing: Work clothes/overalls, waterproofs, steel toes capped boots/wellingtons.
Health requirements: Should be reasonably fit. Anti-tetanus innoculation recommended.
Costs: Travel to pick-up point in Scotland. Camp costs start at £50 (£35 unwaged, retired, student).
Benefits: Accommodation + food provided.
Training: Training given on the job.
Supervision: Staff supervision and camp leaders.
Interviews: Applicants are not interviewed.
Charity number: SCO07410
UK placements: Scotland (Aberdeen City, Aberdeenshire, Angus, Argyll and Bute, Ayrshire – East, Ayrshire – North, Ayrshire – South, Clackmannanshire, Dumfries and Galloway, Dunbartonshire – East, Dunbartonshire – West, Dundee City, Edinburgh, Falkirk, Glasgow City, Highland, Inverclyde, Lanarkshire – North, Lanarkshire – South, Lothian – East, Lothian – West, Midlothian, Moray, Perth and Kinross, Renfrewshire, Renfrewshire – East, Scottish Borders, Shetland Islands, Stirling, Western Isles).

THOMAS-HAUS BERLIN FUR HEILPADOGOGIK UND SPRACHTHERAPIE e.V.

Peter-Lenné-Str. 42,
D-14195 Berlion (Dahlem)
Germany
T: 00 49 30 832 64 53
F: 0043 30 832 9242
E: info@thomas-haus-berlin.de
Contact: The Director

Thomas-Haus Berlin für Heilpädogogik und Sprachtherapie is a Camphill curative therapeutic centre for young children with special needs.

Number of projects: 1 UK: 0
Starting months: January–December
Time required: 52 weeks
Age: 21–99
Causes: Children, Disabled (learning).
Activities: Agriculture/Farming, Caring (general, day and residential), Catering, Community Work, Gardening/Horticulture, Group Work, Social Work, Work Camps – Seasonal.
Qualifications: Need students who have experience.
Worldwide placements: Europe (Germany).

TIME FOR GOD SCHEME, THE

2 Chester House
Pages Lane
Muswell Hill
London
N10 1PR UK
T: +44 (0) 208 883 1504
F: +44 (0) 208 365 2471
E: OfficeTFG@cs.com
W: www.timeforgod.org
Contact: Roger Taylor/Tracy Phillips

The Time for God Scheme offers 9–12 month volunteer placements for Christian young people aged 18–25. Opportunities include working with churches and community projects, the elderly, mentally ill, ex-offenders, disabled children, youth and homeless. Volunteers are supported by field staff.
The TFG programme established 33 years ago operates by matching young people to church and community projects working with a variety of client groups in numerous settings throughout the UK and more recently abroad. TFG helps young people develop new skills, take a year out from education, serve God in a new way, explore a vocation or simply try something new. Throughout the UK, Europe and the USA, Asia, Africa, Australia. ⓑ

Number of projects: Various UK: 150
Starting months: Jan, Sep

Time required: 40–52 weeks
Age: 18–25
Causes: Addicts/Ex-Addicts, AIDS/HIV, Children, Disabled (learning and physical), Elderly People, Health Care/Medical, Inner City Problems, Offenders/Ex-Offenders, Poor/Homeless, Teaching – Nursery, Unemployed, Young People.
Activities: Administration, Campaigning, Caring (general, day and residential), Community Work, Computers, Cooking, Counselling, Group Work, Manual Work, Marketing/Publicity, Music, Outdoor Skills, Religion, Social Work, Sport, Teaching, Theatre/Drama, Training, Visiting/Befriending.
Placements: 200
When to apply: 2–8 months in advance.
Work alone/with others: Both.
Qualifications: Committed Christians or honestly exploring Christian faith.
Health requirements: Nil.
Costs: Home church contributes approximately £600 towards training costs.
Benefits: We pay for day-to-day living costs + £25 per week. Various accommodation from lodging with a family to hostel.accommodation.
Training: TFG provides 3 4–day residential training conferences for all volunteers with opportunities for worship, bible study, reflection, training and a monthly spiritual development programme.
Supervision: Supervisor in placement gives weekly supervision. Pastoral support and placement visits by field officers ensure the volunteer is well supported.
Interviews: We interview all applicants who attend one of our briefing days which take place throughout the year.
Charity number: 206163
Worldwide placements: Africa (Ghana); North America: (USA); Central America (Guatemala); South America (Argentina, Uruguay); Asia (India, Thailand); Australasia (Australia); Europe (Austria, Belgium, Denmark, Finland, France, Germany, Hungary, Ireland, Italy, Netherlands, Norway, Sweden).
UK placements: England (throughout); Scotland (Edinburgh, Stirling); Wales (throughout).

TIPHERETH CAMPHILL IN EDINBURGH

Torphin Holding
49 Torphin Road
Edinburgh
EH13 0PQ UK
T: 0131 441 2055
F: 0131 441 2055
E: tiphereth@gmx.co.uk
W: www.camphill.org.uk
Contact: Vicky Syme

Tiphereth is part of the Camphill movement, where we work to create a community in which people, some of whom have learning difficulties, can learn and work with others in a healthy social relationship based on mutual care and respect. Camphill is inspired by Christian ideals and is based on the acceptance of the spiritual uniqueness of each human being, regardless of disability, religion or racial background. Tiphereth is a small Camphill community on the outskirts of Edinburgh. It consists of two house communities and day-activities for people with special needs of the wider community. The Pentlands group does conservation work in the hills and we run a local community-composting project. Each co-worker is asked to enter fully into the life of the community, which entails housework, cooking, participation in cultural and leisure activities and also day-activities (e.g. gardening, weaving, crafts and therapeutic activities). Wages are not paid to those of us who live in the Community. This would be seen as a divisive factor between the co-workers and those in need of care. The needs of co-workers who have committed themselves for a longer time are met from shared community resources. Although each co-worker has one free day a week, we do not operate a shift system, as it would be counter productive to the creation of a consistent and harmonious atmosphere. Our way of life is demanding, challenging and very rewarding. Depending on the nature of offence, we may be able to place volunteers with an offending background, individually assessed. On the outskirts of Edinburgh city, half an hour bus ride from city centre. 🗎

Number of projects: Many UK: Many
Starting months: January–December
Time required: 26–52 weeks
Age: 18–75
Causes: Conservation, Disabled (learning and physical), Environmental Causes, Wildlife, Young People.
Activities: Arts/Crafts, Caring (general, day and residential), Community Work, Conservation Skills, Cooking, Gardening/Horticulture, Manual Work, Music, Social Work, Theatre/Drama.
Placements: 6–8
When to apply: Apply 6 months before you wish to come, but applications can be accepted much later according to current vacancy situation.
Work alone/with others: Work with others.
Qualifications: A reasonable to good level of English. Good health, an open, willing and positive attitude and lots of energy. No restrictions, but it would be the volunteer's responsibility to apply for any relevant visas.

Equipment/clothing: Warm, waterproof outdoor clothing and footwear.
Health requirements: All volunteers must sign a statement to say they are in good physical health/mental health.
Costs: Travel costs to and from the community, for one year placements. Return fare to Tiphereth will be paid by us.
Benefits: Board and lodging, personal toiletry items, pocket money of £120 /month, plus holiday allowance.
Training: In house training from other experienced co-workers begins immediately and is always available.
Supervision: Due to the work being more 'a way of life' there is always someone experienced to talk to and share with. We have a strong support and supervision structure.
Interviews: None.
Charity number: SCO 17483
UK placements: Scotland (Edinburgh).

TLHOLEGO DEVELOPMENT PROJECT

P O Box 1668
Rustenburg 0300
North West Province South Africa
T: 00 27 14 592 7090
F: as above
E: tlholego@iafrica.com
W: www.sustainable-futures.com
Contact: Mr Paul Cohen

Tlholego Development Project provides a rural educational environment based on ecological principles, with the purpose of training people in the design and implementation of sustainable land use and village settlements. Tlholego is a living model village for those ecological principles, consisting of a comunity of 50+ members, many of whom were formerly disadvantaged under the apartheid regime. These principles are continually refined and improved through the community's activities and experiences. Volunteers play an active part in the community, not only living alongside its members, but assisting in tending the permaculture garden, in the building and maintaining of the buildings constructed using sustainable building technologies, and in the community decision making processes. It is an opportunity to be an active part, rather than an observer, of a vibrant developing rural community. Tlholego Development Project also operates a series of workshops covering permaculture, eco-village design, building using sustainable building technology and landcare through the keyline design and earthworks engineering design system. The leading authorities in their field facilitate these workshops. Volunteers are automatically able to attend these workshops. Volunteers with an offending background would be considered individually. vildev@iafrica.com 120kms north-west of Johannesburg. ♿ 📖

Number of projects: 1 UK: 0
Starting months: January–December
Time required: 4–24 weeks
Age: 16–25
Causes: Environmental Causes, Heritage, Young People.
Activities: Agriculture/Farming, Building/Construction, Development Issues, Fundraising, Gardening/Horticulture.
Placements: 2
When to apply: All year – as early as possible before starting.
Work alone/with others: Both.
Health requirements: Nil.
Costs: All travel and personal expenses. Prefer volunteers that can contribute in part for their food and accommodation ($6–10 per day).
Benefits: Food and basic accommodation. Living and learning experience.
Training: No pre-placement training given.
Supervision: Project directors supervise.
Interviews: Prospective volunteers are not interviewed.
Worldwide placements: Africa (South Africa).

TOC H

1 Forest Close
Wendover
Aylesbury
Buckinghamshire HP22 6BT UK
T: 01296 623911
F: 01296 696137
E: info@toch.org.uk
W: www.toch.org.uk
Contact: Projects Office

Toc H was conceived in 1915 just behind the front lines in Flanders where it ran a house for all ranks for rest and recreation where, in the midst of all the horror and futility of the trenches, men discovered friendships which crossed the normal barriers of rank and class. And they discovered peace, hope and God. At the end of the Great War the international Toc H movement sprang up, open to men and women from all walks of life and committed to the same principles experienced in Talbot House: friendship – to love widely, service – to build bravely, fair-mindedness – to think fairly and the kingdom of God – to witness humbly. Throughout the Second World War Toc H was active across the world in providing creature comforts and friendships for service men and women. Over the last 80 years Toc H has brought together thousands of people. All discover extraordinary friendships; work

together serving their community; welcome, listen and learn from those with very different opinions; and, through the challenge of testing the Christian way by trying it, discover a faith to live by. Volunteers with an offending background are accepted. ♿

Number of projects: 54 UK: 50
Starting months: January–December
Time required: 1–2 weeks
Age: 16–70
Causes: Children, Conservation, Disabled (learning and physical), Elderly People, Environmental Causes, Inner City Problems, Offenders/Ex-Offenders, Poor/Homeless, Unemployed, Work Camps – Seasonal.
Activities: Arts/Crafts, Building/Construction, Caring (general, day and residential), Community Work, Conservation Skills, Counselling, Fundraising, Group Work, Manual Work, Outdoor Skills, Religion, Summer Camps, Training, Visiting/Befriending, Work Camps – Seasonal.
Placements: 500
When to apply: All year.
Work alone/with others: With others in a group of usually 8–12 persons of mixed ages.
Qualifications: No restrictions but EU member countries are favoured.
Equipment/clothing: Not unless notified by project leader before commencement of project.
Health requirements: No.
Costs: Registration fee £20 non members £15 members, plus possible supplementary fee.
Benefits: Travel bursary for low waged/unemployed. Board and lodging.
Training: Usually no pre-placement training.
Supervision: 2 leaders over 18 sharing responsibility. All new leaders trained in accordance with our guidelines. Project support groups/regional committees as back-up.
Interviews: No interviews – we operate a 'first come, first served' policy – sight unseen but references required for work with children.
Charity number: 211042
Worldwide placements: Africa (South Africa, Zimbabwe); Australasia (Australia); Europe (Belgium).
UK placements: England (Bedfordshire, Berkshire, Buckinghamshire, Cheshire, Co Durham, Cumbria, Derbyshire, Devon, Essex, Hampshire, Hertfordshire, London, Norfolk, Northamptonshire, Oxfordshire, Somerset, Staffordshire, Suffolk, Tyne and Wear, West Midlands, Wiltshire, N. Yorkshire, S. Yorkshire, W. Yorkshire); Scotland (Ayrshire – East, Ayrshire – North, Falkirk, Glasgow City, Lanarkshire – North, Lanarkshire – South, Renfrewshire); Wales (Gwynedd, Swansea).

TOPS DAY NURSERIES

Leigh Road
Wimborne
Dorset BH21 2BX UK
T: 01202 841691 or 882829
F: 01202 841691
E: CherylHadland@aol.com
W: www.wimbornetops.co.uk
Contact: Cheryl Hadland

TOPS provides a childcare service to the community, offering 56 (Parkstone) + 50 (Wareham) + 112 (Bournemouth) + 42 (Wimborne) + 60 (Winchester) places for children aged 6 weeks to 8 years. Volunteers can help with: playing with the children, reading stories 1:1, inside and outside, helping with swimming and/or tumble tots, and trips further afield e.g. farms, monkey world; helping to provide a clean, tidy, safe environment including preparation for/clearing up after meals; help with photocopying, filing, children's work. We have lots of pets (birds, rabbits, guinea pigs, hamsters, fish) on site that need handling and care too.
Alternative addresses:
1 Carey Road
Wareham
Dorset
Telephone 01929 555051

Royal Bournemouth Hospital
East Castle Lane
Bournemouth
Dorset
Telephone 0589 244182

Royal Hampshire Hospital
Winchester,
Hants. &
Telephone: 01962 825066

Number of projects: 1 UK: 1
Starting months: January–December
Time required: 1–52 weeks
Age: 16 plus – no upper limit
Causes: Animal Welfare, Children, Teaching/assisting, (nursery).
Activities: Administration, Arts/Crafts, Caring – Day, Community Work, Computers, Cooking, First Aid, Fundraising, Group Work, Music, Teaching, Technical Skills, Theatre/Drama.
Placements: 10
When to apply: All year.
Work alone/with others: With others.
Qualifications: Police check and Ofsted forms completed on first day. GBH/ABH/drugs/child abuse will disallow.
2 references must be provided.
Health requirements: Nil.
Costs: Food and accommodation costs.
Benefits: Training on site, beacon work based training provider.

Training: Induction training on site.
Supervision: Nursery/NVQ assessors are supervisors.
Interviews: Two interviews, one with manager and team training assessor, and one with children.
UK placements: England (Dorset, Hampshire).

TOYBOX CHARITY, THE

P O Box 660
Amersham
Buckinghamshire HP6 5YT UK
T: 01494 432591
F: 01494 432593
E: ange@toybox.org
W: www.toybox.org
Contact: Angela Murray

The Toybox Charity is a UK registered charity which rescues street children in Guatemala, giving them a loving home, an education and a hope for the future. A dedicated street team go on to the streets each afternoon and evening providing first aid, friendship and fun to the hundreds of children whose home is the streets. A day centre is open each day too providing a safe place for the street children to come to where they can get food, clean clothes and showers. Toybox also have five loving, small, family-style homes where the street children can learn to be children again, grow up as a family and go to school. We also have two teams working within poor communities in Guatemala to help prevent children becoming homeless. The Toybox gap-year scheme runs from September to August each year. Students travel out to Guatemala early in September and spend three and a half months learning Spanish and working with the street children and those now in our homes. On return to the UK students spend eight months working with Toybox UK, raising awareness of the plight of the street children and the work of Toybox. They spend time speaking in schools, churches and interest groups about their experiences in Guatemala as well as running stalls for Toybox at major Christian events. Volunteers with an offending background may be accepted, depending on the offence. Guatemala City – Toybox Street Child Project.

Number of projects: 2 UK: 1
Starting months: Sep
Time required: 52 weeks
Age: 18–30
Causes: Children, Poor/Homeless, Young People.
Activities: Caring – General, First Aid, International Aid, Marketing/Publicity.
Placements: 6
When to apply: By the end of June.
Work alone/with others: Work with others as part of a team.

Qualifications: No qualifications needed but volunteers need to be Christians. UK applicants only.
Health requirements: No specific Health requirements.
Costs: Approximately £3500 for the year.
Benefits: Pocket money, accommodation and food in Guatemala.
Opportunity to work in a cross-cultural setting. Accommodation provided both in Guatemala and in the UK.
Training: 1 week of orientation in the UK, 1 week of orientation in Guatemala. 4 weeks of Spanish training. 2 weeks of public speaking training in the UK
Supervision: Carefully supervised during the whole year with Toybox.
Interviews: Interviews in Amersham, Bucks.
Charity number: 1084243
Worldwide placements: Central America (Guatemala).
UK placements: England (Buckinghamshire).

TRAILBLAZERS, WALES

c/o Scope
The Wharf
Schooner Way
Cardiff
CF10 4EU UK
T: 02920 461 703
F: 02920 461 705
E: neil.taylor@cwmpascymru.org.uk
Contact: Neil Taylor

Trailblazers is a club which offers membership to young disabled children between 9 and 16 years throughout Wales. As members of the Trailblazers club, the children will have the opportunity to participate in a variety of activities, which might otherwise be inaccessible to them. Membership will be offered to those children who find it difficult to be included in out-of-school activities for a variety of reasons, including physical, emotional, sensory and perceptual impairments. Trailblazers is supported by young adult volunteers who wish to contribute their time and skills to enhance their own development. It is hoped that we will continue providing out of school hours activities. All volunteers are police screened and must attend child protection training, moving and handling training and induction training.
Volunteers with an offending background may be accepted sometimes, depending on the offence. We also manage a befriending scheme, details enclosed. &

Number of projects: 2 UK: 1
Starting months: January–December
Time required: 1–9 weeks
Age: 16 plus – no upper limit
Causes: Children, Disabled (physical), Holidays for Disabled.

Activities: Administration, Arts/Crafts, Caring (general, day and residential), Driving, Fundraising, Group Work, Music, Newsletter/Journalism, Outdoor Skills, Sport, Summer Camps, Theatre/Drama, Visiting/Befriending.
Placements: 70+
When to apply: Any time.
Work alone/with others: With others.
Qualifications: No.
Health requirements: Good in general.
Costs: Nil.
Benefits: All out of pocket expenses are covered. Accommodation arrangements are made and paid for by us.
Training: Child protection and lifting and handling training and also induction.
Supervision: Each new volunteer is supervised by an experienced volunteer enabler.
Interviews: Applicants are interviewed and must now attend training days for child protection and moving and handling.
UK placements: Wales (throughout).

TRAVEL ACTIVE

P. O. Box 107
5800 AC Venray
The Netherlands
T: 00 31 478 551 900
F: 00 31 478 551 911
E: info@travelactive.nl
W: www.travelactive.nl
Contact: Richard Santalla

Travel Active can offer: Work and travel in Europe: working on a farm in Norway or Switzerland, or restoration projects in France, Italy etc. Work and travel in Australia and Canada: conservation programmes.
Volunteer work in Africa, Latin-America and Asia. Volunteers with an offending background may be accepted depending on the situation and the programme. &

Number of projects: 30 UK: 0
Starting months: January–December
Time required: 3–52 weeks
Age: 16–30
Causes: Animal Welfare, Architecture, Children, Conservation, Disabled (physical), Environmental Causes, Poor/Homeless, Unemployed, Wildlife, Work Camps – Seasonal, Young People.
Activities: Administration, Agriculture/Farming, Arts/Crafts, Building/Construction, Catering, Conservation Skills, Forestry, Gardening/Horticulture, Manual Work, Marketing/Publicity, Outdoor Skills, Social Work, Sport, Summer Camps, Work Camps – Seasonal.
Placements: 1000
When to apply: Depends on the programme.
Work alone/with others: Depends on the programme.

Qualifications: Must be citizens of the EU.
Equipment/clothing: Depends on the
programme.
Health requirements: Depends on the
programme.
Costs: Depends on the programme.
Benefits: Depends on the programme – usually
camping places and youth hostels.
Training: Depends on the programme. For
most of the programmes, we organise
orientation programmes in Holland and also in
the desired country.
Supervision: Depends on the programme.
Usually there is supervision in the workplace.
Worldwide placements: Africa (Benin, Côte
d'Ivoire, Ghana, Nigeria, Senegal, South Africa);
North America: (Canada, USA); Central America
(Costa Rica, Guatemala, Mexico); South
America (Argentina, Bolivia, Ecuador, Peru);
Asia (Israel, Nepal); Australasia (Australia);
Europe (Austria, Finland, France, Italy,
Netherlands, Norway, Spain, Switzerland).

TRAVELLERS

7 Mulberry Close
Ferring
West Sussex BN12 5HY UK
T: 01903 502595
F: 01903 500364
E: info@travellersworldwide.com
W: www.travellersworldwide.com
Contact: Phil Perkes

Travellers offers a unique opportunity to live
and work teach in a different and fascinating
ethnic environment with a different lifestyle –
and to experience a different culture from the
'inside'. An unforgettable experience! Do
gratifying and much-needed work in less
advantaged countries – and add an impressive
entry on your CV!. Placements are open to all –
no formal qualifications needed; you don't
need to speak the local language; your travel
arrangements can allow time to explore the
country. This is not a salaried position. The
work is voluntary but all your food and
accommodation for the entire length of your
programme is included in our charge – all you
need is pocket money. What you can do: teach
conversational english or other subjects such as
music, sports, IT, maths etc. Conservation work
on many different projects in many different
countries – (some examples of our choices are
the Moscow Zoo in Russia, dolphin research in
South Africa, and elephant orphanage in Sri
Lanka. Work experience placements in fields
such as journalism, law, medicine, etc. You can
also combine two or more types of placement
(e.g. teaching and conservation) in two or more
countries (e.g. China and South Africa). In Sri
Lanka, you can even do two months teaching

combined with one month in the elephant
orphanage. All placements very flexible and are
tailored to your requirements – you can also
choose your own start and finish dates and you
can also allow extra time to travel around and
explore the country you are in. Travellers
currently offer placements in thirteen
destinations: Argentina, Brazil, China, Cuba,
Ghana, India, Kenya, Malaysia, Nepal, Russia,
South Africa, Sri Lanka and Ukraine and the list
of new countries is growing all the time.
Travellers is a member of The Year Out Group.
Many cities and locations in many countries,
too numerous to mention – all volunteers are
provided with an extensive information book
on their country especially compiled by
Travellers for their volunteers. ♿ 🗎

Number of projects: 100+ UK: 0
Starting months: January–December
Time required: 2–52 weeks
Age: 17 plus – no upper limit
Causes: AIDS/HIV, Animal Welfare,
Archaeology, Children, Conservation, Disabled
(learning and physical), Environmental Causes,
Health Care/Medical, Human Rights, Poor/
Homeless, Teaching/assisting (nursery, primary,
secondary, mature, EFL) Wildlife, Work Camps –
Seasonal, Young People.
Activities: Arts/Crafts, Building/Construction,
Caring (general and day), Catering, Community
Work, Computers, Conservation Skills, DIY,
Gardening/Horticulture, Manual Work,
Marketing/Publicity, Music, Newsletter/
Journalism, Outdoor Skills, Research, Scientific
Work, Sport, Summer Camps, Teaching,
Technical Skills, Theatre/Drama, Work Camps –
Seasonal.
Placements: 800+
When to apply: Placements are available
throughout the year.
Work alone/with others: Mainly with other
volunteers.
Qualifications: Good English for teaching
placements. We accept gap year students before
university, undergraduates or graduates, people
taking a career break or who are retired. Some
scientific background required for research and
science programmes. No restrictions except
volunteers need to speak English if they want to
do teaching or work experience placement, and
reasonable English if they want a conservation
placement.
Equipment/clothing: None required except
when doing photography in Cuba.
Health requirements: Very few restrictions,
providing we are informed prior to the
placement so that adequate care can be taken in
our destinations. There are always doctors on
call.
Costs: Costs range from £895 to £1,795. For
example, £3895 for Ukraine teaching project,

£945 to learn Spanish in Cuba, £1,245 to teach in Sri Lanka. Plus flight costs.

Benefits: Full in country support and back up. All food and accommodation whilst on placement. In most countries travel to and from place of work is provided. In Russia and Ukraine free travel passes in your placement city are provided.

Training: Extensive guideline and notes prior to leaving. Formal inductions in most countries and assistance in all destinations. Volunteers work under supervision and expert guidance. Optional teaching training prior to leaving.

Supervision: You will be supervised and given all the help you need, both at home and in all destinations.

Interviews: Personal interviews where necessary. Extensive telephone interviews and liaison are standard.

Worldwide placements: Africa (Ghana, Kenya, South Africa); Central America (Cuba); South America (Argentina, Brazil); Asia (China, India, Malaysia, Nepal, Sri Lanka, Vietnam); Europe (Russia, Ukraine).

TREE IS LIFE VEGETABLE SOCIETY

c/o Non-Formal Education Division
P. O. Box 6
Walewale
Janga
Northern Region Ghana
T: 00 233 71 22647
F: 00 233 71 23088
Contact: J.B. Ibrahim Tahiru

Our organsiation is known as the Janga Vegetable Project. It was formed in 1992 by volunteers from Janga, in the district of Walewale capital of West Mamprusi. We start in the dry season between months of September to May to cultivate vegetables and fruit along the basin of the river Volta, also tree planting from the month of June to October. Tree is Life Vegetable Society has the following aims and activities:
1. to overcome specific problems that affect the rural youth, e.g. unemployment,
2. to help the people in the rural community to improve upon their living standards through self-generating income,
3. to improve the quality and quantity of vegetables and fruits. e.g. tomatoes, cashew nuts, sunflowers, peanuts and many others,
4. we also aim to link the rural community to the urban people through improved and modern methods of vegetable and fruit production.
It is in the light of the above aims that we find it necessary to mobilise the rural youth for effective work. The Tree is Life Vegetable Society would be more effective with more help.
Alternative address for J.B. Ibrahim Tahiru:

Johnson Farms Complex Ltd, PO Box 14448, Accra, Telephone 021 400271, 021 401515 or 021 401212. Fax 033-21 400593. They would be pleased if any volunteer could help build a church in the area. 🚻 📋

Number of projects: 3 UK: 0
Starting months: Jun
Time required: 2–10 weeks
Age: 16–50
Causes: Animal Welfare, Environmental Causes, Health Care/Medical, Unemployed, Work Camps – Seasonal.
Activities: Agriculture/Farming, Arts/Crafts, Community Work, Development Issues, Forestry, Fundraising, Gardening/Horticulture, Group Work, Marketing/Publicity, Social Work, Sport, Training, Translating, Visiting/Befriending, Work Camps – Seasonal.
Placements: 100
When to apply: By 5th May.
Work alone/with others: With other young volunteers.
Qualifications: No specific qualifications are required. When writing state your fields of interest and the number of years or weeks you can stay.
Equipment/clothing: Depends on the project to be undertaken.
Health requirements: Nil except malarial prophylactics.
Costs: Registration £10, fares to Ghana + £15, subsistence £50 per annum. All allowances and expenses borne by the volunteer.
Benefits: Accommodation and safety are the sole duty of the society.
Supervision: Supervision is done by the organiser.
Interviews: No interviews before arriving at the worksite.
Worldwide placements: Africa (Ghana).

TREKFORCE EXPEDITIONS

34 Buckingham Palace Road
London
SW1W 0RE UK
T: +44 (0) 207 828 2275
T: +44 (0) 207 828 2276
E: info@trekforce.org.uk
W: www.trekforce.org.uk
Contact: Sarah Bruce

Trekforce Expeditions – adventure with a purpose. Trekforce offers you a once in a lifetime opportunity to play your part in sustainable rainforest conservation, scientific and community projects. Expeditions last two months in Central and South America and East Malaysia. Longer programmes of three, four or five months incorporate conservation work, up to one month of language learning and two months of teaching in rural communities. Each

team of volunteers sees through their own project from start to finish, including a 5–10 day trek such as climbing the highest mountain in the country or trekking into unknown areas of the jungle to create a map for a local organisation or community. All projects are planned in co-ordination with our project partners, such as NGOs and scientific research organisations, and as such are always extremely valuable to their local communities. Each volunteer has to fundraise a minimum amount for Trekforce (UK registered charity), with extensive advice and support from the Trekforce staff. If you are looking for a diverse, challenging adventure, come and find out more on one of our introduction days. Visit our web site for more details and to request an information pack, or send an e-mail to info@trekforce.org.uk.
Trekforce is a member of The Year Out Group. Often projects are in remote jungle locations, in areas inaccessible to any traveller or by transport other than foot. Safety is high priority with Trekforce. Full back up and support provided by helicopter and multiple communication equipment on location.

Number of projects: 15 **UK:** 0
Starting months: Jan, Feb, Mar, Apr, May, Jun, Jul
Time required: 8–20 weeks
Age: 18–32
Causes: Animal Welfare, Children, Conservation, Environmental Causes, Teaching/assisting (primary, EFL), Wildlife, Young People.
Activities: Building/Construction, Community Work, Conservation Skills, Development Issues, Forestry, Fundraising, Group Work, International Aid, Manual Work, Outdoor Skills, Scientific Work, Teaching.
Placements: 275
When to apply: All year.
Work alone/with others: Project phase: teams of 15–20 volunteers with two experienced expedition leaders and two medics. Teaching phase: volunteers are placed in pairs in rural communities living with local families.
Qualifications: No qualifications are required, just a good level of fitness and fluency in English. Must have a UK passport or be resident in the UK at time of application and be able to attend training in the UK prior to departure.
Equipment/clothing: A full kit list is issued as part of the comprehensive joining instructions given on signing up. Extensive advice and discounts are offered at the pre-expedition training event in the UK.
Health requirements: Yes.
Costs: £2570 for 8 weeks. £3200 for 3 months. £3800 for 5 months. All fundraising targets exclude the cost of flights and kit insurance. Food and accommodation, personal insurance and project costs are included.

Benefits: Contribution includes all expenses, training, board & accommodation, medical insurance. Trekforce offer some of the toughest and most challenging expeditions of their kind.
Training: Introduction day followed by a two day briefing event three to four months before departing UK. Seven to ten days in-country training is undertaken before the start of their project phase.
Supervision: Fully qualified and experienced UK expedition staff & medical teams supervise. Help & advice provided throughout. Local staff present on project sites to offer specific skills training, such as scientific research or construction work.
Interviews: Introduction days are run in Central London every other Sunday and take place occasionally in North England and Scotland. Trekforce holds a policy of self-selection, subject to medical well-being.
Charity number: 1005452
Worldwide placements: Africa (Kenya, Uganda); Central America (Belize, Guatemala); Asia (Indonesia, Malaysia).

TRELOAR TRUST

Upper Froyle
Alton
Hampshire GU34 4JX UK
T: 01420 526407
F: 01420 23957
E: personnel@treloar.org.uk
W: www.treloar-trust.org.uk
Contact: Catherine Short

Treloar's is a groundbreaking organisation providing first class education, therapy and care for young people with physical disabilities. We have students aged between seven and 24 and our fundamental purpose is simple: to enable people with disabilities to fulfil their potential in every aspect of their lives. Being a volunteer offers the opportunity for practical experience of living with, and caring for young people who, because of disability or illness, require the very special support that we give them. Volunteer posts exist at the school and college. There are opportunities in the classrooms, boarding houses, medical centres, sports or therapy departments. In all cases you will be working along side experienced permanent members of staff. We need volunteers who have a mature approach, are good team players, able to provide personal care relevant to the student's needs and are willing to take on a wide range of tasks. In addition, you should be able to understand and communicate written and verbal English to a good standard. Treloar school and college are both near Alton in Hampshire. Volunteers with an offending background are not accepted, as this is a school/college for extremely vulnerable young people. Holybourne and Froyle, Nr Alton, Hampshire. ♿

Number of projects: 1 **UK:** 1
Starting months: Sep
Time required: 37 weeks
Age: 18–30
Causes: Children, Disabled (physical), Health Care/Medical, Teaching/assisting (primary, secondary), Young People.
Activities: Caring (general, day and residential), Computers, Group Work, Sport, Teaching, Theatre/Drama.
Placements: 34
When to apply: All year.
Work alone/with others: With other permanent staff.
Qualifications: Enthusiasm and commitment. No restrictions but excellent knowledge of English is essential.
Health requirements: Need to be fit and strong.
Costs: Travel costs to and from home at start and end of every term.
Benefits: £49 per week pocket money. Shared accommodation with other volunteers provided.
Training: Pre-placement training given one week before start of term.
Supervision: Volunteers are supervised by permanent members of staff in each department.
Interviews: Interviews take place at Alton and travel costs are provided.
Charity number: 307103
UK placements: England (Hampshire).

TRIFORM CAMPHILL COMMUNITY

20 Triform Road
Hudson
NY 12534 USA
T: 00 1 518.851.9320
F: 00 1 518.851.2864
E: coworker@camphill.org

W: www.triformcamphill.org
Contact: Meg Henderson

Triform Camphill community is an intentional therapeutic community of 60 people, about half of whom are young adults with disabilities. Located on beautiful farmland in upstate New York, Triform offers a unique opportunity to live and work full time with handicapped young people:
– full participation in all aspects of community life
– experience in curative education and social therapy
– work with handicapped young adults in gardening, farming, weaving, artistic and cultural activities, household management, courses and workshops, outings.
– opportunities to travel to nearby places of interest.
Volunteers live in a house, usually with a family, one or two other volunteers and four to six young adults with disabilities. You will have your own bedroom and be able to have some time in the day for yourself, as well as one day off per week. You will be one of a number of international and American volunteers who come for short term stays – e.g. 12-months as well as the long term volunteers who either live here for some years or who regard Triform as their permanent home. We hope you find this information helpful and positive, and we welcome any questions you may have. Triform recognises the great contribution made by short-term volunteers, who bring vibrancy, energy and questions. We appreciate your interest and willingness to participate, and encourage your application. two+ hours north of New York City, three hours from Boston. ♿ 📷

Number of projects: 1 **UK:** 0
Starting months: Jun, Aug
Time required: 6–52 weeks (plus)
Age: 18 plus – no upper limit
Causes: Disabled (learning and physical), Environmental Causes, Young People.

Computers and Commerce in Cape Town

Oliver Ayres' gap year in South Africa encompassed two very different projects and extensive travel. At his first placement in Cape Town he taught computers and commerce to underprivileged black students from rural areas. "It was very rewarding when my students passed comfortably in the final

exams." A second placement at a small private school for more privileged white students "provided a real contrast." Oliver's year in South Africa "was an amazing experience. I had the opportunity to do things that most people my age can only dream of. I feel now that I am better equipped for the life ahead of me."

Activities: Agriculture/Farming, Arts/Crafts, Building/Construction, Caring – General, Catering, Driving, Forestry, Gardening/ Horticulture, Manual Work, Outdoor Skills, Social Work, Teaching, Theatre/Drama, Training, Visiting/Befriending.
Placements: 7–10
When to apply: As early as possible.
Work alone/with others: With others.
Qualifications: Nil – no minimum education or skills requirement necessary.
Equipment/clothing: Work clothes, winter clothes.
Health requirements: Must provide own medical insurance for first 6 months.

Costs: All travel costs.
Benefits: US$100 pocket money per month +$20 for phone bills. After one year $400 vacation money. Accommodation in own room in family home on campus.
Training: Training with long term co-worker, weekly orientation sessions and after 1 year further training in, for example, health/form/weaving.
Supervision: Undertaken by long term co-worker.
Interviews: If we need to interview an applicant the interview would take place in Britain.
Worldwide placements: North America: (USA).

UGANDA VOLUNTEERS FOR PEACE

P.O. Box 3312 Kampala-Uganda
Plot 823
Kiwooya House, Entebbe Road
Mikindye Uganda
T: 256 41 266852
E: Uvpeace@yahoo.co.uk
Contact: Semakula Stuart

Uganda Volunteers for Peace is a full member of CCIVS and Associate Member of ICYE – Federation in Germany. Mission – To promote the active participation of children and young people in peace building and human rights education for sustainable development through workcamps.
Main objective – To promote a culture of peace and human rights education and for you to demonstrate the much-needed solidarity in Uganda.
Main aims – To aid needy communities to help themselves for sustainable development for a better world. ⬧ ⬧

Number of projects: 10 UK: 0
Starting months: Feb, Mar, Apr, May, Jun, Jul, Aug, Sep, Oct, Nov, Dec
Time required: 3–10 weeks
Age: 15–35
Causes: AIDS/HIV, Children, Disabled (learning), Human Rights, Teaching (primary), Work Camps – Seasonal, Young People.
Activities: Administration, Community Work, Counselling, Development Issues, Fundraising, Manual Work, Social Work, Summer Camps, Teaching, Training, Work Camps – Seasonal.
Placements: 12–24
When to apply: Between September and November for following year.
Work alone/with others: Work with others.
Qualifications: No specific qualifications needed.
Health requirements: Volunteers must be vaccinated against malaria and yellow fever.
Costs: Membership US $100, participation $200 to any activity.
Benefits: Lodging, end of placement, £20/month pocket money and newsletter.
Training: Introductory training, languages, culture, project managing and planning.
Supervision: Volunteers are supervised by office staff, co-workers and project contact persons.
Interviews: Volunteers will be interviewed by committee before posted to projects.
Worldwide placements: Africa (Uganda).

UK ARCHAEOLOGY OPPORTUNITIES

1 Barby Road
Rugby
Warwickshire CV22 5DW UK
E: admin@ukarchaeology.org.uk
W: www.ukarchaeology.org.uk
Contact: Sarah MacLean

UK Archaeology Opportunities is a web site dedicated to providing details of volunteer and training excavations in the UK and Ireland.The web site also lists volunteer projects within archaeology and heritage sectors, adult education courses and work experience suggestions. Please contact Sarah MacLean for more information. Throughout the UK and Ireland. ⬧

Number of projects: Varies UK: Varies
Starting months: January–December
Time required: 1–52 weeks
Age: 16 plus – no upper limit
Causes: Archaeology.
Activities: Manual Work, Research.
Placements: Varies.
When to apply: Anytime – as soon as possible
Work alone/with others: With others.
Qualifications: Varies on project.
Equipment/clothing: Varies.
Health requirements: No restrictions.
Costs: Food, accommodation and travel to and from project.
Training: Varies on project.
Supervision: Varies on project.
Interviews: Varies on project.
Worldwide placements: Europe (Ireland).
UK placements: England (throughout); Scotland (throughout); Wales (throughout).

UK NATIONAL INVENTORY OF WAR MEMORIALS

Imperial War Museum
Lambeth Road
London
SE1 6HZ UK
T: +44 (0) 207 416 5281
T: +44 (0) 207 416 5379
E: memorials@iwm.org.uk
W: www.iwm.org.ukl
Contact: Ms Jane Armer

The National Inventory of War Memorials was initiated in 1989 by the Imperial War Museum and the Royal Commission on Historical Monuments of England, which merged with English Heritage in 1999, to create an archive holding information on the estimated 60,000 war memorials in the British Isles. Prior to this, there had been no centralised information on war memorials. The archive covers every conceivable type of memorial, from the frequently-seen community crosses to buildings, lych gates, gardens, hospitals, organs, chapels, windows, etc. All wars are covered, from the Roman occupation to the Gulf War, although, of course, great impetus was given to the construction of memorials by the Great War, largely because of the policy of not re-patriating bodies. Indeed, the building of so many memorials in the 1920s has been described as the largest public art project in history. We have a standard recording form which our fieldworkers use to collate the information. The type of information sought includes details of the exact location, the conflicts it commemorates, the date of its unveiling, its type and materials, dimensions, details of artists or manufacturers, its condition and other background areas of interest. Unfortunately, much of this information is frequently unavailable and we take the general view that any information, even incomplete, is better than none. Essential, however, is the type of memorial and its exact position, ideally with a photograph. So far, with the help of local volunteers, we have records of about 30,000 memorials, half of which have been input on to a computer database. ♿

Number of projects: Many in the UK **UK:** Many
Starting months: January–December
Time required: 1–52 weeks (plus)
Age: 16–25
Causes: Heritage.
Activities: Outdoor Skills, Research.
Placements: about 70
When to apply: All year.
Work alone/with others: Either.
Qualifications: Basic research skills.
Equipment/clothing: Nil. We provide standard War Memorial recording form to record information.
Health requirements: Nil.
Costs: Research expenses. Food and accommodation.
Benefits: Sometimes, at our discretion, we reimburse photographic costs and other expenses.
Training: No pre-placement training but we do provide notes on how to fill out the form and give general information and lists of memorials we have records for.
Supervision: We have regional co-ordinators.
Interviews: Prospective volunteers are not interviewed.
UK placements: England (Bedfordshire, Berkshire, Bristol, Cambridgeshire, Channel Islands, Cheshire, Cornwall, Co Durham,

Derbyshire, Devon, Dorset, Essex, Gloucestershire, Hampshire, Hertfordshire, Isle of Man, Isle of Wight, Kent, Lancashire, Leicestershire, Lincolnshire, Manchester, Merseyside, Norfolk, Northamptonshire, Nottinghamshire, Rutland, Shropshire, Somerset, Staffordshire, Surrey, E. Sussex, W. Sussex, Tyne and Wear, Warwickshire, Wiltshire, E. Yorkshire, N. Yorkshire, S. Yorkshire, W. Yorkshire); Wales (Anglesey, Blaenau Gwent, Bridgend, Caerphilly, Cardiff, Carmarthenshire, Conwy, Denbighshire, Flintshire, Gwynedd, Merthyr Tydfil, Monmouthshire, Neath Port Talbot, Newport, Rhondda, Cynon, Taff, Swansea, Torfaen, Vale of Glamorgan, Wrexham).

UK YOUTH

Kirby House
20–24 Kirby Street
London
EC1N 8TS UK
T: +44 (0) 207 242.4045
T: +44 (0) 207 242.4125
E: info@ukyouth.org
W: www.ukyouth.org
Contact: John Bateman

UK Youth is a national registered charity, which promotes opportunities for young people to develop skills and interests which will help them to become fulfilled adults and effective citizens. It is the largest non-uniformed youth organisation in the United Kingdom supporting a network that reaches more than 700,000 young people in clubs and projects and includes about 45,000 youth workers with 30,000 other volunteers. It initiates a range of projects that young people enjoy, promoting sports and outdoor activities, art, drama and dance, health education, action to improve the environment, community work, international exchanges to name but a few. Our organisation also works with particular disadvantaged groups such as homeless young people or those involved with car crime, drugs, alcohol or solvents. The key aim of all our work is to give young people, whatever their starting point, the skills and information they need to make constructive decisions, and plan and manage their own activities and projects. UK Youth has a busy activity and residential centre in the New Forest, Hampshire. Avon Tyrrell offers a wide variety of courses, activities, sports to 14,000+ young people per annum. We accept volunteers between March and October, working in activities, general cleaning, kitchens, office and estate work. Contact centre manager directly on 01425 672347. Avon Tyrrell residential training centre. ♿ 📖

Number of projects: 1 **UK:** 1
Starting months: Mar, Apr

Time required: 2–12 weeks
Age: 18 plus – no upper limit
Causes: Children, Conservation, Environmental Causes, Holidays for Disabled, Offenders/Ex-Offenders, Teaching (primary), Unemployed, Wildlife, Work Camps – Seasonal, Young People.
Activities: Administration, Catering, Community Work, Conservation Skills, Development Issues, Driving, Forestry, Fundraising, Gardening/Horticulture, Group Work, Manual Work, Outdoor Skills, Sport, Summer Camps, Teaching, Theatre/Drama, Work Camps – Seasonal.
Placements: 2–20
Work alone/with others: With the rest of the staff of 40.
Qualifications: Experience working with young people.
Equipment/clothing: Wet weather gear, good boots.
Health requirements: Good.
Costs: Travel costs to Avon Tyrrell plus contribution for food.
Benefits: Good experience, free tuition and accommodation. Single person or shared room.
Training: On-site training for specific tasks.
Supervision: Each volunteer is assigned a supervisor.
Interviews: CV and references must be sent first.
Charity number: 306066
UK placements: England (throughout); Scotland (throughout); Northern Ireland (throughout); Wales (throughout).

ULSTER WILDLIFE TRUST

3 New Line
Crossgar
Downpatrick
Co. Down BT30 9EP N. Ireland
T: 028 4483 0282
F: 028 4483 0888
E: info@ulsterwildlifetrust.org
W: www.ulsterwildlife.org
Contact: Eileen McDonald

Ulster Wildlife Trust was founded in 1978 by a number of people who identified the need for a voluntary organisation, which could actively seek to 'conserve the natural habitats of Northern Ireland'. Since then the Trust has grown to become the largest locally based conservation organisation of Northern Ireland. It is the aspiration of the Trust to help everyone to recognise that a healthy environment, rich in wildlife and managed on sustainable principles, is essential for continued human existence. The aims of the Trust are to protect species and habitats, both common and rare, manage 26 nature reserves for wildlife and promote a wider understanding of wildlife issues through communication, education and

training. The Ulster Wildlife Trust is a partner in a 46 strong national network of Wildlife Trusts. The combined influence of this partnership is a membership of 355,000 and a network of 2,500 nature reserves throughout the United Kingdom. There are a number of ways in which volunteers can participate such as through weekend events on nature reserves and work experience placements, as well as longer-term volunteer posts in a number of areas, including practical conservation and education. Volunteers with the Trust gain a wide range of skills and experiences in practical management at the Trust's nature reserves. Long-term volunteers in conservation can undertake training for National Vocational Qualification (NVQ) in Environmental Conservation, which includes pesticide application, chainsaw and brushcutter use and leading visitor walks, as well as use of computerised programs such as GIS, CMS and Recorder. Areas of work include practical habitat management, site monitoring, flora/fauna surveys, management planning and report writing. The reserves team work at the 26 reserves in N. Ireland. The education team deliver programmes at schools and community groups throughout the province. Centres also at Bog Meadows, W. Belfast (urban reserve) and Co Antrim (hill farm and tree nursery).

Number of projects UK: 4
Starting months: January–December
Time required: 1–52 weeks (plus)
Age: 16 plus – no upper limit
Causes: Conservation, Environmental Causes, Wildlife, Young People.
Activities: Administration, Agriculture/Farming, Conservation Skills, Forestry, Fundraising, Gardening/Horticulture, Marketing/Publicity, Research, Scientific Work, Teaching.
Placements: 40
When to apply: All year.
Work alone/with others: Both.
Qualifications: None. A genuine interest in conservation is an advantage.
Equipment/clothing: Casual work clothes, waterproofs, stout boots for outdoor work. Protective safety gear is provided.
Health requirements: Anti-tetanus innoculation recommended. General good health is an advantage for reserve work.
Costs: Accommodation.
Benefits: Out of pocket expenses, training opportunities.
Training: All volunteers receive training to enable them to carry out their tasks safely. Health and safety and first aid training. NVQ level 2 training for longer term volunteers.
Supervision: Named officer.
Interviews: Casual.
UK placements: Northern Ireland (throughout).

UNA EXCHANGE

International Youth Service
The Temple of Peace
Cathays Park
Cardiff
CF10 3AP UK
T: 029 2022 3088
F: 029 2066 5557
E: info@unaexchange.org
W: www.unaexchange.org
Contact: Sam Powell

UNA Exchange sends international volunteers overseas to work on community based in over 60 countries worldwide. Volunteers live and work in an international group, alongside people from many different cultures on projects lasting between 2 to 3 weeks. Longer-term individual placements of up to a year are also available in Europe, through the EVS (European Voluntary Service) programme. International volunteer projects are organised all year round, but the majority run during the summer months. They provide the opportunity for cultural exchange through working with local people and volunteers from other countries. The work involved varies widely, depending on the project, but does not usually require specific skills or qualifications. In addition to our overseas programme we also organise projects in Wales, and there are opportunities for people interested in leading projects. We organise a yearly training course to prepare leaders to co-ordinate groups of international volunteers every Easter. UNA Exchange has been organising volunteer exchanges since 1973 and was originally part of the Wales branch of the UNA (United Nations Association). Now an independent charity, UNA Exchange is part of the Welsh Centre of International Affairs based in Cardiff. ☒ ▤

Number of projects: 1500+ UK: 35
Starting months: January–December
Time required: 2–56 weeks
Age: 14–70
Causes: AIDS/HIV, Archaeology, Architecture, Children, Conservation, Disabled (learning and physical), Elderly People, Environmental Causes, Heritage, Inner City Problems, Poor/Homeless, Refugees, Teaching/assisting, Work Camps – Seasonal, Young People.
Activities: Arts/Crafts, Building/Construction, Community Work, Conservation Skills, Cooking, Development Issues, Forestry, Gardening/Horticulture, Group Work, Manual Work, Music, Outdoor Skills, Research, Social Work, Sport, Summer Camps, Teaching, Theatre/Drama, Training, Work Camps – Seasonal.
Placements: 600
When to apply: March – July for the majority of projects, but you can apply throughout the year.

Work alone/with others: With others.
Qualifications: Nil except age – generally 18+ (14+ for some). Some projects require language proficiency. No nationality restrictions. Volunteers living outside the UK can apply through one of our partner organisations nearest them.
Equipment/clothing: Sleeping bag. Strong footwear on environmental projects.
Health requirements: E111 usually required.
Costs: Volunteers pay travel costs to and from project (this varies according to the country) plus £50–£140 registration fee, depending on the project. Some projects have an additional fee charged by the hosting organisation.
Benefits: Food and accommodation are provided by partner organisation overseas or in Wales. Volunteers with less opportunities (e.g. long-term unemployed) may be eligible for financial support. Varies according to the project. Ranges from tents to hotel rooms.
Training: Optional 1-day training for Eastern Europe/North Africa/Turkey or first-time vols. Mandatory weekend training for rest of Africa, C. and S. America, and Asia (except Japan and S. Korea). Training programme for project leaders for our projects in Wales.
Supervision: All projects have at least one trained leader.
Interviews: For projects outside Europe and North America, volunteers are asked to attend an orientation weekend in Cardiff where they discuss their project choices with programme staff.
Charity number: 700760
Worldwide placements: Africa (Botswana, Burkina Faso, Côte d'Ivoire, Ghana, Kenya, Lesotho, Malawi, Morocco, Mozambique, Namibia, Senegal, South Africa, Swaziland, Tanzania, Togo, Tunisia, Uganda, Zambia, Zimbabwe); North America: (Canada, Greenland, USA); Central America (Guatemala, Mexico); South America (Argentina, Bolivia, Brazil, Chile, Ecuador); Asia (Bangladesh, Cambodia, China, India, Indonesia, Japan, Korea (South), Nepal, Philippines, Thailand, Turkey, Vietnam); Europe (Albania, Armenia, Austria, Azerbaijan, Belarus, Belgium, Bosnia-Herzegovina, Bulgaria, Croatia, Czech Republic, Denmark, Estonia, Finland, France, Germany, Greece, Hungary, Ireland, Italy, Latvia, Lithuania, Netherlands, Poland, Portugal, Romania, Russia, Slovakia, Slovenia, Spain, Switzerland, Turkey, Ukraine, Yugoslavia).
UK placements: Wales (throughout).

UNION REMPART

1 rue des Guillemites
75004 Paris
France
T: 00 33 1 42 71 96 55

F: 00 33 1 42 71 73 00
E: contact@rempart.com
W: www.rempart.com
Contact: Antoine Monpert

Union Rempart needs volunteers to help restore and preserve various castles, fortresses, churches, chapels, abbeys, monasteries, farms, ancient villages, Gallo-Roman amphitheatres and underground passages on the 140 sites organised by Rempart each year during holidays. Work includes masonry, stone cutting, sculpture, coating, woodwork, carpentry, interior decorating, restoration and clearance work. Opportunities for swimming, tennis, riding, water sports, cycling, climbing, rambling, exploring the region, crafts, music, cinema and taking part in local festivities. Each volunteer can choose the camp in which he/she would like to take part.

Number of projects: 130 **UK:** 0
Starting months: Feb, Mar, Apr, May, Jun, Jul, Aug, Sep, Oct, Nov
Time required: 1–52 weeks
Age: 14 plus – no upper limit
Causes: Archaeology, Conservation, Heritage, Work Camps – Seasonal.
Activities: Building/Construction, Conservation Skills, Gardening/Horticulture, Manual Work, Sport, Technical Skills, Theatre/Drama, Training, Work Camps – Seasonal.
Placements: 3,500
When to apply: To take part in a summer work camp – application from April until the start of the work camp.
Work alone/with others: Work in groups.
Qualifications: Some knowledge of French but no experience in restoration needed.
Equipment/clothing: Sleeping bag, workclothes, strong work boots, swimsuit and pocket money.
Health requirements: Anti-tetanus injection.
Costs: Approx €6 per day covers board and accommodation.
Training: No pre-placement training.
Supervision: Every workcamp has leaders, some of them for technical work and others for pedagogical aspects.
Interviews: Applicants should phone each camp director for interview before applying.
Worldwide placements: Europe (France).
UNIPAL (Universities' Educational Trust for Palestinians)

BCM UNIPAL

London
WC1N 3XX UK
T: 01227 272590
F: 01227 272590
E: info@unipal.org.uk
W: www.unipal.org.uk
Contact: Brenda Hayward

UNIPAL sends volunteers to take part in short-term projects during July and August in the Israeli-occupied West Bank and Gaza Strip, as well as with Palestinian communities elsewhere. Projects involve teaching English. Volunteers must be at least 20 years old and applicants should send a stamped self-addressed envelope to the above address before the end of February. Applicants with an offending background are not accepted. 🖹

Number of projects: 3 **UK:** 0
Starting months: Jul
Time required: 5 weeks
Age: 20 plus – no upper limit
Causes: Children, Teaching (secondary, mature, EFL), Young People.
Activities: Summer Camps, Teaching.
Placements: 20–30
When to apply: Before the end of February.
Work alone/with others: With others.
Qualifications: A Levels. TEFL qualification and experience preferred. Must be a native speaker of English.
Equipment/clothing: Sleeping bag, modest summer clothes.
Health requirements: Immunisations required.
Costs: Short term: £380. This price includes flights from the UK, insurance, food, accommodation and teaching materials.
Benefits: Short-term: board and lodging provided. Flights, insurance, food, board all paid for.
Training: There are briefings in April and June for those selected.
Interviews: Interviews take place in London and are held before the Easter vacation.
Charity number: 325007
Worldwide placements: Asia (Lebanon, Palestinian Authority).

UNITED WAY OF ST CROIX

14 Orange Grove Shopping Mall
Christiansted
St Croix Virgin Islands
E: uwi@unitedway.org
Contact: Anne Hutchinson

United Way of St Croix promotes and has information about volunteering in St Croix. It may well be able to put volunteers in touch with organisations which are not yet listed on the WorldWide Volunteering database.

Starting months: January–December
Time required: 1–52 weeks (plus)
Age: 16 plus – no upper limit
Causes: Addicts/Ex-Addicts, AIDS/HIV, Animal Welfare, Archaeology, Architecture, Children, Conservation, Disabled (learning and physical), Elderly People, Environmental Causes, Health Care/Medical, Heritage, Holidays for Disabled, Human Rights, Inner City Problems,

Offenders/Ex-Offenders, Poor/Homeless, Refugees, Teaching/assisting (nursery, primary, secondary, mature, EFL) Unemployed, Wildlife, Work Camps – Seasonal, Young People.
Activities: Accountancy, Administration, Agriculture/Farming, Arts/Crafts, Building/Construction, Campaigning, Caring (general, day and residential), Catering, Community Work, Computers, Conservation Skills, Cooking, Counselling, Development Issues, DIY, Driving, First Aid, Forestry, Fundraising, Gardening/Horticulture, Group Work, International Aid, Library/Resource Centres, Manual Work, Marketing/Publicity, Music, Newsletter/Journalism, Outdoor Skills, Religion, Research, Scientific Work, Social Work, Sport, Summer Camps, Teaching, Technical Skills, Theatre/Drama, Training, Translating, Visiting/Befriending, Work Camps – Seasonal.
Costs: Varies according to the project.
Worldwide placements: Central America (Virgin Islands).

UNITY NORWOOD RAVENSWOOD

25 Bourne Court
Southend Road
Woodford Green
Essex IG8 8HD UK
T: +44 (0) 208 550 6114
F: +44 (0) 208 551 3951
E: norwoodravenswood@nwrw.org
Contact: Raina Gee

Unity Norwood Ravenswood is a play and youth service for children and young people of mixed abilities aged between 5 and 18. Our aim is to provide integrated activities through our weekly clubs, holiday schemes and residential holidays, whilst maintaining a safe and stimulating environment. We offer a balanced programme to meet individual needs which may include integration into mainstream provisions. Unity has four age groups: 5-8's, 8-11's, 11-14's and 14-18's. Volunteers can be involved in the care of a young person and/or planning and running the activity at one of the clubs. There are programmed day schemes during all school holidays, and a holiday in the UK for the 8-11's and 11-18's, during the summer holiday. There is always a new experience for a Unity member to enjoy. Volunteers with an offending background may be accepted depending on the offence. Hendon, Northwest London and Ilford, Essex. 🔲 📄

Number of projects UK: 4
Starting months: January–December
Time required: 4–52 weeks (plus)
Age: 16 plus – no upper limit
Causes: Children, Disabled (learning and physical), Young People.
Activities: Arts/Crafts, Caring (general and day), Cooking, Music.

Placements: 50
When to apply: All year.
Work alone/with others: With others.
Qualifications: Willingness to work with children + young people and ability to communicate. Must be EC residents.
Equipment/clothing: Casual old clothing.
Health requirements: Some.
Costs: Nil.
Benefits: Approved travel, board and lodging (residentials). Out of pocket expenses.
Training: Training is provided to all volunteers. These sessions include emergency first aid, lifting and handling people, programming skills, child centred care, etc.
Interviews: Applicants are interviewed at local offices in Redbridge or Hendon.
Charity number: 1059050
UK placements: England (Berkshire, Essex, Hertfordshire, London).

UNIVERSAL CONNEXIONS

Douglas Primary School
Ayr Road
Douglas
South Lanarkshire ML11 0QA UK
T: 01555 851166
Contact: Tom Penman

Volunteers with offending backgrounds may not be accepted. 📄

Number of projects: 1 UK: 1
Starting months: January–December
Time required: 1–52 weeks
Age: 18 plus – no upper limit
Causes: Children, Teaching/assisting (secondary), Unemployed, Young People.
Activities: Administration, Arts/Crafts, Community Work, Computers, Counselling, Development Issues, DIY, Driving, First Aid, Fundraising, Group Work, Music, Newsletter/Journalism, Outdoor Skills, Research, Social Work, Sport, Summer Camps, Teaching, Technical Skills, Theatre/Drama, Training, Visiting/Befriending.
Placements: 5
When to apply: All year.
Work alone/with others: It varies but mostly with others.
Equipment/clothing: If special Equipment/clothing is required it can be supplied.
Health requirements: Nil.
Costs: Nil.
Benefits: Food and accommodation when working away from project and travel costs.
Training: As required.
Supervision: Yes volunteers are supervised.
Interviews: Interviews take place.

Arrangements can be made to suit the volunteer.
Charity number: SC 020206
UK placements: Scotland (Ayrshire – East, Ayrshire – North, Ayrshire – South, Glasgow City, Lanarkshire – North, Lanarkshire – South, Renfrewshire).

UNIVERSITY FOR THE STUDY OF HUMAN GOODNESS

3983 Old Greensboro Road
Winston-Salem
North Carolina 27101 USA
T: 00 1 336 761 8745
F: 00 1 336 722 7882
E: inquiry@ufhg.org
W: www.ufhg.org
Contact: Joanna White

University for the Study of Human Goodness – Expand your capacity to serve. Soul–centred education is a year-long service learning opportunity for students of all ages seeking to discover deeper meaning and purpose in life and to improve interpersonal relationships skills, while increasing and enhancing entrepreneurial and leadership skills within a co-operative group effort. Outcomes include clearer thinking, greater objectivity and common sense, practical life skills, better communication skills, financial savvy and time management and all while invoking and discovering more joy, love, compassion in life, and a greater sense of connectedness to others. Volunteers/students may enter the programme in January or July. Opportunities for co-op's and internships are available at other times during the year. All of the faculty and administrative staff of the University for the Study of Human Goodness serve without financial compensation, and are all volunteers. Qualified full-time, live-in students receive full room, board and tuition at no cost as part of the university's service to humanity. Our programme is a service learning centre designed to train world servers. A world server is someone who can join any service group or organisation anywhere in the world and through their example, make a difference. The programme combines three elements, service, study, and reflection. It empowers students of all ages to realise their potential while making a positive impact on those around them. The full time programme requires a full year commitment with a minimum of 45 hours per week of applied service learning in our service laboratory, a restaurant where all profits go to a charity and on our campus. Students participate in all phases of restaurant work/management and maintenance of the campus. In addition to applied service, students attend six hours of classes per week on service learning, servant leadership, service entrepreneurship, communication skills, organisational management skills and responsibility. Through the intensity of the year programme, students emerge with the capacity to remain positive, productive and effective no matter the circumstances. Year long programme begins in January and mid July each year. ♿

Number of projects: 4 UK: 0
Starting months: Jan, Jul
Time required: 26–52 weeks
Age: 16–75
Causes: AIDS/HIV, Children, Disabled (learning and physical), Elderly People, Health Care/Medical.
Activities: Administration, Building/Construction, Caring (general, day and residential), Computers, Cooking, Gardening/Horticulture, Manual Work.
Placements: 100
When to apply: All year – application process takes 4–6 wks includes references and personal interview.
Work alone/with others: With others.
Qualifications: Must speak fluent English.
Health requirements: Nil.
Costs: Air fares, travel, insurance, pocket money and all expenses.
Benefits: Food and lodging is provided. Full scholarship for tuition is provided.
Training: Excellent training is provided to all who volunteer.
Supervision: Excellent supervision is provided to all who volunteer.
Interviews: Applicants for volunteer projects are interviewed by telephone and e-mail.
Worldwide placements: North America: (USA).

UNIVERSITY RESEARCH EXPEDITIONS PROGRAM (UREP)

University of California
One Shields Ave
Davis, CA
95616-8813 USA
T: 00 1 530 757 3529
F: 00 1 530 757 3537
E: urep@ucdavis.edu
W: http://urep.ucdavis.edu
Contact: Erin Bishop

UREP brings together students, teachers, and other members of the public with University of California researchers to participate in field research expeditions around the globe. Disciplines studied include animal studies, anthropology, archaeology, arts, conservation, culture, earth sciences, ecology and plant studies.

Number of projects: 25 UK: 0
Starting months: Jan, Feb, Mar, Apr, May, Jun, Jul, Aug, Sep

Time required: 1–52 weeks
Age: 16 plus – no upper limit
Causes: Animal Welfare, Archaeology, Conservation, Environmental Causes, Heritage, Wildlife.
Activities: Arts/Crafts, Conservation Skills, Development Issues, Outdoor Skills.
Placements: 200+
When to apply: March 15th
Work alone/with others: With others.
Qualifications: Curiosity, adaptability and a willingness to share project costs.
Equipment/clothing: Varies.
Health requirements: Project participants should be mentally and physically healthy.
Costs: Equal share of project's costs (£350–£800) + travel to site.
Benefits: The cost covers all equipment including meals and accommodation.
Worldwide placements: Africa (Kenya, Malawi, Mali, South Africa); North America: (Canada, USA); Central America (Belize, Virgin Islands); South America (Bolivia, Brazil, Chile, Ecuador, Peru); Asia (India, Indonesia, Laos, Thailand); Australasia (Australia); Europe (Germany, Russia).

UPPER CANNING SOUTHERN WENGONG CATCHMENT TEAM

P O Box 51
Armadale
Western Australia
T: 00 61 8 9399 0622
F: 00 61 8 9399 0184
Contact: Colleen Martin

The Upper Canning Southern Wengong Catchment Team is a community group interested in the conservation of the Upper Canning and Southern Rivers. The team has obtained funding support from local and state government to carry out on-ground works which aim to restore the rivers. Projects include tree planting, weed pulling/spraying, shopping centre and show displays, yellow fish drain stencilling, newletter publications, school talks, water quality monitoring, habitat surveys, creating rock rittles and ponds in rivers and research. Armadale, Western Australia. 🖺

Number of projects: 15 **UK:** 0
Starting months: January–December
Time required: 1–52 weeks (plus)
Age: 14 plus – no upper limit
Causes: Conservation, Environmental Causes, Wildlife.
Activities: Community Work, Conservation Skills, Forestry, Gardening/Horticulture, Group Work, Marketing/Publicity, Newsletter/Journalism, Outdoor Skills, Research.
Placements: 30
When to apply: All year.

Work alone/with others: It is possible to organise placements with other young volunteers.
Qualifications: Own transport.
Equipment/clothing: Nil – hat, sunscreen and closed shoes.
Health requirements: Nil.
Costs: Travel, board and lodging.
Training: On site if required.
Supervision: On-site co-ordinator.
Interviews: Interviews take place at the city of Armadale Council Offices.
Worldwide placements: Australasia (Australia).

UPPER NENE ARCHAEOLOGICAL SOCIETY

Toad Hall,
86 Main Road
Hackleton
NorthamptonNN7 2AD UK
T: 01604 870312
E: unarchsoc@aol.com
Contact: Mrs D.E. Friendship-Taylor

The Upper Nene Archaeological Society oversees the excavation of a Romano-British villa and underlying Iron Age settlement. Volunteers are required to help with trowelling and a variety of excavation and post-excavation procedures.

Number of projects: 1 **UK:** 1
Starting months: Aug
Time required: 2–3 weeks
Age: 16 plus – no upper limit
Causes: Archaeology.
Activities: Administration, Conservation Skills, Research, Scientific Work.
Placements: 25
When to apply: February – July
Work alone/with others: With others.
Qualifications: English speaking.
Equipment/clothing: Mason's pointing trowel, all other equipment supplied. Clothing for all weathers.
Health requirements: Reasonably fit. Not suitable for severe asthmatics or anyone with severe respiratory problems.
Costs: Specified contribution towards everyday excavation expenses.
Benefits: Basic campsite.
Charity number: 286966
UK placements: England (Northamptonshire).

USDA FOREST SERVICE

P.O. Box 96090
Room 1010 RPE/HRP
Washington DC
20090-6090 USA
T: 00 1 703 235 8855
E: webmaster@fs.fed.us
Contact: The Volunteer Co-ordinator

The USDA Forest Service maintains 19 national forests in Oregon and Washington. Volunteers are needed to maintain trails, campgrounds, wildlife and timber. They are also required to help with recreation, range activities, office work, interpretation and the visitor information services. 🔊

Number of projects: 1
Starting months: January–December
Time required: 1–52 weeks
Age: 14 plus – no upper limit
Causes: Conservation, Environmental causes.
Activities: Administration, Conservation Skills, Forestry, Manual Work, Outdoor Skills, Translating.
When to apply: All year.
Work alone/with others: With others.
Qualifications: English speaking. Those under 18 years of age need the written permission of their parents.
Costs: Travel, accommodation for short-term volunteers.
Benefits: Food and incidental expenses reimbursed. Accommodation for long-term volunteers.
Worldwide placements: North America: (USA).

USPG AND THE METHODIST CHURCH – EXPERIENCE EXCHANGE PROGRAMME

The United College of the Ascension
Weoley Park Road
Selly Oak
Birmingham
B29 6RD UK
T: +44 (0) 121 472 1667
F: +44 (0) 121 472 4320
E: uca@sellyoak.ac.uk
Contact: Mandy Quayle

USPG and The Methodist Church – The Experience Exchange Programme enables people over 18 to work alongside local people in church based projects such as schools, community development programmes and hostels for six months to a year. No specific skills are required although applicants should be flexible, adaptable and open to new ideas. Those with specific skills can be placed accordingly. Placements are constantly being reviewed and new ones set up. Through living in another culture participants experience new challenges and opportunities and discover much about themselves. Participants are strongly encouraged to share what they learn from their experience on their return. The Experience Exchange Programme is one of two volunteer programmes run jointly by the United Society for the Propagation of the Gospel (USPG) and the Methodist Church. Both USPG and the Methodist Church are involved in supporting the mission of the church

worldwide through the exchange of people, prayer, resources and ideas. Volunteers with an offending background would be considered but there are no guarantees. Africa, Asia, the Caribbean, South and Central America and some European placements. 🔊 📄

Number of projects: 1 **UK:** 0
Starting months: Jan, Feb, Aug, Sep, Oct, Nov, Dec
Time required: 27–52 weeks
Age: 18–70
Causes: AIDS/HIV, Children, Disabled (physical), Elderly People, Health Care/Medical, Human Rights, Poor/Homeless, Refugees, Teaching/assisting (nursery, primary, secondary, mature, EFL) Unemployed, Young People.
Activities: Administration, Agriculture/Farming, Arts/Crafts, Building/Construction, Caring – General, Community Work, Computers, Counselling, Development Issues, DIY, Driving, International Aid, Manual Work, Music, Newsletter/Journalism, Religion, Social Work, Sport, Teaching, Technical Skills, Translating, Visiting/Befriending.
Placements: 25
When to apply: Before middle of June for September start.
Work alone/with others: Usually individual placements but working with others locally.
Qualifications: Christian commitment, flexibility and an ability to learn from a new experience.
Equipment/clothing: Varies according to placement.
Health requirements: Health clearance to ensure individual can endure the climate of the placement.
Costs: Varies – usually £2,000–£2,500.
Interviews: Interviews take place in London and exploration weekends in Birmingham.
Charity number: 234518
Worldwide placements: Africa (Angola, Botswana, Egypt, Gambia, Ghana, Kenya, Lesotho, Madagascar, Malawi, Namibia, South Africa, Tanzania, Zambia, Zimbabwe); Central America (Barbados, Belize, Saint Vincent/Grenadines, Trinidad and Tobago); South America (Brazil, Chile, Guyana, Uruguay); Asia (Bangladesh, India, Israel, Japan, Korea (North), Pakistan, Philippines, Sri Lanka); Europe (Estonia, Poland).

USPG AND THE METHODIST CHURCH – ROOT GROUPS INTERNATIONAL

The United College of the Ascension
Weoley Park Road
Selly Oak
Birmingham
B29 6RD UK
T: +44 (0) 121 472 1667
F: +44 (0) 121 472 4320

E: uca@sellyoak.ac.uk
Contact: Mandy Quayle

USPG and The Methodist Church – Root Groups International are for people, aged 18–30, who are looking for a challenge as they try to discover how Christianity should affect their lifestyle and attitudes. Participants from all parts of the world church live together in community. They live and work alongside local communities, often in areas of high unemployment. The groups work in partnership with a local church exploring a way of mission that is practical and challenging. Activities vary widely according to personality and placement: they often include elements of youthwork, befriending the lonely and disadvantaged, worship and bible study, and volunteering at local community centres. In all their work, Root Groups are building relationships with their local community and developing links between church and community. Root Groups International is one of two Short Term Experience Programmes run jointly by the United Society for the Propagation of the Gospel (USPG) and the Methodist Church. USPG is a mission agency of the Anglican church. Both USPG and the Methodist Church are involved in supporting the mission of the church worldwide through the exchange of people, prayer, resources and ideas. Volunteers with an offending background would be considered but there are no guarantees. Placements vary each year – usually inner city. ♿ ▤

Number of projects: 5–6 UK: 3–4
Starting months: Sep, Oct
Time required: 45–52 weeks
Age: 18–30
Causes: Addicts/Ex-Addicts, Children, Disabled (learning and physical), Elderly People, Human Rights, Inner City Problems, Poor/Homeless, Teaching/assisting (nursery), Unemployed, Young People.
Activities: Administration, Arts/Crafts, Campaigning, Caring (general and day), Community Work, Counselling, Group Work, Music, Religion, Social Work, Sport, Teaching, Theatre/Drama, Training, Visiting/Befriending.
Placements: 10
When to apply: Before end of June for September start.
Work alone/with others: With others.
Qualifications: Christian commitment and a willingness to try anything once.
Health requirements: In good health.
Costs: Root Groups are self-supporting and members staying in the UK work part time to fund the group. Those joining an overseas group would be required to raise £2,500 through trust funds etc.
Interviews: Interviews and exploration weekends take place in Birmingham.
Charity number: 234518
Worldwide placements: Africa (Zambia, Zimbabwe); Central America (Belize).
UK placements: England (throughout); Scotland (throughout); Northern Ireland (throughout); Wales (throughout).

V

VAE KENYA

Bell Lane Cottage
Pudleston
Leominster
Herefordshire HR6 0RE UK
T: 01568 750329
F: 01568 750636
E: vaekenya@hotmail.com
W: www.vaekenya.co.uk
Contact: Simon Harris

VAE is a personal organisation that places about twenty young volunteers as teachers in very poor, rural schools around the town of Gilgil in Kenya. We only use schools that are under-resourced and under-staffed ensuring that the maximum benefit is made of the volunteers' capabilities and ensuring that there is a full time job for them to do. We expect volunteers to teach a full timetable and take part in all out of school activities. Volunteers are housed in local accommodation around their schools, none of which have electricity or water. All volunteers employ a house girl. VAE has a long-term strategy for each of its schools, supported by two UK registered charities. HSK (Harambee Schools Kenya) funds educational materials and infrastructure. LLSF (Langalanga Scholarship Fund) provides opportunities for secondary education to the brightest pupils who could not otherwise afford it. VAE has strong links with Gilgil street-boys, and provides them with health care and job opportunities. This has been an extremely successful project. We also help spread government-backed initiatives such as family planning, HIV/AIDS education, and conservation issues. We have seven full time staff based in a central house that acts as office, hotel, conference centre or sometimes convalescent area. It is also a place where visitors may stay. VAE only looks for teachers who will be committed to improving the educational standards of children who come from poor, self-sufficient peasant backgrounds. Education for most is their one chance to break the cycle of poverty. There are opportunities to travel during school holidays. We may be able to place volunteers with an offending background, depending on offence. Rural schools within a ten kilometer radius of the town of Gilgil, Kenya. 🔲

Number of projects: 25-30 UK: 15-20
Starting months: Jan

Time required: 12–26 weeks
Age: 18 plus – no upper limit
Causes: AIDS/HIV, Children, Health Care/Medical, Poor/Homeless, Teaching (primary, secondary), Young People.
Activities: Building/Construction, Community Work, Development Issues, First Aid, Fundraising, International Aid, Library/Resource Centres, Manual Work, Outdoor Skills, Social Work, Sport, Teaching.
Placements: 20
When to apply: Preferably before August.
Work alone/with others: Sometimes with others.
Qualifications: At least three good 'A' Levels. UK citizens only.
Health requirements: Need to be healthy.
Costs: Circa £3,100 for six months, this includes air fare, insurance, accommodation and salary.
Benefits: Air fare, insurance, accommodation and salary are included in cost. Rural African houses (no electricity or water), made from local materials, e.g. mud.
Training: One week in country training, then numerous follow up sessions.
Supervision: European director in Kenya most of the time. VAE has seven full time staff also.
Interviews: All volunteers are interviewed in mutually convenient place.
Charity number: 1078592
Worldwide placements: Africa (Kenya).

VALLERSUND GÅRD

N-7167 Vallersund
Norway
T: 00 47 725 27740 (9am 12noon)
F: 00 47 725 27895
E: info@vallersund-gaard.com
Contact: The Director

Vallersund Gård is a Camphill village community with handicapped adults and ex drug addicts.

Number of projects: 1 UK: 0
Starting months: January–December
Time required: 1–52 weeks
Age: 14 plus – no upper limit
Causes: Addicts/ex-addicts, Children, Disabled (learning).
Activities: Caring – General, Community Work, Group Work, Social Work, Visiting/Befriending.
Worldwide placements: Europe (Norway).

VALLEY AND VALE ARTS PROJECT

The Sardis Media Centre
Heol Dewi Sant
Betws
Bridgend
Mid GlamorganCF32 8SU UK
T: 01656 729185 or 729246
F: 01656 729185
E: mail@valleyandvale.co.uk
W: www.valleyandvale.co.uk
Contact: Alex Bowen

Valley and Vale Community Arts is a not-for-profit organisation, which has been working in South Wales since 1981. We offer arts and media as tools for individual and community development. We run workshops, tailor-made projects and events in dance, forum theatre, video, animation, photography, visual art, digital art and multi-media. We prioritise working with individuals or groups who are often excluded or marginalised from mainstream provision. Betws and Bridgend, South Wales, Cardiff, Swansea and Neath Port Talbot. 🔊

Number of projects: 1 UK: 1
Starting months: January–December
Time required: 1–52 weeks
Age: 14 plus – no upper limit
Causes: Addicts/Ex-Addicts, AIDS/HIV, Children, Disabled (learning and physical), Elderly People, Environmental Causes, Human Rights, Inner City Problems, Offenders/Ex-Offenders, Poor/Homeless, Refugees, Unemployed, Young People.
Activities: Arts/Crafts, Community Work, Counselling, Development Issues, Fundraising, Group Work, Music, Social Work, Theatre/Drama, Training.
Placements: Varies.
When to apply: All year.
Work alone/with others: Both.
Qualifications: Nothing specific.
Equipment/clothing: We have our own to use.
Health requirements: Good health. We are also accessible for wheelchair users and have placements for people with disabilities – learning and/or physical.
Costs: Food and accommodation must be arranged/paid for by volunteer. Travel may be with staff but also may have to be arranged/paid for by volunteer.
Benefits: Social skills, confidence, community arts development work, arts and media skills development, understanding of community arts ethos, working with people often excluded or marginalised, working on issue-based arts projects. We can help find cheap hostel accommodation in Cardiff, but volunteers will have to pay for this.
Training: Provided.
Supervision: Yes.

Interviews: Informal meeting.
UK placements: Wales (Bridgend, Cardiff, Neath Port Talbot, Swansea).

VALUED INDEPENDENT PEOPLE

49 Templeton Crescent
Girrawheen
Western Australia
T: 00 61 8 924 72517
F: 00 61 8 924 72516
E: vip@iinet.net.au
Contact: Margaret Walsh

Valued Independent People provides a flexible, home and neighbourhood, daytime occupation community access and participation service to people with a disability according to their needs. We also provide occasional emergency respite for consumers. We provide an intensive alternative to employment service, under the Post School Options Programme, to school leavers who live either at home with families or in hostels, according to individual needs. Activities include community access, e.g. newspaper deliveries, horseriding, bowling, shopping, dining out, movies, picnics, swimming, library or centre based activities e.g. craft, music, cooking, exercise, independent living skills, sensory stimulation. The organisation is funded by the state government, managed by an independent board of management and staffed by 'facilitators' or carers, some of whom are 'social trainers' i.e. with a human services qualification. North-West Metropolitan area, Perth, WA. 🔊

Number of projects: 2 UK: 0
Starting months: January–December
Time required: 1–52 weeks
Age: 16–65
Causes: Disabled (learning and physical).
Activities: Caring – Day, Community Work.
Placements: 10
When to apply: All year.
Work alone/with others: With other young volunteers and experienced staff.
Qualifications: Interest in working with people with disability.
Health requirements: Nil.
Costs: Fares to Perth, board and lodging.
Benefits: A$5 a day for reimbursement of expenses. Own accommodation.
Training: Normal training provided to all staff and volunteers.
Supervision: Volunteers always work with experienced staff.
Worldwide placements: Australasia (Australia).

VEEP NEPAL

New Baneshwor
Kathmandu
GPO 8975 EPC 5233 Nepal

T: +977 1 4497282
E: info@veepnepal.org.np
W: www.veepnepal.org.np
Contact: Surendra Joshi

VEEP Nepal is a non-profitable, non-governmental social development organisation which is working in rural areas of Nepal. It aims to tap the youth, children and community people to make them involved in national development as well as to acheive its goals basically in the field of raising environment awareness, health and sanitation awareness, educational development and the activities concerned with real people's needs. We have many rural locations in Nepal where we can place volunteers anywhere for one to five months. Volunteer opportunities exist in teaching conversation in English in the local school, creating awareness about basic health issues, environmental issues, sanitation issues, building business skills and self-confidence. We may be able to place volunteers with an offending background, depending on offence. 📖

Number of projects: 1 UK: 0
Starting months: January–December
Time required: 1–20 weeks
Age: 18–75
Causes: Environmental Causes, Health Care/Medical, Teaching (nursery, primary, secondary, EFL).
Activities: Community Work, Computers, Fundraising, Gardening/Horticulture, Group Work, International Aid, Library/Resource Centres, Outdoor Skills, Research, Social Work, Summer Camps, Teaching, Training.
Placements: Varies.
When to apply: Between the first and fifteenth of each month.
Work alone/with others: Work with others.
Qualifications: English language is necessary.
Equipment/clothing: Sleeping bag, hiking boots, flip flops, fleece jacket, lightweight cotton clothes, waterproofs, sarong for women, mosquito/repellent net, suncream, water purification kit, first aid kit, flashlight and penknife. See web site for full list.
Health requirements: Diptheria, tetanus, polio, Hepatitis A & B, typhoid, rabies, Japanese B, tuberculosis and a course of malaria tablets.
Costs: Flights.
Benefits: Accommodation and food plus small stipend, see web site for more details. Volunteers stay with local families in village and eat Nepalese food.
Training: Training is provided – first phase in basic Nepali language, cultural information, entertainment and second phase of training is conducted in local village practising teaching, classroom observation, community interface to prepare for placement.

Supervision: Supervised at all times.
Interviews: None.
Charity number: 202/059/0606 Govt.Regd no. SWC NO.13952
Worldwide placements: Asia (Nepal).

VENTURE SCOTLAND

Norton Park
57 Albion Road
Edinburgh
EH7 5QY UK
T: 0131 475 2395
F: 0131 475 2396
E: info@venturescotland.org.uk
W: www.venturescotland.com
Contact: Peter Johnson

Venture Scotland volunteers take groups of 16–30 year olds on residential weekends and weeks, who would not normally get the opportunity to go away on this type of break, e.g. the unemployed or homeless. We focus on personal and social development through working together on various outdoor and conservation activities. Volunteers with an offending background are accepted providing it does not compromise the 'working with young adults' aspect. We do not offer year out placements. Kinlochetive Bothy, Glencoe.

Number of projects: 1 UK: 1
Starting months: Jan, Feb, Mar
Time required: 1–52 weeks
Age: 21–60
Causes: Addicts/Ex-Addicts, Conservation, Environmental Causes, Inner City Problems, Offenders/Ex-Offenders, Poor/Homeless, Unemployed, Young People.
Activities: Administration, Building/Construction, Community Work, Computers, Conservation Skills, Cooking, Driving, First Aid, Fundraising, Group Work, Manual Work, Marketing/Publicity, Newsletter/Journalism, Outdoor Skills, Training.
Placements: 60
When to apply: All year – induction February – April.
Work alone/with others: With others.
Qualifications: Applicants based in Scotland preferably. First aid, youthwork, outdoor and lifesaving qualifications are desirable.
Equipment/clothing: Sleeping bag, heavy duty waterproofs, boots, torch, hat/gloves.
Health requirements: Reasonable for working outdoors.
Costs: £20 membership fee/£10 concession.
Benefits: Receive training, learn new skills and meet new people.
Training: Induction training provided between February and April each year.

Supervision: Each programme has a leader responsible for supervision. All supervised by director.
Interviews: Interviews take place at our office.
Charity number: ED8089MEB
UK placements: Scotland (throughout).

VENTURECO WORLDWIDE LTD

The Irongard
64 66 The Market Place
Warwick
Warwickshire CV34 4SD UK
T: 01926 411 122
F: 01926 411 133
E: Mail@Ventureco-worldwide.com
W: www.ventureco-worldwide.com
Contact: Mr Mark Davison

VentureCo Worldwide provide exciting four month programmes in South America, Central America, West Africa, Indochina and the Himalayas that form a focus for a career break or gap year. Each programme consists of three phases: language course and cultural orientation, aid project work and a long range expedition. In South America expect to learn/improve Spanish, care for orphans and trek to Machu Picchu. In Asia we learn about Indian culture, survey the tiger population and trek to Everest base camp. In West Africa we work with orphaned primates such as chimps and gorillas, and trek to Timbuktu. Overall budget for the four months is in the region of £4,000 (including return flights). Volunteers with offending backgrounds are accepted. VentureCo is a member of The Year Out Group. Full details available after offer of a place. 📖

Number of projects: 8 **UK:** 0
Starting months: Jan, Feb, Mar, Apr, Jun, Sep, Oct, Nov, Dec
Time required: 15–16 weeks
Age: 17–35
Causes: Animal Welfare, Children, Conservation, Environmental Causes, Health Care/Medical, Poor/Homeless, Teaching/assisting, Wildlife, Work Camps – Seasonal, Young People.
Activities: Agriculture/Farming, Arts/Crafts, Caring – General, Community Work, Conservation Skills, Cooking, Development Issues, Forestry, Group Work, International Aid, Manual Work, Outdoor Skills, Social Work, Sport, Theatre/Drama, Visiting/Befriending, Work Camps – Seasonal.
Placements: 200
When to apply: As early as possible.
Work alone/with others: With other young volunteers and local communities.
Qualifications: No specific qualifications other than the desire to be part of a group and to get involved.

Equipment/clothing: Yes – full details available in a booklet.
Health requirements: Full details available after offer of a place.
Costs: Overall budget in the region of £4,500.
Benefits: Develop foreign language skills, understand the plight of developing countries and gain leadership experience. Full board. All camping equipment provided on expedition.
Training: UK build up weekend ten weeks before departure. VentureCo leaders provide ongoing training during the Venture.
Supervision: One guide accompanies team throughout. One expedition leader joins for expedition.
Interviews: Interviews take place in Warwick.
Worldwide placements: Africa (Cameroon, Gabon, Mali, Niger, Nigeria); Central America (Belize, Cuba, Dominican Republic, Guatemala, Mexico); South America (Argentina, Bolivia, Chile, Ecuador, Peru, Venezuela); Asia (Cambodia, China, India, Laos, Nepal).

VEREINIGUNG JUNGER FREIWILLIGER eV (VJF)

Hans-Otto-Str.
Berlin
10407 Germany
T: 00 49 30 42850603
F: 00 49 30 42850604
E: office@vjf.de

VJF organises international workcamps, most of which are social or ecological projects, but there are also special programmes which focus on issues such as history or archaeology. In most cases volunteers have to do easy manual work on the camps. VJF places 400 international volunteers a year and 300 German volunteers. Please apply through UNA-International Youth Exchange Wales, Concordia, International Voluntary Service or Quaker International Social Projects. All four have entries in this directory. 📖

Number of projects: 1 **UK:** 0
Starting months: May, Jun, Jul, Aug, Sep
Time required: 2–4 weeks
Age: 18–30
Causes: Conservation, Environmental Causes.
Activities: Conservation Skills.
Placements: 400
When to apply: As early as possible.
Work alone/with others: With others.
Equipment/clothing: Outdoor working clothes.
Health requirements: Good health.
Costs: Application fee to the sending organisation + travel expenses.
Benefits: Accommodation.
Training: Yes.
Supervision: Supervised.

Interviews: Via telephone, application form from sending organisation.
Worldwide placements: Europe (Germany).

VIDARÅSEN LANDSBY
N 3240 Andebu
Norway
T: 00 47 3344 41 00 (9.00am 3.00pm)
F: 00 47 3344 01 91
E: vidarasen@camphill.no
Contact: The Director

Vidaråsen Landsby is a Camphill village community. 🗎

Number of projects: 1 UK: 0
Starting months: January–December
Time required: 52 weeks
Age: 14 plus – no upper limit
Causes: Disabled (learning).
Activities: Agriculture/Farming, Arts/Crafts, Caring – Residential, Gardening/Horticulture.
When to apply: All year.
Work alone/with others: With others.
Health requirements: Nil.
Costs: Travel.
Benefits: Food and accommodation.
Training: Yes.
Supervision: Yes.
Interviews: Over telephone.
Worldwide placements: Europe (Norway).

VIGYAN SHIKSHA KENDRA
Vigyan Shiksha Kendra
R.K. Temple Campus
Katra-Krishna Ganj
Banda
Tindwari210128 India
T: 00 91 5192 24587
E: vskbanda@yahoo.com
W: http://geocities.com/vsk_banda
Contact: Dr Bharatendu Prakash

Vigyan Shiksha Kendra was set up in 1974 with an aim to research and improve traditional systems and seed farming techniques. Five to ten hardworking volunteers are needed for four plus months. Projects include training of farmers, artisans and village youth, and publishing a rural newspaper.
– We organise traditional health practitioners and train the next generation. We run an Ayurvedic hospital.
– We organise women and train them for self-employment.
– We work towards self-reliant education for children.
– We are working to establish a medicinal garden including a nursery and we encourage farmers and women-groups to cultivate herbs organically.
– We plan to set up an institute of

environmental engineering and management to prepare an environment-friendly, sustainable society.
– We explore value based ancient knowledge systems in order to promote universal brotherhood, non-violence and peace for the whole humanity Rural area in south-eastern district of Banda, part of U.P. State. 🗎

Number of projects: 3–4 UK: 0
Starting months: January–December
Time required: 20–30 weeks
Age: 18–30
Causes: Animal Welfare, Children, Conservation, Elderly People, Environmental Causes, Health Care/Medical, Heritage, Teaching/assisting (primary, secondary, EFL), Work Camps – Seasonal, Young People.
Activities: Agriculture/Farming, Arts/Crafts, Campaigning, Community Work, Computers, Conservation Skills, Counselling, Development Issues, First Aid, Forestry, Gardening/ Horticulture, Group Work, Library/Resource Centres, Manual Work, Music, Newsletter/ Journalism, Research, Scientific Work, Social Work, Teaching, Technical Skills, Theatre/ Drama, Training, Work Camps – Seasonal.
Placements: 5–10
When to apply: All year.
Work alone/with others: With others.
Qualifications: Scientific, technical or medical background desirable. Above all, commitment is essential. Some knowledge of Hindi desirable.
Health requirements: Volunteer must be in very good health.
Costs: Travel and personal necessities.
Benefits: Board and lodging. Simple vegetarian food as we eat here.
Training: Not necessary – prior knowledge of Hindi language is desirable.
Supervision: We have a built-in process of supervision.
Worldwide placements: Asia (India).

VILLAGE CAMPS INC.
Department 840
Rue de la Morache 14
CH-1260 Nyon
Switzerland
T: 00 41 22 990 9405
F: 00 41 22 990 9494
E: personnel@villagecamps.ch
W: www.villagecamps.com
Contact: Rebecca Meaton

Village Camps need volunteers to work 12 hours a day in summer and winter holiday camps. Experience in working with young people, sports and organisational ability are also necessary. Must have a desire to live and work with young people of various nationalities. Also staff are required with certification in ski-ing, canoeing, rock climbing, teaching, sailing, archery, swimming, football, arts/crafts, outdoor pursuits and nursing.

Summer: Switzerland, UK, France, Austria
Winter: Switzerland.
Number of projects: 10 **UK:** 1
Starting months: Feb, May, Jun, Jul, Aug, Dec
Time required: 2–8 weeks
Age: 21–60
Causes: Children, Conservation, Environmental Causes, Health Care/Medical, Teaching/assisting (nursery, primary, secondary, EFL), Wildlife, Young People.
Activities: Administration, Arts/Crafts, Caring (general, day and residential), Catering, Community Work, Computers, Conservation Skills, Cooking, Counselling, Development Issues, Driving, International Aid, Music, Newsletter/Journalism, Outdoor Skills, Research, Sport, Summer Camps, Teaching, Theatre/Drama, Training, Translating.
Placements: 300
When to apply: February – May (summer camps), July – December (winter camps).
Work alone/with others: With others in a community of 40. Must get along with others.
Qualifications: Good sports (parallel skiers: winter) speak English, knowledge of French/Spanish/Italian/German is a bonus but not essential.
Health requirements: Must be in good health.
Costs: Nil.
Benefits: Pocket money + food, accommodation, ski pass in winter and accident insurance.
Training: Full 7 day in house training a week before work starts.
Supervision: We have trained management staff who oversee and supervise volunteers.
Interviews: We interview by phone.
Worldwide placements: Europe (Austria, France, Netherlands, Switzerland).
UK placements: England (Sussex – West).

VILLAGE EDUCATION PROJECT (KILIMANJARO)

Mint Cottage
Prospect Road
Sevenoaks
Kent TN13 3UA UK
T: 01732 459799
E: info@kiliproject.org
W: www.kiliproject.org
Contact: Katy Allen

Village Education Project (Kilimanjaro) was set up as a UK registered charity in 1994. The overall aim is to improve the education of primary school children by renovating government school buildings, providing books and teaching aids, and sponsoring in-service teacher training. The gap year teaching project

is one of the charity's projects. The students help to teach English in village schools. Students are encouraged to provide extra curricular activities such as sport, art and music for their pupils who are between 7 and 14 years old. The students accompany parties of children on school outings to a National Park and to the coast. Students live in their own village house, and their life in the village involves lots of walking each day up and down the lush countryside of Kilimanjaro's slopes. School holidays provide an opportunity for further travel – Zanzibar being a favourite destination. Katy Allen, the project leader, lived in Kilimanjaro for three years and now visits the region for at least four months each year, and is there to meet the gap year students and help them to settle in to their village and their schools, giving advice and guidance. They have at all times the full support of the local community and church, and specifically of the ex-head of a local school now seconded to work for the charity. Volunteers with an offending background are not accepted. Kilimanjaro – Marangu area.

Number of projects: 1 **UK:** 0
Starting months: Jan
Time required: 32–48 weeks
Age: 18–25
Causes: Teaching/assisting (primary, EFL).
Activities: Arts/Crafts, Sport, Teaching.
Placements: 8+
When to apply: September (18 months ahead of departure date).
Work alone/with others: Both.
Qualifications: Clear speech. No nationality restrictions but British passport holders preferred.
Health requirements: Nil.
Costs: £2,000 (subject to change) fee + insurance and subsistence.
Benefits: Return air ticket, village accommodation in Kilimanjaro.
Training: A pre-departure two week training course is given in Sevenoaks, Kent.
Supervision: On arrival students are met by Katy Allen and introduced to the village. Dilly Mtui, working for the charity, has responsibility when Katy returns to the UK.
Interviews: Interviews take place in Sevenoaks, Kent.
Charity number: 1041672
Worldwide placements: Africa (Tanzania).

VILLAGES YOUTH PROJECT, THE

21 Bridlington Street
Hunmanby
Filey
North Yorkshire YO14 0JR UK
T: 01723 891521
E: woollypost@ukonline.co.uk
Contact: Mike Woolridge

The Villages Youth Project operates in Hunmanby, Muston, Reighton, Speeton, Wold Newton and surrounding villages. It is a youthwork project initiated by local churches and local people of Hunmanby and those in surrounding villages. This project began in 1989. The project was developed to meet the needs and help address the real problems facing young people in rural areas such as unemployment and homelessness, isolation and boredom. During the last five years the project volunteers have converted a double decker bus for use as a youth centre to work with the young people in the villages. They have come across young people who have problems relating to drugs, alcohol, gambling, homelessness, health issues, teenage pregnancies and juvenile offending. As well as providing recreational facilities on the bus, there has been liaison with police, courts and other organisations to help support young people with the various difficulties of meeting the needs of young people. What are its aims? The overall objectives of the Villages Youth Project: (a) to provide facilities for meeting the needs of young people aged 11–25 in Hunmanby, Muston, Reighton, Speeton, Wold Newton and the surrounding area; (b) to offer support and assistance to young people to enable them to make informed choices in the areas of education, health, training, independence and recreation so that their conditions of life may be improved and they may develop their physical, mental and spiritual capacities so as to grow to full maturity as individuals and members of society. Villages of Hunmanby, Reighton, Speeton, Wold Newton, Muston and surrounding area. 🚻 📄

Number of projects: 1 **UK:** 1
Starting months: January–December
Time required: 12–52 weeks
Age: 19 plus – no upper limit
Causes: Conservation, Environmental Causes, Unemployed, Young People.
Activities: Administration, Arts/Crafts, Conservation Skills, Counselling, Development Issues, Driving, Fundraising, Group Work, Outdoor Skills, Religion, Visiting/Befriending.
Placements: 8
When to apply: All year.
Work alone/with others: With others.
Qualifications: Any relative to working with young people.
Health requirements: Nil.
Costs: Food and accommodation.
Benefits: Travel costs.
Training: If required.
Supervision: Yes.
Interviews: Interviews take place at project office.
UK placements: England (N. Yorkshire).

VINCENTIAN SERVICE CORPS

7800 Natural Bridge Road
St Louis
Missouri 63121 USA
T: 00 1 (314) 382 2800 ext 291
F: 00 1 (314) 382 8392
E: vsccentral@juno.com
W: www.vscorps.org
Contact: The Director

The Vincentian Service Corps/Central is part of the national Vincentian Service Corps. The other office is in New York. We invite men and women, 20 years and older to serve the poor for one year. The VSC/Central is sponsored by the Daughters of Charity of the Midwest and all placements from our office are in the central area of the United States. Our volunteers (members) serve in many aspects of social work, health care, education and parish ministry. We offer a one-year programme each year. Applications must be made at least three months ahead. Application forms are available upon request. It is with this application that we can learn the applicant's background, interests, education, family history, medical history and experiences. We ask for five personal references that we follow up for their recommendation regarding the applicant's ability to work in the programme. Evaluations are conducted twice a year with input from the member and from the work supervisor. We strive to place members in community settings whenever possible or preferred. Proximity to Daughters of Charity or Vincentian Priests is always a part of the assignment to ensure their inclusion in the Vincentian family. Because of the difficulty of getting a visa for the USA, we ask applicants from outside the USA to apply for their visa as soon as possible. Volunteers with offending backgrounds are not accepted. 📄

Number of projects: 1 **UK:** 0
Starting months: Jan, Aug
Time required: 52 weeks
Age: 22–65
Causes: AIDS/HIV, Children, Disabled (physical), Elderly People, Health Care/Medical, Human Rights, Inner City Problems, Poor/Homeless, Refugees, Teaching/assisting (nursery, primary, mature, EFL), Young People.
Activities: Building/Construction, Caring (general, residential), Community Work, Computers, Fundraising, Religion, Social Work, Teaching.
Placements: 7
When to apply: At least 3 months in advance.
Work alone/with others: Both.
Qualifications: All applicants must speak very good English because they will be in positions of leadership or role models for those they serve. Spanish is also useful.

Health requirements: Good health.
Costs: Fares to St Louis.
Benefits: Accommodation + $100 per month + $100 per month for food + health insurance and 3 renewal weekends during the year.
Training: There is a week of orientation at the beginning of the programme introducing the member to the charisma of the Vincentian family, to service, community living, cultural diversity and living gospel values.
Supervision: Yes.
Interviews: Interviews are by telephone.
Worldwide placements: North America: (USA); Australasia (New Zealand).

VISIONS IN ACTION

2710 Ontario Road NW
Washington
DC 20009 USA
T: 00 1 202 625 7402
F: 00 1 202 588 9344
E: visions@igc.org
W: www.visionsinaction.org
Contact: Signe Anderson, Annabel Khouri

Visions in Action is an international non-profit organisation founded in 1988 out of the conviction that much can be learned from and contributed to the developing world, by working as part of a community of volunteers committed to achieving social and economic justice. Volunteers are placed with non-profit development organisations, research institutes and media in accordance to their skills, interests and experience. We have volunteers in Uganda, Tanzania, South Africa, Burkina Faso, Zimbabwe and Mexico, in both rural and urban settings. They work in such diverse fields as business management, law, health care, environmental concerns, journalism, youth and children's programmes, scientific research, women's issues, housing, agriculture, building and manual trades, democratisation, human rights and social justice. Volunteers interact on a daily basis with host country nationals and development professionals. They work within the local culture while participating as members of the international development community. Participants in the Visions in Action programme support the following tenets: Grassroots approach: development occurs best when we are as close as possible to the standard of living of those we are trying to assist. Therefore, a modest, low overhead, grassroots approach is taken in all that Visions does. Voluntarism: there is much that can be done in the spirit of true voluntarism – giving of oneself and making personal sacrifices for the betterment of others, expecting nothing in return. Community development occurs best in a community of inspired, informed individuals,

living together and supporting one another throughout the volunteer experience. Self reliance: participants are self-reliant, mirroring the same type of self-reliance that those in developing countries are trying to achieve. Social justice: all of our efforts are directed at achieving social and economic justice for those in the developing world. ⑤

Number of projects: Numerous **UK:** 0
Starting months: Jan, Jun, Jul, Sep, Oct, Dec
Time required: 26–52 weeks
Age: 19–75
Causes: Addicts/Ex-Addicts, AIDS/HIV, Animal Welfare, Archaeology, Architecture, Children, Conservation, Disabled (learning and physical), Elderly People, Environmental Causes, Health Care/Medical, Heritage, Holidays for Disabled, Human Rights, Inner City Problems, Offenders/Ex-Offenders, Poor/Homeless, Refugees, Teaching/assisting (nursery, primary, secondary, mature, EFL) Unemployed, Wildlife, Work. Camps – Seasonal, Young People.
Activities: Administration, Agriculture/Farming, Caring – General, Community Work, Conservation Skills, Development Issues, International Aid, Newsletter/Journalism, Research, Social Work, Training, Work Camps – Seasonal.
Placements: 65
When to apply: At least 90 days before departure.
Work alone/with others: Work for local nonprofit organisations (not with other volunteers).
Qualifications: University degree or equivalent work experience for all programmes except 6 month S. Africa and Mexico programmes and Tanzania summer programme.
Equipment/clothing: No specific equipment. Clothing depends on programme.
Health requirements: Must be in good general health.
Costs: Programme fees which average US$4,400 for one year + travel and some additional pocket money.
Benefits: Housing, monthly stipend, medical insurance and training in development and the local language. Group house in major cities with other volunteers.
Training: A thorough one-month orientation in-country, including local language training, homestays, visits to development projects and guest speakers.
Supervision: Volunteers are supervised by staff at local development organisations.
Interviews: Interviews by phone.
Charity number: 52-1659822
Worldwide placements: Africa (Burkina Faso, South Africa, Tanzania, Uganda, Zimbabwe); Central America (Mexico).

VISWADARSANAM

Feny Land
Nariyapuram – 689 513
Pathanamthitta District
Kerala India
T: 00 91 473 350543
E: viswadarsanam@yahoo.com
Contact: Mr Umesh Babu

Viswadarsanam is a voluntary organisation
located in Kerala in South India. It started on
World Environment Day, 5th June 1987. Our
aim is to make nature truly natural and human
lives more cheerful and thus bring health,
happiness and peace to society to prevent
further deterioration of natural wealth and
promote a sustainable utilisation of natural
resources for human welfare. Essentially we are
an environmental organisation. The activities
included are the following:
1. Establishing a development centre for
humanity and nature.
2. Preparing newsletters, books, information
sheets and audio visuals.
3. Conducting guided educative wilderness
trips, nature walks and trekking for interested
groups. Our interests also extend into rural
development, cottage industry, art and cultural
heritage, flora and fauna, travel and tourism.
We need administrative volunteers for planning
and implementation of long and short-term
projects such as nature camps, environmental
programmes and green health programmes.
Volunteers also help with international
correspondence, computer work and
publication of a souvenir handbook to cover a
decade of work at Viswadarsanam. We need
volunteers for alternative life style
experiments/holistic way of life. We need
volunteers for teaching spoken English to the
local school and university students. Apart from
work involvement, the volunteers will get the
opportunity to relax with cultural programmes,
interact with local people, travel the
countryside, and trek nature trails. There are
forests and rivers nearby. There is also the
opportunity to experience local fairs and
festivals. There are numerous sites in the area.
See the Viswadarsanam home district handbook
for more information about the area. Sightseeing trips to experience Kerala will be
arranged upon request. The asset of
Viswadarsanam is the grace of kind-hearted and
service-minded people. Their might is our
strength. Volunteers are welcome to stay and
acclimatise before committing. Kerala State in S.
India, Pathanamthitta District, Vallicode
Panchayath Nariyapuram village. 🔲

Number of projects: 5 UK: 0
Starting months: January–December
Time required: 1–12 weeks

Age: 18–60
Causes: Animal Welfare, Conservation,
Environmental Causes, Health Care/Medical,
Heritage, Human Rights, Teaching/assisting
(EFL), Wildlife, Work Camps – Seasonal.
Activities: Administration, Agriculture/Farming,
Arts/Crafts, Building/Construction,
Campaigning, Community Work, Conservation
Skills, Cooking, Development Issues, Forestry,
Fundraising, Gardening/Horticulture, Group
Work, Manual Work, Marketing/Publicity,
Newsletter/Journalism, Outdoor Skills,
Teaching, Work Camps – Seasonal.
Placements: 40–50
When to apply: All year.
Work alone/with others: With other
volunteers.
Qualifications: Post A-level or university
preferred. Above all social commitment and
dedication. Any skill is particularly welcome
such as computer knowledge, photography and
cinematography, arts and crafts, language
ability and/or project planning.
Equipment/clothing: Raincoat, sleeping bag,
mosquito net, torch etc.
Health requirements: Good health, not been
in contact with any infectious diseases.
Costs: Registration fee £10. £40 per week, £140
for one month, £350 for 3 months. Travel to
India.
Benefits: The cost covers board and lodging.
Training: Training in local customs and
manners.
Supervision: Maximum supervision by the
camp directors.
Interviews: Selection by application form, then
informal induction on arrival.
Charity number: Q 915
Worldwide placements: Asia (India).

VLAAMS STEUNPUNT VRIJWILLIGERSWERK vzw – BELGIUM

Marie-Joselaan 73
2600 Berchem
Belgium
T: 00 32 3 218 59 01
F: 00 32 3 218 45 23
E: info@vsvw.be
W: www.vrijwilligerswerk.be
Contact: Raf De Zutter/Eva Hambach

Vlaams Steunpunt voor Vrijwilligerswerk vzw
promotes and has information about
volunteering in Belgium. It may well be able to
put volunteers in touch with organisations
which are not yet listed on the WorldWide
Volunteering database.

Starting months: January–December
Time required: 1–52 weeks (plus)
Age: 16 plus – no upper limit
Causes: Addicts/Ex-Addicts, AIDS/HIV, Animal

Welfare, Archaeology, Architecture, Children, Conservation, Disabled (learning and physical), Elderly People, Environmental Causes, Health Care/Medical, Heritage, Holidays for Disabled, Human Rights, Inner City Problems, Offenders/ Ex-Offenders, Poor/Homeless, Refugees, Teaching/assisting (nursery, primary, secondary, mature, EFL) Unemployed, Wildlife, Work Camps – Seasonal, Young People.
Activities: Accountancy, Administration, Agriculture/Farming, Arts/Crafts, Building/Construction, Campaigning, Caring (general, day and residential), Catering, Community Work, Computers, Conservation Skills, Cooking, Counselling, Development Issues, DIY, Driving, First Aid, Forestry, Fundraising, Gardening/Horticulture, Group Work, International Aid, Library/Resource Centres, Manual Work, Marketing/Publicity, Music, Newsletter/Journalism, Outdoor Skills, Religion, Research, Scientific Work, Social Work, Sport, Summer Camps, Teaching, Technical Skills, Theatre/Drama, Training, Translating, Visiting/Befriending, Work Camps – Seasonal.
Costs: Varies according to the project.
Worldwide placements: Europe (Belgium).

VOLUNTARY SERVICE BELFAST (VSB)

34 Shaftesbury Square
Belfast
Antrim BT2 7DB N. Ireland
T: 028 9020 0850
F: 028 9020 0860
E: jim@vsb.org.uk
W: www.vsb.org.k
Contact: Jim Woods

The VSB Volunteer Centre is concerned with promoting, supporting and developing voluntary activity within the Greater Belfast, Castlereagh, North Down and Ards areas. It provides the link between people interested in voluntary work, and organisations or individuals who can benefit from the services provided by the volunteers. Volunteering is about becoming involved in the community to benefit others, by doing something because you want to. You do not have to possess special skills or experience, but it helps to be patient, tolerant, understanding and reliable. Volunteers with an offending background are accepted but generally placed where they can be closely supervised – at least to begin with. It depends on the nature of the offence. We are unlikely to recruit sex offenders for any type of placement. All UK projects are based in Northern Ireland. ♿ 📷

Number of projects: 505+ UK: 500+
Starting months: January–December
Time required: 12–52 weeks (plus)
Age: 16 plus – no upper limit
Causes: Addicts/Ex-Addicts, AIDS/HIV,

Children, Conservation, Disabled (learning and physical), Elderly People, Environmental Causes, Heritage, Poor/Homeless, Unemployed, Wildlife, Young People.
Activities: Administration, Arts/Crafts, Campaigning, Caring – General, Community Work, Conservation Skills, Counselling, DIY, Driving, Fundraising, Gardening/Horticulture, Group Work, International Aid, Manual Work, Marketing/Publicity, Research, Visiting/ Befriending.
Placements: 1000+
When to apply: One month prior to starting.
Work alone/with others: Both.
Health requirements: No specific requirements.
Costs: Accommodation.
Benefits: Travel costs up to £3 per day. Lunch allowance of £1.50 per day.
Training: Provided as required.
Supervision: Ongoing.
Interviews: Interviews take place in our head office in Lisburn Road.
Charity number: XN48736
Worldwide placements: Africa (South Africa); South America (Peru); Asia (India, Israel, Japan); Europe (Bulgaria, Germany, Romania).
UK placements: Northern Ireland (Antrim, Belfast City, Down).

VOLUNTARY WORKCAMPS ASSOCIATION OF GHANA

P.O. Box 1540
Accra
Ghana
T: 00 233 21 663486
F: 00 233 21 665960
E: volu@gppo.africaonline.com.gh
W: www.volu.org
Contact: Pastor Chris Hyame

Voluntary Workcamps Association of Ghana organises workcamps in the rural areas of Ghana for international volunteers. Campers work about seven hours a day, mostly unskilled manual digging, clearing bush, mixing cement or building. The projects are mostly roads, schools, street drains, latrines, hospitals or clinics, social centres, bridges etc. in villages and small towns which villagers themselves are carrying out through voluntary communal labour. In some camps there is a programme of educational work for girls among the village women. The function of the camps is not to do the work for the people but to help them to help themselves by working with them. In selecting and arranging the projects we co-operate closely with some government departments. ♿ 📷

Number of projects: 12–20 UK: 0
Starting months: Jan, Jun, Jul, Aug, Sep, Oct, Dec

Time required: 3–52 weeks
Age: 16–45
Causes: Children, Conservation, Disabled (physical), Environmental Causes, Work Camps – Seasonal.
Activities: Agriculture/Farming, Building/Construction, Community Work, Conservation Skills, Forestry, Group Work, Manual Work, Outdoor Skills, Social Work, Summer Camps, Work Camps – Seasonal.
Placements: 1500
When to apply: February.
Work alone/with others: With others – 25–50 per camp.
Equipment/clothing: Working clothes, boots, gloves, torch, raincoat, mosquito net + repellent, sleeping bag, water purifier.
Health requirements: Volunteers should be physically strong.
Costs: Subscription fee of approx. £120 and travel. (£180 for 2 camps).
Benefits: Accommodation, administration expenses and food at campsite.
Training: Briefing on arrival. Work does not need any formal training.
Supervision: Leaders are chosen for the camps.
Interviews: No interview.
Worldwide placements: Africa (Ghana).

VOLUNTARY WORKCAMPS ASSOCIATION OF NIGERIA

P.O. Box 2189
53 Iseyin Str.
Palmgrove
Lagos
Nigeria
T: 00 234 1 880877
E: kolagaran@yahoo.com
Contact: Kolawole Aganran

Voluntary Workcamps Association of Nigeria organises workcamps centred around community projects for youths of different cultural backgrounds and nationalities throughout Nigeria. Between 120 and 150 volunteers per year participate in the workcamps; the work is mainly skilled and unskilled manual labour. This includes bricklaying, carpentry, sports, games, excursions, debates and discussions. We also undertake short and medium term programmes in the year. The usual length of placement is between one and two months (i.e. July to September). Application forms are available at US$20 for volunteers to receive the brochure and placement for the camps. Only applications received with the fee before the month of May will be considered. 🖹

Number of projects: 1 UK: 0
Starting months: Jul, Aug
Time required: 4–8 weeks
Age: 18 plus – no upper limit

Causes: Environmental Causes, Health Care/Medical, Poor/Homeless, Work Camps – Seasonal, Young People.
Activities: Building/Construction, Community Work, DIY, Sport, Work Camps – Seasonal.
Placements: 40
When to apply: Before May.
Work alone/with others: With others.
Qualifications: Knowledge of English.
Health requirements: Volunteers must be physically fit.
Costs: US$20 for application form. US$200 registration fee + travel and upkeep.
Benefits: Board and lodging.
Training: Pre-camping orientation is available three days before the programme.
Supervision: Yes.
Interviews: No.
Worldwide placements: Africa (Nigeria).

VOLUNTARY YEAR

Stora Sköndal
128 85 Sköndal
Sweden
T: 00 46 8 605 0927
E: elisa@sssd.se
Contact: Elisabeth Rydstrom

Number of projects: 1 UK: 0
Starting months: January–December
Time required: 40–52 weeks
Age: 18–25
Causes: Addicts/Ex-Addicts, AIDS/HIV, Animal Welfare, Archaeology, Architecture, Children, Conservation, Disabled (learning and physical), Elderly People, Environmental Causes, Health Care/Medical, Heritage, Holidays for Disabled, Human Rights, Inner City Problems, Offenders/Ex-Offenders, Poor/Homeless, Refugees, Teaching/assisting (nursery, primary, secondary, mature, EFL) Unemployed, Wildlife, Work Camps – Seasonal, Young People.
Activities: Community Work, Religion.
Worldwide placements: Europe (Sweden).

VOLUNTEER 21 – KOREA

Pangbae-bon-dont 779-1 3f
Seochu-gu
Seoul
S. Korea
T: 00 82 2 599 6576
F: 00 82 2 599 6580
E: volun@peacenet.or.kr
W: www.vol21.peacenet.or.kr
Contact: Dr Kang-Hyun Lee

Volunteer 21 promotes and has information about volunteering in South Korea. It may well be able to put volunteers in touch with organisations which are not yet listed on the WorldWide Volunteering database.

Starting months: January–December
Time required: 1–52 weeks (plus)
Age: 16 plus – no upper limit
Causes: Addicts/Ex-Addicts, AIDS/HIV, Animal Welfare, Archaeology, Architecture, Children, Conservation, Disabled (learning and physical), Elderly People, Environmental Causes, Health Care/Medical, Heritage, Holidays for Disabled, Human Rights, Inner City Problems, Offenders/Ex-Offenders, Poor/Homeless, Refugees, Teaching/assisting (nursery, primary, secondary, mature, EFL) Unemployed, Wildlife, Work Camps – Seasonal, Young People.
Activities: Accountancy, Administration, Agriculture/Farming, Arts/Crafts, Building/Construction, Campaigning, Caring (general, day and residential), Catering, Community Work, Computers, Conservation Skills, Cooking, Counselling, Development Issues, DIY, Driving, First Aid, Forestry, Fundraising, Gardening/Horticulture, Group Work, International Aid, Library/Resource Centres, Manual Work, Marketing/Publicity, Music, Newsletter/Journalism, Outdoor Skills, Religion, Research, Scientific Work, Social Work, Sport, Summer Camps, Teaching, Technical Skills, Theatre/Drama, Training, Translating, Visiting/Befriending, Work Camps – Seasonal.
Costs: Varies according to the project.
Worldwide placements: Asia (Korea (South)).

VOLUNTEER ACTION AND DEVELOPMENT CENTRE OF THE NCSS – Singapore

11 Penang Lane
Singapore 238485
Singapore
F: 00 65 339 6859
E: ncssdmva@singnet.com.sg
Contact: Lynda Soong

The Volunteer Action and Development Centre (VACD) of The National Council of Social Services promotes and has information about volunteering in Singapore. It may well be able to put volunteers in touch with organisations which are not yet listed on the WorldWide Volunteering database.

Starting months: January–December
Time required: 1–52 weeks (plus)
Age: 16 plus – no upper limit
Causes: Addicts/Ex-Addicts, AIDS/HIV, Animal Welfare, Archaeology, Architecture, Children, Conservation, Disabled (learning and physical), Elderly People, Environmental Causes, Health Care/Medical, Heritage, Holidays for Disabled, Human Rights, Inner City Problems, Offenders/Ex-Offenders, Poor/Homeless, Refugees, Teaching/assisting (nursery, primary, secondary, mature, EFL) Unemployed, Wildlife, Work Camps – Seasonal, Young People.

Activities: Accountancy, Administration, Agriculture/Farming, Arts/Crafts, Building/Construction, Campaigning, Caring (general, day and residential), Catering, Community Work, Computers, Conservation Skills, Cooking, Counselling, Development Issues, DIY, Driving, First Aid, Forestry, Fundraising, Gardening/Horticulture, Group Work, International Aid, Library/Resource Centres, Manual Work, Marketing/Publicity, Music, Newsletter/Journalism, Outdoor Skills, Religion, Research, Scientific Work, Social Work, Sport, Summer Camps, Teaching, Technical Skills, Theatre/Drama, Training, Translating, Visiting/Befriending, Work Camps – Seasonal.
Costs: Varies according to the project.
Worldwide placements: Asia (Singapore).

VOLUNTEER CANADA

330 Gilmour Street
Ottawa
Ontario K2P 0P6 Canada
T: 00 1 613 231 4371
F: 00 1 613 231 6725
E: volunteer.canada@sympatico.ca
W: www.volunteer.ca
Contact: Stephanie Smith

Volunteer Canada is the national organisation that promotes volunteering and has information about volunteering in Canada. It may well be able to put volunteers in touch with organisations which are not yet listed on the WorldWide volunteering database.

Teaching/assisting (nursery, primary, secondary, mature, EFL) Unemployed, Wildlife, Work Camps – Seasonal, Young People.
Activities: Accountancy, Administration, Agriculture/Farming, Arts/Crafts, Building/Construction, Campaigning, Caring (general, day and residential), Catering, Community Work, Computers, Conservation Skills, Cooking, Counselling, Development Issues, DIY, Driving, First Aid, Forestry, Fundraising, Gardening/Horticulture, Group Work, International Aid, Library/Resource Centres, Manual Work, Marketing/Publicity, Music, Newsletter/Journalism, Outdoor Skills, Religion, Research, Scientific Work, Social Work, Sport, Summer Camps, Teaching, Technical Skills, Theatre/Drama, Training, Translating, Visiting/Befriending, Work Camps – Seasonal.
Costs: Varies according to the project.
Worldwide placements: Europe (Yugoslavia).

VOLUNTEER CENTER – Bulgaria

3 Tzar Assen Str.
Varna 9002
Bulgaria
T: 00 359 52 226224
F: 00 359 52 600138
E: oscvn@tnt.bg
Contact: Diyan Dimitrov

Volunteer Center promotes and has information about volunteering in Bulgaria. It may well be able to put volunteers in touch with organisations which are not yet listed on the WorldWide volunteering database.

Starting months: January–December
Time required: 1–52 weeks (plus)
Age: 16 plus – no upper limit
Causes: Addicts/Ex-Addicts, AIDS/HIV, Animal Welfare, Archaeology, Architecture, Children, Conservation, Disabled (learning and physical), Elderly People, Environmental Causes, Health Care/Medical, Heritage, Holidays for Disabled, Human Rights, Inner City Problems, Offenders/Ex-Offenders, Poor/Homeless, Refugees, Teaching/assisting (nursery, primary, secondary, mature, EFL) Unemployed, Wildlife, Work Camps – Seasonal, Young People.
Activities: Accountancy, Administration, Agriculture/Farming, Arts/Crafts, Building/Construction, Campaigning, Caring (general, day and residential), Catering, Community Work, Computers, Conservation Skills, Cooking, Counselling, Development Issues, DIY, Driving, First Aid, Forestry, Fundraising, Gardening/Horticulture, Group Work, International Aid, Library/Resource Centres, Manual Work, Marketing/Publicity, Music, Newsletter/Journalism, Outdoor Skills, Religion, Research, Scientific Work, Social Work, Sport, Summer Camps, Teaching, Technical

Starting months: January–December
Time required: 1–52 weeks (plus)
Age: 16 plus – no upper limit
Causes: Addicts/Ex-Addicts, AIDS/HIV, Animal Welfare, Archaeology, Architecture, Children, Conservation, Disabled (learning and physical), Elderly People, Environmental Causes, Health Care/Medical, Heritage, Holidays for Disabled, Human Rights, Inner City Problems, Offenders/Ex-Offenders, Poor/Homeless, Refugees, Teaching/assisting (nursery, primary, secondary, mature, EFL) Unemployed, Wildlife, Work Camps – Seasonal, Young People.
Activities: Accountancy, Administration, Agriculture/Farming, Arts/Crafts, Building/Construction, Campaigning, Caring (general, day and residential), Catering, Community Work, Computers, Conservation Skills, Cooking, Counselling, Development Issues, DIY, Driving, First Aid, Forestry, Fundraising, Gardening/Horticulture, Group Work, International Aid, Library/Resource Centres, Manual Work, Marketing/Publicity, Music, Newsletter/Journalism, Outdoor Skills, Religion, Research, Scientific Work, Social Work, Sport, Summer Camps, Teaching, Technical Skills, Theatre/Drama, Training, Translating, Visiting/Befriending, Work Camps – Seasonal.
Costs: Varies according to the project.
Worldwide placements: North America: (Canada).

VOLUNTEER CENTER BELGRADE, THE

Volunterski Centar
Zmaj Jovina 34
11000 Belgrade
(Yugoslavia) Serbia & Monte Negro
T: 00 381 11 3283306
F: 00 381 11 3283306
E: volonter@crnps.org.yu
W: www.crnps.org.yu
Contact: Jelena Pavlovic

The Volunteer Center Belgrade promotes and has information about volunteering in Yugoslavia. It may well be able to put volunteers in touch with organisations which are not yet listed on the WorldWide volunteering database.

Alternative e-mail addresses:
jpavlovic@crnps.org.yu.
Starting months: January–December
Time required: 1–52 weeks (plus)
Age: 16 plus – no upper limit
Causes: Addicts/Ex-Addicts, AIDS/HIV, Animal Welfare, Archaeology, Architecture, Children, Conservation, Disabled (learning and physical), Elderly People, Environmental Causes, Health Care/Medical, Heritage, Holidays for Disabled, Human Rights, Inner City Problems, Offenders/Ex-Offenders, Poor/Homeless, Refugees,

Skills, Theatre/Drama, Training, Translating, Visiting/Befriending, Work Camps – Seasonal.
Costs: Varies according to the project.
Worldwide placements: Europe (Bulgaria).

VOLUNTEER CENTER – Lithuania

Zemaites Str 21
Room 201
2009 Vilnius
Lithuania
T: 00 370 2 31 06 32
E: info@savanoris.lt
Contact: Gintaras M. Razaitis, MD

Volunteer Center promotes and has information about volunteering in Latvia. It may well be able to put volunteers in touch with organisations which are not yet listed on the WorldWide volunteering database.

Starting months: January–December
Time required: 1–52 weeks (plus)
Age: 16 plus – no upper limit
Causes: Addicts/Ex-Addicts, AIDS/HIV, Animal Welfare, Archaeology, Architecture, Children, Conservation, Disabled (learning and physical), Elderly People, Environmental Causes, Health Care/Medical, Heritage, Holidays for Disabled, Human Rights, Inner City Problems, Offenders/Ex-Offenders, Poor/Homeless, Refugees, Teaching/assisting (nursery, primary, secondary, mature, EFL) Unemployed, Wildlife, Work Camps – Seasonal, Young People.
Activities: Accountancy, Administration, Agriculture/Farming, Arts/Crafts, Building/Construction, Campaigning, Caring (general, day and residential), Catering, Community Work, Computers, Conservation Skills, Cooking, Counselling, Development Issues, DIY, Driving, First Aid, Forestry, Fundraising, Gardening/Horticulture, Group Work, International Aid, Library/Resource Centres, Manual Work, Marketing/Publicity, Music, Newsletter/Journalism, Outdoor Skills, Religion, Research, Scientific Work, Social Work, Sport, Summer Camps, Teaching, Technical Skills, Theatre/Drama, Training, Translating, Visiting/Befriending, Work Camps – Seasonal.
Costs: Varies according to the project.
Worldwide placements: Europe (Lithuania).

VOLUNTEER CENTER – Plovdiv – BULGARIA

17 Avksentiy Veleshki Street Floor 1
Ivan Vazov Library
4000 Plovdiv
Bulgaria
T: 00 359 32 62 4824
F: 00 359 32 63 1995
E: os_plovdiv@rakursy.com
Contact: Angelina Pelova

Volunteer Center – Plovdiv promotes and has information about volunteering in Bulgaria. It may well be able to put volunteers in touch with organisations which are not yet listed on the WorldWide volunteering database.

Starting months: January–December
Time required: 1–52 weeks (plus)
Age: 16 plus – no upper limit
Causes: Addicts/Ex-Addicts, AIDS/HIV, Animal Welfare, Archaeology, Architecture, Children, Conservation, Disabled (learning and physical), Elderly People, Environmental Causes, Health Care/Medical, Heritage, Holidays for Disabled, Human Rights, Inner City Problems, Offenders/Ex-Offenders, Poor/Homeless, Refugees, Teaching/assisting (nursery, primary, secondary, mature, EFL) Unemployed, Wildlife, Work Camps – Seasonal, Young People.
Activities: Accountancy, Administration, Agriculture/Farming, Arts/Crafts, Building/Construction, Campaigning, Caring (general, day and residential), Catering, Community Work, Computers, Conservation Skills, Cooking, Counselling, Development Issues, DIY, Driving, First Aid, Forestry, Fundraising, Gardening/Horticulture, Group Work, International Aid, Library/Resource Centres, Manual Work, Marketing/Publicity, Music, Newsletter/Journalism, Outdoor Skills, Religion, Research, Scientific Work, Social Work, Sport, Summer Camps, Teaching, Technical Skills, Theatre/Drama, Training, Translating, Visiting/Befriending, Work Camps – Seasonal.
Costs: Varies according to the project.
Worldwide placements: Europe (Bulgaria).

VOLUNTEER CENTRE – Latvia

Mukusales Str
33–9 Riga
Latvia 1004
E: bcentrs@hotmail.com
Contact: Girta Ratniece

Volunteer Centre promotes and has information about volunteering in Latvia. It may well be able to put volunteers in touch with organisations which are not yet listed on the WorldWide Volunteering database.

Starting months: January–December
Time required: 1–52 weeks (plus)
Age: 16 plus – no upper limit
Causes: Addicts/Ex-Addicts, AIDS/HIV, Animal Welfare, Archaeology, Architecture, Children, Conservation, Disabled (learning and physical), Elderly People, Environmental Causes, Health Care/Medical, Heritage, Holidays for Disabled, Human Rights, Inner City Problems, Offenders/Ex-Offenders, Poor/Homeless, Refugees, Teaching/assisting (nursery, primary, secondary, mature, EFL) Unemployed, Wildlife, Work Camps – Seasonal, Young People.

Activities: Accountancy, Administration, Agriculture/Farming, Arts/Crafts, Building/ Construction, Campaigning, Caring (general, day and residential), Catering, Community Work, Computers, Conservation Skills, Cooking, Counselling, Development Issues, DIY, Driving, First Aid, Forestry, Fundraising, Gardening/Horticulture, Group Work, International Aid, Library/Resource Centres, Manual Work, Marketing/Publicity, Music, Newsletter/Journalism, Outdoor Skills, Religion, Research, Scientific Work, Social Work, Sport, Summer Camps, Teaching, Technical Skills, Theatre/Drama, Training, Translating, Visiting/Befriending, Work Camps – Seasonal.
Costs: Varies according to the project.
Worldwide placements: Europe (Latvia).

VOLUNTEER CENTRE – Poland

Nowolipie 9/11 Str
00–150 Warsaw
Poland
T: 00 48 22 635 27 73
F: 00 48 22 635 46 02
E: wolontar@medianet.com.pl
Contact: Maglorzata Ochman

Volunteer Centre promotes and has information about volunteering in Poland. It may well be able to put volunteers in touch with organisations which are not yet listed on the WorldWide Volunteering database.

Starting months: January–December
Time required: 1–52 weeks (plus)
Age: 16 plus – no upper limit
Causes: Addicts/Ex-Addicts, AIDS/HIV, Animal Welfare, Archaeology, Architecture, Children, Conservation, Disabled (learning and physical), Elderly People, Environmental Causes, Health Care/Medical, Heritage, Holidays for Disabled, Human Rights, Inner City Problems, Offenders/ Ex-Offenders, Poor/Homeless, Refugees, Teaching/assisting (nursery, primary, secondary, mature, EFL) Unemployed, Wildlife, Work Camps – Seasonal, Young People
Activities: Accountancy, Administration, Agriculture/Farming, Arts/Crafts, Building/ Construction, Campaigning, Caring (general, day and residential), Catering, Community Work, Computers, Conservation Skills, Cooking, Counselling, Development Issues, DIY, Driving, First Aid, Forestry, Fundraising, Gardening/Horticulture, Group Work, International Aid, Library/Resource Centres, Manual Work, Marketing/Publicity, Music, Newsletter/Journalism, Outdoor Skills, Religion, Research, Scientific Work, Social Work, Sport, Summer Camps, Teaching, Technical Skills, Theatre/Drama, Training, Translating, Visiting/ Befriending, Work Camps – Seasonal
Costs: Varies according to the project.
Worldwide placements: Europe (Poland).

VOLUNTEER CENTRE – South Africa

c/o Somerset Hospital
Helen Bowden Building
Private Bag
Green Point 805, 1
South Africa
T: 00 27 21 418 1116
F: 00 27 21 418 3707
E: volcent@iafrica.com
Contact: Deline van Boom

The Volunteer Centre promotes and has information about volunteering in South Africa. It may well be able to put volunteers in touch with organisations which are not yet listed on the WorldWide Volunteering database.

Starting months: January–December
Time required: 1–52 weeks (plus)
Age: 16 plus – no upper limit
Causes: Addicts/Ex-Addicts, AIDS/HIV, Animal Welfare, Archaeology, Architecture, Children, Conservation, Disabled (learning and physical), Elderly People, Environmental Causes, Health Care/Medical, Heritage, Holidays for Disabled, Human Rights, Inner City Problems, Offenders/ Ex-Offenders, Poor/Homeless, Refugees, Teaching/assisting (nursery, primary, secondary, mature, EFL) Unemployed, Wildlife, Work Camps – Seasonal, Young People.
Activities: Accountancy, Administration, Agriculture/Farming, Arts/Crafts, Building/ Construction, Campaigning, Caring (general, day and residential), Catering, Community Work, Computers, Conservation Skills, Cooking, Counselling, Development Issues, DIY, Driving, First Aid, Forestry, Fundraising, Gardening/Horticulture, Group Work, International Aid, Library/Resource Centres, Manual Work, Marketing/Publicity, Music, Newsletter/Journalism, Outdoor Skills, Religion, Research, Scientific Work, Social Work, Sport, Summer Camps, Teaching, Technical Skills, Theatre/Drama, Training, Translating, Visiting/Befriending, Work Camps – Seasonal.
Costs: Varies according to the project.
Worldwide placements: Africa (South Africa).

VOLUNTEER CENTRE FOUNDATION – Hungary

Margit krt 44
Budapest
H-1027 Hungary
T: 00 36 1 351 0303 ext 610
F: 00 36 1 351 0303 ext 645
E: onkenteskozpont@freemail.hu
W: www.onkentes.hu
Contact: Andras F. Toth

The mission of the Volunteer Centre is to promote and spread the idea of volunteerism by serving as an information and resource centre in Hungary. It seeks to connect individuals with NGOs and thus strengthen solidarity in Hungarian society. The Volunteer Centre strengthens and promotes volunteer action in Hungary by providing various services for all those interested (individuals, NGOs, government and business), and thus to improve the performance of the different actors involved in volunteer work in Hungary as well as encourage participation in community life.

Starting months: January–December
Time required: 1–52 weeks (plus)
Age: 18 plus – no upper limit
Causes: Addicts/Ex-Addicts, AIDS/HIV, Animal Welfare, Archaeology, Architecture, Children, Conservation, Disabled (learning and physical), Elderly People, Environmental Causes, Health Care/Medical, Heritage, Holidays for Disabled, Human Rights, Inner City Problems, Offenders/Ex-Offenders, Poor/Homeless, Refugees, Teaching/assisting (nursery, primary, secondary, mature, EFL) Unemployed, Wildlife, Work Camps – Seasonal, Young People.
Activities: Accountancy, Administration, Agriculture/Farming, Arts/Crafts, Building/Construction, Campaigning, Caring (general, day and residential), Catering, Community Work, Computers, Conservation Skills, Cooking, Counselling, Development Issues, DIY, Driving, First Aid, Forestry, Fundraising, Gardening/Horticulture, Group Work, International Aid, Library/Resource Centres, Manual Work, Marketing/Publicity, Music, Newsletter/Journalism, Outdoor Skills, Religion, Research, Scientific Work, Social Work, Sport, Summer Camps, Teaching, Technical Skills, Theatre/Drama, Training, Translating, Visiting/Befriending, Work Camps – Seasonal.
Costs: Varies according to the project.
Worldwide placements: Europe (Hungary).

VOLUNTEER DEVELOPMENT AGENCY

4th Floor
58 Howard Street
Belfast
BT1 6PG N. Ireland
T: 028 9023 6100
F: 028 9023 7570
E: Kellie@volunteering-ni.org
W: www.volunteering-ni.org
Contact: Wendy Osborne

The Volunteer Development Agency promotes and develops volunteer involvement as a valuable and integral part of life by:
1. Promoting a positive climate for volunteering.
2. Developing and supporting standards of practice for involving volunteers.
3. Developing the capacity of the volunteering infrastructure, and
4. Influencing public policy.

The Volunteer Development Agency was set up to promote volunteering and to improve the quality of volunteer involvement across all sectors. It was established as an independent charitable company in 1993. The Agency is a membership organisation consisting of some 320 members from the voluntary and statutory sectors. Membership is open to any organisation or individual working with volunteers or interested in volunteering.

Starting months: January–December
Time required: 1–52 weeks (plus)
Age: 16 plus – no upper limit
Causes: Addicts/Ex-Addicts, AIDS/HIV, Animal Welfare, Archaeology, Architecture, Children, Conservation, Disabled (learning and physical), Elderly People, Environmental Causes, Health Care/Medical, Heritage, Holidays for Disabled, Human Rights, Inner City Problems, Offenders/Ex-Offenders, Poor/Homeless, Refugees, Teaching/assisting (nursery, primary, secondary, mature, EFL) Unemployed, Wildlife, Work Camps – Seasonal, Young People.
Activities: Accountancy, Administration, Agriculture/Farming, Arts/Crafts, Building/Construction, Campaigning, Caring (general, day and residential), Catering, Community Work, Computers, Conservation Skills, Cooking, Counselling, Development Issues, DIY, Driving, First Aid, Forestry, Fundraising, Gardening/Horticulture, Group Work, International Aid, Library/Resource Centres, Manual Work, Marketing/Publicity, Music, Newsletter/Journalism, Outdoor Skills, Religion, Research, Scientific Work, Social Work, Sport, Summer Camps, Teaching, Technical Skills, Theatre/Drama, Training, Translating, Visiting/Befriending, Work Camps – Seasonal.
Costs: Varies according to the project.
UK placements: Northern Ireland (throughout).

VOLUNTEER DEVELOPMENT SCOTLAND (VDS)

Stirling Enterprise Park
Stirling
FK7 7RP UK
T: 01786 479593
F: 01786 449285
E: information@vds.org.uk
W: www.vds.org.uk
Contact: George Thompson

Volunteer Development Scotland (VDS) serves as the National Centre of Excellence for volunteer development. Our mission is to maximise the positive impacts of volunteering on individuals, groups and organisations in Scotland.

Starting months: January–December
Time required: 1–52 weeks (plus)
Age: 16 plus – no upper limit

Causes: Addicts/Ex-Addicts, AIDS/HIV, Animal Welfare, Archaeology, Architecture, Children, Conservation, Disabled (learning and physical), Elderly People, Environmental Causes, Health Care/Medical, Heritage, Holidays for Disabled, Human Rights, Inner City Problems, Offenders/Ex-Offenders, Poor/Homeless, Refugees, Teaching/assisting (nursery, primary, secondary, mature, EFL) Unemployed, Wildlife, Work Camps – Seasonal, Young People.
Activities: Accountancy, Administration, Agriculture/Farming, Arts/Crafts, Building/Construction, Campaigning, Caring (general, day and residential), Catering, Community Work, Computers, Conservation Skills, Cooking, Counselling, Development Issues, DIY, Driving, First Aid, Forestry, Fundraising, Gardening/Horticulture, Group Work, International Aid, Library/Resource Centres, Manual Work, Marketing/Publicity, Music, Newsletter/Journalism, Outdoor Skills, Religion, Research, Scientific Work, Social Work, Sport, Summer Camps, Teaching, Technical Skills, Theatre/Drama, Training, Translating, Visiting/Befriending, Work Camps – Seasonal.
Costs: Varies according to the project.
UK placements: Scotland (throughout).

VOLUNTEER GALAPAGOS

House of Ecuador
58 Sprinfield Park Avenue
Chelmsford
Essex CM2 6EN UK
T: 0845 1249338
F: 01245 602952
E: info@volunteergalapagos.org
W: www.volunteergalapagos.com
Contact: Jeremy Leys

Volunteer Galapagos is actively looking for great and diverse personalities. Your background and age do not matter as long as you are ready to share, learn, listen, give and live a truly genuine experience in the Galapagos Islands. The Galapagos Volunteer programme aims to offer first hand experience to international students, specialising in various areas on one of the islands of the archipelago. The programme caters for anyone from any field interested in contributing to the development of the local community for at least one month and up to one year. We are offering a wide range of vacancies, from teaching to fishing, from events organising to nursing, from scientific research to marketing tasks. We will make sure we find a position that suits you. We are unable to place volunteers with an offending background. 🖹

Number of projects: 3 UK: 0
Starting months: Jan
Time required: 4–52 weeks

Age: 18–85
Causes: Animal Welfare, Architecture, Children, Conservation, Disabled (learning and physical), Elderly People, Environmental Causes, Health Care/Medical, Heritage, Poor/Homeless, Teaching/assisting (nursery, primary, secondary, EFL), Unemployed, Wildlife.
Activities: Accountancy, Administration, Agriculture/Farming, Arts/Crafts, Building/Construction, Campaigning, Caring (general, day and residential), Catering, Community Work, Computers, Conservation Skills, Cooking, Counselling, Development Issues, DIY, Driving, First Aid, Forestry, Fundraising, Gardening/Horticulture, Group Work, International Aid, Library/Resource Centres, Marketing/Publicity, Music, Newsletter/Journalism, Outdoor Skills, Research, Scientific Work, Social Work, Sport, Summer Camps, Teaching, Technical Skills, Theatre/Drama, Training, Translating, Visiting/Befriending.
Placements: 8
When to apply: Any time.
Work alone/with others: With others.
Qualifications: Your background does not matter as long as you are willing to share, learn, listen, give and live a truly genuine experience.
Health requirements: None.
Costs: Volunteers to cover travel. We ask you to be open minded and not to expect American or European cuisine. Cost for first month – US $49.70 per day. Additional month is US$15.70 per day.
Benefits: Food, accommodation included in costs. Stay in naval base, or in an independent house provided by the Albatross Foundation.
Training: Training is provided.
Supervision: Supervision undertaken by the Albatross Foundation working in the island for over 20 years.
Interviews: Interviews held via telephone, or face to face if numbers in one location are justified.
Worldwide placements: South America (Argentina, Bolivia, Brazil, Chile, Colombia, Ecuador, Falkland Islands, French Guiana, Guyana, Paraguay, Peru, South Georgia, Suriname, Uruguay, Venezuela).

VOLUNTEER MISSIONARY MOVEMENT

Hope Park
Liverpool
L16 9JD UK
T: 0151 291 3438
E: vmm@hope.ac.uk
W: www.vmm.cjb.net
Contact: Alice Davidson

The Voluntary Missionary Movement (VMM) is a lay Christian, community based association. Its central purpose is to challenge, enable and support lay Christians to participate in the

Church's mission of promoting justice and integral human development. The origins of VMM are in the Roman Catholic tradition and membership is open to Christians of all traditions who share its vision of mission and development. VMM achieves its purpose primarily through recruiting, training and sending lay Christians with professional, pastoral or technical skills to share their lives and skills in projects usually linked with the local church in a number of developing countries. VMM is concerned to build partnerships overseas with those who share its vision. VMM also promotes greater awareness at home on issues of justice and development and a greater awareness within the Church of the role of lay people in its life and mission. Through various means it also offers support to those members it sends overseas and members in the home country. VMM finds its inspiration in the teachings on social justice in the gospel. Its ethos, identity, aims and strategy are outlined in the constitutional documents of the movement. Volunteers are not involved in the project planning stage but some maybe involved in the management. The partner usually does project planning and management. Volunteers should be prepared to give their time for a minimum of one year – generally a two year duration, and allow time for recruitment and any necessary language training. We are unable to accept volunteers with an offending background. ⑤

Number of projects: several **UK:** 0
Starting months: January–December
Time required: 52 weeks (plus)
Age: 21–70
Causes: AIDS/HIV, Children, Disabled (learning and physical), Elderly People, Human Rights, Poor/Homeless, Refugees, Teaching (nursery, primary, secondary, mature), Young People.
Activities: Accountancy, Administration, Agriculture/Farming, Arts/Crafts, Building/Construction, Caring – Residential, Community Work, Computers, Counselling, Development Issues, Fundraising, Gardening/Horticulture, Social Work, Teaching, Technical Skills, Training.
Placements: 45–50
When to apply: Any time but please allow up to six months for recruitment process and three months if language training is necessary.
Work alone/with others: Not necessarily with other volunteers.
Qualifications: Professional/technical skills with accredited qualifications. Volunteers must hold an EU passport.
Health requirements: Volunteers should be in good health.

Costs: Travel costs to attend interview and for the introduction weekend.
Benefits: Travel to project, lodging and insurance.
Training: Three weeks preparation training.
Supervision: None, with the exception of an annual visit.
Interviews: Interviews are held in the regional office.
Charity number: 1078695
Worldwide placements: Africa (Kenya, Tanzania, Uganda, Zambia).

VOLUNTEER NEPAL

GPO Box # 11535
Dhapasi, Kathmandu
Nepal
T: 00 977 1 377623/377696
F: 00 977 1 377696
E: cdnnepal@wlink.com.np
W: www.volunteernepal.org.np
Contact: Rajesh Shrestha

Volunteer Nepal is the name of a promising programme aiming to introduce participants in individually differentiated grades to Nepal's diverse geographical and cultural environment and to promote general inter-cultural understanding through experiential learning in Nepal. We are dedicated to the promotion of worldwide understanding of cultural differences. Volunteer Nepal is engaged in service to humanity right on the spot. This is perfect for volunteers who are interested in more than pure vacation-stay. This programme is designed for those people who wish to visit Nepal and contribute their time and skills to benefit the community people as well as learn Nepalese culture and customs by living as a member of a Nepali family and doing volunteer work in various fields. By participating in this programme, it is hoped that participants will experience personal growth as well as open communication channels among different countries and cultures. Other starting dates can be arranged. Nepal is a country of amazing extremes where one can find compacted within its small area a roster of the highest mountains on earth, a repertoire of enchanting cultures and exquisite temples, thick tropical jungles holding a wealth of wildlife, thundering rivers swollen by the snow of Himalayas, and most of all, the friendliest people you have ever met. As diverse as the land on which they live, the people of Nepal represent distinct cultures and races, speaking a variety of tongues and practising different religions. A delightful similarity is that they all speak the language of courtesy, and hospitality is a national culture. Volunteers with an offending background are accepted. ▤

Number of projects: 3 **UK:** 0
Starting months: Feb, Mar, Apr, Aug, Sep, Oct
Time required: 8–16 weeks
Age: 18–65
Causes: AIDS/HIV, Conservation, Disabled (physical), Environmental Causes, Health Care/Medical, Poor/Homeless, Teaching/assisting (nursery, primary, secondary, EFL), Young People.
Activities: Administration, Agriculture/Farming, Arts/Crafts, Community Work, Computers, Conservation Skills, Driving, Fundraising, Group Work, Manual Work, Music, Social Work, Sport, Teaching, Technical Skills, Training.
Placements: 75
When to apply: Two and half months before the progamme commencement date.
Work alone/with others: With others and individually.
Qualifications: Minimum A level (High School Diploma), language requirement is English.
Equipment/clothing: It would be better to bring some school supplies, which helps the volunteer participants to cope with the students in school.
Health requirements: Nil.
Costs: Entrance fee US$/euro 50, Reg. US$ euro/650, Return air fare to Nepal. Visa fee. Personal money.
Benefits: Accommodation – breakfast and dinner for the whole programme. Free trekking (village excursion), rafting, jungle safari, intensive Nepali, homestay, lectures, cross-cultural orientation, meditation, study tour and cultural activities.
Training: 2 weeks pre-service training is provided. This includes homestay, Nepali language training, lectures, cross-cultural orientation, orientation tour, practise teaching, class observation, schooling system and so on.
Supervision: Volunteers are supervised by their host organisation and constant communication is carried out by us CDN Nepal.
Interviews: Prospective volunteers are not interviewed.
Charity number: 5663/110
Worldwide placements: Asia (Nepal).

VOLUNTEER TASK FORCE INC.

194 Loftus Street
North Perth
6006 Western Australia
T: 00 61 8 9328 5388
F: 00 61 8 9328 5385
E: Task1@Smartchat.net.au
Contact: Christa Riegler

Volunteer Task Force Inc has been operating for 30 years. We are a registered charitable organisation with Public Benevolent Institution (PBI) status. We recruit, train and manage

volunteers to perform gardening, home maintenance and voluntary transport for the frail aged, those on disability pensions and their carers. The aim of our programme is to provide services so these clients can remain in their own homes for as long as possible and not have to go into a nursing home or hostel. We have 85 volunteers, five full time and three part time employees. Volunteers with an offending background are accepted with the exception of theft, violent or sexual offences. Two thirds of the metropolitan city of Perth, capital city of Western Australia. 🚹 📄

Number of projects: 1 **UK:** 0
Starting months: January–December
Time required: 1–52 weeks (plus)
Age: 17–80
Causes: Disabled (physical), Elderly People.
Activities: Community Work, Manual Work, Outdoor Skills.
Placements: 80–90
When to apply: Any time, Monday to Friday 9am–4pm. Call to make an appointment.
Work alone/with others: With other young and older volunteers.
Qualifications: All skills and qualifications, honesty, reliability. No nationality restrictions but English language proficiency.
Equipment/clothing: Covered shoes, hat + longsleeved shirt for protection from sun, insects, and irritating plants.
Health requirements: Volunteers are required to manage their own health condition, e.g. schizophrenia, depression.
Costs: Flights to Australia, board and lodging.
Benefits: Re-imbursement of local fares to and from agency and lunch money.
Training: Orientation day at the agency on the first day and on-going on-the-job training.
Supervision: Supervised by a trained, paid staff member.
Interviews: Prospective volunteers are interviewed at the agency, given a volunteer handbook and asked to read the literature and sign an enrolment form, accepting mutual duty of care obligations between volunteer employer and employee.
Charity number: 18037
Worldwide placements: Australasia (Australia).

VOLUNTEER WELLINGTON

PO Box 24130
Manners Street
Wellington
New Zealand
T: 00 64 4 499 4570
F: 00 64 4 499 3907
E: vw@volunteerwellington.org.nz
W: www.volunteerwellington.org.nz
Contact: The Managers

Volunteering Wellington promotes and has information about volunteering in New Zealand. It may well be able to put volunteers in touch with organisations which are not yet listed on the WorldWide Volunteering database. ☒

Number of projects: Wellington only **UK:** 0
Starting months: January–December
Time required: 1–52 weeks (plus)
Age: 16 plus – no upper limit
Causes: Addicts/Ex-Addicts, AIDS/HIV, Animal Welfare, Archaeology, Architecture, Children, Conservation, Disabled (learning and physical), Elderly People, Environmental Causes, Health Care/Medical, Heritage, Holidays for Disabled, Human Rights, Inner City Problems, Offenders/Ex-Offenders, Poor/Homeless, Refugees, Teaching/assisting (nursery, primary, secondary, mature, EFL) Unemployed, Wildlife, Work Camps – Seasonal, Young People.
Activities: Accountancy, Administration, Agriculture/Farming, Arts/Crafts, Building/Construction, Campaigning, Caring (general, day and residential), Catering, Community Work, Computers, Conservation Skills, Cooking, Counselling, Development Issues, DIY, Driving, First Aid, Forestry, Fundraising, Gardening/Horticulture, Group Work, International Aid, Library/Resource Centres, Manual Work, Marketing/Publicity, Music, Newsletter/Journalism, Outdoor Skills, Religion, Research, Scientific Work, Social Work, Sport, Summer Camps, Teaching, Technical Skills, Theatre/Drama, Training, Translating, Visiting/Befriending, Work Camps – Seasonal.
Placements: 1000
When to apply: By appointment any time.
Work alone/with others: Both.
Qualifications: Across the spectrum.
Health requirements: Across the spectrum.
Costs: Reimbursement of out of pocket expenses.
Benefits: Work experience, new networks, contributing to community.
Training: Yes.
Supervision: Yes.
Interviews: Yes.
Worldwide placements: Australasia (New Zealand).

VOLUNTEERING AUCKLAND

186 Manukau Road
Auckland
New Zealand
T: 00 64 9 520 7009
F: 00 64 9 522 1111
E: akvolctr@kiwilink.co.nz
Contact: Cheryll Martin

Volunteering Auckland (1989) is a unique organisation dedicated to the aim of fostering volunteerism in the greater Auckland area and

ensuring a positive experience for volunteers. It aims also to increase public awareness of volunteerism, its benefits and its values to the community. Volunteering Auckland assists registered NFP Community Agencies with the management of their volunteer programmes by offering access to corporate volunteers – the projects undertaken are usually for a half to a full day as a team building exercise for corporate personnel. Volunteering Auckland is also active in the national and international forum, representing the interests of its registered agencies at conferences, workshops and government projects. Volunteering Auckland has approximately 200 not for profit, non governmental agencies registered with it who are looking for volunteers to enhance their services. Volunteering Auckland advertises around the city and in local papers to attract people like you to come in for an interview. We interview you to find out what type of volunteer activity you would like to get involved in, match you up with a voluntary position within an agency, then arrange an appointment for you, where they will explain in more detail about the position on offer. If the position is not suitable and you require other options you are able to contact Volunteering Auckland by phone, as once we have your details in the computer there is no need for you to visit us in person. This also applies if you require volunteer work in the future, or encounter any problems in your volunteer work. On behalf of our agencies we ask for at least six months' commitment as the agency can spend a lot of time and energy in training you for your position. It is a policy at some of our registered agencies that a conviction check may be required, in particular if the agency is dealing with children, the elderly or vulnerable clients. Volunteering is about: HEART, GIVING BACK TO THE COMMUNITY, MAKING A DIFFERENCE. And most important FUN! Voluntary activity takes as little as ONE hour per week. It is not a lot! You can volunteer during the day, in the evenings or on the weekend … The time required, however, for your voluntary activity is dependent on the type of position you are looking for. We trust that you will enjoy your volunteer experience and help us to help you 'make a difference'!
Starting months: Feb, Mar, Apr, May, Jun, Jul, Aug, Sep, Oct, Nov
Time required: 24–52 weeks (plus)
Age: 16 plus – no upper limit
Causes: Addicts/Ex-Addicts, AIDS/HIV, Animal Welfare, Archaeology, Architecture, Children, Conservation, Disabled (learning and physical), Elderly People, Environmental Causes, Health

Care/Medical, Heritage, Holidays for Disabled, Human Rights, Inner City Problems, Offenders/Ex-Offenders, Poor/Homeless, Refugees, Teaching/assisting (nursery, primary, secondary, mature, EFL) Unemployed, Wildlife, Work Camps – Seasonal, Young People.
Activities: Accountancy, Administration, Agriculture/Farming, Arts/Crafts, Building/ Construction, Campaigning, Caring (general, day and residential), Catering, Community Work, Computers, Conservation Skills, Cooking, Counselling, Development Issues, DIY, Driving, First Aid, Forestry, Fundraising, Gardening/Horticulture, Group Work, International Aid, Library/Resource Centres, Manual Work, Marketing/Publicity, Music, Newsletter/Journalism, Outdoor Skills, Religion, Research, Scientific Work, Social Work, Sport, Summer Camps, Teaching, Technical Skills, Theatre/Drama, Training, Translating, Visiting/Befriending, Work Camps – Seasonal.
When to apply: Whenever you decide you want to give your time, energy and skills to our community – telephone us for an appointment.
Work alone/with others: Volunteering is flexible – with projects to suit individuals, groups and families too.
Qualifications: No particular qualifications are necessary, however a willing heart is essential. With over 140 different nationalities and ethnic groups now living in Auckland, our volunteers are multi-national.
Health requirements: Most positions require a general level of health and fitness.
Costs: It is free to register with Volunteering Auckland. Accommodation and food costs to be met by volunteer.
Benefits: Volunteering is all about giving your time to help somebody or something – to help your community. Whatever your situation – supporting a worthwhile cause through volunteering can give you a lot in return.
Training: Most positions registered with us have orientation training and some require specialised training. Information on application.
Worldwide placements: Australasia (New Zealand).

VOLUNTEERING AUSTRALIA

Suite 2/33
Queens Road
Melbourne
Victoria 3004 Australia
T: 00 61 3 9820 4100
F: 00 61 3 9820 1206
E: volaus@infoxchange.net.au
W: www.volunteeringaustralia.org
Contact: Sha Cordingley

Volunteering Australia promotes and has information about volunteering in Australia. It may well be able to put volunteers in touch with organisations which are not yet listed on the WorldWide Volunteering database.

Starting months: January–December
Time required: 1–52 weeks (plus)
Age: 16 plus – no upper limit
Causes: Addicts/Ex-Addicts, AIDS/HIV, Animal Welfare, Archaeology, Architecture, Children, Conservation, Disabled (learning and physical), Elderly People, Environmental Causes, Health Care/Medical, Heritage, Holidays for Disabled, Human Rights, Inner City Problems, Offenders/ Ex-Offenders, Poor/Homeless, Refugees, Teaching/assisting (nursery, primary, secondary, mature, EFL) Unemployed, Wildlife, Work Camps – Seasonal, Young People.
Activities: Accountancy, Administration, Agriculture/Farming, Arts/Crafts, Building/Construction, Campaigning, Caring (general, day and residential), Catering, Community Work, Computers, Conservation Skills, Cooking, Counselling, Development Issues, DIY, Driving, First Aid, Forestry, Fundraising, Gardening/Horticulture, Group Work, International Aid, Library/Resource Centres, Manual Work, Marketing/Publicity, Music, Newsletter/Journalism, Outdoor Skills, Religion, Research, Scientific Work, Social Work, Sport, Summer Camps, Teaching, Technical Skills, Theatre/Drama, Training, Translating, Visiting/Befriending, Work Camps – Seasonal.
Costs: Varies according to the project.
Worldwide placements: Australasia (Australia).

VOLUNTEERING CANTERBURY

Box 13 – 698
141 Hereford Street
Christchurch 8031
New Zealand
T: 0064 3366 2442
F: 0064 3366 0117
E: vc@volcan.org.nz
W: www.volcan.org.nz
Contact: Ruth Gardner

Volunteering Canterbury promotes, supports and upholds the integrity of voluntary work which is done of one's own free will, unpaid for the common good Aroha k te Takata a Rohe. They provide information about volunteering in Canterbury, New Zealand. It may well be able to put volunteers in touch with organisations which are not yet listed on the WorldWide Volunteering database.

Starting months: January–December
Time required: 1–52 weeks (plus)
Age: 16 plus – no upper limit

Causes: Addicts/Ex-Addicts, AIDS/HIV, Animal Welfare, Archaeology, Architecture, Children, Conservation, Disabled (learning and physical), Elderly People, Environmental Causes, Health Care/Medical, Heritage, Holidays for Disabled, Human Rights, Inner City Problems, Offenders/ Ex-Offenders, Poor/Homeless, Refugees, Teaching/assisting (nursery, primary, secondary, mature, EFL) Unemployed, Wildlife, Work Camps – Seasonal, Young People.
Activities: Accountancy, Administration, Agriculture/Farming, Arts/Crafts, Building/ Construction, Campaigning, Caring (general, day and residential), Catering, Community Work, Computers, Conservation Skills, Cooking, Counselling, Development Issues, DIY, Driving, First Aid, Forestry, Fundraising, Gardening/Horticulture, Group Work, International Aid, Library/Resource Centres, Manual Work, Marketing/Publicity, Music, Newsletter/Journalism, Outdoor Skills, Religion, Research, Scientific Work, Social Work, Sport, Summer Camps, Teaching, Technical Skills, Theatre/Drama, Training, Translating, Visiting/Befriending, Work Camps – Seasonal.
When to apply: At any time. Details of positions available can be seen on our web site.
Qualifications: For most positions volunteers will need to have a sufficient standard of English to be easily understood on the telephone.
Costs: No cost to volunteers.
Worldwide placements: Australasia (New Zealand).

VOLUNTEERING IRELAND

Coleraine House
Coleraine Street
Dublin 7
Republic of Ireland
T: 00 353 1 872 2622
F: 00 353 1 872 2623
E: info@volunteeringireland.com
W: www.volunteeringireland.com
Contact: Sandra Velthuis

Volunteering Ireland promotes, supports and facilitates volunteering in the Republic of Ireland. Although we involve some volunteers in our own work, the vast majority of potential volunteers are placed with outside organisations. Our volunteer placement services focus primarily on the central Dublin area, although we may be able to put people in contact with organisations outside this area. If board and lodging are required, we have a list of organisations which provide such volunteering opportunities on our web site and on a free factsheet.

Starting months: January–December
Time required: 1–52 weeks (plus)

Age: 16 plus – no upper limit
Causes: Addicts/Ex-Addicts, AIDS/HIV, Animal Welfare, Archaeology, Architecture, Children, Conservation, Disabled (learning and physical), Elderly People, Environmental Causes, Health Care/Medical, Heritage, Holidays for Disabled, Human Rights, Inner City Problems, Offenders/ Ex-Offenders, Poor/Homeless, Refugees, Teaching/assisting (nursery, primary, secondary, mature, EFL) Unemployed, Wildlife, Work Camps – Seasonal, Young People.
Activities: Accountancy, Administration, Agriculture/Farming, Arts/Crafts, Building/ Construction, Campaigning, Caring (general, day and residential), Catering, Community Work, Computers, Conservation Skills, Cooking, Counselling, Development Issues, DIY, Driving, First Aid, Forestry, Fundraising, Gardening/Horticulture, Group Work, International Aid, Library/Resource Centres, Manual Work, Marketing/Publicity, Music, Newsletter/Journalism, Outdoor Skills, Religion, Research, Scientific Work, Social Work, Sport, Summer Camps, Teaching, Technical Skills, Theatre/Drama, Training, Translating, Visiting/Befriending, Work Camps – Seasonal.
Placements: 1400 in 2002
Costs: Varies according to the project.
Worldwide placements: Europe (Ireland).

VOLUNTEERING WAIKATO – NEW ZEALAND

2nd Floor Caro Street Community Building
PO Box 19-111
Hamilton
New Zealand
T: 00 64 7 839 3191
F: 00 64 7 839 7987
E: volunteeringwaikato@xtra.co.nz
Contact: Sue Chapman

Volunteering Waikato promotes and has information about volunteering in New Zealand. It may well be able to put volunteers in touch with organisations which are not yet listed on the WorldWide Volunteering database.

Starting months: January–December
Time required: 1–52 weeks (plus)
Age: 16 plus – no upper limit
Causes: Addicts/Ex-Addicts, AIDS/HIV, Animal Welfare, Archaeology, Architecture, Children, Conservation, Disabled (learning and physical), Elderly People, Environmental Causes, Health Care/Medical, Heritage, Holidays for Disabled, Human Rights, Inner City Problems, Offenders/ Ex-Offenders, Poor/Homeless, Refugees, Teaching/assisting (nursery, primary, secondary, mature, EFL) Unemployed, Wildlife, Work Camps – Seasonal, Young People.
Activities: Accountancy, Administration, Agriculture/Farming, Arts/Crafts, Building/

Construction, Campaigning, Caring (general, day and residential), Catering, Community Work, Computers, Conservation Skills, Cooking, Counselling, Development Issues, DIY, Driving, First Aid, Forestry, Fundraising, Gardening/Horticulture, Group Work, International Aid, Library/Resource Centres, Manual Work, Marketing/Publicity, Music, Newsletter/Journalism, Outdoor Skills, Religion, Research, Scientific Work, Social Work, Sport, Summer Camps, Teaching, Technical Skills, Theatre/Drama, Training, Translating, Visiting/Befriending, Work Camps – Seasonal.
Costs: Varies according to the project.
Worldwide placements: Australasia (New Zealand).

VOLUNTEERS FOR OUTDOOR COLORADO

600 South Marion Parkway
Denver
Colorado 80209 USA
T: 00 1 303 715 1010 ext.13
F: 00 1 303 715 1212
E: voc@voc.org
W: www.voc.org
Contact: Wendy Hodges

Volunteers for Outdoor Colorado (VOC) is a non-profit organisation formed in 1984 to engage volunteers in improving Colorado's public lands. Each year VOC performs between 10 and 12 weekend outdoor service projects. These projects vary in size from 75 to 1,000 volunteers. We travel all over the state to find fun, interesting and worthwhile service projects for our volunteers. VOC provides all the tools, crew leading and food for these projects. VOC also serves as a clearinghouse for other volunteer opportunities and internships around the state of Colorado. Included in the VOC network are hundreds of volunteer opportunities with agencies such as the National Park Service, US Forest Service, Bureau of Land Management and Colorado State Parks and other non-profit organisations. Positions vary from one time events to summer long internships. Volunteers should visit our web site for the most current information on volunteer positions throughout the year. Individuals or groups wishing to pursue any of these volunteer possibilities should contact our office by phone, fax, e-mail, postal mail, or visit our web site (www.voc.org). The projects are contained in the VOC projects section and the other volunteers opportunities are contained in the VOC Network section. Instructions for how to use the Network are located on the web site. Volunteers with an offending background are accepted. ♿ 📄

Number of projects: 400+ only Colorado **UK:** 0
Starting months: January–December

Time required: 1–26 weeks
Age: 14–80
Causes: Archaeology, Conservation, Environmental Causes, Wildlife, Young People.
Activities: Building/Construction, Community Work, Conservation Skills, Forestry, Gardening/Horticulture, Group Work, Manual Work, Outdoor Skills, Scientific Work, Training.
Placements: 4000+
When to apply: All year.
Work alone/with others: Depends on the position. On VOC projects always with others.
Qualifications: Depends on the position.
Equipment/clothing: Volunteers must have their own transportation and overnight gear if they are planning on camping out on a VOC project. Accommodations and necessary equipment for VOC Network opportunities varies for each position.
Health requirements: Depends on the position.
Costs: Depends on the project.
Benefits: Some positions offer housing, stipend, travel allowance.
Training: Depends on the position.
Supervision: Depends on the position.
Interviews: Prospective volunteers may be interviewed, depending on the project.
Worldwide placements: North America: (USA).

VSO

317 Putney Bridge Road
London
SW15 2PN UK
T: +44 (0) 20 8780 7500
F: +44 (0) 20 8780 7300
E: enquiry@vso.org.uk
W: www.vso.org.uk
Contact: Heidi Rothwell

VSO is an international development charity that works through volunteers. VSO enables people aged 17–70 to share their skills and experience with communities and organisations across the developing world. We passionately believe we can make a difference in tackling poverty and disadvantage by helping people realise their potential. Placements are in education, health, natural resources, technical trades, engineering, business, communications and social development. Over 1,900 volunteers work in 71 countries in Africa, Asia, Eastern Europe and the Pacific. Standard VSO placements overseas are usually for one to two years. VSO youth programmes offer shorter placements. Volunteers must be willing to work for a modest living allowance. Volunteers with an offending background are accepted. ♿ 📄

Number of projects: 1800 **UK:** 0
Starting months: Jan, Feb, Apr, May, Sep
Time required: 26–52 weeks (plus)

Age: 17–70
Causes: AIDS/HIV, Children, Conservation, Disabled (learning and physical), Environmental Causes, Health Care/Medical, Inner City Problems, Teaching/assisting (primary, secondary, mature), Teaching (EFL), Wildlife, Young People.
Activities: Accountancy, Administration, Agriculture/Farming, Arts/Crafts, Building/Construction, Catering, Community Work, Computers, Conservation Skills, Forestry, Fundraising, Gardening/Horticulture, Library/Resource Centres, Marketing/Publicity, Music, Newsletter/Journalism, Research, Social Work, Sport, Teaching, Technical Skills, Training.
Placements: 900
When to apply: All year – only on standard application form.
Work alone/with others: Either.
Qualifications: Mainstream programme – usually requires professional qualification and relevant work experience.
Youth programmes – interest in working in the UK and overseas communities – qualifications not important.
Health requirements: Yes.
Costs: Negligible.
Benefits: Modest living allowance, accommodation, health insurance, travel costs, training.
Training: All volunteers receive training suitable to their placement overseas.
Supervision: Varies.
Interviews: Interviews take place in London, Netherlands or Canada.
Charity number: 313757
Worldwide placements: Africa (Cameroon, Eritrea, Ethiopia, Gambia, Ghana, Guinea-Bissau, Kenya, Malawi, Mozambique, Namibia, Nigeria, Rwanda, South Africa, Tanzania, Uganda, Zambia, Zimbabwe); Central America (Belize); South America (Guyana); Asia (Bangladesh, Bhutan, Cambodia, China, India, Indonesia, Kazakhstan, Laos, Maldives, Mongolia, Nepal, Pakistan, Philippines, Sri Lanka, Thailand, Vietnam); Australasia (Kiribati, Papua New Guinea, Solomon Islands, Tuvalu, Vanuatu); Europe (Albania, Bosnia-Herzegovina, Bulgaria, Estonia, Hungary, Latvia, Lithuania, Macedonia, Romania, Russia, Slovakia).

VWOP – Nepal

G.P.O. Box 11969
Kathmandu
Nepal11969 Nepal
T: 00 977 1488 773
F: 00 977 1416 144
E: vwop2000@hotmail.com
Contact: B.R. Dumre

VWOP provides voluntary jobs in remote and urban areas of Nepal teaching in schools, farm work, health and environment work throughout the year. Volunteers may implement their own ideas/programmes/activities, invest in education, agriculture, livestock, health, environment etc. in rural areas of Nepal. Experience not essential. Interested volunteers gain first hand experience of living and working with local people and participate in cultural activities, exploring parts of Nepal, and engaging in trekking, whitewater rafting, sightseeing etc. Volunteers stay with local families sharing their home and food and amenities.

Number of projects: 3 UK: 0
Starting months: January–December
Time required: 2–20 weeks
Age: 15–40
Causes: Children, Conservation, Environmental Causes, Health Care/Medical, Poor/Homeless, Teaching/assisting (nursery, primary, secondary, mature, EFL) Young People.
Activities: Agriculture/Farming, Arts/Crafts, Community Work, Conservation Skills, First Aid, Gardening/Horticulture, Music, Research, Social Work, Sport, Teaching, Technical Skills, Theatre/Drama, Training.
Placements: 50
When to apply: Approximately 1month prior to starting date.
Work alone/with others: Work with other volunteers.
Qualifications: No. English language ability is enough.
Equipment/clothing: None needed other than winter/summer clothes.
Health requirements: We are unable to accept volunteers with transferable diseases.
Costs: Volunteers have to pay registration fee – US$20, organisation fee $50, accommodation and food $50/month.
Training: Orientation of local environment and culture.
Supervision: Supervision is undertaken by a member of the organisation occasionally.
Interviews: No.
Worldwide placements: Asia (Nepal).

WAR ON WANT

37–39 Great Guildford Street
London
SE1 OES UK
T: +44 (0) 207 620 1111
T: +44 (0) 207 261 9291
E: drudkin@waronwant.org
W: www.waronwant.org
Contact: David Rudkin

War on Want was established over 50 years ago. It is a membership organisation working with project partners overseas. It does not administer relief aid but financial support for long-term development programmes. It also believes in the need to raise awareness in Britain about the causes of world poverty. This is essential in order to promote the fundamental changes in international policies that are needed before a permanent improvement in the lives of the world's poor can be made. As with all charities, volunteers are used extensively at War on Want. They are required only at our London office, primarily for administrative support. However, there are occasional campaign-based tasks, e.g. attending conferences, representing WOW at NGO meetings etc. 🖐

Number of projects: 19+ UK: 0
Starting months: January–December
Time required: 4–52 weeks
Age: 21–75
Causes: Human Rights, Inner City Problems, Young People.
Activities: Administration, Campaigning, Computers, Development Issues, Fundraising, International Aid.
Placements: 20
When to apply: All year.
Work alone/with others: Both.
Qualifications: Excellent English, A levels or computer skills or willingness to learn quickly.
Costs: Accommodation costs.
Benefits: £4.50 for lunch plus travel costs.
Training: Briefing but most training is on the job.
Supervision: All volunteers allocated one member of staff or supervisor.
Charity number: 208724
Worldwide placements: South America (Brazil).
UK placements: England (London).

WARWICKSHIRE ASSOCIATION OF YOUTH CLUBS

Arno House
63 Willes Road
Leamington Spa
Warwickshire CV31 1BN UK
T: 01926 450156
F: 01926 313328
E: info@wayc.org.uk
W: www.wayc.org.uk
Contact: William Clemmey

Warwickshire Association of Youth Clubs is an association of 115 youth clubs working with over 9,000 young people and over 900 youth workers in Warwickshire, Coventry and Solihull. We were established as a charity in 1954 to meet the needs of youth organisations working with young people up to the age of 25. We also work directly with young people, regardless of race, creed, sex or disability. We are affiliated to Young Warwickshire and to UK Youth. The main duties and responsibilities are:
1. To help with the delivery and development of the youth work amongst affiliated clubs and groups of young people throughout Coventry, Warwickshire and Solihull. This will be done in close collaboration with the staff.
2. To establish relationships and a style of working that will enable the young people to: find out about themselves and realise their abilities and potential; develop and maintain relationships with others; actively participate in the decision making processes of the programme, resource allocation, etc.; identify, understand, confront and challenge attitudes, behaviour and practices which discriminate against any individual, or group based on race, gender, disability, economic circumstances, belief or sexuality; raise and explore issues relevant to them; experience new challenges in a supportive and comfortable environment; recognise the social, political and legal structures which affect their lives and examine strategies in order to challenge and in turn effect or change those structures.
3. When needed to provide reports of your work. You will help to monitor and evaluate the work with young people, staff members and the council of management.
4. To work in partnership with the statutory youth and community services in Coventry, Solihull and Warwickshire and youth workers in the voluntary and maintained sectors.
5. To be responsible for keeping within any budget that is allocated to you. You will be held accountable for such expenditure.

6. To take a full part in the staff development programme offered by the Association.
7. To carry out any other duties as agreed with the executive director that relates to the work of the Association
We are able to support and provide Youth Achievement Award and First Gear Course opportunities. We also run a Millennium Volunteers Programme for 16–24 year olds. Our events and competitions programme includes: netball, pool, ice skating, dance, five-a-side football and unihoc. Young people are also involved in international youth work. In Easter 2001 we were involved in a quadrilateral youth exchange with Russia, Denmark and Belarus. Our environmental 'Springboard' project offers young people the opportunity to explore environmental issues and take part in action that means something to them. We have a new 12-berth narrowboat Dream Catcher which can be borrowed by youth groups, schools and disabled groups. We are seeking volunteer helmsmen for this. Our database of experts enables youngsters to take part in a variety of sports and arts workshops and projects whatever their location Coventry, Solihull, Leamington Spa, Nuneaton, Warwick, Kenilworth, Rugby, Stratford etc. 🚹 📄

Number of projects: 4 UK: 3
Starting months: January–December
Time required: 1–52 weeks (plus)
Age: 16–70
Causes: Young People.
Activities: Administration, Arts/Crafts, Computers, Driving, Fundraising, Group Work, Marketing/Publicity, Music, Newsletter/Journalism, Outdoor Skills, Sport, Summer Camps, Theatre/Drama, Training.
Placements: 120
When to apply: Any time of year, preferably at least a month in advance.
Work alone/with others: Both.
Qualifications: No qualifications although an interest in youth work is needed.
Equipment/clothing: Normal clothes.
Health requirements: Health requirements.
Costs: None although you would need to find accomodation, food etc.
Benefits: Travel costs.
Training: We offer training.
Supervision: We supervise our workers.
Interviews: We would interview candidates before appointment.
Charity number: 1056035
UK placements: England (Warwickshire, West Midlands).

WARWICKSHIRE WILDLIFE TRUST

Brandon Marsh Nature Centre
Brandon Lane
Coventry
Warwickshire CV3 3GW UK

T: 024 7630 8975
F: 024 7663 9556
E: PDickin@warkswt.cix.co.uk
Contact: Phil Dickin

Warwickshire Wildlife Trust is the leading local environmental charity, dedicated to protecting wildlife and natural habitats throughout Warwickshire, Coventry and Solihull. It is one of 47 independent trusts forming the Wildlife Trusts – the largest body in the UK concerned with all aspects of nature conservation. The Trust manages over 50 nature reserves totalling over 2,000 acres, including woodlands, meadows and wetlands. Practical work on these reserves is carried out by a network of local volunteers. The Trust also works to protect wildlife by campaigning on nature conservation issues, by liaising with other organisations, individuals and community groups, and by promoting a greater awareness of conservation to the general public. The Trust promotes wildlife education in schools, colleges and local communities through talks, exhibitions and guided walks. The Trust's junior membership is part of the national environment club – Wildlife Watch – which provides projects for members and affiliated schools, so involving them directly with environmental issues.
The Trust's flagship Nature Centre at Brandon Marsh just outside Coventry was opened by Sir David Attenborough in 1992. Its 200 acres of pools and wetlands are now visited by over 25,000 people each year, including over 5,000 children on organised educational activities. The Centre is open every day from 9–5 (10–5 at weekends). In addition to income from membership, the Trust raises funds by sponsorship, grants, donations and legacies. The Trust is organised through a Council of Trustees elected from its members, who provide the overall direction for the development of the Trust. On a day-to-day basis conservation work is carried out by a staff of 32, based at the Trust offices at Brandon Marsh Nature Centre. Volunteers with an offending background may be accepted but not for work with children. 🚹

Number of projects: 50+ UK: 50+
Starting months: January–December
Time required: 1–52 weeks (plus)
Age: 14 plus – no upper limit
Causes: Animal Welfare, Children, Conservation, Environmental Causes, Heritage, Inner City Problems, Teaching/assisting (primary, secondary, mature), Unemployed, Wildlife, Young People.
Activities: Administration, Arts/Crafts, Campaigning, Community Work, Conservation Skills, Development Issues, Forestry, Fundraising, Gardening/Horticulture, Group Work, Library/Resource Centres, Manual Work, Marketing/Publicity, Newsletter/Journalism,

Outdoor Skills, Research, Scientific Work, Teaching, Training.
Placements: 20
When to apply: All year.
Work alone/with others: With others.
Equipment/clothing: Loaned.
Health requirements: Nil.
Costs: Accommodation.
Benefits: Travel costs and expenses reimbursed.
Training: Depends on the person and the opportunity we offer.
Supervision: All volunteers are closely supervised. Responsibility will be given to individuals who have shown a clear ability to take on responsibility.
Interviews: Interviews take place at Brandon Marsh Nature Centre.
Charity number: 209200
UK placements: England (Warwickshire, West Midlands).

WATERWAY RECOVERY GROUP – CANAL CAMPS

P.O. Box 114
Rickmansworth
WD3 1ZY UK
T: 01923 711114
F: 01923 897000
E: enquiries@wrg.org.uk
W: www.wrg.org.uk
Contact: Enquiries Officer

In helping to restore one of Britain's derelict canals, you will have the opportunity to do a hundred and one things that you have never done before and earn yourself a place in canal restoration history! You will be meeting all sorts of new people, having a lively social life in the evenings and you could find yourself doing any, if not all of the following: restoring industrial archaeology; demolishing old brickwork structures; bricklaying and pouring concrete; driving a dumper truck; clearing a lock chamber of 'orrible black slimy silt; helping to run a major national waterways festival; cooking for 20 hungry volunteers; clearing vegetation and felling trees. For a worthwhile and fun-filled week with about 20 or so like-minded people, all you need is to be reasonably fit, over 17, and able to cope with the basic facilities of village hall accommodation. No skills or previous experience required, just a willingness to get involved and have fun!

Number of projects: 30 **UK:** 30
Starting months: January–December
Time required: 1–22 weeks
Age: 17–70
Causes: Archaeology, Conservation, Environmental Causes, Heritage, Work Camps – Seasonal.

Activities: Building/Construction, Conservation Skills, Forestry, Manual Work, Outdoor Skills, Summer Camps, Work Camps – Seasonal.
Placements: 1,000
When to apply: All year.
Work alone/with others: With others.
Qualifications: Volunteers not resident in the UK must be over 21 and for site safety reasons must have a working knowledge of English.
Equipment/clothing: Outdoor working clothes, strong work or wellington boots (steel toe capped), sleeping bag.
Health requirements: Reasonable fitness.
Costs: £35 per week towards food and accommodation or £5 per day.
Benefits: Accommodation in village halls or similar.
Training: All training is provided at the camp although there is an optional annual training weekend.
Supervision: Each residential camp has leaders responsible for supervising the work tasks.
Interviews: Applicants are not interviewed.
Charity number: 212342
UK placements: England (Buckinghamshire, Cornwall, Derbyshire, Devon, Essex, Gloucestershire, Herefordshire, Hertfordshire, Leicestershire, Lincolnshire, Shropshire, Somerset, Staffordshire, Suffolk, Surrey, E. Sussex, W. Sussex, Wiltshire, Worcestershire, N. Yorkshire, W. Yorkshire).

WEC INTERNATIONAL

Bulstrode
Oxford Road
Gerrards Cross
BuckinghamshireSL9 8SZ UK
T: 01753 884631
F: 01753 278166
E: trek.bulstrode@talk21.com
W: www.wectrekuk.org
Contact: Sheila Kilkenny

WEC International is an interdenominational mission agency with workers in many countries around the world. Our aim is to share the Gospel with people who have never heard it. As well as church-related activities, workers are involved in community development projects, rehabilitation programmes, medical work, teaching (primary, secondary and teaching English as a second language), administration and working with children. Small numbers of volunteers are needed for various tasks in a number of countries to help long-term personnel.

Number of projects: 50+ **UK:** 3
Starting months: January–December
Time required: 4–36 weeks
Age: 18–70
Causes: Addicts/Ex-Addicts, AIDS/HIV, Children, Health Care/Medical, Poor/Homeless,

Refugees, Teaching/assisting (nursery, primary, secondary, EFL), Unemployed, Young People. **Activities:** Accountancy, Administration, Agriculture/Farming, Arts/Crafts, Building/Construction, Caring – General, Catering, Community Work, Computers, Cooking, Counselling, Development Issues, DIY, Driving, First Aid, Library/Resource Centres, Manual Work, Music, Outdoor Skills, Religion, Research, Social Work, Sport, Summer Camps, Teaching, Technical Skills, Theatre/Drama, Training, Translating, Visiting/Befriending, Work Camps – Seasonal.
Placements: 40+
When to apply: At least 4 months in advance.
Work alone/with others: Individuals join permanent team in host country, teams consist of 4–10.
Qualifications: Evangelical Christians. Teachers, maintenance/mechanical and general help/medical doctors, nurses, obstetricians, midwives/secretaries/computer specialists. Must be UK resident.
Equipment/clothing: Information from country of service.
Health requirements: Good health is necessary.
Costs: All costs are paid by the volunteers.
Benefits: Arranged at each location by host group.
Training: WEC Trek has 5 days training for all participants. All volunteers are required to attend an orientation course before final acceptance for any position.
Supervision: The leader of each placement has full responsibility for supervision.
Interviews: Interviews take place at WEC HQ, Gerrards Cross or at the nearest WEC base in the UK.
Charity number: 237005
Worldwide placements: Africa (Burkina Faso, Chad, Côte d'Ivoire, Equatorial Guinea, Gambia, Ghana, Guinea, Guinea-Bissau, Senegal, Sierra Leone, South Africa); Central America (Mexico); South America (Brazil); Asia (Japan, Taiwan, Thailand); Australasia (Australia, Fiji, New Zealand); Europe (Albania, Bulgaria, France, Spain).
UK placements: England (Buckinghamshire, Lancashire, West Midlands).

WELSHPOOL AND LLANFAIR LIGHT RAILWAY

The Station
Llanfair
Caereinion
Welshpool
Powys SY21 0SF UK Wales
T: 01938 810441
E: info@wllr.org.uk
Contact: Frank Cooper

Welshpool and Llanfair Light Railway is a restored Edwardian railway in beautiful Mid-Wales countryside. 🌐

Number of projects: 1 UK: 1
Starting months: January–December
Time required: 1–52 weeks
Age: 16–80
Causes: Conservation, Heritage.
Activities: Building/Construction, Conservation Skills, Forestry, Manual Work, Outdoor Skills, Summer Camps, Technical Skills.
Placements: 350
When to apply: All year.
Work alone/with others: With others.
Equipment/clothing: Overalls, steel capped work boots.
Health requirements: Fit, healthy, no medication which may affect work ability.
Costs: Travel, board, lodging and pocket money.
Benefits: Subsidised accommodation – no pocket money. Youth hostel style.
Training: As required, depending on actual job.
Supervision: We have paid management and 'regular' volunteer supervisors.
Charity number: 1000378
UK placements: Wales (Powys).

WEST YORKSHIRE YOUTH ASSOCIATION

Investing in Success Project
Kettlethorpe Youth Centre
Standbridge Lane
Kettlethorpe
WF2 7NW UK
T: 01924 256686
F: 01924 242306
E: headoffice@wyya.co.uk
Contact: Andy Clow

The West Yorkshire Youth Association has always made the needs and welfare of young people central to the activities and organisation since its inception in 1907. Now it is a dynamic organisation running nine projects. We are looking to continue that development as we build on our work to meet the needs of many young people, within cities, rural communities and on a county wide basis. The Association works to provide opportunities and support for young people in training and employment, housing, the arts, involvement in the community, sports and outdoor pursuits and the running of a residential centre open to all young people. In order that we can convert ideas and needs into reality we work with communities, local authorities and trusts to continue to meet more of the needs and develop the aspirations of young people across West Yorkshire. Volunteers with an offending background may be accepted depending on the role and the offence. 🌐 📷

Number of projects: 9 UK: 9
Starting months: January–December
Time required: 1–52 weeks
Age: 16 plus – no upper limit
Causes: Young People.
Activities: Arts/Crafts, Outdoor Skills, Sport.
When to apply: All year.
Work alone/with others: With others.
Health requirements: Nil.
Costs: Accommodation.
Benefits: Depending on budgets of individual
projects.
Training: If needed.
Supervision: Yes.
Interviews: Applicants are interviewed at the
base/office of the particular project.
Charity number: 519883
UK placements: England (W. Yorkshire).

WESTERN AUSTRALIAN AIDS COUNCIL

664 Murray Street
West Perth
6005 Australia
T: 00 61 8 9482 0000
F: 00 61 8 9482 0001
E: waac@waaids.com
W: www.waaids.com
Contact: Volunteer Co-ordinator

The West Australian AIDS Council needs the
support of volunteers. Without this support,
vital services would not be able to function.
HIV/AIDS affects the lives of hundreds of
people in Western Australia. We need your
support to continue to help people living with
HIV/AIDS and to prevent the further
transmission of HIV. Support services:
volunteers help to improve the quality of life
for people living with HIV/AIDS. Volunteers
provide transport and other practical assistance
in the home, as well as emotional support.
Qualified practitioners of complementary
therapies such as massage, volunteer their skills
in our Living Well Programme. Volunteers of
support services give approximately four hours
per week with the majority of volunteer work
occurring during weekdays. Community
education: volunteers play a vital role in
improving the general communities'
understanding and knowledge of HIV/AIDS and
accompanying issues. Education on safer
practices aims to prevent the further
transmission of HIV. There are a number of
ways volunteers can make a difference in their
community. Some of these include providing
resources, information and referrals on the
AIDSline, and through the Needle and Syringe
Exchange Programme. Volunteers can also
provide informative presentations to schools
and other community groups. Weekday work is
available with some weekend and after hours
work also available. Peer education: volunteers

reduce the impact and further transmission of
HIV/AIDS through their work with men who
have sex with men. There are plenty of
opportunities to become involved in the
community. Volunteers provide outreach
services, groups and workshops and a telephone
information and referral service. Peer Education
programmes mostly operate in the evening,
with limited weekday work available. Freedom
centre: volunteers provide support and
information to young people with same sex
attractions through a youth drop in centre.
Shifts are available in the evenings and
volunteers must be 27 years old or under. Perth
Metropolitan Area.

Number of projects: 15 UK: 0
Starting months: January–December
Time required: 26–52 weeks (plus)
Age: 18 plus – no upper limit
Causes: Addicts/Ex-Addicts, AIDS/HIV, Young
People.
Activities: Administration, Caring – Day,
Community Work, Fundraising,
Visiting/Befriending.
Placements: 300
When to apply: When the volunteer arrives in
Perth.
Work alone/with others: With other young
volunteers.
Qualifications: Own transport occasionally.
Volunteer training day required by some projects.
Health requirements: Nil.
Costs: Training course A$30.
Benefits: Out of pocket expenses reimbursed.
Training: 4–5 days training provided.
Supervision: Yes.
Interviews: Yes.
Worldwide placements: Australasia (Australia).

WESTON SPIRIT

5th Floor
Cotton House, Old Hall Street
Liverpool
MerseysideL3 9WS UK
T: 0151 258 1066
F: 0151 258 1388
E: info@westonspirit.org.uk
W: www.westonspirit.org.uk
Contact: Sally Neale

Weston Spirit works in the inner city areas of
the UK offering disengaged young people a real
alternative to problems such as unemployment,
drugs, alcohol misuse, homelessness and abuse,
amongst other things. Our aim is to encourage
young people predominantly aged 15–18 years
from major British cities to reassess their
attitude and their role within the communities
in which they live.
Recruitment: talks are carried out in youth
training centres, schools, youth clubs, through

outreach workers and word of mouth, as well as referrals from the social, careers and probation services. Any young person aged between 15–18 years and living within commuting distance of a city centre base is eligible for the programme. Intro day: interested individuals attend a day of activities which include team building, discussions and ice breaking exercises before participating in a residential course. Residential experience: a week-long intensive course towards the development of team building values, community involvement and inter-personal skills. This is the foundation of the Weston Spirit membership. Membership: continued development in their home area through a positive programme of activities run from a city base. These include educational, training and employment opportunities, group work and social awareness, enterprise skills and project work, counselling and community involvement. Weston Spirit also offers short courses to young people aged 13–25 across the UK which include working with young offenders. Projects: Reach for the Sky Roadshow, travelling UK to provide young people with exciting personal development opportunities. Up2U Awards – giving young people across the UK opportunity to have a say and vote for community awards. Training for adults through trading company (Weston Spirit Trading Ltd). Volunteers with an offending background are accepted – depending on offence. 🔊

Number of projects: 9 **UK:** 9
Starting months: January–December
Time required: 1–52 weeks
Age: 14–25
Causes: Inner City Problems, Offenders/Ex-Offenders, Poor/Homeless, Unemployed, Young People.
Activities: Administration, Community Work, Cooking, Counselling, Driving, Fundraising, Group Work, Library/Resource Centres, Marketing/Publicity, Training.
Placements: 20
When to apply: All year.
Work alone/with others: Both.
Qualifications: No special qualifications.
Health requirements: Nil.
Costs: Cost of weekly visits to drop-in centres.
Benefits: Most expenses are paid by Weston Spirit.
Training: Yes, and induction.
Supervision: Yes.
Interviews: Interviews are conducted in relevant city centre base or national office.
Charity number: 327937
UK placements: England (Berkshire, London, Manchester, Merseyside, Nottinghamshire, Tyne and Wear, West Midlands, N. Yorkshire, W. Yorkshire); Northern Ireland (Belfast City); Wales (Cardiff, Merthyr Tydfil).

WEYMOUTH CANOE LIFEGUARDS

WOEC
Knightsdale Road
Weymouth
Dorset UK
E: info@weymouthlifeguards.co.uk
W: www.weymouthlifeguards.co.uk
Contact: Paul Seys

Weymouth Canoe Lifeguards are a group of volunteers operating off Weymouth beach on the Dorset coast. We mainly cover events during the summer months and occasionally cover nationally as part of the BCU Lifeguards. Dorset coast. 📄

Number of projects: 1 **UK:** 1
Starting months: January–December
Time required: 1–52 weeks
Age: 14 plus – no upper limit
Causes: Children, Health Care/Medical, Young People.
Activities: Community Work, First Aid, Fundraising, Group Work, Outdoor Skills, Sport.
Placements: 80
When to apply: All year round.
Work alone/with others: With others.
Qualifications: Not to start with but all lifeguard qualifications are obtainable.
Equipment/clothing: Wetsuit etc.
Health requirements: N/A.
Costs: £12 a year membership. Any accommodation costs.
Training: Full, regular lifeguard training is undertaken. Volunteers train approx. 3–4 times a week.
Supervision: When involved in rescue covers there is always a senior lifeguard present. All training sessions are adequately supervised.
Interviews: Yes, at the address in Weymouth.
UK placements: England (Dorset).

WILD ANIMAL RESCUE FOUNDATION OF THAILAND

235 Sukhumvit SO1 31
Bangkok
10110 Thailand
T: (662) 261 9670, 662 0898, 261 9672
F: (662) 261 9670
E: war@warthai.org
W: www.warthai.org
Contact: Khun Pornpen Payakkaporn

The Wild Animal Rescue Foundation of Thailand is a non-profit making organisation dedicated to preventing the maltreatment of wild animals, relieving their suffering and providing a secure and caring environment in which they can live. WAR seeks the help and advice of local and international experts in the rehabilitation of animals back to the wild. WAR also works in conjunction with government and non-governmental agencies in informing people about the need to preserve and protect the environment.

Currently Wild Animal Rescue Foundation operates two wildlife sanctuaries that are focused on providing appropriate housing and care for wild animals in need. Many that are with the Foundation are former pets who, as they matured, were not wanted by their owners. Some have been found abandoned while others have been saved from slaughter. The Foundation's aim is to return the animals to the wild. Unfortunately mature wild animals that have lived almost their entire lives in captivity lack the skills needed to survive on their own. Also those who are disabled or have been traumatised by their experiences with humans are unsuitable for release. These creatures will spend the rest of their lives in one of the sanctuaries where they receive all the care and attention they need. Candidates suitable for return to the wild go through a rehabilitation programme where they learn how to become self-reliant before they are set free. In addition to the sanctuaries WAR also provides assistance at Lopburi Zoo which is operated by the Thai Military and is involved in the protection of the habitats of sea turtles during the egg laying and hatching season. Lopburi Zoo – Lopburi City Central, Thailand. Gibbon Rehabilitation Project – Phuket Island, South West Thailand. The Sea Turtle and Dugong Research Project Ranong – Southern Thailand. Wild Animal Resue and Education Centre, Ranong – Southern Thailand.

Number of projects: 4 **UK:** None
Starting months: January–December
Time required: 3–52 weeks (plus)
Age: 18 plus – no upper limit
Causes: Animal Welfare, Conservation, Teaching/assisting, Wildlife.
Activities: Building/Construction, Campaigning, Fundraising, Manual Work, Teaching.
Placements: 70
When to apply: All year.
Work alone/with others: With other volunteers.
Qualifications: Ability to communicate in English.
Equipment/clothing: Clothing for very hot and at times very wet conditions.
Health requirements: Applicants must be in good general health.
Costs: Travel and subsistence costs registration fee.
Benefits: Shared accommodation in small bungalow type buildings or traditional huts, water and electricity are provided.
Training: On site training.

Supervision: Supervision given by Thai staff and animal handlers.
Interviews: No.
Worldwide placements: Asia (Thailand).

WILD AT HEART

Office Suite 7A Cowell Park
47 Old Main Road
Hillcrest
3610 Kwazulu/Natal South Africa
T: 27 31 765 1818
F: 27 31 765 1818
E: claude@wah.co.za
W: www.wah.co.za
Contact: Tracey

Wild at Heart is actively involved in African conservation. Our various projects which include wildlife rehabilitation centres, monkey sanctuary, reptile parks, wildlife trauma clinics and game farms all benefit from the many skilled and helpful volunteers we receive from around the world. Volunteers participate in every type of activity and workload such as feeding animals, taking care of injured wildlife, tracking elephants and much more. We may be able to place volunteers with an offending background. South Africa, Kruger National Park region.

Number of projects: 13 **UK:** 0
Starting months: January–December
Time required: 2–12 weeks
Age: 18 plus – no upper limit
Causes: Animal Welfare, Conservation, Environmental Causes, Wildlife.
Activities: Agriculture/Farming, Community Work, Conservation Skills, Group Work, Outdoor Skills, Research.
Placements: 1000
When to apply: Any time.
Work alone/with others: Work with others.
Qualifications: Nothing specific.
Equipment/clothing: Natural coloured clothing.
Health requirements: No restrictions.
Costs: Programme fees and travel costs. Please contact us for latest costs.
Benefits: Accommodation and food included in programme cost.
Training: All field guide and animal handling training provided.
Supervision: Project leaders supervise volunteers.
Interviews: No interview.
Worldwide placements: Africa (South Africa).

WILDERNESS TRUST, THE

The General's Orchard
The Ridge, Little Baddow
Chelmsford
Essex CM3 4SX UK

T: 01245 221565
F: 01245 221565
E: info@wilderness-trust.org
W: www.wilderness-trust.org
Contact: Jo Roberts

The Wilderness Trust is a UK charity. Its aims are to provide environmental education through experiential learning, conservation by addressing the urgent need for conservation of wild areas in the UK and abroad through lobbying on all levels, and youth development by arranging youth expeditions to wilderness areas. South Africa: volunteering opportunities in South Africa are available and can be arranged through the Trust. These include:
1. 4–12 week placement at Ben Lavin Reserve in the Northern Province. This inspiring programme continues to grow, with a steady supply of Wilderness Trust volunteers making a contribution to this reserve near the Zimbabwe border in South Africa. Work involves all aspects of running a small reserve and includes management, maintenance and conservation projects. Volunteers can work for a period of six weeks to three months. Ben Lavin is a showcase of community involvement as it was recently handed back to the local Manavhela clan as part of the government sponsored 'right to buy' scheme. The clan in turn have expressed a desire to continue in partnership with previous owners, the Wildlife and Environment Society of Southern Africa, and aim to use the reserve as a centre of learning and excellence in environment. This makes the volunteer programme even more unique involving participation in an important and innovative initiative for the new South Africa. Money raised from the programme will be used to invest in community and education programmes and volunteers can feel that contribution will live on once they have left. The reserve is malaria free and does not have dangerous big game.
2. Three-week youth expeditions to South Africa. These take place during the long UK summer holidays. The programmes include a game rangers course, community and cultural activity, adventure training and walking wilderness trails in designated wilderness areas. Expeditions can be arranged for specific school, college, universities or other youth organisations. Individuals may bid to attend one of the annual open expeditions. Special journeys may be arranged for those with limited physical abilities.
3. The Trust has access to land owned by the Duke of Westminster in northwest Scotland. Wilderness trails are organised for youth leadership, marginalised youth and adults.

4. The Trust has connections with wilderness organisations in Canada, the USA, northern Norway and Italy. Introductions can be given to those who apply to the Trust for opportunities to take part in wilderness trails in those countries.
Cost, dates and placement availability can be obtained on request. Shamwari – Eastern Cape, South Africa.
Ben Lavin – Northern Province, South Africa.
Wilderness expeditions – South Africa.
Scotland – Sutherland. 🦽 📄

Number of projects: 1 UK: 1
Starting months: Jan, Feb, Mar, Apr, May, Jun, Jul, Aug, Sep, Oct, Nov
Time required: 1–16 weeks
Age: 16–70
Causes: Conservation, Disabled (physical), Environmental Causes, Holidays for Disabled, Inner City Problems, Offenders/Ex-Offenders, Wildlife, Young People.
Activities: Community Work, Conservation Skills, Development Issues, Outdoor Skills.
Placements: 40–50
When to apply: All year.
Work alone/with others: With others.
Equipment/clothing: Kit list sent with joining instruction.
Health requirements: Reasonably fit, able to carry a rucksack and walk up to 10 miles a day. Must be prepared to live and sleep in the open on wilderness trails.
Costs: Trail costs including accommodation available on request. All overseas work is self-funding.
Training: On site.
Supervision: Provided by permanent staff or qualified wilderness trail guides on site.
Interviews: Are required for Ben Lavin and expedition placements.
Charity number: 1005826
Worldwide placements: Africa (South Africa); North America (Canada, USA); Europe (Germany, Italy, Norway).
UK placements: Scotland (Aberdeenshire, Angus, Fife, Highland, Moray); Wales (Conwy).

WILDFOWL AND WETLANDS TRUST (WWT)

Slimbridge
Gloucestershire GL2 7BT UK
T: 01453 891900 ext 137
F: 01453 891941
E: anna.weeks@wwt.org.uk
W: www.wwt.org.uk
Contact: Anna Weeks

The Wildfowl and Wetlands Trust is a registered charity whose aim is to preserve and protect wetlands through programmes of scientific study, education and the operation of nine visitor centres around the UK. Volunteers are needed at the visitor centres to help with a variety of practical conservation tasks including: grounds wardening (planting, weeding, trimming etc), reserve management, looking after the birds at the centres (feeding, making nest boxes etc) and reserve wardening (feeding, making nest boxes etc). Additionally, volunteers are also needed to work in the visitor centre working on the information desk, helping with school parties, manning the observation tower, selling membership and grain. We particularly need this help at weekends. Volunteers also help in the education department through teaching and helping with holiday activities. There is also the opportunity to learn a lot about the unique environments of the wetlands themselves and we provide full training, social events and interesting and varied work. Slimbridge, Arundel, Dumfriesshire, Co. Down, Llanelli, Ormskirk and Washington Tyne and Wear + Barnes London. &

Number of projects: 9 UK: 9
Starting months: January–December
Time required: 12–52 weeks (plus)
Age: 16 plus – no upper limit
Causes: Animal Welfare, Conservation, Disabled (learning), Environmental Causes, Holidays for Disabled, Offenders/Ex-Offenders, Poor/ Homeless, Refugees, Teaching/assisting (primary, secondary, mature), Unemployed, Wildlife.
Activities: Administration, Arts/Crafts, Campaigning, Community Work, Conservation Skills, DIY, Gardening/Horticulture, Manual Work, Marketing/Publicity, Newsletter/ Journalism, Outdoor Skills, Scientific Work, Teaching, Training.
Placements: 20+
When to apply: All year.
Work alone/with others: Both.
Qualifications: Driving licence is useful.
Equipment/clothing: Outside gear – waterproof coat and wellies are useful although we can provide these. All essential uniform supplied free of charge.
Health requirements: Need to be fit and healthy for outdoor work but we should be able to find a suitable placement for volunteers of all abilities.
Costs: Own food. If not full time, accommodation and petrol. Free accommodation for full-time placements (on a first come first served basis).
Benefits: For full-time volunteers there is limited space in hostel at Slimbridge which is free. Discount in the on site shop and restaurant. Free uniform. Volunteer social and training programmes.

Training: General induction given at commencement of placement plus more specific training as required.
Supervision: Work alongside other staff with a line manager who supervises and delegates. Overall volunteer co-ordinator as a support role.
Interviews: Interviews take place at the respective WWT Centre.
Charity number: 1030884
UK placements: England (Cambridgeshire, Gloucestershire, Lancashire, London, Norfolk, Sussex – West, Tyne and Wear); Scotland (Dumfries and Galloway); Northern Ireland (Down); Wales (Pembrokeshire).

WILDLIFE TRUST FOR BEDS, CAMBS, NORTHANTS AND PETERBOROUGH

3B Langford Arch
London Road
Sawston, Cambridge
Cambridgeshire CB2 4EE UK
T: 01223 712405
F: 01223 712412
E: lodonnell@cambswt.cix.co.uk
W: www.wildlifetrust.org.uk/bcnp
Contact: Lindsey O'Donnell

The Wildlife Trust for Bedfordshire, Cambridgeshire, Northamptonshire and Peterborough is a voluntary organisation totally committed to protecting the local countryside and its inhabitants. Our concern is for wildlife of all types, rare and common, ranging from orchids to otters, barn owls to badgers, securing their survival for future generations. Our vitally important work will ensure the existence of our precious countryside and the many endangered species currently under threat. Our Wildlife Trust is part of a nation-wide network of local trusts dedicated to all aspects of wildlife protection. It is because of this dedication that the wildlife trusts collectively manage 2,000 nature reserves which include some of the most important sites for wildlife in the UK. Our effectiveness comes from working in partnership with local communities with the common purpose of conserving the countryside. In Bedfordshire, Cambridgeshire and Northamptonshire we manage over 137 nature reserves, screen planning applications and fight to save sites where there is a threat to the survival of wildlife. The trust has 17,300 members throughout its three counties. Volunteers with an offending background may be accepted for certain jobs but not those working with children.

Number of projects: 1 UK: 1
Starting months: January–December
Time required: 1–52 weeks (plus)
Age: 14–80
Causes: Conservation, Environmental Causes, Wildlife.

Activities: Administration, Conservation Skills, Forestry, Manual Work, Marketing/Publicity, Newsletter/Journalism, Outdoor Skills.
Placements: 1,000
When to apply: All year.
Work alone/with others: With others.
Qualifications: Nil. Training/advice given where necessary.
Equipment/clothing: If outside – outdoor clothing/waterproofs/boots if appropriate. Safety gear provided if necessary.
Health requirements: Depends on task – general good health preferred.
Costs: Travel costs. Accommodation and food.
Training: All training is given on the job.
Supervision: It is the responsibility of the person taking on the volunteers to supervise them. By the nature of the job, it cannot be close supervision.
Interviews: Applicants are not interviewed.
Charity number: 11000412
UK placements: England (Bedfordshire, Cambridgeshire, Northamptonshire).

WILDLIFE TRUST FOR BIRMINGHAM AND THE BLACK COUNTRY, THE

28 Harborne Road
Edgbaston
Birmingham
B15 3AA UK
T: +44 (0) 121 454 1199
F: +44 (0) 121 454 6556
E: wendy.b@bbcwildlife.org.uk
W: www.bbcwildlife.org.uk
Contact: Wendy Burnett

The Wildlife Trust for Birmingham and Black Country is an independent voluntary nature conservation organisation. It is a member of the Wildlife Trusts, a national partnership of 47 county trusts. Volunteers are needed to help in the office, help in the horticulture nursery, the environment education centre or to help outposted project officers. There may also be opportunities to undertake ecological survey. 🔊

Number of projects: 5+ **UK:** 4 + office
Starting months: January–December
Time required: 1–52 weeks
Age: 21–65
Causes: Conservation, Environmental Causes, Wildlife.
Activities: Conservation Skills, Gardening/Horticulture, Manual Work, Outdoor Skills.
Placements: 30
When to apply: All year.
Work alone/with others: With others.
Qualifications: Practical and office skills useful. For ecological survey relevant qualifications necessary.

Equipment/clothing: Smart casual for office. Work clothes, waterproofs, stout boots for outdoor work.
Health requirements: Any medical conditions (illness, allergy or physical disability) that may require treatment/medication or which affects the volunteer working with machinery must be notified to us in advance.
Costs: Food and accommodation.
Benefits: Travel costs. We would try to help with funding accommodation.
Training: Some in-house training if and when available and if funds allow.
Supervision: Work is undertaken under the supervision of the relevant member of staff.
Interviews: Interviews held at our office are essential.
Charity number: 513615
UK placements: England (West Midlands).

WILDLIFE TRUST of SOUTH AND WEST WALES, THE

The Welsh Wildlife Centre
Cilgerran
Cardigan
SA43 2TB UK
T: 01239 621212
F: 01239 613211
E: wildlife@wtww.co.uk
W: www.wtww.co.uk
Contact: Rachel Wood

The Wildlife Trust of South and West Wales manages Skomer Island which is a National Nature Reserve. The island is internationally famous for its seabird colonies. Our volunteers help us with a wide variety of tasks, including the repair and maintenance of buildings, hides and footpaths, and at appropriate times may help with scientific work, bird surveys and generally contribute to the island's records. Help will also be needed to meet the boats which bring day visitors to the island, collecting landing fees and patrolling the reserve. We are very keen to have help from good birdwatchers during the last week of May and the first two weeks of June as during this time a great deal of seabird census work is carried out. Volunteers with an offending background are not accepted for long-term periods. 📖

Number of projects: 1 **UK:** 1
Starting months: Mar, Apr, May, Jun, Jul, Aug, Sep, Oct
Time required: 1–2 weeks
Age: 16–90
Causes: Conservation, Environmental Causes.
Activities: Conservation Skills, DIY, Group Work, Manual Work, Outdoor Skills, Scientific Work.
Placements: 110
When to apply: 1 September for the following year.

Work alone/with others: With others.
Qualifications: Nil – interest in natural history an advantage.
Equipment/clothing: Stout walking boots, waterproof clothing and bedding (pillow case, sheet and duvet).
Health requirements: Good general health.
Costs: Everything free except that volunteers need to bring their own food.
Benefits: Accommodation and travel from mainland to Skomer.
Training: Introductory talk and health and safety talk given on arrival.
Supervision: Under direct supervision of island warden and assistant warden.
Interviews: Applicants are not interviewed.
Charity number: 227996
UK placements: Wales (Pembrokeshire).

WILTSHIRE WILDLIFE TRUST

Elm Tree Court
Long Street
Devizes
Wiltshire SN10 1NJ UK
T: 01380 725670
F: 01380 729017
E: wio@wiltshirewildlife.org
W: www.wiltshirewildlife.org
Contact: Wildlife Information Officer

The Wiltshire Wildlife Trust is the largest voluntary organisation in the county concerned with nature conservation and the environment. The Trust manages over 40 nature reserves which include wildlife habitats such as woodland, chalk downland, wildflower rich hay meadows, watermeadows and streams. With expert and skilled staff, and volunteers the Trust is the charity best able to protect Wiltshire and Swindon's wildlife. The Trust works with landowners, local authorities, statutory agencies, local communities, schools and youth groups and businesses to achieve its vision of a sustainable future for wildlife and people. The Trust is heavily involved in sustainability work which will have an effect on biodiversity and the quality of people's lives. Although much of our work depends on the financial support of over 11,000 members, just as important is the enormous contribution of time given by volunteers. Training and support given to volunteers. Volunteers who work with children will need to undertake necessary vetting to ensure they are suitable to work with this vulnerable group. The Trust offices are at Swindon and Salisbury as well as Devizes. &

Number of projects: 1 UK: 1
Starting months: January–December
Time required: 4–52 weeks (plus)
Age: 16–75
Causes: Children, Conservation, Environmental

Causes, Teaching/assisting (primary, secondary), Wildlife, Young People.
Activities: Administration, Agriculture/Farming, Arts/Crafts, Campaigning, Community Work, Conservation Skills, First Aid, Forestry, Fundraising, Gardening/Horticulture, Manual Work, Marketing/Publicity, Newsletter/Journalism, Outdoor Skills, Research, Scientific Work, Teaching, Training.
Placements: 1,000 aprox
When to apply: All year.
Work alone/with others: With others.
Health requirements: Nil.
Costs: Travel to work. Food and accommodation.
Benefits: All reasonable expenses reimbursed.
Training: Any necessary training is carried out.
Supervision: Volunteers are supervised by a Trust member of staff or key volunteers.
Interviews: Interviews are conducted at the Devizes head office or at our offices in Swindon or Salisbury.
Charity number: 266202
UK placements: England (Wiltshire).

WINANT CLAYTON VOLUNTEER ASSOCIATION

Davenant Centre
179 Whitechapel Road
London
E1 1DU UK
T: +44 (0) 207 375 0547
E: wcva@dircon.co.uk
W: www.wcva.dircon.co.uk
Contact: Louise Douglas

Winant Clayton Volunteers travel as a group to east coast USA in late June to undertake two months community/social work, followed by two and a half weeks travel. Placements are with different groups: the homeless, elderly, children, HIV/AIDS, mental health etc. The work is full-time, up to 40 hours per week over five days. It can be challenging and exhausting but the rewards are great, and there is a real opportunity to make a valuable contribution to people in need. Volunteers are supervised and given support by our US board, which, like the UK committee, is made up of returned volunteers. It is a reciprocal scheme, with a similar group of US volunteers coming to volunteer each summer in the East End of London. Ability to be flexible and open-minded is more important than qualifications. Some volunteers fundraise towards their costs and are supported in this by Winant Clayton. Candidates from the East End of London and Irish candidates may be able to apply for a bursary. Volunteers with an offending background may be accepted – minor offences to be cleared with the US Embassy. USA – east coast and New York City. &

Number of projects: 25 UK: 15
Starting months: Jun, Jul, Aug, Sep
Time required: 12 weeks
Age: 19–80
Causes: AIDS/HIV, Children, Disabled (learning and physical), Elderly People, Health Care/ Medical, Inner City Problems, Poor/Homeless, Young People.
Activities: Caring – Day, Community Work, Counselling, Social Work.
Placements: 20
When to apply: End of January.
Work alone/with others: Both alone and with others.
Qualifications: UK + Irish passports essential, volunteer work and/or social community work experience desirable.
Equipment/clothing: General.
Health requirements: Reasonable level of mobility and fitness required.
Costs: Air fare + insurance + visa + travel expenses + possible small administration fee for a police check (disclosure).
Benefits: Food, accommodation and pocket money while on placement.
Training: 2-day orientation in London, 1 day in New York and induction at work placement.
Supervision: Volunteers have supervisor at their project. In addition they have an American 'Link' for support, as well as the New York based Winant Clayton co-ordinator.
Interviews: Interviews take place in London during February. Occasionally we are able to hold regional interviews.
Charity number: 296101
Worldwide placements: North America: (USA).
UK placements: England (London).

WIND SAND AND STARS

6 Tyndale Terrace
London
N1 2AT UK
T: +44 (0) 207 359 7551
T: +44 (0) 207 359 4936
E: office@windsandstars.co.uk
W: www.windsandstars.co.uk
Contact: Liz Dempsey

Wind Sand and Stars is a small company that specialises in projects and journeys in the desert and mountain regions of Sinai. Each summer we organise an expedition for young people combining desert travel and adventure with the opportunity to work on projects with the local Bedouin people and to develop expedition and leadership skills. 🔣 📄

Number of projects: 3–5 UK: 0
Starting months: Jun, Jul, Aug
Time required: 4 weeks
Age: 16–25

Causes: Environmental Causes.
Activities: Community Work, Group Work, Outdoor Skills, Research.
Placements: 20–25
When to apply: October – April.
Work alone/with others: With others.
Qualifications: Good level of fitness and stamina. An Egyptian visa is required.
Equipment/clothing: Tough, light desert clothing and some camping equipment.
Health requirements: A medical form will be provided for completion.
Costs: Approximately £2,000.
Benefits: Support given for fundraising activities. Work/travel in desert environment – sleep under the stars.
Training: One day pre-departure training.
Supervision: Qualified leaders.
Interviews: Prospective applicants are occasionally interviewed at our office.
Worldwide placements: Africa (Egypt).

WINGED FELLOWSHIP TRUST

Angel House
20–32 Pentonville Road
London
N1 9XD UK
T: +44 (0) 207 833 2594
T: +44 (0) 207 278 0370
E: admin@wft.org.uk
W: www.wft.org.uk
Contact: Marina Tsakiridou

The Winged Fellowship provides respite for carers and quality holidays for people with severe physical disabilities. We would not be able to cope without the much appreciated help of our volunteers. Our volunteers are asked to be the hands and feet of our disabled guests and to be their companions and friends. The tasks they undertake include:
1. Helping one of the guests wash and dress in the mornings.
2. Helping feed those who need assistance.
3. Transferring people from wheelchair to the toilet and vice-versa, or from their wheelchair to an ordinary chair.
4. Accompanying them in a group on outings to places of interest, the theatre or shopping.
5. Serving meals.
6. Generally assisting in the every day running of the centres.
Volunteers work long hours and the work is physically and emotionally very demanding but we hope also interesting and rewarding. Many of our volunteers return again and again. There are opportunities for volunteers to work in Europe on the Overseas and Discovery Holidays programme but these volunteers are only selected after completing voluntary work with Winged Fellowship in the UK. We require references before accepting any volunteer.

Volunteers with an offending background may be accepted but not offences against the person or sexual offences. 🖔

Number of projects: 10 approximately **UK:** 5
Starting months: Feb, Mar, Apr, May, Jun, Jul, Aug, Sep, Oct, Nov, Dec
Time required: 1–2 weeks
Age: 16–75
Causes: Children, Disabled (learning and physical), Elderly People, Holidays for Disabled.
Activities: Arts/Crafts, Caring (general, residential), Fundraising, Sport.
Placements: 4500
When to apply: All year.
Work alone/with others: With others.
Qualifications: Must be able to speak and understand spoken English. No restrictions but we do not assist volunteers to obtain visas to enter Britain.
Health requirements: Reasonably fit.
Costs: Pocket money only.
Benefits: Free board and lodging up to £50. Travel expenses refunded.
Training: Written information and induction training, on-going support, supervision and feedback sessions.
Supervision: Constant access to professional staff. Buddy system of supervision.
Interviews: Interviews do not take place – if a volunteer is found to be unsuitable they will be asked to leave.
Charity number: 295072
UK placements: England (Essex, Hampshire, Merseyside, Nottinghamshire).

WINGED FELLOWSHIP TRUST – HOLIDAYS

Shap Road
Kendal
CumbriaLA9 6NZ UK
T: +44 (0) 1539 735080
F: +44 (0) 1539 735567
E: holidays@wft.org.uk
W: www.wft.org.uk
Contact: Heather Rothwell

Winged Fellowship Trust – Holidays department runs activity and hobby holidays for blind people, in many cases providing opportunities and experiences that are outside the scope of their everyday lives. A sighted guide is needed on a one to one basis for each visually impaired person on almost all occasions. WFT Holidays would be very grateful to hear from anyone who would be prepared to help. The activities themselves vary considerably and are based both in Britain and abroad. They vary from sunbathing in Tenerife to sightseeing in Jerusalem, from ballroom dancing courses in Chester to riding a tandem in the Cotswolds. Sighted holiday guides have to work reasonably hard – it's not a cheap holiday. The most important attributes for a guide are, perhaps, common sense and the ability to communicate. Days can be long and demanding and often start with assisting at breakfast and continue through to the social activities in the evening. WFT Holidays needs sighted holiday guides of all ages. In return for the help and assistance, costs are subsidised. If you feel you can spare a little time to help others, if you would like to see a brochure or want to discuss the idea, please telephone 01539 735080. 🖔

Number of projects: 100 approx. **UK:** 70 approx.
Starting months: January–December
Time required: 1–3 weeks
Age: 18–85
Causes: Holidays for Disabled, Work Camps – Seasonal.
Activities: Caring (general, day and residential), Cooking, Driving, Group Work, Music, Outdoor Skills, Sport, Summer Camps, Theatre/Drama, Training, Visiting/Befriending, Work Camps – Seasonal.
Placements: 1,000
When to apply: All year.
Work alone/with others: With others.
Qualifications: Not necessarily though all skills can be helpful.
Health requirements: Good general health.
Costs: Dependent on the project but club membership required for volunteers: £18 over l8.
Benefits: Dependent on the project. Depends on type of holiday but typically 2-star hotels, guest houses. Half board.
Training: One day training course as available, video guidance, leaflet guidance, telephone guidance if required.
Supervision: A group leader suitably qualified for the activity accompanies all groups.
Interviews: Applicants are not interviewed but a written reference is required.
Worldwide placements: Africa (Egypt); North America: (USA); Asia (China, Hong Kong, Israel, Jordan, Nepal, Singapore, Sri Lanka, Thailand); Europe (Andorra, Austria, Cyprus, France, Greece, Italy, Malta, Norway, Portugal, Spain).
UK placements: England (throughout); Scotland (throughout); Northern Ireland (throughout); Wales (throughout).

WOMANKIND WORLDWIDE

32–37 Cowper Street
London
EC2A 4AW UK
T: +44 (0) 207 549 5700
T: +44 (0) 207 549 5701
E: info@womankind.org.uk
W: www.womankind.org.uk
Contact: Sarah Hibberd

Womankind Worldwide is the UK charity which assists women in developing countries in their efforts to overcome poverty and ill health, to gain access to education and training, to eliminate violence and to take greater control of their lives. Our vision is of a society, just, equitable and peaceful, in which women are equal partners in determining the values, direction and governance of society at all levels both national and international, for the benefit of all. Our guiding principles are: listen to women's own needs; respect their knowledge and experience; take a broad view of development and be imaginative and responsive in our support; encourage women to use all their skills and develop those skills; work in partnership with women; co-operate with organisations with similar aims; support a wide range of women's projects; collaborate with men working towards women's advancement. All volunteering places are in our London office and there are no opportunities to volunteer abroad. 🦽 📄

Number of projects: 19 **UK:** 1
Starting months: January–December
Time required: 12–52 weeks (plus)
Age: 24–40
Causes: Human Rights, Inner City Problems, Young People.
Activities: Administration, Development Issues, First Aid, Library/Resource Centres, Marketing/Publicity, Newsletter/Journalism, Research, Translating.
Placements: 20
When to apply: All year.
Work alone/with others: Both.
Qualifications: English essential. Spanish desirable. Computer skills, writing skills, database if possible.
Health requirements: Nil.
Costs: Food and accommodation.
Benefits: Travel expenses (up to London area Zone IV) and £3 lunch.
Training: None.
Supervision: The line manager responsible for the area of work supervises the volunteer.
Interviews: Interviews are conducted in our office.
Charity number: 328206
UK placements: England (London).

WOMEN'S ENVIRONMENTAL NETWORK

P O Box 30626
London
E1 1TZ UK
T: +44 (0) 20 7361 481 9004
F: +44 (0) 20 7361 481 9144
E: info@wen.org.uk
W: www.wen.org.uk
Contact: Ann Link

WEN is a unique, vital and innovative campaigning organisation, which represents women and campaigns on issues which link women, environment and health. We are a non-profit membership organisation. Women taking action for a healthier planet is a community fund supported project to set up a self-sustaining network of local groups (UK wide) to take action on links between the environment and human health, eg. breast cancer and hormone disrupting chemicals in cosmetics and household products. Waste prevention campaign initiated the Waste Minimisation Act 1998, which gives local authorities powers to promote measures to reduce waste. We inform councils and individuals on alternatives to wasteful products and packaging, and were involved with a waste prevention project at Spitalfields Market. The Taste of a Better Future campaign encourages people to grow their own organic foods and supports growing groups. The real nappy project/campaign promotes the use of 'real' nappies to replace the use of disposable nappies. National office in Tower Hamlets, East London. 🦽

Number of projects: 5 **UK:** 5
Starting months: January–December
Time required: 6–52 weeks (plus)
Age: 20 plus – no upper limit
Causes: Environmental Causes.
Activities: Administration, Campaigning, Group Work, Marketing/Publicity, Newsletter/Journalism, Research.
Placements: Depends.
When to apply: All year.
Work alone/with others: Both.
Qualifications: Good written English, adaptability. Other specific skills are required at times.
Health requirements: Nil.
Costs: Food and accommodation.
Benefits: £3 for cost of lunch and £3–£4 travel per day if total of 6 hours are worked.
Training: An induction for half a day.
Supervision: Volunteer will be supervised by campaign co-ordinator.
Interviews: After sending a CV, prospective volunteers will need to attend an interview in London.
UK placements: England (London).

WOMEN'S ROYAL VOLUNTARY SERVICE

Milton Hill House
Milton Hill
Steventon, Abingdon
Oxfordshire OX13 6AF UK
T: 01235 442961
F: 01235 861166
E: enquiries@wrvs.org.uk
W: www.wrvs.org.uk
Contact: Sophia Lewis

WRVS is one of the most active voluntary organisations. It aims to help people maintain independence and dignity in their homes and communities, particularly in later life. It also provides on site support for those affected and made vulnerable by disasters such as floods, rail and plane accidents. A network of around 100,000 volunteers, 13,000 of whom are men, support the organisation throughout Britain. To find out about our work in communities across England, Scotland and Wales visit our web site www.wrvs.org.uk. Applications to be a WRVS volunteer can be made online via our web site, or by telephoning 0845 601 4670. 🖆 🖹

Number of projects: 5,000 UK: 5,000
Starting months: January–December
Time required: 1–52 weeks
Age: 14–75
Causes: Children, Elderly People, Offenders/Ex-Offenders, Poor/Homeless.
Activities: Administration, Caring (general, day and residential), Catering, Community Work, Cooking, Driving, Social Work, Training, Visiting/Befriending.
Placements: 7500
When to apply: All year.
Work alone/with others: With others.
Qualifications: Varied.
Costs: Nil. Out of pocket expenses of volunteering are met. Accommodation costs if needed.
Benefits: Travel costs.
Training: Relevant training provided, usually at project.
Supervision: Supervision of young volunteers will meet good practice guidelines appropriate for the project.
Interviews: Interview. Two references required.
UK placements: England (throughout); Scotland (throughout); Wales (throughout).

WOODLAND TRUST, THE

Autumn Park
Dysart Road
Grantham
Lincolnshire NG31 6LL UK
T: 01476 581111
E: volunteers@woodland-trust.org.uk
W: www.woodland-trust.org.uk
Contact: Merle Dekanski

The Woodland Trust is Britain's largest conservation organisation concerned solely with the acquisition and management of woodland. The Trust protects Britain's heritage of native and broad leaved trees by acquiring existing woodland and open land on which to plant trees for the future, and by managing those woods in perpetuity. This ownership ensures that the woods are open to all for quiet, informal recreation and that they remain integral parts of familiar landscapes providing habitats for wildlife benefit. Opportunities for volunteering include tree planting, path and weed clearance. Volunteers are also required to act as speakers to inform the public about Woodland Trust, photograph woods/species, survey flora, fauna and visitors, undertake research and develop new ways to raise funds in order to purchase threatened woodland. 🖆

Number of projects: Varies UK: Varies
Starting months: January–December
Time required: 1–48 weeks
Age: 16–75
Causes: Conservation, Environmental Causes, Wildlife.
Activities: Administration, Arts/Crafts, Conservation Skills, Forestry, Fundraising, Manual Work, Newsletter/Journalism, Outdoor Skills, Research, Translating.
Placements: Unknown.
When to apply: All year.

Conserving Leatherback Turtles in Costa Rica

Sally Wade embarked on a six month placement in Costa Rica having identified GAP Challenge through WorldWide Volunteering. With nine other students she took part in a variety of conservation projects. One in particular was on a protected beach for leatherback turtle nesting. Sally's diary records, "We do two shifts a night patrolling for nesting turtles and help to measure and tag the turtles and count the number in the clutch." One night there were eight turtles on the beach at once. She was pleased to have "made a difference to the conservation work. I urge anyone who is thinking about taking a year out to go for it!"

Work alone/with others: Either, depending on experience.
Qualifications: Depends on the task.
Equipment/clothing: Warm waterproof clothing with stout shoes or boots for practical work. For some tasks access to IT equipment is an advantage.
Health requirements: Depends on the task.
Costs: Accommodation and food.
Benefits: Travel expenses depending on project.
Training: None.
Supervision: None.
Interviews: Yes at project.
Charity number: 294344
UK placements: England (throughout); Scotland (throughout); Northern Ireland (Antrim, Armagh, Derry/Londonderry, Down, Fermanagh, Tyrone); Wales (throughout).

WOODLARKS CAMP SITE TRUST

Kathleen Marshall House
Tilford Road,
Farnham
Surrey GU10 3RN UK
T: 01252 716279
E: woodlarks1@aol.com
W: www.woodlarks.org.uk
Contact: Mrs Jane Cook

Woodlarks Camp Site Trust offers the opportunity for children and adults with disabilities to have a traditional camping holiday as part of an organised group on our peaceful wooded campsite. Facilities include a heated outdoor swimming pool, a trampoline, archery, barbecue and campfire sites, and an aerial runway. The Trust provides for six week-long camps that are open to public application and which depend on volunteers to assist the campers. Each camp is aimed at a specific group and is organised by a different camp leader. Adventurers for boys aged 10–18 (male volunteers only).
Explorers for girls aged 10–18 (female volunteers only).
Odyssians for men and women aged 18 to 35.
Pathfinders for women aged over 18 (female volunteers only).
Pioneer 1 for men aged over 18 (female volunteers are accepted).
Pioneer 11 for men aged over 18 (male and female volunteers accepted).
Volunteers are normally taken on for a period of one week (the duration of a single camp), but some do stay for longer.
When the campsite is closed (between October and April) there are often opportunities for skilled volunteers to assist in the maintenance and repair of the facilities. Those interested should contact the Honorary Secretary. ⑤

Number of projects: 1 UK: 1

Starting months: May, Jun, Jul, Aug, Sep
Time required: 1 week
Age: 14–75
Causes: Children, Disabled (physical), Holidays for Disabled.
Activities: Caring – Residential, Summer Camps.
Placements: 500 of all ages.
When to apply: January – April.
Work alone/with others: With others.
Equipment/clothing: Sleeping bag, torch, waterproof gear.
Health requirements: Physical health necessary for physically demanding work.
Costs: Camps charge different amounts normally in the region of £30–£100.
Benefits: Tents.
Training: Yes if required.
Supervision: Yes at all times.
Interviews: Camp leaders may wish to interview prospective volunteers at the site.
Charity number: 305148
UK placements: England (Surrey).

WORCESTERSHIRE LIFESTYLES

Woodside Lodge
Lark Hill Road
Worcester
Worcs WR5 2EF UK
T: 01905 350686
F: 01905 350684
E: worcslifestyles@care4free.net
Contact: Nicola Boho

Worcestershire Lifestyles is an independent registered charity established in 1991 to assist people with disabilities to exercise freedom of choice, extend their horizons and make decisions about the lifestyle they wish to enjoy. Lifestyles recruits volunteer workers, on behalf of social services, to provide full-time support and assistance to people with disabilities to enable them to lead the independent lifestyle of their choice, in the counties of Worcestershire and Herefordshire. Volunteers work on a one-to-one basis to assist individuals or families to undertake everyday tasks and pursuits, for example: personal assistance; sharing leisure pursuits; shopping; cooking. Volunteers are: people who have just left school/college looking for a worthwhile experience; people taking time out to develop themselves or decide on their career path; people who need relevant experience for their chosen career, for example, nursing, social work, probation work, occupational therapist, speech therapist or physiotherapy. Volunteers must be able to make a commitment of at least four months.
Volunteers with an offending background may be accepted. This depends on the offence as volunteers usually work on a one-to-one basis with someone with a disability.
Minicom contact number: 01905-350635. ⑤

Number of projects: 1 UK: 1
Starting months: January–December
Time required: 18–52 weeks (plus)
Age: 17 plus – no upper limit
Causes: Disabled (learning).
Activities: Caring (general and day).
Placements: up to 80
When to apply: All year.
Work alone/with others: Sometimes alone and sometimes with other volunteers.
Qualifications: Good spoken English. Caring, honest, reliable and adaptable. Only visa restrictions. Providing the volunteer can obtain a visa allowing them to be a full-time volunteer with us, they will be considered for a placement.
Equipment/clothing: No specific equipment or clothing required.
Health requirements: Volunteers need to be both mentally and physically fit.
Costs: No costs (volunteers from abroad must pay their own travel costs to England).
Benefits: Volunteers receive weekly pocket money of £60.23. Return fares from home to the project at the start and finish of placement, within the UK. Bonus paid on satisfactory completion of agreed commitment. Invaluable experience and references. Free accommodation provided.
Training: Moving and handling training provided by Social Services. New volunteers shadow existing volunteers.
Supervision: Volunteers are supervised by Social Services volunteer supervisors.
Interviews: Volunteers resident in the UK are interviewed in Worcester. Overseas volunteers are asked to complete a more detailed application form.
Charity number: 1068883
UK placements: England (Herefordshire, Worcestershire).

WORDSWORTH TRUST, THE

Dove Cottage
Grasmere
Cumbria LA22 9SH UK
T: +44 (0) 1539 435544
F: +44 (0) 1539 435748
E: c.kay@wordsworth.org.uk
W: www.wordsworth.org.uk
Contact: Catherine Kay

The Wordsworth Trust is a busy heritage attraction in the English Lake District with 70–80,000 visitors per year. The main activities involving volunteers are giving guided tours of Dove Cottage (home of the poet William Wordsworth 1799–1808), working in the ticket/gift shop/ reception in the Wordsworth Museum. Volunteers can also become involved behind the scenes, for example in administration, education, collections

management – this depends on their own interests. The Trust also runs a contemporary arts programme, which includes exhibitions and a season of poetry readings. Volunteers with an offending background may be accepted – depending on the offence. 🖹

Number of projects: 1 UK: 1
Starting months: Mar, Jun, Oct
Time required: 6–52 weeks
Age: 16 plus – no upper limit
Causes: Heritage.
Activities: Library/Resource Centres.
Placements: 15
When to apply: All year.
Work alone/with others: With other young volunteers.
Qualifications: Good English is essential.
Health requirements: Nil.
Costs: Rent and subsistence.
Benefits: Subsistence allowance (equivalent to job-seekers' allowance). Rented room in on-site accommodation.
Training: Induction training and on the job training.
Supervision: Integrated working with paid staff members, line manager for projects.
Interviews: On site – unless travel constraints make this impossible.
UK placements: England (Cumbria).

WORKAWAY

C/Bodeguerros 5
11140 CoNil de la Frontera
Cadiz
Spain
E: info@workaway.info
W: www.workaway.info
Contact: David Burton

Workaway.info is a site set up to promote fair exchange between budget travellers, language learners or culture seekers with families, individuals or organisations who are looking for help with a range of varied and interesting activities. We hold a database of hosts throughout the world. Volunteers are expected to work for five hours per day in exchange for food and accommodation. We are unable to accept volunteers with an offending background. Spain, France, New Zealand, South America. 🖺

Number of projects: many UK: several
Starting months: January–December
Time required: 1–52 weeks
Age: 16 plus – no upper limit
Causes: Animal Welfare, Archaeology, Architecture, Children, Conservation, Elderly People, Environmental Causes, Health Care/Medical, Heritage, Human Rights, Poor/Homeless, Teaching/assisting (EFL), Wildlife, Young People.

Activities: Accountancy, Administration, Agriculture/Farming, Arts/Crafts, Building/Construction, Campaigning, Caring (general, day and residential), Catering, Community Work, Computers, Conservation Skills, Cooking, Counselling, Development Issues, DIY, Driving, First Aid, Forestry, Fundraising, Gardening/Horticulture, Group Work, International Aid, Library/Resource Centres, Manual Work, Marketing/Publicity, Music, Newsletter/Journalism, Outdoor Skills, Religion, Research, Scientific Work, Social Work, Sport, Summer Camps, Teaching, Technical Skills, Theatre/Drama, Training, Translating, Visiting/Befriending, Work Camps – Seasonal.
Placements: 200
When to apply: Any time.
Work alone/with others: Both.
Qualifications: Varies from project to project. No restrictions as long as appropriate visas and travel documents are held.
Equipment/clothing: Varies from project to project.
Health requirements: Varies from project to project.
Costs: €15 subscription.
Benefits: Work for 5 hours/day in exchange for food and accommodation.
Training: Varies.
Supervision: Varies.
Interviews: No.
Worldwide placements: Australasia (Australia, New Zealand); Europe (France, Spain).

WORLD ASSEMBLY OF YOUTH (WAY)

Ved Ballahoj 4 e
Bronshoj
Copenhagen
DK – 2700 Denmark
T: 00 45 3160 7770
F: 00 45 3160 5797
E: way@inform-bbs.dk
Contact: Mr Heikki Pakarinen

WAY recognises the Universal Declaration of Human Rights as the basis of its action and services and works for the promotion of youth and youth organisations in programme areas such as: democracy, environment, human rights, population, health, drugs, community development, and leadership training. ▣

Number of projects: 10 UK: 0
Starting months: January–December
Time required: 26–52 weeks
Age: 20–30
Causes: Young People.
Activities: Administration, Computers, Development Issues, Group Work, Library/Resource Centres, Newsletter/Journalism, Training, Translating.

Placements: 2–3
When to apply: All year.
Work alone/with others: Both.
Qualifications: Fluent English, Spanish or French.
Health requirements: Good health essential. Travelling in the tropics is required.
Costs: No costs.
Benefits: Accommodation and 3,000DK per month. Travel costs to Denmark reimbursed.
Training: Offered.
Supervision: Yes.
Worldwide placements: Europe (Denmark).

WORLD CHALLENGE EXPEDITIONS

Black Arrow House
2 Chandos Road
London
NW10 6NF UK
T: +44 (0) 208 728 7200
F: +44 (0) 208 961 1551
E: welcome@world-challenge.co.uk
W: www.world-challenge.co.uk
Contact: Nicola Stopforth

World Challenge Expeditions (WCE) was established to provide educational adventure opportunities for young people. World Challenge Expeditions have been organising expeditions and gap year placements throughout the developing world for over 15 years. The ethos behind every programme is challenge, participation and environment and every participant is encouraged to take on as much responsibility as they can. The entire expedition or placement process encourages the development of skills for life, such as leadership, teamwork and decision making. There are four programmes run by World Challenge Expeditions; Leadership Challenge (UK-based four or seven-day activity expeditions), First Challenge (eight-day adventures to Poland, Morocco, Romania, Spain and Greece), Gap Challenge (six-weeks to nine-month work placements in 10 countries around the world (see Gap Challenge section for details)) and Team Challenge. Team Challenge is the core programme of WCE. A typical team consists of approximately fifteen 16–18 year olds together with their teacher and a WCE leader and assistant leader, who during the four to six week expedition take part in a physically challenging itinerary and a cultural project phase. Under the guidance of their Leaders, the students take control of all aspects of their expedition, including budget, travel and catering, taking it in turns to act as group leader. Each Team Challenge expedition is the culmination of 18 months of preparation. Teams spend this time researching and planning their itinerary, whilst raising their funds towards the overall cost. Throughout this period, they work closely with an overseas operations manager from World Challenge Expeditions. The expert knowledge that these managers can provide combines with the introduction of the money management programme. In 2002 alone, over 40,000 students participated in one or more of World Challenge Expeditions progammes within the UK and to more than 40 destinations in the developing world including Nepal, Bolivia, Mongolia and Malaysia.

Number of projects: Many **UK:** Expedition in UK may include project work.
Starting months: Apr, Jun, Jul, Sep
Time required: 1–36 weeks
Age: 14–24
Causes: Children, Conservation, Disabled (learning and physical), Environmental Causes, Health Care/Medical, Inner City Problems, Poor/Homeless, Teaching/assisting (primary, secondary, EFL), Wildlife, Young People.
Activities: Agriculture/Farming, Building/Construction, Community Work, Conservation Skills, Forestry, Fundraising, Manual Work, Social Work, Teaching, Work Camps – Seasonal.
Placements: 50,000 + in UK + overseas
Work alone/with others: School teams. Individuals in groups.
Equipment/clothing: Information provided on suitable clothing for expeditions.
Health requirements: All applicants are asked to disclose pre-existing conditions.
Costs: Varies according to programme, destination and length of expedition. Generally includes all training, travel insurance (excluding Gap Challenge), in country costs, 24 hour emergency London back-up.
Benefits: Accommodation.
Training: Team Challenge: During the 15–18 month programme culminating in a 4–6 week expedition. Teams learn how to plan their expedition, raise their funds through a money management programme and also attend training and skills courses.
Supervision: Each team is accompanied by qualified leaders. There is also a 24-hour emergency back-up support from World Challenge Expeditions HQ in London.
Worldwide placements: Africa (Botswana, Kenya, Madagascar, Malawi, Morocco, Namibia, South Africa, Tanzania, Uganda, Zambia); North America: (Canada); Central America (Belize, Costa Rica, Guatemala, Honduras, Mexico); South America (Argentina, Bolivia, Brazil, Ecuador, Guyana, Peru, Venezuela); Asia (Indonesia, Jordan, Kyrgyzstan, Malaysia, Mongolia, Nepal, Pakistan, Thailand, Tibet, Turkey, Vietnam); Australasia (Australia); Europe (Greece, Poland, Romania, Spain, Turkey).
UK placements: England (Derbyshire); Wales (Monmouthshire).

WORLD EXCHANGE

St Colm's International House
23 Inverleith Terrace
Edinburgh
EH3 5NS UK
T: 0131 315 4444
F: 0131 315 2222
E: we@stcolms.org
W: www.worldexchange.org.uk
Contact: Rev. Robert S. Anderson

World Exchange sends 50 volunteers each year to work in the developing world and also assists congregations or groups planning their own short term visits and exchanges. Placements are arranged through partner churches and agencies of the Church of Scotland, the Catholic Church, the Scottish Episcopal Church and United Reform Church UK. We take volunteers of all denominations, experiences and of all ages. Main supported projects are in Malawi and India, with additional projects in Pakistan, Lebanon, Rwanda, Caribbean and Guatamala. Volunteers work in health, education, development, church/community and administration according to their skills and experiences. Volunteers are expected to raise up to £2500 for the World Exchange travel fund. This pays for travel insurance, preparation courses before departure, debriefing weekend upon return and contributes to costs while the volunteer is overseas. (Other overseas costs are borne by the host organisation.) In our volunteer placements we hope there is something of value for the volunteers themselves, for the host and for the British churches. The time as a volunteer should be a time of growth in terms of both maturity and faith. 🔊

Number of projects: 50 **UK:** 0
Starting months: Jan, Jul, Aug, Sep
Time required: 12–50 weeks
Age: 18 plus – no upper limit
Causes: AIDS/HIV, Children, Health Care/Medical, Human Rights, Poor/Homeless, Teaching/assisting (primary, secondary, mature), Teaching (EFL), Work Camps – Seasonal, Young People.
Activities: Accountancy, Administration, Agriculture/Farming, Arts/Crafts, Building/Construction, Community Work, Computers, Conservation Skills, Development Issues, Music, Religion, Social Work, Teaching, Technical Skills, Theatre/Drama, Work Camps – Seasonal.
Placements: 50
When to apply: All year.
Work alone/with others: Both.
Qualifications: Member of a Scottish Church or the United Reformed Church UK. British only.
Equipment/clothing: None is required beyond the personal equipment of commitment and enthusiasm.

Health requirements: Have to pass a medical. We aim to be as inclusive as possible.
Costs: Raising up to £2,500 towards costs. After this all your overseas costs and your air fares are met.
Benefits: The cost includes travel, accommodation, allowance and insurance. NI is not paid. Accommodation varies from placement to placement, often self catering in own flat or house.
Training: We provides preparation courses which are held twice a year before departure.
Supervision: We provide support while volunteers are overseas.
Interviews: Interviews are held in Edinburgh.
Worldwide placements: Africa (Egypt, Kenya, Malawi); Central America (Trinidad and Tobago); Asia (India, Lebanon, Pakistan); Australasia (Kiribati).

WORLD HORIZONS

Centre for the Nations
North Dock
Llanelli
Dyfed SA15 2LF UK
T: 01554 750005
E: ndock@worldhorizons.org
Contact: The Director

Number of projects: 1 UK: 0
Starting months: January–December
Time required: 1–52 weeks (plus)
Age: 14 plus – no upper limit
Causes: Conservation, Environmental Causes.
Activities: Community Work, Conservation Skills, Outdoor Skills.
UK placements: Wales (Swansea).

WORLD LAND TRUST

Blyth House
Bridge Street
Halesworth
Suffolk IP19 8AB UK
T: 01986 874422
F: 01985 874425
E: kirsty@worldlandtrust.org
W: www.worldlandtrust.org
Contact: Kirsty Forbes

The World Land Trust is an international conservation charity based in Halesworth, Suffolk. A small team of six employees manage and administrate a range of overseas projects in which land is purchased and protected from destruction. In the first ten years of our existence, we have saved over 250,000 acres of endangered habitat in Argentina, Belize, Costa Rica, Ecuador, the Philippines and England. So, although our projects are global, the day to day work is all done from Halesworth and this is where most volunteers are based. The world land trust volunteer programme involves two different aspects: part time volunteers and full time internships. Part time volunteers tend to be local people who wish to get involved for a couple of hours a week and assist with various of the Trust's activities. Full time internships (six month placements) have been designed for new graduates who are pursuing a career in consevation and require first hand experience and further training in conservation management. The trust internship programme is a rolling programme, and information can be found on our web site, under 'Getting Involved' section. ⓖ ▣

Number of projects: 3 UK: 1
Starting months: January–December
Time required: 4–26 weeks
Age: 21–99
Causes: Conservation, Environmental Causes, Heritage, Teaching (secondary), Wildlife.
Activities: Accountancy, Administration, Agriculture/Farming, Arts/Crafts, Campaigning, Computers, Conservation Skills, Development Issues, Forestry, Fundraising, Library/Resource Centres, Marketing/Publicity, Newsletter/Journalism, Research, Teaching.
Placements: 5–10
When to apply: All year.
Work alone/with others: Both.
Qualifications: A good level of literacy and numeracy. Potential interns are required to hold a degree (or equivalent) in ecology, conservation or related subject.
Equipment/clothing: Interns are required to be computer literate, training in other office equipment is available for all volunteers.
Health requirements: Non-smoking policy.
Costs: Accommodation and travel to and from the office.
Benefits: Travel and lunch expenses up to a maximum of £10 per day. Support in the form of references, CV development and job search. Interns receive valuable hands-on experience in conservation as well as formal and informal training. We help in finding rented accommodation.
Training: Part time volunteers are given training when relevant. Full time interns are given relevant training throughout 6 month placement.
Supervision: Volunteers are never left unsupervised and have a manager to go to at all times.
Interviews: Usually in London or Halesworth.
Charity number: 1001291
Worldwide placements: Central America (Belize, Turks and Caicos Islands); South America (Argentina, Ecuador); Asia (Philippines).
UK placements: England (Gloucestershire, Suffolk).

WORLD VISION UK

World Vision House
599 Avebury Boulevard
Central Milton Keynes
Buckinghamshire MK9 3PG UK
T: 01908 841023
F: 01908 841025
E: kenny.wickens@worldvision.org.uk
W: /studentchallenge
Contact: Kenny Wickens

The student challenge is aimed at students between 19 and 29 years of age and takes place for five weeks over the summer vacation. It seeks to help you understand issues of development from a Christian perspective. Due to World Vision's network of offices throughout the world and many years of development expertise, we are able to offer a unique student experience in the Eastern Europe, the Middle East, Africa and Asia. Placement examples: World Vision is working among Palestinian people for justice and peace. As the peace process flounders World Vision is seeking to draw people together in order to bring about reconciliation. After a one week orientation in Jerusalem your work placement will take place in a Palestinian community. It will involve working with children in a nearby refugee camp and helping to develop Bethlehem Bible College. You may be asked to do a number of other tasks. You do not have to be an expert, just flexible and keen. Malawi is the world's fifth poorest country. World Vision is working to help alleviate crippling poverty in both a rural and urban setting in Ghana and to bring freedom to those bound by poverty. You will receive one week's orientation in Accra, Ghana's capital. There you will meet development specialists, politicians, church leaders and human rights experts. You will then begin a two week placement in local villages where you will help build classrooms with the rest of the community and work with children from that area. In the Philippines you will meet men and women who are working with the poor as an expression of their service to God. They have given their lives to working with the poor and their faith takes its expression in words and actions. You will experience an holistic conception of development that does not ignore an individual's spiritual needs but sees them as a central component towards developing the person. You will have a life-changing experience working with the urban poor of the Philippines.

Number of projects: 5 **UK:** 0
Starting months: Jun
Time required: 4–5 weeks
Age: 19–29
Causes: Children, Human Rights, Poor/Homeless, Refugees.
Activities: Building/Construction, Community Work, Development Issues, Fundraising, Group Work, International Aid, Religion, Research, Sport, Summer Camps, Teaching.
Placements: 20–30
When to apply: Before April.
Work alone/with others: With others in a team.
Qualifications: Experience in areas of interest (academic and experience).
Equipment/clothing: Each location differs.
Health requirements: Full medical prior to posting.
Costs: Self funded £900–£1,400.
Benefits: Organisation caters for day to day living costs. All accommodation is paid for as part of the programme – guest houses, local families.
Training: We hold a $2\frac{1}{2}$ day orientation each spring. For Palestine we hold a one week orientation in Jerusalem.
Supervision: Volunteers will be supervised by World Vision in the project country.
Interviews: 2 hour interview in Milton Keynes.
Charity number: 285908
Worldwide placements: Africa (Ghana, Malawi, Zambia); Asia (Bangladesh, Israel, Philippines); Europe (Armenia).

WORLD YOUTH MILLENNIUM AWARDS

VSO
317 Putney Bridge Road
London
SW15 2PN UK
T: +44 (0) 20 8780 7500
F: +44 (0) 20 8780 7300
E: enquiries@vso.org.uk
W: www.vso.org.uk
Contact: Enquiries Department

World Youth Millennium Awards exchange programme gives 17–25 year olds the chance to live and work with another young person from a developing country for six months, spending three months in the UK and another three overseas. Teams are made up of nine young people from the UK and nine from a developing country. Participants live with their counterpart in a local host family and work together as volunteers on a community placement in both countries. As well as doing work of practical benefit to local communities, the programme also aims to stimulate solidarity between youth in the UK and in the developing countries and promote strong and active participation in civil society in each of the countries involved. We run exchanges with Sri Lanka, India, Thailand, Tanzania, Ghana, Nigeria and South Africa. Host communities in the UK can be anywhere in Scotland, Wales, Northern Ireland or England. World Youth is meant to reflect the diversity of the UK population, in terms of social and ethnic diversity, region, gender, disability and age. For example, we welcome applications from young people who do not plan to go on to further education, as well as those who are or will be going to university. Supported by the VSO and the Prince's Trust, and funded by the Millennium Commission, the scheme covers everything from medical costs, training and travel to visas, food and accommodation and a basic allowance. Advice and support is also given to help the young volunteers to raise £500 in their local community before the programme starts. Volunteers with an offending background will be accepted. ⑤

Number of projects: 10 **UK:** 10
Starting months: Jan, Jul, Nov
Time required: 24 weeks
Age: 17–25
Causes: AIDS/HIV, Children, Conservation, Disabled (learning and physical), Elderly People, Holidays for Disabled, Poor/Homeless, Teaching/assisting, Young People.
Activities: Building/Construction, Caring – General, Community Work, Conservation Skills, Development Issues, Group Work.
Placements: 180
When to apply: 6 months before programme starts.
Work alone/with others: Work with others.
Qualifications: Volunteers need to be a British resident and have the right to live and work in UK. An NI number is also required.
Health requirements: Must be physically and mentally fit for a challenging six month programme including three months overseas.
Costs: At the moment there are no costs incurred to volunteers, however they raise at least £500 before starting the programme.
Benefits: All food, accommodation and travel costs are covered, personal allowance (£15/week in the UK). There is no end of placement grant.
Training: Extensive training before, during and after the programme.
Supervision: A project supervisor is responsible for the team.
Interviews: There is an assessment day (with group activities and a short interview) held in London.
Worldwide placements: Africa (Ghana, Nigeria, South Africa, Tanzania); Asia (India, Sri Lanka, Thailand).
UK placements: England (throughout).

WORLDTEACH

Center for International Development
Harvard University
79 John F. Kennedy Street
Cambridge
Massachusetts 02138 USA

T: 00 1 (617) 495 5527
F: 00 1 (617) 495 1599
E: info@worldteach.org
W: www.worldteach.org
Contact: Ellen Whitman

Based in Cambridge, Massachusetts, WorldTeach is a non-profit organisation which sends volunteers overseas to teach English in developing countries. Working in educational settings ranging from primary schools to adult education centres, WorldTeach volunteers teach English as a foreign language and, in some cases, maths and science. Outside traditional school settings, volunteers develop curriculum and provide contextualised English training for guides working in national parks and reserves in Honduras, Mexico, Guatemala and Honduras. There are year-long opportunities in Costa Rica, Ecuador, the Marshall Islands and Namibia, six month programmes in China, and nature guide training programmes. We also have a summer programme open to undergraduates in Namibia, Ecuador and Costa Rica. Pre departure information provided upon acceptance. ⑤

Number of projects: 9 **UK:** 0
Starting months: Jan, Mar, Apr, Jun, Aug, Sep, Dec
Time required: 8–52 weeks
Age: 18 plus – no upper limit
Causes: AIDS/HIV, Conservation, Environmental Causes, Teaching/assisting (primary, secondary, mature, EFL).
Activities: Community Work, International Aid, Teaching, Training.
Placements: 120–200
When to apply: Any time but approx. 4 months in advance – rolling admissions. You will need time to fundraise if necessary. We accept applications until 2 months prior to programme departure.
Work alone/with others: Summer – with others.
Nature guide training – with others.
Others – individual placements.
Qualifications: Native English fluency required. Bachelors degree (except summer programme), 25 hrs teaching English experience or TEFL course after acceptance recommended.
Equipment/clothing: Nothing special.
Health requirements: Health examination.
Costs: From US$3990–$5990 incl. airfare from US, health insurance, one week – one month training, year long support, room and board.
Benefits: Accommodation with family or in apartment + small living allowance. Either a homestay or apartment/dormitory arrangements.
Training: There is a 3–4 week orientation on arrival (includes language lessons, training on

how to teach English, and cross cultural adjustment sessions) for year long and semester volunteers; summer volunteers receive one week of orientation.

Supervision: A field co-ordinator resides in each country to offer orientation and year long support to our volunteers.

Interviews: Interviews are in Cambridge, Massachusetts or for candidates who do not live near Cambridge, interviews are with returned WorldTeach volunteers in your area when possible.

Worldwide placements: Africa (Namibia); Central America (Costa Rica, Honduras, Mexico, Panama); South America (Ecuador); Asia (China); Australasia (Marshall Islands).

WWOOF – Australia

W Tree, via Buchan
Victoria 3885 Australia
T: 00 61 3 515 50218
F: 00 61 3 515 50342
E: wwoof@wwoof.com.au
W: www.wwoof.com.au
Contact: Garry Ainsworth

WWOOF is a form of cultural exchange in which volunteers live and work as a family to learn about organic farming and gardening, as well as about life in Australia. Working for 3–6 hours a day in exchange for board and lodging is the basis of all WWOOFing. The hosts are mostly people who are involved in alternative lifestyles, and most of them are organic growers, many practise permaculture and biodynamics. Work includes gardening, planting trees, woodcutting, weeding, cooking – anything!

Number of projects: 1 UK: 0
Starting months: January–December
Time required: 1–52 weeks
Age: 16 plus – no upper limit
Causes: Conservation, Environmental Causes, Wildlife.
Activities: Agriculture/Farming, Building/Construction, Conservation Skills, Forestry, Gardening/Horticulture, Manual Work, Outdoor Skills.
Placements: 10,000
When to apply: About 2 weeks prior to starting.
Work alone/with others: Yes with other young volunteers.
Equipment/clothing: Work clothes, sun hat, sun screen and good boots.
Health requirements: Nil.
Costs: To book costs £21 (AUD$55.00) for one and £24.50 (AUD$65.00) for 2 people travelling together. This includes $5 for postage out of Australia.
Benefits: Volunteers stay in people's homes and work in exchange for food and lodging.

Training: None.
Supervision: Supervised by the host farmer.
Interviews: Prospective volunteers are not interviewed.
Worldwide placements: Australasia (Australia).

WWOOF – Canada

4429 Carlson Road
Nelson
British Columbia VIL 6X3 Canada
T: 00 1 250 354 4417
F: 00 1 250 354 4417
E: wwoofcan@shaw.ca
W: www.wwoof.ca/www.wwoofusa.com
Contact: John Vanden Heuvel

WWOOF (World Wide Opportunities on Organic Farms) is a very popular and successful programme in which hundreds of UK young people have participated. It has been a wonderful way to meet Canadians, live with a family (total integration!), see Canada and pick up valuable life skills and experiences. You can choose from 450 farms and homesteads. (Separate booklet for USA and Hawaii). Please send $5 (cash) to cover postage and $30 cash with application. Alternative web site or www.wwoofusa.com/hawaii. Right across Canada, East Coast to West Coast, across the States and the Hawaiian islands.

Number of projects: 600+ UK: 0
Starting months: January–December
Time required: 1–26 weeks
Age: 17–70
Causes: Animal Welfare, Children, Conservation, Environmental Causes, Teaching (primary, secondary, EFL).
Activities: Agriculture/Farming, Building/Construction, Conservation Skills, Forestry, Gardening/Horticulture, Manual Work, Teaching.
Placements: 2,000+
When to apply: All year.
Work alone/with others: With others.
Qualifications: Only a willingness to try to the best of one's ability. No restrictions as long as you can easily obtain a tourist visa.
Equipment/clothing: Good footwear and sleeping bag.
Health requirements: Provide own medical insurance.
Costs: Travel costs + registration $30 (cash), city-host/lodging and meals while travelling. Approx £200 per 1, 2, 3 months.
Benefits: Board/lodging and a wonderful experience.
Training: At the farm.
Supervision: Supervised by your host.
Interviews: Volunteer applicants are not interviewed.
Worldwide placements: North America: (Canada, USA).

WWOOF – New Zealand

P O Box 1172
Nelson
New Zealand
T: 00 64 3 544 9890
F: 00 64 3 544 9890
E: a+j@wwoof.co.nz
W: www.wwoof.co.nz
Contact: Jane and Andrew Strange

WWOOF (Willing Workers on Organic Farms) has as its aims:
– to enable people to learn first hand organic growing techniques.
– to enable town-dwellers to experience living and working on a farm.
– to show alternative ways of life.
– to improve communication within the organic movement.
– to help develop confidence in becoming self-sufficient.
– to meet interesting people and make useful contacts.
WWOOF – NZ provides the opportunity for you to live and experience life on New Zealand organic properties. You learn organic farming methods by helping on the farm and having 'hands-on' experience. Usually you live with the family and are expected to join in and co-operate with the day to day activities. The success of WWOOF depends on mutual co-operation. There is a variety of properties spread throughout NZ, including farms, market gardens, communities and ventures in self-sufficiency in which organic growing plays some part. Currently there are over 600 host farms. Volunteers with an offending background are not accepted if the conviction is of a serious nature. 🖻

Number of projects: 1 UK: 0
Starting months: January–December
Time required: 1–52 weeks
Age: 16 plus – no upper limit
Causes: Conservation, Environmental Causes, Heritage.
Activities: Agriculture/Farming, Arts/Crafts, Building/Construction, Conservation Skills, Cooking.
Placements: 3000
When to apply: All year.
Work alone/with others: 50% of the time with other young volunteers.
Qualifications: Enthusiasm is the prime requisite. Must be able to enter the country without a special invitation.
Equipment/clothing: Sturdy shoes and work clothes.
Health requirements: Nil.
Costs: £12 membership fee.
Benefits: Full board and lodging.
Training: Written guidelines are given.

Supervision: Volunteers may be left to work alone – but not usually for extended periods.
Interviews: Prospective volunteers are not interviewed.
Worldwide placements: Australasia (New Zealand).

WWOOF – Togo

BP 25
Agou Nyogbo
Togo
T: 47.10.30
F: 47.10.12
E: wwooftogo@hotmail.com
Contact: Prosper Komla Agbeko

WWOOF (Willing Workers on Organic Farms) – Togo. Every summer we organise an adventure camp on Bethel, the highest mountain in Togo, which includes walking trips, reforestation, discovering wild vegetation and tropical species. You are invited to return to the rural life with Jeunesse en Action. You can experience a completely calm and dark night except for the light of the moon and stars, cook over wood fires, and learn about African family life. Volunteers are also needed all year to help work on organic farms in all areas on Togo.
Aims of WWOOF:
To get first-hand experience of organic farming and growing.
To get into the countryside.
To help the organic movement.
To make contact with other people in the organic movement.
NB Please send two international reply coupons with each letter. Letters received without will not be answered. 🖻

Number of projects: 3 UK: 0
Starting months: January–December
Time required: 3–52 weeks
Age: 17–80
Causes: Animal Welfare, Children, Conservation, Environmental Causes, Health Care/Medical, Heritage, Poor/Homeless, Teaching/assisting (nursery, EFL), Unemployed, Wildlife, Work Camps – Seasonal, Young People.
Activities: Agriculture/Farming, Arts/Crafts, Building/Construction, Caring – General, Community Work, Conservation Skills, Counselling, Development Issues, DIY, First Aid, Forestry, Fundraising, Gardening/Horticulture, Group Work, International Aid, Library/Resource Centres, Manual Work, Marketing/Publicity, Research, Sport, Summer Camps, Teaching, Training, Work Camps – Seasonal.
Placements: 20–30
When to apply: 30 days in advance.
Work alone/with others: With others.
Qualifications: French or English speaking.

Equipment/clothing: Workclothes, mosquito net and cream, suncream, torch, sleeping bag.
Health requirements: Water filters, anti-malarial pills and anti-diarrhoea pills.
Costs: All travel, FF150 inscription+ FF150/wk board. Summer camp FF250/wk, FF900/month. Accommodation in tents.
Benefits: Nil financial because Togo is so poor with a very low standard of living.
Training: If required.
Supervision: Yes.
Charity number: 3939
Worldwide placements: Africa (Togo).

WWOOF – UK

P O Box 2675
Lewes
BN7 1RB UK
T: 01273 476286
F: 01273 476286
E: hello@wwoof.org
W: www.wwoof.org.uk
Contact: Fran Whittle

WWOOF UK (World Wide Opportunities on Organic Farms) is a world wide exchange network where bed, board and practical experience are given in return for work. Stays of varied length are possible. WWOOF provides excellent opportunities for organic training, changing to a rural life, cultural exchange and being part of the organic movement. WWOOF aims are: to get first hand experience of organic farming and growing; to give practical assistance to producers of organic food; to get into the countryside; to make contact with other people in the organic movement; to form links and foster understanding between city and rural dwellers; to facilitate inter-cultural understanding between people of different nationalities. 🖑

Number of projects: 250 UK: 250
Starting months: January–December
Time required: 2–52 weeks (plus)
Age: 16 plus – no upper limit
Causes: Conservation, Environmental Causes, Wildlife.
Activities: Agriculture/Farming, Building/Construction, Conservation Skills, Development Issues, Forestry, Gardening/Horticulture, Group Work.
Placements: 5000
When to apply: Not more that 6 months before wishing to start. Application form by post, s.a.e., or application forms to print off from www.wwoof.org.uk
Work alone/with others: Sometimes alone and sometimes with other young people.
Qualifications: A desire to work hard, take the rough with the smooth, to learn, to give and take and to care for the environment and

people. Nationality restrictions only by visa requirements.
Equipment/clothing: Bad/good weather clothing, strong boots, gloves, sleeping bag for short stays.
Costs: Membership fee £15. A good day's work in exchange for bed and board. Volunteer pays travel costs.
Benefits: Board and lodging.
Training: On the job training, working alongside host.
Supervision: Varies from host to host, task to task.
Interviews: No interviews.
UK placements: England (throughout); Scotland (throughout); Northern Ireland (throughout); Wales (throughout).

WWOOF/FIOH

P.O. Box TF 154
Trade Fair Site
Accra
Ghana
T: 00 233 21 716091
F: 00 233 21 716091
E: kingzeeh@yahoo.co.uk
Contact: Kenneth Nortey

WWOOF/FIOH is affiliated to WWOOF. Voluntary farm workers work on both organic and traditional farms. Work includes weeding with a hoe or cutlass and harvesting of food and cash crops including maize, cassava, oranges, cocoa etc. Volunteers also needed to teach English, French, science, music and mathematics – mostly in primary and secondary schools. Placements throughout the year. Volunteers with skills in bicycle repairs and maintenance are invited to work in a bicycle repair workshop. The workshop trains apprentices to repair bicycles. Street children are trained here and are assisted with tools and some funds to set up wayside bicycle repair works. All volunteers are offered the security of arriving to pre-arranged work and family. This allows you to integrate more easily, without the stress of having to find a position. Available: two summer work-camps (July and August). NB Applicants to send three international reply coupons (IRCs) available at Post Offices, for enquiries and programme details and each time they write. We have established a Bicycle Institute. The schools and the Bicycle Institute need more volunteers. An appeal to volunteers to bring library books (reading and any other books), bicycle tools and parts for repair work – we use foot pumps. At the vocational/technical institute we offer courses in tie and dye and Batik textile printing projects. Volunteers can take part in these activities to acquire these skills. We need used computers to start computer studies at the Institute. We are working with another organisation called the

World Hunger Relief Inc. We are involved in a very big organic agricultural projects to help reduce hunger in Ghana and around the world. Throughout Ghana.

Number of projects: 7 UK: 0
Starting months: January–December
Time required: 1–12 weeks
Age: 18–65
Causes: Conservation, Teaching/assisting (nursery), Work Camps – Seasonal.
Activities: Agriculture/Farming, Arts/Crafts, Catering, Community Work, Computers, Conservation Skills, Development Issues, Music, Social Work, Summer Camps, Teaching, Theatre/Drama, Training, Work Camps – Seasonal.
Placements: 50
When to apply: One month in advance.
Work alone/with others: With others usually.
Qualifications: Nil but vols. with teaching, organic farm or bicycle repair experience especially welcome.
Equipment/clothing: Working/wellington boots, hand gloves (garden), mosquito net (c. $10 in Ghana).
Health requirements: Yellow fever vaccination.
Costs: Programme fee: US$30 for farm placements, $200 for teaching, $300 for each workcamp. Board: £5 per week.
Benefits: Accommodation free usually.
Training: Volunteers are taken through all basics for each project.
Supervision: Supervision is offered by the co-ordinator and the farm manager at all times.
Interviews: No interview is needed.
Charity number: G.717
Worldwide placements: Africa (Côte d'Ivoire, Ghana, Nigeria, Togo).

WYCLIFFE BIBLE TRANSLATORS

Recruitment UK
Horsleys Green
High Wycombe
Buckinghamshire HP14 3XL UK
T: 01494 682256
F: 01494 682300
E: recruitment_uk@wycliffe.org
W: www.wycliffe.org.uk
Contact: Tom, Chris or Hilary

Wycliffe is an international Christian mission agency, focusing on Bible translation for the world's minority languages. We are also involved in a range of related activities, such as linguistic analysis, literacy and community development. We recently adopted a new vision statement: 'By the year 2025, together with partners worldwide, we aim to see a Bible translation programme begun in all remaining languages that need one'. With somewhere over 2000 languages still needing analysis and Bible translation, this is a huge challenge. What could you do? We have a variety of long and short-term opportunities and recruit people with a wide variety of skills. Those with linguistic ability are of course always welcome. However we are equally keen to recruit teachers, IT specialists, mathematicians (yes honest!), administrators, theologians and those with good management skills. If your skills are not on this list, but you're still interested, please contact us anyway! Our total list of opportunities is much longer. If you'd like to find out more about some of the specific opportunities we offer, then please visit our web site www.wycliffe.org.uk. We suggest you start with the 'about us' section, and then 'getting involved' and 'go' pages. 🗎

Number of projects: 1,000+ UK: 2
Starting months: January–December
Time required: 6–52 weeks
Age: 17–65
Causes: Children, Human Rights, Teaching/assisting (nursery, primary, secondary, mature, EFL).
Activities: Accountancy, Administration, Building/Construction, Community Work, Computers, Development Issues, Fundraising, Library/Resource Centres, Manual Work, Marketing/Publicity, Outdoor Skills, Religion, Research, Summer Camps, Teaching, Technical Skills, Training, Translating, Visiting/Befriending.
Placements: >100
When to apply: Any time – by the end of April for summer placements.
Work alone/with others: Not usually with other young volunteers.
Qualifications: Foreign languages (esp. French) and/or 1 other skill (computer, secretarial, teacher etc) are useful but not essential.
Equipment/clothing: Yes – full advice will be given, depending on destination country.
Health requirements: Must be able to cope with the demands of placement – often in tropical conditions.
Costs: Participants pay own costs incl. travel, vaccinations, insurance, + minimal living costs.
Benefits: We do not pay salaries as a voluntary organisation. Volunteers are responsible for raising their own funds, usually from churches, family and friends. We do give some help and advice on how to do this. Accommodation is arranged ahead of time. Varies on location.
Training: As part of your preparations we will invite you to a Window On Wycliffe course at the Wycliffe Centre. This programme is specially designed to help you cope with some of the situations you may face overseas and introduce you to the world of Wycliffe.
Supervision: Supervised by senior members –

usually on an individual basis.

Interviews: Interviews take place at High Wycombe or by area representative.

Worldwide placements: Africa (Benin, Burkina Faso, Cameroon, Central African Republic, Chad, Congo Dem Republic, Congo Republic, Côte d'Ivoire, Gambia, Ghana, Kenya, Liberia, Mali, Mozambique, Niger, Nigeria, Senegal, Tanzania, Togo, Uganda); North America: (USA); Central America (Mexico); South America (Brazil, Peru); Asia (Philippines); Australasia (Papua New Guinea, Solomon Islands, Vanuatu); Europe (Germany, Hungary, Russia).

UK placements: England (Buckinghamshire, Devon); Scotland (Edinburgh); Northern Ireland (Belfast City).

Y

YANADI EDUCATION SOCIETY (YES)

D.No.7-16-174
Srinagar 8th Lane
Guntur
A.P.522 002 India
T: 0091 863 358545
E: yestribal@yahoo.com
Contact: Mr T.R. Jayachandar

The Yanadi Education Society was established in 1953 to empower the Yanadi community (which is on the lowest rung of the ladder of the tribal communities) in educational, social, cultural and economic fields. Our main activities are: organising the Yanadi and other tribal communities by conducting motivation camps; conducting awareness programmes in the targeted villages; establishing educational institutions and hostels for the tribal children; promoting technical and information technology among the educated; conducting medical and health camps in the targeted villages; promoting cultural heritage and cultural values of the tribal people; establishing libraries and study centres; forming women's self help groups; establishing charitable institutions like old age homes, children's homes. We do not accept volunteers with an offending background. Guntur Region, Andhra Pradesh.

Number of projects: 2 UK: 0
Starting months: Jun
Time required: 1–52 weeks (plus)
Age: 16–25
Causes: Addicts/Ex-Addicts, Elderly People, Environmental Causes, Health Care/Medical, Teaching/assisting (nursery, primary, secondary), Young People.
Activities: Campaigning, Caring – General, Community Work, Conservation Skills, First Aid, Group Work, Social Work, Sport, Teaching, Training, Work Camps – Seasonal.
Placements: 60
When to apply: By March.
Work alone/with others: With other young volunteers.
Qualifications: Basic education required and English. The local language is Telugu.
Equipment/clothing: No special equipment required.
Health requirements: Good health essential.
Costs: No costs other than travel.
Benefits: Accommodation provided.
Training: Leadership training is given.
Supervision: Our director, Mr Jayachandar supervises all the voluntary activities.

Interviews: Interviews at our office.
Worldwide placements: Asia (India).

YMCA

640 Forest Road
London
E17 3DZ UK
T: +44 (0) 208 509 4525
F: +44 (0) 208 521 1772
W: www.ymca.org.uk
Contact: Sue Claydon

YMCA volunteering opportunities are based in autonomous local units. The range of work in the UK includes accommodation for the homeless; sport, recreation and fitness; outdoor education, working with children and young people; specialist services for the disadvantaged and vulnerable in society. The YMCA is a Christian organisation, open to all irrespective of gender, race or faith but requires all volunteers to, at least, be in sympathy with the Christian basis of the movement. Most major cities in the UK. 🖰 🖺

Number of projects: 250 UK: 250
Starting months: January–December
Time required: 1–52 weeks
Age: 16 plus – no upper limit
Causes: Addicts/Ex-Addicts, Children, Disabled (learning and physical), Inner City Problems, Offenders/Ex-Offenders, Poor/Homeless, Young People.
Activities: Administration, Caring (general, residential), Catering, Community Work, Computers, Cooking, Counselling, Development Issues, Driving, Fundraising, Group Work, Music, Social Work, Sport, Summer Camps, Theatre/Drama, Training.
Placements: 60+
When to apply: All year.
Work alone/with others: With others.
Qualifications: As most of the volunteer positions require criminal background disclosures, it may not be possible in these cases, to accept applications from non UK citizens. Hence would only require UK residents.
Equipment/clothing: Supplied if required for specialist volunteering job.
Health requirements: Good health.
Costs: Nil.
Benefits: Personal development and training, accommodation, pocket money (varies).
Training: As required.
Supervision: Yes.
Interviews: Interviews normally take place on site.

UK placements: England (Bedfordshire, Berkshire, Bristol, Buckinghamshire, Cambridgeshire, Channel Islands, Cheshire, Cornwall, Co Durham, Cumbria, Derbyshire, Devon, Dorset, Essex, Gloucestershire, Hampshire, Herefordshire, Hertfordshire, Isle of Man, Kent, Lancashire, Leicestershire, Lincolnshire, London, Manchester, Merseyside, Norfolk, Northamptonshire, Northumberland, Nottinghamshire, Oxfordshire, Rutland, Shropshire, Somerset, Staffordshire, Suffolk, Surrey, E. Sussex, W. Sussex, Tyne and Wear, Warwickshire, West Midlands, Worcestershire, E. Yorkshire, N. Yorkshire, S. Yorkshire, W. Yorkshire); Scotland (throughout); Northern Ireland (throughout); Wales (throughout).

YMCA (Union Chretienne de Jeunes Gens)

Secretariat General
18 Bd Mobutu Sese Seko
BP 02
Lomé
Togo
T: (228) 227 88 38
F: (228) 227 95 80
E: ucjg-ymca@netcom.tg
Contact:

UCJG-Togo is an international Christian voluntary organisation dedicated to improving the standard of living in Togo. The organisation is involved in a wide range of activities offering many opportunities for volunteers. As well as organising summer workcamps, the organisation runs education and training programmes, community development programmes, environmental projects, cultural programmes and biblical study retreats.

Number of projects: 1 **UK:** 0
Starting months: January–December
Time required: 4 weeks
Age: 14 plus – no upper limit
Causes: Children, Poor/Homeless, Teaching/assisting, Young People.
Activities: Community Work, Group Work, Social Work.
Work alone/with others: With others.
Qualifications: None.
Health requirements: Good health.
Costs: US$350+ covers board and accommodation. Travel costs.
Benefits: The cost covers board and accommodation usually in YMCA hostels.
Training: Usually none.
Supervision: Most supervision is with experienced and even specialised managers.
Worldwide placements: Africa (Togo).

YORK STUDENT COMMUNITY ACTION

The Student Centre
University of York
Heslington
York
North Yorkshire YO10 5DD UK
T: 01904 433133
F: 01904 434664
E: su-ysca@york.ac.uk
W: www.ysca.org.uk/camp
Contact: Tory Nelson Parker

York Student Community Action runs camps for disadvantaged children from the Yorkshire area, during the summer and Easter school holidays. The children are referred to us by welfare organisations as those 'in desperate need of a break'. The children come from a multitude of different backgrounds and

situations, including young carers for their parents, those with behavioural difficulties, siblings of children with behavioural difficulties, those suffering from parental neglect and those from low-income backgrounds. The camp provides both children and parents with a greatly needed break. The children are taken to Hinderwell, a tiny village in Yorkshire for a week of residential camp. Activities include trips to the cinema, bowling, swimming, canoeing, to the seaside and to a theme park. Volunteers are required who have patience and wish to help these children and their parents, whilst developing themselves. Volunteers are fully trained and closely supervised whilst on camp. North east coast.

Number of projects: 7 **UK:** 7
Starting months: Mar, Apr, Jun, Jul
Time required: 1–3 weeks
Age: 18–30
Causes: Children, Disabled (learning), Poor/ Homeless, Young People.
Activities: Arts/Crafts, Catering, Driving, First Aid, Group Work, Music, Outdoor Skills, Sport, Summer Camps.
Placements: 100
When to apply: 2 months before.
Work alone/with others: With others.
Qualifications: Love of children, patience, willingness to adapt to challenging situations. Good knowledge of English.
Equipment/clothing: Rucksack, boots and waterproofs if possible + sleeping bag if wanted. Warm clothing and swimming costume.
Health requirements: Nil.
Costs: Nil except travel costs to York.
Benefits: Accommodation and food.
Training: 2-day training programme covering child protection, challenging behaviour, general child-training.
Supervision: All in groups supervised by a group leader. All group leaders supervised by the community action officer.
Interviews: No interview. Application forms are sent to interested volunteers.
UK placements: England (Derbyshire, N. Yorkshire).

YORKSHIRE WILDLIFE TRUST

10 Toft Green
York
YO1 1JT UK
T: 01904 659570
F: 01904 613467
E: yvettehollings@yorkshirewt.cix.co.uk
W: www.yorkshire-wildlife-trust.org.uk
Contact: Yvette Hollings

Yorkshire Wildlife Trust is a member of the Wildlife Trusts, a national partnership of 47 County Trusts. The aims of the Trust are primarily to: promote nature conservation in the community; acquire and manage nature reserves for wildlife and for people; monitor biological and geological resources; liaise with local authorities to promote regard for nature conservation; offer practical advice on nature conservation to landowners. Please note that the requirements, criteria, selection and support sections only outline our nature reserves volunteer programmes. We do have other opportunities for getting involved, which change fairly regularly so volunteers are advised to contact office for further information. It is the Trust's policy to involve all sectors of the community, of all ages, backgrounds, abilities and disabilities towards these ends. Volunteers require no previous experience just lots of enthusiasm. If they desire, they can go on to participate more fully assisting with the organisation and running of activities/projects. Volunteers with an offending background may be accepted – each case separately assessed. Variable. &

Number of projects: 10 **UK:** 10
Starting months: January–December
Time required: 1–52 weeks (plus)
Age: 14 plus – no upper limit
Causes: Conservation, Environmental Causes, Wildlife.
Activities: Conservation Skills.
Placements: 350
When to apply: Any time.
Work alone/with others: Both.
Equipment/clothing: Casual work clothes, waterproofs, stout boots for outdoor work. Protective safety gear is provided.
Health requirements: Anti-tetanus innoculation recommended.
Costs: Food, accommodation and travel.
Benefits: Out of pocket expenses.
Training: On the job training – task specific.
Supervision: On-site.
Interviews: None needed.
UK placements: England (E. Yorkshire, N. Yorkshire, S. Yorkshire, W. Yorkshire).

YOUNG DISABLED ON HOLIDAY

Flat 4, 62 Stuart Park
Corstorphine
Edinburgh
EH12 8YE UK
T: 0131 339 8866
E: aliwalker1@aol.com
Contact: Alison Walker

The Young Disabled on Holiday organisation runs a wide range of interesting holidays in the UK and abroad purely for the young with an age limit for both disabled and helpers of 18–35. In addition to holidays at fixed locations there are boating and camping trips. Activities on the holidays include discotheques, swimming, horseriding, wheelchair sports, barbecues and banquets. Please send s.a.e. for information.

Number of projects: 2 **UK:** 2
Starting months: Jan, May, Jun, Jul, Aug, Sep
Time required: 1–52 weeks
Age: 18–35
Causes: Disabled (physical), Holidays for Disabled, Young People.
Activities: Caring – General.
Placements: 45
When to apply: From Jan onwards.
Work alone/with others: Both.
Qualifications: Patience, be fit and willing to work as a team.
Health requirements: Must be generally fit.
Costs: 50% of cost of holiday abroad; 50% of cost of UK holiday.
Benefits: Half board. Stay with holiday-maker at holiday destination e.g. hotel, camp site.
Training: None.
Supervision: 2 holiday organisers supervise.
Interviews: Applicants are not interviewed – send CV and complete application.
Charity number: 200644
Worldwide placements: North America: (USA); Asia (Turkey); Europe (France, Ireland, Netherlands, Spain, Turkey).
UK placements: England (throughout); Scotland (throughout); Wales (throughout).

YOUNG POWER IN SOCIAL ACTION (YPSA)

House # 2, Road # 1, Block # B
Chandgaon R/A
Chittagong – 4212
Bangladesh
T: 00 880 31 653088 ext. 123
F: 00 880 31 650145
E: ypsa@abnetbd.com
Contact: Md. Arifur Rahman

Young Power in Social Action [YPSA] is a voluntary organisation working with social development issues, which has been running in the southern part of Bangladesh since 1985. The majority of the work focuses on women and children, adolescents and youth. Some of their projects include non formal primary education for poor children, community based rehabilitation of people with disabilities, advocacy, reforestation, health and sanitation, STD treatment, mother and child care and micro-credit finance for women and youths etc. YPSA has a strong network with likeminded organisations at home and abroad. YPSA has a Centre for Youth and Development (YPSA-CYD) which aims to work for and with young people for their development. YPSA also leads a networking group of youth organisations called

Pro Youth Network. YPSA organises individual volunteer placements, internships and workcamps for national and international volunteers who are interested in participating in their development projects. Volunteers can participate in both short and long term periods. YPSA won the International Youth Peace Prize from Bolivia for its outstanding social activities in 1999. Volunteers with an offending background (including drug addiction and smoking) are not accepted. Chittagong, Bangladesh's 2nd largest city in the southern part. It is the port city of Bangladesh. ▤

Number of projects: 1 **UK:** 0
Starting months: January–December
Time required: 12–24 weeks
Age: 18–35
Causes: Disabled (learning and physical), Environmental Causes, Health Care/Medical, Teaching/assisting (primary, EFL), Work Camps – Seasonal, Young People.
Activities: Administration, Agriculture/Farming, Community Work, Computers, Development Issues, Forestry, Fundraising, Gardening/Horticulture, Manual Work, Newsletter/Journalism, Research, Social Work, Teaching, Training, Work Camps – Seasonal.
Placements: 10
When to apply: All year.
Work alone/with others: With other young volunteers.
Qualifications: At least 'A' level. No restrictions providing you can obtain a visa.
Equipment/clothing: Modest dress and/or sub-continental dress is preferred.
Health requirements: Innoculation as recommended by your doctor.
Costs: Return travel to Bangladesh + registration and administrative fee of US$100. Small contribution need for host family.
Benefits: Free board and lodging, local transport and local sight-seeing with a guide. A single room with a single bed with a host family.
Training: An orientation course on YPSA and its ongoing projects and local culture.
Supervision: Volunteers are directed and supervised by the chief executive of YPSA.
Interviews: Prospective volunteers are not interviewed.
Worldwide placements: Asia (Bangladesh).

YOUTH ACCOMMODATION CENTRES INTERNATIONAL

188 St Lucia Street
Valetta
VLT 06 Malta
E: myha@keyworld.net
Contact: Manwel Cutajar

Interested persons are asked to send three international reply coupons for programme and an application form. ♿

Number of projects: 1 UK: 0
Starting months: Jan, Feb, Mar, Apr, May, Jun, Jul, Aug, Sep, Oct, Nov
Time required: 2–8 weeks
Age: 16–50
Causes: Young People.
Activities: Fundraising, Newsletter/Journalism.
Placements: 10
When to apply: All year.
Work alone/with others: Alone.
Qualifications: Enthusiasm, initiative.
Health requirements: Clean bill of health.
Costs: Deposit and postage expenses + travel costs to/from Malta, local transport and food.
Benefits: Free youth hostel accommodation.
Training: On site.
Supervision: On site.
Interviews: Prospective volunteers are not interviewed. A commission selects applications.
Worldwide placements: Europe (Malta).

YOUTH ACTION

Youth House
Unit 1, 38 Hangingroyd Lane
Hebden Bridge, W. Yorkshire
HX7 7DD UK
T: 01422 842308
F: 01422 842308
E: youthaction@wyya.co.uk
Contact: Larraine Longbottom

Youth Action aims to create dynamic groups of young people who can be a driving force for inspired action and leadership in the community. This involves young people in voluntary community action and activity responding to local community needs. We aim to offer an accredited training package of personal development. The project works with the 14–21 age group from a cross section of social backgrounds. 📖

Number of projects: 1 UK: 1
Starting months: January–December
Time required: 1–52 weeks
Age: 21–25
Causes: Young People.
Activities: Arts/Crafts, Campaigning, Community Work, Computers, Fundraising, Group Work, Newsletter/Journalism, Outdoor Skills, Theatre/Drama.
Placements: 1
When to apply: All year.
Work alone/with others: With an adult worker.
Qualifications: Motivation, leadership qualities and commitment.
Health requirements: Nil.
Costs: Food and accommodation.

Benefits: All costs paid by project.
Training: As required.
Supervision: Yes.
UK placements: England (W. Yorkshire).

YOUTH ACTION FOR PEACE

8 Golden Ridge
Freshwater
Isle of Wight PO40 9LE UK
T: 01983 752557
F: 01983 756900
E: yapuk@ukonline.co.uk
W: www.yap-uk.org
Contact: Cedric Medland

The international branches of Youth Action for Peace co-ordinate hundreds of projects each year, mainly within Europe. The variety of work undertaken on these projects is enormous, ranging from conservation in rural France, restoration of historic buildings in Italy, development construction and conservation in Africa or Asia and disarmament action in Germany. The projects allow you to serve in an area of need, whilst working in a community atmosphere with other volunteers and local people. There is also a great opportunity to get to know a particular region and its culture. The majority of projects last two to four weeks with 10 to 20 participants. They are normally held in the months from June to September, but a few projects happen in the winter and spring too. Knowing a foreign language is not essential. Volunteers with an offending background are accepted. ♿

Number of projects: 1088 UK: 5
Starting months: January–December
Time required: 1–52 weeks
Age: 16 plus – no upper limit
Causes: Archaeology, Architecture, Children, Conservation, Disabled (learning and physical), Elderly People, Environmental Causes, Health Care/Medical, Heritage, Human Rights, Inner City Problems, Poor/Homeless, Refugees, Teaching/assisting (primary), Wildlife, Work Camps – Seasonal, Young People.
Activities: Agriculture/Farming, Arts/Crafts, Building/Construction, Campaigning, Community Work, Conservation Skills, Forestry, Gardening/Horticulture, Group Work, International Aid, Library/Resource Centres, Manual Work, Music, Social Work, Sport, Summer Camps, Teaching, Theatre/Drama, Work Camps – Seasonal.
Placements: 70
When to apply: From March onwards. Send first and second class stamps on a stamp addressed envelope. For winter projects please apply from December onwards.
Work alone/with others: With others.

Qualifications: No skills but English is desirable. Official language on camps abroad is often English.
Equipment/clothing: Sleeping bag, sleeping mat, working clothes.
Health requirements: Nil.
Costs: Travel costs to and from the project vary. Registration fee in UK £95. Membership fee £25 or £10. Extra fee for projects in Africa, Asia or Latin America and training fee. This is stated on programme descriptions.
Benefits: Food and accommodation are provided. In some funded programmes all costs are covered.
Training: Training weekends for specified destinations.
Supervision: Volunteers are supervised by responsible volunteer co-ordinators of the hosting organisation.
Interviews: Applicants are not usually interviewed but for specified destinations interviews take place in various offices.
Worldwide placements: Africa (Egypt, Ghana, Kenya, Morocco, Senegal, Sierra Leone, South Africa, Tanzania, Togo, Uganda, Zimbabwe); North America: (Canada, Greenland, USA); Central America (Honduras, Mexico); South America (Brazil, Chile, Ecuador, Peru); Asia (Bangladesh, Cambodia, India, Israel, Japan, Korea (South), Mongolia, Nepal, Palestinian Authority, Philippines, Thailand, Turkey); Europe (Armenia, Austria, Belarus, Belgium, Croatia, Czech Republic, Denmark, Estonia, France, Germany, Greece, Hungary, Italy, Lithuania, Netherlands, Poland, Portugal, Romania, Russia, Slovakia, Spain, Turkey, Ukraine, Yugoslavia).
UK placements: England (Essex, Somerset, West Midlands, N. Yorkshire).

YOUTH ACTION FOR PEACE – DEUTSCHLAND

Christlicher Friedensdient e.V. (YAP-cfd)
Rendelerstraße 9-11
60385 Frankfurt
Germany
T: 00 49 69 45 90 71
F: 00 49 69 46 12 13
E: yap-cfd@t-online.de
Contact: Nikolaus Ell

Youth Action for Peace – Deutschland conducts international workcamps on ecological and peace projects for volunteers. Volunteers work in children's centres, on conservation projects etc. which require light manual work and occasionally campaigning activities. Ample time is provided for the discussion of questions which arise from the work and for leisure activities. Volunteers with offending backgrounds are accepted if they accept our conditions.

Applications must not be made to Germany. Please apply only to our English branch:
YAP/Methold House
North Street,
Worthing, W. Sussex BN1 1DU
T: 01903 528619
F: 01903 528611.

Starting months: Jun, Jul, Aug, Sep
Time required: 2–3 weeks
Age: 18–26
Causes: Conservation, Environmental Causes.
Activities: Campaigning, Conservation Skills, Manual Work.
Placements: 200
When to apply: As early as possible.
Work alone/with others: With others.
Equipment/clothing: Details on request.
Health requirements: In good health.
Costs: Travel.
Benefits: Board and lodging provided – accommodation is basic low standard.
Training: Training is given to German volunteers.
Supervision: International volunteers are supervised by team leaders.
Interviews: Applicants are not interviewed.
Worldwide placements: Africa (Egypt, Ghana, Morocco, Togo, Tunisia, Zambia); Central America (Cuba, Honduras, Mexico); South America (Peru); Asia (India, Israel, Japan, Jordan, Lebanon, Syria); Europe (Germany, Russia).

YOUTH AND STUDENT CND (Campaign for Nuclear Disarmament)

162 Holloway Road
London
N7 8DQ UK
T: +44 (0) 207 607 3616 or 0207 700 2393
T: +44 (0) 207 700 2357
E: info@youthstudentcnd.org.uk
W: www.youthstudentcnd.org.uk
Contact: Heather

We will accept volunteers for anything from one week to a year. There is a variety of mostly office based work. In summer, there is also campaigning, stall holding and bar work to be done at festivals. Mainly London.

Number of projects: 1 UK: 0
Starting months: January–December
Time required: 1–52 weeks
Age: 14–25
Causes: Environmental Causes, Young People.
Activities: Administration, Campaigning, Computers, Fundraising, Group Work, Marketing/Publicity, Newsletter/Journalism.
When to apply: All year.
Work alone/with others: With others.
Health requirements: Nil.

Costs: Accommodation.
Benefits: Travel expenses and lunch. None provided.
Training: Basic (as required).
Supervision: Part-time, help available from other office workers if needed.
Interviews: Informal.
UK placements: England (Cambridgeshire, London, Manchester, Oxfordshire).

YOUTH CHALLENGE INTERNATIONAL

305–20 Maud Street
Toronto
M5V 2M5 Canada
T: 416 504 3370
F: 416 504 3376
E: youthmanager@yci.org
W: www.yci.org
Contact: Shauna Houlton

Youth Challenge International combines development, health education and environmental research with adventurous projects carried out by teams of volunteers aged 18–30 years. Volunteers represent several countries and all walks of life. Conditions are basic and work schedules are demanding. An experienced staff team ensures projects are dynamic and results-oriented. Self-discovery, personal growth and community development are key elements. Projects include: Aquaducts, wells and schools – live and work alongside community members, improve schools, health posts and water supplies. Rainforest projects – work with local park rangers to preserve and reclaim rainforest, help biologists study and collect environmental data. Health promotion – travel with local professionals to help deliver workshops on primary healthcare, water treatment or HIV/AIDS prevention; help doctors perform sight restoring cataract surgery. Youth skills summits – organise exciting summits; bring together hundreds of indigenous youth from small rural villages. There may be placements for those with an offending background depending on offence. Costa Rica, Guyana, Vanuatu.

Number of projects: 10 **UK:** 0
Starting months: Feb, May, Jun, Jul, Sep, Dec
Time required: 5–10 weeks
Age: 18–30
Causes: AIDS/HIV, Children, Conservation, Environmental Causes, Health Care/Medical, Teaching/assisting (nursery, primary, secondary, mature), Young People.
Activities: Building/Construction, Community Work, Conservation Skills, Development Issues, Group Work, Manual Work, Teaching.
Placements: 200
When to apply: As soon as possible.
Work alone/with others: Work with others.

Qualifications: Must have a certificate in first aid and be able to swim 200 meters. Most nationalities accepted.
Equipment/clothing: Volunteers need a backpack and a first aid kit.
Health requirements: All volunteers must be medically cleared by our nurse.
Costs: Programme fees range from US $2,685–$3485 plus airfare.
Benefits: Once in country, all costs are covered. Basic accommodation in groups of 8–15.
Training: 2 day pre-departure training is given.
Supervision: Each groups is with 2 group leaders who will supervise all staff.
Interviews: Volunteers are interviewed over telephone.
Worldwide placements: Central America (Costa Rica); South America (Guyana).

YOUTH CLUB FOR NATURE CONSERVATION

P.O. Box AD 130
Cape Coast
Ghana
T: 00233 24 364844
E: ycnc@hotvoice.com
W: www.mandatethefuture.org/ghana
Contact: Eunice Tiwaa Boakye

The Youth Club for Nature Conservation is a non-profit youth service charitable environmental conservation organisation, dedicated to the conservation of biodiversity to secure improved livelihood conditions for all people. This is done through educating young people and women in communities and educational institutions on ecological issues, restoration strategies, pilot projects and support for sustainable community participatory development programmes, through the provision of voluntary services of youth experts in varying fields of community and natural resources management. Current projects/initiatives include – nutrition for quality health – empowers communities through training workshops, supply of farming/gardening equipment, support, cultivation, improving and maintaining germplasm in their local food crops, organic farming and exchanging their problems, strategies and ideas. Community participatory apiculture – to conserve and secure alternative sustainable livelihood for rural subsistence farming communities. Eco-library and training/resource centre – to collate, process, train/educate and empower stakeholders especially the young people and women. Mandate the future Ghana – an ICT based development programme working on ideas, wants and needs, achievements, desires and viewpoints of grassroots youth groups on issues affecting them throughout Ghana. We may be able to place volunteers with an offending background depending on offence. In Southern Ghana comprising the central, eastern, western, Ashanti and Volta regions. Placements can be arranged in other regions with partner organisations. 🔊 📄

Number of projects: 5 UK: 0
Starting months: January–December
Time required: 4–52 weeks
Age: 15–45
Causes: Conservation, Environmental Causes
Activities: Building/Construction, Conservation Skills, Forestry, International Aid, Manual Work, Outdoor Skills.
Placements: 65–100
When to apply: Three months in advance of preferred start date.
Work alone/with others: Varies.
Qualifications: Ability to speak the English language and most importantly, commitment to serve needy communities to achieve sustainable livelihood.
Equipment/clothing: Protective clothing with assignments involving field work.
Health requirements: No restrictions.
Costs: Travel costs, subsistence and registration for association with project or project placement.
Benefits: Board and lodging near to the project site.
Training: There is an induction programme before all project placements, with tours to familiarise volunteers with their chosen area. Taught ethics of community service in Ghana and conservation skills.
Supervision: All volunteers are supervised and work with a local project co-ordinator, who is in touch with conditions in that community.
Interviews: Prospective volunteers must submit their CV, with what they want to do on their chosen project, their proposal for a new project (if applicable) and the benefit to be derived from their service.

YOUTH FEDERATION

17 Castle Street
Chester
Cheshire CH1 2DS UK
T: 01244 325867
F: 01244 317506
E: youthfed@aol.com
Contact: David Packwood

Cheshire and Wirral Youth Federation needs volunteers to work in various youth clubs, youth projects and communities and to assist with a wide ranging programme of youth activities. There are some opportunities to work with Federation HQ team; other opportunities to work with a local youth group or project. The Federation will try to match people with the appropriate placement. Much work takes place during evenings, weekends and holidays. Unless the volunteer has financial support it is best to place local young people with local projects. We now have four volunteer development workers based in Chester, East Cheshire, Walton and Wirral. Their role is to recruit, select and induct volunteers. They will also offer training and continue mentor support. Other opportunities exist with the Millennium Volunteers project. Projects also take place in art and drama, as well as with rural youth groups. Volunteers with offending backgrounds accepted depending on the offence. 🔊

Starting months: January–December
Time required: 1–52 weeks
Age: 14–70
Causes: Addicts/Ex-Addicts, Disabled (learning and physical), Elderly People, Inner City Problems, Offenders/Ex-Offenders, Poor/Homeless, Unemployed, Young People.
Activities: Administration, Arts/Crafts, Community Work, Counselling, Driving, Fundraising, Group Work, Music, Newsletter/Journalism, Outdoor Skills, Research, Social Work, Sport, Summer Camps, Visiting/Befriending.
Placements: 2,000
When to apply: All year.
Work alone/with others: With others.
Qualifications: Dependent on project – enthusiasm and energy.
Health requirements: Nil.
Costs: Board and lodging.
Benefits: Expenses reimbursed and help to find accommodation if needed.
Training: 6-week induction training.
Supervision: All volunteers are supervised on a monthly basis by development workers.
Interviews: Interviews take place in Chester.
Charity number: 506539
UK placements: England (Cheshire, Merseyside).

YOUTH HOSTELS ASSOCIATION (ENGLAND AND WALES)

P. O. Box 6030
Matlock
DerbyshireDE4 3XA UK
T: 01629 822074
E: recruitment@yha.org.uk
W: www.yha.org.uk
Contact: Edwina Edwards

16–25 year olds can volunteer for activities such as hostel and grounds maintenance. Alternatively countryside work, fundraising, publicity and promotion professional services. All skills and interests welcomed. For more information contact the national volunteer co-ordinator at the above address for a volunteering in YHA information pack. Long-term volunteering available for project work. Hostel wardening at small self-catering youth hostels.

Number of projects UK: 1
Starting months: January–December
Time required: 1–52 weeks
Age: 14 plus – no upper limit
Causes: Conservation, Environmental Causes, Heritage, Unemployed, Wildlife.
Activities: Administration, Building/Construction, Catering, Computers, Conservation Skills, DIY, Forestry, Fundraising, Gardening/Horticulture, Group Work, Manual Work, Marketing/Publicity, Newsletter/ Journalism, Outdoor Skills, Translating.
When to apply: All year.
Work alone/with others: Both.
Qualifications: All skills and interests welcomed. No restrictions but must be resident in the UK.
Equipment/clothing: Depends on the activity.
Health requirements: No restrictions.
Costs: Food and travel costs.
Benefits: Some expenses reimbursed, usually accommodation and food. Opportunity to self-develop through new challenges.
Training: Available as necessary.
Supervision: Yes.
Interviews: Tele-interviews conducted by volunteer co-ordinators. Volunteers must complete a volunteer registration form.
Charity number: 301657
UK placements: England (throughout); Wales (Caerphilly, Cardiff, Conwy, Denbighshire, Monmouthshire, Newport, Pembrokeshire, Powys).

YOUTH SYNERGY FOR TOMORROW (SYJED)

103 Av. Nicolas Grunitzky
B.P. 7097
Lomé
Togo
T: +228 (2) 213681
F: +15072624345
E: syjed@hotmail.com
W: www.syjed.fr.fm
Contact: Mr Jean-Claude Adzalla-Koma

Youth Synergy for Tomorrow (SYJED) is a youth voluntary organisation for development. Every summer we organise international workcamps where young volunteers from all over the world come together and work at the community level on various humanitarian and development projects. Our aim is to promote peace and tolerance for better human development. Through the years, the SYJED has grown and now we offer any volunteer opportunity for students or workers of any age. We have partnered with Volontariat Francophone (VF) to offer opportunities for our prospective volunteers with other French speaking countries. We have opportunities in the following fields: community, association

and NGO, trade unions, women's co-operative and organisations, youth organisations, health, schools and new technologies. ♿

Number of projects: 28 **UK:** 0
Starting months: January–December
Time required: 3–52 weeks
Age: 16 plus – no upper limit
Causes: AIDS/HIV, Children, Environmental Causes, Health Care/Medical, Human Rights, Teaching/assisting (primary), Work Camps – Seasonal, Young People.
Activities: Summer Camps, Work Camps – Seasonal.
Placements: 140
When to apply: Any time.
Work alone/with others: With others.
Qualifications: No qualifications needed for summer camps. For other volunteering opportunities, some qualifications will be needed. Remember our motto is to 'bring volunteering opportunities to everyone'.
Health requirements: Malarial prophylactics.
Costs: All travel to and within Togo, a registration fee of $170 for the three weeks workcamp. For other vol. opportunities, some extra will be needed and some waived. Contact us.
Benefits: Food and accommodation provided during summer workcamps.
Training: At some workcamps (health/AIDS, FGM sensitivity) training is given to the volunteers before the camp activities start. Some other training available.
Supervision: Volunteers are under supervision of local staff or chairman.
Interviews: No interviews are required.
Worldwide placements: Africa (Togo).

YOUTH WITH A MISSION

Highfield Oval
Ambrose Lane
Harpenden
HertfordshireAL5 4BX UK
T: 01582 463216
F: 01582 463213
E: enquiries@oval.com
W: www.ywam-england.com
Contact: Public Relations Manager

Youth With A Mission is an international, interdenominational Christian missionary organisation working in over 132 nations worldwide. YWAM was founded in 1960 and is committed to training people to care for those in need, through short term relief and long term community development projects. Our desire for those who work with us is that they 'know God and make Him known'. As a volunteer on one of YWAM's short term projects, you will get the opportunity to share your Christian faith with those you meet, take part in building and development projects, work alongside permanent staff in urban community work in cities such as Amsterdam and London. You will be able to work with children in orphanages and on the street in some of the poorest of the world's cities. We need people who have a wide variety of skills from cooks to secretaries, people who are willing to have a hands on experience, to work in a team with other volunteers in order to get the job done. ♿

Number of projects: 100's **UK:** 20
Starting months: Jan, Apr, Jun, Jul, Sep
Time required: 1–52 weeks
Age: 14 plus – no upper limit
Causes: Addicts/Ex-Addicts, AIDS/HIV, Children, Health Care/Medical, Human Rights, Inner City Problems, Offenders/Ex-Offenders, Poor/Homeless, Teaching – Primary, Young People.
Activities: Accountancy, Administration, Building/Construction, Catering, Community Work, Computers, Cooking, Group Work, Manual Work, Music, Religion, Summer Camps, Teaching, Theatre/Drama, Training.
Placements: 1,000's worldwide.
When to apply: 2–6 months before start date.
Work alone/with others: With teams.
Qualifications: Christian faith and to be a member of a church.
Equipment/clothing: Nothing specific – Bible.
Health requirements: Depends on location but generally, no.
Costs: Anyone considering work with YWAM or participating in a short term project will need to raise financial support to cover all costs.

Costs vary approx. £3,000 for 6 months, approx. £150 for two weeks.
Benefits: The cost covers food, board, travel etc.
Training: We have training weekends for short-term outreaches or placements are part of a training school.
Supervision: All volunteers come under the leadership structure of our organisation.
Interviews: Prospective volunteers may be interviewed – depending on the length of placement.
Charity number: 264078
Worldwide placements: Africa (Ghana, Kenya, Malawi, Mali, Mauritania, Morocco, Mozambique, Nigeria, South Africa, Tanzania, Uganda, Zimbabwe); North America: (Canada, USA); Central America (Barbados, Mexico); South America (Bolivia, Brazil, Colombia, Paraguay); Asia (Cambodia, China, Hong Kong, India, Indonesia, Nepal, Philippines, Singapore, Thailand); Australasia (Australia, New Zealand); Europe (Albania, Bosnia-Herzegovina, Croatia, Cyprus, Denmark, France, Ireland, Italy, Lithuania, Moldova, Netherlands, Norway, Portugal, Romania, Russia, Slovakia, Spain, Sweden, Switzerland, Turkey, Ukraine).
UK placements: England (Cumbria, Derbyshire, Devon, Herefordshire, Hertfordshire, London, Merseyside, Nottinghamshire, E. Sussex, W. Sussex, Warwickshire); Scotland (Ayrshire – East, Ayrshire – North, Ayrshire – South, Edinburgh, Glasgow City, Renfrewshire); Northern Ireland (Down); Wales (Cardiff, Rhondda, Cynon, Taff, Vale of Glamorgan).

Z

ZARTONK-89 NGO

Sebastia 104
Yerevan
375032 Armenia
T: (+374) 773128
F: (+374) 544015
E: zartnk-89@netsys.am
W: http://www.ngoc.am/NGOS/Zartonk-89/zartonk.htm
Contact: Susanna Grigoryan

Zartonk-89 (which acts in Republic of Armenian) is a non-governmental organisation (NGO) founded in 1989 and registered as an NGO with the Ministry of Justice in 1995. Since its foundation, the NGO has been actively engaged in the promotion of health, education, environment and social assistance for needy segments of rural and urban populations in Armenia. The active support creativity of our partners and local volunteers has made it possible to extend its presence to other regions of Armenia. There are branches of our NGO all over the country. Our mission is to improve the lives of parentless, needy and refugee children and youth in Armenia. We implement various educational, social and health projects focused on improving the mental, physical and social skills of youth and on building their self esteem. In addition we have implemented several development projects that benefit entire communities. Our projects range from summer camps and basic education programmes for parentless and needy children to basic hygienic education for elementary school children and first aid training for rural villagers. In addition, we have installed flour mills in agricultural regions to create work places. From an organisational viewpoint, our NGO has a collegial management. The NGO board is directly responsible for electing the NGO president, vice president and secretary respectively. The operational work lies with the NGO staff, which comprises some permanent staff and volunteer members. Our modest resources have allowed us to establish and maintain partnerships with other sister organisations abroad whose support for our NGO activities has been active and consistent. The support, for instance, of the Catholic Committee against Hunger and Development in France is worth mentioning. Zartonk-89 actively monitors the issues it has undertaken as part of its vision. This monitoring allows the organisation to conduct brainstorming sessions for the identification and generation of new project proposals. We are unable to place volunteers with an offending background. Projects throughout Armenia – Yerevan, Armavir, Lory, Syunik, Shirak and Gegharkunik.

Number of projects: 12 UK: 0
Starting months: January–December
Time required: 1–52 weeks (plus)
Age: 18–40
Causes: AIDS/HIV, Children, Disabled (physical), Environmental Causes, Health Care/Medical, Human Rights, Poor/Homeless, Teaching (nursery, primary, EFL), Unemployed, Wildlife, Young People.
Activities: Agriculture/Farming, Building/Construction, Catering, Community Work, Computers, Development Issues, First Aid, Fundraising, International Aid, Social Work, Summer Camps, Training, Translating.
Placements: 25
When to apply: On going.
Work alone/with others: Work with others.
Qualifications: No specific requirements, just a willingness to help. Certain skills would be very useful depending on the project, but are not essential – computer, Internet, building, fundraising skills, proposal writing and knowledge of Armenian, Russian and French.
Equipment/clothing: Depends on the project. If the individual is volunteering online, a computer and Internet connection would help. Volunteers coming to Armenia should bring clothes appropriate to the weather. Winters are cold and summers are very hot.
Health requirements: Volunteers planning to travel to Armenia should take the necessary precautions as recommended by their respective governments. Tetanus, Hepatitis A and B vaccines are usually recommended.
Costs: Depends on the project and where the volunteer plans travel from. To the extent that it is possible, Zartonk-89 will provide volunteers with food and living arrangements. Other fees may be applicable – accommodation.
Benefits: We will try to find accommodation, sometimes this has to be paid for by the volunteer. Wherever possible, we will provide volunteers with food.
Training: Depends on the project.
Supervision: Depends on the project, but generally supervision will be provided by members of the organisation.
Interviews: Volunteers are interviewed via e-mail.
Charity number: 01B 000641
Worldwide placements: Europe (Armenia).

Index by Worldwide Placement

Index by Cause